Fodor's Affordable Caribbean

New Edition

"The Fodor's series puts a premium on showing its readers a good time."
—Philadelphia Inquirer

"Concentrates on life's basics . . . without skimping on literary luxuries."
—New York Daily News

"Good helpmates for the cost-conscious traveler."
—Detroit Free Press

"These books succeed admirably; easy to follow and use, full of cost related information, practical advice and recommendations . . . maps are clear and easy to use."
—Travel Books Worldwide

"The books can help you fill the gap between deprivation and ostentation when you travel."
—Dawson Sentinel

Parts of this book appear in *Fodor's Caribbean*

Fodor's Travel Publications, Inc.
New York • Toronto • London • Sydney • Auckland

ISBN 0-679-02948-6

Fodor's Affordable Caribbean

Editor: Melanie A. Sponholz
Editorial Contributors: Pamela Acheson, Robert Andrews, Robert Blake, Hannah Borgeson, Gail Gillen de Haas, Barbara Hults, Dawn Lawson, Kristen Perrault, Marcy Pritchard, Melissa Rivers, Linda K. Schmidt, Mary Ellen Schultz, M.T. Schwartzman, Kate Sekules, Jordan Simon, Dinah Spritzer, Jane E. Zarem
Creative Director: Fabrizio La Rocca
Cartographer: David Lindroth
Cover Photograph: S. Achernar/Image Bank

Design: Vignelli Associates

Special Sales

Fodor's Travel Publications are available at special discounts for bulk purchases for sales promotions or premiums. Special editions, including personalized covers, excerpts of existing guides, and corporate imprints, can be created in large quantities for special needs. For more information contact your local bookseller or write to Special Markets, Fodor's Travel Publications, 201 East 50th Street, New York, NY 10022. Inquiries from Canada should be directed to your local Canadian bookseller or sent to Random House of Canada, Ltd., Marketing Department, 1265 Aerowood Drive, Mississauga, Ontario L4W 1B9. Inquiries from the United Kingdom should be sent to Fodor's Travel Publications, 20 Vauxhall Bridge Road, London SW1V 2SA.

MANUFACTURED IN THE UNITED STATES OF AMERICA
10 9 8 7 6 5 4 3 2 1

Contents

Maps and Plans

How This Guide Will Save You Money

If you're one of the rock-bottom-budget travelers who sleep on park benches to save money and would never, ever dress up for duck à l'orange at Jean-Louis, then look to another guidebook for your travel information.

But if you're among those who budget some of the finer things into their traveling life, if you would stay home before spending a night in a hostel dormitory with strangers, and if you're willing to pay a little more for crisp sheets, a firm bed, a soft pillow, and a really superb dining experience every now and again, read on. It's for you that Fodor's team of savvy, budget-conscious writers and editors have prepared this book.

We share your traveling style and your champagne tastes, and we know that saving money is all about making choices. Some of us do it by sticking to public transportation and picnic lunches. Others spend more on a hotel with amenities but don't care about fancy meals. Still others take the hostel route in order to go on a shopping spree.

In this guide, we've tried to include enough options so that all of you spend time and money in the ways you most enjoy. The hotels we suggest are good values, and there are no dives, thank you—only clean, friendly places with an acceptable level of comfort, convenience, and charm. We also recommend a range of inexpensive and moderately priced restaurants where you can eat well in pleasant surroundings. We'll also tell you about the best local shopping and how to golf, scuba, sail, and more without breaking the bank.

As for planning what to see and do, you'll find the same lively writing and authoritative background information available in Fodor's renowned Gold Guides.

Please Write to Us

Everyone who has contributed to *Affordable Caribbean* has worked hard to make the text accurate. All prices and opening times are based on material supplied to us at press time, and Fodor's cannot accept responsibility for any errors that may have occurred. The passage of time always brings changes, so it's a good idea to call ahead to confirm information when it matters—particularly if you're making a detour to visit specific sights or attractions. When making reservations at a hotel or inn, be sure to mention if you have a disability or are traveling with children, if you prefer a private bath or a certain type of bed, or if you have specific dietary needs or any other concerns.

Do let us know about your trip. Did you enjoy the restaurants we recommended? Was your hotel comfortable and were the museums you visited worthwhile? Did you happen upon a treasure that we haven't included? We would love to have your feedback, positive and negative. If you have suggestions or complaints, we'll look into them and revise our entries when it's the right thing to do. So please send us a letter or postcard (we're at 201 East 50th Street, New York, New York 10022). We look forward to hearing from you. In the meantime, have a wonderful trip!

Karen Cure
Editorial Director

Fodor's Choice for Budget Travelers

No two people will agree on what makes a perfect vacation, but it's fun and helpful to know what others think. We hope you'll have the chance to experience some of Fodor's Choices yourself while visiting the Caribbean. For detailed information about each entry, refer to the appropriate chapter in this guidebook.

Beaches

Shoal Bay, Anguilla

Palm Beach, Aruba

Seven Mile Beach, Grand Cayman

Negril, Jamaica

Anse du Gouverneur, St. Barts

Magens Bay, St. Thomas, U.S. Virgin Islands

Trunk Bay, St. John, U.S. Virgin Islands

Diving/Snorkeling

Reefs around Bonaire

Virgin Gorda, British Virgin Islands

Cayman Islands (especially Sting Ray City)

Southern Coast of Curaçao

Scott's Head, Dominica

Saba's pinnacles

St. Vincent

Reefs around Speyside, Tobago

Turks and Caicos Islands' reefs

Buck Island Reef, St. Croix, U.S. Virgin Islands

Hiking

Washington/Slagbaai National Park, Bonaire

Morne Diablotin, Dominica

Parc Naturel, Basse-Terre, Guadeloupe

Bamboo Forest, Montserrat

Dunn's River Falls, Jamaica

El Yunque Rain Forest, Puerto Rico

The Quill, St. Eustatius

National Park, St. John

Hotels

Boscobel Beach (for families), Jamaica (*$$*)

Fort Recovery, Tortola, British Virgin Islands (*$$*)

Relais Caraibes, Martinique (*$$*)

Passangrahan Royal Guest House, St. Martin (*$–$$*)

Admiral's Inn, Antigua (*$*)

Maho Bay Camp, St. John (*$*)

Bruce Bowker's Carib Inn, Bonaire (*$*)

Restaurants

Bon Appetit, Aruba (*$$*)

Ile de France, Barbados (*$$*)

Le Balata, Guadeloupe (*$$*)

Le Coq Hardi, Martinique (*$$*)

Veni Mange, Trinidad (*$–$$*)

Niggy's Montserrat (*$*)

Roy's, Anguilla (*$*)

Turtle Pier Bar & Restaurant, St. Maarten (*$*)

Skyworld, Tortola, British Virgin Islands (*¢–$*)

Jerk Centres on Boston Beach, Jamaica (*¢*)

Lolo snack stands, St. Martin (*¢*)

Value Vacations

Villa rental, Montserrat

Campground, St. John

Parador, Puerto Rico

Dive package, Bonaire

Bare-boat charter, British Virgin Islands (for experienced sailors)

Plantation-house hotel, Nevis (off-season)

The Caribbean

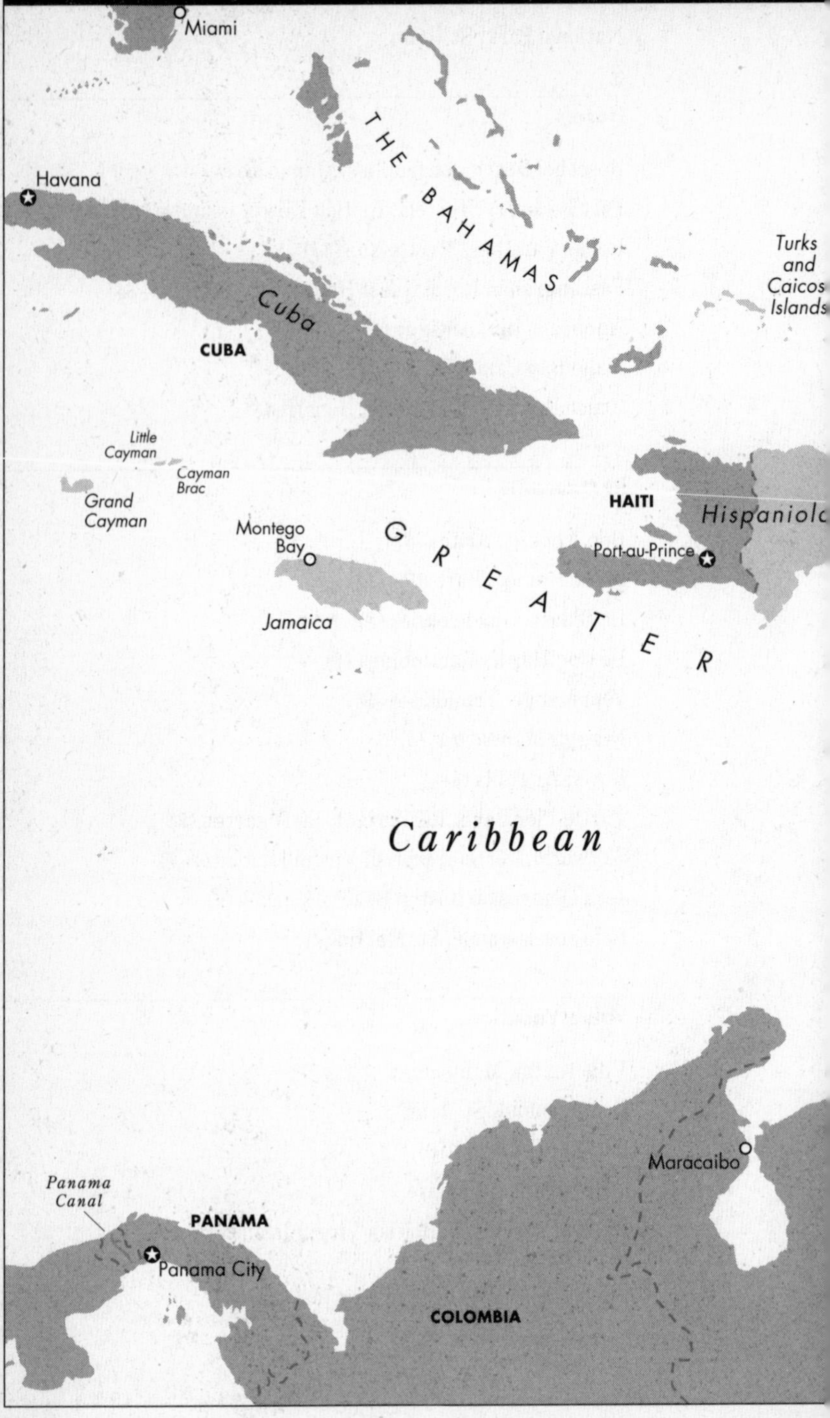

Miami

THE BAHAMAS

Havana

Turks and Caicos Islands

Cuba

CUBA

Little Cayman

Cayman Brac

Grand Cayman

HAITI

Hispaniola

Montego Bay

GREATER

Port-au-Prince

Jamaica

Caribbean

Maracaibo

Panama Canal

PANAMA

Panama City

COLOMBIA

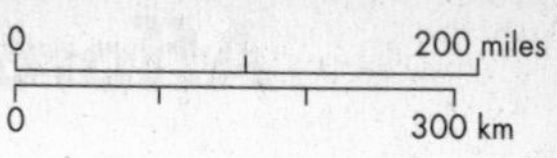
0
200 miles
0
300 km
N
ATLANTIC OCEAN
DOMINICAN REPUBLIC
Santo Domingo
San Juan
Puerto Rico
St. John
St. Thomas
Virgin Gorda
Tortola
St. Croix
Anguilla
St. Maarten/
St. Martin
St. Barthélemy
Saba
Barbuda
St. Eustatius
St. Kitts
Nevis
Antigua
Montserrat
Marie Galante
Guadeloupe
LEEWARD ISLANDS
ANTILLES
Dominica
Martinique
WINDWARD ISLANDS
Sea
St. Lucia
Barbados
St. Vincent
The Grenadines
Grenada
Tobago
Trinidad
LESSER ANTILLES
Aruba
Bonaire
Curaçao
Caracas
VENEZUELA

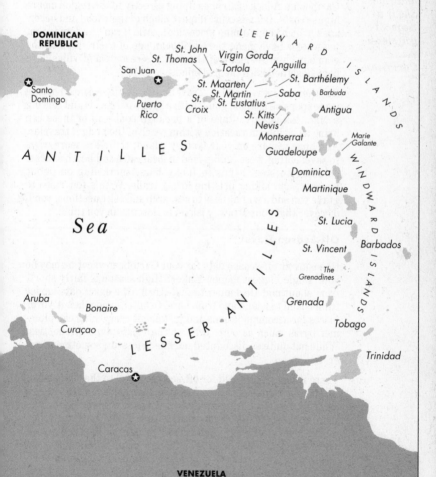

Making Your Vacation Affordable

By Jane Hershey

Jane Hershey's work has appeared in Good Housekeeping, US, *and* Elle. *She is a frequent traveler to the Caribbean.*

What traveler hasn't dreamed of a vacation in this Caribbean, with its near-perfect weather, stunning beaches, exotic cultures, and multitude of outdoor activities? Sadly, the cost of paradise can be a rude awakening. Many of these islands are expensive—some shockingly so. It's telling that some of our island chapters list hotels costing under $125 a night in a budget category—not out of line when you consider that hotel rates of $600 a night are common on these islands. There are reasons for the hefty price tags you find in the Caribbean. A lack of airlines flying directly to the region means higher costs. Islands must import much of their food and beverages, which keeps dining prices high. And it can't be denied that jet-setters have made the Caribbean one of their stops on the glamour circuit—many of the region's resorts and villas have been designed with them in mind.

But there are ways to save. Traveling in the off-season, choosing less expensive islands, going with a group of friends and renting a villa, taking advantage of a package deal—all of these can bring a Caribbean vacation within reach of the budget traveler. And once you are on your fantasy island, there are more ways to save: eating West Indian food in local cafés and beach shacks, listening to steel bands in funky bars, snorkeling on public beaches, and hiking pristine forest trails. With a few rules to guide you and a willingness to research and ask questions, you'll discover that your faraway island is closer than you think.

Off-Season Travel

Choosing an off-season date for your Caribbean vacation may be your single biggest money-maker. High season is fairly short, from about mid-December to mid-April, (the exact date varies from island to island and from hotel to hotel), and when it's over prices for accommodations and just about everything can plummet by as much as 50%, even at the most deluxe properties. While not quite as discounted, airline prices are sometimes lower, too.

There is much to be said for off-season travel to the Caribbean. Without the prime-time crowds, it's easier to rent a car, enjoy a local historic site, or find a deserted beach without the prime-time crowds. While temperatures are fairly constant year-round, brief storms are almost likely to occur in January as they are in August. (The one time of the year many travelers avoid is September and October—hurricane season.) In the drier summer months you'll find fewer mosquitoes and other flying nuisances. The water tends to be calmer and clearer, which means better snorkeling and sailing. Spring and summer are also when many Caribbean countries hold local festivals, such as St. Thomas's Frenchtown Carnival in June and Antigua's Windsurfing Week and calypso competition in July.

Besides the region's traditional low season, the Caribbean has other small "windows" during high season, when hotels that face sharp drops in occupancy quietly lower their rates for a week or so. A common window occurs in early January, right after New Year's; another is at the end of January, right before the February surge of visitors. Dates and price decreases vary among hotels and islands; a good travel agent can be useful in helping you find deals. (*see* Travel Agents, *below*). Note that rates are fairly stable year-round at city hotels that cater to business travelers and small inns and B&Bs with already-rock-bottom prices. But be sure to ask: Many are willing to negotiate during slack periods.

Choice of Destination

Your choice of island is vital in determining affordability. The Caribbean consists of many nations, and in some ways they differ from one another as much as, say, France differs from Holland, or the United Kingdom from the United States. Prices can differ as dramatically. Some islands, such as St. Barts and Antigua, tend to attract a jet-set clientele, so their hotel and restaurant prices are higher than those on popular family and couple-oriented destinations such as the U.S. Virgin Islands, Jamaica, and Puerto Rico. Not that these and other islands don't have world-class facilities, or that there are no budget lodgings on expensive islands; it's just that larger islands tend to pay more attention to the needs of a wider spectrum of the vacation market. You'll notice that the price charts for Dining and Lodging in each of our island chapters differ greatly from one another: What's moderately priced in Puerto Rico, for instance, may be considered inexpensive on Antigua. Aim for a specific atmosphere rather than a specific island. Laid-back, casual elegance isn't only found on pricey islands like Anguilla; look for it in the many charming, small hotels tucked into intimate bays and hillsides on unknown "treasure islands" like Saba or Dominica. Our Finding Your Place in the Sun chart (*see below*) categorizes each island in terms of cost.

Setting Priorities

Deciding what's most important to you can save a surprising amount of money. If activity-filled informality is what you're seeking, steer clear of destinations and resorts that emphasize fine dining and elegant atmosphere, or you'll likely end up paying for someone else's bone china and imported caviar. If golf and tennis aren't your games, put your dollars where the best diving, snorkeling, or beach-combing are found. All that turf—whether astro or natural—costs a fortune in upkeep and staffing, and you end up paying for facilities you may not even use.

If you prefer an active vacation, it's wise to research which properties and destinations offer the best values. Various hotels and airlines offer many sports-specific packages. Many hotels in some countries, like Jamaica, feature rafting and horseback riding. Other hotel and all-inclusive companies have properties catering to dive enthusiasts. (If you prefer not to use a package, think about taking the least expensive room available and cutting back on extra luxuries so you'll have more money for your sport.)

Lodging

Unless you go camping, your accommodations will almost certainly be the most expensive portion of your trip. Here are savvy ways to save.

Hotels Sometimes it makes sense to deal with a larger hotel or resort, even though the initial price tag looks higher. Even in season, these facilities usually have rooms to fill, and they can be more flexible about upgrades and discounts on food, drink, and activities. Smaller, independent properties can't afford to be as generous.

Is a popular resort going through a change of management or redecoration? If you're willing to put up with minor nuisances like staff training and repainting, you might take advantage of special rates. Just make certain that the rock drill won't be outside your door at 6 AM and that the swimming pool will be filled.

How important is an oceanfront room to you? Many properties have a category for rooms that are off the beach. Amenities in these rooms, often referred to as "mountain" or "garden" view, are similar to those on the ocean, but rates can be 50% less, even in high season.

There are also ways to save if you take your family. A number of hotel chains have children's day camps and teen programs. Most of these programs are free to guests; some charge a small amount for meals and excursions. Many chains (and individual properties) allow children under 18 to stay free in their parent's room. Some have low-price children's menus and other discounts. Do not hesitate to ask about such offers when you book—you may be pleasantly surprised, even in high season.

All-Inclusives All-inclusives—where guests pay one preset price that covers room, meals, and all activities—have a reputation for being expensive, and many are. But some can actually help you save money, particularly if you plan on an active vacation with plenty of sports, recreation, eating, and drinking. If nothing else, you'll know up front exactly how much your vacation will cost. The popularity of these resorts has mushroomed over the past decade, and now all-inclusives for every taste and budget have emerged. Some cater to sports enthusiasts, others are designed especially for families. Still others emphasize romantic tranquillity and comparative luxury at an affordable price. Evaluate carefully the personality of the all-inclusive you are considering, and find out exactly what's included before you book. Some resorts throw in everything down to the last rum punch and paddleboat; others require separate payment for drinks, as at Club Meds, or certain menu items. Better rooms or rooms with better views will cost you more at some all-inclusives. Remember that affordably priced all-inclusives will not offer the same levels of comfort and service as all-inclusives charging three times as much.

Apartment and Villa Rentals Many couples and families are discovering the pleasures of renting a private or semiprivate villa. In fact, many resorts are developing such options as part of their facilities. Most villas are upscale properties, often with several bedrooms, a pool, a gourmet kitchen, elaborate home entertainment system, a cook, maid—even a car. Although weekly high-season rates at such posh digs can seem like a king's ransom, prices drop dramatically in the off-season. If you share the cost among more than one couple or family, some of the rentals are quite affordable. On St. Barts and Montserrat, villas are cheaper and more attractive than many hotels.

Even if you don't plan to travel with a group, rental cottages and houses can still be affordable. Just keep in mind that you will probably need your own car (many villas are in remote settings far from beaches and grocery stores), and will have to do your own cooking (or at least, make your own coffee if you choose to eat out), and wash your own beach towels. In general, renting lower-priced properties requires a slightly adventurous and independent spirit. If you're the type that won't let less-than-perfect plumbing or faded furnishings interfere with your enjoyment of glorious sunsets and a secluded pool, this route may be your ticket to paradise. For a list of companies offering villa rentals throughout the Caribbean, *see* Apartment and Vila Rentals in Chapter 1, Essential Information. *See also* Lodging in island chapters for additional companies on specific islands.

Camping Ecological awareness has sparked a renewed interest in camping vacations, and even if you're not on a budget, it can be one of the most delightful ways to vacation in the Caribbean. However, camping is not an option on all islands. Many have no campgrounds or camp sites, and some forbid or discourage independent campers on beaches and protected forest areas. What camping exists comes in all stripes. At **Cinnamon Bay,** on St. John, U.S. Virgin Islands, you can get cabins, linens, and personal barbeque grills, or opt for simpler accommodations at lower rates. **Mojacasabe,** on Puerto Rico, has a pool and beach. Other islands have nothing more than sites where you can pitch a tent. For those who enjoy camping with a group, the **Sierra Club** (Outing Dept., 730 Polk St., San Francisco, CA 94109, tel. 415/776–2211) and **American Youth Hostels** (Box 37613, Washington, DC 20013–7613, tel. 202/783–6161) offer hiking, biking, and other tours that involve camping. A growing number of specialty tour operators combine camping with archaeological or ecological tourism. A good source of information on such companies is the advertising sections of Caribbean specialty magazines, such as *Caribbean Travel & Life,* or publications like *Outdoors*. *See also* Lodging in island chapters for campgrounds on specific islands.

Guest Houses and B&Bs Although this form of lodging is not as developed as in Europe or the United States, it does exist in the Caribbean—with wildly differing degrees of quality. Some properties may not meet your standards of comfort and hygiene, while others can be sparkling, well-run establishments—with the bonus of warmth and charm you find only in privately owned establishments. It's best to approach B&Bs and guest houses here with a flexible attitude about things like private baths and modern furnishings. Those who do are rewarded with accommodations that almost always cost less than all but the most bare-bones hotel rooms.

To investigate this option, start by looking at advertising sections in reputable travel monthlies or major newspapers (the Sunday *New York Times* travel section, for instance, features weekly listings). Note that most B&Bs do not accept credit cards; ask when you book and make your initial deposit. For more information about guest houses and B&Bs on a particular island, *see* Lodging in each island chapter.

Special Deals

Smart travelers never pay the full rate for anything. They know that a little research will yield packages, limited offers, and all kinds of ways to save.

Doing Your Homework **Magazines** such as *Caribbean Travel & Life* and *Islands* not only run in-depth articles on Caribbean destinations, but also have large advertising sections full of hotels, property rentals, and group and special-interest travel opportunities. In addition, general-interest travel magazines usually do at least one annual issue on Caribbean travel. There are also a number of Caribbean travel newsletters. Look for some of their advertisements in magazines, or check your local library.

Most national and regional **newspapers** carry regular travel sections, usually on Sunday. Check the ads for packages offered by chain agencies such as **Empress** and **Liberty** and airlines such as **American, United,** and **BWIA.** Larger newspapers have large sections of small ads; these include dozens of villa and condominium companies and smaller hotels, along with a few fairly sizable properties, such as Puerto Rico's **Palmas Del Mar.** Many of the rates are highly competitive, even during high season.

Travel Agents These can be the budget traveler's best friend when it comes to finding quality bargains. Agents have access to one or more airline computer booking systems that allow them to see a broad spectrum of flights and fares. Experienced agents also know which properties are offering special packages; which have changed management, policy, or price structures to your advantage or disadvantage; and who's actively looking for business during high and low seasons. They can also be more aggressive than most individual travelers when it comes to striking a hard bargain. A good agent is personally familiar with the destinations and type of travel you have in mind. However, the more specific information you can be about your budget, priorities, and preferences for lodging, meals, sports, and atmosphere, the more helpful an agent can be.

Packages Both airlines and hotel packages include accommodations. Airline packages also include airfare and may include car rental and other options. Hotel packages seldom include airfare but usually pile on extras like champagne breakfasts and free use of sports facilities. Either can mean significant savings over the same components purchased separately, but you must be prepared to use a calculator and compare costs: Sometimes making your own arrangements can be cheaper.

Airline packages frequently work with hotels at all price levels. You can usually have your pick of properties and room types, especially during low season. Airline packages also take care of airport transfers—which can be costly on some islands. For a list of airlines offering packages to the Caribbean, *see* Independent Packages in Chapter 1, Essential Information.

Hotel packages include the popular honeymoon variety, with extra pampering like breakfast in bed and complimentary cocktails on arrival. Some of the best include massages, sunset sailing trips, and even a free round of golf. These packages frequently incorporate a better class of rooms (and baths). Often the best time to book this type of deluxe package is during low season. Caribbean hotels also offer tennis, golf, diving, sailing, and other sports packages. For a list of hotel chains with properties in the Caribbean that offer packages, *see* Independent Packages in Chapter 1, Essential Information. In addition, individual properties throughout the book may be featuring package deals when you call to book; be sure to inquire.

Discount Flights Most major U.S. carriers have only limited flights to the region; thus cheap airfares are few and far between. Nevertheless, options such as airline packages, charter flights, and discount travel clubs do offer some hope. For information on researching **discount flights,** *see* Cutting Flight Costs in Chapter 1, Essential Information.

Money-Saving Tips

- Choose a less-expensive island. (*See* our Finding Your Place in the Sun chart.)
- Choose islands that offer activities such as hiking and snorkeling, rather than those catering primarily to golfers or tennis buffs.
- Take advantage of hotels that offer cheaper rates for garden-view, rather than ocean-view, rooms. Ask about other discounts at hotels when you call. Find out if a hotel is undergoing renovations, and ask for a rate reduction. At expensive properties, ask whether smaller rooms are available at a lower price, even if not advertised.
- If you are traveling with more than one couple or with a large family, consider renting a condominium or villa.
- Go camping.
- Research airline packages and hotel packages.
- If you are traveling with children, find out which hotels offer special programs and rates. In low season, try to negotiate a standard suite with sofabed or larger accommodation for the price of a regular room. Many such units come with their own wet bars, microwaves, and other cooking equipment.
- Check your frequent flier miles and combine this low airfare with a land-only package. Some flier programs have hotel and car rental discounts, too. Read all fine print to check restrictions.

Island Finder

	Cost of Island	Number of rooms	Nonstop flights	Cruise ship port	U.S. dollars accepted	Historic sites	Natural beauty	Lush	Arid	Mountainous	Rain forest	Beautiful beaches	Good roads
Anguilla	$$$	978			●				●			●	
Antigua & Barbuda	$$$$	3317	●	●	●	●	●		●		●	●	
Aruba	$$	6150	●	●	●		●		●			●	●
Barbados	$$	5580	●	●	●	●						●	●
Bonaire	$$	803	●		●								●
British Virgin Islands	$$$	1224		●	●	●	●	●	●	●	●	●	
Cayman Islands	$$$$	3453	●	●	●				●			●	●
Curaçao	$$	2200	●	●	●	●							●
Dominica	$	757					●	●		●	●		
Dominican Republic	$	28,000	●			●		●		●		●	
The Grenadines	$	500					●	●		●	●	●	
Grenada	$$$	1428		●	●	●	●	●		●	●	●	
Guadeloupe	$$	7798		●		●	●	●		●	●		●
Jamaica	$$$	18,935	●	●	●		●	●		●		●	●
Martinique	$$$	6960	●	●			●	●		●	●		●
Montserrat	$$	710		●	●		●	●		●	●		
Nevis	$$$	400			●	●	●	●		●		●	
Puerto Rico	$	8581	●	●	●	●	●	●	●	●	●	●	●
Saba	$	138			●		●			●			●
St. Barthélemy	$$$$	715		●	●		●			●		●	●
St. Eustatius	$	83			●	●				●	●		
St. Kitts	$$	1200			●		●	●		●	●	●	●
St. Lucia	$$	2919	●	●	●		●	●		●	●		
St. Martin/St. Maarten	$$$	5300	●	●	●			●		●		●	●
St. Vincent	$$	730			●	●	●	●		●	●		
Trinidad	$	1600	●								●		
Tobago	$$	1100	●						●		●	●	
Turks and Caicos	$$$	1139	●		●				●			●	
U.S. Virgin Islands:													
St. Croix	$$	1142		●	●	●		●		●			●
St. John	$$	763		●	●		●	●		●		●	●
St. Thomas	$$	3217	●	●	●					●		●	●

Public transportation	Fine dining	Local cuisine	Shopping	Music	Casinos	Nightlife	Diving and Snorkeling	Sailing	Golfing	Hiking	Ecotourism	Villa rentals	All-inclusives	Campgrounds	Luxury resorts	Secluded getaway	Good for families	Romantic hideaway
	●	●	●	●			●					●	●		●	●		●
●	●	●	●		●	●	●	●	●				●		●		●	
●	●	●	●	●	●	●	●	●	●	●			●		●		●	●
●	●	●	●	●		●	●		●	●		●	●		●		●	
					●		●	●		●	●				●			
●	●	●	●	●		●	●	●		●	●	●	●	●	●	●	●	●
	●		●			●	●		●		●	●	●		●		●	
●	●	●	●		●	●	●	●		●							●	
		●								●	●					●		●
●		●			●	●	●		●	●		●	●		●		●	
●		●					●	●		●	●	●	●		●	●	●	●
	●	●	●	●		●	●	●	●	●		●	●		●	●	●	●
●	●	●	●		●	●	●	●		●	●	●		●		●		
●	●	●	●	●		●	●	●	●	●	●	●	●	●	●		●	●
●	●	●	●	●	●	●	●	●	●	●		●		●				
●	●	●					●	●	●	●	●	●				●	●	
	●	●		●			●	●	●	●					●	●		●
●	●	●	●	●	●	●	●	●	●	●	●	●		●	●	●	●	●
		●					●			●	●	●			●	●		●
	●	●	●			●	●	●				●			●	●		●
		●					●			●	●					●		
	●	●	●	●	●	●	●	●	●	●			●		●	●	●	●
●	●	●	●	●		●	●	●	●	●		●	●		●	●	●	●
●	●	●	●		●	●	●	●	●			●	●		●		●	●
●		●		●			●	●		●	●				●	●	●	●
●		●		●		●	●		●						●		●	
		●		●		●	●		●							●		
							●	●	●	●	●		●		●	●		●
●	●	●	●			●	●		●	●	●				●			
	●	●					●			●	●	●		●	●	●	●	●
●	●	●	●			●	●	●	●			●	●		●			

- Use a travel agent to help you find the best deals, including lesser-known or new properties with introductory rates.
- It's not uncommon for associations, such as university alumnae groups, to offer discounted airline tickets to members; check with yours.
- If you're not participating in a meal plan at your hotel, eat your main meal at lunch and go light on dinner. Check out local cafés; on larger islands, save at chain restaurants such as Pizza Hut. Or, at midday, consider a picnic or lunch at a roti stand or other casual spot.
- If your room has a kitchen, buy local produce and cook at least one dinner.
- In bars, stick with the local rum punch and avoid imported wines, liquors, soft drinks, or juices. Better yet, buy your rum and mixers at a convenience store and make your own.
- Rent a moped instead of a car on islands that have suitable roads. (Be sure to rent helmets, too.)
- Take minivans instead of private cabs on the islands that have them.
- Compare the cost of guided island tours with that of a rental car for a day. Prices are comparable on some islands. On many, car rental is less. Surprisingly, on some islands a guided tour—especially on a smaller island that takes only half a day to see—is less.
- Bring your own snorkeling gear, tennis racket and balls, and other portable sports equipment.
- Shop wisely. Look only for legitimate bargains or unique finds like spices at local markets. Bargains on luxury items like cameras and jewelry *can* be found at duty-free ports, but you'll need to do your homework before your trip: Check stateside prices on items you intend to buy before you leave home. Put all purchases on a credit card—if there's a dispute later, the card company can help.
- Make local phone calls from a pay phone. For long-distance calls, make sure your hotel allows you to use your discount calling card.
- Choose local nightlife, such as a steel band at a small bar, over a hotel casino or cabaret show.
- Think off-season.
- Remember that you're on vacation. This is a time to cut your costs, but not your losses. It's no bargain if you can't relax and have fun, too.

1 Essential Information

Important Contacts

No single travel resource can give you every detail about every topic that might interest or concern you at the various stages of your journey—when you're planning your trip, while you're on the road, and after you get back home. The following organizations, books, and brochures will supplement the information in *Fodor's Affordable Caribbean*. For related information, including both basic tips on visiting the Caribbean and background information on many of the topics below, study Smart Traveling A to Z, the section that follows Important Contacts A to Z.

Air Travel

For information on airports and major airlines serving the Caribbean from the U.S., see individual island chapters.

For inexpensive, no-frills flights, contact **Carnival Air Lines** (tel. 800/824–7386), which serves the Caicos, Nassau, and Puerto Rico, and **Kiwi International** (tel. 800/538–5494), based in Newark and New York, serving San Juan.

From the U.K. **British Airways** (tel. 0345/222–747 or 0345/222–111) and **British West Indian Airways** (tel. 0171/839–9333) offer direct flights from London to the Caribbean.

Complaints To register complaints about charter and scheduled airlines, contact the U.S. Department of Transportation's **Office of Consumer Affairs** (400 7th St. NW, Washington, DC 20590, tel. 202/366–2220 or 800/322–7873).

Publications For general information about charter carriers, ask for the Office of Consumer Affairs' brochure **"Plane Talk: Public Charter Flights."** The Department of Transportation also publishes a 58-page booklet, **"Fly Rights"** ($1.75; Consumer Information Center, Dept. 133-B, Pueblo, CO 81009).

For other tips and hints, consult the Consumers Union's monthly **"Consumer Reports Travel Letter"** ($39 a year; Box 53629, Boulder CO 80322, tel. 800/234–1970) and the newsletter **"Travel Smart"** ($37 a year; 40 Beechdale Rd., Dobbs Ferry, NY 10522, tel. 800/327–3633); ***The Official Frequent Flyer Guidebook,*** by Randy Petersen ($14.99 plus $3 shipping; 4715-C Town Center Dr., Colorado Springs, CO 80916, tel. 719/597–8899 or 800/487–8893); ***Airfare Secrets Exposed,*** by Sharon Tyler and Matthew Wonder (Universal Information Publishing; $16.95 plus $3.75 shipping from Sandcastle Publishing, Box 3070-A, South Pasadena, CA 91031, tel. 213/255–3616 or 800/655–0053); and ***202 Tips Even the Best Business Travelers May Not Know,*** by Christopher McGinnis ($10 plus $3 shipping; Irwin Professional Publishing, Box 52927, Atlanta, GA 30355, tel. 708/789–4000 or 800/634–3966).

Better Business Bureau

For local contacts in the home town of a tour operator you may be considering, consult the **Council of Better Business Bureaus** (4200 Wilson Blvd., Arlington, VA 22203, tel. 703/276–0100).

Boat Travel

For a list of suggested boat charter companies, *see* Tour Operators, *below*.

Car Rental

For information on car rental agencies and costs in the Caribbean, see individual island chapters.

Rental Wholesalers Contact the **Kemwel Group** (106 Calvert St., Harrison, NY 10528, tel. 914/835-5555 or 800/678-0678).

Children and Travel

Flying Look into **"Flying with Baby"** ($5.95 plus $1 shipping; Third Street Press, Box 261250, Littleton, CO 80126, tel. 303/595-5959), cowritten by a flight attendant. **"Kids and Teens in Flight,"** free from the U.S. Department of Transportation's Office of Consumer Affairs, offers tips for children flying alone. Every two years the February issue of ***Family Travel Times*** (*see* Know-how, *below*) details children's services on three dozen airlines.

Know-how ***Family Travel Times,*** published 10 times a year by Travel with Your Children (TWYCH, 45 W. 18th St., New York, NY 10011, tel. 212/206-0688; annual subscription $55), covers destinations, types of vacations, and modes of travel.

The ***Family Travel Guides*** catalogue ($1 postage; tel. 510/527-5849) lists about 200 books and articles on family travel. ***Traveling with Children—And Enjoying It,*** by Arlene K. Butler ($11.95 plus $3 shipping; Globe Pequot Press, Box 833, 6 Business Park Rd., Old Saybrook, CT 06475, tel. 203/395-0440, 800/962-0973 in CT, or 800/243-0495) helps plan your trip with children, from toddlers to teens. Also check ***Take Your Baby and Go! A Guide for Traveling with Babies, Toddlers and Young Children,*** by Sheri Andrews, Judy Bordeaux, and Vivian Vasquez ($5.95 plus $1.50 shipping; Bear Creek Publications, 2507 Minor Ave., Seattle, WA 98102, tel. 206/322-7604 or 800/326-6566). Also from Globe Pequot are ***Recommended Family Resorts in the United States, Canada, and the Caribbean,*** by Jane Wilford with Janet Tice ($12.95), and ***Recommended Family Inns of America*** ($12.95). Travel with Your Children (*see above*) also publishes ***Cruising with Children*** ($22).

Lodging Hotels and resorts that offer special programs for children include:

In Aruba, the **Aruba Sonesta Hotel, Beach Club & Casino** (tel. 800/766-3782); in Puerto Rico, the **Hyatt Regency Cerromar Beach** and the **Hyatt Dorado Beach** (tel. 800/233-1234), and the **El San Juan** (tel. 800/468-2818); in Jamaica, **SuperClubs Boscobel Beach** (tel. 800/858-8009); in St. Thomas in the U.S. Virgin Islands, the **Stouffer Grand Beach Resort** (tel. 809/775-1510); in Nevis, **Four Seasons** (tel. 800/332-3442); and **Club Med** (tel. 800/258-2633) in the Dominican Republic and St. Lucia.

Tour Operators Contact **Rascals in Paradise** (650 5th St., Suite 505, San Francisco, CA 94107, tel. 415/978-9800 or 800/872-7225).

If you're outdoorsy, look into **Ecology Tours** (c/o the Audubon Center of the North Woods, Box 530, Sandstone, MN 55072, tel. 612/245-2648), which mix travel and nature study, and the **American Museum of Natural History** (79th St. and Central Park W., New York, NY 10024, tel. 212/769-5700 or 800/462-8687).

Cruising

To find out which ships are sailing where and when they depart, contact the **Caribbean Tourism Organization** (20 E. 46th St., 4th floor, New York, NY 10017, tel. 212/682-0435). The **Cruise Lines International Association** (CLIA) publishes a useful pamphlet entitled "Cruising Answers to Your Questions"; to order a copy, send a self-addressed business-size envelope with 55¢ postage to CLIA (500 5th Ave., Suite 1407, New York, NY 10110).

Customs

U.S. Citizens The **U.S. Customs Service** (Box 7407, Washington, DC 20044, tel. 202/927–6724) can answer questions on duty-free limits and publishes a helpful brochure, "Know Before You Go." For information on registering foreign-made articles, call 202/927–0540.

Canadians Contact **Revenue Canada** (2265 St. Laurent Blvd. S, Ottawa, Ontario, K1G 4K3, tel. 613/993–0534) for a copy of the free brochure **"I Declare/Je Déclare"** and for details on duties that exceed the standard duty-free limit.

U.K. Citizens **HM Customs and Excise** (Dorset House, Stamford St., London SE1 9NG, tel. 0171/202–4227) can answer questions about U.K. customs regulations and publishes **"A Guide for Travellers."**

For Travelers with Disabilities

Complaints To register complaints under the provisions of the Americans with Disabilities Act, contact the U.S. Department of Justice's **Public Access Section** (Box 66738, Washington, D.C. 20035, tel. 202/514–0301, TDD 202/514–0383, fax 202/307–1198).

Lodging **Divi Hotels** (tel. 800/367–3484), which has six properties in the Caribbean, runs one of the best dive programs for the disabled at its resort in **Bonaire.** The facility is equipped with ramps; guest rooms and bathrooms can accommodate wheelchairs; and the staff is specially trained to assist divers with disabilities.

Organizations *For Travelers with Hearing Impairments* Travelers with hearing impairments should contact the **American Academy of Otolaryngology** (1 Prince St., Alexandria, VA 22314, tel. 703/836–4444, fax 703/683–5100, TTY 703/519–1585). The academy can give advice on travel.

For Travelers with Mobility Problems Contact the **Information Center for Individuals with Disabilities** (Fort Point Pl., 27–43 Wormwood St., Boston, MA 02210, tel. 617/727–5540, 800/462–5015 in MA, TTY 617/345–9743); **Mobility International USA** (Box 10767, Eugene, OR 97440, tel. and TTY 503/343–1284, fax 503/343–6812), the U.S. branch of an international organization based in Belgium (*see below*) that has affiliates in 30 countries; **MossRehab Hospital Travel Information Service** (1200 W. Tabor Rd., Philadelphia, PA 19141, tel. 215/456–9603, TTY 215/456–9602); the **Society for the Advancement of Travel for the Handicapped** (347 5th Ave., Suite 610, New York, NY 10016, tel. 212/447–7284, fax 212/725–8253); the **Travel Industry and Disabled Exchange** (TIDE, 5435 Donna Ave., Tarzana, CA 91356, tel. 818/344–3640, fax 818/344–0078); and **Travelin' Talk** (Box 3534, Clarksville, TN 37043, tel. 615/552–6670, fax 615/552–1182).

For Travelers with Vision Impairments Contact the **American Council of the Blind** (1155 15th St. NW, Suite 720, Washington, DC 20005, tel. 202/467–5081, fax 202/467–5085) or the **American Foundation for the Blind** (15 W. 16th St., New York, NY 10011, tel. 212/620–2000, TTY 212/620–2158).

In the United Kingdom, contact the **Royal Association for Disability and Rehabilitation** (RADAR, 12 City Forum, 250 City Rd., London EC1V 8AF, tel. 0171/250–3222) or **Mobility International** (Rue de Manchester 25, B1070 Brussels, Belgium, tel. 00–322–410–6297), a clearinghouse of travel information for people with disabilities.

Publications Several free publications are available from the U.S. Information Center (Box 100, Pueblo, CO 81009, tel. 719/948–3334): **"New Horizons for the Air Traveler with a Disability"** (address to Dept. 355A), describing legally mandated changes; the pocket-size **"Fly Smart"**

(Dept. 575B), good on flight safety; and the Airport Operators Council's worldwide **"Access Travel: Airports"** (Dept. 575A).

The 500-page ***Travelin' Talk Directory*** ($35; tel. 615/552–6670) lists people and organizations who help travelers with disabilities. For specialist travel agents worldwide, consult the ***Directory of Travel Agencies for the Disabled*** ($19.95 plus $2 shipping; Twin Peaks Press, Box 129, Vancouver, WA 98666, tel. 206/694–2462 or 800/637–2256).

Travel Agencies and Tour Operators The Americans with Disabilities Act requires that travel firms serve the needs of all travelers. However, some agencies and operators specialize in making group and individual arrangements for travelers with disabilities, among them **Access Adventures** (206 Chestnut Ridge Rd., Rochester, NY 14624, tel. 716/889–9096), run by a former physical-rehab counselor; **Travel Trends** (2 Allan Plaza, 4922–51 Ave., Box 3581, Leduc, Alberta T9E 6X2, tel. 403/986–9000), which has group tours and is especially good for cruises; **Tomorrow's Level of Care** (Box 470299, Brooklyn, NY 11247, tel. 718/756–0794 or 800/932–2012), which offers nursing services and medical equipment. In addition, many of the operators and agencies listed below (*see* Tour Operators) can also arrange vacations for travelers with disabilities.

For Travelers with Hearing Impairments One agency is **International Express** (7319-B Baltimore Ave., College Park, MD 20740, tel. TDD 301/699–8836, fax 301/699–8836), which arranges group and independent trips.

For Travelers with Mobility Impairments A number of operators specialize in working with travelers with mobility impairments: **Accessible Journeys** (35 W. Sellers Ave., Ridley Park, PA 19078, tel. 610/521–0339 or 800/846–4537, fax 610/521–6959), a registered nursing service that arranges vacations; **Hinsdale Travel Service** (201 E. Ogden Ave., Suite 100, Hinsdale, IL 60521, tel. 708/325–1335 or 800/303–5521), a travel agency that will give you access to the services of wheelchair traveler Janice Perkins; and **Wheelchair Journeys** (16979 Redmond Way, Redmond, WA 98052, tel.206/885–2210), which can handle arrangements worldwide.

For Travelers with Developmental Disabilities Contact the nonprofit **New Directions** (5276 Hollister Ave., Suite 207, Santa Barbara, CA 93111, tel. 805/967–2841), for travelers with developmental disabilities and their families as well as the general-interest operations above.

Discount Clubs

Options include **Entertainment Travel Editions** (fee $25–$48, depending on destination; Box 1068, Trumbull, CT 06611, tel. 800/445–4137); **Great American Traveler** ($49.95 annually; Box 27965, Salt Lake City, UT 84127, tel. 800/548–2812); **Moment's Notice Discount Travel Club** ($25 annually, single or family; 425 Madison Ave., New York, NY 10017, tel. 212/486–0503); **Privilege Card** ($74.95 annually; 3391 Peachtree Rd. NE, Suite 110, Atlanta GA 30326, tel. 404/262–0222 or 800/236–9732); **Travelers Advantage** ($49 annually, single or family; CUC Travel Service, 49 Music Sq. W, Nashville, TN 37203, tel. 800/548–1116 or 800/648–4037); and **Worldwide Discount Travel Club** ($50 annually for family, $40 single; 1674 Meridian Ave., Miami Beach, FL 33139, tel. 305/534–2082).

Electricity

Send a self-addressed, stamped envelope to the **Franzus Company** (Customer Service, Dept. B50, Murtha Industrial Park, Box 142, Beacon Falls, CT 06403, tel. 203/723–6664) for a copy of the free brochure "Foreign Electricity Is No Deep Dark Secret."

Gay and Lesbian Travel

Organizations The **International Gay Travel Association** (Box 4974, Key West, FL 33041, tel. 800/448–8550), a consortium of 800 businesses, can supply names of travel agents and tour operators.

Publications The premier international travel magazine for gays and lesbians is **Our World** ($35 for 10 issues; 1104 N. Nova Rd., Suite 251, Daytona Beach, FL 32117, tel. 904/441–5367). The 16-page monthly "Out & About" ($49 for 10 issues; tel. 203/789–8518 or 800/929–2268) covers gay-friendly resorts, hotels, cruise lines, and airlines.

Tour Operators Cruises and resort vacations are handled by **R.S.V.P. Travel Productions** (2800 University Ave. SE, Minneapolis, MN 55414, tel. 800/328–RSVP) for gays, **Olivia** (4400 Market St., Oakland, CA 94608, tel. 800/631–6277) for lesbian travelers. For mixed gay and lesbian travel, contact **Atlantis Events** (8335 Sunset Blvd., West Hollywood, CA 90069, tel. 800/628–5268). **Toto Tours** (1326 W. Albion Suite 3W, Chicago, IL 60626, tel. 312/274–8686 or 800/565–1241) has group tours worldwide.

Travel Agencies The largest agencies serving gay travelers are **Advance Travel** (10700 Northwest Freeway, Suite 160, Houston, TX 77092, tel. 713/682–2002 or 800/695–0880); **Islanders/Kennedy Travel** (183 W. 10th St., New York, NY 10014, tel. 212/242–3222 or 800/988–1181); **Now Voyager** (4406 18th St., San Francisco, CA 94114, tel. 415/626–1169 or 800/255–6951); and **Yellowbrick Road** (1500 W. Balmoral Ave., Chicago, IL 60640, tel. 312/561–1800 or 800/642–2488). **Skylink Women's Travel** (746 Ashland Ave., Santa Monica, CA 90405, tel. 310/452–0506 or 800/225–5759) works with lesbians.

Health Issues

Finding a Doctor For members, the **International Association for Medical Assistance to Travellers** (IAMAT, 417 Center St., Lewiston, NY 14092, tel. 716/754–4883; 40 Regal Rd., Guelph, Ontario N1K 1B5, tel. 519/836–0102; 1287 St. Clair Ave., Toronto, Ontario M6E 1B8, tel. 416/652–0137; 57 Voirets, 1212 Grand-Lancy, Geneva, Switzerland; membership free) publishes a worldwide directory of English-speaking physicians meeting IAMAT standards.

Medical-Assistance Companies Contact **International SOS Assistance** (Box 11568, Philadelphia, PA 19116, tel. 215/244–1500 or 800/523–8930; Box 466, Pl. Bonaventure, Montréal, Québec H5A 1C1, tel. 514/874–7674 or 800/363–0263); **Medex Assistance Corporation** (Box 10623, Baltimore, MD 21285, tel. 410/296–2530 or 800/573–2029); **Near Services** (Box 1339, Calumet City, IL 60409, tel. 708/868–6700 or 800/654–6700); and **Travel Assistance International** (1133 15th St. NW, Suite 400, Washington, DC 20005, tel. 202/331–1609 or 800/821–2828). Because these companies also sell death-and-dismemberment, trip-cancellation, and other insurance coverage, there is some overlap with the travel-insurance policies sold by the companies listed under Insurance, *below.*

Insurance

Travel insurance covering baggage, health, and trip cancellation or interruptions is available from **Access America** (Box 90315, Richmond, VA 23286, tel. 804/285–3300 or 800/284–8300); **Carefree Travel Insurance** (Box 9366, 100 Garden City Plaza, Garden City, NY 11530, tel. 516/294–0220 or 800/323–3149); **Near Services** (Box 1339, Calumet City, IL 60409, tel. 708/868–6700 or 800/654–6700); **Tele-Trip** (Mutual of Omaha Plaza, Box 31716, Omaha, NE 68131, tel. 800/228–9792); **Travel Guard International** (1145 Clark St., Stevens Point, WI 54481, tel. 715/345–0505 or 800/826–1300); **Travel Insured International** (Box 280568, East Hartford, CT 06128-0568, tel. 203/

528–7663 or 800/243–3174); and **Wallach & Company** (107 W. Federal St., Box 480, Middleburg, VA 22117, tel. 703/687–3166 or 800/237–6615).

In the U.K. The **Association of British Insurers** (51 Gresham St., London EC2V 7HQ, tel. 0171/600–3333; 30 Gordon St., Glasgow G1 3PU, tel. 0141/226–3905; Scottish Provident Bldg., Donegall Sq. W, Belfast BT1 6JE, tel. 01232/249176; and other locations) gives advice by phone and publishes the free **"Holiday Insurance,"** which sets out typical policy provisions and costs.

Lodging

Apartment and Villa Rental Among the companies to contact are **At Home Abroad** (405 E. 56th St., Suite 6H, New York, NY 10022, tel. 212/421–9165); **Europa-Let** (92 N. Main St., Ashland, OR 97520, tel. 503/482–5806 or 800/462–4486); **Property Rentals International** (1008 Mansfield Crossing Rd., Richmond, VA 23236, tel. 804/378–6054 or 800/220–3332); **Rent-a-Home International** (7200 34th Ave. NW, Seattle, WA 98117, tel. 206/789–9377 or 800/488–7368); **Unusual Villas & Island Rentals** (101 Tempsford La., Penthouse 9, Richmond, VA 23226, tel. 800/768–0280); **Vacation Home Rentals Worldwide** (235 Kensington Ave., Norwood, NJ 07648, tel. 201/767–9393 or 800/633–3284); **Villas and Apartments Abroad** (420 Madison Ave., Suite 1105, New York, NY 10017, tel. 212/759–1025 or 800/433–3020); and **Villas International** (605 Market St., Suite 510, San Francisco, CA 94105, tel. 415/281–0910 or 800/221–2260). Members of the travel club **Hideaways International** ($99 annually; 767 Islington St., Portsmouth, NH 03801, tel. 603/430–4433 or 800/843–4433) receive two annual guides plus quarterly newsletters and arrange rentals among themselves.

Home Exchange Principal clearinghouses include **HomeLink International/Vacation Exchange Club** ($60 annually; Box 650, Key West, FL 33041, tel. 305/294–1448 or 800/638–3841), which gives members four annual directories, with a listing in one, plus updates; and **Loan-a-Home** ($35–$45 annually; 2 Park La., Apt. 6E, Mount Vernon, NY 10552-3443, tel. 914/664–7640), which specializes in long-term exchanges.

Money Matters

ATMs For specific foreign **Cirrus** locations, call 800/424–7787; for foreign Plus locations, consult the **Plus** directory at your local bank.

Currency Exchange If your bank doesn't exchange currency, contact **Thomas Cook Currency Services** (41 E. 42nd St., New York, NY 10017, or 511 Madison Ave., New York, NY 10022, tel. 212/757–6915 or 800/223–7373 for locations) or **Ruesch International** (tel. 800/424–2923 for locations).

Wiring Funds Funds can be wired via **American Express MoneyGram**℠ (tel. 800/926–9400 from the U.S. and Canada for locations and information) or **Western Union** (tel. 800/325–6000 for agent locations or to send using MasterCard or Visa, 800/321–2923 in Canada).

Passports and Visas

U.S. Citizens For fees, documentation requirements, and other information, call the **Office of Passport Services** information line (tel. 202/647–0518).

Canadians For fees, documentation requirements, and other information, call the Ministry of Foreign Affairs and International Trade's **Passport Office** (tel. 819/994–3500 or 800/567–6868).

U.K. Citizens For fees, documentation requirements, and to get an emergency passport, call the **London Passport Office** (tel. 0171/271–3000).

Phone Matters

For local access numbers abroad, contact **AT&T** USA Direct (tel. 800/874–4000), **MCI** Call USA (tel. 800/444–4444), or **Sprint** Express (tel. 800/793–1153).

Photo Help

The **Kodak Information Center** (tel. 800/242–2424) answers consumer questions about film and photography.

Senior Citizens

Educational Travel The nonprofit **Elderhostel** (75 Federal St., 3rd Floor, Boston, MA 02110, tel. 617/426–7788), for people 60 and older, has offered inexpensive study programs since 1975. The nearly 2,000 courses cover everything from marine science to Greek myths and cowboy poetry. Fees for two- to three-week international trips—including room, board, and transportation from the United States—range from $1,800 to $4,500.

Organizations Contact the **American Association of Retired Persons** (AARP, 601 E St. NW, Washington, DC 20049, tel. 202/434–2277; $8 per person or couple annually). Its Purchase Privilege Program gets members discounts on lodging, car rentals, and sightseeing, and the AARP Motoring Plan furnishes domestic trip-routing information and emergency road-service aid for an annual fee of $39.95 per person or couple ($59.95 for a premium version). AARP also arranges group tours and cruises through AARP Travel Experience from American Express (400 Pinnacle Way, Suite 450, Norcross, GA 30071, tel. 800/927–0111 or 800/745–4567).

For other discounts on lodgings, car rentals, and other travel products, along with magazines and newsletters, contact the **National Council of Senior Citizens** (membership $12 annually; 1331 F St. NW, Washington, DC 20004, tel. 202/347–8800) and **Mature Outlook** (subscription $9.95 annually; 6001 N. Clark St., Chicago, IL 60660, tel. 312/465–6466 or 800/336–6330).

Publications ***The 50+ Traveler's Guidebook: Where to Go, Where to Stay, What to Do,*** by Anita Williams and Merrimac Dillon ($12.95; St. Martin's Press, 175 5th Ave., New York, NY 10010, tel. 212/674–5151 or 800/288–2131), offers many useful tips. **"The Mature Traveler"** ($29.95; Box 50820, Reno, NV 89513), a monthly newsletter, covers travel deals.

Students

I.D. Cards Get the **International Student Identity Card** (ISIC) if you're a bona fide student or the **International Youth Card** (IYC) if you're under 26. In the United States, the ISIC and IYC cards cost $16 each and include basic travel-accident and illness coverage, plus a toll-free travel hot line. Apply through the Council on International Educational Exchange (*see* Organizations, *below*). Cards are available for $15 each in Canada from **Travel Cuts** (187 College St., Toronto, Ontario M5T 1P7, tel. 416/979–2406 or 800/667–2887) and in the United Kingdom for £5 each at student unions and student travel companies.

Organizations A major contact is the **Council on International Educational Exchange** (CIEE, 205 E. 42nd St., 16th Floor, New York, NY 10017, tel. 212/661–1450) with locations in Boston (729 Boylston St., 02116, tel. 617/266–1926), Miami (9100 S. Dadeland Blvd., 33156, tel. 305/670–9261), Los Angeles (1093 Broxton Ave., 90024, tel. 310/208–3551), 43 other college towns nationwide, and the United Kingdom (28A Poland St., London W1V 3DB, tel. 0171/437–7767). Twice a year, it publishes *Student Travels* magazine. The CIEE's Council Travel Service offers domestic air passes for bargain travel within the United States and is the exclusive U.S. agent for several student-discount cards.

Campus Connections (325 Chestnut St., Suite 1101, Philadelphia, PA 19106, tel. 215/625–8585 or 800/428–3235) specializes in discounted accommodations and airfares for students. The **Educational Travel Centre** (438 N. Frances St., Madison, WI 53703, tel. 608/256–5551) offers rail passes and low-cost airline tickets, mostly for flights departing from Chicago.

In Canada, also contact **Travel Cuts** (*see above*).

Tour Operators

Among the companies selling packages to the Caribbean, the following have a proven reputation, are nationally known, and offer plenty of options.

Contact **American Airlines Fly AAway Vacations** (tel. 800/321–2121); **Delta Dream Vacations** (tel. 800/872–7786); **Domenico Tours** (750 Broadway, Bayonne, NJ 07002, tel. 201/823–8687 or 800/554–8687); and **Globetrotters** (139 Main St., Cambridge, MA 02142, tel. 800/999–9696 or 617/621–9911). **Gogo Tours,** based in Ramsey, New Jersey, sells packages only through travel agents. **Club Med** (tel. 800/258–2633) sells packages that include charter air to its family, couples, and singles resorts throughout the Caribbean.

For packages to Jamaica, Antigua, or the U.S. Virgin Islands, try **Continental Airlines' Grand Destinations** (tel. 800/634–5555). For packages to Puerto Rico or Grand Cayman, call **United Vacations** (tel. 800/328–6877). For a greater selection of properties in the Cayman Islands, try **Cayman Airtours** (tel. 800/247–2966).

Regional operators specialize in putting together packages for travelers from their local area. Arrangements may include charter or scheduled air. Contact **Apple Vacations** (25 Northwest Point Blvd., Elk Grove Village, IL 60007, tel. 708/640–1150 or 800/365–2775); **Friendly Holidays** (1983 Marcus Ave., Lake Success, NY 11042, tel. 516/338–1200 or 800/221–9748); **Travel Impressions** (465 Smith St., Farmingdale, NY 11735, tel. 516/845–7000 or 800/224–0022); and **Trans National Travel** (2 Charlesgate W., Boston, MA 02215, tel. 617/262–0123 or 800/262–0123).

From the U.K. Packages to the Caribbean are available from **Caribbean Connection** (Concorde House, Forest St., Chester CH1 1QR, tel. 0244/341131), with a 100-page catalogue devoted to Caribbean holidays; **Caribtours** (161 Fulham Rd., London SW3 6SN, tel. 0171/581–3517), another Caribbean specialist; **Kuoni Travel** (Kuoni House, Dorking, Surrey RH5 4AZ, tel. 0306/742222); and **Tradewinds Faraway Holidays** (Station House, 81/83 Fulham High St., London SW6 3JP, tel. 0171/731–8000).

Theme Trips

Adventure **All Adventure Travel** (5589 Arapahoe #208, Boulder, CO 80303, tel. 800/537–4025) can book biking, hiking, kayaking, diving, rafting, and many other adventures throughout the Caribbean. **American Wilderness Experience** (Box 1486, Boulder, CO 80306, tel. 303/444–0099 or 800/444–0099) and **Ocean Voyages** (1709 Bridgeway, Sausalito, CA 94965, tel. 415/332–4681) offer adventure cruises on motor yachts and catamarans for scuba divers, snorkelers, and kayakers.

Diving Leading dive packagers to the Caribbean include **Tropical Adventures** (111 2nd Ave., North Seattle, WA 98109, tel. 206/441–3483 or 800/247–3483) and **Go Diving** (5610 Rowland Rd. #100, Minnetonka, MN 55343, tel. 800/328–5285). For a dive vacation aboard a live-aboard boat, try **Sea & Sea Travel Service** (50 Francisco St. #205, San Francisco, CA 94133, tel. 415/434–3400 or 800/DIV–XPRT).

Golf Packages including accommodations, confirmed tee-times, greens fees, lessons, and sometimes airfare are offered by **GolfTrips** (Box 2314, Winter Haven, FL 33883-2314, tel. 813/324–1300 or 800/428–1940).

Health **Spa-Finders** (91 5th Ave., New York, NY 10003, tel. 800/ALL–SPAS) represents spas on many Caribbean islands.

Horseback Riding For individually customized packages to Jamaica, call **FITS Equestrian** (685 Lateen Rd., Solvang, CA 93463, tel. 805/688–9494 or 800/600–3487).

Learning Vacations **Earthwatch** (680 Mount Auburn St., Watertown, MA 02272, tel. 617/926–8200) recruits volunteers to serve in its EarthCorps as short-term assistants to scientists on research expeditions in an array of scientific fields. The **Smithsonian Institution's Study Tours and Seminars** (1100 Jefferson Dr. SW, Room 3045, Washington, DC 20560, tel. 202/357–4700) run natural-history cruises and scuba diving programs. Natural-history cruises are also available from the **National Audubon Society** (700 Broadway, New York, NY 10003, tel. 212/979–3066).

Singles **Grammercy's SingleWorld** (401 Theodore Fremd Ave., Rye, NY 10580, tel. 914/967–3334 or 800/223–6490) has cruises to the Caribbean on dozens of major cruise ships.

Yacht Charters For crewed or uncrewed charters, try **Lynn Jachney Charters** (Box 302, Marblehead, MA 01945, tel. 617/639–0787 or 800/223–2050); **Huntley Yacht Vacations** (210 Preston Rd., Wernersville, PA 19565, tel. 610/678–2628 or 800/322–9224); **The Moorings** (19345 US HWY 19 North, 4th floor, Clearwater, FL 34624, tel. 813/538–8760 or 800/437–7880); **Russell Yacht Charters** (404 Hulls Hwy., Suite 175, Southport, CT 06490, tel. 203/255–2783 or 800/635–8895); and **Sail Away** (15605 S.W. 92 Ave., Miami, FL 33157, tel. 305/253–SAIL or 800/SAILAWAY).

Organizations The **National Tour Association** (546 E. Main St., Lexington, KY 40508, tel. 606/226–4444 or 800/682–8886) and **United States Tour Operators Association** (USTOA, 211 E. 51st St., Suite 12B, New York, NY 10022, tel. 212/750–7371) can provide lists of member operators and information on booking tours.

Publications Consult the brochure **"Worldwide Tour & Vacation Package Finder"** from the National Tour Association (*see above*) and the Better Business Bureau's **"Tips on Travel Packages"** (publication No. 24-195, $2; 4200 Wilson Blvd., Arlington, VA 22203).

Travel Agencies

For names of reputable agencies in your area, contact the **American Society of Travel Agents** (1101 King St., Suite 200, Alexandria, VA 22314, tel. 703/739–2782).

Visitor Information

Almost all islands have a U.S.–based tourist board, listed with its name and address under Important Addresses in the individual island chapters that follow; they're good sources of general information, up-to-date calendars of events, and listings of hotels, restaurants, sights, and shops. The **Caribbean Tourism Organization** (20 E. 46th St., New York, NY 10017–2452, tel. 212/682–0435 in the U.S.; Vigilant House, 120 Wilton Rd., London SW1V 1JZ, tel. 0171/233–8382 in the U.K.) is another good resource.

U.S. Government Travel Briefings

The U.S. Department of State's Overseas Citizens Emergency Center (Room 4811, Washington, DC 20520; enclose SASE) issues **Consular Information Sheets,** which cover crime, security, political climate, and health risks as well as embassy locations, entry requirements, currency regulations, and other routine matters. For the latest information, stop in at any U.S. passport office, consulate, or embassy; call the interactive hot line (tel. 202/647–5225, fax 202/647–3000); or, with your PC's modem, tap into the Bureau of Consular Affairs' computer bulletin board (tel. 202/647–9225).

Weather

For current conditions and forecasts, plus the local time and helpful travel tips, call the **Weather Channel Connection** (tel. 900/932–8437; 95¢ per minute) from a touch-tone phone.

Smart Travel Tips

The more you travel, the more you know about how to make trips run like clockwork. To help make your travels hassle-free, Fodor's editors have rounded up dozens of tips from our contributors and travel experts all over the world, as well as basic information on visiting the Caribbean. For names of organizations to contact and publications that can give you more information, *see* Important Contacts A to Z, *above.*

Air Travel

If time is an issue, **always look for nonstop flights,** which require no change of plane. If possible, **avoid connecting flights,** which stop at least once and can involve a change of plane, although the flight number remains the same; if the first leg is late, the second waits.

Cutting Costs The Sunday travel section of most newspapers is a good source of deals.

Major Airlines The least-expensive airfares from the major airlines are priced for round-trip travel and are subject to restrictions. You must usually **book in advance and buy the ticket within 24 hours** to get cheaper fares, and you may have to **stay over a Saturday night.** The lowest fare is subject to availability, and only a small percentage of the plane's total seats are sold at that price. It's good to **call a number of airlines, and when you are quoted a good price, book it on the spot**—the same fare on the same flight may not be available the next day. Airlines generally allow you to change your return date for a $25–$50 fee, but most low-fare tickets are nonrefundable. However, if you don't use it, you can apply the cost toward the purchase price of a new ticket, again for a small charge.

Consolidators Consolidators, who buy tickets at reduced rates from scheduled airlines, sell them at prices below the lowest available from the airlines directly—usually without advance restrictions. Sometimes you can even get your money back if you need to return the ticket. Carefully read the fine print detailing penalties for changes and cancellations. If you doubt the reliability of a consolidator, **confirm your reservation with the airline.**

Charter Flights Charters usually have the lowest fares and the most restrictions. Departures are limited and seldom on time, and you can lose all or most of your money if you cancel. (The closer to departure you cancel, the more you lose, although sometimes you will be charged only a small fee if you supply a substitute passenger.) The flight may be canceled for any reason up to 10 days before departure (after that, only if it is physically impossible to operate). The charterer may also revise the itinerary or increase the price after you have bought the ticket, but only if the new arrangement constitutes a "major change" do you have the right to a refund. Before buying a charter ticket, **read the fine print** about the company's refund policies. Money for charter flights is usually paid into a bank escrow account, the name of which should be on the contract, and if you don't pay by credit card, **make your check payable to the carrier's escrow account** (unless you're dealing with a travel agent, in which case, his or her check should be payable to the escrow account). The U.S. Department of Transportation's Office of Consumer Affairs has jurisdiction.

Charter operators may offer flights alone or with ground arrangements that constitute a charter package. You typically must book charters through your travel agent.

Aloft

Airline Food If you hate airline food, **ask for special meals when booking.** These can be vegetarian, low-cholesterol, or kosher, for example; commonly prepared to order in smaller quantities than standard catered fare, they can be tastier.

Smoking Smoking is banned on all flights within the U.S. of less than six hours' duration and on all Canadian flights; the ban also applies to domestic segments of international flights aboard U.S. and foreign carriers. Delta has banned smoking system-wide. On U.S. carriers flying to destinations in the Caribbean, a seat in a no-smoking section must be provided for every passenger who requests one, and the section must be enlarged to accommodate such passengers if necessary as long as they have complied with the airline's deadline for check-in and seat assignment. If smoking bothers you, request a seat far from the smoking section.

Foreign airlines are exempt from these rules but do provide no-smoking sections. British Airways has banned smoking; some nations have banned smoking on all domestic flights, and others may ban smoking on some flights. Talks continue on the feasibility of broadening no-smoking policies.

Boat Travel

If you are an experienced sailor, **consider a bare-boat charter**; this can be an affordable and fun way to see the Caribbean, particularly during the off-season. Indeed, off-season prices for even crewed charters can fit your budget when the cost is divided among several couples. As always, be sure to find out exactly what is included in the price. To find the boat that matches your needs and budget, **consult an established charter broker** (*see* Tour Operators *in* Important Contacts A to Z, *above*).

Bus Travel

Although public transportation is practically nonexistent in much of the Caribbean, you can find reliable bus systems on some of the larger islands, such as Barbados. Most are not recommended for touring an island, but you can **use local buses for short trips** where they are available. In general, traveling by public transportation requires a more flexible attitude and a willingness to endure erratic schedules and crowded, sometimes dilapidated vehicles. For local color, however, it can't be beat.

Cameras, Camcorders, and Computers

Laptops Before you depart, **check your portable computer's battery,** because you may be asked at security to turn on the computer to prove that it is what it appears to be. At the airport, you may prefer to **request a manual inspection,** although security X-rays do not harm hard-disk or floppy-disk storage. Also, **register your foreign-made laptop with U.S. Customs.** If your laptop is U.S.-made, call the consulate of the country you'll be visiting to find out whether or not it should be registered with local customs upon arrival. You may want to **find out about repair facilities at your destination** in case you need them.

Photography If your camera is new or if you haven't used it for a while, **shoot and develop a few rolls of film** before you leave. Always **store film in a cool, dry place**—never in the car's glove compartment or on the shelf under the rear window.

Every pass of your film through an X-ray machine increases the chance of clouding. To protect it, carry it in a clear plastic bag and **ask for hand inspection at security.** Such requests are virtually always honored at U.S. airports, and usually are accommodated abroad. Don't depend on a lead-lined bag to protect film in checked luggage—the airline may increase the radiation to see what's inside.

Video Before your trip, **test your camcorder, invest in a skylight filter to protect the lens, and charge the batteries.** (Airport security personnel may ask you to turn on the camcorder to prove that it's what it appears to be). The batteries of most newer camcorders can be recharged with a universal or worldwide AC adapter charger (or multivoltage converter), usable whether the voltage is 110 or 220. All that's needed is the appropriate plug.

Videotape is not damaged by X-rays, but it may be harmed by the magnetic field of a walk-through metal detector, so **ask that videotapes be hand-checked.** Although most Caribbean islands operate on the National Television System Committee video standard (NTSC), used by the United States and Canada, Guadeloupe and Martinique use the Secam standard. On these islands, you will not be able to view your tapes through the local TV set or view movies bought there in your home VCR. Blank tapes bought in the Caribbean can be used for camcorder taping, but they are pricey. Some U.S. audiovisual shops convert foreign tapes to U.S. standards; contact an electronics dealer to find one near you.

Children and Travel

The Caribbean islands and their resorts are increasingly sensitive to the needs of families. Children's programs are part of all major new hotel developments. Baby food is easy to find, but except at major hotels you may not find such items as high chairs and cribs.

Baby-sitting For recommended local sitters, **check with your hotel desk.**

Driving If you are renting a car, **arrange for a car seat when you reserve.** Sometimes they're free.

Flying Always **ask about discounted children's fares.** On international flights, the fare for infants under age 2 not occupying a seat is generally either free or 10% of the accompanying adult's fare; children ages 2 through 11 usually pay half to two-thirds of the adult fare. On domestic flights, children under 2 not occupying a seat travel free, and older children currently travel on the lowest applicable adult fare. Some routes, including some in the Caribbean, are considered neither international nor domestic and have still other rules.

Baggage In general, the adult baggage allowance applies for children paying half or more of the adult fare. Before departure, **ask about carry-on allowances** if you are traveling with an infant. In general, those paying 10% of the adult fare are allowed one carry-on bag, not to exceed 70 pounds or 45 inches (length + width + height) and a collapsible stroller; you may be allowed less if the flight is full.

Safety Seats According to the FAA, it's a good idea to **use safety seats aloft.** Airline policy varies. U.S. carriers allow FAA-approved models, but airlines usually require that you buy a ticket, even if your child would otherwise ride free, because the seats must be strapped into regular passenger seats. Foreign carriers may not allow infant seats, may charge the child's rather than the infant's fare for their use, or may require you to hold your baby during takeoff and landing, thus defeating the seat's purpose.

Facilities When making your reservation, **ask for children's meals or a freestanding bassinet** if you need them; bassinets are available only to those with seats at the bulkhead, where there's enough legroom. If you don't need a bassinet, **think twice before requesting bulkhead seats**—the only storage for in-flight necessities is in the inconveniently distant overhead bins.

Lodging Most hotels allow children under a certain age to stay in their parents' room at no extra charge, while others charge them as extra adults; be sure to **ask about the cut-off age.**

Cruises

To get the best deal on a cruise, **consult a cruise-only travel agency.** Remember that brochure rates are just "list prices," so it pays to **shop around for the best deal** and **book early** to get an extra discount.

Customs and Duties

On Arrival Exact customs regulations vary slightly from island to island; see the individual country chapters for details.

Back Home
In the U.S. You may bring home $600 worth of foreign goods duty-free if you've been out of the country for at least 48 hours and haven't used the $600 exemption, or any part of it, in the past 30 days. This exemption, higher than the standard $400 allowance, applies to two dozen countries included in the Caribbean Basin Initiative. If you visit a CBI country and a non-CBI country, such as Martinique, you may still bring in $600 worth of goods duty-free, but no more than $400 can be from the non-CBI country. Travelers returning from the U.S. Virgin Islands are entitled to a $1,200 duty-free allowance. If your travel included the U.S.V.I. and another country—say, the Dominican Republic—the $1,200 allowance still applies, but at least $600 worth of goods must be from the U.S.V.I.

Travelers 21 or older may bring back one liter of alcohol duty-free, provided the beverage laws of the state through which they reenter the United States allow it. In addition, 100 non-Cuban cigars and 200 cigarettes are allowed, regardless of your age. Antiques and works of art more than 100 years old are duty-free.

Duty-free, travelers may mail packages valued at up to $200 to themselves and up to $100 to others, with a limit of one parcel per addressee per day (and no alcohol or tobacco products or perfume valued at more than $5); outside, identify the package as being for personal use or an unsolicited gift, specifying the contents and their retail value. Mailed items do not count as part of your exemption.

In Canada Once per calendar year, when you've been out of Canada for at least seven days, you may bring in C$300 worth of goods duty-free. If you've been away less than seven days but more than 48 hours, the duty-free exemption drops to C$100 but can be claimed any number of times (as can a C$20 duty-free exemption for absences of 24 hours or more). You cannot combine the yearly and 48-hour exemptions, use the C$300 exemption only partially (to save the balance for a later trip), or pool exemptions with family members. Goods claimed under the C$300 exemption may follow you by mail; those claimed under the lesser exemptions must accompany you.

Alcohol and tobacco products may be included in the yearly and 48-hour exemptions but not in the 24-hour exemption. If you meet the age requirements of the province through which you reenter Canada, you may bring in, duty-free, 1.14 liters (40 imperial ounces) of wine or liquor *or* 24 12-ounce cans or bottles of beer or ale. If you are 16 or older, you may bring in, duty-free, 200 cigarettes, 50 cigars or cigarillos, and 400 tobacco sticks or 400 grams of manufactured tobacco. Alcohol and tobacco must accompany you on your return.

An unlimited number of gifts valued up to C$60 each may be mailed to Canada duty-free. These do not count as part of your exemption. Label the package "Unsolicited Gift—Value under $60." Alcohol and tobacco are excluded.

In the U.K. From countries outside the EU, including those in the Caribbean, you may import duty-free 200 cigarettes, 100 cigarillos, 50 cigars or 250 grams of tobacco; 1 liter of spirits or 2 liters of fortified or sparkling wine; 2 liters of still table wine; 60 milliliters of perfume; 250 milliliters of toilet water; plus £136 worth of other goods, including gifts and souvenirs.

Dining

Unless you've chosen a money-saving meal plan at your hotel, seek out informal restaurants and casual cafés and **sample the island's local Creole and West Indian specialties.** Don't be afraid of the barbecue stands found on most islands; the food is usually fresh, cheap, and tasty. On larger islands such as St. Thomas and Jamaica, if all you need is something quick and cheap, you can always resort to American fast-food stops. The restaurant reviews in the chapters that follow indicate only when reservations are necessary or advised. Since dining is usually informal throughout the region, we have mentioned attire only when something more elegant or formal than casual dress is called for.

For Travelers with Disabilities

The Caribbean has not progressed as far as other areas of the world in accommodating travelers with disabilities, and very few attractions and sights are equipped with ramps, elevators, or wheelchair-accessible rest rooms. However, major new properties are beginning to do their planning with the needs of travelers with mobility problems and hearing and visual impairments in mind. Wherever possible in our lodging listings, we indicate whether special facilities are available.

When discussing accessibility with an operator or reservationist, **ask hard questions.** Are there any stairs, inside *or* out? Are there grab bars next to the toilet *and* in the shower/tub? How wide is the doorway to the room? To the bathroom? For the most extensive facilities, meeting the latest legal specifications, **opt for newer accommodations,** which more often have been designed with access in mind. Older properties or ships must usually be retrofitted and may offer more limited facilities as a result. Be sure to **discuss your needs before booking.**

Cruises Cruising is one of the best ways for wheelchair users to visit the Caribbean. Newer ships have been designed with accessiblity in mind, and virtually all older ships have been retrofitted to some degree. Try to **find a ship that docks** rather than dropping anchor and tendering passengers ashore. Getting in and out of the tender can be difficult for passengers with mobility problems, especially in choppy seas.

Discount Clubs

Travel clubs offer members unsold space on airplanes, cruise ships, and package tours at as much as 50% below regular prices. Membership may include a regular bulletin or access to a toll-free hot line giving details of available trips departing from three or four days to several months in the future. Most also offer 50% discounts off hotel rack rates. Before booking with a club, **make sure the hotel or other supplier isn't offering a better deal.**

Health Concerns

Few real hazards threaten the health of a visitor to the Caribbean. The small lizards that seem to have overrun the islands are harmless, and poisonous snakes are hard to find, although you should exercise caution while bird-watching in Trinidad. The worst problem may well be a tiny sand fly known as the "no-see-um," which tends to appear after a rain, near wet or swampy ground, and around sunset. If you feel particularly vulnerable to insect bites, **bring along a good repellent.**

Sunburn or sunstroke can also be serious problems. Even people who are not normally bothered by strong sun should head into this area with a long-sleeve shirt, a hat, and long pants or a beach wrap. These are essential for a day on a boat but are also advisable for midday at the beach and whenever you go out sightseeing. **Use sunblock, limit your exposure, and be sure to drink enough liquids.**

Since health standards vary from island to island, inquire about local conditions before you go. No special shots are required for most destinations; where they are, we have made note of it.

Divers' Alert Scuba divers take note: **Do not fly within 24 hours of scuba diving.**

Insurance

Travel insurance can protect your investment, replace your luggage and its contents, or provide for medical coverage should you fall ill during your trip. Most tour operators, travel agents, and insurance agents sell specialized health-and-accident, flight, trip-cancellation, and luggage insurance as well as comprehensive policies with some or all of these features. Before you make any purchase, **review your existing health and homeowner's policies** to find out whether they cover expenses incurred while traveling.

Baggage Airline liability for your baggage is limited by the terms of your ticket (*see* Packing for the Caribbean, *below*). Insurance for losses exceeding the terms of your airline ticket can be bought directly from the airline at check-in for about $10 per $1,000 of coverage; note that it excludes a rather extensive list of items, shown on your airline ticket.

Flight You should **think twice before buying flight insurance.** Often purchased as a last-minute impulse at the airport, it pays a lump sum when a plane crashes, either to a beneficiary if the insured dies or sometimes to a surviving passenger who loses eyesight or a limb. Supplementing the airlines' coverage described in the limits-of-liability paragraphs on your ticket, it's expensive and basically unnecessary. Charging an airline ticket to a major credit card often automatically entitles you to coverage and may also embrace travel by bus, train, and ship.

Health If your own health insurance policy does not cover you outside the United States, **consider buying supplemental medical coverage.** It can provide from $1,000 to $150,000 worth of coverage for medical and/or dental expenses incurred as a result of an accident or illness during a trip. These policies also may include a personal-accident, or death-and-dismemberment, provision, which pays a lump sum ranging from $15,000 to $500,000 to your beneficiaries if you die or to you if you lose one or more limbs or your eyesight, and a medical-assistance provision, which may either reimburse you for the cost of referrals, evacuation, or repatriation and other services, or automatically enroll you as a member of a particular medical-assistance company. (*See* Health Issues in Important Contacts A to Z, *above.*)

For U.K. Travelers You can buy an annual travel-insurance policy valid for most vacations during the year in which it's purchased. If you go this route, make sure it covers you if you have a preexisting medical condition or are pregnant.

Trip Without insurance, you will lose all or most of your money if you must cancel your trip due to illness or any other reason. Especially if your airline ticket, cruise, or package tour is nonrefundable and cannot be changed, it's essential that you **buy trip-cancellation-and-interruption insurance.** When considering how much coverage you need, look for a policy that will cover the cost of your trip plus the nondiscounted price of a one-way airline ticket should you need to return home early. Read the fine print carefully, especially sections defining "family member" and "preexisting medical conditions." Also **consider default or bankruptcy insurance,** which protects you against a supplier's failure to deliver. However, such policies often do not cover default by a travel agency, tour operator, airline, or cruise line if you bought your tour and the coverage directly from the firm in question.

Lodging

Plan ahead and reserve a room well before you travel to the Caribbean. If you have reservations but expect to arrive later than 5 or 6 PM, advise the hotel, inn, or guest house in advance. Also be sure to **find out what the rate quoted includes**—use of sports facilities and equipment, airport transfers, and the like—and whether it operates on the **European Plan** (EP, with no meals), **Continental Plan** (CP, with Continental breakfast), **Breakfast Plan** (BP, with full breakfast), **Modified American Plan** (MAP, with two meals), or **Full American Plan** (FAP, with three meals), or is **All-inclusive** (with three meals, all facilities, and drinks unless otherwise noted). Some hotels neglect to mention you'll be paying a tax and service charge on top of the quoted rate. A Full American Plan may be ideal for travelers on a budget who don't want to worry about additional expenses, but those who enjoy a different dining experience each night will prefer to book rooms on a European Plan. Since many hotels insist on a Modified American Plan, particularly during high season, find out whether you can exchange dinners for lunch. In lodging reviews throughout the book, we have indicated what meal plans are available in each review's service information.

Decide whether you want a hotel on the leeward side of the island (with calm water, good for snorkeling) or on the windward (with waves, for good surfing). Inquire about the view; in most cases you pay more to look at the ocean than at the garden or another part of the property. Also **find out how close the property is to a beach;** at some hotels you can walk barefoot from your room onto the sand; others are across a road or are a 10-minute drive away. This information is essential to help you determine whether you must rent a vehicle to get to the beach (unless your hotel provides a shuttle).

Air-conditioning is not a necessity on all islands, most of which are cooled by trade winds. Even many super-deluxe hideaways known for their "barefoot elegance" have rooms cooled exclusively by trade winds and ceiling fans. **Ask for a second-floor or corner room to enjoy stronger breezes and better cross ventilation.**

Apartment and Villa Rentals If you want a home base that's roomy enough for a family and comes with cooking facilities, **consider a furnished rental.** It's generally cost-wise, too, although not always—some rentals are luxury properties (economical only when your party is large). Home-exchange directories do list rentals—often second homes owned by prospective house swappers—and some services search for a house or apartment for you (even a castle if that's your fancy) and handle the paperwork. Some send an illustrated catalogue and others send photographs of specific properties, sometimes at a charge; up-front registration fees may apply.

Home Exchange If you would like to find a house, an apartment, or other vacation property to exchange for your own while on vacation, **become a member of a home-exchange organization,** which will send you its annual directories listing available exchanges and will include your own listing in at least one of them. Arrangements for the actual exchange are made by the two parties to it, not by the organization (*see* Lodging *in* Important Contacts A to Z, *above*).

Medical Assistance

No one plans to get sick while traveling, but it happens, so **consider signing up with a medical-assistance company.** These outfits provide referrals, emergency evacuation or repatriation, 24-hour telephone hot lines for medical consultation, dispatch of medical personnel, relay of medical records, cash for emergencies, and other personal and legal assistance.

Money and Expenses

ATMs Cirrus, Plus and many other networks connecting automated-teller machines operate internationally. Chances are that you can **use your bank card at ATMs** to withdraw money from an account and get cash advances on a credit-card account if your card has been programmed with a personal identification number, or PIN. Before leaving home, **check in on frequency limits** for withdrawals and cash advances. Also **ask whether your card's PIN must be reprogrammed** for use in the Caribbean. Four digits are commonly used overseas. Note that Discover is accepted only in the United States.

On cash advances you are charged interest from the day you receive the money, whether from a teller or an ATM. Although transaction fees for ATM withdrawals abroad may be higher than fees for withdrawals at home, Cirrus and Plus exchange rates are excellent because they are based on wholesale rates only offered by major banks.

Traveler's Checks Whether or not to buy traveler's checks depends on where you are headed; **take cash to rural areas and small towns, traveler's checks to cities.** The most widely recognized are American Express, Citicorp, Thomas Cook, and Visa, which are sold by major commercial banks for 1%–3% of the checks' face value—it pays to **shop around.** Both American Express and Thomas Cook issue checks that can be countersigned and used by you or your traveling companion. So you won't be left with excess foreign currency, **buy a few checks in small denominations** to cash toward the end of your trip. Record the numbers of the checks, cross them off as you spend them, and keep this information separate from your checks.

Wiring Money You don't have to be a cardholder to send or receive funds through MoneyGram℠ from American Express. Just go to a MoneyGram agent, located in retail and convenience stores and in American Express Travel Offices. Pay up to $1,000 with cash or a credit card, anything over that in cash. The money can be picked up within 10 minutes in the form of U.S. dollar traveler's checks or local currency at the nearest MoneyGram agent, or, abroad, the nearest American

Express Travel Office. There's no limit, and the recipient need only present photo identification. The cost runs from 3% to 10%, depending on the amount sent, the destination, and how you pay.

You can also send money using Western Union. Money sent from the United States or Canada will be available for pickup at agent locations in 100 countries within 15 minutes. Once the money is in the system, it can be picked up at any one of 25,000 locations. Fees range from 4% to 10%, depending on the amount you send.

Packages and Tours

A package or tour to the Caribbean can make your vacation less expensive and more convenient. Firms that sell tours and packages purchase airline seats, hotel rooms, and rental cars in bulk and pass some of the savings on to you. In addition, the best operators have local representatives to help you out at your destination.

A Good Deal? The more your package or tour includes, the better you can predict the ultimate cost of your vacation. Make sure you know exactly what is included, and **beware of hidden costs.** Are taxes, tips, and service charges included? Transfers and baggage handling? Entertainment and excursions? These can add up.

Most packages and tours are rated deluxe, first-class superior, first class, tourist, or budget. The key difference is usually accommodations. If the package or tour you are considering is priced lower than in your wildest dreams, **be skeptical.** Also, **make sure your travel agent knows the hotels** and other services. Ask about location, room size, beds, and whether the facility has a pool, room service, or programs for children, if you care about these. Has your agent been there or sent others you can contact?

Buyer Beware Each year consumers are stranded or lose their money when operators go out of business—even very large ones with excellent reputations. If you can't afford a loss, take the time to **check out the operator**—find out how long the company has been in business, and ask several agents about its reputation. Next, **don't book unless the firm has a consumer-protection program.** Members of the United States Tour Operators Association and the National Tour Association are required to set aside funds exclusively to cover your payments and travel arrangements in case of default. Nonmember operators may instead carry insurance; look for the details in the operator's brochure—and the name of an underwriter with a solid reputation. Note: When it comes to tour operators, **don't trust escrow accounts.** Although there are laws governing those of charter-flight operators, no governmental body prevents tour operators from raiding the till. Next, **contact your local Better Business Bureau and the attorney general's office** in both your own state and the operator's; have any complaints been filed? Last, **pay with a major credit card.** Then you can cancel payment, provided that you can document your complaint. Always **consider trip-cancellation insurance** (*see* Insurance, *above*).

Big vs. Small An operator that handles several hundred thousand travelers annually can use its purchasing power to give you a good price. Its high volume may also indicate financial stability. But some small companies provide more personalized service; because they tend to specialize, they may also be experts on an area.

Using an Agent Travel agents are an excellent resource. In fact, large operators accept bookings only through travel agents. But it's good to **collect brochures from several agencies,** because some agents' suggestions may be skewed by promotional relationships with tour and package firms that reward them for volume sales. If you have a special interest, **find an agent with expertise in that area;** the American Society of

Travel Agents can give you leads in the United States. (Don't rely solely on your agent, though; agents may be unaware of small-niche operators, and some special-interest travel companies only sell direct).

Single Travelers Prices are usually quoted per person, based on two sharing a room. If you are traveling solo, you may be required to pay the full double occupancy rate. Some operators eliminate this surcharge if you agree to be matched up with a roommate of the same sex, even if one is not found by departure time.

Packing for the Caribbean

Pack light, because baggage carts are nonexistent at most Caribbean airports and luggage restrictions are tight, particularly on small island-hopper planes.

Dress on the islands is light and casual. Bring loose-fitting clothes made of natural fabrics to see you through days of heat and high humidity. Take a coverup for the beaches, not only to protect you from the sun but also to wear to and from your hotel room. Bathing suits and immodest attire are frowned upon off the beach on many islands. A sun hat is advisable, but you don't have to pack one, since inexpensive straw hats are available everywhere. For shopping and sightseeing, bring walking shorts, jeans, T-shirts, long-sleeve cotton shirts, slacks, and sundresses. You'll need a light sweater for protection from the trade winds and at higher altitudes. Evenings are casual but "casual" can range from really informal to casually elegant, depending on the establishment; jacket and tie are rarely required except in the fancier casinos and in the very fancy restaurants.

You'll want an umbrella during the rainy season; leave the plastic or nylon raincoats at home, since they're extremely uncomfortable in hot, humid weather. **Bring suntan lotion and film from home;** they're much more expensive on the islands. You'll need insect repellent, too, especially if you plan to walk through rain forests or visit during the rainy season. Bring an extra pair of eyeglasses or contact lenses in your carry-on luggage, and if you have a health problem, **pack enough medication** to last the trip or have your doctor write a prescription using the drug's generic name, because brand names vary from country to country (you'll then need a prescription from a doctor in the country you're visiting). **Don't put prescription drugs or valuables in luggage to be checked,** for it could go astray. To avoid problems with customs officials, carry medications in original packaging. Also don't forget the addresses of offices that handle refunds of lost traveler's checks.

Electricity The general rule in the Caribbean is 110 and 120 volts AC, and the outlets take the same two-prong plugs found in the United States, but **you may need an adaptor on some of the French and British islands.** Hotels sometimes have 110-volt outlets for low-wattage appliances marked "For Shavers Only" near the sink; don't use them for high-wattage appliances like blow-dryers. If your laptop computer is older, carry a converter; new laptops operate equally well on 110 and 220 volts, so you need only an adapter.

Luggage Free airline baggage allowances depend on the airline, the route, and the class of your ticket; ask in advance. In general, on domestic flights and on international flights between the United States and foreign destinations, you are entitled to check two bags—neither exceeding 62 inches, or 158 centimeters (length + width + height), or weighing more than 70 pounds (32 kilograms). A third piece may be brought aboard; its total dimensions are generally limited to less than 45 inches (114 centimeters), so it will fit easily under the seat in front of you or in the overhead compartment. In the United States, the Federal Aviation Administration gives airlines broad latitude to limit carry-on allowances and tailor them to different aircraft and operational conditions. Charges for excess, oversize, or overweight pieces vary.

If you are flying between two foreign destinations, note that baggage allowances may be determined not by piece but by weight—generally 88 pounds (40 kilograms) in first class, 66 pounds (30 kilograms) in business class, and 44 pounds (20 kilograms) in economy. If your flight between two cities abroad *connects* with your transatlantic or transpacific flight, the piece method still applies.

Safeguarding Your Luggage Before leaving home, **itemize your bags' contents** and their worth, and label them with your name, address, and phone number. (If you use your home address, cover it so potential thieves can't see it.) Inside your bag, **pack a copy of your itinerary.** At check-in, **make sure that your bag is correctly tagged** with the airport's three-letter destination code. If your bags arrive damaged or not at all, file a written report with the airline before leaving the airport.

Passports and Visas

If you don't already have one, **get a passport.** While traveling, **keep one photocopy of the data page** separate from your wallet and leave another copy with someone at home. If you lose your passport, promptly call the nearest embassy or consulate, and the local police; having the data page can speed replacement.

See individual island chapters for specific passport and visa requirements. Some islands require passports; others do not.

Renting a Car

Renting a car in the Caribbean can be a cost-effective choice if you plan to do a lot of sightseeing or if you're staying at a budget property far from the beach. If you plan to spend most of your time at a beachside resort, however, it may not pay—especially if the property has a free shuttle service into town. But whether you need wheels for a day or for two weeks, it pays to look into the options available and **compare costs.** In general, a full day's guided tour on a Caribbean island is more expensive than a single day of car rental, but not always: Car rental costs can vary widely from island to island (from $30 a day up to $80), and there are also gas and local driving license purchases to be considered. On a smaller island, where a drive of a few hours is sufficient to see the sights, you may find half-day tours are comparable or even cheaper than renting your own car. And although guided tours usually charge per person, many private taxi drivers charge the same price for up to four people in a single cab. If you're with a group, you may find that hiring a cab and driver is actually the cheapest way to see the island.

Cutting Costs To get the best deal, **book through a travel agent and shop around.** When pricing cars, **ask where the rental lot is located.** Some off-airport locations offer lower rates—even though their lots are only minutes away from the terminal via complimentary shuttle. You may also want to **price local car-rental companies,** whose rates may be lower still, although service and maintenance standards may not be up to those of a national firm. Also **ask your travel agent about a company's customer-service record.** How has it responded to late plane arrivals and vehicle mishaps? Are there often lines at the rental counter, and, if you're traveling during a holiday period, does a confirmed reservation guarantee you a car?

Always **find out what equipment is standard** at your destination before specifying what you want; **do without automatic transmission or air-conditioning** if they're optional.

Insurance When you drive a rented car, you are generally responsible for any damage or personal injury that you cause as well as damage to the vehicle. Before you rent, **see what coverage you already have** under the terms of your personal auto-insurance policy and credit cards. For about $14 a day, rental companies sell insurance, known as a collision damage waiver (CDW), that eliminates your liability for damage to the car; it's always optional and should never be automatically added to your bill.

Requirements Whether or not your own driver's license will suffice varies from island to island. See individual chapters for details.

Surcharges Note that some rental agencies charge extra if you return the car before the time specified on your contract. To avoid a hefty refueling fee, **fill the tank just before you turn in the car.**

Senior-Citizen Discounts

To qualify for age-related discounts, **mention your senior-citizen status up front** when booking hotel reservations, not when checking out, and before you're seated in restaurants, not when paying your bill. Note that discounts may be limited to certain menus, days, or hours. When renting a car, **ask about promotional car-rental discounts**—they can net lower costs than your senior-citizen discount.

Shopping

Many Caribbean ports of call are duty-free, but **don't assume that duty-free means cheap.** It pays to know the standard prices stateside and to comparison shop. You may do better at your local store's clearance sale (especially if you live in the New York area). In general, you'll realize the most substantial savings (often 25%–50% off) on items manufactured outside the United States. **Local crafts usually make the best buys and gifts.** Seek out crafts markets, and remember that bargaining is expected. Some of the indigenous items to look for are spices in Grenada; rums in Jamaica, Barbados, and Martinique; *santos* in Puerto Rico; straw work in Dominica; and Saba lace on Saba. Shells, batiks, and locally made bay rum fragrances are other possibilities. Even if some of these items *seem* pricey, they're usually a fraction of the stateside cost (assuming you can find them).

Students on the Road

The Caribbean is not as far out of a student's budget as you might expect. Many islands have fine camping facilities, inexpensive guest houses, and small no-frills hotels. You're most likely to meet students from other countries in the French and Dutch West Indies, where many go on holiday or sabbatical. Puerto Rico, Jamaica, Grenada, and Dominica, among others, have large resident international student populations at their universities.

To save money, **look into deals available through student-oriented travel agencies.** To qualify, you'll need to have a bona fide student I.D. card. Members of international student groups also are eligible. *See* Students *in* Important Contacts A to Z, *above.*

Telephones

Long-Distance The long-distance services of AT&T, MCI, and Sprint make calling home relatively convenient and let you avoid hotel surcharges; typically, you dial an 800 number in the United States and a local number abroad). Before you go, **find out the local access codes** for your destinations.

When to Go

The Caribbean "season" has traditionally been a winter one, usually extending from December 15 to April 14. This "season" exists because northern weather is at its worst, not because the Caribbean weather is at it's best. In fact, winter is when the Caribbean is at its windiest. However, the winter months are the most fashionable, the most expensive, and the most popular, and most hotels are heavily booked. You have to **make your reservations at least two or three months in advance.** You may want to **travel in the summer** (after April 15) when hotel prices drop 20%–50%. Saving money isn't the only reason to visit the Caribbean during the off-season. Temperatures in summer are only a few degrees warmer than in winter. It used to be that there were also fewer fellow travelers, but the summer is growing ever busier, and more and more hotels and restaurants are staying open year-round. September, October, and November are the least crowded months, but hotel facilities can be limited and some restaurants will be closed. Reservations, however, can be easy to get, even at top establishments. You won't have the beaches completely to yourself but they will be less crowded.

The flamboyant flowering trees are at their height in summer, and so are most of the flowers and shrubs of the West Indies. In May, June, and July, the water is clearer for snorkeling and smoother for sailing in the Virgin Islands and the Grenadines.

Climate The Caribbean climate is fairly constant. The average year-round temperature for the region is 78°F–85°F. The extremes of temperature are 65°F low, 95°F high, but as everyone knows, it's the humidity, not the heat, that makes you suffer, especially when the two go hand in hand. You can count on downtown shopping areas being hot at midday any time of the year, but air-conditioning provides some respite. Stay near the beaches, where water and trade winds can keep you cool, and shop early or late in the day.

High places can be cool, particularly when the Christmas winds hit Caribbean peaks (they come in late November and last through January). Since most Caribbean islands are mountainous (notable exceptions being the Caymans, Aruba, Bonaire, and Curaçao), the altitude always offers an escape from the latitude. Kingston (Jamaica), Port-of-Spain (Trinidad), and Fort-de-France (Martinique) swelter in summer; climb 1,000 feet or so, though, and everything is fine.

Hurricanes occasionally sweep through the Caribbean, and officials on many islands are not well equipped to warn locals, much less tourists. Check the news daily and keep abreast of brewing tropical storms by reading stateside papers if you can get them. The rainy season, usually in fall, consists mostly of brief showers interspersed with sunshine. You can watch the clouds come over, feel the rain, and remain in your lounge chair for the sun to dry you off. A spell of overcast days is "unusual," as everyone will tell you.

Generally speaking, there's more planned entertainment in winter. The peak of local excitement on many islands, most notably Trinidad, St. Vincent, and the French West Indies, is Carnival.

2 Anguilla

Updated by Pamela Acheson

Beach lovers become giddy when they first see Anguilla (rhymes with vanilla) from the air and spot the blindingly white beaches and neon blue and aquamarine waters that rim this scrubby piece of land. The highest point on the dry, limestone isle is 213 feet above sea level, and there are neither streams nor rivers, only saline ponds used for salt production. If you don't like beaches, you won't find a lot to do here. There are no glittering casinos, fascinating historic sites, or nightclubs and no duty-free shops stuffed with irresistible buys (although you're only about 30 watery minutes away from the bustle of St. Martin/St. Maarten's resorts and casinos).

Anguilla is noted for expensive, luxurious enclaves that exist to pamper. But the island also offers a wide range of affordable guest houses, apartments, and small hotels, many right on the water. You can swim, do some diving, practice your backhand, catch up on your reading, compare the relative merits of the beaches, or just find one that suits you and sink down on it to worship the sun.

Anguilla is the most northerly of the Leeward Islands, lying between the Caribbean Sea and the Atlantic Ocean. Stretching from northeast to southwest, it's about 16 miles long and only 3 miles across at its widest point. *Anguilla* means "eel" in Italian, but the Spanish *anguila* or French *anguille* (both of which also mean "eel") may have been the original name. Archaeological evidence shows that the island was inhabited as long as 2,000 years ago by Indians who named the island Malliouhana, a more mellifluous title that's been adopted by some of the island's shops and resorts.

In 1631, the Dutch built a fort here, but no one has been able to locate its site. English settlers from St. Kitts colonized the island in 1650, after which there were the obligatory Caribbean battles between the English and the French, and in 1688 the island was attacked by a party of "wild Irishmen," some of whom settled on the island. But Anguilla's primary discontent was over its status vis-à-vis the other British colonies, particularly St. Kitts. In the 18th century, Anguilla, as part of the Leeward Islands, was administered by British officials in Antigua. In 1816, Britain split the islands into two groups, one of them composed of Anguilla, St. Kitts, Nevis, and the British Virgin Islands and administered by a magistrate in St. Kitts. For more than 150 years thereafter various island units and federations were formed and disbanded, with Anguilla all the while simmering over its subordinate status and enforced union with St. Kitts. Anguillans twice petitioned for direct rule from Britain, and twice were ignored. In 1967, when St. Kitts, Nevis, and Anguilla became an associated state, the mouse roared, kicked St. Kitts policemen off the island, held a self-rule referendum, and for two years conducted its own affairs. In 1968, a senior British official arrived and remained for a year working with the Anguilla Council. A second referendum in 1969 confirmed the desire of the Anguillans to remain apart from St. Kitts–Nevis, and the following month a British "peacekeeping force" parachuted down to the island, where it was greeted with flowers, fluttering Union Jacks, and friendly smiles. When the paratroopers were not working on their tans, they helped a team of royal engineers improve the port and build roads and schools. Today Anguilla elects a House of Assembly and its own leader to handle internal affairs, while a British governor is responsible for public service, the police, and judiciary and external affairs.

The territory of Anguilla includes a few islets or cays, such as Scrub Island to the east, Dog Island, Prickly Pear Cays, Sandy Island, and Sombrero Island. The island's population numbers about 8,000, predominantly of African descent but also including descendants of Europeans, especially the Irish. Historically, because the limestone land was hardly fit for agriculture, Anguillans have had to seek work on neighboring islands. Until recently, the primary means of employment were fishing and boat building. Today, tourism has become the growth industry of the island's stable economy. But the government is determined to keep Anguilla's tourism growing at a slow and cautious pace to protect the island's natural resources and beauty.

What It Will Cost These sample prices, meant only as a general guide, are for high season. A ¢ guest house or apartment for two will cost about $90 per night. Dinner at a $ restaurant (which will be quite casual) will be about $20 for two. A rum punch, glass of wine, or other cocktail is about $3; a beer at a local bar costs $2.50. Car-rental rates are reasonable here, about $35–$45 per day. Taxis are expensive; the trip from Sandy Ground or Road Bay to the Valley is around $15. A sailing excursion, with snorkeling and lunch provided, is around $40. Snorkel equipment rents for about $6.

Before You Go

Tourist Information Contact the very helpful **Anguilla Tourist Information and Reservation Office** (c/o Medhurst & Associates, 775 Park Ave., Huntington, NY 11743, tel. 516/425–0900, or 800/553–4939; fax. 516/425–0903). In the United Kingdom, contact the **Anguilla Tourist Office** (3 Epirus Rd., London SW6 7UJ, tel. 0171/937–7725).

Arriving and Departing

By Plane **American Airlines** (tel. 800/433–7300) is the major airline with nonstop flights from the United States to its hub in San Juan, from which the airline's **American Eagle** flies three times daily (twice offseason) to Anguilla, with good connections to flights from the continental U.S. **Windward Islands Airways** (Winair; tel. 809/775–0183) wings in daily from St. Thomas and at least three times a day from St. Maarten's Juliana Airport. **LIAT** (tel. 809/465–2286) comes in from St. Kitts and Antigua. **Air Anguilla** (tel. 809/497–2643), has regularly scheduled daily flights from St. Thomas, St. Maarten, and

Tortola. It also provides air-taxi service on request from neighboring islands, as does **Tyden Air** (tel. 809/497–2717).

From the Airport At **Wallblake Airport** you'll find taxis lined up to meet the planes. A trip from the airport to Sandy Ground will cost about $8. Fares, which are government regulated, should be listed in brochures the drivers carry. If you are traveling in a group, the fares apply to the first two people; each additional passenger adds $3 to the total. Tipping is welcome. There are no buses or shuttles.

By Boat Ferries run frequently between Anguilla and St. Martin. They leave from Blowing Point on Anguilla every half hour from 7:30 to 5 and from Marigot on St. Martin every half hour from 8 to 5:30. There are also evening ferries that leave from Blowing Point at 6 and 9:15 and from Marigot at 7 and 10:45. You pay the $9 one-way fare ($11 evenings) on board and a $2 departure tax before boarding. Don't buy a round-trip ticket, because it restricts you to the boat on which it is purchased. On very windy days the 20-minute trip can be bouncy, and if you suffer from motion sickness, you may want medication. An information booth outside the customs shed in Blowing Point is usually open daily from 8:30 to 5, but sometimes the attendant wanders off.

From the Docks Taxis are always waiting to pick passengers up at the Blowing Point landing. It costs $12 to get to the Mallиouhana Hotel, $15 to the Cap Juluca Hotel, and $17 to the most distant hotels. Rates are fixed by the government; the taxi driver should have a list of these. There are no buses or shuttles.

Passports and Visas U.S. and Canadian citizens need proof of identity. A passport is preferred (even one that has expired within the last five years). A photo ID, along with a birth certificate (original with raised seal), a voter registration card, or a driver's license is also acceptable. Visitor's passes are valid for stays of up to three months. British citizens must have a passport. All visitors must also have a return or ongoing ticket.

Language English, with a West Indian lilt, is spoken on Anguilla.

Precautions The manchineel tree, which resembles an apple tree, shades many beaches. The tree bears poisonous fruit, and the sap from the tree causes painful blisters. Avoid sitting beneath the tree, because even dew or raindrops falling from the leaves can blister your skin.

Be *sure* to take along insect repellent—mosquitoes are all over the place.

Anguilla is a quiet, relatively safe island, but there's no point in tempting fate by leaving your valuables unattended in your hotel room, on the beach, or in your car.

Staying in Anguilla

Important Addresses **Tourist Information:** The **Anguilla Tourist Office** (The Social Security Bldg., The Valley, tel. 809/497–2759) is open weekdays 8–noon and 1–4.

Emergencies **Police** and **Fire:** Emergency is now 911. (For non-emergencies dial 809/497–2333.) **Hospital:** There is a 24-hour emergency room at the new **Princess Alexandra Hospital** (Stoney Ground, tel. 809/497–2551). **Ambulance:** Call 809/497–2551. **Pharmacies:** The **Government Pharmacy** (tel. 809/497–2551) is in the Princess Alexandra Hospital; the **Paramount Pharmacy** (Waterswamp, tel. 809/497–2366) is open Monday–Saturday 8:30–8:30 and has a 24-hour emergency service.

Currency Legal tender here is the Eastern Caribbean dollar (E.C.$), but U.S. dollars are widely accepted. (You'll often get change in E.C. dollars.) The E.C. is fairly stable relative to the U.S. dollar, hovering between E.C. $2.60 and $2.70 to U.S. $1. Credit cards are not always accepted, and it's hard to predict where you'll need cash. Some resorts will only settle in cash; others will accept personal and traveler's checks. Be sure to carry lots of small bills; change for a $20 bill is often difficult to obtain. Note: Prices quoted are in U.S. dollars unless indicated otherwise.

Taxes and Service Charges The government imposes an 8% tax on accommodations. A 10% service charge is added to all hotel bills and most restaurant bills. If you're not certain about the restaurant service charge, ask. If you are particularly pleased with the service, you can certainly leave a little extra. Tip taxi drivers 10% of the fare. The departure tax is $10 at the airport, $2 by boat.

Getting Around There are rumors on Anguilla about public transportation, but for now, if you don't rent a car, you'll probably have to rely on taxis to take you significant distances. Hitchhiking is common and considered safe here.

Taxis The somewhat stiff taxi rates are regulated by the government and there are fixed fares from point to point. Posted rates are for one to two people; each additional person pays $3. The fare from the airport and from Blowing Point Landing to most hotels ranges from $8 to $15.

Rental Cars This is your best bet for maximum mobility, if you're comfortable driving on the left. For the most part, Anguilla's roads are narrow, paved (in a manner of speaking) two-laners, and many of the beaches are reachable only via ghastly dirt roads. Watch out for the four-legged critters that amble across the road, and observe the 30 mph speed limit. To rent a car you'll need a valid driver's license and a local license, which can be obtained for $6 at any of the car-rental agencies. Among the agencies are **Avis** (tel. 809/497–6221 or 800/331–2112), **Budget** (tel. 809/497–2217 or 800/527–0700), **Connors (National)** (tel. 809/497–6433 or 800/328–4567), and **Island Car Rental** (tel. 809/497–2723). Count on $35–$45 per day's rental, plus insurance. Motorcycles and scooters are available for about $30 per day from **R & M Cycle** (tel. 809/497–2430).

Telephones and Mail To call Anguilla from the United States, dial area code 809 + 497 + the local four-digit number. International direct-dial is available on the island. **Cable & Wireless** (Wallblake Rd., tel. 809/497–3100) is open weekdays 8–6, Saturday 9–1, Sunday and holidays 10–2 and sells Caribbean Phone Cards ($5, $10, $20 denominations) for use in specially marked phone booths. The card can be used for local calls and calls to other islands. You can also use the card to call the United States and, in this case, bill the call to a MasterCard or Visa. Inside the departure lounge at the Blowing Point Ferry and at the airport, there is an AT&T USADirect access telephone for collect or credit card calls to the United States. To make a local call (E.C. 25¢) on the island, dial the four-digit number.

Airmail letters to the United States cost E.C. 60¢; postcards, E.C. 25¢.

Opening and Closing Times Banks are open Monday–Thursday 8–3 and Friday 8–5. Shopping hours are variable. No two shops seem to have the same hours, but many are open between 10 and 4. Call, or ask at the tourist office for opening and closing times, or adopt the island way of doing things; if they're not open when you stop by, stop by again.

Guided Tours A round-the-island tour by taxi will take about 2½ hours and will cost $40 for one or two people, $5 for each additional passenger. The cost is about the same as a full-day's car rental.

Bennie's Tours (Blowing Point, tel. 809/497–2788), and **Mallouhana Travel and Tours** (The Valley, tel. 809/497–2431) put together personalized package tours on and around the island.

Exploring Anguilla

Numbers in the margin correspond to points of interest on the Anguilla map.

Exploring on Anguilla means deciding which beach is best, with perhaps a time-out for lunch at one of the resorts along the way. For this, a rental car or scooter is necessary. Since Anguilla is relatively flat, bikes are an excellent way to tour, although the cost for two people nearly equals that of a rental car. Guided tours are another possibility (*see above*), but these cost the same for a couple of hours as does a rental car for the day.

There are only a few roads on the island, but none of them is marked, so it's still pretty easy to get lost your first time out. Having a map, and checking it frequently against passing landmarks, is essential. If you have not collected maps and brochures from the tourist booths either at the airport or on the boat ferry, then make the Tourist Office in The Valley your first stop on the island. The island is sprinkled with salt ponds and small villages, the most important of which is The Valley, where administrative offices, banks, a few boutiques, guest houses, eateries, and markets are located. Take a look at the island's historic house, then go beachcombing.

1 **Wallblake House** is a plantation house that was built around 1787 by Will Blake (Wallblake is probably a corruption of his name). Legends of murders, invasions by the French in 1796, and high living surround the house. Now owned and used by the Catholic Church, the plantation has spacious rooms, some with tray ceilings edged with handsome carving. On the grounds are an ancient vaulted stone cistern and an outbuilding called the Bakery, which was used not for bread-making but for baking turkeys and hams. The oven measures 12 feet across and rises 3 feet up through a stepped chimney. *Cross Roads, The Valley. Call Father John, tel. 809/497–2405, to make an appointment to tour the plantation.*

From the **Wallblake House** follow the sign to the Cottage Hospital, and you'll come to a dirt road that leads to **Crocus Bay** and several strips of white-sand beaches.

Head northeast out of The Valley, following the occasional marker to Shoal Bay and its beautiful beach. As you approach the coast at
2 **Shoal Bay,** you'll pass near **The Fountain,** where Arawak petroglyphs have been discovered. Presently closed to the public, the area is being researched by the Anguilla Archaeological and Historical Society. The AAHS (tel. 809/497–2767) plans to open a museum in the former Customs House in The Valley. The next stretch of this road is a bumpy mess. Hang in there. The beach is worth the trip.

Backtrack on the road from Shoal Bay and take your first real left. In about 2 miles you'll reach the fishing village of **Island Harbour,** where you'll see colorful, handcrafted fishing boats pulled up on the shore.

Two miles farther east, the fishing village of **Island Harbour** nestles in its sheltered cove.

Follow rutted dirt roads from Island Harbour to the easternmost tip of the island. On the way to the aptly named **Scrub Island** and **Little Scrub Island** off the eastern tip of Anguilla, you'll pass Captain's Bay, with its isolated beach, on the north coast.

You can also choose to bypass the east end of the island, because there isn't much to see there. From Island Harbour, a paved road leads south, skirts Savannah Bay on the southeast coast, and contin-
3 ues to **Sandy Hill Bay.**

Four miles down the coast, beyond the Long Salt Pond, is **Forest Bay,** a fit place for scuba diving. South of Forest Bay lies **Little Harbour,** with a lovely horseshoe-shape bay and the splendid **Cinnamon Reef Beach Club.**

From Little Harbour, follow the paved road past Wallblake Airport,
just outside The Valley, and turn left on the main road. After about a
mile, bear right, following signs for Sandy Ground, then continue
4 for another two miles to **Sandy Ground,** one of the most active and
most developed of the island's beaches. It is home to the **Mariners
Hotel, Tamariain Watersports,** a dive shop, a commercial pier, and
several small guest houses and restaurants. A ferry leaves frequently from here for Sandy Island, 2 miles offshore.

If you backtrack from Sandy Ground to the main road you were on
5 and continue south, you'll pass (at the light) the turnoff to **Blowing
Point Harbour,** where you'll have docked if you arrived by ferry from
Marigot in St. Martin.

The main paved road travels more or less down the center of the island. Teeth-jarring dirt roads lead to the coasts, the beaches, and some of the best resorts on the island.

On the south coast, west of Blowing Point, is the crescent-shape home of **Rendezvous Bay,** the island's first hotel, built in 1959. Farther south, you'll pass turnoffs to a number of fancy resorts, all on beautiful beaches open to the public. Turnoffs on the left-hand side will take you to the **Casablanca Resort** and to **Cap Juluca,** which is on beautiful **Maunday's Bay.** Turnoffs on the right head to **Meads Bay,** where you'll find the **Malliouhana** and the **Frangipani Beach Club,** and to **Barnes Bay** and Coccoloba Plantation. At the very end of the road you'll come to beautiful **Shoal Bay West** and the striking architecture of **Cove Castles.**

Beaches

The island's big attractions are its beaches. All are free to the public and all are white sand. Nude bathing is a no-no. Most of the island's beaches are on coral reefs that are great for snorkeling. Most apartment complexes and guest houses are within a 15-minute walk of the nearest beach, if not actually on it. You *will* need a car to go beach-hopping.

One of the prettiest beaches in the Caribbean, **Shoal Bay** is a 2-mile L-shape beach of talcum-powder-soft white sand. There are beach chairs, umbrellas, a backdrop of sea-grape and coconut trees, and for seafood and tropical drinks there's Trader Vic's, Uncle Ernie, and the Round Rock. Souvenir shops for T-shirts, suntan lotion, and the like abound. Head to Shoal Bay for good snorkeling in the offshore coral reefs, and visit the water-sports center to arrange diving, sailing, and fishing trips.

Island Harbor, another busy beach, is shaded by coconut trees and lined with colorful fishing boats. Depart from here for **Scilly Cay,** a three-minute motorboat ride away. You can get snorkeling equipment on the ferrying motorboat, but at times the waters are too rough to see much. On Scilly Cay there is a beach bar that serves drinks and grilled lobster and seafood.

The reward for traveling along an inhospitable dirt road via four-wheel drive is complete isolation at **Captain's Bay** on the northeastern end of the island. The surf slaps the sands with a vengeance, and the undertow is quite strong here. Wading is the safest water sport.

Mimi Bay is a difficult-to-reach, isolated, half-mile beach east of Sea Feathers Bay. But the trip is worth it. When the surf is not too rough, the barrier reef makes for great snorkeling.

Also not far from Sea Feathers is **Sandy Hill,** a base for fishermen. Here you can buy fresh fish and lobster right off the boats and snor-

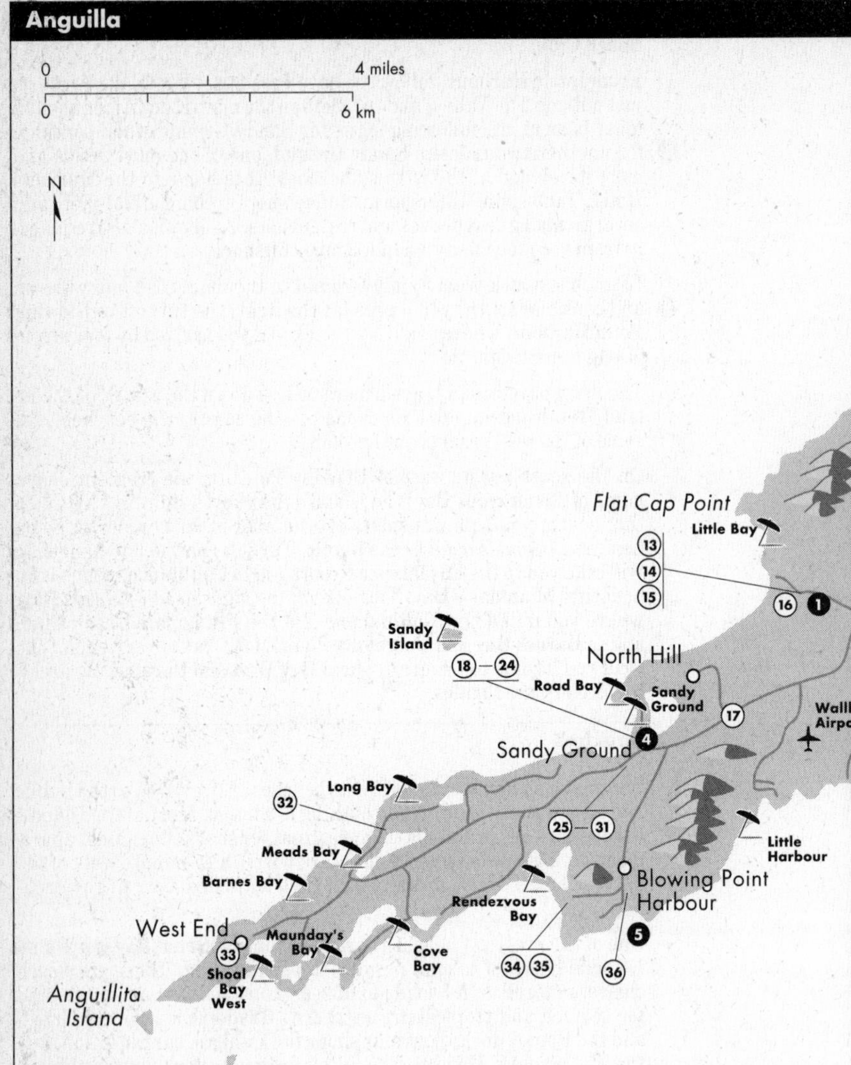

Exploring

Blowing Point Harbour, **5**

The Fountain, **2**

Sandy Ground, **4**

Sandy Hill Bay, **3**

Wallblake House, **1**

Dining

Aquarium, **25**

Arlo's, **26**

Chillie's, **18**

Cross Roads, **14**

Hill Street Snack Bar, **13**

Johnno's, **19**

La Fontana, **10**

Lucy's Harbour View Restaurant, **27**

The Old House, **17**

Pepper Pot, **15**

Riviera Bar and Restaurant, **20**

Roy's, **16**

Short Curve, **28**

Smitty's, **6**

Smuggler's Grill, **37**

Tropical Penguin, **24**

Uncle Ernie's, **11**

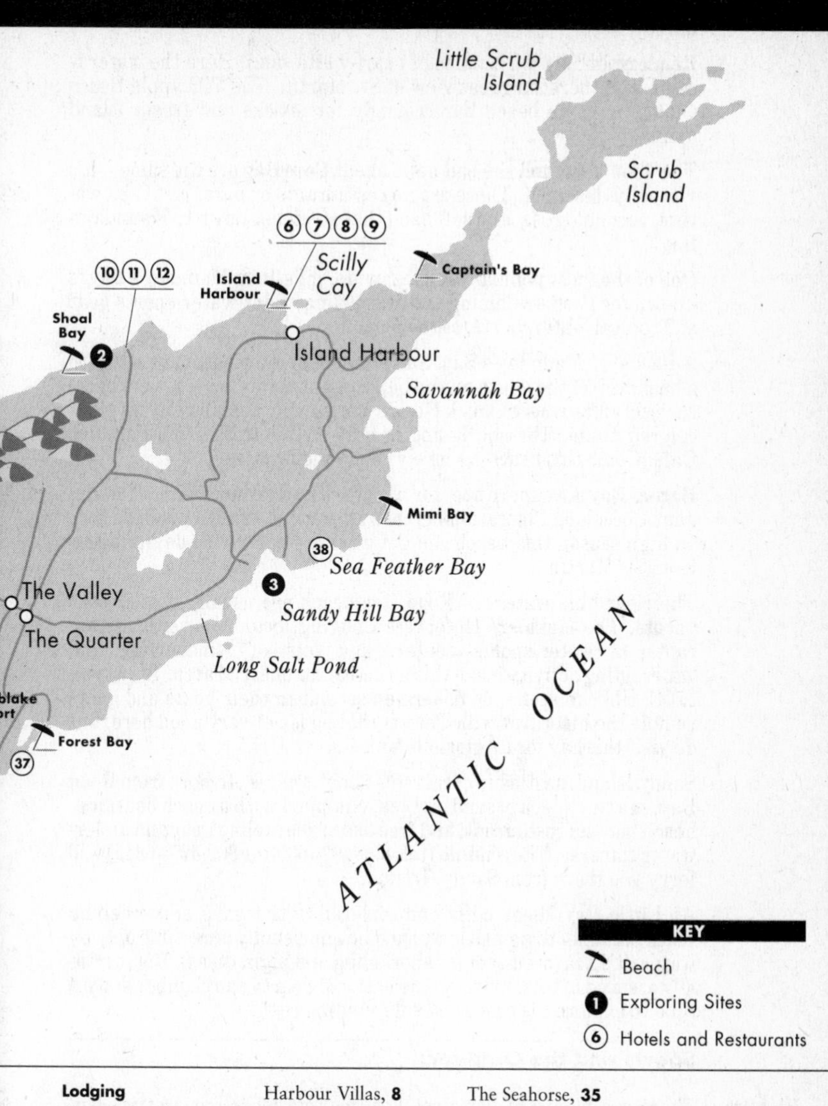

Lodging
Arawak Beach Resort, **9**
Blue Waters Inn, **33**
Easy Corner Villas, **29**
Ferryboat Inn, **36**
Harbour Lights, **7**
Harbour Villas, **8**
Inter-Island Hotel, **30**
La Palma, **21**
La Sirena, **32**
Mariners, **22**
Rainbow Reef, **38**
Rendezvous Bay Hotel, **34**
The Seahorse, **35**
Shoal Bay Villas, **12**
Skiffles Villas, **31**
Sydan's, **23**

kel in the warm waters. Don't plan to sunbathe—the beach is quite narrow here.

Rendezvous Bay is 1½ miles of pearl-white sand. Here the water is calm, and there's a great view of St. Martin. The Pineapple Beach Club's open-air beach bar is handy for snacks and frosty island drinks.

The good news and the bad news about **Cove Bay** are the same—it's virtually deserted. There are no restaurants or bars, just calm waters, coconut trees, and soft sand that stretches down to Maunday's Bay.

One of the most popular beaches, wide, mile-long **Maunday's Bay** is known for good swimming and snorkeling. Rent water-sports gear at Tropical Watersports (*see below*).

Adjacent to Maunday's Bay, **Shoal Bay West** is a pleasant beach with a backdrop of the white stucco buildings of Cove Castles, a set of futuristic villas where Chuck Norris has a home, set apart by its pink-colored stone. The snorkeling is best in the area of the Paradise Cafe. Comb this beach for lovely conch shells as well.

Barnes Bay is a superb spot for windsurfing and snorkeling. The elegant Coccoloba Plantation perches above and offers a poolside bar. In high season this beach can get a bit crowded with day-trippers from St. Martin.

The clear blue waters of **Road Bay** beach are usually dotted with yachts. The Mariners Hotel (*see* Lodging, *below*), several restaurants, a water-sports center, and lots of windsurfing and waterskiing activity make this an active commercial area. It's a typical Caribbean scene, as fishermen set out in their boats and goats ramble the littoral at will. The snorkeling is not very good here, but do visit this bay for its glorious sunsets.

Sandy Island, nestled in coral reefs about 2 miles offshore from Road Bay, is a tiny speck of sand and sea, equipped with a beach boutique, beach bar and restaurant, and free use of snorkeling gear and underwater cameras. The ***Shauna*** (tel. 809/497–6395 or 809/497–6845) will ferry you there from Sandy Ground.

At **Little Bay** sheer cliffs embroidered with agave and creeping vines plummet to a small gray sand beach, usually accessible only by water (it's a favored spot for snorkeling and night dives). But, virtually assured of total privacy, the hale and hearty can clamber down a rope to explore the caves and surrounding reef.

Sports and the Outdoors

Bicycling There are plenty of flat stretches, making wheeling pretty easy. Bikes can be rented (for about $15–$20 a day) at **Boothes** (tel. 809/497–2075) and at **Boo's Cycle Rental** (809/497–2323), where you can also rent mopeds and scooters. **Multiscenic Tours** (tel. 809/497–5810) rents mountain bikes.

Fitness Lest you go flabby lolling around on the beach, you'll find exercise equipment, aerobics, and martial arts instruction at **Highway Gym** (George Hill Rd., tel. 809/497–2363). A day pass costs $8.

Tennis Hotel guests have priority, but occasionally resorts will rent out an empty court, usually at $30–$40 an hour. If you're determined to play, there are two courts at the **Carimar Beach Club** (tel. 809/497–6881), two lighted courts at **Coccoloba Plantation** (tel. 809/497–6871), four courts at **Cap Juluca** (tel. 809/497–6666), four (two lighted) championship courts at **Malliouhana** (tel. 809/497–6111), two Deco Turf tournament courts at **Cinnamon Reef** (tel. 809/497–2727), and two courts at **Fountain Beach and Tennis Club** (tel. 809/497–6395). Tennis is also available on single courts at **Cove Castles**

(tel. 809/497–6801), **Mariners** (tel. 809/497–2671), **Masara** (tel. 809/497–3200), **Rendezvous Bay** (tel. 809/497–6549), **Pelicans** (tel. 809/497–6593), **Sea Grapes** (tel. 809/497–6433), and **Spindrift Apts.** (tel. 809/497–4164).

Sea Excursions Picnic, swimming, and diving excursions to Prickly Pear, Sandy Island, and Scilly Cay are available through **Sandy Island Enterprises** (tel. 809/497–6395), **Enchanted Island Cruises** (tel. 809/497–3111), **Suntastic Cruises** (tel. 809/497–3400), and **Tropical Watersports** (tel. 809/497–6666 or 809/497–6779). Prices average $20–$40 per person, depending on the activity and whether meals or drinks are included. Use of snorkeling equipment is usually free. **Princess Soya** (tel. 809/497–2671) offers snorkeling trips and half-day sails on a 50-foot catamaran, starting at $30 per person. Fishing trips can be arranged through Elbert or Trevor Richardson in Long Bay (tel. 809/497–6397). Local fisherman Rollin Ruan (tel. 809/497–3394) is a font of knowledge and will take you out on one of his boats for a half- or full-day excursion, including snorkeling and refreshments; cost ranges from $20 to $40 per person.

Water Sports The major resorts offer complimentary Windsurfers, paddleboats, and water skis to their guests. If your hotel has no water-sports facilities, you can get in gear at **Tropical Watersports** at Cap Juluca Resort (tel. 809/497–6666 or 809/497–6779) or **Tamariain Watersports** (tel. 809/497–2020). Tamariain Watersports also has PADI instructors, short resort courses, and more than a dozen dive sites, including several spectacular wrecks and reefs. Single-tank dives are $40; snorkel-gear rental, $6.

Shopping

Shopping tips are readily available in the informative free publications *Anguilla Life* and *What We Do in Anguilla*, but you have to be a really dedicated shopper to peel yourself off the beach and poke around in Anguilla's few shops.

Stop at **Beach Stuff** (Back St., South Hill, tel. 809/497–6814) for a good selection of inexpensive but very fashionable sportswear and swimwear. **The Valley Gap** (Shoal Bay Beach, tel. 809/497–2754) is the place for local crafts, T-shirts, and swimwear. **Vanhelle Boutique** (Sandy Ground, tel. 809/497–2965) stocks gift items and Brazilian swimsuits for men and women. **Java Wraps** (George Hill Rd., tel. 809/497–5497), a small branch of the Caribbean-wide chain, carries superb batik clothing for the whole family. **Oluwakemi's Afrocentric Boutique** (Lansome Rd., The Valley, tel. 809/497–5411) sells books, sandals, umbrellas, jewelry, T-shirts, hats, and all manner of clothing; they'll be happy to sew to order.

A wide selection of island crafts are found at **Anguilla Arts and Crafts Center** (The Valley, tel. 809/497–2200). **Alicea's Place** (The Quarter, tel. 809/497–3540) sells locally made ceramics and pottery. At **New World Gallery** (The Valley, tel. 809/407–5950) you can usually view an exhibit and also browse for art, jewelry, textiles, and antiquities. Visit **Scruples Gift Shop** (Social Security Bldg., tel. 809/497–2800) for simple gift items such as shells, handmade baskets, wooden dolls, hand-crocheted mats, lace tablecloths, and bedspreads. **Devonish Cotton Gin Art Gallery** (The Valley, tel. 809/497–2949) displays and sells the work of several prominent local artists, including the wood, stone, and clay creations of Courtney Devonish, an internationally known potter and sculptor. **Cheddie's Carving Shop** (The Cove, tel. 809/497–6027), just down the road from Coccoloba Plantation, showcases Cheddie's own work—wonderfully textured, fanciful creatures fashioned from various woods, including mahogany, walnut, and driftwood. Even the whimsically carved desk and balustrade in his studio testify to his vivid imagination.

Many artists hold open studios; the tourism board can provide brochures.

Dining

Anguilla is one of those islands where the restaurants tend to fall into two categories: those serving very expensive Continental cuisine and those dishing up budget Caribbean fare. Even with careful ordering you generally can't keep the former within a low budget, but at the latter you'll enjoy delicious food and good company at affordable prices. Luckily, the handful or so of restaurants that fall into the reasonable middle price range are excellent. Call ahead—in the winter to make a reservation, and in the summer and fall to see if the place you've chosen is open. Most restaurants not affiliated with a hotel tack an additional 5% on to the service charge if you pay by credit card.

If you're cooking in, **Vista Food Market** (South Hill, tel. 809/497–2804) is usually well stocked. If you plan to picnic (on the beach or in your room), try the **Fat Cat** (George Hill, tel. 809/497–2307) for escargots to go, as well as takeout quiche, soups, chili, chicken, and conch dishes. **Amy's Bakery** (Blowing Point, tel. 809/497–6775) turns out homemade pies, cakes, tarts, cookies, and breads.

Highly recommended restaurants are indicated by a star ★.

Category	Cost*
$$	$25–$35
$	$15–$25
¢	under $15

**per person, excluding drinks, service, and 8% sales tax*

$$ ★ **La Fontana.** Northern Italian dishes at this small restaurant have spicy island touches, thanks to the Rastafarian chef. Pasta possibilities include *fettuccine al limone* (with a sauce of black olives, lemon, parmesan, and butter), pasta with lobster and fresh herbs, and a daily Rasta pasta special, such as linguine with tomatoes and shrimp. Also on the menu are grilled duck, steak, fish, and chicken, and a fantastic lobster dish cooked with black olives, capers, and tomatoes. *Fountain Beach hotel, Shoal Bay, tel. 809/497–3492. Reservations accepted. AE, MC, V. Closed Wed. and Sept.*

$$ **Lucy's Harbour View Restaurant.** A swinging gate forms the entrance to this terrace restaurant. Sweeping sea views and Lucy's delicious whole red snapper are the specialties here; curried and Creole dishes, such as conch and goat, are also favored selections. Be sure to try the sautéed potatoes (be very sparing with the tableside hot sauce!). A reggae band plays on Wednesday and Friday nights. *South Hill, tel. 809/497–6253. Reservations accepted. No credit cards. Closed Sun.*

$$ **Riviera Bar & Restaurant.** The chef here has created an unusual menu of French, Creole, and Asian specialties—French cheeses, homemade pâté, sushi, oysters sautéed in soy sauce and sake, and dolphinfish in a spicy Creole sauce are typical offerings. The grilled lobster and fish soup à la Provençale are highly recommended. The beachside setting is relaxed and informal, and there's a very happy Happy Hour from 6 to 7 daily. Live bands play here frequently in season. *Sandy Ground, tel. 809/497–2833. Reservations advised in season. AE, V.*

$$ ★ **Smuggler's Grill.** Visit this romantic, somewhat-out-of-the-way restaurant on Forest Bay to sample one of its 10 different preparations of fresh Anguillan lobster. The chef has based the recipes on cuisines from around the world, including French, Southeast Asian, In-

dian, and Tunisian. The menu also includes escargot, onion soup, and other French bistro fare, and a good selection of steaks and chops. The salad bar is amply stocked. *Forest Bay, tel. 809/497–3728. MC, V. Closed Sun. and Aug.–Sept. No lunch.*

$–$$ ★ **Arlo's.** This popular Italian restaurant serves the best pizza on the island. If you don't want pizza as a main course, share one as an appetizer, then choose from a list of entrées that includes spaghetti Bolognese, lasagna, tortellini du jour, various preparations of fettuccine, and veal or chicken parmigiana. There's always a nightly appetizer and entrée special. The hilltop setting overlooks the sea; you can dine indoors or on the terrace. *South Hill, tel. 809/497–6810. MC, V. Closed Sun. and Sept.–Oct. No lunch.*

$–$$ ★ **The Old House.** Guests enjoy the relaxing atmosphere at this lovely restaurant on a hill near the airport. Tables are covered with white and green tablecloths and are decorated with fresh flowers, even at breakfast, when those in the know order island fruit pancakes. For lunch or dinner try the conch simmered in lime juice and wine, curried local lamb with pigeon peas and rice, or Anguillan fish cooked in a pot with limes, garlic, and tomatoes. *George Hill, tel. 809/497–2228. Reservations advised. AE, D, MC, V.*

$ **Aquarium.** An upstairs terrace, the Aquarium is all gussied up with gingerbread trim, bright blue walls, and red tablecloths. The lunch menu lists sandwiches and burgers. Stewed lobster, curried chicken, barbecued chicken, and mutton stew are offered at night. This is a popular spot with locals. *South Hill, tel. 809/497–2720. Reservations accepted. No credit cards. Closed Tues.*

$ ★ **Roy's.** The dainty pink-and-white-covered deck belies the rowdy reputation of Roy and Mandy Bosson's pub, an Anguillan mainstay and one of the island's best buys. The menu's most popular items are Roy's fish-and-chips, cold English beer, pork fricassee, and a wonderful chocolate rum cake. Sunday's lunch special is roast beef and Yorkshire pudding. A faithful clientele gathers in the lively bar. *Crocus Bay, tel. 809/497–2470. Reservations accepted. MC, V. Closed Mon. No lunch Sat.*

$ **Tropical Penguin.** This is the newest addition to the bars and restaurants scattered along the shores at Sandy Ground. The yachting crowd and landlubbers alike head here for light lunches of salads, sandwiches, or hamburgers and come back at dinnertime for grilled chicken, pasta dishes, and fresh fish. *Sandy Ground, tel. 809/497-2253. No credit cards. Closed Sat.*

¢–$ **Chillies.** For a change of pace, stop in this beach bar for killer margaritas and surprisingly decent Tex-Mex fare, including chili potato soup and seafood quesadillas. Dishes tend to be bland unless you request otherwise. *Sandy Ground, tel. 809/497–3171. AE, MC, V.*

¢–$ **Cross Roads.** Millie Philip's roadside bar features hearty breakfasts and, at lunch, seafood salads, fish, and chicken—all satisfying fare at low prices. *Wallblake, The Valley, tel. 809/497–2581. No credit cards.*

¢–$ **Hill Street Snack Bar.** Stop here for great hamburgers and giant portions of West Indian specialties—oxtail, lamb chops, and fresh local fish served with peas and rice. *George Hill, tel. 809/497–2487. No credit cards.*

¢–$ ★ **Johnno's.** Performances by the island band Dumpa and the AnvVibes make this *the* place to be on Sunday afternoons, but the grilled or barbecued lobster, kingfish, snapper (all of which Johnno catches himself), and chicken are good anytime. This is a classic Caribbean beach bar, attracting a funky eclectic mix, from locals to movie stars. *Sandy Ground, tel. 809/497–2728. No credit cards.*

¢–$ **Short Curve.** You'll get tasty homemade sea moss, maubey (a drink made from the bark of a tree) and ginger beer, steamy fish soup, delectable stewed chicken, and other island specialties at this quiet spot off the main road. Huge portions are dressed with mounds of rice and peas, fresh potato salad, and greens. *South Hill, tel. 809/497–6600. No credit cards.*

¢–$ **Smitty's.** The tempting aroma of barbecue wafts through this small, trellised shack on the sand overlooking colorful Island Harbour. Try the succulent local lobster or juicy ribs. Smitty's rocks with live music Thursdays and Sundays. *Island Harbour, tel. 809/497–4300. No credit cards.*

¢ **Pepper Pot.** Cora Richardson's small eatery in the center of town serves some of the best *rotis* on the island. Here these Trinidadian specialties are made of boneless chicken, *tania* (a local vegetable), celery, pepper, onion, garlic, and peas, all wrapped in dough and baked. Dumpling dinners, lobster, whelk, and conch are also good choices. *The Valley, tel. 809/497–2328. Reservations accepted. No credit cards.*

¢ **Uncle Ernie's.** No one is saying whether this beach shack is named after the "wicked" character in the rock opera *Tommy,* but it does serve a mean ribs and coleslaw for $6 and ice cold beer for a buck. Lots of regulars call it home. *Shoal Bay, no telephone. No credit cards.*

Lodging

Even in the island's lowest season (mid-June–mid-September), standard room rates at luxury resorts are expensive. Note that the high ranges in our price chart reflect the realities of this tony island. Yet unlike some expensive islands that have few or no options for the budget traveler, Anguilla does offer some affordable smaller properties. Guest houses here are usually simple, locally owned properties, with few if any of a larger hotel's amenities and facilities, but they often represent substantial savings. As a rule, lodgings clustered around Sandy Ground, Shoal Bay, and Island Harbour represent the best value, if only for the shops and restaurants within walking distance. The more expensive hotels have air-conditioning; cheaper apartments and guest houses often substitute ceiling fans. Ask the **Tourist Office** (tel. 809/497–2759) for its Inns of Anguilla list. When you call to reserve a room in a resort, be sure to inquire about special packages.

Highly recommended lodgings are indicated by a star ★.

Category	Cost*
$$	$150–$225
$	$80–$150
¢	under $80

**All prices are for a standard double room for two, excluding 8% tax and a 10% service charge. To estimate rates for hotels offering MAP, add about $35–$40 per person per day to the above price ranges. For all-inclusives, add about $75–$100 per person per day.*

Hotels *$$* **Arawak Beach Resort.** Built on the site of an ancient Arawak village, this waterfront resort is perhaps the first in the Caribbean to showcase the Amerindian heritage of the region. Hexagonal, breezy, two-story villas are furnished with hand-carved replicas of Amerindian furniture. The restaurant serves Caribbean and Amerindian food, utilizing cassava, papaya, plantains, and other traditional island crops, some of which grow right in the restaurant's courtyard. A small museum displays artifacts uncovered during construction. Canoes are available in addition to the usual water sports. Although the hotel beach is not one of Anguilla's best, Scilly Cay and its beautiful beaches are just a minute away by launch. This is a no-smoking property; alcoholic beverages are not served, but you may bring your own. *Box 98, Island Harbour, tel. 809/497–4888, fax 809/497–*

4898. 10 rooms, 3 junior suites, 1 luxury suite. Facilities: restaurant, pool, museum, boutique, all water sports. AE. EP.

$$ ★ **La Sirena.** You'll find one of the island's best values at this personable, well-run hotel overlooking Meads Bay. La Sirena doesn't have the chic elegance of Malliouhana (its ultraluxurious neighbor), but it lets you stay just down the beach for about a third of the cost. Choose one of the five spacious villas (a new three-bedroom villa was just completed) or one of the 20 guest rooms. The decor is typical Caribbean—rattan furniture and pastel-printed fabrics. Rooms are cooled by ceiling fans. The restaurant is on the second floor and open to the sea breezes. A new Swiss chef prepares French cuisine with a Caribbean flair. *Box 200, Meads Bay, tel. 809/497–6827 or 800/331–9358; in NY, 212/251–1800; fax 809/497–6829. 20 rooms, 5 villas. Facilities: restaurant, bar, 2 pools, picnic and snorkeling equipment, car rental. AE, MC, V. EP, MAP.*

$$ **Mariners.** Honeymooners and businesspeople on retreat make up much of the clientele of this popular casual resort. It's set at the far end of the beach at Sandy Ground, one of Anguilla's busiest stretches of sand, a short stroll from a number of beach bars and restaurants. The pervasive West Indian style of the Mariners includes the charm of 19th-century gingerbread cottages, and the occasional annoyance of service that, while friendly, is so laid-back it verges on lackadaisical. Accommodations vary considerably in size and price range, from deluxe two-bedroom, two-bath cottages with full kitchens to small rooms with twin beds, minibars, and shower baths. All units are light and airy, with tile floors, white rattan, and bright prints. Charter the resort's Boston whaler for picnics, snorkeling, and fishing trips. The Thursday-night barbecue and Saturday West Indian night in the beachfront restaurant are popular island events. *Box 139, Sandy Ground, tel. 809/497–2815, 809/497–2671, or 800/223–0079; fax 809/497–2901. 25 1-bedroom suites, 25 studios. Facilities: 2 restaurants, 2 bars, Jacuzzi, laundry service, boutique, pool, lighted tennis court, water-sports center. AE, MC, V. EP, MAP, FAP, all-inclusive (drinks not included).*

$$ **Shoal Bay Villas.** Palm trees and 2 miles of splendid sand surround this small condominium hotel. Units are brightly decorated in pink and blue, with painted rattan furniture; all but the poolside doubles have fully equipped kitchens. There's no air-conditioning, but all rooms have ceiling fans. The Reefside Beach Bar is an informal open-air restaurant open for breakfast, lunch, and dinner. All water sports can be arranged, and meal and room packages can be tailored to fit your needs. Children are not allowed during the winter. *Box 81, Shoal Bay, tel. 809/497–2051 or 800/722–7045; in NY, 212/535–9530; in Canada, 416/283–2621; fax 809/497–3631. 2 studios, 2 2-bedroom units, 7 1-bedroom units, 2 poolside doubles. Facilities: restaurant, bar, pool. AE, MC, V. EP, BP, MAP.*

$–$$ ★ **Rendezvous Bay Hotel.** Anguilla's first resort, which opened more than 20 years ago, sits amid 60 acres of coconut groves on the fine white sand of Rendezvous Bay, just a mile from the ferry dock. The main building is rather undecorated and has a breezy, broad front patio. Owner Jeremiah Gumb has turned the lounge into a showcase for his elaborate electric train set, complete with tunnels and multiple tracks. The original guest rooms are about 100 yards from the beach and are quite simple, with one double and one single bed, a private shower bath, Haitian art on the walls, and ceiling fans (no air-conditioning). New two-story villas are along the wide beach or on the more rocky stretches of the coast that offer excellent snorkeling. Inside are spacious, air-conditioned one-bedroom suites, decorated in natural wicker and pastel prints, with refrigerators or kitchenettes. The suites are quite affordable and can be joined to form larger units. *Box 31, Rendezvous Bay, tel. 809/497–6549; in the United States, 908/738–0246 or 800/274–4893; in Canada, 800/468–0023; fax 809/497–6026. 20 rooms, 24 1-bedroom villa suites. Facili-*

ties: restaurant, lounge, game and TV room, 2 tennis courts, water-sports center. No credit cards. EP, MAP.

$ ★ **Ferryboat Inn.** This small family-run complex is an enjoyable bargain. It's just a short walk from the ferry dock, on a small beach. Simply furnished but spacious one- and two-bedroom apartments are decorated with white or pastel fabrics. All have full kitchens, dining areas, cable TV, and ceiling fans. The two-bedroom beach house is air-conditioned. All rooms and the open-air restaurant look out across the water to views of hilly St. Martin, which is stunning at night, when it's covered with sparkling lights. Marjorie McClean, the owner and manager, is eager to please. *Box 189, Blowing Point, tel. 809/497-6613, fax 809/497-3309. 6 1- and 2-bedroom apartments, 1 beach house (air-conditioned). Facilities: restaurant, bar. V. EP.*

$ **Inter-Island Hotel.** Rooms and two small one-bedroom apartments at this modest establishment are simply furnished with wicker and rattan. There is no air-conditioning, but some rooms have a breezy open balcony. Most rooms have refrigerators and all have cramped shower bathrooms that define the term "water closet." The homey restaurant serves hearty breakfasts and offers heaping servings at its West Indian dinners. The nearest beach is a two-minute drive away. *Box 194, The Valley, tel. 809/497-6259 or 800/223-9815; in Canada, 800/468-0023; fax 809/497-5381. 12 rooms, 2 1-bedroom apartments. Facilities: restaurant, bar, TV lounge, transportation to beach ½ mi away. AE, D, MC, V. EP.*

Guest Houses

¢ **La Palma.** This pink-and-white private home may be plain, but it's right on Road Bay. The immaculate white terrace gleams, the doors are a lovely carved mahogany, and owner Marie Richardson's welcome couldn't be warmer. She's a superb cook, too: Reserve at least one night in her sweet dollhouse of a restaurant to feast on the likes of pumpkin soup and baked chicken smothered in onions. The one-bedroom apartment and one of the three tidy rooms include a kitchenette. *Sandy Ground, tel. 809/497-3260. 3 studios, 1 1-bedroom apartment. Facilities: restaurant, bar. AE. EP.*

Villa and Apartment Rentals

Private villas are generally not affordable on Anguilla. Apartment complexes, while modest, are clean, well-run, and often tastefully furnished. The Tourist Office has a complete listing of vacation rentals. You can also contact **Sunshine Villas** (Box 142, Blowing Point, tel. 809/497-6149) or **Property Real Estate Management Services** (Box 256, George Hill, tel. 809/497-2596), which represents more moderate choices. Housekeeping accommodations are plentiful and well organized. The following are a selection:

$$ ★ **Blue Waters Inn.** These glistening white, Moorish-style buildings sit at the far end of a spectacular beach, within walking distance of several excellent restaurants. Sunny one- and two-bedroom units (the latter just slipping into the high end of this price category) are decorated with pastel fabrics and have white tile floors, dining areas, full kitchens, and terraces. *Box 69, Shoal Bay West, tel. 809/497-6292, fax 809/497-3309. 9 apartments. AE, MC, V.*

$$ **Easy Corner Villas.** These one-, two-, and three-bedroom apartments with kitchens are adequately furnished and have well-equipped kitchens with microwaves. Only three of the units are air-conditioned; all have only shower baths. Number 10 is a deluxe two-bedroom villa. The location, on a bluff overlooking Road Bay, means you have to walk five minutes to the beach, but the price is right. *Box 65, South Hill, tel. 809/497-6433, 809/497-6541, or 800/223-8815. 17 units. AE, MC, V.*

$$ **Rainbow Reef.** Three seaside acres provide a dramatically beautiful setting for this group of villas. Each self-contained unit has two bedrooms, a fully equipped kitchen, a spacious dining and living area, and a large gallery overlooking the sea. A gazebo with beach furniture and barbecue facilities perches right above the beach. *Box 130,*

Sea Feather Bay, tel. 809/497–2817 or 708/325–2299. 14 units. No credit cards.

$$ ★ **Skiffles Villas.** These self-catering villas, perched on a hill overlooking Road Bay, are usually booked a year in advance. The one-, two-, and three-bedroom apartments have fully equipped kitchens, floor-to-ceiling windows, and pleasant porches. *Box 82, Lower South Hill, tel. 809/497–6619, 219/642–4855, or 219/642–4445. 5 units. Facilities: pool. No credit cards.*

$ **Harbour Villas.** The area surrounding this property is less developed than other hotel locations on Anguilla and bursting with local flavor. However, it's across the street from and overlooks all the activity of Island Harbour and its small beach. Charming Mediterranean-style villas have a full kitchen, a shower bath, and an appealing, homey decor. *Island Harbour, tel. 809/497–4393. 16 villas. No credit cards.*

$ **The Seahorse.** These cozy, secluded cottages overlook Rendezvous Bay, arguably Anguilla's most exquisite beach. Each apartment has a kitchenette, a shower bath, and a private ocean-view terrace. *Cul de Sac, tel. 809/497–6751. 5 1-bedroom apartments. No credit cards.*

$ **Sydan's.** These pleasant, clean efficiencies are a tremendous bargain. Each has a kitchenette and shower bath and is comfortably furnished. Road Bay, with all its bustling activity, is just across the street. *Sandy Ground, tel. 809/497–3180. 6 studios. Facilities: gift shop. AE, MC, V.*

¢–$ **Harbour Lights.** These pretty, slightly weathered blue-and-white buildings front their own tiny private beach. The units are nothing special, but are breezy and pleasant, with kitchenettes and shower baths. *Island Harbour, tel. 809/497–4435. 4 1-bedroom apartments. No credit cards.*

Off-Season Bets If you're in luck, the deluxe, sumptuous **Cap Juluca** (Maunday's Bay, tel. 809/497–6666) or **Malliouhana** (Mead's Bay, tel. 809/497–6111) may offer a special package during the off-season (April 15–December 15). You'll have a chance to experience pampering and elegance usually reserved for royalty, rock stars, and Rothschilds. The tranquil, lovely villas at **Cinnamon Reef Beach Club** (Little Harbour, tel. 809/497–2727) can also sneak into our $$ category during low season.

Nightlife

Much of the music and entertainment on Anguilla occurs at some of the least expensive bars and restaurants. Also, although a single drink at one of the luxury resorts may run $6, it often comes with excellent entertainment.

The **Mayoumba Folkloric Group**, a group made up of the best performers in the Anguilla Choral Circle, performs complete song-and-dance skits depicting Antillean and Caribbean culture with African drums and a string band. They appear every Thursday night at **La Sirena** (Meads Bay, tel. 809/497–6827). Be on the lookout for Bankie Banx, Anguilla's own reggae superstar. He has his own group called New Generations. If you're lucky, you'll catch him playing solo at the **Malliouhana** (Meads Bay, tel. 809/497–6111) during cocktail hours. You'll appreciate his true talent—no electronics here, just a remarkable voice and great guitar playing. Other local groups include Keith Gumbs and The Mellow Tones, Spraka, Megaforce, Joe and the Invaders, Dumpa and the AnvVibes, and Sleepy and the All-Stars, a string-and-scratch band. Steel Vibrations, a pan band, often entertains at barbecues and West Indian evenings. Most of the major hotels feature some kind of live entertainment almost nightly in season. A Calypso combo plays most nights at **Cinnamon Reef Beach Club** (Little Harbour, tel. 809/497–2727). **The Mariners** (Sandy Ground, tel. 809/497–2671) has regularly scheduled Thursday-night barbecues and Saturday-night West Indian parties, both with live entertainment by local groups. During high season,

Pimms and **Chatterton's** (Cap Juluca, tel. 809/497–6666) have live music at dinner. Things are pretty loose and lively at **Johnno's** beach bar (tel. 809/497–2728) in Sandy Ground, which has live music and alfresco dancing Wednesday and Saturday nights and Sunday afternoons, when it feels as if the entire island population is in attendance. The **Dragon's Disco** (South Hill, tel. 809/497–2687) is a hot spot on weekends after midnight. The **Coconut Paradise** restaurant (Island Harbour, tel. 809/497–4150) has nightly entertainment ranging from disco to limbo. For soft dance music after a meal, go to **Lucy's Palm Palm** (tel. 809/497–2253) at Sandy Ground. There is usually a live band on Tuesday and Friday evenings. Sunday is the big night in restaurants. In addition to the above, **Uncle Ernie's** (Shoal Bay, no tel.), **Round Rock** (Shoal Bay, tel. 809/497–2076), and **Smitty's** (Island Harbour, tel. 809/497–4300) swing all day and well into the night.

3 Antigua

Updated by Jordan Simon

One could spend an entire year—and a leap year, at that—exploring the beaches of Antigua (pronounced an-*tee*-ga); the island has 366 of them, many with snow-white sand. All the beaches are public, and many are backed by lavish resorts offering sailing, diving, windsurfing, and snorkeling. These resorts have given Antigua a reputation as one of the most expensive islands in the Caribbean.

The largest of the British Leewards, Antigua is where Lord Horatio Nelson headquartered during his forays into the Caribbean to do battle with the French and pirates in the late 18th century, and there is still a decidedly British atmosphere here, with Olde English public houses that will raise the spirits of Anglophiles. Since becoming independent from Great Britain in 1981, however, Antigua has gone Floridian in a big way. Large resorts catering to an international (mostly North American and European) package-tour clientele have proliferated. Club Antigua, for instance, is the largest resort in the eastern Caribbean: 470 rooms and 16 villas and still growing. Not all of these large, mainly all-inclusive resorts are affordable in high season, though, despite their democratic feel. If you're traveling to Antigua in the winter, you'll find better value in the smaller, self-catering hotels, particularly around St. John's and English Harbour. Good guest house and B&B accommodations here are rare. On the other hand, budget dining is plentiful at small restaurants and cafés, especially in St. John's.

Antigua is still a place with a rich history and a strong sense of national identity. Its cricketers, like the legendary Viv Richards, arguably the greatest batsman the game has ever seen, are famous throughout the Caribbean. English Harbour, on the southeast end of the island, is steeped in the history of the colonial era and Lord Horatio Nelson. Nelson's Dockyard is Antigua's answer to Williamsburg, Virginia: a carefully restored gem of British Georgian architecture that still evokes a vanished era and the world-famous admiral who gave it its name. For history buffs, English

Harbour and the surrounding villages and historic sites offer much of interest.

Those who want beaches, nightlife, and resorts should head for Dickenson Bay, at the northwest end of the island. It's here that a lively tourist trade has grown up, centered on the bustling capital of St. John's. You can parasail and waterski, bounce across the azure water on an inflatable rubber banana, lie in a Jacuzzi, or sip piña coladas at a swim-up bar as you listen to Bob Marley and the Wailers. Swingers and singles abound, as do restaurants, discos, and casinos. The least-developed part of the island is in the southwest, in the shadow of Antigua's highest mountain, Boggy Peak. At Fry's Bay and Darkwood Beach, visitors will find long, unspoiled beaches and, on weekends, Antiguan families who come to swim and picnic under the tamarind trees. Antigua's sister island of Barbuda, about 30 miles to the north, offers shelling, diving, and snorkeling for day-trippers from Antigua.

What It Will Cost These sample prices, meant only as a general guide, are for high season. A ¢ hotel is about $60 a night; a bed-and-breakfast for two, about $50; and a modest two-bedroom villa, about $900 a week. Expect to pay around $200 a night for a $$ hotel. A ¢ restaurant meal will be $6–$10; a sandwich lunch is about $5. A rum punch here costs around $3.50, a glass of house wine anywhere from $3 to $5, and a beer is about $1.50. Car rental here is expensive—about $50 a day, plus $12 for a temporary license. It's $6 for a taxi from St. John's to Dickenson Bay; from St. John's to English Harbour is $18. A single-tank dive averages $40, while snorkel equipment rents for about $10 a day.

Before You Go

Tourist Information Contact the **Antigua and Barbuda Tourist Offices** (610 5th Ave., Suite 311, New York, NY 10020, tel. 212/541–4117; 25 S.E. 2nd Ave., Suite 300, Miami, FL 33131, tel. 305/381–6762; 60 St. Clair Ave. E, Suite 304, Toronto, Ontario M4T 1N5, Canada, tel. 416/961–3085; Antigua House, 15 Thayer St., London W1M 5LD, England, tel. 0171/486–7073).

Arriving and Departing

By Plane **American Airlines** (tel. 800/433–7300) has daily direct service from New York and Miami, as well as several flights from San Juan that connect with flights from more than 100 U.S. cities. **BWIA** (tel. 800/JET–BWIA) has direct service from New York, Miami, and Toronto; **Air Canada** (tel. 800/422–6232) from Toronto; **British Airways** (tel. 800/247–9297) from London; and **Lufthansa** (tel. 800/645–3880) from Frankfurt. **LIAT** (tel. 809/462–0701) has daily flights from Antigua to Barbuda, 15 minutes away, as well as to down-island destinations.

V.C. Bird International Airport is, on a much smaller scale, to the Caribbean what O'Hare is to the Midwest. When several wide-bodies are sitting on the runway at the same time, all waiting to be cleared for takeoff, things can get a bit congested.

From the Airport Taxis meet every flight, and drivers will offer to guide you around the island. The taxis are unmetered, but rates are posted at the airport and drivers are required to carry a rate card with them. The fixed rate from the airport to St. John's (20 minutes) is $12 in U.S. currency (although drivers often *quote* Eastern Caribbean dollars); from the airport to English Harbour (30 minutes), $24; and from St. John's to the Dockyard, $40 round-trip.

Passports and Visas U.S. and Canadian citizens need only proof of identity. A valid passport is most desirable, but a birth certificate is acceptable provided it has a raised or embossed seal and has been issued by a county or state (not a hospital) *and* provided that you also have some type of photo identification, such as a driver's license. A driver's license by itself is *not* sufficient. British citizens need a passport. All visitors must present a return or ongoing ticket.

Language Antigua's official language is English.

Precautions Some beaches are shaded by manchineel trees, whose leaves and applelike fruit are poisonous to touch. Most of the trees are posted with warning signs and should be avoided; even raindrops falling from them can cause painful blisters. If you should come in contact with one, rinse the affected area and contact a doctor.

Throughout the Caribbean, incidents of petty theft are increasing. Leave your valuables in the hotel safe-deposit box; don't leave them unattended in your room or on the beach. Also, the streets of St. John's are fairly deserted at night, so it's not a good idea to wander out alone.

Staying in Antigua

Important Addresses **Tourist Information:** The **Antigua and Barbuda Department of Tourism** (Thames and Long Sts., St. John's, tel. 809/462–0480) is open Monday–Thursday 8–4:30, Friday 8–3. There is also a tourist-information desk at the airport, just beyond the immigration checkpoint. The tourist office gives limited information. You may have more success with the **Antigua Hotels Association** (Long St., St. John's, tel. 809/462–3703), which also provides assistance.

Emergencies **Police:** tel. 809/462–0125. **Fire:** tel. 809/462–0044. **Ambulance:** tel. 809/462–0251. **Hospital:** There is a 24-hour emergency room at the 210-bed **Holberton Hospital** (Hospital Rd., St. John's, tel. 809/462–0251/2/3). **Pharmacies: Joseph's Pharmacy** (Redcliffe St., St. John's, tel. 809/462–1025), **City Pharmacy** (St. Mary's St., St. John's, tel. 809/462–1363), and **Health Pharmacy** (Redcliffe St., St. John's, tel. 809/462–1255).

Currency Local currency is the Eastern Caribbean dollar (E.C.$), which is tied to the U.S. dollar and fluctuates only slightly. At hotels, the rate is E.C. $2.60 to U.S. $1; at banks, it's about E.C. $2.70. American dollars are readily accepted, although you will usually receive change in E.C. dollars. Be sure you understand which currency is being used, since most places quote prices in E.C. dollars. Most hotels, restaurants, and duty-free shops take major credit cards, and all accept traveler's checks. It's a good idea to inquire at the Tourist Office or your hotel about current credit-card policy. Note: Prices quoted are in U.S. dollars unless indicated otherwise.

Taxes and Service Charges Hotels collect a 7% government room tax and add a 10% service charge to your bill. In restaurants, a 10% service charge is usually added to your bill, and it's customary to leave another 5% if you are pleased with the service. Taxi drivers expect a 10% tip. The departure tax is $10.

Getting Around Antigua is a fairly large island, as Caribbean islands go (it's a 40-minute drive from Dickenson Bay to English Harbour, for instance). You will need at least one very full day, and preferably two, to really explore. Roads are extensive but not particularly good. Driving is on the left-hand side. The standard forms of transportation are cab and private car. There is no public bus service as such. If you are staying at an all-inclusive resort, you will probably only leave your accommodation once or twice for shopping or a sightseeing excursion. Almost all resorts and hotels either have their own stretch of beach or are within walking distance of one. Hitchhiking is not encouraged on Antigua.

Taxis Taxis are abundant on Antigua, and you won't have to look far to find one. Most hotels and resorts have their own cab drivers. In St. John's, there is a busy taxi stand, appropriately near the King's Casino, in the Heritage Quay complex. Taxis are unmetered, but rates are fixed by the government and drivers are required to carry a rate sheet. A cab from resorts in Dickenson Bay to St. John's costs $6; from St. John's to English Harbour, $18.

Public Transportation There is no scheduled bus service on Antigua. However, an extensive network of privately owned minibuses (mostly 16-seater Nissans) connects the main centers of St. John's and English Harbour with the rest of the island. These are mostly used by local people traveling to work or to shop, but they do offer a cheap, if unreliable, alternative to cabs.

Cross-island buses leave from St. John's at the West Bus Station at the end of Market Street and travel by three different routes. One route travels via the village of All Saints to English Harbour. Another services the southwest coast, via Ebenezer and Johnson's Point. A third goes to the southeast coast via the village of Philip's. Buses from the East Bus Station in St. John's, on Independence Avenue, service points east, passing via Potter's and Seeton's to Pineapple Beach. Fares are computed by distance, but are low (St. John's to English Harbour costs E.C. $4). There are no set timetables and no fixed bus stops (just flag down the bus). Most depart St. John's and the villages early, about 6:30 AM, and return as needed, usually about two hours later.

Rental Cars To rent a car, you'll need a valid driver's license and a temporary permit ($12), which is available through the rental agent. Rentals average about $50, in season, per day, with unlimited mileage. Most agencies provide both automatic and stick shift and both right- and left-hand-drive vehicles. If you plan to drive, be careful! Not only is driving on the left, but Antiguan roads are also generally unmarked and full of potholes. Jeeps ($55 per day)are also available from most of the rental agencies. Among the agencies are **Budget** (St. John's, tel. 809/462–3009 or 800/648–4985), **National** (St. John's, tel. 809/462–2113 or 800/468–0008), **Carib Car Rentals** (Hodges Bay, tel. 809/462–2062), **Hertz** (St. John's, also Jolly Harbour, tel. 809/462–4114), **Dollar** (St. John's, tel. 809/462–0362), and **Avis** (at the airport or the St. James's Club, tel. 809/462–2840).

Telephones and Mail To call Antigua from the United States, dial 1, then area code 809, then the local seven-digit number (and cross your fingers for luck). Many numbers are restricted from receiving incoming international calls. In addition, the telephone system is primitive, and even local connections crackle. Few hotels have direct-dial telephones, but connections are easily made through the switchboard. A local call costs E.C. 25¢. Recently introduced is the phone card, to be used in new public telephones, that permits the placing of local and overseas telephone calls. You may purchase the phone card from most hotels or from a post office. Some phone card booths can now access Sprint and MCI. In addition, there are several **Boatphones** scattered throughout the island at major tourist sites; simply pick up the receiver and the operator will take your credit card number (any major card) and assign you a PIN (personal identification number). Calls using your PIN are then charged to that credit card.

To place a call to the United States, dial 1, the appropriate area code, and the seven-digit number. AT&T's USADirect is available only from a few designated telephones, such as those at the airport departure lounge, the cruise terminal at St. John's, the English Harbour Marina, the Pineapple Beach Club, and the Sugar Mill Hotel. To place an interisland call, dial the local seven-digit number.

In an emergency, you can make calls from **Cable & Wireless (WI) Ltd.** (42–44 St. Mary's St., St. John's, tel. 809/462–9840, and Nelson's Dockyard, English Harbour, tel. 809/463–1517).

Airmail letters to North America cost E.C. 60¢; postcards, E.C. 40¢. The post office is at the foot of High Street in St. John's.

Opening and Closing Times In general, shops are open Monday–Saturday 8:30–noon and 1–4. Some close at noon on Thursday and Saturday. Duty-free shops that cater to tourists often have flexible hours. Banks are open Monday–Thursday 8–2 and Friday 8–4.

Guided Tours The cheapest way to see the island is to rent a car for the day (*see above*). But if you don't want to brave left-hand driving and potholed roads, elect for a guided tour. Nearly all **taxi drivers** on Antigua double as guides; a four-hour island tour costs about $70, though prices are usually negotiable. Every major hotel has a reliable cabbie on call. Tour operators include **Bryson's Travel** (St. John's, tel. 809/462–0223); **Alexander, Parrish Ltd.** (St. John's, tel. 809/462–0387); and **Antours** (St. John's, tel. 809/462–4788).

Tropikelly (tel. 809/461–0383) and **Estate Safari Adventure** (tel. 809/462–4713) offer tours to the "wilds" of Antigua's interior, where there are few marked trails and roads are rough. Both operators charge about $55 per person and show you deserted plantation houses, rain-forest trails, and ruined sugar mills and forts. The luxuriant tropical forest around the island's highest point, Boggy Peak, is especially worth seeing. The cost of the tour includes lunch, and if you're with Estate Safari, snorkeling at a secluded beach.

Exploring Antigua

Numbers in the margin correspond to points of interest on the Antigua (and Barbuda) map.

St. John's

1 The capital city of **St. John's,** home to some 40,000 people (nearly half the island's population), lies at sea level on the northwest coast of the island. Stop in at the Tourist Bureau, at the corner of Long and Thames streets, to pick up free map and island brochures.

Cross Long Street and walk one block north and one block east to Church Street. The **Museum of Antigua and Barbuda** is a "hands-on history" opportunity. Signs say Please Touch, with the hope of welcoming both citizens and visitors into Antigua's past. Exhibits interpret the history of the nation from its geological birth to political independence in 1981. There are fossil and coral remains from some 34 million years ago, a life-size Arawak house, models of a sugar plantation, a wattle-and-daub house, and a minishop with handicrafts, books, historical prints, and paintings. The colonial building that houses the museum is the former courthouse, which dates from 1750. *Church and Market Sts., tel. 809/462–1469. Admission free. Open weekdays 8:30–4, Sat. 10–1.*

Walk two blocks east on Church Street to the **Anglican Cathedral of St. John the Divine.** The church sits on a hilltop, surrounded by its churchyard. At the south gate, there are figures of St. John the Baptist and St. John the Divine, said to have been taken from one of Napoleon's ships and brought to Antigua. The original church on this site was built in 1681 and replaced by a stone building in 1745. An earthquake destroyed that church in 1843, and the present building dates from 1845. With an eye to future earthquakes, the parishioners had the interior completely encased in pitch pine, hoping to forestall heavy damage. The church was elevated to the status of cathedral in 1848. *Between Long and Newgate Sts., tel. 809/461–0082. Admission free.*

Recross Long Street, walk one block south, and turn right on High Street. At the end of High Street, you'll see the **Cenotaph,** which honors Antiguans who lost their lives in World Wars I and II.

Retrace your steps seven blocks to the **Westerby Memorial,** which was erected in 1888 in memory of the Moravian bishop George Westerby. One block south of the memorial is **Heritage Quay,** a multimillion-dollar shopping complex that keeps expanding. Two-story

Exploring
Curtain Bluff, **11**
Devil's Bridge, **15**
Dows Hill Interpretation Center, **9**
English Harbour, **6**
Falmouth, **5**
Fig Tree Drive, **10**
Fort George, **4**
Fort James, **2**
Harmony Hall, **16**
Indian Town, **14**
Liberta, **3**
Megaliths of Greencastle Hill, **12**
Nelson's Dockyard, **7**
Parham, **13**
St. John's, **1**
Shirley Heights, **8**

Dining
Admiral's Inn, **40**
Big Banana-Pizzas on the Quay, **33**
Brother B's , **27**
Calypso, **29**
Crazy Cactus Cantina, **34**
Home, **32**
Ital, **30**
La Dolce Vita, **35**
Lemon Tree, **26**
Lobster Pot, **19**
Redcliffe Tavern, **31**
Russell's, **25**
Shirley Heights Lookout, **41**

Lodging
Admiral's Inn, **40**
Antigua Beachcomber Hotel, **17**
Banana Cove, **42**
Barrymore Beach Club, **20**
Catamaran Hotel, **38**
Club Antigua, **37**
Falmouth Beach Apartments, **39**
Island Inn, **23**
Lord Nelson Beach Hotel, **18**
Murphy's Place, **28**
Sand Haven Hotel, **22**
Spanish Main, **36**
Sunset Cove, **21**
Yepton Beach Resort, **24**

Antigua

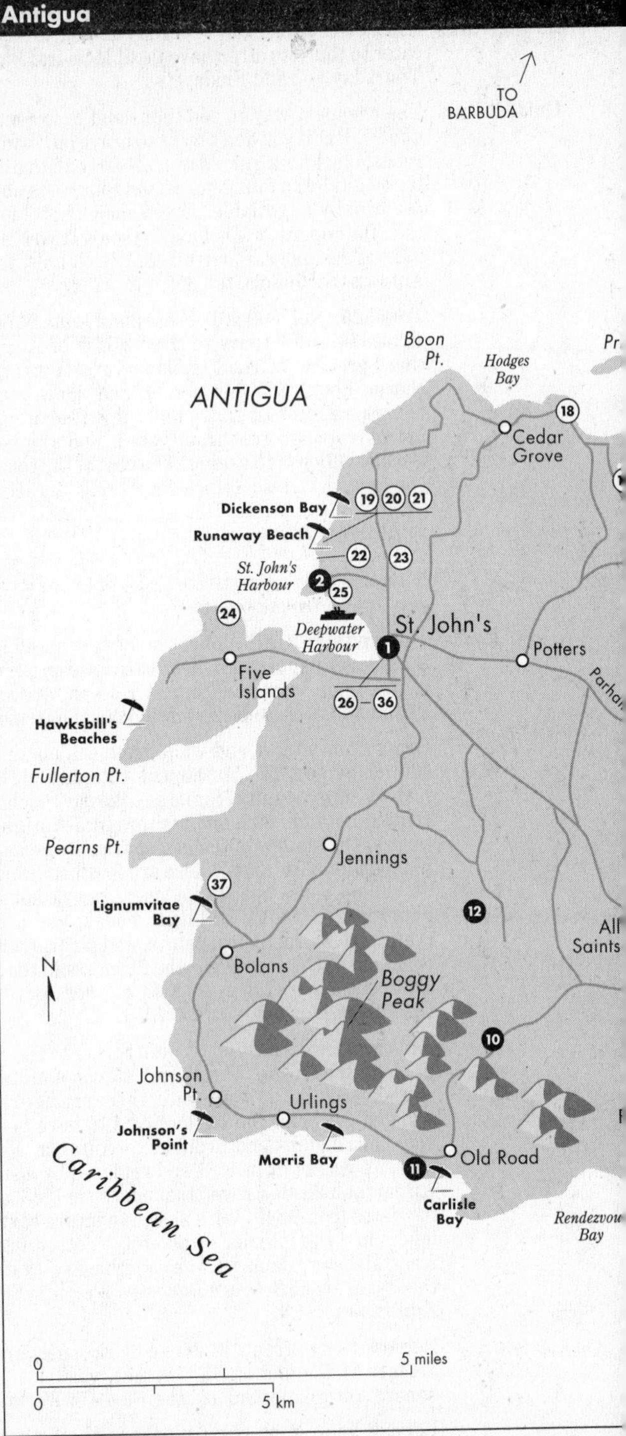

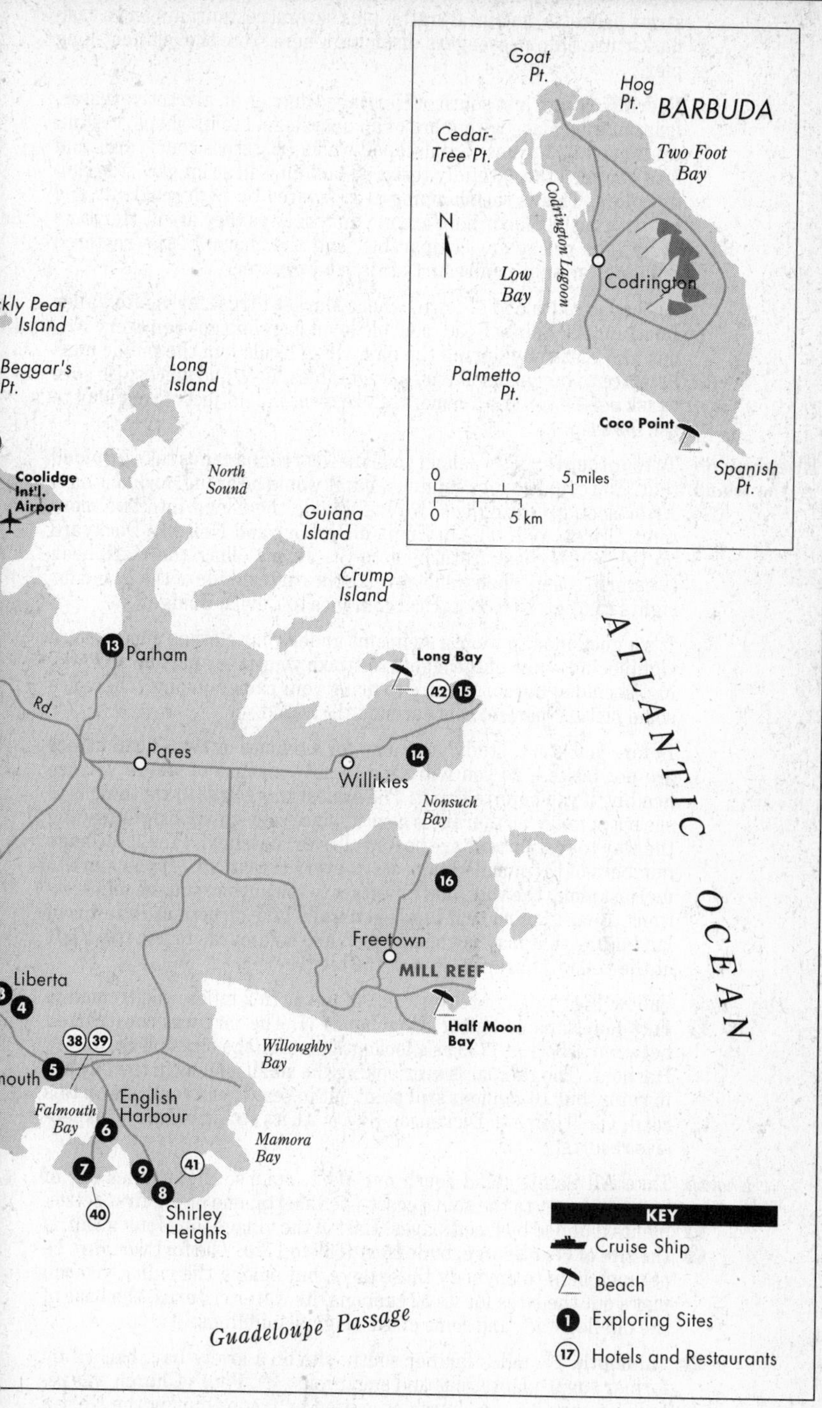

BARBUDA
Goat Pt.
Hog Pt.
Cedar-Tree Pt.
Two Foot Bay
Codrington Lagoon
Codrington
Low Bay
Palmetto Pt.
Coco Point
Spanish Pt.
0 5 miles
0 5 km
N
ckly Pear Island
Beggar's Pt.
Long Island
Coolidge Int'l. Airport
North Sound
Guiana Island
Crump Island
ATLANTIC OCEAN
Parham
Rd.
Long Bay
Pares
Willikies
Nonsuch Bay
Freetown
MILL REEF
Half Moon Bay
Liberta
Willoughby Bay
nouth
Falmouth Bay
English Harbour
Mamora Bay
Shirley Heights
Guadeloupe Passage
KEY
Cruise Ship
Beach
Exploring Sites
Hotels and Restaurants

buildings showcase stores specializing in duty-free goods, sportswear, T-shirts, imports from down-island (paintings, T-shirts, straw baskets), and local crafts, plus several restaurants and a casino. Cruise-ship passengers disembark here from the 500-foot-long pier.

Redcliffe Quay, just south of Heritage Quay, is an attractive waterfront marketplace with more of an upscale feel to its shops, restaurants, and boutiques. Landscaped walks crisscross courtyards and lead between the carefully restored buildings in a riot of cotton candy colors. This is the shopping area favored by both residents and return guests. Goods here are not duty-free as they are at Heritage Quay, but prices are comparable, and the charm of the restored buildings around small courtyards is far greater.

At the far south end of town, where Market Street forks into Valley Road and All Saints Road, a whole lot of haggling goes on every Friday and Saturday during the day, when locals jam the public **marketplace** to buy and sell fruits, vegetables, fish, and spices. Be sure to ask before you aim a camera, and expect the subject of your shot to ask for a tip.

Elsewhere on the Island

To tour the rest of the island you'll need to rent a car or take a guided tour. You could do it by minibus, but it would be a long, arduous day. After seeing Fort James, we will divide the island into two more tours. First, we'll take in English Harbour and Nelson's Dockyard on the south coast, returning to St. John's along the Caribbean (western) coast. Then we'll travel to the eastern side of the island for sights ranging from historical churches to Devil's Bridge.

It's a good idea to wear a swimsuit under your clothes while you're sightseeing—one of the sights to strike your fancy may be an enticing, secluded beach. Be sure to bring your camera along. There are some picture-perfect spots around the island.

Before you start, study your map for a minute or two. Road names are not posted, so you will need to have a sense of where you are heading if you hope to find it. The easiest way to get to anything is to see if a popular restaurant is near it, since easy-to-spot signs leading the way to restaurants are posted all over the island. (You'll see huge numbers of them nailed to posts at every crossroad.) If you start to feel lost along the way, don't hesitate to ask anyone you see for directions. Bear in mind that locals generally give directions in terms of landmarks that may not seem much like landmarks to you (turn left at the yellow house, or right at the big tree).

Fort James

2 Follow Fort Road northwest out of town. In 2 miles, you'll come to **Fort James,** named after King James II. The fort was constructed between 1704 and 1739 as a lookout point for the city and St. John's Harbour. The ramparts overlooking the small islands in the bay are in ruins, but 10 cannons still point out to sea. If you continue on this road, you'll come to Dickenson Bay, with its string of smart, expensive resorts.

English Harbour

3 4 Take All Saints Road south out of St. John's. Eight miles out of town—almost to the south coast—is **Liberta,** one of the first settlements founded by freed slaves. East of the village, on Monk's Hill, is the site of **Fort George,** built from 1689 to 1720. The fort wouldn't be of much help to anybody these days, but among the ruins, you can make out the sites for its 32 cannons, its water cisterns, the base of the old flagstaff, and some of the original buildings.

5 **Falmouth,** 1½ miles farther south, sits on a lovely bay, backed by former sugar plantations and sugar mills. **St. Paul's Church** was rebuilt on the site of a church once used by troops during the Nelson period.

6 **English Harbour** lies on the coast, just south of Falmouth. This is the most famous of Antigua's attractions. In 1671, the governor of the Leeward Islands wrote to the Council for Foreign Plantations in London pointing out the advantages of this land-locked harbor, and by 1704, English Harbour was in regular use as a garrisoned station.

In 1784, 26-year-old Horatio Nelson sailed in on HMS *Boreas* to serve as captain and second in command of the Leeward Island Station; he made frequent stops there for a period of three years.

The Royal Navy abandoned the station in 1889, and it fell into a state of decay. The Society of the Friends of English Harbour began restoring it in 1951, and on Dockyard Day, November 14, 1961,
7 **Nelson's Dockyard** was opened with much fanfare.

The dockyard is reminiscent, albeit on a much smaller scale, of Williamsburg, Virginia. Within this compound are crafts shops, hotels, and restaurants. It is a hub for oceangoing yachts and serves as headquarters for the annual Sailing Week Regatta. A lively community of mariners keeps the area active in season. Beach lovers tend to stay elsewhere on the island, but visitors who enjoy history and who are part of (or like being around) the nautical scene often choose one of the hotels in the area of English Harbour. One of the Dockyard's former storehouses is now the beautifully restored and very British **Copper and Lumber Store Hotel.** Another fine hostelry, the **Admiral's Inn,** started out as a pitch-and-tar store built of bricks that had been used as ballast in British ships. If you're a landlubber but want to experience the thrill of seeing the area from the water, the *Horatio Nelson* offers 20-minute guided cruises (Dockyard Divers, tel. 809/464–8591) The tour costs $6 per person, and the boat leaves every half hour from 9 to 5 daily.

The **Admiral's House Museum** has several rooms displaying ship models, a model of English Harbour, silver trophies, maps, prints, and Nelson's very own telescope and tea caddy. *English Harbour, tel. 809/463–1053 or 809/463–1379. Admission: $2. Open daily 8–6.*

On a ridge overlooking the dockyard is **Clarence House** (tel. 809/463–1026), built in 1787 and once the home of the duke of Clarence. Princess Margaret and Lord Snowdon spent part of their honeymoon here in 1960, and Queen Elizabeth and Prince Philip have dined here. It is now used by the governor-general; visits are possible when he is not in residence. Slip a tip to the caretaker, who will give you a fascinating tour; the place is worth a visit. As you leave the dockyard, turn right at the crossroads in English Harbour and drive
8 to **Shirley Heights** for a spectacular view of English Harbour. The heights are named for Sir Thomas Shirley, the governor who fortified the harbor in 1787.

9 Not far from Shirley Heights is the new **Dows Hill Interpretation Center,** with viewing platforms for sweeping views of the English Harbour area. Inside you can view a cheery but rather bland multimedia presentation on the island's history and culture, from the days of the Amerindians to the present. *For more information, contact the Parks Department, tel. 809/460–1053. Admission: E.C. $15. Open daily 9–5.*

Drive back up to Liberta. Four and a half miles north of town, oppo-
10 site the Catholic church, turn left and head southwest on **Fig Tree Drive.** (Forget about plucking figs; *fig* is the Antiguan word for banana.) This drive takes you through the rain forest, which is rich in mangoes, pineapples, and banana trees. This is also the hilliest part of the island—**Boggy Peak,** to the west, is the highest point, rising to 1,319 feet. Fig Tree Drive runs into Old Road, which leads down
11 to **Curtain Bluff,** an unforgettable sight. At the tip of a tiny outcropping of land, between Carlisle Bay and Morris Bay, it offers dramat-

ic views of the wonderful color contrasts where the waters of the Atlantic Ocean meet those of the Caribbean Sea. From here, the main road sweeps along the southwest coast, where there are lovely beaches and spectacular views. The road then veers off to the northeast and goes through the villages of Bolans and Jennings.

12 From Jennings, a road turns right to the **Megaliths of Greencastle Hill,** an arduous climb away (you'll have to walk the last 500 yards). Some say the megaliths were set up by humans for the worship of the sun and moon; others believe they are nothing more than unusual geological formations.

The East End St. John's is 6 miles northeast of Jennings. To explore the other half of the island, take Parham Road east out of St. John's. Three and a half miles to the east, you'll see on your left the now-defunct sugar refinery. Drive 2 miles farther and turn left on the side road that
13 leads 1¼ miles to the settlement of **Parham. St. Peter's Church,** built in 1840 by Thomas Weekes, an English architect, is an octagonal Italianate building whose facade was once richly decorated with stucco, though it suffered considerable damage during the earthquake of 1843.

Backtrack and continue east on Parham Road for about three-quarters of a mile, to a fork in the road. One branch veers to the right in a southeasterly direction toward Half Moon Bay, and the other continues toward the northeast coast. The latter route runs through the village of Pares. If you have the time, take the marked dirt road on your right shortly after the village to **Betty's Hope,** Antigua's first sugar plantation, founded in 1650. You can tour the twin windmills and view exhibits relating to the island's sugar era. It isn't much now, but the private trust overseeing the restoration has ambitious plans. Continue along the main road through the village of Willikies
14 to **Indian Town,** a national park, where archaeological digs have revealed evidence of Carib occupation.

15 Less than a mile farther along the coast is **Devil's Bridge,** a natural formation sculpted by the crashing breakers of the Atlantic at Indian Creek. The bluffs took their name from the slaves who committed suicide there in the 18th century because they believed they had the devil in them. Surf gushes out through blowholes that were carved by the breakers.

Backtrack again to Parham Road and take the fork that runs southeast. You'll travel 9 miles to Half Moon Bay. Just before the coast are the village of **Freetown** and the **Mill Reef area,** where many pre-Columbian discoveries have been made.

16 **Harmony Hall,** northeast of Freetown (follow the signs), is an interesting art gallery. A sister to the Jamaican gallery near Ocho Rios, Jamaica, Harmony Hall is built on the foundation of a 17th-century sugar-plantation great house. Artists Graham Davis and Peter and Annabella Proudlock, who founded the Jamaican gallery, teamed up with local entrepreneur Geoffrey Pidduck to create an Antiguan art gallery specializing in high-quality West Indian art. A large gallery is used for one-man shows, and another exhibition hall displays watercolors. A small bar and a restaurant outside under the trees are open in season. *Brown's Mill Bay, tel. 809/463–2057. Open daily 10–6.*

Beaches

Antigua's beaches are public, and many are dotted with resorts that provide water-sports equipment rentals and a place to grab a cool drink. Sunbathing topless or in the buff is strictly illegal.

Antigua **Dickenson Bay** has a lengthy stretch of powder-soft white sand and a host of hotels (the Siboney, Sandals, Antigua Beach Village, and

Halcyon Cove) that cater to water-sports enthusiasts. Don't come here seeking solitude.

The white sand of **Runaway Beach,** just south of Dickenson Bay, is home to the Barrymore Beach Club and the Runaway Beach Club, so things can get crowded. Refresh yourself with hot dogs and beer at the Barrymore's Satay Hut.

Five Islands Peninsula, in the northwest, has four secluded beaches of fine tan sand and coral reefs for snorkeling.

Johnson's Point is a deliciously deserted beach of bleached white sand on the southwest coast.

A large coconut grove adds to the tropical beauty of **Carlisle Bay,** a long snow-white beach over which the estimable Curtain Bluff resort sits. Standing on the bluff of this peninsula, you can see the almost blinding blue waters of the Atlantic Ocean drifting into the Caribbean Sea.

Half Moon Bay is a three-quarter-mile crescent of sand on the eastern end of the island; it's a prime area for snorkeling and windsurfing. Half Moon Bay Hotel will let you borrow gear with a refundable deposit.

Long Bay, on the far eastern coast, has coral reefs in water so shallow that you can actually walk out to them. Here is a lovely beach, as well as the Long Bay Hotel and the rambling Pineapple Beach Club.

Barbuda **Coco Point,** on Barbuda, is an uncrowded 8-mile stretch of white sand. Barbuda, encircled by reefs and shipwrecks, is great for scuba diving.

Sports and the Outdoors

Almost all the resort hotels can come up with fins and masks, Windsurfers, Sunfish, catamarans, and other water-related gear (*see* Lodging, *below*).

Bicycling Biking hasn't caught on here. Distances are comparatively large, and the terrain away from the coast is arid and sparsely vegetated. **Sun Cycles** (tel. 809/461–0324), in St. John's, rents bikes for about $20 a day.

Fitness Center The **Benair Fitness Club** (Country Club Rd., Hodges Bay, tel. 809/462–1540) has fitness equipment, a Jacuzzi, aerobic classes, and a juice bar. The **Lotus Health Centre** (Dickenson Bay, tel. 809/462–2231) offers spa treatments, including Swedish massage, foot reflexology, and various kinds of facials. The adjacent **Fitness Shack** (tel. 809/462–5223) has extensive fitness equipment and aerobic classes.

Golf There is an 18-hole course at **Cedar Valley Golf Club** (tel. 809/462–0161), and a nine-hole course at **Half Moon Bay Hotel** (tel. 809/460–4300). An 18-hole round will cost $50.

Scuba Diving Antigua doesn't have the most spectacular diving in the Caribbean, though there are a number of exciting sites, including the Sunken Rock and the wreck of the Mimosa. Captain A. G. Fincham, a British ex-merchant seaman, runs a shipshape shop at **Dockyard Divers** (tel. 809/464–8591). As well as offering resort courses and PADI/NAUI certification, he leads day trips for certified divers and has dive packages. Other specialists include **Dive Antigua** (tel. 809/462–3483) and **Dive Runaway** (tel. 809/462–2626). Average price for a single-tank dive is $40. Snorkel equipment rents for about $10 a day.

Sea Excursions **Wadadli Cats** (tel. 809/462–4792) makes trips to Bird Island and Barbuda on its three sleek catamarans. Prices range from $60–$75 and include soft drinks and a barbecue on the beach. The ***Jolly Roger*** (tel. 809/462–2064) has a "fun cruise," complete with "pirate" crew, limbo dancing, plank walking, and other pranks. ***Paradise I*** (tel. 809/462–4158) is a 45-foot Beneteau yacht that offers lunch or sunset cruises. ***Kokomo Cats*** (tel. 809/462–7245) offers several different cruises, including one to deserted beaches, one to English Harbour, and one to gaze at the sunset.

Tennis Many of the larger resorts have their own tennis courts. The **St. James's Club** (tel. 809/460–5000) has seven (five lighted for night play); **Sandals** (tel. 809/462–0267) has two; **Halcyon Cove** (tel. 809/462–0256) four (lighted); and **Curtain Bluff** (tel. 809/462–8400), four Har-Tru and a grass court. For nonguests, court fees are about $30 an hour. The **Temo Sports Complex** (Falmouth Bay, tel. 809/463–1781) has floodlit courts, glass-backed squash courts, showers, a sports shop, and a small restaurant. Squash-court rental is E.C. $30 for 40 minutes; tennis is E.C. $30 an hour.

Waterskiing Many all-inclusive resorts provide this free to guests; others will make arrangements through local outfitters. Dickenson Bay is the center for waterskiing (watch out you don't collide with an inflatable banana). **Wadadli Watersports** (tel. 809/462–4792) and **Halcyon Cove Watersports** (tel. 809/462–0256) will whiz you around for $20 a half-hour.

Windsurfing The **High Wind Centre** (tel. 809/462–3094) at the Lord Nelson Hotel is *the* spot for serious board sailors, run by expert Patrick Scales. Rentals are also available at **Wadadli Watersports** (tel. 809/462–4792) and **Hodges Bay Club** (tel. 809/462–2300); most major hotels offer boardsailing equipment. Equipment rental averages $20 an hour.

Shopping

If you haven't already seen enough designer clothes, Gucci bags, and Louis Vuitton suitcases back home, you can get your fill at **Heritage Quay.** Cruise-ship passengers must pass through this complex when they arrive on the island. The small shops around the historic **Redcliffe Quay** section of St. John's are better, but prices are comparable to those in the United States. Other tourist shops in St. John's are on **St. Mary's, High,** and **Long streets.** At the other end of the scale, endless street stalls sell garish T-shirts and cheap jewelry. High-quality crafts are few and far between, but try some of the following:

Janie Easton designs many of the original finds in her **Galley Boutique** (the main shop in a historic building in English Harbour, tel. 809/462–1525), and her prices are reasonable. Trinidadian Natalie White sells her sculptured cushions and wall hangings, all hand-painted on silk and signed, from her home-studio (tel. 809/463–2519) and from her **Craft Originals Studio** on the Coast Road. Artist-filmmaker Nick Maley, with his wife, Gloria, has turned the **Island Arts Galleries** (Alton Pl., on Sandy La., behind the Hodges Bay Club, tel. 809/461–3332; Heritage Quay, tel. 809/462–2787) into a melting pot for Caribbean artists. **Harmony Hall** (at Brown's Bay Mill, near Freetown, tel. 809/460–4120) is the Antiguan sister to the original Jamaica location. In addition to "Annabella Boxes," books, and cards, there are pottery and ceramic pieces, carved wooden fantasy birds, and an ever-changing roster of exhibits. John and Katie Shears have opened **Seahorse Studios** (at Cobbs Cross, en route to English Harbour, tel. 809/463–1417), presenting the works of good artists in a good setting. **Bona** (Redcliffe Quay, tel. 809/462–2036) presents antiques, select crystal and porcelain, leaf-of-lettuce pottery from Italy, and "wedding frogs" from Thailand, collected during the world travels of owners Bona and Martin Macy. **The Handicraft Centre** (High and Thames Sts., St. John's, tel. 809/462–0639) specializes in islands products like straw bags, mahogany warri boards, pottery and hand-painted T-shirts and sundresses. **La Boutique Africaine** (36 St. Mary's St., St. John's, tel. 809/462–

0119) is the place for Kenyan soapstone sculpture and woven bags, Masai flasks, Ibo ebony combs, exquisite ivory chess sets, colorful batiks—even Tibetan wall hangings at surprisingly good prices. The **CoCo Shop** (St. Mary's St., tel. 809/462–1128) is a favorite haunt for Sea Island cotton designs, Daks clothing, and Liberty of London fabrics. **Karibbean Kids** (Redcliffe Quay, tel. 809/462–4566) has great gifts for youngsters. A "must" buy at the **Map Shop** (St. Mary's St., tel. 809/462–3993) for those interested in Antiguan life, is the paperback *To Shoot Hard Labour (The Life and Times of Samuel Smith, an Antiguan Workingman)*; it costs $12, but you won't regret spending it. Also check out any of the books of Jamaica Kincaid, whose works on her native Antigua have won international, albeit controversial, acclaim.

Dining

Travelers on a budget can save on the many West Indian fast-food and street-food options on Antigua, especially in St. John's. Inexpensive restaurants, most serving local cuisine, Chinese food, or an international (mainly Italian) mix, are also easy to find. At Fort James, just outside St. John's, a group of cheerfully painted **fish-and-chip stalls** near the water serve lunch on weekends. And a delightful operation called the **Pumpkin Runner** is a mobile van that sets up shop on a St. John's street corner and turns out lip-smacking local food. Local specialties include *funghi* (pronounced foon-ji), a cornmeal and okra paste usually served with swordfish and pumpkin; *ducana,* a boiled dumpling filled with grated sweet potato and coconut; goatwater, or kiddi (goat), stew, a rich, soupy mix seasoned with cloves; *souse,* pig's trotters cooked with hot peppers, onions, and lime juice; pepper pot, a hearty mix of oxtail, beef chunks, and "any other meat you have," simmered overnight; or spinach, *eddo* (a local potatolike vegetable), and okra cooked with salted meat. A typical breakfast snack, costing about E.C. $3, is freshly baked bread covered in melted cheese and butter.

In St. John's, **Speedy Joe's,** on Nevis Street, and **Big Bite,** on Long Street, have a good selection of sandwiches, *rotis* (West Indian sandwiches of curried meat or chicken wrapped in pastry), and fresh juices. **Billigan's,** on Camacho Avenue, and the **A & A Ice Cream Parlor,** on St. Mary's Street, have a menu of local dishes. At **Jap's Snack Shop,** a tiny bakery-cum-café on Vivien Richards Street, the legendary Viv Richards still comes for his funghi and swordfish whenever he returns to the island. In **Redcliffe Quay,** several attractive cafés serve sandwiches, quiches, and the like, good with passion fruit juice or homemade ginger beer.

For those who'll be cooking, the biggest supermarkets are in St. John's, including **Dew's,** on Long Street, and **Food City.** At the **public market** on Independence Avenue (open Fri. and Sat. 6 AM–2 PM), you'll find a large selection of local fruits and vegetables, as well as fresh fish (snapper, swordfish, grunt, mullet), meat, and poultry. Other stalls sell local products, radios, and cassettes (good calypso music).

At the other end of the scale from budget cafés and restaurants are the island's sophisticated, expensive dining rooms serving fine Continental and American cuisine. If you decide to give any of these a try, you'll need to make reservations (in high season). Restaurants listed below do not require reservations unless stated otherwise.

Most menu prices are listed in E.C. dollars; some are listed in both E.C. and U.S. dollars. Be sure to ask if credit cards are accepted and in which currency the prices are quoted. Prices below are in U.S. dollars.

What to Wear Inquire about dress, as some places require a jacket and tie in winter; in listings below, dress is casual unless stated otherwise. Beach attire is a no-no, even at lunch.

Highly recommended restaurants are indicated by a star ★.

Category	Cost*
$$	$20–$30
$	$10–$20
¢	under $10

**per person, excluding drinks, service, and 7% sales tax*

$$ ★ **Admiral's Inn.** Known as the Ad to yachtsmen around the world, this historic inn in the heart of English Harbour is a must for Anglophiles and mariners. At the bar inside, you can sit and soak up the centuries under dark, timbered wood (the bar top even has the names of sailors from Nelson's fleet carved into it), but most guests sit on the terrace under shady Australian gums to enjoy the splendid views of the harbor complex and Clarence House opposite. Specialties include curried conch, fresh snapper with equally fresh limes, and lobster thermidor. The pumpkin soup is the best on the island. *Nelson's Dockyard, tel. 809/460–1027. Reservations required. AE, MC, V.*

$$ **Home.** When Carl Thomas came back to his native Antigua after years in New York, he decided to open a restaurant in his boyhood home, a '50s bungalow in a quiet suburb of St. John's. So he completely refurbished the original house, knocked down walls to create one large space, and planted an herb and vegetable garden. Modern unfinished pine furniture and polished wood floors give the place an airy atmosphere. Unusual ceramic candlesticks adorn the tables, and walls are hung with African and Caribbean art (Carl's own watercolors are in the rest room). The menu, which Carl dubs "Caribbean haute cuisine," is ambitious for Antigua. Unfortunately, the quality is quite uneven. Carl could use a stronger hand with his seasonings. Grouper in herb sauce and simpler offerings are more successful than such intriguing dishes like molasses pepper steak. Don't miss the smoked fish, a house specialty, and bread pudding with whisky sauce. *Gambles Terr., St. John's, tel. 809/461–7651. Reservations advised in high season. AE, MC, V.*

$$ **Lemon Tree.** This air-conditioned, art deco restaurant, on the second floor of a historic building in the old part of St. John's, is a smart, upbeat eating place, popular with cruise-ship guests. There's live music every night, varying from soft classical piano to funky reggae. The menu is eclectic, mixing minipizzas and ribs with beef Wellington, Cornish hen, lobster, vegetarian crepes, very spicy Cajun garlic shrimp, and pasta dishes. For those who like Mexican food, the Lemon Tree offers unbeatable burritos, as well as chili, nachos, and fajitas. *Long and Church Sts., St. John's, tel. 809/462–1969. Weekend reservations advised. AE, DC, MC, V. Closed Sun. No lunch Sat.*

$$ ★ **Redcliffe Tavern.** Every item on the tavern's part northern Italian, part Continental, part Creole menu is wonderfully fresh. The dinner menu includes delicious pastas, marinated grilled chicken, fresh local lobster, spicy Creole crab puffs, and a smoked salmon and shellfish terrine in lime mousseline. The lunch menu also lists salads, sandwiches, and hamburgers. The dining room is on the second floor of a beautifully restored colonial warehouse set amid the courtyards of Redcliffe Quay. Brick and stone walls are decorated with pieces of antique water-pumping equipment that still bear their English maker's crests. Salvaged from all over the island, the beautiful old machines, with their flywheels and pistons, have been imaginatively integrated into the restaurant's structure (one supports the buffet bar, for instance). You can also dine on the treetop-level terrace. *Redcliffe Quay, St. John's, tel. 809/461–4557. AE, MC, V.*

$$ **Shirley Heights Lookout.** This restaurant is set in an 18th-century fortification high on a bluff, with a breathtaking view of English Harbour below. The first-floor pub opens onto the lookout point. Upstairs, there's a cozy, windowed dining room with hardwood floors and beamed ceilings. Pub offerings include burgers, sandwiches, and barbecue, while upstairs you can order the likes of pumpkin soup and lobster in lime sauce. If you like to be at the center of things, come here Sunday around 3 PM or Thursday around 3:30 PM, when locals, yachters, and visitors troop up the hill for the barbecue. Enlivened by steel-band and reggae music, it lasts well into the evening. *Shirley Heights, tel. 809/463–1785. Reservations required in season. AE, MC, V.*

$–$$ **Calypso.** The St. John's professional set frequents this cheerful outdoor spot. At lunchtime it is packed with smartly dressed lawyers and government functionaries smoking cigars and chatting over traditional Caribbean food. Tables are arranged under green umbrellas on a sunny trellised patio dominated by the remains of a brick kiln. Specials change every day, but you can usually count on stewed lamb, grilled lobster, and baked chicken served with rice, dumplings, and funghi. *Redcliffe St., St. John's, tel. 809/462–1965. AE, MC, V. Dinner Fri. only. Closed Sun.*

$–$$ **Crazy Cactus Cantina.** Overgrown plants festooned with Christmas lights, Carnival masks, straw lamp shades, hurricane oil lanterns and menus painted on paddles dress up this Mexican eatery. The owner-chef is a Brit who's lounged on many a south-of-the-border beach, and he serves up lethal margaritas and excellent nachos, enchiladas, and chimichangas. It's not nearly as fiery as purists might like, but things heat up on Latin nights (usually Saturday, but call ahead to make sure), which feature sensational salsa and merengue bands. *All Saint's Rd., St. John's, tel. 809/462–1183. MC, V.*

$–$$ **La Dolce Vita.** This Italian charmer in Redcliffe Quay is a cool oasis, with crisp white napery and wooden planters and chianti flasks everywhere. Nothing wildly innovative here, just good, solid standards like pasta carbonara, bolognese, Alfredo, and puttanesca; chicken or veal milanese; and yummy pizzas (try the unusual tuna or lobster if you're feeling adventurous). The bountiful salads are also reliable. *Redcliffe Quay 16, tel. 809/462–2016. AE, D, MC, V.*

$–$$ **Russell's.** Russell Hodge, the vivacious owner, had the brilliant idea of restoring a part of Fort St. James, with its gorgeous views of the bay and headlands, and converting it into an open-air restaurant. Potted plants and faux-Victorian gas lamps lend a romantic aura to the cool stone-and-wood terrace. The menu—all delectable local specialties with an emphasis on seafood—is listed on the blackboard. You might start with definitive conch fritters or whelks in garlic butter, then try an excellent snapper Creole. Live jazz is a lure Sunday nights. Russell's sister Valerie owns the estimable Shirley Heights Lookout (*see above*), and sister Patsy operates the delightful Pumpkin Runner, a fast food van dispensing savory local dishes every night in St. John's. The Hodges might well be Antigua's first family of food. *Fort James, tel. 809/462–5479. AE, DC.*

$ ★ **Big Banana-Pizzas on the Quay.** This tiny, often crowded spot is tucked into one side of a beautifully restored warehouse with broad plank floors and stone archways. It serves some of the best pizza on the island, topped with traditional and not-so-traditional items. There are also delectable specials like conch salad. It's a busy lunch and dinner spot, and there is live entertainment some evenings. *Redcliffe Quay, St. John's, tel. 809/462–2621. AE, MC, V.*

¢ **Brother B's.** It's impossible to miss this funky restaurant in the appropriately named Soul Alley; a yellow-painted wooden fence and hand-painted boards advertise its fare. This is the place to try such local specialties as pepper pot; funghi; *pelleau*, a seasoned rice dish with chicken, meat, and peas; saltfish; ducana; and bull's foot soup, a

Caribbean variant of a 19th-century dish from Manchester, England. *Soul Alley, St. John's, tel. 809/462–0616. No credit cards.*

¢ **Ital.** Kimba, the owner of this tiny backstreet café (also known as the Best Health Vegetarian Restaurant), is a man with a mission. An earnest, imposing-looking Rastafarian with a mass of dreadlocks piled under his cap and a beard down to his navel, he presides over his four tables in the shade of a lemon tree with almost biblical authority, preparing food in keeping with his philosophy. No animal products or cooking oil (only coconut butter) are used. Tofu, rice, barley, and local cassava bread figure prominently. Everything is cooked in clay pots, and the "Ital-juices" (carrot, papaya, mango) are all fresh-squeezed. For E.C. $20 he will cook you all you can eat under faded pictures of Haile Selassie, Marcus Garvey, and a print bearing the inscription "Behold the conquering lion of Judah." As you can gather, this place is seriously alternative. *Lower Newgate St., St. John's, no phone. No credit cards. Closed Sun. No dinner.*

Lodging

The dominant form of accommodation on Antigua is the large resort catering to an international clientele. Despite the package-tour feel of a lot of these places, they are not cheap, at least not during high season. Those that are moderately priced are included below; more expensive ones drop their rates dramatically during the summer (*see* Off-Season Bets, *below*). Most of these larger hotels and resorts are located on or within walking distance of a beach; you won't need a car if you'll be eating at your hotel. Those seeking cheaper alternatives should know that guest houses and B&Bs, with a few notable exceptions (*see below*) are rare on Antigua, as are villa and apartment rentals. Don't count on these budget properties being on a beach. If you're looking for active nightlife and opportunities to meet other island guests, you'll want to stay in one of the hotels in Dickenson Bay, where properties are close together and St. John's is just a five-minute cab ride away.

Highly recommended lodgings are indicated by a star ★.

Category	Cost*
$$	$160–$240
$	$85–$160
¢	under $85

**All prices are for a standard double room for two, excluding 7% tax and 10% service charge. To estimate rates for hotels offering MAP, add about $45 per person per day to the above price ranges. For all-inclusives, add about $80–$100 per person per day.*

Hotels

$$ **Barrymore Beach Club.** Situated on Runaway Bay, this mid-priced resort offers standard rooms or one-bedroom apartments, both with kitchens, in two-story, condominium-style buildings. Decor is appealing, with beige tile floors, louvered windows, rattan furniture, and striped fabrics. The gardens, with hibiscus and bougainvillea plants much in evidence, are well maintained. Although individual units are generously spaced from one another, the standard rooms are small for two people and tend to be rather airless. Another drawback is the cramped beach here. But the resort is quiet and attractive, and there's a small, reasonably priced restaurant nearby. The staff is extremely cordial. *Box 1574, Runaway Bay, tel. 809/462–4101; in NY, 212/545–8467; in Canada, 800/668–2779; fax 809/462–4140. 36 units. AE, MC, V. EP.*

$$ **Club Antigua.** This sprawling, all-inclusive resort is in one of the least attractive parts of the island. The nearby saltwater lagoon, a mosquito breeding ground, has been dredged to create a vast mari-

na and condominium complex. With 470 rooms and 16 villas, it is the largest resort on Antigua and threatens to get even larger. The resort caters to a fun-loving, budget clientele (the cruise on the resort's repro pirate ship is a notorious drinking binge), many of whom come from Europe. The rooms are the size of a monk's cell (10 by 13 feet), music blares everywhere, and you'll have to face long queues in the dining hall for meals, but the sports facilities are extensive and the nearby beaches, as everywhere on the island, are attractive. Although the architecture has a sterile Southwest adobe-style look, the rooms are actually rather pretty, with terra-cotta floors and fresh pastel fabrics. For a few extra dollars, you can get a junior suite almost twice the size. Always inquire about special packages, which offer a much better rate. Throw out the all-inclusive deal and you'd be paying ¢ to $ prices. If you want a cheap, all-inclusive vacation and don't expect too much savoir vivre, this will be your best bet on Antigua. The management also runs the related Jolly Harbour Beach Resort, which offers very fairly priced self-contained two-bedroom villas; you may be able to arrange reciprocal privileges if you stay there instead. *Box 744, St. John's, tel. 809/462–0061or 800/223–9815, fax 809/462–4900. 470 rooms, 16 villas. Facilities: 3 restaurants, 4 bars, disco, pool, 8 tennis courts, movie room, shops, car-rental desk, water-sports center, excursion boat. AE, MC, V. All-inclusive.*

$$ **Yepton Beach Resort.** This Swiss-designed, full-service, all-suites resort is set on Hog John Bay on the Five Islands peninsula, not far from St. John's. The Mediterranean-style white-stucco buildings are situated so that accommodations have views on one side of the resort's own attractive beach and on the other side of a lagoon dotted with pelicans and egrets. Some of the rooms are two-room suites, with a bedroom and large living-room-cum-kitchenette. Others are studios, with a folding Murphy bed and kitchenette. By putting together a double bedroom and a studio, you can also make an apartment that sleeps four. All rooms are air-conditioned. Live reggae, calypso, and jazz groups appear three nights a week. Many different packages are available. *Box 1427, St. John's, tel. 809/462–2520 or 800/361–4621, fax 809/462–3240. 38 units. Facilities: restaurant, 2 tennis courts, pool, water sports. AE, MC, V. EP, MAP.*

$ ★ **Admiral's Inn.** This lovingly restored 18th-century Georgian inn is the centerpiece of the magnificent Nelson's Dockyard complex. Once an engineers' office and warehouse (the bricks were originally used as ballast for British ships), the Admiral's Inn reverberates with history. The best rooms are upstairs in the main building. They have the original timbered ceilings complete with iron braces, hardwood floors, and massive, whitewashed brick walls. Straw mats from Dominica on the floors and views through wispy Australian gums to the sunny harbor beyond complete the effect. The rooms in the garden annex are smaller and tend to be a little airless. The best-kept secret here is The Loft, a simple, timbered space upstairs in a separate building that used to be the dockyard's joinery. It has two big bedrooms, an enormous kitchen, and a magnificent view from the timbered living room onto the busy harbor. The inn's boat ferries guests to a nearby beach. Be aware that the inn sits smack in the middle of a bustling daytime tourist attraction. The same owners run the simply furnished, breezy, self-contained Falmouth Beach Apartments (*see below*). *Box 713, St. John's, tel. 809/460–1027 or 800/223–5695and 800/223–9815, fax 809/460–1534. 14 rooms, 1 2-bedroom apt. Facilities: restaurant, pub, complimentary beach shuttle and access to water sports at Falmouth Beach Apts. AE, MC, V. EP, MAP.*

$ **Antigua Beachcomber Hotel.** The advantages of this small, plain hotel are its beachfront location, affordability, and proximity to the airport (the occasional jet does scream by while you're sunning). All rooms have a safe, a phone, and cable TV; most have a patio or balcony. Six also have air-conditioning; beachfront rooms add a kitchenette. Decor is basic—just solid color linens and tropical paintings—but the property is kept clean and tidy. *Winthrops Bay, Coolidge, Box 10, tel. 809/462–3100, fax 809/462–2110. 28 rooms. Facilities: restaurant, bar, game room, pool. AE, D, DC, MC, V. EP, MAP.*

★ **Catamaran Hotel.** Renovation in 1989 was careful to retain the historical ambience of this plantation-style house, with its attractive apricot, white, and black trim and wraparound veranda supported on white, classical-style pediments. The property sits on the water at Falmouth Harbour, on a beach lined with palm and almond trees. The best rooms are the eight first-floor suites, with four-poster beds, full baths, kitchenettes, and private balconies. None of the rooms has air-conditioning, TV, or telephone. English Harbour is only a 2-mile, $6 cab ride away, and a nearby supermarket stocks provisions for cooking. There's also a restaurant (under different management), Captain Bruno's, serving à la carte meals and good pizzas. This low-key, low-priced, tranquil resort offers excellent value. *Box 958, Falmouth, tel. 809/460–1036, fax 809/460–1506. 16 rooms. Facilities: restaurant, bar, marina, shops. AE, MC, V. EP.*

$ **Island Inn.** The meticulously manicured garden and airy reception area gleaming with white tile and rattan indicate how well-maintained this homey property is. Rooms are spotless, with fresh flowers daily. Each of the standard rooms has a safe, a TV, and a private patio. Efficiencies are a better deal: For only $10 more, they include air-conditioning and a kitchenette. The beach (either Runaway Bay or Dickenson Bay) is a 15-minute walk away; your stay includes one free round-trip ride. A pool was slated for completion for the 1995/96 season (ask when you make reservations). *Anchorage Road, Box 1218, tel. 809/462–4065, fax 809/462–4066. 10 units. Facilities: restaurant, bar. AE, D, DC, MC, V. EP, MAP.*

$ ★ **Lord Nelson Beach Hotel.** This small, weathered mom-and-pop resort is run by the Fullers, expatriate Americans who have been here since 1949. As they have a vast, extended family of their own, it's a perfect place for children to scamper about and explore. If you don't mind a bit of chipped paint and organized chaos, you'll love it, too. In recent years it's become a mecca for windsurfers, who like its windsurfing boards, easy access to the water, and dedicated professional staff. The best rooms here are in a two-story, apricot-colored building that looks directly onto the property's own horseshoe-shaped beach. Each room is a slightly different hodgepodge. One has beautiful tiled floors and an ornately carved bed from Dominica that is so high you almost need to be a pole-vaulter to get into it. Several others have four-poster beds, antique armoires, and vivid local still lifes. Guests eat in the timbered dining room, which is draped with fishnets and dominated by a replica of the boat in which Captain Bligh was cast off from the *Bounty*; expect hearty dishes such as stuffed pork chops, wahoo, and snapper. As the resort is fairly isolated (5 miles from St. John's), figure into your budget about E.C. $25 for cab fare to any meal you have elsewhere. *Box 155, St. John's, tel. 809/462–3094, fax 809/462–0751. 16 rooms. Facilities: restaurant, bar, dive shop, windsurfing. AE, MC, V. EP, MAP, FAP. Closed Sept.*

¢–$ **Sand Haven Hotel.** Sand Haven was a run-down property before the enterprising Paul and Carol Lightfoot and Peter Rose purchased it in 1994. Now it's a jewel in the rough that's a property to watch. Rooms come in all shapes, sizes, and styles. All qualify as beachfront and have full bath, ceiling fan, fridge, and patio. The four largest also offer cable TV. Decor is a mishmash, mostly in light floral patterns; throw rugs cover the unattractive concrete floors. A constant breeze stirs the wind chimes at the captivating new restaurant, Spice of Life, which overlooks the floodlit beach and serves an artful blend of Indian and Creole cuisine, emphasizing fresh seafood. The bar is a prime spot to watch beautiful sunsets. *Runaway Bay, Box 2456, tel. 809/462–4438, fax 809/462–4491. 14 rooms. Facilities: restaurant, 2 bars. AE, MC, V. EP, MAP.*

Guest Houses and B&Bs

$ **Murphy's Place.** Mrs. Murphy, a hard-working, talkative woman, started taking guests into her home, a modern bungalow on the outskirts of St. John's, to pay for her children's education. Now she gets calls from places like Miami from people begging for a room. The units, in a plain wooden annex hung with yellow bella flowers, are of two kinds: Singles each have a double bed, a shower, and a fan; two-bedroom units have a large living-room area and a well-equipped kitchen. The furnishings are simple enough, but Mrs. Murphy sews many of the curtains and bedspreads herself and takes a lot of trouble seeing that everything is shipshape and clean. On a patio festooned with plants, she serves afternoon tea for those who want it and a pancake breakfast on Saturday. As a result, the guest book is full of the signatures of (mostly young) people from all over the world. The beach is about 3 miles away. *Box 491, St. John's, tel. 809/461–1183. 4 rooms. Facilities: patio. No credit cards. EP.*

¢ **Spanish Main.** Congenial owners Valerie and David converted this beautiful historic wooden house into a comfy guest house. The unadorned rooms have wonderful high ceilings and old wood paneling. All have clean, cramped shower baths and ceiling fans. Those in front open onto a common balcony and can be noisy. The largest rooms rent for $55, but there are three "singles" that go for $35 and "We negotiate," claim Valerie and David. The downstairs restaurant specializes in both Indian and Creole food. The nearest beaches are a 15-minute drive. *Independence Avenue, St. John's, Box 2881, tel. 809/462–0660. 9 rooms. Facilities: restaurant, bar. No credit cards. EP.*

Villa and Apartment Rentals

Few villas designed for vacationers have been built on Antigua. Instead, the island has a number of condominium- and apartment-style resorts. Units in many of these have limited cooking facilities or Pullman kitchens.

$–$$ **Sunset Cove.** Accommodations in this complex on Dickenson Bay are in white, two-story blocks, festooned with bougainvillea. Units range from standard rooms (barely enough space to squeeze past the end of the bed) to studios to villas, which are basically a room and studio combined and can sleep four. The best suites are ocean-view (forget what the brochure says about the views of the others; they look across at the suites opposite). All units come with air-conditioning, ceiling fans, TVs, VCRs, and microwave ovens. Many units are very close together, and you may end up hearing a good bit of your neighbor's holiday, too. But the property is attractive, well-maintained, and uncrowded, and a little beach of white coral sand is only a stone's throw away. Rooms and studios are $; villas $$. *Runaway Bay, Box 1262, St. John's, tel. 809/462–3762 or 800/766–6016, fax 809/462–2684. 33 units. Facilities: pool, maid service, bar. AE, DC, MC, V. EP.*

$ **Banana Cove.** These one- and two-bedroom self-contained apartments are set in a relatively secluded part of Antigua, near Devil's Bridge. The units are airy and appealing, with hardwood floors, island prints, and bright pastel fabrics. Each has a complete kitchen and bath, a small terrace, and remarkably large closets. The best buys are the two-bedroom suites with pool views (ocean view is nearly twice as expensive). The beach is a small spit of land, but Long Bay is a short drive. *Dian Bay, Box 1389, tel. 809/463–2003 or 800/223–9815, fax 809/463–2425. 30 units. Facilities: pool, restaurant, bar. AE, MC, V. EP.*

$ **Falmouth Beach Apartments.** This is the sister hotel of the Admiral's Inn at English Harbour. The best accommodations are in an attractive colonial-style house at the water's edge on the hotel's own small palm-lined beach. These units are basically one large room—a bedroom-living-room-kitchenette combination—and a bathroom with a shower. All open onto the house's timbered wraparound veranda with a view of the water and the hilly peninsula opposite. Since the beach is very sheltered, it is perfect for toddlers and small children who are learning to swim. There are no telephones or TVs and no air-conditioning. (The upstairs units catch the breezes better.) Other rooms are located in four modern buildings perched on the hillside and have a separate kitchen, a bedroom with twin beds, and a bathroom with shower. Decor is the standard rattan and beige tiles, jazzed up by old maps or striking paintings. All apartments have daily maid service. This quiet and simple place is truly a good value. *Box 713, Falmouth Harbour, tel. 809/460–1094 or 800/223–5695, fax 809/460–1534. 28 rooms. Facilities: sailing. AE, MC, V. EP.*

Off-Season Bets The following properties offer substantial reductions in the off-season, making them particularly good choices: **The Copper and Lumber Store Hotel** (Box 184, St. John's, tel. 809/463–1058), whose smaller rooms qualify as $$ even in high season; **Halcyon Cove Beach Resort and Casino** (Box 251, St. John's, tel. 809/462–0256 or 800/223–1588); the **Inn at English Harbour** (Box 187, St. John's, tel. 809/463–1014); the **Royal Antiguan Resort** (Deep Bay, St. John's, tel. 809/462–3733); **Sandals** (Box 147, St. John's, tel. 809/462–0267 or 800/726–3257); and **Siboney Beach Club** (Box 222, St. John's, tel. 809/462–0806 or 800/533–0234), which just misses being entirely $$ in high season.

Nightlife

Most of Antigua's evening entertainment centers on the resort hotels, which feature calypso singers, steel bands, limbo dancers, and folkloric groups on a regular basis. Check with the Tourist Board for up-to-date information.

Shirley Heights Lookout (Shirley Heights, tel. 809/463–1785) does Sunday-afternoon and Thursday evening barbecues that continue into the night with music and dancing. It's a favorite local spot for residents, visitors, and the ever-changing yachting crowd. (It also has the best gossip on the island!) **Hemingway's** (St. Mary's St., St. John's, tel. 809/462–2783), a restaurant serving West Indian fare, is a popular gathering spot for Yuppie locals. **The Verandah** (St. Mary's St., St. John's, tel. 809/462–5677) attracts an appreciative local crowd for live music Friday and Saturday nights. **Russell's** (Fort James, tel. 809/462–5479) presents live jazz combos on Sunday nights. The **Crazy Cactus Cantina** (All Saints Road, tel. 809/462–1183) holds frequent Latin nights, when the sensuous rhythms of live merengue and salsa hold sway. On Wednesday nights, **Colombo's** (Galleon Beach Club, English Harbour, tel. 809/460–1452) is the place to be for live reggae, and the **Lemon Tree Restaurant** (Long and Church Sts., St. John's, tel. 809/461–1969) swings every night but Sunday in season until at least 11 PM. The crowd at **Millers by the Sea** (Dickenson Bay, tel. 809/462–2393) spills over onto the beach for its ever-popular happy hour and live nightly entertainment. This is the place to come and dance on the beach way into the night. The ***Jolly Roger*** (from Dickenson Bay, tel. 809/462–2064) gets a boisterous group for its Saturday night cruises. Head out on this replica of a pirate ship for a four-hour sail under the stars with a barbecue, open bar, and dancing to live island music.

Casinos There is usually no cover charge at casinos on Antigua, and casual dress is fine. There are four major casinos, as well as several holes-in-the-wall that feature mainly one-armed bandits. The "world's largest slot machine" as well as gaming tables are at the **King's Casino** (tel. 809/462–1727), at Heritage Quay. Slot machines and gaming tables attract gamblers to the **Flamingo** (Michaels Mount, tel. 809/462–1266). The **St. James's Club** (Mamora Bay, tel. 809/463–1113) has a private casino with a European ambience. The casino at the **Royal Antiguan Resort** (tel. 809/462–3733) is an Atlantic City–style casino.

Discos **The Lime** (Redcliffe Quay, St. John's, tel. 809/462–2317) opens at 10:30 PM on Friday and Saturday and draws a frenetic mix of locals and visitors. **The Web** (Old Parham Rd., St. John's, tel. 809/462–3186) and **Grasshopper** (Airport Rd., no phone) attract a somewhat rowdier, more heavily local crowd.

4 Aruba

Updated by Barbara Hults

Imagine Aruba as one big Love Boat cruise, with quite a few casinos to enliven the night or unburden your wallet. Most of its 38 hotels sit side by side down one major strip along the southwestern shore, with restaurants, exotic boutiques, fiery floor shows, and glitzy casinos right on their premises. Nearly every night there are organized theme parties, treasure hunts, beachside barbecues, and fish fries with steel bands and limbo dancers.

Here, in a land whose symbol is a tree (the divi-divi) that is bent over like the ones Dorothy saw before her house took off to Oz, what's new? Why, smashing new golf and tennis clubs! Robert Trent Jones never saw wind like this before. But his designers have compensated, and so take your clubs and racket when you go.

The "A" in the ABC Islands, Aruba is small—only 19.6 miles long and 6 miles across at its widest point, approximately 70 square miles. Once a member of the Netherlands Antilles, Aruba became an independent entity within the Netherlands in 1986, with its own royally appointed governor, a democratic government, and a 21-member elected Parliament. With education, housing, and health care financed by an economy based on tourism, the island's population of 70,337 recognizes visitors as valued guests. The national anthem proclaims, "The greatness of our people is their great cordiality," and this is no exaggeration. Waiters serve you with smiles and solid eye contact, English is spoken everywhere, and hotel hospitality directors appear delighted to serve your special needs. Good direct air service from the United States makes Aruba an excellent choice for even a short vacation.

The island's distinctive beauty lies in its countryside—an almost extraterrestrial landscape full of rocky deserts, divi-divi trees, cactus jungles, secluded coves, and aquamarine vistas with crashing waves. With its low humidity and average temperature of 82°F, Aruba has the climate of a paradise; rain comes mostly during November. Sun, cooling trade winds, friendly and courteous service, modern and efficient amenities, and 11 modern casinos are Aruba's strong suit and help fill its more than 7,000 hotel rooms.

Budget-minded travelers have much to celebrate. Aruba has a cheap, safe, and reliable bus system; abundant fast-food franchises; and a glut of overbuilding that's kept room rates stable for the past few years. Although standard high-season rates for large resort hotels and time-share units here are pricey (you generally need to spend at least $150 a night), these complexes offer numerous package deals in the high season, as well as much discounted rates in low season. In addition, the island has several small apartment hotels and guest houses with rock-bottom rates. Check with the airlines for package deals, which, especially from Easter to just before Christmas, are hard to beat.

What It Will Cost These sample prices, meant only as a general guide, are for high season. Moderately priced hotels and time-share units cost $150–$185 a night. Small ¢ apartment hotels offer basic, air-conditioned lodging for under $85 a night. Dinner at a $ restaurant costs $15–$20 or less; at a ¢ restaurant, about $12; and cheaper still at the many fast-food spots around the island. All-you-can-eat buffets have also become popular, charging around $10 per person. A rum punch costs about $2.50; a glass of wine or other cocktail, $3.50; and a glass of beer, $2. Car rental averages $30–$35 a day. Taxi rates are fixed; from the airport to your hotel, figure about $12–$16, depending upon your hotel's location. Round-trip bus fare from hotels along Eagle and Palm beaches to Oranjestad is $1.50. A single-tank dive is about $30. Snorkel equipment rents for around $9 a day.

Before You Go

Tourist Information Contact the **Aruba Tourism Authority** (1000 Harbor Blvd., Weehawken, NJ 07087, tel. 201/330–0800 or 800/862–2782, fax 201/330–8757; 2344 Salezdo St., Miami, FL 33134, tel. 305/567–2720, fax 305/567–2721; 86 Bloor St. W, Suite 204, Toronto, Ontario, Canada M5S 1M5, tel. 416/975–1950).

Arriving and Departing

By Plane Aruba is 2 1/2 hours from Miami and 4 hours from New York. Flights leave daily to Aruba from New York-area airports and Miami International airport, with easy connections from most American cities. **Air Aruba** (tel. 800/882–7822), the island's official airline, flies nonstop to Aruba daily from Miami and five days a week from Newark. Twice-weekly service has begun from Baltimore. **American Airlines** (tel. 800/433–7300) offers daily nonstop service from both Miami International and New York's JFK International airport. American also offers economical packages to Aruba, especially in off-season (summer). **ALM** (tel. 800/327–7230), the major airline of the Dutch Caribbean islands, flies five days a week nonstop from Miami to Aruba; two nonstop and two direct flights a week leave out of Atlanta with connecting services (throughfares) to most major U.S. gateways tied in with Delta. Air Aruba and ALM also have connecting flights to Caracas, Bonaire, Curaçao, and St. Maarten as well as other Caribbean islands. ALM also offers a Visit Caribbean Pass for interisland travel. From Toronto and Montreal, you can fly to Aruba on American Airlines via San Juan. American also has connecting flights from several U.S. cities via San Juan. VIASA (tel. 800/486–4272), the Venezuelan carrier, has Monday and Thursday nonstop flights out of Houston.

From the Airport Aruba has one airport, Queen Beatrix International, about 3½ miles from downtown Oranjestad. There is no public transportation to the hotels. A taxi to properties at Eagle Beach will run about $12 for up to four people; to Palm Beach, $16. Some hotels include transfers in their package rates. If you're staying at a small guest house, it's advisable to rent a car at the airport.

Passports and Visas U.S. and Canadian residents need only show proof of identity—a valid passport, birth certificate, naturalization certificate, green card, valid nonquota immigration visa, or a valid voter registration card. All other nationalities must submit a valid passport.

Precautions Aruba is a party island, but only up to a point. A police dog sniffs for drugs at the airport.

The strong trade winds are a relief in the subtropical climate, but don't hang your bathing suit on a balcony—it will probably blow away. Help Arubans conserve water and energy: Turn off air-conditioning when you leave your room, and keep your faucets turned off.

Staying in Aruba

Important Addresses **Tourist Information:** The **Aruba Tourism Authority** (L. G. Smith Blvd. 172, Eagle Beach, Aruba, tel. 297/8–21019, fax 297/8–34702; or in Oranjestad at A. Schutte Str. 2, tel. 297/8–23778), has free brochures and guides who are ready to answer any questions.

Emergencies **Police:** tel. 100. **Hospital:** Horacio Oduber, tel. 24300. **Pharmacy:** Botica del Pueblo, tel. 21254. **Ambulance** and **fire:** tel. 115. All hotels have house doctors on call 24 hours a day; call the front desk.

Currency Arubans happily accept U.S. dollars virtually everywhere, so there's no real need to exchange money, except for necessary pocket change (cigarettes, soda machines, or pay phones). The currency used, however, is the Aruban florin (AFl), which at press time exchanged to the U.S. dollar at AFl 1.78 for cash, AFl 1.80 for traveler's checks, and to the Canadian dollar at AFl 1.30. The Netherlands Antilles florin (used in Bonaire and Curaçao) is not accepted in Aruba. Major credit cards and traveler's checks are widely accepted, but you will probably be asked to show identification when cashing a traveler's check. Prices quoted here are in U.S. dollars unless otherwise noted.

Taxes and Service Charges Hotels charge a 5% government room tax and usually add an 11% service charge to room bills. Restaurants usually add a 15% service charge to your bill. There is no sales tax in Aruba. The departure tax is $12.50.

Getting Around Aruba is small and easy to explore. Car rentals are reasonably priced, and navigation is simple: It's hard to get lost when all you have to do is follow the pointing divi-divi trees back to hotel row along Palm Beach. If you're staying at one of the larger hotels or time-shares, you'll already be on the beach, and Aruba's safe, cheap, and reliable bus system will shuttle you into town and back. We recommend renting a car for a day to explore the island, longer if you are staying somewhere away from the beach. A few rental car agencies offer one day free with a three-day or longer rental.

Taxis A dispatch office is located at **Alhambra Bazaar and Casino** (tel. 297/8–21604 or 297/8–22116); you can also flag down taxis on the street. Since taxis do not have meters, rates are fixed and should be confirmed before your ride begins. All Aruba's taxi drivers have participated in the government's Tourism Awareness Programs and have received their Tourism Guide Certificate. An hour's tour of the island by taxi will run you about $30 with a maximum of four people per car.

Rental Cars You'll need a valid U.S. or Canadian driver's license to rent a car, and you must be able to meet the minimum age requirements of each rental service, implemented for insurance reasons. Jeeps are wonderful for exploring off the beaten path, but they're twice as expensive as a basic rental car. Local rental car agencies are cheaper than well-known major companies. Their rates average $30–$35 a day (less if you rent for three or more days) for a Nissan Sentra or a Toyota Tercel; air-conditioning is an unnecessary option. Three reputable local agencies, with several locations including one at the airport, are: **Hedwina Car Rental** (airport, tel. 297/8–37393; Fortheuvelstraat, tel. 297/8–26442), **Optima** (tel. 297/8–36263 or 297/8–35622), and **Marcos** (tel. 297/8–65889). Gas runs about $2.75 for an imperial gallon (5 liters). For a small car, plan on $25 a week for gas.

If you prefer to rent from a major company, contact **Avis** (Kolibristr. 14, tel. 297/8–28787; airport tel. 297/8–25496), **Budget Rent-A-Car** (Kolibristr. 1, tel. 297/8–28600; airport tel. 297/8–25423; at Divi resorts tel. 297/8–35000), **Hertz, De Palm Car Rental** (L. G. Smith Blvd. 142, Box 656, tel. 297/8–24545; airport tel. 297/8–24886), **Dollar Rent-a-Car** (Grendeaweg 15, tel. 297/8–22783; airport tel. 297/8–25651; Manchebo tel. 297/8–26696), **National** (Tank Leendert 170, tel. 297/8–21967; airport tel. 297/8–25451; Holiday Inn tel. 297/8–63600), and **Thrifty** (airport tel. 297/8–35335).

Scooter Rentals More economical than car rental, scooters cost about $15–$20 a day for a 50cc single-seater, $18–$25 for an 80cc double-seater. Rates are lower with two-day or longer rentals, and it's worth calling several services to get the best rate. The following offer free pickup and drop-off service at your hotel: **Semver Cycle Rentals** (tel. 297/8–66851), **Ron's Motorcycle Rental** (tel. 297/8–62090), **George's Cycle Center** (tel. 297/8–25975), and **Pardo's** (tel. 297/8–24573 or 297/8–23524).

Buses For inexpensive trips between the beach hotels and Oranjestad, buses run hourly. One-way fare is 90¢; round-trip fare is $1.50, and exact change is preferred. In Oranjestad, the main terminal is located on South Zoutmanstraat, next to Fort Zoutman and just behind the yellow government building on L. G. Smith Boulevard (the one across from the Seaport Village shopping mall). Public buses run approximately every 20 minutes from 7:30 AM to 11 PM Monday–Saturday, less frequently on Sunday. Contact the Aruba Tourism Authority (tel. 297/8–21019) for a bus schedule or inquire at the front desk of your hotel. A free Shopping Tour Bus (you'll know it by its wild colors) departs every hour beginning at 9:15 AM and ending at 3:15 PM from the Holiday Inn, making stops at all the major hotels on its way toward Oranjestad. Be aware that you'll have to find your own way back to your hotel.

Telephones and Mail To dial direct to Aruba from the United States, dial 011–297–8, followed by the number in Aruba. Local and international calls in Aruba can be made via hotel operators or from the Government Long Distance Telephone, Telegraph, and Radio Office, **SETAR** (tel. 297/8–37138), which has branches in the post office building in Oranjestad and in front of the Hyatt Regency Hotel, adjacent to the hotel's parking lot. You can also send telegrams and faxes from SETAR. When dialing locally in Aruba, simply dial the five-digit number. A local telephone call costs AFl 25¢. To reach the United States, dial 001, then the area code and number.

You can send an airmail letter from Aruba to anywhere in the world for AFl 1, a postcard for AFl 70¢.

Opening and Closing Times Shops are generally open Monday–Saturday 8–6. Most stores stay open through the lunch hour, noon–2. Many stores open when cruise ships are in port on Sunday and holidays. Nighttime shopping at the Alhambra Bazaar runs 5–midnight. Bank hours are weekdays 8–noon and 1:30–4. The Aruba Bank at the airport is open Saturday 9–4 and Sunday 9–1.

Guided Tours

Orientation Most of Aruba's highways are in excellent condition, but guided tours save time and energy. **De Palm Tours** (L. G. Smith Blvd. 142, tel. 297/8–24400, 297/8–24545, or 800/766–6016, fax 297/8–23012) offers a basic 3½-hour tour that hits the island's high spots. Wear tennis or hiking shoes (there'll be optional climbing), and note that the air-conditioned bus can get cold. The tour, which begins at 9:30 AM, picks you up in your lobby and costs $17.50 per person. **Aruba Friendly Tours** (tel. 297/8–25800) offers guided 3½-hour sightseeing tours to the island's main sights twice a day ($20).

Special-Interest Although not inexpensive, these tours take you off the beaten track, offer good photo opportunities, and lend insight into the island's architectural, botanical, and environmental history. **Corvalou Tours** (tel. 297/8–21149) offers unusual excursions for specialized interests. The Archaeological/Geological Tour involves a four- to six-hour field trip through Aruba's past, including the huge monoliths and rugged, desolate north coast. Also available are architectural, bird-watching, and botanical tours. The fee for all tours is $40 per person, $70 per couple, with special prices for parties of five or more.

For a three-in-one tour of prehistoric Indian cultures, volcanic formations, and natural wildlife, contact archaeologist Eppie Boerstra of **Marlin Booster Tracking, Inc.,** at Charlie's Bar (tel. 297/8–45086 or 297/8–41513). The fee for a six-hour tour is $35 per person, including a cold picnic lunch and beverages. Tours can be given in English, Dutch, German, French, and Spanish.

Hikers will enjoy a guided three-hour trip to remote sites of unusual natural beauty, accessible only on foot. The fee is $25 per person, including refreshments and transportation; a minimum of four people is required. Contact **De Palm Tours** (*see above*).

Private Safaris Educational Tours (tel. 297/8–34869) offers adventure safaris by land cruiser into Aruba's interior. The half-day ($30) and full-day ($40) tours explore the island's history, geology, and wildlife.

Watapana Tours (tel. 297/8–35191) organizes daytime swim and snorkel tours and nighttime tours of the nightclubs.

Boat Cruises **Pelican Watersports** (tel. 297/8–31228) offers morning brunch cruises for sailing and snorkeling and afternoon sailings for $25 per person, including meals. **De Palm Tours** (*see above*) offers 1½-hour glass-bottom boat tours for $15 a person, moonlight or sunset party cruises for $25 a person, and three-hour sailing and snorkeling cruises with sandwiches and an open bar for $22.50 a person. **Red Sail Sports** (tel. 297/8–24500) offers four-hour snorkel, sail, and lunch cruises, with an open bar, aboard a 53-foot catamaran; sunset sails; party sails; and even a romantic dinner cruise, at prices that range from $27.50 to $49.50 a person.

Exploring Aruba

Numbers in the margin correspond to points of interest on the Aruba map.

Oranjestad

1 Aruba's charming Dutch capital, **Oranjestad,** is best explored on foot. Take a bus from your hotel to the **Port of Call Marketplace,** a new shopping mall. After exploring the boutiques and shops, head up L. G. Smith Boulevard to the colorful **Fruit Market,** located along the docks on your right.

Stop in for lunch at the **Bali Floating Restaurant,** where you can enjoy *rijsttafel* (a buffet of Indonesian foods served over rice) or sip a cool drink and watch the fishermen bringing in their catch (*see* Dining, *below*).

Continue walking along the harbor until you come to **Seaport Village,** a festive shopping, dining, and entertainment mall. Next door (one block southwest) is **Wilhelmina Park,** a small grove of palm trees and flowers overlooking the sea.

Cross L. G. Smith Boulevard to Oranjestraat and walk one block to **Fort Zoutman,** one of the island's oldest buildings. It was built in

1796 and used as a major fortress in the skirmishes between British and Curaçao troops. The Willem III Tower, named for the Dutch monarch of that time, was added in 1868. The fort's Historical Museum displays centuries' worth of Aruban relics and artifacts in an 18th-century Aruban house. *Oranjestr., tel. 297/8–26099. Admission: $1. Open weekdays 9–noon and 1–4.*

Turn left onto Zoutmanstraat and walk two blocks to the **Archeology Museum,** where there are two rooms of Indian artifacts, farm and domestic utensils, and skeletons. *Zoutmanstr. 1, tel. 297/8–28979. Admission free. Open weekdays 7:30–noon and 1–4:30.*

From here, cross the street to the Protestant Church. You're now on Wilhelminastraat. Walk one block and turn right on Kazernestraat. On your right side is the **Strada Complex I** and on your left, **Strada Complex II.** Both are shopping malls, and both are excellent examples of Dutch Colonial architecture. Behind Strada Complex II is the **Holland Aruba Mall,** a new shopping complex built to resemble a Dutch Colonial village. Upstairs is an international food court.

At the intersection of Kazernestraat and Caya G. F. Betico Croes, turn right. This is Oranjestad's main street. When you come to Hendrikstraat, turn left and continue walking until you come to the **Saint Francis Roman Catholic Church.** Next to the church is the **Numismatic Museum,** displaying coins and paper money from more than 400 countries, including some from ancient Greece and Rome. *Iraussquilnplein 2-A, tel. 297/8–28831. Admission free. Open weekdays 8:30–noon and 1–4:30.*

Diagonally across from the church is the **post office,** where you can buy colorful Aruban stamps. Next door is the SETAR, where you can place overseas phone calls.

The Countryside

The "real Aruba"—what's left of a wild, untamed beauty—can be found only in the countryside. About 170 species of birds can be found—little parrots and sugarbirds, herons, and fish eagles. Either rent a car, take a sightseeing tour, or hire a cab for $30 an hour (for up to four people). The main highways are well paved, but on the north side of the island some roads are still a mixture of compacted dirt and stones. A four-wheel-drive vehicle will allow you to explore the unpaved interior. An occasional iguana or cormorant may make an appearance. Traffic is sparse, and you can't get lost. If you do lose your way, just follow the divi-divi trees (because of the direction of the trade winds, the trees are bent toward the leeward side of the island, where all the hotels are).

Few beaches outside the hotel strip have refreshment stands, so take your own food and drink. And one more caution: Note that there are *no* public bathrooms—anywhere—once you leave Oranjestad, except in the infrequent restaurant.

East to San Nicolas

For a shimmering vista of blue-green sea, drive east on L. G. Smith Boulevard toward San Nicolas, on what is known as the Sunrise side
of the island. Past the airport, you'll soon see the towering 541-foot
2 peak of **Hooiberg** (Haystack Hill). If you have the energy, climb the
562 steps up to the top for an impressive view of the city.

Turn left where you see the drive-in theater (a popular hangout for
Arubans). Drive to the first intersection, turn right, and follow the
3 curve to the right to **Frenchman's Pass,** a dark, luscious stretch of
highway arbored by overhanging trees. Local legend claims the
French and native Indians warred here during the 17th century for
4 control of the island. Nearby are the cement ruins of the **Balashi**
Gold Mine (take the dirt road veering to the right)—a lovely place to picnic, listen to the parakeets, and contemplate the towering cacti. A magnificent gnarled divi-divi tree guards the entrance.

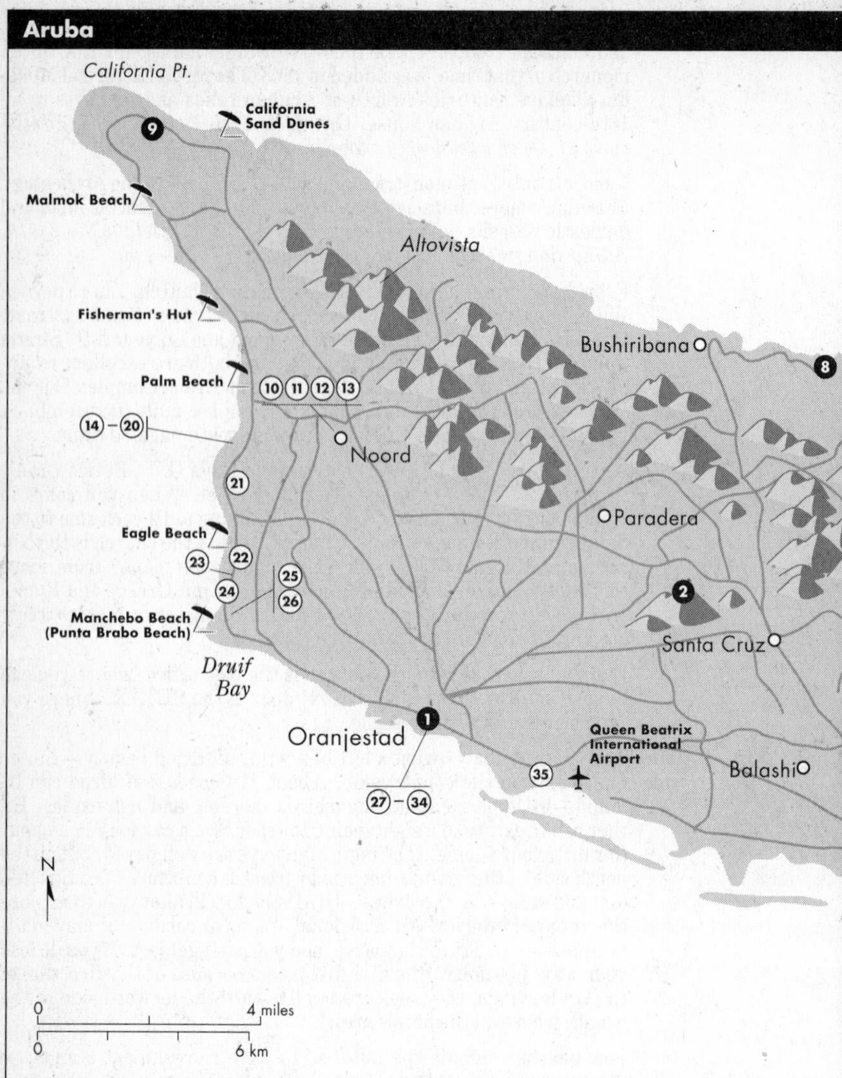

Exploring
Balashi Gold Mine, **4**
California Lighthouse, **9**
Frenchman's Pass, **3**
Guadirikiri/Fontein caves, **7**
Hooiberg (Haystack Hill), **2**
Natural Bridge, **8**
Oranjestad, **1**
San Nicolas, **6**
Spanish Lagoon, **5**

Dining
Bali Floating Restaurant, **27**
Bon Appetit, **15**
Boonoonoonoos, **28**
Brisas del Mar, **36**
Buccaneer Restaurant, **29**
Captain's Table, **20**
Coco Plum, **34**
La Paloma, **13**
Mi Cushina, **37**
The Old Cunucu House, **20**
Olé, **14**
Papiamento, **21**

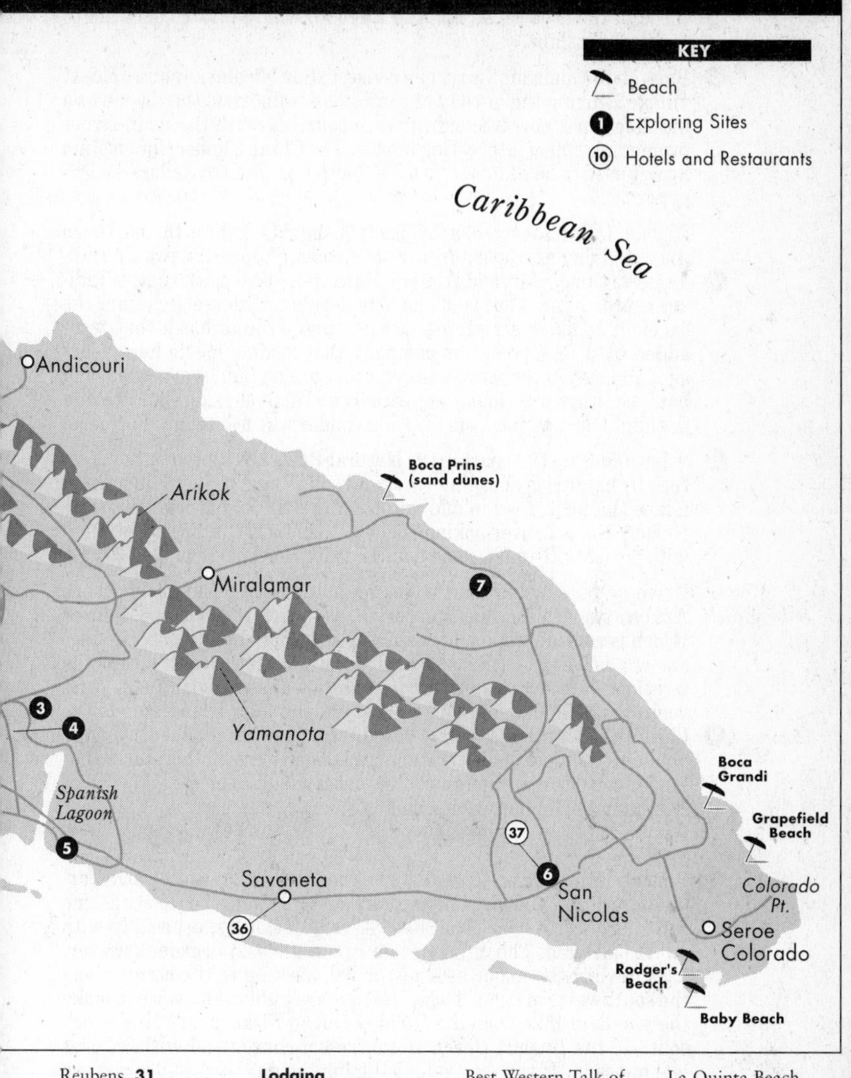

Reubens, **31**
Roseland, **25**
The Steamboat, **16**
Talk of the Town Restaurant, **35**
Twinklebone's House of Roastbeef, **11**
The Waterfront, **32**

Lodging
Amsterdam Manor Beach Resort, **23**
Aruba Beach Club, **26**
Aruba Hilton Hotel & Casino, **17**
Aruba Palm Beach Hotel & Casino, **18**
Best Western Talk of the Town Resort, **35**
Cactus Apartments, **10**
Coconut Inn, **12**
La Cabana All Suite Beach Resort & Casino, **22**
La Quinta Beach Resort, **24**
The Mill Resort, **19**
Sonesta Resorts at Seaport Village, **30**
Vistalmar, **33**

Backtrack all the way to the main road, past the drive-in, and drive
5 through the area called **Spanish Lagoon,** where pirates once hid to
repair their ships.

6 Back on the main highway, pay a visit to **San Nicolas,** Aruba's oldest village. During the heyday of the Exxon refineries, the town was a bustling port; now it's dedicated to tourism, with the main-street promenade full of interesting kiosks. The **China Clipper Bar** on Main Street used to be a famous "whore" bar frequented by sailors docked in port.

Anyone looking for geological exotica should head for the northern
coast, driving northwest from San Nicolas. Stop at the two old Indi-
7 an caves **Guadirikiri** and **Fontein.** Both were used by the native Indi-
ans centuries ago, but you'll have to decide for yourself whether the "ancient Indian inscriptions" are genuine—rumor has it they were added by a European film company that made a movie here years ago. You may enter the caves, but there are no guides available, and bats are known to make appearances. Wear sneakers and take a flashlight or rent one from the soda vendor who has set up shop here.

8 A few miles up the coast is the **Natural Bridge,** sculpted out of coral rock by centuries of raging wind and sea. To get to it, you'll have to follow the main road inland and then the signs that lead the way. Nearby is a café overlooking the water and a souvenir shop stuffed with trinkets, T-shirts, and postcards for reasonable prices.

West of Palm Beach

Drive or take a taxi west from the hotel strip to Malmok, where Aruba's wealthiest families reside. Open to the public, **Malmok Beach** is considered one of the finest spots for shelling, snorkeling, and windsurfing (*see* Beaches, *below*). Right off the coast here is the wreck of the German ship *Antilla,* which was scuttled in 1940—a favorite haunt for divers. At the very end of the island stands the
9 **California Lighthouse,** now closed, which is surrounded by huge
boulders that look like extraterrestrial monsters; in this stark landscape, you'll feel as though you've just landed on the moon.

Beaches

Beaches in Aruba are legendary in the Caribbean: white sand, turquoise waters, and virtually no garbage, for everyone takes the "no littering" sign—"No Tira Sushi"—very seriously, especially with an AFl 500 fine. The influx of tourists in the past decade, however, has crowded the major beaches, which back up to the hotels along the southwestern strip. These beaches are public, and you can make the two-hour hike from the Holiday Inn on Fisherman's Hut Beach south to the Bushiri Beach Hotel free of charge and without ever leaving sand. If you go strolling during the day, make sure you are well protected from the sun—it scorches fast. Luckily, there's at least one covered bar (and often an ice-cream stand) at virtually every hotel you pass. If you take the stroll at night, you can hotel-hop for dinner, dancing, gambling, and late-night entertainment. On the northern side of the island, heavy trade winds make the waters too choppy for swimming, but the vistas are great and the terrain is wonderfully suited to sunbathing and geological explorations. Most of the major hotels are on the beach or within a few minutes' walk. The only exception is the **Sonesta Hotel,** which provides free transportation to its private beach. The public bus runs from town to Eagle, Palm, and Manchebo beaches; fare is 90¢ one way; $1.50 round-trip. You can also take the bus to the Holiday Inn and walk to Fisherman's Hut Beach. A car is necessary to get to the other beaches listed below. Among the finer beaches are:

Baby Beach. On the island's eastern tip, this semicircular beach bordering a bay is as placid as a wading pool and only 4 to 5 feet deep—

perfect for tots and terrible swimmers. Thatched shaded areas are good for cooling off.

Grapefield Beach. On the north side of San Nicolas, this gorgeous beach is perfect for professional windsurfing.

Boca Prins. Near the Fontein Cave and Blue Lagoon, this beach is about as large as a Brazilian bikini, but with two rocky cliffs and tumultuously crashing waves, it's as romantic as you get in Aruba. This is not a swimming beach, however. Boca Prins is famous for its backdrop of enormous vanilla sand dunes. Most folks bring a picnic lunch, a beach blanket, and sturdy sneakers.

Malmok Beach. On the southwestern shore, this lackluster beach borders shallow waters that stretch out 300 yards from shore, making it perfect for beginners learning to windsurf.

Fisherman's Hut. Next to the Holiday Inn, this beach is a windsurfer's haven. Take a picnic lunch (tables are available) and watch the elegant purple, aqua, and orange Windsurfer sails struggle in the wind.

Palm Beach. Once called one of the 10 best beaches in the world by the *Miami Herald,* this is the center of Aruban tourism, offering the best in swimming, sailing, and fishing. During high season, however, it's a sardine can.The high-rise hotels are directly on the beach here.

Eagle Beach. Across the highway from what is quickly becoming known as Time-Share Lane is Eagle Beach on the southern coast. Not long ago, it was a nearly deserted stretch of pristine sands dotted with the occasional thatched picnic hut. Now that the new time-share resorts have been completed, this beach is one of the more hopping on the island.

Manchebo Beach (formerly Punta Brabo Beach). In front of the Manchebo Beach Resort, this impressively wide stretch of white powder is where officials turn a blind eye to those who wish to sunbathe topless. Elsewhere on the island, topless sunbathing is not permitted.

Sports and the Outdoors

Bowling The **Eagle Bowling Palace** (Pos Abou, tel. 297/8–35038) has 12 lanes, a cocktail lounge, and snack bar. The cost is $8.25 a game from 10 AM to 3 PM, $10.25 a game from 3 PM to 2 AM, and $1.20 for shoe rentals. Open 10 AM–2 AM.

Golf A new 18-hole, par-71 golf course, **Tierra del Sol,** has opened on the northwest coast near the California Lighthouse. It was designed by Robert Trent Jones to reflect Aruba's desertlike terrain, with divi-divi trees and cactus. Four separate playing environments include dry/stone, cacti, dunes, and beach. The highest green is 98 feet above sea level. The course is managed by the Hyatt Resorts Caribbean. The **Aruba Golf Club** (Golfweg 82, near San Nicolas, tel. 297/8–42006) has a nine-hole course with 25 sand traps, roaming goats, and lots of cacti. There are 11 Astroturf greens, making 18-hole tournaments a possibility. The clubhouse contains a bar, storage rooms, workshop, and separate men's and women's locker rooms. The course's official U.S. Golf Association rating is 67; greens fees are $7.50 for nine holes, $10 for 18 holes. There are no caddies, but golf carts are available.

Land Sailing Carts with a Windsurfer-type sail are rented at **Aruba SailCart** (Bushiri 23, tel. 297/8–35133) at $15 (single seater) and $20 (double seater) for 30 minutes of speeding back and forth across a dirt field. The sport is new to Aruba and thrilling for land-bound sailors. Anyone can learn the rudiments of driving the cart in just a few minutes.

Rentals are available from 10 AM–7 PM; food and drinks are served until 10 PM.

Miniature Golf Two elevated 18-hole minigolf courses surrounded by a moat are available at **Joe Mendez Adventure Golf** (Eagle Beach, tel. 297/8–76625). There are also paddleboats and bumper boats, a bar, and a snack stand. Fees are $6 for a round of minigolf, $5 for 30 minutes of paddleboating, and $5 for 10 minutes of bumper boating.

Snorkeling and Scuba Diving With visibility up to 90 feet, Aruban waters are excellent for snorkeling in shallow waters, and scuba divers will discover exotic marine life and coral. Certified divers can go wall diving, reef diving, or explore wrecks sunk during World War II. The *Antilla* shipwreck—a German freighter sunk off the northwest coast of Aruba near Palm Beach—is a favorite spot with divers and snorkelers.

Pelican Watersports (J. G. Emanstr. 1, Oranjestad, tel. 297/8–31228 or 297/8–63600), **Red Sail Sports** (L. G. Smith Blvd. 83, tel. 297/8–24500 or 800/255–6425) and **De Palm Tours** (L. G. Smith Blvd. 142, tel. 297/8–24545 or 297/8–24400) are the island's three largest water-sports operators. All offer snorkeling trips that cost $15–$19 a person, including equipment. They also offer beginner dive courses and day and night dives. Prices vary among operators, so call around. Beginner courses ("resort" courses) range from $60 to $80 a person. Single-tank dives average $30; two-tank dives, $50, and night dives are about $35. Prices include tanks and weight belts; if you need to rent additional equipment, figure on an extra $15–$25.

Many operators also offer package dives and PADI-certification courses. They include **Red Sail Sports, Aruba Pro Dive** (Ponton 88, tel. 297/8–25520), and **Mermaid Sports Divers** (Manchebo Beach Resort, tel. 297/8–35546 or 800/223–1108.)

Tennis Aruba's winds add a certain challenge to the best of swings, but world-class tennis has just arrived, thanks to the **Aruba Racquet Club** (tel. 297/8–60215). The $1.4 million club was designed by Stan Smith Design International and is located near the Aruba Marriott, which at press time was scheduled to open in the summer of 1995.

Windsurfing **Pelican Watersports** (J. G. Emanstr. 1, tel. 297/8–31228) rents equipment and offers instruction with a certified Mistral instructor. Stock boards and custom boards rent for $30 per two hours, $55 per day. **Red Sail Sports** (L. G. Smith Blvd. 83, tel. 297/8–24500 or 800/255–6425) offers two-hour beginner lessons for $44 and advanced lessons for $33 per hour. It also offers Fanatic board and regular windsurfing board rentals by the hour, day, and week.

Windsurfing instruction and board rental are also available through **Sailboard Vacation** (L. G. Smith Blvd. 462, tel. 297/8–21072), **Roger's Windsurf Place** (L. G. Smith Blvd. 472, tel. 297/8–21918), and **De Palm Tours** (L. G. Smith Blvd. 142, Box 656, tel. 297/8–24545).

Shopping

Caya G. F. Betico Croes—Aruba's chief shopping street—makes for a pleasant diversion from the beach and casino life. Major credit cards are welcome virtually everywhere, U.S. dollars are accepted almost as often as local currency, and traveler's checks can be cashed with proof of identity. Shopping malls have arrived in Aruba, so when you finish walking the main street, stop in at a mall to browse through the chic new boutiques.

Many shops sell duty-free merchandise such as jewelry, perfume, hand-embroidered linens, watches, china, and crystal. Others sell name-brand designer clothing. The best bargains are island crafts, both those made on Aruba and those imported from Latin America and other Caribbean islands. Several souvenir and crafts stores are full of Dutch porcelains and figurines, as befits the island's Netherlands heritage. Dutch cheese is a good buy (you are allowed to bring up to one pound of hard cheese through U.S. customs), as are hand-embroidered linens and any products made from the native plant aloe vera—sunburn cream, face masks, and skin refresheners. Since there is no sales tax, the price you see on the tag is the price you pay. But one word of warning: Don't pull any bargaining tricks. Arubans consider it rude to haggle.

One good craft store is **Artesania Arubiano** (L. G. Smith Blvd. 142, next to the Aruba Tourism Authority, tel. 297/8–37494), where you'll find charming Aruban home-crafted pottery, silk-screened T-shirts and wall hangings, and folklore objects. **Mopa Mopa** (L. G. Smith Blvd 47, tel. 297/8–37125) is a most unusual store that sells objects that look hand-painted but aren't. The buds of the Mopa Mopa tree are boiled down to a resin, to which natural plant colors are added. It is stretched and tiny pieces are cut and layered to form intricate designs with a translucent, stained-glass effect. The birds and butterflies, pins and boxes, figures of campesinos or mothers with child make wonderful gifts not found elsewhere. Inexpensive souvenirs can also be found at the **Bon Bini Festival** (*see* Nightlife, *below*) craft stalls.

Shopping Malls

Seaport Village Mall (located on L. G. Smith Blvd., tel. 297/8–23754) is landmarked by the Crystal Casino Tower. This covered mall is located only five minutes away from the cruise terminal. It has more than 130 stores, boutiques, and perfumeries, with merchandise to meet every taste and budget. The arcade is lined with tropical plants and caged parrots, and the casino is located just at the top of the escalator.

There are several other shopping malls in Oranjestad, all of which are worth visiting. The **Holland Aruba Mall** (Havenstr. 6, right downtown) houses a collection of smart shops and eateries. Nearby are the **Strada I** and **Strada II,** two small complexes of shops in tall Dutch buildings painted in pastels.

Port of Call Marketplace (L. G. Smith Blvd. 17) features fine jewelry, perfumes, duty-free liquors, batiks, crystal, leather goods, and fashionable clothing.

Dining

If your hotel room or apartment has a kitchen, save money by making breakfast and lunch and eating it, island-style, on your terrace. For American brands and good quality meats, shop at **Pueblo** (L. G. Smith Blvd. 156). Other grocery stores include **Ling & Sons** (Weststr. 29), **Favorito Supermercado** (Hendrikstr. 28), and **Kong Hing** (Havenstr. 16).

Aruba's restaurants serve a cosmopolitan variety of cuisines, although most menus are specifically designed to please American palates—you can get fresh surf and New York turf almost anywhere. Make the effort to try Aruban specialties—*pan bati* is a delicious beaten bread that resembles a pancake, and plantains are similar to cooked bananas.

For good or for bad, fast food has arrived in Aruba. For those who are homesick, there's McDonald's, Kentucky Fried Chicken, Burger King, and Wendy's. For breakfast and lunch, the restaurants in the hotels tend to be more expensive than the ones in town, although on Sundays, it may be difficult to find any other kind of restaurant that's open before dinner. Some hotels offer several food plans, which you can purchase either in advance or upon arrival. But before you purchase a Full American Plan (FAP), which includes breakfast, lunch, and dinner, remember that Aruba has numerous excellent and reasonably priced restaurants from which to choose and that eating at different places can be part of the fun of a vacation.

What to Wear Dress ranges from casual to elegant, but even the finest restaurants require at the most only a jacket for men and a sundress for women. The air-conditioning does get cold, so don't go bare-armed. And anytime you plan to eat in the open air, remember to douse yourself first with insect repellent—the mosquitoes can get unruly, especially in July and August, when the winds drop.

Highly recommended restaurants are indicated by a star ★.

Category	Cost*
$$	$20–$30
$	$15–$20
¢	under $15

**per person for a main course only, excluding drinks and 15% service*

$$ **Bali Floating Restaurant.** Floating in its own Oriental houseboat anchored in Oranjestad's harbor, the Bali has one of the island's best rijsttafel dinners. It costs $39 for two people. Bamboo rooftops and Indonesian antiques add to the charm of this popular restaurant. The service is slow, but well meaning. Happy hour is 6–8 PM. *L. G. Smith Blvd., Oranjestad, tel. 297/8–22131. AE, MC, V.*

$$ ★ **Bon Appetit.** With its white tablecloths, clay-potted plants, low lighting, and warm-looking wood beams, this restaurant glows like a beautiful tan—but it's the savory smells that hook you. The international cuisine wins acclaim—*Gourmet* magazine once requested the recipe for *keshi yena,* baked cheese stuffed with meat and condiments. Generous portions of seafood and beef (especially the gargantuan prime rib) fill the plates of this midpriced restaurant. The kitchen won a Dutch award for being the cleanest in Aruba. Leave room for the flaming Max dessert, named after owner and charming host Max Croes. *Palm Beach 29, tel. 297/8–65241. Reservations advised. AE, D, DC, MC, V. Closed Sun. No lunch.*

$$ **Buccaneer Restaurant.** Imagine you're in a sunken ship—fishnets and turtle shells hang from the ceiling, and through the portholes you see live sharks, barracudas, and groupers swimming by. That's the Buccaneer, a virtual underwater grotto snug in an old stone building, flanked by heavy black chains and boasting a fantastic 5,000-gallon saltwater aquarium, plus 12 more porthole-size tanks. The surf-and-turf cuisine is prepared by the chef-owners with European élan, and the tables are always full. Order the fresh catch of the day or more exotic fare, such as shrimp with Pernod; smoked pork cutlets with sausage, sauerkraut, and potatoes; or the turtle steak with a light cream sauce. Go early (around 5:45 PM) to get a booth next to the aquariums. *Gasparito 11-C., Oranjestad, tel. 297/8–26172. AE, MC, V. Closed Sun. No lunch.*

$$ **Olé.** Spain comes alive within the coral stone walls of this romantic restaurant. Waiters and waitresses croon Spanish love songs table side to the melodic music of a classical guitarist, while an illuminated waterfall tumbles into a moat just outside. The ambience makes up for the limited menu. Order some sangria, share a few tapas, and then split a paella for two. Honeymooners will want to request, in advance, the sole table on the private terrace overlooking the waterfall. *Hyatt Regency Aruba Resort, L. G. Smith Blvd. 85, tel. 297/8–61234. Reservations required. AE, DC, MC, V.*

$$ **Papiamento.** Longtime restaurateurs Lenie and Eduardo Ellis decided Aruba needed a bistro that was cozy yet elegant, intimate, and always romantic. So they converted their 130-year-old home into just such a spot. Guests can feast sumptuously indoors surrounded

by antiques, or outdoors in a patio garden decorated with enormous ceramics (designed by Lenie) and filled with ficus and palm trees adorned with lights. The service is impeccable at this family-run establishment. The chef utilizes flavors from both Continental and Caribbean cuisines to produce favorites that include seafood and meat dishes. Try the Dover sole, the Caribbean lobster, shrimp and red snapper cooked table side on a hot marble stone, or the "claypot" for two—a medley of seafoods prepared in a sealed clay pot. *Washington 61, Noord, tel. 297/8–64544. Reservations advised. AE, MC, V. No lunch.*

$$ **Talk of the Town Restaurant.** Here you'll find candlelight dining and some of the best steaks in town: The owner comes from a family of Dutch butchers. This fine restaurant is also a member of the elite honorary restaurant society, Chaine de Rotisseurs. Saturday night is all-you-can-eat prime rib night ($18.95), but seafood specialties, such as the crabmeat crepes and the escargots à la bourguignonne, are popular, too. The poolside grill stays open until 2 AM. *L. G. Smith Blvd. 2, Oranjestad, tel. 297/8–23380. AE, DC, MC, V.*

$$ **Twinklebone's House of Roast Beef.** Prime rib with Yorkshire pudding is the kitchen's pride, but there's a full international menu with dishes named after local friends and residents. There is a cabaret here twice nightly (call ahead): The chef leaves the stove to sing Aruban tunes with the maître d', and the owner, hostess, and waiters also break into song and encourage the patrons to join in. *Turibana Plaza, Noord 124, tel. 297/8–69800 or 297/8–26780. Reservations advised. AE, MC, V. Closed Sun.*

$$ **The Waterfront.** At this happening harborside eatery you can sit on the wide patio and people-watch, or choose the air-conditioned indoors beneath huge murals of mermaids, dolphin, manatees, and tropical fish. Choose a live lobster from the tank at the entrance and have it steamed, broiled, stuffed with crabmeat, or served *fra diablo*. There's also Alaskan king crab, garlic crab, snow crab, and fresh fish grilled over an open fire. Breakfast is served, too. *Seaport Village, tel. 297/8–35858. Reservations advised. AE, MC, V.*

$–$$ **Boonoonoonoos.** The name—say it just as it looks!—means extraordinary, which is a bit of hyperbole for this Austrian-owned Caribbean bistro in the heart of town, but in the fiercely competitive Aruban restaurant business, you gotta have a gimmick. The specialty here is Pan-Caribbean cuisine. The decor is simple, but the tasty food, served with hearty portions of peas and rice and plantains, makes up for the lack of tablecloths, china, and crystal. The roast chicken Barbados is sweet and tangy, marinated in pineapple and cinnamon and simmered in fruit juices. The Jamaican jerk ribs (a 300-year-old recipe) are tiny but spicy, and the satin-smooth hot pumpkin soup drizzled with cheese and served in a pumpkin shell may as well be dessert. The place is small, and the tables are close together: Skip it when it's crowded, since the service and the quality of the food deteriorate. *Wilhelminastr. 18A, Oranjestad, tel. 297/8–31888. Reservations advised. AE, V. Closed Sun. No lunch.*

$–$$ ★ **Brisas del Mar.** This friendly 10-table place overlooking the sea makes you feel as if you're dining in an Aruban home. Old family recipes use traditional indigenous ingredients like the aromatic *yerbiholé* leaf and the sizzling Mme. Jeanette pepper. Try the smashing steamy fish soup (which would do a Marseillaise proud), *keri keri* (shredded fish kissed with annatto seed), or some of the best pan bati on the island. The brightly hued fishing boats bobbing in the harbor attest to the freshness of the food. It's so good, it justifies the taxi ride needed to reach it—10 miles east of Oranjestad in the town of Savaneta. *Savaneta 22A, tel. 297/8–47718. Reservations advised. AE, D, MC, V. Closed Mon.*

$–$$ **Captain's Table.** Within La Cabana All Suite Beach Resort is this gem offering everything from health salads and herbal teas to barbecued Sunset burgers and grilled T-bone steaks. A special treat is the weekend prime rib special, served with a baked potato and salad for $14. Breakfast is an all-you-can-eat for $8. *L. G. Smith Blvd. 250, tel. 297/8–39000. AE, DC, MC, V. Closed Mon.*

$–$$ ★ **La Paloma.** "The Dove" is a no-frills, low-key neighborhood joint decorated with hanging plants and chianti bottles, and it's usually packed. The cuisine is international and Italian, but you can order conch stew with pan bati and fried plantains. Caesar salad and minestrone soup are house specialties. This is not the place for a romantic interlude; come for the family atmosphere, American-style Italian food, and reasonable prices. *Noord 39, tel. 297/8–32770. AE, MC, V. Closed Tues.*

$–$$ **The Old Cunucu House.** On a small estate in a residential neighborhood, three minutes from the high-rise hotels, this 74-year-old white stucco home with slanting roofs, wood beams, and a terracotta courtyard filled with bougainvillea has been converted to a seafood-and-international restaurant of casual élan. Dine on red snapper, almond-fried shrimp with lobster sauce, Cornish hen, New York sirloin, or beef fondue à deux. An Aruban trio sings and plays background music every Friday, and on Saturday evening a mariachi band serenades the patrons. Happy hour is 5 to 6 PM. *Palm Beach 150, tel. 297/8–61666. Reservations advised. AE, DC, MC. Closed Mon.*

$ **Coco Plum.** Fresh fruit drinks, seafood, and hearty Aruban dishes are the specialties at this pleasant and casual alfresco eatery. The average price for a filling breakfast or lunch is $6. For dinner, try the fish soup followed by red snapper *crioyo* (a sauce of sweet peppers, onions, and tomatoes) or *keshi yena* (baked cheese stuffed with meat and condiments). *Caya G. F. Betico Croes 100, tel. 297/8–31176. No credit cards. Open Mon.–Sat. 7:30–7.*

$ **Mi Cushina.** The menu at "My Kitchen" lists such Aruban specialties as *sopi di mariscos* (seafood soup) and *kreeft stoba* (lobster stew). The walls are hung with antique farm tools, coffee bags, and old family photos, and there's a small museum devoted to the aloe vera plant. You'll need a car to get here, about a mile from San Nicolas. *Cura Cabai 24, San Nicolas, tel. 297/8–48335. Reservations advised. AE, MC, V. Closed Tues.*

$ **The Steamboat.** The motto of this large, well-lit restaurant with nautical decor is "eat as much as you wish, and never come out hungry." Breakfast ($6.95; served until noon) and dinner ($14.95) are all-you-can-eat buffets (children under nine eat for half price). Dinner includes a huge salad and dessert bar. Sunday and Thursday are barbecue nights, with chicken, spare ribs, corn on the cob, and rice. Deli sandwiches are served until 4 AM. A 15% gratuity is added to all bills. *J. E. Irausquin Blvd. 370 (across from the Americana Aruba hotel), tel. 297/8–66700. AE, MC, V.*

¢ **Reubens.** Stop by for Aruban and Indonesian food as well as deli favorites. This clean coffee shop is open for breakfast and lunch only. There's live music some weekends. *Seaport Village, tel. 297/8–66565. No credit cards. No dinner.*

¢ **Roseland.** This former nightclub in the Alhambra Casino complex now dedicates itself to serving copious buffets to hungry tourists. There are different specials for every night of the week. A mere $10.95 buys you all you can eat, including 20 salads and four desserts; children under 10 eat free. *L. G. Smith Blvd. 93, tel. 297/8–35000, ext. 469. AE, DC, MC, V. No lunch.*

Lodging

Most of the hotels in Aruba are located west of Oranjestad along L. G. Smith Boulevard. Most include a host of facilities—drugstores, boutiques, health spas, beauty parlors, casinos, restaurants, pool bars, and gourmet delis. Rates are steep throughout the island, and, unfortunately, the rooms to be had for $100 a night or less are often disappointing. You may want to splurge on a hotel with full facilities (around $150–$185 a night). Most hotels offer packages, and these are considerably less expensive than the one-night rate. Off-season, roughly mid-April to mid-December, rates drop from 30% to 45%. You should also check with American Airlines and other tour operators for inexpensive vacation packages.

If you don't mind very basic accommodations, you can save money by staying at one of the island's small guest houses or small apartment hotels. These often have kitchen facilities. Especially in high season (winter), these may be your most affordable option, costing as little as $50 a night. Several are listed below; contact the Tourism Authority (*see* Tourist Information *in* Before You Go, *above*) for a complete list. Be sure to ask for a written confirmation of any reservations you make at these properties.

Aruba also has an abundance of time-share resorts, which are booked more or less the same as a hotel room but often with a one-week minimum. Time-share accommodations are generally in apartment/condominium-type complexes, but often with the addition of restaurants, shops, and sports facilities. Price-wise, they can be reasonable off-season, especially considering that you can easily cook your own meals in a time-share.

Do not arrive in Aruba without a reservation; many hotels are booked months in advance, especially in the winter season. Hotel restaurants and clubs are open to all guests on the island, so you can visit other properties no matter where you're staying. Most hotels, unless specified, do not include meals in their room rates. There are no bed-and-breakfasts or campgrounds on Aruba.

Highly recommended lodgings are indicated by a star ★.

Category	**Cost***
$$	$150–$185
$	$85–$150
¢	under $85

**All prices are for a standard double room for two, excluding 5% tax and 11% service charge. To estimate rates for hotels offering MAP/FAP, add about $30–$40 per person per day to the above price ranges. For all-inclusives, add about $65 per person per day.*

Resort Hotels

$$ **Aruba Palm Beach Hotel & Casino.** Formerly a Sheraton, this pink, eight-story Moorish palazzo even has pink-swaddled palm trees dotting its drive. The lobby, with its impressive grand piano, is a haze of pink and purple, underlaid with cool marble. The large backyard sunning grounds are a well-manicured tropical garden, with a fleet of pesky parrots guarding the entrance. The oversize guest rooms are cheerfully decorated in either burgundy and mauve or emerald and pink. Each has a walk-in closet, color cable TV, and a tiny balcony and overlooks either the ocean, the pool, or the gardens. For a peaceful meal, eat alfresco in the rock-garden setting of the Seawatch Restaurant. For live music, try the Players Club lounge, open nightly until 3 AM. Every Wednesday there's a popular limbo and steel band show and barbecue party around the pool for $23 per person. *L. G. Smith Blvd. 79, Palm Beach, tel. 297/8–63900; in FL, 305/539–0033; fax 297/8–61941. 202 rooms. Facilities: 2 restaurants, pizza parlor, coffee shop, disco, TV, shops, casino, 2 lighted tennis courts, water sports, tour desk, beauty salon. AE, DC, MC, V. EP, MAP.*

$$ **Sonesta Resorts at Seaport Village.** For the most part, these two luxury hotels in Oranjestad are out of our price range, but the lowest room rates just sneak into the top end of our $$ category. If falling out of bed and onto a beach isn't important to you, then Sonesta's in-town location is ideal—especially if you like to shop, eat, and gamble. There are actually two hotels, the new one with suites and

the older (1992) with rooms. This modern resort stands out amid the Dutch architecture of Oranjestad. In one lobby, sleek low couches wrap around pink stucco pillars while glass elevators rise above the circular deep-water grotto; brilliantly hued toucans and parrots squawk at you from their baroque cages; and motor skiffs board guests headed for the resort's 40-acre private island. The 300 tropical green-and-pink guest rooms and suites are spacious and modern, with tiny balconies, cable TV, hair dryers, safe-deposit boxes, and stocked minibars. The free daily "Just Us Kids" program offers children ages 5 to 12 supervised activities, including kite flying, bowling, movies, storytelling, and field trips. For adults there are free casino classes, volleyball, and beach bingo. The gourmet restaurant, L'Escale, is one of Aruba's most creative—and expensive. The neighboring Crystal Casino houses the Caribbean's largest $1 slot machine. Dancers should head for the Desires Lounge, where there's live entertainment every night except Sunday. *L. G. Smith Blvd. 82, tel. 297/8–36000, 800/766–3782, or 800/343–7170, fax 297/8–34389. Sonesta Resort & Casino, 300 rooms; Sonesta Suites & Casino, 275 suites. Facilities: 4 restaurants, 4 bars, minispa and fitness center, pool, 40-acre private island with water-sports center, 2 casinos, nightclub, 85 shops, children's program, tour desk, beauty salon. AE, DC, MC, V. EP.*

$ ★ **Best Western Talk of the Town Resort.** Originally a run-down chemical plant, Talk of the Town was transformed by Ike and Grete Cohen into a top-notch budget resort. It gets its name from the excellent on-premises restaurant (*see* Dining, *above*). There are two other restaurants here, and various meal plans let you try all three. A huge pool is at the center of the two-story motel-like structure, with most of the rooms overlooking the charming Spanish-style courtyard. Some accommodations have kitchens and all offer TVs, air-conditioning, and minifridges. Though the resort is on the outskirts of Oranjestad, there is a beach just across the street, where you have the run of the Surfside Beach Club, complete with pool, two Jacuzzis, snack bar, and a water-sports and dive center. *L. G. Smith Blvd. 2, Oranjestad, tel. 297/8–23380 or 800/233–1108, fax 297/8–32446. 63 rooms. Facilities: 3 restaurants, nightclub, cable TV, facilities exchange with Manchebo Beach Resort, gift shop, beach club, 2 pools, 3 Jacuzzis, snack bar, water-sports and dive center. AE, MC, V. EP, BP, MAP.*

Time-Share Resorts

$$ **Aruba Beach Club.** This attractive low-rise property is almost exclusively a time-share resort, although a handful of rooms remain regular hotel rooms. The open-air lobby leads to a patio, gardens, and pool, with the beach only a few steps beyond. Action centers on the pool bar, with a clientele that's mostly American, mostly young-to-middle-aged couples with children. The pastel rooms are more basic than luxurious, even though they're refurbished every two years. Each has a kitchenette and a balcony. Guests may use all the facilities at the Casa Del Mar resort next door. *L. G. Smith Blvd. 53, Punta Brabo Beach, tel. 297/8–23000 or 800/223–6510, fax 297/8–26557. 131 studio and 1-bedroom suites. Facilities: 2 restaurants, cocktail lounge, pool bar, ice-cream parlor, satellite TV, adults' and children's pools, 2 lighted tennis courts, children's playground, baby-sitting. AE, MC, V. EP.*

$$ **La Cabana All Suite Beach Resort & Casino.** At the top end of Eagle Beach, across the road from the sand, is Aruba's largest time-sharing condominium/hotel complex. The original four-story building faces the beach and forms a horseshoe around a huge free-form pool complex with a water slide, poolside bar, outdoor café, and water-sports center. One-third of the rooms have a full sea view; two-thirds have a partial view. All the oddly configured, but comfortable, rooms—studios or one-bedroom suites—come with a fully equipped kitchenette, a small balcony, and a Jacuzzi, and all have air-conditioning and ceiling fans. Suites have interconnecting doors

so that three may be linked together to form two- and three-bedroom units. The ground-floor living rooms do not offer as much privacy as those on higher floors because they look out onto the pool area. The Grand Suites, in back of the original structure (some have sea views), opened in 1993, doubling the number of suites and making this the largest hotel in the Caribbean. However, the gracious staff makes it seem like a resort one-third its size. The resort has much to offer: a modern fitness and health center, an ice cream and espresso shop, a budget restaurant, a small grocery store, several shops, and an activities center in the main complex. Shuttle buses run guests over to the upscale casino, the Caribbean's largest, where the hotel has another three restaurants and the *rouge et noir* Tropicana nightclub, with comedians and Las Vegas–style shows. *L. G. Smith Blvd. 250, tel. 297/8–79000 or 800/835–7193; in NY, 212/251–1710; fax 297/8–77208. 803 suites. Facilities: 5 restaurants, 3 bars, casino, racquetball, squash and tennis courts, health and fitness center. AE, DC, MC, V. EP, MAP.*

$$ **The Mill Resort.** Two-story, red-roof buildings flank the open-air common areas of this small condominium hotel, which opened in September 1990. Unlike time-share resorts, this hotel sells each unit to an individual, who then leases the unit back to the resort for use as a hotel room. The decor is soft, country French, with a delicate rose-and-white color scheme, white wicker furniture, and wall-to-wall silver carpeting. The junior suites feature a king-size bed, sitting area, and kitchenette. The studios have a full kitchen, but only a queen-size convertible sofa bed and a tiny bathroom. There's no kitchen in the hedonistic Royal Den, but there's a marble Jacuzzi tub big enough for two. This resort is popular both with couples seeking a quiet getaway and families vacationing with small children. There's no restaurant on the premises, but the Old Mill Restaurant is next door. There are also (to the relief of many guests) no bars, no tour desk, and no organized evening activities. Action can be found at the nearby large resorts, and the beach is only a five-minute walk away. *L. G. Smith Blvd. 330, Palm Beach, tel. 297/8–67700, fax 297/8–67271. 89 apartment-style rooms; suites are available by combining units. Facilities: pool, kiddie pool, mini food market, baby-sitting, car rental, 2 lighted tennis courts, fitness center, pool snack bar. AE, DC, MC, V. EP.*

$–$$ **Amsterdam Manor Beach Resort.** This attractive gabled russet- and mustard-color hotel looks like part of a Dutch colonial village by the ocean. You feel as if you're stepping back three centuries the moment you walk through the gate. Rooms are furnished either in Dutch modern or quaint provincial style, and range from smallish studios with a balcony, cable TV, and kitchenette to deluxe two-bedroom suites with a Jacuzzi and full kitchen. Alas, this cozy enclave and its lovely pool with a waterfall are intruded upon by the noise of traffic from Palm Beach Road. At least that glorious beach is just across the street. *L. G. Smith Blvd. 252, tel. 297/8–71492, fax 297/8–71463. 73 units. Facilities: restaurant, bar, minimarket, pool. MC, V. EP.*

$–$$ **La Quinta Beach Resort.** Across the road from Eagle Beach is this moderately priced time-share complex with a friendly staff. The efficiency and one-bedroom units were completed in 1993 and are small but well designed and stylish, with full cooking facilities, TVs, and hair dryers in the tiled bathrooms. One-, two-, and three-bedroom units also have sofa beds and VCRs; some also have a Jacuzzi. *Eagle Beach, tel. 297/8–75010 or 800/223–9815, fax 297/8–76263. Facilities: bar, 2 pools, cable TV, tennis courts. AE, DC, MC, V. EP.*

Small Apartment Hotels

$ **Vistalmar.** There's no beach, but the sea is just across the street, along with a swimming pier; guests can also use the beach from the Best Western Talk of the Town Resort. Units are air-conditioned one-bedroom apartments with a full kitchen, living room/dining

room, and decent-sized sun porch. There are TVs but no phones in the rooms. The drawback to this small hotel is its distance from town, making a rental car a necessity. *A.O. Yarzagaray, Bucutiweg 28, tel. 297/8–28579. 8 rooms. Facilities: laundry room. EP.*

¢ **Cactus Apartments.** A fence of tall cacti surrounds this mustard-color apartment hotel. Public buses stop nearby, but a car is highly recommended, especially because the property is not on the beach. All units are air-conditioned, with beige tile floors, a kitchenette, tiny bathroom (shower only), color TV, and double bed. There's no pool and only one public telephone, but there's daily maid service and washer and dryer facilities. It's no more than a clean, cheap place to sleep, but for $50 a night ($40 if you stay for more than a week) in high season, it's hard to do better. *Jacinto Tromp, Matadera 5, Noord, tel. 297/8–22903, fax 297/8–20433. 13 units. EP.*

¢ **Coconut Inn.** It's best to have a car if you're staying at this budget hotel, a five-minute drive inland from hotel row on Palm Beach. Request one of the "superior studio" rooms in the two-story white building and accept no substitute, as the rest of the rooms are old, musty, dark, and lacking in cheer. All superior studios are air-conditioned, with one double bed, a second bed meant for a small child, a bathroom with tiled shower, color TV, kitchenette, and small balcony or patio. The public bus stops a short walk away. *Angelo Rojer, Noord 31, tel. 297/8–66288, fax 297/8–65433. 24 rooms. EP.*

Off-Season Bets Some of the best off-season rates can be found by requesting off-season packages from hotels or harilines. Try, for example, **Sonesta Resorts at Seaport Village** (*see above*), **Playa Linda Beach Resort** (L. G. Smith Blvd. 87, Palm Beach, tel. 297/8–*61000 or 800/346–7084), and the **Radisson Aruba Caribbean Resort & Casino** (L. G. Smith Blvd. 81, Palm Beach, tel. 297/8–66555 or 800/777–1700).

Nightlife

Casinos Casinos are all the rage in Aruba. At last count there were 11. The crowds seem to flock to the newest of the new: As we go to press, the Marriott is planning its 1995 summer entry into this hotbed of high rollers. The Crystal Casino at the Sonesta enjoyed the business until the Hyatt Regency's ultramodern gaming room stole the show (the marquee above the bar at this casino opens to reveal a live band). Then it was the wildly popular **Royal Cabana Casino**—largest in the Caribbean—in La Cabana All Suite Beach Hotel (L. G. Smith Blvd. 250, tel. 297/8–79000) with its sleek interior, multitheme three-in-one restaurant, and showcase Tropicana nightclub. Smart money's on the just-opened **Hilton Casablanca Casino,** quietly elegant with a Bogart theme (Iraùsquin Blvd. 77, tel. 297/8–64466). One place where you'll always find some action is the **Alhambra Casino** (L. G. Smith Blvd. 93, Oranjestad, tel. 297/8–35000), where a "Moorish slave" gives every gambler a hearty handshake upon entering.

The **Holiday Inn**'s casino (L. G. Smith Blvd. 230, tel. 297/8–63600) is open 19 hours a day, with an adjacent New York–style deli open until 5 AM. The **Americana Aruba Beach Resort & Casino** (L. G. Smith Blvd. 83, tel. 297/8–64500) opens daily at 1 PM for slots, 5 PM for all games. The **Aruba Palm Beach Hotel Casino** (L. G. Smith Blvd. 79, tel. 297/8–63900) opens at 10 AM for slots, 6 PM for all games. You can also woo Lady Luck at the Sonesta Hotel's **Crystal Casino** (L. G. Smith Blvd. 82, tel. 297/8–36000), where the action is nonstop from 10 AM to 4 AM for slots; 1 PM to 4 AM for the gaming tables. And there's the expanded **Hyatt Regency's Copacabana Casino** (L. G. Smith Blvd. 85, tel. 297/8–61234), a 10,000-square-foot complex with a Carnival in Rio theme and live entertainment. Low-key gambling can be found at the new waterside **Seaport Casino** (L. G. Smith Blvd. 9, tel. 297/8–35600).

Disco and Dancing Arubans usually start partying late, and action doesn't start till around midnight, mostly on the weekends. At **Papas & Beer** (L. G. Smith Blvd. 184, tel. 297/8–60300), whose purple-and-pink neon signs can be seen lighting up the night from as far away as hotel row, live bands perform nightly, waiters in funky costumes do dance routines under flickering strobe lights, video screens flash, and food and drinks are served almost round-the-clock. Another popular nightclub is **Blue Wave** (Shellstr., tel. 297/8–38856) with live bands on Saturday nights and a "Ladies Night" drawing in the crowds on Thursday. For a young adult–style "amusement park," stop in at **La Visage** (L. G. Smith Blvd. 152A, tel. 297/8–33418), the disco for the young set, both Arubans and tourists. Jazz lovers may prefer the quiet piano bar atmosphere of **La Nota** (Emmastr. 7, tel. 297/8–32739), which remains lively from around 10 PM until it closes at 2 AM.

One truly different evening out is **Chiva Parranda** (tel. 297/8–37643), which means "bus out on the town." Every Wednesday and Thursday at 6:30 PM, this nightlife tour boards up to 40 people on a hand-painted 1947 Ford bus and whisks them off to the five hot local night-spots and a restaurant. The $49.50-per-person price includes a drink at each rum shop and a three-course dinner. You're picked up (and poured off) at your hotel. As your affable host remarks, "I finally learned how to cash in on being a party animal." Party animals can prowl farther now, with the **Cucunu,** a bus that offers them the chance to taste the pleasures of country bars. No dinner, but a snack and "jungle juice" is served aboard, for $29.50. It takes place Tuesday and Saturday from 8 till 12 PM. You're picked up and (fortunately, we'd guess) dropped off after the country crawl.

Specialty Theme Nights One of the unique things about Aruba's nightlife is the number of specialty theme nights offered by the hotels: At last count there were more than 30. Each "party" features dinner and entertainment, followed by dancing. For a complete list, contact the Aruba Tourism Authority (tel. 297/23778 or 297/8–21019).

An Aruban must is the **Bon Bini Festival,** held every Tuesday evening from 6:30 to 8:30 PM in the outdoor courtyard of the Fort Zoutman Museum. *Bon Bini* is Papiamento for "welcome," and this tourist event is the Aruba Institute of Culture and Education's way of introducing you to all things Aruban. Stroll by the stands of Aruban foods, drinks, and crafts, or watch Aruban entertainers perform Antillean music and folkloric dancing. A master of ceremonies explains the history of the dances, instruments, and music. It's a fun event, and a good way to meet other tourists. Look for the clock tower. *Oranjestraat, tel. 297/8–22185. Admission: Afl2 adults, Afl1 children.*

Weekend evenings are lively all over town, so the theme-night pickings are fewer. The best ones are Divi Aruba Beach Resort's **Beach BBQ and Caribbean Party** (L. G. Smith Blvd. 93, tel. 297/8–23300) on Saturday nights and the Mexican fiesta **Fajitas and 'ritas** (L. G. Smith Blvd. 85, tel. 297/8–61234) held Friday nights at the beachside Palms Restaurant in the Hyatt Regency.

Theater **Aladdin Theater** (L. G. Smith Blvd. 93, tel. 297/8–35000), a cabaret tucked into the Alhambra Bazaar, hosts a variety of shows, including Broadway musicals.

Tropicana (L. G. Smith Blvd. 250, tel 297/8–39000), La Cabana All Suite's cabaret theater and nightclub, features first-class Las Vegas–style revues and a special comedy series every weekend.

Twinklebone's House of Roast Beef (Noord 124, tel. 297/8–26780) does serve succulent prime rib and the like. But it's best known for the fun cabaret put on by the staff twice nightly. Customers eat it up.

5 Barbados

Updated by Jane E. Zarem

Genuinely proud of their country, the quarter million Bajans (Barbadians) on Barbados welcome visitors as privileged guests. Barbados is fine for people who want nothing more than to offer their bodies to the sun, yet travelers who want to discover Caribbean island life and culture will also find it ideal.

You can pay a lot for a vacation on Barbados, but you don't have to. This large island has everything from superluxury resorts to tiny B&Bs for $30 a night. Restaurants serving Continental cuisine are expensive, but travelers on a budget can opt for West Indian fare from local cafés. This is also an island where you can get around easily by bus. For a small fare, hop aboard, rub shoulders with other straphangers, and get acquainted with diverse sights and attractions.

Barbados is 21 miles long, 14 miles wide, and relatively flat; the highest point is Mt. Hillaby, at 1,115 feet. Beaches along the tranquil West Coast—in the lee of the northwest trade winds—are backed by first-class resorts. More hotels are situated along the beaches on the South Coast. British and Canadian visitors often favor the posh hotels of St. James Parish, on the West Coast. Americans (couples more often than singles) tend to gravitate toward the large South Coast resorts. The south is also where you'll find smaller, less expensive hotels and guest houses. Since this area is compact, especially around St. Lawrence, you can walk to neighboring restaurants and local nightspots without relying on taxis. Beaches are lovely in both areas.

To the northeast are rolling hills and valleys covered by acres of impenetrable sugarcane. The Atlantic surf pounds gigantic boulders along the rugged East Coast, where the Bajans themselves have vacation homes. Elsewhere on the island, linked by almost 900 miles of good roads, are small villages, historic plantation houses, stalactite-studded caves, a wildlife preserve, and the Andromeda Gardens, one of the most attractive small tropical gardens in the world.

No one is sure whether the name *Los Barbados* ("the bearded ones") refers to the beardlike root that hangs from the island's fig trees or to the bearded natives who greeted the Portuguese "discoverer" of the island in 1536. The name Los Barbados was still current almost a century later when the British landed—by accident—in what is now Holetown in St. James Parish. They colonized the island in 1627 and remained until it achieved independence in 1966.

Barbados has retained a very British atmosphere. Afternoon tea is a ritual at numerous hotels. Cricket is the national sport (a religion, some say), producing some of the world's top players. Polo is played in winter. The British tradition of dressing for dinner is firmly entrenched; although jackets are not expected at $$ restaurants, they are not out of place. Sundresses are suitable for women. A daytime stroll in a swimsuit is as inappropriate in Bridgetown as it would be on New York's 5th Avenue. Yet the island's atmosphere is hardly stuffy. When the car you ordered for noon doesn't arrive until 12:30, you can expect a cheerful response, "He okay, mon, he just on Caribbean time."

What It Will Cost These sample prices, meant only as a general guide, are for high season. Expect to pay around $80 and up at a small hotel close to the sea. A guest house costs anywhere from $30–$50 a night, while a room at a B&B can be as low as $25 a night. A $$ dinner can cost as much as $40 a person, but more careful selection from a menu can keep the price to around $12. A generous plateful of curry with rice from a local café will be $5 or less. Wine is imported and therefore expensive. Local Banks beer is good and reasonably priced at $1.50. Local rum, notably Mount Gay and Cockspur, is excellent and, at $4.50 a bottle, a steal. Cars rent for $60–$65 a day. Taxis are expensive—an average trip between your hotel and Bridgetown will cost about $5. Public transportation is efficient and a bargain—BDS $1.50 (about U.S. 75¢) for any distance. A single-tank dive is about $40; multiple dives will save you money. Snorkel-equipment rental is about $5 a day.

Before You Go

Tourist Information Contact the **Barbados Tourism Authority** (800 2nd Ave., New York, NY 10017, tel. 212/986–6516 or 800/221–9831, fax 212/573–9850; 3440 Wilshire Blvd., Suite 1215, Los Angeles, CA 90010, tel. 213/380–2198, fax 213/384–2763). **In Canada:** 5160 Yonge St., Suite 1800, N. York, Ontario M2N 6L9, tel. 416/512–6569 or 800/268–9122, fax 416/512–6851; 615 René Levesque Blvd., Suite 460, Montreal, Québec H3B 1P5, tel. 514/861–0085, fax 514/861–7917. **In the United Kingdom:** 263 Tottenham Court Rd., London W1P 9AA, tel. 0171/636–9448, fax 0171/637-1496.

Arriving and Departing

By Plane Grantley Adams International Airport in Barbados is a Caribbean hub. There are daily flights from New York via San Juan, and **American Airlines** (tel. 800/433–7300) and **BWIA** (tel. 800/538–2942) both have nonstop flights from New York and direct flights from Miami. From Canada, **Air Canada** (tel. 800/776–3000) connects from Montreal through New York or Miami and flies nonstop from Toronto. From London, **British Airways** (tel. 800/247–9297) has nonstop service and BWIA connects through Trinidad.

Flights to St. Vincent, St. Lucia, Trinidad, and other islands are scheduled on **LIAT** (tel. 809/495–1187) and BWIA; Air St. Vincent/Air Mustique links Barbados with St. Vincent and the Grenadines.

From the Airport Airport taxis are not metered. A large sign at the airport announces the fixed rate to each hotel or area, stated in both Barbados and U.S. dollars (about $20 to the West Coast hotels, $13 to the South Coast ones). You can also catch a bus into Bridgetown (BDS $1.50), then transfer to another for West Coast and South Coast hotels.

Passports and Visas To enter Barbados, U.S. and Canadian citizens need proof of citizenship and a return or ongoing ticket. Acceptable proof of citizenship is a valid passport or an original birth certificate and a photo ID; a voter registration card or baptismal certificate is not acceptable. British citizens need a valid passport.

Language English is spoken everywhere, often accented with the phrases and lilt of a Bajan dialect.

Precautions Beach vendors of coral jewelry, handcrafts, and other items will not hesitate to offer you their wares. The degree of persistence varies, and sharp bargaining is expected on both sides. One hotel's brochure gives sound advice: "Please realize that encouraging the beach musicians means you may find yourself listening to the same three tunes over and over for the duration of your stay."

The water on the island is plentiful and safe to drink in both hotels and restaurants. It is naturally filtered through 1,000 feet of pervious coral. Insects aren't much of a problem on Barbados, but if you plan to hike or spend time on secluded beaches, it's wise to use insect repellent. The little green apples that fall from the large branches of the manchineel tree may look tempting, but they are poisonous to eat and toxic to the touch. Even taking shelter under the tree when it rains can give you blisters. If you do come in contact with one, go to the nearest hotel and have someone there phone for a physician. Don't invite trouble by leaving valuables unattended on the beach or in plain sight in your room, and don't pick up hitchhikers.

Staying in Barbados

Important Addresses **Tourist Information:** The **Barbados Tourism Authority** is on Harbour Road in Bridgetown (tel. 809/427–2623, fax. 809/426–4080). Hours are weekdays 8:30–4:30. There are also information booths, staffed by Board representatives, at Grantley Adams International Airport and at Bridgetown's Cruiseship Terminal.

Emergencies **Emergency and Police:** tel. 112. **Ambulance**: tel. 115. **Fire department:** tel. 113. **Scuba diving accidents:** Divers' Alert Network (DAN; tel. 809/684–8111 or 809/684–2948). **24 hr. decompression chamber:** Barbados Defence Force, St. Ann's Fort, Garrison, St. Michael Parish, tel. 809/436–6185.

Currency One Barbados dollar (BDS $1) equals about U.S. 50¢. Because the value of the Barbados dollar is pegged to that of the U.S. dollar, the ratio remains constant. Both currencies and the Canadian dollar are accepted everywhere on the island. Prices quoted throughout this chapter are in U.S. dollars unless noted otherwise.

Taxes and Service Charges At the airport you must pay a departure tax of BDS $25 (U.S. $12.50) in either currency before leaving Barbados.

A 5% government tax is added to hotel bills, and a 10% service charge is added to your hotel bill and to most restaurant checks; any additional tip recognizes extraordinary service. When no service charge is added, tip maids $1 per room per day, waiters 10% to 15%, taxi drivers 10%. Airport porters and bellboys expect BDS $2 (U.S. $1) per bag. There is no sales tax.

Getting Around Barbados has almost 900 miles of good roads, and it's easy to get around by taxi or bus. A rental car is not critical to your mobility. Another inexpensive option is to rent a bicycle and explore on your own, at least in the vicinity of your hotel.

Taxis Taxis operate at a fixed hourly rate of BDS $32. For short trips, the rate per mile (or part thereof) should not exceed BDS $2.50. From Bridgetown to Crane Beach the fare is BDS $35; from Bridgetown to

Harrison's Cave, it's BDS $30. The most expensive fare, from the southern part of the island to the north, is BDS $55. Always settle on a price before you enter the taxi, and agree on whether it's in U.S. or Barbados dollars. Taxis outside the major hotels are less open to negotiation. One to five persons may travel at the same rate.

Buses Blue buses with a yellow stripe are public; yellow buses with a blue stripe are privately owned. They travel the same routes and are all inexpensive (fixed fare of BDS $1.50, exact change appreciated), plentiful, reliable, and usually packed. Buses leave from Bridgetown for destinations throughout the island approximately every 30 minutes. North- and westbound buses use the terminals at Lower Green Street and Princess Alice Highway; southbound buses leave from the Fairchild Street Bus Terminal. Destinations are marked over the front windshield. Bus stops are marked TO CITY and OUT OF CITY. You need to flag buses down; they do not stop automatically for those standing at the stop.

Privately owned minibuses also operate for the same fixed fare. Most of these ply shorter routes and usually keep to the coastal roads. Board these at the terminals at Temple Yard, Probyn Street, and River Road in Bridgetown. Routes are usually painted on the side of the vehicles and their destination displayed on a card in the bottom left-hand corner of the windshield.

Rental Cars It's a pleasure to explore Barbados by car, provided you take the time to study a good map and don't mind asking directions frequently. The more remote roads are in good repair, yet few are well lighted at night; and night falls quickly—at about 6 PM. Even in full daylight, the tall sugarcane fields lining a road can make visibility difficult. Use caution: Pedestrians are everywhere. And remember, traffic keeps to the left.

To rent a car you must have an international driver's license, obtainable at the airport and major car-rental firms for BDS $10 (U.S. $5) if you have a valid driver's license. More than 40 offices rent minimokes for $35–$60 a day plus insurance (about $215 a week), usually with a three-day or four-day minimum; cars with automatic shift are $60–$65 a day, or approximately $260-$300 a week. Gas costs about $3 a gallon. The speed limit, in keeping with the pace of life, is 60 kph (37 mph) in the country, 40 kph (21 mph).

The principal car-rental firms are **National** (Bush Hall, St. Michael, tel. 809/426–0603), **Dear's Garage** (Christ Church, tel. 809/429–9277 or 809/427–7853), **Sunny Isle** (Worthing, tel. 809/435–7979), **Sunset Crest Rentals** (St. James, tel. 809/432–1482), and **P&S Car Rentals** (St. Michael, tel. 809/424–2052).

Bicycles You can rent bikes for about BDS $17–$25 a day from numerous outlets. In Hastings, try **M.A. Williams Bicycle Rentals** (tel. 809/427–3955). On Rockley Main Road in Christ Church, **Fun Seekers Inc.** rents both bikes and motorscooters (tel. 809/435–8206).

Operating a motorscooter requires an international driver's license—and some skill and daring. Rental costs are about $16 a day for a single-seater and $31 for a two-seater.

Telephones and Mail The area code for Barbados is 809. Except for emergency numbers, all phone numbers have seven digits and begin with 42 or 43. A local call costs BDS 10¢.

An airmail letter from Barbados to the United States or Canada costs BDS 90¢ per half-ounce; an airmail postcard costs BDS 65¢. Letters to the United Kingdom are BDS $1.10; postcards are BDS 70¢.

Opening and Closing Times Stores are open weekdays 9–5, Saturday 8–1. Some supermarkets are open daily 8–6. Banks are open Monday–Thursday 8–3, Friday 8–5.

Guided Tours

Barbados has a lot to see. A half- or full-day bus or taxi tour, which can be arranged by your hotel, is a good way to get your bearings. The price varies according to the number of attractions included; an average full-day tour costs between $40 and $50 per person.

L.E. Williams Tour Co. (tel. 809/427–1043) offers an 80-mile island tour for about $50 a person. A bus picks you up between 8:30 and 9:30 AM and takes you through Bridgetown, the St. James beach area, past the Animal Flower Cave, Farley Hill, Cherry Tree Hill, Morgan Lewis Mill, the East Coast, St. John's Church, Sam Lord's Castle, Oistin's fishing village, and to St. Michael Parish, with drinks along the way and a West Indian lunch at the Atlantis Hotel in Bathsheba.

Highland Outdoor Tours (Canefield, St. Thomas Parish, tel. 809/438–8069) specializes in adventure trips to the island's seldom-seen natural wonders. Visitors have the option of half-day or full-day horseback treks (including a bareback ride in the surf), scenic hiking expeditions, and tractor-drawn jitney rides through some of Barbados's great plantations. Prices range from $25 to $100 per person and include refreshments and transportation to and from your hotel.

Alternatively, customize your own tour by hiring a taxi. Most drivers enthusiastically narrate their island's history and can give you off-the-cuff insights to local attractions. You will need to agree upon where you want to go and for how long in order to settle on a price somewhere in the region of $60 for a half-day tour (this is per car, not per person, so four people traveling together will save money).

Exploring Barbados

The Barbados National Trust, headquartered at 10th Avenue, Belleville, St. Michael (tel. 809/426–2421), has designed **The Heritage Passport,** a 50% discounted admission to Barbados's most popular attractions and historic sites. A Full Passport includes 16 sites and costs $35; a Mini-Passport includes 5 sites and costs $12. Children under 12 are admitted free if accompanied by a passport holder (maximum two children per passport). Passports may be purchased at hotels, Trust headquarters, or at the sites.

Bridgetown

Numbers in the margin correspond to points of interest on the Bridgetown map.

Bridgetown is a bustling city, complete with rush hours and traffic congestion. You'll avoid hassle by taking a bus to town and touring on foot. Sightseeing will take only an hour or so, and the shopping area is compact.

In the center of town, overlooking the picturesque harbor known as
1 the Careenage, is **Trafalgar Square**. Its monument to Lord Horatio
Nelson predates Nelson's Column in London's Trafalgar Square by more than two decades. Several blocks inland, on Synagogue Lane, the **Jewish Synagogue** (tel. 809/426–5792) dates back to 1654 and has recently been restored to its original purpose as a house of prayer.

Facing Trafalgar Square are the **House of Assembly** and the **Parliament**. A series of stained-glass windows depicting British monarchs, from James I to Queen Victoria, adorn these Victorian government buildings. Like so many smaller structures in Bridgetown, they stand beside a growing number of modern office build-
2 ings. The principal shopping area, **Broad Street,** leads west from
Trafalgar Square. Bridgetown is a major Caribbean free port.

3 The picturesque **Careenage,** a finger of sea that provided early
Bridgetown with a natural harbor, is where working schooners were careened (turned on their sides) to be scraped of barnacles and repainted. Today the Careenage serves mainly as a berth for pleasure

yachts and charter boats and a gathering place for locals and tourists.

Although no one has proved it conclusively, George Washington, on
his only visit outside the United States, is said to have worshiped at
4 **St. Michael's Cathedral.** The structure, east of Trafalgar Square,
was nearly a century old when he visited in 1751 and has been destroyed by hurricanes and rebuilt twice, in 1780 and 1831. The two bridges over the Careenage are the Chamberlain Bridge and the Charles O'Neal Bridge, both of which lead to Highway 7.

5 East of St. Michael's Cathedral, **Queen's Park** is home to one of the
largest trees in Barbados: an immense baobab more than 10 centur-
6 ies old. The historic **Queen's Park House,** former home of the commander of the British troops, has been converted into a theater—with an exhibition room on the lower floor—and a restaurant. Queen's Park is a long walk from Trafalgar Square; you may want to take a taxi. *Open daily 9–5.*

7 About a mile south of Bridgetown on Highway 7, the **Barbados Museum** has artifacts and mementos of military history and everyday life in the 19th century. You'll see cane-harvesting implements, lace wedding dresses, ancient (and frightening) dentistry instruments, and slave sale accounts kept in a spidery copperplate handwriting. Wildlife and natural-history exhibits, a well-stocked gift shop, and a good café are also here, in what used to be the military prison. *Hwy. 7, Garrison Savannah, tel. 809/427–0201. Admission: BDS $10 adults, BDS $5 children under 12. Open Mon.–Sat. 9–5, Sun. 2–6.*

Central Barbados

Numbers in the margin correspond to points of interest on the Barbados map.

1 An interesting place for swimmers and snorkelers is the **Folkstone Marine Park & Visitor Centre,** north of Holetown. While Folkstone has a land museum of marine life, the real draw is the underwater snorkeling trail around Dottin's Reef, with glass-bottom boats available for use by nonswimmers. A dredge barge sunk in shallow water is home to myriad fish, and it and the reef are popular dive sites. Huge sea fans, soft coral, and the occasional giant turtle are sights to see.

2 Highway 2 will take you to **Harrison's Cave.** These pale-gold limestone caverns, complete with subterranean streams and a 40-foot waterfall, are considered to be among the finest cave systems in the region. Open since 1981, the caves are so extensive that tours are made by electric tram (hard hats are provided, but all that may fall on you is a little dripping water). *Tel. 809/438–6640. Admission: BDS $15 adults, BDS $7.50 children. Reservations advised. Open daily 9–6.*

3 The nearby **Welchman Hall Gully,** a part of the National Trust in St. Thomas, gives you another chance to commune with nature. Here are acres of labeled flowers and trees, the occasional green monkey, and great peace and quiet. *Tel. 809/438–6671. Admission: BDS $10 adults, BDS $5 children. Open daily 9–5.*

4 Continue along Highway 2 to reach the **Flower Forest,** 8 acres of fragrant flowering bushes, canna and ginger lilies, and puffball trees, and more than a hundred species of flora. The tranquil setting also offers beautiful views of Mt. Hillaby. *Tel. 809/433–8152. Admission: BDS $10. Open daily 9–5.*

Go back toward Bridgetown and take Highway 4 and smaller roads
5 to **Gun Hill** for a view so pretty it seems almost unreal: Shades of green and gold cover the fields all the way to the horizon, the picturesque gun tower is surrounded by brilliant flowers, and the white limestone lion behind the garrison is a famous landmark. Military

Exploring
Andromeda Gardens, **6**
Animal Flower Cave, **10**
Barclay's Park, **7**
Barbados Wildlife Reserve, **11**
Chalky Mount Potteries, **8**
Codrington Theological College, **15**
Farley Hill, **12**
Flower Forest, **4**
Folkstone Marine Park & Visitor Centre, **1**
Gun Hill, **5**
Harrison's Cave, **2**
Pie Corner, **9**
Ragged Point Lighthouse, **14**
St. Nicholas Abbey, **13**
Welchman Hall Gully, **3**

Dining
Atlantis Hotel, **43**
Bonito Bar & Restaurant, **44**
Brown Sugar, **25**
Chefette, **18**
David's Place, **33**
Fathoms, **20**
Ile de France, **29**
Josef's, **35**
La Maison, **17**
Nico's, **19**
Ocean View Hotel, **27**
Pisces, **40**
Plantation, **37**
Rose and Crown, **22**
Waterfront Cafe, **24**

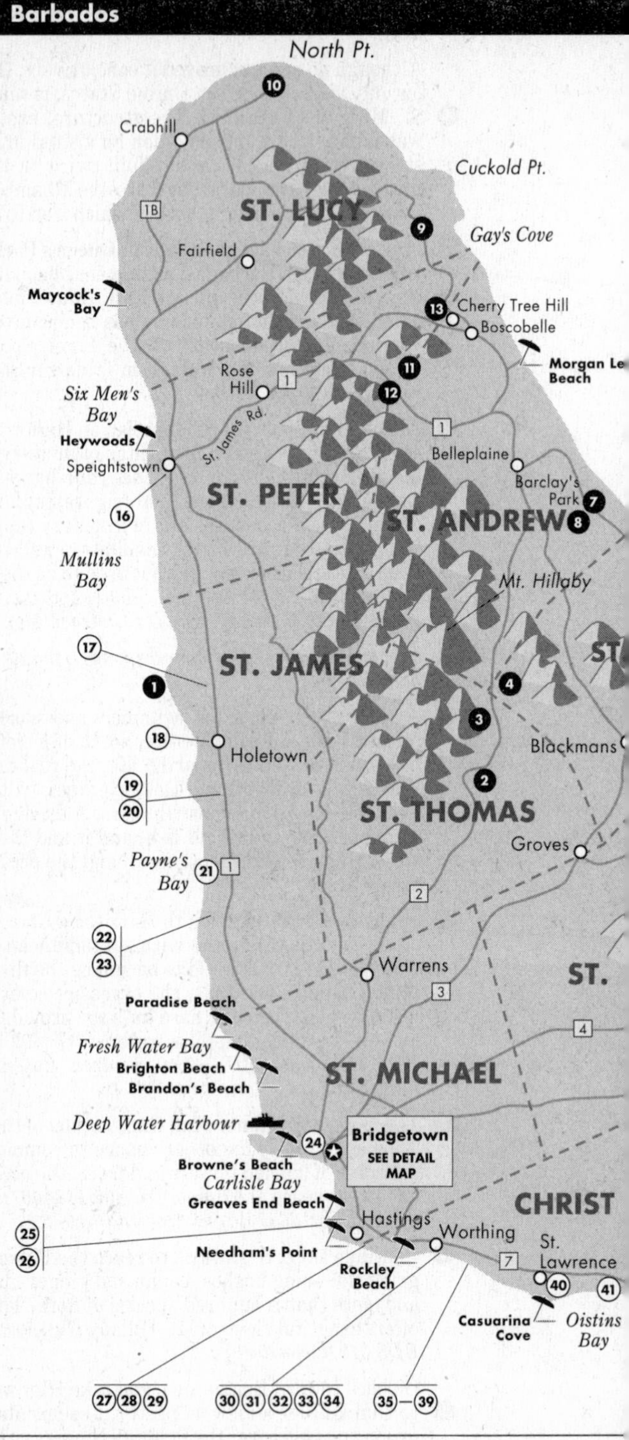

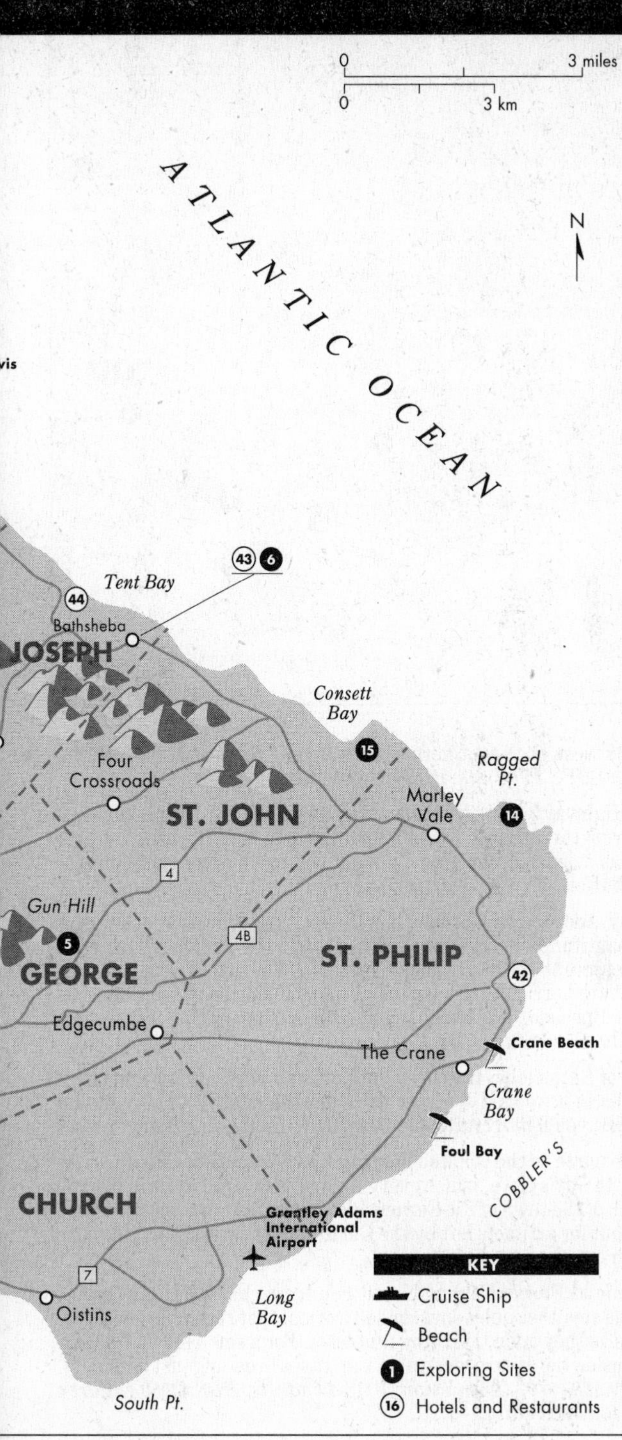

Lodging

Accra Beach Hotel, **28**
Atlantis Hotel, **43**
Barbados Beach Village, **23**
Barbados Hilton, **26**
Benston Windsurfing Club Hotel, **41**
Casuarina Beach Club, **39**
Little Bay Hotel, **36**
Marriott's Sam Lord's Castle, **42**
Ocean View Hotel, **27**
Pegwell Inn, **30**
Rio, **34**
Sandridge Beach Hotel, **16**
Sandy Beach Hotel, **31**
Sichris Hotel, **32**
Smuggler's Cove, **21**
Southern Palms, **38**

Barbados Museum, **7**
Broad Street, **2**
Careenage, **3**
Queen's Park, **5**
Queen's Park House, **6**
St. Michael's Cathedral, **4**
Trafalgar Square, **1**

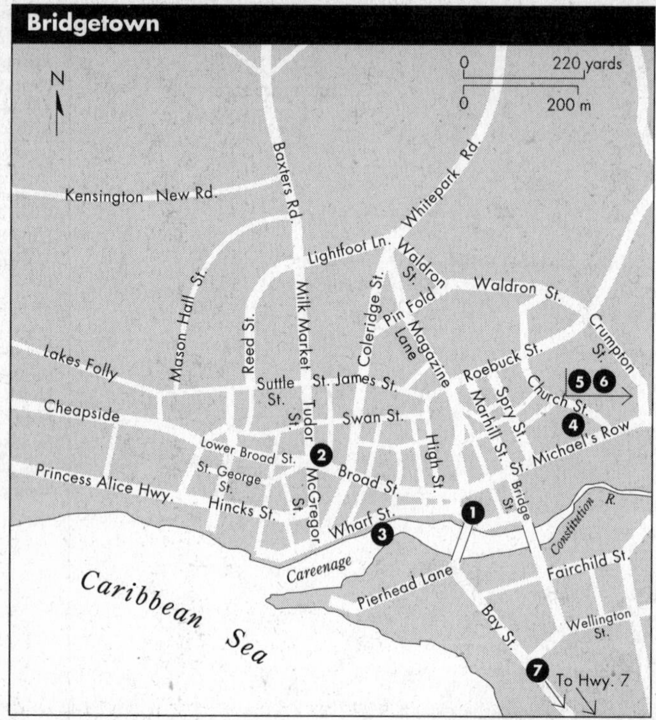

invalids were once sent here to convalesce. *Tel. 809/429–1358. Admission: BDS $5 adults, BDS $2.50 children.*

The East Coast Take Highway 3 across the island to Bathsheba and the phenomenal view from the **Atlantis,** one of the oldest hotels in Barbados, where you may need help getting up from the table after sampling the lunch buffet.

6 Nearby **Andromeda Gardens** is a fascinating collection of unusual and beautiful plant specimens from around the world, cultivated in beds set into the cliffs overlooking the sea. The plants were collected by the late horticulturist Iris Bannochie and are now administered by the Barbados National Trust. *Tel. 809/433–9384. Admission: BDS $10. Open daily 9–5.*

7 North of Bathsheba, **Barclay's Park** offers a similar view and picnic
8 facilities in a wooded seafront area. At the nearby **Chalky Mount Potteries,** you'll find craftspersons making and selling their wares.

A drive north to the isolated Morgan Lewis Beach (*see* Beaches, *below*) or to Gay's Cove, which every Bajan calls Cove Bay, will put you
9 in reach of the town of **Pie Corner.** Pie Corner is known not for baked goods but for artifacts left by the Carib and Arawak tribes who once lived there.

10 The **Animal Flower Cave** at North Point, reached by Highway 1B, displays small sea anemones, or sea worms, that resemble jewel-like flowers as they open their tiny tentacles. For a small fee you can explore inside the cavern and watch the waves breaking just outside it. *Tel. 809/439–8797. Admission: BDS $3 adults, BDS $1.50 children under 12. Open daily 9–4.*

North-Central Barbados The attractions of north-central Barbados may easily be combined with the tour of the East Coast.

11 The **Barbados Wildlife Reserve** can be reached on Highway 1 from Speightstown on the West Coast. The reserve is home to herons, land turtles, a kangaroo, screeching peacocks, innumerable green monkeys, geese, brilliantly colored parrots, and a friendly otter. The fauna are not in cages, so step carefully and keep your hands to yourself. The preserve has been much improved in recent years with the addition of a giant walk-in aviary and natural-history exhibits. Terrific photo opportunities are everywhere. *Tel. 809/422–8826. Admission: BDS $15 adults, BDS $10 children under 12 with adult. Open daily 10–5.*

12 Just to the south is **Farley Hill**, a national park in northern St. Peter Parish; the rugged landscape explains why they call this the Scotland area. The imposing ruins of a once-magnificent plantation great house are surrounded by gardens, lawns, an avenue of towering royal palms, and gigantic mahogany, whitewood, and casuarina trees. Partially rebuilt for the filming of *Island in the Sun,* the structure was later destroyed by fire. *Admission: BDS $2 per car; walkers free. Open daily 8:30–6.*

13 **St. Nicholas Abbey**, near Cherry Tree Hill, was named for a former owner and is the oldest (ca. 1650) great house in Barbados. It's well worth visiting for its stone and wood architecture in the Jacobean style. Fascinating home movies, made by the present owner's father, record scenes of Bajan town and plantation life in the 1920s and 1930s. There are no set showing times; you need only ask to see them. *Tel. 809/422–8725. Admission: BDS $2.50. Open weekdays 10–3:30.*

The South Shore

Driving east from Bridgetown on Highways 4 and 4B, you'll note the
many **chattel houses** along the route. The property of tenant farmers, these ever-expandable houses were built to be dismantled and
moved when necessary. When you reach the coast, you'll see the ap-
14 propriately named **Ragged Point Lighthouse,** where the sun first
shines on Barbados and its dramatic Atlantic seascape. About 4
miles to the northwest, in the eastern corner of St. John Parish, the
15 coralstone buildings and serenely beautiful grounds of **Codrington
Theological College,** founded in 1745, stand on a cliff overlooking
Consett Bay.

Beaches

Barbados is blessed with beautiful Caribbean beaches dotted with tall palms and shaded by leafy mahogany trees. All beaches are open to the public. (Access to hotel beaches may not always be public, but you can walk onto almost any beach from another one.)

West Coast Beaches

The West Coast has the stunning coves and white-sand beaches that are dear to postcard publishers—plus calm, clear water for snorkeling, scuba diving, and swimming. Beaches begin in the north at **Almond Beach Village** (about a mile of sand) and continue almost unbroken to Bridgetown at **Brighton Beach**, a popular spot with locals. The afternoon clouds and sunsets are breathtaking from any of the beaches along the West Coast.

While beaches here are seldom crowded, the West Coast is not the place to find isolation. Owners of private boats stroll by, offering waterskiing, parasailing, and snorkel cruises. There are no concession stands per se, but hotels welcome nonguests for terrace lunches (wear a cover-up). Picnic items and necessities can be bought at the Sunset Crest shopping center in Holetown.

Good spots for swimming include **Paradise Beach**; **Brandon's Beach,** a 10-minute walk south; **Browne's Beach,** in Bridgetown; and **Greaves End Beach,** south of Bridgetown at Aquatic Gap, between the Grand Barbados Beach Resort and the Barbados Hilton in St. Michael Parish.

South Coast Beaches The heavily traveled south coast of Christ Church Parish is much more built up than the St. James Parish coast in the west; here you'll find condos, high-rise hotels, beach parks, many places to eat and shop, and the traffic (including public transportation) that serves them. These busier beaches generally draw a younger, more active crowd. The quality of the beach itself is consistently good, the reef-protected waters safe for swimming and snorkeling.

Needham's Point, with its lighthouse, is one of Barbados's best beaches, crowded with locals on weekends and holidays. Two others are in the St. Lawrence Gap area, near **Casuarina Cove.** The **Benston Windsurfing Club Hotel** in Maxwell caters specifically to windsurfing aficionados, though most hotels and resorts provide boards or rent them for a nominal fee.

As you move toward the Atlantic side of the island, the waves roll in bigger and faster. **Crane Beach** has been a popular swimming beach for years; the waves at the nearby Crane Hotel are a favorite with bodysurfers. (But remember that this is the ocean, not the Caribbean, and exercise caution.)

Nearby **Foul Bay** lives up to its name only for sailboats; for swimmers and alfresco lunches, it's lovely.

North Coast Beaches Those who love wild natural beauty will want to head north up the East Coast highway. With secluded beaches and crashing ocean waves on one side, rocky cliffs and verdant landscape on the other, the windward side of Barbados won't disappoint anyone who seeks dramatic views. But be cautioned: Swimming here is treacherous and *not* recommended. The waves are high, the bottom tends to be rocky, and the currents are unpredictable. Limit yourself to enjoying the view and watching the surfers—who have been at it since they were kids.

A worthwhile, little-visited beach for the adventurous who don't mind trekking about a mile off the beaten track is **Morgan Lewis Beach,** on the coast east of Morgan Lewis Mill, the oldest intact windmill on the island. Turn east on the small road that goes to the town of Boscobelle (between Cherry Tree Hill and Morgan Lewis Mill), but instead of going to the town, take the even less-traveled road (unmarked on most maps; you will have to ask for directions) that goes down the cliff to the beach. What awaits is more than 2 miles of unspoiled, uninhabited white sand and sweeping views of the Atlantic coastline. You may see a few Bajans swimming, sunning, or fishing, but for the most part, you'll have privacy.

Return to your car and cross the island's north point on the secondary roads until you reach the West Coast. About a mile west from the end of Highway 1B is **Maycock's Bay,** an isolated area in St. Lucy Parish about 2 miles north of Almond Beach Village, the island's northernmost resort complex.

Sports and the Outdoors

Golfing Barbadians love golf, and golfers love Barbados. The **Royal Westmoreland Golf Club** (tel. 809/422–4653), a challenging Robert Trent Jones 18-hole course that meanders through the 480-acre Westmoreland Sugar Estate and overlooks the scenic West Coast, was brand-new for the 1995 season. The 7th hole on the championship course at the prestigious **Sandy Lane Club** (tel. 809/432–1145) is famous for both its elevated tee and its incredible view. **Club Rockley Barbados** (tel. 809/435–7873), on the South Coast, has a 9-hole course. **Almond Beach Village** (tel. 809/522–4900), the former Heywoods Resort on the northwest corner of the island, has a 9-hole course. The **Belair Par-3** (tel. 809/423–4653) course is on the rugged East Coast, near Sam Lord's Castle. All are open to nonguests. Greens fees range from $12.50 for 9 holes at Belair to $120 for 18 holes at Sandy Lane.

Hiking and Walking Hilly but not mountainous, the interior of Barbados is ideal for hiking. The **Barbados National Trust** (Belleville, St. Michael, tel. 809/426–2421) sponsors free 5-mile walks year-round on Sunday, from 6:30 AM to about 9:30 AM and from 3:30 PM to 5:30 PM, as well as special moonlight hikes when the heavens permit. Newspapers announce the time and meeting place (or you can call the Trust).

Jogging The **Hash House Harriers** is an international running group that organizes relaxed jogs each week. Contact John Carpenter (tel. 809/429–5151 days or 809/429–3818 evenings).

Sea Excursions The West Coast is the area for scuba diving, sailing, and lunch-and-rum cruises on the red-sailed ***Jolly Roger*** "pirate" party ship (Fun Cruises, tel. 809/436–6424). Somewhat more sedate sailing experiences can be had on the ***Wind Warrior*** (tel. 809/427–7245) and the ***Secret Love*** (tel. 809/432–1972). Cruises cost about $50 per person.

Scuba Diving Many dive shops provide instruction (three-hour beginner's "resort" courses and weeklong certification courses) followed by a shallow dive, usually on Dottin's Reef. Trained divers can explore reefs, wrecks, and the walls of "blue holes," the huge circular depressions in the ocean floor. Not to be missed by certified, guided divers is the *Stavronikita,* a 368-foot Greek freighter that was deliberately sunk at about 125 feet. Hundreds of butterfly fish hang out around its mast, and the thin rays of sunlight that filter down through the water make exploring the huge ship a wonderfully eerie experience. The cost for a single-tank dive on Barbados is approximately $40. Multiple dives are discounted. Equipment other than tank and weights costs extra.

At **The Dive Shop, Ltd.** (Grand Barbados Beach Resort, tel. 809/426–9947), experienced divers can participate in deep dives to old wrecks to look for bottles and other artifacts (and you can usually keep what you find). **Exploresub Barbados** (St. Lawrence Gap, Christ Church, tel. 809/435–6542) offers a full range of daily dives. **Dive Boat Safari** (Barbados Hilton, tel. 809/427–4350) offers full diving and instruction services.

Snorkeling Snorkeling gear can be rented for about BDS $10 (U.S. $5) from nearly every hotel.

Squash and Tennis Squash courts can be reserved at the **Club Rockley Barbados** (tel. 809/435–7880) and **Barbados Squash Club** (Marine House, Christ Church, tel. 809/427–7913). Most hotels have tennis courts that can be reserved day and night. Be sure to bring your whites; appropriate dress is expected on the court. Fees average BDS $30 (U.S. $15), and guests of the hotel have first dibs.

Surfing The best surfing is available on the East Coast, and most wave riders congregate at the Soup Bowl, near Bathsheba. An annual international surfing competition is held on Barbados every October.

Waterskiing Waterskiing is widely available, often provided along St. James and Christ Church by the private speedboat owners. Cost is about BDS $35 (U.S. $18) for 15 minutes. Inquire at your hotel, which can direct you to the nearest Sunfish sailing and Hobie Cat rentals as well.

Windsurfing Windsurfing boards and equipment are often guest amenities at the larger hotels and can be rented by nonguests. The best place to windsurf is on the southeastern coast of the island, at Silver Sands and Silver Rock Beach.

Shopping

Traditionally, Broad Street and its side streets in Bridgetown have been the center for shopping action. Hours are generally weekdays 9–5 and Saturday 8–1. Many stores have an in-bound (duty-free) department where you must show your travel tickets or a passport in order to buy duty-free goods. Bridgetown stores have values on fine bone china, crystal, cameras, stereo and video equipment, jewelry, perfumes, and clothing. But these luxury items tend to be expensive, even without taxes. You are advised to check stateside prices before deciding upon a purchase here: The item may be cheaper at home.

Island handicrafts are everywhere: woven mats and place mats, dresses, dolls, handbags, shell jewelry. The **Best of Barbados** shops (Mall 34 in Bridgetown, tel. 809/436–1416; and 6 other locations) offer the highest-quality arts and crafts, both "native-style" and modern designs. A resident artist, Jill Walker, sells her watercolors and prints here. **Coffee & Cream Gallery** (Paradise Village, St. Lawrence Gap, tel. 809/428–2708) displays and sells artwork of all types by local artists.

At the **Pelican Village Handicrafts Center** (tel. 809/426–4391) on the Princess Alice Highway near the Cheapside Market in Bridgetown, in a cluster of conical shops, you can watch goods and crafts being made before you purchase them. Rugs and mats made from pandanus fiber and khuskhus grass are good buys.

For native Caribbean arts and crafts, including items from Barbados and elsewhere in the region, visit the **Verandah Art Gallery** (Broad St., Bridgetown, tel. 809/426–2605).

Best 'N The Bunch (St. Lawrence Gap, tel. 809/428–2472) is a wildly colored chattel house at The Chattel House Village and its own best advertisement. Here the expertly crafted jewelry of Bajan David Trottman is sold at reasonable prices.

Dining

Restaurant prices are generally high on Barbados. Continental fare is standard at restaurants here, and for this you'll pay $25 and up per person for dinner. The better hotels and restaurants of Barbados have employed chefs trained in New York and Europe to attract and keep their sophisticated clientele. Gourmet dining here usually means fresh seafood, beef, or veal with finely blended sauces. Fortunately, many of these restaurants offer the same cuisine at lunch for about half the cost.

Budget diners will fare much better with the native West Indian cuisine. You can enjoy delicious fried flying fish, for example, for less than $10 at local restaurants. Small cafés typically offer zesty goat curry with rice for under $5. The island's West African heritage brought rice, peas, beans, and okra to its table, the staples that make a perfect base for slowly cooked meat and fish dishes. Many side dishes are cooked in oil (the pumpkin fritters can be addictive). Be cautious at first with the West Indian seasonings; like the sun, they are hotter than you think.

Most menus include dolphinfish, kingfish, snapper, and flying fish prepared every way imaginable. Shellfish abound; so does steak. For breakfast and dessert, you'll find mangoes, soursop, papaya (pawpaw), and, in season, "mammy apples," a softball-size, thick-skinned fruit with giant seeds.

Cou-cou is a mix of cornmeal and okra with a spicy Creole sauce made from tomatoes, onions, and sweet peppers; it is often served with steamed flying fish. Pepper-pot stew, a hearty mix of oxtail, beef chunks, and "any other meat you may have," is simmered overnight and flavored with *cassareep*, a preservative and seasoning that gives the stew its dark, rich color. *Christophines* and *eddoes* are tasty, potato-like vegetables that are often served with curried shrimp, chicken, or goat. *Buljol* is a cold salad of shredded, raw codfish, marinated with tomatoes, onions, sweet peppers, and celery.

Callaloo soup is made from okra, crabmeat, the spinachlike vegetable that gives the dish its name, and seasonings. You'll find that many restaurants create their own versions of these traditional dishes.

Among the liquid refreshments of Barbados, in addition to the omnipresent Banks Beer and Mount Gay rum, are **falernum**, a liqueur concocted of rum, sugar, lime juice, and almond essence, and **mauby**, a refreshing nonalcoholic beerlike drink made by boiling bitter bark and spices, straining the mixture, and sweetening it.

Increasingly, hotels here are offering MAP plans or are becoming all-inclusive; but if no meals are included in your hotel rate, take advantage of the island's grocery stores, found in every neighborhood and stocked with local and imported foods. Convenience stores in shopping plazas located along the coast road are another option.

What to Wear Barbados's British heritage and large resident population keep the island's dress code modest. Although this does not always mean a tie and jacket, you'll find that jeans, shorts, and beach shirts are frowned upon at dinnertime.

Highly recommended restaurants are indicated by a star ★.

Category	Cost*
$$	$25–$40
$	$15–$25
¢	under $15

**per person, excluding drinks and 5% service charge*

$$ **Brown Sugar.** A special-occasion atmosphere prevails at Brown Sugar, which is set in a restored West Indian wooden house across the road from the Grand Barbados Beach Resort outside Bridgetown. Dozens of ferns and hanging plants decorate the breezy multilevel restaurant. An extensive and authentic West Indian lunch buffet—everything from cou-cou to pepper-pot stew—served between noonand 2:30, is popular with local businessmen and reasonably priced. The dinner menu adds entrées such as Creole orange chicken and homemade desserts, including angel food chocolate mousse cake, passion fruit or nutmeg ice cream, and lime cheesecake with guava sauce. *Bay St., Aquatic Gap, St. Michael Parish, tel. 809/426-7684. Reservations advised. AE, DC, MC, V. No lunch Sat.*

$$ ★ **Fathoms.** The newest property of veteran restaurateurs Stephen and Sandra Toppin is open seven days a week for lunch and dinner, with 22 well-dressed tables scattered from the inside dining rooms to the patio's ocean edge. Dinner may bring a grilled lobster, island rabbit, jumbo baked shrimp, or cashew-crusted kingfish. Fathoms is casual by day, candlelit by night. *Payne's Bay, St. James Parish, tel. 809/432-2568. Dinner reservations advised. AE, MC, V.*

$$ ★ **Ile de France.** French owners Martine (from Lyon) and Michel (from Toulouse) Gramaglia have adapted the pool and garden areas of the Windsor Arms Hotel and turned them into an island "in" spot. White latticework opens to the night sounds, soft taped French music plays, and a single, perfect hibiscus dresses each table. Specialties include foie gras, tournedos Rossini, lobster-and-crepe flambé, and filet mignon with a choice of pepper, béarnaise, or champignon sauce. This is the one place on the island where you can eat decent French food. Even if the prices here strain your budget, your taste buds will reassure you that all is not lost. *Windsor Arms Hotel, Hastings, Christ Church Parish, tel. 809/435-6869. Reservations required. No credit cards. Closed Mon. No lunch.*

$$ **Josef's.** Swede Nils Ryman created a menu from the unusual combination of Caribbean and Scandinavian fare. Blackened fish, rolled in

Cajun spices and seared in oil, and toast Skagen, made from diced shrimp blended with mayonnaise and fresh dill, are menu favorites. Stroll around the garden before moving to the alfresco dining room downstairs or to the simply decorated room upstairs for a table that looks out over the sea. *Waverly House, St. Lawrence Gap, Christ Church Parish, tel. 809/435–6541. Reservations advised. AE, DC, MC, V.*

$$ ★ **La Maison.** The elegant atmosphere in the colonial-style Balmore House is created by English country furnishings and a paneled bar opening onto a seaside terrace for dining. The award-winning gourmet cuisine is nothing less than superb. A French chef from the Loire Valley creates seafood specials, including a flying-fish parfait appetizer. Passion-fruit ice cream is a dessert special. *Holetown, St. James Parish, tel. 809/432–1156. Reservations advised. AE, D, MC, V. Closed Mon.*

$$ ★ **Ocean View Hotel.** Barbados's oldest restaurant, the dining room of this elegant, pink, grande dame hotel is dressed in fresh fabrics, with great bunches of equally fresh flowers and sparkling crystal chandeliers. Bajan dishes are served for lunch and dinner, and the Sunday-only Planter's luncheon buffet offers course after course of traditional dishes—callaloo, cou-cou, flying fish, and more. There's a cabaret and dancing on weekend evenings. *Hastings, Christ Church Parish, tel. 809/427–7821. Reservations advised. AE, MC, V.*

$$ **Pisces.** Fish is the way to go at this eatery at the water's edge in lively St. Lawrence Gap. Flying fish, dolphinfish, crab, kingfish, shrimp, prawns, and lobster are prepared any way from charbroiled to sautéed. There are also some chicken and beef dishes. Other items include conch fritters, tropical gazpacho, and seafood terrine with mango sauce. Enjoy dining alfresco, in a contemporary setting filled with hanging tropical plants and twinkling white lights. *St. Lawrence Gap, Christ Church Parish, tel. 809/435–6564. Reservations advised. AE, MC, V. No lunch.*

$$ **Plantation.** The Bajan buffet on Wednesday and the entertainment on Wednesday, Friday, and Saturday are big attractions here. The Plantation is in a renovated Barbadian residence surrounded by spacious grounds above the Southwinds Resort. French and Bajan cuisine is served either indoors or on the terrace. *St. Lawrence Gap, Christ Church Parish, tel. 809/428–5048. Reservations advised. AE, MC, V. No lunch.*

$$ **Rose and Crown.** A variety of fresh seafood is served in this casual eatery, but it's the lobster that's high on diners' lists. Indoors is a paneled bar; outdoors are tables on a wraparound porch. *Prospect, St. James Parish, tel. 809/425–1074. Reservations advised. AE, MC, V. No lunch. Closed Sat.*

$ **Atlantis Hotel.** While the surroundings may be simple, the seemingly endless buffet and the magnificent ocean view make this restaurant a real find. Owner-chef Enid Maxwell serves up an enormous Bajan buffet daily, where you're likely to find pickled souse (marinated pig parts and vegetables), pumpkin fritters, spinach balls, pickled breadfruit, fried "fline" (flying) fish, roast chicken, pepperpot stew, and West Indian–style okra and eggplant. Among the homemade pies are an apple and a dense coconut. *Bathsheba, St. Joseph Parish, tel. 809/433–9445. Reservations advised. AE.*

$ ★ **David's Place.** Come here for first-rate food in a first-rate location—a black-and-white Bajan cottage overlooking St. Lawrence Bay. Baxters Road chicken, local flying fish, pepper-pot, curried shrimp, and other entrées are served with homemade cheesebread. Dessert might be banana pudding, coconut-cream pie, carrot cake with rum sauce, or cassava pone. *Worthing Main Rd., St. Lawrence Gap, Christ Church Parish, tel. 809/435–6550. Reservations advised. AE, MC, V.*

$ **Nico's.** Expatriates and tourists gather at this intimate second-floor bistro in Holetown. An oval bar surrounded by stools stands in the middle of the room, with the tables on the perimeter and a few more on the terrace above the street. Drop by for drinks and socializing, and order a snack (the fried Camembert is good); or try something more substantial, such as seafood thermidor. *2nd St., Holetown, St. James Parish, tel. 809/432–6386. MC, V.*

¢ **Bonito Bar & Restaurant.** When you tour the rugged East Coast, plan to arrive in Bathsheba at lunchtime and stop at Mrs. Enid Worrell's Bonito Bar for a wholesome West Indian meal. The view of the Atlantic coast from the second-floor dining room of this rather plain restaurant is magnificent. Lunch might be a choice of fried fish, baked chicken, or beef stew, accompanied by vegetables and salads fresh from the family garden. If your timing is right, she may have homemade cheesecake for dessert. Be sure to try the fresh fruit punch—with or without rum. The Bajan luncheon buffet, on Sunday from 1–3, is popular with residents and visitors alike. *Coast Road, Bathsheba, St. Joseph Parish, tel. 809/433–9034. No credit cards.*

¢ **Chefette.** Sometimes you just want a quick bite to eat, with no hassle and no frills—and change from a $10 bill. Chefette is the local fast-food chain, with eateries in several locations on the island. Roasted or barbecued chicken and ribs, spicy rotis, beef burgers, baked potatoes, fries, rice, and salads will whet your appetite then satisfy your hunger. They're open from 11 to 11 in most locations—some have drive-through windows. *Marhill St. (tel. 809/429–5216), Broad St. (tel. 809/436–6381), and Harbour Rd. (tel. 809/426–3043) in Bridgetown; Oistins (tel. 809/428–2223) and Rockley (tel. 809/435–6709 or 809/435–6602) in Christ Church Parish; Holetown (tel. 809/432–0430) in St. James Parish. No credit cards.*

¢ **Waterfront Café.** Located on the Careenage, a sliver of sea in Bridgetown, this is the perfect place to enjoy a drink, snack, or meal, and there's live music nightly. Locals and tourists gather at outdoor café tables for sandwiches, salads, fish, steak-and-kidney pie, and casseroles. The pan-fried flying-fish sandwich is especially tasty. In the evening, from the brick and mirrored interior, you can gaze through the arched windows, enjoy the cool trade winds and let time pass. The café is open until midnight. *Bridgetown, St. Michael Parish, tel. 809/427–0093. MC, V. Closed Sun.*

Lodging

The southern and western shores of Barbados are lined with lodgings of every size and price, from superluxury resorts to B&Bs and rental apartments. Besides looking at rates, budget travelers should consider location when choosing their hotel. Those north of Bridgetown, in the parishes of St. Peter, St. James, and St. Michael, tend to be self-contained resorts that carry a high price tag. Furthermore, the stretches of empty road between them do not encourage strolling to a neighborhood bar or restaurant. In contrast, the area southeast of Bridgetown, in Christ Church Parish, contains both expensive and inexpensive hotels that cluster near or along the busy strip known as St. Lawrence Gap, where small restaurants, bars, and nightclubs abound.

In addition to hotels, Barbados has a range of alternative accommodations. Guest houses, best described as small hotels with meals provided on request, provide simple lodgings at $30–$50 a double per night. B&Bs are another option. About 20 are listed with the **Barbados Tourism Authority** (tel. 809/427–2623); roughly half are in Christ Church Parish. B&Bs here tend to be humble rooms in family homes; prices start at about $25 a night. Finally, apartment and home rentals are becoming increasingly popular among visitors to the island (*see* Villa and Apartment Rentals, *below*).

Hotels listed are grouped here by location—West Coast, which is north of Bridgetown; South Coast, east of Bridgetown; and a couple of properties in the remote southeast and East Coast. You'll notice that most of the affordable hotels in Barbados are on the South Coast.

Highly recommended lodgings are indicated by a star ★.

Category	Cost*
$$	$130–$225
$	$80–$130
¢	under $80

**All prices are for a standard double room for two, excluding 5% government tax and 10% service charge. To estimate rates for hotels offering MAP/FAP, add about $35–$45 per person per day to the above price ranges.*

Hotels and Resorts

West Coast

Barbados Beach Village. An informal, lively atmosphere prevails here. It's one of the least expensive places on the famous St. James Coast. Choose from single rooms, one-bedroom suites, or duplex villas; suites and villas have kitchenettes and private balconies. The beachside patio restaurant serves international and local cuisine, and there's a pool bar and nightclub. *Fitts Village, Hwy. 1, St. James Parish, tel. 809/425–1440, fax 809/424–0996. 89 rooms. Facilities: restaurant, pool, disco, minimart, tennis, water sports. AE, DC, MC, V. EP. $$*

Barbados Hilton. This large resort, just five minutes from Bridgetown, is for those who like activity and plenty of people around. Expect to rub shoulders with seminar attendees and conventioneers. You may detect an odor from the nearby oil refinery. Attractions here include an atrium lobby, a 1,000-foot-wide, man-made beach with full water sports, and lots of shops. All rooms and suites have balconies; unfortunately, those within our price category face the gardens, not the sea. *Needham's Point, St. Michael Parish, tel. 809/426–0200, fax 809/436–8646. 183 rooms, 2 suites. Facilities: restaurant, lounge, pool, tennis courts, health club. AE, DC, MC, V. EP. $$*

Smugglers Cove. The studio and one-bedroom accommodations in this small beachfront hotel are simple and cozy, but you'll be surrounded by glamorous St. James hotels and share the same sea view—at a fraction of the price. All rooms have kitchenettes, and there's a restaurant and bar. *Paynes Bay, St. James Parish, tel. 809/432–1741, fax 809/432–1749. 14 studios, 7 one-bedroom suites. Facilities: restaurant, bar, beach, pool. AE, V. EP. $–$$*

Sandridge Beach Hotel. Friendliness and conviviality abound at this small beachfront resort. It's near quaint Speightstown, Barbados's second city, on the northern edge of the fashionable West Coast. Accommodations are in standard hotel rooms or suites with a kitchenette. Complimentary water sports include windsurfing, sailing, snorkeling and glass-bottom-boat rides. Sandy's, the hotel restaurant, oofers a full menu and a barbecue buffet, with entertainment on Monday and Thursday nights. *Road View, St. Peter Parish, tel. 809/422–2361, fax 809/422–2965. 52 rooms. Facilities: restaurant, bar, beach, pool, water sports. AE, D, DC, MC, V. EP, MAP, FAP, CP, BP. $*

South Coast

Casuarina Beach Club. This luxury apartment hotel on 900 feet of pink sand takes its name from the casuarina pines that surround it. The quiet setting provides a dramatic contrast to those of other South Coast resorts. The bar and restaurant are on the beach. A new reception area includes small lounges where you can get a dose of TV—there aren't any in the guest rooms. The rooms and two-bedroom suites face the beach, pool, or garden; some have kitchenettes. Scuba diving, golf, and other activities can be arranged. The

Casuarina Beach is especially popular with those who prefer self-catering holidays in a secluded setting, yet want to be close to nightlife and shopping of St. Lawrence Gap. Children under 12 can stay free with a parent. *Dover, Christ Church Parish, tel. 809/428–3600, fax 809/428–1970. 134 units. Facilities: restaurant, bar, pool, tennis, minimarket, duty-free shop. AE, D, MC, V. EP. $$*

Sandy Beach Hotel. On a wide, sparkling white beach, this comfortable hotel has a popular poolside bar and the Beachfront Restaurant, which serves a West Indian buffet Tuesday and Saturday nights. Although the hotel is in the top end of our $$ price category, you can offset costs by preparing your own meals (all rooms have kitchenettes) and by skipping a car rental (St. Lawrence Gap, with restaurants and entertainment, is within walking distance). Water sports, which cost extra, include scuba-diving certification, deep-sea fishing, harbor cruises, catamaran sailing, and windsurfing. *Worthing, Christ Church Parish, tel. 809/435–8000, fax 809/435–8053. 89 units. Facilities: restaurant, bar, beach, pool. AE, D, DC, MC, V. EP. $$*

Southern Palms. A plantation-style hotel on a 1,000-foot stretch of sandy beach near the Dover Convention Center, Southern Palms is popular with business travelers as well as beach lovers. Italian statues and fountains add a European flair to the otherwise Caribbean atmosphere. Each wing of the hotel has its own small pool. *St. Lawrence Gap, Christ Church Parish, tel. 809/428–7171, fax 809/428–7175. 92 rooms. Facilities: 2 pools, duty-free shop, small conference center, miniature-golf course, tennis court, dining room, water sports. AE, D, DC, MC, V. EP. $$*

Accra Beach Hotel. Rockley Beach, one of Barbados's most beautiful South Coast beaches, is the setting for this hotel. Its 21 luxury studio apartments have fully equipped kitchenettes and private balconies with an ocean view. Other rooms are comfortably furnished with twin beds; some have balconies. All studios have been recently renovated with new carpets and tiling. Guests gather for alfresco dining by the pool in the evenings. Nightlife, shopping, and sports activities are close by. *Rockley, Christ Church Parish, tel. 809/435–8920, fax 809/435–6794. 52 rooms. Facilities: dining room, lounge, beach bar, water-sports center. AE, MC, V. EP. $*

Benston Windsurfing Club Hotel. A small hotel that began as a gathering place for windsurfing enthusiasts, the Benston is now a complete school and center for the sport. The rooms are spacious and sparsely furnished to accommodate the active young crowd that chooses this bare-bones hotel right on the beach. The bar and restaurant overlook the water, and other restaurants are within walking distance. All sports can be arranged, but windsurfing (learning, practicing, and perfecting it) is king. *Maxwell Main Rd., Christ Church Parish, tel. 809/428–9095, fax 809/435–8954. 14 rooms. Facilities: restaurant, bar, entertainment. AE, MC, V. EP. $*

Sichris Hotel. The Sichris is a real find. More attractive inside than than it is from the road, it's a comfortable and convenient self-contained resort. It's minutes from Bridgetown and a five-minute walk to the beach. The air-conditioned one-bedroom suites are smallish but have kitchenettes and private balconies. The pool is quite small and, literally, a hot spot—it's encircled by low white buildings that reflect the sun's rays. *Worthing, Christ Church Parish, tel. 809/435–7930, fax 809/435–8232. 24 rooms. Facilities: pool, restaurant, bar. AE, DC, MC, V. EP. $*

★ **Ocean View.** One of the best-kept secrets on the island, this unique hideaway with its 40 rooms and suites is a stopping place for celebrities on their commute to private villas in Mustique. Owner John Chandler places his antiques throughout his three-story grande dame nestled against the sea (the beach is not good for swimming), adds great bouquets of tropical flowers everywhere, and calls it home. Rooms vary considerably, and their charm depends on whether you appreciate the eclectic furnishings. Smaller, sparsely furnished rooms fall into our ¢ category, while larger rooms stretch into the upper reaches of our $ range. A car is not essential here, since the property is on the main coastal road: Restaurants are within walking distance, and popular beaches are a short bus ride away. Those who enjoy this old colonial-style building for what it is and don't mind the lack of modern amenities will be happiest here. Cat lovers will be wooed by the owner's pets, which drape themselves over lounge chairs. On weekends during high season, the restaurant has a buffet dinner with cabaret show and dancing. *Hastings, Christ Church Parish, tel. 809/427–7821, fax 809/427–7826. 31 rooms. Facilities: restaurant, bar, pool, cabaret. AE, MC, V. EP. ¢–$*

Little Bay Hotel. This small hotel just a five-minute walk from great beaches is a find. Three one-bedroom apartments have fully equipped kitchens; seven hotel rooms have refrigerators. All rooms have ceiling fans and breathtaking views of St. Lawrence Bay. Room 100—a corner unit with a small sitting room and a balcony overlooking the bay—is a favorite. The popular restaurant is open to the bay and features delicious seafood. You can watch TV in the small lounge. Nightlife is a stroll away. *St. Lawrence Gap, Christ Church Parish, tel. 809/435–7246, fax 809/435–8574. 10 rooms. Facilities: restaurant, bar. AE, V. EP. ¢*

Pegwell Inn. You need only cross the street to get to the beach from this small, friendly guest house. The four guest rooms have twin beds and private baths. Coffee- and tea-making facilities are available, and you can pick up picnic supplies from the food plaza next door. There are dozens of restaurants in nearly St. Lawrence Gap. Prices are low and are cut in half for children under 12. *Welches, Christ Church Parish, tel. 809/428–6150. 4 rooms. Facilities: restaurant, bar. No credit cards. EP. ¢*

Rio. Mr. and Mrs. Harding run this small family-owned inn 3 miles outside Bridgetown and within walking distance of the beach. Inexpensive restaurants, food shops, pubs, and nightclubs are all within walking distance. Rooms are not large, but rates are rock bottom. *St. Lawrence Gap, Christ Church Parish, tel. 809/428–1546. 7 doubles with bath, 2 singles with shared bath. No credit cards. EP. ¢*

Southeast and East Coast

Marriott's Sam Lord's Castle. The "castle" is actually a sprawling great house. It's set on the Atlantic coast about 14 miles east of Bridgetown and surrounded by 72 acres of grounds, gardens, and beach. The rooms, most in buildings angling off the main house toward the beach, are conventionally furnished in international Marriott style. Only the standard doubles facing the gardens are within our $$ price category. The beach fronts ocean waters with large breakers and is a mile long. There are also three freshwater pools. The hotel is miles from any other resort or activity, but the two restaurants, evening entertainment, and even a few slot machines are designed to keep everyone busy. *Long Bay, St. Philip Parish, tel. 809/423–7350, fax 809/423–5918. 234 rooms. Facilities: 3 restaurants, beach, 3 pools, 7 lighted tennis courts, entertainment. AE, DC, MC, V. EP, MAP, FAP. $$*

Atlantis Hotel. If you'd rather skip the international tourist scene, consider this modest, somewhat out-of-the-way hotel. It's in a pastoral location, overlooking a majestically rocky Atlantic coast. You'll need your own wheels here (a bike will do for the energetic), because the nearest swimming beach with sand is a good 15-minute ride away. Spartan rooms feature little more than a bed, writing table, and a couple of chairs. The restaurant (*see* Dining, *above*) serves bountiful Bajan buffets, and the congenial atmosphere is welcome indeed. *Bathsheba, St. Joseph Parish, tel. 809/433–9445. 8 rooms. Facilities: restaurant. AE. EP. ¢*

Rental Homes and Apartments

These are a popular option on Barbados. Apartments range from studios to two-bedroom units. **Husband Heights Apartments** (Hotel Management Services, Hastings, Christ Church Parish, tel. 809/

429–9039) manages units with rates of $20–$100 per person per day in Christ Church Parish.

Villas and private homes are available for rent south of Bridgetown in the Hastings–Worthing area, along the St. James Parish coast, and in St. Peter Parish. Rentals are available through Barbados realtors, including **Alleyne, Aguilar & Altman** (Rosebank, St. James Parish, tel. 809/432–0840), **Bajan Services** (St. Peter Parish, tel. 809/422–2618), and **Ronald Stoute & Sons Ltd.** (St. Philip Parish, tel. 809/423–6800). In the United States, contact **At Home Abroad** (tel. 212/421–9165) or **Villa Vacations** (tel. 617/593–8885 or 800/800–5576). The **Barbados Tourism Authority** has a listing of rental properties and prices.

Off-Season Bets During the off-season (mid-April–mid-December), hotel prices tumble as much as 50%. Barbados receives less rain than some other southern Caribbean islands, making it a good choice for an autumn vacation. (Be aware, however, that some properties discount less dramatically during the shoulder season, from November to mid-December.) Although some properties, such as Glitter Bay and Sandy Lane, still charge more than $300–$500 a night in the off-season, other glamorous resorts do become affordable. **Treasure Beach** (Payne's Bay, St. James Parish, tel. 809/432–1346, fax 809/432–1094) has 24 one-bedroom suites, a delightful beach, a good restaurant, and a cozy, intimate atmosphere. The seven-acre **Colony Club** (Box 429, Bridgetown, Hwy. 1, St. James Parish, tel. 809/422–2335, fax 809/422–1726), a cottage colony on the beach, has rooms with private patios and a dining room and cocktail terrace that curve along the beach. One of our most highly recommended hotels is the **Crane Beach Hotel** (Crane Bay, St. Philip Parish, tel. 809/423–6220, fax 809/423–5343), on a remote hilltop overlooking the dramatic Atlantic coast. A Roman-style pool with columns separates the main house from the dining room. The beach, a beautiful stretch of sand thumped by waves, is reached by descending about 200 steps.

The Arts and Nightlife

The Arts **Barbados Art Council.** The gallery shows drawings, paintings, and other art, with a new show about every two weeks. *2 Pelican Village, Bridgetown, tel. 809/426–4385. Admission free. Open weekdays 10–5, Sat. 9–1.*

Nightlife When the sun goes down, the musicians come out, and folks go limin' in Barbados (anything from hanging out to a chat-up or jump-up). Competitions among reggae groups, steel bands, and calypso singers are major events, and tickets can be hard to come by—but give it a try.

Island residents have their own favorite nightspots. The most popular one is still **After Dark** (St. Lawrence Gap, Christ Church Parish, tel. 809/435–6547), with the longest bar on the island, a jazz-club annex, and an outdoor area where headliners appear.

Harbour Lights claims to be the "home of the party animal," and most any night features live music with dancing under the stars. *On the Bay, Marine Villa, Bay St., St. Michael Parish, tel. 809/436–7225.*

Another "in" spot, **Front Line** (Wharf St., tel. 809/429–6160) at the Wharf in Bridgetown, attracts a young crowd for its reggae music.

Disco moves are made on the floor at the **Hippo Disco** in the Barbados Beach Village Hotel (St. James Parish, tel. 809/425–1440), and above it, where dancers gyrate until the early hours of the morning.

A late-night (after 11) excursion to **Baxter Road** is de rigueur for midnight Bajan street snacks, local rum, great gossip, and good lie-telling. **Enid & Livy's** and **Collins** are just two of the many long-standing favorites. The later, the better.

Bars and Inns Barbados supports the rum industry in more than 1,600 "rum shops," simple bars where people (mostly men) congregate to discuss the world's ills, and in more sophisticated inns where you'll find world-class rum drinks and the island's renowned Mount Gay and Cockspur rums. The following offer welcoming spirits: **The Ship Inn** (St. Lawrence Gap, Christ Church Parish, tel. 809/435–6961), **The Coach House** (Paynes Bay, St. James Parish, tel. 809/432–1163), and **Harry's Oasis** (St. Lawrence Gap, Christ Church Parish, no phone). **Bert's Bar** at the Abbeville Hotel (Rockley, Christ Church Parish, tel. 809/435–7924) serves the best daiquiris in town—any town. Also try **The Boat Yard** (Bay Street, Bridgetown, tel. 809/436–2622), **The Waterfront Cafe** (Bridgetown, tel. 809/427–0093), **The Warehouse** (Bridgetown, tel. 809/436–2897), and **Boomers Restaurant & Lounge** (St. Lawrence Gap, Christ Church Parish, tel. 809/428–8439).

6 Bonaire

Updated by Barbara Hults

Bonaire's lure is, to an extent, more underwater than above. A mecca for divers, the island enjoys one of the most unspoiled reef systems in the world. The water is so clear that you can lean over a dock and look the fish straight in the eye. The island itself is a stark desert, perfect for the rugged individualist who is turned off by the overcommercialized high life of the other Antillean islands. It doesn't hold much for connoisseurs of fine cuisine, shopping maniacs, or beachcombers. What it does have is a spectacular array of exotic wildlife—from fish to fowl to flowers—that will keep nature-watchers awestruck for days. Bonaire is the kind of place where you'll want to rent a Jeep and go dashing off in search of the wild flamingo, the wild iguana, or even the wild yellow-winged parrot called the Bonairian lora.

Kudos for the preservation of the 112-square-mile isle go to the people and government of Bonaire. They've also made a tremendous effort to maintain the beauty of the island's waters. In 1970, with the help of the World Wildlife Fund, they developed the Bonaire Marine Park—a model of ecological conservation. The underwater park includes, roughly, the entire coastline, from the high-water tidemark to a depth of 200 feet, all of which is protected by strict laws. Because the Bonairians are determined to keep their paradise intact, any diver with a reckless streak is firmly requested to go elsewhere.

While several upscale and expensive hotels have been built here, Bonaire remains rich in reasonably priced inns, guest houses, small hotels, and inexpensive apartments. Fast food has not arrived on this sleepy island, but you can control food costs here by choosing lodgings with a kitchen and cooking your meals. Scuba diving is an expensive sport, but with so many excellent dive sites just offshore, you can stick to beach diving and forego the more expensive boat dives. All of the island's dive operators offer boat-dive packages, which offer substantial savings over the price of individual boat dives. At night, find out which hotel has a band playing and drop in to listen for free. On Bonaire, you're always welcome. With only 11,665 inhabitants, the island has a feeling of a small community with a gentle pace.

What It Will Cost These sample prices are meant only as a general guide, and are estimates for high season. A decent room on Bonaire can cost as little as $50 a night. Apartments with kitchens run a bit more, but can be found for $60–$90 a night. Two couples traveling together can rent a two-bedroom, two-bath villa with a fully equipped kitchen for about $150 a night. Because most of the food on Bonaire is imported, prices tend to be high; try to stick to local places and order dishes such as the fish of the day with rice, fried plantains, and vegetables, which can run as low as $5. Expect to pay about $2.50 for a rum punch, $3 for a cocktail, and $2 for a beer. Car rental begins at about $31 a day and includes unlimited mileage. A taxi from the airport to your hotel costs $8–$12 for up to four passengers; fare from most hotels into town is about $6–$8. Snorkel-gear rental costs from $5 to $11 a day. Six full days of unlimited shore diving, which includes tanks, air, and weight belts, ranges from $80–$110. Individual boat dives cost from $15 to $40, depending on the dive operator. A week of unlimited shore dives plus six boat dives costs about $170. Your best bet is to check around and choose a package and price that fit your needs.

Before You Go

Tourist Information Contact the **Bonaire Government Tourist Office** (10 Rockefeller Plaza, Suite 900, New York, NY 10022, tel. 212/956–5911 or 800/826–6247, fax 212/838–3407; in Canada: 512 Duplex Ave., Toronto, Ontario M4R 2E3, tel. 416/484–4864) for advice and information on planning your trip.

Arriving and Departing
By Plane **ALM** (tel. 800/327–7230) and **Air Aruba** (tel. 800/882–7822) will get you to Bonaire. ALM has eight direct flights (through Curaçao) a week, two nonstop flights a week from Miami, and five flights a week from Atlanta through Curaçao, with connecting service (through-fares) to most U.S. gateways tied in with Delta and other airlines, making ALM Bonaire's major airline. ALM also flies to Caracas, Aruba, Curaçao, and St. Maarten, as well as other Caribbean islands, using Curaçao as its Caribbean hub. Air Aruba flies six days a week from Newark and daily from Miami to Aruba with connecting service to Bonaire. American Airlines (tel. 800/433–7300) offers daily flights from New York to Aruba, but you must connect to Bonaire through ALM or Air Aruba. ALM also offers a Visit Caribbean Pass, which allows easy interisland travel.

From the Airport Bonaire's Flamingo Airport is tiny, but you'll appreciate its welcoming ambience. The customs check is perfunctory if you are arriving from another Dutch isle; otherwise you will have to show proof of citizenship, plus a return or ongoing ticket. There is no public transportation to the hotels, but rental cars and taxis are available; cab fare costs $8–$12 for up to four people to most hotels. Try to arrange the pickup through your hotel. Most air, land, and dive packages booked from the United States include airport transfers.

Passports and Visas U.S. and Canadian citizens need offer only proof of identity, so a passport, notarized birth certificate, or voter registration card will suffice. British subjects may carry a British visitor's passport, available from any post office. All other visitors must carry an official passport. In addition, any visitor who steps onto the island must have a return or ongoing ticket and is advised to confirm that reservation 48 hours before departure.

Language The official language is Dutch, but few speak it, and even then only on official occasions. The street language is Papiamento, a mixture of Spanish, Portuguese, Dutch, English, African, and French—full of colorful Bonairian idioms that even Curaçaoans sometimes don't get. You'll light up your waiter's eyes, though, if you can remember to say masha danki (thank you). English is spoken by most people working at the hotels, restaurants, and tourist shops.

Precautions Divers who plan to rent a car and go shore diving on their own should buy the excellent "Guide to the Bonaire Marine Park," available at dive shops around the island, which specifies the level of diving skill required for 44 sites. No matter how beautiful a beach may look, heed all warning signs regarding the rough undertow. Listen carefully to the Marine Park orientation and always dive with a buddy. Take plenty of mosquito repellent and use it liberally, especially at night, or if hiking in the National Park. Also take plenty of sunscreen and reapply it often. Other musts are a hat, sunglasses, and an extra T-shirt to cover your back while snorkeling. While crime is almost unheard of on Bonaire, thefts do occur, and valuables do disappear from unlocked cars. Lock your car and leave your money, credit cards, jewelry, and passport in your hotel safe. If you're taking a camera, be sure to carry it, or lock it in your car's trunk.

Staying in Bonaire

Important Addresses **Tourist Information:** The **Tourism Corporation of Bonaire** (Kaya Libertador Simon Bolivar 12, tel. 599/7–8322 or 599/7–8649, fax 599/7–8408).

Emergencies **Police:** For assistance call 7–8000. In an emergency, dial 11. **Ambulance:** tel. 14. **Hospitals: St. Franciscus Hospital,** Kralendijk (tel. 599/7–8900).

Currency The great thing about Bonaire is that you don't need to convert your American dollars into the local currency, the Netherlands Antilles florin (NAf; also called guilder). U.S. currency and traveler's checks are accepted everywhere, and the difference in exchange rates is negligible. Banks accept U.S. dollar banknotes at the official rate of NAf 1.78 to the U.S. dollar, traveler's checks at NAf 1.80. The rate of exchange at shops and hotels ranges from NAf 1.75 to NAf 1.80. The guilder is divided into 100 cents. Note: Prices quoted here are in U.S. dollars unless indicated otherwise.

Taxes and Service Charges Hotels charge a room tax of $4.10 per person, per night, and many add a 10%–15% maid service charge to your bill. Most restaurants add a 10% service charge to your bill. There's no sales tax on purchases in Bonaire. Departure tax when going to Curaçao is $5.75. For all other destinations it's $10.

Getting Around There's no public transportation on Bonaire, but hitchhiking is considered a respectable way to get around. You can ask someone for a lift or stick out your thumb at a passing vehicle. You can also zip about the island in a car or a Suzuki Jeep. Scooters and bicycles, which are also available, are less practical but can be fun, too. Just remember that there are many miles of unpaved road; the roller-coaster hills at the national park require strong stomachs; and during the rainy season, mud—called Bonairian snow—is unpleasant. All traffic stays to the right.

Rental Cars **Budget** rents cars, Suzuki minivans, and Jeeps at its six locations, but reservations can be made only at the head office (tel. 599/7–8300, ext. 225). Pickups are at the airport (tel. 599/7–8315) and at several hotels. It's always a good idea to make reservations (fax 599/7–8865 or 599/7–8118; in the U.S., tel. 800/472–3325). Prices range from $31 a day for a Volkswagen to $60 a day for an automatic, air-conditioned four-door sedan. Other agencies are **Avis** (tel. 599/7–5795, fax 599/7–5791), **Dollar Rent-A-Car** (tel. 599/7–5588, at the airport; tel. 599/7–8888; fax 599/7–7788), **Sunray** (tel. 599/7–5230, fax 599/7–4888), and **AB Car Rental** (tel. 599/7–8980 or 599/7–5410, fax

599/7–5034). There is also a government tax of $2 per day per car rental.

Scooters Two-seater scooters are available from **Bonaire Bicycle & Motorbike Rental** (tel. 599/7–8226) and **S.F. Wave Touch** (tel. 599/7–4246) for about $26 a day and $165 a week.

Bicycles Bicycling is a safe way to get around Kralendijk. Bring a water bottle to safeguard against dehydration, and wear plenty of sunscreen. For exploring the National Park, however, a car or Jeep is recommended. **Bonaire Bicycle & Motorbike Rental** (tel. 599/7–8226) rents bicycles for $15 a day. **Captain Don's Habitat** (tel. 599/7–8290 or 599/7–8913) rents mountain bicycles for $6 per day plus a $250 deposit. **Harbour Village Beach Resort** (tel. 599/7–7500) occasionally rents bikes to nonguests for $11 a day.

Taxis Taxis are unmetered; they have fixed rates controlled by the government. A trip from the airport to your hotel will cost $6 to $10 for up to four passengers. A taxi from most hotels into town costs between $4 and $6. Fares increase from 7 PM to midnight by 25% and from midnight to 6 AM by 50%. Call **Taxi Central Dispatch** (tel. 599/7–8100 or dial 10), or inquire at your hotel.

Telephones and Mail It's difficult for visitors to Bonaire to get involved in dramatic, heart-wrenching phone conversations or in *any* phone discussions requiring a degree of privacy: Only about one-third of the major hotels have phones in their rooms, so calls must be made from hotel front desks or from the central telephone company office in Kralendijk. Telephone connections have improved, but static is still common. To call Bonaire from the United States, dial 011–599–7 + the local four-digit number. When making inter-island calls, dial the local four-digit number. Local phone calls cost NAf 25¢.

Airmail postage rates to North America are NAf 1.75 for letters and NAf 90¢ for postcards; to Britain, NAf 2.50 for letters and NAf 1.25 for postcards.

Opening and Closing Times Stores in the Kralendijk area are generally open Monday through Saturday 8–noon and 2–6. On Sundays and holidays and any other days that cruise ships happen to arrive, most shops open for a few extra hours. Most restaurants are open for lunch and dinner, but few not affiliated with hotels are open for breakfast.

Guided Tours **Bonaire Sightseeing Tours** (tel. 599/7–8778, fax 599/7–8118) will chauffeur you around the island on various tours, among them a two-hour Northern Island Tour ($13) that visits the 1,000 steps; Goto Lake; and Rincon, the oldest settlement on the island; and a two-hour Southern Island Tour ($13) that covers Akzo Salt Antilles N.V., a modern salt-manufacturing facility where flamingos gather; Lac Bay; and the oldest lighthouse on the island. A half-day tour ($19) visits sites in both the north and south. For $30, you can take a half-day tour of Bonaire's Washington/Slagbaai National Park (entrance fee included), 13,500 acres of majestic scenery, wildlife, unspoiled beaches, and tropical flora. A full-day tour of the park costs $50. Day trips to Curaçao are offered for $125 per person and include round-trip airfare and transfers, an island tour of Curaçao, and lunch. Ayubi's Tours (tel. 599/7–5338) also offers several half- and full-day island tours. Taxi drivers are usually knowledgeable enough about the island to conduct half-day tours; they charge about $60 for a northern-route tour and $40 for a southern-route tour.

Exploring Bonaire

Numbers in the margin correspond to points of interest on the Bonaire map.

Kralendijk Bonaire's capital city of **Kralendijk** (population: 2,500) is five min-
1 utes from the airport and a short walk from Bruce Bowker's Carib

Inn and the Club Flamingo. There's really not much to explore here, but there are a few sights worth noting in this small, very tidy city.

Kralendijk has one main drag, J.A. Abraham Boulevard, which turns into **Kaya Grandi** in the center of town. Along it are most of the island's major stores, boutiques, restaurants, duty-free shops, and jewelry stores (*see* Shopping and Dining, *below*).

Walk down the narrow waterfront avenue called Kaya C.E.B. Hellmund, which leads straight to the **North** and **South piers.** In the center of town, stop in at the new Harborside Mall, which has 13 chic boutiques. Along this route you will see **Fort Oranje,** with cannons pointing to the sea.

The elegant white structure that looks like a tiny Greek temple is the **Fish Market,** where local fishermen sell their early-morning haul, along with vegetables and fruits.

Elsewhere on the Island

Two tours, north and south, are possible of the 24-mile-long island; both will take from a few hours to a full day, depending upon whether you stop to snorkel, swim, dive, or lounge. If you like to explore at your own pace, you'll need to rent a car. While it's possible to see the whole island in one whirlwind day, it's more enjoyable to pack a swimsuit and snorkel gear and take your time over two or more days. In dry weather, a scooter is fine for exploring the southern end of Bonaire. If you prefer to leave the driving to others and like to hear anecdotal information about what you're seeing, a guided tour will be more to your liking (*see* Guided Tours, *above*).

South Bonaire

The trail south from Kralendijk is chock-full of icons—both natural and man-made—that tell the minisaga of Bonaire. Heading south along the Southern Scenic Route, the first icon you'll come to is the unexpected symbol of modernism—the towering 500-foot antenna
2 of **Trans-World Radio,** one of the most powerful stations in Christian broadcasting. From here, evangelical programs and gospel music are transmitted daily in five languages to all of North, South, and Central America, as well as to the entire Caribbean.

3 Keep on cruising past the salt pans until you come to the **salt flats,** voluptuous white drifts that look something like huge mounds of vanilla ice cream. Harvested twice a year, the "ponds" are owned by the Akzo Salt Antilles N.V. company, which has reactivated the 19th-century salt industry with great success. Keep a lookout for the three 30-foot obelisks—white, blue, and red—that were used to guide the trade boats coming to pick up the salt.

Along the sea just a bit farther south is **Pink Beach,** a half-mile-long stretch of incredibly soft sand that derives its name from the delicate pink hue of the sand at the shoreline (*see* Beaches, *below*). Flamingoes may be seen here, for it's near the 135-acre flamingo sanctuary—an exclusive breeding ground for some 10,000 birds. Nesting flamingoes are easily frightened, so the sanctuary is off limits to tourists. The birds can be seen best near the slave huts at Rode Pan (*see below*).

Next, you might want to head east to the **Maracultura Foundation** (tel. 599/7–8595), where you can visit an aquaculture research center that is experimenting with methods of farming fish, shrimp, and conch. Another option is to go south, where the gritty history of the salt industry is revealed in **Rode Pan,** the site of two groups of tiny slave huts. During the 19th century, the salt workers, imported slaves from Africa, worked the fields by day, then crawled into these huts at night to sleep. Each Friday afternoon, they walked seven hours to Rincon to spend the weekend with their families, returning each Sunday to the salt pans. In recent years, the government has restored the huts to their original simplicity. Only very small people will be able to go inside, but take a walk around and put your head in for a look.

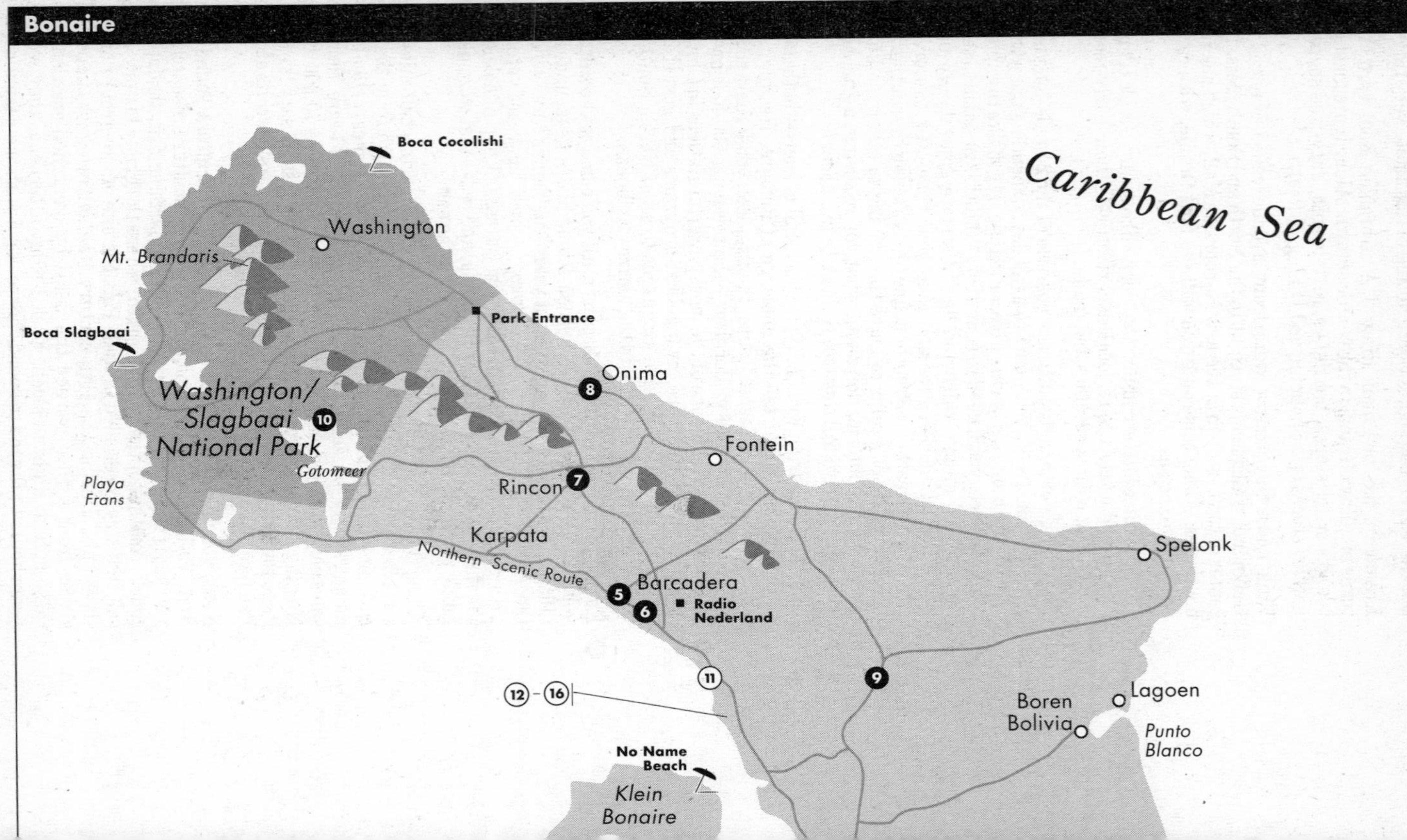
Bonaire
Caribbean Sea
Boca Cocolishi
Washington
Mt. Brandaris
Park Entrance
Boca Slagbaai
Onima
8
Washington/
Slagbaai
National Park
10
Fontein
Gotomeer
Playa
Frans
Rincon
7
Karpata
Northern Scenic Route
Spelonk
Barcadera
5
6
Radio
Nederland
11
9
12 - 16
Lagoen
Boren
Bolivia
Punto
Blanco
No Name
Beach
Klein
Bonaire

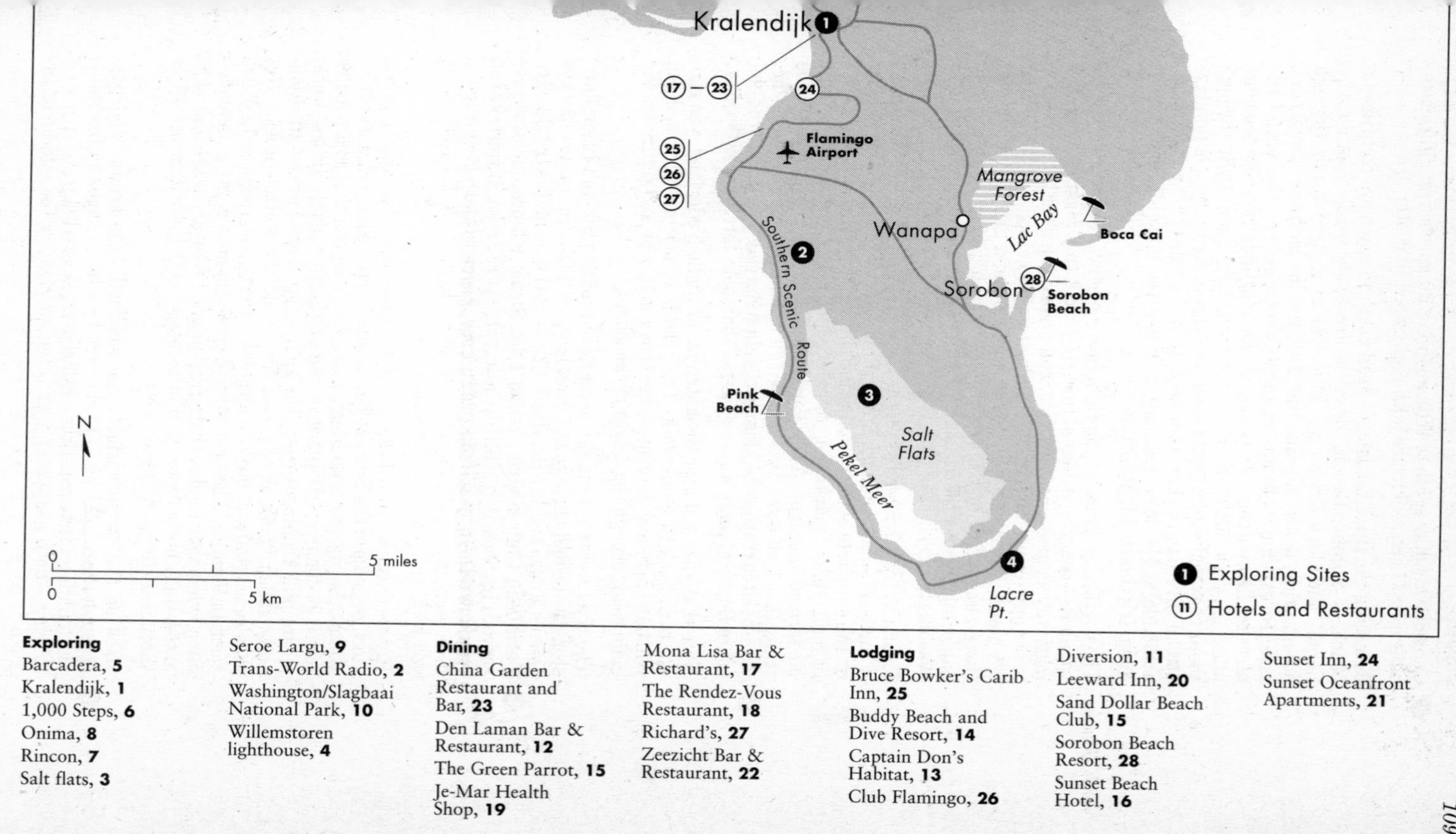
Kralendijk
17 — 23
24
Flamingo Airport
25
26
27
Mangrove Forest
Wanapa
Lac Bay
Boca Cai
Southern Scenic Route
Sorobon
28
Sorobon Beach
Pink Beach
Salt Flats
Pekel Meer
Lacre Pt.
N
0
5 miles
0
5 km
Exploring Sites
Hotels and Restaurants
Exploring
Barcadera, 5
Kralendijk, 1
1,000 Steps, 6
Onima, 8
Rincon, 7
Salt flats, 3
Seroe Largu, 9
Trans-World Radio, 2
Washington/Slagbaai National Park, 10
Willemstoren lighthouse, 4
Dining
China Garden Restaurant and Bar, 23
Den Laman Bar & Restaurant, 12
The Green Parrot, 15
Je-Mar Health Shop, 19
Mona Lisa Bar & Restaurant, 17
The Rendez-Vous Restaurant, 18
Richard's, 27
Zeezicht Bar & Restaurant, 22
Lodging
Bruce Bowker's Carib Inn, 25
Buddy Beach and Dive Resort, 14
Captain Don's Habitat, 13
Club Flamingo, 26
Diversion, 11
Leeward Inn, 20
Sand Dollar Beach Club, 15
Sorobon Beach Resort, 28
Sunset Beach Hotel, 16
Sunset Inn, 24
Sunset Oceanfront Apartments, 21

4 Continue heading south to **Willemstoren,** Bonaire's first lighthouse, built in 1837 and still in use (although closed to visitors).

Rounding the tip of the island, head north to two more picturesque beaches—**Sorobon Beach,** where the dress code reads "Clothing Optional" and **Boca Cai** at Lac Bay. The road here winds through otherworldly desert terrain, full of organ-pipe cacti and spiny-trunk mangroves—huge stumps of saltwater trees that rise out of the marshes like witches. At Boca Cai, you'll be impressed by the huge piles of conch shells discarded by local fishermen. (Sift through them; they make great gifts—but pack them carefully.) On Sundays at Cai, live bands play from noon to 4, and there's beer and food available at the local restaurant. When the mosquitoes arrive at dusk, it's time to hightail it home.

North Bonaire

The northern tour takes you right into the heart of Bonaire's natural wonders—desert gardens of towering cacti, tiny coastal coves, dramatically shaped coral grottoes, and plenty of fantastic panoramas. A snappy excursion with the requisite photo stops will take about 2½ hours, but if you pack your swimsuit and a hefty picnic basket (forget about finding a Burger King), you could spend the entire day exploring this northern sector, including a few hours snorkeling in Washington Park.

Head out from Kralendijk on the Kaya Gobrenador N. Debrot until it turns into the Northern Scenic Route, a one-lane, one-way street on the outskirts of town. Following the route northward, look closely for a yellow marker on your left just past the towering Radio Nederland antennas. A few yards ahead, you'll discover some stone steps that lead down into a cave full of stalactites and vegetation.
5 Once used to trap goats, this cave, called **Barcadera,** is one of the oldest in Bonaire; there's even a tunnel that looks intriguingly spooky.

Note that once you pass the antennas of Radio Nederland, you cannot turn back to Kralendijk. The road becomes one-way, and you will have to follow the cross-island road to Rincon and return via the main road through the center of the island.

The road weaves through spectacular eroded pink-and-black limestone walls and eerie rock formations with fanciful names like the Devil's Mouth and Iguana Head. Opposite the turnoff to the Bonaire
6 Caribbean Club is a site called **1,000 Steps,** a limestone staircase carved right out of the cliff on the left side of the road. If you take the trek down them, you'll discover a great place to snorkel and scuba dive. Actually, you'll only climb 67 steps, but it feels like 1,000 when you walk up them carrying scuba gear.

If you continue toward the northern curve of the island, the green storage tanks of the Bonaire Petroleum Corporation become visible. Follow the sign to **Goto Meer,** a saltwater lagoon that is a popular flamingo hangout. Bonaire is one of the few places in the world where pink flamingos nest. The spiny-legged creatures—affectionately called "pink clouds"—at first look like swizzle sticks. But they're magnificent birds to observe—and there are about 15,000 of them in Bonaire. The best time to catch them at home is January–June, when they tend to their gray-plumed young. For the best view of these shy birds, take the dirt access road to the left, which slices through a virtual jungle of cacti.

Back on the paved surface, the road will loop around and pass
7 through **Rincon,** a well-kept cluster of pastel cottages and century-old buildings that constitute Bonaire's oldest village. Watch your driving—both goats and dogs often sit right in the middle of the main drag.

Rincon was the original Spanish settlement on the island: It became home to the slaves brought from Africa to work on the plantations and salt fields. Superstition and voodoo lore still have a powerful impact here, more so than in Kralendijk, where they work hard at suppressing the old ways. Rincon has a couple of local eateries, but the real temptation is **Prisca's Ice Cream** (tel. 599/7–6334), to be found at her house on Kaya Komkomber.

Pass through Rincon on the road that heads back to Kralendijk, but
8 take the left-hand turn before Fontein to **Onima.** Small signposts direct the way to the **Indian inscriptions** found on a 3-foot limestone ledge that juts out like a partially formed cave entrance. Look up to see the red-stained designs and symbols inscribed on the limestone, said to have been the handiwork of the Arawak Indians when they inhabited the island centuries ago.

Backtrack to the main road and continue on to Fontein and then to
9 **Seroe Largu,** the highest point on the southern part of the island. During the day, a winding path leads to a magnificent view of Kralendijk's rooftops and the island of Klein Bonaire; at night, the twinkling city lights below make this a romantic stop.

Washington/Slagbaai National Park

Once a plantation producing divi-divi trees (whose pods were used for tanning animal skins), aloe (used for medicinal lotions), charcoal, and goats, **Washington/Slagbaai National Park** is now a model of
10 conservation, designed to maintain fauna, flora, and geological treasures in their natural state. Visitors may easily tour the 13,500-acre tropical desert terrain along the dirt roads. As befits a wilderness sanctuary, the well-marked, rugged roads force you to drive slowly enough to appreciate the animal life and the terrain. A four-wheel-drive vehicle is a must. (Think twice about coming here if it rained the day before—the mud you may encounter will be more than inconvenient.) If you are planning to hike, bring a picnic lunch, camera, sunscreen, and plenty of water. There are two different routes: The long one, 22 miles (about 2½ hours), is marked by yellow arrows; the short one, 15 miles (about 1½ hours), is marked by green arrows. Goats and donkeys may dart across the road, and if you keep your eyes peeled, you may catch sight of large, camouflaged iguanas in the shrubbery.

Bird-watchers are really in their element here. Right inside the park's gate, flamingos roost on the salt pad known as **Salina Mathijs,** and exotic parakeets dot the foot of **Mt. Brandaris,** Bonaire's highest peak at 784 feet. Some 130 species of colorful birds fly in and out of the shrubbery in the park. Keep your eyes open and your binoculars at hand. (For choice beach sites in the park, *see* Beaches, *below.*) Swimming, snorkeling, and scuba diving are permitted, but visitors are requested not to frighten the animals or remove anything from the grounds. There is absolutely no hunting, fishing, or camping allowed. A useful guidebook to the park is available at the entrance for about $6. *Admission: $5 adults, $1 children under 15. The park is open daily 8–5, but you must enter before 3:30.*

Beaches

Beaches in Bonaire are not the island's strong point. Don't come expecting Aruba-length stretches of glorious white sand. Bonaire's beaches are smaller, and though the water is indeed blue (several shades of it, in fact), the sand is not always white. You can have your pick of beach in Bonaire according to color: pink, black, or white.

All Bonaire's beaches are open to the public, and good places to swim can be found all along the island's west coast. If you're staying in the vicinity of Kralendijk, you can walk or hitch a ride to beaches at the **Harbour Village Beach Resort** or the **Sunset Beach Hotel.** Another option is to take a water taxi (available from several hotels and dive shops for $12 round-trip) over to **No Name Beach** on Klein Bonaire. Here, with a picnic basket and snorkeling gear, you can play king of the dune in style. Except for a few forgotten sneakers, there is absolutely nothing on Klein Bonaire, so remember to take whatever you'll need along. And don't miss the boat back home.

Hermit crabs can be found along the shore at **Boca Cocolishi,** a black-sand beach in Washington/Slagbaai Park on the northeast coast. The dark hues of tiny bits of dried coral and shells that form the basin and beach give the sand an unusual look. Located on the windward side of the island, the water is too rough for anything more than wading; however, the spot is perfect for an intimate picnic *à deux*. To get there, take the Northern Scenic Route to the park, then ask for directions at the gate.

Also inside Washington Park is **Boca Slagbaai,** a beach of coral fossils and rocks, with interesting coral gardens just offshore that make for fine snorkeling. Bring scuba boots or canvas sandals to walk into the water because the "beach" is rough on bare feet. The gentle surf makes it an ideal place for picnicking or swimming, especially for children.

You'll need a car or strong legs to bicycle south to **Pink Beach,** where the sand has a pinkish tint that takes on a magical shimmer in the late-afternoon sun. The water is suitable for swimming, snorkeling, and scuba diving. Take the Southern Scenic Route on the western side of the island, past the Trans-World Radio station, close to the slave huts. A favorite hangout for Bonairians on the weekend, it is virtually deserted during the week.

For uninhibited sun worshipers who'd rather enjoy the rays in the altogether, the private "clothes-optional" **Sorobon Beach Resort** offers calm water, soft clean sand, and refreshing tropical breezes. Nonguests are welcome, but must purchase a $15 day resort pass at the entrance gate.

Boca Cai is across Lac Bay, which is an ideal spot for windsurfing.

Sports and the Outdoors

Scuba Diving Bonaire has some of the best reef diving this side of Australia's Great Barrier Reef. The island is unique primarily for its incredible dive sites; it takes only 5–25 minutes to reach your site, the current is usually mild, and although some reefs have very sudden, steep drops, most begin just offshore and slope gently downward at a 45° angle. General visibility runs 60 to 100 feet, except during surges in October and November. An enormous range of coral can be seen, from knobby brain and giant brain coral to elkhorn, staghorn, mountainous star, gorgonian, and black coral. You're also likely to encounter schools of parrotfish, surgeonfish, angelfish, eels, snappers, and groupers. Beach diving is excellent just about everywhere on the leeward side of the island.

The well-policed Bonaire Marine Park, which encompasses the entire coastline around Bonaire and Klein Bonaire, remains an underwater wonder because visitors take the rules here seriously. Do not even think about (1) spearfishing, (2) dropping anchor, or (3) touching, stepping on, or collecting coral. Divers must pay an admission charge of $10, for which they receive a colored plastic tag (to be attached to an item of scuba gear) entitling them to one calendar year of unlimited diving in the Marine Park. The fees are used to maintain the underwater park. Tags are available at all scuba facilities and from the Marine Park headquarters in the Old Fort in Kralendijk (tel. 599/7–8444). To help preserve the reef, all dive operations on Bonaire now offer free buoyancy-control, advanced-buoyancy control, and photographic buoyancy-control classes. Check with any dive shop for the schedule.

There is a **hyperbaric decompression chamber** next to the hospital in Kralendijk (tel. 599/7–8187 or 599/7–8900 for emergencies).

Dive Operations Bonaire hotels frequently offer dive packages, which include accommodations, boat trips, shore diving, air, and use of tanks. Ask the Bonaire tourist office for a brochure describing the various packages. Organized tours are not necessary on Bonaire, as many dive sites are easily accessible from shore and clearly marked by yellow stones on the roadside. Most of the hotels listed in this guide have dive centers. The competition for quality and variety is fierce. Before making a room reservation, inquire about specific dive/room packages that are available. The prices for unlimited shore diving (you pay for tanks and weights), boat dives, and rental equipment vary with each dive facility, so it pays to comparison shop. For instance, snorkel-equipment rental costs $5 a day at Bruce Bowker's Carib Inn Dive Shop, but $11 a day at Great Adventure's Bonaire (at the Harbour Village Beach Resort). Scuba-gear rental ranges from $20 to $40 a day, again depending on the dive shop. **Peter Hughes Dive Bonaire** (Club Flamingo, tel. 599/7–8285 or 800/367–3484), **Sand Dollar Dive and Photo** (Sand Dollar Beach Club, Kaya Gobrenador Debrot 79, tel. 599/7–8738), and **Habitat Dive Center** (Captain Don's Habitat, Kaya Gobrenador Debrot 103, tel. 599/7–8290 or 800/327–6709; fax 599/7–8240) are all PADI five-star dive facilities qualified to offer both PADI and NAUI certification courses. Sand Dollar Dive and Photo is also qualified to certify dive instructors. Other centers include **Bonaire Scuba Center** (Black Durgon Inn; in the U.S., write to Box 775, Morgan, NJ 08879, or call 908/566–8866 or 800/526–2370), **Buddy Dive Resort** (Kaya Gobrenador N. Debrot 85, tel. 599/7–5080), **Dive Inn** (close to South Pier, Kaya C.E.B. Hellmund, tel. 599/7–8761), **Neal Watson's Bonaire Undersea Adventures** (Coral Regency Resort, Kaya Gobrenador Debrot 90, tel. 599/7–5580 or 800/327–8150), **Great Adventures Bonaire** (Harbour Village Beach Resort, tel. 599/7–7500 or 800/424–0004), and **Bruce Bowker's Carib Inn Dive Center** (Bruce Bowker's Carib Inn, tel. 599/7–8819, fax 599/7–5295).

Americans Jerry Schnabel and Suzi Swygert of **Photo Tours N.V.** (Kaya Grandi 68, tel. 599/7–8060) specialize in teaching and guiding novice-through-professional underwater photographers. They also offer land-excursion tours of Bonaire's birds, wildlife, and vegetation. **Dee Scarr's Touch the Sea** (Box 369, tel. 599/7–8529) is a personalized (two people at a time) diving program that provides interaction with marine life; it is available to certified divers.

Dive Sites The "Guide to the Bonaire Marine Park" lists 44 sites that have been identified and marked by moorings. In the past few years, however, an additional 42 designated mooring and shore diving sites have been added through a conservation program called Sea Tether. Guides associated with the various dive centers can give you more complete directions. The following are a few popular sites to whet your appetite; these and selected other sites are pinpointed on our Bonaire Diving map.

Take the track down to the shore just behind Trans-World Radio station; dive in and swim south to **Angel City,** one of the shallowest and most popular sites in a two-reef complex that includes **Alice in Wonderland.** The boulder-size green and tan coral heads are home to black margates, Spanish hogfish, gray snappers, and the large, purple tube sponges.

Calabas Reef, located off the Club Flamingo, is the island's most popular dive site. All divers using the hotel's facilities take their warm-up dive here where they can inspect the wreck sunk by Don Stewart for just this purpose. The site is replete with Christmas-tree sponges and fire coral adhering to the ship's hull. Fish life is frenzied, with the occasional octopus putting in an appearance.

You'll need to catch a boat to reach **Forest,** a dive site off the coast of Klein Bonaire, so named for the abundant black-coral forest found

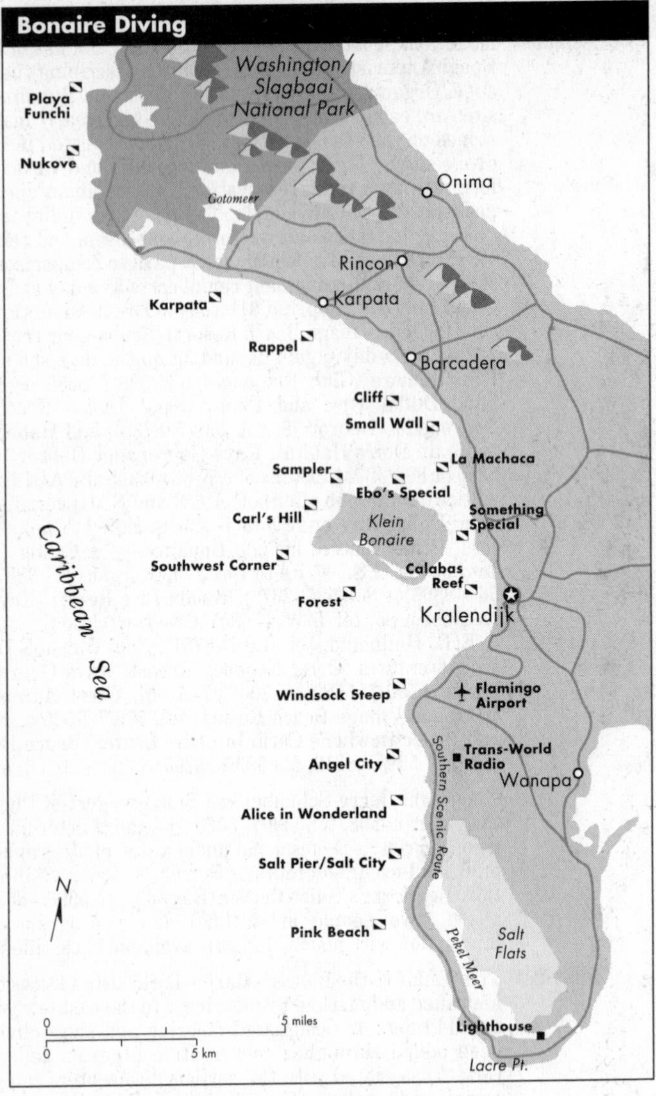

there. Responsible for occasional currents, this site gets a lot of fish action, including what's been described as a "friendly" spotted eel that lives in a cave.

Small Wall is one of Bonaire's only complete vertical wall dives. Located off the Black Durgon Inn, it is one of the island's most popular night diving spots. Access is made by boat (Black Durgon guests can access it from shore). The 60-foot wall is frequented by sea horses, squid, turtles, tarpon, and barracudas and has dense hard and soft coral formations; it also allows for excellent snorkeling.

Rappel, near the Karpata Ecological Center, is one of the most spectacular dives. The shore is a sheer cliff, and the lush coral growth is home to an unusual variety of marine life, including orange sea horses, squid, spiny lobsters, and a spotted trunkfish named Sir Timothy that will befriend you for a banana or a piece of cheese.

Something Special, just south of the entrance of the marina, is famous for its garden eels, which slither around the relatively shallow sand terrace.

Windsock Steep, situated in front of the small beach opposite the airport runway, is an excellent first-dive spot and a popular place for snorkeling close to town.

Snorkeling Don't consider snorkeling the cowardly diver's sport; in Bonaire the experience is anything but elementary. For only $8–$11 per day, you can rent a mask, fins, and snorkel at any hotel with a watersports center (see Lodging, below). The better spots for snorkeling are on the leeward side of the island, where you have access to the reefs.

Tennis Tennis is available free to guests at the **Sunset Beach Hotel, Club Flamingo,** and the **Sand Dollar Beach Club.** Nonguests can play for free during the day at the **Club Flamingo** and even take the free tennis clinics on Tuesday and Wednesday mornings (8:30–10). At night, there's an hourly charge.

Waterskiing Call **Goodlife Watersport** at 599/7–4588) to arrange a lesson.

Windsurfing Lac Bay, a protected cove on the east coast, is ideal for windsurfing. Novices will find it especially comforting, since there's no way to be blown out to sea. **Windsurfing Bonaire,** known locally as "Jibe City," (fax 599/7–5363; U.S. representative, 800/748–8733) offers courses for beginning to advanced board sailors. Lessons cost $20; board rentals start at $20 an hour; $40 for a half day. There are free regular pickups at all the hotels at 9 AM and 1 PM; ask your hotel to make arrangements.

Sea Excursions You can also see the island by boat. The 56-foot ***Samur*** (tel. 599/7–5433), an authentic Siamese junk built in Bangkok, offers a four-hour sail, snorkel, and swim cruise to Klein Bonaire for $35 a person, including lunch; a five-hour trip that includes a barbecue on Klein Bonaire's beach is $45. Prices also include as much rum, vodka, and soft drinks as you can handle, snorkel gear, and plenty of food. A two-hour sunset cruise for $25 (half price for children 5–12) is also available. The 37-foot trimaran ***Windwood*** (tel. 599/7–8285) also offers half-day sail, swim, and snorkel cruises to Klein Bonaire four mornings a week. The $29 cost includes snacks, an open bar, and snorkel gear. The two-hour happy hour sunset cruise costs $19 a person; the late-afternoon sunset snorkel tour is $22.50 per person. Glass-bottom boat tours are offered aboard the ***Bonaire Dream*** (no phone). The 1½-hour trip ($15 adults, $7.50 children) leaves Monday–Saturday from the Harbour Village Marina.

Shopping

You can get to know all the shops in Bonaire in a matter of a few hours, but sometimes there's no better way to enjoy some time out of the sun and sea than to go shopping, particularly if your companion is a dive fanatic and you're not. Almost all the shops are situated on the Kaya Grandi or in adjacent streets and tiny malls. There are several snazzy boutiques worth a browse. One word of caution: Buy as many flamingo T-shirts as you want, but don't plan to take home anything made of goatskin or tortoiseshell; they are not allowed into the United States. There are no outdoor crafts markets on Bonaire, but some of the better stores carrying unusual handicrafts or reasonably priced Dutch items are listed below.

Stop at the Bonaire Shopping Gallery at 33 Kaya Grandi for a host of nice shops: **Aries Boutique** (tel. 599/7–8091) is a good place to look for 18-carat gold and for Delft china and Dutch gourmet items; **Kibrahacha Souvenir and Gifts** (tel. 599/7–8434) features wall hangings, exotic shells and driftwood, embroidered dresses, and Dutch curios; and **Littman Gifts** (tel. 599/7–8091) is the place for batik cloth by the yard, European costume jewelry, T-shirts, framed underwater pictures, wooden divers, and glass flamingos are also sold.

Caribbean Arts and Crafts (38-A Kaya Grandi, tel. 599/7–5051) is a welcome newcomer to Bonaire's shopping scene. Here you'll find Mexican onyx, papier-mâché clowns, woven wall tapestries, painted wooden fish and parrots, straw bags, and hand-blown glass vases. Things Bonaire (Kaya Grandi 38C, tel. 599/7–8423) offers T-shirts, shorts, colorful earrings, batik dresses, souvenirs, and guidebooks. A government-funded crafts center, Fundashon Arte Industri Bonairiano (J.A. Abraham Blvd., Kralendijk, next to the post office, no phone) offers locally made necklaces of black coral in a variety of colors, hand-painted shirts and dresses, and the "fresh craft of the day." At the Club Flamingo, Ki Bo Ke Pakus, or What Do You Want? (tel. 599/7–8239) has attractive bikinis, dashikis, and pareos.

Dining

Gourmets aren't sneaking off to Bonaire for five-star cuisine, but with a healthy variety of dining experiences, visitors should not go home hungry. Happily, fresh local dishes are generally the most reasonably priced menu items. Sample a restaurant's fresh catch of the day—snapper, wahoo, grouper, tuna, swordfish—prepared over the grill or panfried in a Creole sauce (usually, a spicy sauce of sweet peppers, tomatoes, and onions). Other favorites are goat stew, stewed conch, fried conch, and *nasi goreng*, an Indonesian meat and rice dish. Most local meals include *funghi* (a polentalike dish), sweet potatoes, and fried plantains. Local appetizers include Kadushi soup, made from the flesh of the Kadushi cactus; iguana soup (available only when someone has caught one of the fleet-footed lizards); and fish soup. Besides the restaurants listed below, budget local food can be found in town at **Julius Place** (Kaya L.D. Gerharts, tel. 599/7–5544) and **La Sonrisa** (Kaya Grande 13, tel. 599/7–5017). The three Chinese restaurants in town also offer budget fare. **Cozzoli's Pizza** (Harbourside Mall, Kralenkijk, tel. 599/7–5195) serves New York–style pizza and is as close as Bonaire comes to a fast-food eatery.

Many accommodations on Bonaire have kitchens. Several larger apartment resorts, such as Sand Dollar Beach Club, will, upon advance request, stock an arriving guest's refrigerator with breakfast basics. Supermarkets on Bonaire tend to be small and carry a limited number of items. Fresh fish, fruit, and vegetables can be found at the harborside **Fish Market** on Caya C.E.B. Hellmund in Kralendijk. **Sand Dollar Grocery** (Sand Dollar Shopping Center; open daily 8–6) has everything from diapers to Dewars on the shelves, plus frozen precooked meals in the freezer. Guests of Bruce Bowker's Carib Inn usually shop at **Joke's Minimarket** (Kaya Suecia 23), located just across the street. Other popular markets include **Korona Supermarket** (Kaya Korona 89) and **Supermarket Montecatini** (Kaya Grandi 51).

Most restaurants add a 10% service charge to the bill. If not, you should tip your waiter 10%–15%. Hotel restaurants tend to be more pricey than the restaurants in town.

Highly recommended restaurants are indicated by a star ★.

Category	Cost*
$$	$15–$20
$	$10–$15
¢	under $10

**Per person, excluding drinks and service. There is no sales tax.*

$$ **Den Laman Bar & Restaurant.** A 6,000-square-foot aquarium provides the backdrop to this casual, nautically decorated, sea-breeze-cooled restaurant. Eat indoors next to the glass-enclosed "ocean show" (request a table in advance) or outdoors on the noisier patio overlooking the sea. Pick a fresh Caribbean lobster from the tank, or order red snapper Creole, which is a hands-down winner. Homemade cheesecake is a draw. *77 Gobrenador Debrot, next to the Sunset Beach Hotel, tel. 599/7–8599. Reservations advised. AE, MC, V. No lunch.*

$$ ★ **The Rendez-Vous Restaurant.** The terrace of this café, draped with a canopy of electric stars, is the perfect place to watch the world of Bonaire go by as you fill up on warm freshly baked French bread with garlic butter, hearty homemade soups, seafood, steaks, and vegetarian specialties. Or munch on light pastries accompanied by steamy espresso. *3 Kaya L.D. Gerharts, tel. 599/7–8454. Reservations advised. AE. Closed Tues. No lunch.*

$$ ★ **Richard's.** Animated and congenial owner Richard Beady's alfresco eatery on the water is casually romantic and has become the most recommended restaurant on the island—a reputation that's well deserved. Richard, originally from Boston, sets the tone by personally checking on every table. Although the menu is limited, the food is consistently excellent, catering to American palates with flavorful, not spicy, preparations. Among the best dishes are conch *alajillo* (fillet of conch with garlic and butter), shrimp primavera, and grilled wahoo. Filet mignon béarnaise satisfies those seeking something other than creatures of the deep. For a touch of seafood, start with the fish soup, a tasty broth with chunks of the catch of the day. A new pier lets you arrive by boat. The Sunset Happy Hour is popular with locals. *60 J.A. Abraham Blvd., a few houses away from Bruce Bowker's Carib Inn, tel. 599/7–5263. Reservations advised. AE, MC, V. Closed Mon. No lunch.*

$–$$ **The Green Parrot.** This family-run restaurant, on the dock of the Sand Dollar Beach Club, features the biggest hamburgers and the best strawberry margaritas on the island. Try the onion-string appetizer, which consists of onion rings shaped into a small bread loaf. Bagels with cream cheese, char-grilled steaks, Creole fish, and barbecue chicken and ribs are also served. This is where you'll find both American expatriates and tourists hanging out. It's also a good place for viewing the setting sun. Entertainment at the Saturday barbecue is usually the Trio Dinamico. Food is served from 8 AM to 10 PM. The pool bar is open from 11 to 7. *Sand Dollar Beach Club, tel. 599/7–5454. Reservations advised in high season. AE, MC, V.*

$–$$ **Zeezicht Bar & Restaurant.** Zeezicht ("sea view"; pronounced zay-*zeekt*) is one of the better restaurants in town that is open for three meals a day. At breakfast you'll get basic American fare with an Antillean touch, such as a fish omelet. Dinner is either on the terrace overlooking the harbor or in the homey, rough-hewn main room. Locals are dedicated to this hangout, especially for the seviche, conch sandwiches, snails in hot sauce, and Zeezicht soup (full of conch, fish, shrimp, and oysters). After dessert, stop in the garden to see the monkey and the parrots. Happy hour features live entertainment. *10 Kaya Corsow, across from Karel's Beach Bar, tel. 599/7–8434. AE, MC, V.*

¢–$ **Mona Lisa Bar & Restaurant.** This restaurant offers authentic Dutch fare, along with a few Indonesian dishes, at unbeatable prices. Ask the Dutch chef for suggestions. The specialty here is pork tenderloin satay drizzled with a special peanut-butter sauce. Somehow, Mona Lisa has become renowned for fresh vegetables, though God knows where they come from, since nearly everything in Bonaire has to be imported. This is a late-night hangout for local schmoozing and light snacks, which are served until about 2 AM. *15 Kaya Grandi, tel. 599/7–8718. MC, V. Closed Sun.*

¢ **China Garden Restaurant and Bar.** Despite its name, this place has an everything-you-could-ever-want menu, from American sandwiches to shark's-fin soup, steaks, lobster, even omelets. But Cantonese dishes are still the specialty. Try the goat Chinese-style, anything in black-bean sauce, or one of the sweet-and-sour dishes. Lots of locals turn up between 5 PM and 7 PM to have a drink and watch the latest in sports on the bar's cable TV. The decor is brightened with Chinese lanterns and scarlet tablecloths. *47 Kaya Grandi, tel. 599/7–8480. Reservations advised in high season. AE, DC, MC, V. Closed Tues.*

¢ **Je-Mar Health Shop.** Bonaire's answer to the health craze, this tiny shop serves tofu burgers and salads alongside aisles of health food products. Decor is nonexistent. It's open weekdays 7–7. *Kaya Grandi, tel. 599/7–5012. MC, V. Closed weekends.*

Lodging

Bonaire is not an inexpensive island in high season, but budget vacations can be arranged out of season. Before making reservations, ask the Bonaire Government Tourist Office in New York about special dive packages, or check with the airlines and hotels to see what the latest offers are. They can be exceptional. Hotels on Bonaire cater primarily to avid divers who spend their days under water and come up for air only for evening festivities. Hence, hotel facilities tend to be modest, with small swimming pools and limited service. Groomed sandy beaches are less important to these hotels than efficient dive shops. In the last few years, several apartment complexes have been built, offering modern amenities at moderate prices. But even rooms in many affordable resorts here offer the same fully equipped kitchens found in apartment complexes—together with the facilities of a full-scale hotel. Most of the true budget properties on Bonaire are older than the more recently built complexes, but many have undergone renovations that include air-conditioning, modern bathrooms, microwave ovens in kitchens, and upgraded furnishings. Unlike budget accommodations on many other islands, Bonaire's guest houses are often within walking distance of a beach.

Most hotels, apartment resorts, guest houses, and villas are located along the west coast just north or south of Kralendijk. Large hotels offer several meal plans, with a full American breakfast (BP) averaging $9 a person, and a breakfast and dinner plan (MAP) costing about $35 per person per day. Only one hotel, the Club Flamingo, offers an all-inclusive option, with all meals, drinks, and dives included in the value-oriented package. Always ask for a hotel's package rate, as it usually includes breakfast, airport transfers, some diving, taxes, service charges, and gratuities at a rate that is less than à la carte prices. High season runs from mid-December until mid-April, with prices reduced anywhere from 15% to 30% the rest of the year.

Highly recommended lodgings are indicated by a star ★.

Category	Cost*
$$	$110–$150
$	$80–$110
¢	under $80

**All prices are for a standard double room for two in high season, excluding a $4.10 per-person, per-night government room tax and a 10%–15% service charge. To estimate rates for hotels offering MAP, add about $35 per person per day to the above price ranges. For all-inclusives, add about $70 per person per day.*

Hotels and Resorts

$$ ★ **Captain Don's Habitat.** With its recent (1992) expansion and massive renovation, the Habitat, once a sort of extended home of Captain Don Stewart, the island's wildest sharpshooting personality, can no longer pass itself off as a mere guest house for divers. Stewart's Curaçaon partners have poured money into this resort, adding a set of upscale rooms (junior suites) and then a long row of private villas (the Hamlet section) that rank among the island's best: All are spacious, with ocean-view verandas, full kitchens, and stylish appointments. The rooms in the original 11 cottages are also spacious but in need of refurbishing. The atmosphere at the Habitat is laid-back and easygoing, with the emphasis on the staff's personal warmth rather than on spic-and-span efficiency. This is also one of few dive resorts that welcomes families. The beachfront property units—with glorious views of Klein Bonaire—are spaced widely apart, and the grounds have been landscaped with rocks and cacti. Be sure to meet Captain Don, who shows up twice a week just to say hello, shoot the breeze, and tell his incredible tales, most of which are actually true. A full dive center with seven boats, complete with a resident photo pro, rounds out the picture. *Kaya Gobrenador Debrot 103, Box 88, tel. 599/7–8290, fax 599/7–8240. U.S. representative: Habitat North American, tel. 800/327–6709. 11 cottages, 11 villas, 16 rooms. Facilities: restaurant, 2 bars, gift shop, pool, cruises, baby-sitting, laundry facilities, bicycles, dive center, photo labs. AE, DC, MC, V. EP, MAP, FAP.*

$$ **Club Flamingo.** The Club Flamingo is the closest thing you'll find to a small village on Bonaire—a plantation-style resort that will serve your every need. Unfortunately, only the standard category accommodations fall into our $$ price range, and these are in sore need of new furnishings and fresh paint. Despite showing signs of age, the resort still has an excellent dive facility and an upbeat activities program. Many guests choose the all-inclusive option, a good value for serious divers. The dive facility, Dive Bonaire, was founded by world-class expert Peter Hughes and features some of the best photo labs in the Caribbean. Several rooms are accessible to travelers using wheelchairs, and the dive operation even has specially trained masters who teach scuba diving to individuals with disabilities and dive with them. The on-premise tennis pro offers free clinics every Tuesday and Wednesday morning, there's a daily activities program, live bands perform several nights a week, and the island's only casino—billed as the world's only barefoot gaming center—is here as well. The all-inclusive package offers great value for the price. *J.A. Abraham Blvd., tel. 599/7–8285, fax 599/7–8238. U.S. representative: Divi Hotels, tel. 800/367–3484. 105 rooms, 40 time-share units. Facilities: 2 restaurants, 3 bars, 2 pools, 2 dive shops, casino, lighted tennis court, Jacuzzi, 2 car-rental desks, tour desk, jewelry store, boutique. AE, D, MC, V. EP, MAP, all-inclusive.*

$$ ★ **Sand Dollar Beach Club.** These elegant, spacious time-share apartments combine a European design with a tropical rattan decor, though this varies according to the individual owner's taste. Each has cable TV, air-conditioning, a full kitchen, a large bathroom, a queen-size sofa bed, and a private patio or terrace that looks out to the sea (though the views from the ground-floor units are ob-

structed by foliage). Some units also have telephones. This American enclave is popular with serious divers and their families. There's daily maid service, and the maids will even do your laundry for $4 a load. There's an on-premise PADI five-star dive center, a limited activities club for children, and two lighted tennis courts. There is a beach, but it's minuscule and disappears at high tide. The resort's waterfront Green Parrot restaurant serves breakfast, lunch, and dinner, and there's a grocery store for those who like to cook. *Kaya Gobrenador Debrot 79, tel. 599/7–8738, fax 599/7–8760. 77 studio, 1-, 2-, and 3-bedroom units and 8 2-bedroom town houses. Facilities: restaurant, bar, dive center, photo lab, pool, 2 lighted tennis courts, outdoor showers, strip shopping center, grocery/convenience store. AE, DC, MC, V. EP, MAP, FAP.*

$$ **Sorobon Beach Resort.** Here's the perfect place for acting out all your *Swept Away* fantasies. The Sorobon is a secluded cluster of cottages on a lovely private sandy beach at Lac Bay, on the southeast shore. This delightfully unpretentious small resort is for "naturalists" who take its "clothing-optional" motto literally. Guests are a fair mix of Europeans and Americans. The chalets are arranged in a "V" shape to give the resort more openness and the guests direct access to the beach. Each chalet consists of two small one-bedroom units, each with simple light-wood Scandinavian furnishings, an older-style kitchen, and a shower-only bath. In keeping with the get-away-from-it-all concept, there's no air-conditioning, TV, or telephone. A daily shuttle will take you to town. Relax sitting around full-moon bonfires, playing Ping-Pong, or enjoying a shiatsu massage, all right on the beach. The heady windsurfing in Lac Bay, a result of the unbeatable combo of shallow bay and strong trade winds, draws raves. Restaurant, bar, volleyball, a nature-oriented book and video library, even a telescope to view the stunning night skies are all for the asking. But act blasé when the manager arrives wrapped in a towel. *Box 14, tel. 599/7–8080 or 800/828–9356, fax 599/7–5363. 25 cottages. Facilities: restaurant, bar, kitchenettes, library. AE, MC, V. EP.*

$$ **Sunset Beach Hotel.** In 1990 a group of businessmen purchased this hotel (then called the Bonaire Beach Hotel) and began renovations. New beds and drapes were brought in, walls painted, and wood floors polished. Each sizable room got a digital safety vault, direct-dial telephone, remote-control color TV, minirefrigerator, and coffeemaker. Age, however, has its drawbacks, and here the drawback is the location of the original buildings: They are all set back from the shore, giving even the best rooms only garden views. And in spite of the new amenities, the old-looking rooms and bathrooms lack brightness and appeal. Still, the 12 acres encompass one of the island's better hotel beaches (in contrast to the swimming pool, which is tiny), a miniature golf course, a water-sports concession that offers more than any other on the island, and a romantic thatch-roof restaurant overlooking the sea. Unfortunately, the food is not the island's best, and although the service is super-friendly, it is not always efficient. Divers come for the complete scuba center, Dive Inn, which has three dive boats. You can also rent Sunfish, Windsurfers, and snorkeling gear, or go parasailing or boogie boarding. The Bonairian theme night, with native buffet, folkloric dance show, steel band, and dancing waitresses, costs $20 per person. *Kaya Gobrenador Debrot 75, Box 333, tel. 599/7–8448, fax 599/7–8118. U.S./Canada representative: tel. 800/333–1212, 800/344–4439, or 800/223–9815. 142 rooms, 3 1-bedroom suites. Facilities: restaurant, bar/lounge, pool, 3 hot tubs, dive center, water-sports center, water taxi to Klein Bonaire, miniature golf, shuffleboard, 2 lighted tennis courts, game room, tour desk, gift shop, car rental. AE, D, DC, MC, V. EP, MAP.*

¢ **Buddy Beach and Dive Resort.** Those who eschew luxury, requiring only basic amenities with matching rates, enjoy this growing complex situated on the beach. The original 10 apartments are tiny but clean, with a kitchenette, tile floors, twin beds, a sofa bed, and a shower-only bathroom. In keeping with the no-frills style, the five units on the ground level have no air-conditioning and no TV; the five second-floor units have air-conditioning. In the 20 new luxury units, guests have a choice of a studio, or a one- to three-bedroom apartment, all with sea views, TV, air-conditioned bedrooms, full kitchen, plus dishwasher and microwave. A dive operation and pool are also on the premises. *Kaya Gobrenador Debrot , Box 231, tel. 599/7–8065 or 800/786–3483, fax 599/7–8647. 10 apartments, 20 studio and 1- to 3-bedroom condominium units. Facilities: pool with bar, dive shop. AE, MC, V. EP.*

Guest Houses The **Tourism Corporation of Bonaire** (Kaya Libertador Simon Bolivar 12, Kralendijk, Bonaire, Dutch Caribbean, tel. 599/7–8322 or 599/7–8649, fax 599/7–8408) will mail or fax a list of guest houses and bungalows offering rooms for rent.

¢ ★ **Bruce Bowker's Carib Inn.** American diver Bruce Bowker started his small diving lodge out of a private home, continually adding onto and refurbishing the air-conditioned inn, about a mile from the airport. New rattan furnishings, cable TVs, completely renovated kitchens, and a family-style atmosphere have turned his homey hostelry into one of the island's best bets, albeit one that gets booked far in advance by repeat guests. Bowker knows everybody by name and loves to fill special requests. The two units with no kitchen have a refrigerator and an electric kettle, but for more involved dining, you'll have to leave the premises—there's no restaurant. Richard's (*see* Dining, *above*) is nearby. Those who prefer to cook can shop for supplies at the grocery store just across the street. Nervous virgin divers will enjoy Bowker's small scuba classes (one or two people); PADI certification is available. You'll have to drive about a mile to the nearest beach. *Box 68, tel. 599/7–8819, fax 599/7–5295. U.S. representative: ITR, tel. 800/223–9815 or 212/545–8649. 9 units. Facilities: pool, scuba classes, dive center, retail dive store. AE, MC, V. EP.*

¢ **Leeward Inn.** American owners Don and Ditta Balstra have restored this 80-year-old guest house and modernized its five rooms. Guests come for the friendly service and the inexpensive meals at the on-site Harthouse Café as well as for the budget-priced, basic accommodations. The pastel-painted rooms have light tile floors, twin beds, white Formica furnishings, and modern bathrooms (shower only, except for one room). There are no TVs, no phones, and no air-conditioning (ceiling fans and tropical breezes keep things cool). The location, just three short blocks from the heart of Kralendijk, is a block from the sea and a 10-minute walk to the Club Flamingo beach. *Kaya Grandi 60, Kralendijk, tel. 599/7–5516, fax 599/7–5517. 4 rooms, 1 suite. Facilities: restaurant, dive shop. AE, MC, V. EP.*

¢ **Sunset Inn.** This pleasant property has seven rooms, a community kitchen, and a small public beach across the street. The Dive Inn dive shop is adjacent to the guest house and offers guests dive packages as well as PADI instruction. The five rooms are smallish and basic, with showers, color TVs, refrigerators, and air-conditioning. The two suites are roomier. *Kaya C.E.B. Hellmund 29, tel. 599/7–8448 or 800/344–4439, fax 599/7–8118. 7 units. AE, MC, V. EP.*

Villa and Apartment Rentals Island villa and apartment rentals run the gamut from apartments in resort hotels to efficiency units to stand-alone houses rented by the week. Generally resort hotel units (*see* Hotels and Resorts, *above*) cost more, but they offer on-site facilities that may be worth the extra price. Two families traveling together will find a wide selection of properties to choose from. The **Tourism Corporation of Bonaire** (tel. 800/826–6247) can help locate guest houses and smaller rental apartments.

$$ **Sunset Oceanfront Apartments.** One- and two-bedroom apartments that overlook the sea are available at this small complex with pool,

located just a three-minute walk from downtown Kralendijk. All of the apartments have color TV, air-conditioned bedrooms, and small kitchenettes with refrigerator and microwave oven. *Kaya Lodewijk D. Gerarts 22, Kralendijk, tel. 599/7–8291 or 800/344–4439, fax 599/7–8865. 12 units. Facilities: pool. AE, MC, V.*

$ **Diversion.** The Dutch owners decided Bonaire needed modern, amenity-laden apartments geared toward divers with thin wallets but a yen for the upscale, so they built these seven one-bedroom apartments north of hotel row in 1991. For about $950 a week (minimum one-week stay), you get a medium-sized apartment overlooking the sea, daily maid service, unlimited scuba air tanks and weight belts, plus a minivan for driving to the island's gold mine of shore diving. Each apartment comes with a fully equipped kitchen, a porch, a lockable "wet room" for scuba gear, telephone, cable TV, an air-conditioned bedroom, and a sofa bed in the living room. *Box 104, Kralendijk, tel. 599/7–8659 or 599/7–8427, fax 599/7–5327. 7 one-bedroom units. MC, V.*

Off-Season Bets Between mid-April and mid-December is low season on Bonaire, and the time when hotel rates go down by as much as 30%. Two people traveling together can stay in a spacious one-bedroom unit for less than $135 a night at the **Coral Regency** (Kaya Gobrenador Debrot 90, tel. 599/7–5580; in the U.S., tel. 800/327–8150) or in a one-bedroom unit at the **Sand Dollar Beach Club** (*see above*) sometimes as low as $170 per night.

The Arts and Nightlife

The Arts Slide shows of underwater scenes keep both divers and nondivers fascinated in the evenings. Dee Scarr, a dive guide, presents the fascinating "Touch the Sea" show Monday night at 8:45, from the beginning of November to the end of June, at **Captain Don's Habitat** (tel. 599/7–8290). Check with the Habitat for other shows throughout the week. **Sunset Beach Hotel** (tel. 599/7–8448) offers a free one-hour slide show every Wednesday evening at 7. The **Club Flamingo** (tel. 599/7–8285) offers a free underwater video, "Discover the Caribbean," on Sunday night at 7.

The best singer on the island is guitarist **Cai-Cai Cecelia,** who performs with his duo Monday night at the **Club Flamingo,** Wednesday night at **Sunset Beach Hotel,** and Thursday night at **Captain Don's Habitat.** He sings his own compositions, as well as Harry Belafonte classics. A local duo also sings and plays music every Thursday night at the **Club Flamingo.** The Kunuku Band plays every Friday and Sunday for happy hour at **Captain Don's Habitat.** The M & M Duo also entertains three nights a week at the Chibi Chibi Restaurant at the **Club Flamingo.**

Nightlife Most divers are exhausted after they finish their third, fourth, or fifth dive of the day, which probably explains why there's only one disco in Bonaire. Nevertheless, **E Wowo** (Kralendijk, at the corner of Kaya Grandi and Kaya L. D. Gerharts, no phone) is usually packed in high season, so get there early. The name E Wowo means "eye" in Papiamento and is illustrated with two flashing op-art eyes on the wall. Recorded music is loud, and the large circular bar seats a lot of action. The cover charge varies according to the season.

The popular bar **Karel's** (tel. 599/7–8434), on the waterfront across from the Zeezicht Restaurant, sits on stilts above the sea and is *the* place for mingling with islanders, dive pros, and tourists, especially Friday and Saturday nights, when there's live music.

Mi Ramada (Rincon, tel. 599/7–6338) is a hopping joint, splashed with neon colors and adorned with everything from license plates to creatively carved driftwood, that serves fine local Creole food to the accompaniment of top bands from all three ABC islands. Friday and

Saturday nights are party time, when Bonairians gather along the main street of Kralendijk to dance to informal bands that set up on the sidewalk.

The island has only one casino. It's at the **Club Flamingo** and opens at 8 PM and is closed on Sunday.

7 The British Virgin Islands

Tortola, Virgin Gorda, and Outlying Islands

Updated by Pamela Acheson

Serene, seductive, and spectacularly beautiful even by Caribbean standards, the British Virgin Islands are happily free of the runaway development that has detracted from the charm of so many West Indian islands. The pleasures to be found here are of the understated sort—sailing around the multitude of tiny nearby islands; diving to the wreck of the RMS *Rhone*, sunk off Salt Island in 1867; exploring the twisting passages and sunlit grottoes of Virgin Gorda's famed Baths; and settling down on some breeze-swept terrace to admire the sunset. There are just over 50 islands in the archipelago. Tortola, about 10 square miles, is the largest of the British islands, and Virgin Gorda, with 8 square miles, ranks second. Scattered around them are the islands of Jost Van Dyke; Great Camanoe; Norman; Peter; Salt; Cooper; Dead Chest; the low-lying, coral Anegada; and others.

Some of the most luxurious and expensive resorts in the Caribbean are scattered throughout the B.V.I. In addition, yacht owners and those on expensive private charters make up a significant portion of the B.V.I.'s visitors, furthering the islands' reputation as a genteel, costly destination. Nevertheless, there are a number of reasonably priced hotels and restaurants here. Many—though not all—accommodations are on or near beaches, and some include cooking facilities, so renting a car or eating out aren't always necessities. Sailors will discover bare-boat charters at affordable rates. There are even a handful of campgrounds in the B.V.I., a relatively uncommon phenomenon in the Caribbean. Nightlife, too (what there is of it) can be a bargain. Many local bands and singers perform at informal open-air bars and restaurants; it's possible to hear great music for the price of a drink.

The lack of direct-air flights from the mainland United States helps the British islands retain the endearing qualities of yesteryear's Caribbean. One first has to get to Puerto Rico, 60 miles to the west, or to nearby St. Thomas in the United States Virgin Islands, and catch a small plane to the little airports on Beef Island/Tortola and Virgin Gorda. Many of the travelers who return year after year prefer arriving by water. Sailing has always been a popular activity in the B.V.I. The first arrivals here were a seafaring tribe, the Siboney Indians. Christopher Columbus was the first European to visit, during his second voyage to the New World, in 1493. In the ensuing years, the Spaniards passed through these waters seeking gold and preying on passing galleons crammed with Mexican and Peruvian gold, silver, and spices. Among the most notorious of these predatory men were Blackbeard Teach; Bluebeard; Captain Kidd; and Sir Francis Drake, who lent his name to the channel that sweeps through the two main clusters of the B.V.I.

In the 17th century, these colorful cutthroats were replaced by the Dutch, who were soon sent packing by the British. They established a plantation economy and brought in African slaves to work the cane fields while the plantation owners and their families reaped the benefits. When slavery was abolished in 1838, the plantation economy quickly faltered, and the majority of the white population returned to Europe. The islands dozed, a forgotten corner of the British empire, until the early 1960s. In 1966, a new constitution, granting greater autonomy to the islands, was approved.

What It Will Cost These sample prices, meant only as a general guide, are for high season. A $ hotel will be about $100 a night; a ¢ hotel room can be had for about $60. A two-bedroom villa rents for around $250 a night—$125 per couple if shared. Dinner at a ¢ restaurant will cost about $9; a sandwich lunch is around $6. Expect to pay a hefty $3 for a beer at a restaurant, and a similar price for a glass of house wine or a rum punch. Four-wheel-drive vehicles rent for $40–$50 a day. Taxis are expensive here: A trip from Road Town to Cane Garden Bay on Tortola is about $15; on Virgin Gorda, it's $20 from Spanish Town to Leverick Bay. A single-tank dive averages $60; daily snorkel equipment rents for about $10.

Before You Go

Tourist Information Information about the B.V.I. is available through the **British Virgin Islands Tourist Board** (370 Lexington Ave., Suite 416, New York, NY 10017, tel. 212/696–0400 or 800/835–8530) or at the **British Virgin Islands Information Office** in San Francisco (1686 Union St., Suite 305, San Francisco, CA 94123, tel. 415/775–0344, 800/922–4873 in CA, or 800/232–7770). British travelers can write or visit the **BVI Information Office** (110 St. Martin's La., London WC2N 4DY, tel. 0171/240–4259).

Arriving and Departing

By Plane No nonstop service is available from the United States to the B.V.I.; connections are usually made through San Juan, Puerto Rico, or St. Thomas, U.S.V.I. Airlines serving both San Juan and St. Thomas include **American** (tel. 800/433–7300), **Continental** (tel. 800/231–0856), and **Delta** (tel. 800/323–2323). **Key Airlines** (tel. 800/786–2386) flies to St. Thomas from major cities through its Savannah, Georgia, hub on Thursdays and Sundays. From San Juan, **American Eagle** (tel. 800/433–7300) flies to Tortola. Regularly scheduled service between the B.V.I. and most other Caribbean islands is provided by **Leeward Islands Air Transport** (LIAT; tel. 809/495–1187). Many Caribbean islands can also be reached via **Gorda Aero Service** (Tortola, tel. 809/495–2271), a charter service.

From the Airport There is no bus service from the airports, and taxis (often in the form of minivans and open-air safari buses) are expensive. Fares are officially set, but can seem confusing. It's best to tell the taxi driver the number in your group and your destination and to make sure you understand the price before you get in the taxi (if the amount seems out of line, go to a different driver). Fare from the Beef Island/Tortola airport to Wickham's Cay I in Road Town (20 minutes) is a flat fee

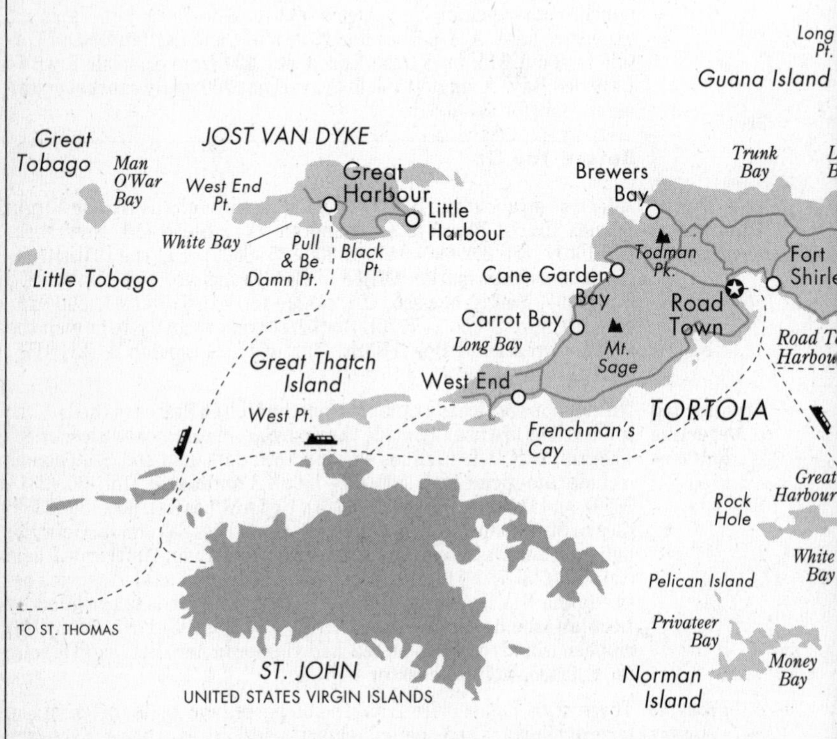
ATLANTIC
Long Pt.
Guana Island
Great Tobago
Man O'War Bay
JOST VAN DYKE
West End Pt.
Great Harbour
Little Harbour
Trunk Bay
Brewers Bay
White Bay
Pull & Be Damn Pt.
Black Pt.
Todman Pk.
Little Tobago
Cane Garden Bay
Road Town
Carrot Bay
Long Bay
Mt. Sage
Great Thatch Island
West End
West Pt.
TORTOLA
Frenchman's Cay
Great Harbour
Rock Hole
White Bay
Pelican Island
TO ST. THOMAS
Privateer Bay
Money Bay
Norman Island
ST. JOHN
UNITED STATES VIRGIN ISLANDS

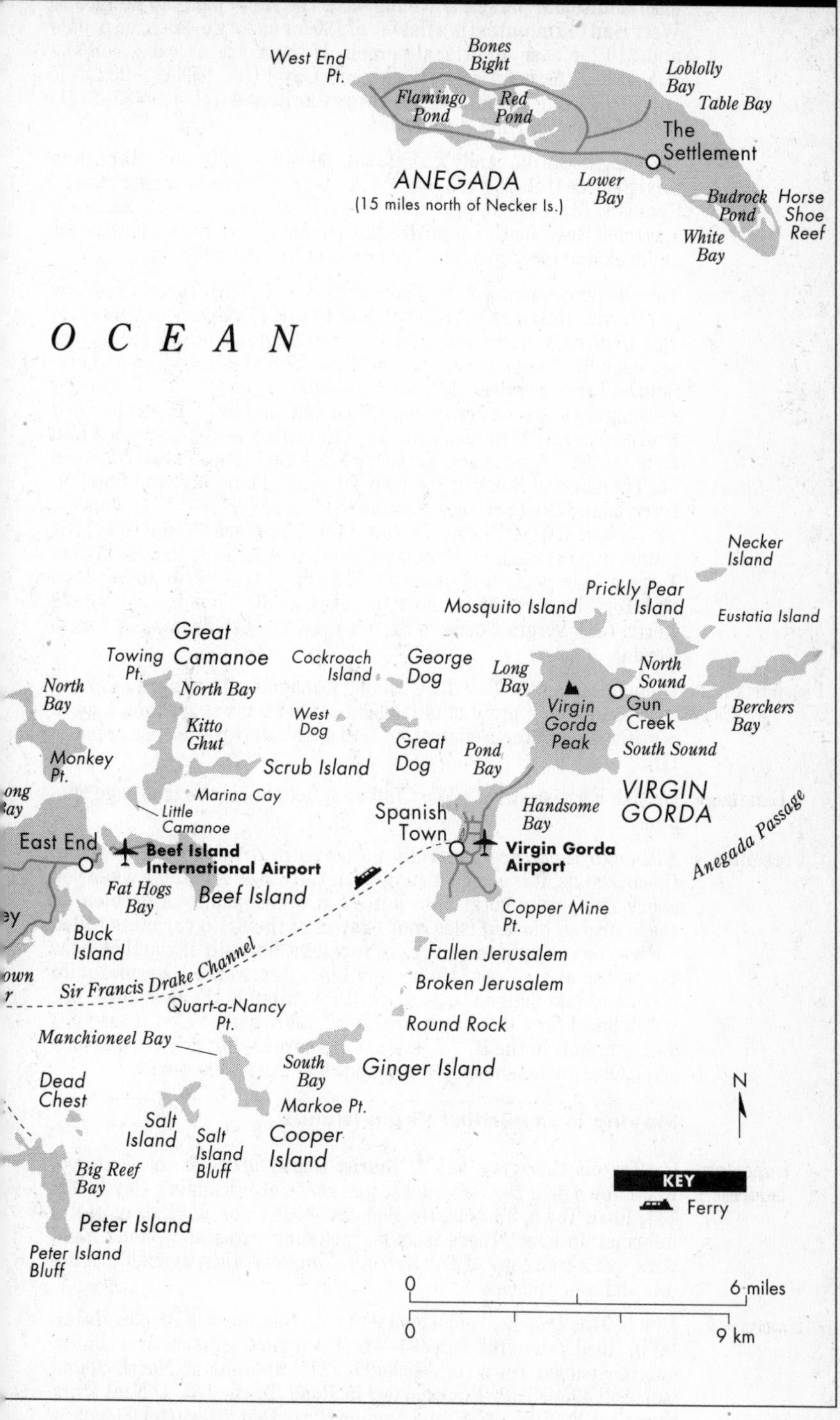

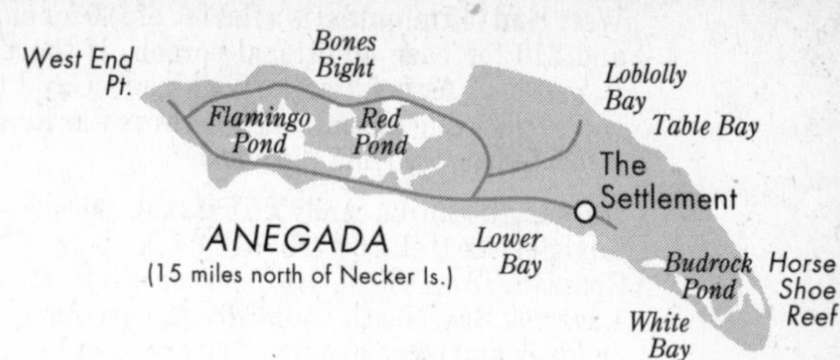
West End Pt.
Bones Bight
Loblolly Bay
Table Bay
Flamingo Pond
Red Pond
The Settlement
ANEGADA
(15 miles north of Necker Is.)
Lower Bay
Budrock Pond
Horse Shoe Reef
White Bay
O C E A N
Necker Island
Prickly Pear Island
Mosquito Island
Eustatia Island
Great Camanoe
Towing Pt.
Cockroach Island
George Dog
Long Bay
North Sound
North Bay
North Bay
West Dog
Virgin Gorda Peak
Gun Creek
Bercher's Bay
Kitto Ghut
Great Dog
Pond Bay
South Sound
Monkey Pt.
Scrub Island
VIRGIN GORDA
Marina Cay
Little Camanoe
Spanish Town
Handsome Bay
Anegada Passage
East End
Beef Island International Airport
Virgin Gorda Airport
Fat Hogs Bay
Beef Island
Copper Mine Pt.
Buck Island
Fallen Jerusalem
Sir Francis Drake Channel
Broken Jerusalem
Quart-a-Nancy Pt.
Manchioneel Bay
Round Rock
South Bay
Ginger Island
Dead Chest
Markoe Pt.
Salt Island
Salt Island Bluff
Cooper Island
Big Reef Bay
Peter Island
Peter Island Bluff
N
KEY
Ferry
0
6 miles
0
9 km

of $15 for one, two, or three people traveling together and $5 for each additional person traveling with the same party. The fare to West End (45 minutes) is a flat fee of $30 for one, two, or three people and $10 for each additional person. If there are no cabs, call the **B.V.I. Taxi Association** at Wickham's Cay I (tel. 809/494–2322). If you're planning to rent a car, **Airways Car Rental** (tel. 809/495–2161) is located across from the airport.

On Virgin Gorda, **Andy's Taxi** (tel. 809/495–5252) and **Mahogany Taxi Service** (tel. 809/495–5469) take people from the airport to the Spanish Town/Yacht Harbour area for $2 per person. Rates to Leverick Bay/North Sound are $20 a person, with reduced rates for children and large groups. Drivers meet incoming flights.

By Boat Various ferries connect St. Thomas, U.S.V.I., with Tortola and Virgin Gorda. **Native Son, Inc.** (tel. 809/495–4617), operates three ferries (***Native Son, Oriole,*** and ***Voyager Eagle***), and offers service between St. Thomas and Tortola (West End and Road Town) daily. **Smiths Ferry Services** (tel. 809/494–4430 or 809/494–2355) carries passengers between downtown St. Thomas and Road Town and West End on Monday through Saturday, offers daily service between Red Hook on St. Thomas and Tortola's West End, and travels between St. Thomas and Spanish Town on Tuesday, Thursday, and Sunday. **Inter-Island Boat Services' *Sundance II*** (tel. 809/776–6597) connects St. John and West End on Tortola daily. Fares are $17 one-way, $32 round-trip between St. Thomas (Charlotte Amalie or Red Hook) and Tortola (any port); $16 one-way, $28 round-trip between St. John and Tortola; and $45 round-trip between St. Thomas and Virgin Gorda ($25 Virgin Gorda to St. Thomas, $20 St. Thomas to Virgin Gorda).

Passports and Visas Upon entering the B.V.I., U.S. and Canadian citizens are required to present some proof of citizenship, if not a passport then a birth certificate or voter-registration card with a driver's license or photo ID.

Language British English, with a West Indian inflection, is the language spoken.

Precautions Although there are generally no perils in drinking the water in these islands, it is a good idea to ask if the water is potable when you check in to your hotel. Mosquitoes, are not usually a problem in these breeze-blessed isles, but beware of the little varmints called no-see-ums. Apply some type of repellent liberally if you'll be near the water at twilight. No-see-um bites itch worse than mosquito bites and take longer to go away. Prevention is the best cure, but witch hazel (or a dab of gin or vodka) offers some relief if they get you. Animals in the B.V.I. are not dangerous, but can be road hazards. Give goats, sheep, horses, and cows the right-of-way.

Staying in the British Virgin Islands

Important Addresses On Tortola there is a **B.V.I. Tourist Board Office** at the center of Road Town near the ferry dock, just south of Wickham's Cay I (Box 134, Road Town, Tortola, tel. 809/494–3134). For all kinds of useful information about these islands, including rates and phone numbers, get a free copy of *The Welcome Tourist Guide*, available at hotels and other places.

Emergencies Dial 999 for a medical emergency. On Tortola there is **Peebles Hospital** in Road Town (tel. 809/494–3497). Virgin Gorda has two clinics, one in Spanish Town (tel. 809/495–5337) and one at North Sound (tel. 809/495–7310). **Pharmacies:** in Road Town, **J.R. O'Neal Drug Store** (tel. 809/494–2292) and **Lagoon Plaza Drug Store** (tel. 809/494–2498); in Spanish Town, **Medicure** (tel. 809/495–5182).

Currency British though they are, the B.V.I. use the U.S. dollar as the standard currency.

Taxes and Service Charges Hotels collect a 7% accommodations tax, which they will add to your bill along with a 10% service charge. Restaurants may put a similar service charge on the bill, or they may leave it up to you. For those leaving the B.V.I. by air, the departure tax is $8; by sea it is $5. There is no sales tax. Some merchants add a charge for credit-card purchases.

Getting Around

Boat Ferries run between Tortola and Virgin Gorda (both North Sound and Spanish Town), Jost Van Dyke, and Peter Island. All make two or three daily runs, unless otherwise noted. **Speedy's Fantasy** (tel. 809/495–5240) makes the run between Road Town, Tortola, and Spanish Town, Virgin Gorda daily. Fares are $10 one-way, $19 round-trip. Running daily between Virgin Gorda's North Sound (Bitter End Yacht Club) and Beef Island/Tortola are **North Sound Express** (tel. 809/494–2746) boats. Fares are $18 one-way, $36 round-trip. There are also daily boats between Tortola's CSY Dock just east of Road Town and Peter Island. Fare is $10 round-trip (free if you're having dinner on Peter Island; seven runs daily; tel. 809/494–2561 for schedule). **Jost Van Dyke Ferry Service** (809/495–2997) makes the Jost Van Dyke–Tortola run daily via the *When* ferry. Fare is $7 one-way, $14 round-trip.

Cars Driving on Tortola and Virgin Gorda is not for the timid. Roller-coaster roads with breathtaking ascents and descents and tight turns that give new meaning to the term hairpin curves are the norm. It's a challenge well worth trying, however; the ever-changing views of land, sea, and neighboring islands are among the most spectacular in the Caribbean. Most people will strongly recommend renting a four-wheel drive vehicle. Driving is on the left side of the road. Speed limits are 30–40 mph outside town and 10–15 mph in residential areas. A valid B.V.I. driver's license is required and can be obtained for $10 at car rental agencies. You must be at least 25 and have a valid driver's license from another country to get one.

Four-wheel-drive vehicles can be rented for around $45 per day; passenger cars for around $35 a day. There is often a slightly discounted weekly rate. Rental agencies on Tortola include **Avis** (Botanic Station, tel. 809/494–3322), **Budget** (Wickham's Cay I, tel. 809/494–2639), **Hertz** (West End, tel. 809/495–4405), and **National** (Nanny Cay, tel. 809/494–3197). In Spanish Town on Virgin Gorda, try **Mahogany Rentals** (tel. 809/495–5469) or **Andy's Taxi and Jeep Rental** (tel. 809/495–5252).

Taxis Taxis are generally expensive in the B.V.I., with the exception of the $2 taxi-shuttles between Virgin Gorda's airport and the Spanish Town/Yacht Harbour area. On Tortola, expect to pay a flat rate of $15 for one, two, or three people ($5 each additional passenger) from Road Town to Cane Garden Bay, to Long Bay, and to West End. On Virgin Gorda, expect to pay $20 (for the first three people) from Spanish Town to Leverick Bay. On Tortola, there is a B.V.I. Taxi Association stand in Road Town near the ferry dock (tel. 809/494–2875) and Wickhams Cay I (tel. 809/494–2322); there's one on Beef Island at the airport (tel. 809/495–2378). You can also usually find a taxi at the Sopers Hole ferry dock, West End, where ferries from St. Thomas arrive. On Virgin Gorda, Mahogany or Andy's (*see above*) also provide taxi service.

Buses On Tortola, **Scato's Bus Service** (tel. 809/494–2365) makes daily runs from Road Town (opposite the ferry dock) to Cane Garden Bay, Sebastians, West End, and back to Road Town. The fare is $3 one-way; if you tell the driver when you want to return, he'll make sure you get picked up. Call for schedules. There are no buses on Virgin Gorda.

Mopeds and Bicycles On Virgin Gorda, **Honda Scooter Rental** (tel. 809/495–5212) rents mopeds and bikes.

Telephones and Mail The area code for the B.V.I. is 809. To call anywhere in the B.V.I. once you've arrived, dial only the last five digits. A local call from a public pay phone costs 25¢. Pay phones are frequently on the blink, but using them is often easier with a **Caribbean Phone Card,** available in $5, $10, and $20 denominations. The cards are sold at most major hotels and many stores and can be used all over the Caribbean. For credit-card or collect long-distance calls to the United States, look for special USADirect phones that are linked to an AT&T operator, or dial 111 from a pay phone and charge the call to your MasterCard or Visa. U.S.A. Direct and pay phones can be found at most hotels and in towns.

There are post offices in Road Town on Tortola and in Spanish Town on Virgin Gorda. Postage for a first-class letter to the United States is 35¢ and for a postcard 20¢. (It might be noted that postal efficiency is not first-class in the B.V.I.) For a small fee, **Rush It** in Road Town (809/494–4421) or Spanish Town (809/495–5821) offers most U.S. mail and UPS services via St. Thomas the next day.

Opening and Closing Times Stores are generally open Monday–Saturday 9–5. Bank hours are Monday–Thursday 9–2:30 and Friday 9–2:30 and 4:30–6.

Guided Tours For a 2½-hour tour around most of Tortola, get in touch with the **B.V.I. Taxi Association** (Wickham's Cay I, tel. 809/494–2875 or 809/494–2322; airport, tel. 809/495–2378). Tours are $45 for a minimum of three people; $12 for each additional person. **Travel Plan Tours** (tel. 809/494–2872) provides special tours for large groups. They charge $25 a person and have a 12 person minimum. **Style's Taxi Service** (tel. 809/494–2260 during the day or 809/494–3341 at night) also handles large groups but sometimes makes regular runs during high season to various beaches for $5 a person. Pickup is at the Chase Manhattan Bank in Road Town. Guided tours around the entire island of Virgin Gorda cost $30 for two people and can be arranged through **Andy's Taxi and Jeep Rental** (tel. 809/495–5252) or **Mahogany Rentals and Island Tours** (tel. 809/495–5469).

Exploring Tortola

Numbers in the margin correspond to points of interest on the Tortola map.

You can easily explore all of Tortola (or Virgin Gorda) in a single day with a rental car; this will even leave you time for a swim here and a snack there. If you'd rather do it in several concentrated hours or would prefer not to navigate the steep hills on your own, you can opt for a guided tour (*see* Guided Tours, *above*); the costs of car rentals or guided tours are roughly the same. The drives on Tortola are dramatic, with dizzying roller-coaster dips and climbs and glorious views. Distractions are the real danger here, from the glittering mosaic of azure sea, white skies, and emerald islets to the ambling cattle and goats grazing roadside.

Before setting out on your tour of Tortola, you may want to devote an hour or so to strolling down Main Street and along the waterfront
1 in **Road Town,** the laid-back island capital. Locals don't use street names much because they know where everything is, so if you ask directions, ask how to get to such-and-such restaurant or store, rather than how to find the street. Start at the General Post Office facing **Sir Olva Georges Square,** across from the ferry dock and customs office. The hands of the clock atop this building permanently point to 10 minutes to 5, rather appropriate in this drowsy town where time does seem to be standing still.

The eastern side of Sir Olva Georges Square is open to the harbor, and a handful of elderly Tortolans can generally be found enjoying the breeze that sweeps in from the water here. The General Post Office and government offices occupy two other sides of the square, and small shops line the third side. From the front of the post office, follow Main Street to the right past a number of small shops housed in traditional pastel-painted West Indian buildings with high-pitched, corrugated tin roofs, bright shutters, and delicate fretwork trim.

On the left, about half a block from the post office, you'll encounter the **British Virgin Islands Folk Museum.** Founded in 1983, the museum has a large collection of artifacts from the Arawak Indians, some of the early settlers of the islands. Of particular interest are the triangular stones called *zemis*, which depict the Arawak gods Julihu and Yuccahu. The museum also has a display of bottles, bowls, and plates salvaged from the wreck of the RMS *Rhone*, a British mail ship sunk off Salt Island in a hurricane in 1867. *Main St., no phone. Admission free. Open Mon., Tues., Thurs., Fri. 10–4, Sat. 10–1, though hours may vary.*

From Main Street, turn right onto Challwell Street, cross Waterfront Drive, and proceed a few hundred yards to Wickham's Cay to admire the boats moored at **Village Cay Marina.** Enjoy a broad view of the wide harbor, home of countless sailing vessels and yachts, and a base of the well-known yacht-chartering enterprise the Moorings. You'll find a **B.V.I. Tourist Board** office to serve you right here, as well as banks, a post office, and more stores and boutiques.

When you've finished wandering about Wickham's Cay, take Fishlock Road up to the courthouse and make a right to get back on Main Street. At the police station, turn left onto Station Avenue and follow it to the **J.R. O'Neal Botanic Gardens.** These 2.8 acres of lush gardens include hothouses for ferns and orchids, special gardens of medicinal herbs and plants, and plants and trees indigenous to the seashore. A number of flower shows and special events are held here during the year. *Station Ave., tel. 809/494–4557. Admission free. Open Mon.–Sat. 8–4, Sun. noon–5.*

Retrace your steps to Sir Olva Georges Square to pick up your car. From Road Town, head southwest along Waterfront Drive. Follow the coastline for 5 miles or so of the easiest driving in the B.V.I.: no hills; little traffic; lots of curves to keep things interesting; and the lovely, island-studded channel on your left. At Sea Cows Bay the road bends inland just a bit to pass through a small residential area, but it soon rejoins the water's edge. Sir Francis Drake Channel provides a kaleidoscope of turquoise, jade green, and morning-glory blue on your left, and further entertainment is provided by pelicans diving for their supper. The next development you come to is **Nanny Cay.** Jutting out into the channel, this villagelike complex, with brightly painted buildings trimmed with lacy wood gingerbread, also contains a marina that can accommodate more than 200 yachts. A bar and restaurant, Peg Leg's Landing, offers a good place to stop for a soft drink and a view.

From Nanny Cay the route continues westward as St. John, the smallest of the three main U.S.V.I., comes into view across the channel. The road curves into West End past the ruins of the 17th-
2 century Dutch **Fort Recovery,** a historic fort 30 feet in diameter, on the grounds of Fort Recovery Villas. There are no guided tours, but the public is welcome to stop by. The road ends at **Sopers Hole.** The waterfront here is dominated by the boat terminal and customs office that service the St. Thomas/St. John/Tortola ferries. Turn around and head back, taking your very first right over a bridge, fol-
3 lowing signs to **Frenchman's Cay,** and bear right on the other side of the bridge. There's a marina and a captivating complex of pastel-

Tortola

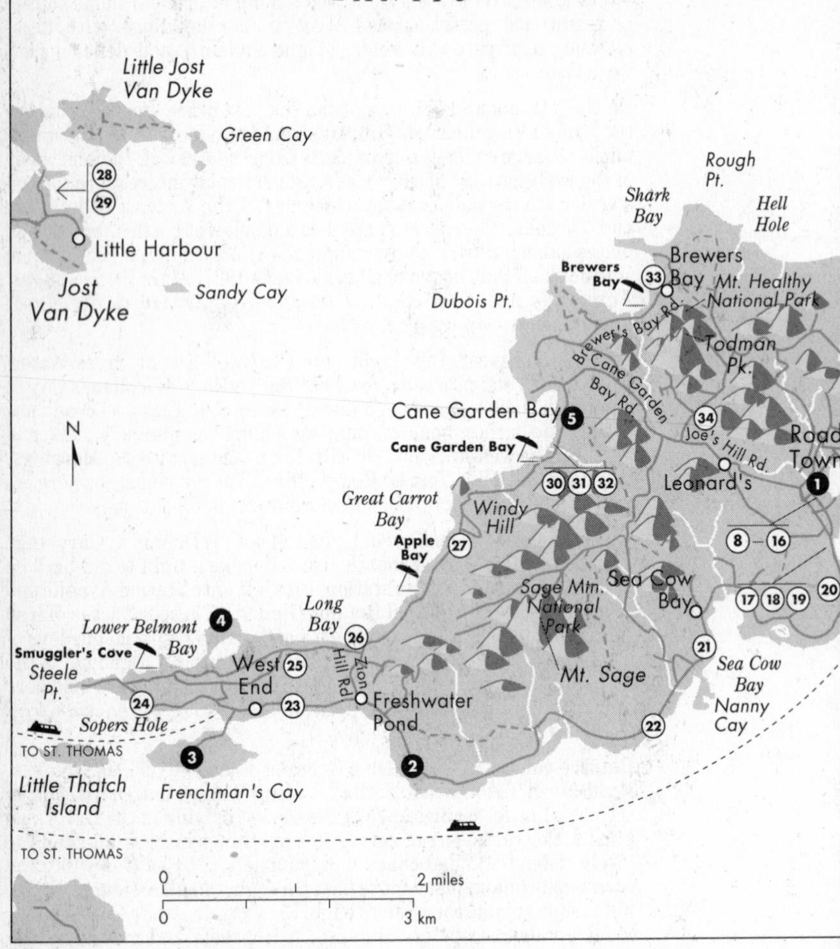

Exploring
Beef Island, **6**
Belmont Point, **4**
Cane Garden Bay, **5**
Fort Recovery, **2**
Frenchman's Cay, **3**
Queen Elizabeth II Bridge, **7**
Road Town, **1**

Dining
The Apple, **27**
C and F Restaurant, **16**
The Fishtrap, **14**
Hungry Sailor Garden Cafe, **8**
Jolly Roger, **24**
Marlene's, **13**
Midtown Restaurant, **9**
Pusser's Pub, **10**
Rhymer's, **30**
Skyworld, **34**
The Struggling Man, **21**
Virgin Queen, **11**
The Whiz, **12**

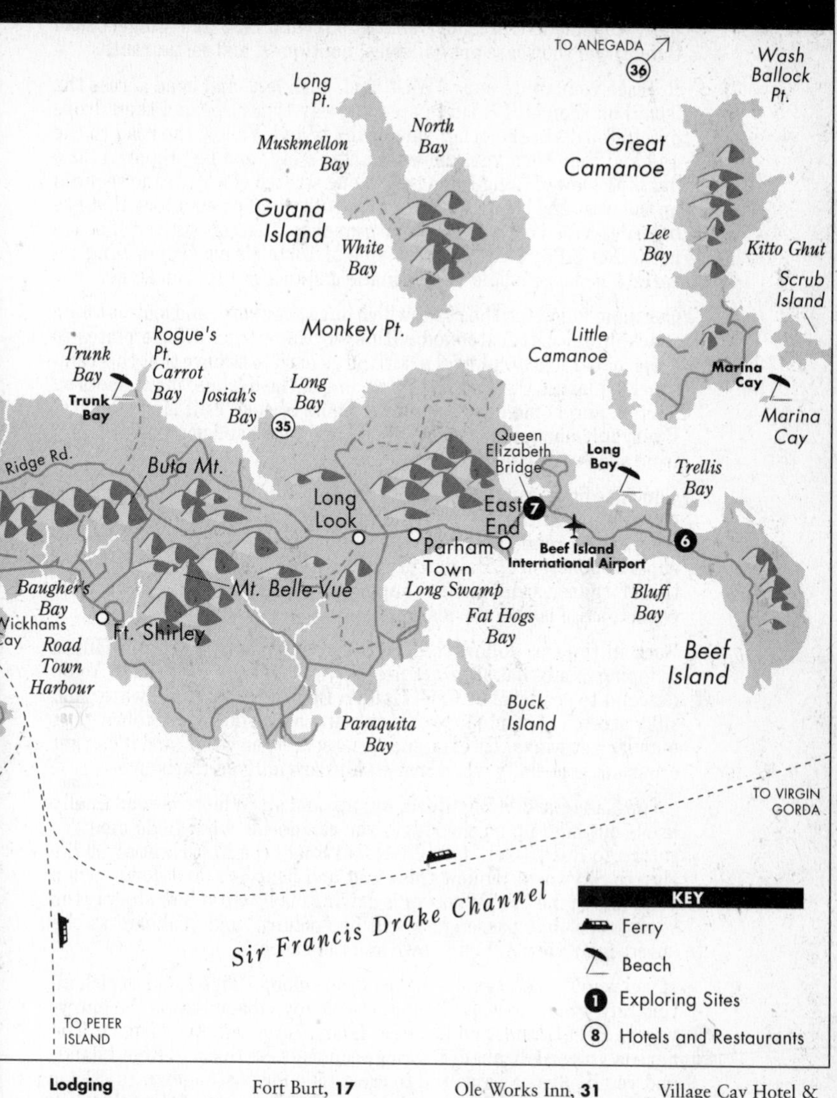

Lodging
Anegada Beach Campground, **36**
Brewer's Bay Campground, **33**
B.V.I. Aquatic Hotel, **23**
Cane Garden Bay Beach hotel, **32**
Fort Burt, **17**
Fort Recovery, **22**
Hotel Castle Maria, **18**
Jolly Roger Inn, **24**
Josiah's Bay Cottages, **35**
Maria's by the Sea, **19**
Ole Works Inn, **31**
Rockview Holiday Homes, **25**
Sea View Hotel, **20**
Sebastian's on the Beach, **26**
Tula's Enchanted Garden, **28**
Village Cay Hotel & Manna, **15**
White Bay Campground, **29**

hued, West Indian–style buildings with shady second-floor balconies, colonnaded arcades, shuttered windows, and gingerbread trim; these showcase art galleries, boutiques, and restaurants.

Retrace your route out of West End, turn left, and head across the island on Zion Hill Road, a steep byway that rises and then drops precipitously to the other side of the island. Follow the road to the end and then turn left, drive up a steep hill, and be prepared for a dazzling view of Long Bay, a mile-long stretch of white sand secured
4 on the west end by **Belmont Point,** a sugar-loaf promontory that has been described as "a giant green gumdrop." On this stretch of beach is the Long Bay Beach Resort, one of Tortola's more appealing resorts. The large island visible in the distance is Jost Van Dyke.

Continue following the road, which hugs the shore, and look out for a shack on the left festooned with everything from license plates to crepe paper leis to colorful graffiti. It's hard to believe that this ramshackle place is the *Bomba Shack,* one of the liveliest night spots on Tortola and home of the famous Bomba Shack "Full Moon" party. Every full moon, bands play here all night long and people flock here from all over Tortola and from other islands.

Continue on to Apple Bay and the **Sugar Mill Hotel.** You may want to have dinner in the 350-year-old mill that now serves as the hotel's main dining room, and take a look at owners Jeff and Jinx Morgan's superb collection of Haitian primitive art. With any luck you'll meet the Morgans, a delightful couple with a seemingly inexhaustible repertoire of island stories.

Back in the car, follow the North Coast Road over Windy Hill, a gripping climb that affords splendid vistas of the sea and sky. You'll
5 descend to sea level at **Cane Garden Bay:** Its crystalline water and silky stretch of sand make this enticing beach one of Tortola's most popular getaways. Its existence is no secret, however, and it can get crowded, especially when cruise ships are in Road Harbour.

Go up Cane Garden Bay Road, up, up, and up. When the road finally levels out high up on the ridge, you can decide what to do next. To return to Road Town, take Joe's Hill Road, the first right after the sign to Skyworld. Follow this right and bear left (and down) when you come to the "Y." Whoever is driving may gasp at how steeply the road drops, but passengers will be "oohing" and "aahing" at the spectacular view of Road Town and the harbor.

If you want to keep exploring, continue along Ridge Road, which ultimately winds up at East End, the sleepy village that is the entry-
6 way to **Beef Island,** and the Beef Island International Airport. The
7 narrow **Queen Elizabeth II Bridge** connects Tortola and Beef Island, and you'll have to pay a toll to cross (50¢ for passenger cars, $1 for vans and trucks). It's worth it if only for the sight of the toll-taker extending a tin can attached to the end of a board through your car window to collect the fee. If you like interesting seashells, **Long Bay** on Beef Island has them for the picking.

From East End, proceed southwest on Blackburn Highway to Sir Francis Drake Highway, then west along the coast back to Road Town.

Exploring Virgin Gorda

Numbers in the margin correspond to points of interest on the Virgin Gorda map.

Virgin Gorda's main settlement, located on the island's southern
1 wing, is **Spanish Town,** a peaceful village so tiny that it barely qualifies as a town at all. Also known as The Valley, Spanish Town is home to a marina, a small cluster of shops, a couple of car-rental agencies,

and the ferry slip. At the **Virgin Gorda Yacht Harbour** you can enjoy a stroll along the dock front or do a little browsing in the shops there.

If you're driving, be prepared to stop and ask for directions, because many roads are unmarked. Turn right from the marina parking lot onto Lee Road and head through the more populated, flat countryside of the south for about 10 minutes. Continue past the Fischer's
2 Cove Beach Hotel on your right and look for signs for **the Baths,** Virgin Gorda's most celebrated site. Giant boulders, brought to the surface eons ago by a vast volcanic eruption, are scattered about the beach and in the water. The size of small houses, the rocks form remarkable grottoes. Climb between these rocks to swim in the many pools. Early morning and late afternoon are the best times to visit, since The Baths and the beach here are usually crowded with day-trippers visiting from Tortola.

If it's privacy you crave, follow the shore north for a few hundred yards to reach several other quieter bays—Spring, The Crawl, Little Trunk, and Valley Trunk—or head south to Devil's Bay. These beaches have the same giant boulders as those found at the Baths—but not the same crowds.

Back in the car, retrace your route along Lee Road until you reach the southern edge of Spanish Town. Take a right onto Millionaire Road and proceed to a T-intersection, then make another right and
3 follow Copper Mine Road, part of it unpaved, to **Copper Mine Point.** Here you will discover the ruins of a copper mine established here 400 years ago and worked first by the Spanish, then by English miners until the early 20th century. This is one of the few places in the B.V.I. where you won't see islands along the horizon.

Pass through town and continue north to **Savannah Bay** and **Pond Bay,** two pristine stretches of sand that mark the thin neck of land connecting Virgin Gorda's southern extension to the larger north-
4 ern half. The view from this scenic elbow, called **Black Rock,** is of the Sir Francis Drake Channel to the north and the Caribbean Sea to the south. The road forks as it goes uphill. The unpaved left prong winds past the Mango Bay Club resort (and not much else) to Long Bay and not quite to Mountain Point. To continue exploring, take the road on the right, which winds uphill and looks down on beautiful South Sound.

You'll see steps and a small sign (the sign is sometimes missing) on
5 the left for the trail up to the 265-acre **Virgin Gorda Peak National Park** and the island's summit at 1,359 feet. It's about a 15-minute hike up to a small clearing, where you can climb a ladder to the platform of a wooden observation tower. The view at the top is dazzling, if somewhat tree-obstructed. A bit farther on, the road forks again. The right fork leads to **Gun Creek,** where launches pick up passengers for the Bitter End, Biras Creek, and Drake's Anchorage, three of Virgin Gorda's upscale resorts.

The left fork will bring you to **Leverick Bay.** There is a resort here, with a cozy beach and marina, a restaurant, a cluster of shops, and some luxurious hillside villas to rent, all a little like a tucked-away tropical suburb. Low-gear your way up one of the narrow hillside roads (you're not on a driveway, it only seems that way) to one of those topmost Leverick dwellings, where you can park for a moment. Out to the left, across Blunder Bay, you'll see **Mosquito Island,** home of Drake's Anchorage Resort; the hunk of land straight ahead is **Prickly Pear,** which has been named a national park to protect it from development. At the neck of land to your right, across from Gun Creek, is **Biras Creek Hotel,** and around the bend to the north of that you'll see the Danish-roof buildings of the **Bitter End Yacht Club and Marina.** Between the Bitter End and Prickly Pear
6 you should be able to make out **Saba Rock,** home of one of the Caribbean's best-known diving entrepreneurs, Bert Kilbride—a colorful

Virgin Gorda

Exploring
The Baths, **2**
Black Rock, **4**
Copper Mine Point, **3**
Eustatia Sound, **7**
Saba Rock, **6**
Spanish Town, **1**
Virgin Gorda Peak National Park, **5**

Dining
The Bath and Turtle, **12**
The Crab Hole, **13**
Mad Dog, **8**
Pusser's Leverick Bay, **17**
Teacher's Pet Ilma's, **10**

Lodging
Fischer's Cove Beach Hotel, **11**
Guavaberry Spring Bay Vacation Homes, **9**
Leverick Bay Resort, **18**
Mango Bay Resort, **15**
Paradise Beach Resort, **16**
The Wheelhouse, **14**

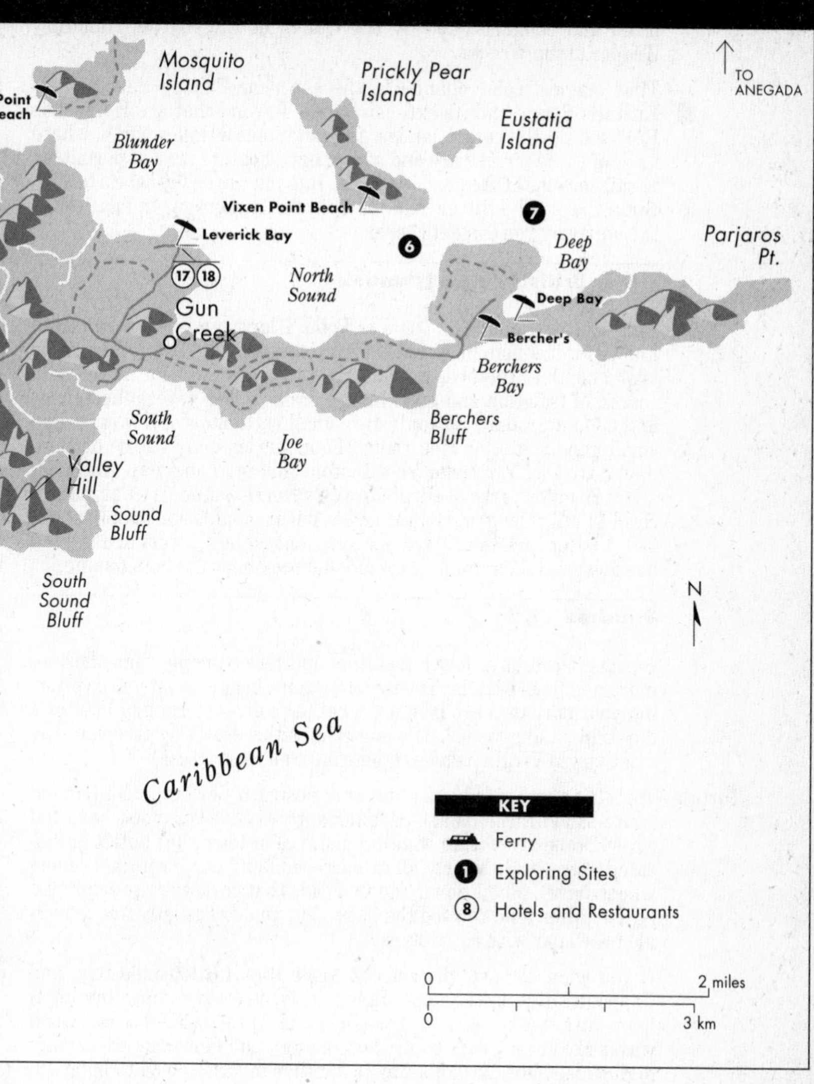
Mosquito Island
Prickly Pear Island
TO ANEGADA
Point Beach
Eustatia Island
Blunder Bay
Vixen Point Beach
7
Leverick Bay
6
Deep Bay
Parjaros Pt.
17 18
North Sound
Gun Creek
Deep Bay
Bercher's
Berchers Bay
South Sound
Berchers Bluff
Joe Bay
Valley Hill
Sound Bluff
South Sound Bluff
N
Caribbean Sea
KEY
Ferry
1 Exploring Sites
8 Hotels and Restaurants
0
2 miles
0
3 km

character who knows where all the wrecks are and who is recognized and commissioned by the Queen of England as Honorary Keeper of the Wrecks.

That magical color change in the sea near Prickly Pear reveals
7 **Eustatia Sound** and its extensive reef. Beyond that are Horseshoe Reef and the flat coral island of Anegada some 20 miles north, where most of those wrecks are and where bare-boaters are not permitted to sail because of the perilous reefs. But you can easily take a boat to Biras Creek, the Bitter End, or Drake's Anchorage. In fact, that's the only way you can get there.

Other British Virgin Islands

Just across from Road Town is **Peter Island,** an 1,800-acre island known for its eponymous exclusive resort. **Jost Van Dyke,** the sizable island north of Tortola's western tip, is a good choice for travelers in search of isolation and good hiking trails; it has several hostelries and a campground, but only two small settlements, few cars, and small generators for electricity. Four ferries daily (three on Sunday) go to Jost Van Dyke from Tortola; fare is $7 one-way. **Anegada,** about 20 miles north of Virgin Gorda's North Sound, is a flat mass of coral 11 miles long and 3 miles wide with a population of only about 250. Visitors are chiefly scuba divers, snorkelers, lovers of deserted beaches, and fishermen, some of whom come for the bonefishing.

Beaches

Beaches here have fewer facilities and fewer people than those of more populous islands. Try to get out on a boat at least one day during your stay in these islands, whether a dive-snorkeling boat or a day-trip sailing vessel. It's sometimes the best way to get to the most virgin Virgin beaches (some have no road access).

Tortola Tortola's north side has a number of postcard-perfect, palm-fringed white-sand beaches that curl luxuriantly around turquoise bays and coves. None are within walking distance of town, but hotels are located on several. Nearly all are accessible by car (preferably four-wheel drive), albeit down bumpy roads that corkscrew precipitously. Facilities tend toward the basic, but you can usually find a humble beach bar with rest rooms.

If you want to surf, the area of **Apple Bay, Little Apple Bay, and Cappoon's Bay** is the spot. Sebastian's, the very appealing hotel here, caters especially to those in search of the perfect wave. Good waves are never a sure thing, but January and February are usually high times here. **Josiah's Bay** is another favored place to hang 10. The water at **Brewers Bay** is good for snorkeling. There's a campground here, but in the summer you'll find almost nobody around. The beach and its old sugar mill and rum-distillery ruins are just north of Cane Garden Bay (up and over a steep hill), just past Luck Hill.

Beautiful **Cane Garden Bay** is Tortola's most popular beach and one of the B.V.I.'s best-known anchorages. The informal Cane Garden Bay Beach Hotel is here. You can rent sailboards and such, and for noshing or sipping you have a choice of going to Stanley's Welcome Bar; Rhymer's; The Wedding; or Quito's Gazebo, where local recording star Quito Rhymer sings island ballads four nights a week.

Long Bay (East) on Beef Island offers scenery that draws superlatives and is visited only by a knowledgeable few. The view of Little Camanoe and Great Camanoe islands is appealing, and if you walk around the bend to the right, you can see little Marina Cay and Scrub Island. Take the Queen Elizabeth II Bridge to Beef Island and watch for a small dirt turnoff on the left before the airport.

Drive across that dried-up marsh flat—there really is a beach (with interesting seashells) on the other side.

Long Bay (West) is a stunning mile-long stretch of white sand, and the road that leads to it offers panoramic views of the bay (bring your camera). Long Bay Beach Resort sits along part of it, but the whole beach is open to the public. The water is not as calm as that at Cane Garden or Brewer's Bay, but it is still very swimmable.

After bouncing your way to beautiful **Smuggler's Cove** (Lower Belmont Bay), you'll really feel as if you've found a hidden paradise (although don't expect to be alone on weekends). Have a beer or toasted cheese sandwich, the only items on the menu, at the extremely casual snack bar. There is a fine view of the island of Jost Van Dyke, and the snorkeling is good.

About the only thing you'll find moving at **Trunk Bay** is the surf. It's directly north of Road Town, midway between Cane Garden Bay and Beef Island, and you'll have to hike down a *ghut* (gully) from the high Ridge Road.

Virgin Gorda The best beaches are most easily reached by water, although they are accessible on foot, usually after a moderately strenuous hike of 10 to 15 minutes.

Anybody going to Virgin Gorda must experience swimming or snorkeling among its unique boulder formations. But why go to **the Baths,** which is usually crowded, when you can catch some rays just north at **Spring Bay** beach, which is a gem, and, a little farther north, at **the Crawl?** Both are easily reached from The Baths on foot or by swimming.

Leverick Bay is a small, busy beach-cum-marina that fronts a resort restaurant and pool. Don't come here to be alone, but if you want a lively little place and a break from the island's noble quiet, take the road north and turn left before Gun Creek. The view of Prickly Pear Island is a plus, and there's a dive facility right here to motor you out to beautiful Eustatia Reef just across North Sound.

It's worth going out to **Long Bay** (near Virgin Gorda's northern tip, past the Diamond Beach Club) for the snorkeling (Little Dix Bay resort has outings here). Going north from Spanish Town, go left at the fork near Pond Bay. Part of the route there is dirt road.

The North Shore has many nice beaches. From Biras Creek or Bitter End you can walk to **Bercher's** and **Deep Bay** beaches. Two of the prettiest beaches in North Sound are accessible only by boat: Mosquito Island's **Hay Point Beach** and Prickly Pear's **Vixen Point Beach.**

Savannah Bay is a lovely long stretch of white sand, and though it may not always be deserted, it seems wonderfully private for a beach just north of Spanish Town (on the north side of where the island narrows, at Black Rock). From town it's about 30 minutes on foot.

Other Islands Beaches on other islands, reachable only by boat, include Jost Van Dyke's **Great Harbour** and **White Bay; Marina Cay;** Peter Island's **Big Reef Bay, White Bay,** and **Dead Man's Bay;** Mosquito Island's **Limetree Beach, Long Beach,** and **Honeymoon Beach;** and Cooper Island's **Manchineel Bay.** Farther off, and reachable by plane as well as boat, is beach-ringed, reef-laced **Anegada.**

Sports and the Outdoors

Horseback Riding On Tortola, equestrians should get in touch with **Shadow Stables** (tel. 809/494–2262) or Mr. Thomas at his **Ellis Thomas Riding School** (809/494–4442).

Sailboarding One of the best spots for sailboarding is at Trellis Bay on Beef Island. **Boardsailing B.V.I.** (Trellis Bay, Beef Island, tel. 809/495–2447) has rentals, private lessons, and group rates. Rentals are $20 the first half hour, $15 the second half hour, and $55 for the day. On Virgin Gorda, The **Nick Trotter Sailing School** (Bitter End Yacht Club, North Sound, tel. 809/495–2745 or 800/872–2392) rents boards for two hours for $25, $10 each additional hour, and offers three-hour beginner courses for $50; a brush-up one-hour course is $25.

Sailing/ Boating The B.V.I. offer some of the finest sailing waters in the world, with hundreds of boats available for charter—with or without crew—as well as numerous opportunities for day sails. Bare-boating is an affordable option for competent sailors if split among three or four couples. For sailors interested in renting a bare boat, contact **The Moorings** (1305 U.S. 19 S, Suite 402, Clearwater, FL 34624, tel. 800/535–7289). Based in Road Town, it is the largest operator in the islands and offers day sails as well as boat rentals.

A day sail or theme cruise is a must on the beautiful waters surrounding these islands. Although the cost per person may seem steep, it usually includes snorkel equipment rental, lunch or snacks, and sometimes drinks. The speedy ***Island Hopper*** (tel. 809/495–4870) leaves from Prospect Reef (but will pick up elsewhere for $5 extra per person) and takes a maximum of eight people virtually anywhere they want to go in the B.V.I. for beach or snorkeling trips. Cost is $35 per person half-day, $65 full-day. If you want the slower pace of sailboat, the 80-foot ***White Squall*** (Road Town, tel. 809/494–2564) offers a full day of snorkeling, beaching, barbecue lunch, sodas, and rum punch for $70 a person (lower off-season). The catamaran ***Patouche II*** (Wickham's Cay I, Road Town, tel. 809/496–0222) takes people on half-day snorkeling cruises to Norman Island for $48 per person, and offers half-day sunset sails with snorkeling and hors d'oeuvres for $58 a person. On Virgin Gorda, call **Harrigan's Rent-A-Boat** (Yacht Harbour, tel. 809/495–5542).

Scuba Diving and Snorkeling The famed wreck of the RMS *Rhone*, off Salt Island, is reason enough to dive during your B.V.I. stay. For snorkelers, perhaps the most popular spot is at the famed Baths on Virgin Gorda. Dive and snorkel sites also abound near the smaller islands of Norman, Peter, Cooper, Ginger, the Dogs, and Jost Van Dyke; the North Sound area of Virgin Gorda; Brewer's Bay and Frenchman's Cay on Tortola; and the wreck-strewn waters off Anegada. In addition to renting equipment, many of the dive operators here also offer instruction, hotel/dive packages, and snorkeling excursions. On Tortola, contact **Baskin-in-the-Sun** (Box 108, Road Harbour, tel. 809/494–2858 or 800/233–7938) or **Underwater Safaris Ltd.** (Box 139, Road Town, tel. 809/494–3235 or 800/537–7032). **Dive BVI** (VG Yacht Harbour, tel. 809/495–5513 or 800/848–7078) has locations at Leverick Bay and Spanish Town on Virgin Gorda and on Peter Island and offers special dive packages in conjunction with most of the Virgin Gorda hotels listed in this chapter. A single-tank dive from these operators costs about $60. Snorkel equipment rents for about $10.

Tennis Several resorts on Tortola have tennis courts for guests' use. Nonguests may use courts at **Prospect Reef** (Road Town, tel. 809/494–3311). On Virgin Gorda, nonguests can use the courts at **Biras Creek** (tel. 809/494–3555). Court fees average $5–$10 an hour.

Shopping

The British Virgins are not known as a shopping haven, and what there is is not cheap. Although you won't find many bargains, the shops listed below offer unusual and reasonably priced items.

Shopping Districts Most of the shops and boutiques on Tortola are clustered on and off Road Town's **Main Street** and at the **Wickhams Cay** shopping area adjacent to the Marina. There is also an ever-growing group of art, jewelry, clothing, and souvenir stores at **Sopers Hole** on Tortola's West End. On Virgin Gorda, there's a scattering of shops in the minimall adjacent to the bustling yacht harbor in Spanish Town.

Specialty Stores
Jewelry

Felix Gold and Silver Ltd. (Main St., Road Town, tel. 809/494–2406) handcrafts exceptionally fine jewelry in its on-site workshop. Choose from island or nautical themes or have something custom-made (in most cases, within 24 hours). **Samarkand** (Main St., Road Town, tel. 809/494–6415) features handmade gold and silver pendants, earrings, bracelets, and pins.

Local Crafts

Artists at **Caribbean Handprints** (Main St., Road Town, tel. 809/494–3717) create silk-screened fabric and sell it by the yard or fashioned into dresses, shirts, pants, bathrobes, beach cover-ups, and beach bags. Local artist display their works at the **Virgin Gorda Craft Shop** (Virgin Gorda Yacht Harbour, no phone). Choose among West Indian jewelry and crafts styled in straw, shells, and other local materials, or pick up clothing and paintings by Caribbean artists.

Textiles

Zenaida (Cutlass House, Wickham's Cay, Road Town, tel. 809/494–2113) displays the fabric finds of Argentinean Vivian Jenik Helm, who travels through South America, Africa, and India in search of batiks, hand-painted and hand-blocked fabrics, and interesting weaves. You can choose from her fabulous pareus and wall hangings, unusual bags, belts, sarongs, scarves, and ethnic jewelry.

Dining

Dining in the B.V.I. can be quite affordable if you are willing to stay out of fancy restaurants and sample local cuisine. On Tortola, there is a wide range of lunch and dinner choices, including hearty buffets. If you plan to cook, you'll find several excellent take-out places and grocery stores in Road Town. Stick with the local supermarkets rather than the more expensive yacht provisioning stores. **Bobby's Supermarket** (Wickham's Cay I) sells take-out and baked goods as well as grocery items. **Riteway** (Road Town and Pasea Estate) sells liquor and wine as well as groceries; the Pasea location usually has the island's best selection of vegetables. **Roadtown Wholesale Cash & Carry** (Pasea Estate) sells items in bulk at discount prices; consider it if you are traveling with a large family or group. Even at the supermarkets, expect high prices. Liquor is cheap, but beer and soda are very expensive. (If you are traveling with children, pack several gallon packages of their favorite drink mix.)

On more remote Virgin Gorda there are fewer restaurants to choose from, but it is still possible to eat out inexpensively. Groceries are more limited and more expensive than on Tortola. The **Commissary and Ship Store** (Yacht Harbour) and the smaller **Buck's Food Market** (Yacht Harbour and Leverick Bay) are your best bets.

Highly recommended restaurants are indicated by a star ★.

Category	Cost*
$$	$15–$25
$	$10–$15
¢	under $10

**per person for a three-course meal, excluding drinks and service; there is no sales tax in the B.V.I.*

Tortola
$$

The Apple. This small, inviting restaurant is in a West Indian house. Soft candlelight creates a relaxed atmosphere for diners as they sample fish steamed in lime butter, conch or whelks in garlic sauce, and other local seafood dishes. There is a traditional West Indian barbecue and buffet every Sunday evening from 7 to 9. The excellent lunch menu includes a variety of sandwiches, meat and vegetarian lasagna, lobster quiche, seafood crepes, and croissants with ham and Swiss or spinach and feta. *Little Apple Bay, tel. 809/495–4437. Reservations accepted. No credit cards.*

$$ **C and F Restaurant.** Just outside Road Town, on a side street past the Moorings, is one of the island's most popular restaurants. Crowds head here for the best barbecue in town (chicken, fish, and ribs), fresh local fish prepared any way you wish, and excellent curries. Sometimes you have to wait for a table, but it is worth it. *Purcell Estate, tel. 809/494-4941. No reservations. No lunch. AE, MC, V.*

$$ **The Fish Trap.** Dine alfresco at this restaurant, which serves grilled local fish, steaks, and chicken. Friday and Saturday there's a barbecue with a terrific salad bar; Sunday prime rib is the special. *Columbus Centre, Wickham's Cay I, Road Town, tel. 809/494–2636. Reservations accepted. AE, MC, V. Closed Sun. lunch.*

$$ ★ **Virgin Queen.** The sailing and rugby crowd and locals gather here to play darts, drink beer, and eat Queen's Pizza (on the expensive side, but touted as the best pizza in the Caribbean) or some of the excellent West Indian and English fare. The list of daily specials might include bangers and mash, shepherd's pie, barbecued chicken or fish, or stuffed chicken with peas and rice. Although some dishes are expensive, many lunch and dinner specials are under $10, and portions are hearty. *Fleming St., Road Town, tel. 809/494–2310. No reservations. No credit cards. Closed Sun.*

$–$$ **Rhymer's.** Located at Cane Garden Bay Beach Hotel, this casual beachfront restaurant features all-you-can-eat buffets that include barbecued ribs, conch, and other West Indian specialties on Tuesday, Saturday, and Sunday evenings for $15 a person. *Cane Garden Bay, tel. 809/495–4639. MC, V.*

$ ★ **Skyworld.** This well-known restaurant with a spectacular view of the B.V.I. is expensive for dinner, but has quite reasonable lunch specials, many in the $5–$8 range. Sandwiches are served on delicious freshly baked bread. After lunch, visit the observation deck atop the restaurant for the 360-degree view of numerous islands and cays. *Ridge Rd., tel. 809/494–3567. AE, MC, V.*

$ **The Struggling Man.** Barely more than a roadside shack, this pleasant place with raffish candy-cane decor offers striking views of Drake's Channel, and simple, tasty West Indian specialties. *Sea Cow Bay, tel. 809/494–4163. No reservations. No credit cards.*

¢–$ **Hungry Sailor Garden Café.** This patio restaurant is an offshoot of the adjoining and more expensive Captain's Table. Its blackboard menu includes close to 20 selections, most under $10. Good bets include shepherd's pie, flying fish, hamburgers, and Caesar salad. *Wickham's Cay I, tel. 809/494–3885. AE, MC, V.*

¢–$ **Jolly Roger.** A young boating crowd comes here day and night for pizza (also available for take-out), cheeseburgers, conch fritters, and nightly West Indian specials. The barbecues on Friday and Saturday nights (entrées $8.50–$13) feature live music. *West End, tel. 809/495–4559. MC, V.*

¢–$ **Midtown Restaurant.** Locals frequent this coffee shop for breakfast, lunch, and dinner. The menu of West Indian specialties includes conch, whelk, salt fish, pork, and mutton. *Main St., Road Town, tel. 809/494–2764. No credit cards.*

¢–$ **Pusser's Pub.** This boisterous pub is open from late morning until late evening and serves English-style meat pies, pizza, deli sandwiches, and some Mexican items. Thursday night is "nickel beer night." *Waterfront Dr., Road Town, tel. 809/494–2467. AE, MC, V.*

¢ **Marlene's.** This take-out shop is open all day selling cakes, pastries, West Indian baked or fried pâtés (meat baked in pastry dough), spicy rotis (curries wrapped in a West Indian version of a tortilla), and sandwiches. *Wickham's Cay I, Road Town, tel. 809/494–4634. No credit cards.*

¢ **The Whiz.** This small, cafeteria-style restaurant has daily specials, sandwiches, and salads. Take-out is also available. *At the Round-A-Bout, Road Town, no phone. No credit cards. Closed Sun.*

Virgin Gorda

$$ ★ **The Bath and Turtle.** You can really sit back and relax at this informal patio tavern with its friendly staff. Choose from the simple menu's burgers, well-stuffed sandwiches, pizzas, pasta dishes, and daily specials. Live entertainment is presented on Wednesday and Sunday nights. *Virgin Gorda Yacht Harbour, tel. 809/495–5239. Reservations accepted. MC, V.*

$–$$ **The Crab Hole.** Callaloo soup, salt fish, stewed goat, rice and peas, green bananas, curried chicken rotis, and other West Indian specialties are the draw at this homey hangout. *The Valley, tel. 809/495–5307. Reservations accepted. No credit cards.*

$–$$ **Pusser's Leverick Bay.** It's a bit of a drive unless you are staying in Leverick Bay, but this restaurant and beach bar has nightly specials that can be very reasonably priced, such as Wednesday's Mexican Enchilada Night. Call ahead to see what's on. *Leverick Bay, tel. 809/495–7369. AE, MC, V.*

$ **Mad Dog.** Just before the circular drive to the Baths is this casual spot. Drop by for BLTs, hamburgers, hot dogs, and delicious frozen drinks. *The Valley, tel. 809/495–5830. No credit cards.*

$ **Teacher's Pet Ilma's.** This little hole-in-the-wall offers delightful local atmosphere and delicious native-style family dinners. *The Valley, tel. 809/495–5355. Reservations required. No credit cards. No lunch.*

Lodging

The number of rooms in the B.V.I. is small compared with other destinations in the Caribbean. What is available is often in great demand, and the prices are not low; the top-of-the-line resorts here are among the most expensive in the Caribbean. Nevertheless, these islands also have a number of affordable properties, as well as some moderately priced rentals and even a few campgrounds. The modest hotels we recommend are clean and well-kept, but rooms may seem a little on the bare side.

Road Town hotels don't have beaches, but all have pools and are within walking distance of grocery stores, restaurants, nightlife, and shopping. Bus service is available to a number of beaches around the island. Hotels outside Road Town are relatively isolated, but some are on or near a beach. If you stay at one of these, you can do without a car for most of your trip, but if you like to explore or want to visit deserted beaches (some of the island's best are off the beaten track), you'll want to rent a car for at least several days. On Virgin Gorda, you can manage without a car if you're staying in the Spanish Town area, but you may be walking up to a mile or more to shops, restaurants, or beaches.

Highly recommended lodgings are indicated by a star ★.

Category	Cost*
$$	$130–$180
$	$75–$130
¢	under $75

**All prices are for a standard double room for two in high season, excluding 7% hotel tax and 10% service charge. To estimate rates for hotels offering MAP/FAP, add about $35 per person per day to the above price ranges.*

Hotels
Tortola

Sebastian's on the Beach. Airy white rooms, simply decorated with floral-print curtains and bedspreads, have either terraces or balconies, some with great ocean views. Bathrooms only have stall showers, and there is no air-conditioning; but ceiling fans and louvered windows keep the rooms cool, and you are lulled sleep to the sound of the ocean. The nonbeachfront rooms lack views and can be noisy, but they are just as big and are quite a bit cheaper than the beachfront rooms. The restaurant here is excellent. *Box 441, Road Town, tel. 809/495–4212, fax 809/495–4466. 26 rooms. Facilities: restaurant, bar, beach, water sports, commissary. AE. EP. $$*

Fort Burt. Set on a hill overlooking Road Harbour, the hotel is built within the walls of a Dutch fort dating from 1666. Guest rooms are rather threadbare, with a hodgepodge of furniture styles. It's at the edge of town, away from beaches, but there is a pool. *Box 187, Road Town, tel. 809/494–2587. 7 rooms. Facilities: restaurant, bar, pool. AE, MC, V. EP, MAP. $*

★ **Fort Recovery.** Built around the remnants of a Dutch fort, this appealing group of one- to four-bedroom bungalows stretches along a small beach facing Sir Francis Drake Channel. The grounds are bright with tropical flowers. All units have fully equipped kitchens and sliding glass doors that open onto patios facing the ocean. Bedrooms are air-conditioned; living rooms (not air-conditioned) are suitable as an additional bedroom for one child. *Box 239, Road Town, tel. 809/495–4467, fax 809/495–4036. 10 units. Facilities: commissary. AE, MC, V. EP. $*

Hotel Castle Maria. You can walk to from Road Town to this simple three-story hotel. Some rooms have kitchenettes, balconies, and air-conditioning. All have refrigerators and cable TV. *Box 206, Road Town, tel. 809/494–2553. 30 rooms. Facilities: restaurant, bar, pool. AE, MC, V. EP. $*

Maria's by the Sea. Perched like a sandpiper on the edge of Road Harbour, this simple hotel is an easy walk from in-town restaurants. The small rooms are decorated with white rattan furniture, floral-print bedspreads, and locally done murals. All rooms have kitchenettes and balconies, some of which offer harbor views. A freshwater pool is available for cooling dips. *Box 206, Road Town, tel. 809/494–2595. 14 rooms. Facilities: restaurant, bar, pool. AE, MC, V. EP. $*

★ **Ole Works Inn.** Local recording star Quito Rhymer owns this exceptionally charming inn. It's on one of Tortola's most beautiful beaches. A steeply pitched roof and lots of glass, wood, and island stone add a contemporary flair to what was once an old sugar mill. Attractive rooms have ceiling fans, air-conditioning, and refrigerators. *Cane Garden Bay, tel. 809/495–4837. 8 rooms, 1 honeymoon tower. Facilities: TV in lobby. MC, V. CP. ¢–$*

BVI Aquatic Hotel. The rates here are remarkably reasonable, but don't expect many extras at this unpretentious place. All rooms do come equipped with kitchenettes. You'll need a car if you're staying here; it's a bit out of the way, though the village of West End isn't too far to walk. There's a beach of sorts, but it's small and rocky. *Box 605, West End, tel. 809/495–4541. 14 rooms. Facilities: bar, restaurant. No credit cards. EP. ¢*

Cane Garden Bay Beach Hotel. One of the Caribbean's most beautiful beaches is right at the doorstep of this hotel. The rooms are bare and dark, with brown-tile floors, blue-green walls, and multicolor bedspreads. However, they are air-conditioned and have balconies, TVs, phones, and kitchenettes. The warm waters of Cane Garden Bay beckon, and a wealth of water activities will keep you outdoors. The beach bar and terrace restaurant attract locals, day-trippers, and charter-boat types, so the atmosphere is always lively. *Box 570, Cane Garden Bay, tel. 809/495–4639. 25 rooms. Facilities: restaurant, bar, water sports. AE, MC, V. EP. ¢*

Jolly Roger Inn. This inn is set at the harbor's edge of Sopers Hole. The seven rooms are small but clean and brightly painted in tropical pastels. There is no air-conditioning, but rooms are well ventilated. A restaurant (*see* Dining, *above*) fronts the building and has live music several nights a week. It's a good spot if you like to be in the midst of the action, but a bad one if you crave the water, because it has no beach or pool. *West End, tel. 809/495–4559. 6 rooms, 2 with bath, 4 with shared bath. Facilities: restaurant, bar, dinghy dock. AE, MC, V. EP. ¢*

Sea View Hotel. You can walk to many restaurants and shops from this hotel on the outskirts of Road Town, but you'll need a car to get to the beach. The modest three-story building contains rooms and studios with cable TV, but no air-conditioning. Ten rooms have kitchenettes. *Box 59, Road Town, tel. 809/494–2483. 28 units. Facilities: pool. No credit cards. EP. ¢*

Virgin Gorda

★ **Guavaberry Spring Bay Vacation Homes.** These unusual hexagonal cottages are perched on stilts. You'll feel like you're in a tree house, amid the swaying branches and chirping birds. One- and two-bedroom units are situated on a hill, a short walk from a tamarind-shaded beach and not far from the mammoth boulders and cool basins of the Baths. Although two-bedroom units fall into our $$ range, they become a bargain when split between two couples. *Box 20, Virgin Gorda, tel. 809/495–5227, fax 809/495–7367. 10 one-bedroom units, 6 two-bedroom units. Facilities: commissary. No credit cards. EP. $–$$*

Leverick Bay Resort. The 16 hillside rooms of this small hotel are decorated in pastels and hung with original art. All rooms have refrigerators, balconies, and lovely views of North Sound. Four two-bedroom condos are also available. A Spanish Colonial–style main building houses a restaurant operated by Pusser's of Tortola. A dive operation, crafts shop, commissary, coin-operated laundry, and beauty salon are also on-site. *Box 63, tel. 809/495–7421, fax 809/495–7367. 16 rooms, 4 2-bedroom condos. Facilities: restaurant, bar, marina, pool, shopping arcade, water sports. AE, D, MC, V. EP. $–$$*

Fischer's Cove Beach Hotel. Simply furnished, two-unit cottages, some oddly shaped to catch the sea breezes, are set amid somewhat unkempt gardens. The restaurant here offers a choice of Continental cuisine or such West Indian classics as crispy conch fritters, red snapper, and funghi, a polentalike side dish. *Box 60, The Valley, tel. 809/495–5252. 22 rooms. Facilities: restaurant, bar, disco, water sports. AE, MC, V. EP. $*

Mango Bay Resort. Sparkling white villas framed by morning glories and frangipani, handsome contemporary Italian decor, and a gorgeous ribbon of golden sand that all but vanishes at high tide make this an idyllic retreat. Even for Virgin Gorda it's a study in isolation. *Box 1062, Virgin Gorda, tel. 809/495–5672. 8 villas. Facilities: water sports. No credit cards. EP. $*

Paradise Beach Resort. These one-, two-, and three-bedroom beachfront suites and villas were originally intended to be part of the Mango Bay Resort and are consequently remarkably similar to that property. Units are handsomely decorated in Caribbean pastels. Jeep rental is included in the daily rate. *Box 534, Virgin Gorda, tel. 809/495–5871. 9 units. Facilities: water sports. No credit cards. EP. $*

The Wheelhouse. This hotel is conveniently close to the Virgin Gorda Marina and shopping center, and half a mile from the nearest beach. Rooms, in a cinder-block building, are air-conditioned but small. The restaurant and bar can get noisy. *Box 66, tel. 809/495–5230. 12 rooms. Facilities: restaurant, bar. AE, MC, V. CP. $*

Campgrounds

All have bathroom and showers on the premises.

Anegada Beach Campground. Tents and bare sites are available on a beautiful stretch of white sand on this remote coral island. Various tent sizes range from $20 to $36 a day. Bare sites are $10. *Anegada, tel. 809/495–8038. Facilities: snack bar, snorkel-equipment rental, commissary. No credit cards. ¢*

Brewers Bay Campground. Both prepared ($20) and bare sites ($7) are located on Brewers Bay, one of Tortola's prime snorkeling spots. Check out the ruins of the distillery that gave the bay its name. *Box 185, Road Town, Tortola, tel. 809/494–3463. Facilities: bar, restaurant, commissary, water sports, baby-sitters available. No credit cards. ¢*

Tula's Enchanted Garden. Located in Little Harbour on the tiny island of Jost Van Dyke, Tula's offers both tents ($10) and bare ($4 a person) sites. *Little Harbour, Jost Van Dyke, tel. 809/495–9566 or 809/775–3073. Facilities: snack bar, restaurant, commissary. No credit cards. ¢*

White Bay Campground. Located on the east end of White Bay is this collection of bare sites ($7 a person per night), equipped sites ($25 for lamp, bed, and ice chest inside a tent), and cabins ($35 a night.) *White Bay, Jost Van Dyke, tel. 809/495–9312. Restaurant open for lunch. No credit cards. ¢*

Villa and Apartment Rentals

Villas are available in a wide range of prices in the B.V.I., and the less expensive ones, most of which are on Virgin Gorda, can be downright cheap if you split the cost among several families.

Tortola

Josiah's Bay Cottages. These out-of-the-way hexagonal cottages with one and two bedrooms are furnished in tropical prints and have large picture windows, kitchens, and roomy balconies. It's a five-minute walk from here to the beach, but you'll need a car to go anywhere else. *Box 306, tel. 809/494–6186. 9 units. Facilities: pool. AE, MC, V. $$*

Rockview Holiday Homes. Although most of their properties are luxury, this company has several more modest villas on the hillside along the northwest side of the island. None of these villas has a pool, but some are a short drive from a beach, and many have truly stunning views. *Box 263, tel. 809/494–2550. 30 1- and 2-bedroom villas. AE, MC, V. $$*

Virgin Gorda

Guavaberry Spring Bay. The managers of these popular hexagonal cottages (*see above*) also handle one-, two-, and three-bedroom villas, some with private pools, in The Valley area of Virgin Gorda. Prices start in the $$ range, but some units are very expensive. *Box 20, tel. 809/495–5227. No credit cards. $$*

Virgin Gorda Villa Rentals. This company manages villas all over Virgin Gorda, from Leverick Bay to the southern tip of the island. Many villas have private swimming pools; all boast spectacular views. *Box 63, tel. 809/495–7421. AE, D, MC, V. $–$$*

Off-Season Bets

Virtually every property in the B.V.I., including its most exclusive resorts, offers reduced rates off-season. Top-of-the-line properties including **Biras Creek Hotel** (tel. 809/494–3555); **Bitter End Yacht Club** (tel. 809/494–2746); **Drake's Anchorage** (tel. 809/494–2254 or 800/624–6651); **Little Dix Bay Resort** (tel. 809/495–5555); and **Peter Island Hotel and Yacht Harbour** (tel. 809/494–2561 or 800/346–4451) offer a number of off-season packages. If you are willing to travel in the fall (when the weather can be quite beautiful though somewhat unpredictable), you can find truly exceptional price reductions—most of which are never publicized. It's best to call the hotel directly for these, about a month before you want to visit, and ask if any special rates or packages are available.

Nightlife

Check the *Limin' Times*, which is published weekly, for current schedules. Generally, in season, schedules are close to what is listed below.

On Tortola, live bands play at **Pusser's Landing** (Sophers Hole, tel. 809/494–4554) Thursday through Sunday, the **Jolly Roger** (West End, tel. 809/495–4559) Friday and Saturday, **Sebastian's** (Apple Bay, tel. 809/495–4214) Saturday and Sunday, and **Bomba's Shack**

(Apple Bay, tel. 809/495–4148) on Sunday, Wednesday, and every full moon. At **Quito's Gazebo** (Cane Garden Bay, tel. 809/495–4837), B.V.I. recording star Quito Rhymer sings island ballads. **Stanley's Welcome Bar** (Cane Garden Bay, tel. 809/495–4520) gets rowdy when crews stop by to party. On Virgin Gorda, **Andy's Chateau de Pirate** (Fischer's Cove Beach Hotel, The Valley, tel. 809/495–5252) has live music and dancing on the weekends, and **The Bath and Turtle** has local bands Wednesday and Sunday evenings. One of the busiest nocturnal spots in the B.V.I. is little Jost Van Dyke. Check out **Rudy's Mariner Rendezvous** (tel. 809/495–9282), **Foxy's Tamarind** (tel. 809/495–9258), and **Sydney's Peace and Love** (tel. 809/495–9271).

8 Cayman Islands

Grand Cayman, Cayman Brac, Little Cayman

Updated by Melissa Rivers

The venerable old *Saturday Evening Post* dubbed them "the islands that time forgot." But the past decade has changed all that: The Cayman Islands, a British Crown colony that includes Grand Cayman, Cayman Brac, and Little Cayman, are now one of the Caribbean's hottest destinations.

Your dollars will go farther on other Caribbean islands than they do here. In Grand Cayman, which enjoys a high level of prosperity, the U.S. dollar is worth 80 Cayman cents, and the cost of living is 20% higher than in the United States. However, not everyone on the island earns a banker's salary—despite the 554 offshore banks in George Town, Grand Cayman's capital—and an affordable vacation *is* possible here.

If you're willing to do some homework before your trip, cook some of your dinners, and forego expensive pastimes like parasailing, Grand Cayman is well worth considering, especially for families and groups. Most of the available rooms are in condos; four or more people sharing an apartment or villa bring down lodging costs considerably. Plan an off-season summer visit, and prices dip another 20%–40%. Grand Cayman rewards the budget traveler with gorgeous beaches, pleasant accommodations, low crime, genuinely welcoming locals, and some of the best scuba diving in the hemisphere.

Island-hopping among the Caymans costs only about $99 for day trips, but you'll need to rent a car or moped to get around on the sister islands. Gung-ho scuba divers who have no use for shopping or lolling on wide sandy beaches will prefer Little Cayman (Jacques Cousteau called Bloody Bay Wall one of the world's best dives). Cayman Brac has modern, comfortable hotels and lovely beaches. It offers dive excursions to nearby Little Cayman, as well as good spelunking in numerous caves. Both islands offer good value.

What It Will Cost These price estimates, meant only as a general guide, are for high season. A $ hotel on Grand Cayman is about $90–$110 a night. A villa or apartment rental (usually two bedrooms or more) will cost $225 and up. A $ restaurant dinner is $9–$12. A picnic lunch or pub hamburger will be around $4.75; fast food, $3–$4. A rum punch costs about $4 at most restaurants, as does (surprisingly) a beer. A glass of wine is a little less. Car rental averages $48. A cab from the airport to Seven Mile Beach will be $10–$15; from George Town to Seven Mile Beach, about $8. A single-tank dive costs $35–$40. Snorkel equipment rents for about $15 a day.

Before You Go

Tourist Information For the latest information on activities and lodging, write or call any of the following offices of the **Cayman Islands Department of Tourism** (6100 Waterford Bldg., 6100 Blue Lagoon Dr., Suite 150, Miami, FL 33126-2085, tel. 305/266–2300; 2 Memorial City Plaza, 820 Gessner, Suite 170, Houston, TX 77024, tel. 713/461–1317; 420 Lexington Ave., Suite 2733, New York, NY 10170, tel. 212/682–5582; 9525 West Bryn Mawr Ave., Suite 160, Rosemont, IL 60018, tel. 708/678–6446; 3440 Wilshire Blvd., Suite 1202, Los Angeles, CA 90010, tel. 213/738–1968; 234 Eglinton Ave. E, Suite 306, Toronto, Ontario M4P 1K5, tel. 416/485–1550; Trevor House, 100 Brompton Rd., Knightsbridge, London SW3 1EX, tel. 0171/581–9960).

Don't fail to study the annually updated "Rates and Facts" booklet, available from any tourist office. You'll find a wealth of detailed information and prices on accommodations, sports, taxi and transportation rentals, plus maps and general information. (Restaurant listings are in a separate brochure.)

Arriving and Departing

By Plane **Cayman Airways** (tel. 800/422–9626) flies nonstop to Grand Cayman from Miami two or three times daily, from Tampa four times a week, and from Houston and Atlanta three times a week. **American Airlines** (tel. 800/433–7300) has daily nonstop flights from Miami. **Northwest** (tel. 800/447–4747) has regularly scheduled nonstop flights from Miami and Detroit. **U.S. Air** (tel. 800/428–4322) flies daily nonstop from Tampa and three times a week from Pittsburgh and Charlotte, North Carolina. **British Airways** (tel. 800/247–9297) offers direct flights from Gatwick on a varying seasonal schedule. **Cayman Airtours** (tel. 800/247–2966) offers package deals. Air service from Grand Cayman to Cayman Brac and Little Cayman is offered via Cayman Airways and **Island Air** (809/949–5152 or 800/922–9606). Flights land at Owen Roberts Airport, Gerrard-Smith Airport, or Edward Bodden Airfield. **Airport Information**: For flight information, call 809/949–5252.

From the Airport A taxi from the airport on Grand Cayman to central Seven Mile Beach costs $10–$15; Seven Mile Beach to George Town is $8. Some hotels offer free pickup. Car rentals are also available.

Passports and Visas American and Canadian citizens do not have to carry passports, but they must show some proof of citizenship, such as a birth certificate or voter registration card, plus a return ticket. British and Commonwealth subjects do not need a visa, but must carry a passport.

Language English is spoken everywhere; all local publications are in English as well.

Precautions Locals make a constant effort to conserve fresh water, so don't waste a precious commodity. Caymanians also strictly observe and enforce laws which prohibit collecting or disturbing endangered animal and plant life and historical artifacts found throughout the islands and surrounding marine parks; simply put, take only pictures and don't stand on reefs.

Penalties for drug and firearms importation and possession of controlled substances include large fines and prison terms.

Theft is not widespread, but be smart: Lock up your room and car and secure valuables as you would at home. Outdoors, marauding blackbirds called "ching chings" have been known to carry off jewelry if it is left out in the open.

There are several poisonous plants on the island—the Maiden Plum, the Lady Hair, and the manchineel tree. If in doubt, don't touch. The leaves and applelike fruit of the manchineel are poisonous to touch and should be avoided; even raindrops falling from them can cause painful blisters.

Staying in the Cayman Islands

Important Addresses **Tourist Information**: The main office of the **Department of Tourism** is located in the Harbour Center (N. Church St., tel. 809/949–0623). Information booths are at the airport (tel. 809/949–2635); in the George Town Craft Market, on Cardinal Avenue, open when cruise ships are in port (tel. 809/949–8342); and in the kiosk at the cruise ship dock in George Town (no phone). There is also an island-wide tourist hot line (tel. 809/949–8989). For complete tourist information and free assistance in booking island transportation, tours, charters, cruises, and other activities, you can contact the **Tourist Information and Activities Service** (tel. 809/949–6598, fax 809/947–6222) day or night.

Emergencies **Police and Hospitals**: 911. **Ambulance**: 555. **Pharmacy**: Island Pharmacy (tel. 809/949–8987) in West Shore Centre on Seven Mile Beach. **Divers' Recompression Chamber**: Call 809/949–4234 or 555.

Currency Although the American dollar is accepted everywhere, you'll save money if you go to the bank and exchange U.S. dollars for Cayman Island (C.I.) dollars, which are worth about $1.20 each. The Cayman dollar is divided into a hundred cents with coins of 1¢, 5¢, 10¢, and 25¢, and notes of $1, $5, $10, $25, $50, and $100. There is no $20 bill. Prices are often quoted in Cayman dollars, so it's best to ask. All prices quoted here are in U.S. dollars unless otherwise noted.

Taxes and Service Charges Hotels collect a 6% government tax and add a 10% service charge to your bill. Many restaurants add a 10%–15% service charge. There is no sales tax. At press time, the departure tax was C.I. $8.

Getting Around If your accommodations are along Seven Mile Beach, you can walk or bike to the shopping centers, restaurants, and entertainment spots along West Bay Road. George Town is small enough to see on foot. If you're touring Grand Cayman by car, there's a well-maintained road that circles the island; it's hard to get lost. If you want to see the sights or simply get away from the resort, you'll need a rental car or moped on Little Cayman and Cayman Brac; your hotel can make the arrangements for you. Otherwise, airport transfers are included in most resort rates, and many resorts offer bicycles for local sightseeing.

Taxis Taxis offer island-wide service. Fares are determined by an elaborate rate structure set by the government, and although it may seem pricey for a short ride, cabbies rarely try to rip off tourists. Ask to see the chart if you want to double-check the quoted fare. **A.A. Transportation** (tel. 809/949–7222), **Cayman Cab Team** (tel. 809/947–1173), and **Holiday Inn Taxi Stand** (tel. 809/947–4491) offer 24-hour service.

Rental Cars Grand Cayman is relatively flat and fairly easy to negotiate if you're careful of traffic. To rent a car, bring your current driver's license, and the car-rental firm will issue you a temporary permit ($5). Most firms have a range of models available, from compacts to Jeeps to minibuses. Rates range from $35 to $55 a day. The major agencies have offices in a plaza across from the airport terminal, where you can pick up and drop off vehicles. Just remember, driving is on the left.

Car-rental companies are **Ace Hertz** (tel. 809/949–2280 or 800/654–3131), **Budget** (tel. 809/949–5605 or 800/527–0700), **Cico Avis** (tel. 809/949–2468 or 800/331–1212), **Coconut** (tel. 809/949–4037 or 800/262–6687), **Dollar** (tel. 809/949–4790), **Economy** (tel. 809/949–9550, **Soto's 4X4** (tel. 809/945–2424), and **Thrifty** (tel. 809/949–6640 or 800/367–2277).

Bicycles and Scooters

When renting a motor scooter or bicycle, don't forget the sunblock and that driving is on the left. Bicycles ($10–$15 a day) and scooters ($25–$30 a day) can be rented from **Bicycles Cayman** (tel. 809/949–5572), **Cayman Cycle** (tel. 809/947–4021), and **Soto Scooters** (tel. 809/947–4363).

Telephones and Mail

For international dialing to Cayman, the area code is 809. To call outside, dial 0, then 1, then the area code and number. You can call anywhere, anytime, through the cable and wireless system and local operators. To make local calls, dial the seven-digit number. To place credit card calls, dial 110.

Beautiful stamps are available at the main post office in downtown George Town and at the philatelic office in West Shore Plaza. Both are open weekdays from 8:30 to 3:30 and Saturday 8:30 to 11:30. Sending a postcard to the United States, Canada, the Caribbean, or Central America costs C.I.15¢. An airmail letter is C.I.30¢ per half ounce. To Europe and South America, the rates are C.I.20¢ for a postcard and C.I.40¢ per half ounce for airmail letters.

Opening and Closing Times

Banking hours are generally Monday–Thursday 9–2:30 and Friday 9–1 and 2:30–4:30. Shops are open weekdays 9–5, and on Saturday in George Town from 10 to 2; in outer shopping plazas, from 10 to 5. Shops are usually closed on Sunday except in hotels.

Guided Tours

Land Tours

Guided day tours of the island can be arranged with **A.A. Transportation Services** (tel. 809/949–7222; ask for Burton Ebanks), **Majestic Tours** (tel. 809/949–7773), **Reids Premier Tours** (tel. 809/949–6531), **Rudy's Travellers Transport** (tel. 809/949–3208), and **Tropicana Tours** (tel. 809/949–0944). Half-day tours average $25–$45 a person and generally include a visit to the Turtle Farm and Hell in West Bay, drives along Seven Mile Beach and through George Town, and time for shopping downtown. In addition to those stops, full-day tours, which average $50–$65 per person and include lunch, also visit Bodden Town to see pirate caves and graves and the East End to see blow holes on the ironshore (calcified coral ledge) and the site of the famous Wreck of the Ten Sails.

Water Tours

The most impressive sights are underwater. It may be worth the splurge to take a trip with **Atlantis Submarines** (tel. 809/949–7700). Their $2.8 million sub takes 48 passengers, a driver, and a guide down along the Cayman Wall to depths of up to 100 feet for close up views of the abundant, colorful marine life—huge barrel sponges, corals of extraterrestrial-like configurations, strange eels, and schools of beautiful and beastly fish. Night dives are quite dramatic, because the artificial lights of the ship make the colors more vivid than they are in daytime excursions. Costs range from around $60–$80 per person for trips from 45 minutes to an hour in length. The company also operates private trips on a research submersible that reaches depths of 800 feet. In the **Seaworld Explorer** (tel. 809/949–8534), passengers sit before windows in the hull of the boat just five feet below the surface observing divers who swim around with food, attracting fish to the craft. The cost of this hour-long trip is $29; $19 for children 2–12.

Guided snorkeling trips, available through **Charter Boat Headquarters** (tel. 809/947–4340), **Captain Eugene's Watersports** (tel. 809/949–3099), and **Kirk Sea Tours** (tel. 809/949–6986), usually include stops at Stingray City Sandbar, Coral Garden, and Conch Bed, the top snorkel sites. Full-day trips include lunch prepared on the boat or the shore and cost less than $40 per person; half-day trips average $25. Glass-bottom-boat trips cost around $23 and are available through **Aqua Delights** (tel. 809/947–4786), **Cayman Mermaid** (tel. 809/949–8100), and **Kirk Sea Tours** (tel. 809/949–6986).

Sunset sails, dinner cruises, and other theme (dance, booze, pirate, etc.) cruises are available aboard the ***Jolly Roger*** (tel. 809/949–8534), a replica of a 17th Century Spanish galleon, ***Blackbeard's Nancy*** (tel. 809/949–8988), a 1912 tops'l schooner, and the ***Spirit of Ppalu*** (tel. 809/949–1234), a 65-foot glass-bottom catamaran. Party cruises typically run between $15 and $50 per person.

Exploring the Cayman Islands

Numbers in the margin correspond to points of interest on the Grand Cayman and the Cayman Brac and Little Cayman maps.

George Town

1 Begin exploring **George Town** at the **Cayman Islands National Museum** on Harbour Drive, slightly south of the Cruise Ship Dock Gazebo. Built in 1833, this building was used as a courthouse, a jail (where the gift shop is now), a post office, and a dance hall before being reopened in 1990 as a museum. It is small but fascinating, with excellent displays and videos illustrating the history of Cayman plant, animal, human, and geological life. Pick up a walking tour map of George Town at the museum gift shop before leaving. *Harbour Dr., tel. 809/949–8368. Admission: $5, students and senior citizens $2.50. Open weekdays 9–5, Sat. 10–4.*

From the museum, turn right onto Harbour Drive for a leisurely stroll along the waterfront. The circular gazebo is where visitors from the cruise ships disembark. Diagonally across the street is the **Elmslie Memorial United Church,** named after Scotsman James Elmslie, the first Presbyterian missionary to serve in the Caymans. The church was the first concrete block building built in the Cayman Islands. Its vaulted ceiling, with wood arches and sedate nave, reflect the quietly religious nature of island residents.

Continue north on Harbour Drive (which becomes North Church Street) past the **War Memorial** erected in memory of the Caymanian Royal Navy volunteers who died in defense of Great Britain during World Wars I and II. Next you come to **Fort George Park,** established to preserve the stone wall remnants of the circa-1790 fort, reputedly one of the smallest ever built in the Caribbean.

Backtrack and turn left onto **Fort Street,** a main shopping street where you'll find the People's Boutique, the Kennedy Gallery, and a whole row of jewelry shops featuring black coral, gold and silver, gemstones, and treasure coins—Peter Davey, Bernard Passman, Smith's, Savoy Jewellers, and the Jewellery Centre.

At the end of the block is the heart of downtown George Town. At the corner of Fort Street and **Edward Street,** notice the small clock tower dedicated to Britain's King George V and the huge fig tree manicured into an umbrella shape. Here too is a new statue (unveiled in 1994) of national hero James Bodden, the father of Cayman tourism. Across the street is the **Cayman Islands Legislative Assembly Building** next door to the 1919 **Peace Memorial Building.**

Turning right on Edward Street, you'll find the charming **library,** built in 1939; it has English novels, current newspapers from the United States, and a small reference section. It's worth a visit just for the Old World atmosphere and a look at the shields depicting Britain's prominent institutions of learning that decorate the ceiling beams. Across the street is the **courthouse.** Down the next block enter the "financial district," where banks from all over the world have offices.

Straight ahead is the **General Post Office,** also built in 1939, with its strands of decorative colored lights and some 2,000 private mailboxes on the outside. (Mail is not delivered on the island.) Behind the post office is **Elizabethan Square,** a shopping and office complex on Shedden Road that houses various food, clothing, and souvenir establishments. The courtyard, with benches around a pleasant garden and fountain, is a good place to rest your feet.

Leave Elizabethan Square via Shedden Road, walking past Anderson Square and Caymania Freeport. Turn right back onto Edward Street, then left at the Royal Bank of Canada onto **Cardinal Avenue.** This is the main shopping area. On the right is the chic Kirk Freeport Plaza, known for its duty-free luxury items. Turn left on **Harbour Drive** and make your way back to Shedden Road, passing the English Shoppe, a souvenir outlet that looks more as if it belongs on Shaftesbury Avenue in London than in the West Indies, and Artifacts, with its maritime antiques.

2 The **Cayman Maritime Treasure Museum,** a quick taxi ride away on West Bay Road, in front of the Hyatt Regency, is a real find. Dioramas show how Caymanians became seafarers, boat builders, and turtle breeders. An animated figure of Blackbeard the Pirate spins salty tales about the pirates and buccaneers who "worked" the Caribbean. Since the museum is owned by a professional treasure-salvaging firm, it's not surprising that there are a lot of artifacts from shipwrecks. *West Bay Rd., tel. 809/947–5033. Admission: $5 adults, $3 children 6–12. Open Mon.–Sat. 9–5.*

The Outer Districts

To see the rest of the island, rent a car or scooter, or take a guided tour (*see above*). A full-day guided tour (sufficient to see the major sights) is comparable in cost to a single day of car rental and lunch. The flat road that circles the island is in good condition, with clear signs; you'd have to work to get lost here. Venturing away from the Seven Mile Beach strip, you'll encounter the more down-home character of the islands.

At the northwest end of the island is the **West Bay** community, home to numerous gingerbread-trimmed homes of historic interest (a walking tour brochure is available from the tourist office). One such
3 home is the **Old Homestead,** formerly known as the West Bay Pink House, and probably the most photographed home in Grand Cayman. This picturesque pink-and-white Caymanian cottage was built in 1912 of wattle and daub around an ironwood frame, and tours, led by cheery Mac Bothwell who grew up in the house, present a nostalgic and touching look at life in Grand Cayman before the tourism and banking boom. *West Bay Rd., tel. 809/949-7639. Admission: $5. Open Mon.–Sat. 8–5.*

4 The **Cayman Island Turtle Farm,** started in West Bay in 1968, is the most popular attraction on the island today, with some 200,000 visitors a year. There are turtles of all ages, from ping-pong-ball-size eggs to day-old hatchlings to huge 600-pounders that can live to be 100 years old. The Turtle Farm was set up both as a conservation and a commercial enterprise; it releases about 5% of its stock back out to sea every year, harvests turtles for local restaurants, and exports the by-products. (Note: U.S. citizens cannot take home any turtle products because of a U.S. regulation banning their import.) In the adjoining café, you can sample turtle soup or turtle sandwiches while looking over an exhibit about turtles. *West Bay Rd., tel. 809/949–3893. Admission: $5 adults, $2.50 children 6–12. Open daily 8:30–5.*

The other area of West Bay that is of brief interest is the tiny village
5 of **Hell,** which is little more than a patch of incredibly jagged rock

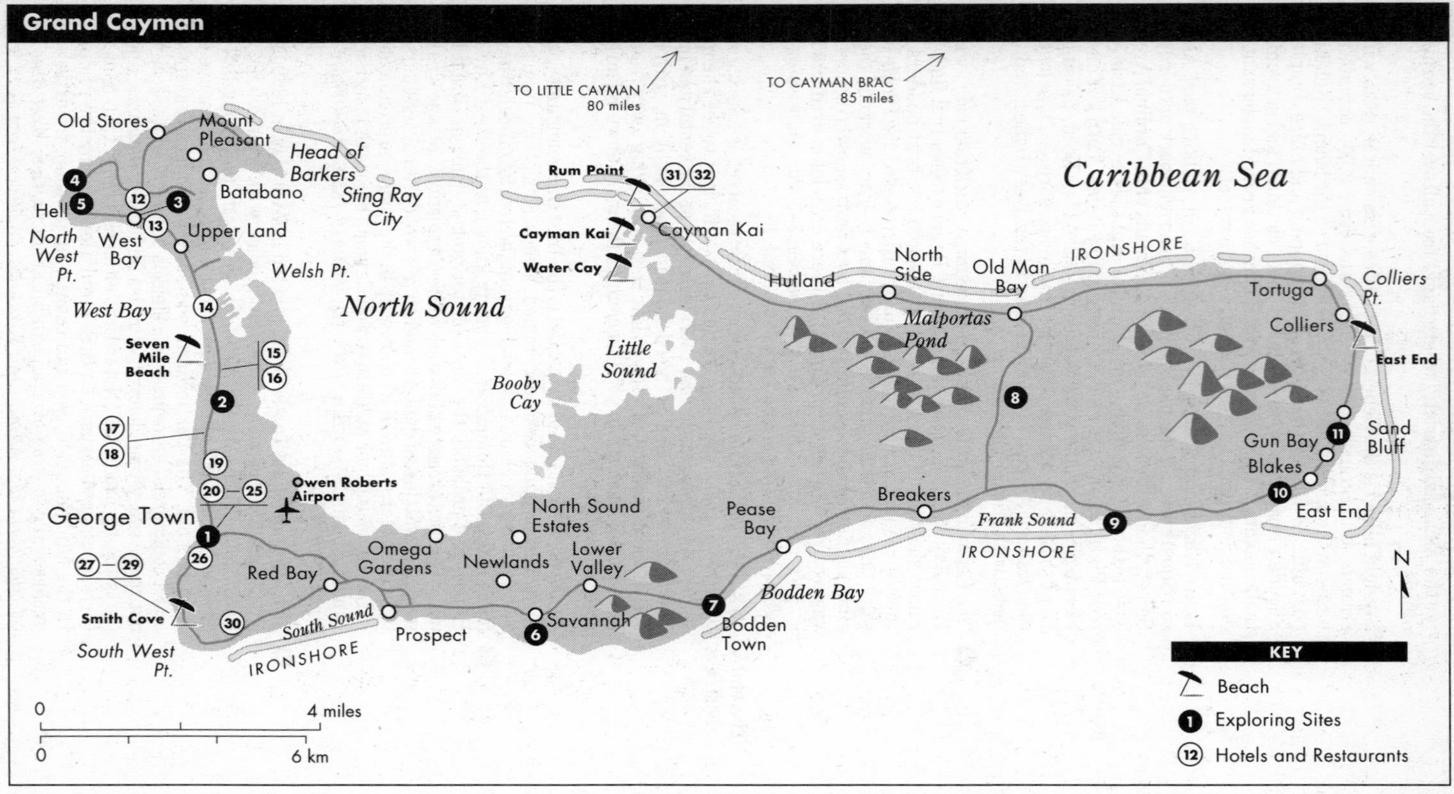
Grand Cayman
TO LITTLE CAYMAN 80 miles
TO CAYMAN BRAC 85 miles
Caribbean Sea
Old Stores
Mount Pleasant
Head of Barkers
Batabano
Sting Ray City
Hell
North West Pt.
West Bay
Upper Land
Welsh Pt.
West Bay
North Sound
Seven Mile Beach
Rum Point
Cayman Kai
Water Cay
Cayman Kai
Little Sound
Booby Cay
Hutland
North Side
Old Man Bay
IRONSHORE
Malportas Pond
Tortuga
Colliers Pt.
Colliers
East End
Sand Bluff
Gun Bay
Blakes
East End
Owen Roberts Airport
George Town
North Sound Estates
Omega Gardens
Newlands
Lower Valley
Pease Bay
Breakers
Frank Sound
IRONSHORE
Red Bay
Smith Cove
South West Pt.
South Sound
IRONSHORE
Prospect
Savannah
Bodden Bay
Bodden Town
0 4 miles
0 6 km
N
KEY
Beach
Exploring Sites
Hotels and Restaurants

Cayman Brac and Little Cayman

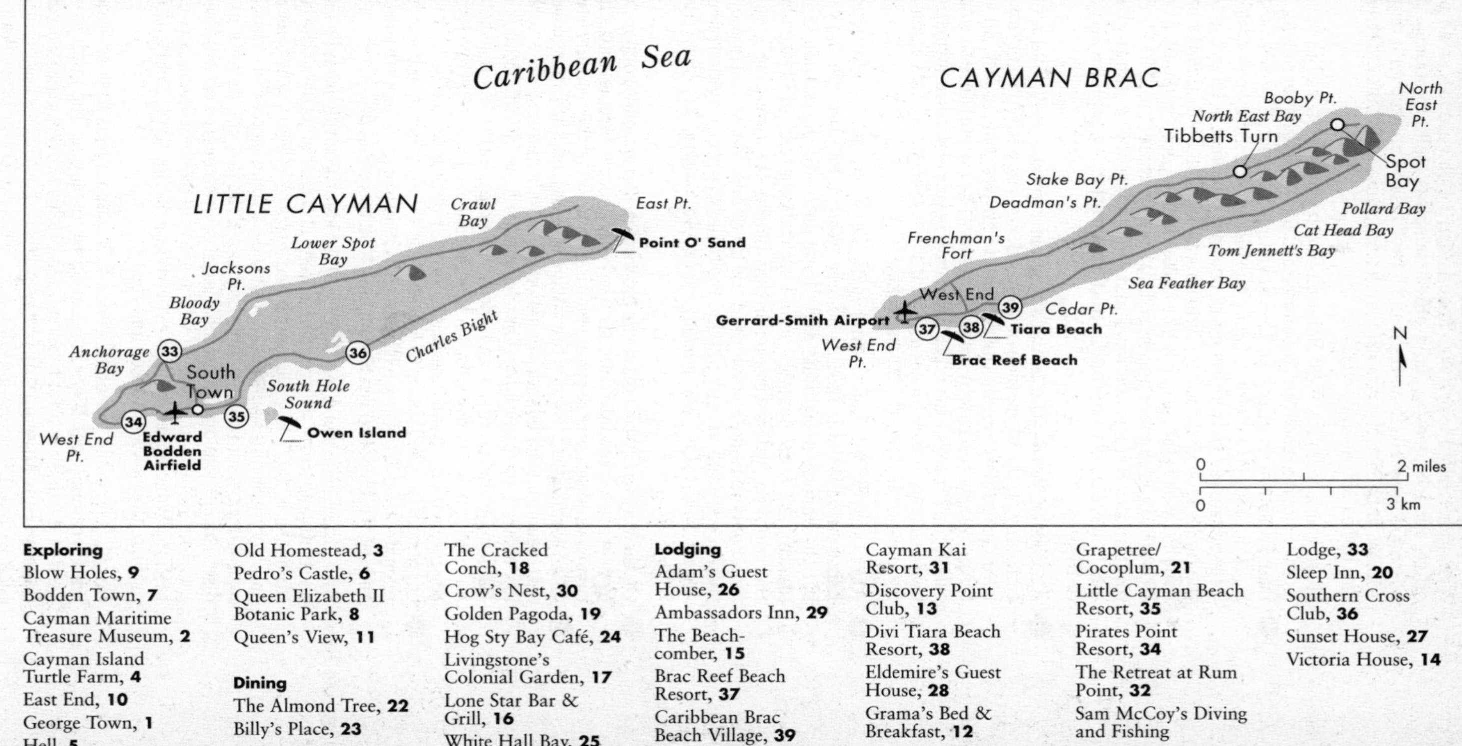

Exploring
Blow Holes, **9**
Bodden Town, **7**
Cayman Maritime Treasure Museum, **2**
Cayman Island Turtle Farm, **4**
East End, **10**
George Town, **1**
Hell, **5**
Old Homestead, **3**
Pedro's Castle, **6**
Queen Elizabeth II Botanic Park, **8**
Queen's View, **11**

Dining
The Almond Tree, **22**
Billy's Place, **23**
The Cracked Conch, **18**
Crow's Nest, **30**
Golden Pagoda, **19**
Hog Sty Bay Café, **24**
Livingstone's Colonial Garden, **17**
Lone Star Bar & Grill, **16**
White Hall Bay, **25**

Lodging
Adam's Guest House, **26**
Ambassadors Inn, **29**
The Beach-comber, **15**
Brac Reef Beach Resort, **37**
Caribbean Brac Beach Village, **39**
Cayman Kai Resort, **31**
Discovery Point Club, **13**
Divi Tiara Beach Resort, **38**
Eldemire's Guest House, **28**
Grama's Bed & Breakfast, **12**
Grapetree/ Cocoplum, **21**
Little Cayman Beach Resort, **35**
Pirates Point Resort, **34**
The Retreat at Rum Point, **32**
Sam McCoy's Diving and Fishing Lodge, **33**
Sleep Inn, **20**
Southern Cross Club, **36**
Sunset House, **27**
Victoria House, **14**

formations called iron hore. The big attraction here is a small post office, which does a land-office business selling stamps and postmarking cards from Hell, and lots of T-shirt and souvenir shops. Almost unbelievably, a nearby nightclub, called the Club Inferno, is run by the McDoom family.

Head south to South West Point on South Church St. and then east
as the road becomes South Sound Road for a straight shot along the
6 island's southern edge. In the Savannah district, **Pedro's Castle,**
built in 1780, lays claim to being the oldest structure on the island. Legends linked to this structure abound, but what is known is that the building was struck by lightning in 1877 and left in ruins until bought by a restaurateur in the 1960s. Gutted once again by fire in 1970, the building was purchased by the government in 1991 for restoration as a historic landmark and remains cordoned off by a chain-link fence, closed to the public until restoration is complete (perhaps in 1996).

7 At **Bodden Town**—the island's original capital—you'll find an old cemetery on the shore side of the road. Graves with A-frame structures are said to contain the remains of pirates, but, in fact, may be those of early settlers. A curio shop serves as the entrance to what's called the **Pirate's Caves,** partially underground natural formations that are more hokey (decked out with fake treasure chests and mannequins in pirate garb) than spooky.

8 At Frank Sound Road, turn left (north) to get to the **Queen Elizabeth II Botanic Park,** a 60-acre wilderness preserve showcasing the variety of habitats and plants native to the islands. Signs identify the flora along the mile-long walking trail. Halfway along the trail is a walled compound that houses the rare blue iguana, found only in remote sections of the Caymans. You will also see native orchids, and, if you're lucky, the brilliant green Cayman parrot. *Frank Sound Rd., tel. 809/947–9462. Admission: $3. Open daily 7:30–5:30.*

9 On the way to East End are the **blow holes,** a great photo opportunity as waves crash into the fossilized coral beach, forcing water into
caverns and sending geysers shooting up through the ironshore (cal-
10 cified coral ledge). Next is the village of **East End,** the first recorded
settlement on the island. Its major claim to fame these days is that
it's where a renowned local musician called the "Fiddle Man," aka
Radley Gourzong, lives and occasionally performs his distinctive
form of music (more akin to Louisiana's backwater zydeco than
reggae) with his band, the Happy Boys. Further on, as the highway
11 curves north, you'll come to **Queen's View** lookout point and a monument dedicated by Queen Elizabeth in 1994 to commemorate the legendary **Wreck of the Ten Sails** which took place just off shore.

Cayman Brac

Brac, the Gaelic word for "bluff," aptly identifies this island's most distinctive feature, a rugged limestone cliff that runs down the center of the island's 12-mile length and soars to 140 feet at its eastern end. Lying 89 miles northeast of Grand Cayman, accessible via Cayman Airways and Island Air, Cayman Brac is a spelunker's paradise: You can explore the island's large **caves** (namely Peter's, Great, Bat, and Rebeka's), some of which are still used for hurricane protection. Wear sneakers for exploring, not flip-flops; some of the paths to the caves are steep and rocky.

Only 1,200 people live on this island, in communities such as Watering Place and Spot Bay. In addition to displaying the implements used in the daily lives of Bracers in the 1920s and '30s, the two-room **Cayman Brac Museum** (tel. 809/948–2622) showcases a few oddities, such as a 4,000-year-old Viking ax. The variety of Brac flora includes unusual orchids, mangoes, papaya, agave, and cacti. The endangered Cayman Brac parrot is most easily spotted in the **Parrot Preserve** on Major Donald Drive (also known as Lighthouse Rd.);

this 6-mile dirt road also leads to a beacon light on ironshore cliffs that offer the best panoramic view of North East Point and the open ocean. Parts of the island are unpopulated, so you can explore truly isolated areas both inland and along the shore. Two hotels that cater to divers and a rental condo complex are located on the southwest coast. Swimming is possible, but unlike Seven Mile Beach, the bottom is rocky and clogged with turtle grass.

Little Cayman Only 7 miles away from Cayman Brac is Little Cayman Island, which has a population of about 50 (only 20 or so full-timers) on its 12 square miles. This is a true hideaway: few phones, fewer shops, no nightlife—just spectacular diving, great fishing, and laid-back camaraderie. Visitor accommodations are mostly in small lodges. In addition to privacy, the real attractions of Little Cayman are diving in spectacular **Bloody Bay,** off the north coast, and fishing, which includes angling for tarpon and bonefish. Birders will enjoy the **Governor Gore Bird Sanctuary,** established in 1994 and home to 5,000 pairs of red-footed boobies (the largest colony in the Western Hemisphere) and 1,000 magnificent frigate birds.

And if Little Cayman ever gets too busy, there is one final retreat—**Owen Island,** which is just 200 yards offshore. Accessible by rowboat, it is in the middle of a blue lagoon and has a sandy beach. Take your own picnic if you plan to spend the day.

Beaches

Grand Cayman You may read or hear about the "dozens of beaches" of these islands, but that's more exaggeration than reality. Grand Cayman's west coast, the most developed area of the entire colony, is where you'll find its famous **Seven Mile Beach** (actually 5½ miles long) and its expanses of powdery white sand. The beach is litter-free and sans peddlers, so you can relax in an unspoiled, hassle-free (if somewhat crowded) atmosphere. This is also Grand Cayman's busiest vacation center, and most of the island's accommodations, restaurants, and shopping centers are on this strip. You'll find headquarters for the island's aquatic activities in various places along the strip (*see* Sports and the Outdoors, *below*).

Smith Cove, off South Church Street in George Town, south of the Grand Old House, is a popular bathing spot with residents on weekends.

The best shore-entry snorkeling locations are off the ironshore south of George Town at **Eden Rock** (tel. 809/949–7243) and **Parrot's Landing** (tel. 809/949–7884); north of town, at the reef just off the **West Bay Cemetery** on Grand Cayman's west coast; and in the reef-protected shallows of the island's north and south coasts, where coral and fish life are much more varied and abundant.

Other good beaches include **East End,** at Colliers, by Morritt's Tortuga Club, which can be lovely when free of the seaweed tossed ashore by trade winds. Seldom discovered by visitors unless they're staying there are the beautiful beach areas of **Cayman Kai** (which was undergoing some development at press time), **Rum Point,** and, even more isolated and unspoiled, **Water Cay.** These are favored hideaways for residents and popular Sunday picnic spots.

Cayman Brac The resorts and rental condos on the **southwest coast** have fine small beaches, better for sunning than for snorkeling because of the abundance of turtle grass in the water. Excellent snorkeling can be found immediately offshore of the now-defunct **Buccaneer's Inn** on the north coast.

Little Cayman The beaches of **Point o' Sand,** on the eastern tip, and **Owen Island,** off the south coast, are exquisite, isolated patches of powder that are great for sunbathing and worth a minisplurge to reach by car, bike, or boat.

Sports and the Outdoors

Diving and Snorkeling To say the Cayman Islands are a scuba diver's paradise is not overstating the case. Jacques Cousteau called Bloody Bay (off Little Cayman) one of the world's top dives, and the famed Cayman Wall, off Grand Cayman, ranks up there as well. Pristine water (often exceeding 100-foot visibility), breathtaking coral formations, and plentiful and exotic marine life await divers. Snorkeling here is also wonderful, with countless shallow, offshore reefs. A must-see here is **Stingray City,** which has been called the best 12-foot dive (or snorkel) in the world. Here dozens of stingrays, which have become tame from being fed first by fishermen and now by divers, suction squid off divers' outstretched palms and gracefully swim and twist around the divers in the shallow waters.

Divers are required to be certified and possess a "C" card or take a short resort or full certification course. A certification course, including classroom, pool, and boat sessions as well as checkout dives, takes four to six days and costs \$350–\$400. A short resort course usually lasts a day and costs about \$80–\$100. It introduces the novice to the sport and teaches the rudimentary skills needed to make a shallow, instructor-monitored dive.

All dive operations on Cayman are more than competent; among them are **Aquanauts** (tel. 809/945–1990 or 800/357–2212), **Bob Soto's** (tel. 809/947-4631 or 800/262–7686), **Don Foster's** (tel. 809/949–5679 or 800/833–4837), **Eden Rock** (tel. 809/949–7243), **Parrot's Landing** (tel. 809/949–7884 or 800/448–0428), **Red Sail Sports** (tel. 809/949–8745 or 800/ 255–6425), and **Sunset Divers** (tel. 809/949–7111 or 800/854–4767). Request full information on all operators from the Department of Tourism (*see* Before You Go, *above*). A single-tank dive averages \$45; a two-tank dive about \$55. Snorkel equipment rental runs from \$5 to \$15 a day, so consider purchasing your own before you come.

On Cayman Brac, **Brac Aquatics** (tel. 809/949–1429 or 800/544–2722) and **Divi Tiara** (tel. 809/948–1553) offer scuba and snorkeling. On Little Cayman, contact **Paradise Divers** (tel. 809/948–0004 or 800/450–2084), **Reef Divers** (tel. 809/948–1033), **Sam McCoy's Fishing & Diving** (tel. 809/949–2891 or 800/626–0496), or the **Southern Cross Club** (tel. 800/899–2582). Each hotel also has its own instructors.

Golf The **Grand Cayman–Britannia** golf course (tel. 809/949–8020), next to the Hyatt Regency, was designed by Jack Nicklaus. The course is really three in one—a nine-hole par 70 regulation course, an 18-hole par 57 executive course, and a Cayman course (played with a Cayman ball that goes about half the distance of a regulation ball). Greens fees range from \$40 to \$80. Golf carts (\$15–\$25) are mandatory.

Windier, and therefore more challenging, is **The Links at Safe Haven** (tel. 809/949-5988), Cayman's first 18-hole championship golf course. The Roy Case–designed par 71, 6,519-yard course also features an aqua driving range (the distance markers and balls float), a two-story clubhouse, locker rooms, a pro shop, a patio bar with live jazz happy hours on weekends, and a fine restaurant serving Continental and Caribbean cuisine daily for lunch and dinner. Greens fees run to \$60. Golf carts (\$15–\$20 per person) are mandatory.

Water Sports Water skis, Windsurfers, Hobie Cats, and jet skis are available at many of the aquatic shops along Seven Mile Beach (*see* Diving, *above*).

Shopping

Grand Cayman has two money-saving attributes—duty-free merchandise and the absence of a sales tax. Prices on imported merchandise—English china, Swiss watches, French perfumes, and Japanese cameras and electronic goods—are often lower than elsewhere, but not always. To make sure you get a bargain, come prepared with a price list of items you are thinking of buying and comparison shop. Unusual jewelry can also be found, ranging from authentic sunken treasure and ancient coins made into necklaces and pins to relatively inexpensive rings and earrings made from semiprecious stones, coral, and seashells. **Tortuga Rum Company's** (tel. 809/949–7701 or 949–7866/7) scrumptious rum cake makes a great souvenir.

Good Buys
Arts and Crafts

Debbie van der Bol runs an arts-and-crafts shop called **Pure Art** (tel. 809/949–9133) on South Church Street and at the Hyatt Regency (tel. 809/947–5633). She sells watercolors, wood carvings, and lacework by local artists, as well as her own sketches and cards. Original prints, paintings, and sculpture with a tropical theme are found at **Island Art Gallery** (tel. 809/949–9861) in the Anchorage Shopping Center in George Town. The **Kennedy Gallery** (tel. 809/949–8077) in West Shore Center and on Fort Street in George Town, features primarily limited-edition pastel watercolors of typical Cayman scenes by Robert E. Kennedy.

The **Heritage Crafts Shop** (tel. 809/949–7093), near the harbor in George Town, sells local crafts and gifts. The **West Shore Shopping Center,** on Seven Mile Beach near the Radisson, offers good-quality island art, beachwear, ice cream, and more. The **Queen's Court Shopping Center,** on Seven Mile Beach close to town, was just opening at press time and promises to offer an array of souvenirs, crafts, and gifts.

Black Coral

Black coral products are exquisite and a popular choice. However, environmental groups discourage tourists from purchasing any coral that is designated as endangered species, because the reefs are not always harvested carefully. If you feel differently, there are a number of local craftsmen who create original designs and finish their own work. The coral creations of **Bernard Passman** (Fort St., George Town, tel. 809/949–0123) won the approval of the English royal family. Beautiful coral pieces are also found at **Richard's Fine Jewelry** (Harbour Dr., George Town, tel. 809/949–7156), where designers Richard and Rafaela Barile attract their fair share of celebrities.

Dining

Among Caribbean destinations, the Caymans are second only to the French islands for fine gourmet dining and prices to match. West Indian fare in local restaurants offers the best value. The following tips will cut costs.

You can skip lunch if you eat enough breakfast at the huge all-you-can-eat buffet at the **Holiday Inn Grand Cayman** (tel. 809/947–4444); cost is about $10. The **Wholesome Bakery** (tel. 809/949–7588), on the waterfront in George Town, offers full bacon-and-egg or waffle breakfasts for about $5. Enjoy fine dining and save almost 50% over dinner prices when you lunch at **Hemingway's** (tel. 809/949–1234), **Lantana's** (tel. 809/947–5595), and other fine restaurants. (Be sure to reserve.) Try **Champion House** (tel. 809/949–7882) on Eastern Avenue for large takeout portions of local dishes such as spicy beef stew, conch, breadfruit salad, cassava, and yams. A huge plateful ($6–$8) can be refrigerated for dinner.

Happy hours in West Bay Road hotels and restaurants offer discounted drinks and free hors d'oeuvres some weeknights (call ahead to check) between 5 and 7 or 8; graze enough, and you've replaced dinner. Try the **Cracked Conch** (tel. 809/947–5217) Tuesday through Friday evenings, **Sunset House** (tel. 809/949–7111) on Thursday, and **Clarion Grand Pavilion** (tel. 809/947–5656) and **Indies Suites** (tel. 809/947–5025) on varying weeknights. Other weekly all-you-can-eat feeds of fajitas, seafood, or fish are listed in Friday's *Caymanian Compass*, available everywhere.

For the occasional quick, cheap meal, there are always the fast-food joints: On Seven Mile Beach you'll find Burger King, Pizza Hut, Subway, KFC, Domino's, TCBY Yogurt, and Wendy's. The latter offers an all-you-can-eat salad bar, including pastas and Mexican food, for about $8.

Although Grand Cayman's supermarkets are somewhat more expensive than those in the United States, some now offer salad bars and deli takeout salads for around $4 a pound—perfect for picnics or eating in. Try **Kirk's, Foster's Food Fair,** and **Hurley's,** all along Seven Mile Beach. Note that supermarket munchies such as potato chips and nachos cost about triple what they do stateside.

Many restaurants automatically add a gratuity to your bill. If you're not sure, just ask; otherwise, you'll be tipping twice. Highly recommended restaurants are indicated by a star ★.

Category	Cost*
$$	$20–$30
$	$10–$20
¢	under $10

**per person, excluding drinks and service*

$$ ★ **Crow's Nest.** With the ocean right in its backyard, this secluded seafood restaurant, located about a 15-minute drive south of George Town, is a great spot for snorkeling as well as lunching. The shark du jour, herb-crusted dolphinfish with lobster sauce, and shrimp and conch dishes are excellent, as is the chocolate fudge rum cake. *South Sound Rd., tel. 809/949–9366. Reservations advised. AE, MC, V. No lunch Sun.*

$$ **Golden Pagoda.** The well-known Chinese restaurant in the Caymans features Hakka-style cooking. Among its specialties are Moo goo gai pan, butterfly shrimp, and chicken in black-bean sauce. Take-out (takie-outie, they call it) is available, and they now offer showy Japanese teppanyaki dinners (minimum two persons) Tuesday through Saturday night. *West Bay Rd., tel. 809/949–5475. Reservations required for Japanese dinner. AE, MC, V. No lunch weekends.*

$$ **Livingstone's Colonial Gardens.** From the vine- and palm-shrouded terrace and jungle-motif dining room to waiters in safari shorts and pith helmets, the theme here is Colonial Africa. The menu features jungle greens (salads), Congo-tizers (appetizers), missionary's hot pot (soups), and an English carving board. Vegetarians will appreciate the assortment of suitable dishes here. *West Bay Rd., near the Clarion Grand Pavilion, tel. 809/947–5181. Reservations accepted. AE, MC, V.*

$$ **White Hall Bay.** Formerly the Cook Rum, the White Hall Bay has moved across the street to a restored waterfront Caymanian house, but it hasn't lost any of its casual ambience and charm. The hearty West Indian menu includes turtle and conch stews, salt beef and beans, crab backs, and pepper-pot stew. Follow up with dessert specials, such as cook rum cake and coconut cream pie. *N. Church St., tel. 809/949–8670. AE, D, MC, V.*

$–$$ ★ **The Cracked Conch.** Specialties of this popular, often crowded seafood restaurant, the originator of cracked (tenderized and panfried) conch, include conch fritters, conch chowder, spicy Cayman-style snapper, turtle steak, and other seafood offerings. The key lime pie is divine. Locals flock here on weekdays for the low-priced lunch buffet—hot entrée, soup, and salad for C.I. $6.50. The bar, a prime local hangout, has karaoke, dive videos, and great happy hour specials. *West Bay Rd. near the Hyatt, tel. 809/947–5217. MC, V.*

$ **The Almond Tree.** Looking for authentic island atmosphere in modern Grand Cayman? This eatery combines architecture from the South Seas isle of Yap with bones, skulls, and bric-a-brac from Africa, South America, and the Pacific. Sample good-value seafood entrées, including turtle steak and fresh grouper, with all-you-can-eat entrées for C.I. $11 on Wednesday and Friday. *N. Church St., tel. 809/949–2893. Dinner reservations advised. AE, MC, V. Closed Sun.*

$ ★ **Hog Sty Bay Café.** Lots of socializing goes on in the casual atmosphere of this English-style café on the harbor in George Town. A simple menu of sandwiches, hamburgers, and Caribbean dishes will satisfy you for lunch and dinner. Many believe the conch fritters served here are the best in town. Come and watch the sun set from the seaside patio or for the weekday happy hour. *N. Church St., tel. 809/949–6163. AE, MC, V.*

¢–$ **Billy's Place.** Who comes to the Caribbean without trying jerk food? Billy's, the yellow and blue diner in the Kirk Super Market parking lot, is the place to do it in Grand Cayman. In addition to hearty servings of jerk chicken, pork, goat, shrimp, conch, fish, lobster, and burgers, you can order Indian *pakoras* (vegetable fritters), tandoori chicken or shrimp, and several curried selections. Service tends to be abrupt, but the crowds don't seem to mind. *N. Church St., tel. 809/949–0470. AE, D, MC, V. Closed Sun.*

¢–$ **Lone Star Bar & Grill.** This very casual sports bar offers indoor and outdoor seating at tables covered with red-and-white checkered cloths. The menu is mostly Tex-Mex, with most dishes under $10. The bar is open daily until 1 AM. *Seven Mile Beach, tel. 809/947–5175. AE, MC, V.*

Lodging

Although it takes work to make the Caymans an affordable destination, the wide range of accommodations on Grand Cayman gives you a head start. You'll get a better rate at most properties if you book for a stay of a week or more. Money-saving packages (everything from honeymoon trips to air/hotel deals) are offered through hotels and through **TourScan, Inc.** (tel. 800/962–2080 or 203/655–8091) and **Cayman Airtours** (tel. 800/247–2966).

Most of the hotels on Grand Cayman are on or very near Seven Mile Beach. Those that aren't either have their own beach—sometimes rocky coral, sometimes sand—or have a beach nearby (within a 10-minute walk). All hotels on Cayman Brac and Little Cayman are on the beach. More than half of the Caymans' rooms are in condominiums rather than hotels, with daily rates ranging from $215 all the way to $565 during high season. Traveling with another couple brings the cost well into our $$ price range and below. Most properties offer accommodations with kitchens. Shopping the well-stocked supermarkets and cooking your own meals further cuts costs.

Most of the larger hotels along Seven Mile Beach don't offer meal plans. The smaller properties that are more remote from the restaurants usually offer MAP or FAP. **Cayman Islands Reservation Service:** 800/327–8777.

Highly recommended lodgings are indicated by a star ★.

Category	Cost*
$$	$160–$200
$	$110–$160
¢	under $110

**All prices are for a standard double room for two, excluding 6% tax and a 10% service charge. To estimate rates for hotels offering MAP/FAP, add about $40 per person per day to the above price ranges.*

Grand Cayman *Hotels*

★ **Sleep Inn.** This two-story Choice Hotels affiliate is a stroll from Seven Mile Beach, close to the airport and just a mile from George Town's shops. Air-conditioned rooms are motel-modern, with peaches-and-cream pastels and modern wood furnishings. The Dive Inn dive shop is here, as are tours and car and motorcycle rentals. *Box 30111, Grand Cayman, tel. 809/949–9111, fax 809/949–6699. 124 rooms. Facilities: pool, whirlpool, poolside bar and grill, water-sports shop, boutique. AE, D, MC, V. EP. $–$$*

Sunset House. Low-key and laid-back describe this resort with sparse, motel-style rooms on the ironshore south of George Town, 4 miles from Seven Mile Beach. A congenial staff, popular bar, and seafood restaurant are pluses, but it's the diving that attracts most guests. Full dive services include free waterside lockers, two- and three-tank dives at the better reefs around the island, and Cathy Church's U/W Photo Center. There are also excellent dive packages. It's a five-minute walk to a sandy beach, 10 minutes to George Town. *Box 479, S. Church St., Grand Cayman, tel. 809/949–7111 or 800/854–4767, fax 809/949–7101. 59 rooms. Facilities: restaurant, bar, dive shop and underwater photo center, fresh and seawater pools, whirlpool. AE, D, DC, MC, V. EP, BP, MAP. $–$$*

Cayman Kai Resort. Nestled next to a coconut grove, each sea lodge has a full kitchen, dining and living areas, and a screened-in porch overlooking the ocean. The hotel is on a beach at the north-central tip of the island—quite remote. You need a car to get anywhere, but many guests are content to stay put and dive. Not all of the rooms have air-conditioning, so be sure to request it if it's important to you. *Box 201, North Side, tel. 809/947–9055 or 800/223–5427, fax 809/947–9102. 17 suites. Facilities: restaurant, 2 bars. AE, MC, V. EP. $*

Ambassadors Inn. This peach-pink, motel-like property is just across the road from the ironshore, a mile south of town on the southwest tip of the island. A large patio with open-air and indoor dining (breakfast and lunch) faces the swimming pool; the area is shaded by a gigantic sea-grape tree. The talking green parrot says "hello" as you return from your computer-assisted daily dive trip (maximum 12 divers). Simple, smallish rooms have private baths (shower only), pink and green flowered bedspreads, and scuffed furniture, but if you can live with the semi-rustic nature of the place, Ambassador's Inn is a great bargain. Gung-ho divers return repeatedly for the great diving, the casual atmosphere, and the camaraderie. *Box 1789, Grand Cayman, tel. 809/949–7577 or 800/648–7748, fax 809/949–7050. 18 rooms. Facilities: restaurant, bar, pool, dive facilities. AE, MC, V. EP. ¢*

Condominiums and Villas

The **Cayman Islands Department of Tourism** (6100 Blue Lagoon Dr., Suite 150, Miami, FL 33126, tel. 305/266–3200) provides a complete list of condominiums and small rental apartments in the $$ range. Many of these are multibedroom units that become affordable when shared by two or more couples. Rates are higher during the winter season, and there may be a three- or seven-night minimum, so check before you book. The following complexes bear a marked similarity to one another. All are equipped with fully stocked kitchens, telephones, satellite television, air-conditioning, living and dining areas, and patios, and are individually decorated (most following a pastel tropical scheme). Differences arise in property amenities and proximity to town. All are well-maintained and directly on the beach, though you will need a car for grocery shopping. **Cayman Islands Reservation Service** (6100 Blue Lagoon Dr., Suite 150, Miami, FL 33126, tel.800/327–8777), **Cayman Villas** (Box 681, Grand Cayman, tel. 809/947–4144 or 800/235–5888, fax 809/949–7471), and **Hospitality World Ltd.** (Box 30123, Grand Cayman, tel. 809/949–8098 or 800/232–1034, fax 809/949–7054) can also make reservations.

The Beachcomber. Set in the middle of Seven Mile Beach, each of the simply furnished apartments in this older condo community has a view of the ocean from a private, screened patio. There is a grocery store just across the street and countless shopping and dining outlets within walking distance, so once you're here, you don't really need a car. The Beachcomber reef is just offshore for snorkeling, and palapas on the beach provide shade when the sun gets a bit too warm. *Box 1799, Seven Mile Beach, Grand Cayman, tel. 809/947–4470, fax 809/947–5019. 23 units. Facilities: pool, beach huts, outdoor grills, laundry facilities. AE, MC, V. $$*

Discovery Point Club. At the quiet, far north end of Seven Mile Beach in West Bay, this complex offers the same lovely beach with more peace and seclusion and is within walking distance of great snorkeling in the protected waters of Cemetery Reef. You'll need a car to pick up groceries or see the sights in George Town (6 miles away). The individually decorated, fully furnished one- and two-bedroom apartments have all the amenities, and outside are tennis courts, a hot tub, and a pool for relaxation. Kids 12 and under are free during the off season (Apr.–Dec.). *Box 439, West Bay, Grand Cayman, tel. 809/947–4724, fax 809/947–5051. 45 units. Facilities: pool, hot tub, 2 tennis courts, outdoor grills, laundry facilities. AE, MC, V. $$*

Grapetree/Cocoplum. A half-mile from George Town on Seven Mile Beach, these sister condo units are adjacent to one another. Grapetree's two-bedroom, two-bath units are carpeted, with traditional wicker furnishings and beige and brown decor. Cocoplum's units are similar, with Caribbean pastel prints; its grounds have more plants and trees. The two share two pools and tennis courts. *Box 1802, Seven Mile Beach, Grand Cayman, tel. 809/949–5640 or 800/635–4824, fax 809/949–0150. 51 units. Facilities: 2 pools, 2 tennis courts, outdoor grills. AE, MC, V. $$*

The Retreat at Rum Point. It has its own narrow beach with casuarina trees, far from the madding crowd, on the north central tip of Grand Cayman, 27 miles from town. Up to six people can rent a two-bedroom villa here. Two or three people are comfortable in the one-bedroom units. Spacious rooms have blue-lavender upholstered furniture. There are dive facilities nearby, where you can take advantage of the superb offshore diving, including the famed North Wall. You'll be stranded without a car; it's a 35-minute drive to George Town or the airport. *Box 46, North Side, Grand Cayman, tel. 809/947–9535 or 800/423–2422, fax 809/947–9058. 23 units. Facilities: restaurant, bar, pool, 2 tennis courts, exercise room, sauna, racquetball court, laundry facilities. MC, V. $$*

Victoria House. The one-, two-, and three-bedroom units in this squarish white building have white tile floors and white walls, and are decorated with muted Caribbean prints and rattan furniture. You may choose from a range of activities, including tennis and water sports. The Victoria is 3 miles north of town on a quiet stretch of Seven Mile Beach; if you're an early riser, you may catch a glimpse of giant sea turtles on the sand. *Box 30571, Seven Mile Beach (near West Bay), Grand Cayman, tel. 809/947–4233, fax 809/947–5328. 25 units. Facilities: scuba, snorkeling, tennis court, hammocks, laundry facilities. AE, MC, V. $$*

Guest Houses and B&Bs Away from the beach and short on style and facilities, these nevertheless offer rock-bottom prices (all fall well below our $ category), a friendly atmosphere, and your best shot at getting to know the locals. Rooms are clean and simple, often with cooking facilities, and most have a private bathroom. Many establishments have outdoor grills and picnic tables for guest use. A rental car is recommended. These places do not accept personal checks or credit cards, but do take reservations through the **Cayman Islands Reservation Service:** tel. 800/327–8777.

Adam's Guest House. The rooms and 2-bedroom apartment in this '50s-style ranch house are bright and spotless. Each is air-conditioned, has a small kitchenette with microwave, toaster oven, and minifridge, and has a private entrance. Owners Tom and Olga Adam are well-traveled, warm, and interesting. Their hospitality—along with their dog and exotic birds—make this a real home away from home. The house is a mile south of George Town, so you can easily walk to shops and restaurants. The beach is 4 miles away, but Smith Cove Bay, with its wonderful snorkeling, is just one mile south, and dive facilities are within a 10-minute walk. *Box 312, Melnac Ave. (near the Seaview Hotel), Grand Cayman, tel. 809/949–2512 or tel./fax 809/949–0919. 5 units. Facilities: outdoor grill and picnic tables. No credit cards or personal checks. EP. ¢*

Eldemire's Guest House. Grand Cayman's first guest house is a mile from town and a half-mile from pretty Smith Cove beach. A rambling ranch house, it has large, simple, spotless guest rooms and three studio apartments. All units are decorated in pastel pink and blue and have private baths and ceiling fans, but no TV or phone. You can use the kitchen to cook meals, and each guest gets some fridge space. Eighty-four-year-old owner Erma E. clearly loves her work, which includes dispensing island lore and local recipes for coconut jelly and honey chicken wings. The house has a large screened porch, and the plant-filled yard has a picnic table and barbecue pit. It's a 15-minute drive to Seven Mile Beach. *Box 482, on South Church St., Grand Cayman, tel. 809/949–5387, fax 809/949–6987. 7units. Facilities: outdoor grill and picnic tables. No credit cards or personal checks. EP. ¢*

Grama's Bed & Breakfast. Graham and Madge Ebanks offer simple rooms with air-conditioning and ceiling fans in a remodeled two-story house. There are hot plates in rooms, and an outdoor grill for guest use. Private screened patios overlook a freshwater pool, and the secluded, residential location offers a taste of real Caymanian life. A car is needed to get anywhere other than Seven Mile Beach, a few blocks away. It's 8 miles to town or the airport. *Box 198, Crescent Close off Town Hall Crescent in West Bay, Grand Cayman, tel. 809/949–3798. 5 rooms. Facilities: pool, outdoor grill. No credit cards or personal checks. BP. ¢*

Cayman Brac *Hotels* **Brac Reef Beach Resort.** Designed, built, and owned by Bracer Linton Tibbets, the resort lures divers and vacationers who come to savor the special ambience of this tiny island. The recently (1994) renovated with rooms, with balconies, and the pool, pretty beach, snorkeling, guest bicycles, new dive shop, and two-story covered dock are additional reasons to stay here. The modest all-inclusive package rates include three buffet meals daily, all drinks, airport transfers, and taxes and services charges. *Box 56, Cayman Brac, tel. 809/948–7323, 813/323–8727 in FL or 800/327–3835, fax 809/948–7207. 40 rooms. Facilities: restaurant, bar, pool, hot tub, dive shop, lighted tennis court, bicycles, photo center. AE, D, MC, V. EP, MAP, FAP, all-inclusive. $–$$*

Divi Tiara Beach Resort. This older resort is dedicated to divers. It has an excellent diving facility complemented by the Divi chain's standards: tile floors, rattan furniture, louvered windows, balconies, and ocean views (from most rooms). A shuttle takes guests across the island to a great snorkeling spot. Kids 16 and under stay free in their parents' room. *Box 238, Cayman Brac, tel. 809/948–1553, fax 809/948–7316; in the U.S., 919/419–3484 or 800/801–5550, fax 919/419–2075. 70 rooms. Facilities: restaurant, bar, pool, lighted tennis court, volleyball, dive shop, water-sports center, underwater photo shop, snorkeling, fishing. AE, MC, V. EP, MAP, FAP, all-inclusive. $–$$*

Condominiums and Villas

★ **Caribbean Brac Beach Village.** This small condo complex built in 1992 enjoys the same pretty beach as the other resorts, but for the money you get a two-bedroom, two-and-a-half-bath, fully furnished apartment right on the beach. Kids 11 and under stay free with their parents, making this a family money saver. Beige walls and rattan furniture, white tile floors, and pastel floral prints give the units a bright, airy look. With advance notice, the management company will stock your kitchen with groceries and arrange for dive packages, rental cars, and maid service (each at minimal additional cost). A pool, restaurant, bar, gift shop, and six more condos were scheduled for addition during a 1995 expansion. *Box 4, Stake Bay, Cayman Brac, tel. 809/948–2265 or 800/791–7911, fax 809/948–2206. 16 rooms. Facilities: pier, laundry room. MC, V. EP. $$*

Little Cayman

Hotels

★ **Little Cayman Beach Resort.** This two-story property, on the south side of the island, opened in early 1993. Considerably less rustic than those of other Little Cayman resorts, the air-conditioned, water-view rooms here have modern furnishings in jewel-tone tropical colors. The dining room overlooking the bar area seats 50 for family-style buffet meals. Double hammocks are slung under beach palapas. The resort offers diving and fishing packages and also caters to bird-watchers and soft adventure ecotourists. Paddleboats, sailboats, kayaks, a complete dive operation, tennis, and free bicycles provided for exploring the island keep guests busy. All-inclusive packages are available for both divers and nondivers and include three meals daily, all alcoholic and soft drinks, airport transfers, taxes, and gratuities. *Blossom Village, Little Cayman, tel. 809/948–1033 or 800/327–3835, fax 809/948–1045. 32 rooms. Facilities: restaurant, bar, dive shop, pool, hot tub, tennis court, gift shop, deep-sea fishing charters, bicycles, dive packages available. AE, D, MC, V. EP, MAP, FAP, all-inclusive. $–$$*

★ **Pirates Point Resort.** The guest-house feel of this comfortably informal resort generates almost instant comeraderie among the guests, and many come back year after year. The charming, individually decorated rooms have tiled floors, white rattan and wicker furnishings, ceiling fans, and louvered windows. Owner Gladys Howard, a native Texan, leads nature walks and is a Cordon Bleu chef; her small restaurant is open to nonguests, too. "Relaxing" rates (for nondivers) include the mouthwatering meals and wine; all-inclusive rates include meals, alchoholic beverages, two daily boat dives, fishing, and picnics on uninhabited Owen Island. *Little Cayman, tel. 809/948–1010 or 800/654–7537, fax 809/948–1011. 10 rooms. Facilities: restaurant, bar, bikes, dive operation, fishing, complimentary airport transfers. MC, V. FAP, all-inclusive. $–$$*

Sam McCoy's Diving and Fishing Lodge. Be prepared for an ultracasual experience: This is an ordinary family house with very simple bedrooms and baths. There's no bar or restaurant per se; guests just eat at a few tables outdoors or with Sam and his family in the dining room. Fans like it for its owner's infectious good nature, the superb diving and snorkeling right offshore, and the family atmosphere. "Relaxing" rates (for nondivers) include three meals a day and airport transfers; all-inclusive rates also include beach and boat diving. Sam's son, Chip, is the most experienced local fishing guide on the island; his bonefishing trips are around $20 an hour. *Little Cayman, tel. 809/948–0026 or 800/626–0496, fax 809/948–0026. 6 rooms. Facilities: pool, beach barbecue. No credit cards. FAP, all-inclusive. $–$$*

Southern Cross Club. Diving and fishing (deep-sea, light-tackle, bottom, and bone-fishing) are the draw at this older retreat. The rooms, in cottages spread along a pretty beach, have a simple white-on-white decor with wicker furniture, ceiling fans (no air-conditioning), and painted cement floors. A motorboat makes trips to the beaches of uninhabited Owen Island nearby. Three family-style meals a day are included in the rates. There's been a lot of turn over in staff and management lately, and service is suffering for it. *Little Cayman, tel. 809/948–1099 or 800/899–2582; in the U.S., 317/636–9501, fax 317/636–9503. 10 rooms. Facilities: restaurant, beach bar, bicycles, diving and fishing packages, snorkeling, complimentary airport transfers. No credit cards. FAP. $*

Off-Season Bets **TourScan, Inc.** (tel. 203/655–8091 or 800/962–2080) offers discount packages that include hotel and airfare for 53 properties in the Caymans, from simple to luxury resort, during both high and low seasons. Other plans and packages may be available through individual hotels. Study the "Rates and Facts" brochure from the Tourism Board and call or fax properties directly for complete information.

Nightlife

Each of the island hotspots attracts a different clientele. The **Holiday Inn** (tel. 809/947–4444) offers something for everyone: **Coconuts** (tel. 809/ 947–5757), the hotel's original comedy club, features young American stand-up comedians who entertain year-round every Wednesday through Sunday. Crowds also gather poolside, where the island-famous "Barefoot Man" sings and plays four nights a week. Dancing is spontaneous and welcome, and it's a great spot to people-watch.

Long John Silver's Nightclub (tel. 809/949–7777), at the Treasure Island Resort on Seven Mile Beach, is a spacious, tiered club that is usually filled to capacity when the island's top bands playthere. **Island Rock Nightclub** (Falls Shopping Center, Seven Mile Beach, tel. 809/947–5366), a popular disco and bar with occasional live bands, had been converted to a teen club at press time, but may revert to an adult club during high season; call to check before venturing out. Latest to hit the hotspot list is **Rumheads** (tel. 809/949–7169), featuring nightly drink specials, live entertainment, and theme nights; the youngish crowd can get pretty rowdy, and brawls aren't exactly out of the ordinary here.

Locals and visitors frequent the **Cracked Conch** (West Bay Rd., near the Hyatt, tel. 809/947–5217) for karaoke, classic dive films, and the great happy hour with hors d'oeuvres Tuesday–Friday evenings.

For current entertainment, look at the freebie magazine, *What's Hot*, or check the Friday edition of the *Caymanian Compass* for listings of music, movies, theater, and other entertainment possibilities.

9 Curaçao

Updated by Barbara Hults

Curaçao is an island for explorers. Its charming Dutch capital, underwater park, Seaquarium, floating market, and dozens of little cove beaches give it a taste of everything, and it is apt to please most tastes. Thirty-five miles north of Venezuela and 42 miles east of Aruba, Curaçao is the largest of the islands in the Netherlands Antilles. The sun smiles down on the island, but it's never stiflingly hot: The gentle trade winds are a constant source of refreshment. Water sports attract enthusiasts from all over the world, and some of the best reef diving is here. Though the island claims 38 beaches, it doesn't have long stretches of sand or enchanting scenery. Arid countryside, rocky coves, and a sprawling capital situated around a natural harbor make up the much of the island. Until recently, the economy was based not on tourism but on oil refining and catering to offshore corporations seeking tax hedges. Although tourism has become a major economic force in the past five years or so, with millions of dollars invested in restoring old colonial landmarks and modernizing hotels, Curaçao's atmosphere remains comparatively low-key—offering an appealing alternative to the commercialism found on many other Caribbean islands.

Budget travelers are benefiting from the recent attention to tourism. Many inexpensive resorts, hotels, and apartment units have sprung up. Visitors who put cuisine ahead of ambience will enjoy the many Antillean eateries that serve hearty local dishes at easy-on-the-wallet prices. A number of good Chinese restaurants serve first-class Cantonese food, and there are always the fast-food standbys such as Burger King, McDonald's, KFC, and Pizza Hut. In the evening, many of the bigger resorts have two-for-the-price-of-one happy hours, with live music and free snacks; a night of bingo costs only a few dollars.

What It Will Cost The sample prices below are meant only as a general guide and are estimates for high season. A two-bedroom villa rental can run about $200 a night. A hearty meal for one at the covered market behind the post office is about $4; at a Chinese restaurant, $8; at a seafood restaurant, $15 and up. Cocktails average $3 here, while a beer is around $2. A taxi into town from most hotels will run $6, while a bus costs around NAf 50¢. Car rentals begin at $33 a day during high season, but the average cost is more like $46 a day. Snorkel gear costs between $7 and $10 a day.

Before You Go

Tourist Information Contact the **Curaçao Tourist Office** (400 Madison Ave., Suite 311, New York, NY 10017, tel. 212/751–8266 or 800/332–8266, fax 212/486–3024; 330 Biscayne Blvd., Suite 808, Miami, FL 33132, tel. 305/374–5811 or 800/445–8266, fax 305/374–6741) for information.

Arriving and Departing

By Plane **American Airlines** (tel. 800/624–6262) flies direct daily from Miami. **ALM** (tel. 800/327–7230), Curaçao's national airline, maintains frequent service from Miami and Atlanta. For Atlanta departures, ALM has connecting services (throughfares) to most U.S. gateways with Delta. ALM also offers a Visit Caribbean Pass, allowing easy interisland travel. **Air Aruba** (tel. 800/882–7822) has daily direct flights to Curaçao (flights make brief stops in Aruba) from both Miami and Newark airports. Air Aruba also has regularly scheduled service to Curaçao from Miami, Newark, and Baltimore, and to Aruba and Bonaire. **E Liner Airways** (tel. 599/9–697270 or 599/9–604773) has started interisland service, including sightseeing and a beach tour of Aruba and of Bonaire.

From the Airport Buses do run from the **International Airport Curaçao** into Willemstad, but unless you're staying in town, you will have to switch buses at either the Punda or Otrobanda Terminal to get to your hotel. The majority of hotels are located only a 15- to 20-minute drive from the airport, and a taxi will run $10 to $12 for up to four people. Be sure to agree on the fare, in U.S. dollars, before departure. Hotels located more than a half hour from town usually provide free airport transfers for their guests; transfers are included in most packages.

Passports and Visas U.S. and Canadian citizens traveling to Curaçao need only proof of citizenship and a valid photo ID. A voter's registration card or a notarized birth certificate (not a photocopy) will suffice—a driver's license will *not*. British citizens must produce a passport. All visitors must show an ongoing or return ticket.

Language Dutch is the official language, but the vernacular is Papiamento—a mixture of Dutch, Portuguese, Spanish, African, French, and English. Developed during the 18th century by Africans, Papiamento evolved in Curaçao as the mode of communication between landowners and their slaves. These days, however, English, as well as Spanish and Dutch, is studied by schoolchildren. Anyone involved with tourism—shopkeepers, restaurateurs, and museum guides—speaks English. A Spanish phrase book will be helpful.

Precautions Mosquitoes on Curaçao do not seem as vicious and bloodthirsty as they do on Aruba and Bonaire, but that doesn't mean they don't exist. To be safe, keep perfume to a minimum, be prepared to use insect repellent before dining alfresco, and spray your hotel room at night—especially if you've opened a window.

If you plan to go into the water, beware of long-spined sea urchins, which can cause pain and discomfort if you come in contact with them. Do not eat—or even touch—any of the little green applelike fruits of the manchineel tree: They're poisonous. In fact, steer clear of the trees altogether; raindrops or dewdrops dripping off the leaves can blister your skin. If contact does occur, rinse the affected area with water and, in extreme cases, get medical attention. Usually, the burning sensation won't last longer than two hours.

Staying in Curaçao

Important Addresses **Tourist Information:** The **Curaçao Tourism Development Foundation** has three offices on the island where multilingual guides are ready to answer questions. You can also pick up maps, brochures, and a copy of "Curaçao Holiday." The main office is located in Willemstad at Pietermaai 19 (tel. 599/9–616000); other offices are in the Waterfort Arches (tel. 599/9–613397), across from the Van Der Valk Plaza Hotel, and at the airport (tel. 599/9–686789).

Emergencies **Police** or **Fire:** tel. 114. The **Main Police Station** number is 599/9–611000. **Hospitals:** For medical emergencies, call **St. Elisabeth's Hospital** (tel. 599/9–624900) or an ambulance (tel. 112). **Pharmacies: Botica Popular** (Madurostraat 15, tel. 599/9–611269), or ask at your hotel for the nearest one.

Currency U.S. dollars—in cash or traveler's checks—are accepted nearly everywhere, so there's no need to worry about exchanging money. However, you may need small change for pay phones, cigarettes, or soda machines. The currency in the Netherlands Antilles is the guilder, or florin as it is also called, indicated by an fl. or NAf. on price tags. The U.S. dollar is considered very stable; the official rate of exchange at press time was NAf1.75 to U.S. $1. Note: Prices quoted here are in U.S. dollars unless indicated otherwise.

Taxes and Service Charges Hotels collect a 7% government tax and add a 12% service charge to the bill; restaurants add 10%–15%. The airport departure tax is U.S. $10; $5.75 if your destination is Bonaire.

Getting Around

Taxis Curaçao's taxis are easily identified by the signs on their roofs and the letters "TX" after the license number. Drivers have an official tariff chart. Taxis tend to be moderately priced, but since there are no meters, you should confirm the fare with the driver before departure. The fare from Willemstad to the hotels in Piscadera Bay is about $5; to the hotels by the Seaquarium, about $7. There is an additional 25% surcharge after 11 PM. Taxis are readily available at hotels; in other cases, call Central Dispatch at tel. 599/9–616711. Since crossing the Queen Juliana Bridge by cab can easily double your fare from town to your hotel, save money by beginning your ride from the same side of the canal as your hotel: Just stroll across the Queen Emma floating bridge and *then* get your cab.

Rental Cars You can rent a car from **Budget** (tel. 599/9–683420), **Avis** (tel. 599/9–681163), **Dollar** (tel. 599/9–690262), or **National Car Rental** (tel. 599/9–683489) at the airport or have it delivered free to your hotel. Rates typically range from about $46 a day for a Toyota Starlet to about $73 for a four-door sedan. If you're planning to do country driving or rough it through Christoffel Park, a Jeep is best. All you'll need is a valid U.S. or Canadian driver's license. Scooters ($20), mopeds ($15), and bikes ($12.50) can be rented from **Easy Going** (tel. 599/9–695056).

Shuttle Vans All the major hotels outside of town offer free shuttle service into Willemstad. Shuttles coming from the Otrabanda side leave you at Rif Fort. From there it's a short walk north to the foot of the Queen Emma pontoon bridge. Shuttles coming from the Punda side leave you near the main entrance to Fort Amsterdam. Check the schedule with your hotel's front desk clerk, as the shuttles do not run every hour, and be sure to ask the driver for the return schedule from town back to your hotel.

Buses Yellow public buses, called convoys, are available from about 6 AM until 11:30 PM. At least six main routes can be used for sightseeing or beachcombing. Buses leave either from the Punda Bus Terminal at the downtown market place or the Otrabanda Bus Terminal located under the overpass. At press time, the fare was about Naf50¢ one-way. You'll need florins, so be sure to have enough coins. A number of private vans also function as buses. They list their destinations onb a card on the dashboard and show the word "Bus" on their license plates. Hail one from a bus stop, but be sure to check the route with the driver. The minimum fare for these private buses is NAf .50. The **Punda to Hato** bus runs hourly from 6:15 AM and stops at the Senior Liqueur Factory, the zoo and botanical gardens, Landhuis Brievengat, and the Hato Caves. The **Punda to Dominquito** bus departs hourly from 7:35 AM and stops at the Bolivar Museum, the Seaquarium, and the Jan Thiel Beach Club. The **Otrabanda to Wespunt** bus stops at Landhuis Ascension, Christoffel Park, and Westpunt beach. For prices and schedules, contact the **ABC Bus Company** (tel. 599/9–684733).

Telephones and Mail Phone service through the hotel operators in Curaçao is slow, but direct-dial service, both on-island and to the United States, is fast and clear. Hotel operators will put the call through for you, but if you make a collect call, do check immediately afterward that the hotel does not charge you as well. To call Curaçao direct from the United States, dial 011–599–9 plus the number in Curaçao. To place a local call on the island, dial the six-digit local number. A local call from a pay phone costs NAf .25. An airmail letter to anywhere in the world costs NAf 2.50, a postcard NAf 1.25.

Opening and Closing Times Most shops are open Monday to Saturday 8–noon and 2–6. Banks are open weekdays 8–3:30.

Guided Tours You don't really need a guide to show you downtown Willemstad—it's an easy taxi, bus, or free shuttle van ride from most major hotels and small enough for a self-conducted walking tour (follow the one outlined in the free tourist booklet "Curaçao Holiday"). To see the rest of the island, however, a guided tour can save you time and energy, though it is easy to cover the island yourself in a rented car. Most hotels have tour desks where arrangements can be made with reputable tour operators. For very personal, amiable service, try **Casper Tours** (tel. 599/9–653010 or 599/9–616789). For $25 per person, you'll be escorted around the island in an air-conditioned van, with stops at the Juliana Bridge, the salt pans, Knip Bay for a swim, the grotto at Boca Tabla, and lunch at Jaanchi Christiaan's, which is famous for its native cuisine. **Taber Tours** (tel. 599/9–376637) offers a 3½-hour city and country tour ($10) that includes visits to the Curaçao Liqueur Factory, the Curaçao Museum, and a shopping center. A full-day tour includes a visit to the Seaquarium and a snorkel trip; it costs $25 per person. Sightseeing by taxi costs $20 an hour for up to four people.

Boat Tours **Taber Tours** (tel. 599/9–376637) offers a two-hour sunset cruise ($29.50 for adults, $20 for children under 12), with a feast of French bread, cheese, and wine. One-hour morning, afternoon, and evening cruises of Santa Anna Harbor are offered aboard the **M/S *Hilda Veronica*** (tel. 599/9–611257; cost: $7 adults, $4 children). A snorkeling, sailing, and lunch cruise to Klein Curaçao, an offshore island, is offered aboard the ***Miss Anne*** (tel. 599/9–671579; cost: $40), as are moonlight cruises for $15 per person and sunset cruises for $18, both including drinks.

Exploring Curaçao

Numbers in the margin correspond to points of interest on the Curaçao map.

Willemstad 1 The capital city, **Willemstad,** is a favorite cruise stop for two reasons: The shopping is considered among the best in the Caribbean, and a quick tour of most of the downtown sights can be managed within a six-block radius. Santa Anna Bay slices the city down the middle: On one side is the Punda, and on the other is the Otrabanda (literally, the "other side"). Think of the Punda as the side for tourists, crammed with shops, restaurants, monuments, and markets.

Otrabanda is less touristy, with lots of narrow winding streets full of private homes notable for their picturesque gables and Dutch-influenced designs.

There are three ways to make the crossing from one side to the other: (1) drive or take a taxi over the Juliana Bridge; (2) traverse the Queen Emma pontoon bridge on foot; or (3) ride the free ferry, which runs when the bridge is open for passing ships.

Our walking tour of Willemstad starts at the **Queen Emma Pontoon Bridge,** affectionately called the Lady by the natives. During the hurricane season in 1988, the 700-foot floating bridge practically floated right out to sea; it was later taken down for major reconstruction. If you're standing on the Otrabanda side, take a few moments to scan Curaçao's multicolored "face" on the other side of Santa Anna Bay. Spiffy rows of town houses combine the gabled roofs and red tiles of the island's Dutch heritage with the gay colors unique to Curaçao. The architecture makes a cheerful contrast to the stark cacti and the austere shrubbery dotting the countryside. Millions of dollars have been poured into restoring old colonial landmarks and upgrading and modernizing hotels. If you wait long enough, the bridge will swing open (at least 30 times a day) to let the seagoing ships pass through. The original bridge, built in 1888, was the brainchild of the American consul Leonard Burlington Smith, who made a mint off the tolls he charged for the bridge. Initially, the charge was 2¢ per person for those wearing shoes, free to those crossing barefoot. Today it's free to everyone.

Take a breather at the peak of the bridge and look north to the 1,625-foot-long **Queen Juliana Bridge,** completed in 1974 and standing 200 feet above water. That's the bridge you drive over to cross to the other side of the city, and although the route is time-consuming (and more expensive if you're going by taxi), the view from the bridge is worth it. At every hour of the day, the sun casts a different tint over the city, creating an ever-changing panorama; the nighttime view, rivaling Rio's, is breathtaking.

When you cross the Pontoon Bridge and arrive on the Punda side, turn left and walk down the waterfront, along **Handelskade.** You'll soon pass the ferry landing. Now take a close look at the buildings you've seen only from afar; the original red tiles of the roofs came from Europe and arrived on trade ships as ballast.

Walk down to the corner and turn right at the customs building onto Sha Caprileskade. This is the bustling **floating market,** where each morning dozens of Venezuelan schooners arrive laden with tropical fruits and vegetables. Fresh mangoes, papayas, and exotic vegetables vie for space with freshly caught fish and herbs and spices. It's probably too much to ask a tourist to arrive by 6:30 AM when the buying is best, but there's plenty of action to see throughout the afternoon. Any produce bought here, however, should be thoroughly washed before eating.

Keep walking down Sha Caprileskade. Head toward the Wilhelmina Drawbridge, which connects Punda with the once-flourishing district of **Scharloo,** where the early Jewish merchants first built stately homes. Scharloo is now a red-light district.

If you continue straight ahead, Sha Caprileskade becomes De Ruyterkade. Soon you'll come to the post office, which will be on your left. Behind it is the **Old Market** (Marche), where you'll find local women preparing hearty Antillean lunches. For $4–$6 you can enjoy such Curaçaon specialties as *funghi* (a polentalike dish), *keshi yena* (Edam cheese stuffed with a spicy meat or seafood mixture), goat stew, fried fish, peas and rice, and fried plantains. After lunch, return to the intersection of De Ruyterkade and Columbusstraat and turn left.

Curaçao

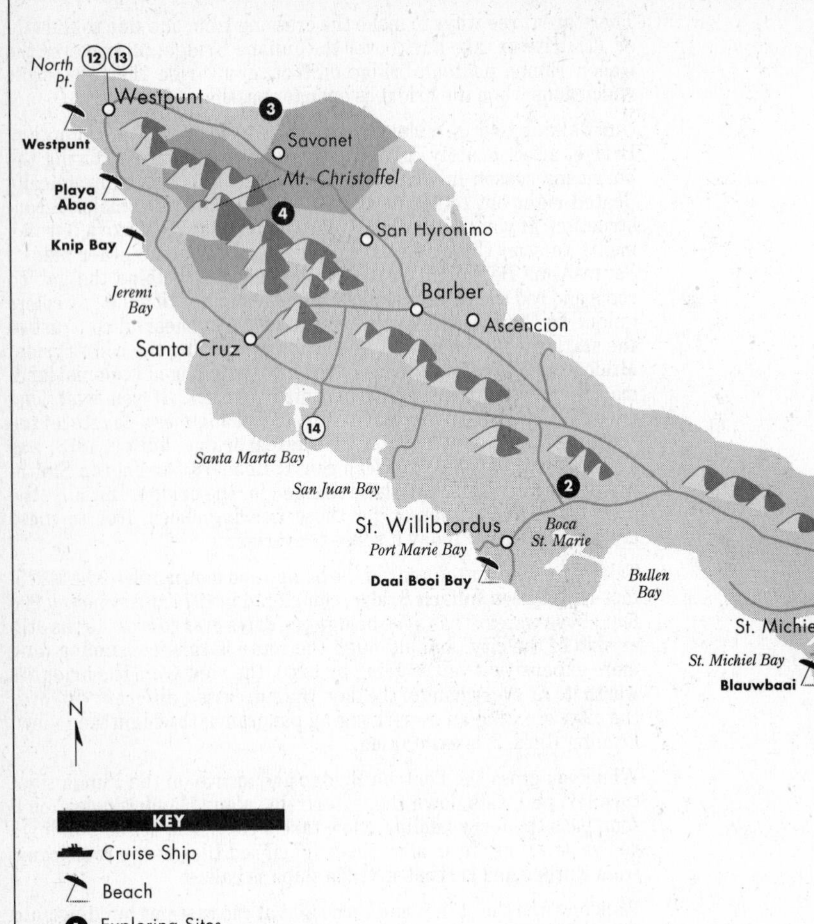

Exploring
Amstel Brewery, **8**
Boca Tabla, **3**
Caracas Bay, **11**
Christoffel Park, **4**
Curaçao Seaquarium, **5**
Curaçao Underwater Marine Park, **6**
Hato Caves, **10**
Landhuis Brievengat, **9**
Landhuis Jan Kock, **2**
Senior Liqueur Factory, **7**
Willemstad, **1**

Dining
Belle Terrace, **20**
Bon Appetit, **24**
Cozzoli's Pizza, **21**
El Marinero, **23**
Fort Waakzaamheid, **17**
Garuda Indonesian Restaurant, **15**
Golden Star Restaurant, **28**
Grill King, **19**
Guacamaya Steakhouse, **25**
Jaanchi Christiaan's Restaurant, **12**
Rijsttafel Indonesia Restaurant, **27**

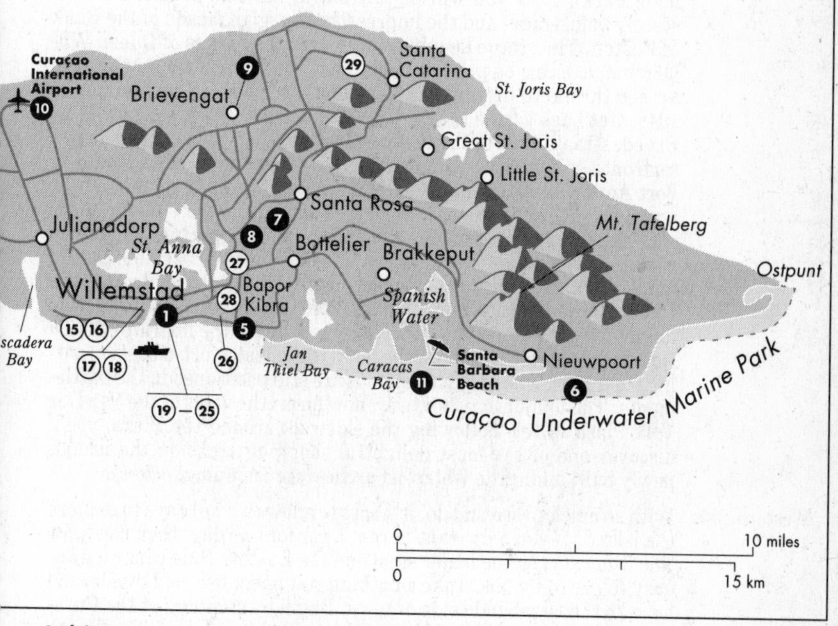

Lodging

Avila Beach Hotel, **20**

Club Seru Coral, **29**

Coral Cliff Resort and Casino, **14**

Holiday Beach Hotel and Casino, **16**

Landhuis Daniel, **13**

Lions Dive Hotel & Marina, **26**

Otrabanda Hotel & Casino, **18**

Van Der Valk Plaza Hotel and Casino, **22**

Walk up Columbusstraat to the **Mikveh Israel-Emmanuel Synagogue,** founded in 1651 but built in 1732 and the oldest temple still in use in the Western Hemisphere. One of the most important sights in Curaçao, it draws 20,000 visitors a year. Enter through the gates around the corner on Hanchi Snoa and ask the front office to direct you to the guide on duty. A unique feature is the brilliant white sand covering the synagogue floor, a remembrance of Moses leading his people through the desert; the Hebrew letters on the four pillars signify the names of the Four Mothers of Israel: Sarah, Rebecca, Rachel, and Leah. The fascinating Jewish Cultural Museum (tel. 599/9–611633, admission $2) in the back displays Jewish antiques (including a set of circumcision instruments) and artifacts from Jewish families collected from all over the world. The gift shop near the gate has excellent postcards and commemorative medallions. *Hanchi Di Snoa 29, tel. 599/9–611067. Open weekdays 9–11:45 AM and 2:30–5 PM. English and Hebrew services conducted by an American rabbi are held Fri. at 6:30 PM and on Sat. at 10 AM. Jacket and tie.*

Continue down Columbusstraat and cross Wilhelminaplein (Wilhelmina Park). Now you will be in front of the courthouse, with its stately balustrade, and the impressive Georgian facade of the Bank of Boston. The statue keeping watch over the park is of Queen Wilhelmina, a deceased popular monarch of the Netherlands, who gave up her throne to her daughter Juliana after her Golden Jubilee in 1948. Cut back across the park and turn left at Breedestraat. Take Breedestraat down to the Pontoon Bridge, then turn left at the waterfront. At the foot of the bridge are the mustard-colored walls of **Fort Amsterdam.** Take a few steps through the archway and enter another century. The entire structure dates from the 1700s, when it was actually the center of the city and the most important fort on the island. Now it houses the governor's residence, the Fort Church, the ministry, and several other government offices. Next door is the **Plaza Piar,** dedicated to Manuel Piar, a native Curaçaoan who fought for the independence of Venezuela under the liberator Simon Bolívar. On the other side of the plaza is the **Waterfort,** a bastion dating from 1634. The original cannons are still positioned in the battlements. The foundation, however, now forms the walls of the Van Der Valk Plaza Hotel. Following the sidewalk around the Plaza, you'll discover one of the most delightful shopping areas on the island, newly built under the **Waterfort arches** (*see* Shopping, *below*).

Western Side

With so much to see and do, it's best to allow two full days to explore the island. If you only want to rent a car for one day, then use it for this itinerary, as the major sights on the Eastern Side itinerary are easy to get to by bus. Take a bathing suit and a few cold drinks and head to the Otrabanda side of town. Begin by stopping at the **Curaçao Museum** (tel. 599/9–623873), located behind the Holiday Beach Hotel on Van Leeuwenhoekstraat. Built in 1853 and restored in 1942, it houses a collection of Indian artifacts as well as colonial and historical island memorabilia. Then turn back to the highway and head northwest until the road merges with Westpunt Highway (Weg Naar Wespunt). For a splendid view, and some unusual island ghost tales, follow this road to the intersection at Cunucu Abao, then veer
2 left onto Weg Naar San Willibrordo until you come to **Landhuis Jan Kock** (tel. 599/9–648087), located across from the salt pans. Since the hours are irregular, be sure to call ahead to arrange a tour of this reputedly haunted mid-17th-century plantation house, or stop by on Sunday mornings, when the proprietor occasionally opens the small restaurant behind her home and serves delicious Dutch pancakes.

Continuing north on this road, you'll come to the village of Soto. From here the road leads to the northwest tip of the island, through landscape that Georgia O'Keeffe might have painted—towering cacti, flamboyant dried shrubbery, and aluminum-roof houses. Throughout this *cunucu,* or countryside, you'll see native fishermen

hauling in their nets, women pounding cornmeal, and an occasional
donkey blocking traffic. Landhouses, plantation houses from centuries past, dot the countryside, though most are closed to the public. Their facades, though, can often be glimpsed from the highway.
Stop at Playa Abao, Knip Bay, or Westpunt for a swim. Rounding
the northwest tip of the island, the road becomes Wespunt Highway
3 again and heads south to **Boca Tabla,** where the sea has carved a
magnificent grotto. Safely tucked in the back, you can watch and listen to the waves crashing ferociously against the rocks. A short dis-
4 tance farther is **Christoffel Park,** a fantastic 4,450-acre garden and
wildlife preserve with the towering Mt. Christoffel at its center.
Open to the public since 1978, the park consists of three former plantations with individual trails that take about 1 to 1½ hours each to traverse. You may drive your own car (heavy-treaded tires) or rent a Jeep with an accompanying guide ($15). Start out early (by 10 AM the park starts to feel like a sauna), and if you're going solo, first study the *Excursion Guide to Christoffel Park*, which is sold at the front desk of the elegant if dilapidated Landhuis Savonet (the plantation house turned Natural History Museum); it outlines the various routes and identifies the flora and fauna found here. No matter what route you take, you'll be treated to interesting views of hilly fields full of prickly-pear cacti, divi-divi trees, bushy-haired palms, and exotic flowers that bloom unpredictably after April showers. There are also caves and ancient Indian drawings. For the strong of heart: Walk through the bat caves on the Savonet route (marked in blue); you'll hear bat wings rustling in the corners and see a few scary but nonpoisonous scorpion spiders scuttling over the walls. Make sure you're wearing the proper shoes; the ground is covered with guano (bird and bat droppings) that almost seems alive because of the millions of harmless mites. It's not all a shop of horrors, though—if you make it to the last chamber, you may see a magnificent white-faced barn owl that nests in the cave fissures.

As you drive through the park, keep a lookout for tiny deer, goats, and other small wildlife that might suddenly dart in front of your car. The snakes you could encounter—the whip snake and the minute silver snake—are not poisonous. White-tailed hawks may be seen on the green route, white orchids and crownlike passion flowers on the yellow route.

Climbing up the 1,239-foot Mt. Christoffel on foot is an exhilarating experience and a definite challenge to anyone who hasn't grown up scaling the Alps. The guidebook claims the round-trip will take you one hour, and adolescent Curaçaoan boys do make a sport of racing up and down, but it's really more like 2½ (sweaty) hours for a reasonably fit person who's not an expert hiker. And the last few feet are deadly. The view from the peak, however, *is* thrilling—a panorama of the island, including Santa Marta Bay and the tabletop mountain of St. Hieronymus. On a clear day, you can even see the mountain ranges of Venezuela, Bonaire, and Aruba. *Savonet, tel. 599/9–640363. Admission: $5 adults, $3 children 6–15. Open Mon.–Sat. 8–5, Sun. 6–3.*

Eastern Side

To explore the eastern side of the island, take the coastal road — Martin Luther King Boulevard—out from Willemstad past the zoo and botanical gardens (neither is exceptional) about 2 miles to Bapor Kibra. There you'll find the Seaquarium and the Underwater Park.

5 The **Curaçao Seaquarium** is *the* place to see the island's underwater treasures without getting your feet wet. It's now more fun than ever, thanks to the *Seaworld Explorer,* a semisubmersible submarine that leaves from near the Seaquarium entrance (4:30 PM) to take its daily hour-long tour of the coral reefs and submerged wrecks offshore, with their kaleidoscope of fish who are happy to emerge when the diver empties their daily meal into the water. Queen angelfish, yellowtail snapper, porcupine fish, and the ever-popular barracuda are

among the denizens. The craft, with a barge top that submerges only five feet underwater, has wide glass windows in the submerged section, which extends down to about 100 feet. Call for reservations 24 hours in advance (tel. 599/7–604892; $29 adults, $19 children under 12), and get your ticket before going into Seaquarium.

Don't neglect the Seaquarium itself. It's the world's only public aquarium where sea creatures are raised and cultivated totally by natural methods. Where else can you hand-feed a shark (or watch a diver do it)? The new section called Animal Encounters consists of several large, open water enclosures that bring you face to face with a variety of jaws. If you want to snorkel among them, you're welcome. In one pool, snorkelers and divers swim freely with stingrays, tarpon, groupers, and such. In the other, Shark Encounter, divers and snorkelers can feed sharks by hand in perfect safety, they say, through thick mesh fencing that separates diver and shark. In between these two busy tanks is an underwater observatory where you can watch, if shark feeding isn't your hobby. The cost is $50 for divers, $30 for snorkelers, which includes admission to Seaquarium, and food for the sharks. Reservations for Animal Encounters must be made 24 hours in advance.

You can spend several hours in Seaquarium, mesmerized by the 46 tanks full of more than 400 varieties of exotic fish and vegetation found in the waters around Curaçao, including sharks, lobsters, turtles, corals, and sponges. Look out for the over-5-foot-long mascot, Herbie the lugubrious jewfish. Four sea lions from Uruguay are the most recent pride of the aquarium. If you get hungry, stop at the excellent Italian restaurant or the steak house-cum-Mexican eatery. There are also glass-bottom-boat tours, fun feeding shows, and a viewing platform overlooking the wreck of the steamship SS *Oranje Nassau*, which sank in 1906 and now sits in 10 feet of water. A nearby 495-yard man-made beach of white sand is well suited to novice swimmers and children, and bathroom and shower facilities are available. A souvenir shop sells some of the best postcards and coral jewelry on the island. *Tel. 599/9–616666. Admission: $6 adults, $3 children. Open daily 9 AM–10 PM.*

❻ **Curaçao Underwater Marine Park** (tel. 599/9–618131) consists of about 12½ miles of untouched coral reefs that have been granted the status of national park. Mooring buoys have been placed at the most interesting dive sites on the reef to provide safe anchoring and to prevent damage to the reef. Several sunken ships await visitors in the deep. The park stretches along the south shore from the Princess Beach Hotel in Willemstad to the eastern tip of the island.

❼ Located on Salina Arriba, in the Landhouse Chobolobo, the **Senior Liqueur Factory** (tel. 599/9–613526) distills and distributes the original Curaçao liqueur. Don't expect to find a massive factory—it's just a small showroom in the open-air foyer of a beautiful 17th-century landhouse. There are no guides, but you can read the story of the distillation process on posters, and you'll be graciously offered samples in various flavors. If you're interested in buying—the orange-flavored chocolate liqueur is fantastic over ice cream—you can choose from a complete selection, which is bottled in a variety of fascinating shapes, including Dutch ceramic houses.

❽ In nearby Salina you can take a free tour of the **Amstel Brewery**, which offers insights into the world's only beer made from distilled seawater. Free tours (followed by all-you-can-drink beer tastings) are held Tuesday and Thursday mornings at 10 AM. *Closed June 15–Aug. 6.*

❾ **Landhuis Brievengat** (tel. 599/9–378344) is a 10-minute drive northeast of Willemstad, near the Centro Deportivo sports stadium. On the last Sunday of the month (from 10 AM to 3 PM), this old estate holds an open house with crafts demonstrations and folkloric shows. You can see the original kitchen still intact, the 18-inch-thick walls, fine antiques, and the watchtowers, once used for lovers' trysts. The restaurant, which is open only on Wednesday and Friday, serves a fine rijsttafel. Every Friday night starting at 9 a party is held on the wide wraparound terrace, with two bands and plenty to drink.

Head northwest toward the airport (take a right onto Gosieweg, follow
the loop right onto Schottegatweg, take another right onto Jan
Norduynweg, a final right onto Rooseveltweg, and follow the signs) to
10 the island's newest attraction, **Hato Caves.** Hourlong guided tours
wind down into the various chambers: the Water Pools, Voodoo Chamber, Wishing Well, Fruit Bats' Sleeping Quarters, and Curaçao Falls, where a stream of silver joins with a stream of gold (they're colored by lights) and is guarded by a limestone "dragon" perched nearby. Hidden lights illuminate the limestone formations and gravel walkways. It's one of the better Caribbean caves open to the public. *Tel. 599/9–680378. Admission: $4.25 adults, $2.75 children. Open Tues.–Sun. 10–5. Closed Mon.*

Wind southward past Spanish Water, where you'll pass several private yacht clubs that attract sports anglers from all over the world for international tournaments. And make a stop at **Santa Barbara
Beach,** especially on Sundays, when the atmosphere approaches
11 party time (*see* Beaches, *below*). **Caracas Bay,** off Bapor Kibra, is a
popular dive site, with a sunken ship so close to the surface that even snorkelers can balance their flippers on the helm.

Beaches

Curaçao has some 38 beaches, but unfortunately, many are extremely rocky and litter-strewn. Instead of long, powdery stretches of sand, you'll discover the joy of inlets: tiny bay openings to the sea marked by craggy cliffs, exotic trees, and scads of interesting pebbles. If your hotel, apartment, or guest house doesn't have a beach, you can hop a bus to one that does. Your front desk clerk can tell you which bus to take and when it runs, or you can call the **ABC Bus Company** (*see* Buses *in* Getting Around, *above*). All of the major hotels have a beach, although some are teeny and others are manmade. Nonguests are supposed to pay the hotels a beach fee, but often there is no one there to collect.

Hotels with the best beach properties include the new **Sonesta Beach Hotel** (impressively long), the **Princess Beach** (impressively sensuous), and the **Coral Cliff Resort** (impressively deserted).

One of the largest, more spectacular beaches on Curaçao is **Blauwbaai** (Blue Bay). There's plenty of white sand and lots of shady places, showers, and changing facilities, but since it's a private beach, you'll pay an entrance fee of about $2.50 per car. Take the road that leads north, past the Holiday Beach Hotel and the Curaçao Caribbean, toward Julianadorp. At the end of the stretch of straight road, a sign will instruct you to bear left for Blauwbaai and the fishing village of St. Michiel. The latter is a good place for diving.

Starting from the church of St. Willibrordus, signs will direct you to **Daai Booi Bay,** a sandy shore dotted with thatched shelters. The road to this public beach is a small paved highway flanked on either side by thick, lush trees and huge organ-pipe cacti. The beach is curved, with shrubbery rooted into the side of the rocky cliffs—a great place for swimming.

Knip Bay has two parts: Big (Groot) Knip and Little (Kleine) Knip. Only Little Knip is shaded with trees, but these are manchineels, so steer clear of them. Also beware of cutting your feet on beer-bottle caps. Both have alluring white sand, but only Big Knip has changing facilities as well as several tiki huts for shade, and calm turquoise waters that are perfect for swimming and lounging. The protected cove, flanked by sheer cliffs, is usually a blast on Sundays, when there is live music. To get there, take the road to the Knip Landhouse, then turn right. Signs will direct you. In between the big and the little bay is a superb scenic route.

Playa Abao, northwest of Knip Bay, has crystal-clear turquoise water and a small beach. Sunday afternoons are crowded and festive. There's a snack bar and public toilets.

Westpunt, on the northwest tip of the island, is shady in the morning. It doesn't have much sand, but you can sit on a shaded rock ledge. On Sunday, watch the divers jump from the high cliff. The bay view is worth the trip. For lunch, stop at Jaanchi Christiaan's nearby (*see* Dining, *below*).

Santa Barbara, on the eastern tip of the island, is popular with families. It has changing facilities and a snack bar, but charges a small entrance fee, usually around $3.35 per car.

Sports and the Outdoors

Golf Visitors are welcome to play golf at the **Curaçao Golf and Squash Club** (tel. 599/9–373590) in Emmastad. The nine-hole course offers a challenge because of the stiff trade winds and the sand greens. Greens fees are $15. Golf clubs and pull carts are available for rent. *Open 8–12:30.*

Jogging The **Rif Recreation Area,** locally known as the *corredor*, stretches from the water plant at Mundo Nobo to the Curaçao Caribbean Hotel along the sea. It consists of more than a mile of palm-lined beachfront, a wading pond, and a jogging track with an artificial surface, as well as a big playground. There is good security and street lighting along the entire length of the beachfront.

Tennis Most hotels (including Sonesta Beach, Curaçao Caribbean, Las Palmas, Princess Beach, and Holiday Beach) offer well-paved courts, illuminated for day and night games, but these are only open to hotel guests. Your only option if you're not staying at one of these is the **Santa Catherina Sports and Country Club** (tel. 599/9–677028). Forty-five minutes of court time costs $7 during the day, $10 after 6 PM.

Water Sports Curaçao has facilities for all kinds of water sports, thanks to the government-sponsored **Curaçao Underwater Marine Park** (tel. 599/9–618131), which includes almost a third of the island's southern diving waters. Scuba divers and snorkelers can enjoy more than 12½ miles of protected reefs and shores, with normal visibility from 60 to 80 feet (up to 150 feet on good days). With water temperatures ranging from 75° to 82°F, wet suits are generally unnecessary. No coral collecting, spearfishing, or littering is allowed. An exciting wreck to explore is the SS *Oranje Nassau*, which ran aground more than 80 years ago and now hosts hundreds of exotic fish and unusually shaped coral.

Most hotels either offer their own program of water sports or will be happy to make arrangements for you. An introductory scuba resort course usually runs about $50–$65.

Underwater Curaçao (tel. 599/9–618131) offers complete vacation/dive packages in conjunction with the Lions Dive Hotel & Marina, as well as private and group lessons and dive excursions. A single dive costs $33. Its fully stocked dive shop, located between the Lions Dive Hotel and the Curaçao Seaquarium, offers equipment for sale or rent. Take a dive/snorkeling trip on the *Coral Sea*, a 40-foot twin diesel yacht-style dive boat. Landlubbers can see beneath the sea aboard the *Coral View*, a monohull flat-top glass-bottom boat that makes four excursions a day. The 30-minute ride costs $5.50 per person and requires a minimum of five people.

Seascape (tel. 599/9–625000, ext. 177), at the Curaçao Caribbean Hotel and Casino, specializes in snorkeling and scuba diving trips to reefs and underwater wrecks in every type of water vehicle—from pedal boats and water scooters to water skis and Windsurfers. A six-dive package costs $155 and includes unlimited beach diving plus one free night dive. Snorkeling gear costs about $5 an hour or $10 a day to rent. Die-hard fishermen and those in quest of a full-body tan will enjoy the day trip to Little Curaçao, the "clothes optional" island between Curaçao and Bonaire, where the fish are reputed to be lively: Plan on $25 per person.

Peter Hughes Diving (tel. 599/9–367888, ext. 5047), at the Princess Beach Hotel rents equipment and conducts diving and snorkeling trips.

Coral Cliff Diving (tel. 599/9–642822) offers scuba certification courses ($320), a one-week windsurfing school ($170), a one-week basic sailing course ($255), and a full schedule of dive and snorkeling trips to Curaçao's southwest coast. It also rents pedal boats, Hobie Cats, and underwater cameras.

For windsurfing, check out the **Curaçao High Wind Center** (Princess Beach Hotel, tel. 599/9–614944). Lessons cost $20 an hour.

Shopping

Curaçao is not the shopper's haven that most guidebooks make it out to be. If you're looking for bargains on Swiss watches, cameras, crystal, or electronic equipment, do some comparison shopping back home and come armed with a list of prices. You can find some excellent buys on French perfumes and jewelry, especially gold. For many years, Curaçao catered to hordes of Venezuelan shoppers who adored American goods. In recent years, European merchandise has made inroads, but most of it is expensive designer clothing from Italy, Spain, and France. You are expected to declare expensive purchases at U.S. Customs.

Shopping Areas Most of the shops are concentrated in one place—**Punda**—in downtown Willemstad, within about a six-block area. The main shopping streets are **Heerenstraat, Breedestraat,** and **Madurostraat. Heerenstraat** and **Gomezplein** are pedestrian malls, closed to traffic, and their roadbeds have been raised to sidewalk level and covered with pink inlaid tiles.

The hippest shopping area lies under the **Waterfort arches,** along with a variety of restaurants and bars. One of our two favorite shops under the arches is **Bamali** (tel. 599/9–612258), which sells Indonesian batik clothing, leather bags, and charming handicrafts. Our other favorite at Waterfort is **Clarisa & Laura Kemper** (tel. 599/9–618313), which specializes in exquisite leather and silk creations.

Good Buys **La Zahav N.V.** (Curaçao International Airport, tel. 599/9–689594) is one of the best places to buy gold jewelry—with or without diamonds, rubies, and emeralds—at true discount prices. The shop is located in the airport transit hall, just at the top of the staircase. **Boutique Liska** (Schottegatweg Oost 191-A, tel. 599/9–613111) is where local residents shop for smart women's fashion. **Toko Zuikertuintje** (Zuikertuintjeweg, tel. 599/9–370188), a supermarket built on the original 17th-century Zuikertuintje Landhuis, is where most of the local elite shop. Enjoy the free tea and coffee while you stock up on all sorts of European and Dutch delicacies. Shopping here for a picnic is a treat in itself. **Clog Dance** (De Rouvilleweg 9B, tel. 599/9–623280) sells not only Dutch clogs but also a medley of good Dutch products.

Arts and Crafts At **Gallery 86** (2-N Bloksteeg, tel. 599/9–613417) a large collection of watercolors by local artists depicts landhouses and island scenes.

Native crafts and curios are on hand at **Fundason Obra di Man** (Bargestraat 57, tel. 599/9–612413). Particularly impressive are the posters of Curaçao's architecture. **Arawak Clay/Craft Products** (Industry Park, Brievgat; Cruise Terminal, Otrabanda; tel. 599/9–377658) sells island-made ceramics such as tiles, plates, ashtrays, mugs, and tiny replicas of landhouses.

Dining

Restaurateurs in Curaçao believe in whetting appetites with a variety of cuisines and intriguing ambiences: Dine under the boughs of magnificent old trees, in the romantic gloom of wine cellars in renovated landhouses, or on the ramparts of 18th-century forts. Curaçaoans partake of some of the best Indonesian food in the Caribbean, and they also find it hard to resist the French, Swiss, Dutch, and Swedish delights.

Even at budget prices, good food is abundant. In the Old Covered Market behind the post office in Willemstad, you can lunch on a large plate of grilled fish or chicken over rice, with plantains and vegetables, for $4–$6. Fast-food spots in the center of town are another option: Choose from Burger King, Pizza Hut, KFC, or McDonald's. There are six Chinese restaurants serving Cantonese food, with lots of dishes under $10. Other good bets are the clean, no-frills local eateries serving Dutch/Curaçaon specialties; for $7–$9 you can get a dinner of pork chops, shrimp *criollo* (a spicy tomato-based sauce), goat stew, or fresh grilled kingfish served with funghi (a polentalike dish), plantains, vegetables, and rice. At Indonesian restaurants, a 16-course rijsttafel (smorgasbord of meats, chicken, fish, and vegetables) that will quell the hungriest appetite is served at your table for about $14 a person.

If you're cooking in, you'll find plenty of supermarkets and minigrocery stores on Curaçao. If you purchase your fruits or vegetables from either the floating market or the market behind the post office (*see* Exploring Willemstad, *above*), be sure to wash all produce well. You can also buy fresh fish at both markets. Meat is best purchased from a butcher or supermarket. The latter include: **Mangusa Supermarket** (Seru Mangusa 1), **Mini Market Jandoret** (Jandoret 62), **Bello Horizonte** (Aztekenweg 17), and **Broadway Supermarket** (Ontarioweg 1).

Even at ¢ restaurants, reservations are always helpful, and are advised during winter. Dress in restaurants is almost always casual, but if you feel like putting on your finery, there will be a place for you.

Highly recommended restaurants are indicated by a star ★.

Category	Cost*
$$	$15–$25
$	$10–$15
¢	under $10

**per person, excluding drinks and service*

$$ **Belle Terrace.** Tucked into the quaint Avila Beach Hotel, this seaside patio restaurant sits beneath the boughs of an ancient tree. Candlelit dinners on crisp white linen add to the romance, as palms sway obligingly and waves whisper. Specials change nightly and range from such Curaçao dishes as keshi yena and *sopito* (fish and coconut soup) to salted boiled breast of duck and filet mignon. In between stops at the creative salad bar, watch the fish jumping out of the sea—they fly up to 20 feet. *Avila Beach Hotel, Penstraat 130–*

134, tel. 599/9–614377. Reservations required. AE, DC, MC, V. No lunch.

$$ ★ **El Marinero.** Owner and "captain" Luis Chavarria presides over a nautically attired waitstaff at his friendly eatery. The decor carries on the theme, with the bow of a boat jutting out from one wall. The service is efficient, and the food is excellent. The chef whips up one superb seafood dish after another, including such delicacies as shellfish soup, seviche, paella, and conch. The sea bass Creole-style is delicious, as is the garlic lobster. *Schottegatweg Noord 87-B, tel. 599/9–379833. Reservations advised. AE, DC, MC, V.*

$$ **Fort Waakzaamheid.** High on a hill overlooking Willemstad and the harbor, this fort was captured by Captain Bligh of HMS *Bounty* two centuries ago. Now it is controlled by an Irishman, Tom Farrel, who operates an open-air restaurant and bar in the evening. The atmosphere is informal, and the food is primarily barbecued seafood and steaks decorated with your own makings from a salad bar. You will be equally well greeted if you go just for cocktails and snacks—and the sunsets are magnificent. There are early bird specials from 5 to 7 PM. *Berg Domi, tel. 599/9–623633. Located off the main highway on the Otrabanda side of the suspension bridge. Reservations advised. AE, V. No lunch.*

$$ **Guacamaya Steakhouse.** The portions here are hearty, the chef knows what *rare* means, and there's even a small selection of seafood to satisfy the noncarnivore in the crowd. A large papier-mâché parrot sits on a brass perch, waiters stroll by in Bermuda shorts and safari hats, and the drink of the house—a *guacamaya*—is a tall, iced concoction the color of foliage. Try the chateaubriand or the tenderloin medallions. There's also steak tartare and a mixed skewer of chicken, pork, and beef kebabs. *Schottegatweg-West 365, tel. 599/9–689208. Reservations required. AE, DC, MC, V. Closed Mon.*

$$ **Rijsttafel Indonesia Restaurant.** An antique rickshaw guarding the entrance sets the mood for this tranquil spot. No steaks or chops here, just one dish after another of exotic delicacies that make up the traditional Indonesian banquet called rijsttafel. Choose from 16 to 25 traditional dishes that are set buffet-style around you. You can also order from an à la carte menu, which includes fried noodles, fresh jumbo shrimp in garlic, and combination meat-and-fish platters. Desserts are nearly mystical: A "ladies only" ice cream comes with a red rose, and the coconut ice cream comes packed in a coconut shell. The walls are hung with beautiful Indonesian puppets ($25–$40) that make stunning gifts. *Mercurriusstraat 13–15, Salinja, tel. 599/9–612606. Reservations required. AE, DC, MC, V. No lunch Sun.*

$–$$ **Garuda Indonesian Restaurant.** The rijsttafel here features 19 trays of traditional vegetable, chicken, meat, fish, and shrimp dishes, each with its own sauce. The ocean breezes, bamboo and rattan decor, and Far Eastern music add to the feeling of being a guest in a foreign land. Save room for a dessert of *spekkok*, a multilayered pastry with nuts that will melt in your mouth. *Next to the Curaçao Caribbean Hotel, tel. 599/9–626519. Reservations advised. AE, DC, MC, V. Closed Mon. No lunch weekends.*

$ **Grill King.** Locals and tourists crowd this casual, no-frills waterfront eatery, especially on weekends, when a keyboardist provides entertainment. The sea crashing against the rocks below makes an exciting backdrop to a meal of succulent seafood or flame-broiled meats. Try the grilled conch with a shrimp cocktail appetizer, the wahoo in criollo sauce, or the Danish-style, baby-back ribs. Service is a bit slow but always pleasant. *Waterfort Arches, tel. 599/9–616870. Reservations advised. AE, D, DC, MC, V. No lunch Sun.*

¢–$ **Bon Appetit.** This Dutch coffee shop in the heart of the shopping district is a popular breakfast and lunch spot. The fare is reasonably priced, the portions are large, and the service is friendly and pleasant. Try the Dutch pancakes with pineapple. *Hanchi di Snoa 4, tel. 599/9–616916. AE, DC, MC, V. Closed Sun.*

¢ **Cozzoli's Pizza.** Fast, cheap, hearty New York–style pizzas are offered here, along with calzones, sausage rolls, and lasagna. It is right in the middle of downtown Willemstad. *Breedestraat 2, tel. 599/9–617184. No credit cards.*

¢ ★ **Golden Star Restaurant.** This place looks and feels more like a friendly roadside diner than a full-fledged restaurant, but the native food is among the best in town. Owner Marie Burke turns out such Antillean specialties as *bestia chiki* (goat stew), shrimp Creole, and delicately seasoned grilled conch, all served with generous heaps of rice, fried plantains, and avocado. Steaks and chops are among the other options. *Socratestraat 2, tel. 599/9–654795. AE, DC, MC, V.*

¢ **Jaanchi Christiaan's Restaurant.** Tour buses make regular lunch stops at this open-air restaurant for the mouthwatering local dishes. The main-course specialty is a hefty platter of freshly caught fish with potatoes and vegetables. Curaçaoans joke that Jaanchi's iguana soup is "so strong it could resurrect the dead"—truth is, it tastes just like chicken soup, only better. But Jaanchi, Jr., says if you want iguana, you must order in advance "because we have to go out and catch them." He's not kidding. *Westpunt 15, tel. 599/9–640126. AE, DC, MC, V.*

Lodging

Package rates, which can be arranged through a travel agent, are available at most hotels. Curaçao has a number of excellent-value hotels priced at around $100 a night. For this price—maybe half of what you'd pay on more expensive islands—you get a pleasant room at a full-service hotel with a restaurant, a water-sports center, and a beach. It's possible to pay much less for a room in a small guest house or inn—around $50 a night—but know that you'll be taking a huge drop in quality. These properties generally have stark rooms, off-beach locations (though not always), and few facilities—you'll have to leave the property to get everything from snorkel gear to breakfast.

Hotels here tend to be in three main areas: On the beaches of Piscadera Bay (a few minutes west of the Otrabanda side of Willemstad); on the Bapor Kibra beachfront (an eight-minute drive from the Punda side of Willemstad); and in the Westpunt area at the northwest tip of the island. Beaches are within walking distance at all three locations. Almost every hotel in Curaçao participates in the tourist board–promoted "Break Away" package, which offers a number of extras for not much more money than room rates. If you're a diver, be sure to ask any hotel you call about scuba packages. Almost every hotel outside of Willemstad offers free shuttle service into town. There are no campgrounds on Curaçao and, so far, no all-inclusive resorts.

Highly recommended lodgings are indicated by a star ★.

Category	Cost*
$$	$120–$160
$	$85–$120
¢	under $85

**All prices are for a standard double room for two and include tax and service charges. To estimate rates for hotels offering MAP/FAP, add about $20–$30 per person per day to the above price ranges.*

Hotels *$$* ★ **Avila Beach Hotel.** The royal family of Holland and its ministers stay at this 200-year-old mansion overlooking the ocean for three good reasons: the privacy, the personalized service, and the austere elegance. The reception area is cooled by whirring fans and graced with brass lanterns, porcelain statuary, and a baby grand, suggesting colonial plantation living at its ultimate. The original guest rooms (in the mansion) are charming but basic-looking, with hardwood or tile floors and small baths with showers only. Most guests will prefer the newer La Belle Alliance section, on its own beach adjacent to the main property. These Mediterranean-style yellow-and-gold low-rise buildings, with Dutch red-gabled roofs and lighted walkways, hold 45 rooms and 18 one- and two-bedroom apartments. All of these rooms have either balconies or patios with sea views. Half of the rooms are equipped with kitchenettes; all of the apartments have full kitchens. Although this section lacks the old-world ambience of the original structure, the accommodations are larger and have more modern amenities. The restaurant has a unique outdoor dining area shaded by an enormous tree. The Danish chefs, who specialize in local fare and weekly smorgasbord, also smoke their own fish and bake their own bread. Recent additions include a new café/jazz club with an open-air sea view, a tennis court, and a conference room. The double quarter-moon-shape beach is enchanting. Many consider this hotel the best buy on the island and a welcome change from the new mega-resorts. *Box 791, Penstraat 130134, Willemstad, tel. 599/9–614377 or 800/448–8355, fax 599/9–611493. 59 rooms, 18 apartments. Facilities: restaurant, bar, coffee shop, tennis court, baby-sitting, cable TV, shuttle bus to city center. AE, DC, MC, V. EP.*

$$ **Holiday Beach Hotel and Casino.** This ex–Holiday Inn is a four-story, 27-year-old, U-shape, aquamarine-color building surrounding a pool area. Over the past four years, the rooms have been completely renovated and refurnished in a beige, emerald, and rose color scheme, with bleached wood and rattan furniture. All have TV, shower and bath, and balcony. Half the rooms face the parking lot; most of the others face the pool area, and only a few have sea views. The air-conditioned lobby is spacious to permit the assembly of tour groups, and one of the island's largest casinos, Casino Royale, is off to the lobby's left. The hotel's outstanding feature is its crescent beach, quite large for Curaçao and dotted with palm trees. There's also a water-sports concession and a tiki-hut beach bar. Guests are encouraged to join in the voluminous daily selection of activities. The lobby bar happy hour is one of the most popular on the island. Although this is an older property, the renovation, along with the friendly service, makes it a good choice for people seeking good value on a middle-of-the-road budget. *Box 2178, Otrabanda, Pater Euwensweg, Willemstad, tel. 599/9–625400, fax 599/9–624397. 200 rooms. Facilities: 2 bars, pool, water-sports concession, playground, 2 tennis courts, beauty shop, boutique, drugstore, gift shop, car-rental agent, baby-sitting, casino. AE, DC, MC, V. EP.*

$ **Lions Dive Hotel & Marina.** This recent addition to the Curaçao vacation scene is a hop, skip, and plunge away from the Seaquarium. The pink-and-green caravansary is set next to a quarter-mile of private beach. The rooms are airy, modern, and light-filled, with tile floors, large bathrooms, and lots of windows. A pair of French doors leads out to a spacious balcony or terrace, and every room has a view of the sea. The Sunday-night happy hour is especially festive, with a local merengue band playing poolside. By midnight, however, the only sound to be heard is the whir of your room's air conditioner. Pluses include a young, attractive staff who are eager to please and a scuba center that's top-notch. Dive packages are offered with Underwater Curaçao, and most, if not all, of the guests are dive enthusiasts. *Bapor Kibra, Curaçao, tel. 599/9–618100, fax 599/9–618200. 72 air-conditioned rooms. Facilities: restaurant, terrace bar, pool, scuba diving center with 2 dive boats, water-sports concession, video-rental shop. AE, DC, MC, V. CP.*

$ **Otrabanda Hotel & Casino.** Views of passing ships, the Punda, and the floating bridge give the Otrabanda a charming outlook. New in 1991, this city hotel is across the harbor from downtown Willemstad.

The management appears more interested in keeping the locals gambling in the ground-floor casino than in attracting visitors to the small but clean and simple rooms. But with double rooms at $105 during high season, it offers good value. There's a generous breakfast buffet each morning. *Breedestradt (Oost), Otrabanda, tel. 599/9–627400, fax 599/9–627299. 45 rooms. Facilities: restaurant, bar, coffee shop, casino. AE, V. CP.*

$ **Van Der Valk Plaza Hotel and Casino.** "Please don't touch the passing ships" is the slogan of the Van Der Valk Plaza, the only hotel in the world with marine-collision insurance. The ships do come close to the island's first high-rise hotel, built into the massive walls of a 17th-century fort at the entrance of Willemstad's harbor. At the Plaza, you give up beachfront (you have beach privileges at major hotels, however) for walking access to the city's center. Consequently, it's a business traveler's oasis, complete with secretarial service, fax and telex machines, and typing and translation services. The ramparts rising from the sea offer a fantastic evening view of the twinkling lights of the city. A new, enlarged casino has been completed, the fine restaurants are a splendid place to watch the ships anchor in the harbor, and the lobby is now a vision in marble, with handsomely upholstered furniture, vaulting trees, and a winding lagoon and waterfall. Regrettably, the rooms are sorely lacking in style and decor. One hundred and thirty-five of the rooms are in the tower, many with a sea view and some with balconies. All rooms have cable TV, air-conditioning, and a minifridge. *Box 229, Plaza Piar, Willemstad, tel. 599/9–612500, fax 599/9–616543. 254 rooms. Facilities: 2 restaurants, 3 bars, coffee shop, pool, casino, room service, business services, dive shop, drugstore, gift shop, car-rental agent, tour desk, pool. Baby-sitter and house physician on call. AE, DC, MC, V. CP.*

¢ **Coral Cliff Resort & Casino.** Seclusion and rustic simplicity are everything here. A 45-minute ride from the center of Willemstad, the grounds of the resort boast a beach so enticing that it even attracts native islanders seeking a weekend retreat. (The beach is open to the public for a $5 admission charge.) The resort exudes a European atmosphere—wood beams accent the lavender, mint, olive, and teal colors—and is very popular with Dutch tourists. Guests used to luxurious or amenity-laden resorts will find the rooms stark and in sore need of modernizing. However, all are air-conditioned, have spectacular views of the sea, and are equipped with satellite TVs, direct-dial phones, and old but functional kitchenettes. The hotel recently installed a children's playground and miniature golf course, a tennis court, and slot machines in the bar. All guests receive complimentary airport transfers. *Box 3782, Santa Marta Bay, tel. 599/9–641820 or 800/344–1212, fax 599/9–641781. 35 units. Facilities: restaurant, bar, pool, casino, car-rental agent, marina, water-sports center, miniature golf, playground, tennis court, PADI 4-star dive shop. AE, DC, MC, V. EP, BP, MAP, FAP.*

¢ **Landhuis Daniel.** Dating back to 1630, this plantation house was never a farm, but served as an inn for travelers going east or west on the island. The property, at the west end of the island, has a restaurant, a pool, and a dive center as well. Rooms are nicely furnished. A few have private baths; only one is air-conditioned, but the trade winds usually take care of excessive heat at night. *Weg naar Westpunt, tel. 599/9 –648400. 9 rooms. Facilities: restaurant, pool, dive center. No credit cards. EP.*

Villa and Apartment Rentals

As a rule, Curaçao's rental villas and cottages are not on the beach, although there are a few in the Westpunt area that overlook the sea and are a short walk from the water. For a complete list of rental units available, contact the **Curaçao Tourism Development Foundation** (Pietermaii 19, Willemstad, Curaçao, Netherland Antilles, tel. 599/9–616000, fax 599/9–612305). Most villas and cottages cater to Europeans used to basic amenities and a no-frills atmosphere. Air-conditioning is not a standard feature, so be sure to request it. One top-notch apartment complex is listed below.

¢–$$ **Club Seru Coral.** This modern resort complex with bungalows and studio apartments opened in 1992 on Curaçao's east coast. The grounds feature both desert and tropical landscaping. Bungalows have two bedrooms, bath, fully equipped kitchen, and a combination dining/living room. The compact studio apartments are comparable to large hotel rooms with complete kitchenettes. All accommodations are air-conditioned and have tile floors, twin beds, patios, color TVs, phones, radios, and safe-deposit boxes. There's a restaurant and pool here, and guests have tennis privileges at the Santa Catherina Sports Club, located 2½ miles away. Free pickup from the airport is provided, but since the resort is off the beach and a good 9 miles from town, a rental car is advised. *Koraal Partier 10, tel. and fax 599/9–678276. 41 units. Facilities: restaurant, bar, pool, children's pool, room service, car-rental desk, satellite TV, games room, baby-sitting, small grocery and liquor store, daily maid service. AE, D, DC, MC, V.*

Guest Houses and Inns Curaçao has a number of small budget hotels, guest houses, and inns charging less than $50 a day in high season. Many are off the beaten track and have few, if any, facilities, other than rooms with kitchenettes. Request a list from the Tourism Development Foundation (*see* Villa and Apartment Rentals, *above*), along with a detailed island map so that you can locate each place. If you're worried about what you might end up with, first book a hotel and then inspect your room at the guest house before deciding to stay there.

Off-Season Bets Prices at Curaçao's top hotels decrease by about 30% from mid-April to mid-December. Full-service resorts with excellent off-season rates in our $$ category include the new **Sonesta Beach Hotel & Casino** (Box 6003, Piscadera Bay, tel. 599/9–368800 or 800/766–3782, fax 599/9–627502); and the **Princess Beach Hotel and Casino** (M.L. King Blvd. 8, tel. 599/9–367888 or 800/327–3286, fax 599/9–614131).

Nightlife

Friday is the big night out, with rollicking happy hours, most with live music, at several hotels, most notably the Holiday Beach and Avila Beach (*see* Lodging, *above*). The once-a-month open house at Landhuis Brievengat (*see* Exploring Curaçao, Eastern Side, *above*) is a great way to meet interesting locals—it usually offers a folkloric show, snacks, and local handicrafts. Every Friday night the landhouse holds a big party with two bands. Check with the tourist board for the schedule of folkloric shows at various hotels. The Sonesta Beach, Van Der Valk Plaza, Curaçao Caribbean, Holiday Beach, Otrabanda, and Princess Beach hotels all have casinos that are open 1 PM–4 AM.

The Salinja district is the spot for clubbing: You'll find everything from merengue to house. **The Pub** (Salinja 144A, tel. 599/9–612190) is a crowded, energetic dancing-and-drinking club. It's the place for the loud, the hip, the young, and the wanna-bes checking on the latest Curaçao fads. The dress is casual to funky, so leave your heels at home. Open Friday 8 PM–4 AM, Saturday 9 PM–4 AM, Monday–Thursday and Sunday 9 PM–3 AM.

Considered the most colorful disco in town, **Facade** (Lindbergweg 32, Salina, tel. 599/9–614640) is about as hip as Curaçao gets. It's dark and cool, with huge bamboo chairs for lounging. The men cruise and the women are dressed to kill. There are two disco floors with flashing lights and an intense aural assault, sometimes from a live band. It's packed on Thursday, Friday, and Saturday nights from 10 PM to

4 AM. Friday happy hour is from 6 to 8 PM and 10 to 11PM. Facade is closed Tuesday.

L'Aristocrat (Lindbergweg-Salina, tel. 599/9–614353) attracts the more mature crowd seeking late-night pleasures, and on Saturday night the line to get in stretches down the block. Inside, the trendy clientele gyrates to a heavy beat while silent large-screen TVs flash sensual images. This is the place to see and be seen. There's a $9 cover charge, and it's open Friday and Saturday 10 PM to 4 AM; closed Monday.

Rum Runners (Otrobanda Waterfront, De Rouvilleweg 9, tel. 599/9–623038) is another casual hot spot. This well-lit indoor/outdoor bar and eatery serves up tapas in an atmosphere that's reminiscent of a college fraternity hall. There's music nightly. The crowd stays until about midnight, after which the majority switch to **Facade, The Pub,** or **L'Aristocrat.**

10 Dominica

Updated by Jordan Simon

The national motto emblazoned on the coat of arms of the Commonwealth of Dominica reads *"Après Bondi, c'est la ter."* It is a French-Creole phrase meaning "After God, it is the land." On this unspoiled isle, the land is indeed the main attraction: It turns and twists, towers to mountain crests, then tumbles to falls and valleys. It is a land that the Smithsonian Institution called a giant plant laboratory, unchanged for 10,000 years. Indeed, after a heavy rain you half expect to see things grow before your very eyes; the island is a virtual rainbow in entirely green hues.

The grandeur of Dominica (pronounced dom-in-*ee*-ka) is not manmade. This untamed, ruggedly beautiful land, located in the eastern Caribbean between Guadeloupe to the north and Martinique to the south, is a 305-square-mile nature retreat; 29 miles long and 15 miles wide, the island is dominated by some of the highest elevations in the Caribbean and is laced with 365 rivers, "one for every day of the year." Much of the interior is covered by a luxuriant rain forest, a wild place where you almost expect Tarzan to swing howling by on a vine. Straight out of Conan Doyle's *Lost World*, everything here is larger than life, from the towering tree ferns to the enormous insects. This exotic spot is home to such unusual critters as the Sisserou (or Imperial) parrot and the red-necked (or Jacquot) parrot, neither of which is found anywhere else in the world.

Dominica's rugged mountains and abundant forests and rivers have held the island back from rapid economic development. And the lack of good beaches has hindered the growth of tourism. Consequently, with the exception of imported items, costs here are among the lowest in the Caribbean. Hotel prices are less than on most other islands (but then, even its best hotels are almost basic by Caribbean resort standards), and for the most part prices remain steady year-round. Only a few hotels are close to the beach, but Dominica is not an island for magnificent beaches, nor for casinos or piña coladas or glitzy resorts. Instead, it's an island for explorers, hikers, and divers. Many of its accommodations are in secluded rain-forest and hill settings with few amenities or activities. Guests are independent types who make their own itineraries, usually chock-full of exploring the magnificent countryside.

The island is home to the last remnants of the Carib Indians, whose ancestors came paddling up from South America more than a thousand years ago. The fierce, cannibalistic Caribs kept Christopher Columbus at bay when he came to call during his second voyage to the New World. Columbus turned up at the island on Sunday, November 3, 1493. In between Carib arrows he hastily christened it Dominica (Sunday Island), and then sailed on. In 1805, the island became a British colony and remained so until November 3, 1978, when it became a fully independent republic, officially called the Commonwealth of Dominica. There are about 82,000 people living on the island, and they are some of the friendliest people in all of the Caribbean.

What It Will Cost These sample prices, meant only as a general guide, are for high season. For a standard double room at a $$ hotel, expect to pay about $110. Dinner at a $ restaurant costs about $12. Beer prices at restaurants start at $1.50. Wine is prohibitive, but local rum is cheap; a rum punch at a restaurant costs about $2.50. Taxis are no bargain, at about $1 a mile, and because sites are scattered over the island, transportation costs mount. There is infrequent bus service that's less convenient, but a lot cheaper: A ride from Roseau in the southwest to Woodford Hill in the northeast is about $3.50. Car rental begins at $35 a day; rentals of three or more days will save you money. A single-tank dive is about $40, and snorkel equipment rents for $5–$6 a day.

Before You Go

Tourist Information Contact the **Caribbean Tourism Organization** (20 E. 46th St., New York, NY 10017, tel. 212/682–0435). In the United Kingdom, contact the **Dominica Tourist Office** (1 Collingham Gardens, London SW5 0HW, tel. 0171/835–1937 or 0171/370–5194).

Arriving and Departing

By Plane No major airlines fly into Dominica (although **American** may begin service in late 1995), but **LIAT** (tel. 809/462–0700) connects with flights from the United States on Antigua, Barbados, Guadeloupe, Martinique, St. Lucia, and San Juan, Puerto Rico. **Air Martinique** (tel. 809/448–2181) flies from Fort-de-France, and **Air Guadeloupe** (tel. 809/448–2181) from Pointe-à-Pitre. **BWIA** (tel. 809/462–0363) connects from Antigua, **Winair** (tel. 809/448–2181) from St. Maarten, and **Air BVI** (tel. 809/774–6500) from Tortola, B.V.I. **Nature Island Express** (tel. 809/449–2309) provides service to and from Barbados, St. Lucia, and St. Maarten daily.

From the Airport **Canefield Airport** (about 3 miles north of Roseau) handles only small aircraft and daytime flights; landing here can be a hair-raising experience for those uneasy about flying. Cab fare is about $8 to Roseau. **Melville Hall Airport,** on the northeast coast, handles larger planes; although interesting, the 90-minute drive through the island's rain forest to Roseau is bumpy, exhausting, and costs about $50 by private taxi or $17 per person by co-op cab.

By Boat The **Caribbean Express** (Fort-de-France, Martinique, tel. 596/60–12–38) has scheduled service Monday, Wednesday, Friday, and Saturday from Guadeloupe in the north to Martinique in the south, with stops at Les Saintes and Dominica. Fares run approximately 25% below economy airfares.

Passports and Visas The only entry requirements for U.S. or Canadian citizens are proof of citizenship, such as a driver's license or passport, and an ongoing or return airline ticket. British citizens are required to have passports, but visas are not necessary.

Language The official language is English, but most Dominicans also speak a French-Creole patois.

Precautions Be sure to bring insect repellent. Bring along pills for motion sickness; the roads twist and turn dramatically, and the local drivers barrel across them at a dizzying pace. If you plan to hike even the simplest trail, bring along extra clothing and hiking boots or athletic sneakers to change into; trails are very rugged and often very muddy.

Staying in Dominica

Important Addresses **Tourist Information:** Contact the main office of the **Division of Tourism** (National Development Corp., Valley Rd., Roseau, tel. 809/448–2045). The tourist desk at the **Old Market Plaza** (Roseau, tel. 809/448–2186) is open Monday 8–5, Tuesday–Friday 8–4, Saturday 9–1. The offices at **Canefield Airport** (tel. 809/449–1242) and **Melville Hall Airport** (tel. 809/445–7051) are open weekdays 6:15–11 AM and 2–5:30 PM.

Emergencies **Police, Fire, and Ambulance:** Call 999. **Hospitals: Princess Margaret Hospital** (Federation Dr., Goodwill, tel. 809/448–2231 or 809/448–2233). **Pharmacies: Jolly's Pharmacy** (12 King George V St., Roseau, tel. 809/448–3388).

Currency The official currency is the Eastern Caribbean dollar (E.C.$), but U.S. dollars are accepted everywhere. At banks the rate is officially tied to the U.S. dollar, at a rate of E.C. $2.60 to U.S. $1. Local prices, especially in shops frequented by tourists, are often quoted in both currencies, so be sure to ask. Prices quoted here are in U.S. dollars unless noted otherwise.

Taxes and Service Charges Hotels collect a 5% government tax; restaurants a 3% tax. Most hotels and restaurants add a 10% service charge to your bill. Taxi drivers appreciate a 10% tip. The departure tax is $10, or E.C. $25.

Getting Around

Rental Cars If it doesn't bother you to drive on the left over potholed mountainous roads with hairpin curves, rent a car and strike out on your own. Daily car-rental rates begin at $35 (weekly about $190), plus collision damage at $6 a day, and personal accident insurance at $2 a day, and you'll have to put down a deposit and purchase a visitor's driving permit for E.C. $20. You can rent a car from **Anselm's Car Rental** (3 Great Marlborough St., Roseau, tel. 809/448–2730), **Avis** (4 High St., Roseau, tel. 809/448–2481), **S.T.L. Rent-A-Car** (Goodwill Rd., Roseau, tel. 809/448–2340 or 809/448–4525), **Valley Rent-A-Car** (Goodwill Rd., Roseau, tel. 809/448–3233), or **Wide Range Car Rentals** (79 Bath Rd., Roseau, tel. 809/448–2198). **Budget Rent-A-Car** (Canefield Industrial Estate, Canefield, tel. 809/449–2080) offers daily rates, three-day specials, and weekly and monthly rates.

By Taxi Taxis have fixed rates, though a little negotiation is always possible (except from the airport). A typical fare within Roseau is $5; a trip from Roseau to Portsmouth is $45. Taxis are hard to find after 6 PM, so you should make prior arrangements with a cabbie.

Telephones and Mail To call Dominica from the United States, dial area code 809 and the local access code, 44, followed by the five-digit local number. On the island, you need to dial only the five-digit number. A local call costs E.C. 25¢. Direct telephone, telegraph, telefax, teletype, and telex services are via **Cable & Wireless (West Indies) Ltd.** Card phones are becoming more common here. You can purchase the cards at the Cable & Wireless office and other locations. All pay phones are equipped for local and overseas dialing.

First-class (airmail) letters to the United States and Canada cost E.C. 95¢; postcards cost E.C. 50¢.

Opening and Closing Times Business hours are weekdays 8–1 and 2–4, Saturday 8–1. Banks are open Monday–Thursday 8–3, Friday 8–5.

Guided Tours A variety of hiking and photo safari tours is conducted by **Dominica Tours** (tel. 809/448–2638) in sturdy four-wheel-drive vehicles. Prices range from $15 to $100 per person, depending upon the length of the trip and whether picnics and rum punches are included. There are also boat tours that include snorkeling, swimming, and rum or fruit drinks. **Rainbow Rover Tours** (tel. 809/448–8650) are conducted in air-conditioned Land Rovers. You can take in the island for a half or full day at a cost of $30–$60, which includes food and drink. **Ken's Hinterland Adventure Tours** (tel. 809/448–4850) provides tours in vans with knowledgeable guides and can design expeditions to fit your needs. Prices vary according to the tour; an afternoon hike to the Valley of Desolation costs $30 and includes transportation to and from your hotel.

Any taxi driver will be happy to offer his services as a guide for $18 an hour, with tip extra. It's a good idea to get a recommendation from your hotel manager or the Dominica Division of Tourism? (*see* Tourist Information, *above*) before selecting a guide and driver. A tour to introduce you to the ruggedness of the island's terrain and its flora can be managed in four hours, but if you want to travel around the island, plan on seven.

Exploring Dominica

Numbers in the margin correspond to points of interest on the Dominica map.

The island's mountainous interior means getting anywhere takes longer than you think. Although you can get a quick overview of the island in one day of touring by car, you should supplement this with specialized hiking and sightseeing tours. The highways ringing the island's perimeter have been upgraded in recent years; but more remote destinations remain somewhat inaccessible, and it's wise to hire a car and driver or take an escorted tour.

Roseau All the hotels and virtually all the island's population are on the leeward, or Caribbean, side of the island. Twenty thousand or so inhab-
1 itants reside in **Roseau** (pronounced rose-*oh*). This noisy ragged town on the flat delta of the Roseau River is reminiscent of a more tattered version of New Orleans' French Quarter. A new waterfront and pier have upgraded the coastal side of town, but Roseau, which is one of the poorest capitals in the Caribbean, lacks the grand colonial architecture and the regal layout typical of the region. Walking through town, you will notice the French West Indian construction of most homes and shops—small wood-and-stone or wood-and-concrete shanties, many with balustrades and French doors. One impressive sight, on Victoria Street, is the **Fort Young Hotel,** originally built as a fort in the 18th century. Directly across the street is the **state house;** the **public library** and the **old court house** are both nearby.

The National Park Office, fittingly located in the 40-acre Botanical Gardens in Roseau, can provide tour guides and a wealth of printed information. *Tel. 809/448–2401, ext. 417. Open Mon. 8–1 and 2–5, Tues.–Fri. 8–1 and 2–4.*

Head north to Woodbridge Bay Harbour and stroll along the harbor, where you can watch bananas, citrus, and spices being loaded onto ships.

Elsewhere on the Island **Morne Trois Pitons** is a blue-green hill of three peaks, the highest of which is 4,403 feet. The mountain is usually veiled in swirling mists
2 and clouds, and the 16,000-acre national park over which it looms is awash with cool mountain lakes, waterfalls, and rushing rivers.

Ferns grow 30 feet tall, and wild orchids sprout from trees. Sunlight leaks through green canopies, and a gentle mist rises over the jungle floor.

The road from the capital to the Morne Trois Pitons National Park runs through the **Roseau River Valley** toward Laudat. About 5 miles out of Roseau, the Wotton Waven Road branches off toward the
3 **sulphur springs,** where you'll see the belching, sputtering, and gurgling release of hot springs along a river and nearby field—evidence of the area's restless volcanic activity. Double back and continue up the road to Laudat, taking the next side road to the spectacular twin
4 **Trafalgar Falls.** The road ends at **Papillote Wilderness Retreat** (*see* Dining, *below*, and Lodging, *below*). Both are visible from a viewing platform that is an easy hike from Papillote's driveways—guides there will happily show you the way. If you're in decent shape and possess agility and balance, it's worth hiking up the riverbed to the cool pools at the bases of both falls. The taller of the two is where hot, orange-colored sulfuric and ferric waters mix with the crash of cold river water; taking a dip is an exhilarating experience.

Again, double back to the main road from Roseau and continue to
5 **Laudat,** a small mountaintop village about 7 miles from Roseau and a good starting point for a venture into the park. Two miles northeast
6 of Laudat, at the base of **Morne Micotrin** (4,006 feet), you'll find **Freshwater Lake,** and farther on, **Boeri Lake,** which is fringed with greenery and has purple hyacinths floating on its surface.

Laudat is the starting point for the most talked about—and most
7 treacherous—hike in Dominica: the trek to **Boiling Lake** and the **Valley of Desolation.** You should only go with a guide (*see* Hiking *in* Sports and the Outdoors, *below*) and will have to leave at about 8 AM for this steep and slippery, all-day, 6-mile (round-trip) trek. You will return covered with mud, nicks, and scrapes; exhausted; and satisfied that you've seen one of the world's true wonders. Guides keep small groups of hikers (six to eight maximum) under their eye at all times. This is for serious hikers only: Make sure you're in excellent condition, and bring your own drinking water. The lake, the world's second-largest boiling lake, is like a caldron of gurgling gray-blue water. It is 210 feet wide, and the temperature of the water ranges from 180°F to 197°F. Its depth is unknown. It is believed that the lake is not a volcanic crater but a flooded fumarole—a crack through which gases escape from the molten lava below.

The Valley of Desolation lies below Boiling Lake, and it lives up to its name. Harsh sulfuric fumes have destroyed virtually all the vegetation in what was once a lush forested area. Hikers in the Valley of Desolation are advised to stay on the trail to avoid breaking through the crust that covers the hot lava below.

You'll have to backtrack to Roseau and head north toward the Pont
8 Casse rotary to reach **Emerald Pool.** At the rotary, follow signs for Castle Bruce for about 3½ miles until you come to the trail that leads to Emerald Pool. Lookout points along this short (about a 20-minute walk) trail provide sweeping views of the windward (Atlantic) coast and the forested interior. Emerald Pool is a swirling, fern-bedecked basin into which a 50-foot waterfall splashes. This is the most accessible of Dominica's natural wonders—and fittingly its least wondrous.

A good map and steady nerves are necessary for driving along the rugged, ragged windward coast. A few miles east of Pont Casse there is a fork in the road where a right turn will take you to the southeast coast and a left, to the northeast coast.

If you head back from the Emerald Pool toward Pont Casse and turn left at the intersection a couple of miles before the rotary, the road
9 leads to **Rosalie,** where there is a river for swimming, a black-sand

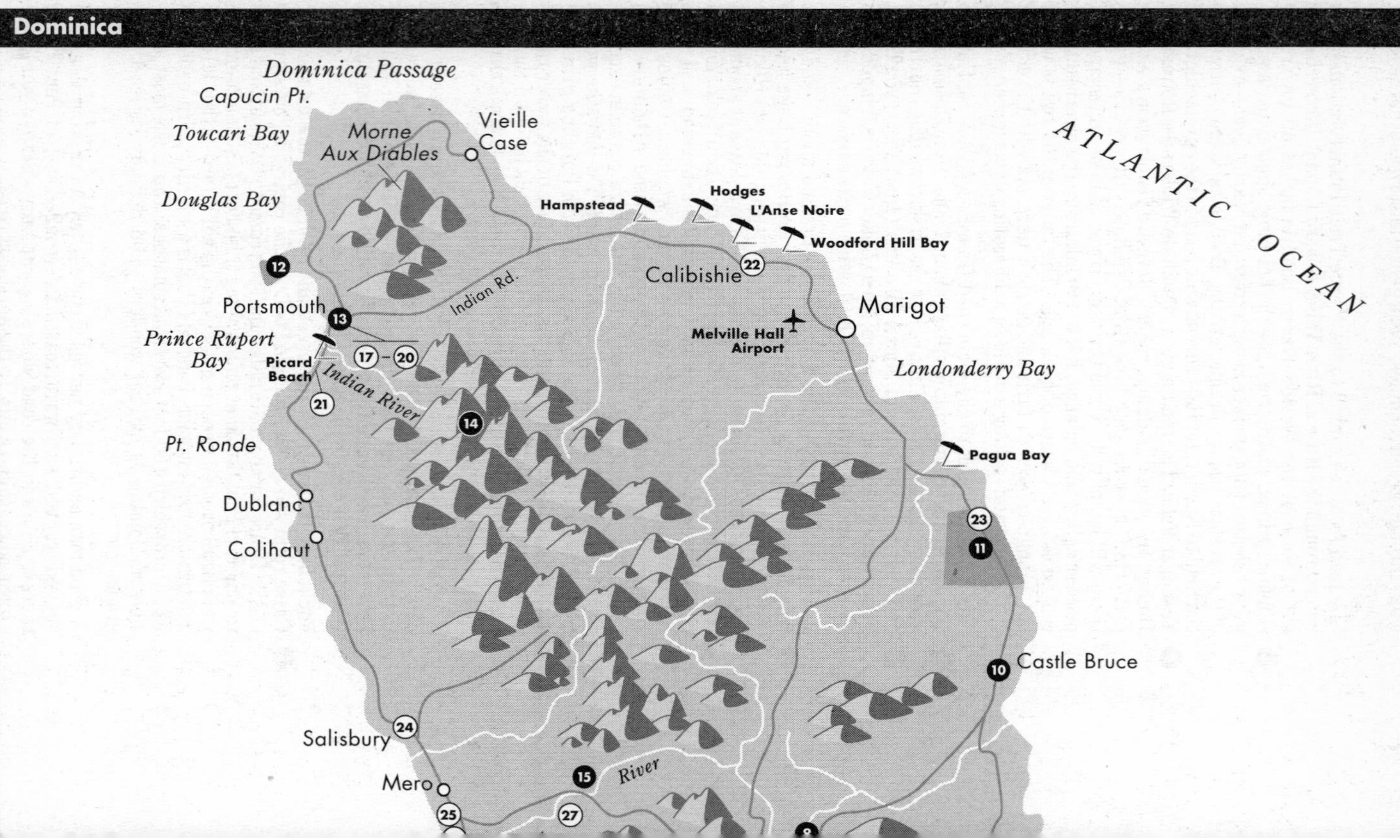
Dominica
Dominica Passage
Capucin Pt.
Toucari Bay
Morne Aux Diables
Vieille Case
ATLANTIC OCEAN
Douglas Bay
Hampstead
Hodges
L'Anse Noire
Woodford Hill Bay
12
Calibishie
22
Indian Rd.
Portsmouth
13
Marigot
Melville Hall Airport
Prince Rupert Bay
Picard Beach
17 – 20
Londonderry Bay
Indian River
21
14
Pt. Ronde
Pagua Bay
Dublanc
Colihaut
23
11
Castle Bruce
10
Salisbury
24
Mero
15
River
25
27

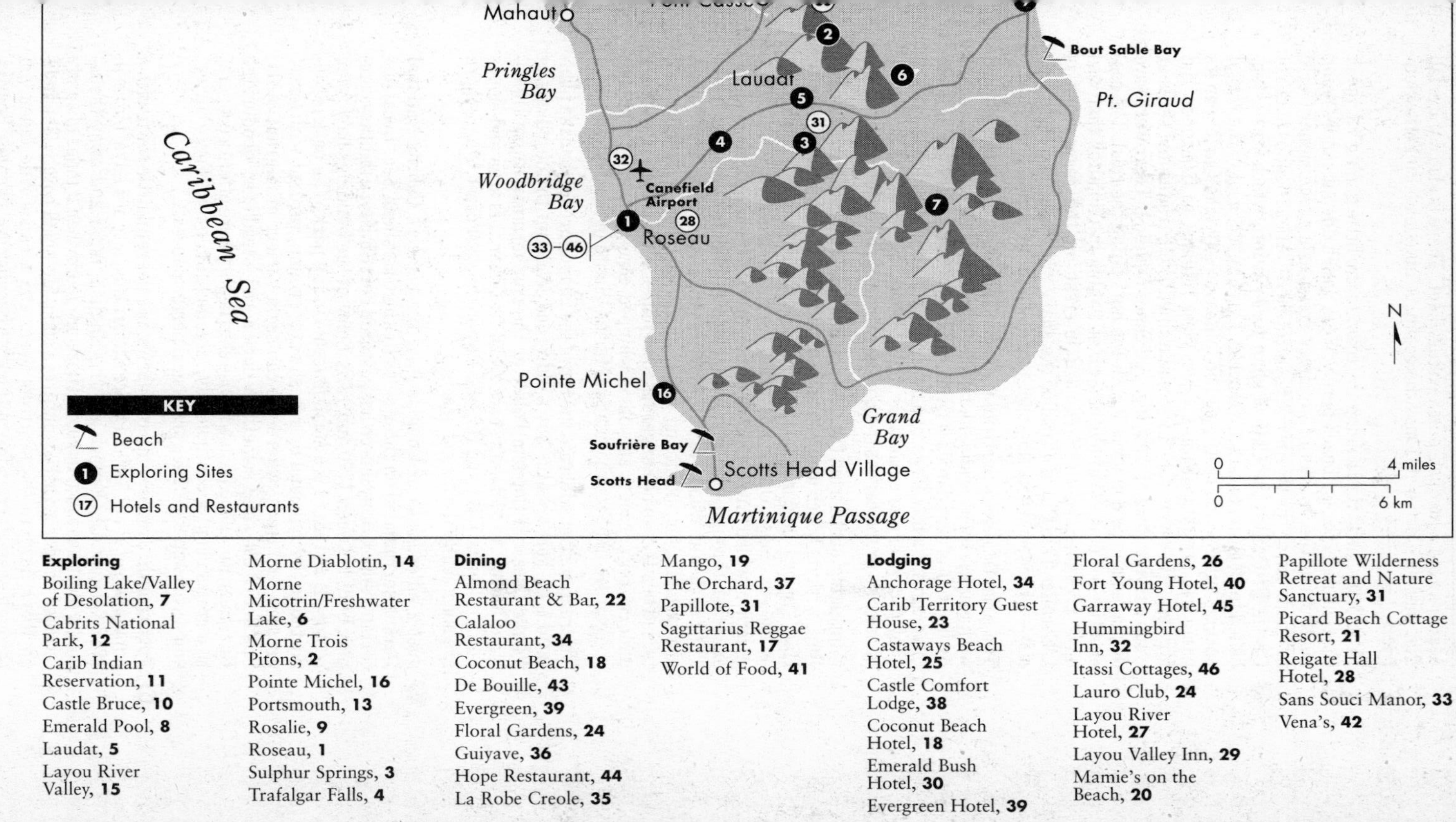

Exploring
Boiling Lake/Valley of Desolation, **7**
Cabrits National Park, **12**
Carib Indian Reservation, **11**
Castle Bruce, **10**
Emerald Pool, **8**
Laudat, **5**
Layou River Valley, **15**
Morne Diablotin, **14**
Morne Micotrin/Freshwater Lake, **6**
Morne Trois Pitons, **2**
Pointe Michel, **16**
Portsmouth, **13**
Rosalie, **9**
Roseau, **1**
Sulphur Springs, **3**
Trafalgar Falls, **4**

Dining
Almond Beach Restaurant & Bar, **22**
Calaloo Restaurant, **34**
Coconut Beach, **18**
De Bouille, **43**
Evergreen, **39**
Floral Gardens, **24**
Guiyave, **36**
Hope Restaurant, **44**
La Robe Creole, **35**
Mango, **19**
The Orchard, **37**
Papillote, **31**
Sagittarius Reggae Restaurant, **17**
World of Food, **41**

Lodging
Anchorage Hotel, **34**
Carib Territory Guest House, **23**
Castaways Beach Hotel, **25**
Castle Comfort Lodge, **38**
Coconut Beach Hotel, **18**
Emerald Bush Hotel, **30**
Evergreen Hotel, **39**
Floral Gardens, **26**
Fort Young Hotel, **40**
Garraway Hotel, **45**
Hummingbird Inn, **32**
Itassi Cottages, **46**
Lauro Club, **24**
Layou River Hotel, **27**
Layou Valley Inn, **29**
Mamie's on the Beach, **20**
Papillote Wilderness Retreat and Nature Sanctuary, **31**
Picard Beach Cottage Resort, **21**
Reigate Hall Hotel, **28**
Sans Souci Manor, **33**
Vena's, **42**

beach, an old aqueduct, and a waterwheel. There is also a waterfall that dashes down a cliff into the ocean. A hike leads to **Petite Soufrière.**

From here, head north along the coast to the little fishing village of
10 **Castle Bruce.** On the beach here you can watch dugout canoes being
made from the trunks of gommier trees using traditional Carib
methods (after the tree is cut it's stretched). About 6 miles north of
11 Castle Bruce lies the **Carib Indian Reservation,** which was estab-
lished in 1903 and covers 3,700 acres. Don't expect a lot in the way of ancient culture and costume. The folks who gave the Caribbean its name live pretty much like other West Indians, as fishermen and farmers. However, they have maintained their traditional skills at wood carving, basket weaving, and canoe building. Their wares are displayed and sold in little thatch-top huts lining the road. The reservation's Roman Catholic church at Salibia has an altar that was once a canoe. Another point of interest on the reservation is **L'Escalier Tête Chien** ("trail of the snake staircase" in Creole patois)—a hardened lava flow that juts down to the ocean.

The Atlantic here is particularly fierce and roily, the shore marked with countless coves and inlets. The Carib still tell wondrous colorful legends of the island's origins. La Roche Pagua, they say, is home to a fragrant white flower; bathe in its petals and your loved one will obey your every command. By night, Londonderry Islets metamorphose into grand canoes to take the spirits of the dead out to sea.

Continuing north from the reservation, you'll go past lovely **Pagua Bay,** with its beach of dark sand. A bit farther along, near Melville Hall Airport, is **Marigot,** the largest (population: 5,000) settlement on the east coast. On the northeast coast, steep cliffs rise out of the Atlantic, which flings its frothy waters over dramatic reefs, and rivers crash through forests of mangroves and fields of coconut trees. The beaches at **Woodford Hill, Hampstead, L'Anse Noir,** and **Hodges** are excellent for snorkeling and scuba diving, though all this wind-tossed beauty can be dangerous to swimmers, since there are strong underwater currents as well as whipped-cream waves. From here you can see the French island of Marie Galante in the distance.

The road continues across the top of the island through banana plantations to Portsmouth, but a side road leads up to the village of **Vieille Case** and **Capucin Pointe** at the northernmost tip of the island. **Morne Aux Diables** soars 2,826 feet over this area and slopes down to **Toucari Bay** and **Douglas Bay** on the west coast, where there are spectacular dark-sand beaches.

12 Just 2 miles south of Douglas Bay, the 250-acre **Cabrits National Park** is surrounded on three sides by the Caribbean Sea. Local historian Lennox Honychurch has restored **Fort Shirley,** a military complex built between 1770 and 1815. Some of the buildings have been restored, and there is a small museum in the park. The park is connected to the mainland by a freshwater swamp, verdant with ferns, grasses, and trees, where you can see a variety of migrant birds. Smaller cruise ships sometimes dock here instead of at Woodbridge Bay, near Roseau. The new cruise ship facility here offers a cooperative crafts shop, a continuously screened film about Fort Shirley, and occasional live dance or musical performances.

13 **Portsmouth,** 2 miles south of Cabrits, is a peaceful little town with a population of about 5,000. **Prince Rupert Bay,** site of a naval battle in 1782 between the French and the English, is far and away the island's most beautiful harbor. There are more than 2 miles of sandy beaches fringed with coconut trees and a few small hotels. The **Indian River** flows to the sea from here, and a canoe ride takes you through an exotic rain forest thick with mangrove swamps. Board a rowboat for total tranquillity, to be able to hear fish jumping and ex-

otic birds calling. The guides here are notoriously overeager: Choose carefully or ask your hotel to recommend someone.

Just south of Indian River is **Pointe Ronde,** the starting point for an
14 expedition to **Morne Diablotin,** at 4,747 feet the island's highest
summit. This is not an expedition you should attempt alone; the uninhabited interior is an almost impenetrable primeval forest. You'll need a good guide (*see* Hiking *in* Sports and the Outdoors, *below*), sturdy shoes, a warm sweater, and firm resolve.

Heading back to Roseau, the west-coast road dips down through the little villages of **Dublanc** (with a side road off to the Syndicate Estate), **Colihaut,** and **Salisbury** before reaching the mouth of the
15 Layou River. The **Layou River Valley** is rich with bananas, cacao, cit-
rus fruits, and coconuts. The remains of Hillsborough Estate, once a rum-producing plantation, are here. The river is the island's longest and largest, with deep gorges, quiet pools and beaches, waterfalls and rapids—a great place for a full day's outing of swimming and shooting the rapids, or just sunning and picnicking.

The road at the bend near Dublanc that leads to the Syndicate Estate also leads to the 200-acre site of **Project Sisserou.** This protected site has been set aside with the help of some 6,000 schoolchildren, each of whom donated 25¢ for the land where the endangered Sisserou parrot (found only in Dominica) flies free. At last estimate, there were only about 60 of these shy and beautiful birds, covered in rich green feathers with a mauve front.

Just south of Roseau the road forks, with a treacherous prong leading east to **Grand Bay,** where bay leaves are grown and distilled. If
16 you continue due south from Roseau, you'll go through **Pointe
Michel,** settled decades ago by Martinicans who fled the catastrophic eruption of Mont Pelée. The stretch all the way from Roseau to Scotts Head at the southernmost tip of the island has excellent beaches for scuba diving and snorkeling.

Beaches

Don't come to Dominica in search of powdery white-sand beaches. The travel-poster beaches do exist on the northeast coast, but this is still an almost totally undeveloped area. The beaches that most visitors see are of dark sand, evidence of the island's volcanic origins. The best beaches are found at the mouths of rivers and in protected bays. Scuba diving, snorkeling, and windsurfing are all excellent here.

Layou River has the best river swimming on the island, and its banks are great for sunbathing.

Picard Beach, on the northwest coast, is the island's best beach. Great for windsurfing and snorkeling, it's a 2-mile stretch of brown sand fringed with coconut trees. The Picard Beach Cottage Resort and Coconut Beach hotels are along this beach.

Pagua Bay, a quiet, secluded beach of dark sand, is on the Atlantic coast.

Woodford Hill Bay, Hampstead, L'Anse Noir, and **Hodges,** all on the northeast coast, are excellent beaches for snorkeling and scuba diving. Strong underwater currents discourage swimmers.

In the southeast, near La Plaine, **Bout Sable Bay** is not much good for swimming, but the surroundings are stirringly elemental: towering red cliffs challenge the rollicking Atlantic.

The beaches south of Roseau to **Scotts Head** at the southernmost tip of the island are good for scuba diving and snorkeling because of the dramatic underwater walls and sudden drops.

The scuba diving is excellent at **Soufrière Bay,** a sandy beach south of Roseau. Volcanic vents puff steam into the sea; the experience has been described as "swimming in champagne."

Sports and the Outdoors

Hiking Trails range from the easy to the arduous. For the former, all you'll need are sturdy, rubber-soled shoes and an adventurous spirit.

For the hike to Boiling Lake or the climb up Morne Diablotin you will need hiking boots, a guide, and water. Guides will charge about \$30–\$35 per person and can be contacted through the Division of Tourism or the Forestry Division (tel. 809/448–2401 or 809/448–2638).

Scuba Diving *Skin Diver* magazine recently ranked Dominica among the top five Caribbean dive destinations. There's no shore diving here, so you'll have to hook up with a dive shop to make boat arrangements. **Dive Dominica** (Castle Comfort, tel. 809/448–2188, fax 809/448–6088), with three boats, is one of the best dive shops in Dominica, run by owners Derek and Ginette Perryman, NAUI-approved instructors. They offer snorkeling and resort dives for beginners and, for the advanced set, dives on drop-offs, walls, and pinnacles—by day or night. The owners of the **Dominica Dive Resorts, Waitukubuli** (there are two: one at the Anchorage Hotel, tel. 809/448–2638, the other at the Portsmouth Beach Hotel, tel. 809/445–5142), are PADI-certified and offer both resort courses and full certification. The **Castaways Beach Hotel,** 11 miles north of Roseau, has diving at its water-sports center (tel. 809/449–6245 or 800/525–3833). The latest addition to the scene is **Nature Island Dive** (Soufrière, tel. 809/449–8181), run by three friendly couples, one local, one American, one British/American. They also offer sea kayaking and mountain bike tours and rentals. Future plans include building a casual dive resort that will incorporate old plantation ruins on the hill overlooking the bay. The going rate at all of the above is about \$40 for a single-tank dive, \$65 for a two-tank dive, or \$90 for a resort course with two open-water dives.

Snorkeling Major island operators rent equipment for about \$5–\$6 a day: **Anchorage Hotel** (tel. 809/448–2638), **Castaways Beach Hotel** (tel. 809/449–6245), **Coconut Beach Hotel** (tel. 809/445–5393), and **Picard Beach Cottage Resort** (tel. 809/445–5131).

Swimming River swimming is extremely popular on Dominica, and the best river to jump into is the Layou River (*see* Exploring Dominica, *above*). *See also* Beaches, *above,* for our pick of the best beaches for swimming, snorkeling, or surfing.

Shopping

Gift Ideas The distinctive handicrafts of the Carib Indians include traditional baskets made of dyed *larouma* reeds and waterproofed with tightly woven *balizier* leaves. These crafts are sold on the reservation, as well as in Roseau's shops. Dominica is also noted for its spices, hot peppers, bay rum, and coconut-oil soap; its vetiver-grass mats are sold all over the world. All of these items represent good value.

Starbrite Industries (Canefield Industrial Estate, tel. 809/449–1006) makes great candles, including some in the shape of the Dominican parrot, cupids, and trees. It's open weekdays 8–4. The **Old Mill Culture Centre and Historic Site** (Canefield Rd., no phone) presents exhibits on the historical, cultural, and political development of Dominica. In addition, the center exhibits and sells wood carvings by a master carver, Louis Desire, and those of his students—all lovingly carved from Dominican woods. The center is open weekdays 9–1 and 2–4. There are gift shops at Papillote (wonderful wooden bowls) and Floral Gardens (domestic goods and crafts). (*See* Lodging, *below.*)

Stop in at **Caribana Handcrafts** (31 Cork St., Roseau, tel. 809/448–2761) for ceramics, woodcarvings, and baskets. **Fadelle's** (28 Kennedy Ave., Roseau, tel. 809/448–2686) offers still more straw and woodwork, as well as soaps, sauces, and perfumes. You can watch the local ladies weaving in the back room at **Tropicrafts** (41 Queen Mary St., Roseau, tel. 809/448–2747; Bay St., Portsmouth, tel. 809/445–5956), where you'll find woodcarvings, rum, hot sauces, and local perfumes, in addition to traditional Carib baskets, hats, and woven mats. **Balisier** (35 Great George St., no phone) is the spot for charming sunbonnets, carnival dolls, island jewelry, and hand-painted T-shirts. A local priest runs **Dominica Pottery** (Bayfront St. and Kennedy Ave., Roseau, no phone), whose products are fashioned with various local clays and glazes.

The government actively promotes and encourages local artisans and helped open the new **NDFD Small Business Mini Mall** (9 Great Marlborough St., Roseau, tel. 809/448–0412). Among the more notable booths are **Linx Jewelry,** where Dyanna handpaints T-shirts and creates unusual African-influenced earrings, bracelets, necklaces and pins from coconut husks, seashells, clay, wood, and pods; **Caribbean Perfumes,** fragrant with teas, scents, and potpourri from vanilla to vetiver; and the **Blow Kalbass Healing Center,** which hawks natural products touted to cure everything from acne to rheumatism (locals swear by the skin creams, clay baths, and hair pomade).

Proof that the old ways live on in Dominica can be found by the number of herbal doctors setting up shop in the streets of Roseau. One stimulating memento of your visit might be rum steeped with Bois Bandé (scientific name Richeria Grandis), a tree whose bark is reputed to have aphrodisiacal properties. You can find it at Tropicrafts, although it's cheaper in the supermarkets (try **Whitchurch** on Kennedy Ave.). Macoucherie distills the best-known elixir.

Dining

Except in Roseau, most restaurants on Dominica are attached to hotels. But even here, you'll have ample opportunity to sample the local cuisine; indeed, you'll be hard-pressed to find anything else. Menus are remarkably similar throughout the island, although preparations differ. Produce and fish are mostly from local sources, and meals usually consist of meat, chicken, or fish in a Creole sauce, served with sweet green plantains, ushkush yams, breadfruit, and dasheen (a tuber similar to the potato and called taro elsewhere)—these and other staples are known as ground provisions. On virtually every menu you'll find "mountain chicken"—a euphemism for a large toad called *crapaud.* Two rare delicacies for the intrepid diner are *manicou* (a small opossum) and the tender, gamey *agouti* (a large, indigenous rodent); both are best smoked or stewed. Few restaurants are expensive here.

Highly recommended restaurants are indicated by a star ★.

Category	Cost*
$$	$20–$30
$	$10–$20
¢	under $10

**per person, excluding drinks, service, and 3% sales tax*

$$ **De Bouille.** The upscale attractive dining room at the Fort Young Hotel—with its stone walls and wood-raftered ceiling—is usually filled with the businesspeople who frequent the hotel. The Indian chef adds a touch of his homeland cuisine to Continental and Dominican dishes (the special may be mountain chicken tandoori). The menu includes callaloo and pumpkin soup, grilled lobster, steak, and curried chicken. The three-course executive menu is a steal at E.C. $40 it might feature such inventive entrees as fricassee of rabbit or braised tuna florentine. The atmospheric Balas Bar across the hall, overlooking the pool, offers inexpensive, filling bar eats such as grilled chicken, pizza, and club sandwiches. *Fort Young Hotel, Roseau, tel. 809/448–5000. Reservations recommended. AE, MC, V.*

$$ **Evergreen.** Enjoy a relaxing meal on a large, airy, seaside terrace overlooking the sea. It's decorated with bright tropical prints, crystal teardrop chandeliers, and a striking art deco-ish bar in stark gray, black, and white. Delicious dinners include a choice of soup and salad; entrées of chicken, fish, and beef are served with local fruits and vegetables, such as kushkush and plantains. Homemade desserts include fresh fruit, cake, and ice cream. *Evergreen Hotel, Roseau, tel. 809/448–3288. Reservations advised. AE, V, MC.*

$$ ★ **Floral Gardens.** You may feel as if you're eating in a private home at this warm, welcoming restaurant with its wood paneling, roughhewn timber beams, and vetiver mats. The food is delectable. This is the place to sample local specialties such as crapaud and agouti. Finish it off with luscious homemade coconut or rum raisin ice cream. *Floral Gardens Motel, Concord, tel. 809/445–7636. Reservations advised in high season. AE, MC, V.*

$$ **Guiyave.** Have a drink at the second-floor bar and then repair to the table-filled balcony for a scrumptious lunch. Spareribs, lobster, rabbit, and mountain chicken are offered, along with homemade beef or chicken patties, spicy *rotis* (Caribbean burritos), and a variety of light snacks and sandwiches. This restaurant is noted for its fresh tropical fruit juices (cherry, guava, and passion fruit) and its homemade pies, tarts, and cakes. *15 Cork St., Roseau, tel. 809/448–2930. No credit cards. No dinner.*

$$ ★ **La Robe Creole.** The eclectic à la carte menu here includes lobster and conch crepes, charcoal-grilled fish and meats, barbecued chicken, and a selection of salads. Callaloo and crab soup, made with dasheen and coconut, is a specialty. A good way to keep the tab down is to order appetizers as your main course; otherwise, this restaurant should be considered a splurge choice. The dining room is a cozy place, with wood rafters, ladder-back chairs, and colorful madras tablecloths. The downstairs take-out annex, The Mouse Hole, is an inexpensive place to stock up for your picnic. *3 Victoria St., Roseau, tel. 809/448–2896. Reservations advised. AE. Closed Sun.*

$$ **Mango.** Vases overflowing with fresh flowers and a beautiful mural depicting the Indian River enliven this unassuming new restaurant frequented by locals. Diners enjoy both the comparatively refined ambience and Peter Pascal's solid home-cooking. The *lambi* (conch) is tender as can be, the goat colombo has quite a kick, and the mountain chicken is succulent. This is one of the few places where you can find *breego*, a tiny flavorful conch. *Bay Street, Portsmouth, tel. 809/445–3099. No credit cards.*

$$ **The Orchard.** A spacious, unadorned dining room opens onto a pleasant, covered courtyard, surrounded by latticework. Chef Joan Cools-Lartique whips up Creole-style coconut shrimp, lobster, black pudding, mountain chicken, callaloo soup with crabmeat, and other island delicacies, as well as an assortment of sandwiches, for the changing menu. *31 King George V St., Roseau, tel. 809/448–3051. AE, D, MC, V.*

$$ **Papillote.** The indefatigable Anne Jean-Baptiste has constructed a beautiful new stone-and-tile restaurant. Fans of the original needn't worry: The botanical gardens are still right outside, a hot-spring

pool still bubbles merrily (just the spot to savor a lethal rum punch before or after dinner) and it's just as popular with birds, butterflies—and tour groups—as ever. Try the bracing callaloo soup, dasheen puffs, chicken rainforest (marinated with papaya and wrapped in banana leaves) and, if they're on the menu, the succulent *bouk* (tiny, delicate river shrimp). *Papillote Wilderness Retreat, tel. 809/448–2287. AE, D, MC, V.*

$–$$ **Almond Beach Restaurant & Bar.** If you're visiting one of the island's northeast beaches, stop here for a lunch of callaloo soup, lobster, or octopus. Select from tantalizing fruit juices, including guava, passion fruit, tangerine, soursop, and papaya, or one of the bewitching spiced rums, steeped for more than two months in various herbs and spices. Try the *pweve* (patois for pepper), the aniselike *nanie,* or *lapsenth,* a violet-scented pick-me-up and digestif. The setting and ambience are delightful: Murals painted by local artists adorn the back wall, and you dine in a series of gazebos overlooking the Atlantic. The genial owners, Mr. and Mrs. Joseph, are experts in local culture and custom and often arrange a traditional *bélé* dance performance or *jing ping* (a type of folk music featuring the accordion, the *quage* [a kind of washboard instrument], drums, and a boom boom [a percussive instrument]) concert on busy weekends. *Calibishi, tel. 809/445–7783. AE, D, MC, V.*

$–$$ **Calaloo Restaurant.** Up the stairs of a verandaed building on a busy Roseau street is this small, informal eatery decorated with local crafts. Mrs. Marge Peters is the vivacious hostess, who holds court at the postage stamp–sized bar. She takes great pride in age-old cooking traditions and uses only the freshest local produce. (What she does with breadfruit alone—roasted slabs, puffs, creamy velouté, juice, pie—could fill a cookbook.) Changing lunch and dinner specials, served with heaping helpings of provisions such as pumpkin, plantain, yams, and yucca, might include pepper-pot soup, curried conch, or the signature crab callaloo, fragrant with cumin, coconut cream, lime, clove and garlic. Most everything here is homemade, including juices (try the sea moss—"puts lead in your pencil") and ice cream (the soursop is marvelous). *63 King George V St., Roseau, tel. 809/448–3386. No credit cards.*

$ **Coconut Beach.** This casual, low-key beachfront restaurant and bar is popular with visiting yacht owners (moorings are available), students from the nearby medical school, and anyone interested in an afternoon on a stretch of white-sand beach. Fresh tropical drinks and local seafood dishes are the specialty here; sandwiches and rotis are also served. *Coconut Beach Hotel, Portsmouth, tel. 809/445–5393. AE, D, MC, V.*

¢–$ **Hope Restaurant.** The owners did their best to cheer up the unprepossessing interior, painting the walls a bright turquoise and strewing fresh flowers around the three cramped dining rooms. But you don't come here for the ambience. You come for genuine Creole cooking at rock bottom prices. Mountain chicken (E.C. $35) and agouti (E.C. $25) are served with generous sides of provisions for barely half the price charged at fancier restaurants. Savory pork, goat, and chicken are even cheaper. Hope provides local flavor in every sense of the phrase: It's filled with old men playing dominoes and cabbies whose runs have just ended (they always know a good deal). It's open every day for breakfast, lunch, and dinner. *15 Steber St., Roseau, tel. 809/448–2019. No credit cards.*

¢–$ **World of Food.** Sit in the garden of the late Jean Rhys, the Dominican-born novelist who won Britain's Royal Literary Award. The spot has been turned into a garden bistro serving rotis, sandwiches, and other light meals. Locals come here in the evening, attracted by the girls who hang around the dance floor next door. *Field La., off Queen Mary St., Roseau, tel. 809/448–6125. No credit cards.*

¢ **Sagittarius Reggae Restaurant.** Astrological paraphernalia covers the walls of this place. The johnnycakes have Egg McMuffins beat by a country mile, and the fruit juices are sublime. Weekends, a disc jockey blasts reggae and soca, transforming the restaurant into a hopping club. *Portsmouth, no phone. No credit cards.*

Lodging

Most hotels here are locally owned, and standards are often not up to what many Caribbean travelers have come to expect. Rooms may be dark, bathrooms far from luxurious, and linens a bit threadbare at some properties. On the plus side, prices are low and owners are usually extremely warm and hospitable. It pays to compare rates and call for hotel brochures, as everything from bare-bones motels to charming hilltop properties is comparably priced here.

The only beachfront hotels are in the Portsmouth area, the one exception being the Castaways on Mero Beach outside Roseau. Roseau's seaside facilities have splendid Caribbean views but are beachless. Since you're on this lush, tropical island, try to spend at least two nights at one of the wonderful nature retreats set in the rain forest: These are Dominica's greatest assets, at least where lodging is concerned.

Most hotels offer an MAP plan; considering the uniformity of Dominica's restaurants and the difficulty getting around, this option makes sense. Dominica is one of the few Caribbean islands that knows no high or low seasons in terms of lodging prices (although this may change as tourism increases). Nevertheless, you may be able to negotiate better rates than those posted when you call for reservations during the summer.

Highly recommended lodgings are indicated by a star ★.

Category	Cost*
$$	$110–$150
$	$65–$110
¢	under $65

**All prices are for a standard double room for two, excluding 5% tax, 3% sales tax, and a 10%–15% service charge. To estimate rates for hotels offering MAP, add about $20 per person per day to the above price ranges.*

$$ **Castaways Beach Hotel.** A young crowd, many of them divers, flocks to this beachfront hotel in Mero, 11 miles north of Roseau. Daytime activity centers on its mile-long, dappled gray beach; evenings, the focus is on the restaurant and terrace, which are attractive, although the food leaves something to be desired. The festive Sunday brunch with live music packs them in. Rooms are spacious and have balconies overlooking the beach. However, it's hard to tell that they were refurbished in 1992, since they are dark, a bit musty, and decorated in 1970s colors and styles. Some have air-conditioning and cable TV. Good-value dive packages are offered. *Box 5, Roseau, tel. 809/449–6245 or 800/626–0581, fax 809/449–6246. 27 rooms. Facilities: restaurant, 2 bars, beach, tennis court, water-sports center, scuba, dive packages. AE, MC, V. EP, MAP.*

$$ **Evergreen Hotel.** A recent expansion added six bright, modern rooms with balconies and an airy bar and restaurant with terrace to this small hotel 2 miles from downtown Roseau. Although the squeaky-clean new annex is somewhat lacking in authentic island charm, it's still where you want to stay. Air-conditioned rooms have bright print fabrics, rattan furnishings, cable TV, large shower baths, and lovely sea views. Other new additions include a pool, Italian ceramic tiles in the public areas, and a small garden. The older building, a stone-and-wood structure with a red roof, has more character. Rooms here are less expensive but are plain and lack sea

views. Public rooms contain paintings and wood carvings by noted local artist Carl Winston. The restaurant is excellent and another good reason to stay here. *Box 309, Roseau, tel. 809/448–3288, fax 809/448–6800. 16 rooms. Facilities: 2 restaurants, bar, pool. AE, MC, V. CP, MAP.*

$$ ★ **Fort Young Hotel.** Once the island's main military installation, Fort Young is now Roseau's top downtown hotel. The fort was built in the late 1700s, and Dominican paintings and prints from that era decorate the massive stone walls. The cliffside setting offers dramatic views; it's worth paying extra for a room facing the ocean. Rooms have small balconies, air-conditioning, ceiling fans, shower baths, cable TV, and modern furnishings. *Box 519, Roseau, tel. 809/448–5000, fax 809/448–5006. 33 rooms. Facilities: restaurant, bar, pool, entertainment, disco. AE, MC, V. EP.*

$$ **Garraway Hotel.** This rather garish lime green structure in downtown Roseau by the waterfront is Dominica's first international standard business hotel. The owner proudly compares it to a Ramada or Marriott. It's an apt comparison. Rooms are large and decorated mainly in soft seashell colors like seafoam, coral and powder blue; all have direct-dial phones, cable TVs and air-conditioning. Suites have sitting rooms of varying sizes and sofa beds. The higher floors survey a colorful jumble of rooftops that seems straight from a Chagall canvas. Local paintings and vetiver mats add a distinctive touch to the decor of the public spaces. The Garraway is rather tasteful and intimate for a business hotel. Still, those seeking true Dominican flavor are better off in a small inn or guest house. An additional 17 rooms are slated to be completed in late 1995. The restaurant specializes in creative Creole cuisine. *Bay Front, Box 789, Roseau, tel. 809/449–8800, fax 809/449–8807. 20 rooms, 11 suites. Facilities: restaurant, bar, Jacuzzi, conference room. AE, MC, V. EP.*

$$ ★ **Lauro Club.** From the dining room's bright linen napery, cheerful wall mural, and fresh flowers to the cottages' bold colors and contemporary furniture, the Lauro Club has a neat European feel that, oddly enough, works well in the Caribbean. Each unit has a sitting area, a daybed, and a kitchenette on the large veranda, but none has a TV or air-conditioning. Six units have direct sea views; the other four are up the hill a bit but still catch a glimpse of the water. Below are a swimming pool and a sandy beach area; a long wooden staircase that twists down to the ocean. The Club is in Salisbury, between Roseau and Portsmouth and about 13 miles from each, so you'll probably need to rent a car. *Box 483, Roseau, tel. 809/449–6602, fax 809/449–6603. 10 units. Facilities: restaurant, bar, pool. AE, MC, V. EP, MAP.*

$$ **Picard Beach Cottage Resort.** Eight small wood cottages dot the grounds of this former coconut plantation on the island's northwest coast. Units have a simple, rustic appeal, with louvered windows, locally made furniture, small porches, and kitchenettes. The restaurant serves large breakfasts as well as lunch and dinner. The beach is right out your door, and you can use the pool at the Portsmouth Beach Hotel next door. The place is a bit overpriced, but offers what are probably the best rooms in Portsmouth. *Box 34, Roseau, tel. 809/445–5131; in the U.S., 800/424–5500, fax 809/445–5599. 8 cottages. Facilities: restaurant, bar, beach, pool, dive center with scuba, snorkeling, and windsurfing. AE, MC, V. EP.*

$$ **Reigate Hall Hotel.** It is known as the fanciest hotel in Dominica, but, unfortunately, the service and standards at Reigate Hall have deteriorated of late, and the property is not as impeccably maintained as in the past. The lovely stone-and-wood dwelling is perched high on a steep wooded cliff, a mile above Roseau and the ocean. Rooms have locally made furnishings, air-conditioning, and private balconies; the higher-priced rooms 17 and 18 have sea views. Some rooms have exposed brick, beam ceilings, and antiques; others have wet bars and refrigerators. Room amenities and arrangement are

sort of a hodgepodge, with every room a bit different. The restaurant is expensive for a full meal; count on at least $30 a person unless you forgo dessert and coffee. The nearest swimming beach is a $10 cab ride away, so you may find lazing around the pool more convenient. *Reigate, tel. 809/448–4031; in the U.S., 800/223–9815; in Canada, 800/468–0023, fax 809/448–4034. 14 rooms, 2 suites, 1 apartment. Facilities: restaurant, 2 bars, pool, sauna. AE, MC, V. EP, MAP.*

$$ ★ **Sans Souci Manor.** Three luxury apartments and one bungalow sit in a prosperous suburb high above Roseau. All units have clay-tile floors, locally made wood-and-wicker furniture, fully equipped kitchens, large verandas with sweeping views of Roseau and the hills, and museum-quality Caribbean and Latin American art. Urbane owner John Keller hosts a sophisticated crowd of Americans and Europeans, many of them repeat visitors. Dinners—for those who wisely opt for the MAP plan—are three-course affairs prepared by Mr. Keller, a gourmet cook, and served house-party style on his plant-filled terrace. Management will help make car rental and tour arrangements, or you can hire the property's own car and driver. Transfers from Canefield Airport are included in the rates, which are a jaw-dropping $105 a night (EP). *Box 373, St. Aroment, Roseau, tel. 809/448–2306, fax 809/448–6202. 3 apartments, 1 bungalow. Facilities: dining, honor bar, pool, airport transfers. AE, MC, V. EP. MAP.*

$–$$ **Anchorage Hotel.** Years of wear have taken their toll on this hotel although it still becomes an active scene during the season. Make sure you reserve one of the renovated rooms, which have clay-tile floors and madras fabrics, in the two-story galleried section; don't bother with any of the other dark, lifeless units. Downtown Roseau is a 10-minute walk away, but the nearest beach requires a $5 cab ride. The hotel is headquarters for Dominica Tours (*see* Guided Tours *in* Staying in Dominica, *above*). *Box 34, Roseau, tel. 809/448–2638, fax 809/448–5680. 36 rooms. Facilities: restaurant, bar, pool, squash court. AE, D, MC, V. EP, MAP, FAP.*

$–$$ **Castle Comfort Lodge.** This small dive lodge, sandwiched between the Anchorage and Evergreen hotels and run by the enthusiastic Derek and Ginette Perryman, wins a loyal following for its first-rate dive shop and excellent-value dive packages. Rooms are nothing special, although the five oceanfront units are more modern and cheerful than many you will find on the island. The back rooms are smaller but have cable TV and phone. As a bonus, the home-cooked meals are bountiful and delicious. The Perrymans can also arrange various inland adventures and nature walks. *Box 63, Roseau, tel. 809/448–2188, fax 809/448–6088. 10 rooms. Facilities: restaurant, dive shop. AE, MC, V. EP, MAP.*

$ **Coconut Beach Hotel.** This continually expanding Portsmouth hotel received a much-needed face-lift in 1994. The original self-contained beachfront units have been brightened with frilly floral linens, still life paintings, and vases of fresh flowers daily, but baths here are bare and depressing, and amenities are nonexistent (only those staying a week get utensils to use in their kitchenettes). The newer suites are simple, fresh, white-tiled affairs with air-conditioning and full bath to compensate for the lack of ocean view and access. All units have cable TVs. The hotel fronts the island's best beach, lovely Picard. Another plus is an open-air bar and restaurant where a crowd of yachties (moorings are available here) and locals keeps things lively, aided and abetted by the friendly, laid-back staff. *Box 37, Roseau, tel. 809/445–5393, fax 809/445–5693. 22 rooms. Facilities: restaurant, bar, dive shop, yacht moorings. AE, D, MC, V. EP, MAP.*

$ ★ **Hummingbird Inn.** This simple hilltop retreat is just a short drive from Roseau and Canefield Airport. Two hillside bungalows with outstanding Caribbean views hold 10 rooms. Interiors are simple—white walls, terra-cotta-tile floors, and peaked wooden ceilings.

Varnished wooden hurricane windows can be left open all night to let in fresh breezes and the sounds of tree frogs and the ocean a few hundred yards below. There's no air-conditioning and no TVs or phones. Ceiling fans were added in 1994. Other nice touches include handmade quilts, hammocks slung strategically on the wraparound terraces, and tables fashioned out of the trunks of local gommier trees. One large suite also has a four-poster bed and a kitchen. The Hummingbird's cook is perhaps the best of any guest house on Dominica, and nonguests can arrange for dinner here if they call a day in advance. *Box 60, Roseau, tel. or fax 809/449–1042. 9 rooms, 1 suite. Facilities: restaurant, bar. AE, MC, V. EP, MAP.*

$ ★ **Itassi Cottages.** The brochure pretty well lives up to its promise: ". . . for discerning travelers who are not necessarily loaded." These three self-contained cottages can hold from two to six people each. They're much homier than most island lodgings, with a mix of antiques, straw mats, beautiful handmade floral bedspreads, calabash lamps, and wraparound porches with hammocks and sweeping views of Roseau, Scotts Head, and the Caribbean. These are ideal for long-term stays. Each has a kitchen, ceiling fans, and cable TV, and there is a shared laundry facility. Grounds are beautifully landscaped and include a tennis court. *Box 319, Roseau, tel. 809/448–4313, fax 809/448–3045. 3 cottages. Facilities: kitchens, laundry facility, tennis court. AE, MC, V.*

¢–$ **Layou Valley Inn.** Tamara Holmes and her late husband built this tasteful house in the foothills of the national park, under the peaks of Morne Trois Pitons. She's a Russian who once translated for NASA but now devotes her talents to the kitchen, where she whips up excellent Creole food, as well as the occasional French or Russian specialty—coq au vin or chicken Kiev. The rooms are simple and clean, and the sunken lounge (an oasis of hand-hewn mosaics, stone floors, exquisite woodcarvings, and lush hanging plants) and glass-fronted dining area are comfortable, attractive areas where guests mingle. Unless you plan on going nowhere (which suits some guests just fine), you'll need a car—even buses pass only infrequently. *Box 196, Roseau, tel. 809/449–6203, fax 809/448–5212. 10 rooms. Facilities: restaurant, bar, swimming in mountain rivers, guided climbs to the Boiling Lake at extra cost. AE, MC, V. EP, MAP.*

¢–$ ★ **Papillote Wilderness Retreat and Nature Sanctuary.** Picture a magical retreat in the middle of a rain forest: Lush greenery abounds, geese and guinea fowl ramble the grounds, surreal stone animals crop up everywhere, a nearby river beckons you to take a dip, and 200-foot Trafalgar Falls is a short hike from your room. Papillote Wilderness Retreat claims this spectacular natural setting, as well as a bubbling hot-spring pool and owner Anne Jean-Baptiste's botanical garden. She has cultivated a mind-boggling assortment of plants and flowers, which she may graciously use to brew you a soothing herbal infusion—bergamot to combat insomnia or l'oiselles for a cold. Rooms are not as spectacular as their surroundings; they're low-ceilinged, bare, and somewhat dark, with a rustic, log-cabin feel. The restaurant serves good, moderately priced meals. *Box 67, Roseau, tel. 809/448–2287, fax 809/448–2286. 10 rooms. Facilities: restaurant, bar, gift shop. AE, DC, MC, V. EP, MAP.*

¢ **Carib Territory Guesthouse.** Caribs Charles and Margaret Williams own this very basic wayside house and live on the premises with their children. There are eight very bare and inexpensive bedrooms. The three that were added in 1994 have their own baths and are the comfiest. You can also get lunch and a cold drink, not to mention a good selection of Carib crafts. Call the Williamses in advance and schedule a half-day or full-day walk with Charles through the territory. *Crayfish River, Carib Territory, tel. 809/445–7256. 8 rooms (5 with shared bath). Facilities: restaurant, bar, gift shop, TV room. AE, D, MC, V. EP, MAP.*

¢ **Emerald Bush Bar–Restaurant–Bush Hotel–Nature Park.** Peter Kaufmann and his friendly dogs are the proprietors of this diversion a short drive from the Emerald Pool, where you can stop for a glass of fresh juice or a rum punch, wander along a couple hours' worth of unbelievably lush trails, or spend the night in an A-frame cottage that is barely a cut above camping (rooms cost as little as $18 per night). The list of nonamenities is long: no electricity, no phone, no TV, etc. Be prepared to rough it—but this is one of the most beautiful settings in Dominica. The bar and restaurant are open only until about sundown. *Castle Bruce Rd., mailing address: Box 277, Roseau, tel. 809/448–4545, fax 809/448–7954. 8 rooms. Facilities: restaurant, bar, pool. AE, MC, V. EP, MAP.*

¢ **Floral Gardens.** This motel looks like a Swiss Chalet—complete with latticed windows and flower boxes—plonked down on the edge of Dominica's rain forest reserve on the island's windward side. Although rooms are carefully decorated with island crafts and homey fabrics, they are small and dark, with a slightly claustrophobic feel. New, larger units overlooking the beautiful Layou River were completed in 1994; 10 more "luxury suites" are on the drawing board. The restaurant here (*see* Dining, *above*) is a favorite among residents and tour groups, and the hotel's location is convenient for river bathing, hiking, and relaxing on northeast coast beaches. Congenial O.J. Seraphin, the former interim prime minister, is the enterprising owner. Never content to leave things alone, he's added an exquisite natural waterfall pool and botanical garden, and plans to expand his already large gift shop into six galleries, each one showcasing a different island craft or product, from pottery to potpourri. *Concord, tel. and fax 809/445–7636. 18 rooms. Facilities: restaurant, gift shop. AE, MC, V. EP, MAP.*

¢ ★ **Mamie's on the Beach.** This basic motel is indeed right on Picard Beach; the second story rooms share a terrace that overlooks the ocean. The large, cheerful rooms—all with fans and private baths (shower only)—have sky-blue walls and rainbow linens; most also have a TV and three beds, which makes this a good bet for families with small children. The adjoining restaurant serves savory local cuisine. Altogehter, Mamie's is an amazing bargain. *Prince Rupert Bay, Portsmouth, tel. and fax 809/445–4295. 8 rooms. Facilities: restaurant, bar. MC, V. EP, MAP.*

¢ **Vena's.** Adjoining the World of Food restaurant is this boardinghouse-style hotel that's full of local color. Vena herself is a character. You'll need a sense of humor to stay here and join in the partying that goes on in the downstairs lounge on weekends. Rooms are tiny and very basic, but so is the $20-a-night price tag. *48 Cork St., Roseau, tel. 809/448–3286. 17 rooms, most with shared bath. Facilities: restaurant next door. No credit cards. EP.*

Cottage and Apartment Rentals

The **Dominica Division of Tourism** (Box 293, Roseau, Dominica, West Indies, tel. 809/448–2045) has a list of rental apartments, as well as hotels and guest houses, with rates. The selection ranges from small, concrete cottages ($400 a week) to more comfortable, attractive units at more than twice the price. Although rentals typically allow you to cut costs by preparing your own meals, this is not always the case on Dominica: Imported foods in grocery stores are expensive, and some rental units here don't even have kitchens. Considering that you will also need a car to get supplies and to get around, it may not make economic sense unless you are traveling with a large family or another couple. In addition to Itassi Cottages, Picard Beach Cottage Resort and Sans Souci Manor (*see above*), other recommended fully outfitted properties are the rambling, historic **Pointe Baptiste Guest House** (Calibishie, tel. 809/445–7322), whose three bedrooms are ideal for large families or small groups, and the rustic, spare-but-pleasant **Chez Ophelia Cottages** (Copthall, Box 152, Roseau, tel. 809/448–3061, fax 809/448–3433) on a hill overlooking Roseau.

Nightlife

Discos If you're not too exhausted from mountain climbing, swimming, and the like, you can join the locals on weekends at **The Warehouse** (tel. 809/449–1303), outside Roseau toward the airport, or the **Night Box** (Goodwill Rd., no phone), which attracts a rowdier clientele. Another favorite with locals is the easygoing **Good Times** (2 miles north of Roseau in Checkhall, tel. 809/449–1660), a reggae bar with an outdoor patio and a sizable crowd on weekends. Indeed, Checkhall is known as a partying spot, so much so that cabbies cruise the streets for passengers well into the wee hours.

Nightclubs When the moon comes up, most visitors go down to the dining room in their resident hotel for the music or chat offered there, which is always liveliest on weekends. The Fort Young has upscale entertainment, as do many of the better hotels—the Castaways, Anchorage, Garraway, and Reigate Hall in particular.

The **Shipwreck,** in the Canefield Industrial area (tel. 809/449–1059), has live reggae and taped music on weekends, and a Sunday bash that starts at noon and continues into the night.

The best insider's spot is definitely **Wykie's La Tropical** (51 Old St., Roseau, tel. 809/448–8015). This classic Caribbean hole-in-the-wall is a gathering spot for the island's movers and shakers, especially during Friday's happy hours (from 5 to 7), when they nibble on stewed chicken or black pudding, then stay on for a local calypso band or some jing ping. Another resident favorite is **Lenville** (tel. 809/446–6598), a very basic rum shop with barbecued chicken and dancing, in the village of Coulivistrie.

11 Dominican Republic

Updated by Jordan Simon

Sprawling over two-thirds of the island of Hispaniola, the Dominican Republic is the spot where European settlement of the Western Hemisphere really began. Santo Domingo, its capital, is the oldest continuously inhabited city in this half of the globe, and history buffs who visit have difficulty tearing themselves away from the many sites that boast of antiquity in the city's 16th-century Colonial Zone. Sunseekers head for the beach resorts of Puerto Plata, Samaná, and La Romana; at Punta Cana, beachcombers tan on the Caribbean's longest stretch of white-sand beach. The highest peak in the West Indies is here: Pico Duarte (10,128 feet) lures hikers to the central mountain range. Ancient sunken galleons and coral reefs divert divers and snorkelers.

Columbus happened upon this island on December 5, 1492, and on Christmas Eve his ship, the *Santa María*, was wrecked on the Atlantic shore. He named it La Isla Española ("the Spanish island"). Santo Domingo, on the south coast where the Río Ozama spills into the Caribbean Sea, was founded in 1496 by Columbus's brother Bartholomew and Nicolás de Ovando, and during the first half of the 16th century, it became the bustling hub of Spanish commerce and culture in the New World.

Hispaniola (a derivation of La Isla Española) has had an unusually chaotic history, replete with bloody revolutions, military coups, yellow-fever epidemics, invasions, and bankruptcy. The country has been relatively stable since the early 1970s, and administrations have been staunch supporters of the United States. American influence looms large in Dominican life. If Dominicans do not actually have relatives living in the United States, they know someone who does; and many speak at least rudimentary English. Still, it is a vibrantly Latin country whose Hispanic flavor contrasts sharply with the culture of the British, French, and Dutch islands in the Caribbean.

Dominican towns and cities are generally not quaint, neat, or particularly pretty. Poverty is everywhere, but the country is also alive and chaotic, sometimes frenzied, sometimes laid-back. Dominicans love music—there is dancing in the streets every summer at Santo Domingo's Merengue Festival—and they have a well-deserved reputation for being one of the friendliest people in the region. The island's tourist zones are as varied as they come—from extravagant Casa de Campo and the manicured hotels of Playa Dorada to the neglected streets of Jarabacoa in its gorgeous mountain setting and the world-weary beauty of the Samaná peninsula.

Along with Haiti, Dominica, Saba, and St. Eustatius, the Dominican Republic is one of the least expensive destinations in the Caribbean. Low wages combined with an excess of hotel rooms keep lodging costs down. With still more hotels under construction, prices aren't likely to climb in the near future. The island's resort hotels tend to be huge, self-contained properties designed to lure package-tour groups rather than independent travelers. Booking a weekly package through your travel agent will cost considerably less than booking a stay yourself on a per-night basis. One- to two-week packages combining airfare and accommodations are a popular means of visiting the Dominican Republic. These packages give you bargain prices, but there are a few drawbacks. Your selection of hotels is limited, and you may be locked into a hotel meal plan, which limits your opportunities to sample the local cuisine.

Since most resort hotels are on or within walking distance of an idyllic beach, renting a car is not vital. You may want a car for a day or two to do some exploring. Taxis or guided tours are other options. It's almost impossible to explore the entire country in one visit. If you're interested in exploring the island's historical sites, as well as lounging on its beaches, you may want to divide your visit between Santo Domingo, the nation's capital, and Puerto Plata, where many of the major beach resorts are located. An efficient, air-conditioned bus fleet operates between the two areas, and American Airlines sometimes offers flights that arrive in Santo Domingo and depart from Puerto Plata (*see* Arriving and Departing, *below*).

What It Will Cost These sample prices, meant only as a general guide, are for high season. The American dollar receives a very favorable rate of exchange in the Dominican Republic, so costs for locally produced items and services are among the least expensive in the Caribbean. A ¢ hotel in Puerto Plata or Santo Domingo is no more than $40 a night. Even the luxury hotels in Santo Domingo start their prices for a double room at around $100, and a moderately priced all-inclusive resort will run about $200 a couple. A simple meal of grilled fish or rice and chicken will be less than $5 at a small restaurant, and a large bottle of beer adds only another $1.25. A rum punch costs around $2; a glass of Bordeaux, $4.50.

Imported goods, on the other hand, are expensive. This is reflected in car rentals, which can be as much as $70 a day for a compact. A two-hour taxi tour of Santo Domingo will cost around $20. With the exception of an efficient, air-conditioned bus service between Santo Domingo and Puerto Plata for $6, public transportation tends to be infrequent and unreliable. A single-tank dive costs about $30; snorkel equipment rents for about $4 a day.

Before You Go

Tourist Information Contact the **Dominican Republic Department of Tourism** (Dominican Consulate, 1 Times Sq., 11th Floor, New York, NY 10036, tel. 212/768–2480; 2355 Salzedo Ave., Suite 305, Coral Gables, FL 33134, tel. 305/444–4592; 1464 Crescent St., Montreal, Québec, Canada H3A 2B6, tel. 514/933–6126). The best source of information is the **Dominican Tourist Information Center** in Santo Domingo (tel. 800/

752–1151). Be prepared to wait at least two weeks for requested materials.

Arriving and Departing

By Plane

The Dominican Republic has two major international airports: Las Américas International Airport, about 20 miles outside Santo Domingo, and La Unión International Airport, about 15 miles east of Puerto Plata on the north coast. **American Airlines** (tel. 800/433–7300) has the most extensive service to the Dominican Republic. It flies nonstop from New York and Miami to Santo Domingo and Puerto Plata and offers connections to both Santo Domingo and Puerto Plata from San Juan, Puerto Rico. American Eagle has two flights a day from San Juan to La Romana and several flights weekly to Punta Cana. **Continental** (tel. 800/231–0856) flies nonstop from New York to Puerto Plata, and from Newark, New Jersey to Santo Domingo. It also offers connecting service from Puerto Plata to Santo Domingo. **Carnival** (tel. 800/437–2110) offers daily service to Santo Domingo from New York, Miami, and Orlando. At press time, **United** (tel. 800/241–6522) was planning to initiate service from Miami to Santo Domingo and Puerto Plata. Minneapolis-based **TransGlobal Tours** (tel. 800/338–2160) offers weekly charters from the Twin Cities to Puerto Plata.

Several regional carriers serve neighboring islands. **ALM** (tel. 800/327–7230) connects Santo Domingo to St. Maarten and Curaçao. There is also limited domestic service available from La Herrera Airport in Santo Domingo to smaller airfields in La Romana, Samaná, and Santiago. At press time the new Barahona International Airport was slated to open by late 1995 (but this is Caribbean time); it will handle large jet aircraft, mostly charters and domestic flights.

The remodeled and enlarged Las Américas (Santo Domingo) and La Unión (Puerto Plata) facilities are sophisticated by Latin American standards. Still, overworked customs and immigration officials are often less than courteous, and luggage theft is rife. Try to travel with carry-on luggage, and keep a sharp eye on it. Porters are licensed, but if you can manage your own bags, we advise you to do so. Be prepared for a daunting experience as you leave customs. However, some order is being imposed—taxis now line up and *usually* charge officially set rates. If you have arranged for a hotel transfer, a representative should be waiting for you in the immigration hall.

From the Airport

Taxis are available at the airport, and the 25-minute ride into Santo Domingo averages R.D. $250 (about U.S. $20). Taxi fares from the Puerto Plata airport average R.D. $200 (U.S. $16) to the town center and R.D. $230 (U.S. $18) to the Playa Dorado hotels. There is no bus service, but you can often team up with another traveler and share a taxi.

Passports and Visas

U.S. and Canadian citizens must have either a valid passport or proof of citizenship, such as an original (not photocopied) birth certificate, and a tourist card. Legal residents of the United States must have an alien registration card (green card), a valid passport, and a tourist card. British citizens need only a valid passport; no entry visa is required. The requisite tourist card costs $10, and you should be sure to purchase it at the airline counter when you check in, and then fill it out on the plane. You can purchase the card on arrival at the airport, but you'll encounter long lines. Keep the bottom half of the card in a safe place because you'll need to present it to immigration authorities when you leave. There is also a U.S. $10 departure tax (payable only in U.S. dollars).

Language

Before you travel to the Dominican Republic, you should know at least a smattering of Spanish. Guides at major tourist attractions and front-desk personnel in the major hotels speak a fascinating form of English, though they often have trouble understanding tourists. Traffic signs and restaurant menus, except at popular tourist establishments, are in Spanish. Using smiles and gestures will help, but a nodding acquaintance with the language or a phrase book is more useful.

Precautions Beware of the *buscones* at the airports. They offer to assist you, and do so by relieving you of your luggage and disappearing with it. Also avoid the black marketeers, who will offer you a tempting rate of exchange for your U.S. dollars. If the police catch you changing money on the street, they'll haul you off to jail (the *calabozo*). Also, buy amber only from reputable shops. The attractively priced piece offered by the street vendor is more than likely plastic. Guard your wallet or pocketbook in Santo Domingo, especially around the Malecón (waterfront boulevard), which seems to teem with pickpockets.

Staying in the Dominican Republic

Important Addresses **Tourist Information:** The **Secretary of Tourism** is in Santo Domingo in a complex of government offices at the corner of Avenida Mexico and Avenida 30 de Maizo (Oficinas Guberbamentales Bldg. D, tel. 809/221—4660, fax 809/682–3806). Unless you are seeking special assistance, it is not worth making the trek here for the limited materials offered to tourists. There's also a tourist office in Puerto Plata (Playa Long Beach, tel. 809/586–3676). Both offices are officially open weekdays 9–2:30, but the Puerto Plata office often opens late and closes early.

Emergencies **Police:** In Santo Domingo, call 711; in Puerto Plata, call 586–2804; in Sosúa, call 571–2233. However, do not expect too much from the police, aside from a bit of a hassle and some paperwork that they will consider the end of the matter. In general, the police and bureaucrats take a hostile approach to visitors.

Hospitals: Santo Domingo emergency rooms that are open 24 hours are **Centro Médico Universidad Central del Este** (UCE) (Av. Máximo Gómez 68, tel. 809/221–0171), **Clínica Abreu** (Calle Beller 42, tel. 809/688–4411), and **Clínica Gómez Patino** (Av. Independencia 701, tel. 809/685–9131). In Puerto Plata, you can go to **Clínica Dr. Brugal** (Calle José del Carmen Ariza 15, tel. 809/586–2519). In Sosúa, try the **Centro Médico Sosúa** (Av. Martinez, tel. 809/571–3949).

Pharmacies: Pharmacies that are open 24 hours are, in Santo Domingo, **San Judas Tadeo** (Av. Independencia 57, tel. 809/689–6664); in Puerto Plata, **Farmacia Deleyte** (Av. John F. Kennedy 89, tel. 809/586–2583).

Currency The coin of the realm is the Dominican peso, which is divided into 100 centavos. It is written R.D. and fluctuates relative to the U.S. dollar. At press time, U.S. $1 was equivalent to R.D. $12.50. Always make certain you know in which currency any transaction is taking place (any confusion will probably not be to your advantage). There is a growing black market for hard currency, so be wary of offers to exchange U.S. dollars at a rate more favorable than the official one. Prices quoted here are in U.S. dollars unless noted otherwise.

Taxes and Service Charges Hotels and restaurants add a service charge (15% in hotels, 10% in restaurants) and 8% government tax. Although hotels add the service charge, it is customary to leave a dollar per day for the hotel maid. At restaurants and nightclubs you may want to leave an additional 5%–10% tip for a job well done. Taxi drivers expect a 10% tip. Skycaps and hotel porters expect at least five pesos per bag. U.S. visitors must buy a $10 tourist card before entering the Dominican Republic. All foreign visitors must pay a $10 departure tax. Both must be paid in U.S. dollars.

Getting Around
Taxis Taxis, which are government regulated, line up outside hotels and restaurants. The taxis are unmetered, and the minimum fare within Santo Domingo is about R.D. $50 (U.S. $4), but you can bargain for

less if you order a taxi away from the major hotels. Hiring a taxi by the hour and with any number of stops is R.D. $125 (U.S. $10) per hour with a minimum of two hours. Be sure to establish the time that you start; drivers like to advance the time a little. You should also be certain that it is clearly understood in advance which currency is to be used in the agreed-upon fare. Taxis can also drive you to destinations outside the city. Rates are posted in hotels and at the airport. If you're negotiating, the going rate is R.D. $5 per kilometer. Sample fares from Santo Domingo are R.D. $1,000 (U.S. $80) to La Romana and R.D. $1,900 (U.S. $152) to Puerto Plata. Round-trips are considerably less than twice the one-way fare. Call **Taxi Anacaona** (tel. 809/530–4800), **Taxi la Paloma** (tel. 809/531–6892), **Taxi Raffi** (tel. 809/689–5468), and **Centro Taxi** (tel. 809/685–9248).

In a separate category are radio taxis, which are convenient if you'd like to schedule a pickup—and a wise choice if you don't speak Spanish. The fare is negotiated over the phone when you make the appointment. The most reliable company is **Apolo Taxi** (tel. 809/541–9595). The standard charge is R.D. $100 per hour during the day, R.D. $120 at night, no minimum, with as many stops as you like.

Avoid unmarked street taxis—there have been numerous incidents of assaults and robberies, particularly in Santo Domingo.

Buses *Públicos* are small blue-and-white or blue-and-red cars that run regular routes, stopping to let passengers on and off. The fare is R.D. $2. Competing with the públicos are the *conchos* or *colectivos* (privately owned buses), whose drivers tool around the major thoroughfares, leaning out of the window or jumping out to try to persuade passengers to climb aboard. It's a colorful, if cramped, way to get around town. The fare is about R.D. $1. Privately owned air-conditioned buses make regular runs to Santiago, Puerto Plata, and other destinations. Avoid night travel because the country's roads are full of potholes. You should make reservations by calling **Metro Buses** (Av. Winston Churchill; in Santo Domingo, call 809/566–7126; in Puerto Plata, 809/586–6062; in Santiago, 809/587–4711) or **Caribe Tours** (Av. 27 de Febrero at Leopoldo Navarro, tel. 809/221–4422). One-way bus fare from Santo Domingo to Puerto Plata is R.D. $75 (U.S. $6). *Voladores* ("fliers") are vans that run from Puerto Plata's Central Park to Sosúa and Cabarete a couple of times each hour for R.D. $10. They don't run on a reliable schedule and are not always labeled with their destination.

Motorbike Taxis Known as *motoconchos*, these bikes are a popular and inexpensive way to get around such tourist areas as Puerto Plata, Sosúa, and Jarabacoa. Bikes can be flagged down both on the road and in town; rates vary from R.D. $3 to R.D. $20, depending on distance.

Rental Cars You'll need a valid driver's license from your own country and a major credit card and/or cash deposit. Cars can be rented at the airports and at many hotels. Among the known names are **Avis** (tel. 809/535–7191), **Budget** (tel. 809/562–6812), **Hertz** (tel. 809/221–5333), and **National** (tel. 809/562–1444). Rates average U.S. $70 and up per day, depending upon the make and size of the car. Driving is on the right side of the road. Many Dominicans drive recklessly, often taking their half of the road out of the middle, but they will flash their headlights to warn against highway patrols.

If for some unavoidable reason you must drive on the narrow, unlighted mountain roads at night, exercise extreme caution. Many local cars are without headlights or taillights, bicyclists do not have lights, and cows stand by the side of the road. Traffic and directional signs are less than adequate, and unseen potholes can easily break a car's axle. The 80-kph (50-mph) speed limit is strictly enforced. Finally, keep in mind that gas stations are few and far between in some of the remote regions. Police are known to supplement their income by stopping drivers on various pretexts and eliciting a "gift." Locals give R.D. $20–R.D. $40.

Telephones and Mail To call the Dominican Republic from the United States, dial area code 809 and the local number. Connections are clear and easy to make. Fortunately, service from the Dominican Republic is much improved. There is direct-dial service to the United States; dial 1, followed by area code and number.

Airmail postage to North America for a letter or postcard costs R.D. $5; to Europe, R.D. $10, and may take up to three weeks to reach the destination.

Opening and Closing Times Regular office and shop hours are weekdays 8–12:30 and 2:30–5, Saturday 8–noon. Government offices are open weekdays 7:30–2:30. Banking hours are weekdays 8:30–4:30.

Guided Tours If you are staying in the Puerto Plata area and wish to visit Santo Domingo, it's easy enough to take the public bus, book your own hotel, and walk your way through Santo Domingo's old quarter yourself. For destinations outside Santo Domingo, however, you may find a guided tour helpful. The country is large, and tours—unlike those on smaller Caribbean islands—will go to specific areas rather than circumnavigating the island.

Prieto Tours (tel. 809/685–0102 or 809/688–5715) operates Gray Line of the Dominican Republic. It offers half-day bus tours of Santo Domingo, nightclub tours, beach tours, tours to Cibao Valley and the Amber Coast, and other itineraries. A half-day sightseeing tour of the capital is R.D. $200 (U.S. $16).

Turinter (tel. 809/685–4020) tours include dinner and a show or casino visit, a full-day tour of Samaná, as well as specialty tours (museum, shopping, fishing).

Apolo Tours (tel. 809/586–5329) offers a full-day tour of Playa Grande and tours to Santiago (including a casino tour) and Sosúa. It will also arrange transfers between your hotel and the airport and will customize trips along the north coast, including making hotel bookings. One tempting two-day trip goes from Puerto Plata along the Amber Coast to Samaná; the $100-a-person cost includes one night's lodging and dinner.

Cafemba Tours (tel. 809/586–2177) runs various tours of the Cibao Valley and the Amber Coast, including Puerto Plata, Sosúa and Río San Juan.

Caribbean Jeep Safaris (tel. 809/571–1924) is an English-speaking outfit that runs Jeep tours in the mountains behind Puerto Plata and Sosúa, ending up at the Carabete Adventure Park, where you can swim in an underground pool and explore caves with Taino rock paintings. Buffet lunch and unlimited drinks are included in the R.D. $600 price.

Exploring the Dominican Republic

Numbers in the margin correspond to points of interest on the Santo Domingo map.

The Dominican Republic is a large country, made larger by the narrow, often potholed and congested roads. Few tourists try to see it all on their first visit. More often, they will explore only an area that can be managed in a day's outing. All of the touring described below may be accomplished by public transportation, but the only regularly scheduled air-conditioned buses are those that run through the Cibao Valley between Santo Domingo and Puerto Plata.

The historic heart of Santo Domingo is easily explored on foot, though you may need a taxi for a few far-flung sights. For touring elsewhere, your options are to rent a car for a day or two, hire a car and driver (at not much additional cost), or take an organized tour (*see* Guided Tours, *above*). If you don't mind driving, a car will give you the most freedom. A guided tour gives you the least freedom, but is the cheapest option.

Santo Domingo

We'll begin our tour where Spanish civilization in the New World began, in the 12-block area of **Santo Domingo** called the Colonial Zone. This historical area is now a bustling, noisy district with narrow cobbled streets, shops, restaurants, residents, and traffic jams. Ironically, all the noise and congestion make it somehow easier to imagine this old city as it was when the likes of Columbus, Cortés, Ponce de León, and pirates sailed in and out, and colonists were settling themselves in the New World. Tourist brochures boast that "history comes alive here"—a surprisingly truthful statement.

Be aware that wearing shorts, miniskirts, and halters in churches is considered inappropriate. (Note: Hours and admission charges are erratic; check with the tourist office for up-to-date information.)

One of the first things you'll see as you approach the Colonial Zone is
a statue only slightly smaller than the Colossus of Rhodes, staring
1 out over the Caribbean Sea. It is **Montesina,** the Spanish priest who
came to the Dominican Republic in the 16th century to appeal for human rights for Indians.

2 **Parque Independencia,** on the far western border of the Colonial Zone, is a big city park dominated by the marble and concrete **Altar de la Patria.** The impressive mausoleum was built in 1976 to honor the founding fathers of the country (Duarte, Sánchez, and Mella).

3 To your left as you leave the square, the **Concepción Fortress,** within the old city walls, was the northwest defense post of the colony. *Calle Palo Hincado at Calle Isidro Duarte, no phone. Admission free. Open Tues.–Sun. 9–6.*

From Independence Square, walk eight blocks east on Calle El
4 Conde and you'll come to **Parque Colón.** The huge statue of Columbus dates from 1897 and is the work of French sculptor Gilbert. On
the west side of the square is the **old Town Hall** and on the east, the
Palacio de Borgella, residence of the governor during the Haitian occupation of 1822–44 and presently the seat of the Permanent Dominican Commission for the **Fifth Centennial of the Discovery and**
Evangelization of the Americas. Gallery spaces house architectural
and archaeological exhibits pertaining to the fifth centennial.

Towering over the south side of the square is the coral limestone fa-
5 cade of the **Catedral Santa María la Menor, Primada de América,** the
first cathedral in America. Spanish workmen began building the cathedral in 1514 but left off construction to search for gold in Mexico.
The church was finally finished in 1540. Its facade is composed of a
mix of architectural styles, from late Gothic to Plateresque (the latter known for intricately carved stonework). Inside, the high altar is
made of beaten silver, and in the Treasury there is a magnificent collection of gold and silver. Some of its 14 lateral chapels serve as
mausoleums for noted Dominicans, including Archbishop Meriño,
who was once president of the Dominican Republic. Of interest is the
Chapel of Our Lady of Antigua, which was reconsecrated by Pope
John Paul II in 1984. In the nave are four baroque columns, carved to
resemble royal palms, which for more than four centuries guarded
the magnificent bronze and marble sarcophagus containing (say Dominican historians) the remains of Christopher Columbus. The sarcophagus has recently been moved to the Columbus Memorial
Lighthouse (*see below*)—only the latest in the Great Navigator's
posthumous journeys. *Calle Arzobispo Meriño, tel. 809/689–1920.*
Admission free. Open Mon.–Sat. 9–4; Sun. masses begin at 6 AM.

When you leave the cathedral, turn right, walk to Columbus Square,
and turn left on Calle El Conde. Walk one more block and turn right
on Calle Hostos and continue for two more blocks. You'll see the
6 ruins of the **Hospital de San Nicolás de Bari,** the first hospital in the
New World, which was built in 1503 by Nicolás de Ovando. *Calle
Hostos, between Calle de Las Mercedes and Calle Luperón, no
phone.*

Continue along Calle Hostos, crossing Calle Emiliano Tejera. Up the
hill and about mid-block on your left you'll see the majestic ruins of
7 the **San Francisco Monastery.** Constructed between 1512 and 1544,
the monastery contained the church, chapel, and convent of the Franciscan order. Sir Francis Drake's demolition squad significantly damaged the building in 1586, and in 1673 an earthquake nearly finished the job, but when it's floodlit at night, the old monastery is indeed a dramatic sight.

Walk east for two blocks along Calle Emiliano Tejera. Opposite the
8 Telecom building on Calle Isabel la Católica, the **Casa del Cordón** is
recognizable by the sash of the Franciscan order carved in stone over the arched entrance. This house, built in 1503, is the Western Hemisphere's oldest surviving stone house. Columbus's son Diego Colón, viceroy of the colony, and his wife lived here until the Alcázar was finished. It was in this house, too, that Sir Francis Drake was paid a ransom to prevent him from totally destroying the city. The house is now home to the Banco Popular. *Corner of Calle Emiliano Tejera and Calle Isabel la Católica, no phone. Admission free. Open weekdays 8:30–4:30.*

Walk one block east along Calle Emiliano Tejera to reach the impos-
9 ing **Alcázar de Colón,** with its balustrade and double row of arches.
The Renaissance structure has strong Moorish, Gothic, and Isabelline (an ornamental, late-Gothic style) influences. The castle of Don Diego Colón, built in 1514, was painstakingly reconstructed and restored in 1957. Forty-inch-thick coral limestone walls were patched and shored with blocks from the original quarry. There are 22 rooms, furnished in a style to which the viceroy of the island would have been accustomed—right down to the dishes and the viceregal shaving mug. Many of the period paintings, statues, tapestries, and furnishings were donated by the University of Madrid. *Just off Calle Emiliano Tejera at the foot of Calle Las Damas, tel. 809/687–5361. Admission: R.D. $10. Open Mon. and Wed.–Fri. 9–5, Sat. 9–4, Sun. 9–1. Closed Tues.*

10 Across from the Alcázar, **La Atarazana** (the Royal Mooring Docks) was once the colonial commercial district, where naval supplies were stored. There are eight restored buildings, the oldest of which dates from 1507. It now houses crafts shops, restaurants, and art galleries.

11 To reach the **Santa Bárbara Church,** go back to Calle Isabel la Católica, turn right, and walk several blocks. This combination church and fortress, the only one of its kind in Santo Domingo, was completed in 1562. *Av. Mella, between Calle Isabel la Católica and Calle Arzobispo Meriño, no phone. Admission free. Open weekdays 8–noon. Sun. masses begin at 6 AM.*

Retrace your steps to Calle Isabel la Católica, go south to Calle de
12 Las Mercedes, turn left, and walk one block right to **Calle Las
Damas,** where you'll make a right turn to the New World's oldest street. The "Street of the Ladies" was named after the elegant ladies of the court who, in the Spanish tradition, promenaded in the evening.

On your left you'll see a sundial dating from 1753 and the **Casa de los Jesuitas,** which houses a fine research library for colonial history as

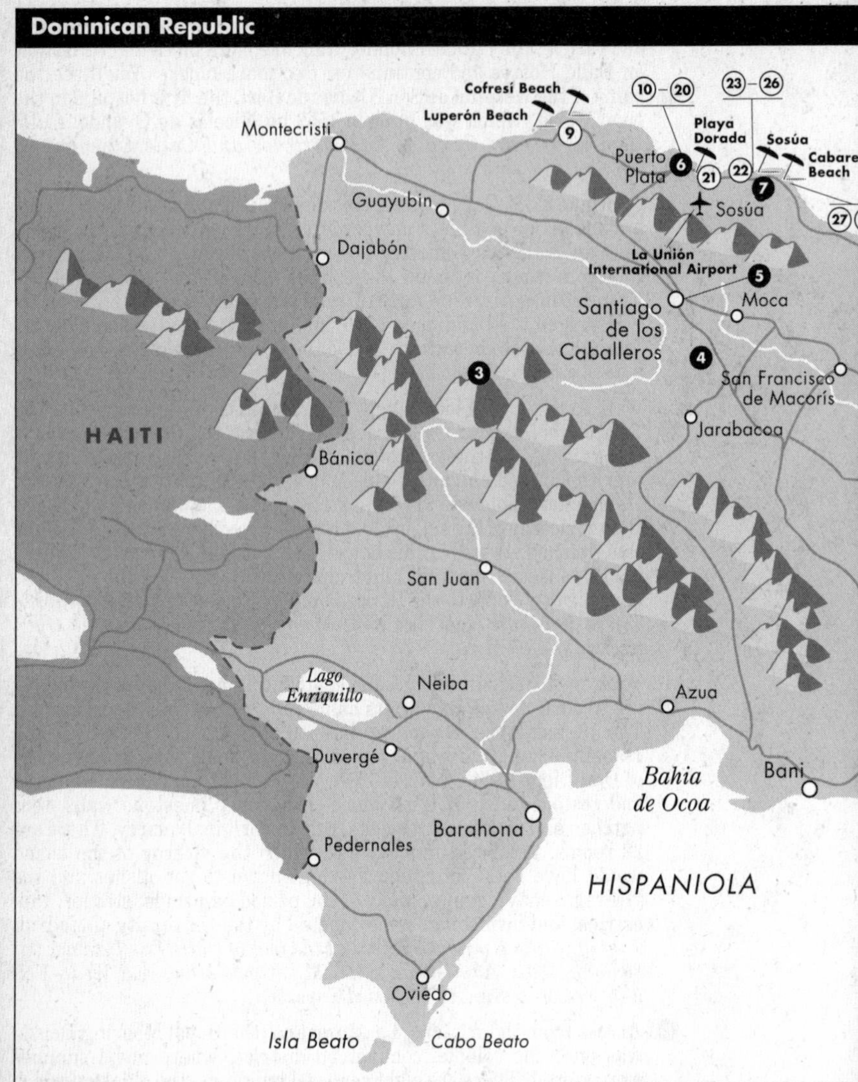

Exploring
Altos de Chavón, **2**
E. Leon Jimenez Tabacalera, **5**
La Vega Vieja, **4**
Parque de los Tres Ojos, **1**
Pico Duarte, **3**
Puerto Plata, **6**
Samaná, **8**
Sosúa, **7**

Dining
Another World, **10**
Café del Sol, **43**
Café de France, **46**
Café St. Michel, **37**
Caribae, **23**
De Armando, **11**
El Conuco, **39**
Fonda de la Atarazana, **35**
Guajiro's Caribbean Cafe, **24**
Hemingway's, **21**
La Bahía, **36**
Lina, **33**
Ludovino's and Joaquin's, **38**
Mesón de la Cava, **34**
Neptuno's Club, **42**
Roma II, **15**
Villa Casita, **44**

Lodging
Cabarete Beach Hotel, **27**
Capella Beach Hotel, **40**
Caribbean Village Club and Resort, **14**
Club Marina, **26**
Club

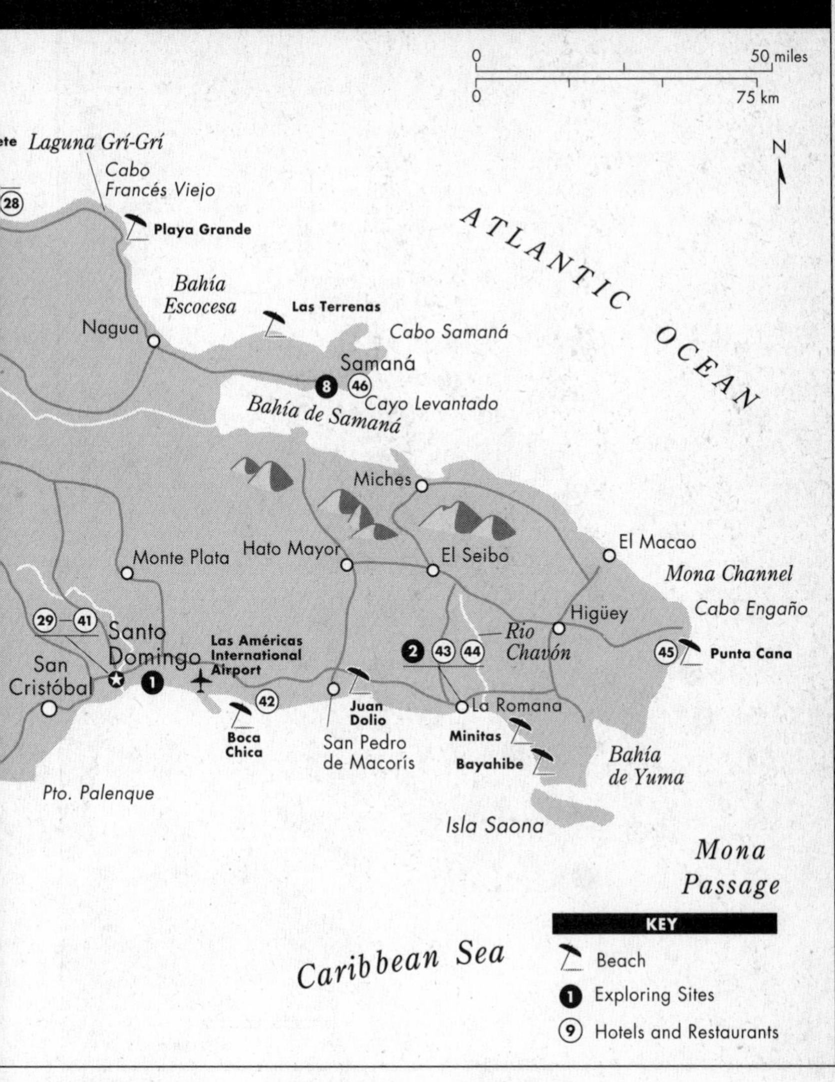

0
50 miles
0
75 km
N
Laguna Grí-Grí
Cabo Francés Viejo
28
Playa Grande
ATLANTIC OCEAN
Bahía Escocesa
Las Terrenas
Nagua
Cabo Samaná
Samaná
8
46
Cayo Levantado
Bahía de Samaná
Miches
Hato Mayor
El Seibo
El Macao
Monte Plata
Mona Channel
Higüey
Cabo Engaño
29
41
Santo Domingo
Las Américas International Airport
2
43
44
Rio Chavón
45
Punta Cana
San Cristóbal
1
42
Juan Dolio
La Romana
Boca Chica
San Pedro de Macorís
Minitas
Bayahibe
Bahía de Yuma
Pto. Palenque
Isla Saona
Mona Passage
KEY
Beach
Exploring Sites
Hotels and Restaurants
Caribbean Sea

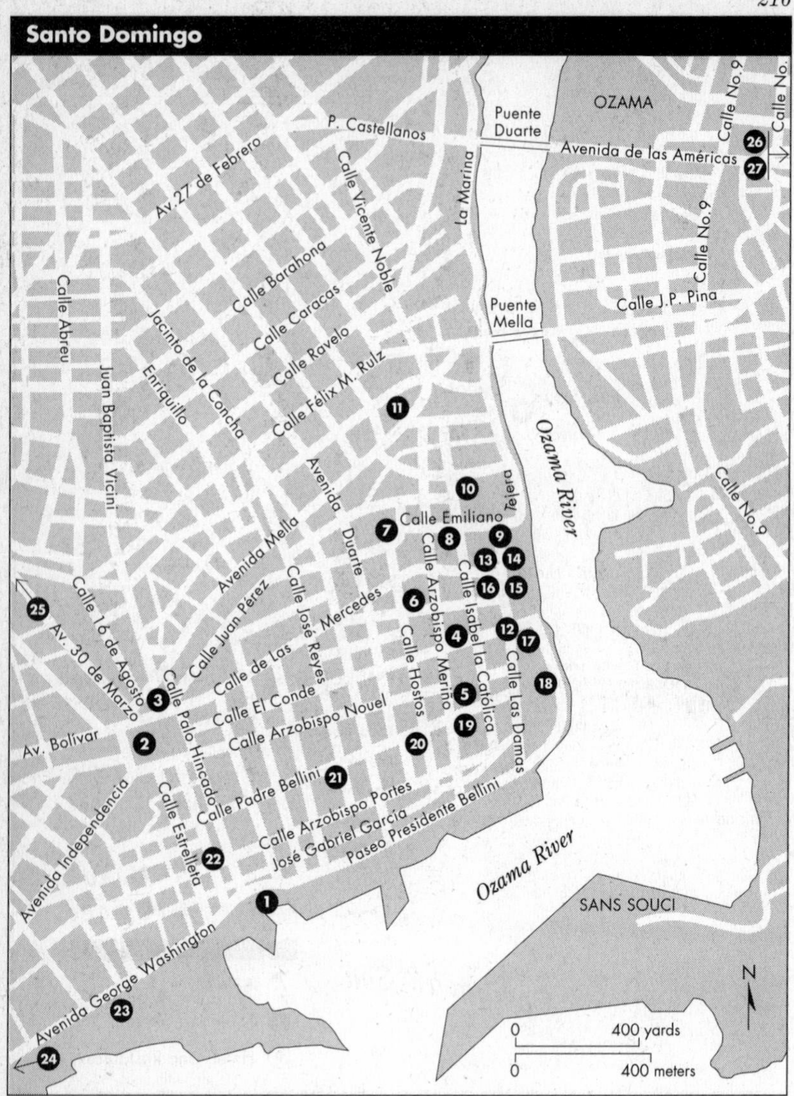

Acuario Nacional, **26**
Alcázar de Colón,**9**
Calle Las Damas, **12**
Capilla de los Remedios, **14**
Casa de Bastidas, **17**
Casa de Tostado, **19**
Casa del Cordón, **8**
Catedral Santa María la Menor, **5**
Concepción Fortress, **3**
El Faro a Colón, **27**
Hospital de San Nicolás de Bari, **6**
Hostal Palacio Nicolás de Ovando, **15**
Iglesia y Convento Domínico, **20**
Jardín Botánico Nacional Dr. Rafael M. Moscoso, **25**
La Atarazana, **10**
La Iglesia de Regina Angelorum, **21**
Malecón, **23**
Montesina, **1**
Museo de las Casas Reales, **13**
National Pantheon, **16**
Parque Colón, **4**
Parque Independencia, **2**
Plaza de la Cultura, **24**
Puerta de la Misericordia, **22**
San Francisco Monastery, **7**
Santa Bárbara Church, **11**
Torre del Homenaje, **18**

well as the Institute for Hispanic Culture. *Admission free. Open weekdays 8–4:30.*

13 Across the street is the **Museo de las Casas Reales** (Museum of the Royal Houses). The collections in the museum are displayed in two early 16th-century palaces that have been altered many times over the years. Exhibits cover everything from antique coins to replicas of the *Niña*, the *Pinta*, and the *Santa María*. There are statue and cartography galleries, coats of armor and coats of arms, coaches and a royal courtroom, gilded furnishings, and Indian artifacts. The first room of the former Governor's Residence has a wall-size map marking the routes sailed by Columbus's ships on expeditions beginning in 1492. *Calle Las Damas, corner Calle Mercedes, tel. 809/682–4202. Admission: R.D. $10. Open Tues.–Sat. 9–4:45, Sun. 10–1.*

14 Across the street is the **Capilla de los Remedios** (Chapel of Our Lady of Remedies), which was originally built as a private chapel for the family of Francisco de Dávila. Early colonists also worshiped here before the completion of the cathedral. Its architectural details, particularly the lateral arches, are evocative of the Castilian-Romanesque style. *Calle Las Damas, at the foot of Calle Mercedes, no phone. Admission free. Open Mon.–Sat. 9–6; Sun. masses begin at 6 AM.*

15 Just south of the chapel on Calle Las Damas, the **Hostal Palacio Nicolás de Ovando** (*see* Lodging, *below*), now a highly praised hotel, was once the residence of Nicolás de Ovando, one of the principal organizers of the colonial city.

16 Across the street from the hotel looms the massive **National Pantheon.** The building, which dates from 1714, was once a Jesuit monastery and later a theater. Rafael Trujillo had it restored in 1955 with an eye toward being buried there. (He is buried instead at Père Lachaise in Paris.) An allegorical mural of his 1961 assassination is painted on the ceiling above the altar, where an eternal flame burns. The impressive chandelier was a gift from Spain's Generalissimo Francisco Franco. *Calle Las Damas, near the corner of Calle Mercedes, no phone. Admission free. Open Mon.–Sat. 10–5.*

Continue south on Calle Las Damas and cross Calle El Conde. Look
17 on your left for the **Casa de Bastidas,** where there is a lovely inner courtyard with tropical plants and temporary exhibit galleries. *Calle Las Damas, just off Calle El Conde, no phone. Admission free. Open Tues.–Sun. 9–5.*

18 You won't have any trouble spotting the **Torre del Homenaje** (Tower of Homage) in the Fort Ozama. The fort sprawls two blocks south of the Casa de Bastidas, with a brooding crenellated tower that still guards the Ozama River. The fort and its tower were built in 1503 to protect the eastern border of the city. The sinister tower was the last home of many a condemned prisoner. *On Paseo Presidente Bellini, overlooking Río Ozama, no phone. Admission: R.D. $10. Open Tues.–Sun. 8–7.*

When you leave the fortress, turn left off Calle Las Damas onto
19 Calle Padre Bellini. A two-block walk will bring you to **Casa de Tostado.** The house was built in the first decade of the 16th century and was the residence of writer Don Francisco Tostado. Its twin Gothic windows are the only ones that are still in existence in the New World. It now houses the **Museo de la Familia Dominicana** (Museum of the Dominican Family), which features exhibits on the well-heeled Dominican family in the 19th century. *Calle Padre Bellini, near Calle Arzobispo Meriño, tel. 809/689–5057. Admission: R.D. $10. Open Thurs.–Tues. 9–2.*

Walk two blocks west on Calle Padre Bellini to the corner of Avenida
20 Duarte. The graceful building with the rose window is the **Iglesia y Convento Domínico** (Dominican Church and Convent), founded in

1510. In 1538, Pope Paul III visited here and was so impressed with the lectures on theology that he granted the church and convent the title of university, making it the oldest institution of higher learning in the New World. *Calle Padre Bellini and Av. Duarte, tel. 809/682–3780. Admission free. Open Tues.–Sun. 9–6.*

Continue west on Calle Padre Bellini for two blocks, and at the cor-
21 ner of Calle José Reyes you'll see another lovely church, **La Iglesia de
Regina Angelorum** (Church of Regina Angelorum), which dates
from 1537. The church was damaged during the Haitian regime,
from 1822 to 1844, but you can still appreciate its Baroque dome,
Gothic arches, and traceries. *Corner of Calle Padre Bellini and
Calle José Reyes, tel. 809/682–2783. Admission free. Open Mon.–
Sat. 9–6.*

Walk four blocks west on Calle Padre Bellini, turn left on Calle Palo
22 Hincado, and keep going straight till you reach the **Puerta de la Misericordia** (Gate of Mercy), part of the old wall of Santo Domingo. It
was here on the plaza, on February 27, 1844, that Ramón Mata
Mella, one of the country's founding fathers, fired the shot that began the struggle for independence from Haiti.

Parque Independencia separates the old city from the new. Avenidas 30 de Marzo, Bolívar, and Independencia traverse the park and mingle with avenues named for George Washington, John F. Kennedy, and Abraham Lincoln. Modern Santo Domingo is a sprawling, noisy city with a population of close to 2 million.

Avenida George Washington, which is lined with tall palms and Las
Vegas–style tourist hotels, breezes along the Caribbean Sea. The
23 Parque Litoral de Sur, better known as the **Malecón,** borders the avenue from the colonial city to the Hotel Santo Domingo, a distance of
about 3 miles. The seaside park, with its cafés and places to relax, is
a popular spot, but beware of pickpockets.

Avenida Máximo Gómez comes down from the north. Take a right
turn on it, cross Avenida Bolívar, and you'll come to the landscaped
24 lawns, modern sculptures, and sleek buildings of the **Plaza de la
Cultura.** Among the buildings are the **National Theater** (tel. 809/
687–3191), which stages performances in Spanish; the **National Library,** in which the written word is Spanish; and museums and art
galleries, whose notations are also in Spanish. The following museums on the plaza are open Tuesday–Saturday from 10 to 5, and admission to each is R.D. $10: The **Museum of Dominican Man** (tel.
809/687–3622) traces the migrations of Indians from South America
through the Caribbean islands. The **Museum of Natural History** (tel.
809/689–0106) examines the flora and fauna of the island. In the **Gallery of Modern Art** (tel. 809/682–8260), the works of 20th-century
Dominican and foreign artists are displayed.

25 North of town in the Arroyo Hondo district is the **Jardín Botánico
Nacional Dr. Rafael M. Moscoso** (Dr. Rafael M. Moscoso National
Botanical Gardens), the largest garden in the Caribbean. Its 445
acres include a Japanese garden, a "great ravine," a glen, a gorgeous display of orchids, and an enormous floral clock. You can tour
the gardens by train, boat, or horse-drawn carriage. *Arroyo
Hondo, no phone. Admission: R.D. $2. Open daily 10–6.*

In the 320-acre **Parque Zoológico Nacional** (National Zoological Park), not far from the Botanical Gardens, animals roam free in natural habitats. There is an African plain, a children's zoo, and what the zoo claims is the world's largest birdcage. *Av. Máximo Gómez at Av. de los Proceres, tel. 809/562–2080. Admission: R.D. $10. Open daily 10–6.*

Now head east and cross the Rí Ozama at Puente Duarte. Take
26 Avenida de las Američas to the **Acuario Nacional** (National Aquarium). The largest aquarium in the Caribbean, with an impressive col-

lection of tropical fish and dolphins, its construction was a controversial public expenditure. *In the Sans Souci district on Av. de las Américas. Admission: R.D. $10. Open daily 10–6.*

27 Follow the signs to the nearby **El Faro a Colón** (Columbus Memorial Lighthouse). This striking lighthouse monument and museum complex dedicated to the Great Navigator is shaped like a pyramid cross. Completed in 1992, its inauguration was set to coincide with the 500th anniversary of Christopher Columbus's landing on the island. Along with its showpiece laser-powered lighthouse, the complex holds the tomb of Columbus (recently moved there after 400 years in the Catedral Santa María la Menor) and six museums featuring exhibits related to Columbus and early exploration of the New World. One museum focuses on the long, rocky, and often controversial history of the lighthouse memorial itself and another on the Great Navigator's posthumous peregrinations (Cuba, Spain, and the Dominican Republic have all laid claim to—and hosted—his remains, which even today are a subject of controversy). *Av. España, tel. 809/591–1492. Admission: R.D. $5, children under 12 R.D. $1. Open Tues.–Sun. 9–4.*

The East Coast

Numbers in the margin correspond to points of interest on the Dominican Republic map.

Continue east on Las Américas Highway toward La Romana, about a two-hour drive along the southeast coast. All along the highway to Romana are small resort-hotel complexes where you can find refreshments or stay overnight. About 1½ miles outside the capital,
1 you'll come to the **Parque de los Tres Ojos** (Park of the Three Eyes). The "eyes" are cool blue pools peering out of deep limestone caves, and it's actually a four-eyed park. If you've a mind to, you can look into the eyes more closely by climbing down into the caves.

About 20 minutes east of the city is **Boca Chica Beach,** popular because of its proximity to the capital. Another 45 minutes or so farther east is the city of **San Pedro de Macorís,** where the national sport and the national drink are both well represented. Some of the country's best *béisbol* games are played in **Tetelo Vargas Stadium,** which you can see off the highway to your left. The **Macorís Rum distillery** is on the eastern edge of the city. Outside town is Juan Dolio, another beach popular with *capitaleños.*

The two big businesses around La Romana used to be cattle and sugarcane. That was before Gulf & Western created (and subsequently sold) the **Casa de Campo** resort, which is a very big business, indeed, and **Altos de Chavón,** a re-creation of a 16th-century village and art colony on the resort grounds.

Casa de Campo means "house in the country," and, yes, you could call it that. This particular "house" is a resort that sprawls over 7,000 acres, accommodates some 3,000 guests, and offers two public golf courses (one of them, a teeth-clencher called Teeth of the Dog, has seven holes that skirt the sea), 16 tennis courts, horseback riding, polo, archery, trap shooting, and every imaginable water sport. Oscar de la Renta designed much of the resort and has a boutique in Altos de Chavón. He also owns a villa at Casa de Campo.

2 **Altos de Chavón** sits on a bluff overlooking the Río Chavón, about 3 miles east of the main facility of Casa de Campo. You can drive there easily enough, or you can take one of the free shuttle buses from the resort. In this re-creation of a medieval Spanish village there are cobblestone streets lined with lanterns, wrought-iron balconies, and courtyards swathed with bougainvillea. More than a museum piece, this village is a place where artists live, work, and play. There is an art school, affiliated with New York's Parsons School of Design; a disco; an archaeological museum; five restaurants; and a 5,000-seat outdoor amphitheater (used about four times a year) where Frank

Sinatra and Julio Iglesias have entertained. The focal point of the village is **Iglesia St. Stanislaus,** which is named after the patron saint of Poland in tribute to the Polish Pope John Paul II, who visited the Dominican Republic in 1979 and left some of the ashes of St. Stanislaus behind.

From here the road continues east to Punta Cana and Bávaro, glorious beaches on the sunrise side of the island. On the way, you'll pass through Higuey, an undistinguished collection of ramshackle buildings notable only for its controversial church, which resembles a pinched McDonald's arch and was consecrated by Pope John Paul II in 1984.

The Cibao Valley

This tour can be made by bus (fare: R.D. $70/U.S. $6), though you won't see as much: Although the bus does stop briefly in Santiago de los Caballeros, you have to get off and take a local bus from there if you want to see La Vega. Strictly as a means of transport from Santo Domingo to Puerto Plata, however, a bus is ideal.

The road north from Santo Domingo, known as Autopista Duarte, cuts through the lush banana plantations, rice and tobacco fields, and royal poinciana trees of the Cibao Valley. All along the road there are stands where, for a few centavos, you can buy ripe pineapples, mangoes, avocados, *chicharrones* (either fried pork rinds or
3 chicken pieces), and fresh fruit drinks. To the west is **Pico Duarte,** at 10,128 feet the highest peak in the West Indies.

In the heart of the Cibao is La Vega. Founded in 1495 by Columbus, it is the site of one of the oldest settlements in the New World. The inquisitive will find the tour of the ruins of the original settlement,
4 **La Vega Vieja** (The Old La Vega), a rewarding experience. About 3 miles north of La Vega is **Santo Cerro** (Holy Mount), site of a miraculous apparition of the Virgin and therefore of many local pilgrimages. The **Convent of La Merced** is there, and the views of the Cibao Valley are breathtaking. The new town boasts a remarkable church of its own, **Concepcíon de la Vega,** constructed in 1992 to commemorate the 500th anniversary of the discovery (and evangelization) of America. The unusual modern Gothic style—all curvaceous concrete columns, arches and buttresses—is striking indeed.

La Vega is also justly celebrated for its Carnival, featuring the haunting, disturbing *diablos cojuelos*—"devil masks." These papier mâché creations are incredibly intricate, fanciful gargoyle demons painted in surreal colors with real cows' teeth contributing eerie authenticity. The skill is usually passed down for generations; artisans work in dark, cramped studios throughout the area. The studio closest to downtown is that of José Luis Gomez. Ask any local (tip them 10–20 pesos) to guide you to his atelier. He speaks no English, but will show you the stages of mask development. He sells the masks, which make extraordinary wall hangings, for U.S. $50–$60, a great buy considering the craftsmanship.

About 144 kilometers (90 miles) north of the capital, you'll come to
5 the industrial city of **Santiago de los Caballeros,** where a massive monument honoring the Restoration of the Republic guards the entrance to the city. Many past presidents were born in Santiago, and it is currently a center for processing tobacco leaf. You can gain an appreciation of the art and skill of Cuban cigar-making with a tour of **E. Leon Jimenez Tabacalera** (tel. 809/563–1111). The best hotel in town is the **Gran Almirante.**

The Amber Coast

The Autopista Duarte ultimately leads (in three to four hours from Santo Domingo) to the Amber Coast, so called because of its large, rich, and unique deposits of amber. The coastal area around Puerto Plata is a region of splashy resorts. The north coast boasts more than 70 miles of beaches with condominiums and villas going up fast.

6 **Puerto Plata,** although now quiet and almost sleepy, was a dynamic city in its heyday. Visitors can get a feeling for this past in the magnificent Victorian **Glorieta** (Gazebo) in the central **Parque Independencia.** Next to the park, the recently refurbished **Catedral de San Felipe** recalls a simpler, colonial past. On Puerto Plata's own Malecón, the **Fortaleza de San Felipe** protected the city from many a pirate attack and was later used as a political prison. The fort is most dramatic at night.

Puerto Plata is also the home of the **Museum of Dominican Amber,** a lovely galleried mansion and one of several tenants in the Tourist Bazaar. The museum displays and sells the Dominican Republic's national stone. Semiprecious, translucent amber is actually fossilized pine resin that dates back about 50 million years, give or take a few millennia. The north coast of the Dominican Republic has the largest deposits of amber in the world (the only other deposits are found in Germany and the former Soviet Union), and jewelry crafted from the stone is the best-selling item on the island. *Calle Duarte 61, tel. 809/586–2848. Admission: R.D. $15. Open Mon.–Sat. 9–5.*

Southwest of Puerto Plata (follow the signs from the Autopista), you can take a cable car (when it is working) to the top of **Mt. Isabel de Torres,** which soars 2,600 feet above sea level. On the mountain there is a botanical garden, a huge statue of Christ, and a spectacular view. The cable was first laid in 1754, although rest assured that it's been replaced since then. Lines can be long, and once on top of the mountain you may wonder if it was worth the time. Don't eat at the restaurant at the top—the food is awful. *No phone. Cable car operates Tues. and Thurs.–Sun. 8–6. Round-trip is R.D. $20.*

Back on the main road (Autopista), proceed another 6 miles east to
7 **Sosúa,** a small community settled during World War II by 600 Austrian and German Jews. After the war, many of them returned to Europe or went to the United States, and most of those who remained married Dominicans. Only a few Jewish families reside in the community today, and there is only one small, one-room synagogue. The flavor of the town is decidedly Spanish. (Note: The roads off the Autopista are horribly punctured with potholes.)

Sosúa has become one of the most frequently visited tourist destinations in the country, favored by French Canadians and Europeans. Hotels and condos are going up at breakneck speed. It actually consists of two communities, **El Batey** and **Los Charamicos,** which are separated by a cove and one of the island's prettiest beaches. The sand is soft and white, the water crystal clear and calm. The walkway above the beach is packed with tents filled with souvenirs, pizzas, and even clothing for sale—a jarring note in this otherwise idyllic setting.

Continue east on the Autopista past **Cabarete,** a popular windsurfing haunt, and **Playa Grande.** The powdery white beach remains miraculously undisturbed and unspoiled by development.

The Autopista rolls along eastward and rides out onto a "thumb" of
8 the island, where you'll find **Samaná.** Back in 1824, a sailing vessel called the *Turtle Dove*, carrying several hundred escaped American slaves from the Freeman Sisters' Underground Railroad, was blown ashore in Samaná. The escapees settled and prospered, and today their descendants number several thousand. The churches here are Protestant; the worshipers live in villages called Bethesda, Northeast, and Philadelphia; and the language spoken is an odd 19th-century form of English.

The wealth of marine life in the surrounding waters is beginning to attract more specialty tourists. Sportfishing at Samaná is considered to be among the best in the world. In addition, about 3,000 humpback whales winter off the coast of Samaná from December to

March. Major whale-watching expeditions like those out of Massachusetts are being organized and should boost the region's economy without scaring away the world's largest mammals.

Samaná makes a fine base for exploring the area's natural splendors. Most hotels on the peninsula arrange tours to the **Los Haitises National Park,** a remote unspoiled rain forest with limestone knolls, crystal lakes, mangrove swamps teeming with aquatic birds, and caves stippled with Taino petroglyphs. **Las Terrenas,** a remote stretch of beautiful, nearly deserted beaches on the north coast of the Samaná peninsula, is barely known to North American tourists, although French Canadians and Europeans, especially Germans, have begun making the long trek to this latter-day hippie haven that also attracts surfboarders and windsurfers. There are several modest seafood restaurants (the best is **Boca Fina,** no phone), a dusty main street in the town of Las Terrenas, a small airfield, the comparatively grand all-inclusive **El Portillo Beach Club** (tel. 809/688–5785), and several congenial hotels right on the beach at Punta Bonita. If you're seeking tranquillity and are happy just hanging out drinking beer and soaking up sun, this is the place for you. The road from Samaná, even though it is longer and not paved, is a lot less strenuous than coming over the hills from Sanchez.

Beaches

The Dominican Republic has more than 1,000 miles of beaches, including the Caribbean's longest strip of white sand—Punta Cana. Many beaches are accessible to the public and may tempt you to stop for a swim. Be careful: Some have dangerously strong currents. Most of the nation's coastline is paralleled by a road, so access to these beaches is easy. You'll need a car to visit those away from your hotel, because public transportation is unreliable.

Boca Chica is the beach closest to Santo Domingo (2 miles east of Las Américas Airport, 21 miles from the capital), and it's crowded with city folk on weekends. This beach was once a virtual four-lane highway of fine white sand. "Progress" has since cluttered it with plastic beach tables, chaise longues, pizza stands, and beach cottages for rent. But the sand is still fine, and you can walk far out into clear blue water, which is protected by natural coral reefs that help keep the big fish at bay.

About 20 minutes east of Boca Chica is another beach of fine white sand, **Juan Dolio.** The Metro Hotel and Marina, the all-inclusive Decameron, Villas del Mar Hotel, and Punta Garza Beach Club are on this beach.

Moving counterclockwise around the island, you'll come to the La Romana area, with its miniature **Minitas** beach and lagoon, and the long white-sand, palm-lined crescent of **Bayahibe** beach, which is accessible only by boat. La Romana is the home of the 7,000-acre Casa de Campo resort, so you're not likely to find any private place in the sun here.

The gem of the Caribbean, **Punta Cana** is a 20-mile strand of pearl-white sand shaded by trees and coconut palms. Located on the easternmost coast, it is the home of several top resorts.

Las Terrenas, on the north coast of the Samaná peninsula, looks like something from *Robinson Crusoe:* Tall palms list toward the sea, away from the mountains; the beach is narrow but sandy, and best of all, there is nothing man-made in sight—just vivid blues, greens, and yellows.

Playa Grande, on the north coast, is a long stretch of powdery sand that is slated for development. The new Playa Grande Hotel has already disturbed the solitude. With this exception, the entire northeast coast seems like one unbroken golden stretch, unmaintained and littered with kelp, driftwood, and the occasional beer bottle. If you don't mind the lack of facilities and upkeep, you have your pick of deserted beaches.

The ideal wind and surf conditions of **Cabarete Beach,** also on the north coast, have made it an integral part of the international windsurfing circuit.

Farther west is the lovely beach at **Sosúa,** where calm waters gently lap at long stretches of soft white sand. Unfortunately the backdrop here is a string of tents, with hawkers pushing cheap souvenirs. You can, however, get snacks and rent water-sports equipment from the vendors.

On the north Amber Coast, still-developing **Puerto Plata** is about to outdo San Juan's famed Condado strip. The beaches are of soft beige or white sand, with lots of reefs for snorkeling. The Atlantic waters are great for windsurfing, waterskiing, and fishing expeditions.

About an hour west of Puerto Plata lies **Luperón Beach,** a wide white-sand beach fit for snorkeling, windsurfing, and scuba diving. The Luperón Beach Resort is handy for rentals and refreshments.

Sports and the Outdoors

Although there is hardly a shortage of outdoor activities here, the resorts have virtually cornered the market on sports, including every conceivable water sport. Some hotels, particularly all-inclusives, offer their facilities only to guests. You can check with the tourist office for more details. Listed below is a mere smattering of the island's athletic options:

Bicycling Pedaling is easy on pancake-flat beaches, but there are also steep hills in the Dominican Republic. Bikes are available at **Villas Doradas** (Playa Dorada, Puerto Plata, tel. 809/586–3000), **Dorado Naco** (Dorado Beach, tel. 809/586–2019), **Jack Tar Village** (Puerto Plata, tel. 809/586–3800), and **Hotel Cofresi** (Puerto Plata, tel. 809/586–2898). Be aware that cars, buses, and trucks can make biking hazardous on some roads. You'll be charged for any bike damage. Count on a $15 daily rental fee.

Boating Small-boat sailing is limited, though most resort hotels have a few tattered sailing dinghies for rent at about R.D. $100 (U.S. $8) an hour. Hobie Cats and paddleboats are available at **Heavens** (Playa Dorada, tel. 809/586–5250). Check also at **Casa de Campo** (La Romana, tel. 809/523–3333) and **Club Med** (Punta Cana, tel. 809/567–5228).

Golf **Casa de Campo** has two 18-hole Pete Dye courses that are open to the public and a third for the private use of villa owners. These are among the best in the Caribbean; greens fees at the two public courses are $50 (including cart). The **Bávaro Beach** resort complex shares an 18-hole course. The **Playa Dorada** hotels have their own 18-hole Robert Trent Jones–designed course; there is also a nine-hole course nearby at the **Costambar.** Guests in Santo Domingo hotels are usually allowed to use the 18-hole course at the **Santo Domingo Country Club** on weekdays—*after* members have teed off. There is a nine-hole course outside of town, at Lomas Lindas. A new Pete Dye course is under construction outside Santo Domingo.

Scuba Diving and Snorkeling Ancient sunken galleons, undersea gardens, and offshore reefs are the lures here, although the Dominican Republic offers less for the diver than many other Caribbean islands. For equipment and trips, contact **Mundo Submarino** (Santo Domingo, tel. 809/566–0344).

Tennis There must be a million nets laced around the island, and most of them can be found at the large resorts (*see* Lodging, *below*). If your hotel does not have courts, you can usually reserve court time at another nearby resort hotel (not at all-inclusive properties), for approximately $14 an hour.

Windsurfing Between June and October, **Cabarete Beach** offers what many consider to be optimal windsurfing conditions: wind speeds at 20–25 knots and 3-to 15-foot waves. The Professional Boardsurfers Association has included Cabarete Beach in its international windsurfing slalom competition. The novice is also welcome to learn and train on modified boards stabilized by flotation devices. **CaribBIC Windsurfing Center,** on Caberete Beach (tel. 800/635–1155 or 800/243–9675), offers accommodations, equipment, training, and professional coaching. Most hotels have Windsurfers for rent at R.D. $120 (U.S. $10).

Shopping

The hot ticket in the Dominican Republic is amber jewelry. This island has the world's largest deposits of amber, and the prices here for the translucent, semiprecious stone are unmatched. The stones, which range in color from pale lemon to dark brown, are actually petrified resin from coniferous trees that disappeared from Earth about 50 million years ago. The most valuable stones are those in which tiny insects or small leaves are embedded. (Don't knock it till you've seen it.)

In the crafts department, hand-carved wooden rocking chairs are big sellers, and they are sold unassembled and boxed for easy transport. La Vega is famous for its *diablos cojuelos* (devil masks) and Santiago for its cigars, which rival the best Havanas (*see* Exploring, *above*). Look also for the delicate ceramic lime figurines that symbolize the Dominican culture.

Bargaining is both a game and a social activity in the Dominican Republic, especially with street vendors and at the stalls in El Mercado Modelo. Vendors are disappointed and perplexed if you don't haggle. They also tend to be tenacious, so unless you really have an eye on buying, don't even stop to look—you may get stuck buying a souvenir just to get rid of an annoying vendor.

Shopping Districts **El Mercado Modelo** in Santo Domingo is a covered market in the Colonial Zone bordering Calle Mella. The restored buildings of **La Atarazana** (across from the Alcázar in the Colonial Zone) are filled with shops, art galleries, restaurants, and bars. The main shopping streets in the Colonial Zone are **Calle El Conde,** which has been transformed into an exclusively pedestrian thoroughfare, and **Calle Duarte.** (Some of the best shops on Calle Duarte are north of the Colonial Zone, between Calle Mella and Av. de las Américas.) **Plaza Criolla** (corner of Av. 27 de Febrero and Av. Anacaona) is filled with shops that sell everything from scents to nonsense. Duty-free shops selling liquors, cameras, and the like are at the **Centro de los Héroes** (Av. George Washington), the **Hotel El Embajador,** the **Santo Domingo Sheraton,** and at **Las Américas Airport.** The two major commercial malls in Santo Domingo are **Unicentro** (406 Av. Abraham Lincoln) and **Plaza Central** (Avs. Bolívar and 27 de Febrero). The latter includes such top boutiques as **Jenny Polanco**, **Nicole B,** and **Benetton**, which includes a coffeehouse on its second level with rotating exhibit by up-and-coming young artists.

In Puerto Plata, the seven showrooms of the **Tourist Bazaar** (Calle Duarte 61) are in a wonderful old galleried mansion with a patio bar. Another cluster of shops is at the **Plaza Shopping Center** (Calle Duarte at Av. 30 de Marzo). A popular shopping street for jewelry and local souvenirs is **Calle Beller.**

In **Altos de Chavón,** art galleries and shops are grouped around the main square.

Good Buys

Amber/Jewelry **Ambar Tres** (La Atarazana 3, Colonial Zone, Santo Domingo, tel. 809/688–0474) carries a wide selection of the Dominican product.

Dominican Art In Santo Domingo, the **Arawak Gallery** (Av. Pasteur 104, tel. 809/685–1661) specializes in pre-Columbian artifacts and contemporary pottery and paintings. **Galería de Arte Nader** (La Atarazana 9, Colonial Zone, tel. 809/688–0969) showcases top Dominican artists in a variety of medias. **Novo Atarazana** (Atarazana 21, tel. 809/689–0582) has a varied assortment of artifacts made by locals.

Visit the stalls of **El Mercado Modelo** in the Colonial Zone for a dizzying selection of Dominican crafts. **El Conde Gift Shop** (Calle El Conde 153, Santo Domingo, tel. 809/682–5909) is the spot for exquisite mahogany carvings.

In Puerto Plata, **Macaluso's** (Calle Duarte 32, tel. 809/586–3433) specializes in Dominican and Haitian paintings and wood carvings. The **Collector's Corner Gallery and Gift Shop** (Plaza Shopping Center, Calle Duarte at Av. 30 de Marzo, no phone) offers a wide range of souvenirs, including amber.

In Santiago, try **Artesanía Lime** (Autopista Duarte, km 2½, Santiago, tel. 809/582–3754) for mahogany carvings, as well as Carnival masks.

Dining

Dining out is a favorite form of entertainment for Dominicans, and they tend to dress up for the occasion. Most restaurants begin serving dinner around 6 PM, but the locals don't generally turn up until 9 or 10. There are French, Italian, and Chinese restaurants, as well as those serving traditional Dominican fare. Dining doesn't have to be expensive in the Dominican Republic, so long as you keep away from beef. Freshly caught fish is usually your best bet. A simple rice-and-beans lunch (*moro de habichuelas*) is cheap and filling. To save money, don't eat every meal in a full-service restaurant. Small stands and more casual restaurants offer tasty roast pork and goat dishes that cost less than $2. One Dominican fast-food chain has become all the rage for harried capitaleños on the go: *Nosotros Empanadas.* Most of the 17 outlets are in Santo Domingo, serving up burgers and empanadas into the wee hours. Regrettably, many local restaurants in heavily touristed areas such as the Amber Coast are closing, victims of the all-inclusive craze. But Santo Domingo's Malecón and Puerto Plata's Long Beach offer a series of stands and pizzerias that also represent great value. Santo Domingo's best pizzeria is attached to the excellent *Vesuvio* (tel. 809/689–2141), many of whose affordable pastas can be purchased in this casual annex. For snacking, you'll find luscious local fruit—mangoes, citrus fruits, passion fruit, and papaya—sold on the streets everywhere. Grocery stores here are not so exciting. There is little variety, and even some staples you would expect to see on the shelves may be missing.

Some favorite local dishes you should sample are paella, *sancocho* (a thick stew usually made with five different meats, though sometimes as many as seven), *arroz con pollo* (rice with chicken), *plátanos* (plantains) in all their tasty varieties, and tortilla *de jamón* (filled with a spicy ham omelet). Country snacks include *chicharrones* (fried pork rinds) and *galletas* (flat biscuit crackers). Many a meal is topped off with *majarete*, a tasty cornmeal custard. Presidente, Bohemia, and Quisqueya are the local beers, Bermúdez and Brugal the local rums. To end a meal, sip the dark brown aged rum known as *añejo* over ice. Wine is on the expensive side because it has to be imported. Dominicans like their coffee strong (decaffeinated coffee is rare); if you're not of like mind, you may want to bring your own.

The dress code tends to be more formal in Santo Domingo, both at lunch and dinner, with long pants and dresses suggested. In resort areas, shorts and beach wraps are acceptable at lunch; for dinner, especially at gourmet restaurants, long pants, skirts, and collared shirts are the norm. Ties are not required anywhere.

Highly recommended restaurants are indicated by a star ★.

Category	Cost*
$$	$20–$30
$	$10–$20
¢	under $10

**per person, excluding drinks, 10% service charge, and 8% sales tax*

The Amber Coast

$$ **Another World.** It defines hokey and kitschy. The brochures exhort you to "spend an unforgettable evening with Stuart and his charming mother Jeanette, from Miami, Florida, in their 120-year-old restored Victorian 'haunted' farmhouse." (Stuart is a former singer/actor known to belt his rendition of "My Way." Jeanette calls the ghosts their "friendly boarders.") And then there's the minizoo, including a 350-pound Bengal tiger, a honey bear, and a capuchin monkey appropriately named Hanky Panky. The food selection is straight from Noah's Ark as well: frogs' legs tempura, river prawns, escargots, rabbit, and quail are just a few choices from the enormous—and surprisingly well-prepared—menu. Free pickup and return to Puerto Plata hotels, as well as complimentary hors d'oeuvres and cordials make this a pitch difficult to resist. *Puerto Plata, tel.809/543–8116. Reservations advised. MC, V. No lunch.*

$$ **De Armando.** You may feel that you're dining in a proper old relative's dining room in this charmingly old-fashioned eatery. In a pretty aqua-and-white house, the dining room has high-backed embroidered chairs, crisp white napery, and dark-wood tables. Steak, seafood, and Continental dishes are all served here: Try the snapper in green peppercorn sauce or sea bass in champagne mushroom velouté. A guitar trio provides the musical portion of your meal. *Av. Mota 23, at Av. Separación, tel. 809/586–3418. Reservations required. MC, V.*

$–$$ **Caribae.** Aquariums teeming with all kinds of sea creatures decorate the dining room of this warm, unassuming spot. You can choose your own lobster, shrimp, and oysters for the barbecue. Costs are low because this health-conscious restaurant raises its own shrimp at a farm and grows its own 100% organic vegetables. *Camino Libre 70, Sosúa, tel. 809/571–3138. MC, V.*

$ **Guajiro's Caribbean Cafe.** Visit this casual Sosúa eatery for some of the best inventive local cuisine in the area. Try the green plantain soup or *yuca* (an island tuber) in *mojo* (a lime, garlic, olive oil marinade) to start, then *pollo à la merengue* (sweet and spicy coriander chicken) or *filetillo saltado* (catch of the day, usually kingfish, in *sofrito*, a savory sauce of garlic and green pepper rouged with tomato). For a filling meal order the cubano sandwich bursting with roast pork, ham, cheese and pickles. Thatching, nautical paraphernalia dangling from the rafters, rough-hewn wooden tables and chairs, and traditional straw hats, shirts and machetes hanging on the walls give the place a rustic country feel. Latin jazz nights are scheduled regularly and draw a rollicking crowd. *Calle Pedro Clisande, El Batey, Sosúa, tel. 809/571–2161. No reservations. AE, MC, V.*

¢ **Hemingway's.** This tropical variation on an English pub (maybe they should have called it Maugham's) is a cool retreat with polished hardwood floors and tables, nautical paraphernalia, trellises, and a sizable aquarium. Food is strictly of the happy-hour variety: burgers, chicharrones de pollo (we call them chicken McNuggets—theirs

are tastier), and "wings from hell." But you can't beat beers and cuba libres for R.D. $20! *Playa Dorada Plaza, no phone. AE, MC, V.*

¢ **Roma II.** Surprisingly delicious pizzas, cooked in a wood-burning oven, come from this unassuming wooden shack. The pizza dough and pasta are made fresh daily. Other specialties include spaghetti *con pulpo* (with octopus), *filete chito* (steak with garlic), and a host of other pastas and special sauces. *Corner Calle E. Prudhomme and Calle Beller, tel. 809/586–3904. No reservations. No credit cards.*

Boca Chica
$–$$ **Neptuno's Club.** This breezy seaside eatery is little more than a shack perched above the water, seemingly held together by the barnacles of marine memorabilia. While you can order good local preparations of chicken and pork, it goes without saying that seafood reigns supreme. Try the Neptuno's fish casserole in coconut water or kingfish in béchamel sauce. *Boca Chica Beach, tel. 809/523–4703. MC, V. Closed Mon.*

La Romana
$$ **Café del Sol.** At this outdoor café in a re-created medieval Spanish village, 3 miles east of Casa de Campo, you can lunch quite inexpensively on pizza, a light salad, or quiche while gazing at the distant mountain range. Dinner here is more elaborate and more expensive. *Altos de Chavón, tel. 809/523–3333, ext. 2346. No reservations. AE, DC, MC, V.*

$$ **Villa Casita.** Candles, muted lights, and piano music give this small restaurant a romantic feel. The chef specializes in creative Dominican cooking. Start with octopus vinaigrette, spinach crepes, or pasta with anchovies and clams before feasting on sea bass or local lobster. Meat eaters fare slightly less well with steak or—the better choice—veal rollantine. The polished wood bar is a nice place for cognac and coffee. *Francisco Richer 71, La Romana, tel. 809/556–2808. Reservations suggested. AE, MC, V.*

Samaná
$$ **Café de France.** Local aficionados swear the beef here (try the fillet in mushroom or peppercorn sauce) is among the best in the Dominican Republic. Seafood here is also dependable: One standout is shrimp (or grouper) in garlic-coconut sauce. The small bistro is on the waterfront and is simply decorated, with white stucco walls and red tablecloths. An even more casual annex serves knockout pizzas. *Malecon, Samaná, no phone. Reservations advised (stop by the restaurant). MC, V.*

Santo Domingo
$$ ★ **Lina.** Lina was the personal chef of Trujillo, and she taught her secret recipes to the chefs of this stylish contemporary restaurant, still a favorite of Santo Domingo movers and shakers. Brass columns, mirrored ceilings, planters, art naïf, Villeroy and Boch china, and a pianist tickling the ivories set the elegant tone. The extensive menu favors Continental and haute Dominican dishes. Paella is the best-known specialty (so hearty you won't need an appetizer or dessert), but other offerings include filet mignon Roquefort, red snapper in coconut or almond cheese sauce, and a casserole of mixed seafood flavored with Pernod. *Gran Hotel Lina, Av. Máximo Gómez at Av. 27 de Febrero, tel. 809/686–5000. Reservations required. Jacket required. AE, DC, MC, V.*

$$ **Mesón de la Cava.** The capital's most unusual restaurant is more than 50 feet below ground in a natural cave complete with stalagmites and stalactites. You must descend a circular staircase, ducking rock protrusions, to dine on Continental standards like prime fillet with Dijon flambé, and tournedos Roquefort. Seafood preparations tend to be more adventurous, such as red snapper poached in white wine and coconut sauce, but the food takes a back seat to the spectacular setting. You'll need to order the less expensive chicken and seafood dishes and perhaps forgo an appetizer or dessert to keep your meal within our $$ range. There is live music and dancing nightly until 1 AM, although sometimes you may wish they'd stop playing Jackson Five renditions and allow a majestic silence to fall over the

cathedralesque grotto. *Av. Mirador del Sur, tel. 809/533–2818. Reservations required. Jacket required. AE, DC, MC, V.*

$–$$ **Café St. Michel.** The decor is rather odd, sort of a contemporary indoor take on a gazebo, but the menu of French bistro–style dishes and local fare keeps diners coming back. Cream of pumpkin soup and steak tartare are specialties. Desserts include a prizewinning chocolate torte and spectacular soufflés. *Av. Lope de Vega 24, tel. 809/562–4141. Reservations advised. Jacket required. AE, MC, V.*

$–$$ **Fonda de la Atarazana.** Dinner and dancing on the brick patio of a 17th-century building in the Colonial Zone make for a very romantic evening. Try the kingfish, shrimp, or chicharrones de pollo. *La Atarazana 5, tel. 809/689–2900. AE, MC, V. Weekend reservations advised.*

¢–$ ★ **El Conuco.** Conuco means countryside—and it's hard to believe that this open-air thatched hut, alive with hanging plants, hibiscus, and frangipani and decorated with basketry, sombreros, license plates, and graffiti, is smack in the center of Santo Domingo. This is a superb place to sample typical Dominican cuisine, from *la bandera* (white rice, kidney beans, and stewed beef duplicating the colors of the flag) to a magnificent, delicately flaky *bacalao de la comai* (cod in white cream sauce with garlic and onions). The ambience is always celebratory; waiters occasionally take to makeshift drum sets to accompany the merengue tapes. *152 Casimiro de Moya, tel. 809/221–3231. MC, V.*

¢–$ **La Bahía.** The catch of the day is always tops at this unpretentious spot. Try the kingfish in coconut sauce or the *espaguettis à la canona* (spaghetti heaped with seafood). The conch, which appears in a variety of dishes, is also good. For starters, try the *sopa palúdica*, a thick soup made with fish, shrimp, and lobster and served with tangy garlic bread. The decor strikes a nautical note, with fishing nets and seashells. *Av. George Washington 1, tel. 809/682–4022. No reservations. AE, MC, V.*

¢ ★ **Ludovino's** and **Joaquin's.** Shacks and stands serving cheap eats for people on the run are a Dominican tradition, as much a part of the culture and landscape as the Colonial Zone. Two such shacks have become legends in Santo Domingo; both are located in working-class districts outside the normal tourist loop. El Palacio de los Yaniqueques (everyone calls it Ludovino's after the nutty owner) is famed for its johnnycakes—fried dough stuffed with everything from chicken to seafood. You pay the cashier when you order and get a free thimbleful of strong, sweet coffee while you wait for your food. Joaquin's serves up the best pork sandwich—laden with onions, tomatoes, pickles, and seasonings—in the Western World (yes, even Texas barbecue takes a back seat). The price for a filling meal? Two bucks at either. *Ludovino's: 19 Summer Wells, no phone. Open daily 7 AM–8 PM. Joaquin's: Av. Abraham Lincoln and Max Henríquex Ureña St., no phone. Open nightly 7 PM–2 AM.*

Lodging

The Dominican Republic has the largest hotel inventory in the Caribbean. Puerto Plata alone has 9,000 rooms and hosts 250,000 tourists a year. There are already so many adjoining resorts that when you go out for a stroll you have to flag landmarks to find your way back to the one where your luggage is. What the island's hotels lack in charm, they make up for in low rates. Even many of the larger resorts and all-inclusives here are affordable.

More and more hotels in the Dominican Republic are becoming all-inclusives. These are often a good choice, since restaurants and sports facilities within walking distance of hotels are scarce. If you take an EP plan at a hotel, you may find yourself eating your meals there anyway, without the savings provided by an MAP or all-inclusive plan. Note that our prices are based on room-only rates.

Small hotels at the bottom end of our ¢ category tend to have pretty dingy rooms and are often in urban centers, away from the better beaches. What you save on accommodations may be offset by the cost of the car you'll need to rent. Rental properties are almost nonexistent in the Dominican Republic, except for the high-priced luxury villas at Casa de Campo.

Santo Domingo's hotels, while often providing rooms with views of the Caribbean, are at least 30 minutes away by car from any beach where you would want to swim. All of the other hotels listed are on the beach or close to the water. Those hotels on Playa Dorado that do not front the beach have shuttle buses that go there; in any case you are never more than a 10-minute walk away.

Highly recommended lodgings are indicated by a star ★.

Category	Cost*
$$	$80–$120
$	$50–$80
¢	under $50

**All prices are for a standard double room for two, excluding 15% service charge and 8% tax. To estimate rates for hotels offering MAP/FAP, add about $20–$30 per person per day to the above price ranges. For all-inclusives, add about $40–$45 per person per day.*

The Amber Coast

$$

Caribbean Village Club and Resort. Rooms in the newer Royale building have kitchenettes and cable TV and are simply decorated in peach tones. The older Tropicale is a series of small houses with connecting skywalks. Rooms here are more like miniapartments, perfect for families, all with terrace or balcony, kitchenette, small sitting area, marble floors, and light pastel decor. One free-form pool has a swim-up terrace. The beach is a 10-minute hike away, but there's free shuttle service. The hotel's La Tortuga restaurant, a snack bar, and water-sports facilities are right on the sand. Nightly entertainment and dancing take place in the patio lounge and lobby bar. The staff genuinely works hard to compensate for the off-beach location. *Playa Dorada, tel. 809/586–5350, fax 809/320–5386. 310 rooms, 26 suites. Facilities: 3 restaurants, 3 bars/lounges, grill, 2 pools, 2 lighted tennis courts, minimart, disco, child care, beach club and water-sports center, medical clinic, shopping arcade, access to golf course. AE, MC, V. CP, MAP.*

$$ ★

Flamenco Beach Resort, Villas Doradas, and **Playa Dorada Beach Resort.** Guests can use the facilities at all three of these hotels, which are lined up one after the other on the mile-long white-sand beach. They're all known for their lively nightlife and variety of social and sports programs, but the similarities end there. Rooms at the older, all-inclusive Playa Dorada are dowdy and sadly in need of refurbishment. Service is efficient but unenthusiastic. Villas Doradas, also all-inclusive, is a step up. Rooms are decorated in earth tones (a refreshing change of pace) and hung with abstract paintings, and all have cable TV, safe, and minibar. The Chinese restaurant here is surprisingly good. The newer Flamenco is the real jewel. The glorious public spaces include cobblestone and Andalusian brick floors, hand-painted tiles, stuccoed walls, and antique carved doors. There are four magnificent restaurants including Via Veneto, a lively trattoria, and the gourmet Spanish El Cortijo. The main free-form pool (with swim-up bar) is designed to resemble a lake, complete with waterfall and lapping waves. Rooms and suites have tasteful hardwood furnishings, terra-cotta floors, bright floral upholstery, minibar, cable TV, and a balcony or terrace. Club Miguel Angel is a hotel within a hotel offering premium concierge service. The only thing missing at the Flamenco is an ocean view.

Flamenco: Playa Dorada, Puerto Plata, tel. 809/320–5084, fax 809/320–6319. 518 units. Facilities: 4 restaurants, 3 bars, pizzeria, 2 pools, water-sports center, 2 lighted tennis courts, shopping arcade. Villas Doradas: Box 1370, Puerto Plata, tel. 809/320–3000, fax 809/320–4790. 207 rooms. Facilities: 5 restaurants, 2 bars, pool, water-sports center, car rental, 3 tennis courts, gift shop. Playa Dorada: Box 272, Puerto Plata, tel. 809/586–3988 or 800/423–6902, fax 809/320–1190. 252 rooms, 1 suite. Facilities: 4 restaurants, 2 bars, pool, disco, casino, ice-cream parlor, access to golf course, tennis courts, horseback riding, bikes, jogging trail, water-sports center. AE, DC, MC, V. EP, MAP, FAP (Flamenco), all-inclusive (Playa and Villas Dorada).

$$ **Heavens.** It's all fun and games at this all-inclusive property. From exercise to merengue lessons, Heavens caters to the young (not the young at heart), and children are welcome, too. This is one of Playa Dorado's smaller resorts; buildings seem to jostle each other for space, and the pool area is densely packed with chaise longues. The decor is dominated by stylized palm trees in rattan, cloth, and metal, which help liven up the claustrophobic rooms. The Rainbow Restaurant is the only Dominican eatery to offer a no-smoking area. Locals frequent the high-tech Andromeda disco, but ask for a room away from it—things can get noisy. *Box 576, Playa Dorada, Puerta Plata, tel. 809/586–5250 or 800/835–7697, fax 809/320–4733. 150 rooms and suites. Facilities: 2 restaurants, disco, bar, cable TV, pool, horseback riding, water aerobics, windsurfing, sailing, snorkeling and scuba, merengue lessons. AE, MC, V. All-inclusive.*

$$ **Jack Tar Village.** At this link in the all-inclusive chain of JTVs, everything, including drinks and golf greens fees, is included in the cost of your accommodations. Accommodations are in Spanish-style villas set back from the beach in a large landscaped garden. You can request a room closer to the beach or golf course, or a quieter one away from all the action. Villas 1–12 are the noisiest; 71–74 the most isolated. Units in the two-story villas are rather ordinary, with ugly red or green naugahyde chairs. Request one in a single-story villa: Though these lack patios, they have a fresher, wicker-and-pastel decor. All units have cable TV, safe, direct-dial phone and air-conditioning. Although the place is most popular with couples of all ages (especially American), it has a fine child care facility. One of the restaurants specializes in theme buffets, another in Caribbean-inspired Continental; the third, Elaine's is at the casino. There is free transportation to town, but the all-inclusive deal will probably keep you on the premises. *Box 368, Playa Dorada, tel. 809/586–3800 or 800/999–9182, fax 809/320–4161. 280 rooms, 4 suites. Facilities: 3 restaurants, 5 bars, 2 pools, hot tub, gym, sauna, massage, shops, beauty parlor, child care, casino, night club, golf, horseback riding, 4 lighted tennis courts, water-sports center. AE, MC, V. All-inclusive.*

$$ **Playa Chiquita.** A broad breezeway leads from the registration desk, past the free-form pool with swim-up bar and shallow children's section, right to the delightful private cove. The rooms have a contemporary tropical decor, with pastel upholstery, rattan furnishings, and terra-cotta floors. All have cable TVs, double or king-size beds, and wet bars; most have a patio or balcony. The recently added casino has proved wildly popular with locals and tourists alike. *Sosúa, tel. 809/689–6191 or 800/922–4272, fax 809/571–2460. 90 rooms. Facilities: restaurant, coffee shop, pool, gift shop, nightclub, casino, water sports. MC, V. EP, MAP.*

$$ ★ **Puerto Plata Beach Resort and Casino.** More of a village than a resort, Puerto Plata's 7 acres hold cobblestone pathways, colorful gardens, and rooms and suites in 23 two- and three-story buildings. During high season, only the standard doubles are within our $$ range. During the summer, the one-bedroom suites also fall within this price category. Accommodations have terra-cotta floors and a primarily mint and jade decor, with cable TV, minifridge, and bal-

cony or terrace. An activities center sets up water-sports clinics, rents bicycles, and so forth. The resort also caters to the little ones, with children's games and enclosures for them at the shallow end of the pool. Bogart's is the glitzy disco. Ylang-Ylang, named after the evening flower that blooms here, is a highly rated gourmet restaurant and catering service. This resort is just outside of town and a ways from Playa Dorada, which will be an added attraction to some. *Box 600, Av. Malecón, Puerto Plata, tel. 809/586–4243 or 800/223–9815, fax 809/586–4377. 170 rooms, 46 suites. Facilities: 4 restaurants, bar, pool, outdoor Jacuzzi, horseback riding, casino, gift shop, nightclub, 4 lighted tennis courts, water-sports center. AE, MC, V. MAP. All-inclusive.*

$–$$ **Cabarete Beach Hotel.** This delightful small hotel is set right on a tantalizing curve of golden sand ideal for windsurfing and swimming (the surrounding reef protects it from fierce breakers). Deluxe rooms (in the $$ category) are those with full ocean view and air-conditioning. Standards (in the $ category) are slightly smaller and noisier, and only some have air-conditioning. All rooms are decorated with bright framed prints and blond woods and have such charming touches as rocking chairs. The lovely terrace restaurant is known for its bountiful breakfast buffets of luscious homemade breads, muffins and pastries. The Tropical Bar—a riot of painted gourds and coconuts, colorful murals and thatching—prides itself on its eight fresh fruit juices daily and more than 50 exotic libations. The BIC Windsurf Center (though not part of the hotel) is right next door. The staff is unfailingly helpful and courteous. *Cabarete, tel. 809/571–0755, fax 809/571–0831. 24 rooms. Facilities: restaurant, bar, gift shop. AE, MC, V. EP, MAP.*

$–$$ **Hotel Cofresi.** Rooms here are rather basic and somewhat cramped, but the staff is courteous and the setting is breathtaking. The resort is built on the reefs along the Atlantic, and the sea spritzes its waters into the peaceful man-made lagoon and pools along the beach. Most rooms have cable TV, hair dryer, safe, and kitchenette. There are jogging and exercise trails, paddleboats for the lagoon, scuba-diving clinics, and evening entertainment, including a disco. The restaurants specialize in flavorful Dominican fare. *Box 327, Costambar, tel. 809/586–2898, fax 809/586–8064. 145 rooms, 5 suites. Facilities: 2 restaurants, 2 bars, disco, nightclub, 3 pools (1 saltwater), game room, bicycling, horseback riding, paddleboats, 2 lighted tennis courts, water-sports center. AE, MC, V. All-inclusive.*

$–$$ **Punta Goleta Beach Resort.** This bare-bones all-inclusive resort is set on 100 acres of unruly tropical vegetation. It's across the road from Cabarete beach, where windsurfing is king. The buildings are a showy apricot and jade with lacy gingerbread trim, but rooms are unexceptional in typical soft pastels. All rooms are air-conditioned, and most have terraces or patios. There is a lot of activity—volleyball in the pool or on the beach, frog and crab racing, board games, merengue lessons, and boating on the lagoon. Villas are quite expensive. The uninterested staff is lethargic at best but the resort still offers fairly good value. *Box 318, Cabarete, tel. 809/571–0700, fax 809/571–0707. 126 rooms, 10 villas. Facilities: 2 restaurants, 4 bars, disco, jogging track, pool, lagoon, horseback riding, golf, tennis, water-sports center. AE, DC, MC, V. All-inclusive.*

$–$$ ★ **Sosúa by the Sea.** Sosúa offers some of the best buys on the Amber Coast, including this hotel. Aside from three superior suites, all units (studios or one-bedroom apartments) fall into this price category when you include the cost of the mandatory MAP. All of the fresh spacious accommodations, decorated in pleasing seashell colors with wicker and rattan furnishings, have air-conditioning, satellite TV, safe, refrigerator, and direct-dial phone. For $10 more, the one-bedroom apartments are the best buy, especially for families, since they have a sofa bed in the living room and a kitchenette. Children under seven stay free. The hotel shares a rock-bordered golden

strand with several other small hotels, and a water-sports center is right down the beach. The only drawback is the lack of ocean view. *Sosúa, Box 361, Puerto Plata, tel. 809/571–3222, fax 809/571–3020. 81 units. Facilities: 2 restaurants, bar, pool, hot tub, water-sports center, gift shop, boutique, beauty salon, massage parlor. AE, MC, V. MAP.*

¢–$ **Hotel Montemar.** If you don't mind the lackadaisical upkeep—some rooms have soiled or burned carpets and broken tiles—the Montemar is a good choice for a cost-conscious holiday. It's on the Malecón, between Puerto Plata and Playa Dorada, a five-minute walk from the town's Long Beach. Prices are low, there's a daily schedule of activities, and transportation is provided to the beaches of Playa Dorada. All rooms have air-conditioning, cable TV, safe, direct-dial phone, and private bath. Small standard rooms lack an ocean view. A staff of hotel-school trainees give the place an appealingly warm atmosphere. *Box 382, Puerto Plata, tel. 809/586–2800 or 800/332–4872, fax 809/586–2009. 95 rooms. Facilities: restaurant, bar, pool, 2 tennis courts, beach club, boutique, gift shop, beauty parlor. AE, MC, V. All-inclusive.*

¢ ★ **Club Marina.** This is a wonderfully unusual budget option. Eduardo de Lora, a master stained-glass craftsman, designed the charming beige-stucco-and-red-tile hotel. Everything displays his creative touch: The pool is landscaped with rocks, giving it a natural grotto feel, and spiral staircases are embedded with shards of glass (there are no exposed edges!). The rooms themselves are plain but impeccably neat, with a well-worn integrity. The blue-and-white tiles, lilac bedspreads, and closets painted jade green brighten them up. The restaurant serves wonderful home cooking, and its prices are sensational. All units have cable TV, private bath, and small French balcony. The beach is a five-minute walk. The hotel is owned by the beachfront Casa Marina resort, and although you're paying only half as much as guests there ($50–$65 per person depending on season), you get the use of all its facilities. *Alejo Martínez St., Sosúa, tel. 809/571–3939. 36 rooms. Facilities: restaurant, pool. AE, MC, V.*

¢ **Hostal Jimessón.** One of the few hotels in downtown Puerto Plata, the Jimessón is a gingerbread-trimmed, century-old clapboard house that looks like it came straight from New Orleans. There are rocking chairs on the front porch, and the parlor houses a veritable museum of antique grandfather clocks, Victrolas, and mahogany and wicker furniture. Other superb, homey touches include a live parrot, hanging plants, and the owners' genuine hospitality. Unfortunately, air-conditioned guest rooms, in a newer concrete addition in back, share none of the main house's charm; they have tiny, cramped bathrooms and are furnished with only a bed and table. Although the house is only a few city blocks from the seafront, the better beaches are a couple of miles away. The numerous and varied restaurants of Puerto Plata are within easy walking distance. *Calle John F. Kennedy 41, Puerto Plata, tel. 809/586–5131, fax 809/586–6313. 22 rooms. Facilities: bar, cable TV. AE, MC, V. EP.*

¢ **The Latin Quarter.** This small hotel is in the middle of Puerto Plata's Malecón, a minute's walk from Long Beach. The rooms are a bit dark and musty, but are air-conditioned, have a phone, and are decorated with bright floral linens and comfortable rattan and wicker furniture. There is a large pool, as well as a tennis court (that may or may not be maintained). The biggest drawback is noise: The rooms get a lot of traffic noise, and the disco here is extremely popular with locals, who merengue well into the night. *Malecón (mailing address: Beller 7), Puerto Plata, tel. 809/586–2588, fax 809/586–1828. 52 rooms. Facilities: restaurant, 2 bars, disco, pool, 1 tennis court. AE, MC, V.*

Boca Chica/ Juan Dolio *$$* **Capella Beach Hotel.** This new deluxe resort opened in 1994 on a section of Juan Dolio Beach it ostentatiously calls Villas Del Mar, and it's striving to become the top southern-coast destination, with the exception, of course, of Casa de Campo. It's built on a grand scale, with beautiful tile and mosaic work in the elegant public spaces and a hodgepodge of architectural styles from Victorian (white colonnaded porticoes) to Moorish (arches and red-tile roofs) to South Pacific (two of the restaurants sit in cathedralesque thatched huts). Rooms are large and handsomely appointed with ceramic lamps, pictures of local plants, and pink and mint-green fabrics. Most have balconies and huge walk-in closets; some have ocean views. Unfortunately, the service does not yet meet exacting international standards, the food is not as good as it might be, and the property already requires upkeep (bathrooms seem rather cheaply done and elevators have stained carpets). Nonetheless, the vast array of amenities and facilities is bound to please travelers seeking something a cut above most Dominican resorts, especially at the surprisingly reasonable rates. *Villas Del Mar, Box 4750, Santo Domingo, tel. 809/526–1080 or 800/468–3571, fax 809/526–1088. 261 rooms, 21 suites. Facilities: 3 restaurants, 3 bars, 2 pools, 2 lighted tennis courts, fitness center, water-sports center, game room, shopping arcade, nightly entertainment. AE, D, MC, V. EP, MAP.*

Punta Cana *$$* **Club Mediterranée.** Everything but hard liquor is included in the price you pay for a stay at this 70-acre facility on the Punta Cana beach. Its air-conditioned, double-occupancy rooms are in three-story beach and coconut-grove buildings. Each has twin beds and a bathroom with shower; the decor features pastels and rattan furnishings. The two large, open-air restaurants specialize in theme buffets and Continental fare. There's a disco on the beach, plus the whole spectrum of Club Med activities, from archery to yoga. *Punta Cana, tel. 809/687–2767 or 800/258–2633, fax 809/565–2558; in NY, tel. 212/750–1670. 332 rooms. Facilities: 2 restaurants, bar, disco, pool, 14 tennis courts (6 lighted), golf driving range and putting green, archery, boccie ball, volleyball, boat rides, soccer, ping-pong, aerobics classes, water-sports center. AE, MC, V. All-inclusive (drinks not included).*

Samaná *$$* ★ **Gran Bahía.** This luxury all-inclusive resort is built at the water's edge in an area yet to be spoiled with overdevelopment. Indeed, the place hasn't yet caught on and has lowered its prices, barely sneaking into our $$ category. It's worth the splurge. The grand yet welcoming reception area and three-story white colonnaded atrium surround a spectacular fountain flanked with numerous cozy nooks for cocktails or reading. The modern colonial Victorian has graceful verandas and balconies looking out over the pool and the sea beyond. The superb views make breakfast on your room's private terrace a treat. The large guest rooms have tiled floors and are decorated with cheerful floral prints and pastel watercolor paintings. Dining alfresco is pleasant, although you would be wise to stay with the fresh seafood rather than try the meat dishes. The delightfully European ambience here appeals to a select, chic crowd. *Box 2024, Santo Domingo, tel. 809/538–3111 or 800/372–1323, fax 809/538–2764. 98 rooms. Facilities: 2 restaurants, bar, pool, 2 tennis courts, gym, archery, 9-hole golf course, beauty salon, boutique, whale-watching arranged. AE, MC, V. All-inclusive.*

Santo Domingo *$$* **Gran Hotel Lina and Casino.** The whitewashed modern cinder-block structure of this hotel gives little hint of its stylish, exquisite interior, which gleams with marble floors, mirrored brass colonnades, and striking modern art. The rather plain rooms, mostly in dusky rose, are air-conditioned with double beds, minifridges, huge marble baths, and cable TVs, and exude a staid secure ambience. The staff is friendly and helpful. *Box 1915, Santo Domingo, tel. 809/686–5000 or 800/942–2461, fax 809/686–5521. 205 rooms, 15 suites. Facil-*

ities: restaurant, piano bar, casino, nightclub, coffee shop, health club, 2 tennis courts, pool. AE, DC, MC, V. EP, MAP, FAP.

$$ **Hotel El Embajador and Casino.** This hotel radiates an air of faded gentility; it seems caught in a '50s time warp—Hollywood's idea of a top hotel in an exotic locale. But though the exterior needs sprucing up, the public rooms are imposing by Dominican standards. The bedrooms are spacious but spare, with tatty carpeting, old-fashioned desks and wardrobes, and bare walls. All have minibar, cable TV, and private balcony with either a mountain or an ocean view (choose the latter). An executive concierge floor is good for business travelers. The Jardin de Jade serves marvelous Chinese food. The pool is open to the public and is a popular weekend gathering place for resident foreigners. You can try your luck at the casino, or just listen to the live bands that play there throughout the day and night. *Av. Sarasota 65, Santo Domingo, tel. 809/221–2131 or 800/457–0067, fax 809/532–4494. 304 rooms, 12 suites. Facilities: 2 restaurants, 2 bars, casino, pool, free transport to beach, 4 tennis courts (1 lighted), shopping arcade. AE, DC, MC, V. EP, MAP.*

$ ★ **Hostal Palacio Nicolás de Ovando.** The oldest hotel in the New World, and one of the few in the Colonial Zone, was home to the first governor in the early 1500s. The decor is Spanish, with carved mahogany doors, beamed ceilings, tapestries, arched colonnades, and three courtyards with splashing fountains. The spartan air-conditioned rooms are reminiscent of monks' cells but have views of the port, the pool, or the Colonial Zone. Dominican specialties are served in the restaurant. This is Santo Domingo's only hotel with the charm of antiquity; with prices at the low end of this category, it's the city's most delightful bargain. Its disadvantage is its location: At nighttime, the area can be deserted and unpleasant for walking alone. *Calle Las Damas 44, Apdo. 89-2, Santo Domingo, tel. 809/687–3101, fax 809/686–5170. 55 rooms. Facilities: restaurant, bar, TV, pool. AE, MC, V. EP.*

$ ★ **Hotel Hispañiola.** This hotel is older and less costly than its sister hotel, the Hotel Santo Domingo, next door. It draws a younger, more active crowd, who gather at the disco and the casino, which is filled with striking paintings, stained glass, and towering floral arrangements. There are two restaurants here, Las Cañas and La Pizetta, as well as the very dark, very intimate, and very red Hispañiola Bar, which has a small dance area. Air-conditioned guest rooms are spacious and decorated with chintz, wicker, blond woods, and local crafts, but they're a tad worn. The staff is helpful and will take the time to advise you on your travel plans. A slight drawback is the hotel's location at the opposite end of the Malecón to the historic quarter, and a good 10-minute walk to most of the action. *Avs. Independencia and Abraham Lincoln, tel. 809/535–1511 or 800/223–6620, fax 809/535–4050. 163 rooms, 2 suites. Facilities: 2 restaurants, bar, pool, disco, casino, 3 tennis courts. AE, DC, MC, V. EP, MAP.*

¢ **Hotel Cervantes.** Its location, in the heart of the capital's residential district, five blocks from the Malecón, has made this modern four-story hotel popular with businessmen and tourists who want inexpensive, clean, and functional accommodations. All rooms have air-conditioning, either a king-size bed or two queen-size beds, and a small sitting area with a table and chairs. The decor is pastel-modern. The hotel's restaurant prides itself on its steaks and other meats, and the front office staff cheerfully provides advice on what to see and do in the capital. *Calle Cervantes 202, Santo Domingo, tel. 809/686–8161, fax 809/686–5754. 180 rooms. Facilities: restaurant, pool, sauna, barber shop, free parking. AE, DC, MC, V. EP.*

Off-Season Bets Although Santo Domingo hotel prices remain fairly constant year-round, beach resorts drop rates by up to 40% during the off-season. Some of the island's top hotels become affordable at this time, among them Playa Dorada's **Paradise Beach Resort and Club** (Box

337, Playa Dorada, tel. 809/586–3663 or 800/752–0836, fax 809/320–4858). This well-designed property, a cluster of low-rise buildings with white tile roofs and latticed balconies, offers its all-inclusive package for a price that just misses our $$ category during high season; it's also one of only four Playa Dorada resorts that actually front the beach. Another resort that skirts our $$ category in high season is the **Bávaro Beach Resort** (Higüey, tel. 809/682–2162 or 800/336–6612, fax 809/682–2169), a complex of five hotels situated on the glorious 20-mile stretch of Punta Cana beach, with a wide variety of daily activities, an 18-hole golf course, and several bars and restaurants. You may also wish to investigate discounts at the huge **Casa de Campo** complex (Box 140, La Romana, tel. 809/523–3333 or 800/223–6620, fax 809/523–8548), where certain summer packages make double rooms affordable.

The Arts and Nightlife

Get a copy of the magazine *Vacation Guide* and the newspaper *Touring*, both of which are available free at the tourist office and at hotels, to find out what's happening around the island. Also look in the *Santo Domingo News* and the *Puerto Plata News* for listings of events. The monthly *Dominican Fiesta!* also provides up-to-date information.

Casinos These are the raison d'être for many visitors to the island. There's no cover charge in the casinos, and everyone from high-stakes rollers to those with a few quarters frequents them. Most of the casinos are concentrated in the larger hotels of Santo Domingo, but there are others here and there, and all offer blackjack, craps, and roulette. Casinos are open daily 3 PM–4 AM. You must be 18 to enter, and jackets are required. In Santo Domingo, the most popular casinos are in the Jaragua (Av. Independencia, tel. 809/686–2222), the Embajador (Av. Sarasota, tel. 809/533–2131), the Gran Hotel Lina (Av. Máximo Gómez, tel. 809/686–5000), the Naco Hotel (Av. Tiradentes 22, tel. 809/562–3100), and the Hispañiola (Av. Independencia, tel. 809/535–1511)

Cafés **Café Atlántico** (J. A. Aybar at Abraham Lincoln, tel. 809/565–1841) is responsible for bringing happy hour and Tex-Mex cooking to the Dominican Republic. (Its sister restaurant of the same name is a hot spot in Washington, D.C.) Usually young, very lively, and very friendly, the late-afternoon yuppie crowd comes for the music, the food, the exotic drinks, and the energetic atmosphere.

Exquesito (Av. Tiradentes 8, tel. 809/541–0233) is in a striking setting that mixes traditional Dominican decor with deconstructivist provincial Italian. The fare includes French cheeses, Italian antipasti, and a local version of deli. Talk, relax, and try the fondue at this top gathering spot that appeals to the young and terminally hip.

A recent annex to the Café St. Michel, the **Grand Café** (Av. Lope de Vega 26, tel. 809/562–4141) attracts a relaxed local crowd. You can escape the music by going upstairs to the Tree House. The menu is informal and generally light, but try the Creole oxtail.

The **Museo del Jamon** (La Atarazana 9, no phone) is a casual boîte (with displays on curing ham, hence the name) that is popular Thursday and Sunday evenings after 10 for its folkloric dance shows, with the brilliantly lit Alcázar as a thrilling backdrop.

Music and Dance An active and frenzied young crowd dances to new wave; house; and, of course, merengue at **Alexander's** club (Av. Pasteur 23, tel. 809/685–9728). The neon palm tree outside **Bella Blue** (Av. George Washington 165, tel. 809/689–2911) beckons nightbirds to this Malecón dance club, where the crowd is definitely over 21, and no jeans are allowed.

Happy hours are joyous indeed at Santo Domingo's big hotels, with two-for-one drinks and rollicking bands. A favorite of locals for live music featuring local merengue bands, **Las Palmas** (Hotel Santo Domingo, Av. Independencia at Abraham Lincoln, tel. 809/535–1511) has a happy hour from 6 to 8 PM. The newest sensation is **Guacara Taina** (655 Rómulo Betancourt Ave., tel. 809/530–2666), a cultural center/disco set in a cave. It hosts folkloric dances by day and becomes the city's hottest nightspot in the late evening. Said to be the world's only disco grotto, it boasts two dance floors, three bars, and lots of nooks and crannies. An aptly named club, **Tops** (Plaza Hotel, Av. Tiradentes, tel. 809/541–6226) offers excellent views of the city. Located on the 12th floor of the hotel, it features a variety of special events, from lingerie fashion shows to the latest bands. When all the partying is over, capitaleños will guide you to **La Aurora** (Av. Hermanos Deligne, tel. 809/685–6590), a lush after-hours supper club. Savor typical dishes, even sancocho, at four in the morning. Here you'll see not only the party goers but also the musicians who entertained them. It's a spot of preference for Santo Domingo's hottest band, 4:40.

Nearly every hotel in Puerto Plata has a disco and frequent live entertainment. Among the most popular spots are **La Roca Club** (Sosúa, tel. 809/571–2179), **Crazy Moon** (Paradise Beach Club, tel. 809/320–3663), and **Andromeda** (Heavens, tel. 809/586–5250).

12 Grenada

Updated by Jane E. Zarem

Grenada, 21 miles long and 12 miles wide, is bordered by dozens of beaches and secluded coves, crisscrossed by nature trails, and filled with spice plantations, tropical forests, and select hotels that cling to hillsides and overlook the sea.

Known as the Isle of Spice, Grenada is a major producer of nutmeg, mace, cinnamon, cocoa, and many other common household spices. The pungent aroma of spices fills the air at the outdoor markets, where they're sold from large burlap bags; in the restaurants, where chefs believe in using them liberally; and in the pubs, where cinnamon and nutmeg are sprinkled on the rum punches. If the Irish hadn't beaten them to the name, Grenadians might have called their land the Emerald Isle, for the lush rain forests and the thick vegetation on the hillsides give it a great, green beauty that few Caribbean islands can match.

Located in the Eastern Caribbean 90 miles north of Trinidad, Grenada is the most southerly of the Windward Islands. It is a nation composed of three inhabited islands and a few uninhabited islets: Grenada island is the largest of the three, with 120 square miles and about 91,000 people; Carriacou, 16 miles north of Grenada, has 13 square miles and a population of about 5,000; and Petit Martinique, 5 miles northeast of Carriacou, has 486 acres and a population of 700. Although Carriacou and Petit Martinique are popular for day trips and fishing and snorkeling excursions, most of the tourist action is on Grenada. Here, too, you will find the nation's capital, St. George's, and its largest harbor, St. George's Harbour.

Although Grenada's tourism industry is undergoing an expansion, it is a controlled expansion. No building can stand taller than a coconut palm, and new construction on the beaches must be at least 165 feet from the high-water mark. Even with the increase in tourism, the island is able to maintain its original West Indian flavor. Hotels, resorts, and restaurants remain, for the most part, small and family-owned by people who get to know their guests and pride themselves on giving personalized service.

Grenada is somewhat lower on the price spectrum than many Caribbean resort islands. Even if you stay in Grand Anse, the area around the most celebrated of the island's beaches, you'll find some moderately priced, well-maintained hotels. Alternatively, consider even less-expensive apartment hotels, guest houses on small coves, inexpensive hotels close to St. George's, or inns on Carriacou. For all properties, be sure to inquire whether beaches and restaurants are within walking distance, or plan to use public transportation; the high cost of car rental and gas on Grenada can outweigh the savings of remote hotels. Most accommodations on Grenada are open year-round, often dropping their rates by as much as 40% during the off season. Group packages, too, are common here.

Dining on Grenada need not be expensive either. Relatively cheap eateries are as common as pricey restaurants, and you don't have to pay a lot to take advantage of the island's remarkable produce. Public transportation, not available on all Caribbean islands, can convey you around the island's perimeter for anywhere between E.C. $1 and E.C. $6. There are drawbacks, of course: Schedules are unpredictable (you'd never be able to rely on a ride back to your hotel from St. George's after dinner, for example); seating arrangements are, well, cuddly; and some of the local drivers like to challenge accepted properties of physics. Still, for the open-minded and adventuresome, it's fun and cheap.

What It Will Cost These sample prices, meant only as a general guide, are for high season. You can stay one-night at a ¢ hotel for $40 or pay up to $150 for a room just steps away from Grand Anse Beach. A $ dinner for one averages about $15. A fast-food meal is $4–$6; a sandwich lunch, about $2.50–$3.50. Rum punch is about $2 here, while a Carib beer is $1.60. A taxi ride from St. George's to Grand Anse is $7; the public bus, 37¢. Rental cars with standard transmission cost about $50 a day. Jeeps and automatic-drive vehicles are around $5 more. A gallon of gas is about $2.60. A single-tank dive costs about $40; snorkel-equipment rental is $5–$10 a day.

Before You Go

Tourist Information Contact the **Grenada Board of Tourism:** in the United States (820 2nd Ave., Suite 900D, New York, NY 10017, tel. 212/687–9554 or 800/927–9554, fax 212/573–9731); in Canada (Suite 820, 439 University Ave., Toronto, Ontario M5G 1Y8, tel. 416/595–1339, fax 416/595–8278); or in the United Kingdom (1 Collingham Gardens, Earl's Court, London SW5 0HW, tel. 0171/370–5164 or 0171/370–5165, fax 0171/370–7040).

Arriving and Departing

By Plane **American Airlines** (tel. 800/334–7400) has daily flights during high season from major U.S. and Canadian cities via their San Juan hub; **BWIA** (tel. 800/327–7401 or 800/538-2942 in Miami) flies from New York, Miami, Toronto, and London to Barbados, where **LIAT** (Leeward Islands Air Transport, tel. 809/440–2796 or 809/440–2797) has connecting flights to Grenada. **Air Canada** (tel. 800/776–3000) flies from Toronto to Barbados, as well. LIAT has scheduled service between Grenada and Carriacou and also serves Trinidad, St. Lucia, Martinique, Antigua, Dominica, Guadeloupe, and Venezuela.

From the Airport Taxis are available at Point Salines International Airport to take you to your hotel. Rates to St. George's and the hotels of Grand Anse and L'Anse aux Epines are about $10–$12. In Eastern Caribbean currency, this amounts to about E.C. $25–E.C. $35. Some of the less centrally located hotels offer a free airport pickup, so inquire when you make your reservations. Unfortunately, there's no public transportation from the airport, so unless you've made arrangements in advance of your arrival, plan to take a cab.

Passports and Visas Passports are not required of U.S., Canadian, and British citizens, provided they have two proofs of citizenship (one with photo) and a return air ticket. A passport, even an expired one, is the best proof of citizenship. A driver's license with photo *and* an original birth certificate or voter registration card will also suffice.

Language English is the official language of Grenada.

Precautions Secure your valuables in the hotel safe. Avoid walking late at night in the Grand Anse/L'Anse aux Epines hotel districts; it's dark enough to run into things, maybe even into one of the cows that graze silently by the roadside. Starving mosquitos adore tourists, especially after heavy rains; bring repellent.

Staying in Grenada

Important Addresses **Tourist Information:** The **Grenada Board of Tourism** is located on the Carenage in St. George's (tel. 809/440–2001, fax 809/440–6637). It has maps, brochures, and information on accommodations, tours, and other services.

Emergencies **Police and Fire:** Call 911. **Ambulance:** In St. George's, Grand Anse, and L'Anse aux Epines, call 434. For other areas, check with your hotel. **Hospital: St. George's Hospital** (tel. 809/440–2051, 809/440–2052, 809/440–2053). **Pharmacies: Gitten's** (Halifax St., St. George's, tel. 809/440–2165; after hours, 809/440–2340) and **Gitten's Drugmart** (Grand Anse, tel. 809/444–4954; after hours, 809/440-2340) are both open weekdays and Saturday 9–8, Sunday and public holidays 9–noon. **Parris' Pharmacy Ltd.** (Victoria St., Grenville, tel. 809/442–7330), on the windward side of the island, is open Monday–Wednesday and Friday 9–4:30, Thursday 9–1, and Saturday 9–7.

Currency Grenada uses the Eastern Caribbean (E.C.) dollar. At press time the exchange rate in banks was E.C. $2.67 to U.S. $1. Be sure to ask which currency is referred to when you make purchases and business transactions; prices are often quoted in E.C. dollars. Money can be exchanged at any bank or hotel. However, hotels are unable by law to give foreign currency in change or on departure. U.S. currency and traveler's checks are widely accepted. Most hotels and major restaurants accept credit cards. Prices quoted here are in U.S. dollars unless indicated otherwise.

Taxes and Service Charges Hotels add an 8% government tax; restaurants add a 10% tax. In addition, hotels and some restaurants add a 10% service charge to your bill. If not, a 10%–15% gratuity at mealtime should be added for a job well done.

The departure tax is E.C. $35 (about U.S. $13) for adults and E.C. $17.50 (about U.S. $6.50) for children ages 5 to 12. Children under 5 are exempt.

Getting Around

Buses Privately owned minivans ply the winding road between St. George's and Grand Anse Beach, where many of the hotels are located. Hail one anywhere along the way, pay E.C. $1, and hold on to your hat. They pass by frequently from about 6 AM to 8 PM daily except Sundays and public holidays. You can get anywhere on the island by minivan for E.C. $1–E.C. $6—a bargain by any standard—but be prepared for packed vehicles, unpredictable schedules, and some hair-raising maneuvers on mountainous roads and byways.

Taxis Taxis—also in the form of minivans, though without the crush of passengers—are plentiful, and rates set by the government are posted at the hotels and at the pier on the Carenage in St. George's. The trip from the Carenage to Grand Anse is about $7; to L'Anse aux Epines, count on a $12 fare; to the golf course, $6. A surcharge of

33.3% is added to all fares for rides taken between 6 PM and 6 AM. Cabs are plentiful at all hotels, at the cruise passenger welcome center, and on the Carenage.

For trips outside St. George's, you'll be charged E.C. $4.25 (U.S. $1.60) a mile for the first 10 miles, and E.C. $3.60 (U.S. $1.35) a mile thereafter.

Most tourists use taxis liberally, but to save money you should confine their use to getting back to your hotel after dark. For a guided tour of the island, you're better off pricewise using an established tour agency (*see* Guided Tours, *below*) than a taxi and driver.

Boats Twice a week, boats depart the Carenage in St. George's for Carriacou. Trips take about four hours; cost is $20 round-trip. Call 809/443–7179 or 809/443–8209.

Rental Cars Driving here is not a leisurely venture. The main coastal road is winding and often steep and narrow. Driving is on the left side of the road. To rent a car, you will need a valid driver's license, with which you may obtain a local permit from the traffic department (at the fire station on the Carenage) or some car-rental firms, at a cost of E.C. $30. Rental cars cost about $50 a day or $260 a week with unlimited mileage. A Jeep or automatic-drive car runs about $55 a day, and $285 a week. Gas costs about $2.60 per gallon. Your hotel can arrange a rental for you. Car-rental agencies in St. George's are numerous. **David's** (tel. 809/444–3399 or 809/440–3038, fax 809/444–4404) maintains four offices: Point Salines International Airport, Grenada Renaissance Hotel, Rex Grenadian Hotel, and the Limes in Grand Anse. **Avis** is at Spice Isle Rental (tel. 809/440–3936 or 809/440–2624; after hours 809/444–4563; fax 809/440–4110) on Paddock and Lagoon roads in St. George's. In the True Blue area, call **McIntyre Bros. Ltd.** (tel. 809/444–3944 or 809/444–2901; after hours, 809/443–5319).

Telephones and Mail Grenada can be dialed directly from the United States and Canada. The area code is 809. Long-distance calls from Grenada can be dialed directly from pay phones and most hotel rooms. The price of a local call from a pay phone is E.C. 25¢. Public booths at many locations accept U.S. quarters as well as E.C. 25¢ and E.C.$1 coins.

Airmail rates for letters to the United States and Canada are E.C. 75¢ for a half-ounce letter and E.C. 35¢ for a postcard.

Opening and Closing Times Store are generally open 8–4 weekdays, 8–1 on Saturday. Most are closed Sunday. Banks are open Monday–Thursday 8–1:30 or 2, Friday 8–5. The main post office, on Lagoon Road in St. George's, is open 8–3:30 weekdays.

Guided Tours **New Trends Tours** (Siesta Apartment Hotel, Grand Anse, tel. 809/444–1236, fax 809/444–4836) offers a wide selection of tours, as does **Arnold's Tours** (611 Archibald Ave., St. George's, tel. 809/440–0531 or 809/440–2213, fax 809/440–4118). Both agencies will customize their offerings for individual clients, but "Around the Island" is typically a seven-hour trip up the west coast to a spice plantation at Gouyave, then to the Mascoll plantation house, Morne Fendue, for lunch. The return route is through the east-coast town of Grenville and across scenic St. David's Parish. The tour costs about $35 per person.

A number of tour operators in St. George's offer standard four-hour tours, which include the town of St. George's, scenic Westerhall Point, a trip across the island to the Atlantic side, a small fishing village, a sugar-processing factory, and Grand Anse Beach. The half-day excursion should run you about $25 or less. **Spiceland Tours** (the Carenage, tel. 809/440–5180) offers several five- and seven-hour island tours, from an "Urban/Suburban" tour of St. George's and the

South Coast to an "Emerald Forest Tour" highlighting Grenada's natural beauty.

To get a taste of Grenada's gorgeous interior, hook up with **Henry's Safari Tours** (tel. 809/444–5313, fax 809/444–4847), which offers tours ranging from three to seven hours. Henry will take you anywhere, and at whatever pace you wish. You can pay up to $100 if you're on your own; join three or more people, however, and the cost per person drops to $15–$35.

Exploring Grenada

Numbers in the margin correspond to points of interest on the Grenada (and Carriacou) map.

A half-day guided tour makes a good introduction to Grenada and will familiarize you with the island's highlights. If you find yourself intrigued with a particular spot, you can probably return via public transportation, walk (depending upon distances), or combine the two. You may want to rent a car for an additional day to beach-hop or return to a favorite site, but keep in mind the steep daily rental rate and price of gas. Be prepared for challenging driving conditions even on the major coastal road that circles the island. (For more information, *see* Guided Tours and Getting Around, *above.*)

Our first itinerary is a walking tour of St. George's. It's easy and fun; you should have time to cover everything in a day and still enjoy a seafood lunch on the Carenage. The East Coast and West Coast tours are driving tours that require more than a day to complete, but budget travelers can combine highlights from both tours and visit them via public transportation or in a single day of driving. The Grand Anse tour includes beach, boutiques, restaurants, and nightlife in an easily traversed area.

St. George's

Grenada's capital city and major port is one of the most picturesque and authentic West Indian towns in the Caribbean. Pastel warehouses cling to the curving shore along the Carenage, the horseshoe-shaped harborside thoroughfare. Rainbow-color houses rise
1 above it and disappear into steep green hills. A walking tour of **St. George's** can be made in about two hours, particularly with the help of the Grenada Board of Tourism's free brochure, "Historical Walking Tour of St. George's," which directs you to 21 points of historical interest. Pick it up at their office on the Carenage, next to the cruise passenger welcome center (*see below*).

Start on the **Carenage,** the capital's main thoroughfare that bounds three sides of St. George's Harbour. Cruise ships and windjammers dock at the pier, at the eastern end of the Carenage next to the **Welcome Center** and **Grenada Board of Tourism** office. The **Delicious Landing** restaurant (tel. 809/440–3948), with outdoor tables, is at the western end. In between are the **National library,** a number of warehouses and small **shops,** and two more good restaurants: **Rudolf's** and **The Nutmeg** (*see* Dining, *below*). The Nutmeg has a huge open window that provides a great view of the harbor.

You can reach the **Grenada National Museum** by walking along the west side of the Carenage and taking Young Street west to Monckton Street. The museum has a small, interesting collection of archaeological and colonial artifacts and recent political memorabilia. *Young and Monckton Sts., tel. 809/440–3725. Admission: $1 adults, 25¢ children under 18. Open weekdays 9–4:30; Sat. 10–1:30.*

Continue walking west along Young Street past tile-roofed warehouses, turn left at the Traffic Police Control Station onto Cross Street, and you'll reach the **Esplanade,** the thoroughfare that runs along the ocean side of town. (The fastest way between the Carenage and the Esplanade is through the **Sendall Tunnel**, slightly

Exploring
Annandale Falls and Visitors' Centre, **9**
Bay Gardens, **2**
Concord Falls, **3**
Dougaldston Estate, **4**
Grand Bacolet Bay, **6**
Grand Etang National Park, **8**
Grenville, **7**
St. George's, **1**
St. George's University Medical School, **10**
Westerhall, **5**

Dining
The Boatyard, **28**
Coconut's Beach, **16**
Cot Bam, **18**
La Sagesse, **30**
Mamma's, **13**
Mt. Rodney Estate, **11**
The Nutmeg, **14**
Rudolf's, **15**
Scrapers (Carriacou), **31**
South Winds, **17**
Rick's Café/Sugar & Spice, **22**
Tabanka, **23**
Tropicana, **12**

Lodging
Blue Horizons Cottage Hotel, **19**
Caribbee Inn (Carriacou), **33**
Cassada Bay Resort (Carriacou), **34**
The Flamboyant Hotel and Cottages, **20**
Gem Holiday Beach Resort, **24**
La Sagesse Nature Center, **30**
No Problem Apartments, **25**
Petit Bacaye, **29**
Siesta, **21**
Scrapers Bay View Holiday Cottages (Carriacou), **31**
Silver Beach Resort (Carriacou), **32**
South Winds Cottages, **17**
Tropicana, **12**
True Blue, **27**
Wave Crest Holiday Apartments, **26**

Grenada (and Carriacou)

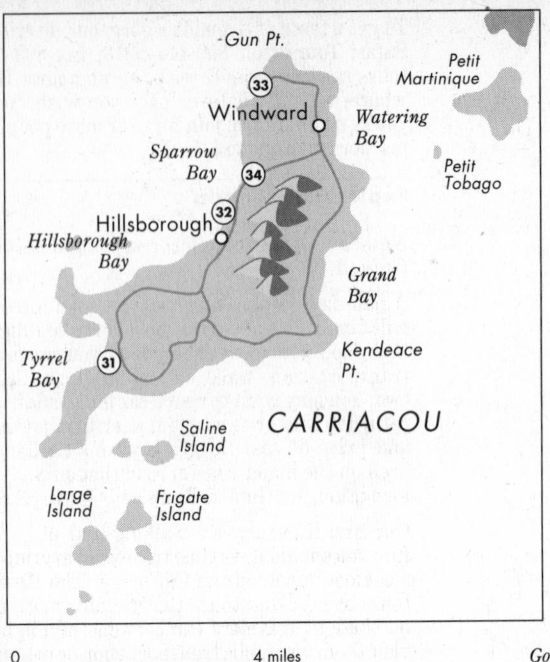

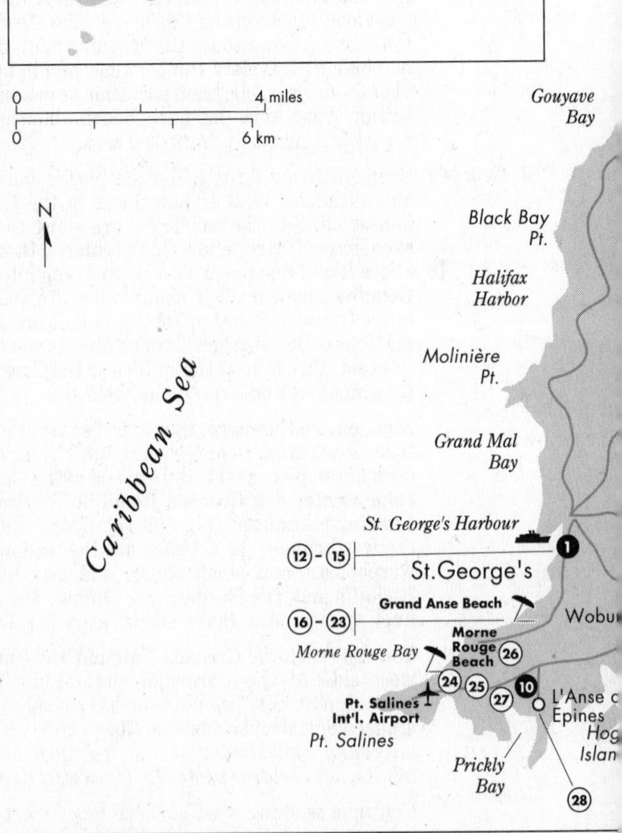

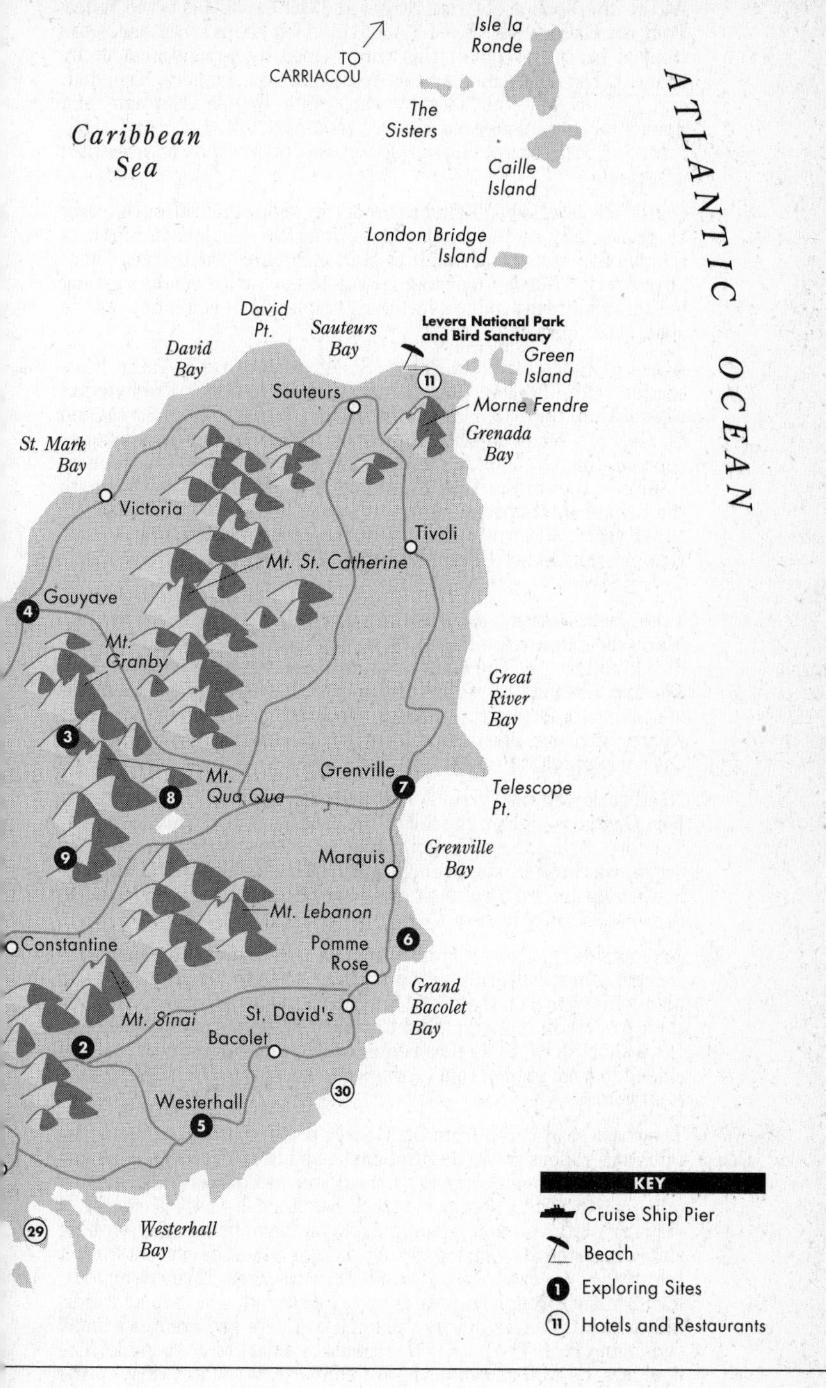
TO
CARRIACOU
Isle la Ronde
The Sisters
Caille Island
London Bridge Island
Caribbean Sea
ATLANTIC OCEAN
David Pt.
Sauteurs Bay
David Bay
Levera National Park and Bird Sanctuary
Green Island
Sauteurs
Morne Fendre
Grenada Bay
St. Mark Bay
Victoria
Tivoli
Mt. St. Catherine
Gouyave
Mt. Granby
Great River Bay
Mt. Qua Qua
Grenville
Telescope Pt.
Marquis
Grenville Bay
Mt. Lebanon
Constantine
Pomme Rose
Grand Bacolet Bay
Mt. Sinai
St. David's
Bacolet
Westerhall
Westerhall Bay
KEY
Cruise Ship Pier
Beach
Exploring Sites
Hotels and Restaurants

north of Fort George. Take it if you're too tired to walk up the steep hill.)

At the intersection of Cross Street and the Esplanade is the **Yellow Poui Art Gallery** (tel. 809/440–3001), which keeps irregular hours (tourist brochures put it this way: "Open by appointment or by chance). The studio displays art from Grenada, Jamaica, Trinidad, and Guyana and canvases by expatriate British, German, and French artists. *Shopping hours: weekdays 9:15–12:15 and 1:15–3:15, Sat. 9:15–12:15; closed Sun. Appointments may be scheduled after hours.*

On the Esplanade you'll find a row of tiny shops that sell such treats as guava jelly and coconut fudge. Take the Esplanade north to Granby Street and turn right to **Market Square.** The market comes alive every Saturday morning from 8 to noon with vendors selling baskets and fresh produce, including tropical fruit you can eat on the spot. Don't miss it!

Walk up Granby Street to Halifax Street, and turn left. At the intersection of Halifax and Church streets is **St. Andrew's Presbyterian Church,** built in 1830. Follow Church Street east to Gore Street and **St. George's Anglican Church,** built in 1828. It's lined with plaques representing Grenada in the 18th and 19th centuries. Continue up Church Street to the **York House,** built around 1800. Now home to the Senate and Supreme Court, it's open to the public for unstructured visits. Return to Market Square and turn left to reach **St. George's Methodist Church,** built in 1820, on Green Street near Tyrrel Street.

Take Tyrrel Street east to the corner of Park Lane to see the **Marryshow House.** Built in 1917, it combines Victorian and West Indian architecture. The Marryshow also houses the **Marryshow Folk Theatre,** Grenada's first cultural center. Plays, West Indian dance and music, and poetry readings are presented here on occasion. *Tyrrel St., near Bain Alley, tel. 809/440–2451. Admission free. Open weekdays 8:30–4:30, Sat. 9–1.*

Head back west on Tyrrel Street and turn left onto Church Street. **Fort George** is high on the hill at the southern tip of Church Street. The fort, rising above the point that separates the harbor from the ocean, was built by the French in 1705. The fort now houses the police headquarters. *Church St., no phone. Admission free. Open daily during daylight hours.*

2 Just outside St. George's, in the suburb of St. Paul's, **Bay Gardens** is a private horticultural paradise where 450 species of flowers and plants that grow on the island are cultivated in patterns that mimic their growth in the wild. Eight acres of paths are open to visitors. It's a short drive by taxi or rental car, or you can request it be included in your guided tour. *Admission $1. Open daily during daylight hours.*

The West Coast

3 The coast road north from St. George's winds past soaring mountains and valleys covered with banana and breadfruit trees, palms, bamboo, and tropical flowers. You can stop at **Concord Falls,** about 8 miles north of St. George's, which has a small visitors' center, a viewing platform, and a changing room for donning your bathing suit (admission $1). During the dry months when the currents aren't too strong, you can take a dip under the cascades. If you're up to it, hike 2 miles through tropical forest to a second, spectacular waterfall, which thunders down over huge boulders and creates a small swimming pool. The path is clear, but it's smart to use a guide. The boulders, as well as the path, are slippery as you get close to the falls, and maneuvering can be tricky.

About 15 minutes farther north is the town of **Gouyave,** center of the nutmeg industry. A tour of the three-story **Nutmeg Processing Sta-**

tion, which turns out 3 million pounds of Grenada's most famous export per year, makes a fragrant and fascinating half hour. *Gouyave, no phone. Admission $1. Open weekdays 10–1 and 2–4.*

4 **Dougaldston Estate,** at the edge of town, has a spice factory where you can see cocoa, nutmeg, mace, cloves, cinnamon, and other spices laid out on giant trays to dry in the sun. Pick up a bag of cinnamon bark, cloves, bay leaves, mace or nutmeg for $2. *Gouyave, no phone. Admission $1. Open weekdays 9–4.*

The East Coast

Start your tour at **Westerhall,** a residential area about 5 miles southeast of St. George's, known for its beautiful villas, gardens, and pan-
5 6 oramic views. From here, take a dirt road north to **Grand Bacolet
Bay,** a jagged peninsula on the Atlantic where the surf pounds
against deserted beaches. A little more than 2 miles north is
7 **Grenville,** the island's second-largest city. From here you can watch
schooners set sail for the outer islands. As in St. George's, Saturday
is market day, and the town fills with local people doing their shopping for the week. Cooking enthusiasts may want to see the town's
spice-processing factory, which is open to the public.

If you take the interior route back to St. George's, you'll get a full
sense of the lush, mountainous nature of the island. Only one paved
road cuts across the island. Leaving Grenville and heading for St.
George's, you'll wind upward through the rain forest until you're
surrounded by mist. Then you'll descend onto the sunny hillsides. In
8 the middle of the island is **Grand Etang National Park.** The area is a
bird sanctuary and forest reserve where you can fish and hike. Crater Lake, in the crater of an extinct volcano here, is a 13-acre glass-
like expanse of cobalt-blue water. *Main interior road, halfway
between Grenville and St. George's, tel. 809/442–7425. Admission
$1. Open weekdays 8–4.*

9 At **Annandale Falls and Visitors' Centre,** a mountain stream cascades 50 feet into a pool surrounded by such exotic tropical flora as liana vines and elephant ears. This is a good swimming and picnic spot. *Main interior road, 15 min east of St. George's, tel. 809/440–2452. Suggested donation: $1. Open daily 9–5.*

Grand Anse and the South End

Most of the island's hotels and its nightlife are in Grand Anse or the
adjacent community of L'Anse aux Epines, which means Cove of
Pines. The **Grand Anse Shopping Centre** has a supermarket/liquor
store, clothing store, shoe store, fast-food joint, and several small
10 gift shops with good-quality souvenirs. At press time, **St. George's
University Medical School** was planning to vacate its prime location
on Grand Anse Beach, consolidating the school at its new campus in
True Blue.

True Blue, a residential area on a picturesque cove between Grand Anse and L'Anse aux Epines can be reached from the Grand Anse Road by turning left onto an unnamed road just before you reach the airport.

Grenada's Grenadines

Carriacou, Petit Martinique, and a handful of uninhabited specks that comprise the nation of Grenada are north of Grenada island and part of the Grenadines, an archipelago of 32 tiny islands and cays.

Carriacou is a little island (13 square miles) with a lot of punch. With more than 100 rum shops and only one gasoline station, this island hideaway will bring the fastest metabolism down to a quiet purr. Carriacou exudes the kind of ebullient spirit and goodwill that you want in a Caribbean retreat but usually find only in a travel brochure. Come here if you want peace. Don't bother if you want luxurious amenities, or if you would suffer coldly a parrot on your breakfast table!

Hillsborough is Carriacou's main town. Rolling hills cut a wide swath through the island's center, from Gun Point in the north to

Tyrrel Bay in the south. In February, fun lovers are drawn to Carriacou for Carnival festivities. In August, the Carriacou Regatta attracts yachts and sailing vessels from throughout the Caribbean. LIAT has several daily flights between Grenada and Carriacou (flying time is about 18 minutes), and schooners leave from St. George's Harbour twice a week (*see* Getting Around, *above*). Since getting to Carriacou is not cheap, you may want to consider staying on this little island for a few days. Room rates for the spartan accommodations here are rock bottom, and finding budget dining is easy. Carriacou is a wonderful place to hang out if you really want to relax. Moreover, the quality of the scuba diving and snorkeling here may surpass that of the larger island.

Beaches

Grenada has some 80 miles of coastline, 65 bays, and 45 white-sand beaches—many in secluded little coves. All the beaches are public and within an easy minibus ride of St. George's. Most are located on the Caribbean, south of St. George's in the Grand Anse and L'Anse aux Epines areas, where most of the hotels are clustered. Virtually every hotel, apartment complex, and residential area has its own beach or tiny cove.

The loveliest and most popular beach is **Grand Anse,** about a 10-minute ride from St. George's. It's a gleaming, 2-mile curve of sand with clear, gentle surf. You'll find rougher waters and shorter stretches of sand at **L'Anse aux Epines,** but the windward side of the island has its advantages: Rainfall is slightly less, and the little cove beaches are less populated.

Morne Rouge Beach is on the Caribbean side, about 1 mile south of Grand Anse Bay and 3 miles south of St. George's Harbour. The beach forms a half-mile-long crescent and has a gentle surf excellent for swimming. A small café serves light meals during the day. In the evening, there's the disco, Fantazia 2001 (*see* Nightlife, *below*).

Levera National Park and Bird Sanctuary is at the northern tip of the island, where the Caribbean meets the Atlantic. The southernmost Grenadines are visible in the distance. The surf is rougher here than on the Caribbean beaches, but it is great for body surfing or watching the waves roll in. In 1991, this area, with its thick mangroves for food and protection, became an official sanctuary for nesting seabirds and seldom-seen tropical parrots. Also of interest here are fine Arawak ruins and petroglyphs. Facilities include a visitor center, changing rooms, a small amphitheater, and a gift shop.

Sports and the Outdoors

Bicycling Level ground is rare in Grenada, but that doesn't stop the aerobically primed. What's more, 15-speed mountain bikes are cheaper to rent than four-wheel-drive vehicles and can get you to a lot of the same places. Try **Ride Grenada** (L'Anse aux Epines, tel. 809/444–1157). Caution: Sharing the narrow, winding roads with fast-moving vehicles can be hazardous.

Diving and Snorkeling **Dive Grenada** on Grand Anse Beach (Grenada Renaissance Resort, tel. 809/444–4371 or 809/444–4372, ext. 638, fax 809/444–4800) and **Grand Anse Aquatics Ltd.** (Coyaba Beach Resort, tel. 809/444–4129) offer scuba and snorkeling trips to reefs and shipwrecks. Single-tank dives are $40; dives to the *Bianca C*, a 600-foot cruise ship that caught fire and sank in waters 100 feet deep, are $55; snorkeling trips, $18. They also offer diving instruction, including resort courses for novices. Head for Carriacou for mind-bending marine beauty. **Silver Beach Diving** (Silver Beach Resort, tel. 809/443–7882, fax 809/443–7165), near Hillsborough, offers scuba diving at more than 20 sites.

Snorkel-equipment rental on Grenada costs between $5 and $10 per day. **The Moorings** (*see* Sailing, *below*) rents gear for $40 a week. Beginners will be happy bobbing up and down the waters at Grand Anse, but the more experienced should inquire about outlying spits, islands, and shipwrecks where more colorful and abundant underwater life appears.

Golf The **Grenada Golf and Country Club** in Grand Anse (tel. 809/444–4128) has a nine-hole course. Greens fees are E.C. $7. Your hotel will make arrangements for you.

Hiking Grenada has a mountainous, volcanically-formed terrain, and inland regions are covered with riots of lush, green, tropical growth. You'll need a guide for interior jaunts. Trails aren't always marked, and you may find yourself blazing through tangled jungle mass or sliding down muddy slopes on your derrière. **Henry's Safari Tours** (*see* Guided Tours, *above*) offers lower rates for three or more in a group.

Sailing The **Moorings' Club Mariner Watersports Center** (tel. 809/444–4439 or 809/444–4549), at the Secret Harbour Hotel, offers a full-day sail for $40 a person and a half-day sail to Calivigny Island for $25 a person. A trip to Hog Island is $15 a person, lower for groups of five or more. Costs include snorkel-equipment rental, but you're expected to bring your own lunch and drinks. For qualified sailors, the Moorings offers a 23.5-foot Beneteau for $30 an hour; a 21-foot Impulse for $25 an hour, and a 15-foot Precision for $20 an hour. For $15 an hour, you can get a little dinghy with an outboard engine. The major hotels on Grand Anse Beach have water-sports centers where you can rent small sailboats, Windsurfers, Jet Skis, aqua bikes, and Sunfish.

Tennis Several hotels have tennis courts that are free to their guests, but most of these are at properties that are out of our price ranges. If there are no courts where you're staying, you can play at the public tennis courts at Grand Anse or pay a court rental fee at a resort. (Count on an average hourly rate of $10.)

Shopping

The best souvenirs of Grenada are little spice baskets filled with cinnamon, nutmeg, mace, bay leaf, vanilla, and ginger. You can find them in practically every shop, but your best bet is the Saturday morning market in downtown St. George's. Bananas are a steal here, and big, palm-tied bundles of cinnamon bark resembling cords of wood cost about $2. *Note: Do not take photographs of individuals at the market without asking their permission.* Vendors who stroll the beach in Grand Anse sell spice baskets, as well as fabric dolls, T-shirts, hats and baskets woven from green palm, and coral jewelry. (Environmental groups discourage tourists from buying coral.)

Good Buys
St. George's Stick to island handicrafts. While even some of these can be expensive, many are reasonably priced. **Tikal** (Young St., tel. 809/440–2310) carries mainly premium-priced goods, but you can find mahogany walking sticks for $19, brightly colored batik shorts for $26, tiny handmade dolls for $3, and colorful note cards for a dollar or two. **Spice Island Perfumes** on the Carenage (tel. 809/440–2006) has shelves of T-shirts, spice baskets ($3.25), and hand-painted cotton caftans. At the far end of the Carenage, White Cane Industries (tel. 809/444–2014) stocks bargain baskets, hats, and spectacularly colored rag rugs, all handwoven locally by blind craftspeople.

Grand Anse Try **Imagine** (Grand Anse Shopping Complex, tel. 809/444–4028) for assorted island creations. Woven hats and baskets are reasonably priced here. Those who don't consider $15–$20 for a pair of pierced earrings to be an extravagance can find lovely West Indian jewelry here.

Dining

Restaurants here come in all price ranges. You'll find entrées priced anywhere from $4 to $20. Unlike most Caribbean islands, which have a scarcity of fresh produce, Grenada has everything from cabbages and tomatoes to bananas, mangoes, papaya (pawpaw), plantains, melons, *callaloo* (similar to spinach), breadfruit, oranges, tangerines, limes, *christophines* (similar to squash), avocados—the list is endless. Fresh seafood of all kinds, including lobster and shrimp, is also plentiful. Conch, known here as *lambi*, is very popular and appears on most menus in some form, usually as a stew. Be sure to try one of the exotic ice creams made from guava or nutmeg. Almost all the Grenadian restaurants serve local dishes, which are varied enough to be continually interesting. Rum punches are served everywhere, but no two places make them exactly alike. The local beer, Carib, is also very popular and quite good.

If you're renting a self-contained unit and want to save money by cooking, ply your way through the crowds at the Saturday morning market in St. George's for fresh fruits and vegetables, or stop in at the **Marketing Board,** on Young Street in St. George's, for fresh produce, hot sauces, and spices. Then look over the selection at **D'Green Grocers,** on the main road between the Grand Anse Shopping Complex and Le Marquis mall, where everything except the apples is fresh and locally harvested. You can stock up on paper products here, too. **Foodland** (Lagoon Rd., St. George's) and **Food Fair** (at the Carenage and in Grand Anse) are larger but somewhat more expensive. Stay away from the marine minimarkets unless you're desperate: They cater to yachtsmen who aren't pinching pennies.

Highly recommended restaurants are indicated by a star ★.

Category	Cost*
$$	$20–$40
$	$10–$20
¢	under $10

**per person, excluding drinks, service, and 10% sales tax*

Grenada

$$ **The Boatyard.** Embassy personnel and expatriates fill this lively restaurant, which sits smack in the middle of a marina. Burgers, fish-and-chips, and deep-fried shrimp are served at lunchtime. At dinner you may order club steaks, lobster, and different types of meat and seafood brochettes. In season there's disco music on Friday night, a steel band on Saturday, and live jazz on Sunday. *L'Anse aux Epines, tel. 809/444–4662. MC, V. Closed Mon.*

$$ ★ **Coconut's Beach, The French Restaurant.** Take local seafood, add butter, wine, and Grenadian herbs, and you have excellent French Creole cuisine. Throw in a beautiful setting at the northern end of Grand Anse Beach, and this little cottage becomes a delightful spot for lunch or dinner. Entrées range in price from $5 to $25. Choose lambi curry, fish Creole, steak, chicken, or lobster prepared in a variety of ways. Splurge on lobster ginger boy (half a lobster stir-fried with ginger, chili and soy sauce); it gets raves. In season, there's a beach barbecue with live music each Wednesday, Friday and Sunday night. *Grand Anse Beach, tel. 809/444–4644. Reservations advised. Free transportation arranged. AE, MC, V.*

$$ **The Nutmeg.** Fresh seafood is the specialty at this restaurant. Try the grilled turtle steaks, lobster, or shrimp, or just enjoy a drink, a chicken roti, and a great view of the harbor. *The Carenage, St. George's, tel. 809/440–2539. AE, D, MC, V.*

$$ **Rudolf's.** This informal pub offers fine West Indian fare, as well as sandwiches and burgers. Skip the attempts at haute cuisine

"Viennoise" or "Parisienne," and enjoy the crab back, lambi, and delectable nutmeg ice cream. This is *the* place for eavesdropping on local gossip. The rum punches are lethal—even for Grenada. *The Carenage, St. George's, tel. 809/440-2241. No credit cards. Closed Sun.*

$$ **South Winds.** From the glassed-in terrace of this popular restaurant you get a splendid view of St. George's Harbour in the distance. Choose Continental or Caribbean cuisine, including stuffed crab back, lambi chowder, coconut shrimp (dipped in shredded coconut and deep-fried), or Gems of the Island (lobster, conch, and shrimp in a Creole sauce). Entrées range from about $4.50 for lambi stew to $22.50 for grilled lobster with avocado. Complimentary transportation from your hotel is provided. An adjoining sports bar has a big-screen cable TV. *Grand Anse, above South Winds Cottages, tel. 809/444-4810. Reservations advised. AE, MC, V. No lunch.*

$–$$ **La Sagesse.** A perfect spot to soothe the most frazzled of souls, this open-air restaurant and beach bar is on a secluded cove 20 minutes from Grand Anse. Come for a swim, a hike, and a meal—or just a meal! Select from sandwiches, salads, or lobster for lunch. Lambi, smoked marlin or dolphinfish, fillet of grouper, and tuna steak are joined on the dinner menu by a daily vegetarian special. Transportation to and from your hotel is provided. *La Sagesse Nature Center, St. David's, tel. 809/444-6458. Reservations advised. AE, MC, V.*

$–$$ ★ **Tabanca at Journey's End.** Dine on the open terrace overlooking the sea and St. George's Harbour. Sunbathers are lured to this bistro from Grand Anse Beach, just below, for luncheon of sandwiches, omelets, seafood specialties, and crisp salads. Fillet of kingfish mimosa wins raves, Carib beer is on tap, and the special rum punch hits the spot. Dinners of steak, fish, and lobster are delicious. Fabulous homemade desserts—tortes and other pastries—are inspired by the Austrian heritage of the owner. *Grand Anse, tel. 809/444-1300. AE, D, DC, MC, V. Closed Tues.*

$ ★ **Mamma's.** One of Mamma's daughters will set generous helpings of local specialties before you—roast turtle, lobster salad, christophine salad, cabbage salad, or fried plantain, as well as such exotica as armadillo, opossum, and sea urchin. Sixteen to 19 native dishes are served family style at a fixed E.C. $45 per person. *Lagoon Rd., St. George's, tel. 809/440-1459. Reservations required. No credit cards.*

$ ★ **Mount Rodney Estate.** Although it's in the far north and a one-hour drive from St. George's, this makes a perfect lunch stop when touring the island. The house, built in the 1870s, has a magnificent view of the Grenadines. A full luncheon includes rum or fruit punch, soup or salad, chicken or fish entrée, and dessert of fruit or ice cream. It's served in the breezy gazebo on weekdays from noon to 3 PM for a fixed price of E.C. $40. Afterwards, enjoy touring the home and six acres of gardens at leisure. Reservations are essential, as lunch is restricted to 30 guests per day. *Sauteurs, St. Patrick's, tel. 809/442-9420. Reservations required. No credit cards. No dinner. Closed weekends.*

$ **Tropicana.** This busy restaurant is directly opposite St. George's Inner Harbour, at the roundabout on the main road. The open-air bar faces the waterfront. The place attracts a large business and interisland clientele. One of the two brothers who own Tropicana was a chef in a Chinese restaurant in Trinidad, so the extensive menu combines West Indian and Chinese cuisine. You can get takeout, too. Entrées range from $4 to $17. Fridays and Saturdays are barbecue nights, with grilled chicken, ribs, pork chops, or fish for $7 to $10. *Lagoon Rd., St. George's, tel. 809/440-1586. Reservations advised in season. AE, MC, V.*

¢ **Cot Bam.** "Club on the Beach at Morne Rouge" is right on Grand Anse Beach next to the Coyaba Beach Resort, within walking distance of all the Grand Anse hotels. The casual atmosphere of this bar-restaurant-nightclub, with its tin roof and bamboo railings, makes it a great place to kick back and relax. You can stroll in wearing shorts, after a long day at the beach, to dance or chat the night away. Order a chicken roti served with coleslaw for E.C. $6 and a Carib beer, and you're set for the evening. The staff is a delight. *Grand Anse, tel. 809/444–2050. AE.*

¢ **Rick's Café & Sugar and Spice Ice Cream Parlour.** This is a favorite of both medical students and mothers with ice cream–addicted offspring. It's a quick, easy-on-the-wallet stop in the Grand Anse shopping center, and the food is fair to middling. Pizza by the slice is about $1.30, and a ham-and-cheese sub goes for $1.70. Ice cream is dished up in your choice of 14 tropical flavors. *Grand Anse Shopping Complex, tel. 809/444–4597. No credit cards. Closed Mon. No lunch Sun.*

Carriacou
¢–$ **Scraper's.** Good things are happening at Tyrrel Bay. Scraper's serves up lobster, conch, and an assortment of fresh catches, along with a simple spirit and decor seasoned with occasional calypsonian serenades (owner Steven Gay "Scraper" is a pro). Order a rum punch and exercise your right to do nothing. Lunch is a bargain: A big bowl of callaloo soup and a cheeseburger cost about $5. *Tyrrel Bay, Carriacou, tel. 809/443–7403. AE, D, MC, V.*

Lodging

Grenada has a healthy number of affordable accommodations. Even in Grand Anse there are a few moderately priced hotels right on the beach. Another option is to stay at an apartment hotel, which allows you to save on meals and taxes. Granted, you may not be sitting on the sand at some of these places, but an easy five- or 10-minute amble will get you there. The high cost of car rental and gas prices here can outweigh the savings at more remote accommodations. Campgrounds are virtually nonexistent on Grenada, and most villa rentals creep into the extravagant range (with some exceptions; *see below*).

Summertime is the time to really save here; prices are discounted 20%–40%. The availability of meal plans (listed in the service information of each review, *below*) can vary with the season; assume those specified apply year-round unless otherwise noted.

Highly recommended lodgings are indicated by a star ★.

Category	Cost*
$$	$100–$150
$	$50–$100
¢	under $50

**All prices are for a standard double room for two, excluding 8% tax and a 10% service charge. To estimate rates for hotels offering MAP, add about $25–$45 per person per day to the above price ranges.*

Hotels
Grenada
★ **Blue Horizons Cottage Hotel.** Spice Island Inn's sister hotel is an especially good value. Each comfortable, air-conditioned suite has a kitchenette, private terrace, TV, phone, and hair dryer. Handsome mahogany furniture is set off by white walls and cool, tiled floors. Palms stud the large, sunny lawn around the swimming pool. Grand Anse beach, where the Spice Island Inn sprawls along 1,600 feet of sand, is a short walk down the hill. Water sports are free for guests of either hotel. Guests may eat at Blue Horizon's La Belle Creole or at Spice Island. *Box 41, Grand Anse, St. George's, tel. 809/444–4316, 809/444–4592 or 800/223–9815 in the U.S., fax 809/444–2815. 32 suites with terraces. Facilities: restaurant, 2 bars, lounge, pool. AE, MC, V. EP, CP, MAP. $$*

Flamboyant Hotel and Cottages. Not just a good value, the friendly

Flamboyant is also home of the famous Monday-night crab-racing spectacular. The rooms and suites of this Grenadian-owned cross between a hotel and a self-catering resort have one of the island's best views, sweeping over the entire Grand Anse Bay to St George's. All rooms are simply furnished with air-conditioning, minibar, satellite TV, phone, and balcony. One-bedroom suites and two-bedroom cottages each have a kitchen and lounge. You can take a dip in the freshwater pool or continue down a rather steep stairway to the beach. A cabana bar serves snacks and is the site of frequent barbecues. *Box 214, Grand Anse, St. George's, tel. 809/444–4247, fax 809/444–1234. 16 rooms, 20 suites, 2 cottages. Facilities: restaurant, bar, beach bar, pool, satellite TV, free use of snorkeling equipment. AE, D, MC, V. EP, BP, MAP. $$*

★ **True Blue.** Although the "blue" in the inn's name comes from the history of the residential area that was once an indigo plantation, the title could just as easily have come from the beautiful views of blue bay and ocean. Four spacious one-bedroom apartment units are perched cliff-side, among the trees, each with a private veranda overlooking the sea. Three two-bedroom island cottages, nestled in private seaside gardens, are air-conditioned and have ceiling fans. Kitchens in both the apartments and the cottages are large and fully equipped. You can swim in the pool or the bay. Sunsets are spectacular from Indigo's, the inn's deck restaurant. Boaters frequently come for dinner, tying up at the inn's private dock. For a special treat, you can book a day sail on the owner's yacht. *Box 308, Old Mill Ave., True Blue, St. George's, tel. 809/444–2000 or 800/742–4276, fax 809/444–1247. 7 units. Facilities: restaurant, bar, pool, full maid/laundry service daily, docking facilities, yacht charter. AE, MC, V. $$*

Gem Holiday Beach Resort. Couples and families are the main clients of this convenient and reasonably priced resort. It's right on the palm-lined white sandy beach of Morne Rouge Bay and not far from beautiful Grand Anse Beach. Each of the modern suites is air-conditioned and has a fully equipped kitchenette and a balcony overlooking the Caribbean. And for those who love nightlife, Fantazia 2001, the hottest nightclub in town, is right at the doorstep. *Box 58, Morne Rouge Bay, St. George's, tel. 809/444–1189 or 809/444–2288, fax 809/444–1189. 17 apartments. Facilities: restaurant, bar, beach, complimentary entry to nightclub, shuttle to shopping center, snorkeling equipment. AE, MC, V. $*

La Sagesse Nature Center. This is a secluded getaway on a lovely bay 10 miles east of Point Salines International Airport. The grounds include a salt-pond bird sanctuary, thick growths of mangroves, and several hiking trails. A main guest house, recently renovated, has two high-ceilinged suites with kitchenettes, ceiling fans, and hot-water baths. There is also a two-bedroom beach cottage, and two less-expensive rooms are tucked in behind the restaurant. Mike Meranski, the cheerful American owner-manager, will run guests into town for grocery supplies and shopping. *Box 44, St. David's, tel. 809/444–6458, fax 809/444–6458. 6 double rooms. Facilities: restaurant, bar, beach, satellite TV. MC, V. EP. $*

Siesta. This bright white hideaway, nestled into the hillside one block from Grand Anse Beach, is Mediterranean in style, Grenadian in charm. It's convenient to everything that's happening in Grand Anse, but at a fraction of the cost of neighboring hotels with beachfront locations. The rooms and suites are simply but comfortably furnished and are air-conditioned; suites have a kitchenette. Loll on the patio, swim in the piano-shaped pool, or walk 200 yards to the beach. It's a five-minute walk to Grand Anse shops and the bus to St. George's. One child under 12, accompanied by two adults, stays free. *Box 27, Grand Anse, St. George's, tel. 809/444–4645 or 800/742–4276, fax 809/444–4647. 16 rooms, 21 suites. Facilities: restaurant, juice bar, pool. AE, MC, V, EP, MAP. $*

Tropicana. Rooms in this family-run inn are small and simple, but they're tidy and attractive; some have private patios. Don't expect quiet and solitude—Tropicana is located at a traffic circle on the main road, directly across the street from St. George's Inner Harbour. Interisland business travelers and budget-minded vacationers who don't need to be on a beach enjoy its convenience. Buses to downtown St. George's and Grand Anse stop at the door. The popular restaurant serves West Indian and Chinese cuisine (*see* Dining, *above*). *Lagoon Rd., St. George's, tel. 809/440–1586, fax 809/440–9797. 20 rooms. Facilities: restaurant, bar. AE, MC, V., EP, CP, MAP, FAP. ¢*

Carriacou

Silver Beach Resort. Stretches of pristine beach surround this 18-room hotel on Grenada's sister isle. All rooms have private patios and ocean views (but no TVs). The scuba facilities here are the biggest in the Grenadines. The open-air restaurant by the water is the best place on the island for a hearty, early-morning breakfast. *Silver Beach, Carriacou, tel. 809/443–7337, fax 809/443–7165. 12 doubles (2 with kitchenettes), 6 cottages with kitchenettes. Facilities: restaurant, snorkeling, windsurfing, spearfishing, day trip to offshore islets, boutique, scuba certification course, island bus service, transfers from Carriacou airport, car rental. AE, MC, V. EP, CP, MAP. $$*

Caribbee Inn at Prospect. Check out the spectacular view of the Carriacou coast from this small country house, perched on the side of a hill. It's surrounded by a miniature nature reserve, and bird lovers will thrill to the magnificent macaws that fly freely around the grounds. Rooms are spacious and attractively furnished with four-poster beds; some have balconies. A two-bedroom detached villa suitable for four persons can be booked by the week. Home-baked breads and French Creole dishes highlight the meals served in Caribbee's Pepperpot restaurant. *Tel. 809/443–7380, fax 809/443–8142. 8 rooms, honeymoon suite, and 2-bedroom villa. Facilities: restaurant, bar, snorkeling, boating, bicycles, library, courtesy car to airport and town. AE, MC, V. EP, MAP. $–$$*

Cassada Bay Resort. In addition to a breathtaking panorama of the ocean, this resort gives you the use of a private offshore island (a five-minute boat ride from the beach) for snorkeling and windsurfing. Cabins here, on the south side of Carriacou, cascade down the side of a hilltop overlooking the sea and offer an unadorned, but peaceful, sea-sprayed hideaway. *Belmont, Carriacou, tel. 809/443–7494, fax 809/443–7672. 20 doubles. Facilities: restaurant, bar, water-sports center. AE, DC, MC, V. EP, CP, MAP. $*

Apartments

An apartment with kitchen facilities can be a cost-effective alternative for families with children and couples traveling together. Self-catering accommodations range in style from individual palm-thatched cottages to side-by-side poolside efficiencies.

Grenada

No Problem Apartments. You aren't on the beach at this apartment complex, but it's no problem getting there: Free transportation is provided to and from the airport, Grand Anse Beach, and St. George's. Free bicycles are available, too. Each air-conditioned suite has two twin beds and a fully equipped kitchenette; there's a minimart on site. No problem, indeed. *Box 280, True Blue, St. George's, tel. 809/444–4336 or 809/444–4634, fax 809/444–2803. 20 apartments. Facilities: pool, laundry service, baby-sitters, minimart, transportation to airport, town, and beach. AE, MC, V, EP. $*

Petit Bacaye. The only drawback here is the 30-minute drive to Grand Anse and the airport, which means you may want to rent a car for at least part of your stay—unless you really want to luxuriate in seclusion. The lovely cluster of one-bedroom palm-thatched cottages is in a palm grove on Grenada's southern coast. Each cottage has a unique hand-turned bed made of local wood in Petit Bacaye's own workshop, a ceiling fan, fully equipped kitchenette, modern bath, and a veranda. Plan to lie back in your personal hammock and relax: You'll find no TVs, no telephones, and no newspapers. *Box 655, St. George's, tel. 809/443–2552. 4 one-bedroom cottages. Facilities: beach, bar, linens and utensils, maid and laundry service. No credit cards. $*

Wave Crest Holiday Apartments. Owner Joyce Dabrieo takes great pains to keep these 20 sunny units spotless and well-maintained. All accommodations are air-conditioned. Apartments have balconies and full kitchens. The buildings are surrounded by flower gardens. Grand Anse beach is a five-minute walk away. An excellent value. *Box 278, St. George's, tel. 809/444–4116, fax 809/444–4847. 4 rooms, 14 one-bedroom apartments, 2 two-bedroom apartments. AE, D, MC, V. $*

South Winds Holiday Cottages and Apartments. From this steep hillside setting, you get a distant view of St. George's Harbour. Grand Anse Beach is a five-minute walk away. Each of the two-bedroom cottages and one-bedroom apartments has a fully equipped kitchenette and a patio. If you tire of cooking dinner, the restaurant is very good. The sports bar is popular, too. Weekly and monthly rates are available. Special package rates include a rental Jeep or car. *Box 118, Grand Anse, St. George's, tel. 809/444–4310, fax 809/444–4404. 5 two-bedroom cottages, 14 one-bedroom apartments. Facilities: restaurant, sports bar, vehicle rental. AE, DC, D, MC, V. ¢–$*

Carriacou

Scraper's Bay View Holiday Cottages. Though clean and well maintained, this slightly funky property on Tyrrel Bay is not for those who need the antiseptic familiarity of chain hotels (bathroom facilities, for instance, are simply separated from the sleeping area by a curtain). Seven units, four of which have kitchens, are housed in duplex cottages across the road from the bay and beach. You can get along without a car here, though you may feel confined after three or four days. Lively nightlife and cordial hosts await you; Mr. Scraper won't hesitate to tell you he makes the best rum punch in the Caribbean. *Tyrell Bay, Carriacou, tel. 809/443–7403. 7 rooms. Facilities: restaurant/bar, souvenir shop. AE, D, MC, V. EP. ¢*

Off-Season Bets

Many of the premium-priced hotels in Grenada drop their room rates drastically during the summer. All of the following qualify for a $$ listing during the off season: **Coyaba Beach Resort** (Box 336, Grand Anse, St. George's, tel. 809/444–4129), **Grenada Renaissance Resort** (Box 441, Grand Anse, St. George's, tel. 809/444–4371), and **Rex Grenadian** (Point Salines, Box 893, St. George's, tel. 809/444–3333 or 800/255–5859). The same goes for a handful of villas—call **Bain & Bertrand Realtors** (tel. 809/444–2848) in Grenada or **Down Island Rental** (tel. 809/443–8182) in Carriacou for information.

Nightlife

Grenada's nightlife is centered mainly at the resort hotels. During winter, many have steel, reggae, and pop bands in the evenings. **Spice Island Inn, The Calabash, Coyaba,** and the **Grenada Renaissance** are among the most lively, but check out the new **Rex Grenadian,** too (*see* Lodging, *above*). Check with your hotel or the tourist information office to find out where various bands are performing on a given night.

Fantazia 2001 (Gem Apartments premises, Morne Rouge Beach, tel. 809/444–4224) is a popular disco on the beach, where soca and reggae are played, along with international favorites. It's dark and loud and fun, with a mix of locals and tourists. There is a small cover charge (E.C. $5) on Friday and Saturday nights. **Le Sucrier** (The Sugar Mill, Grand Anse, tel. 800/444–1068) is open on Wednesday, Thursday, Friday, and Saturday from 9 PM to 3 AM, and attracts a young crowd with local comedy and a disco on Thursday and "oldies" night on Wednesday. Friday night is "the" night at the **Boatyard Res-**

taurant and Bar (L'Anse aux Epines beach in the Marina, tel. 809/444–4662), from 11 PM till sunup, with international discs spun by a smooth-talkin' local DJ. Check out **Cot Bam** (tel. 809/444–2050) on Grand Anse beach for a night of dancing, dining, and socializing. The place is open until 3 AM on Friday and Saturday, and it definitely hits the spot for visitors who want something simple, lively, and friendly for little money. Don't forget the **Beachside Terrace** (St. George's, tel. 809/444–4247) at the Flamboyant Hotel in Grand Anse. Crab racing on Monday nights, a live steel band on Wednesdays, and a beach barbecue with calypso music on Friday evenings draw an international set who savor a casual, unpretentious environment.

Brave the boat trip to Carriacou, then buy yourself a drink at the **Hillsborough Bar** (Carriacou, tel. 809/443–7932). The bar is a small, white, flat-topped structure on the main street of the island's seat of government, a town populated by no more than about 600 citizens, including owner Edward Primus. Rum flows freely.

13 Guadeloupe

Updated by Jordan Simon

It's a steamy hot Saturday in mid-August. There may be a tropical depression brewing somewhere to the west. It's that time of year. But the mood in Pointe-à-Pitre, Guadeloupe's commercial center, is anything but depressed. Amid music and laughter, women adorned with gold jewelry and dressed in clothes made of the traditional madras and foulard parade through the streets. Balanced on their heads are huge baskets decorated with miniature kitchen utensils and filled with mangoes, papayas, breadfruits, christophines, and other island edibles. The procession wends its way to the Cathédrale de St-Pierre et St-Paul, where a high mass is celebrated. A five-hour feast with music, song, and dance will follow.

The Fête des Cuisinières (Cooks' Festival) takes place annually in honor of St. Laurent, patron saint of cooks. The parading *cuisinières* are the island's women chefs, an honored group. This festival gives you a tempting glimpse of one of Guadeloupe's stellar attractions—its cuisine. The island's more than 200 restaurants serve some of the best food in all the Caribbean.

Guadeloupe looks like a giant butterfly resting on the sea between Antigua and Dominica. Its two wings—Basse-Terre and Grande-Terre—are the two largest islands in the 659-square-mile Guadeloupe archipelago, which includes the little islands of Marie-Galante, La Désirade, and Les Saintes, as well as French St. Martin and St. Barthélemy to the north. Mountainous 312-square-mile Basse-Terre (lowland) lies on the leeward side, where the winds are "lower." Smaller, flatter Grande-Terre (218 square miles) gets the "bigger" winds on its windward side. The Rivière Salée, a 4-mile seawater channel flowing between the Caribbean and the Atlantic, forms the "spine" of the butterfly. A drawbridge over the channel connects the two islands.

If you're seeking resorts and white sandy beaches, your target is Grande-Terre. By contrast, Basse-Terre's Natural Park, laced with mountain trails and washed by waterfalls and rivers, is a 74,100-acre haven for hikers, nature lovers, and anyone yearning to peer into the steaming crater of an active volcano. If you want to get away from it all, head for the islands of Les Saintes, La Désirade, and Marie-Galante.

As a diverse archipelago, Guadeloupe offers vacations of every style and for every budget. Although splashy hotels with every amenity exist here, the island is more about variety than luxury. Self-contained resorts near the beach aren't cheap, but many offer good value if you want to spend your vacation around the pool or on the beach. Guadeloupe also has smaller, less expensive inns (*Relais Créoles*) and small apartments and cottages (*gîtes*). Many of the latter have their own kitchens, which can save you a lot of money, since restaurants here tend to be expensive. It also lets you sample the French goods on the shelves of local supermarkets.

Car rental costs are high here, and on an island as large as Guadeloupe, you'll probably want your own wheels. Driving around the island is the best way to appreciate its diversity. Indeed, diversity's the name of the game here: Night owls and nature enthusiasts, hikers and bikers, scuba divers, sailors, mountain climbers, beachcombers, and hammock potatoes all can indulge themselves in Guadeloupe.

Sugar, not tourism, is Guadeloupe's primary source of income. French is the official language here. But even if your tongue twirls easily around a few French phrases, you will sometimes receive a bewildered response. The Guadeloupeans' Creole patois greatly affects their French pronunciation. However, don't despair—most hotels and many of the restaurants have some English-speaking staff.

What It Will Cost These sample prices, meant only as a general guide, are for high season. Guadeloupe has many small hotels in the $100-a-night range or a little below. Resort hotels on the beach start at about $150. A week's rental of a small apartment may be about $350–$450. Food is wonderful here, and prices show it: It's hard to come away from a good dinner for less than $20 a person without wine. You can save by getting takeout, ordering from the prix fixe menus, and buying picnic fare from local stores, where imported goods are plentiful and affordable (an average-quality bottle of Bordeaux is about $7). A beer is $2.50 and up at a restaurant; a 'ti punch varies from less than $2 in a small café to about $3.50 at a hotel bar. You'll probably need a car to get around; public transportation is limited, and there's lots to see. Plan on about $60 a day. Cab far from the airport to Pointe-à-Pitre is about $11; from Gosier to St-François, about $28. A single-tank dive averages $50; snorkel equipment rental is about $10 a day.

Before You Go

Tourist Information For information contact the **French West Indies Tourist Board** by calling France-on-Call at 900/990–0040 (50¢ per min, 9 AM–7 PM EST), or write to the **French Government Tourist Office** (610 5th Ave., New York, NY 10020; 9454 Wilshire Blvd., Beverly Hills, CA 90212; 645 N. Michigan Ave., Chicago, IL 60611). In Canada contact the French Government Tourist Office (1981 McGill College Ave., Suite 490, Montreal, Québec H3A 2W9, tel. 514/288–4264 or 30 St. Patrick St., Suite 700, Toronto, Ontario M5T 3A3, tel. 416/593–6427). In the United Kingdom, the tourist office can be reached at 178 Piccadilly, London, United Kingdom W1V 0AL, tel. 0171/499–6911.

Arriving and Departing
By Plane **American Airlines** (tel. 800/433–7300) is usually the most convenient, with year-round daily flights from more than 100 U.S. cities direct to San Juan and nonstop connections to Guadeloupe via Amer-

ican Eagle. **Air Canada** (tel. 800/422–6232) flies direct from Montreal and Toronto. **Air France** (tel. 800/237–2747) flies nonstop from Paris and Fort-de-France, and has direct service from Miami and San Juan. **Air Guadeloupe** (tel. 590/82–47–00) flies daily from St. Martin and St. Maarten, St. Barts, Marie-Galante, La Désirade, and Les Saintes. **LIAT** (tel. 212/251–1717) flies from St. Croix, Antigua, and St. Maarten in the north and is your best bet from Dominica, Martinique, St. Lucia, Grenada, Barbados, and Trinidad.

From the Airport You'll land at La Raizet International Airport, 2½ miles from Pointe-à-Pitre. Cabs are lined up outside the airport. The metered fare is about 60F to Pointe-à-Pitre, 90F to Gosier, and 200F to St-François. Fares go up 40% on Sundays and holidays and from 9 PM to 7 AM. For 5F, you can take a bus from the airport to downtown Pointe-à-Pitre. If you plan to rent a car for your entire vacation, you may want to collect it at the airport (*see* Getting Around, *below*).

By Boat Major cruise lines call regularly, docking at berths in downtown Pointe-à-Pitre about a block from the shopping district. **Trans Antilles Express** (tel. 590/83–12–45) and **Transport Maritime Brudey Frères**(tel. 590/90–04–48) provide ferry service to and from Marie-Galante and Les Saintes. The *Jetcat* and *Madras* ferries depart daily from the pier at Pointe-à-Pitre for Marie-Galante starting at 8 AM (check the schedule). The trip takes one hour, and the fare is 160F round-trip. For Les Saintes, Trans Antilles Express connects daily from Pointe-à-Pitre at 8 AM and from Terre-de-Haut at 4 PM. The trip takes 45 minutes and costs 160F round-trip. The *Socimade* (tel. 590/88–48–63) runs between La Désirade and St-François, departing daily at 8 AM and 4 PM. Return ferries depart daily at 3:30 PM. These schedules are subject to change and should be verified through your hotel or at the tourist office. The **Caribbean Express** (tel. 590/83–04–43) operates from Guadeloupe's Pointe-à-Pitre to Dominica and Martinique. The fare to Dominica is 450F, and the ride takes 2½ hours; the fare to Martinique is 450F and takes four hours. The ferry departs from Pointe-à-Pitre at 8 AM four days a week, but check the schedules because they frequently change.

Passports and Visas U.S. and Canadian citizens need only proof of citizenship. A passport is best (even one that expired up to five years ago). Other acceptable documents are a notarized birth certificate with a raised seal (not a photocopy) or a voter registration card accompanied by a government-authorized photo ID. A free temporary visa, good only for your stay in Guadeloupe, will be issued to you upon your arrival at the airport. British citizens need a valid passport but no visa. In addition, all visitors must hold an ongoing or return ticket.

Language The official language is French. Everyone also speaks a Creole patois, which you won't be able to understand even if you're fluent in French. In the major tourist hotels, most of the staff knows some English. However, communicating may be more difficult in the smaller hotels and restaurants in the countryside. Some taxi drivers speak a little English. Arm yourself with a phrase book, a dictionary, patience, and a sense of humor.

Precautions Put your valuables in the hotel safe. Don't leave them unattended in your room or on the beach. Keep an eye out for motorcyclists riding double. They sometimes play the notorious game of veering close to the sidewalk and snatching shoulder bags. It isn't a good idea to walk around Pointe-à-Pitre at night, because it's almost deserted after dark. If you rent a car, always lock it with luggage and valuables stashed out of sight.

The rough Atlantic waters off the northeast coast of Grande-Terre are dangerous for swimming.

Ask permission before taking a picture of an islander, and don't be surprised if the answer is a firm "No." Guadeloupeans are also deeply religious and traditional. Don't offend them by wearing short shorts or swimwear off the beach.

Staying in Guadeloupe

Important Addresses **Tourist Information:** The **Office Départemental du Tourisme** has an office in Pointe-à-Pitre (5 Square de la Banque B.P. 1099, 97181 Cedex, tel. 590/82–09–30). The office is open weekdays 8–5, Saturday 8–noon. There's a tourist information booth at the airport.

Emergencies **Police:** In Pointe-à-Pitre (tel. 590/82–00–17), in Basse-Terre (tel. 590/81–11–55). **Fire:** In Pointe-à-Pitre (tel. 590/83–04–76), in Basse-Terre (tel. 590/81–19–22). **SOS Ambulance:** tel. 590/82–89–33. **Hospitals:** There is a 24-hour emergency room at the main hospital, **Centre Hopitalier de Pointe-à-Pitre** (Abymes, tel. 590/89–10–10). There are 23 clinics and five hospitals located around the island. The tourist office or your hotel can assist you in locating an English-speaking doctor. **Pharmacies:** Pharmacies alternate in staying open around the clock. The tourist office or your hotel can help you locate the one that's on duty.

Currency Legal tender is the French franc, which comprises 100 centimes. At press time, U.S. $1 bought 5.20F and 1£ bought 8.10F, but currencies fluctuate daily. Check the current rate of exchange. Some places accept U.S. dollars, but it's best to change your money into the local currency. Credit cards are accepted in most major hotels, restaurants, and shops, less so in smaller places and in the countryside. Prices are quoted here in U.S. dollars unless otherwise noted.

Taxes and Service Charges A *taxe de séjour* varies from hotel to hotel but never exceeds $1.50 per person, per day. Most hotel prices include a 10%–15% service charge; if not, it will be added to your bill. Restaurants are legally required to include 15% in the menu price. No additional gratuity is necessary. Tip skycaps and porters about 5F. Many cab drivers own their own cabs and don't expect a tip. You won't have any trouble ascertaining if a 10% tip is expected.

Getting Around

Taxis Taxis are metered and fairly pricey. During the day you'll pay about 60F from the airport to Pointe-à-Pitre, about 90F to Gosier, and about 200F to St-François. A 15–20-minute ride from Gosier to St-François costs about 150F. Between 9 PM and 7 AM and on Sundays and holidays, fares increase 40%. If your French is in working order, you can contact radio cabs at 590/82–13–67, 590/82–00–00, and 590/20–74–74.

Buses Modern public buses run from 5:30 AM to 7:30 PM and connect Guadeloupe's major towns to Pointe-à-Pitre. Fares range from 5F to 25F. They stop along the road at bus stops and shelters marked ARRÊTBUS, but you can also flag one down along the route. Although buses are an inexpensive way to get around, they run infrequently, and are especially crowded before and after school.

Vespas or Bikes If you opt to tour the island by bike, you won't be alone. Biking is a major sport here, as well as an inexpensive way to get around. Bike rental averages 50F a day (75F for mountain bikes). On Grand-Terre, the terrain is flat and poses no strain. If you're in reasonably good shape you can use a bike to get from one town to another here. Mountainous Basse-Terre, on the other hand, is best for short bike excursions. For rentals contact **Veló Tout Terrain** (Pointe-à-Pitre, tel. 590/97–85–40), which also offers tours of Basse terre and Marie Galante; **Cyclo-Tours** (Gosier, tel. 590/84–11–34); **Le Flamboyant** (St-François, tel. 590/84–45–51); and **Rent-a-Bike** (Meridien Hotel, St-François, tel. 590/84–51–00). Mountain bikes with 18 speeds are available from **Espace VTT** (St-François, tel. 88–79–91). For information on escorted bike tours, *see* Guided Tours, *below*.

Vespas can be rented at **Vespa Sun** (many locations in Pointe-à-Pitre, tel. 590/82–17–80), and **Equator Moto** (Gosier, tel. 590/90–36–77). A day's rental is about 200F, with a 1000F ($200) deposit or a major credit card.

Rental Cars Your valid driver's license will suffice for up to 20 days, after which you'll need an international driver's permit. Guadeloupe has 1,225 miles of excellent roads (marked as in Europe), and driving around Grande-Terre is relatively easy. On Basse-Terre it will take more effort to navigate the hairpin bends that twist through the mountains and around the eastern shore. Guadeloupeans are skillful drivers, but they do like to drive fast. Cars can be rented at **Avis** (tel. 590/82–33–47 or 800/331–1212), **Budget** (tel. 590/82–95–58 or 800/527–0700), **Hertz** (tel. 590/84–57–94 or 800/654–3131), **Thrifty** (tel. 590/91–55–66), and **Eurorent** (tel. 590/91–42–16). There are rental offices at the airport as well as at the major resort areas. Car rentals cost a bit more on Guadeloupe than on the other islands. Count on about $60 a day for a small rental car. Insist on a Peugeot or Ford rather than a Citroen; the latter seem to break down more easily on rutted roads and in the rain forest.

Telephones and Mail To call from the United States, dial 011 then 590 and the local six-digit number. (To call person-to-person, dial 01–590.) To call the United States from Guadeloupe, dial 19 then 1, then the area code and phone number. It is not possible to place collect or credit card calls to the United States from Guadeloupe. To make calls outside of your hotel, purchase a Telecarte at the post office or other outlets marked TELECARTE EN VENTE ICI. Telecartes look like credit cards and are used in special booths marked TELECOM. Local and international calls made with the cards are cheaper than operator-assisted calls. Coin-operated phones are rare but can be found in restaurants and cafés. To dial locally in Guadeloupe, simply dial the six-digit phone number. A local call costs 1F.

Postcards to the United States cost 3.70F; letters up to 20 grams, 4.60F. Stamps can be purchased at the post office, *café-tabacs*, hotel newsstands, or souvenir shops. Postcards and letters to the United Kingdom cost 3.60F.

Opening and Closing Times Banks are open weekdays 8–noon and 2–4. Credit Agricole, Banque Populaire, and Société Générale de Banque aux Antilles have branches that are open Saturday. During the summer most banks are open 8–3. Banks close at noon the day before a legal holiday that falls during the week. As a rule, shops are open weekdays 8 or 8:30–noon and 2:30–6, but hours are flexible when cruise ships are in town.

Guided Tours There are set fares for taxi tours to various points on the island. The tourist office or your hotel can arrange for an English-speaking taxi driver and even organize a small group for you to share the cost of the tour. One popular itinerary is a six-hour trip from Gosier to Basse-Terre and the Soufrière volcano; cost is approximately $85 per car (not per person).

George-Marie Gabrielle (Pointe-à-Pitre, tel. 590/82–05–38) and **Petrelluzzi Travel** (Pointe-à-Pitre, tel. 590/82–82–30) both offer half- and full-day excursions around the island. A modern bus with an English-speaking guide will pick you up at your hotel. Costs average $60 for a half-day tour, $85 for a full day, including lunch.

Le Relais du Moulin (near Ste-Anne, tel. 590/88–23–96) arranges bicycle tours on Grand-Terre. For more challenging excursions into the mountainous terrain of Basse-Terre, try the **Velo Club V.C.G.F.** (801 Résidence du Port, Pointe-à-Pitre, tel. 590/91–60–31). For information about cycling vacations in Guadeloupe, contact **Brooks Country Cycling and Hiking Tours** (140 W. 83rd St., New York, NY 10024, tel. 212/874–5151).

Parfum d'Aventure (St-François, tel. 590/88–47–62) offers adventure excursions in Basse Terre, including canyoning, canoeing on the Lézarde, sea kayaking, hikes from easy to grueling, and four-wheel drives. The half- and full-day jaunts range from $40–$100 per person, usually including lunch.

Exploring Guadeloupe

Numbers in the margin correspond to points of interest on the Guadeloupe map.

Although a guided tour will take you to many of the sites described below, a rental car will be cheaper (unless there are several of you sharing the cost of a taxi tour). Roads are well marked. Pointe-à-Pitre can be managed on foot.

Pointe-à-Pitre

1 **Pointe-à-Pitre** is a city of some 100,000 people in the extreme southwest of Grande-Terre. It lies almost on the "backbone" of the butterfly, near the bridge that crosses the Salée River. In this bustling, noisy city, with its narrow streets, honking horns, and traffic jams, there is a faster pulse than in many other Caribbean capitals, though at night the city streets are deserted.

Life has not been easy for Pointe-à-Pitre. The city has suffered severe damage over the years as a result of earthquakes, fires, and hurricanes. The most recent damage was done in 1979 by Hurricane Frederic, in 1980 by Hurricane David, and in 1989 by Hurricane Hugo. Standing on boulevard Frébault, you can see on one side the remaining French colonial structures and on the other the modern city. However, downtown is rejuvenating itself while maintaining its old charm. The recent completion of the Centre St-John Perse has transformed old warehouses into a new cruise-terminal complex that consists of a hotel (the Hotel St-John), three restaurants, space for 80 shops, and the headquarters for Guadeloupe's Port Authority.

Stop at the Office of Tourism, in Place de la Victoire across from the quays where the cruise ships dock, to pick up maps and brochures. *Bonjour, Guadeloupe* and *Living in Guadeloupe,* the free visitors' guides, are very useful. Outside the tourist office, stalls take over the sidewalk, selling everything from clothes to kitchen utensils. Across the road alongside the harbor, a gaggle of colorfully dressed women sell fruits and vegetables.

When you leave the office, turn left, walk one block along rue Schoelcher, and turn right on rue Achille René-Boisneuf. Two more blocks will bring you to the **Musée St-John Perse.** The restored colonial "Steamboat Gothic" house is dedicated to the Guadeloupean poet who won the 1960 Nobel Prize in Literature. (Nearby, at 54 rue René-Boisneuf, a plaque marks his birthplace.) The museum contains a complete collection of his poetry, as well as some of his personal effects. There are also works written about him and various mementos, documents, and photographs. *Corner rues Noizières and Achille René-Boisneuf, tel. 590/90–01–92. Admission: 10F. Open Thurs.–Tues. 9–5.*

Rues Noizières, Frébault, and Schoelcher are Pointe-à-Pitre's main shopping streets. In sharp contrast to the duty-free shops is the bustling **marketplace,** which you'll find by backtracking one block from the museum and turning right on rue Frébault. Located between rues St-John Perse, Frébault, Schoelcher, and Peynier, the market is a cacophonous and colorful place where housewives bargain for papayas, breadfruits, christophines, tomatoes, and a vivid assortment of other produce.

Take a left at the corner of rues Schoelcher and Peynier. The **Musée Schoelcher** honors the memory of Victor Schoelcher, the 19th-century Alsatian abolitionist who fought slavery in the French West Indies. The museum contains many of his personal effects, and the exhibits trace his life and work. *24 rue Peynier, tel. 590/82–08–04. Admission: 10F. Open weekdays 8:30–11:30 and 2–5.*

Walk back along rue Peynier past the market for three blocks. You'll come to **Place de la Victoire,** surrounded by wood buildings with balconies and shutters. Many sidewalk cafés have opened up on this revitalized square, making it a good place for lunch or light refreshments. The square was named in honor of Victor Hugues's 1794 victory over the British. The sandbox trees in the park are said to have been planted by Hugues the day after the victory. During the French Revolution, Hugues's guillotine in this square lopped off the head of many a white aristocrat. Today the large palm-shaded park is a popular gathering place. The tourist office is at the harbor end of the square.

Rue Duplessis runs between the southern edge of the park and La Darse, the head of the harbor, where fishing boats dock and fast motorboats depart for the choppy ride to Marie-Galante and Les Saintes.

Rue Bebian is the western border of the square. Walk north along it (away from the harbor) and turn left on rue Alexandre Isaac. You'll see the imposing **Cathedral of St. Peter and St. Paul,** which dates from 1847. Mother Nature's rampages have wreaked havoc on the church, and it is now reinforced with iron ribs. Hurricane Hugo took out many of the upper windows and shutters, but the lovely stained-glass windows survived intact.

Grande-Terre

This round-trip tour of **Grande-Terre** will cover about 85 miles. You may want to visit its sights and towns on several short trips—a bike is an option here—rather than on one long tour. Head south out of Pointe-à-Pitre on Route N4 (named the "Riviera" road in honor of the man-made beaches and resort hotels of Bas-du-Fort). The road goes past the marina, which is always crowded with yachts and cabin cruisers. The numerous boutiques and restaurants surrounding the marina make it popular in the evening.

The road turns east and heads along the coast. In 2 miles you'll sight
2 **Fort Fleur d'Epée,** an 18th-century fortress that hunkers on a hillside behind a deep moat. This was the scene of hard-fought battles between the French and the English. You can explore the well-preserved dungeons and battlements, and on a clear day take in a sweeping view of Iles des Saintes and Marie-Galante.

3 The **Guadeloupe Aquarium,** just past the fort off the main highway, is one of the Caribbean's largest and most modern. *Place Créole (just off Rte. N4), tel. 590/90–92–38. Admission: 38 adults, 20F children, free for children under 5. Open daily 9–7.*

4 **Gosier,** a major tourist center 2 miles farther east, is a busy place indeed, with big hotels and tiny inns, cafés, nightclubs, shops, and a long stretch of sand. The Creole Beach, the Auberge de la Vieille Tour, and the Canella Beach are among the hotels here.

Breeze along the coast through the little hamlet of St-Felix and on to
5 **Ste-Anne,** about 8 miles east of Gosier. Only ruined sugar mills remain from the days in the early 18th century when this village was a major sugar-exporting center. Sand has replaced sugar as the town's most valuable asset. The soft white-sand beaches here are among the best in Guadeloupe. On a more spiritual note, you'll pass Ste-Anne's lovely cemetery with stark-white aboveground tombs.

Don't fret about leaving the beaches of Ste-Anne behind you as you head eastward. The entire south coast of Grande-Terre is scalloped with white-sand beaches. Eight miles along, just before coming to

Exploring
Anse-Bertrand, **13**
Basse-Terre, **23**
Bouillante, **21**
Cascade aux Ecrevisses, **17**
Chutes du Carbet, **28**
Dumanoir Alley, **29**
Edgar-Clerc Archaeological Museum, **10**
Etang As de Pique, **26**
Fort Fleur d'Epée, **2**
Fort Napoléon, **32**
Gosier, **4**
Grand-Bourg, **33**
Guadeloupe Aquarium, **3**
Ilet du Gosier, **34**
La Pointe de la Grande Vigie, **12**
Le Moule, **9**
Les Mamelles, **19**
Les Saintes, **31**
Matouba, **25**
Morne-à-l'Eau, **15**
Parc Archéologique des Roches Gravées, **27**
Parc Tropical de Bras-David, **18**
Pointe-à-Pitre, **1**
Pointe des Châteaux, **7**
Port-Louis, **14**
Porte d'Enfer, **11**
St-Claude, **24**
St-François, **6**
Ste-Anne, **5**
Ste-Marie, **30**
Saut de la Lézarde, **16**
Vieux-Habitants, **22**
Zévalos, **8**
Zoological Park and Botanical Gardens, **20**

Dining
Chez Clara, **35**
Chez Jackye, **39**
Chez Mimi, **77**
Chez Violetta-La Creole, **60**
Folie Plage, **56**
Jardin Gourmand, **58**
L'Amour en Fleurs, **71**
La Canne á Sucre, **54**
La Chaloupe, **79**
La Frite Dorée, **63**
La Grande Pizzeria, **57**
La Paillotte, **85**
La Saladerie, **47**
La Table Creole, **62**
La Touna, **42**
Le Balata, **59**

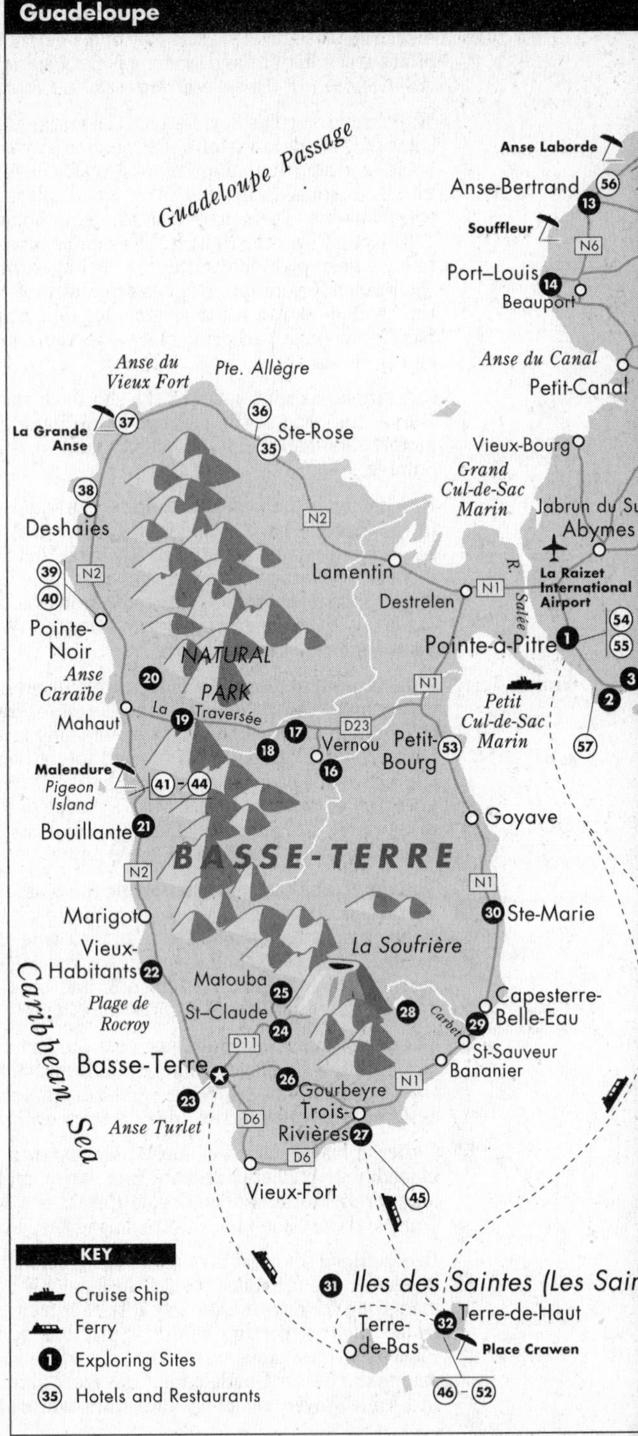

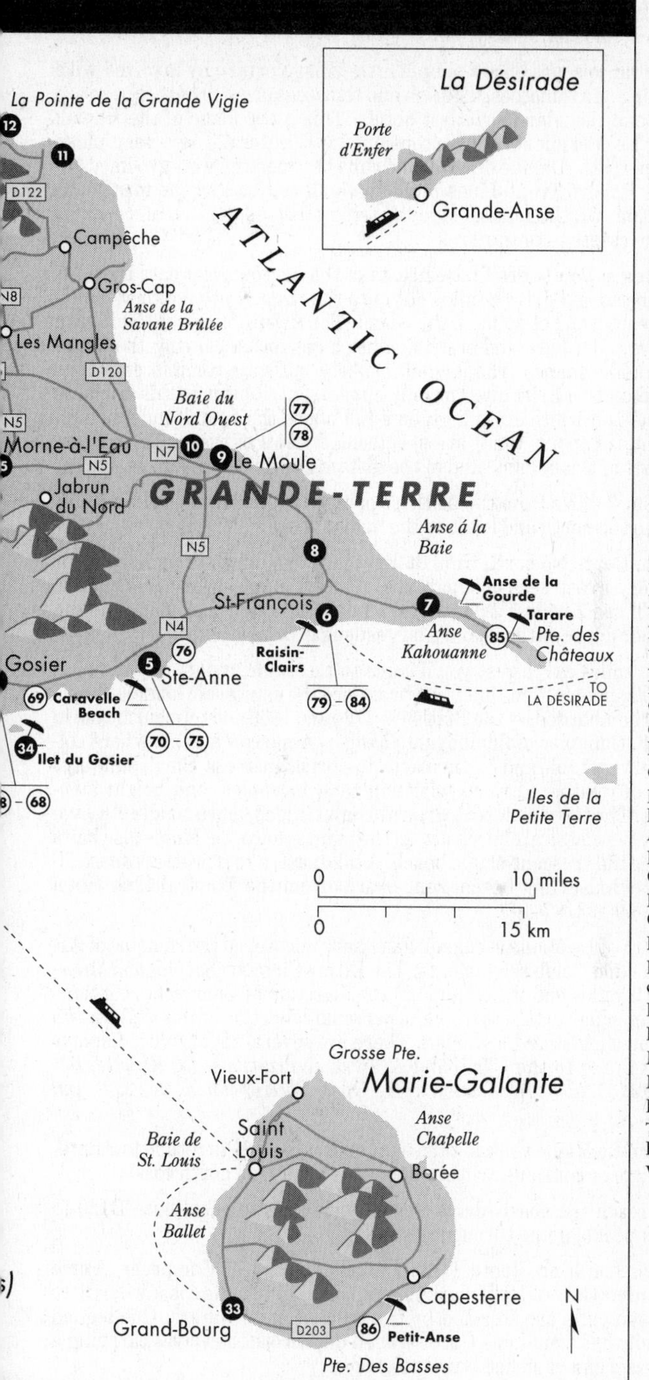

Le Banc de Sable, **46**
Le Corsaire, **61**
Le Flibustier, **70**
Le Karacoli, **37**
Le Normandie, **55**
Le Rocher de Malendure, **41**
Le Sable Blanc, **80**
Le Touloulou, **86**
Le Triangle, **49**
Les Gommiers, **40**
Les Pieds dans l'Eau, **81**
Pizzeria Napoli, **64**
Relais des Iles, **48**
Relais du Moulin, **76**

Lodging

Auberge de la Distillerie, **53**
Bois Joli, **52**
Canella Beach, **65**
Cap Sud Caraibes, **66**
Centre UCPA, **84**
Club Méditerranée La Caravelle, **72**
Domaine de Malendure, **43**
Domaine de Petite Anse, **44**
Fort Royal Touring Club, **38**
Golf Marine Club Hotel, **82**
Grand Anse Hotel, **45**
L' Auberge les Petits Saintes aux Anacardies, **51**
Le Barrière de Corail, **75**
La Sucrerie du Comté, **36**
La Toubana, **73**
Le Domaine de l'Anse des Rochers, **83**
Les Flamboyants, **68**
L' Orchidée, **67**
Marifa, **69**
Mini-Beach, **74**
Relais du Moulin, **76**
Tropical Club Hotel, **78**
Village Creole, **50**

6 the blue-roof houses of **St-François,** you'll come to the Raisins-Clairs beach, another beauty.

St-François was once a simple little village primarily involved with fishing and tomatoes. The fish and tomatoes are still here, but so are some of the island's ritziest hotels. This is the home of the Hamak and Le Méridien's new extension, La Cocoteraie, two very plush properties. Avenue de l'Europe runs between the well-groomed 18-hole Robert Trent Jones municipal golf course and the man-made marina. On the marina side, a string of shops, hotels, and restaurants caters to tourists.

7 To reach **Pointe des Châteaux,** take the narrow road east from St-François and drive 8 miles out onto the rugged promontory that is the easternmost point on the island. The Atlantic and the Caribbean waters join here and crash against huge rocks, carving them into castlelike shapes. The jagged, majestic cliffs are reminiscent of the headlands of Brittany. The only human contribution to this dramatic scene is a white cross high on a hill above the tumultuous waters. From this point there are spectacular views of the south and east coasts of Guadeloupe and of the distant cliffs of La Désirade.

About 2 miles from the farthest point, a rugged dirt road crunches off to the north and leads to the nudist beach Pointe Tarare.

Take Route N5 north from St-François for a drive through fragrant silvery-green seas of sugarcane. About 4 miles beyond St-François
8 you'll see **Zévalos,** a handsome colonial mansion that was once the manor house of the island's largest sugar plantation.

9 Four miles northwest you'll come to **Le Moule,** a port city of about 17,000 people. This busy city was once the capital of Guadeloupe. It was bombarded by the British in 1794 and 1809 and by a hurricane in 1928. Canopies of flamboyants hang over narrow streets where colorful vegetable and fish markets do a brisk business. Small buildings are of weathered wood with shutters, balconies, and bright awnings. The town hall, with graceful balustrades, and a small 19th-century neoclassical church are on the main square. Le Moule also has a beautiful crescent-shape beach. A mile east, a reef protects an excellent windsurfing beach; rent boards from the **Tropical Club Hotel** (tel. 590/93–97–97).

North of Le Moule archaeologists have uncovered the remains of Ar-
10 awak and Carib settlements. The **Edgar-Clerc Archaeological Museum,** 3 miles out of Le Moule in the direction of Campêche, contains Amerindian artifacts from the personal collection of this well-known archaeologist and historian. There are several rooms with displays pertaining to the Carib and Arawak civilizations. *La Rosette, tel. 590/23–57–57. Admission free. Open Thurs.–Tues. 9–12:30 and 2–5.*

From Le Moule you can turn west on Route D101 to return to Pointe-à-Pitre or continue northwest to see the rugged north coast.

To reach the coast, drive 8 miles northwest along Route D120 to Campêche, going through Gros-Cap.

11 Turn north on Route D122 1½ miles north of Campêche. **Porte d'Enfer** (Gate of Hell) marks a dramatic point on the coast where two jagged cliffs are stormed by the wild Atlantic waters. One legend has it that a Madame Coco strolled out across the waves carrying a parasol and vanished without a trace.

12 Four miles from Porte d'Enfer is **La Pointe de la Grande Vigie,** the northernmost tip of the island. Park your car and walk along the paths that lead right out to the edge. There is a splendid view of the Porte d'Enfer from here, and on a clear day you can see Antigua 35 miles away.

13 **Anse Bertrand,** the northernmost village in Guadeloupe, lies 4 miles south of La Pointe de la Grande Vigie along a gravel road. Drive carefully. En route to Anse Bertrand you'll pass another good beach, Anse Laborde. The area around Anse Bertrand was the last refuge of the Caribs. Most of the excitement these days takes place in the St-Jacques Hippodrome, where horse races and cockfights are held.

14 Route N6 will take you 5 miles south to **Port-Louis,** a fishing village of about 7,000. As you come in from the north, look for the turnoff to Souffleur Beach, once one of the island's prettiest, but now a little shabby. The sand is fringed by flamboyant trees whose brilliant orange-red flowers bloom during the summer and early fall. The beach is crowded on weekends, but during the week it's blissfully quiet. The sunsets here are something to write home about.

From Port-Louis the road leads 5 miles south through mangrove swamps and turns inland at Petit Canal. Three miles east of Petit Canal, turn right on the main road. Head 6 miles south to
15 **Morne-à-l'Eau,** an agricultural city of about 16,000 people. Morne-à-l'Eau's unusual amphitheater-shape cemetery is the scene of a moving (and beautiful) candlelight service on All Saints' Day. Take Route N5 out of town along gently undulating hills past fields of sugarcane and dairy farms.

Just south of Morne-à-l'Eau are the villages of **Jabrun du Sud** and **Jabrun du Nord,** which are inhabited by the descendants of the "Blancs Matignon," the whites who hid in the hills and valleys of the Grands Fonds after the abolition of slavery in 1848.

Continue on Route N5 to Pointe-à-Pitre.

Basse-Terre

There is high adventure on the butterfly's west wing, which swirls with mountain trails and lakes, waterfalls, and hot springs. Basse-Terre is the home of the Old Lady, as the Soufrière volcano is called locally, as well as of the capital, also called Basse-Terre.

Guadeloupe's de rigueur tour takes you through the 74,100-acre **Parc Naturel de la Guadeloupe,** a sizable chunk of Basse-Terre. (The park's administrative headquarters is in Basse-Terre, tel. 590/80–24–25.) Before going, pick up a *Guide to the Natural Park* from the tourist office. It rates the hiking trails according to difficulty.

The Route de la Traversée (La Traversée) is a good paved road that runs east–west, cutting a 16-mile-long swath through the park to the west-coast village of Mahaut. La Traversée divides Basse-Terre into two almost equal sections. The majority of mountain trails falls into the southern half. Allow a full day for the following excursion. Wear rubber-soled shoes, and take along both a swimsuit and a sweater, and perhaps food for a picnic. Try to get an early start, to remain ahead of the hordes of cruise-ship passengers that descend on La Traversée and the park for the day. A mountain-bike tour of at least three days is an excellent way to further explore the tropical rain-forest-clad mountains, hiking trails, and deserted beaches.

Begin your tour by heading west from Pointe-à-Pitre on Route N1, crossing the Rivière Salée on the Pont de la Gabare drawbridge. At the Destrelan traffic circle turn left and drive 6 miles south through sweet-scented fields of sugarcane to the Route de la Traversée (a.k.a. D23), where you'll turn west.

As soon as you cross the bridge, you'll begin to see the riches produced by Basse-Terre's fertile volcanic soil and heavy rainfall. La Traversée is lined with masses of thick tree-ferns, shrubs, flowers, tall trees, and green plantains that stand like soldiers in a row.

Five miles from where you turned off Route N1, you'll come to a junction. Turn left and go a little over a mile south to **Vernou.** Many of the old mansions you'll see in this area remain in the hands of the

original aristocratic families, the Bekés (whites in Creole), who can trace their lineage to before the French Revolution. Traipsing along a path that leads beyond the village through the lush forest, you'll
16 come to the pretty waterfall at **Saut de la Lézarde** (Lizard's Leap), the first of many you'll see.

Back on La Traversée, 3 miles farther, you'll come to the next one,
17 **Cascade aux Ecrevisses** (Crayfish Falls). Park your car and walk along the marked trail that leads to a splendid waterfall dashing down into the Corossol River (a fit place for a dip). Walk carefully—the rocks along the trail can be slippery.

18 Two miles farther along La Traversée you'll come to the **Parc Tropical de Bras-David,** where you can park and explore various nature trails. The **Maison de la Forêt** (admission free, open daily 9–5) has a variety of displays that describe (for those who can read French) the flora, fauna, and topography of the Natural Park. There are picnic tables where you can enjoy your lunch in tropical splendor.

Two and a half miles more will bring you to the two mountains
19 known as **Les Mamelles**—Mamelle de Petit-Bourg at 2,350 feet and Mamelle de Pigeon at 2,500 feet. (*Mamelle* means "breast," and when you see the mountains you'll understand why they are so named.) There is a spectacular view of the two mountains, from the pass that runs between them; the vista includes a smaller mountain to the north. From this point, trails ranging from easy to arduous lace up into the surrounding mountains. There's a glorious view from the lookout point, 1,969 feet up the Mamelle de Pigeon. If you're a climber, you'll want to spend several hours exploring this area.

You don't have to be much of a hiker to climb the stone steps leading
20 from the road to the **Zoological Park and Botanical Gardens.** Titi the Raccoon is the mascot of the Natural Park. There are also cockatoos, iguanas, and turtles. The cramped cages are a sorrowful sight (you'll want to liberate the residents immediately), but the setting and views are stunning. A snack bar is open for lunch daily except Monday. *La Traversée, tel. 590/98–83–52. Admission: 30F adults, 20F children. Open daily 9–5.*

On the winding 4-mile descent from the mountains to **Mahaut,** you'll see patches of the blue Caribbean through the green trees. In the village of Mahaut, turn left on Route N2 for the drive south along the coast. In less than a mile you'll come to **Malendure.** The big attraction here is offshore, where **Pigeon Island** sits surrounded by the Jacques Cousteau Marine Reserve. Les Heures Saines and Chez Guy, both on the Malendure Beach, conduct diving trips (*see* Sports and the Outdoors, *below*), and the glass-bottom *Aquarium* and *Nautilus* make daily snorkeling trips to this spectacular site.

21 From Malendure, continue through neighboring **Bouillante,** where
22 hot springs burst up through the earth, and **Vieux-Habitants,** one of the oldest settlements on the island. Pause to see the restored church, which dates from 1650, before driving 8 miles south to the capital city.

23 **Basse-Terre,** the capital and administrative center, is an active city of about 15,000 people. Founded in 1640, it has had even more difficulties than Pointe-à-Pitre. The capital has endured not only foreign attacks and hurricanes but sputtering threats from La Soufrière as well. More than once it has been evacuated when the volcano began to hiss and fume. The last major eruption was in the 16th century. But the volcano seemed active enough to warrant the evacuation of more than 70,000 people in 1975.

The centers of activity are the port and the market, both of which you'll pass along boulevard Général de Gaulle. The 17th-century **Fort St. Charles,** at the extreme south end of town, and the **Cathedral**

of Our Lady of Guadeloupe, to the north, across the Rivière aux Herbes, are worth a short visit. Drive along boulevard Felix Eboue to see the colonial buildings that house government offices. Follow the boulevard to the **Jardin Pichon** to see its beautiful gardens. Stop off at **Champ d'Arbaud,** an Old World square surrounded by colonial
buildings. Continue along the boulevard to the **botanical gardens.** A
24 steep, narrow road leads 4 miles up to the suburb of **St-Claude,** on the slopes of La Soufrière. In St-Claude there are picnic tables and good views of the volcano. You can also get a closer look at the volcano by driving up to the Savane à Mulets. From there leave your car and hike the strenuous two-hour climb (with an experienced guide) to the summit at 4,813 feet, the highest point in the Lesser Antilles. Water boils out of the eastern slope of the volcano and spills into the Carbet Falls.

25 Drive 2 miles farther north from St-Claude to visit **Matouba,** a village settled by East Indians whose descendants still practice ancient rites, including animal sacrifice. If you've an idle 10 hours or so, take off from Matouba for a 19-mile hike on a marked trail through the Monts Caraibes to the east coast.

Descend and continue east on Route N1 for 4 miles to **Gourbeyre.**
26 Visit **Etang As de Pique.** Reaching this lake, 2,454 feet above the town, is another challenge for hikers, but you can also reach it in an hour by car via paved Palmetto Road. The 5-acre lake, formed by a lava flow, is shaped like an *as de pique* (ace of spades).

From Gourbeyre you have the option of continuing east along Route N1 or backtracking to the outskirts of Basse-Terre and taking the roller-coaster Route D6 along the coast. Either route will take you through lush greenery to **Trois-Rivières.**

27 Not far from the ferry landing for Les Saintes is the **Parc Archéologique des Roches Gravées,** which contains a collection of pre-Columbian rock engravings. Pick up an information sheet at the park's entrance. Displays interpret the figures of folk and fauna depicted on the petroglyphs. The park is set in a lovely botanical garden that is off the beaten track for many tourists, so it remains a haven of tranquillity. *Bord de la Mer, Trois-Rivières, tel. 590/92–91–88. Admission: 4F. Open daily 9–5.*

Continue for 5 miles, through banana fields and the village of Bananier, to reach the village of **St-Sauveur,** gateway to the magnifi-
28 cent **Chutes du Carbet** (Carbet Falls). Three of the chutes, which drop from 65 feet, 360 feet, and 410 feet, can be reached by following the narrow, steep, and spiraling Habituée Road for 5 miles up past the **Grand Etang** (Great Pond). At the end of the road you'll have to proceed on foot. Well-marked but slippery trails lead to viewing points of the chutes.

Continue along Route N1 for 3 miles toward **Capesterre-Belle-Eau.**
29 You'll cross the Carbet River and come to **Dumanoir Alley,** lined with century-old royal palms.

Three miles farther along, through fields of pineapples, bananas,
30 and sugarcane, you'll arrive at **Ste-Marie,** where Columbus landed in 1493. In the town there is a monument to the Great Discoverer.

Seventeen miles farther north, you'll return to Pointe-à-Pitre.

Iles des Saintes

This eight-island archipelago, usually referred to as **Les Saintes,** dots the waters off the south coast of Guadeloupe. The islands are
31 Terre-de-Haut, Terre-de-Bas, Ilet à Cabrit, Grand Ilet, La Redonde, La Coche, Le Pâté, and Les Augustins. Columbus discovered the islands on November 4, 1493, and christened them Los Santos in honor of All Saints' Day.

Arrival on Terre-de-Haut requires a choppy 35-minute ferry crossing from Trois-Rivières or a 60-minute ride from Pointe-à-Pitre.

Ferries leave Trois-Rivières at about 8:30 AM (7:30 AM on Sunday) and return about 3 PM. From Pointe-à-Pitre the usual departure time is 8 AM, with return at 4 PM. Check with the tourist office for up-to-date ferry schedules. Round-trip fare from either point is 160F. Check with the tourist office for up-to-date ferry schedules.

Of the islands, only Terre-de-Haut and Terre-de-Bas are inhabited, with a combined population of 3,260. Many of les Saintois, as the islanders are called, are fair-haired, blue-eyed descendants of Breton and Norman sailors. Fishing is the main source of income for les Saintois, and the shores are lined with their fishing boats and *filets bleus* (blue nets dotted with burnt-orange buoys). The fishermen wear hats called *salakos*, which look like inverted saucers or coolie hats. They are patterned after a hat said to have been brought here by a seafarer from China or Indonesia.

With 5 square miles and a population of about 1,500, Terre-de-Haut is the largest island and the most developed for tourism. Its "big city" is Bourg, which boasts one street and a few bistros, cafés, and shops. Clutching the hillside are trim white houses with bright red or blue doors, balconies, and gingerbread frills.

Terre-de-Haut's ragged coastline is scalloped with lovely coves and beaches, including the nudist beach at Anse Crawen. The beautiful bay, complete with sugarloaf, has been called a mini Rio. This is a quiet, peaceful getaway, but it may not remain unspoiled. Tourism is increasing and now accounts for 50% of the economy. Although government plans call for a total of only 250 hotel rooms, the tourist-related industries are making a major pitch for visitors. Consider overnighting to get a true feel for the islands without the day-trippers.

There are three paved roads on the island, but don't even think about driving here. The roads are ghastly, and backing up is a minor art form, choreographed on those frequent occasions when two vehicles meet on one of the steep, narrow roads. There are four minibuses that transport passengers from the airstrip and the wharf and double as tour buses. However, the island is so small you can get around by walking. It's a mere five-minute stroll from the airstrip and ferry dock to downtown Bourg.

32 **Fort Napoléon** is a relic from the period when the French fortified these islands against the Caribs and the English, but nobody has ever fired a shot at or from it. Inside is a museum whose galleries include a collection of 250 modern paintings, heavily influenced by Cubism and Surrealism and hung at odd angles, and an exhaustive exhibit on the important naval Battle of Les Saintes (history buffs may recall Admiral de Grasse from the American Revolution). You can also visit the well-preserved barracks and prison cells, and admire the surrounding botanical gardens, which specialize in cacti of all sizes and descriptions. From the fort you can see Fort Josephine across the channel on the Ilet à Cabrit. *Bourg, no phone. Admission: 15F adults, 5F children 6–12. Open daily 9–12:30.*

For such a tiny place, Terre-de-Haut offers a variety of hotels and restaurants. For details, *see* Dining *and* Lodging, *below*. The **Centre Nautique des Saintes** (Plage de la Coline, tel. 590/99–54–25) and **Espace Plongé Caraibes** (Bourg, tel. 590/99–51–84) rent equipment and lead dive excursions offshore.

Marie-Galante Columbus sighted this flat island on November 3, 1493, the day before he landed at Ste-Marie on Basse-Terre. He named it for his flagship, the *Maria Galanda*, and sailed on.

The ferry departs from Pointe-à-Pitre at 8 AM, 2 PM, and 5 PM with returns at 6 AM, 9 AM, and 3:45 PM. (Schedules often change, especially on the weekends, so check at the tourist office or the harbor offices.)
33 The round trip costs 160F. You'll put in at **Grand Bourg,** the major

city, with a population of about 8,000. A plane will land you 2 miles from Grand Bourg. If your French, or phrase book, is good enough, you can negotiate a price with the taxi drivers for touring the island. There are several places near the ferry landing where you can get an inexpensive meal of seafood with Creole sauce.

Covering about 60 square miles, Marie-Galante is the largest of Guadeloupe's islands. It is dotted with ruined 19th-century sugar mills, and sugar is still one of its major products—the others are cotton and rum. One of the last refuges of the Caribs when they were driven from the mainland by the French, the island is now a favorite retreat of Guadeloupeans, who come on weekends to enjoy the beach at Petit-Anse.

You'll find dramatic coastal scenery, with soaring cliffs such as the Gueule Grand Gouffre (Mouth of the Giant Chasm) and Les Galeries (where millennia of erosion have sculpted a natural arcade) holding an angry ocean at bay, and enormous sun-dappled grottos like Le Trou à Diable, whose underground river can be explored with a guide. Don't miss the **Château Murat** (tel. 590/97–03–79; admission 10F adults, 5F children 6–12, open daily 9:15–5), a restored 17th-century sugar plantation and rum distillery that houses exhibits on the history of rum-making and sugarcane production, as well as the admirable Ecomusée, whose displays celebrate local crafts and customs. And do visit the distilleries, especially Père Labat, whose rum is considered one of the finest in the Caribbean and whose atelier turns out lovely pottery.

If you want to stay over, you can choose from Au Village de Ménard (5 bungalows, tel. 590/97–77–02) in St-Louis, Auberge de l'Arbre à Pain (7 rooms, tel. 590/97–73–69) in Grand Bourg, or Hotel Hajo (6 rooms, tel. 590/97–32–76) in Capesterre. An entertainment complex in Grand Bourg, El Rancho has a 400-seat movie theater, restaurant, terrace grill, snack bar, disco, and a few double rooms.

La Désirade According to legend, La Désirade is the "desired land" of Columbus's second voyage. He spotted the island on November 3, 1493. The 8-square-mile island, 5 miles east of St-François, was for many years a leper colony. The main settlement is Grande-Anse, where there is a pretty church and a hotel called L'Oasis (10 rooms, tel. 590/20–02–12). Nothing fancy, but the restaurant serves excellent seafood. Most of the 1,600 inhabitants are fishermen.

There are good beaches here, notably Souffleur and Baie Mahault, and there's little to do but loll around on them. The island is virtually unspoiled by tourism and is likely to remain so, at least for the foreseeable future.

Three or four minibuses meet the flights and ferries, and you can negotiate with one of them to give you a tour. Ferries depart from St-François daily at 8 and 4. The return ferry departs daily at 3:30. However, be sure to check schedules. Cost is 100F.

Beaches

Guadeloupe's beaches, all free and open to the public, generally have no facilities. For a small fee, hotels allow nonguests to use changing facilities, towels, and beach chairs. You'll find long stretches of white sand on Grande-Terre. On the south coast of Basse-Terre the beaches are gray volcanic sand, and on the northwest coast the color is golden-tan. There are several nudist beaches (noted below), and topless bathing is prevalent at the resort hotels. Note that the Atlantic waters on the northeast coast of Grande-Terre are too rough for swimming. Except for Ilet du Gosier, all beaches are accessible from the road; even the smallest beach is signposted with a track leading to the sands.

34 **Ilet du Gosier** is a little speck off the shore of Gosier where you can bathe in the buff. Make arrangements for water-sports rentals and boat trips to the island (cost: 50F) through the Creole Beach Hotel in Gosier (tel. 590/84–46–46). Take along a picnic for an all-day outing. *Beach closed weekends.*

Some of the island's best beaches of soft white sand lie on the coast of Grande-Terre from Ste-Anne to Pointe des Châteaux. One of the longest and prettiest stretches is just outside the town of Ste-Anne at **Caravelle Beach,** though there are rather dilapidated shacks and cafés scattered about the area. Protected by reefs, the beach makes a fine place for snorkeling. Club Med, with its staggering array of activities, occupies one end of this beach.

Just outside of St-François is **Raisin-Clairs,** home of Le Méridien (tel. 590/88–51–00), which rents Windsurfers, water skis, and sailboats.

Between St-François and Pointe des Châteaux, **Anse de la Gourde** is a beautiful stretch of sand that becomes very popular on weekends. **La Langouste** (tel. 590/88–52–19), a popular lunch spot on the weekends, guards the entrance to the beach.

Tarare is a secluded strip just before the tip of Pointe des Châteaux; many bathe naked there. There is a small bar/café located where you park the car, a four-minute walk from the beach.

Just outside of Deshaies on the northwest coast of Basse-Terre, **La Grande Anse** is a secluded beach of soft beige sand sheltered by palms. There's a large parking area but no facilities other than the Karacoli restaurant, which sits with its "feet in the water," ready to serve you rum punch and Creole dishes.

From here south along the western shore of Basse-Terre, signs point the way to small beaches. By the time you reach Pigeon Island, the sand starts turning gray; as you work your way farther south, it becomes black.

Malendure beach lies on the west coast of Basse-Terre, across from Pigeon Island. Jacques Cousteau called it one of the 10 best diving places in the world. Several scuba operations are based here (*see* Sports and the Outdoors, *below*). There are also glass-bottom boat trips for those who prefer to keep their heads above water.

Souffleur, on the west coast of Grande-Terre, north of Port-Louis, has brilliant flamboyant trees that bloom in the summer. There are no facilities on the beach, but you can buy the makings of a picnic from nearby shops. Be sure to stick around long enough for a super sunset.

Place Crawen, Les Saintes' quiet, secluded beach for skinny-dipping, is a half-mile of white sand on Terre-de-Haut. Facilities are within a five-minute walk at Bois Joli hotel (*see* Lodging, *below*). The other popular beach is **Les Pompierres,** a palm-fringed stretch of tawny sand.

Petit-Anse, on Marie-Galante, is a long gold-sand beach crowded with locals on weekends. During the week it's quiet, and there are no facilities other than the little seafood restaurant, La Touloulou.

Sports and the Outdoors

Bicycling *See* Getting Around, *above*.

Boating All beachfront hotels rent Hobie Cats, Sunfish, pedal boats, motorboats, and water skis. Small boat rental runs about 60F an hour; water skiing is about 75F for 15 minutes.

Golf **Golf Municipal Saint-François** (St-François, tel. 590/88–41–87) has an 18-hole Robert Trent Jones course, an English-speaking pro, a clubhouse, a pro shop, and electric carts for rental. The greens fee is 250F.

Hiking Basse-Terre's Natural Park is laced with fascinating trails, many of which should be attempted only with an experienced guide. Trips for up to 12 people are arranged by **Organisation des Guides de Montagne de la Caraibe (O.G.M.C.)** (Maison Forestière, Matouba, tel. 590/94–29–11). The cost for a four- to five-hour hike is about 100F per person (not including lunch), and you are advised to wear sturdy shoes with strong ankle support.

Horseback Riding Beach rides (50F per hour), picnics, and lessons are available through **Le Criolo** (St-Felix, Gosier, tel. 590/84–04–06).

Scuba Diving The main diving area is the Cousteau Underwater Park off Pigeon Island (west coast of Basse-Terre). Guides and instructors here are certified under the French CMAS rather than PADI or NAUI. To explore the wrecks and reefs, contact **Les Heures Saines** (Malendure, tel. 590/98–86–63) or **Chez Guy et Christian** (Malendure, tel. 590/98–82–43). Both of these outfits arrange dives elsewhere around Guadeloupe. Chez Guy also arranges weekly packages that include accommodations in bungalows. Other leading operations include **Caraibes Plongées** (Gosier, tel. 509/90–44–90) and **Marine Anse Plongée** (Bouillante, tel. 590/98–78–78). On the Isle des Saintes, the **Centre Nautique des Saintes** (Plage de la Coline, Terre-de-Haut, tel. 590/99–54–25) and **Espace Plongé Caraibes** (Bourg, tel. 590/99–51–84) rent dive and snorkel equipment and will arrange dives. A single-tank dive averages 200F–300F.

Sea Excursions and Snorkeling Most hotels rent snorkeling gear for around 50F a day and post information about excursions. The ***King Papyrus*** (Marina Bas-du-Fort, tel. 590/90–92–98) is a catamaran that offers full-day outings replete with rum, dances, and games, as well as moonlight sails. An evening cruise with buffet and drinks is 350F per person. Glass-bottom boats also make 90-minute excursions to Pigeon Island (*see* Scuba Diving, *above*) for 95F a person. The sailing school **Evasion Marine** (locations in St-François and Bas-du-Fort, tel. 590/84–46–67) offers excursions on board the *Ginn Fizz,* the *Ketch,* or the *Sloop*. Prices vary depending on the cruise; a full-day trip to Marie-Galante, for example, is 300F.

Tennis Courts are located at the following hotels: **Auberge de la Vieille Tour** (tel. 590/84–23–23), **Club Méditerranée La Caravelle** (tel. 590/88–21–00), **Golf Marine Club Hotel** (tel. 590/88–60–60), **Le Méridien St-François** (tel. 590/88–51–00), and **Relais du Moulin** (tel. 590/88–23–96). Games can also be arranged through the **St-François Tennis Club** (tel. 590/88–41–87), the **Marina Club** in Pointe-à-Pitre (tel. 590/90–84–08), and the **Tennis League of Guadeloupe** (tel. 590/90–90–97) in Glosier. Courts rent for approximately 75F an hour.

Windsurfing Immensely popular here, windsurfing rentals and lessons are available at all beachfront hotels. Windsurfing buffs congregate at the **UCPA Hotel Club** (tel. 590/88–64–80) in St-François. You can also rent a *planche-à-voile* (a board for windsurfing)—try the **Calinnago** (Pointe de la Verdure, Gosier, tel. 590/84–25–25). Windsurfers rent for 60F an hour; three hours of instruction cost about 250F.

Shopping

You'll find shopping less of a temptation here than it is on Martinique, where the selection is larger and the language less of a barrier. But shopping in Pointe-à-Pitre is fun at the street stalls around the harbor quay, in front of the tourist office, and at the market. The more touristy—and more expensive—shops are down at the Jean-Perse cruise terminal, where an attractive mall is home to two dozen shops. Get an early start—it's hot and sticky by midday.

Many stores offer a 20% discount on luxury items purchased with traveler's checks or, in some cases, major credit cards. You can find good buys on anything French—perfumes, crystal, china, cosmetics, fashions, scarves. As for local handcrafted items, you'll see a lot of junk, but you can also find island dolls dressed in madras, finely woven straw baskets and hats, salako hats made of split bamboo, madras table linens, and wood carvings. And, of course, the favorite Guadeloupean souvenir—rum.

Shopping Areas In Pointe-à-Pitre the main shopping streets are **rue Schoelcher, rue de Nozières,** and **rue Frébault.** The **Jean-Perse Cruise Terminal** in Pointe-à-Pitre has a complex of smart shops that tend to be more expensive than stores in the older part of town. Bas-du-Fort's two shopping districts are the **Mammouth Shopping Center** and the **Marina,** where there are 20 or so boutiques and several restaurants. In **St-François** there are also several shops surrounding the marina. Many of the resorts have fashion boutiques. There are also a number of duty-free shops at Raizet Airport.

Good Buys
Native Crafts For dolls, straw hats, baskets, and madras table linens, try **Au Caraibe** (4 rue Frébault, Pointe-à-Pitre, no phone). Anthuriums and other plants that pass muster at U.S. customs are packaged at **Casafleurs** (42 rue René-Boisneuf, tel. 590/82–31–23, and Raizet Airport, tel. 590/82–33–34). **Mariposa** (13 Galerie du Port, St-François, tel. 590/88–69–38) offers a collection of local crafts. **L'Imagerie Créole** (Bas-du-Fort, tel. 590/90–87–28) carries native-art antiques. For imaginative, thought-provoking paintings and sculpture, visit the **Centre d'Art Haitien** (rue Delgres, Pointe-à-Pitre, tel. 590/82–54–46, and 65 Montauban, Gosier, tel. 590/84–04–84). **L'Atelier de l'Art** (Gosier, Rte. des Hotels, no phone) offers fanciful creations of wood and straw. **Chritiane Boutique** (Blvd. Général de Gaulle, Gosier, tel. 590/84–52–51) offers a mind-boggling jumble ranging from tacky tchotchkes like "fertility" sculptures to sublime art naïf canvases for as little as $20. On Terre de Haut, **Maogany Artisanat** (Bour, tel. 590/99–50–12) sells Yves Cohen's batik and hand-painted T-shirts in luminescent seashell shades. **Pascal Foy** (Rte. à Pompierres, tel. 590/99–52–29) produces stunning homages to traditional Creole architecture: painted houses incorporating collage and objets trouvés that make marvelous wall hangings. Prices begin at $90 and are well worth it. On Terre de Bas, contact **José Beaujour** (tel. 590/99–80–20) for an authentic salako.

Rum and Tobacco **Delice Shop** (45 rue Achille René-Boisneuf, Pointe-à-Pitre, tel. 590/82–98–24) is the spot for island rums and gourmet items from France, from cheese to chocolate. **Comptoir sous Douane** (Raizet Airport, tel. 590/82–22–76) has a good selection of island rums and tobacco.

Dining

The food here is superb. You'll find numerous reasonably priced restaurants serving creative, delicious food, but as a rule dining here is not cheap. Expect to pay about $25 for a good Creole dinner, less for lunch, more (sometimes double) at a formidable French restaurant serving haute cuisine. You may want to budget for at least one splurge meal here. Needless to say, the quality of hotel dining rooms is superior, and you won't suffer if you negotiate a good meal plan rate. Consult the lodging listings for additional recommendations.

Many of Guadeloupe's restaurants feature seafood (shellfish is a great favorite), often flavored with rich herbs and spices à la Creole. Favorite appetizers are *accras* (codfish fritters), *boudin* (highly seasoned pork sausage), and *crabes farcis* (stuffed land crabs). Christophines, squashlike vegetables, are prepared in a variety of ways. Banana-like plantains are often served as a side dish. *Blaff* is a spicy fish stew. Lobster, turtle steak, and *lambi* (conch) are often among the main dishes, and homemade coconut ice cream is a typical dessert. The island boasts 200 restaurants, including those serving classic French, Italian, African, Indian, Vietnamese, and South American fare. The local libation of choice is the *petit punch* ("ti poonch," as it is pronounced)—a heady concoction of rum, lime juice, and sugarcane syrup. The innocent-sounding little punch packs a powerful wallop.

Buying groceries is a pleasure on Guadeloupe, where import items from Europe are widely available and relatively affordable. You can save money on some meals by purchasing takeout for picnics or for eating back at your lodgings. **Match** is the supermarket here; there are three branches in Pointe-à-Pitre, one each in Gosier and St-François. The supermarket at the marina in Bas-du-Fort is also popular, as is a smaller market off av. de l'Europe in St-François. For vegetables and tropical fruits, shop the market on the quay at Pointe-à-Pitre. You'll find minimarkets in the center of every town and village.

Unless you're fluent in French and Creole, you'll want to keep with you a small booklet, "Ti Gourmet Guadeloupe," which lists restaurants, defines menu terms, and gives some indication of prices. The booklet is free from the tourist office and many hotels. Though the French are wont to bare all on the beach, dress is much more decorous in restaurants. Casual is fine for lunch, but beach attire is a no-no. Except at the more laid-back marina and beach eateries, dinner is slightly more formal. Long pants, collared shirts, and skirts or dresses are appreciated, although not required.

For additional savings, bear in mind that most beaches have snack bars serving simple grilled fish and meats or pizza. Look also for mobile vans that set up shop, selling crepes and barbecued chicken. In towns or at the marinas, seek out creperies and saladeries for quick, filling lunches, or grab a boudin Creole or poisson from one of the ladies in the Pointe-à-Pitre market for 5F. Most restaurants offer a prix-fixe menu (also called formule)—sometimes including wine, often with a choice of dishes—that's a tremendous value. Remember that gratuity is usually included (indicated at the bottom of the menu as *service compris*).

Highly recommended restaurants are indicated by a star ★.

Category	Cost*
$$	$25–$35
$	$15–$25
¢	under $15

**per person, excluding drinks*

Grande-Terre

$$ **Jardin Gourmand.** The Acaudal Hotel's dining room is a training ground for student cooks, waiters, and waitresses. The menu changes with the visiting French master chefs and apprentices but usually includes red snapper and lobster prepared in various ways. Exotic Creole courses are sometimes offered: Try the octopus gratinéed with a pink sauce or shark in coconut milk. For dessert the delicious frozen nougat with banana is a good choice. Don't be tempted by the *menu de dégustation*, which is out of our price range. *Acaudal, Montauban, Gosier, tel. 590/84–15–66. Reservations advised. Jacket required. AE, DC, MC, V. No lunch.*

$$ ★ **La Canne à Sucre.** A favorite over the years for its innovative Creole cuisine, La Canne à Sucre has a reputation for being the best restaurant in Pointe-à-Pitre. It has a commanding position at the corner of the quay, in the complex adjacent to the cruise-ship terminal, and hulking ships cast a shadow over the terrace. Take time to admire

the lovely murals of a sugarcane harvest that adorn the building. There are two dining rooms with separate menus. Meals upstairs are more elaborate and twice as expensive, so stick to the main-floor Brasserie. Order such classic bistro dishes as duck à l'orange, grouper in red wine butter, and a puff pastry of skate with saffron sauce. *Quai No. 1, Port Autonome, Pointe-à-Pitre, tel. 590/82-10-19. Reservations advised. AE, MC, V. No lunch Sat.*

$$ ★ **Le Balata.** Dinner will test the budget at this restaurant, but the romance may justify the splurge. The setting is high on a bluff above the main Gosier Bas-du-Fort highway. If you're traveling from Gosier in the direction of Fort-de-France, you'll find the winding, pitted entrance road off the highway, at the Elf gas station. Pretty flowered linens and trellises woven with hanging vines create a pastoral setting. Madame Guynamant presents classic Lyonnaise cuisine with Creole touches. Begin with shellfish in a cucumber sauce or homemade foie gras, then contemplate the catch of the day with parsley butter. A special businessman's lunch is available at 110F, including wine, and there's a 155F dinner menu (no wine). Choose a table by the window (reserve early), and enjoy the magnificent view of Fort Fleur d'Epée. *Rte. de Labrousse, Gosier, tel. 590/90-88-25. Reservations advised. AE, MC, V. Closed Sun. and Aug. No lunch Sat.*

$$ **Le Flibustier.** This rustic hilltop farmhouse is a favorite with staffers from neighboring Club Med. It's a lively, fun place that warms up after 8 PM, when the G.O.s (*general organisateurs*—the staffers who force you to limbo) hold court, smoke up a storm, and serenade attractive guests with ribald ditties. A complete dinner of mixed salad, grilled lobster, coconut ice cream, 'ti punch, and half a pitcher of wine is $48, which is barely over our price limit when you consider that drinks are included. You may also order à la carte off the blackboard menu. *La Colline, Fonds Thézan (between Ste-Anne and St-Felix), tel. 590/88-23-36. No credit cards. Closed Mon. No lunch Sun.*

$-$$ **Chez Violetta–La Creole.** The late Violetta Chaville established this restaurant's à la carte Creole menu when she was head of Guadeloupe's association of cuisinières (female chefs). Her brother has carried on her cooking traditions, dishing up specials such as red snapper in Belle Doudou sauce, a Creole mix of onions, tomatoes, peppers, and spices. The food, while still good, has been eclipsed by other island kitchens, but the restaurant remains a stop on many tourist itineraries and is popular with American visitors. *Eastern outskirts of Gosier Village, tel. 590/84-10-34. No credit cards.*

$-$$ **La Grande Pizzeria.** Open late and very popular, this simple seaside spot serves pizza; pasta; salads; and some Milanese, Bolognese, and other Italian seafood specialties. Keep to the pizzas and you'll have a satisfying meal for less than 90F. The tab may sneak out of the $$ range if you order the veal or other more elaborate dishes, such as the delectable risotto with seafood or tagliatelle with shrimp scampi. Plastic tables and chairs are set on the terrace and spruced up with colorful napery. *Bas-du-Fort, tel. 590/90-82-64. MC, V. No lunch.*

$-$$ **Le Corsaire.** Restaurants on Gosier's main drag and the Route des Hotels leading to the Pointe de la Verdure vie with one another to offer the best value menus. Family-run Le Corsaire rates highly thanks not only to its fine fare at finer prices, but also to its fun-loving ambience. The waitstaff affects a piratical look with ponytails, earrings, and goatees. A *vivier* (lobster tank) and a flamboyant mural of a buccaneer and his ship dominate the decor. Maman is a sweetie, singing out "C'est bon?" from the kitchen and nodding approvingly as you eat. For 99F you get a set menu, which might start with a conch tart or stuffed crab, then segue into beef brochette, octopus fricassee, or chicken colombo. The King Creole menu at 120F nets you a large lobster. You can also order a pizzas for 40F–52F.

Rte. des Hotels, Gosier, tel. 590/84–17–39. AE, MC, V. No lunch Mon.

$ **Chez Mimi.** This intimate boîte is an appealing clutter of handmade butterflies, flower baskets, and hats, plastered with postcards and business cards and splashed with vivid murals. Mimi is as colorful as the decor and the food (try the luscious clam blaff for 70F) is delectable. *81 rue St-Jean, Le Moule, tel 590/23–64–87. No credit cards. Closed Sun.*

$ **Folie Plage.** This lovely spot north of Anse-Bertrand is especially popular with families on weekends. Prudence Marcelin prepares reliable Creole food; superb court bouillon and imaginative curried dishes are among the specialties. There is a children's wading pool here. *Anse Laborde, tel. 590/22–11–17. Reservations advised. No credit cards.*

$ **La Chaloupe.** In tony St-François, you'll find several atmospheric cafés in the marina, specializing in simple grilled meats and fish (figure on about 75F) and tasty pizzas (around 50F). La Chaloupe has a fun, nautical decor, jazzed up with art naïf placemats, batik wall hangings, multihued straw chairs, and a virtual jungle of potted plants. The more exotic dishes—shrimp flamed with old rum in saffron cream sauce—can catapult the tab well into the $$ range. *Marina de St-François, tel. 590/88–52–72. AE, MC, V.*

$ ★ **La Table Creole.** This little terrace eatery is the domain of the affable Carmélite Jeanne, who turns out dazzling Creole cuisine that is deceptively mild yet will heat you up like the noonday sun. Sea urchin gratin, succulent kingfish and snapper blaff, and goat colombo are among her memorable specialties. The menus at 80F and 100F are fabulous bargains. Sprays of fresh flowers spill everywhere you look, and Mme. Jeanne usually dresses colorfully to match. *St-Félix, outside Gosier, tel. 590/84–28–28. MC, V. Closed Sept. No dinner Sun.*

$ **L'Amour en Fleurs.** In this unpretentious little roadhouse, Madame Trésor Amanthe prepares spicy blaffs and a tasty blend of conch, octopus, rice and beans, and court bouillon. Don't miss the homemade coconut ice cream. The place is close to Club Med and very popular with its guests. The weekend-night live comedy offered here is usually awful. *Ste-Anne, tel. 590/88–23–72. No credit cards.*

$ **Le Sable Blanc.** St-François' rue Front-de-Mer teems with affordable eateries. Fishermen literally cruise by displaying their daily catch. Ask to sit upstairs for the ocean views. Le Sable Blanc has more ambience than its neighbors, with bright madras linens and local crafts giving it a cheery touch. The prices are sensational. Choose from six three-course menus ranging in price from 75F to 140F. The solid Creole menu includes the usual standards, from chicken colombo to crayfish fricassee. Live music is a draw weekend nights. *Rue Front-de-Mer, St-François, tel. 590/88–55–95. MC, V. No dinner Sun.*

¢–$ **La Frite Dorée.** Construct a rickety wood-and-reed shack, string up a few green Christmas lights for decor, add a couple of African masks, place some beach umbrellas out front and *voilà*, you have a restaurant. Okay, so the silverware is bent, mangy mutts coming in from the rain nose your feet, and the accras can be oily. But menus at 60F and 75F, a marvelous lobster at 100F, a warm welcome, a lively clientele, and good takeout make this a best bet. *Rte. des Hotels, Pointe de la Verdure, Gosier, no phone. No credit cards.*

¢–$ **Le Normandie.** Don't be put off by the dark, almost seedy interior of this venerable hotel on Pointe-à-Pitre's main square. Instead, sit outside on the terrace, which makes for wonderful people-watching. The restaurant is quite a bargain for lunch (slightly more expensive in the evening). For 40F you can relish an appetizer and entrée, such as roast pork or brochettes of shrimp. There are also menus at 69F and 99F that include dessert and more exotic entrée choices. Pizzas and pastas are other good buys. You can stay here in one of nine air-conditioned rooms, each with a private bath, for about 350F. *Hotel*

Normandie, 14 pl. de la Victoire, Pointe-à-Pitre, tel. 590/82–37–15. MC, V.

¢ **La Paillotte.** La Paillotte couldn't be humbler: a thatched hut, as the name promises, with sand floors and white plastic tables. It offers a delicious 140F lobster menu, and fish and chicken can be had for half that. A beach-combing ambience prevails, with French youths smoking Gauloises and tracing each other's names in the sand with their toes. *Pointe des Chateaux, tel. 590/88–63–61. No credit cards.*

¢ **Les Pieds dans l'Eau.** At the left of the UCPA windsurfing center is this simple, bare-bones restaurant facing the water. Seafoam green walls and a few flowerpots keep it from seeming too dreary. The menu is varied, with Creole dishes, salads, and fish. If you want to splurge on lobster (100F menu), the prices here are lower than anywhere else on the island. For 50F you get a full meal of conch creole or pork colombo, served with heaping helpings of rice, accras, and salad. *Rue du Front-de-Mer, St-François, tel. 590/88–66–02. No credit cards.*

¢ **Pizzeria Napoli.** You'll find this casual eatery on the left-hand side of the main road as you enter Gosier. Sit on the terrace and order up one of the large pizzas, or try one of the fresh pâtés. *Montauban, Gosier, tel. 590/84–32–49. No credit cards.*

Basse-Terre

$$ ★ **Le Rocher de Malendure.** The setting alone—a flower-decked terrace on a bluff overlooking Malendure Bay and Pigeon Island—makes this restaurant worth a special trip for lunch. The best choices on the menu are the fresh fish, but there are also meat dishes, including veal in raspberry vinaigrette and tournedos in three sauces. Even if you don't want a large meal, stop here for a drink and perhaps a plate of accras. The owners, Monsieur and Madame Nouy, also rent out five bungalows at very reasonable prices. *Malendure Beach, Bouillante, tel. 590/98–70–84. DC, MC, V. Weekend reservations advised. No dinner Sun.*

$–$$ ★ **Chez Clara.** Clara Laseur, who gave up a jazz-dancing career in Paris to run her family's seaside restaurant with her mother, dishes out delicious Creole meals. Seating is on the inviting terrace of a gorgeous Creole house adorned with lacy gingerbread trim. Clara takes the orders (her English is excellent), and the place is often so crowded (even in the off-season) with her friends and fans that you may have to wait at the octagonal wooden bar before being seated. The food is worth the wait, however—check the daily specials listed on the blackboard, for example the succulent octopus or sublime ginger carambola sorbet. *Ste-Rose, tel. 590/28–72–99. Reservations advised. MC, V. Closed Wed. and Oct. No dinner Sun.*

$–$$ **La Touna.** If you can't get a table at Le Rocher de Malendure, proceed down the shore to the casual La Touna. Waves wash the edge of this open-fronted restaurant, where a huge lobster sculpture stares down at diners. The fresh fare includes home-smoked local fish, caught by the owner, served with Creole or French sauces. Finish your meal with scrumptious homemade nougat ice cream. *Pigeon, Bouillante, tel. 590/78–70–10. MC, V. Closed Mon. No dinner Sun.*

$–$$ ★ **Le Karacoli.** Lucienne Salcede's rustic seaside restaurant is well established and well regarded. It has its feet firmly planted in the sands of Grande-Anse, a great place for a swim, and Lucienne won't mind if you come in shirtless off the beach. She'll even graciously direct you to a shower (really!), so you don't track up the gleaming tile floors. Order a bottle of muscadet and some delicious Creole specialties, and you're set for a perfect afternoon. Creole boudin is a hot item here (in more ways than one), as are accras. Other offerings include coquilles, court bouillon, fried chicken, and turtle ragout. For dessert, try the banana flambé, heavily perfumed with rum, followed by a homemade *digestif* (after-dinner liqueur). *Grande-Anse, north of Deshaies, tel. 590/28–41–17. MC, V. No dinner Sat.–Tues.*

$ **Chez Jackye.** Jacqueline Cabrion serves Creole and African dishes in her cheerful plant-filled, seaside restaurant. Creole boudin is a house specialty, as are lobster (grilled, vinaigrette, or fricassee), fried crayfish, clam blaff, and goat in port sauce. There's also a wide selection of omelets, sandwiches, and salads. For dessert, try peach melba or banana flambé. The 120F menu will have you waddling out happily. *Anse Guyonneau, Rue de la Bataille, Pte. Noire, tel. 590/98–06–98. AE, MC, V. Closed Sun.*

$ **Les Gommiers.** A changing menu here may list crayfish soup, octopus fricassee, pork chops with banana, goat colombo, paella, and grilled entrecôte. Banana splits and profiteroles are on the dessert list. For lunch, salade Niçoise and other light dishes are offered. Fixed menus at 70F and 100F are sensational values. Lovely peacock chairs grace the bar, and polished wood furnishings and potted plants fill the dining room. *Rue Baudot, Pte. Noire, tel. 590/98–01–79. MC, V. No dinner Sun.–Tues.*

Iles des Saintes, Terre-de-Haut

$$ ★ **Le Banc de Sable.** Jacques and Odette Chan run this superb restaurant. Dine on a charming open-air terrace built into the old stone house or in the tiny garden overlooking the sea. Jacques' father is Chinese and his mother Breton; he artfully blends their native cuisines in such mouthwatering dishes as chicken in ginger, duck in honey, and a *panaché de poissons* (a mix of the day's fresh catch, perhaps tuna, kingfish, and snapper) in sea urchin sauce. For dessert, try the *tarte crouistillante* (crusty pastry brimming with custard and tropical fruits in a passion-fruit coulis). *Bourg, tel. 590/99–54–76. MC, V. No dinner Sun.*

$–$$ **La Saladerie.** This delightful seaside terrace restaurant serves a sophisticated mélange of Creole and Continental dishes. Begin with rilletes of smoked fish, crabes farcis, or a warm crepe filled with lobster, conch, octopus, and fish. House specialties include an assortment of smoked fish served cold and stuffed fish fillet served in a white-wine sauce. The wine list is pleasantly varied. This is the place for a light meal with a fabulous view. *Anse Mirre, tel. 590/99–50–92. MC, V.*

$–$$ ★ **Relais des Iles.** Select your lobster from the vivier and enjoy the splendid view from this hilltop eatery, while your meal is expertly prepared by Bernard Mathieu. Interesting preparations of local vegetables—christophines au gratin, breadfruit purée—accompany each entrée. For dessert, try the melt-in-your-mouth white chocolate mousse. The wine list is excellent. *Rte. de Pompierre, tel. 590/99–53–04. Reservations advised in high season. No credit cards.*

¢–$ **Le Triangle.** Brothers Réné and Pedro Foy turn out delicious conch or octopus fricassee, grilled dorado or kingfish, and other Creole dishes at this breezy seaside terrace adorned with flowerpots and madras linens. *Fond de Curé, Bourg, tel. 590/99–50–50. MC, V. Closed Sun.*

Marie Galante

$ **Le Touloulou.** The ultracasual Le Touloulou, set on the sensuous curve of Petite Anse beach, serves sumptuous seafood at down-to-earth prices. Chef Patrice Pillet's standouts include conch *feuilleté* (in puff pastry) with yams and the very local *bébelé* (tripe with breadfruit, plantains and dumplings). There are good menus at 60F, 90F, and 140F. *Petite Anse, tel. 590/97–32–63. MC, V. Closed Mon. and mid-Sept.–mid-Oct.*

Lodging

Resort hotels on the beach start at about $150 a night here; most of them are clustered around Gosier, Bas-du-Fort, and, more recently, Ste-Anne and St-François. Properties tend to be on the beach, with restaurants and shops within walking distance; a car is necessary only if you wish to explore the rest of the island. Many of the affordable large hotels belong to French chains and cater to tour groups. Expect friendly service but not necessarily individuality or charm. Avoid the temptingly priced hotels in Pointe-Pitre, which are actually overpriced considering the noisy, musty, even seedy accommodations. The lone exception is the **St. John** (tel. 590/82–51–57) in the relatively new cruise terminal. For just under $100, you get a tiny room with air-conditioning, cable TV, safe, and phone, whose art deco touches and dark wood furnishings deliberately evoke a cabin on an elegant cruise ship.

Guadeloupe also has many small hotels (*Relais Créoles*) in the $100-a-night range. These are usually owner-managed, often away from the beach, and without the amenities—tennis courts, pools, room service—of large hotels. Less expensive still are the *gîtes*, which are small apartments, cottages, and rooms in private houses. These can be rented through a central agency (*see* Home and Apartment Rental, *below*). Like Relais Créoles, gîtes tend to be off the beaten track and removed from beaches.

Highly recommended lodgings are indicated by a star ★.

Category	Cost*
$$	$150–$225
$	$75–$150
¢	under $75

**All prices are for a standard double room for two, excluding a* taxe de séjour, *which varies from hotel to hotel, and a 10%–15% service charge. To estimate rates for hotels offering MAP, add about $25–$35 per person per day to the above price ranges. To estimate rates for all-inclusives, add about $40 per person per day.*

Hotels, Resorts, and Inns

$$ **Canella Beach.** In this 150-room resort built to resemble a Creole village, you have a choice of single-level and duplex studios and junior and duplex suites. Each has its own terrace or balcony with a small kitchenette. Ask for a room on the top floor for the best views. Decor is a pleasant departure from pastels, with earth tones complementing the white tile floors and rattan furnishings. Each unit has a phone, and you are assigned your own phone number when you check in, so calls don't have to go through the front desk. Unlike the other Pointe de la Verdure hotels, the Canella Beach enjoys its own semiprivate cove. Water sports are free, and there is a beach bar for refreshments. Set back from the beach are the swimming pool and tennis courts. The staff, with inspiration from Jean-Pierre Reuff, the general manager, is enthusiastic (and sometimes disorganized) and enjoys speaking English. Another plus is the Verandah restaurant, which offers dining indoors with air-conditioning or outdoors cooled by the sea breezes. The menu includes Creole and French dishes; the salad with warm goat cheese makes an excellent light meal or an appetizer. *Pointe de la Verdure, 97190 Gosier, tel. 590/90–44–00 or 800/233–9815, fax 590/90–44–44; in NY, 212/251–1800. 146 rooms. Facilities: restaurant, pool, 4 tennis courts, water sports, excursions arranged to nearby islands. AE, DC, MC, V. EP, MAP.*

$$ **Cap Sud Caraibes.** This is a tiny Relais Créole on a country road between Gosier and Ste-Anne, just a five-minute walk from a quiet beach. English is not the first language here, but every attempt is made to make you feel at home. Individually decorated rooms are air-conditioned, and each has a balcony and an enormous bath. There's a big kitchen that guests are welcome to share. The nearest grocery store is a five-minute walk away. *Gosier 97190, tel. 590/85–96–02, fax 590/85–80–39. 12 rooms. Facilities: bar, snorkeling equipment, airport transfers, dry-cleaning and laundry facilities. AE, MC, V. CP.*

$$ **Club Méditerranée La Caravelle.** This version of the well-known club chain has air-conditioned twin-bed rooms, some with balconies, and 50 secluded acres at the western end of a magnificent white-sand

beach. Nice extras include a volleyball court, calisthenics classes, and a French-English language lab, where you can take French classes and use a tape recorder and headphones to practice. The property draws a fun-loving, younger crowd, most of whom are from France, and serves as the home port for Club Med's sailing cruises. *Ste-Anne 97180, tel. 590/88–21–00 or 800/258–2633, fax 590/88–06–06. 275 rooms. Facilities: restaurant, pub, boutiques, 6 lighted tennis courts (with pro), pool, water-sports center. AE. All-inclusive (drinks extra).*

$$ **Fort Royal Touring Club.** This is by far the most elegant, comfortable lodging on Basse-Terre. The modern white structure overlooks two pristine beaches. Spacious rooms all have TV, air-conditioning, phone, hair dryer, and terrace or balcony with sea views. White tile floors contrast nicely with azure fabrics, and there are handsome wicker and rattan furnishings and mahogany beds. The hotel offers tours into the National Park and plenty of activities, most of them beach-related. *Pointe du Petit Bas-Vent, Deshaies 97126, tel. 590/25–50–00, fax 590/25–50–01. 198 rooms. Facilities: restaurant, bar, 2 pools, 4 lighted tennis courts, 4-hole minigolf, water-sports center including dive shop. AE, MC, V. EP, CP, MAP.*

$$ **Golf Marine Club Hotel.** Near the town's newer shops and restaurants, this small hotel offers a more moderately priced alternative to Hamak and Le Méridien. But the hotel's name overpromises: It is not a club, the municipal golf course is across the street, and it has neither marina nor beach. You must walk two blocks to the nearest public beach. The rooms, however, are pristine and pleasingly decorated in soft blues. Each has a balcony, but those facing the street tend to be noisy, so reserve one looking onto the gardens. A third of the rooms—called mezzanine suites—are out of our $$ price range. On the patio terrace facing the small pool is a relaxed, informal restaurant where meals are served. *Av. de l'Europe, B.P. 204, St-François 97118, tel. 590/88–60–60, fax 590/88–68–98. 42 rooms, 32 suites. Facilities: restaurant, pool, 2 tennis courts. AE, DC, MC, V. CP, MAP.*

$$ **La Toubana.** Red-roof bungalows are sprinkled on a hilltop overlooking the Caravelle Peninsula, arguably the best beach on the island and the most compelling reason to stay here. The bungalows are air-conditioned, and all rooms have private bath, phone, kitchenette, and an ocean view (those with a partial view are cheaper). Despite a recent renovation, the rooms are unexceptional; the weathered wood, simple rattan furnishings, and floral linens give them a rustic feel. The pool is rather small. There's evening entertainment at the dependable French-Creole restaurant, whose specialty, lobster, unfortunately exceeds the $$ range. Pets are welcome. *Box 63, Ste-Anne 97180, tel. 590/88–25–78 or 800/223–9815, fax 590/88–38–90. 32 bungalows. Facilities: restaurant, bar, pool, tennis court, water-sports center. AE, DC, V. CP, MAP.*

$$ **Le Domaine de l'Anse des Rochers.** Although its standard rates exceed our $$ range, package deals are common at this large resort. Its 27 acres are spread along the coast a few miles from St-François. Rooms are either in Creole-style buildings or 34 villas that climb the rise behind them. All rooms have terra-cotta floors, rich russet-patterned bedspreads, ceramic lamps, and original touches like antique radios. Bathrooms are merely functional, but terraces and kitchenettes are pluses. The formal restaurant offers à la carte dining, but most evenings, guests attend the theme buffet dinner at the Blanc Mangé restaurant, where performers entertain on the large piazza. Across the piazza is an open-sided disco, good for late-night revelry. The complex is so large that the trek to the man-made beach at one end can prompt you to use the car. And though Anse des Rochers may not have the best beach on the island, it does boast the largest swimming pool. Dramatically designed, the pool creates the effect of water cascading into the sea. *Anse des Rochers, St-François 97118, tel. 590/93–90–00, fax 590/93–91–00. 356 rooms. Facilities: 2*

restaurants, beach snack bar, pool, disco, minimart, gift shop, car rental, 2 lighted tennis courts, archery, conference rooms. AE, DC, MC, V. EP, CP, MAP.

$$ **Relais du Moulin.** A restored windmill serves as the reception room for this Relais Creole tucked in Châteaubrun, near Ste-Anne. A spiral staircase leads up to a TV/reading room, from which there is a splendid view. Accommodations are in air-conditioned bungalows. Rooms are immaculate but claustrophobic, somehow managing to pack in twin beds, small terraces, and kitchenettes. The hotel is on a small hill, and there is usually a pleasant, cooling breeze. The restaurant, overlooking the restored windmill, is rather expensive but worth the splurge. By day, sunlight floods through large windows, while at night candlelight flickers on crisp white cloths. The nouvelle cuisine served here includes the house specialty: grouper and lobster served with Creole sauce or stuffed with fresh homemade pâté. Crème caramel in coconut sauce is among the sumptuous desserts. A *menu de dégustation* for 220F offers seven courses and is a good way to sample Creole cooking. The beach is a 10-minute hike away. It's best to have your own rental car; bikes are available. The owner-manager speaks English. *Châteaubrun, Ste-Anne 97180, tel. 590/88–23–96 or 800/223–9815, fax 590/88–03–92. 40 rooms. Facilities: restaurant, bar, pool, tennis court, archery. AE, MC, V. CP, MAP.*

$$ **Tropical Club Hotel.** Great windsurfing and swimming are big draws for this hotel on the northeastern coast of Grand-Terre. The golden beach catches cooling trade winds from the Atlantic, but a reef about 100 yards offshore keeps the waves gentle. Set back from the beach is an almond-shaped pool, adjacent to an open-sided dining room that serves French and Creole fare. The guest rooms are in three buildings on a rise at the back of the main hotel building. Each room has a double bed, two bunk beds, TV, air-conditioning, telephone, and fan. The bunk beds are in an entrance annex—ideal for children (those under 21 stay free). The bathroom has a shower only, and the toilet is in a separate area. Every room has a private balcony with a small kitchenette, table and chairs, and a view of the sea. The best views are from the rooms on the top (third) floor. The decor, in tired rattan and seafoam colors, won't win any awards, and the setting is remote, but the property compensates with a host of activities and an energetic staff. *Le Moule, 97160, tel. 590/93–97–97, fax 590/93–97–00. 72 rooms. Facilities: restaurant, bar, pool, windsurfing, pétanque area, gym, boutique, 3 lighted tennis courts nearby. AE, MC, V. CP, MAP.*

$–$$ **L'Orchidée.** Right in the center of Gosier, this hotel is perfect for the businessperson who does not need resort facilities or a beach. Its spotless, air-conditioned studios have a small kitchenette, a balcony, and a direct-dial phone. The decor consists of dark-wood furnishings, teal fabrics, and sparkling white tile floors. On the ground floor a small shop serves morning coffee. Owner-manager Madame Karine Chenaf speaks English and can help you arrange your day. *Blvd. Général de Gaulle 32, Gosier 97130, tel. 590/84–54–20, fax 590/84–54–90. 21 rooms, 3 apartments. Facilities: dining room, boutique, indoor parking, free membership in local recreation center with pool, tennis, water sports. MC, V. EP.*

$ ★ **Auberge de la Distillerie.** This homey country inn is an excellent choice for those who want to be close to the national park and its hiking trails. The 12 rooms in the 19th-century house are individually and charmingly decorated, with wicker furnishings, tile floors, wood beams, ceramic lamps, and local artworks. Apricot, mint, olive, silver, and rose are the dominant colors of the decor. All have air-conditioning, TV, phone, and terrace; some have a fridge. The slightly larger bungalows have larger terraces and open onto the extravagantly overgrown gardens. There's also a rustic wood chalet that sleeps two to four people. The restaurant, noted for its delectable Creole cuisine, is built around the partially enclosed pool. Boat trips on the Lézarde River can be arranged; you can also swim in the river. *Vernou 97170, Petit-Bourg, tel. 590/94–25–91 or 800/223–9815, fax 590/94–11–91. 14 units. Facilities: restaurant, bar, piano bar, pool, bakery. AE, MC, V. EP, CP, MAP.*

$ **Domaine de Malendure.** These peach houses with mint roofs climb the side of a hill and have sensational views of the Ilet Pigeon. It's a pretty steep climb to the units farthest from the reception building. Units have a simple, rustic decor; stucco walls and terra-cotta floors are accented by blond wood and pine furnishings and floral fabrics. All units are air-conditioned and have a balcony, phone, TV, and minibar. It's a five-minute drive down to the beach, but most guests prefer the large pool with its sweeping views of the bay. *Morne Tarare-Pigeon, Bouillante 97132, tel. 590/98–92–12, fax 590/98–47–00. 44 rooms. Facilities: restaurant, bar, pool. MC, V. CP, MAP.*

$ **Domaine de Petite Anse.** The red-roofed ocher buildings of this resort spill down lushly landscaped hills overlooking the ocean. The location is perfect: You're near a beach and close to the National Park. Accommodations are either in hotel rooms or bungalows and are decorated with dark rattan and bright floral fabrics. Rooms are simple and small, but well-outfitted with TV, phone, air-conditioning, safe, and fridge. Be sure to request one with a balcony and sea view (they're the same price). Bungalows have a terrace, full bath, and kitchenette in addition to the amenities listed above. This is one of Guadeloupe's premier spots for an active vacation, and very popular with young French couples and families. The resort is noted for its dive shop and nature tours. The staff, while friendly, speaks limited English. *Plage de Petite Anse, Monchy, Bouillante 97125, tel. 590/98–78–78, fax, 590/98–80–28. 135 rooms, 40 bungalows. Facilities: restaurant, bar, boutique, pool, catamaran, archery, volleyball, water-sports center including sea kayaking and dive shop. AE, DC, MC, V. EP.*

$ **Grand Anse Hotel.** Less than a mile from a black-sand beach and offering spectacular mountain views, this Relais Creole is a good choice for nature lovers. It's also near the ferry landing from which you leave for Les Saintes. Air-conditioned bungalows have shower bath, phone, TV, refrigerator, and small balcony. The heavy polished wood furnishings should achieve antique status in a few years. Water sports and nature hikes can be arranged. *Trois-Rivières 97114, tel. 590/92–90–47, fax 590/92–93–69. 16 bungalows. Facilities: restaurant, bar. MC, V. CP, MAP.*

$ ★ **La Sucrerie du Comté.** The ruins and rusting equipment (including a locomotive) of a 19th-century sugar factory litter the lawns and gardens here, like hulking abstract sculptures. In fact, it is the historically significant grounds, along with the attractive public areas, that are the main attraction of this resort. The interiors of the fine restaurant and bar re-create gracious plantation living, with wood beams, stone walls, lace lamp shades, and towering floral arrangements. The nearest beach is a 10-minute stroll through a tangle of greenery. Twenty-six bungalows duplicate the gingerbread architecture of the turn of the century. Inside, the air-conditioned rooms are small but pretty, with white tile floors, peach walls, and aqua and pale green linens. The enthusiastic French owner, Monsieur Girard Jean-Luc, will have you speaking French in no time, as you try the homemade fruit punches lined up in great jars on the bar in the evening. *Comté de Lohéac, Ste-Rose 97115, tel. 590/28–60–17, fax 590/28–65–63. 50 rooms. Facilities: restaurant, bar, pool, tennis court. AE, DC, MC, V. CP, MAP.*

$ **Marifa.** The studios and duplexes of this spanking new (1994) establishment are appealing and sunny, brightly decorated in mango and turquoise. All are air-conditioned and have a kitchenette, balcony, TV, phone, and safe, as well as nice extras, like a hair dryer in the bathroom. There are two drawbacks: The staff speaks little English, and you need a car to reach the nearest beach or decent restaurant (at press time management was planning to add an eatery by the end of the 1995/96 season). However, the rates are excellent, especially for the duplexes, which can sleep two couples or a family and still make the $ category. *Domaine de Mare Galliard, Gosier 97190, tel. 590/85-96-31, fax 590/85-93-67. 24 units. Facilities: bar, pool. AE, MC, V. CP.*

$ **Mini-Beach.** This small hotel, at the northern end of Ste-Anne's beach, has a welcoming central living and dining area with wicker chairs, hanging plants, and an open-hearth kitchen. There are six simple rooms with private baths and three one-room bungalows. One bungalow is at the water's edge, another is on the beach near the main house, the third is in the gardens. All are very simply furnished, but more than adequate for a beach-combing life. The restaurant is noted for its Creole *cuisine raffiné* (stylish takes on traditional dishes); there is a popular piano concert every Thursday. Ste-Anne's restaurants are nearby. *BP 77, Ste-Anne 97180, tel. 590/88-21-13, fax 590/88-19-29. 9 rooms. Facilities: restaurant. MC, V. CP.*

¢–$ **Les Flamboyants.** This small hotel is located just outside Gosier, with spectacular views from the promontory over the sea and Ilet du Gosier. Choose between rooms in the main building, where *petit déjeuner* (breakfast) is included in the room rate, or pay 40F more for a room with kitchen in one of the bungalows (breakfast not included). You can walk to Gosier restaurants and stores and to the beach. *Chemin Ste-Anne, Gosier 97190, tel. 590/84-14-11, fax 590/84-53-56. 6 rooms, 5 bungalow rooms. Facilities: pool. MC, V. EP, CP.*

¢ **Centre UCPA.** Most of the guests at this small, clean hotel come from France on package vacations, and all of them seem to be windsurfing fanatics: You'll feel most at home if you speak French and share their enthusiasm for the sport. The hotel is off a small beach, with reefs offshore and ideal sailing conditions. Creature comforts are few; fellow guests, young and energetic. *Rue du Front-de-Mer, St-François, tel. 590/88-64-80. 24 rooms. Facilities: restaurant, windsurfing. No credit cards. EP.*

¢ **La Barrière de Corail.** Be prepared for spartan rooms at budget prices. This series of bungalows, most with kitchenettes, offers good value. The beach is only a few yards away, and the shops and restaurants of Ste-Anne are within easy walking distance. *Durivage, Ste-Anne 97180; for reservations, write: Mme. Giroux, MABC, rue Béban, Pointe-à-Pitre 97110, tel. 590/88-20-03. 14 bungalows. MC, V. EP.*

Iles des Saintes

$–$$ ★ **Village Creole.** Baths by Courrèges, dishwashers, freezers, satellite TV, videos, and international direct-dial phones are among the amenities in this apartment hotel. Somewhat isolated, it appeals to the likes of models and high-powered business titans looking for a peaceful retreat. Units are duplexes, with bedrooms upstairs and kitchen/dining areas down. They're decorated simply but chicly, with white tile floors, unvarnished rattan, powder blue accents and framed posters. While the units are identical in size and decor, those on the hill with garden view are the less expensive. Ghyslain Laps, the English-speaking owner, will help you whip up meals in the kitchen. If you'd prefer not to cook, he can provide you with a cook and housekeeper for an extra charge. The waters off the small beach are usually too rough for swimming. *Pte. Coquelet 97137, Terre-de-Haut, tel. 590/99-53-83 (telex 919671), fax 590/99-55-55. 22 duplexes. Facilities: airport shuttle service, daily maid service, scooter and boat rentals, water-sports center. MC, V. EP.*

$ **Bois Joli.** A beautiful setting, right on the bay overlooking the "sugarloaf," is the attraction here. Most of the rooms, either in the inn or one of the bungalows, are air-conditioned but rather drab. The hotel restaurant serves wonderful clams in Creole sauce on a terrace that overlooks the sea. Water sports can be arranged, and the Anse Crawen nudist beach is a five-minute walk away. Pets are allowed. *Terre-de-Haut 97137, tel. 590/99-50-38 or 800/223-9815, fax 590/*

99-55-05. 29 rooms. Facilities: restaurant, bar, pool, airport transfers. MC, V. EP, MAP.

$ ★ **l'Auberge les Petits Saints aux Anacardies.** Ten air-conditioned rooms are tucked into this inn, which is trimmed with trellises and topped by dormers. Each room has twin beds, a phone, and casement windows that open to a splendid view of gardens, hills, and the bay. Some also have sea views (Room 2's is extraordinary), and most have a private bath. A glorious clutter greets you in the reception area, crammed with antiques and objets d'art culled from owners Jean-Paul Coles and Didier Spindler's world travels—porcelain lions, birdcages, cigar-store Indians. Furnishings are a similarly odd assortment of antiques. There's a one-bedroom bungalow next to the main house. Steak au poivre, grilled lobster, and smoked local fish are among the restaurant's offerings. The hotel's private boat makes excursions around the islands. This is one of the most distinctive properties in the archipelago. *La Savane 97137, Terre-de-Haut, tel. 590/99-50-99, fax 590/99-54-51. 10 rooms (9 with private bath). Facilities: restaurant, bar, pool, sauna. AE, MC, V. CP, MAP.*

Home and Apartment Rental For information about villas, apartments, and private rooms in modest houses, contact **Gîtes de France** (Association Guadeloupéenne des Gîtes de France, Office du Tourisme de la Guadeloupe, B.P. 759, Pointe-à-Pitre 97110, tel. 590/91-64-33, fax 590/91-45-40). Rentals average $400 a week and usually require a minimum stay of one week. For additional information about apartment-style accommodations, contact the **ANTRE Association** (tel. 590/88-53-09). You might also consider the plain but fully outfitted rustic wooden bungalows at the **Centre de Vacances de C.G.O.S.H.** (Rivières-Sens, Gourbeyre 97113, tel. 590/81-36-12, fax 590/81-71-41). Local, then foreign, members of the hospital social workers' organization that runs this complex get first crack (and best rates), but nonmembers still pay only $500 a week to stay here. There is a restaurant, boutique, child-care center, and activities desk.

Campgrounds Camping is not well developed on Guadeloupe. The island has two campgrounds with tent sites and shower and toilet facilities: **Camping La Traverse** (Anse de la Grande Plaine, Pointe-Noire 97116, tel. 590/98-21-23) and **Camping Les Sables D'Or** (Plage de Grand Anse, Deshaies 97126, tel. 590/28-44-60).

Off-Season Bets Hotel prices drop by approximately 40% after April 15 and remain bargains until December 15. Among hotels that become more affordable then are **Auberge de la Vielle-Tour** (Gosier 97190, tel. 590/84-23-23, fax 590/84-33-43), with its own small beach, a swimming pool, and some of the best French cuisine on the island; and the action-packed **Le Méridien St-François** (St-François 97118, tel. 590/88-51-00, fax 590/88-40-71), on the beach in St-François.

The Arts and Nightlife

Cole Porter notwithstanding, Guadeloupeans maintain that the beguine began here (the Martinicans make the same claim for their island). Many of the resort hotels feature dinner dancing, as well as entertainment by steel bands and folkloric groups.

Discos A mixed crowd of locals and tourists frequents the discos. Night owls should note that carousing is not cheap. Most discos charge an admission of at least $8, which includes one drink. Drinks cost about $5 each. Some of the enduring hot spots are **Le Foufou** (Hotel Frankel, Bas-du-Fort, tel. 590/84-35-59), the very Parisian **Elysée Matignon** (Rte. des Hôtels, Bas-du-Fort, tel. 590/90-89-05), **Le Caraibe** (Salako, Gosier, tel. 590/84-22-22), **New Land** (Rte. Riviera, Gosier, tel. 590/84-37-91), **Caraibes 2** (Carrefour de Blanchard, Bas-du-Fort, tel. 590/90-97-16), **La Victoria** (Rte. de Bas-du-Fort, tel. 590/90-97-76), and **New Land** (Rte. Riviera, Gosier, tel. 590/84-

37–91). The only disco of note on Basse Terre is the **Espace Vaneau** (Mahaut, Bouillante, tel. 590/98–25–72).

Bars and Nightclubs Generally, nightclubs don't charge a cover, but they can be expensive. **Le Jardin Brésilien** (Marina, Bas-du-Fort, tel. 590/90–99–31) has light music in a relaxed setting on the waterfront. There's nightly entertainment at the **Lele Bar** (Le Méridien, St-François, tel. 590/88–51–00) and **Au Bar du Minuit** (Montauban, Gosier, tel. 590/84–53–77). **Le Figuier Vert** (Mare Galliard, Gosier, tel. 590/85–85–51) offers live jazz Friday and Saturday nights. Right at the pier in Bourg, Terre de Haut, sultry Brazilian chanteuse Nilce Laps holds sway nightly at **Nilce's** (no phone) in a charming waterfront bistro decorated with assorted authentic bistro antiques. Locals also congregate at the **Cafe de la Marina** (tel. 590/99–53–78) after the daytrippers leave; there's always someone playing the Santois version of a bagpipe.

Casinos There are two casinos on the island. Both have American-style roulette, blackjack, and chemin de fer. The legal age is 21. Admission is $10, and you'll need a photo ID. Jacket and tie are not required, but "proper attire" means no shorts. The **Casino de Gosier les Bains** (Gosier, tel. 590/84–18–33) has a bar and restaurant and is open Monday–Saturday 9 PM–dawn. Slot machines open at 10 AM. The **Casino de St-François** (Marina, St-François, tel. 590/88–41–31) has a snack bar and nightclub and is open Tuesday–Sunday 9 PM–3 AM.

14 Jamaica

Updated by Melissa Rivers

The third-largest island in the Caribbean (after Cuba and Puerto Rico), the English-speaking nation of Jamaica enjoys a considerable self-sufficiency based on tourism, agriculture, and mining. Its physical attractions include jungle mountaintops, clear waterfalls, and unforgettable beaches, yet the country's greatest resource may be the Jamaicans themselves. Although 95% of the population trace their bloodlines to Africa, their national origins lie in Great Britain, the Middle East, India, China, Germany, Portugal, South America, and many of the other islands in the Caribbean. Their cultural life is a wealthy one; the music, art, and cuisine of Jamaica are vibrant, with a spirit easy to sense but as hard to describe as the rhythms of reggae or the flourish of the streetwise patois.

In addition to the pleasure capitals of the north coast—Montego Bay and Ocho Rios—Jamaica has a real capital in Kingston. For all its congestion and for all the disparity between city life and the bikinis and parasails to the north, Kingston is the true heart and head of the island. This is the place where politics, literature, music, and art wrestle for acceptance in the largest English-speaking city south of Miami, its actual population of nearly 1 million bolstered by the emotional membership of virtually all Jamaicans.

The first people known to have reached Jamaica were the Arawaks, gentle Indians who paddled their canoes from the Orinoco region of South America about a thousand years after the death of Christ. Then, in 1494, Christopher Columbus stepped ashore at what is now called Discovery Bay. Having spent four centuries on the island, the Arawaks had little notion that his feet on their sand would mean their extinction within 50 years.

The Spaniards were never impressed with Jamaica; their searches found no precious metals, and they let the island fester in poverty for 161 years. When 5,000 British soldiers and sailors appeared in Kingston Harbor in 1655, the Spaniards did not put up a fight. The arrival of the English, and the three centuries of rule that followed, provided Jamaica with the surprisingly genteel underpinnings of its present life—and the rousing pirate tradition, fueled by rum, that enlivened a long period of Caribbean history.

The very British 18th century was a time of prosperity in Jamaica. This was the age of the sugar baron, who ruled his plantation great house and made the island the largest sugar-producing colony in the world. Because sugar fortunes were built on slave labor, however, production became less profitable when the Jamaican slave trade was abolished in 1807, and slavery was ended in 1838.

As was often the case in colonies, a national identity came to supplant allegiance to the British in the hearts and minds of Jamaicans. This new identity was given official recognition on August 6, 1962, when Jamaica became an independent nation with loose ties to the Commonwealth.

In recent years, Jamaica has become synonymous with the all-inclusive resort phenomenon: Pay one price for a hassle-free vacation. Many of these properties are luxurious and high-priced, but the more affordable establishments are a smart choice for active travelers wanting to take advantage of the many sports and other activities offered at all-inclusives. If you can do without sports galore and bountiful cocktails, you'll save more by staying at one of the island's small inns, most of which are right on the beach or offer complimentary shuttle service. If you're willing to rough it, Jamaica has extensive camping facilities, good vantage points for appreciating the island's natural splendor. Fine local eateries help you avoid overpriced hotel restaurants; look for "jerk centers" in every sizable town.

What It Will Cost These sample prices, meant only as a general guide, are for high season. A $ hotel room on the beach is about $100; a $$ all-inclusive resort can be as much as $350 for a couple. Dinner at a $ restaurant, including one cocktail, costs about $20. A jerk pork and chicken lunch is around $5. A rum punch or glass of wine is about $2.50; a Red Stripe beer, $2. Rental car prices here are on the high side—about $80 a day. A taxi ride from the airport to your hotel can cost anywhere from $10 to $30; within town, figure on $1–$5. It's about $10 for a great-house tour, around $3 for admission to a natural attraction. A single-tank dive averages $50; snorkel equipment rents for about $5.

Before You Go

Tourist Information Contact the **Jamaica Tourist Board** (801 2nd Ave., 20th Floor, New York, NY 10017, tel. 212/856–9727, 800/233–4582; fax 212/856–9730; 500 N. Michigan Ave., Suite 1030, Chicago, IL 60611, tel. 312/527–1296, fax 312/527–1472; 1320 S. Dixie Hwy., Suite 1100, Coral Gables, FL 33146, tel. 305/665–0557, fax 305/666–7239; 8214 Westchester, Suite 500, Dallas, TX 75225, tel. 214/361–8778, fax 214/361–7049; 3440 Wilshire Blvd., Suite 1207, Los Angeles, CA 90010, tel. 213/384–1123, fax 213/384–1123. In Canada: 1 Eglinton Ave. E, Suite 616, Toronto, Ontario M4P 3A1, tel. 416/482–7850, fax 416/482–1730. In the United Kingdom: 1–2 Prince Consort Rd., London, SW7 2BZ, tel. 0171/224–0505, fax 0171/224–0551).

Arriving and Departing

By Plane **Donald Sangster International Airport** in Montego Bay (tel. 809/952–3009) is the most efficient point of entry for visitors destined for Montego Bay, Ocho Rios, Runaway Bay, and Negril. **Norman Manley International Airport** in Kingston (tel. 809/924–8231) is better for visitors to the capital or Port Antonio. **Trans Jamaica Airlines** (tel. 809/952–5401 in Montego Bay, 809/924–8850 in Kingston) provides shuttle services on the island. Be sure to reconfirm your departing flight a full 72 hours in advance.

Air Jamaica (tel. 800/523–5585) and **American Airlines** (tel. 212/619–6991 or 800/433–7300) fly nonstop daily from Raleigh-Durham and Miami. Air Jamaica provides the most frequent service from U.S. cities, including Atlanta, Philadelphia, Baltimore, and Orlando. American also flies in from San Juan. **Continental** (tel. 800/231–0856) flies in four times a week from Newark, **Northwest Airlines** (tel. 212/563–7200 or 800/447–4747) has daily direct service to Montego Bay from Minneapolis and Tampa, and **Aeroflot** (tel. 809/929–2251) flies in from Havana. **Air Canada** (tel. 800/776–3000) offers daily service from Toronto and Montreal in conjunction with Air Jamaica, and both **British Airways** (tel. 800/247–9297) and Air Jamaica connect the island with London.

From the Airport All-inclusive resorts provide free transfers from the airport, as do many small hotels when you stay on a special package; always inquire when booking, as the hotel may throw it in if asked. There is no public transportation to and from the airports. Taxi rates are not fixed, but sample fares to popular destinations are posted in public areas. Always set the price in advance, figuring $10–$20 to Kingston or Montego Bay from their respective airports, three or four times that to Negril, Ocho Rios, or Port Antonio. Buses cost around half what a taxi would charge but are slower and often crowded. You get a ticket from any of the tour desks at the airport.

Passports and Visas Passports are not required of visitors from the United States or Canada, but every visitor must have proof of citizenship, such as a birth certificate or a voter registration card (a driver's license is not enough). British visitors need passports but not visas. Each visitor must possess a return or ongoing ticket. Declaration forms are distributed in flight in order to keep customs formalities to a minimum.

Language The official language of Jamaica is English. Islanders usually speak a patois among themselves, a lyrical mixture of pidgin English, Spanish, and various African languages.

Precautions Do not let the beauty of Jamaica cause you to relax the caution and good sense you would use in your own hometown. Never leave money or other valuables in your hotel room; use the safe-deposit boxes that most establishments make available. Carry your funds in traveler's checks, not cash, and keep a record of the check numbers in a secure place. Never leave a rental car unlocked, and never leave valuables even in a locked car. Finally, resist the call of the wild when it presents itself as a scruffy-looking native offering to show you the "real" Jamaica. Jamaica on the beaten path is wonderful enough; don't take chances by wandering far from it. And ignore efforts, however persistent, to sell you a ganja joint.

Staying in Jamaica

Important Addresses **Tourist Information:** The main office of the **Jamaica Tourist Board** is in Kingston (2 St. Lucia Ave., New Kingston, Box 360, Kingston 5, tel. 809/929–9200). There are also JTB desks at both Montego Bay and Kingston airports and JTB offices in all resort areas.

Emergencies **Police, fire, and ambulance:** Police and air-rescue is 119; fire department and ambulance is 110. **Hospitals: University Hospital** at Mona in Kingston (tel. 809/927–1620), **Cornwall Regional Hospital** (Mt. Salem, in Montego Bay, tel. 809/952–5100), **Port Antonio General Hospital** (Naylor's Hill in Port Antonio, tel. 809/993–2646), and **St. Ann's Bay Hospital** (near Ocho Rios, tel. 809/972–2272). **Pharmacies: Pegasus Hotel in Kingston** (tel. 809/926–3690), **McKenzie's Drug Store** (16 Strand St. in Montego Bay, tel. 809/952–2467), and **Great House Pharmacy** (Brown's Plaza in Ocho Rios, tel. 809/974–2352).

Currency The Jamaican government abolished the fixed rate of exchange for the Jamaican dollar, allowing it to be traded publicly and subject to market fluctuations. At press time the Jamaican dollar was worth about J$30 to U.S.$1. Currency can be exchanged at airport bank counters, exchange bureaus, or commercial banks. Prices quoted below are in U.S. dollars unless otherwise noted.

Taxes and Service Charges Hotels collect a 10% government tax on room occupancy. Most hotels and restaurants add a 10% service charge to your bill. If not, a tip is appreciated. The departure tax is J$400, or approximately $14.

Getting Around

Taxis Some but not all of Jamaica's taxis are metered. If you accept a driver's offer of his services as a tour guide, be sure to agree on a price before the vehicle is put into gear. All licensed taxis display red Public Passenger Vehicle (PPV) plates. Cabs can be summoned by telephone or flagged down on the street. Rates are per car, not per passenger, and 25% is added to the metered rate between midnight and 5 AM. Licensed minivans are also available and bear the red PPV plates.

Rental Cars Jamaica has dozens of car-rental companies throughout the island. Because rentals can be difficult to arrange once you've arrived, you must make reservations and send a deposit before your trip. (Cars are scarce, and without either a confirmation number or a receipt you may have to walk.) Best bets are **Avis** (tel. 800/331–1212), **Dollar** (tel. 800/800–4000), **Hertz** (tel. 800/654–3131), and **National** (tel. 800/227–3876). In Jamaica, try the branch offices in your resort area or try **United Car Rentals** (tel. 809/952–3077) or **Jamaica Car Rental** (tel. 809/952–5586). You must be at least 21 years old to rent a car (at least 25 years old at several agencies), have a valid driver's license (from any country), and have a valid credit card. You may be required to post a security of several hundred dollars before taking possession of your car; ask about it when you make the reservation. Rates average $75–$90 a day.

Traffic keeps to the left in Jamaica. Be cautious until you are comfortable with it.

Trains At press time, rail service between Kingston and Montego Bay had been suspended.

Buses Buses are the mode of transportation Jamaicans use most, and consequently buses are *extremely* crowded and slow. They also lack air-conditioning and can get rather uncomfortable. Yet the service is acceptable between major destinations. Schedule or route information is available at bus stops or from the driver. The buses run fairly frequently from Kingston to Port Antonio, and from Montego Bay to Ocho Rios or Negril, but they rarely stick to a timetable. Stops are usually small roadside shelters, with a dilapidated but clearly marked sign.

Telephones and Mail The area code for all Jamaica is 809. Direct telephone, telegraph, telefax, and telex services are available.

At press time, airmail postage from Jamaica to the United States or Canada was J$1.50 for letters, J$1.20 for postcards.

Opening and Closing Times Normal business hours for stores are weekdays 8–4, Saturday 8–1. Banking hours are generally Monday–Thursday 9–2, Friday 9–noon and 2:30–5.

Guided Tours Half-day tours are offered by a variety of operators in the important areas of Jamaica. The best great-house tours include Rose Hall, Greenwood, and Devon House. Plantations to tour are Prospect and Sun Valley. The Appleton Estate Express Tour uses a bus to visit villages, plantations, and a rum distillery. The increasingly popular waterside folklore feasts are offered on the Dunn's, Great, and White rivers. The significant city tours are those in Kingston, Montego Bay, and Ocho Rios. Quality tour operators include **Glamour Tours** (tel. 809/979–8207), **Tropical Tours** (tel. 809/952–1110), **Greenlight Tours** (tel. 809/952–2650), **SunHoliday Tours** (tel. 809/952–5629), and **Jamaica Tours** (tel. 809/952–8074). The highlight of the Hilton High Day Tour (tel. 809/952–3343), which has been dubbed "Up, Up, and Buffet," is a meet the people, experience Jamaican food, and learn some of its history day, all on a private estate (around $65, including transportation). **South Coast Safaris Ltd.** has guided boat excursions up the Black River for some 10 miles (round-trip), into the mangroves and marshlands, aboard the 25-passenger *Safari Queen* and 25-passenger *Safari Princess* (tel. 809/965–2513 or, after 7 PM, 809/962–0220). **Calico Sailing** (tel. 809/952–5860, fax 809/979–0843) offers snorkeling trips and sunset cruises on the waters of Montego Bay; costs are $50 and $25 respectively. The **Touring Society of Jamaica** (tel. and fax 809/975–7158) offers several ecotours, from birding in the Blue Mountains to the natural history of Cockpit Country.

Exploring Jamaica

Numbers in the margin correspond to points of interest on the Jamaica map.

The astonishing diversity of Jamaica's attractions makes renting a car the most desirable way to get to know the island. If you only intend to explore the area near your hotel, you will save money by hiring a taxi or taking a guided tour (*see above*).

Montego Bay

1 The number and variety of its attractions make **Montego Bay,** on the island's northwest corner, the logical place to begin an exploration of Jamaica. Confronting the string of high-rise developments that crowd the water's edge, you may find it hard to believe that little of what is now Montego Bay (the locals call it MoBay) existed before the turn of the century.

Rose Hall Great House, perhaps the greatest in the West Indies in the 1700s, enjoys its popularity less for its architecture than for the legend surrounding its second mistress, Annie Palmer, who was credited with murdering three husbands and a plantation overseer who was her lover. The story is told in two novels sold everywhere in Jamaica: *The White Witch of Rose Hall* and *Jamaica White.* The great house is east of Montego Bay, just across the highway from the Rose Hall resorts. There's a pub on site for snacks and drinks. *Tel. 809/953–2323. Admission: $10 adults, $6 children. Open daily 9–6.*

Greenwood Great House, 15 miles east of Montego Bay, has no spooky legend to titillate visitors, but it's much better than Rose Hall at evoking the atmosphere of life on a sugar plantation. The Barrett family, from which the English poet Elizabeth Barrett Browning was descended, once owned all the land from Rose Hall to Falmouth, and the family built several great houses on it. The poet's father, Edward Moulton Barrett ("the Tyrant of Wimpole Street"), was born at Cinnamon Hill, currently the private estate of country singer Johnny Cash. Highlights of Greenwood include oil paintings of the Barretts, china made especially for the family by Wedgwood, a library filled with rare books printed as early as 1697, fine antique furniture, and a collection of exotic musical instruments. There's a pub on site for snacks and drinks here as well. *Tel. 809/953–1077. Admission: $10 adults, $5 children. Open daily 9–6.*

One of the most popular excursions in Jamaica is rafting on the
2 **Martha Brae River.** The gentle waterway takes its name from that of an Arawak Indian who killed herself because she refused to reveal the whereabouts of a local gold mine to the Spanish. According to legend, she finally agreed to take them there and, on reaching the river, used magic to change its course, drowning herself along with the greedy Spaniards. Her duppy (ghost) is said to guard the mine's entrance to this day. Bookings are made through hotel tour desks. The trip costs just under $40 per raft (two per raft) for the 1½-hour

Jamaica

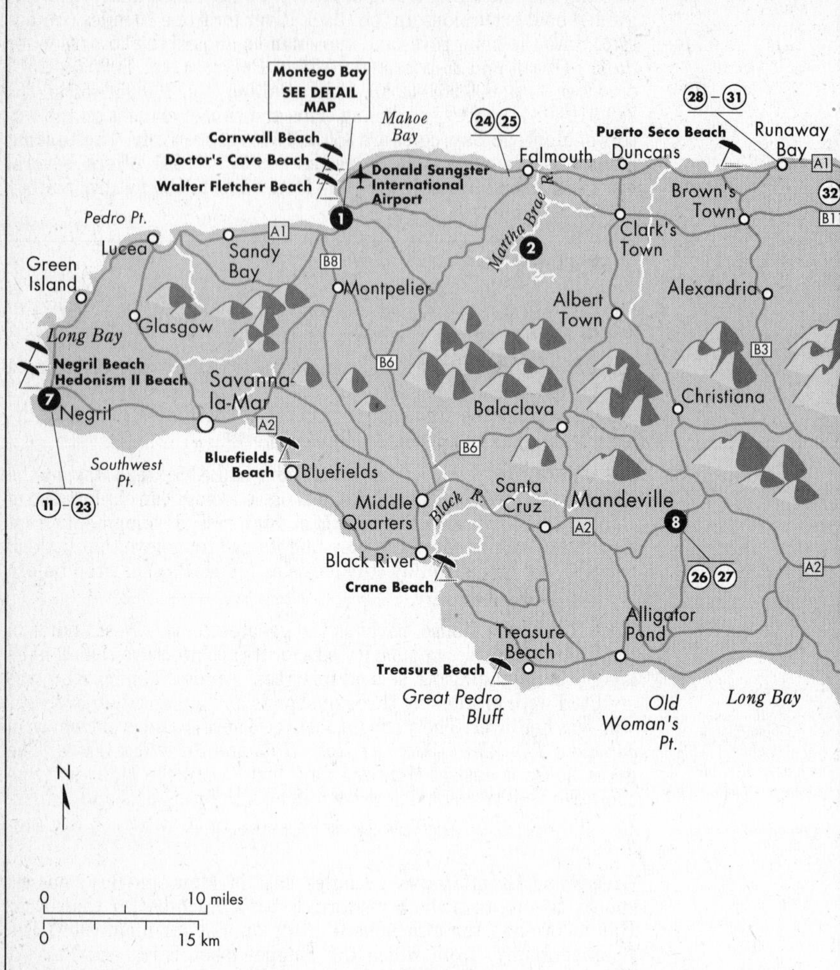

Exploring
Kingston, **9**
Mandeville, **8**
Martha Brae River, **2**
Montego Bay, **1**
Negril, **7**
Ocho Rios, **3**
Port Antonio, **4**
Port Royal, **10**
Rio Grande River, **5**
Somerset Falls, **6**

Dining
Almond Tree, **41**
Café Au Lait, **11**
Chelsea Jerk Centre, **50**
Cosmo's Seafood Restaurant and Bar, **16**
Double V Jerk Centre, **37**
Evita's, **35**
Gloria's Rendezvous, **59**
The Hot Pot, **51**
Hotel Four Seasons, **52**
Ivor Guest House, **58**
The Jade Garden, **57**
Paradise Yard, **17**
Peppers, **53**
The Ruins, **36**
Sweet Spice, **13**
Tan-ya's, **18**

Lodging
Astra Country Inn & Restaurant, **26**
Bonnie View Plantation Hotel, **44**
Boscobel Beach, **43**
Charela Inn, **15**
Club Caribbean, **28**
Club Jamaica Beach Resort, **40**
Couples, **42**
Devine Destiny, **19**

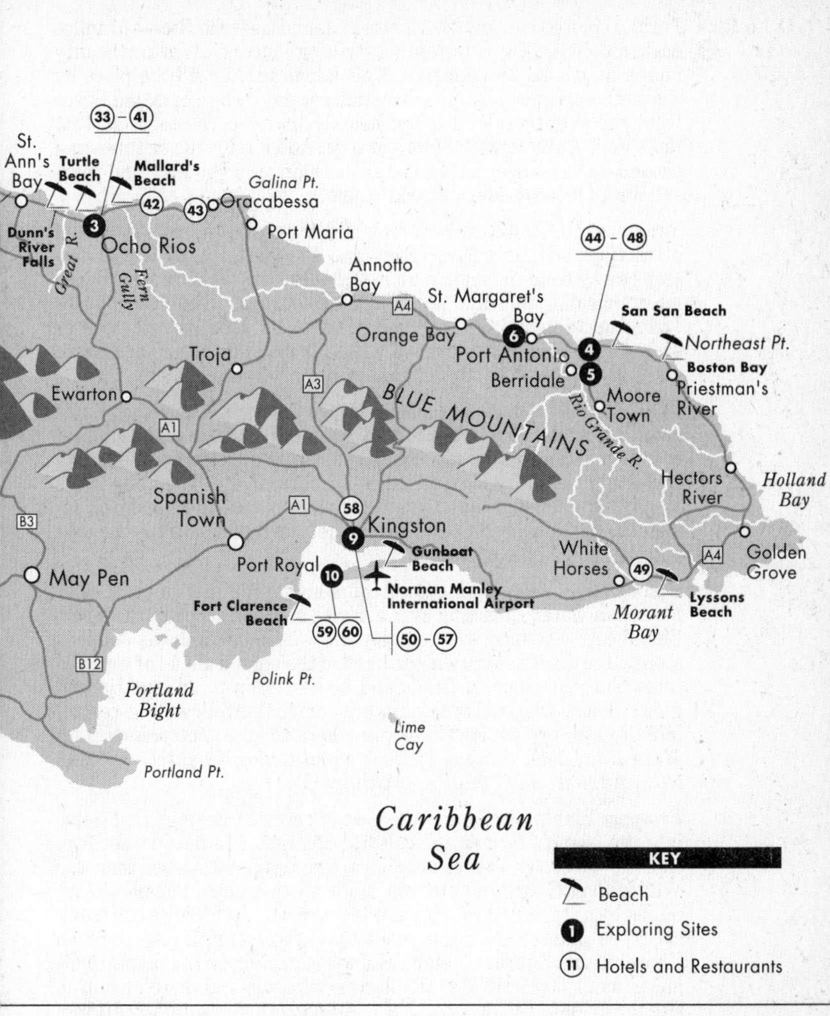

33 - 41
St. Ann's Bay
Turtle Beach
Mallard's Beach
Galina Pt.
42
43
Oracabessa
Dunn's River Falls
3
Ocho Rios
Port Maria
Great R.
Fern Gully
Annotto Bay
44 - 48
A4
St. Margaret's Bay
San San Beach
Orange Bay
6
4
Northeast Pt.
Port Antonio
Boston Bay
Troja
Berridale
5
Priestman's River
Ewarton
A3
BLUE MOUNTAINS
Moore Town
Rio Grande R.
A1
Hectors River
Holland Bay
Spanish Town
A1
58
B3
Kingston
9
Golden Grove
A4
White Horses
Gunboat Beach
Port Royal
10
49
May Pen
Norman Manley International Airport
Lyssons Beach
Fort Clarence Beach
Morant Bay
59 60
50 - 57
B12
Polink Pt.
Portland Bight
Lime Cay
Portland Pt.
Caribbean Sea
KEY
Beach
Exploring Sites
Hotels and Restaurants

river run, about 25 miles from most hotels in Montego Bay. The ticket office, gift shops, a bar/restaurant, and swimming pool are at the top of the river. To make arrangements call 809/952–0889.

Ocho Rios 3

Perhaps more than anywhere else in Jamaica, **Ocho Rios**—67 miles east of Montego Bay—presents a striking contrast of natural beauty and recreational development. The Jamaicans can fill the place by themselves, especially on a busy market day, when cars and buses from the countryside clog the heavily traveled coastal road that links Port Antonio with Montego Bay. Add a tour bus or three and the entire passenger list from a cruise ship, and you may find yourself mired in a considerable traffic jam.

Yet a visit to Ocho Rios is worthwhile, if only to enjoy its two chief attractions—Dunn's River Falls and Prospect Plantation. A few steps away from the main road in Ocho Rios are waiting some of the most charming inns and oceanfront restaurants in the Caribbean. Lying on the sand of what will seem to be your private cove or swinging gently in a hammock with a tropical drink in your hand, you'll soon forget the traffic that's only a brief stroll away.

The dispute continues as to the origin of the name Ocho Rios. Some claim it's from the Spanish for "eight rivers"; others maintain that the name is a corruption of *chorreras*, which describes a seemingly endless series of cascades that sparkle from the limestone rocks along this stretch of coast. For as long as anyone can remember, Jamaicans have favored Ocho Rios as their own escape from the heat and the crowds of Kingston.

Dunn's River Falls is an eye-catching sight: 600 feet of cold, clear mountain water splashing over a series of stone steps to the warm Caribbean. The best way to enjoy the falls is to climb the slippery steps. Don a swimsuit, take the hand of the person ahead of you, and trust that the chain of hands and bodies leads to an experienced guide. Those who lead the climbs are personable fellows who reel off bits of local lore while telling you where to step. *Immediately off Main Rd. (A-1), between St. Ann's and Ochos Rios, tel. 809/974–5015. Admission: $5 adults, $2 children 2–11.*

Prospect Plantation Tour is the best of several offerings that delve into the island's former agricultural lifestyle. It's not just for specialists; virtually everyone enjoys the beautiful views over the White River Gorge and the tour by jitney (a canopied open-air cart pulled by a tractor) through a plantation with exotic fruits and tropical trees planted over the years by such celebrities as Winston Churchill and Charlie Chaplin. Horseback riding on the plantation's more than 1,000 acres is available as is minigolf, and there's a pub on site for drinks. *Tel. 809/974–2058. Admission: $12 adults, children 12 and under free. Open daily 10:30–2.*

Ocho Rios's newest attraction is **Coyaba River Garden and Museum,** which features exhibits from Jamaica's many cultural influences (the national motto is "Out of Many One People"). The museum covers the island's history from the time of the Arawak Indians up to the modern day. The complex includes an art gallery, a crafts shop, and a snack bar, and offers the Moonshine Festival, a dinner-entertainment package on Wednesday and the Jamaica Music Review every Friday night. *Shaw Park Rd., Ochos Rios, tel. 809/974–6235. Admission: $4.50 adults, children 12 and under free. Open daily 8:30–5.*

Port Antonio 4

Every visitor's presence in **Port Antonio** pays homage to the beginnings of Jamaican tourism. Early in the century the first tourists arrived here on the island's northeast coast, 133 miles east of Montego Bay, drawn by the exoticism of the island's banana trade and seeking a respite from the New York winters. The original posters of the shipping lines make Port Antonio appear as foreign as the moon, yet in time it became the tropical darling of a fast-moving crowd and counted Clara Bow, Bette Davis, Ginger Rogers, Rudyard Kipling, J.P. Morgan, and William Randolph Hearst among its admirers. Its most passionate devotee was the actor Errol Flynn, whose spirit still seems to haunt the docks, devouring raw dolphinfish and swigging gin at 10 AM.

Although the action has moved elsewhere, the area can still weave a spell. Robin Moore wrote *The French Connection* here, and Broadway's tall and talented Tommy Tune found inspiration for the musical *Nine* while being pampered at Trident.

A stroll through the town suggests a step into the past. **Queen Street,** in the residential Titchfield area, a couple of miles north of downtown Port Antonio, has several fine examples of Georgian architecture. **DeMontevin Lodge** (21 Fort George St., on Titchfield Hill, tel. 809/993–2604), owned by the Mullings family (the late Gladys Mullings was Errol Flynn's cook), and the nearby **Musgrave Street** (the craft market is here) are in the traditional sea-captain style that one finds along coasts as far away as New England.

The town's best-known landmark is **Folly,** on the way to Trident, a Roman-style villa in ruins on the eastern edge of East Harbor. The creation of a Connecticut millionaire in 1905, the manse was made almost entirely of concrete. Unfortunately, the cement was mixed with seawater, and it began to crumble as it dried. According to local lore, the millionaire's bride took one look at her shattered dream, burst into tears, and fled forever. Little more than the marble floor remains today. After sundown, Folly is a hangout for some of the area's less savory characters and should be avoided (or something like that).

5 Rafting on the **Rio Grande River** (yes, Jamaica has a Rio Grande, too) is a must. This is the granddaddy of the river-rafting attractions, an 8-mile-long swift green waterway from Berrydale to Rafter's Rest. Here the river flows into the Caribbean at St. Margaret's Bay. The trip of about three hours is made on bamboo rafts pushed along by a raftsman who is likely to be a character. You can pack a picnic lunch and eat it on the raft or along the riverbank; wherever you lunch, a vendor of Red Stripe beer will appear at your elbow. A restaurant, bar, and souvenir shops are at Rafter's Rest (tel. 809/993–2778), a pleasant spot to relax, even if you don't want to pay the approximately $40 per two-person raft for the trip.

Another interesting excursion takes you 8 miles west of Port Anto-
6 nio to **Somerset Falls,** a sun-dappled spot crawling with flowering vines; you can climb its 400 feet with some assistance from a concrete staircase. A brief raft ride takes you part of the way. **Athenry Gardens,** a 3-acre tropical wonderland, and **Nonsuch Cave** are some 6 miles northeast of Port Antonio in the village of Nonsuch. The cave's underground beauty has been made accessible by concrete walkways, railed stairways, and careful lighting. *Somerset Falls, tel. 809/993–3740. Admission: $2. Open daily 10–5. Atherny/Nonsuch, tel. 809/993–3740. Admission: $5. Open daily 9–5.*

A short drive east from Port Antonio deposits you at **Boston Bay,** which is popular with swimmers and has been enshrined by lovers of jerk pork. The spicy barbecue was originated by the Arawaks and perfected by runaway slaves called the Maroons. Eating almost nothing but wild hog preserved over smoking coals enabled the Maroons to survive years of fierce guerrilla warfare with the English.

Crystal Springs, about 18 miles west of Port Antonio, has more than 15,000 orchids, and hummingbirds dart among the blossoms, landing on visitors' outstretched hands. Hiking and camping are available here. *Buff Bay, tel. 809/993–2609. Admission: 50¢. Open daily 9–6.*

Negril 7 Situated 52 miles southwest of Montego Bay on the winding coast road, **Negril** is no longer Jamaica's best-kept secret. In fact, it has begun to shed some of its bohemian, ramshackle atmosphere for the attractions and activities traditionally associated with Montego Bay. Applauding the sunset from Rick's Cafe may still be the highlight of a day in Negril, yet increasingly the hours before and after have come to be filled with conventional recreation.

One thing that has not changed around this west coast center (whose only true claim to fame is a 7-mile beach) is the casual approach to life. As you wander from lunch in the sun to shopping in the sun to sports in the sun, you'll find that swimsuits are common attire. Want to dress for a special meal? Slip a caftan over your bathing suit.

Negril's newest attraction is the **Anancy Family Fun and Nature Park** (tel. 809/957–4100), just across the street from the family-oriented Poinciana Beach Resort. Named after the mischievous spider character in Jamaican folktales, the 3-acre site features an 18-hole miniature golf course, go-cart rides, a fishing pond, a nature trail, and three small museums (craft, conservation, and heritage). Another new attraction is the **Negril Hills Golf Club** (tel. 809/957–4638). The 18-hole championship course, designed by Roy Case and Robert Simons, is slated for completion sometime in 1995. At press time, 9 holes were open.

After sunset, activity centers on **West End Road,** Negril's main (and only) thoroughfare, which comes to life in the evening with bustling bistros and earsplitting discos. West End Road leads to the town's only building of historical significance, the **Lighthouse,** built in 1894 and only 100 feet tall. All anyone can tell you about it, however, is that it's been there for a while. Even historians find it hard to keep track of the days in Negril.

Negril today stretches along the coast south from the horse-shoe-shaped **Bloody Bay** (named during the period when it was a whale-processing center) along the calm waters of **Long Bay** to the Lighthouse section and the landmark **Rick's Cafe** (tel. 809/957–4335). Sunset at Rick's is a Negril tradition. Divers spiral downward off 50-foot-high cliffs into the deep green depths as the sun turns into a ball of fire and sets the clouds ablaze with color.

In the 18th century Negril was where the English ships assembled in convoys for the dangerous ocean crossing. Not only were there pirates in the neighborhood, but the infamous Calico Jack and his crew were captured right here, while they guzzled the local rum. All but two of them were hanged on the spot; Mary Read and Anne Bonney were pregnant at the time, and their execution was delayed.

Mandeville 8 More than a quarter of a century after Jamaica achieved its independence from Great Britain, **Mandeville** seems like a hilly tribute to all that is genteel and admirable in the British character. At 2,000 feet above sea level, 70 miles southeast of Montego Bay, Mandeville is considerably cooler than the coastal area 25 miles to the south. Its vegetation is more lush, thanks to the mists that drift through the mountains. The people of Mandeville live their lives around a village green, a Georgian courthouse, tidy cottages and gardens, even a parish church. The entire scene could be set down in Devonshire, were it not for the occasional poinciana blossom or citrus grove.

Mandeville is omitted from most tourist itineraries even though its residents are increasingly interested in showing visitors around. It is still much less expensive than any of the coastal resorts, and its diversions include horseback riding, cycling, croquet, hiking, tennis, golf, bird-watching, and people-meeting. The town itself is characterized by its orderliness. You may stay here several days, or a glimpse of the lifestyle may satisfy you and you'll scurry back to the steamy coast. **Manchester Club** features tennis, nine holes of golf, and well-manicured greens; **Mrs. Stephenson's Gardens** (tel. 809/962–2328) are lovely, with orchids and fruit trees; the natural **Bird Sanctuary** at Marshalls Penn (tel. 809/962–2260) shows off 25 species indigenous to Jamaica; and **Marshall's Penn Great House** offers an array of walking tours. The cool, crisp air will make you feel up to any stroll in Mandeville. Further information on Mandeville is available through the visitors information center at the Astra Country Inn & Restaurant (tel. 809/962–3265 or 800/526–2422).

Kingston

The reaction of most visitors to the capital city, situated on the southeast coast of Jamaica, is anything but love at first sight. In fact,
9 only a small percentage of visitors to Jamaica see it at all. **Kingston,** for the tourist, may seem as remote from the resorts of Montego Bay as the loneliest peak in the Blue Mountains. Yet the islanders themselves can't seem to let it go. Everybody talks about Kingston, about their homes or relatives there, about their childhood memories. More than the sunny havens of the north coast, Kingston is a distillation of the true Jamaica. Parts of it may be dirty, crowded, often raucous, yet it is the ethnic cauldron that produces the cultural mix that is the nation's greatest natural resource. (Note, however, that when the sun sets even Kingstonians beat a quick path out of downtown Kingston, which is considered unsafe after dark.) Kingston is a cultural and commercial crossroads of international and local movers and shakers, art-show openings, theater (from Shakespeare to pantomime), and superb shopping. Here, too, the University of the West Indies explores Caribbean art and literature, as well as science. As one Jamaican put it, "You don't really know Jamaica until you know Kingston."

The first-time business or pleasure traveler may prefer to begin with New Kingston, which glistens with hotels, office towers, apartments, and boutiques. Newcomers may feel more comfortable settling in here and venturing forth from comfort they know will await their return.

Kingston's colonial past is very much alive away from the high rises of the new city. **Devon House,** our first stop, is reached through the iron gates at 26 Hope Road. Built in 1881 and bought and restored by the government in the 1960s, the mansion has period furnishings. Shoppers will appreciate Devon House, for the firm Things Jamaican has converted portions of the space into some of the best crafts shops on the island. On the grounds you'll find one of the few mahogany trees to survive Kingston's ambitious but not always careful development. *Devon House, tel. 809/–929–7029. Admission: $2. Open Tues.–Sat. 9:30–5. Shops open Mon.–Sat. 10–6.*

Once you have accepted the fact that Kingston doesn't look like a travel poster—too much life goes on here for that—you may see your trip here for precisely what it is, the single best introduction to the people of Jamaica. Near the waterfront, the **Institute of Jamaica** is a museum and library that traces the island's history from the Arawaks to current events. The charts and almanacs here make fascinating browsing; one example, famed as the Shark Papers, is made up of damaging evidence tossed overboard by a guilty sea captain and later recovered from the belly of a shark. *12 East St., tel. 809/922–0620. Admission free. Open Mon.–Thurs. 9–5, Fri. 9–4.*

From the institute, push onward to the **University of the West Indies** (tel. 809/927–1660) in the city's Mona section. A cooperative venture begun after World War II by several West Indian governments, the university is set in an eye-catching cradle of often misty mountains. The place seems a monument to the conviction that education and commitment lead to a better life for the entire Caribbean. There's a bar and disco on the campus where you can meet the students.

Jamaica's rich cultural life is evoked at the **National Gallery,** which was once at Devon House and can now be found at Kingston Mall near the reborn waterfront section. The artists represented here may not be household names in other nations, yet the paintings of such intuitive masters as John Dunkley, David Miller, Sr., and David Miller, Jr., reveal a sensitivity to the life around them that transcends academic training. Among other highlights from the 1920s through the 1980s are works by Edna Manley and Mallica Reynolds, better known as Kapo. Reggae fans touring the National Gallery will want to look for Christopher Gonzalez's controversial statue of Bob Marley. *12 Ocean Blvd., tel. 809/922–1561. Admission fees charged for special exhibits. Open weekdays 11–4.*

Reggae fans will also want to see the **Bob Marley Museum.** Painted in Rastafarian red, yellow, and green, this recording studio was built by Marley at the height of his career. The studio has since become the museum, with impromptu tours given by just about anyone who may be around (Bob's famous son, Ziggy, a reggae star in his own right, was the guide on our last visit). Certainly there is much here to help the outsider understand Marley, reggae, and Jamaica itself. The Ethiopian flag is a reminder that Rastas consider the late Ethiopian emperor Haile Selassie to be the Messiah, a descendant of King Solomon and the Queen of Sheba. A striking mural by Everald Brown, *The Journey of Superstar Bob Marley,* depicts the hero's life from its beginnings in a womb shaped like a coconut to enshrinement in the hearts of the Jamaican people. *56 Hope Rd., tel. 809/927–9152. Admission: $4 adults, 50¢ children ages 4–12. Open Mon., Tue., Thurs., and Fri. 9:30–5; Wed. and Sat. 12:30–6.*

Although it's no longer lovingly cared for, the **Royal Botanical Gardens at Hope** is a nice place to picnic or while away an afternoon. Donated to Jamaica by the Hope family following the abolition of slavery, the garden consists of 50 acres filled with tropical trees, plants, and flowers, most clearly labeled for those taking a self-guided tour. Free concerts are given here on the first Sunday of each month. Park in the lot and walk or pay J$50 to drive through the park. *Hope Rd., tel. 809/927–1085. Admission: J$10 adults, J$5 children. Open weekdays 10–5, weekends 10–6.*

Another good picnic spot is the **Rockfort Mineral Baths,** listed on the Jamaica National Heritage Trust after being restored by the Caribbean Cement Company (which is next door). Named for the stone fort set above Kingston Harbour in 1694 by the British to guard against invasion, and for the natural mineral spring that emerged following a devastating earthquake in 1907, this complex draws Kingstonians who come to cool off in the invigorating spring water in the public swimming pool or to unwind tense muscles in private whirlpool tubs. You can also have a massage and visit the juice bar or the cafeteria before staking out your picnic spot on the landscaped grounds. *Kingston (on A-1, just outside town), tel. 809/938–5055. Admission to pool: $J40 adults, $J20 children; private baths start at $J250. Open weekdays 6:30–6, weekends 8–6.*

Unless your visit must be very brief, you shouldn't leave Kingston
10 without a glimpse of "the wickedest city in the world." **Port Royal** has hardly been that since an earthquake tumbled it into the sea in 1692, yet the spirits of Henry Morgan and other buccaneers add a great deal of energy to what remains. The proudest possession of St. Peter's Church, rebuilt in 1726 to replace Christ's Church, is a silver communion plate said to have been donated by Morgan himself. A ferry from the Square in downtown Kingston goes to Port Royal at least twice a day, and the town is small enough to see on foot.

You can no longer down rum in Port Royal's legendary 40 taverns, but you can take in a draft of the past at the **National Museum of Historical Archaeology** and explore the impressive remains of **Fort Charles,** once the area's major garrison. On the grounds is the small **Fort Charles Maritime Museum** and **Giddy House,** an old artillery storehouse that gained its name after being permanently tilted by the earthquake of 1907. Nearby is a graveyard in which rests a man who died twice. According to the tombstone, Lewis Galdy was swallowed up in the great earthquake of 1692, spewed into the sea, rescued, and lived another four decades in "Great Reputation." *Old Naval Hospital, Port Royal, tel. 809/924-8782. Admission: $2 adults, $1 children. Open daily 9:30-5:30.*

Admirers of Jamaica's wonderful coffee may wish to travel to the **Blue Mountains,** to visit **Pine Grove** or the Jablum coffee plant at **Mavis Bank.** Unless you are traveling with a local, do not rent a car and go on your own, as the mountain roads wind and dip, hand-lettered signs blow away, and a tourist can easily get lost—not just for hours, but for days. Pine Grove, a working coffee farm that doubles as an inn, has a restaurant that serves owner Marcia Thwaites's Jamaican cuisine. Mavis Bank is delightfully primitive—especially considering the retail price of the beans it processes. There is no official tour; ask someone to show you around.

Beaches

Jamaica has 200 miles of beaches, some of them still uncrowded. The beaches listed below are public places (there is usually a small admission charge), and they are among the best Jamaica has to offer. In addition, nearly every resort has its own private beach, complete with towels and water sports. Some of the larger resorts (all-inclusives such as Grand Lido or Hedonism II) sell day passes to nonguests. Costing around $50-$70, these include meals and drinks, as well as use of facilities. Most hotels are on beaches or provide a free shuttle. The following beaches have public sections; access is only denied in those areas adjoining major hotels. Generally, the farther west you travel, the lighter and finer the sand.

Doctor's Cave Beach at Montego Bay shows a tendency toward population explosion, attracting Jamaicans and tourists alike; at times it may resemble Fort Lauderdale at spring break. The 5-mile stretch of sugary sand has been spotlighted in so many travel articles and brochures over the years that it's no secret to anyone. On the bright side, Doctor's Cave is well fitted for all its admirers with changing rooms, colorful if overly insistent vendors, and a large selection of snacks.

Two other popular beaches in the Montego Bay area are **Cornwall Beach,** farther up the coast, which is smaller, also lively, with lots of food and drink available and a water-sports concession, and **Walter Fletcher Beach,** on the bay near the center of town. Fletcher offers protection from the surf on a windy day and therefore unusually fine swimming; the calm waters make it a good bet for children, too.

Ocho Rios appears to be just about as busy as MoBay these days, and the busiest beach is usually **Mallards.** The **Jamaica Grande** hotel, formerly the Mallards Beach and Americana hotels, is here, spilling out its large convention groups at all hours of the day. Next door is **Turtle Beach,** which islanders consider the place for swimming in Ocho Rios.

In Port Antonio, head for **San San Beach** or **Boston Bay.** Any of the shacks spewing scented smoke along the beach at Boston Bay will sell you the famous peppery delicacy, jerk pork.

Puerto Seco Beach at Discovery Bay is sunny and sandy.

There are no good beaches in Kingston. Beachgoers can travel outside of the city, but the beaches there, as a rule, are not as beautiful as those in the resort areas. The most popular stretch of sand is **Hellshire Beach** in Bridgeport, about a 20-30 minute drive from Kingston. **Fort Clarence,** a beach in the Hellshire Hills area southwest of the city, has changing facilities and entertainment. Sometimes Kingstonians are willing to drive 32 miles east to the lovely golden **Lyssons Beach** in Morant Bay or, for a small negotiable fee, to hire a boat at the Morgan's Harbor Marina at Port Royal to ferry them to **Lime Cay.** This island, just beyond Kingston Harbor, is perfect for picnicking, sunning, and swimming.

Not too long ago, the 7 miles of white sand at **Negril Beach** offered a beachcomber's vision of Eden. Today much of it is fronted by modern resorts, although the 2 miles of beach fronting Bloody Bay remain relatively untouched. The nude beach areas are found mostly along sections of the beach where no hotel or resort has been built, such as the area adjacent to Cosmo's (*see* Dining, *below*). A few resorts have built accommodations overlooking their nude beaches, thereby adding a new dimension to the traditional notion of "ocean view."

Those who seek beaches off the main tourist routes will want to explore Jamaica's unexploited south coast. Nearest to "civilization" is **Bluefields Beach** near Savanna-La-Mar, south of Negril along the coast. **Crane Beach** at Black River is another great discovery. And the best of the south shore has to be **Treasure Beach,** 20 miles farther along the coast beyond Crane.

Sports and the Outdoors

The Tourist Board licenses all operators of recreational activities, which should ensure you of fair business practices as long as you deal with companies that display the decals.

Golf The best courses are found around Montego Bay at **Tryall** (tel. 809/956–5681), **Half Moon** (tel. 809/953–2560), **Rose Hall** (tel. 809/953–2650), and **Ironshore** (tel. 809/953–2800). Good courses are also found at **Caymanas** (tel. 809/926–8144) and **Constant Spring** (tel. 809/924–1610) in Kingston and at **SuperClubs Runaway Bay** (tel. 809/973–2561) and **Sandals Golf and Country Club** (tel. 809/974–2528), formerly Upton, in Ocho Rios. A nine-hole course in the hills of Mandeville is called **Manchester Club** (tel. 809/962–2403). Great golf and spectacular scenery also go hand in hand at the new **Negril Hills Golf Club** (tel. 809/957–4638) in Negril, which was scheduled to open fully by mid-1995, but has only managed to get half the course (nine holes) up and running so far. **Prospect Plantation** (tel. 809/974–2058) in Ocho Rios and the **Anancy Family Fun and Nature Park** (tel. 809/957–4100) in Negril have 18-hole minigolf courses.

Tennis Many hotels have tennis facilities that are free to their guests, but some will allow nonguests to play for a fee, usually about $7 a person per hour. The sport is a highlight at **Tyrall** (tel. 809/956-5660), **Round Hill Motel and Villas** (tel. 809/952–5150), and **Half Moon Club** (tel. 809/953–2211) in Montego Bay; **Swept Away** (tel. 809/957–4061) in Negril; and **Sans Souci Lido** (tel. 809/974–2353) and **Ciboney** (tel. 809/974–1027) in Ocho Rios.

Water Sports The major areas for swimming, windsurfing, snorkeling, and scuba diving are Negril in the west and Port Antonio in the east. Equipment rental is not cheap, primarily because so many all-inclusives and major resorts offer facilities free to guests. All the large resorts rent equipment for a deposit and/or a fee. Figure on $5 for snorkeling gear, $20 for a half-hour of windsurfing, and $50 for a single-tank dive. Jamaica Tourist Board–licensed dive operators include: **Resort Divers** (Swept Away, Negril, tel. 809/ 957–4061; San Souci Lido, Ocho Rios, tel. 809/974–2353; Jamaica/Jamaica, Runaway Bay, tel. 809/973–2436), **Sun Divers** (Poinciana Beach Resort, Negril, tel. 809/957–4069, and Ambiance Hotel, Runaway Bay, tel. 809/973–2346), **Garfield Dive Station** (Ocho Rios, tel. 809/974–5749), **North Coast Marine** (Half Moon Club, Montego Bay, tel. 809/953–2211), and **Sandals Beach Resort Watersports** (Montego Bay, tel. 809/ 979–0104). All of these operators offer certification courses and dive trips. Most all-inclusive resorts offer free scuba diving to their guests. **Lady Godiva** (San San Beach, Port Antonio, tel. 809/993–3281) offers scuba diving, snorkeling, windsurfing, a glass-bottom boat, and sailing; excursions start at $25 per person.

Shopping

Jamaican crafts take the form of resortwear, hand-loomed fabrics, silk-screening, wood carvings, paintings, and other fine arts.

Jamaican rum is a great take-home gift. So is Tia Maria, Jamaica's world-famous coffee liqueur. The same goes for the island's prized Blue Mountain and High Mountain coffees and its jams, jellies, and marmalades.

A must to avoid are the "crafts" stalls in MoBay and Ocho Rios that are literally filled with "higglers" desperate to sell touristy straw hats, T-shirts, and cheap jewelry. You may find yourself purchasing an unwanted straw something just to get out alive.

Cheap sandals are good buys in shopping centers throughout Jamaica. While workmanship and leathers don't rival the craftsmanship of those found in Italy or Spain, neither do the prices (about $20 a pair). In Kingston, **Lee's** (New Kingston Shopping Centre, tel. 809/ 929–8614) is a good place to sandal-shop; in Ocho Rios, the **Pretty Feet Shoe Shop** (Ocean Village Shopping Centre, tel. 809/974–5040) is a good bet. In Montego Bay, try **Overton Plaza** or **Westgate Plaza.**

Things Jamaican (Devon House, 26 Hope Rd., Kingston, tel. 809/ 929–6602, and 44 Fort St., MoBay, tel. 809/952–5605) has two outlets and two airport stalls that display and sell some of the best native crafts made in Jamaica, with items that range from carved wooden bowls and trays to reproductions of silver and brass period pieces.

Reggae tapes by world-famous Jamaican artists, such as Bob Marley, Ziggy Marley, Peter Tosh, and Third World, can be found easily in U.S. or European record stores, but a pilgrimage to **Randy's Record Mart** (17 N. Parade, Kingston, tel. 809/922–4859) should be high on the reggae lover's list. Also worth checking are the **Record Plaza** (Tropical Plaza, Kingston, tel. 809/926–7645), **Record City** (14 King St., Port Antonio, tel. 809/993–2836), and **Top Ranking Records** (Westgate Plaza, Montego Bay, tel. 809/952–1216). While Kingston is the undisputed place to make purchases, the determined somehow (usually with the help of a local) will find **Jimmy Cliff's Records** (Oneness Sq., MoBay, no phone), owned by reggae star Cliff.

Fine Macanudo handmade cigars make great gifts and are easily carried. They can be bought on departure at Montego Bay airport (call 809/925–1082 for outlet information). Blue Mountain coffee can be found at **John R. Wong's Supermarket** (1–5 Tobago Ave., Kingston, tel. 809/926–4811). The **Sovereign Supermarket** (Sovereign Center, 106 Hope Rd., tel. 809/927–5955) has a wide selection of coffee and other goods; it is somewhat easier to find and is closer to other shopping and dining. You can also look for the magic beans at **Magic Kitchen Ltd.** (Village Plaza, Kingston, tel. 809/926–8894). If the stores are out of Blue Mountain, you may have to settle for High Mountain coffee, the natives' second-preferred brand.

Silk batiks, by the yard or made into chic designs, are at **Caribatik** (A-1, 2 mi east of Falmouth, tel. 809/954–3314), the studio of the late Muriel Chandler. Drawing on patterns in nature, Chandler translated the birds, seascapes, flora, and fauna into works of art.

Sprigs and Things (Miranda Ridge Plaza, Gloucester Ave., MoBay, tel. 809/952–4735) is where artist Janie Soren sells T-shirts featuring her hand-painted designs of birds and animals. She also paints canvas bags and tennis dresses.

Harmony Hall (an 8-minute drive east on A1 from Ocho Rios; tel. 809/975–4222), a restored great house, is where Annabella Proudlock sells her unique wood Annabella Boxes. The covers feature reproductions of Jamaican paintings. Larger reproductions of paintings, lithographs, and signed prints of Jamaican scenes are also for sale, along with hand-carved wooden combs—all magnificently displayed. Harmony Hall is also well known for its year-round art shows by local artists.

Dining

Sampling the island's cuisine introduces you to virtually everything the Caribbean represents. Every ethnic group that has made significant contributions on another island has made them on Jamaica, too, adding to a Jamaican stockpot that is as rich as its melting pot. So many Americans have discovered the Caribbean through restaurants owned by Jamaicans that the very names of the island's dishes have come to represent the region as a whole. Moreover, restaurants specializing in the savory local cuisine, such as the "jerk centers" found in every major town, are invariably less expensive than restaurants serving Continental cuisine. This is especially true in Negril, which caters to a young, carefree crowd. Its West End Road (bush country just 20 years ago) is lined with shacks where it is virtually impossible to order a bad meal—or a weak rum punch.

Outside of informal local eateries, restaurants can be expensive, particularly those with sensational views or located in major hotels. Kingston has the widest selection; its ethnic restaurants offer Italian, French, Rasta natural foods, Cantonese, German, Thai, Indian, Korean, and Continental fare. Most of the restaurants in MoBay and Ocho Rios will provide complimentary transportation when you call for reservations. If you want to sample the food at an all-inclusive resort, you can purchase a day pass (usually $50–$70 a person) that entitles you to full use of the facilities plus meals (sometimes drinks, too).

If you plan to cook where you are staying, the supermarkets with the greatest produce, lowest prices, and widest selection are Kingston's **Lane** and **Poppeen Center** supermarkets (both New Hope Rd.), Ocho Rios's **General Food Supermarket** (Ocean Village Shopping Centre, next to JTB Office), and Negril's **Hi-Lo Supermarket** (Sunshine Arcade). Several daily markets (weekends are best) in Kingston are located near the bus station downtown. Ocho Rios has a good one on weekends that's located near the clock tower on the main road.

Jamaican food represents a cuisine all its own. Here are a few typically Jamaican dishes:

Rice and Peas. A traditional dish, known also as Coat of Arms and similar to the *moros y christianos* of Spanish-speaking islands: white rice cooked with red beans, coconut milk, scallions, and seasoning.

Pepper Pot. The island's most famous soup—a peppery combination of salt pork, salt beef, okra, and the island green known as *callaloo*—it is green, but at its best it tastes as though it ought to be red.

Curry Goat. Young goat cooked with spices is more tender and has a gentler flavor than the lamb for which it was substituted by immigrants from India.

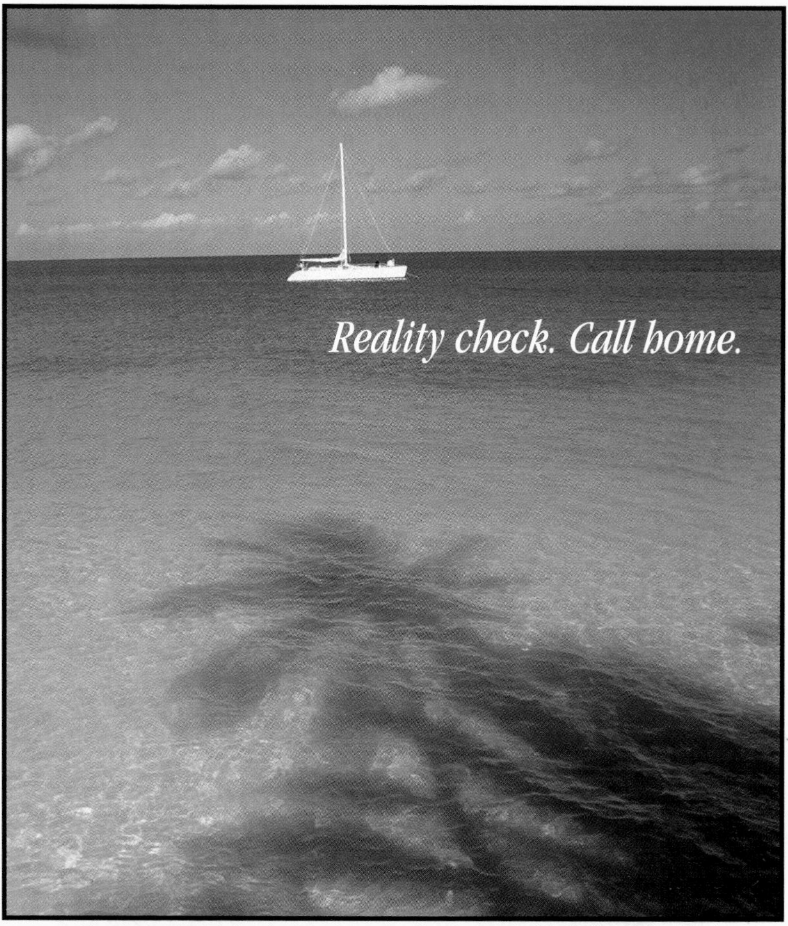

Ackee and Saltfish. Salted fish was once the best islanders could do between catches, so they invented this incredibly popular dish that joins saltfish (in Portuguese, *bacalao*) with ackee, a vegetable (introduced to the island by Captain Bligh of Bounty fame) that reminds most people of scrambled eggs.

Jerk Pork. Created by the Arawaks and perfected by the Maroons, jerk pork is the ultimate island barbecue. The pork (the purist cooks the whole pig) is covered with a paste of hot peppers, pimento berries (also known as allspice), and other herbs and cooked slowly over a coal fire. Many think that the "best of the best" jerk comes from Boston Beach in Port Antonio.

Patties are spicy meat pies that elevate street food to new heights. Although they in fact originated in Haiti, Jamaicans can give patty lessons to anybody.

Dress is casual chic (just plain casual at the local hangouts). People tend to dress up a little for dinner—just because they feel like it—so you may feel more comfortable in nice slacks or a sundress.

Highly recommended restaurants are indicated by a star ★.

Category	Cost*
$$	$20–$30
$	$10–$20
¢	under $10

**per person, excluding drinks and service charge or tip*

Kingston

$$ **Hotel Four Seasons.** The Four Seasons has been pleasing local residents for more than 25 years with its cuisine from the German and Swiss schools as well as local seafood. The setting tries to emulate Old World Europe without losing its casual island character. *18 Ruthven Rd., tel. 809/926–8805. Reservations advised. AE, DC, MC, V.*

$$ **Ivor Guest House.** This elegant yet cozy restaurant has an incredible view of Kingston from 2,000 feet above sea level. Go for dinner, when the view is dramatically caught between the stars and the glittering brooch of Kingston's lights. International and Jamaican cuisine is served. Owner Helen Aitken is an animated and cordial hostess. Afternoon tea here is a treat. *Jack's Hill, tel. 809/977–0033. Reservations required. AE, MC, V. Closed Sept.*

$$ ★ **The Jade Garden.** Located on the third floor of the Sovereign Centre, the Jade Garden, with its shiny black lacquer chairs and views of the Blue Mountains, garners rave reviews for its Cantonese and Thai menu. Favorites include steamed fish in black bean sauce, black mushrooms stuffed with shrimp, and shrimp with lychee. They serve an inexpensive lunch buffet every Friday afternoon (J$460 per person) and dim sum on the last Sunday of each month. *106 Hope Rd., tel. 809/978–3476/9. Weekend reservations advised. AE, MC, V.*

$ ★ **The Hot Pot.** Jamaicans love the Hot Pot for breakfast, lunch, and dinner. Fricassee chicken is the specialty, along with other local dishes, such as mackerel run-down (salted mackerel cooked down with coconut milk and spices) and ackee and salted cod. The restaurant's fresh juices "in season" are the best—tamarind, sorrel, coconut water, soursop, and cucumber. *2 Altamont Terr., tel. 809/929–3906. MC, V.*

$ **Peppers.** This casual outdoor bar is the "in" spot in Kingston, particularly on weekends. Sample the grilled lobster or jerk pork and chicken with the local Red Stripe beer. *31 Upper Waterloo Rd., tel. 809/925–2219. MC, V.*

¢–$ **Gloria's Rendezvous.** This brightly painted, ramshackle Port Royal eatery is wildly popular with Kingston locals escaping the sultry city heat on weekends. Delectable grilled fish and chicken are the draw. *5 Queen St., next to the police station, tel. 809/924–8578. No credit cards.*

¢ **Chelsea Jerk Centre.** This new Kingston restaurant is little more than a cafeteria, with an outdoor terrace that could double as a basketball court. But it doesn't bother those who crowd the tables to munch on superlative jerk pork, chicken, and fish. *7 Chelsea Ave., tel. 809/926–6322. MC, V.*

Montego Bay

$$ **Cascade Room.** Named for the waterfall that dances just outside its tall windows, the Cascade Room is the dressier, candlelit dining room of the Pelican Restaurant (a rather sterile café). Chicken Cordon Bleu, pan-fried shrimp stuffed with crab, smoked marlin, and snapper steamed in butter with scallions, onion, and local spices are highlights from the Continental menu. *Gloucester Ave., tel. 809/952–3171. Reservations advised. AE, DC, MC, V.*

$ **Hemingway's Pub.** The local business community enjoys the pub lunches and dinners at this casual bar and restaurant. The fish-and-chips here is a classic. The terrace is a great place to sit and watch the sun go down. *Miranda Ridge Plaza, Gloucester Ave., tel 809/952–8606/7. No credit cards.*

¢–$ ★ **Le Chalet.** Don't let the French name fool you. This Denny's look-alike, set in a nondescript shopping mall, serves heaping helpings of some of the best Chinese and Jamaican food in MoBay, including succulent curried goat and escoveitch fish (seasoned with onions, tomato, garlic, and peppers). Tasty lobster Cantonese costs only $9. *32 Gloucester Ave., tel. 809/952–5240. AE, MC, V.*

¢ ★ **Pork Pit.** This open-air hangout, across the street from popular Walter Fletcher Beach and not far from the airport, must introduce more travelers to Jamaica's fiery jerk pork than any other place on the island. The Pork Pit is a local phenomenon down to the Red Stripe beer, yet it's accessible in both location and style. Plan to arrive around noon, when the jerk begins to be lifted from its bed of coals and pimento wood. *Gloucester Ave., across from Walter Fletcher Beach, tel. 809/952–1046. No reservations. No credit cards.*

Negril

$$ **Cafe au Lait.** The proprietors of Cafe au Lait are French and Jamaican, and so is the cuisine. Local seafood and produce are prepared with delicate touches and presented in a setting overlooking the sea. *Mirage Resort on Lighthouse Rd., tel. 809/957–4471. Reservations advised. MC, V.*

$$ **Tan-ya's.** This alfresco restaurant is on the edge of the beach at the Seasplash hotel. Jamaican delicacies with an international flavor are served for breakfast, lunch, and dinner. Try the excellent deviled crab backs or the snapper Florentine stuffed with callaloo. *Seasplash Hotel, Norman Manley Blvd., tel. 809/957–4041. AE, DC, MC, V.*

$ ★ **Cosmo's Seafood Restaurant and Bar.** Owner Cosmo Brown has made this seaside open-air bistro a pleasant place to spend a lunch, an afternoon, and maybe stay on for dinner. The fresh fish is the main attraction, and the conch soup that's the house specialty is a meal in itself. There's also lobster (grilled or curried), fish-and-chips, and a catch-of-the-morning. Customers often drop cover-ups to take a beach dip before coffee and dessert and return later to lounge in chairs scattered under almond and sea-grape trees. (There's an entrance fee for the beach alone, but it's less than $1.) *Norman Manley Blvd., tel. 809/957–4330. MC, V.*

¢–$ **Paradise Yard.** Locals enjoy this alfresco restaurant on the Savanna-La-Mar side of the roundabout in Negril. Sit back and relax in the casual atmosphere while eating Jamaican dishes or the house special, Rasta Pasta. Open for breakfast, lunch, and dinner. *White Hall Rd., tel. 809/957–4006. MC, V.*

Dining
Hemingway's Pub, **4**
Le Chalet, **3**
Pork Pit, **5**

Lodging
Atrium at Ironshore, **12**
Cariblue Beach Hotel, **8**
Cascade Room, **2**
Coyaba Beach Resort and Club, **13**
Holiday Inn Rose Hall, **9**
Richmond Hill Inn, **1**
Sandals Inn, **7**
Seacastles, **10**
Toby Inn, **6**
Wyndham Rose Hall, **11**

Montego Bay Dining and Lodging

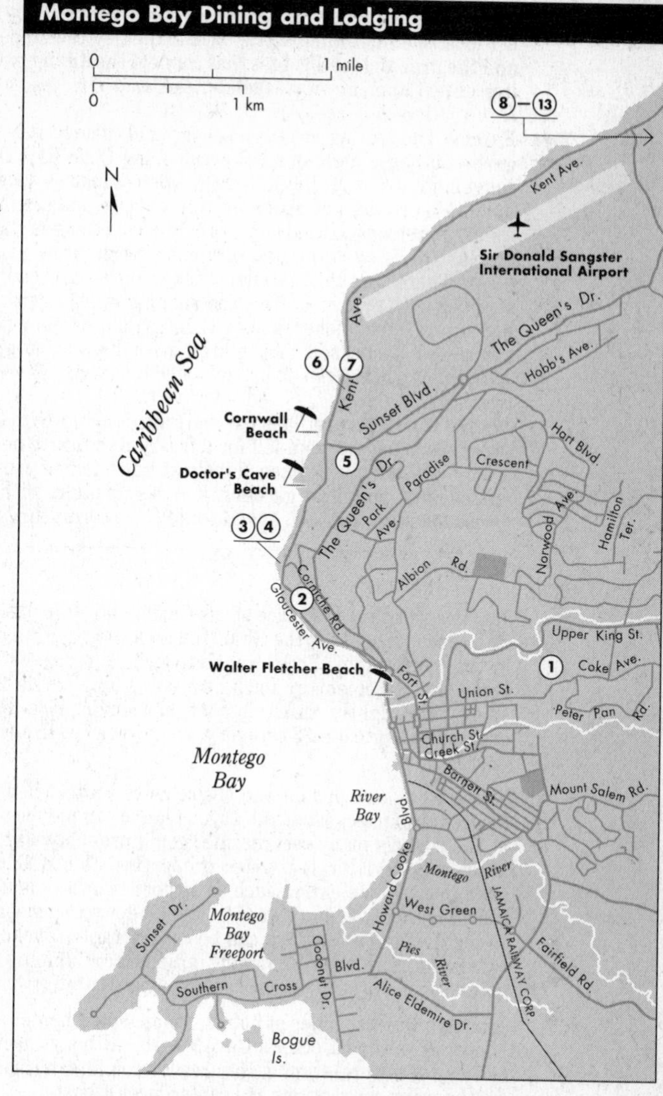

¢–$ **Sweet Spice.** When Paradise Yard is full (it happens) turn to Sweet Spice, immediately next door. This open-air mom-and-pop diner run by the Whytes serves inexpensive, generous plates of conch steak, fried or curried chicken, freshly caught fish, oxtail in brown stew sauce, and other down-home specialties. The fresh juices are quite satisfying. Drop by for breakfast, lunch, or dinner. *1 White Hall Rd., tel. 809/957–4621. MC, V.*

Ocho Rios

$$ ★ **Almond Tree.** One of the most popular restaurants in Ocho Rios, the Almond Tree has a menu of Jamaican and Continental favorites: pumpkin and pepper-pot soups, many wonderful preparations of fresh fish, veal piccata, fondue, spaghetti Bolognese. The swinging rope chairs of the terrace bar and the tables perched above a lovely Caribbean cove are great fun. All but the most expensive seafood dishes fall within our $$ range. *83 Main St., Ocho Rios, tel. 809/974–2813. Reservations required. AE, DC, MC, V.*

$$ **The Ruins.** A 40-foot waterfall dominates the open-air Ruins restaurant, and in a sense it dominates the food as well. Surrender to local

preference and order the Lotus Lily Lobster, a stir-fry of the freshest local shellfish, then settle back and enjoy the tree-shaded deck and the graceful footbridges that connect the dining patios. There's live entertainment on weekends. *DaCosta Dr., tel. 809/974–2442. Reservations advised. AE, D, DC, MC, V.*

$–$$ ★ **Evita's.** The setting here is a sensational, nearly 100-year-old gingerbread house high on a hill overlooking Ocho Rios Bay (but also convenient from MoBay). Large, open windows provide cooling mountain breezes and stunning views of city and sea. More than 18 kinds of pasta are served here, ranging from lasagna Rastafari (vegetarian) to *rotelle alla Eva* (crabmeat with white sauce and noodles). There are also excellent fish dishes—sautéed fillet of red snapper with orange butter, red snapper stuffed with crabmeat—and several meat dishes, among them grilled sirloin with mushroom sauce and barbecued ribs glazed with honey-and-ginger sauce. *Mantalent Inn, Ocho Rios, tel. 809/974–2333. Reservations advised. AE, MC, V.*

¢ **Double V Jerk Centre.** This partially alfresco hut with dirt floor is a great place to park yourself for a frosty Red Stripe beer and fiery, crispy jerk pork or chicken. Lively at lunch (when you can tour the minizoo and botanical garden), it rocks at night with an informal disco. *109 Main Rd., tel. 809/974–2084. No credit cards.*

Lodging

Jamaica was the birthplace of the Caribbean all-inclusive, the vacation concept that took the Club Med idea and gave it a lusty, excess-in-the-tropics spin. From Negril to Ocho Rios, resorts make their strongest statement by including everything, even drinks, water sports, and nightly entertainment, in a single price. There are several that fall into our $$ category, and even a few in our $ and ¢ categories.

Those who don't opt for the all-inclusive route will still find their choices on Jamaica plentiful. If you plan to sample the varied cuisine at the island's many restaurants, you'll probably want to stay in a hotel offering EP rates. Other properties offer MAP or FAP packages that include extras such as airport transfers and sight-seeing tours. Even if you don't want to be tied down to a meal plan, it pays to inquire, as the savings can be considerable. Backpacking types can explore the island's camping options (*see* Camping, *below*). Consider also geography when choosing where to stay:

Montego Bay has miles of hotels, villas, apartments, and duty-free shops set around Doctor's Cave Beach. Although lacking much in the way of cultural stimuli, the area is a comfortable island backdrop for the many conventions and conferences it hosts.

Ocho Rios, on the northwest coast halfway between Port Antonio and Montego Bay, long enjoyed the reputation of being Jamaica's most favored out-of-the-way resort, but the late-blooming Negril has since stolen much of that distinction. Ocho Rios's hotels and villas are all situated within short driving distance of shops and one of Jamaica's most scenic attractions, Dunn's River Falls.

Port Antonio, described by poet Ella Wheeler Wilcox as "the most exquisite port on earth," is a seaside town nestled at the foot of verdant hills toward the east end of the north coast.

Negril, some 50 miles west of Montego Bay, was long a sleepy Bohemian retreat. In the last decade the town has bloomed considerably and added a number of classy all-inclusive resorts (Sandals Negril, Grand Lido, and Swept Away), with a few more on the drawing board. Negril itself is only a small village, so there isn't much of historical significance to seek out. Then again, that's not what brings the sybaritic singles and couples here. The crowd is young, hip, laid-back, and here for the sun, the sand, and the sea.

Mandeville, 2,000 feet above the sea, is noted for its cool climate and proximity to secluded south coast beaches. Most accommodations don't have air-conditioning (it's simply not needed) but are close to golf, tennis, horseback riding, and bird-watching areas.

The smallest of the resort areas, Runaway Bay has a handful of modern hotels and an 18-hole golf course.

Kingston is the most culturally active place on Jamaica. Some of the island's finest hotels are located here, and those high towers are filled with rooftop restaurants, English pubs, serious theater and pantomime, dance presentations, art museums and galleries, jazz clubs, upscale supper clubs, and disco dives. The beaches around the city are not terribly attractive and are sometimes polluted. Hotels here do not run shuttles to better beaches, so if you stay here count on a good 20- to 30-minute drive.

At press time, two new properties were just opening: the luxury all-inclusive, adults-only **Braco Village Resort** (tel. 800/654–1337) in Rio Bueno just west of Runaway Bay, and **Comfort Suites Resort** (tel. 800/228–5150) set on a beautifully landscape hillside in Ocho Rios overlooking the bay and the cruise ship terminal. We were unable to visit the properties in fully operational state, but initial reports have been good. Surprisingly, both fall in our $–$$ range.

Highly recommended lodgings are indicated by a star ★.

Category	Cost EP*	Cost AI**
$$	$150–$225	$225–$300
$	$75–$150	$150–$225
¢	under $75	under $150

**EP prices are for a standard double room for two, excluding 10% tax and any service charge. To estimate rates for hotels offering MAP, add about $30–$40 per person per day to the above price ranges. For FAP, add about $50–$60 per person per day (these rates may include extras).*
***All-inclusive prices are per person, double occupancy, and include tax, service, all meals, drinks, facilities, lessons, airport transfers.*

Falmouth
$$
Trelawny Beach Hotel. The dependable Trelawny Beach resort offers seven stories of pale pink rooms overlooking 4 miles of beach. Off the beaten path, it's run as an all-inclusive resort with an emphasis on families. During the off-season, one child under 15 can stay free with his or her parents. There are daily activities programs for children and adults, a free shopping shuttle into MoBay, and a designated area of beach for nude sunbathing. *Box 54, Falmouth, tel. 809/954–2450 or 800/336–1435, fax 809/954–2149. 350 rooms. Facilities: 2 dining rooms, 4 lighted tennis courts, pool, daily activities, watersports equipment, shopping arcade, beauty salon, disco, nightly entertainment, MoBay shopping shuttle. AE, DC, MC, V. MAP, FAP, all-inclusive.*

$
★
Fisherman's Inn Dive Resort. A charming red-tile-and-stucco building fronts a phosphorescent lagoon at this welcoming, well-run hotel. At night the hotel restaurant offers a free boat ride to diners; dip your hand in the water, and the bioluminescent microorganisms glow. The bright breezy rooms, with pale carpets and walls accented by floral curtains and bedspreads, all face the water. The inn is a good deal, whether you dive (excellent packages are available) or not. Rates include three dives daily and MAP meal plan; nondivers do get a slight discount. *Rock District, tel. 809/954–4078, fax 809/*

954–3427. 12 rooms. Facilities: restaurant, bar, pool, private beach across lagoon, water-sports center/PADI dive shop. AE, MC, V. MAP.

Kingston

$$ **Jamaica Pegasus.** The Jamaica Pegasus is one of two business-class hotels in the New Kingston area. The 17-story complex near downtown has an efficient and accommodating staff, meeting rooms, a top-notch restaurant, a café, Old World decor, a pampering ambience, and an international crowd in the lobby. Other advantages here include an excellent business center, duty-free shops, and 24-hour room service. The rooms, all with balcony and voice-mail, were scheduled to have desperately needed face-lifts in 1995. *81 Knutsford Blvd., Box 333, Kingston, tel. 809/926–3690 or 800/225–5843, fax 809/929–5855. 334 rooms, 16 suites. Facilities: 2 restaurants, 2 bars, coffee shop, boutiques, beauty salon, Olympic-size pool, children's pool, jogging track, health club, 2 lighted tennis courts. AE, DC, MC, V. EP, MAP.*

$$ **Morgan's Harbour Hotel, Beach Club, and Yacht Marina.** A favorite of the sail-into-Jamaica set, this small property has 22 acres of beachfront at the very entrance to the old pirate's town. Done in light tropical prints, the rooms are very basic, but many have a balcony and minifridge. Ask for one in the new wing. Because the hotel is so close to the airport, passengers on delayed or cancelled flights are often bused here to wait. *Port Royal, Kingston, tel. 809/924–8464 or 800/526–2422, fax 809/924–8562. 39 rooms, 6 suites. Facilities: restaurant, pier bar, disco, water-sports center, complimentary airport shuttle, full-service marina, deep sea fishing charters, access to Lime Cay and other cays. AE, MC, V. EP.*

$$ ★ **Wyndham New Kingston.** The high-rise Wyndham New Kingston, the second of Kingston's business beat hotels, underwent major renovations in 1994. All facilities were upgraded, giving everything a pleasant new look, from the expansive marble lobby to the peach, teal, and green decor in well-appointed guest rooms. Lots of extras were thrown in, such as secured-access elevators and in-room hair dryers and coffee/tea setup. Rates include a complimentary massage at the spa and admission to Jonkanoo, the hotel's hot nightclub (*see* Nightlife, *below*). *Box 112, Kingston, tel. 809/926–5430 or 800/526–2422, fax 809/929–7439. 284 rooms, 13 suites, 6 1- and 2-bedroom housekeeping units. Facilities: 2 restaurants, 3 bars, Olympic-size pool, art gallery, shopping arcade, gaming room, 2 lighted tennis courts, health club, beauty salon/spa, nightclub. AE, DC, MC, V. EP, MAP.*

$ **Hotel Four Seasons.** This rambling, converted Edwardian mansion is a bit frayed around the edges, but that only contributes to its shabby, genteel charm. The least expensive rooms have a cramped feel, but those in the "superior" category are spacious and decorated with period antiques. The clientele is an amiable blend of Europeans, honeymooners, and locals. It's a refreshing change of pace from other Kingston accommodations, which tend to be either efficient business hotels or plain guest houses. *18 Ruthven Rd., Kingston 10, tel. 809/926–8805, fax 809/929–5964. 39 rooms. Facilities: restaurant, bar. AE, DC, MC, V. EP, MAP.*

$ ★ **Terra Nova.** Set in the quieter part of New Kingston, one mile from the commercial district and within walking distance of Devon House, is the intimate Terra Nova hotel. Guest rooms are decked out in classical mahogany furniture and fine art. The El Dorado restaurant offers international cuisine and reasonably priced buffets (seafood on Wednesday and Jamaican on Friday). *17 Waterloo Rd., Kingston 10, tel. 809/926–9334, fax 809/929–4933. 35 rooms. Facilities: restaurant, coffee shop, bar, pool. AE, DC, MC, V. EP.*

¢ **Morant Bay Villas.** If you really want to get away from it all, stay at one of these spartan villas in the middle of nowhere, between Kingston and Port Antonio. You'll experience true local flavor (95% of the clientele are Jamaican families) at unbeatable tariffs ($40 and under). Each unit has a private bath, a fan, and a TV. Larger units have kitchenettes; smaller rooms have minifridges. The beach is rocky and poky, but glorious Lyssons is a half-hour walk away. *Morant Bay, St. Thomas, tel. 809/982–2418. 20 units. Facilities: restaurant, bar. No credit cards. EP.*

Mandeville
¢–$ **Astra Country Inn & Restaurant.** Country is the key word in the name of this retreat, which is 2,000 feet up in the mountains. The low price reflects the nature of the very basic rooms here: They define spartan, but are spic-and-span. There is no air-conditioning, but you shouldn't miss it this high in the mountains. The small restaurant is open from 7 AM to 9 PM and serves snacks in addition to breakfast, lunch, and dinner. The food is billed as "home cooking" and emphasizes fresh produce—lots of vegetables and fruit juices. *Ward Ave., Box 60, Mandeville, tel. 809/962–3265 or 800/526–2422, fax 809/962–1461. 20 rooms, 2 housekeeping suites. Facilities: restaurant and bar, swimming pool, sauna, AE, MC, V. EP.*

¢–$ **Mandeville Hotel.** Tropical gardens wrap around the building, and flowers spill onto the terrace where breakfast and lunch are served. Rooms are simple and breeze-cooled; suites have full kitchens. You'll need a car to get around town, go out for dinner, and get to the beach, which is an hour away. *Box 78, Mandeville, tel. 809/962–2460 or 800/233-4582, fax 809/962–0700. 46 rooms, 17 1-, 2-, and 3-bedroom housekeeping suites. Facilities: restaurant, bar, coffee shop, pool, golf privileges at nearby Manchester Club. AE, MC, V. EP.*

Montego Bay
$$ ★ **Coyaba Beach Resort and Club.** Owners Joanne and Kevin Robertson live on the property, interacting with guests daily, giving this $4 million oceanfront retreat the feel of an intimate and inviting country inn. Located just east of Montego Bay, Coyaba is also very family friendly. The plantation-style great house is a successful blend of modern amenities and Old World grace: Guest rooms are decorated with lovely colonial prints and hand-carved mahogany furniture, and sunshine from the tall windows pours over terra-cotta floors and potted plants. Ocean-view rooms are considerably more expensive than those with a mountain view. Airport transfers, banana cake and rum baskets, afternoon tea, and Continental breakfast are part of the package. *Little River P.O., St. James, tel. 809/953–9150 or 800/223–9815, fax 953-2244. 50 rooms. Facilities: restaurant, 2 bars, pool, whirlpool, fitness room, lighted tennis court, masseuse, gift shop, water-sports equipment, scuba diving and fishing charters, golf packages. MC, V. EP.*

$$ **Holiday Inn Rose Hall.** The hotel chain has done much to raise a rundown campground to the level of a full-service property, with activities day and night and many tour facilities (and large tour groups as well). Although the rooms are cheerful enough, the hotel is big and noisy, with drab hallways and public areas. Perhaps the renovations scheduled for late 1995 will have resulted in positive changes. The quietest rooms are those farthest from the pool. The beach is just a sliver. There's live entertainment nightly near the pool and in the bars and restaurants. Kids under 19 stay free; those under 12 eat free as well. *Box 480, Montego Bay, tel. 809/953–2485 or 800/352–0731, fax 809/953–2840. 520 rooms. Facilities: 3 restaurants, 4 bars, pool, water-sports center, exercise room, children's camp, shuffle board, 4 tennis courts (2 lighted), gaming room with slot machines, disco, shops. AE, DC, MC, V. EP, MAP, FAP, all-inclusive.*

$$ **Seacastles.** This apartment resort, with colonnaded verandas alternating with imposing turrets, resembles a cross between Camelot and a West Indian plantation great house. The units are located in six "castles" spread over 14 acres and constructed around a central courtyard with splashing fountain. The studio apartments are smallish and rather plain, but quite adequate; suites have a little more character. The beach is pleasant and tree-shaded. Seacastles is especially popular with Jamaican families. Up to two children under 12 can stay free in their parents' room. *Box 1, Rose Hall, Monte-*

go Bay, tel. 809/953–3250, fax 809/953–3062. 198 studios and housekeeping suites. Facilities: 3 restaurants, 3 bars, pool, 2 lighted tennis courts, water-sports center, complimentary shopping shuttle. AE, DC, MC, V. EP, MAP, FAP.

$$ **Wyndham Rose Hall.** The veteran Wyndham Rose Hall, a self-contained resort built on the 400-acre Rose Hall Plantation, mixes recreation with a top-flight conference setup. A bustling business hotel popular with groups, it has all the resort amenities: tennis courts, golf course, three interconnected pools, a nightclub, a water-sports center, and a shopping arcade. Rooms in shades of deep blue and rose are comfortable but somewhat sterile. A "Kid's Klub" with daily supervised activities is included in the rates. The thin crescent of beach is good for sailing and snorkeling. Indoor and outdoor restaurants serve Continental, Italian, and Jamaican fare. *Box 999, Montego Bay, tel. 809/953–2650 or 800/996–3426, fax 809/953–2617. 489 rooms, 19 suites. Facilities: 4 restaurants, coffee shop, 3 pools, nonmotorized water sports, 6 lighted tennis courts, golf course, nightclub, lounge, fitness center, shopping arcade. AE, DC, MC, V. EP, MAP, all-inclusive.*

$ **The Atrium at Ironshore.** Fifteen moderately priced, fully furnished apartments make up this small complex. Decor varies, but each of the charming units has pastel floral prints, beige tile floors, beige rattan furniture, a patio or balcony, and a private housekeeper/cook on call. Large saltwater tanks full of tropical fish brighten the alfresco dining terrace near the waterfall-fed pool, and you'll often find lively games of darts or skittles underway in the English-style pub. A shopping mall with supermarket, cinema, and several boutiques is within walking distance, but you'll have to take a shuttle to the beach. Children under 12 stay free with their parents. *1084 Morgan Rd., Montego Bay, tel. 809/953–2605, fax 809/952–5641. 15 1½-, 2-, and 3-bedroom housekeeping suites. Facilities: restaurant, pub, pool, laundry facilities, beach and shopping shuttle. AE, DC, MC, V. EP.*

$ **Richmond Hill Inn.** The hilltop Richmond Hill Inn, a quaint, 200-year-old great house originally owned by the Dewars clan, attracts repeat visitors by providing spectacular views of the Caribbean and a great deal of peace, compared with MoBay's hustle. Decor tends toward the dainty and is a bit dated, with frilly lace curtains and doilies, lots of lavenders and mauves, and crushed velvet furniture here and there. A free shuttle will take you to shopping and beaches, about 10–15 minutes away. *Union St., Box 362, Montego Bay, tel. 809/952–3859 or 800/423–4095. 15 rooms, 4 suites. Facilities: terrace dining room, coffee shop, bar, pool, free MoBay shuttle. AE, MC, V. MAP, FAP.*

$ ★ **Sandals Inn.** If you're willing to do without a private beach (there's a public one across the street), you can stay here for much less than the other couples-only Sandals resorts. The inn is more intimate and far more quiet than the other Sandals; it's managed more as a small hotel than a large resort. Full room service is one of the nice touches here not found at the other Sandals properties on Jamaica. The charming rooms are compact; most have balconies facing the pool. Dark carpet contrasts with white lacquered furniture and tropical print fabrics. There's plenty to do here, and you can get in on the action at the other two MoBay Sandals by hopping aboard the free hourly shuttle. The in-town location makes the Inn convenient to shopping and tours. *Box 412, Montego Bay, tel. 809/952–4140 or 800/726–3257, fax 809/952–6913. 52 rooms. Facilities: 2 restaurants, 2 bars, pool, gift shop, lighted tennis court, fitness center, water-sports center. 3-night minimum stay. AE, DC, MC, V. All-inclusive.*

¢–$ **Cariblue Beach Hotel.** This rather dilapidated but ultra-friendly hotel is a favorite with divers. The rooms could use a refurbishment, but they're large and comfortable, and all but a few have an unobstructed ocean view. The stretch of beach is rather paltry, but the nautically minded guests are usually out on the water. The prow-shaped patio of the seafood restaurant is a popular gathering place at happy hour. Kids under 12 stay free in their parents' room. *Ironshore, Box 610, Montego Bay, tel. 809/953–2250, fax 809/952–5018. 20 rooms. Facilities: restaurant, bar, pool, water-sports and dive shop. AE, MC, V. EP, MAP.*

¢ ★ **Toby Inn.** This quiet oasis amid the bustle of downtown MoBay is everything a small budget hotel should be—pleasant, comfortable, and conveniently located. The property is shaded by almond and grapefruit trees filled with chirping birds and is only half a block from the small public beach (major beaches are a five- to 10-minute walk away). The homey rooms are either in balconied buildings surrounding the lively pool area or in cottages set away from the action. The Oriental/Jamaican restaurant is civilized, inexpensive, and very good. *1 Kent Ave., Box 467, Montego Bay, tel. 809/952–4370, fax 809/952–6591. 65 rooms. Facilities: restaurant, bar, 2 pools, boutique, beauty salon. AE, MC, V. EP, MAP.*

Negril

$$ ★ **Hedonism II.** Here is the resort that introduced the Club Med–style all-inclusive to Jamaica. Still wildly successful, Hedonism appeals most to single (60% of guests are), uninhibited vacationers who like a robust mix of physical activities. You can try everything from scuba diving to a trampoline clinic. Wood-trimmed public areas are filled with potted plants (and scantily-clad guests). Handsome guest rooms have modern blond wood furniture. It's too wild for some, party-animal heaven to others. *Box 25, Negril, tel. 809/957–4200 or 800/859–7873, fax 809/957–4289. 280 rooms. Facilities: restaurant, 5 bars, open-air buffet dining room, clothed and nude beaches, pool, 2 hot tubs, water-sports center with scuba diving, fitness center, aerobics, trapeze and trampoline clinics, horseback riding, 6 lighted tennis courts, 2 squash courts, bicycles, basketball, volleyball, game room. AE, DC, MC, V. All-inclusive.*

$$ **Seasplash.** The deluxe, tastefully decorated suites in these Mediterranean-style villas have lovely garden or sea views. Tropical color schemes emphasize lilacs and mauves. This is a good choice for families. Children under 12 stay free with their parents, and they'll be comfortable in the loft or in the living room. Couples will get better value for their vacation dollar elsewhere. *Norman Manley Blvd., Box 123, Negril, tel. 809/957–4041 or 800/254–2786, fax 809/957–4049. 2 rooms, 14 housekeeping suites. Facilities: restaurant, bar, pool, hot tub, boutique, mini-gym. AE, DC, MC, V. EP, MAP, FAP.*

$$ ★ **Swept Away.** Fitness- and health-conscious couples are the target market for this all-inclusive, which emphasizes sports and healthful cuisine. Twenty cottages containing 134 suites are spread along half a mile of drop-dead gorgeous beach. Each cottage has a private inner-garden atrium. The 10-acre sports complex across the road outclasses the competition by a long shot. The Feathers Continental restaurant is open to nonguests. The compound's chefs concentrate on healthful dishes with lots of fish, white meat, fresh fruits, and vegetables. *Long Bay, Negril, tel.809/957–4040 or 800/545–7937, fax 809/957–4060. 134 rooms. Facilities: 2 restaurants, 4 bars, 10 lighted tennis courts, 2 squash courts, 2 racquetball courts, fitness center, spa, jogging track, aerobics room, yoga classes, 2 steam rooms and saunas with plunge pools, 2 hot tubs, pool with lap lanes, water-sports center, golf privileges at Negril Hills. 3-night minimum stay. AE, DC, MC, V. All-inclusive.*

$–$$ **Charela Inn.** Each quiet, elegantly appointed room here has a private balcony or a covered patio. The owners' French-Jamaican roots find daily expression in the kitchen, and there's an excellent selection of wines. The small beach here is part of the glorious 7-mile Negril crescent. Kids under 10 stay free with parents, but they aren't allowed in deluxe rooms. *Box 33, Negril, tel. 809/957–4277 or 800/423–4095, fax 809/957–4414. 35 rooms, 4 suites. Facilities: res-*

taurant, pool, beach, sailboats and windsurfers, day cruise, cocktail party. 5-night minimum stay. MC, V. EP, MAP.

$–$$ ★ **Poinciana Beach Resort.** The management here has created all-inclusive packages with families in mind. A stay at Poinciana includes a "FunPass" to Anancy Park across the street, a supervised children's activity program, a playground, and baby-sitting during meal hours. Up to two children under 14 (one per parent) can stay free. One- and two-bedroom housekeeping suites with kitchens are also a good choice for families. Rooms and suites have cream-colored walls and tile floors. Bright jewel tones in the Jamaican prints that adorn the walls are echoed in the floral bedspreads. One of Jamaica's prettiest palm-speckled sandy beaches awaits, along with a water-sports center (scuba diving costs extra). There are also slot machines, tennis, a sunset cruise, a disco, a sports/piano bar, and a poolside bar with unlimited drinks. The open-air restaurant serves Caribbean cuisine, while the second floor café offers faster fare—burgers, hot dogs, and fries. *Box 44, Negril, tel. 809/957–4100 or 800/468–6728, fax in FL 305/749–6794. 90 rooms including studios, 1- and 2-bedroom housekeeping suites. Facilities: 2 restaurants, nightclub, bar, 2 pools, whirlpool, 2 lighted tennis courts, water-sports center, dive shop, basketball court, volleyball, lawn chess, gaming room, gym, shuffleboard, laundry facility, playground, library, beauty salon, masseuse, grocery store, duty free shops, golf package. AE, MC, V. All-inclusive.*

$ **Negril Cabins.** These timber cottages are nestled amid lush vegetation and towering royal palms. Rooms are unadorned, but natural wood paneling gives them a fresh look. Only superior rooms have air-conditioning; other rooms are cooled by ceiling fans and the breezes that come through the slatted windows. Televisions are also found only in the superior rooms. The gleaming beach is across the road. A most convivial place, the cabins are popular with young Europeans. Reasonably priced dive packages are available, and kids under 16 stay free in their parents' room. *Norman Manley Blvd., Box 118, Negril, tel. 809/957–4350 or 800/382–3444, fax 809/957–4381. 100 rooms. Facilities: 3 restaurants, 3 bars (including piano and swim-up), pool, hot tub, small gym, laundry, dive shop, tennis court, game room, children's program, gift shop. AE, MC, V. EP.*

$ **Negril Gardens.** Towering palms and well-tended gardens surround the pink and white buildings of this hotel. Half of the rooms are beachside, half across the street overlooking the pool; all are attractive, with tile floors and rattan furniture in light colors (no phones or televisions). The beach is nice, and water sports are available. *Box 58, Negril, tel. 809/ 957–4408 or 800/752–6824, fax 809/957–4374. 65 rooms. Facilities: restaurant, 2 bars (including disco), lighted tennis court, small gym, game room, pool, water sports. AE, MC, V. EP, MAP, FAP.*

¢–$ ★ **Devine Destiny.** Lush tropical forest surrounds this terra-cotta tile-roofed resort set 500 yards from the West End cliffs. Spacious guest rooms are decorated in aqua and terra-cotta. All have refrigerators, but there are no phones, radios, or televisions. Some rooms have kitchenettes, some have air-conditioning; some both, some neither. Be sure to give your preferences when making your reservations. Most rooms overlook what the resort claims is the largest pool in Negril. Whether or not the claim is true matters little, for the free-form pool with graceful arched bridges, half-moon swim-up bar, and dining terrace is lovely. Up to two children under 12 stay free with their parents, and there's a game room to keep them occupied. The beach is 20 minutes away on foot, but a daily shuttle makes it easily accessible. *Summerset Rd., (Box 117, West End, Negril), tel. and fax 809/957–9184. 40 rooms. Facilities: 2 restaurants, bar, pool, sundeck, game room, TV room, beach shuttle. AE, MC, V. EP.*

¢ **Thrills.** The beach is a 10-minute drive, a 20-minute bike ride, or a 30-minute walk away from this modest, hopping little inn, but the cliffs just 200 yards from its door are a spectacular site for snorkel-

ing. The spare but pleasant rooms have louvered blinds, private shower baths, and patios, but no phones. *Box 99, Negril, tel. 809/957–4390, fax 809/957–4153. 28 rooms. Facilities: restaurant, bar, disco, pool. MC, V. EP, MAP.*

Ocho Rios

$$ **Boscobel Beach.** This is a parent's dream for a Jamaican vacation, an all-inclusive that makes families feel welcome. The cheery day-care centers, divided by age group, should be a model for the rest of the Caribbean. Thoughtfully, there is an "adults only" section (for when the kids want to get away). Junior suites, refurbished in 1995, have new tile floors, brighter tropical decor, and marble counters in the bathroom. Boscobel only fits into our $$ category for families, since two children (one per parent) under 14 stay free in their parents' room. It's $50 a day for each additional child. There are off-season single-parent packages available as well. Breakfast and lunch are served at long buffets, and snacks are offered all day at the beach bar. Only the adults can dine at Allegro, a romantic Italian restaurant (kids get a supervised dinner elsewhere). Families can dine together at the Pavillion restaurant, which has a Continental menu. *Box 63, Ocho Rios, tel. 809/975–7330 or 800/859–7873, fax 809/975–7370. 208 rooms, half of them junior suites. Facilities: 3 restaurants, 5 bars (including disco and piano), gym, 2 pools, 2 hot tubs, water-sports center with scuba diving, children's activity and nanny care programs, nursery, playground, petting zoo, game room, bicycles, shopping and sightseeing tours, boutique, 4 lighted tennis courts, volleyball, golf greens fees and transportation, aerobics. AE, DC, MC, V. All-inclusive.*

$$ ★ **Couples.** No singles, no children. The emphasis at Couples is on romantic adventure for just the two of you, and the all-inclusive concept eliminates the decision making that can intrude on social pleasure. One-bedroom suites are designed for romance, with two-person hot tubs in the bathroom that peeks through a window at the four-poster king size bed. Continental breakfast is served in bed. The favorite dining spot is Bayside, an open-air restaurant with seating in graceful gazebos that stretch out over the water on stilted platforms. There's a lovely white beach for relaxation or water sports, and a private island, where you can sunbathe in the buff. Couples has the highest occupancy rate of any resort on the island—and perhaps the most suggestive logo as well. There may be a correlation. *Tower Isle, St. Mary, tel. 809/975–4271 or 800/268–7537, fax 809/975–4439. 161 rooms, 11 suites. Facilities: 3 restaurants, 3 bars, 2 pools, 5 whirlpools, island for nude sunbathing, 5 tennis courts (3 lighted), gym, 2 air-conditioned squash courts, water-sports center with scuba diving, horseback riding, nightly entertainment, golf greens fees and transfers, shopping arcade, sunset cruise, sightseeing tour. AE, DC, MC, V. All-inclusive.*

$$ **Sandals Ocho Rios.** The Sandals concept follows its successful formula at yet another couples-only, all-inclusive resort, this one on 12½ acres of beachfront property. The white- and sand-color buildings contrast nicely with the vegetation and the sea. The accommodations are airy, but generic motel decor and white plastic furniture on the balconies create an impersonal atmosphere. Guests enjoy meandering paths through lush foliage, hammocks for two strung between trees, and cozy benches nestled amid flower beds for private stargazing. *Ocho Rios, tel. 809/974–5691 or 800/726–3257, fax 809/974–5700. 237 units. Facilities: 3 restaurants, 4 bars (including 2 swim-ups, piano, and disco), 2 pools, hot tub, 2 lighted tennis courts gym, spa, 2 saunas, game room, basketball court, garden chess, water-sports center with scuba diving, golf greens fees and transportation, sightseeing tour, gift shop. AE, DC, MC, V. All-inclusive.*

$$ **Shaw Park Beach Hotel.** Another popular property, Shaw Park offers a pleasant alternative to downtown high rises. Hallways are dimly lit and uninviting, and rooms are fairly nondescript, but comfortable enough. There's a smallish beach on the property, and the

grounds are colorful and well tended. The Silks disco is a favorite for late-night carousing. Up to two children under 12 stay free in their parents' room. *Cutlass Bay, Box 17, Ocho Rios, tel. 809/974–2552 or 800/243–9420, fax 809/974–5042. 118 rooms. Facilities: restaurant, bar, pool, water sports and dive shop, beach, children's play area, fitness room, library, game/TV room, beauty salon, disco. AE, DC, MC, V. EP.*

$ **The Enchanted Garden.** Twenty stunning acres of gardens, filled with tropical plants and flowers and punctuated with a dramatic series of streams and waterfalls, certainly are enchanting. There is an aviary and a seaquarium where you can enjoy a delicatessen lunch or tea surrounded by tanks of fish and hanging orchids. The futuristic cinder-block villas seem regrettably incongruous amid the natural splendor, but the rooms are comfortable, if somewhat small, and you're never far from the soothing sound of rushing water. There's a free shuttle to the beach, which is several minutes away. *Box 284, Ocho Rios, tel. 809/974–5346 or 800/323–5655, fax 809/974–5823. 112 villa rooms and suites (some housekeeping units), 30 with private plunge pool. Facilities: 5 restaurants, pool, library, spa, disco, gift shop, beauty parlor, aviary, 2 lighted tennis courts, beach shuttle. AE, MC, V. EP, MAP, all-inclusive.*

$ **Jamel Continental.** This spotless, upscale, tropical motel is set on its own beach in a relatively undeveloped area close to all the activities of Ocho Rios and Runaway Bay. The spare units feel more spacious because of the high ceilings; all have a balcony with sea view, dark blue paisley curtains and bedspread, and black and white tile floors. The moderately priced restaurant serves fine local dishes, and the staff is friendly and helpful. *2 Richmond Estate, Priory, St. Ann, tel. 809/972–1031. 17 rooms, 3 suites. Facilities: restaurant, bar, pool, gift shop. MC, V. EP, MAP, FAP.*

¢–$ **Hibiscus Lodge.** This gleaming white building with a blue awning sits amid beautifully manicured lawns laced with trellises and adorned by peacocks, not too far from its tiny private beach. The impeccably neat, cozy rooms all have at least a partial sea view, terrace, and shower-bath, but no phone or TV. This German-run property may be Jamaica's best bargain, attracting a discriminating (and jubilant) crowd. *Box 52, Ocho Rios, tel. 809/974–2676 or 800/526–2422, fax 809/974–1874. 26 rooms. Facilities: restaurant, piano bar, pool, hot tub, lighted tennis court, TV room. AE, DC, MC, V. EP, MAP, FAP.*

¢ ★ **Club Jamaica Beach Resort.** This intimate all-inclusive has been reborn after extensive renovations. There are only 95 rooms here, ensuring guests receive plenty of personal attention from the young, cheerful staff. The rooms are refreshing, with gleaming white tile floors, comfortable modern furnishings, and gem-tone color schemes; more than half look out on the ocean. Guests, identified by their plastic, hospital-style armbands, tend to be active middle-agers and can be seen participating in the resort's daily activities (including nonmotorized water sports on the public beach) and dancing the night away to live entertainment. Children under 12 are not allowed. *Box 342, Turtle Beach, Ocho Rios, tel. 809/974-6632/42 or 800/818–2964, fax 809/974–6644. 95 rooms. Facilities: restaurant and dining terrace, pool bar, cocktail lounge, disco, pool, whirlpool, public beach, water-sports center, daily activities and entertainment, gift shops. AE, MC, V. All-inclusive.*

Port Antonio

$$ **Goblin Hill.** For a while this was known as the Jamaica Hill resort, but it is once again going by its original, evocative name. It's a lush 12-acre estate atop a hill overlooking San San Bay. Each attractively appointed villa comes with its own dramatic view, plus a housekeeper-cook. They are not equipped with phones or TVs. You'll need a car to get to the beach. Excellent villa and car-rental packages are available. The least expensive villas fall into our $ category. *Box 26, Port Antonio, tel. 809/925–8108 or 800/472–1148, fax 809/925–6248. 28*

housekeeping villas. Facilities: bar, pool, beach, 2 lighted tennis courts, water sports, reading and game room, play area, children's activity program, nature trail. AE, MC, V. EP.

$$ ★ **Jamaica Palace.** Built in 1988 to resemble a 17th-century Italian Colonial mansion, this imposing property rises in an expanse of white-pillared marble, with a black-and-white theme continued on the interior, including black lacquer and gilded oversize furniture. Each room has a semicircular bed and original European objets d'art and Oriental rugs; some are more lavish than others. Although the hotel is not on the beach, there is a 114-foot swimming pool shaped like Jamaica. *Box 227, Port Antonio, tel. 809/993–2021 or 800/423–4095, fax 809/993–3459. 24 rooms, 56 suites. Facilities: 2 restaurants, 2 bars, pool, boutiques, lawn chess, beach shuttle, golf packages. AE, MC, V. EP, FAP, MAP.*

$–$$ ★ **Dragon Bay.** Set on a scenic private cove, Dragon Bay is an idyllic grouping of villas surrounded by tropical gardens. The property underwent major renovations in 1994, upgrading the grounds, amenities, and each of the stunning, individually decorated villas. An orchid house was set to be added off the main dining terrace, providing a romantic spot for weddings. Villa 35 has a private pool, a large living room, and two bedrooms with separate sitting rooms that have sofa beds: You could conceivably squeeze two families in. *Box 176, Port Antonio, tel. 809/993–3281/3, fax 809/993–3284. 30 1-, 2-, and 3-bedroom villas. Facilities: restaurant, bar, disco, pool, gym, sauna, private beach. AE, MC, V. EP, MAP, FAP, all-inclusive.*

$ **Bonnie View Plantation Hotel.** Accommodations here are spartan, mattresses are a tad lumpy, and the furnishings a bit frayed. But the hotel certainly lives up to its name: Guests come for the sublime views and air of tranquillity. The nicest rooms (more expensive) are those with private verandas. But you can open your window for a burst of invigorating mountain air, or hang out in the restaurant and savor the unparalleled water panoramas. Beachcombers are forewarned: It's a good 25-minute drive to the ocean. *Box 82, Port Antonio, tel. 809/993–2752 or 800/423–4095, fax 809/993–2862. 20 rooms. Facilities: restaurant, pool, sundeck. AE, DC, MC, V. EP.*

$ **Hotel Mockingbird Hill.** With dogs running around the hillside property and only 10 rooms overlooking the sea and the Blue Mountains, Mockingbird Hill feels more like a cozy bed-and-breakfast than a hotel. Owners Barbara Walker and Shireen Aga run an extremely environmentally sensitive operation: They've used bamboo instead of hardwood for furniture, solar panels to heat water, ceiling fans instead of ozone depleting air-conditioning systems, local produce for meals in their Mille Fleurs dining terrace, and natural landscaping on their 7 acres. They also offer an array of eco-tour options in conjunction with other like-minded community members. The tasteful blue-on-white rooms do not have phones or televisions. *Box 254, Port Antonio, tel. 809/993–3370, fax 809/993–7133. 10 rooms. Facilities: restaurant, bar, pool, TV room, art gallery, art classes. Hiking tours, scuba diving and fishing charters available. MC, V. EP, MAP.*

Runaway Bay

$$ ★ **FDR, Franklyn D. Resort.** Jamaica's first all-suite, all-inclusive resort for families, this fabulous answer to parents' prayers opened in 1990. Upscale yet unpretentious, the pink buildings house spacious and well-thought-out one-, two-, and three-bedroom villas and are grouped in a horseshoe around the swimming pool. Best of all, a "girl Friday" is assigned to each suite, filling the role of nanny, housekeeper, and (when desired) cook. She'll even baby-sit at night for a small charge. Most parents are so impressed that they wish they could take their girl Friday home with them when they leave. Children and teens are kept busy with daylong supervised activities and sports, while parents are free to join in, lounge around the pool, play golf, go scuba diving, or just enjoy uninterrupted time together. Kids under 16 stay and play free with their parents. *Runaway*

Bay, tel. 809/973–3067 or 800/654–1337, fax 809/973–3071. 76 suites. Facilities: 2 restaurants, 4 bars (including disco and piano), pool, water-sports center, clothed and nude beaches, gym, game room, lighted tennis court, miniclub for children with supervised activities, glass-bottom-boat tour, gift and crafts shops. AE, MC, V. All-inclusive.

$ ★ **Jamaica, Jamaica.** This all-inclusive was a pioneer in emphasizing the sheer Jamaican-ness of the island. The cooking is particularly first-rate, with an emphasis on Jamaican cuisine and fresh seafood. Rooms are dominated by carved wooden headboards and a massive Jamaican wooden chair. The happy campers—often Germans, Italians, and Japanese—flock here for the psychedelically colored reef surrounding the beach and the superb golf school. Guests must be over 16. *Box 58, Runaway Bay, tel. 809/973–2436 or 800/859–7873, fax 809/973–2352. 238 rooms, 4 suites. Facilities: 2 restaurants, beach grill, 4 bars (including piano/karakoke, disco, and nightclub), clothed and nude beaches, swimming pool and lap pool, 3 whirlpools, water-sports center, 2 lighted tennis courts, horseback riding, dive center, gym, TV room, game room, sightseeing tours, sundry and gift shops. AE, DC, MC, V. All-inclusive.*

¢–$ **Club Caribbean.** This all-inclusive markets itself to families on a budget. A series of typically Caribbean cottages, half with kitchenette, lines the long but narrow beach. The rooms are very simple and clean, with ceiling fans, worn rattan furnishings, and floral print fabrics, but no phone or TV. Those with air-conditioning cost a bit extra. Ask for one of the new cottages added in late 1994. The place is very popular with European families. Children under six stay free, and 30 cottages have bunk beds instead of kitchenettes. Although most water sports are included, scuba diving costs extra. *Box 65, Runaway Bay, tel. 809/973–3507 or 800/223–9815, fax 809/973–3509. 130 rooms. Facilities: restaurant, 3 bars, pool, shopping arcade, dive center, water sports center, 2 tennis courts, day-care center with children's program, gift shop. AE, MC, V. All-inclusive.*

¢ **H.E.A.R.T. Country Club.** It's a shame more visitors don't know about this place, perched above Runaway Bay and brimming with Jamaica's true character. While training young islanders interested in the tourism industry—H.E.A.R.T. stands for Human Employment And Resource Training—it also provides a quiet and pleasant stay for guests. The employees make an effort to please. Rooms seem somewhat worn around the edges, but are equipped with all the basics and have either an ocean or pretty garden view. The tranquil restaurant serves delicious local and Continental specialties. Kids under 12 stay free with their parents. An excellent beach is a 20-minute hike (uphill coming back) or a five- to 10-minute drive away. *Box 98, St. Ann, tel. 809/973–2671, fax 809/973–2693. 20 rooms. Facilities: restaurant, piano bar, golf, beach shuttle. AE, MC, V. EP, MAP.*

Villa and Apartment Rental

Although Jamaica has some luxurious villas, many more are comfortable, reasonably priced properties. Although a few are located on beaches, most are in the hills, making a car a virtual necessity. Recommended management companies for villas and apartment complexes include **Relax Villa Resort** (Montego Bay, tel. 809/979–0656 or 800/354–7218), **Sunshine Rental Villas** (Ocho Rios, tel. 809/974–5025), and **Jamswing Villas and Condos** (Runaway Bay, tel. 809/973–4847). For a complete listing, contact the **Jamaica Association of Villas and Apartments** (tel. 800/221–8830). Member companies must adhere to certain guidelines.

Camping

There are extensive camping facilities throughout the island, most of them clean, safe, and well-run. The acknowledged leader in the field is **JATCHA** (Jamaica Alternative Tourism Camping and Hiking Association, Box 216, Kingston 7, tel. 809/927–2097). For $15 they'll send information on more than 100 recommended properties, as well as maps and a questionnaire to ascertain your particular needs. Their personalized service will do everything from make reservations to suggesting a tailor-made itinerary.

Off-Season Bets Although exclusive properties such as Tryall and Trident remain out of our price range even during the off-season, several all-inclusives become affordable. In Montego Bay, these include: **Sandals Montego Bay** (Box 100, Montego Bay, tel. 809/952–5510 or 800/726–3257, fax 809/952–0816) and the **Royal Jamaican**(Box 167, Montego Bay, tel. 809/953–2231 or 800/726–3257, fax 809/953–2788). In Negril, try **Sandals Negril** (Box 10, tel. 809/957–4216 or 800/726–3257, fax 809/957–4338).

The Arts and Nightlife

Jamaica—especially Kingston—supports a lively community of musicians. For starters there is reggae, popularized by the late Bob Marley and the Wailers and performed today by son Ziggy Marley, Jimmy Tosh (the late Peter Tosh's son), Gregory Isaacs, the Third World, Jimmy Cliff, and many others. If your experience of Caribbean music has been limited to steel drums and Harry Belafonte, then the political, racial, and religious messages of reggae may set you on your ear; listen closely and you just might hear the heartbeat of the people. Those who already love reggae may want to plan a visit in mid-July to August for the Reggae Sunsplash. The four-night concert at the Bob Marley Performing Center (a field set up with a temporary stage), in the Freeport area of Montego Bay, showcases local talent and attracts such performers as Gladys Knight and the Pips, Steel Pulse, Third World, and Ziggy Marley and the Melody Makers.

Discos and Clubs For the most part, the liveliest late-night happenings throughout Jamaica are in the major resort hotels. Some of the best music will be found in Negril at **De Buss** (tel. 809/957–4405) and of course at the hot, hot spot, **Kaiser's Cafe** (tel. 809/957–4070), as well as the disco at **Hedonism II** (tel. 809/957–4200), and **Compulsion Disco** (tel. 809/957–4416). The most popular spots in Kingston are **Godfather** (Knutsford Blvd., tel. 809/929–5459), **Mingles** at the Courtleigh (tel. 809/929–5321), **Illusions** in the New Lane Plaza (tel. 809/929–2125), **Jonkanoo** in the Wyndham New Kingston (tel. 809/929–3390), and **Mirage** (tel. 809/978–8557), the hot new disco in Sovereign Centre.

In Port Antonio, if you have but one night to disco, do it at the **Roof Club** (11 West St., no phone). On weekends, from elevenish on, this is where it's all happening. If you want to "do the town," check out **CenterPoint** (Folly Rd., tel. 809/993–3377), **Shadows** (40 West St., tel. 809/993–3823), or the Jamaican cultural show on Friday nights at **Fern Hill Club** (tel. 809/993–3222). The principal clubs in Ocho Rios are **Jamaica Me Crazy** at the Jamaica Grande (tel. 809/974–2201), **Acropolis** (70 Main St., tel. 809/ 974–2633), **Silks** in the Shaw Park Beach Hotel (tel. 809/974–2552), and the **Little Pub on Main Street** (tel. 809/974–2324), which produces Caribbean revues. The hottest places in Montego Bay are the **Cave** disco at the Seawinds Beach Resort (tel. 809/952–4070), **Sir Winston's Reggae Club** (Gloucester St., tel. 809/952–2084), and the **Rhythm Nightclub** at the Holiday Inn Rose Hall (tel. 809/953–2485). After 10 PM on Friday nights, the crowd gathers at **Pier 1** on Howard Cooke Boulevard, opposite the straw market (tel. 809/952–2452). Some of the all-inclusives offer a dinner and disco pass from about $50.

15 Martinique

Updated by Jordan Simon

Not for naught did the Arawaks name Martinique *Madinina*, which means "Island of Flowers." This is one of the most beautiful islands in the Caribbean, lush with exotic wild orchids, frangipani, anthurium, jade vines, flamingo flowers, and hundreds of vivid varieties of hibiscus. Trees bend under the weight of such tropical treats as mangoes, papayas, bright red West Indian cherries, lemons, limes, and bananas. Acres of banana plantations, pineapple fields, and waving green seas of sugarcane show the bounty of the island's fertile soil.

The towering mountains and verdant rain forest in the north lure hikers, while underwater sights and sunken treasures attract snorkelers and scuba divers. Martinique appeals as well to those whose idea of exercise is turning over every 10 or 15 minutes to get an even tan or whose adventuresome spirit is satisfied by finding booty in a duty-free shop. Francophiles in particular will find the island enchanting.

The 425-square-mile island is 4,261 miles from Paris, but its spirit (and language) is French, with more than a mere soupçon of West Indian spice. Tangible, edible evidence of that fact is the island's cuisine—a tempting blend of classic French and Creole dishes.

Martinique became an overseas department of France in 1946 and a *région* in 1974, a status not unlike that of an American state vis-à-vis the federal government. The island has benefited from the economic growth in Europe; the standard of living and salaries here are some of the highest in the West Indies. Unfortunately for the budget traveler, this is reflected in the prices. Dining in particular is expensive here, although you get what you pay for: The quality of cuisine here is higher than on many Caribbean islands. You can economize by picnicking. Grocery stores have tempting foods imported from France, and wine is more affordable than on English-speaking islands.

Rental cars and taxis are also costly. If you are planning a beachcombing vacation, choose a small hotel close to the water so you won't need transportation. If your main activity will be exploring, look for lodging away from the beach; the lower cost will help offset the price of car rental.

Despite these high costs, Martinique's hotel prices compare favorably with other Caribbean islands. You can find a number of moderately priced hotels on or near beaches, and many of these offer package deals that make them yet more affordable (always inquire when you call). Downright budget hotels are harder to find, but small apartments, cottages, and rooms in private homes are available through the island's Gîtes de France office. Most of these smaller properties are away from beaches.

What It Will Cost These sample prices, meant only as a general guide, are for high season. Martinique has many small hotels in the $100-a-night range. Resort hotels on the beach start at about $150. A small apartment rents for about $45 a day. Expect to pay at least $20 per person for dinner. Wine is reasonably priced; a recent vintage Médoc is about $7 at the grocery store, and a carafe of house wine at a restaurant can be as low as $8. Local beer is $2.50–$3 at a restaurant; a rum punch ranges from less than $2 at a local rum shop to at least $3.50 at a restaurant. Renting a car will average $60 a day. Taxis are also expensive. Cost from the airport to Fort-de-France is about $15, and about $30 to Pointe du Bout. A *vedette*, or ferry, from Fort-de-France to Pointe du Bout costs 16F (about U.S. $3). A single-tank dive here is around $55, while snorkel equipment rents for about $10 a day.

Before You Go

Tourist Information For information contact the **French West Indies Tourist Board** by calling 800/391–4909, or contact the **French Government Tourist Office, Martinique Promotion Bureau** (444 Madison Ave., New York, NY 10022, tel. 212/757–1125; 9454 Wilshire Blvd., Beverly Hills, CA 90212, tel. 310/271–2358; or 676 N. Michigan Ave., Chicago, IL 60611, tel. 312/751–7800). In Canada, contact the French Government Tourist Office (1981 McGill College Ave., Suite 490, Montreal, Québec H3A 2W9, tel. 514/288–4264; or 1 Dundas St. W, Suite 2405, Toronto, Ontario M5G 1Z3, tel. 416/593–4723 or 800/361–9099). In the United Kingdom the tourist office can be reached at 178 Piccadilly, London, United Kingdom W1V 0AL, tel. 0181/124–4123.

Arriving and Departing

By Plane The most frequent flights from the United States are on **American Airlines** (tel. 800/433–7300), which has year-round daily service from more than 100 U.S. cities to San Juan. From there, the airline's American Eagle flies to Martinique, usually with a stop first at Guadeloupe. **Air France** (tel. 800/237–2747) flies direct from Miami and San Juan; **Air Canada** (tel. 800/422–6232) has service from Montreal and Toronto; **LIAT** (tel. 809/462–0700), with its extensive coverage of the Antilles, flies from Antigua, St. Maarten, Guadeloupe, Dominica, St. Lucia, Barbados, Grenada, and Trinidad and Tobago. **Air Martinique** (tel. 596/51–09–90) has service to and from St. Martin, Dominica, and Guadeloupe. **Council Charter** (tel. 212/661–4546 or 800/765–6065) provides Saturday-Saturday flights out of New York's JFK, and offers flight/lodging packages, during high season.

From the Airport You'll arrive at Lamentin International Airport, which is about a 15-minute taxi ride from Fort-de-France and about 40 minutes from the Trois-Ilets peninsula, the first of many resort areas on the southern beaches, where most of the hotels are located.

Cab fare to Fort-de-France is 70F; 150F to Trois-Ilets. A 40% surcharge is in effect on Sunday and between 8 PM and 6 AM. This means that if you arrive at Lamentin at night, depending on where your hotel is, it may be cheaper to rent a car from the airport than to take a one-way taxi. A bus departs hourly 6–6 to downtown Fort-de-France (cost: 15F).

Passports and Visas U.S. and Canadian citizens must have a passport (an expired passport may be used, as long as the expiration date was no more than five years ago) or proof of citizenship, such as an original (not photocopied) birth certificate or a voter registration card accompanied by a government-authorized photo identification. British citizens are required to have a passport. In addition, all visitors must have a return or ongoing ticket.

Language Many Martinicans speak Creole, a mixture of Spanish and French. Try *sa ou fe* for hello. In major tourist areas you'll find someone who speaks English, but the courtesy of using a few French words, even they are *Parlez-vous anglais?*, is appreciated. The people of Martinique are extremely courteous and will help you through your French. Even if you do speak fluent French, you may have a problem understanding the accent of the country people. Most menus are written in French, so a dictionary is helpful.

Precautions Exercise the same safety precautions you would in any other big city: Leave valuables in the hotel safe-deposit vault and lock your car, with luggage and valuables stashed out of sight. Don't leave jewelry or money unattended on the beach.

Beware of the *mancenillie* (manchineel) trees. These pretty trees with little green fruits that look like apples are poisonous. Sap and even raindrops falling from the trees onto your skin can cause painful, scarring blisters. The trees have red warning signs posted by the Forestry Commission.

If you plan to ramble through the rain forest, be careful where you step. Poisonous snakes, cousins of the rattlesnake, slither through this lush tropical Eden.

Except for the area around Cap Chevalier and the Caravelle Peninsula, the Atlantic waters are rough and should be avoided by all but expert swimmers.

Staying in Martinique

Important Addresses **Tourist Information:** The **Martinique Tourist Office** (Blvd. Alfassa, tel. 596/63–79–60) is open Monday–Thursday 7:30–12:30 and 2:30–5:30, Friday 7:30–12:30 and 2:30–5, Saturday 8–noon. The office's free maps and booklets, "Chouboulonte" and "Martinique Info," are useful. The tourist information booth at Lamentin Airport is open daily until the last flight has landed.

Emergencies **Police:** Call 17. **Fire:** Call 18. **Ambulance:** Call 70–36–48 or 71–59–48. **Hospitals:** There is a 24-hour emergency room at **Hôpital La Meynard** (Châteauboeuf, just outside Fort-de-France, tel. 596/55–20–00). **Pharmacies:** Pharmacies in Fort-de-France include **Pharmacie de la Paix** (corner rue Victor Schoelcher and rue Perrinon, tel. 596/71–94–83) and **Pharmacie Cypria** (Blvd. de Gaulle, tel. 596/63–22–25). **Consulate:** The **United States Consulate** (14 rue Blénac, Fort-de-France, tel. 596/63–13–03).

Currency The coin of the realm is the French franc, which consists of 100 centimes. At press time the rate was 5.30F to U.S. $1, but check the current exchange rate before you leave home. U.S. dollars are accepted in some of the tourist hotels, but for convenience, it's better to convert your money into francs. Banks give a more favorable rate than do hotels. A currency exchange service, **Change Caraibes,** is in the Arrivals Building at Lamentin Airport (tel. 596/51–57–91; open weekdays 7 AM–9 PM, Sat. 8:30–2), which has a more favorable rate, and in Fort-de-France (rue Ernest Deproge, across from the tourist office, tel. 596/60–28–40; open weekdays 8–7, Sat. 8:30–12:30). Note: Prices quoted here are in U.S. dollars unless indicated otherwise.

Major credit cards are accepted in hotels and restaurants in Fort-de-France and the Pointe du Bout areas; few establishments in the countryside accept them. There is a 20% discount on luxury items paid for with traveler's checks or with certain credit cards.

Taxes and Service Charges A resort tax varies from hotel to hotel; the maximum is $1.50 per person per day. Rates quoted by hotels usually include a 10% service charge; some hotels add the 10% to your bill. All restaurants include a 15% service charge in their menu prices.

Getting Around

Taxis Stands are at Lamentin Airport, in downtown Fort-de-France, and at major hotels. Taxis are expensive. Rates are regulated by the government, but local taxi drivers are an independent lot, and prices often turn out to be higher than the minimum "official" rate. The official rate is established at the beginning of each year and is listed in the tourist brochures, available at the airport tourist office. When taxi drivers overcharge, you have little recourse. You can either cause a fuss by contacting the police or show the driver the "officially quoted rate" in the brochure and hope that he accepts it. The cost from the airport to Fort-de-France is about 70F; from the airport to Pointe du Bout, about 150F. A 40% surcharge is in effect between 8 PM and 6 AM and on Sundays.

Buses Public buses and eight-passenger minivans (license plates bear the letters TC) are an inexpensive means of transportation. Buses are always crowded and are not recommended for the timid traveler, especially during rush hours. The routes radiate from Fort-de-France to major towns, including St-Pierre, Basse-Pointe, La Trinité, Le Marin, and Lamentin. In Fort-de-France, the main terminal for the minivans is at Pointe Simon on the waterfront. There are frequent departures from early morning until 8 PM; fares range from $1 to $5.

Ferries Weather permitting, *vedettes* operate daily between Fort-de-France and the Marina Méridien in Pointe du Bout and between Fort-de-France and Anse-Mitan and Anse-à-l'Ane. The Quai d'Esnambuc is the arrival and departure point in Fort-de-France. At press time, the one-way fare was 16F; round-trip, 27F. Either trip takes about 25 minutes. Schedules are listed in the visitors' guide, *Martinique Info*, available at the tourist office.

The **Caribbean Express** (tel. 590/63–12–11) offers daily, scheduled interisland service aboard a 128-foot, 227-passenger motorized catamaran, linking Martinique with Guadeloupe, and Dominica. Fares run approximately 25% below economy airfares.

Bicycles and Motorbikes Bikes and motorbikes can be rented from **Funny** (tel. 596/63–33–05), or **T.S. Location Sarl** (tel. 596/63–42–82), both in Fort-de-France, **Discount** (tel. 596/66–54–37) in Pointe du Bout, and **Scootonnerre** (tel. 596/76–41–12) in Le Diamant. Cost is about $15 a day for bikes; $35 for a small motorbike.

Rental Cars Having a car will make your stay in Martinique much more pleasurable. Although most of the larger hotels are on a beach, you may want to visit other beaches, especially Les Salines, the island's best (*see* Beaches, *below*). Moreover, budget hotels are generally not within walking distance of the water, making a car essential. Martinique has about 175 miles of well-paved and well-marked roads (albeit with international signs). Streets in Fort-de-France are narrow and clogged with traffic; country roads are mountainous with hairpin curves. The Martinicans drive with aggressive abandon, but are surprisingly courteous and will let you into the flow of traffic. When driving up-country, take along the free map supplied by the tourist office. If you want a more detailed map, the "Carte Routière et Touristique" is available at bookstores. There are plenty of gas stations in the major towns, but a full tank of gas will get you all the way around the island with gallons to spare.

A valid driver's license is needed to rent a car for up to 20 days. After that, you'll need an international driver's permit. Major credit cards are accepted by most car-rental agents. Rates are about $60 per day (unlimited mileage). Lower daily rates with per-mile charges, which usually turn out to be higher overall rates, are sometimes available. Question agents closely. Among the many agencies are **Avis** (tel. 596/70–11–60 or 800/331–1212), **Budget** (tel. 596/63–69–00 or 800/527–0700), **Hertz** (tel. 596/60–64–64 or 800/654–3131), and **Europcar/National Car Rental** (tel. 596/51–20–33 or 800/328–4567). Many hotels have a car-rental desk. While Citroens are usually cheaper, they're not as hardy as Peugeots or Fords, which are a better choice if you're driving a lot through the rain forest. Avis and Hertz rent Jeeps. If you book a rental car from the United States at least 48 hours in advance, you can qualify for a hefty discount.

Telephones and Mail

To call Martinique from the United States, dial 011 plus 596 plus the local six-digit number. To place an interisland call, dial the local six-digit number. To call the United States from Martinique, dial 19–1, the area code, and the local number. For Great Britain, dial 19–44, the area code (without the first zero), and the number.

It is not possible to make collect or credit calls from Martinique to the United States. There are few coin telephone booths on the island, and those are usually in hotels and restaurants. Most public telephones now use Telecartes, which are sold in denominations of 50F, 80F, and 100F and may be purchased from post offices, *café-tabacs*, and hotels. These are inserted into the telephone box; units are deducted from your card according to time and distance of each call you make. Long-distance calls made with Telecartes are less costly than are operator-assisted calls.

Airmail letters to the United States cost 4.60F for up to 20 grams; postcards, 3.70F. For Great Britain, the costs are 4.40F and 3.60F, respectively. Stamps may be purchased from post offices, café-tabacs, or hotel newsstands.

Opening and Closing Times

Stores that cater to tourists are generally open weekdays 8:30–6; Saturday 8:30–1. Banking hours are weekdays 7:30–noon and 2:30–4.

Guided Tours

For a personalized tour of the island, ask the tourist office to arrange for a tour with an English-speaking taxi driver. There are set rates for tours to various points on the island; prices are per car, so sharing the ride with two or three others keeps the cost down. The island is so large that you can't begin to see everything in a day. Before opting for a personalized tour, decide what you want to see. The northern part of the island, especially around St-Pierre, is a good choice.

Madinina Tours (tel. 596/61–49–49) offers half- and full-day jaunts, with lunch included in the all-day outings. Boat tours are also available. Madinina has tour desks in most of the major hotels.

Parc Naturel Régional de la Martinique (9 blvd. Général de Gaulle, Fort-de-France 97206, tel. 596/73–19–30) organizes guided hiking tours year-round. Descriptive folders are available at the tourist office.

Exploring Martinique

Numbers in the margin correspond to points of interest on the Martinique map.

The starting point of the tour is the capital city of Fort-de-France, where almost a third of the island's 360,000 people live. From here, we'll tour St-Pierre, Mont Pelée, and other points north; go along the Atlantic coast; and finish with a look at the sights in the south.

Fort-de-France 1

Fort-de-France lies on the beautiful Baie des Flamands on the island's Caribbean (west) coast. With its narrow streets and pastel buildings with ornate wrought-iron balconies, the capital city is reminiscent of the French Quarter in New Orleans. However, where New Orleans is flat, Fort-de-France is hilly. Public and commercial buildings and residences cling to its hillsides behind downtown.

Stop first at the **tourist office,** which shares a building with Air France on the boulevard Alfassa, right on the bay near the ferry landing. English-speaking staffers provide excellent, free material, including detailed maps and an 18-page booklet in English with a series of seven self-drive tours.

Thus armed, walk across the street to **La Savane.** The 12½-acre landscaped park is filled with gardens, tropical trees, fountains, and benches. It's a popular gathering place and the scene of promenades, parades, and impromptu soccer matches. A statue of Pierre Belain d'Esnambuc, leader of the island's first settlers, is upstaged by Vital Dubray's flattering white Carrara marble statue of the Empress Josephine, Napoleon's first wife. Sculpted in a high-waisted Empire gown, Josephine gazes toward Trois-Ilets across the bay, where in 1763 she was born Marie-Joseph Tascher de la Pagerie. Near the harbor is a **marketplace** where high-quality local crafts are sold. Right across from the Savane, you can catch the **ferry** for the beaches at Anse-Mitan and Anse-à-l'Ane and for the 20-minute run across the bay to the resort hotels of Pointe du Bout. The ferry is more convenient than a car for travel between Pointe du Bout and Fort-de-France.

Rue de la Liberté runs along the west side of La Savane. Look for the main post office (rue de la Liberté, between rue Blénac and rue Antoine Siger). Just across rue Blénac from the post office is the **Musée Départementale de Martinique,** which contains exhibits on the pre-Columbian Arawak and Carib periods, including pottery, beads, and part of a skeleton that turned up during excavations in 1972. One exhibit examines the history of slavery; costumes, documents, furniture, and handicrafts from the island's colonial period are on display. *9 rue de la Liberté, tel. 596/71–57–05. Admission: 15F adults, 5F children ages 5–12. Open weekdays 9–1 and 2–5, Sat. 9–noon.*

Leave the museum and walk west (away from La Savane) on rue Blénac, along the side of the post office to rue Victor Schoelcher. There you'll see the Romanesque **St-Louis Cathedral,** the steeple of which rises high above the surrounding buildings. The cathedral has lovely stained-glass windows. A number of Martinique's former governors are interred beneath the choir loft.

Rue Schoelcher runs through the center of the capital's primary shopping district, a six-block area bounded by rue de la République, rue de la Liberté, rue de Victor Severe, and rue Victor Hugo. Stores feature Paris fashions (at Paris prices) and French perfume, china, crystal, and liqueurs, as well as local handicrafts.

Three blocks north of the cathedral, make a right turn on rue Perrinon and go one block. At the corner of rue de la Liberté is the **Bibliothèque Schoelcher,** the wildly elaborate Byzantine-Egyptian-Romanesque–style public library. It's named after Victor Schoelcher, who led the fight to free the slaves in the French West Indies in the 19th century. The eye-popping structure was built for the 1889 Paris Exposition, after which it was dismantled, shipped to Martinique, and reassembled piece by ornate piece on its present location.

Follow rue Victor Severe five blocks west, just beyond the Hôtel de Ville, and you'll come to Place Jose-Marti. The **Galerie de Géologie et de Botanique** at the **Parc Floral et Culturel** will acquaint you with the

Exploring
Ajoupa-Bouillon, **10**
Balata, **9**
Bellefontaine, **3**
Diamond Rock, **18**
Dubuc Castle, **15**
Forêt de Montravail, **19**
Fort-de-France, **1**
La Trinité, **14**
Le Carbet, **4**
Le François, **23**
Le Morne Rouge, **8**
Le Prêcheur, **7**
Le Vauclin, **22**
Les Trois-Ilets, **16**
Leyritz Plantation, **11**
Macouba, **12**
Musée Gauguin, **5**
Petrified Forest, **21**
Pointe du Bout, **17**
St-Pierre, **6**
Ste-Anne, **20**
Ste-Marie, **13**
Schoelcher, **2**

Dining
Athanor, **65**
Au Poissond'Or, **44**
Bidjoul, **51**
Chez Christiane, **52**
Chez Gaston, **33**
Club Nautique, **41**
La Creperie, **31**
La Dunette, **64**
La Factorérie, **27**
La Marina, **45**
La Petite Auberge, **61**
La Villa Creole, **43**
Le Colibri, **25**
Le Coq Hardi, **32**
Le Crew, **34**
Le Diam's, **53**
Le Fromager, **26**
Le Marie Sainte, **35**
Le Second Soufflé, **36**
Le Vieux Galion, **29**
Poï et Virginie, **66**
Pizza Pepe, **54**
Tamarin Plage Restaurant, **50**

Lodging
Auberge de l'Anse-Mitan, **48**
Auberge du Marin, **62**
Baie du Galion, **30**
Bambou, **46**
Chez Eléne, **60**
Club Med/Buccaneer's Creek, **63**
Diamant Les Bains, **57**

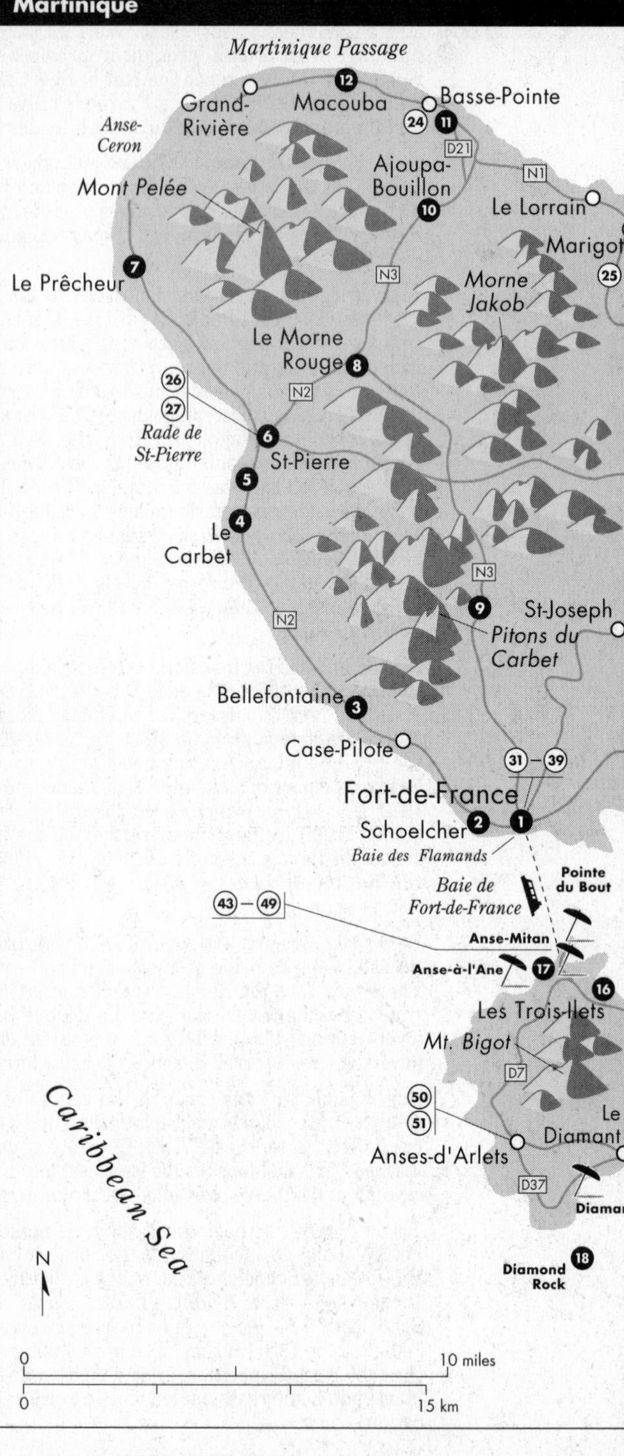

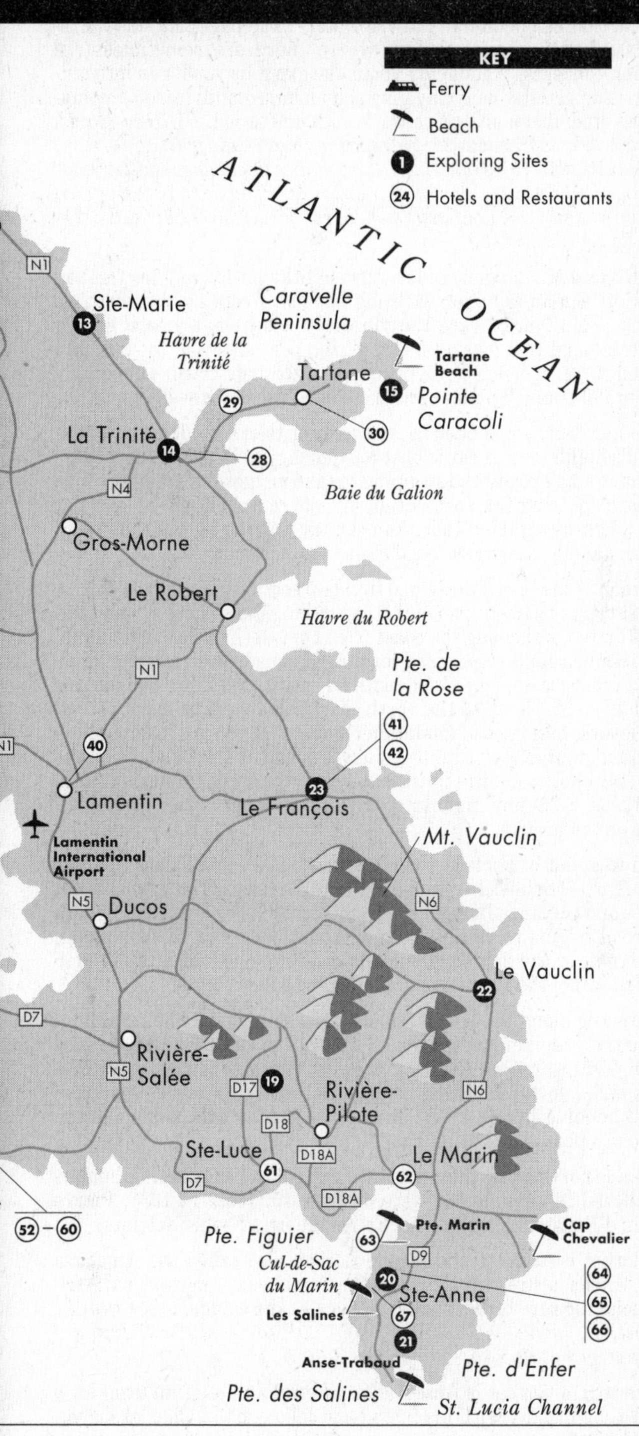
KEY
Ferry
Beach
Exploring Sites
Hotels and Restaurants
ATLANTIC OCEAN
Ste-Marie
Caravelle Peninsula
Havre de la Trinité
Tartane
Tartane Beach
Pointe Caracoli
La Trinité
Baie du Galion
Gros-Morne
Le Robert
Havre du Robert
Pte. de la Rose
Lamentin
Le François
Lamentin International Airport
Mt. Vauclin
Ducos
Le Vauclin
Rivière-Salée
Rivière-Pilote
Ste-Luce
Le Marin
Pte. Marin
Cap Chevalier
Pte. Figuier
Cul-de-Sac du Marin
Ste-Anne
Les Salines
Anse-Trabaud
Pte. d'Enfer
Pte. des Salines
St. Lucia Channel

variety of exotic flora on this island. There's also an aquarium showing fish that can be found in these waters. The park contains the island's official cultural center, where there are sometimes free evening concerts. Wandering about the grounds you'll run into musicians and artists, who may give you an impromptu lesson on playing the steel drum or how to work with driftwood. *Pl. Jose-Marti, Sermac, tel. 596/71–66–25. Admission to grounds free; aquarium: 35F adults, 28F children under 12; botanical/geological gallery: 5F adults, 1F children under 12. Park open daily dawn to 10 PM; aquarium open daily 9–7; gallery open Tues.–Fri. 9:30–12:30 and 3:30–5:30, Sat. 9–1 and 3–5.*

The Rivière Madame meanders through the park and joins the bay at **Pointe Simon,** a major yachting marina. Fronting the river, on Avenue Paul Nardal, are the vibrantly noisy, messy, and smelly vegetable and fish markets. One of the best shows in town occurs around 4 PM, when fishermen return with their catch, effortlessly tossing 100-pound bundles of rainbow-hued fish onto the docks.

The North

From here out, you'll need to rent a car or take a guided tour of the island's highlights. A car is best for touring, as it permits meandering down small roads and stopping to take in views. If there are four or more splitting the cost, a full-day car rental should be cheaper than a half-day guided tour. You can try touring by bus, but you'll end up having to spend several nights on the road.

The tour of the north is divided into two sections: a short day's trip and a long day's (even overnight) excursion. Martinique's "must do" is the drive north along the coast from Fort-de-France to St-Pierre. The 40-mile round-trip to St-Pierre can be made in an afternoon, although there is enough to see to fill an entire day. The drive farther north from St-Pierre to the north coast will appeal primarily to nature lovers, hikers, and mountain climbers. If you are interested in climbing Mont Pelée or hiking, plan to spend at least a night on the road (*see* Sports and the Outdoors, *below,* for guided hikes). Bear in mind that a 20-mile mountain drive takes longer than driving 20 miles on the prairie.

Head west out of Fort-de-France on Route N2. You'll pass through
2 the suburb of **Schoelcher,** home of the University of the French West Indies and Guyana. Just north of Schoelcher is Fond-Lahaye, where the road begins to climb sharply. About 4½ miles farther along, you'll come to the fishing village of **Case-Pilote,** named after a Carib chief to whom the French took kindly and called Pilote.

Continuing along the coastal road, you'll see red-roof houses cling-
3 ing to the green mountainside on the way to **Bellefontaine,** 4 miles north. This is another fishing village, with pastel houses on the hillsides and colorful *gommier* canoes (fishing boats made from gum trees) bobbing in the water. One of the houses here is built in the shape of a boat.

4 Continue north along the coast until you get to **Le Carbet.** Columbus is believed to have landed here on June 15, 1502. In 1635, Pierre Belain d'Esnambuc arrived here with the first French settlers.

Le Carbet is home to the **Zoo de Carbet,** also called the Amazona Zoo, which features animals from the Caribbean, Amazon, and Africa, including rare birds, snakes, wildcats, and caimans. *Le Coin, Le Carbet, tel. 596/78–00–64. Admission: 20F adults, 10F children under 12. Open daily 9–6.*

Just north of Carbet is **Anse-Turin,** where Paul Gauguin lived for a short time in 1887 with his friend and fellow artist Charles Laval.
5 The **Musée Gauguin** traces the history of the artist's Martinique connection through documents, letters, and reproductions of some of the paintings he did while on the island. There is also a display of Martinican costumes and headdresses. *Anse-Turin, Le Carbet, tel.*

596/77–22–66. Admission: 15F adults, 5F children under 12. Open daily 10–5.

From here follow the signs to the **Vallée des Papillons,** a botanical garden and butterfly compound constructed around the 16th-century stone ruins of the Habitation Anse Latouche sugar plantation. You can tour the greenhouse and insectarium, or simply wander the grounds looking for iridescent flashes of color fluttering through the greenery. The best time to view the butterflies is from 10 AM to 3 PM. You can lunch at the excellent on-site restaurant, Le Poids du Roy. *Habitation Anse Latouche, tel. 596/78–19–19. Admission: 30F adults, 10F children under 12. Open daily 9:30–4:15.*

6 Retrace your route back to N2, turn right, and continue to **St-Pierre,** the island's oldest city, which now has a population of about 6,000. At the turn of this century, St-Pierre was a flourishing city of 30,000 and was called the Paris of the West Indies. In spring 1902, nearby Mont Pelée began to rumble and spit out ash and steam. By the first week in May, all wildlife had wisely vacated the area. City officials, however, ignored the warnings, needing voters in town for an upcoming election. At 8 AM on May 8, 1902, the volcano erupted, belching forth a cloud of burning ash with temperatures over 3,600°F. In the space of three minutes, Mt. Pelée transformed the Paris of the West Indies into Martinique's Pompeii. The entire town was destroyed, and its inhabitants were instantly calcified. There was only one survivor, a prisoner named Cyparis, who was saved by the thick walls of his underground cell. (He was later pardoned and for some years afterward was a sideshow attraction at the Barnum & Bailey Circus.) You can wander through the site to see the ruins of the island's first church, built in 1640; the theater; the toppled statues; and Cyparis's cell. The Cyparis Express is a small tourist train that runs through the city, hitting the important sights with a running narrative (in French). *Departures every 45 minutes from Place des Ruines du Figuier (call for exact times), tel. 596/55–50–92. Admission: 30F adults, 10F children under 12. Runs weekdays 9:30–1 and 2:30–5:30.*

The **Musée Vulcanologique** was established in 1932 by American volcanologist Franck Perret. His collection includes photographs of the old town, documents, and a number of relics—some gruesome—excavated from the ruins, including molten glass, melted iron, and contorted clocks stopped at 8 AM, the time of the disaster. *St-Pierre, tel. 596/78–15–16. Admission: 15F adults, 5F children. Open daily 9–5.*

In St-Pierre, Route N2 turns inland toward Morne Rouge, but before going there, you may want to follow the coastal road 8 miles
7 north to **Le Prêcheur.** En route, you'll pass what is called the Tomb of the Carib Indians. The site is actually a formation of limestone hills from which the last of the Caribs are said to have flung themselves to avoid capture by the French. The village of Le Prêcheur was the childhood home of Françoise d'Aubigné, who was later to become the Marquise de Maintenon and the second wife of Louis XIV.

8 Return to St-Pierre and drive 4 miles east on Route N2 to reach **Le Morne Rouge.** Lying on the southern slopes of Mont Pelée, the town of Morne Rouge, too, was destroyed by the volcano. It is now a popular resort spot, with spectacular mountain scenery. This is the starting point for a climb up the 4,600-foot mountain, but you must have a guide (*see* Sports and the Outdoors, *below*).

At this point, you have the option of returning to Fort-de-France or continuing on for a tour of the north and Atlantic coasts.

If you choose to return to the capital, take the Route de la Trace (Rte. N3) south from Le Morne Rouge. The winding, two-lane paved road is one of the Caribbean's great drives, a roller coaster ride snaking through dense tropical rain forests.

9 La Trace leads to **Balata,** where you can see the **Balata Church,** a replica of Sacré-Coeur Basilica in Paris, and the **Jardin de Balata** (Balata Gardens). Jean-Philippe Thoze, a professional landscaper and devoted horticulturalist, spent 20 years creating this collection of thousands of varieties of tropical flowers and plants. There are shaded benches where you can relax and take in the panoramic views of the mountains. *Rte. de Balata, tel. 596/72–58–82. Admission: 30F adults, 10F children. Open daily 9–5.*

From Balata, Route N3 continues 8 miles south to the capital city.

If you've opted to continue exploring the north and Atlantic coasts, take Route N3 north from Morne Rouge. You'll pass through Petite Savane and wind northeast to the flower-filled village of
10 **Ajoupa-Bouillon,** a 17th-century settlement in the midst of pineapple fields.

A mile and a half east of Ajoupa-Bouillon, Route N3 dead-ends at Route N1, which runs north–south. Turn left and head through sugarcane, pineapple, and banana fields toward **Basse-Pointe,** which lies at sea level on the Atlantic coast (about a 3 mi drive). Soon after you turn onto N1, you'll see a small road (D21) off to the left. This
11 road leads to the estimable **Leyritz Plantation,** which has been a hotel for several years. When tour groups from the cruise ships are not swarming over the property, the rustic setting, complete with sugarcane factory and gardens, is delightful. Visit the plantation's **Musée de Poupées Végétales,** which contains a collection of exotic sculptures made by local artisan Will Fenton. He has used bananas, balisier (a tall grass), and other local plants to create the figures of women of French history, all in extravagant period costumes. *Musée de Poupées Végétales, Leyritz Plantation, tel. 596/78–53–92. Admission: 15F. Open daily 7–5.*

Go back to Route N1 and continue north. Just before Basse-Pointe you'll pass a Hindu temple, one of the relics of the East Indians who settled in this area in the 19th century. The view of the eastern slope of Mont Pelée is lovely from here. There's not much to do in Basse-Pointe, although on its outskirts, just before you leave, is the **JM Distillery** (tel. 596/78–92–55; open weekdays 7–noon and 1:30–3:30). It produces fine *rhum vieux,* and a tour and samples are free.

12 Continue down the road to **Macouba** on the coast. From here, the island's most spectacular drive leads 6 miles to **Grand-Rivière,** on the northernmost point. Perched on high cliffs, this village affords magnificent views of the sea, the mountains, and, on clear days, the neighboring island of Dominica. From Grand-Rivière, you can trek 11 miles on a well-marked path that leads through lush tropical vegetation to the beach at Anse-Ceron on the northwest coast. The beach is lovely and the diving is excellent, but the currents are very strong and swimming is not advised.

From Grand-Rivière, backtrack 13 miles to the junction of Routes N1 and N3.

From the junction, continue 10 miles on Route 1 along the Atlantic coast, driving through the villages of Le Lorrain and Marigot to
13 **Ste-Marie,** a town of about 20,000 Martinicans and the commercial capital of the island's north. There is a lovely mid-19th-century church in the town and, on a more earthy note, a rum distillery.

The **Musée du Rhum,** operated by the St. James Rum Distillery, is in a graceful galleried Creole house. Guided tours of the museum take in displays of the tools of the trade and include a visit to the distillery. And, yes, you may sample the product. *Ste-Marie, tel. 596/69–30–02. Admission free. Open weekdays 9–5, weekends 9–1.*

14 **La Trinité,** a northern subprefecture, is 6 miles to the south in a sheltered bay. From La Trinité, the **Caravelle Peninsula** thrusts 8 miles into the Atlantic Ocean. Much of the peninsula is under the auspices of the Regional Nature Reserve and offers places for trekking, swimming, and sailing. This is the home of the **Morne Pavilion,** an open-air sports and leisure center operated by the nature reserve (*see* Sports and the Outdoors, *below*). To reach it, turn right before Tartane on the Spoutourne Morne Pavilion road. The beach at Tartane is popular for its cooling Atlantic breezes.

At the eastern tip of the peninsula, you can root through the ruins of
15 the **Dubuc Castle.** This was the home of the Dubuc de Rivery family, which owned the peninsula in the 18th century. According to legend, young Aimée Dubuc de Rivery was captured by Barbary pirates, sold to the Ottoman Empire, became a favorite of the sultan, and gave birth to Mahmud II.

Return to La Trinité and take Route N4, which winds about 15 miles through lush tropical scenery to Lamentin. There you can pick up Route N1 to Fort-de-France or Route N5 to D7 and the southern resort areas.

The South

The loop through the south is a round-trip of about 100 miles. This excursion will include the birthplace of the Empress Josephine, Pointe du Bout and its resort hotels, a few small museums, and many large beaches. Since you will likely stay in the southern part of the island, you may wish to explore these areas on the days you try out different beaches. You can go from Fort-de-France to Ste-Anne in an hour or less on the highway. Buses ply the road frequently, and you'll see a number of people hitchhiking.

From Fort-de-France, take Route N1 to Route N5, which leads south through Lamentin, where the airport is. A 20-mile drive will bring you to Rivière-Salée, where you'll make a right turn on Route
16 D7 and drive 4½ miles to the village of **Les Trois-Ilets.**

Named after the three rocky islands nearby, it is a lovely little village with a population of about 3,000. It's known for its pottery, straw, and woodworks and as the birthplace of Napoleon's Empress Josephine. On the village square, you can visit the simple church where she was baptized Marie-Joseph Tascher de la Pagerie. To reach the museum and the old sugar plantation where she was born, drive a mile west on Route D7 and turn left on Route D38.

A stone building that held the kitchen of the estate is now home to the **Musée de la Pagerie.** (The main house blew down in the hurricane of 1766, when Josephine was three.) It contains an assortment of memorabilia pertaining to Josephine's life and loves (she was married at 16 in an arranged marriage to Alexandre de Beauharnais). There are family portraits; documents, including a marriage certificate; a love letter written to her in 1796 by Napoleon; and various antique furnishings, including the bed she slept in as a child. *Trois-Ilets, tel. 596/68–38–34. Admission: 15F adults, 3F children. Open Tues.–Sun. 9–5.*

Return to D7 and turn right, passing the D38 turn-off and continuing on to the village of Trois Ilets. The **Maison de la Canne** (at Pointe Vatable, as you leave town) will teach you everything you ever wanted to know about sugarcane. Exhibits take you through three centuries of sugarcane production, with displays of tools, scale models, engravings, and photographs. *Trois-Ilets, tel. 596/68–32–04. Admission: 15F adults, 5F children under 12. Open Tues.–Sun. 9–5:30.*

17 You can reach **Pointe du Bout** and the beach at **Anse-Mitan** by turning right on Route D38 west of Trois-Ilets and just past the **Golf de l'Impératrice Joséphine** (a golf course). This area is filled with resort hotels, among them the Bakoua and the Méridien. The Pointe du

Bout marina is a colorful spot where a whole slew of boats are tied up. The ferry to Fort-de-France leaves from this marina. More than anywhere else on Martinique, Pointe du Bout caters to the vacationer. A cluster of boutiques, ice-cream parlors, and car-rental agencies forms the hub from which restaurants and hotels of varying caliber radiate.

When you return to Route D7, turn right and head west. Less than five miles down the road you will reach **Anse-à-l'Ane,** where there is a pretty white-sand beach complete with picnic tables. There are also numerous small restaurants and inexpensive guest-house hotels here. South from Anse-à-l'Ane, Route D7 turns into a 10-mile roller coaster en route to **Anse-d'Arlets,** a quiet backwater fishing village. You'll see fishermen's nets strung up on the beach to dry and pleasure boats on the water. In recent years, activity has centered on the restaurants and small shops lining the shore. You may want to stop for dinner and a wonderful view of the sunset.

From the center of town, take Route D37 along the coast down to Morne Larcher and on to **Le Diamant,** a small, friendly village with a little fruit-and-vegetable market on its town square. The narrow, twisting, and hilly road offers some of the best shoreline views in Martinique. Be sure to pull to the side at a scenic spot from which
18 you can stare out at **Diamond Rock,** a mile or two offshore.

In 1804, during the squabbles over possession of the island between the French and the English, the latter commandeered the rock, armed it with cannons, christened it HMS *Diamond Rock,* and proceeded to use it as a warship. For almost a year and a half, the British held the rock, bombarding any French ships that came along. The French got wind of the fact that the British were getting cabin fever on their isolated ship-island and arranged a supply of barrels of rum for those on the rock. The French easily overpowered the inebriated sailors, ending one of the most curious engagements in naval history.

Back on the road (D7), it's about 5 miles to the junction of the island's main highway to the south (N5). If you go to the north, you'll be back in Fort-de-France within a half hour. Instead, go south along the coast.

Some 10 miles down the coastline lies **Ste-Luce,** another fishing village with a pretty white beach. From Ste-Luce, you can take Route
19 D17 north 1 mile to the **Forêt de Montravail,** where arrows point the way to Carib rock drawings.

The recently repaved and straightened D7 can quickly take you from Ste-Luce to Ste-Anne. For a more scenic route, say good-bye to Route D7 in Ste-Luce, and hook up with Route D18, which will take you northeast 4 miles to **Rivière-Pilote,** a town of about 12,000 people. From there, Route D18A trickles down south to **Pointe Figuier,** where the scuba diving is excellent. If you have time, stop by the **Ecomusée de Martinique,** despite its name more a historical than a natural museum, whose holdings embrace artifacts from Arawak and Carib settlement through the plantation years. *Anse Figuier, tel. 596/62–79–14. Admission: 15F adults, 5F children under 12. Open Tues.–Sun. 9–5.*

Stay with Route D18A and curve around the beautiful cul-de-sac inlet through **Le Marin.** Just east of Le Marin, turn right on Route D9 and drive all the way down to the sea. En route you'll pass the turnoff to Buccaneer's Creek/Club Med and drive through the pretty vil-
20 lage of **Ste-Anne,** where a Roman Catholic church sits on the square facing a lovely white beach. There are several restaurants here, and a market to buy picnic fixings. Not far away, at the southernmost tip, is the island's best beach, **Les Salines.** It's 1½ miles of soft white sand, calm waters, and relative seclusion (except on weekends).

In sharp contrast to the north, this section of the island is dry. The
soil does not hold moisture for long. A rutted track—suitable for vehicles, but not for queasy stomachs—leads all the way to **Pointe des
Salines** and slightly beyond. The gnarled, stubby trees have given
21 the area the name **Petrified Forest,** in part because the sight is unexpected in a place known as the Island of Flowers.

Backtrack 9 miles to Le Marin. The adventuresome should take a detour a mile before reaching town. Take the small road on your right that leads to **Cap Chevalier.** After less than 2 miles, the road forks. The road to the left dead-ends at a small community and does not justify the 4 miles of driving. The fork to the right, however, runs for about 4 miles to a tiny cove with five or six one-man fishing boats and racks where the fishermen dry their nets. The scene is definitely worth a photograph.

To get out of Cap Chevalier, you must go back toward Le Marin. On
the outskirts of Le Marin, Route N6 branches off to the right and
22 goes north 7 miles to **Le Vauclin,** where it skirts the highest point in
the south, **Mt. Vauclin** (1,654 feet). Le Vauclin is an important fishing port on the Atlantic coast, and the return of the fishermen shortly before noon each day is a big event.

23 Continue north 9 miles on Route N6 to **Le François,** a sizable city of some 16,000 Martinicans. Admission is free to its greatest attraction, the **Habitation Clément** (tel. 596/54–62–07, open daily 9–6), an 18th-century family mansion and rum distillery that together provide a vivid portrait of plantation life. Tastings are included. Le François is also noted for its snorkeling. Offshore are a number of shallow basins called *fond blancs* because of their white-sand bottoms. Boat tours leave from the harbor ($30 per person includes lunch and drinks). You can also haggle with a fisherman to take you out for a while on his boat to indulge in the uniquely Martinican custom of standing waist-deep in the calm water, sipping a ti punch and gossiping.

There is a lovely bay 6 miles farther along at **Le Robert.** You'll also come to the junction of Route N1, which will take you west to Fort-de-France, 12½ miles away.

Beaches

All Martinique's beaches are open to the public, but hotels charge a fee for nonguests to use changing rooms and facilities. There are no official nudist beaches, but topless bathing is prevalent at the large resort hotels. Unless you're an expert swimmer, steer clear of the Atlantic waters, except in the area of Cap Chevalier and the Caravelle Peninsula. The soft, white-sand beaches begin south of Fort-de-France; to the north the beaches are hard-packed gray volcanic sand. The soft white beaches of **Pointe du Bout** are man-made, superb, and lined with luxury resorts.

Anse-Mitan was created by Mother Nature, who placed it just to the south of Pointe du Bout and sprinkled it with golden sand. The waters around this beach offer superb snorkeling opportunities. Small family-owned bistros are half hidden in palm trees nearby.

On the beach at **Anse-à-l'Ane,** you can spread your lunch on a picnic table, browse through the nearby shell museum, and cool off in the bar of the Le Calalou hotel.

Diamant, the island's longest beach (2½ miles), has a splendid view of Diamond Rock, but the waters are sometimes rough and the currents are strong.

Anse-Trabaud is on the Atlantic side, across the southern tip of the island from Ste-Anne. There is nothing here but white sand and the sea.

Les Salines is a 1½-mile cove of soft white sand lined with coconut palms. A short drive south of Ste-Anne, Les Salines is awash with families and children during holidays and on weekends, but quiet and uncrowded during the week even at the height of the winter season. This beach, especially the far end, is peaceful and beautiful. Take along a picnic, including plenty of liquids; there is only one restaurant, Aux Delices de la Mer (tel. 596/62–50–12), close to Pointe des Salines.

Near Les Salines, **Pointe Marin** stretches north from Ste-Anne. A good windsurfing and waterskiing spot, it also has restaurants, campsites, sanitary facilities, and a 10F admission charge. Club Med occupies the northern edge, and Ste-Anne, with several good restaurants, is near at hand.

The Atlantic surf rolls onto **Cap Chevalier,** a windswept beach with hard-packed sand. Swimming here is only for the strong, but the emptiness of the shore appeals to those seeking respite from crowds. Small trees give shade, but there are no refreshment stands.

Sports and the Outdoors

Bicycling The **Parc Naturel Régional de la Martinique** (tel. 596/73–19–30) has designed biking itineraries off the beaten track. Bikes can be rented from **Funny** (tel. 596/63–33–05) and **T.S. Location Sarl** (tel. 596/63–42–82), both located in Fort-de-France, **Discount** (tel. 596/66–54–37) in Pointe du Bout, and **Scootonnerre** (tel. 596/76–41–12) in Le Diamant. VTT (Vélo Tout Terrain), or mountain bikes, specially designed with 18 speeds to handle all terrains, may be rented from **V.T. Tilt** (Anse-Mitan, tel. 596/66–01–01). Average daily cost for a 10-speed bike is 50F; mountain bikes are a few francs more.

Golf At **Golf de l'Impératrice Joséphine** (tel. 596/68–32–81) there is an 18-hole Robert Trent Jones course with an English-speaking pro, a fully equipped pro shop, a bar, and a restaurant. It's in Trois-Ilets, a mile from the Pointe du Bout resort area and 18 miles from Fort-de-France. Greens fees are 300F for 18 holes.

Hiking Inexpensive guided excursions are organized year-round by the **Parc Naturel Régional de la Martinique** (9 blvd. Général de Gaulle, Fort-de-France, tel. 596/73–19–30). The tourist board can also arrange for a guide. The most interesting—and demanding—hikes are in the volcanic, mountainous area around Le Morne Rouge. Terrain is steep and thickly forested. You'll need a guide, especially when low clouds descend and the visibility drops to near zero. Costs vary, but count on 50F for a morning hike. Although you do need a guide to hike inland, you can walk around the island's northern tip between Le Prêcheur and Grand-Rivière—a three- to four-hour hike—on your own.

Sailing Hobie Cats, Sunfish, and Sailfish can be rented by the hour from hotel beach shacks. Sunfish rentals average 75F an hour; Windsurfers, about 60F–100F an hour.

Scuba Diving Among the island's dive operators are **Bathy's Club** (Méridien, tel. 596/66–00–00), **Cressma** (Fort-de-France, tel. 596/61–34–36 or 596/58–04–48), **Club Subaquatique** (Le Port, Case-Pilote, tel. 596/78–73–75), **Okeanos Club** (Diamant, tel. 596/76–21–76), **Planète Bleue** (La Marina, Trois-Ilets, tel. 596/66–08–79), **Sub Diamant Rock** (Novotel, tel. 596/76–42–42), and **Tropicasub** (Anse Latouche, St-Pierre, tel. 596/78–38–03). Single-tank dives start at $55. Snorkel equipment rents for about $10 a day; rental is available at the dive shops listed.

Sea Excursions The glass-bottom boat ***Seaquarium*** (Fort-de-France, tel. 596/61–49–49) and Aquascope (Pointe du Bout, tel. 596/68–36–09), a semisubmersible, do 45- to 60-minute excursions. Costs vary, but an afternoon excursion with snorkeling and a picnic is about 120F. For information on other sailing, swimming, snorkeling, and beach picnic trips, contact **Affaires Maritimes** (tel. 596/71–90–05).

Tennis and Squash In addition to its links, the **Golf de l'Impératrice Joséphine** (Trois-Ilets, tel. 596/68–32–81) has three lighted tennis courts. Leading hotels with courts include the **Le Bakoua** (tel. 596/66–02–02), **Club Med/Buccaneer's Creek** (tel. 596/76–74–52), **Diamant-Novotel** (tel. 596/76–42–42), **La Batelière Hotel** (tel. 596/61–49–49), **Leyritz Plantation** (tel. 596/78–53–92), the **Le Méridien Trois-Ilets** (tel. 596/66–00–00), **Anchorage Hotel** (tel. 596/76–92–32), and **Diamant Marine** (tel. 596/76–46–00). For additional information about tennis on the island, contact **La Ligue Régionale de Tennis** (Petit Manoir, Lamentin, tel. 596/51–08–00). An hour's court time averages 50F for nonguests. There are three squash courts at the modern, aptly named **Squash Hotel** (tel. 596/63–00–01), just outside Fort-de-France.

Shopping

Although it's possible to save money on French fragrances and designer scarves, fine china and crystal, leather goods, and liquors and liqueurs in Fort-de-France, these items won't be cheap (even with the 20% discount on luxury items paid for by traveler's checks or certain major credit cards). Bargain shoppers are better off sticking with local items. Look for Creole gold jewelry, such as loop earrings, heavy bead necklaces, and slave bracelets; white and dark rum; and handcrafted straw goods, pottery, and tapestries. In addition, U.S. Customs allows you to bring some of the local flora into the country.

Good Buys

China and Crystal Look for Lalique, Limoges, and Baccarat at **Cadet Daniel** (72 rue Antoine Siger, Fort-de-France, tel. 596/71–41–48). **Roger Albert** (7 rue Victor Hugo, Fort-de-France, tel. 596/71–71–71) also carries crystal from all the major designers.

Flowers Anthuriums, torch lilies, and lobster claws are packaged for shipment at **MacIntosh** (31 rue Victor Hugo, Fort-de-France, tel. 596/70–09–50, and at the airport, tel. 596/51–51–51). **Les Petites Floralies** (75 rue Blénac, Fort-de-France, tel. 596/71–66–16) is another florist with a wide selection.

Local Handicrafts The **Galerie d'Art** (89 rue Victor Hugo, tel. 596/63–10–62) has some unusual and excellent Haitian art—paintings, sculptures, ceramics, and intricate jewelry cases—at reasonable prices.

Following the peeling roadside signs advertising *ateliers artisanales* (art studios) can yield unexpected treasures, many of them reasonably priced. **Art et Nature** (Ste-Luce, tel. 596/62–59–19) features Joel Gilbert's unique wood paintings, daubed with 20–30 shades of earth and sand. Robert Manscour's **L'Eclat de Verre** (Hwy. N4, outside Gros Morne, tel. 596/58–34–03) specializes in all manner of glittering glassworks. **Victor Anicet** (Monésie, 596/68–25–42) fashions lovely ceramic masks and vases. You can watch the artisans at work at **La Paille Caraibe** (Morne des Esses, 596/69–83–74), weaving straw baskets, mats, hats, and amphorae. While at **Le poterie-briqueterie des Trois-Ilets** (Trois-Ilets, tel. 596/68–17–12) you can watch the creation of pots, vases, and jars patterned after ancient Arawak and Carib traditions.

Just outside Le Diamant is **Atelier Ceramique** (tel. 596/76–42–65). The owners and talented artists, David and Jeannine England, have lived in the Caribbean for more than a decade and are members of the small British expatriate community on the island. Whether or not you like their products—ceramics, paintings, and miscellaneous souvenirs—it's a rare chance to brush up on your English.

Perfumes Dior, Chanel, and Guerlain are among the popular scents at **Roger Albert** (7 rue Victor Hugo, Fort-de-France, tel. 596/71–71–71). Airport minishops sell the most popular scents at in-town prices, so there's no need to carry purchases around.

Rum Rum can be purchased at the various distilleries, including **Duquesnes** (Fort-de-France, tel. 596/71–91–68), **St. James** (Ste-Marie, tel. 596/69–30–02), **Clément** (Le François, tel. 596/54–62–07), and **Trois Rivières** (Ste-Luce, tel. 596/62–51–78).

Dining

As in France, eating well is part of living well. Here you'll find the same interest in food, the same lingering over meals—and the same willingness to pay high prices for memorable cuisine. Notice that a meal in a $$ restaurant costs $30–$50. You'll spend more on dining here than on many Caribbean islands. McDonald's and Burger King have outposts here now, but you'll do better at the many casual snack bars in Fort-de-France or fronting the beaches, where a plate of grilled chicken or fish and fries will set you back as little as 30F, and delicious dessert crepes half that. Many smaller restaurants will prepare a plate of appetizers in lieu of a full meal. As a rule of thumb, at restaurants where reservations are not necessary, it is acceptable to order just an entrée or to substitute appetizers for your main course. At any restaurant where you are advised to make reservations, you are expected to dine well, i.e., three courses plus wine. Most restaurants offer a prix-fixe menu—sometimes including wine, often with a choice of dishes—that represents tremendous value. Ordering the set menu can make even the more expensive restaurants affordable. For additional savings, pick up a copy of the "Ti Gourmet" booklet, available at the tourist office and larger hotels; most of the restaurants listed offer a coupon good for a free drink or a discount.

It used to be argued that Martinique had the best food in all the Caribbean, but many believe this top-ranking position has been lost to some of the other islands of the French West Indies—Guadeloupe, St. Barts, even St. Martin. Nevertheless, Martinique remains an island of restaurants serving classic French cuisine and Creole dishes, its wine cellars filled with fine French wines. Hotel restaurants are predictably good—consult the lodging listings for more recommendations—but some of the best restaurants are tucked away in the countryside, and therein lies a problem. The farther you venture from tourist hotels, the less likely you are to find English-speaking folk. But that shouldn't stop you from savoring the countryside cuisine. The local Creole specialties are *colombo* (curry), *accras* (cod or vegetable fritters), *crabes farcis* (stuffed land crab), *écrevisses* (freshwater crayfish), *boudin* (Creole blood sausage), *lambi* (conch), *langouste* (clawless Caribbean lobster), *soudons* (sweet clams), *blaff* (fish or shellfish plunged into seasoned stock), and *oursin* (sea urchin). The local favorite libation is *le 'ti punch*, a "little punch," concocted of four parts white rum, one part sugarcane syrup (some people like a little more syrup), and a squeeze of lime.

One of the delights of Martinique is grocery shopping for picnic fare or take-out meals. You'll find minimarkets in the center of every town and village, but for a truly mouthwatering experience, visit the **Euromarche** in Lamentin, just off the main Fort-de-France–Rivière highway (N5). This is one of the most complete *hypermarchés* (supermarket) in the Western Hemisphere. Whether you are stocking the larder for a week or planning a simple picnic, you'll be tempted by the breads, pâtés, cheeses, and wines. Choose carefully, and you'll have the makings of a delicious gourmet meal for two that costs less than $15.

Outside of Fort-de-Franc restaurants, dress is casual (anything more is indicated in individual reviews below). Shorts, however, are not appreciated at any restaurant other than alfresco cafés on the beach.

Highly recommended restaurants are indicated by a star ★.

Category	Cost*
$$	$30–$50
$	$20–$30
¢	under $20

**per person, excluding drinks and service*

Anse-d'Arlets
$–$$

Tamarin Plage Restaurant. The lobster *vivier* (tank) middle of the room gives you a clue to the specialty here, but there are other recommendable offerings as well. Fish soup or Creole boudin are good starters, then consider court bouillon, chicken fricassee, and curried mutton. The beachfront bar is a popular local hangout. The hotel across the road, Tamarin Plage, offers six tiny, very basic but sunny rooms for $70 including breakfast. *Anse-d'Arlets, tel. 596/68–67–88. No credit cards.*

¢–$ **Bidjoul.** Many modest restaurants line the small side street that is actually Anse-d'Arlets's main drag. The street borders the water, and fishermen sail right up to the eateries with their latest catch. Bidjoul has a tiny dining room; opt for one of the tables set up under the canopy on the beach across the road. The salads (try the smoked salmon, or the *pecheur*, with tuna, shrimp, crab, and rice) are huge, and the grilled fish as fresh as could be. So, too, is the fish at the neighboring restaurants, but the enthusiasm of Bidjoul's owner makes it stand out. It has become the popular gathering spot for watching the sun set into the Caribbean Sea. *Anse-d'Arlets, tel. 596/68–65–28. No reservations. MC, V.*

Anse-Mitan/ Pte. du Bout
$$
★

La Villa Creole. The steak béarnaise, curries, conch, court bouillon, and other dishes are all superb. However, the real draw here is owner Guy Bruère-Dawson, a popular singer and guitarist who entertains during dinner. The setting is romantic at this very popular place, with ceiling fans whirring and oil lamps flickering on the tables. Ask to be seated in the lush back garden. *Anse-Mitan, tel. 596/66–05–53. Reservations required. AE, DC, V. Closed Sun. No lunch Mon.*

$ **Au Poisson d'Or.** This typical Creole restaurant offers several excellent set menus. You might choose fried conch, poached local fish, fried sea urchin, or scallops sautéed in white wine. The decor is attractive: bamboo walls, straw thatching, madras napery, a veritable jungle of potted plants, and clever paintings of seafood. The only drawback is its position on the "wrong side" of the road, away from the beach. Choose a table in the front area of the terrace to benefit from any passing breezes. *Pointe du Bout, tel. 596/66–01–80. No reservations. No credit cards. Closed Mon.*

¢–$ **La Marina.** Beckoning red-and-white awnings and colorful murals give this breezy terrace a cheerful atmosphere. Views are of the yachts cruising in and out of their berths. Top choices include seafood risotto and lambi fricassee. Tasty pizzas and salads make the best budget options. *Pointe du Bout, no phone. No reservations. AE, MC, V.*

Fort-de-France
$$
★

Le Coq Hardi. Crowds flock here for the best steaks and grilled meats in town. You can pick out your own steak and feel confident that it will be cooked to perfection. Steak tartare is the house specialty, or choose tournedos Rossini (with artichoke hearts, foie gras, truffles, and Madeira sauce), entrecôte Bordelaise, prime rib, or T-bone steaks. For dessert, there's a selection of sorbets, profiteroles, and pear Belle Hélène. *Km 0.6, rue Martin Luther King, tel. 596/71-59-64. Reservations advised. AE, DC, MC, V. Closed Wed. No lunch Sat.*

$ **Chez Gaston.** The Creole menu of this cozy upstairs dining room includes such items as ox-foot soup, conch in parsley sauce, and simmered sea urchins. The brochettes are especially recommended. The kitchen stays open late, and there's a piano bar andsmall dance floor. Downstairs, snacks are served all day. A French phrase book will be very helpful. *10 rue Felix Eboué, tel. 596/71-59-71. No credit cards.*

¢–$ **Le Crew.** Creole and French bistro fare—fish soup, stuffed mussels, snails, country pâté, frogs' legs, tripe, grilled chicken and steak—are served family style in two rustic dining rooms. Portions are ample, and there's a 60F three-course tourist menu that simplifies ordering. *42 rue Ernest Deproge, tel. 596/73-04-14. No credit cards. Closed Sun. No dinner Sat.*

¢–$ ★ **Le Marie Sainte.** Warm wood panelling, exposed beams, colorfully tiled tables, and bright napery create a homey ambience in this wildly popular lunchtime spot. It's worth waiting on the occasional line for scrumptious *daube de poissons* (braised fish), crayfish, and banana beignets. *160 rue Victor Hugo, tel. 596/70-00-30. No credit cards. No dinner. Closed Sun. and Mon.*

¢ **La Crêperie/La Cave du Roi.** Stone walls, heavy wood beams, and candles help recreate an old Norman manor. The crepes, galettes, and cider are delicious. The 50F menu is one of the best buys in town. The crêperie occupies the second floor; on the first is a bar, where there's a cabaret on weekends. *4 rue Garnier Pages, tel. 596/60-62-09. No credit cards. No lunch Sat.–Mon.*

¢ ★ **Le Second Soufflé.** The chef uses fresh produce to make soufflés ranging from aubergine (eggplant) to filet de ti-nain (small green bananas) with chocolate sauce. He also whips up such nonsoufflé items as eggplant ragout and okra quiche. The food echoes the famous Voltaire line painted on the wall: "Tu ne possèdes rien si tu ne digères pas bien" (You have nothing if you don't have good digestion). Even the decor pays tribute to the Martinican table, with colorful murals of fruits and vegetables. With prices around 40F and a wonderful location near the cathedral, this little restaurant is a delightful find. *27 rue Blénac, tel. 596/63-44-11. No reservations. No credit cards. No lunch Sat.*

Le Diamant

$ ★ **Chez Christiane.** Don't be deceived by the seedy front bar (which rocks during pool tournaments and free Friday rum tastings). The back dining room is delightful, with bamboo walls, fresh flowers, and local artist Roland Brival's imaginative paintings of local fauna (he adds texture with shards of green glass). The Creole cuisine is magnificent. The 70F menu might offer boudin, fried fish in caper sauce, and a *coupe glacée* (sundae). Other top choices are a smoky callaloo soup (here called *souple verte aux crabes*), braised ray with ginger, and smoked chicken colombo. *Rue Diamant, tel. 596/76-49-55. Reservations advised. No credit cards.*

$ **Le Diam's.** For an inexpensive meal of anything from crisp, tasty pizzas to grilled fish of the day, this casual, open-sided restaurant facing the village square is hard to beat. More creative preparations include grouper in vanilla, salmon in tarragon sauce, and duck with olives. There's also a 40F children's menu—chopped steak or ham, rice or fries, and ice cream, a rarity on this island. Checkered tablecloths and wicker furniture are the only elements of the simple decor; an overhead fan keeps a breeze going through the dining room. *Place de l'Eglise, tel. 596/76-23-28. No reservations. MC, V. Closed Tues. No lunch Wed.*

¢ **Pizza Pepe.** A jade-colored rattan bar, boldly hued napery, and a few plants enliven this simple seaside terrace. Creative pizzas (the most expensive are $10) include oceanique (crab, onions, olives) and Ingrid (creme fraiche, salmon, olives). You can also get a plate of

roast chicken or grilled shark, with heaping helpings of rice and fresh vegetables, for 60F. *Rue Diamant, tel. 596/76–40–49. No reservations. No credit cards. No lunch Sun. No dinner Mon.*

Le François
$

Club Nautique. Although this little place is not going to turn up in *Architectural Digest,* the food—which comes fresh daily out of the sea—is exquisitely prepared. Have the house specialty drink, a *décollage* (it means "take off" in French—and this potent herb-infused rum will have you jetting sky high), then dig into turtle steak or charcoal-broiled lobster. The restaurant is right on the beach, and boat trips depart from here for snorkeling in the nearby coral reefs. *Le François, tel. 596/54–31–00. AE, DC, MC, V. No dinner Sun.*

Morne-des-Esses
$$
★

Le Colibri. Jules Palladino, a large, gregarious man who clearly loves his food, has established his culinary domain in this spot in the northwestern reaches of the island. Choice seating is at one of the seven tables on the cheerful back terrace. For starters, try *buisson d'écrevisses,* a pyramid of six giant freshwater crayfish accompanied by a tangy tomato sauce flavored with thyme, scallions, and tiny bits of crayfish. This is one of the few places to get traditional *cochon au lait* (suckling pig) and *gibier* (game), such as rabbit in prune sauce and tender, smoky *manicou* (cousin to the opossum). Keep an eye on prices here; some items will push your bill out of our $$ range. *Allée du Colibri, Morne-des-Esses, tel. 596/69–91–95. Reservations required. AE, DC, MC, V. Closed Mon. off-season.*

St-Pierre
$$
★

Le Fromager. This beautiful restaurant is perched high above St-Pierre, with smashing views of the town's red roofs and the sea beyond from the breezy terrace. Dining inside is also pleasant, thanks to the gleaming ecru tile floors, white wicker, polished hardwood furnishings, lace tablecloths, old rum barrels, and potted plants. Superlative choices include crayfish colombo, marinated octopus, and duck fillet with pineapple. You may also opt for the 100F chef's choice menu, which might include avocado vinaigrette and sole sauce pecheur (in a Creole sauce), as well as fruit or crême caramel. *On the road toward Fond St-Denis, tel. 596/78–19–07. Reservations advised in high season. AE, DC, MC, V.*

$

La Factorérie. The food is appealing and the views sweeping at this open-air restaurant alongside the ruins of the Eglise du Fort. Fresh vegetables from the nearby agricultural training school accompany grilled langouste, grilled chicken in a piquant Creole sauce, fricassee de lambi, and the fresh catch of the day. This is a convenient spot to have lunch when visiting St-Pierre, but it is not worth a special trip. *Quartier Fort, St-Pierre, tel. 596/78–12–53. No credit cards. No dinner weekends.*

Ste-Anne
$–$$

La Dunette. Dinner at this restaurant, in the small Ste-Anne hotel of the same name, is served on a plant-hung terrace overlooking the sea. Wrought-iron chairs and tables and bright blue awnings add to the refreshing garden atmosphere. Your choices for lunch or dinner include fish soup, grilled fish or lobster, snapper stuffed with sea urchin, conch fricassee, and several colombos and tandooris. *Ste-Anne, tel. 596/76–73–90. Reservations advised in high season. MC, V. Closed Wed.*

$–$$

Poï et Virginie. Facing the jetty in the center of Ste-Anne is this popular restaurant with bamboo walls, bright art naïf, ceiling fans, and colorful, fresh-cut flowers. The menu is extensive—from meats to fish—but the specialty is the lobster and crab salad. Other noteworthy dishes are lemon chicken in coconut milk, tuna with green peppers, and, for a splurge, crayfish in saffron. Lunchtime is busy, especially on weekends; get here soon after noon if you want a table facing the bay, with views of St. Lucia in the distance. *Rue de Bord de Mer, Ste-Anne, tel. 596/76–72–22. No reservations. AE, DC, MC, V. Closed Mon. No lunch Tues.*

$ **Athanor.** An ambitious menu includes everything from pizza to Creole dishes. Recommended are octopus, blaff, and grilled fish in a shallot-and-rum sauce. Seating is in a plant-filled room, brightened by floral napery and colorful murals, or in a small garden at the back. *Rue de Bord de Mer, Ste-Anne, tel. 596/76–97–60. MC, V.*

Ste-Luce $$ **La Petite Auberge.** This country inn is hidden behind a profusion of tropical flowers, just across the main road from the beach. Fresh seafood is turned into such dishes as *filet de poisson aux champignons* (fish cooked with mushrooms), conch flamed in aged rum, crabes farcis, and fresh langouste in a Creole sauce. Or sample *magret à la mangue* (duck breast with mango), veal stuffed with spinach, or entrecôte Creole. They're all winners. The inn has 12 rooms, all with rustic decor—pink-and-white tile floors, wood paneling, hardwood beds, white wicker furnishings, floral linens—air conditioning, balcony and minifridge, for an unbeatable 330F a night E.P. *Plage du Gros Raisins, Ste-Luce, tel. 596/62–59–70. Reservations advised in high season. AE.*

Tartane $$ **Le Vieux Galion.** This seaside restaurant plays up the nautical theme, with a huge aquarium and murals of old sailing ships complementing fantastic Atlantic views. The crashing surf serenades diners on the terrace. Owner Jean-Pierre Maur does wonders with seafood. Especially memorable are grouper rouged with peppers (reddened by their juices), Tahitian *poisson cru* (marinated raw fish), and conch *à l'armoricaine* with tomato, garlic, creme fraîche, and cognac. *Anse Bellune, Rte. du Tartane, tel. 596/58–20–58. AE, MC, V. Closed Mon. No dinner Sun.*

Lodging

Martinique has a number of moderately priced large resort hotels, designed to accommodate large groups. This may explain the impersonality and lack of charm at many of these hotels, as well as prices that are quite reasonable for the Caribbean. Most are on or near a beach, and many offer attractive packages that are cheaper than their standard room rates; ask about them when you call.

Other affordable options include smaller hotels and inns (*Relais Créoles* and *chambres+ d'hôtes*) and the modest apartments and cottages known as *gîtes*. The latter are simple accommodations, usually available by the week, that range from separate cottages to rooms in a private home to bed-and-breakfast–style properties. The Martinique office of **Gîtes de France** (9 blvd. du Généal-de-Gaulle, BP 1122, Fort-de-France 97248, tel. 596/73–67–92, fax 596/63–55–92) has a list of more than 100 properties and serves as a reservation center. One top recommendation in Anse-d'Arlets is the **Gîte de Mme. Rachel Melinard,** a two-story cottage with superb views of the sea and a well-equipped kitchen, 10 minutes' walk to the nearest swimming beach.

Most of the major hotels are clustered in Pointe du Bout and Anse-Mitan on the Trois-Ilets peninsula, across the bay from Fort-de-France, or in the Le Diamant and Ste-Anne resort areas. You'll find other lodgings—particularly budget properties—scattered around the island.

Many larger hotels offer MAP plan in their weekly rates; if you don't have a car, a meal plan makes economic sense. Even those offering only EP often include buffet breakfast in their package rates. At Relais Créoles, breakfast usually consists of cold cuts, an array of breads, juice, and hot beverages.

Highly recommended lodgings are indicated by a star ★.

Category	Cost*
$$	$125–$180
$	$75–$125
¢	under $75

**All prices are for a standard double room for two in high season, excluding $1.50 per person per night tax and a 10% service charge. To estimate rates for hotels offering MAP, add about $40 per person per day to the above price ranges.*

Hotels and Inns

Anse-Mitan/ Pte. du Bout

Bambou. The young and hardy will enjoy this complex of rustic A-frames with shingled roofs. The cramped rooms, mostly wood-paneled with tile floors and plaid trimmings, are spartan, albeit with such conveniences as air-conditioning, phones, and shower baths. During high season, entertainment is offered five nights a week. You're on the water here (alas, only the large, casual beachfront restaurant has a view), but a five-minute walk brings you to a better beach by Le Bakoua hotel. *Anse-Mitan 97229, tel. 596/66–01–39 or 800/224–4542, fax 596/66–05–05. 118 rooms. Facilities: restaurant and bar, pool, boutique, disco, water-sports center. AE, DC, MC, V. CP, MAP. $$*

★ **PLM Azur La Pagerie.** La Pagerie looks as if it had been plucked out of the Côte d'Azur and planted near the marina in Pointe du Bout. The hotel has small air-conditioned rooms and studios, all with private bath and trim little balcony, and some with kitchenette. The decor is handsome throughout, with dark-wood furnishings, planters, and lace curtains. Although the hotel has no beach or water-sports activities, it is within a short stroll of the resort hotels, restaurants, and activity. Lunch and dinner are served alfresco by the pool. The PLM's lively, cheerful atmosphere has made it a favorite evening watering hole of local expatriates and the sailing crowd. *Pointe du Bout 97229, tel. 596/66–05–30, fax 596/66–00–99. U.S. reservations, 800/221–4542; in NY, 212/757–6500. 98 rooms. Facilities: restaurant, bar, pool. AE, MC, V. EP, MAP. $$*

Auberge de l'Anse-Mitan. Established in 1930, this is the island's oldest family-run inn. Rooms are spartan, but all are air-conditioned and have shower baths. Views are either of the bay or the tropical garden at the back, and some rooms have balconies. Informal meals are served in the large, open-air dining room–terrace. The inn's at the end of the road along the beachfront, and it's peaceful and quiet—particularly if you don't speak French. *Anse-Mitan 97229, tel. 596/66–01–12, fax 596/66–01–05; in Canada, 800/468–0023; in NY, 212/840–6636. 26 rooms. Facilities: restaurant, bar. AE, DC. EP, MAP. $*

Rivage Hotel. You get good value for your money at Maryelle and Jean Claude Riveti's small hotel. The place does have the air of a motor inn circa the Eisenhower years, but it's immaculately maintained, and the studios give you much more room than neighboring hotels at about a third of the cost. Each garden-view unit has air-conditioning, TV, phone, private bath, and either a kitchenette (not always as clean as the rest of the property) or a minifridge. Breakfast and light meals are served in the friendly, informal snack bar. You should have no difficulty communicating: English, Spanish, and French are spoken. The beach is right across the road. *Anse-Mitan 97229, tel. 596/66–00–53, fax 596/66–06–56. 17 rooms. Facilities: snack bar, pool, car rental, poolside barbecue pit. MC, V. EP. ¢*

Basse-Point

★ **Leyritz Plantation.** Sleeping on a former sugar plantation, in the antiques-furnished rooms of the manor house or cottages or in a renovated slave cabin, is certainly a novelty. Leyritz is isolated in the northern part of the island, on 16 acres of lush vegetation, with manicured lawns and stunning views of Mont Pelée. Nicest are the 10 cottage rooms, which have rough wood beams, mahogany four-poster beds, marble-top armoires, secretaries, and other antiques. The slightly larger former slave quarters have eaves, stone-and-stucco walls, more contemporary furnishings, and madras linens. Ironically, it's the newer bungalows that are cramped and lacking in individuality. All accommodations have air-conditioning, TV, phone, and hair dryer. Except for periodic invasions of cruise-ship passengers, it is very quiet here—a sharp contrast to the frenzied level of activity at the hotels in Pointe du Bout. You may not want to spend your entire vacation here, but it makes an interesting overnight stay while visiting the northern part of the island. There's free transportation to the beach, which is about 30 minutes away. *Basse-Pointe 97218, tel. 596/78–53–92, fax 596/78–92–44. 67 rooms. Facilities: restaurant, bar, tennis court, pool. AE, DC, MC, V. CP, MAP. $–$$*

Fort-de-France **Impératrice.** The slightly musty rooms of the Impératrice are in a 1950s five-story building that overlooks La Savane park in the heart of the city. The rooms in the front are either the best or the worst, depending upon your sensibilities: They are noisy, but they overlook the city's center of activity. All rooms have air-conditioning, TV, four-poster bed, and private bath and are decorated with bright Creole prints; 20 have balconies. Children under 8 stay free in the room with their parents, children 8–15 stay at a 50% discount. The hotel also has a popular sidewalk café. *Fort-de-France 97200, tel. 596/63–06–82 or 800/223–9815, fax 596/72–66–30; in Canada, 800/468–0023; in NY, 212/251–1800. 24 rooms. Facilities: restaurant, bar. AE, DC, MC, V. CP. $*

Lafayette. This hotel's claim to fame is its superb second-story restaurant, an oasis of indoor greenery, white latticework, and rich Haitian paintings overlooking the Savane, where you can dine on impeccably prepared Continental fare. If you want to be right in the heart of town, this place is a real find. The choicest rooms are those with French windows. All of the comfortable but rather old-fashioned rooms have heavy wood furnishings, teal linens and floral curtains, and all have a TV and a phone. *5 rue de la Liberté, Fort-de-France 97200, tel. 596/73–80–50 or 800/223–9815, fax 596/60–97–75. 24 rooms. Facilities: restaurant, bar, use of Bakoua Hotel beach facilities. AE, DC, V. CP. $*

Hotel Malmaison. The best bargain in Fort-de-France is this small hotel with white-and-green exterior. It's owned by a Frenchman who's lived on Martinique for 40 years. All rooms have air-conditioning, TV, minibar, and private bath. Decor is an intriguing mishmash: some units have colonial-style beds, mirrored armoires—and red naugahyde chairs, chartreuse linens, and worn burgundy carpets. A few of the higher priced ones have a small living room. For the best value, choose a corner room that has more light and views of the Savane. Beaches are a taxi or ferry ride away. *7 rue de la Liberté, Fort-de-France 97200, tel. 596/63–90–85, fax 596/60–03–93. 20 rooms. MC, V. EP. ¢–$*

La Trinité **Saint Aubin.** This restored coral-color colonial house, with pretty gables and intricate gingerbread trim, is in the countryside above the Atlantic coast. Each modern but musty room has wicker furnishings, air-conditioning, TV, phone, and private bath. Those on the top floor are larger and ideal for families; five second-floor rooms open onto a shared balcony with sweeping views of the sea. This is a peaceful retreat, and only 3 miles from La Trinité, 2 miles from the Spoutourne sports center and the beaches on the Caravelle Peninsula. The inn's restaurant, which serves estimable Creole fare, is closed during June and October. Owner Guy Foret is an engaging host. *Box 52, La Trinité, 97220, tel. 596/69–34–77, 800/223–9815; in Canada, 800/468–0023; in NY, 212/840–6636; fax 596/69–41–14. 15 rooms. Facilities: restaurant, bar, pool. AE, DC, MC, V. CP. $*

Lamentin **Martinique Cottages.** These garden bungalows in the countryside have kitchenettes, terraces, cable TVs, and phones. La Plantation restaurant is a gathering spot for gourmets, and definitely exceeds our price ranges. The beaches are a 15-minute drive away. The cottages are difficult to find; take advantage of the property's airport transfers. *Lamentin 97232, tel. 596/50–16–08, fax 596/50–26–83. 8 rooms. Facilities: restaurant, bar, pool, Jacuzzi. AE, MC, V. EP. ¢–$*

Le Diamant **Diamant Marine.** Miniapartments—one room with bed, kitchenette, and balcony—are in rows of pristine stucco buildings that progress down the hillside to the beach. The rooms are painted in mint, aqua, and periwinkle and decorated with bright abstract prints. The main building, which contains the restaurant, front desk, boutique, and flower shop, is 100 feet above the beach, while the pool is at the bottom of the hill, just above the beach. This arrangement is visually attractive, but the climb up the steps from the pool and beach to the main house and restaurant is strenuous. The hotel caters to French families on tour packages, and the high turnover and large-group clientele contribute to the wear and tear on facilities, although management works hard at maintenance. As at other Marine properties, the staff tends to be youthful and energetic, but things can get impersonal during high season. *Pointe de la Chery, near Diamant, tel. 596/76–46–00 or 800/221–4542, fax 596/76–25–99. 149 rooms. Facilities: restaurant, 2 bars, 2 pools (1 for children), free use of water sports at Novotel, deep-sea fishing, 2 lighted tennis courts, dive shop, boutique, flower shop. AE, DC, MC, V. CP, MAP. $$*

★ **Relais Caraibes.** Of all the hotels on Martinique, this one comes closest to having the individuality and authenticity of a country inn. A note of immediate chic is struck in the thatched public rooms, awash in interior gardens, white wicker furnishings, and antiques ranging from bronze Indian elephants to African masks, culled from the world travels of amiable Parisian owners Monsieur et Madame Senez. Twelve bungalows, decorated in a similar eclectic style, are spread over the manicured grounds, which offer views of the sea and Diamond Rock. Each has a bedroom, a small salon with a sofa bed, a kitchenette, and a bathroom. During high season, the large one-bedroom units cost $190 a night, but standard units remain in our $$ range. There are also three rooms in the main house that have unusual touches like hand-painted headboards, straw birdcages, and Chinese fans. The pool is perched at the edge of the cliff that drops to the sea. The hotel is a mile off the main road, and you need a car to get around. The beach, however, is a short walk away. The restaurant here tends to be expensive at dinner; you may want to travel 2 miles into Diamant for a lighter meal. *Pointe de la Chery, Diamant 97223, tel. 596/76–44–65 or 800/223–9815, fax 596/76–21–20. 15 rooms. Facilities: restaurant, bar, pool, boat, scuba instruction. AE, MC, V. CP, MAP. $$*

★ **Diamant Les Bains.** Although manager Hubert Andrieu and his family go all out to make their guests comfortable, you won't feel quite at home unless you speak at least a little French. A few of the rooms are in the main house, along with the superb and reasonably priced Creole restaurant, but most are in bungalows, some just steps away from the sea (and at the top of the $$ range). The bungalows are lovely, with gleaming white tiles, wood ceilings, local artwork, bright blue fabrics, and olive rattan furnishings. Each has air-conditioning, phone, TV, terrace, and minifridge. The standard rooms are simpler, but still colorful, and are without terrace and fridge. Ask about weekly package rates. *Le Diamant 97223, tel. 596/76–40–14 or 800/223–9815, fax 596/76–27–00; in Canada, 800/468–0023; in NY, 212/251–1800. 24 rooms. Facilities: restaurant, bar, pool, water-sports center. MC, V. CP, MAP. Closed Sept. $–$$*

Plein Sud. The white-and-sapphire buildings of this vacation village are grouped around a courtyard, across the road from the beach. Blue tile floors, rattan and teal-color wicker furniture, and floral fabrics give the one-bedroom apartments a fresh feel. All have kitchenette and terrace or balcony, as well as air-conditioning, phone, and TV. The staff is pleasant. The only drawback is that units, especially those close to the road, can be noisy. *Quartier Dizac, tel. 596/76–26–06, fax 596/76–26–07. Facilities: restaurant, bar, pool, grocery, shops, bank. AE, MC, V. EP. $–$$*

L'Érin Bleu. This homey inn is popular with the dive set. The simple, air-conditioned rooms have white tile floors and tropical print bedspreads. All have panoramic sea views, thanks to the hotel's position atop a cliff. It's a brisk five minute stroll down to the beach and a fine aerobic workout hiking back up. There are also a couple of weight machines for the athletically inclined. The restaurant serves affordable, creatively prepared seafood, and the bar is a delightful place to enjoy a cocktail and the views (the sun's dramatic performance at twilight draws people from miles around). *Route des Anse-d'Arlets, tel. 596/76–41–92, fax 596/76–41–90. 19 rooms. Facilities: restaurant, bar, pool, dive shop, TV room, weight machines. CP, MAP. $*

Chez Elène. At this classic *chambre d'hôte* (guest house), Elène and Dominique Bertin do their best to make you feel at home. The five immaculately kept rooms, some with four-poster beds, are available for only $50 a night. Guests have use of the kitchen, where a refrigerator is set aside for them. There's a three-night minimum and you'll need to reserve up to eight months in advance. The beach is a five-minute walk away. *Anse Cafard, tel. 596/76–41–25, fax 596/76–28–89. 5 rooms. Facilities: kitchen. No credit cards. CP. ¢*

Le François **La Riviera.** Three pretty whitewashed buildings with red tile roofs overlook Le Francois Bay and do indeed look as if they were transported straight from St. Tropez. All rooms have air-conditioning, TV, minibar, phone, and a balcony opening onto breathtaking water views. Decor is contemporary and fresh, mostly in floral patterns. Owner-manager Marie-Anne Prian and her husband Jacques speak English and are most helpful. The restaurant serves marvelous Continental-tinged Creole cuisine; try the blaff of sea urchins or the omelet flamed with aged rum. A long private pier makes La Riviera popular with yachties. *Route du Club Nautique, tel. 596/54–68–54, fax 596/54–30–43. 14 rooms. Facilities: restaurant, bar, boat rentals (canoes free to guests). AE, MC, V. CP, MAP. $*

Le Marin **Auberge du Marin.** John and Véronique Deschamps's bed-and-breakfast on rue Osman Duquesnay is in the former gendarmerie annex, a turn-of-the-century two-story structure now painted pastel. Language will be no problem here, since the Deschampses once lived in Sausalito. You share a bathroom with the other guests on your floor. the small, spartan rooms are not air-conditioned, but sea breezes keep nights cool. There's a small communal kitchen, and an excellent family-style dinner is served nightly. You can walk to the beach. *Le Marin 97290, tel. 596/74–83–88, fax 596/74–76–41. 7 rooms with shared bath. Facilities: restaurant. No credit cards. CP, MAP. ¢*

Ste-Anne **Club Med/Buccaneer's Creek.** Occupying 48 landscaped acres, Martinique's Club Med is an all-inclusive village with plazas, cafés, restaurants, boutique, and a small marina. Air-conditioned pastel cottages contain twin beds and private shower baths. The only money you need spend here is for bar drinks, scuba diving, personal expenses, and excursions into Fort-de-France or the countryside. There's a white-sand beach, a plethora of water sports, and plenty of nightlife. *Pointe Marin 97180, tel. 596/76–72–72, 800/258–2633; in NY, 212/750–1670; fax 596/72–76–02. 300 rooms. Facilities: 2 restaurants and bars, 7 tennis courts (4 lighted), fitness and watersports center, nightclub, disco. AE, MC, V. All-inclusive (except drinks). $$*

Hameau de Beauregard. This pastel-colored, Mediterranean-style village offers self-contained time-share apartments, all with TV, phone, kitchenette, and air-conditioning. One-bedroom units have a sofa bed, making them a good bet for families. Interiors are decorated in jade and bright jungle prints. Most of the activity centers around the pool, though the beach is a short stroll away. *Routes des Salines 97227, tel. 596/76–75–75, fax 596/76–97–13. 90 units. Facilities: restaurant, bar, pool. MC, V. EP, CP, MAP. $$*

La Dunette. This small hotel in Ste-Anne is one of the best buys in this price category. Rooms are not spacious, but they are comfortable, with TVs, air-conditioning, and full baths; make sure yours faces the sea and St. Lucia beyond. The beach in front of the hotel is adequate for a morning dip, but head for Pointe Marin, about a mile away, for more serious sunbathing. An outside patio 50 feet from the water's edge serves as the restaurant (*see* Dining, *above*); there's a small bar for morning coffee and evening aperitifs. A minimarket across the street from the hotel and a vegetable market a block away make assembling a picnic a simple matter. The friendly staff speaks some English. *Ste-Anne 97227, tel. 596/76–73–90, fax 596/76–76–05. 18 rooms. Facilities: restaurant, bar. MC, V. EP. $–$$*

Tartane **Baie du Galion.** This new hotel, a member of the Best Western chain, is on the lovely, wild Caravelle Peninsula. The medium-sized rooms are furnished in a charming Creole style, with polished dark wood furnishings and bright fabrics. All have air-conditioning, TV, phone, safe, fridge, and balcony (50 also have kitchenettes). Hiking is good in the adjacent Nature Reserve. The beach, though on the Atlantic, is relatively good for swimming, and the enormous pool is a focal point for guests. *Anse Tartane 97220, tel. 596/58–65–30 or 800/223–9815, fax 596/58–25–76. 146 rooms. Facilities: restaurant, bar, pool, tennis court. AE, MC, V. BP, MAP. $–$$*

Campgrounds It is acceptable to pitch a tent in designated locations on Martinique. One popular site is at Anse-Mitan (tel. 596/68–31–30); the 70F cost for two people includes access to coin-operated showers. Ste-Anne is another popular site, with a municipal campground (tel. 596/76–72–79) just outside the Club Med. The tourist office (tel. 596/63–79–60) can advise on other locations.

Villas and Apartment Rentals Besides the apartment-style accommodations listed with Gîtes de France (*see above*), units here range from studios to four-bedroom apartments. Weekly rates start at around $300 and climb from there. Contact **Villa Rental Service** (Centrale de Réservation, 20 rue Ernest Deproge, B.P. 823, Fort-de-France 97208, tel. 596/71–56–11, fax 596/63–11–64). **Villages Vacances** (Gros Raisins, 97228 Ste. Luce, tel. 596/62–52–84) is a French organization that operates bungalow villages—usually including a restaurant and pool—whose simple units, outfitted with bath and kitchen, are ideal for families. They're cheapest for organization members, then locals, but even foreign visitors can stay for less than $400 a week. They're reserved far in advance, especially during the French summer holidays.

Off-Season Bets Between April 15 and December 15, you can take advantage of hotel rates that are as much as 40% lower than peak-season prices. Among hotels with rates that decrease dramatically are **Le Bakoua** (Box 589, Fort-de-France, tel. 596/66–02–02 or 800/221–4542, fax 596/66–00–41), often considered Martinique's leading resort hotel; the plush **Diamant Novotel** (Le Diamant 97223, tel. 596/76–42–42 or 800/221–4542); and **Habitation Lagrange** (Marigot 97225, tel. 596/53–60–60, fax 596/53–50–58), a former sugar plantation with a restored 18th-century manor house. Only **Relais Caraibes's** (*see above*) small rooms squeak into our $$ price category during high season, but even the suites at this charming cliffside inn are affordable during the off-season.

The Arts and Nightlife

Be sure to catch a performance of **Les Grands Ballets de Martinique** (tel. 596/63–43–88). The troupe of young, exuberant dancers, singers, and musicians is one of the best folkloric groups in the Caribbean. They perform at Le Bakoua, Le Méridien Trois-Ilets, La Batelière Hotel, Diamant-Novotel and other hotels.

Discos Your hotel or the tourist office can put you in touch with the current "in" places. It's also wise to check on opening and closing times and admission charges. For the most part, the discos draw a mixed crowd of locals and tourists, the young and the not so young. Some of the currently popular places are **Blue Night** (20 blvd. Allègre, Fort-de-France, 596/71–58–43), **Le New Hippo** (24 blvd. Allègre, Fort-de-France, tel. 596/71–74–60), **Le Sweety** (rue Capitaine Pierre Rose, Fort-de-France, no phone), **VonVon** (Méridien, tel. 596/66–00–00), **La Cabane de Pêcheur** (Diamant-Novotel, tel. 596/76–42–42), **L'Oeil** (Petit Cocotte, Ducos, tel. 596/56–11–11), and **Zipp's Dupe Club** (Dumaine, Le François, tel. 596/54–47–06).

Zouk and Jazz Currently the most popular music is the zouk, which mixes the Caribbean rhythm and an Occidental tempo with Creole words. Jacob Devarieux (Kassav) is the leading exponent of this style and is occasionally on the island. More likely, though, you will hear zouk music played by one of his followers at the hotels and clubs. Jazz musicians, like the music, tend to be informal and independent. They rarely hold regular gigs. The **Neptune** (Diamant, tel. 596/76–34–23) is a hot spot for zouk. In season, you'll find one or two combos playing at clubs and hotels, but it is only at **Coco Lobo** (tel. 596/63–63–77, next to the tourist office in Fort-de-France), that there are regular jazz sessions.

Other Music **Las Tapas** (7 rue Garnier Pages, Fort-de-France, tel. 596/63–71–23) presents flamenco or salsa and merengue bands. At Pointe du Bout, **La Villa Creole** (*see* Dining, *above*) is a charming bistro whose owner, Guy Dawson, entertains nightly on the guitar—everything from Brel and Piaf to original ditties. **L'Amphore** (behind the Le Bakoua hotel, tel. 596/66–03–09) is a late-night hangout with a popular piano bar.

Casinos The **Casino Trois-Ilets** (Méridien, tel. 596/66–00–00) is open from 9 PM to 3 AM Monday to Saturday. You must be at least 21 (with a picture ID) to enter, and thereis a 70F admission charge (admission to slot-machine room is free). Try your hand at American and French roulette or blackjack.

16 Montserrat

Updated by Pamela Acheson

Measuring only 11 miles by 8 miles, Montserrat is a small, friendly island that has escaped much of the large-scale development common in other parts of the Caribbean. Mass tourism is rare, package deals almost unheard of. When you see the airstrip, you'll understand why: 747s can't land here. Despite the fact that Montserrat now has a brand-new $30 million seaport, big enough to accommodate small cruise ships, the island still retains its peaceful, unhurried, completely nontouristy atmosphere.

Montserrat is startlingly lush and green, thanks to its fertile, volcanic soil, which is also responsible for the black-sand beaches found on most of the island (although there are some beautiful stretches of "beige" sand on the northwest coast). Three mountain ranges dominate the landscape: Silver Hills to the north; Centre Hills; and the southern range, home to Galway's Soufrière, a 3,000-foot inactive volcano.

The island neither caters to nor discourages the budget traveler. It lacks the exclusive feel and outrageously expensive resorts of some Caribbean islands, but it's not known for particularly cheap hotels or restaurants either. Nevertheless, most accommodations are moderately priced, including some of the rental villas for which the island is known. A healthy handful of small hotels and guest houses offer cheaper alternatives. Activities tend to be inexpensive and sporty; bicycling and hiking are popular. It's the kind of place that attracts independent travelers who want a low-key, away-from-it-all vacation. If you want to pump iron, drink piña coladas, and boogie until dawn, you'll probably be bored. If you like seclusion, nature, peace, and quiet, you'll love it. Despite the island's small size, there are an unusually large number of nature walks, hiking trails, and scenic vistas. This is the island to come to when you want to see rare birds, bubbling volcanic springs, waterfalls, and dense forest.

On the map the island looks like a flint-ax head, with the sharp end pointing north. It was first discovered by Columbus, who sailed past the leeward coast in 1493 and named it after the monastery of Santa Maria de Montserrate near Barcelona. In the 17th century, dissident Irish Catholics fleeing persecution in St. Kitts settled on Montserrat and gave the island its nickname, the Emerald Isle. Place names like Carr's Bay and Kinsale, and surnames like Maloney and Frith, still recall the Irish connection, and though today the island is a British Crown Colony with a resident governor, your passport will be stamped with a shamrock. St. Patrick's Day is also enthusiastically celebrated, albeit to commemorate a major 18th-century slave uprising.

Most visitors arrive at Blackburne Airport on the Atlantic (east) coast and then transfer to the west coast. This is where the best beaches and most of the island's villas and hotels are concentrated, in a 5-by-2 mile area around the capital of Plymouth. As you drive around Montserrat's northern tip from the airport en route to your hotel, you will notice the landscape change from the rocky, windswept Atlantic coast to the luxuriant vegetation of the island's west side, where hibiscus, bougainvillea, giant philodendron, frangipani, avocado, mango, papaya, breadfruit, christophines, coconut palms, and flamboyant trees run riot. Notice, too, the spectacular view unfold across the Caribbean to the mysterious island of Rodondo and, beyond it, to St. Kitts, a sequence of indigo blue peaks on the horizon.

What It Will Cost These sample prices, meant only as a general guide, are for high season. A two-bedroom villa that sleeps four can be found for about $900 a week. A $$ hotel will be around $125 a night, but you can find ¢ (and very basic) hotels for about $30 a night. A B&B will be around $60–$80 for two. A ¢ restaurant dinner ranges from $6 to $8. A rum punch costs anywhere from $2 to $4. A glass of house wine will be $2; a beer, $1–$2. A taxi from the airport to Plymouth runs about $11, from town to the beach it's about $5. Cars rent for $35–$40 a day; mountain bike rental is $25 a day, $140 a week. A single-tank dive will cost about $40; snorkel equipment rents for about $5.

Before You Go

Tourist Information You can get information about Montserrat through the **Caribbean Tourism Organization** (20 E. 46th St., New York, NY 10017, tel. 212/682–0435).

Arriving and Departing

By Plane Although Antigua is not the only gateway, it's the best way to reach Montserrat. **BWIA** (tel. 800/538–2942) flies nonstop on Thursdays and Saturdays (plus Mondays in season) to Antigua from New York and on Thursday, Saturday, and Sunday from Miami; it also has regularly scheduled nonstop service from Toronto, Canada, and Heathrow Airport, London. **American Airlines** (tel. 800/433–7300) has connecting service from a number of U.S. cities through San Juan, Puerto Rico. **Air Canada** (tel. 800/776–3000) offers service from Toronto; **British Airways** (tel. in Britain, 0181/897–4000; in the U.S., 800/247–9297) from Gatwick Airport, London; and **Lufthansa** (tel. 800/645–3880 in the U.S.) transports visitors from Frankfurt via Puerto Rico.

From Antigua's V.C. Bird International Airport, you can make your connections with **LIAT** (tel. 809/491–2200) or **Montserrat Airways** (tel. 809/491–5342 or 809/491–6494) for the 15-minute flight to Montserrat.

You will land on the 3,400-foot runway at Blackburne Airport, on the Atlantic coast, about 11 miles from Plymouth.

From the Airport Taxis meet every flight, and the government-regulated fare from the airport to Plymouth is E.C. $29 (U.S. $11).

Passports and Visas U.S. and Canadian citizens need only proof of citizenship, such as a passport, a notarized birth certificate, or a voter registration card, plus a photo ID, such as a driver's license. A driver's license by itself is *not* sufficient. British citizens must have a passport; visas are not required. All visitors must hold an ongoing or return ticket.

Language It's English with more of a lilt than a brogue. You'll also hear a patois that's spoken on most of the islands.

Precautions Ask for permission before taking pictures. Some residents may be reluctant photographic subjects, and they will appreciate your courtesy.

Most Montserratians frown at the sight of skimpily dressed tourists; do not risk offending them by strolling around in swimsuits.

Staying in Montserrat

Important Addresses **Tourist Information:** The **Montserrat Department of Tourism** (Church Rd., Plymouth, tel. 809/491–2230) is open weekdays 8–noon and 1–4.

Emergencies **Police:** tel. 999 for emergencies or 809/491–2555. **Hospitals:** There is a 24-hour emergency room at **Glendon Hospital** (Plymouth, tel. 809/491–2552). **Pharmacies: Lee's Pharmacy** (Evergreen Dr., Plymouth, tel. 809/491–3274) and **Daniel's Pharmacy** (George St., Plymouth, tel. 809/491–2908).

Currency The official currency is the Eastern Caribbean dollar (E.C.$), often called beewee. At press time, the exchange rate was E.C. $2.70 to U.S. $1. U.S. dollars are readily accepted, but you'll often receive change in beewees. Note: Prices quoted here are in U.S. dollars unless noted otherwise.

Taxes and Service Charges Hotels collect a 7% government tax and add a 10% service charge. Most restaurants add a 10%–15% service charge. If restaurants do not add the service charge, it's customary to leave a 10% or 15% tip. Taxi drivers should be given a 10% tip. The departure tax is E.C. $25 (about U.S. $9).

Getting Around Taxis, private vehicles, or the M11 (a play on the local registration numbers, meaning your own two legs) are the main means of transport on the island. Because the island is small (only 39 square miles), and most of the accommodations are concentrated in a small area on the west coast, biking is also popular. Whatever you choose, you are unlikely to be more than a 10-minute walk from a beach. Even the villas perched on the hillside in the Woodlands district are within walking distance of the sea, although you'll need a car to get to the supermarkets in Plymouth. If you're staying in a hotel, it's not essential to rent a car for your entire stay. Many visitors rent for a day to see the sights, and spend the rest of their time swimming and hiking.

Taxis These are available at the airport, the main hotels, and at the Taxi Stand in Plymouth (tel. 809/491–2261). The distance from your accommodation to Plymouth is likely to be less than 5 miles, so fares are not expensive. The journey from the Vue Point Hotel to Plymouth, for instance, costs E.C. $13; from Woodlands to Plymouth, E.C. $18. The Department of Tourism publishes a list of taxi fares to most destinations.

Car Rentals The island has more than 150 miles of paved (but potholed) roads. If you like to drive, you'll enjoy the switchback hill roads and hairpin curves. Just remember that driving is on the left, and watch out for potholes and the occasional goat. You'll need a valid driver's license, plus a Montserrat license, which is available at the airport or the police station. The fee is E.C. $30 (U.S. $12). Rental cars cost about $35–$40 per day. The smaller companies, whose prices are generally

10%–25% cheaper, will negotiate, particularly off-season. The local Avis outlet is **Pauline Car Rentals** (Plymouth, tel. 809/491–2345 or 800/331–1084). Other agencies are **Budget** (Blackburne Airport, tel. 809/491–6065), **Fenco** (Plymouth, tel. 809/491–4901), **Jefferson's Car Rental** (Dagenham, tel. 809/491–2126), and **Reliable** (Plymouth, tel. 809/491–6990).

Public Transportation There is no public bus service as such; instead, an informal network of privately run minibuses ply the main routes between Plymouth and the villages. They generally start moving early, about 6:30 AM, bringing local people in to work or shop, and then leave town again at 3–4 PM, at the end of the islanders' working day. Outside these times, most service is haphazard, so if you use a minibus to get to Plymouth, you'll probably have to spend all day in town. The main route travels from St. John's, in the north, down the west coast to Plymouth. The main pickup point in Plymouth is the courtyard in front of the Osborne Wholesale Department on Parliament Street; another is at Papa's grocery store on Church Street. (Outside of Plymouth, there are no fixed pickup points; just flag down the vehicle.) Fare for the full route is a mere E.C. $3. The Department of Tourism publishes a list of routes and approximate fares.

Mountain Bikes Montserrat is good mountain-bike country: small, with relatively traffic-free roads and lots of challenging hills to try out all those gears. Potholes will present a constant challenge, as will the heat and steep grades. Even so, biking is a great way to get around this island, where the majority of facilities, shops, and accommodations are concentrated in a small area on the west coast. At **Island Bikes** (Harney St., Plymouth, tel. 809/491–4696), Butch Miller and Susan Goldin, the bustling, can-do Americans who run the outfit, are self-confessed biking junkies and know the island like the backs of their own saddles. Rentals are $25 a day, $140 a week. The couple also conducts guided tours, which include refreshments and a sag wagon for the faint of heart, and can arrange bed-and-bike package tours. They also sponsor two international cycle races each year.

Telephones and Mail To call Montserrat from the United States, dial area code 809 and access code 491 plus the local four-digit number. International direct-dial is available on the island; both local and long-distance calls come through clearly. To call locally on the island, you need to dial the seven-digit number, the first three digits of which are always 491. A local call costs E.C. 25¢.

Airmail letters and postcards to the United States and Canada cost E.C. $1.15 each. Montserrat is one of several Caribbean islands whose stamps are of interest to collectors. You can buy them at the main post office in Plymouth (open Mon., Tues., Thurs. and Fri. 8:15–3:30, Wed. and Sat. 8:15–11:30 AM).

Opening and Closing Times Most shops are open Monday–Saturday 8–5. Banking hours are Monday–Thursday 8–3, Friday 3–5.

Guided Tours Guides are recommended when you are heading to Mount Chance, Galway's Soufrière, and the Great Alps Falls. Prices for two people range from $10 to $30. Guides and tours can be arranged by calling Cecil Cassell, president of the Montserrat Tour Guide Association (tel. 809/491–3160, fax 809/491–2052). Or you can call **John Ryner** (tel. 809/491–2190) and the aptly named **Be-Beep Taylor** (tel. 809/491–3787). Prices (fixed by the Department of Tourism) are E.C. $30 per hour (U.S. $12) or E.C. $130–E.C. $150 (U.S. $50–$58) for a five-hour day tour. Refreshments are extra. For further information, contact the Department of Tourism.

Exploring Montserrat

Numbers in the margin correspond to points of interest on the Montserrat map.

Plymouth About a third of the island's population of 11,000 lives in the capital
❶ city of **Plymouth,** which faces the Caribbean on the southwest coast.
The town is neat and clean, its narrow streets lined with trim Georgian structures built mostly of stones that came from Dorset as ballast on old sailing vessels. Most of the town's sights are set right along the water, and you can easily explore the whole town in less than two hours. On the south side, a bridge over the Fort Ghaut ("gut," or ravine) leads to Wapping, where most of the restaurants are located.

We'll begin at **Government House** on the south side of town just above Sugar Bay. The frilly Victorian house, painted green with white trim and decorated with a shamrock, dates from the 18th century. Beautifully landscaped grounds surround the building, which is the residence of the governor of Montserrat. The grounds are open to visitors Monday, Tuesday, Thursday, and Friday, from 10:30 to 12:30 and are worth a visit.

Follow Peebles Street north and cross the bridge. Just over the bridge, at the junction of Harney, Strand, and Parliament streets, you'll see the **Plymouth Market,** where islanders bring their produce on Friday and Saturday mornings—a very colorful scene of great piles of local vegetables and fruits, and vendors in bright outfits.

From the market, walk along Strand Street for one block to the tall white **war memorial**, a tribute to the soldiers of both World Wars. Next to the monument is the **post office and treasury,** a galleried West Indian–style building by the water, where you can buy stamps that make handsome souvenirs.

Walk away from the water on George Street, which runs alongside the war memorial. The town's main thoroughfare, Parliament Street, cuts diagonally north–south through the town. A left turn onto Parliament Street, at the corner of George Street, will take you to the Methodist church and the courthouse. If you continue straight on George Street, you'll come to the Roman Catholic church. North of the church is the **American University of the Caribbean,** a medical school with many American students.

Elsewhere on the Island The main sights on Montserrat can be seen in a day. Although a guided tour is somewhat more expensive than renting a car (*see* Guided Tours, *above*), it does allow you to see the island through an insider's eyes. A car, on the other hand, gives you more freedom, particularly for lunch and swim stops, and is cheaper.

Tour 1 Take Highway 2, the main road north out of Plymouth. On the outskirts of town there's a stone marker that commemorates the first
❷ colony in 1632. Just north of town is **St. Anthony's Church,** conse-
crated sometime between 1623 and 1666. It was rebuilt in 1730 following one of the many clashes between the French and the English in the area. Two silver chalices displayed in the church were donated by freed slaves after emancipation in 1834. An ancient tamarind tree stands near the church.

Richmond Hill rises northeast of town. Here you will find the
❸ **Montserrat Museum** in a restored sugar mill. The museum contains
maps, historical records, artifacts (including some Arawak and Carib items), and all sorts of memorabilia pertaining to the island's growth and development. *Richmond Hill, tel. 809/491–5443. Admission free (donations accepted). Open Sun. and Wed. 2:30–5 (but call ahead to be sure).*

Take the first left turn past the museum to Grove Road; it will take
❹ you to the **Fox's Bay Bird Sanctuary,** a 15-acre mangrove swamp.
The marked trail through the sanctuary begins right near Fox's Bay beach. Watch for green herons, the rare blue herons, coots, egrets, and kingfishers plus many lizards and iguanas.

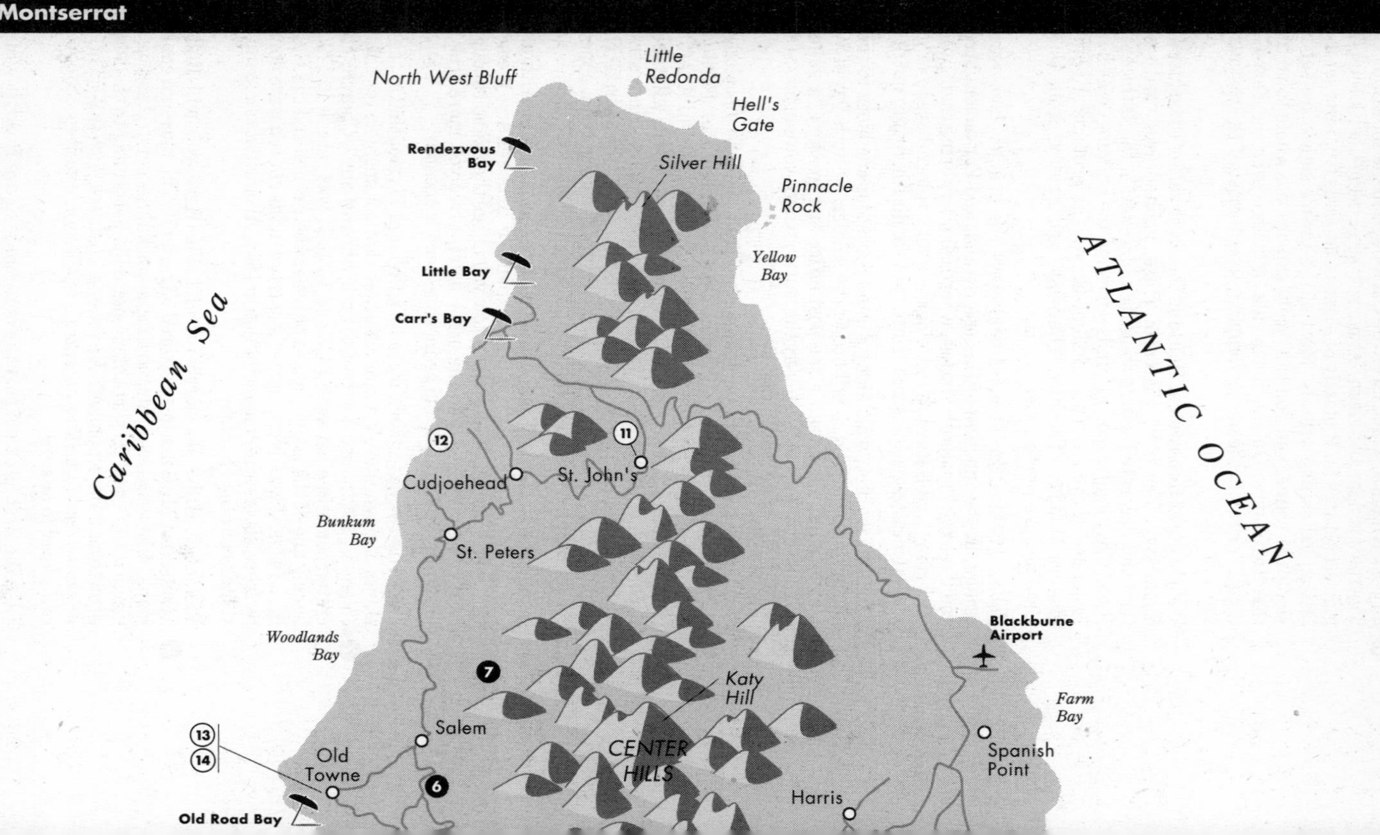
North West Bluff
Little Redonda
Hell's Gate
Rendezvous Bay
Silver Hill
Pinnacle Rock
Yellow Bay
ATLANTIC OCEAN
Little Bay
Carr's Bay
Caribbean Sea
12
11
Cudjoehead
St. John's
Bunkum Bay
St. Peters
Woodlands Bay
Blackburne Airport
7
Katy Hill
Farm Bay
Salem
13
14
Old Towne
CENTER HILLS
Spanish Point
6
Harris
Old Road Bay

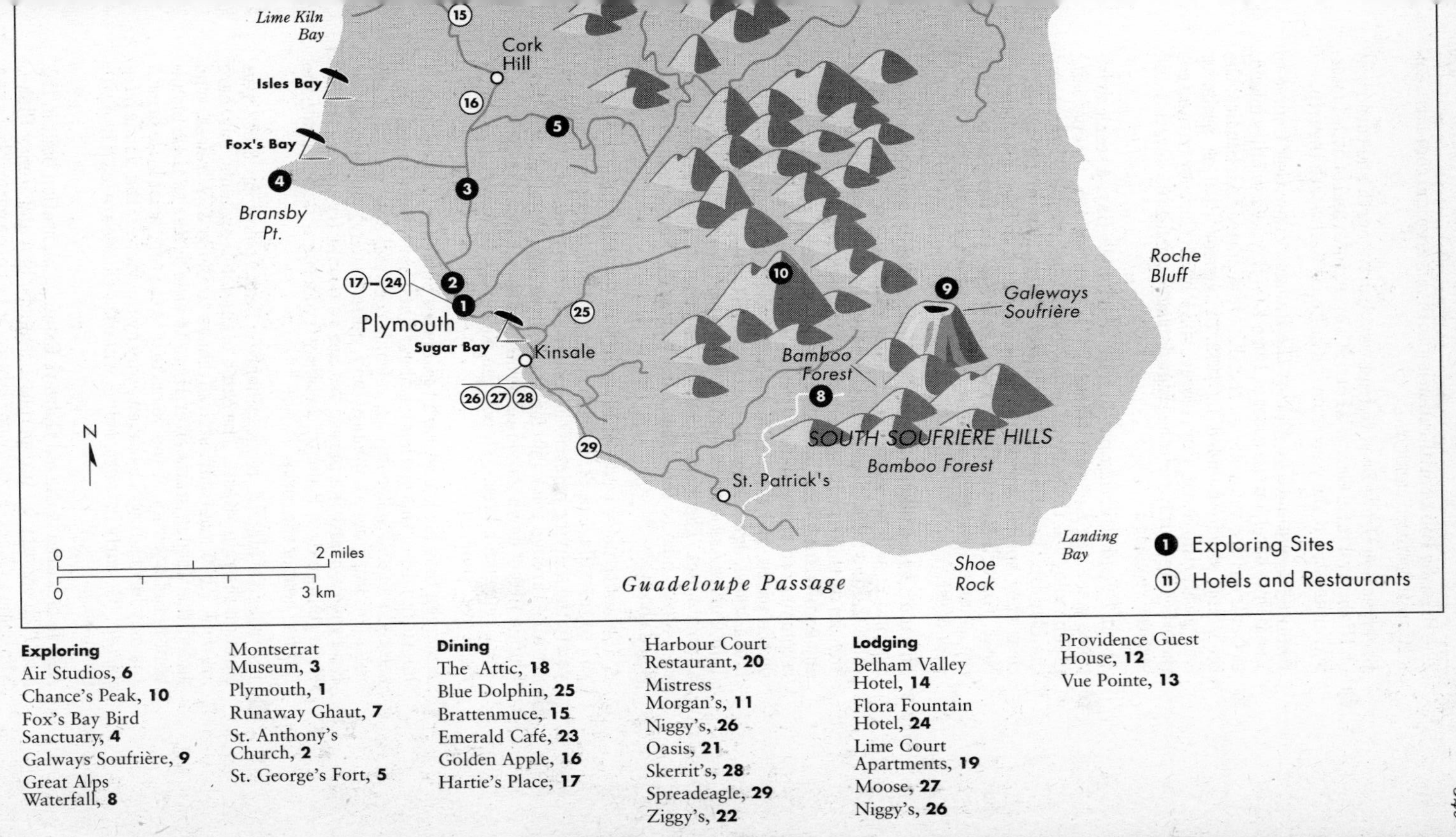
Lime Kiln Bay
Isles Bay
Fox's Bay
Bransby Pt.
Cork Hill
Plymouth
Sugar Bay
Kinsale
Bamboo Forest
Galeways Soufrière
Roche Bluff
SOUTH SOUFRIÈRE HILLS
Bamboo Forest
St. Patrick's
Landing Bay
Shoe Rock
Guadeloupe Passage
N
0 2 miles
0 3 km
Exploring Sites
Hotels and Restaurants
Exploring
Air Studios, 6
Chance's Peak, 10
Fox's Bay Bird Sanctuary, 4
Galways Soufrière, 9
Great Alps Waterfall, 8
Montserrat Museum, 3
Plymouth, 1
Runaway Ghaut, 7
St. Anthony's Church, 2
St. George's Fort, 5
Dining
The Attic, 18
Blue Dolphin, 25
Brattenmuce, 15
Emerald Café, 23
Golden Apple, 16
Hartie's Place, 17
Harbour Court Restaurant, 20
Mistress Morgan's, 11
Niggy's, 26
Oasis, 21
Skerrit's, 28
Spreadeagle, 29
Ziggy's, 22
Lodging
Belham Valley Hotel, 14
Flora Fountain Hotel, 24
Lime Court Apartments, 19
Moose, 27
Niggy's, 26
Providence Guest House, 12
Vue Pointe, 13

The **Bransby Point Fortification** is also in this area and contains a collection of restored cannons.

Backtrack on Grove Road to Highway 2, drive north and turn right
5 on Highway 4 to **St. George's Fort.** It's overgrown and of little historical interest, but the view from the hilltop is well worth the trip.

Highway 2 continues north past the Belham Valley Golf Course to
Vue Pointe hotel, on the coast at Lime Kiln Bay. A few miles inland,
6 at Centre Hills, you will find the site of the former **Air Studios,** the recording studio founded in 1979 by former Beatles producer George Martin. Sting, Boy George, and Paul McCartney have all cut records here, but Hurricane Hugo damaged the facility severely and it never reopened.

About 1½ miles farther north, near Woodland's Bay, a scenic drive
7 takes you along **Runaway Ghaut.** Two centuries ago, this peaceful green valley was the scene of bloody battles between the French and the English. Local legend has it that "those who drink its water clear they spellbound are, and the Montserrat they must obey." Next, you will come to **Carr's Bay, Little Bay,** and **Rendezvous Bay,** the island's three most popular beaches, which are along the northwest coast.

Tour 2 This tour, which takes in Soufrière, the rain forest, and the southern mountains, will be considerably more arduous than the first. It involves hiking from the ends of access roads to the sites themselves. You can do this tour in half a day if you race through it, but if you do any significant hiking or biking, you could easily spend a day. It's recommended that you hire a guide, because there are few markers on the paths, and the access roads are not always easy to find. To find a knowledgeable guide, contact Cecil Cassell at the Montserrat Tour Guides Association, contact the Department of Tourism, or ask at your hotel. The guide's fee will be about $6 per person for the rain-forest hike to the Great Alps Waterfall. Wear sturdy rubber-soled shoes.

A 15-minute drive south of Plymouth on Old Fort Road will bring
you to the village of **St. Patrick's.** From there, a scenic drive takes
you to the starting point of the moderately strenuous 30- to 45-min-
8 ute hike through thick rain forests to **Great Alps Waterfall.** The falls plunge 70 feet down the side of a rock and splash into a shallow pool. For a refreshing break, step in the pool and let the waters cascade right over you.

9 A rugged road leads eastward to **Galways Soufrière,** where another hike is involved, this one lasting about a half hour. Once there, you'll see reddish and yellow-brown volcanic rock and springs and fumaroles of gurgling, bubbling (and quite smelly) molten sulfur. Everyone's heard the phrase "so hot you could fry an egg on it." Here your guide will almost certainly fry an egg to demonstrate the intense heat of the rocks.

10 The island's highest point, **Chance's Peak,** pokes up 3,002 feet through the rain forests. The climb to the top is arduous, but there are now 2,000 makeshift stairs (thanks to Cable & Wireless, who added the wooden stairs after Hugo to ease access to their mountaintop radio tower). If you do make it to the top, what little breath you may have left will be taken away by the view, *if* the clouds have parted. (Go early in the morning, when the clouds are least likely to be there.)

Also in this area is the old **Galways Estate,** a plantation built in the late 17th century by prosperous Irishmen John and Henry Blake, who came to Montserrat from Galway. It has been earmarked as an important archaeological site by the Smithsonian. Amateur archaeologists come here every summer, and the sugar boiling house and parts of both a wind-driven and cattle-driven sugar mill have been partially restored.

Beaches

The sand on the beaches on Montserrat's south coast is of volcanic origin; usually referred to as black, it's actually light to dark gray. On the northwest coast, the sand is beige or white. Black sand absorbs more heat than white, and sandals are recommended. The best of Montserrat's beaches are, like everything else, on the west coast. (The water on the rocky east coast is rough, and the areas are inaccessible.) Most are in lovely little coves surrounded by steep, lush hillsides, where hotels generally perch. In the small, developed area where you will probably be staying, you will rarely be farther than a 10-minute walk from the water.

There are excellent beaches close to the main villa and hotel developments at **Old Road Bay, Isles Bay,** and **Fox's Bay.** Further north, the most popular destinations for swimming and sunning are **Rendezvous Bay** (Montserrat's only white sand beach), **Little Bay,** and **Carr's Bay,** where the sand is beige-gray. Unless you arrive by boat, it's a 30-minute drive from Plymouth over potholed dirt tracks to reach Carr's Bay and Little Bay. From Little Bay, you must hike to Rendezvous Bay. The most pleasant way to reach the northern beaches is by boat (*see* Sports and the Outdoors, *below*).

Sugar Bay, to the south of Plymouth, is a beach of fine gray volcanic sand. The Yacht Club overlooks this beach. The beaches in and around Plymouth itself are adequate, but not the island's best.

Sports and the Outdoors

Most of the sports facilities on Montserrat, apart from hiking and biking, are run from the larger hotels and tend to be expensive for nonguests.

Boating **Captain Martin** (tel. 809/491–5738) takes guests out on his 46-foot trimaran for a full-day sail to the white-sand beach at **Rendezvous Bay** for swimming and snorkeling at the nearby reef. The boat leaves about 10 AM and returns about 5 PM; the cost is $45 and includes an open bar and snorkeling equipment. **Vue Pointe** hotel (tel. 809/491–5210) offers sailing and snorkeling excursions to Rendezvous Bay, Little Bay, and Carr's Bay. The cost is $25 a person and includes a sandwich lunch and snorkeling equipment.

Golf The **Montserrat Golf Course** (tel. 809/491–5220), in the picturesqueBelham Valley, is "slope rated" by the USGA (in other words, it's incredibly hilly) and must be one of the few golf courses that can list gopher holes and iguanas among its hazards. The number of holes (11) is also somewhat eccentric, though by playing a number of them twice, you can get your 18. Four fairways run along the ocean. The rest are uphill and down dale. The greens fee is E.C. $60.

Hiking Small, green, and hilly, Montserrat is an excellent place to hike, assuming you can take the heat. If you want to do an Indiana Jones, then head for the South Soufrière Hills at the southern tip of the island. It is the wildest and most unspoiled part of Montserrat and includes among its highlights the **Bamboo Forest,** a large tract of semi–rain forest inhabited by frogs, numerous plants, and more than 100 species of birds. Among the latter is the national emblem, *iaterus oberi* (Montserrat oriole), also known locally as the Tannia Bird, and which is found nowhere else on earth. You will also see bromeliads, tulip and breadfruit trees, and a plethora of other tropical plants. It is best to go with a guide.

A climb up **Chance's Peak** is well worth the effort. Wooden steps have been laid into the mountainside, and several viewing platforms await at the top. If you're a mountain goat, you can get up and down in two hours, but we recommend bringing a picnic lunch and making a half-day trip of it. Either way you can expect some muscle aches the next day.

A hike to **Galways Soufrière** rewards the intrepid with otherworldly sights from the volcano's crater (*see* Exploring, *above*).

Mountain Biking Montserrat is perfect mountain-bike country (*see* Getting Around, *in* Staying in Montserrat, *above*).

Snorkeling, Scuba Diving, and Water Sports The **Sea Wolf Diving School** (tel. 809/491–7807) in Plymouth and **Aquatic Discoveries** (tel. 809/491–3474 or 3474), located next to the Vue Pointe hotel, both offer one- or two-tank dives, night dives, and instruction from PADI-certified teachers. Costs are about $40 for a one-tank dive and $60 for a two-tank dive. Aquatic Discoveries also offers snorkel tours, whale-watching trips, and deep sea fishing excursions.

Danny Water Sports (tel. 809/491–5645), operating out of the Vue Pointe, offers fishing ($30 an hour), Sunfish sailing ($10 an hour), waterskiing ($10 an hour), and windsurfing ($10 an hour). Both Sea Wolf and Danny Water Sports rent snorkeling equipment ($5–$10 per day).

Tennis There are lighted tennis courts at the **Vue Pointe** hotel (tel. 809/491–5210), the **Montserrat Golf Club** (tel. 809/491–5220), and the **Montserrat Springs Hotel** (tel. 809/491–2481).

Spectator Sports Cricket is the national passion. Cricket and soccer matches are held from February through June in **Sturge Park. Shamrock Car Park** is the venue for netball and basketball games. Contact the Department of Tourism (tel. 809/491–2230) for schedules.

Shopping

Montserrat is one of the few Caribbean islands where a local craft industry has remained (just about) intact. A few good bargains are still to be had, mainly in pottery, straw goods, ceramic jewelry, and jewelry made from shells and coral. The island's most famous product is sea-island cotton, prized for its high quality and softness, but there is a limited amount and it's not cheap. Montserratian stamps are prized by collectors; they can be purchased at the post office or at the Philatelic Bureau, just across the bridge in Wapping. Two lip-smacking local food products are Cassell's hot sauce, available at most supermarkets, and Perk's Punch, an effervescent rum-based concoction manufactured by J.W.R. Perkins, Inc. (tel. 809/491–2596).

Good Buys

Clothes The **Jus' Looking** (George St., Plymouth, tel. 809/491–4076; small branch at airport, open afternoons only, tel. 809/491–4040) boutique features "sculpted," hand-painted pillows from Antigua; painted and lacquered boxes from the Dutch West Indies; Sunny Caribbee's jams, jellies, and packaged spices from the British Virgin Islands (including an Arawak love potion and a hangover cure); special teas; and Caribelle Batik's line of richly colored fabrics, shirts, skirts, pants, and dresses. The shop also has an excellent selection of local poetry and history books. **Montserrat Shirts** (Parliament St., tel. 809/491–2892) has a good selection of men's tropical cotton shirts, plus T-shirts and sandals for the whole family. **Etcetera** (John St., tel. 809/491–3299) is a little shop carrying colorful, lightweight cotton dresses and a small, but fine, selection of local crafts. (If you're lucky, you may see someone making a hat of coconut palm fronds).

The Montserrat Sea Island Cotton Co. (corner of George and Strand Sts., Plymouth, tel. 809/491–7009). Long famous for its cotton creations, this shop has dresses, shirts, and other clothing items plus table linens, much of it made from local sea island cotton.

Crafts The **Tapestries of Montserrat** (Parliament St., tel. 809/491–2520), on the second floor of the John Bull Shop, offers a floor-to-ceiling display of hand-tufted creations—from wall hangings and pillow covers to tote bags and rugs—all with fanciful yarn adornments of flowers, carnival figures, animals, and birds. Owners Gerald and Charlie Handley will even help you create your own design for a small additional fee. At **Carol's Corner** (Vue Pointe hotel, tel. 809/491–5210), Carol Osborne sells everything related to Montserrat—stamps, copper bookmarks, the *Montserrat Cookbook*, Frane Lessac's books of prose, and paintings. Drop by **Dutcher's Studio** (Olveston, tel. 809/491–5253) to see hand-cut, hand-painted objects made from glass, ceramics, and old bottles, and some very appealing ceramic jewelry. If Paula Dutcher is there, ask about the morning iguana feeding at her house. Anywhere from five to 50 reptiles converge on her lawn, sunning themselves and eating hibiscus from your hand. **Island House** (tel. 809/491–3938) on John Street, stocks a fine collection of Haitian art, Caribbean prints, and clay pottery.

Dining

Despite its size, Montserrat offers quite a variety of affordable dining options, from gourmet-quality restaurants to local cafés and bistros. Many of these may look like the proverbial hole-in-the-wall, but if you're lucky you'll be served delicious Caribbean home cooking. The island has a lively assortment of **rum shops**—the Caribbean version of local bars—packed with islanders on Friday nights; you can join in and get a drink and a simple meal. One of the best is the **Cork Hill Rum Shop** in Salem. On Fridays you'll find music, the best spareribs on the island, and chicken and fried fish cooked by local women in their homes and brought to the bar for sale. At the **Treasure Cove,** in the village of Kinsale, a traditional string band featuring guitars, pipes, and tambourines often plays.

For those renting villas, Plymouth has several large, well-stocked supermarkets. The biggest is **Rams Emdee** (Church Rd.). It's run by the same Indian family that manages the Flora Fountain Hotel down the street, which accounts for the store's good selection of Indian foods and spices. Another large, modern store is **Angelo's** (Church Rd.). Most villages, including Kinsale, St. Patrick's, and Salem, have little general stores selling basics like matches, canned goods, fruits and vegetables, and—a staple here—Guinness. **Pete's 24 Hour Bakery** (George St.), which makes delicious rye, whole wheat, and French breads is worth the half-mile trip out of Plymouth. **Economy Bakery** (Church St.; closed Sat.) is also good.

At Plymouth's Strand Street **market** on Saturday morning, the best produce is gone by midday (it opens at 4:30 AM). You'll forget about the grubby buildings when you see the busloads of ample island women in colorful cotton print dresses, the piles of sugarcane, the tempting array of local fruits and vegetables (if you're not sure what something is or how to cook it, just ask!), and the singsong haggling and banter at the stalls.

Montserrat's national dish is goatwater stew, made with goat meat and vegetables, similar to Irish stew. Goat meat has a strong but good flavor. Mountain chicken (*crapaud*, actually enormous frogs) is also a great favorite. Yams, breadfruit, christophines (a kind of squash), limes, mangos, papayas, and a variety of seafood are served in most restaurants. Home-brewed ginger beer, one of the finest traditional drinks of the West Indies, is available at many cafés.

Dress is casual unless otherwise stated. Highly recommended restaurants are indicated by a star ★.

Category	Cost*
$$	$20–$30
$	$10–$20
¢	under $10

**per person, excluding drinks and service*

$$ **Emerald Café.** Dining is relaxed at 10 tables inside and on the terrace, where there are white tables shaded by blue umbrellas. Burgers, sandwiches, salads, and grilled dishes are served at lunchtime. For dinner you can order tournedos sautéed in spicy butter, broiled or sautéed Caribbean lobster, T-bone steak, mountain chicken diable, and giant swordfish steaks. The Island Coconut Pie and other homemade pastries are superb. There's also an ample list of liqueurs and wines, a full bar, and entertainment on weekends. *Wapping, Plymouth, tel. 809/491–3821. Dinner reservations advised in season. MC. Closed Sun.*

$$ **Oasis.** A 200-year-old stone house is the setting for this charming restaurant. You can dine indoors in the intimate bar and lounge, but most choose the outdoor patio, which looks out onto colorful tropical flowers. Calypso mountain chicken, jumbo shrimp Provençale, red snapper with lime butter, and grilled sirloin steak are house specialties. Owners Eric and Mandy Finnamore are also well known for their British-style fish-and-chips. Wapping, Plymouth, tel. 809/491–2328. Reservations advised in season. No credit cards. Closed Wed.

$ **The Attic.** The (formerly) third-story Attic had a sister restaurant on the second story called The Pantry. Compliments of Hurricane Hugo, the Attic ended up in the Pantry, where owners John and Jeanne Fagon decided it would stay! For breakfast, lunch, and dinner, 12 busy tables supply town folk with specialties of ocean perch, pork chops with pantry sauce (made from "whatever's in the pantry"), breaded shrimp, and lobster tail. *Marine Dr., Plymouth, tel. 809/491–2008. No credit cards.*

$ ★ **Blue Dolphin.** It's short on ambience, the chairs are Naugahyde, and the menu's scrawled on a blackboard without prices or descriptions, but the seductive aromas wafting from the kitchen announce that the Blue Dolphin serves some of the best food on the island, including luscious pumpkin fritters, mouthwatering lobster, and meltingly tender mountain chicken. The restaurant is on the northeastern edge of Plymouth. *Amersham, tel. 809/491–3263. No credit cards.*

$ ★ **Brattenmuce.** About 10 minutes by car above the road from Plymouth to Belham Valley, you can't miss the canary-yellow facade and brightly colored croton bushes of this restaurant. The name is a play on the name of the owners, Matt Hawthorne and Bruce Munro, two Canadian expats who have been in Montserrat since 1985. They serve no-frills, North American cuisine—meat loaf and mashed potatoes, pork chops, and chicken cordon bleu. On Wednesday nights they have a Games Night, which is popular with retirees from the North. A three-course meal for E.C. $25 includes free use of the Scrabble boards and Trivial Pursuit. For those who want to stay over, Rogie's, above the restaurant, has simple rooms to let. In the off-season Brattenmuce is open on Wednesday, Friday, and Saturday in the evening. In season, it closes only on Monday. *Belham Valley, tel. 809/419–7564. Reservations advised in high season. No credit cards.*

$ **Golden Apple.** In this large, galleried stone building, you'll be served huge plates of good local cooking. The restaurant's specialty is goatwater stew, which they cook on weekends only, outside over an open fire. Souse; *pelau* (chicken-and-rice curry); conch, stewed or curried; and mountain chicken are also excellent. Tables are covered with cheerful red-and-white checked tablecloths, and the atmosphere is relaxed. A grocery store is adjacent. *Cork Hill, tel. 809/491–2187. No credit cards.*

$ ★ **Niggy's.** In his previous life, the owner was a British character actor in Hollywood. That was before he decided to trade the limelight for a place behind the bar in this extremely popular restaurant (the British governor eats here regularly). The setting is a simple clapboard cottage with yellow bella flowers trailing over the gate, and the food, served at picnic-style benches under a trellis of flowering plants, is excellent and a good value. Try the grilled steaks and chops, shrimp scampi, or one of the pasta specials. Inside at the bar, you'll be regaled with tales of Hollywood, and the whole place feels like a set for a Caribbean remake of *Casablanca*. There's entertainment weekends, and for those who want to stay over, there are two simple but clean rooms in the back. The property is a 10-minute drive from the center of Plymouth. *Kinsale, tel. 809/491–7489. No credit cards. No lunch.*

$ **Spreadeagle.** This is a tiny place that you'll be glad you found if you visit Galway's Soufriere or Great Alps Falls. Peter "Bobb," the owner, keeps beer on ice and serves all sorts of beverages and light snacks. *German's Bay, tel. 809/491–7503. No credit cards. Open 9–5.*

$ ★ **Ziggy's.** On top of a barrel at the entrance to their restaurant, John and Marcia Punter display all the fruits and vegetables that grow on the island, among them ginger, nutmeg, yams, plantain, christophine, and coconuts. This is one of the first clues that what used to be a simple waterfront café and bar has become one of the best bistros on the island. The furnishings are sparse, but the waterside setting is very pleasant, and the menu—everything from curried mutton and rice to lasagna—one of the most varied on the island. *Wapping, Plymouth, tel. 809/491–2237. Reservations advised. No credit cards. Closed Wed.*

¢ **Harbour Court Restaurant.** This simple street café is the best place on the island for granny-watching. At lunchtime, Plymouth's pensioner set comes here for fried chicken or a hamburger. The open-air dining area—only a brown-and-white fence divides it from the street—is simple but clean, with ceiling fans hung from a corrugated roof. The owner, Mr. Watts, is a charming man. His specialty is homemade fruit drinks, including soursop and sorrel. The homemade ginger beer will bring tears to your eyes. On Friday nights there is a steel band. *Plymouth, tel. 809/491–2826. No credit cards.*

¢ **Hartie's Place.** The very pleasant Hartie and her husband lived in New York's Bronx for 20 years before returning here to open this mom-and-pop hamburger restaurant. It's in a wing of their house, about a half mile outside Plymouth on a hill overlooking the sea. The space is small, but clean and well kept; it's become the favorite of students from the American University of the Caribbean, the medical school just up the street. In addition to hamburgers, Hartie dishes up club sandwiches of all kinds—turkey, chicken, ham, etc.—and makes simple Italian dishes, such as spaghetti and meat sauce and lasagna. There's also a big breakfast menu and free delivery around town. Plymouth, tel. 809/491–7576. No credit cards.

¢ **Mistress Morgan's.** Friday and Saturday are goatwater-stew days at Mistress Morgan's, and from 11:30 onward you can join the carloads of locals who make the trek up to the north of the island to eat their fill. Order yourself a hearty bowl of the stew, which costs only E.C. $8 (U.S. $3.50), and plunk yourself down at one of the four picnic tables in the simple, unadorned room. The stew is just the way it should be—with the flesh falling off the bone, brimming with dumplings and innards. If that doesn't sound appetizing, try the souse, baked chicken, or any of the other down-home specialties. *Airport Rd., St. John's, tel. 809/491–5419. No credit cards.*

¢ **Skerrit's.** Leroyd Skerrit has been serving local delicacies—goatwater stew, red snapper, and pig's tail and chicken soup—for nearly a decade at this tiny restaurant, off the beaten track in a safe but run-down neighborhood of Kinsale. A couple of alcove-sized rooms with Formica-topped tables seat no more than 12. The cooking is good, the produce is fresh, and the juices (passion fruit, ginger beer, lime) are thirst-quenching. For E.C. $12 you can eat your fill. *Aymers Ghaut, Kinsale, tel. 809/491-3728. No credit cards. No dinner.*

Lodging

Accommodations on Montserrat are generally small: The two largest hotels, the Vue Pointe and Montserrat Springs, have only 86 rooms between them. The rest are small guest houses. What the island does have are villas—nearly twice as many as hotel rooms. Villas are not only affordable here; given their comforts and conveniences, many prefer them to the hotels (*see* Villa and Apartment Rentals, *below*). Lodging prices tend to fall abruptly from the $150–$200 range to the $40 range, with not much in between. The two mid-price hotels, the Flora Fountain and the Oriole Plaza, are in the center of Plymouth and cater mainly to businesspeople.

Almost all hotels and villa developments are on the milder west coast, where the beaches are. Accommodations in and around Plymouth are within walking distance of a beach (not necessarily the best one). Wherever you stay, you're unlikely to be further than 10 minutes by car from a beach and shops.

Highly recommended lodgings are indicated by a star ★.

Category	Cost*
$$	$75–$150
$	$40–$75
¢	under $40

**All prices are for a standard double room for two, excluding 7% tax and a 10% service charge. To estimate rates for hotels offering MAP, add about $35–$40 per person per day to the above price ranges.*

Hotels

$$ **Flora Fountain Hotel.** This is a hotel for people coming on business (only 35% of the clientele are tourists) or for those who appreciate an old, rambling hotel in the heart of town. The two-story structure has been created around an enormous fountain that's sometimes lighted at night, with small tables scattered in the inner courtyard. There are 18 plainly decorated but adequate rooms, all with tile bath and air-conditioning, and most with balconies. All rooms have phones but not all have TVs, so request one if it's important to you. The restaurant has a chef from Bombay who serves simple sandwiches and fine Indian dishes. Friday night's Indian buffet includes several meat and fish dishes, at least two kinds of rice, vegetable and pork dishes with spices, *raita* (a yogurt sauce), and *samosa* (spicy meat patties). *Box 373, Church Rd., Plymouth, tel. 809/491-6092, fax 809/491-2568. 18 rooms. Facilities: restaurant, bar. AE, D, MC, V. EP, CP, MAP, FAP.*

$$ ★ **Vue Pointe.** The moment you arrive here you feel as though both the staff and the owners, Cedric and Carol Osborne, really care about your well-being. The gracious Monday-night cocktail parties that the Osbornes host at their house, with drinks, delicious homemade hors d'oeuvres, and good conversation, are a perfect example. (Cedric Osborne comes from one of the island's first families and is a mine of information about local goings-on.) The breeze-cooled accommodations include 12 rooms in the main building and 28 hexagonal rondavels that spill down to the gray-sand beach on Old Road Bay. Each rondavel has a large bedroom, cable TV, phone, hair dryer, minifridge, spacious bathroom, and great view. In the main

building a large lounge and bar overlook the pool; the Wednesday-night barbecue, with steel bands and other entertainment, is an event well attended by locals and guests alike. In the adjacent sea-view restaurant, you can have a candlelight dinner of local and international specialties (the chef is one of the most skilled on the island). A 150-seat conference center serves as a theater and disco. For water-sports enthusiasts, there is scuba diving, snorkeling, and fishing. *Box 65, Plymouth, tel. 809/491–5210 or 800/235–0709, fax 809/491–4813. 12 rooms, 28 rondavels. Facilities: restaurant, bar, gift shop, pool, 2 lighted tennis courts, water-sports center. AE, MC, V. EP, MAP.*

$ **Belham Valley Hotel.** On a hillside overlooking Belham Valley and the Belham Valley River, this hotel has a cottage and two apartments (a studio and a newer two-bedroom). All have a stereo, cable TV, a fully equipped kitchen, and a phone; none are air-conditioned. It's the restaurant here that's the big draw, with its lovely views and great food (*see* Dining, *above*). The beach is an eight-minute walk away. *Box 409, Plymouth, tel. 809/491–5553. 3 units. Facilities: restaurant, maid service. AE, MC. EP.*

¢ **Moose.** This budget hotel gets its name from its owner, a former weight lifter, and for a modest fee he'll let you pump iron in his homemade gym (it's the only one on the island). The building is on a rocky beach that's a 10-minute walk from south Plymouth. Rooms, up a flight of wooden steps at the front of the building, are basic, with standing fans and simple, wood-framed beds. Moose's wife, Ida, makes excellent conch fritters and lobster, which she serves at low prices in the simple restaurant downstairs. There are two lively bars in the courtyard at the back, so the rooms are probably not the quietest on the island. *Kinsale, tel. 809/491–3146. 5 rooms. Facilities: restaurant and bar. No credit cards. EP.*

Guest Houses and B&Bs

$$ ★ **Providence Guest House.** On an island where it is almost impossible to find good bed-and-breakfast accommodations, this two-unit guest house, perched on a bluff high above the ocean with spectacular views of St. Kitts and Redonda, stands out. The present owners lovingly restored the former plantation house, and the beautiful stone-and-wood building, with a wraparound veranda, is now one of the finest examples of traditional Caribbean architecture on the island. The two guest rooms—one has a bath as well as a shower and is considerably larger—are on the ground floor and open directly onto the pool area, where gleaming water is edged with tiles from Trinidad. Both rooms have the original timbered ceilings and massive stone walls, which keep them cool in the summer, and are decorated with red quarry tiles and pastel fabrics. If there is any drawback to this idyll, it is the location. The nearest restaurant is 3 miles away in Belham Valley, and the nearest beach is a hike down the hillside. But the owners are willing to make evening meals on request, and they have also installed a kitchenette by the pool, where youcan prepare your own meals. A large breakfast of eggs, oatmeal, and fruits from the garden (in season) is included in the room rate. *Providence Estate House, Montserrat, tel. 809/491–6476. 2 rooms. Facilities: swimming pool, kitchenette, cable TV. No credit cards. CP.*

¢ ★ **Niggy's.** This pretty clapboard cottage with yellow bella flowers trailing over the gate is south of Plymouth (about five minutes by car), and half a mile from a passable beach. It is mostly a restaurant and bar (*see* Dining, *above*). But the owner, a one-time British character actor who gave up a life in Hollywood for the bucolic pleasures of Montserrat, also rents two simple, clean rooms with ceiling fans and showers. Backpackers are frequent guests. *Kinsale, tel. 809/491–7489. No credit cards. CP.*

Villa and Apartment Rental

Montserrat is primarily a villa destination, but many villas are on the expensive side unless you have enough people sharing the cost. One- and two-bedroom villas run between $1000 and $1500 per week, but you can get a four-bedroom villa for $2500 per week.

These villas are generally spacious and upscale and come with a tropical garden, pool, daily maid service, and stunning ocean views. Off-season rates are as much as 50% lower (and usually negotiable), and summer travelers can pick up some true bargains. The best villa developments are on the west coast of the island, within 20 minutes by car of Plymouth. The majority are in the districts of Old Towne, Olveston, and Woodlands. The latter, with its steep hillsides covered in luxuriant vegetation and its magnificent ocean views, is especially noteworthy. Because most villas are in the hills outside Plymouth, you'll need to rent a car, unless you don't mind a 20-minute hike every time you go shopping or to the beach.

Caribbean Connection Plus (tel. 203/261–8603, fax 203/261–8295) is a stateside reservation service for about 50 one- to four-bedroom villas and some condos. They also have an on-island representative to ensure that all goes well.

Isles Bay Plantation (Box 64, Plymouth, tel. 809/491–5248, fax 890/491–5016; in London, tel. and fax 0171/482–1071), known locally as the Beverly Hills of Montserrat, has the crème de la crème of Montserrat's villas. Each house is set on approximately ½ acre of tropical landscaped gardens, has its own 40-foot pool, and is only a 10-minute walk from the beach.

Montserrat Enterprises Ltd (Box 58, Marine Dr., Plymouth, tel. 809/491–2431 ask for Mr. Edwards, fax 809/491–4660) has 22 villas in Old Towne, Woodlands, and Isles Bay.

Neville Bradshaw Agencies (Box 270, Plymouth, tel. 809/491–5270, fax 809/491–5069) has a wide range of villas, mostly in Old Towne and Isles Bay.

Shamrock Villas (Box 180, Plymouth, tel. 809/491–2431) are one- and two-bedroom apartments and town house condominiums in a hillside development minutes from Plymouth.

Off-Season Bets

Montserrat's two finest resort hotels, the **Vue Pointe** (*see above*) and the **Montserrat Springs Hotel and Villas** (Box 259, Plymouth, tel. 809/491–2482) offer reductions of 40% in the off-season. Reasonable villa rates go down further, and some luxury villas become affordable (*see* Villa and Apartment Rental, *above*).

Nightlife

The hotels offer regularly scheduled barbecues and steel bands, and the small restaurants feature live entertainment in the form of calypso, reggae, rock, rhythm and blues, and soul.

Niggy's (Kinsale, tel. 809/491–7489) usually has a vocalist Friday and Saturday nights, and there is often also live jazz on weekends. The **Yacht Club** (Wapping, tel. 809/491–2237) has live island music on Friday, while the **Plantation Club** (Wapping, upstairs over the Oasis, tel. 809/491–2892) is a lively late-night place with taped rhythm and blues, soul, and *soca* (Caribbean music). **La Cave** (Evergreen Dr., Plymouth, no phone), featuring West Indian–style disco and Caribbean and international music, is popular among the young locals. **Nepcoden** (Weekes, no phone), with its ultraviolet lights, peace signs, and black walls, is a throwback to the '60s. In this cellar restaurant you can eat rotis or chicken for $6. **Colors** (Fox's Bay, no phone) is one of the island's most popular nightclubs, with live bands and lots of dancing on weekends.

17 Puerto Rico

Updated by Marcy Pritchard

Puerto Rico, 110 miles long and 35 miles wide, was populated by several tribes of Indians when Columbus landed on the island on his second voyage in 1493. In 1508, Juan Ponce de León, the frustrated seeker of the Fountain of Youth, established a settlement on the island and became its first governor, and in 1521, founded Old San Juan. In 1899, Spain ceded the island to the United States as a result of the Spanish American War, and in 1917, Puerto Ricans became U.S. citizens. In 1952, Puerto Rico became a semiautonomous commonwealth territory of the United States.

No city in the Caribbean is as steeped in Spanish tradition as Puerto Rico's Old San Juan. Built as a fortress in the 16th century the old city is now full of restored buildings, museums, art galleries, bookstores, and 200-year-old houses with balustraded balconies of filigreed wrought iron overlooking narrow cobblestone streets. This Spanish tradition also spills over into the island's countryside, from its festivals celebrated in honor of various patron saints in the little towns to the *paradores,* those homey, inexpensive inns whose concept originated in Spain.

Out in the countryside, amid its quiet colonial towns, lie Puerto Rico's natural attractions. The extraordinary 28,000-acre Caribbean National Forest, more familiarly known as the El Yunque rain forest, is home to more than 240 species of trees. You can hike through forest reserves laced with trails, go spelunking in vast caves, and explore coffee plantations and sugar mills. Puerto Rico also boasts hundreds of beaches with every imaginable water sport and acres of golf courses and tennis courts. Having seen every sight on the island, you can then do further exploring on the islands of Culebra, Vieques, Icacos, and Mona, where aquatic activities, such as snorkeling and scuba diving, prevail.

With its countless small inns and guest houses, inexpensive eateries serving local dishes, and opportunities for camping and hiking,

Puerto Rico is one of the Caribbean's best bets for budget travelers. Beyond the glitzy hotels in San Juan and sprawling resorts out on the island, Puerto Rico's lodgings include affordable, often charming paradors, as well as bed-and-breakfasts and campgrounds. Most hotels stay open year-round, and from mid-April to mid-December, many reduce their rates by as much as 40%. Even those that don't advertise lower rates are often willing to negotiate when you call.

Puerto Rico's restaurants run the gamut, from elegant, expensive establishments to small cafés, roadside kiosks, and standard fast-food places like McDonald's and Pizza Hut. Cafés here are a wonderful value. Often set up near public beaches, they serve authentic local fare such as *empanadillas* (fried pastries stuffed with crabmeat, lobster, or other meats) and all manner of *comida criolla,* a blend of local taste delights.

What It Will Cost These sample prices, meant only as a general guide, are for high season. A ¢ hotel will cost about $40; a guest house, about $50; and a parador, about $60. A ¢ restaurant meal is about $10; snacks for two from a roadside kiosk will be around $7. A glass of beer at a restaurant is about $1.25; a glass of house wine or a piña colada is around $4. Expect to pay about $6 for a six-pack of Medalla beer from the grocery store; $7 for a 750 ml bottle of local rum (26 brands!). Car rental starts at around $30 a day. A taxi from the airport to the Condado Beach area is about $12; from the airport to Old San Juan, around $16. A two-tank dive ranges from $35 to $70. Snorkeling excursions, which include equipment rental and sometimes lunch, start at $25. Snorkel-equipment rental at beaches starts at $5.

Before You Go

Tourist Information Contact the **Puerto Rico Tourism Company** (Box 6334, San Juan, PR 00914, tel. 800/866–7827). Other branches: 575 5th Ave., 23rd Floor, New York, NY 10017, tel. 212/599–6262 or 800/223–6530, fax 212/818–1866; 3575 W. Cahuenga Blvd., Suite 560, Los Angeles, CA 90068, tel. 213/874–5991 or 800/874–1230, fax 213/874–7257; 901 Ponce de Leon Blvd., Suite 604, Coral Gables, FL 33134, tel. 305/445–9112 or 800/815–7391, fax 305/445–9450.

Addresses of representatives in other cities can be obtained by calling the toll-free numbers above.

Overseas offices include 11a West Halkin Street, London SW1X 8JL, United Kingdom (tel. 0171/333–0333).

Arriving and Departing

By Plane The Luis Muñoz Marín International Airport (tel. 809/462–3147), east of downtown San Juan, is the Caribbean hub for **American Airlines** (tel. 800/433–7300). American has daily nonstop flights from New York, Newark, Miami, Boston, Philadelphia, Chicago, Nashville, Los Angeles, Dallas, Baltimore, Hartford, Raleigh-Durham, Washington, D.C., and Tampa; it also provides nonstop service from New York to Aguadilla, and connecting flights through San Juan to Ponce. **Delta** (tel. 800/221–1212) has nonstop service from Atlanta and Orlando, as well as connecting service from major cities. **Northwest** (tel. 800/447–4747) has nonstop flights from Detroit and Minneapolis to San Juan. **TWA** (tel. 800/892–4141) flies nonstop from New York, St. Louis, and Miami. **United** (tel. 800/241–6522) flies nonstop from Miami and Chicago. **USAir** (tel. 800/428–4322) offers nonstop flights from Philadelphia and Charlotte. **Kiwi International Airlines** (tel. 800/538–5494) has nonstop service from Orlando daily except Tuesdays and Wednesdays. Puerto Rico–based **Carnival Airlines** (tel. 800/437–2110) operates daily nonstop flights from New York, Newark, Miami, and Orlando to San Juan, Ponce, and Aguadilla.

Foreign carriers include **Air France** (tel. 800/237–2747), **British Airways** (tel. 800/247–9297), **BWIA** (tel. 800/327–7401), **Iberia** (tel. 800/

772–4642), **LACSA** (tel. 800/225–2272), **LIAT** (tel. 800/468–0482), and **Lufthansa** (tel. 800/645–3880).

Connections between Caribbean islands can be made through **Air Jamaica** (tel. 800/523–5585), **Dominicana Airline** (tel. 800/327–7240), and **Sunaire Express** (tel. 800/595–9501).

From the Airport **Airport Limousine Service** (tel. 809/791–4745) provides minibus service to hotels in the Isla Verde, Condado, and Old San Juan areas at basic fares of $2.50, $3.50, and $4.50, respectively; the fares vary, depending on the time of day and number of passengers. Limousines of **Dorado Transport Service** (tel. 809/796–1214) serve hotels and villas in the Dorado area for $15 per person. Taxi fare from the airport to Isla Verde is about $8–$10; to the Condado area, $12–$15; and to Old San Juan, $18–$20. Be sure the taxi driver starts the meter, or settle on the fare beforehand; you may also be charged a small fee per piece of luggage.

Larger hotels around the island will arrange transportation for you from San Juan to the hotel, but transfers are rarely free. To the Palmas del Mar in Humacao, for instance, the charge is $16 one-way. Your other option if you're staying out on the island is to rent a car, particularly if you intend to explore the island (*see* Getting Around, *below*).

Passports and Visas Puerto Rico is a commonwealth of the United States, and U.S. citizens do not need passports to visit the island. British citizens must have passports. Canadian citizens need proof of citizenship (preferably a passport).

Language Puerto Rico's official languages are Spanish and English. Outside San Juan, it's wise to carry along a Spanish phrase book.

Precautions San Juan, like any other big city and major tourist destination, has its share of crime, so guard your wallet or purse on the city streets. Puerto Rico's beaches are open to the public, and muggings occur at night even on the beaches of the posh Condado and Isla Verde tourist hotels. Don't leave anything unattended on the beach. Leave your valuables in the hotel safe, and stick to the fenced-in beach areas of your hotel. Always lock your car and stash valuables and luggage out of sight. Avoid deserted beaches day or night.

Staying in Puerto Rico

Important Addresses The government-sponsored **Puerto Rico Tourism Company** (Paseo de la Princesa, Old San Juan, Puerto Rico 00902, tel. 809/721–2400) is an excellent source for maps and printed tourist materials. Pick up a free copy of *Qué Pasa*, the official visitors' guide.

Information offices are also found at **Luis Muñoz Marín International Airport** in Isla Verde (tel. 809/791–1014 or 809/791–2551); **La Casita,** near Pier 1 in Old San Juan (tel. 809/722–1709); at the Plaza de Armas in **City Hall** (tel. 809/724–7171 ext. 2392); in the **Covadonga Bus Terminal** (tel. 809/725–1260) across from Pier 4; and in **Condado,** next to the Condado Plaza Hotel (tel. 809/721–2400). Out on the island, information offices are located in **Ponce** (Fox Delicias Mall, 2nd Floor, Plaza Las Delicias, tel. 809/840–5695); **Aguadilla** (Rafael Hernández Airport, tel. 809/890–3315); and in many town's city halls on the main plaza. Offices are usually open weekdays from 8 to noon and 1 to 4:30.

Emergencies **Police, fire, and medical emergencies:** Call 911. **Hospitals:** Hospitals in the Condado/Santurce area with 24-hour emergency rooms are **Ashford Community Hospital** (1451 Av. Ashford, tel. 809/721–2160) and **San Juan Health Centre** (200 Av. De Diego, tel. 809/725–0202). **Pharmacies:** In San Juan, **Walgreens** (1130 Av. Ashford, Condado, tel. 809/725–1510) operates a 24-hour pharmacy. Walgreens also operates more than 30 pharmacies throughout the island. In Old San

Juan, try **Puerto Rico Drug Company** (157 Calle San Francisco, tel. 809/725–2202).

Currency The U.S. dollar is the official currency.

Taxes and Service Charges The government tax on room charges is 7% (9% in hotels with casinos). Some hotels add a service charge (10%–15%) to your bill. Restaurants may add a service charge; when it hasn't been added, a 15%–20% tip is appropriate. There is no departure tax.

Getting Around Puerto Rico's 3,500 square miles is a lot of land to explore. Although it is possible to get from town to town via *público* (*see below*), we don't recommend traveling that way unless your Spanish is good and you know exactly where you're going. The public cars stop in each town's main square, leaving you on your own to reach the beaches, restaurants, paradors, and sightseeing attractions. You'll do much better if you rent a car. The cost is a little lower than a guided tour from San Juan, and having a car allows you to stop, look, swim, and eat at your own pace. Also, the longer you rent, the lower the cost—sometimes down to $21 a day. This is just as well, since a complete tour of Puerto Rico and its outlying islands will take a week or more. If you're staying in the Old San Juan area and don't plan to tour the island, however, you're better off without a car. Parking is miserable and driving worse. Hotels here are within walking distance of restaurants and are a short cab ride from the beach.

Taxis Metered cabs authorized by the Public Service Commission (tel. 809/751–5050) start at $1 and charge 10¢ for every additional 1/10 mile, 50¢ for every suitcase, and $1 for home or business calls. Waiting time is 10¢ for each 45 seconds. Be sure the driver begins the meter.

In and around the San Juan airport and hotel and tourist areas, a typical taxi fare will rarely exceed $20. A cab from Old San Juan to Condado Beach is about $6. From Isla Verde to Old San Juan, expect to pay $14–$17; from Miramar to Condado, around $3–$5. It's possible to charter a taxi for $12–$15 an hour (a drive across Puerto Rico from east to west takes just over two hours; taxi fare from San Juan to Ponce is $125). This may prove an economical option for groups wanting to view area sights. In general, however, taking a taxi from San Juan to other island destinations is a pricey proposition; with rates for rental cars averaging $30 a day, you're better off with your own wheels. You can usually find taxis at each town's main plaza, or have your hotel order one.

Buses The **Metropolitan Bus Authority (AMA)** (tel. 809/250–6064) operates *guaguas* (buses) that thread through San Juan. The fare is 25¢ around San Juan, 50¢ from San Juan to Catano, 75¢ from San Juan to Hato Rey, and 75¢ from Hato Rey to Catano. Buses run in exclusive lanes, *against the traffic* on major thoroughfares, stopping at magenta, orange, and white signs marked PARADA or PARADA DE GUAGUAS. The main terminals are Intermodal Terminal, Calles Marina and Harding, in Old San Juan, and Capetillo Terminal in Rio Piedras, next to the central business district.

Other cities around the island also operate bus services; 25¢ is a standard fare. Traveling by bus is potentially a fun way to do the local scene, and the price is certainly right. However, buses are often crowded, and schedules are less than rigid. Unless your Spanish is good enough to help you figure out why you have ended up nowhere near where you wanted to be, you should consider other means of transportation.

Públicos *Públicos* (public cars) with yellow license plates ending with P or PD scoot to towns throughout the island, stopping in each town's main plaza. The 17-passenger cars operate primarily during the day, with routes and fares fixed by the Public Service Commission. In San

Juan, the main terminals are at the airport and at Plaza Colón on the waterfront in Old San Juan.

Públicos are best for traveling from town center to town center during off-peak times. During rush hours on weekdays (about 8–9 AM and 4–5 PM), públicos are often full; the same is true for weekend travel to popular beaches and recreation areas. Sample fares: San Juan to Fajardo, $3; San Juan to Ponce, $7; San Juan to Rincón, $7; San Juan to Mayaguez, $8; Aguadilla to Mayaguez, $1.75; and Ponce to Cabo Rojo, $5.

Linéas *Linéas* are private taxis you share with three to five other passengers. There are more than 20 companies, each usually specializing in a certain region. Most will arrange door-to-door service. Check local yellow pages listings under Linéas de Carros. They're a cheaper method of transport and a great way to meet people, but be prepared to wait: they usually don't leave until they have a full load.

Trolleys If your feet fail you in Old San Juan, climb aboard the free open-air trolleys that rumble and dip like roller coasters through the narrow streets. Departures are from La Puntilla and from the marina, but you can board anywhere along the route.

Ferries The ferry between Old San Juan (Pier 2) and Cataño costs a mere 50¢ one-way. The ferry runs every half hour from 6 AM to 10 PM. The 400-passenger ferries of the **Fajardo Port Authority** (tel. 809/863–0852), which carry cargo as well as passengers, make the 90-minute between Fajardo and the island of Vieques twice on weekdays and three times on weekends (one-way $2 adults, $1, children 3–12). They make the 90-minute run between Fajardo and the island of Culebra once a day Monday–Thursday and twice a day Friday–Sunday (one-way $2.25 adults, $1 children 3–12).

Rental Cars U.S. driver's licenses are valid in Puerto Rico for three months. All major U.S. car-rental agencies are represented on the island, including **Avis** (tel. 809/721–4499 or 800/331–1212), **Hertz** (tel. 809/791–0840 or 800/654–3131), **Budget** (tel. 809/791–3685 or 800/527–0700), and **National** (tel. 809/791–1805 or 800/328–4567). Local rental companies, sometimes less expensive, include **Caribbean Rental** (tel. 809/724–3980) and **L&M Car Rental** (tel. 809/725–8416). Prices start at about $30 (plus insurance), with unlimited mileage. Discounts are offered for long-term rentals, and some discounts are offered for AAA or 72-hour advance bookings. Most car rentals have shuttle service to or from the airport and the pickup point.

If you plan to drive across the island, arm yourself with a good map and be prepared for unmarked mountain roads. Some car rental agencies distribute free maps when you pick up your car. These maps lack detail, and are usually out-of-date due to new construction. The simplest thing to do is head to the nearest gas station—most of them sell better maps. Good maps are also found at **The Book Store** (255 Calle San José, Old San Juan, tel. 809/724–1815). Many service stations in the central mountains do not take credit cards. Speed limits are posted in miles, distances in kilometers, and gas prices in liters.

Telephones and Mail The area code for Puerto Rico is 809. Since Puerto Rico uses U.S. postage stamps and has the same mail rates (22¢ for a postcard, 32¢ for a first-class letter), you can save time by bringing stamps from home.

Opening and Closing Times Shops are open from 9 to 6 (from 9 to 9 during Christmas holidays). Banks are open weekdays from 8:30 to 2:30 and Saturday from 9:45 to noon.

Guided Tours Old San Juan can be seen either on a self-guided walking tour or on the free trolley. To explore the rest of the city and the island, consider renting a car. (We do, however, recommend a guided tour of the vast El Yunque rain forest.) If you'd rather not do your own driving, there are several tour companies you can call. Most San Juan hotels have a tour desk that can make arrangements for you. The standard half-day tours (at $15–$30) are of Old and New San Juan; Old San Juan and the Bacardi Rum Plant; and Luquillo Beach and El Yunque rain forest. All-day tours ($25–45) include a trip to Ponce, a day at El Comandante Racetrack, or a combined tour of the city and El Yunque rain forest. Out on the island, hotels can either arrange tours for you or refer you to nearby outfits for your arrangements.

Leading tour operators include **Borinquén Tours, Inc.** (tel. 809/725–4990), **Gray Line of Puerto Rico** (tel. 809/727–8080), **Normandie Tours, Inc.** (tel. 809/722–6308), **Rico Suntours** (tel. 809/722–2080 or 809/722–6090), **United Tour Guides** (tel. 809/725–7605 or 809/723–5578), and **Loose Penny Tours** (tel. 809/261–3030).

Boat Tours In San Juan and most coastal towns, you'll find excursion boats that tour the coast and outlying islands. Though price tags for daylong excursions seem steep, the trips are actually a good value, as they usually include a meal, drinks, snorkeling, and sometimes exploring or other activities. You might want to consider one for a splurge. In San Juan, **Castillo Watersports** (tel. 809/791–6195 or 809/726–5752) offers a day sail for $69 a person that includes transfers, lunch, drinks, and snorkeling instructions. **Caribbean School of Aquatics** (tel. 809/728–6606) offers day-sail packages aboard the *Fun Cat* from $69 a person. In Fajardo, **Captain Jayne Sailing Charters** (tel. 809/774–1748) will take you on a six-passenger, 26-foot sailboat to a small, deserted island about 3 miles offshore for snorkeling and exploring. The $60-per-person cost includes transfers from San Juan, lunch, drinks, and snorkeling gear. Also out of Fajardo, the 35-passenger *Spread Eagle* (tel. 809/863–1905) departs at 10 AM for an hour-long sail to outlying islands. The $45 fare includes lunch; transportation from San Juan is an additional $10. Additional boat tour operators can be found by contacting local marinas. In San Juan, try **Club Nautico de San Juan** (tel. 809/722–0177) or **San Juan Bay Marina** (tel. 809/721–8062). In Fajardo, a major center of nautical activity, try **Club Nautico de Puerto Rico** (Isleta Marina, tel. 809/860–2400), **Puerto Chico Marina** (tel. 809/863–0834), **Puerto del Rey** (tel. 809/860–1000), or **Villa Marina** (tel. 809/728–2450). In Humacao, contact the marina at the **Palmas del Mar Resort** (tel. 809/852–6000).

Exploring Puerto Rico

Numbers in the margin correspond to points of interest on the Old San Juan Exploring map.

Old San Juan Old San Juan, the original city founded in 1521, contains authentic and carefully preserved examples of 16th- and 17th-century Spanish colonial architecture, some of the best in the New World. More than 400 buildings have been beautifully restored in a continuing effort to preserve the city. Graceful wrought-iron balconies, decorated with lush green hanging plants, extend over narrow streets paved with blue-gray stones (*adequines*, originally used as ballast for Spanish ships). The old city is partially enclosed by the old walls, dating from 1633, that once completely surrounded it. Designated a U.S. National Historic Zone in 1950, Old San Juan is chockablock with shops, open-air cafés, private homes, tree-shaded squares, monuments, plaques, pigeons, and people. The traffic is awful. Get an overview of the inner city on a morning's stroll (bearing in mind that this "stroll" includes some steep climbs). However, if you plan to immerse yourself in history or to shop, you'll need two or three days.

El Morro and Fort San Cristóbal are described in our walking tour: You may want to set aside extra time to see them, especially if you're an aficionado of military history. UNESCO has designated each fortress a World Heritage Site; each is also a National Historic Site.

Both are administered by the National Park Service; you can take one of its tours or wander around on your own.

Sitting on a rocky promontory on the northwestern tip of the old city
1 is **Fuerte San Felipe del Morro** ("El Morro"), a fortress built by the Spaniards between 1540 and 1783. Rising 140 feet above the sea, the massive six-level fortress covers enough territory to accommodate a nine-hole golf course. It is a labyrinth of dungeons, ramps and barracks, turrets, towers, and tunnels. Built to protect the port, El Morro has a commanding view of the harbor. Its small, air-conditioned museum traces the history of the fortress. *Calle Norzagaray, tel. 809/729–6960. Admission free. Open daily 9:15–6.*

San José Plaza is two short blocks from the entrance to El Morro,
2 but for the moment we'll bypass it and head for the **San Juan Museum of Art and History,** which is a block east of the tour's path but a must. A bustling marketplace in 1855, this handsome building is now a modern cultural center that houses exhibits of Puerto Rican art. Multi-image audiovisual shows present the history of the island; concerts and other cultural events take place in the huge courtyard. *Calle Norzagaray, at the corner of Calle MacArthur, tel. 809/724–1875. Admission free. Open Tues.–Sat. 9–5.*

3 Turn back west toward San José Plaza to **La Casa de los Contrafuertes,** on Calle San Sebastián. This building is also known as the Buttress House because wide exterior buttresses support the wall next to the plaza. The house is one of the oldest remaining private residences in Old San Juan. Inside is the Pharmacy Museum, a re-creation of an 18th-century apothecary shop, and the Latin American Graphic Arts Museum and Gallery, which hosts occasional exhibitions. *101 Calle San Sebastián, Plaza de San José, tel. 809/724–1844. Admission free. Open Tues.–Sat. 9–noon and 1–4:30.*

4 In the center of the plaza, next to the museum, is the **San José Church.** With its series of vaulted ceilings, it is a splendid example of 16th-century Spanish Gothic architecture. The church, which is one of the oldest Christian houses of worship in the Western Hemisphere, was built in 1532 under the supervision of the Dominican friars. The body of Ponce de León, the Spanish explorer who came to the New World seeking the Fountain of Youth, was buried here for almost three centuries before being removed in 1913 and placed in the cathedral (*see below*). *Calle San Sebastián, tel. 809/725–7501. Admission free. Open Mon.–Sat. 8:30–4, Sun. mass at 12:15 PM.*

5 Also on the plaza, take a look through the **Pablo Casals Museum,** which contains memorabilia of the famed cellist, who made his home in Puerto Rico for the last 16 years of his life. The museum holds manuscripts, photographs, and his favorite cellos, in addition to recordings and videotapes of Casals Festival concerts (the latter shown on request). *101 Calle San Sebastián, Plaza de San José, tel. 809/723–9185. Admission free. Open Tues.–Sat. 9:30–5.*

6 Next door is the **Dominican Convent.** Built by Dominican friars in 1523, the convent often served as a shelter during Carib Indian attacks and, more recently, was headquarters for the Antilles command of the U.S. Army. Now home to the Institute of Puerto Rican Culture, the beautifully restored building contains an ornate 18th-century altar, religious manuscripts, artifacts, and art. The institute also maintains a bookshop here. The Convent is the intended future home of the city's museum of fine arts. Classical concerts are occasionally held here. *98 Calle Norzagaray, tel. 809/724–1844. Admission free. Open weekdays 10–5, Sat. 9–5.*

7 From San José Plaza, walk west on Calle Beneficencia to **Casa Blanca.** The original structure on this site, not far from the ramparts of El Morro, was a frame house built in 1521 as a home for Ponce de León. But Ponce de León died in Cuba, never having lived in it, and it

Puerto Rico

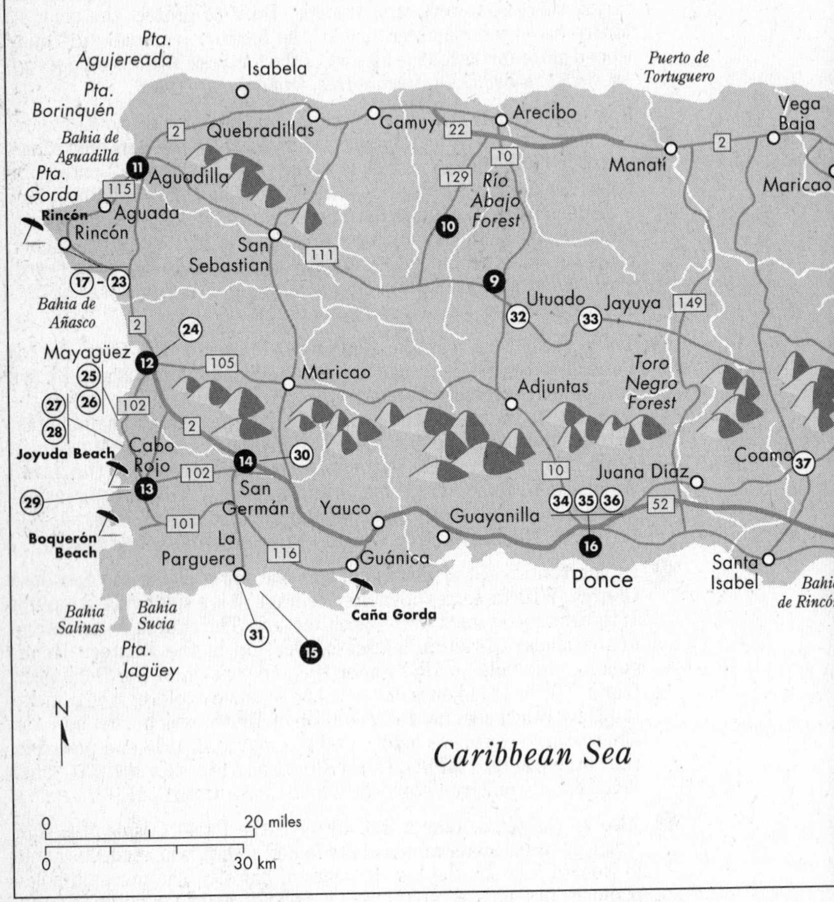

Exploring
Aguadilla, **11**
Bacardi Rum Plant, **3**
Bayamón, **2**
Cabo Rojo, **13**
Caguana Indian Ceremonial Park, **9**
Caparra Ruins, **1**
Carribean National Forest (El Yunque), **4**
Culebra, **8**
Fajardo, **6**
Las Cabezas de San Juan Nature Reserve, **7**
Luquillo Beach, **5**
Mayagüez, **12**
Phosphorescent Bay, **15**
Ponce, **16**
Río Camuy Cave Park, **10**
San Germán, **14**

Dining
The Black Eagle, **17**
El Bohio, **26**
El Molino del Quijote Restaurante, **22**
Fox Delicias Mall, **35**
La Casona de Serafin, **25**
La Rotisserie, **24**

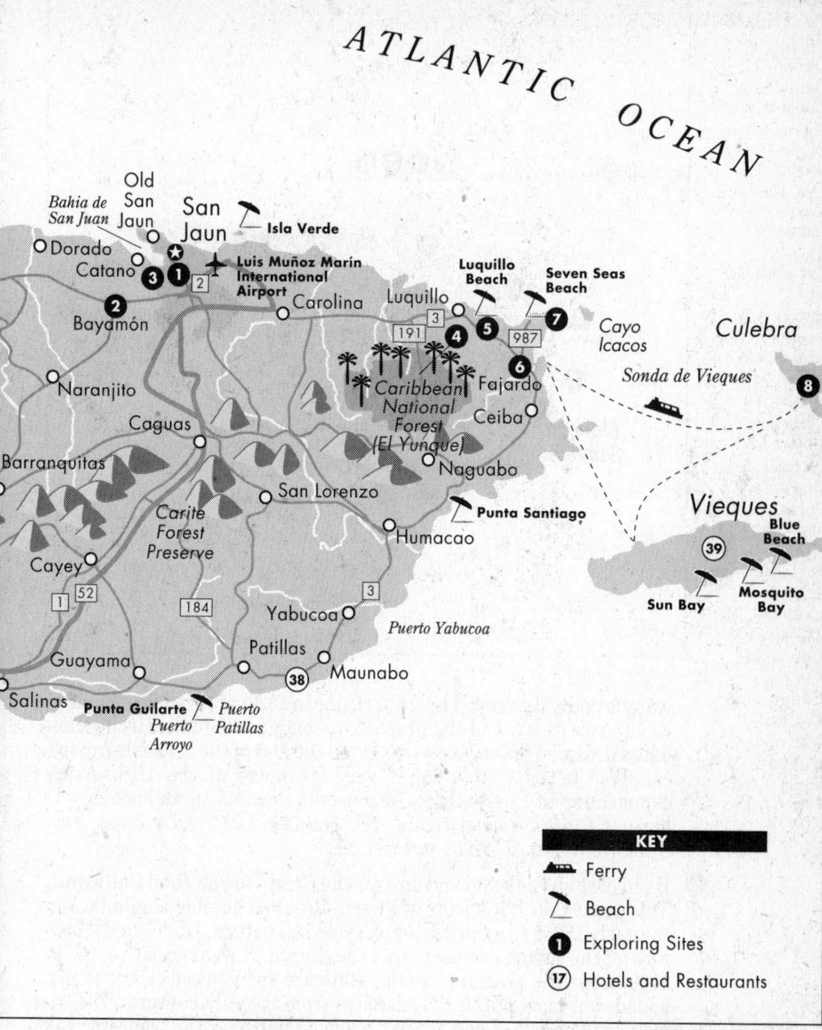

Parador Perichi's, **27**
Pastrami Palace, **23**
Restaurant El Ancla, **34**

Lodging
Beside the Pointe, **18**
Hotel Caribe Playa, **38**
Hotel Joyuda Beach, **28**
Hotel Meliá, **36**
The Lazy Parrot, **21**
Parador Baños de Coamo, **37**
Parador Boquemar, **29**
Parador Casa Grande, **32**
Parador Hacienda Gripiñas, **33**
Parador Oasis, **30**
Parador Perichi's, **27**
Parador Villa Antonio, **20**
Parador Villa Parguera, **31**
Sea Gate, **39**
Villa Cofresi Hotel, **19**

Casa Blanca, **7**
Casa del Libro, **12**
City Hall, **16**
Cristo Chapel, **11**
Dominican Convent, **6**
Fuerte San Felipe del Morro, **1**
La Casa de los Contra-fuertes, **3**
La Fortaleza, **10**
La Intendencia, **15**
Pablo Casals Museum, **5**
Plaza de Armas, **14**
Plaza de Colón, **17**
Plazuela de la Rogativa, **9**
Popular Arts and Crafts Center, **13**
Port, **20**
San Cristóbal, **18**
San José Church, **5**
San Juan Cathedral, **8**
San Juan Museum of Art and History, **2**
Tapia Theater, **19**

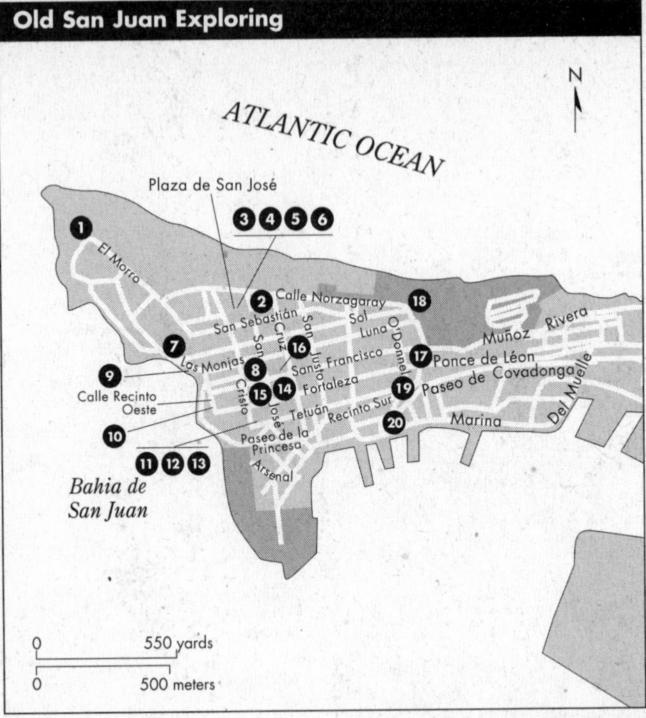

was virtually destroyed by a hurricane in 1523, after which Ponce de León's son-in-law had the present masonry home built. His descendants occupied it for 250 years. From the end of the Spanish-American War in 1898 to 1966, it was the home of the U.S. Army commander in Puerto Rico. A museum devoted to archaeology is here. *1 Calle San Sebastián, tel. 809/724–4102. Admission free. Open Wed.–Sat. 9–noon and 1–4:30.*

8 Head east on Calle Sol and down Calle Cristo to **San Juan Cathedral.** This great Catholic shrine of Puerto Rico had humble beginnings in the early 1520s as a thatch-topped wood structure. Hurricane winds tore off the thatch and destroyed the church. It was reconstructed in 1540, when the graceful circular staircase and vaulted ceilings were added, but most of the church dates from the 19th century. The remains of Ponce de León are in a marble tomb near the transept. *153 Calle Cristo, tel. 809/722–0861. Open daily 8–4. Masses: Sat. 7 PM, Sun. 9 AM and 11 AM, weekdays 12:15 PM.*

Across the street from the cathedral you'll see the Gran Hotel El Convento, which was a Carmelite convent more than 300 years ago. Go west alongside the hotel on Caleta de las Monjas toward the city
9 wall to the **Plazuela de la Rogativa.** In the little plaza, statues commemorate the legend that the British, while laying siege to the city in 1797, mistook the flaming torches of a *rogativa* (religious procession) for Spanish reinforcements and beat a hasty retreat. The monument was donated to the city in 1971 on its 450th anniversary.

10 One block south on Calle Recinto Oeste you'll come to **La Fortaleza,** which sits on a hill overlooking the harbor. La Fortaleza, the Western Hemisphere's oldest executive mansion in continual use, home of 170 governors and official residence of the present governor of Puerto Rico, was built as a fortress. The original primitive structure, built in 1540, has seen numerous changes over a period of three centuries, resulting in the present collection of marble and mahogany,

medieval towers, and stained-glass galleries. Guided tours are conducted every hour on the hour in English, on the half-hour in Spanish. *Tel. 809/721–7000. Admission free. Open weekdays 8:30–5.*

11 At the southern end of Calle Cristo is **Cristo Chapel.** According to legend, in 1753 a young horseman, carried away during festivities in honor of the patron saint, raced down the street and plunged over the steep precipice. A witness to the tragedy promised to build a chapel if the young man's life could be saved. Historical records maintain the man died, though legend contends that he lived. Inside is a small silver altar, dedicated to the Christ of Miracles. *Open Tues. 10–3 and on most Catholic holidays.*

12 Across the street from the chapel, the 18th-century **Casa del Libro** has exhibits devoted to books and bookbinding. The museum's 5,000 books include many rare volumes. *255 Calle Cristo, tel. 809/723–0354. Admission free. Open Tues.–Sat. 11–4:30.*

13 The new **Popular Arts and Crafts Center,** run by the Institute of Puerto Rican Culture, is in a colonial building next door. The center is a superb repository of island crafts, some of which are for sale. *253 Calle Cristo, tel. 809/722–0621. Admission free. Open Mon.–Sat. 9:30–5.*

Follow the wall east one block and head north on Calle San José two
14 short blocks to **Plaza de Armas,** the original main square of Old San Juan. The plaza, bordered by Calles San Francisco, Fortaleza, San José, and Cruz, has a lovely fountain with 19th-century statues representing the four seasons.

15 West of the square stands **La Intendencia,** a handsome three-story neoclassical building. From 1851 to 1898, it was home to the Spanish Treasury; now it is the headquarters of Puerto Rico's State Department. *Calle San José, at the corner of Calle San Francisco, tel. 809/722–2121 ext. 230. Admission free. Tours at 2 and 3 in Spanish, 4 in English. Open weekdays 8–noon and 1–4:30.*

16 On the north side of the plaza is **City Hall,** called the *Alcaldía*, built between 1604 and 1789. In 1841, extensive renovations were made to make the Alcaldía resemble Madrid's city hall, with arcades, towers, balconies, and a lovely inner courtyard. A tourist information center and an art gallery are on the first floor. *Tel. 809/724–7171 ext. 2391. Open weekdays 8–4; tourist office also open Sat. 8–4.*

Four blocks east on the pedestrian mall of Calle Fortaleza, you'll find
17 **Plaza de Colón,** a bustling square with a statue of Christopher Columbus atop a high pedestal. Originally called St. James Square, it was renamed in honor of Columbus on the 400th anniversary of the discovery of Puerto Rico. On the north side of the plaza is a terminal for buses to and from San Juan.

Walk two blocks north from Plaza de Colón to Calle Sol and turn
18 right. Another block will take you to **San Cristóbal,** the 18th-century fortress that guarded the city from land attacks. Even larger than El Morro, San Cristóbal was known as the Gibraltar of the West Indies. *Tel. 809/729–6960. Admission free. Open daily 9–5.*

19 South of Plaza de Colón is the magnificent **Tapia Theater** (Calle Fortaleza at Plaza de Colón, tel. 809/722–0407), named after the famed Puerto Rican playwright Alejandro Tapia y Rivera. Built in 1832, remodeled in 1949 and again in 1987, the municipal theater is the site of ballets, plays, and operettas. Stop by the box office to find out what's showing and if tickets are available.

20 Stroll from Plaza de Colón down to the **port,** where the **Paseo de la Princesa** is spruced up with flowers, trees, benches, and street lamps. Take a seat and watch the boats zip across the water.

San Juan

Numbers in the margin correspond to points of interest on the San Juan Exploring, Dining, and Lodging map.

You'll need to resort to taxis, buses, públicos, or a rental car to reach the points of interest in "new" San Juan.

Avenida Muñoz Rivera, Avenida Ponce de León, and Avenida Fernández Juncos are the main thoroughfares that cross Puerta de Tierra, just east of Old San Juan, to the business and tourist districts of Santurce, Condado, and Isla Verde.

1 In Puerta de Tierra is Puerto Rico's **Capitol,** a white marble building that dates from the 1920s. The grand rotunda, with mosaics and friezes, was completed a few years ago. The seat of the island's bicameral legislature, the Capitol contains Puerto Rico's constitution and is flanked by the modern buildings of the Senate and the House of Representatives. There are spectacular views from the observation plaza on the sea side of the Capitol. Pick up an informative booklet about the building from the House Secretariat on the second floor. *Av. Ponce de León, tel. 809/721–7305 or 809/721–7310. Admission free. Open weekdays 8:30–5.*

At the eastern tip of Puerta de Tierra, behind the splashy Caribe
2 Hilton, the tiny **Fort San Jeronimo** is perched over the Atlantic like an afterthought. Added to San Juan's fortifications in the late 18th century, the structure barely survived the British attack of 1797. Restored in 1983 by the Institute of Puerto Rican Culture, it is now a military museum with displays of weapons, uniforms, and maps. *Tel. 809/724–1844. Admission free. Open Wed.–Sun. 9:30–noon and 1:30–4:30.*

Dos Hermanos Bridge connects Puerta de Tierra with Miramar, Condado, and Isla Grande. Isla Grande Airport, from which you can take short hops to the islands of Vieques and Culebra, is on the bay side of the bridge.

On the other side of the bridge, the Condado Lagoon is bordered by Avenida Ashford, which threads past the high-rise Condado hotels and El Centro Convention Center, and Avenida Baldorioty de Castro Expreso, which barrels all the way east to the airport and beyond. Due south of the lagoon is Miramar, a primarily residential area with fashionable, turn-of-the-century homes and a cluster of hotels and restaurants.

3 **Santurce,** which lies between Miramar on the west and the Laguna San José on the east, is a busy mixture of shops, markets, and offices. The classically designed **Sacred Heart University** is the home of the **Museum of Contemporary Puerto Rican Art.** *Barat Bldg., tel. 809/268–0049. Admission free. Open weekdays 9–4:30, Sat. 10–4.*

4 Internationally acclaimed performers appear at the **Centro de Bellas Artes** (Fine Arts Center). This completely modern facility, the largest of its kind in the Caribbean, has a full schedule of concerts, plays, and operas. *Corner of Av. De Diego and Av. Ponce de León, tel. 809/725–7338.*

South of Santurce is the "Golden Mile"—Hato Rey, the city's bustling new financial hub. Isla Verde, with its glittering beachfront hotels, casinos, discos, and public beach, is to the east, near the airport.

Northeast of Isla Verde, Boca de Cangrejos sits between the Atlantic and Torrecilla Lagoon—a great spot for fishing and snorkeling. Southeast of Miramar, Avenida Muñoz Rivera skirts along the northern side of the mangrove-bordered **San Juan Central Park,** a convenient place for jogging and tennis. The park was built for the 1979 Pan-American Games. *Cerra St. exit on Rte. 2, Santurce, tel. 809/722–1646. Admission free. Open Mon. 2–9:45, Tues.–Fri. 6:30 AM–9:45 PM, weekends 6:30–6.*

San Juan Exploring, Dining, and Lodging

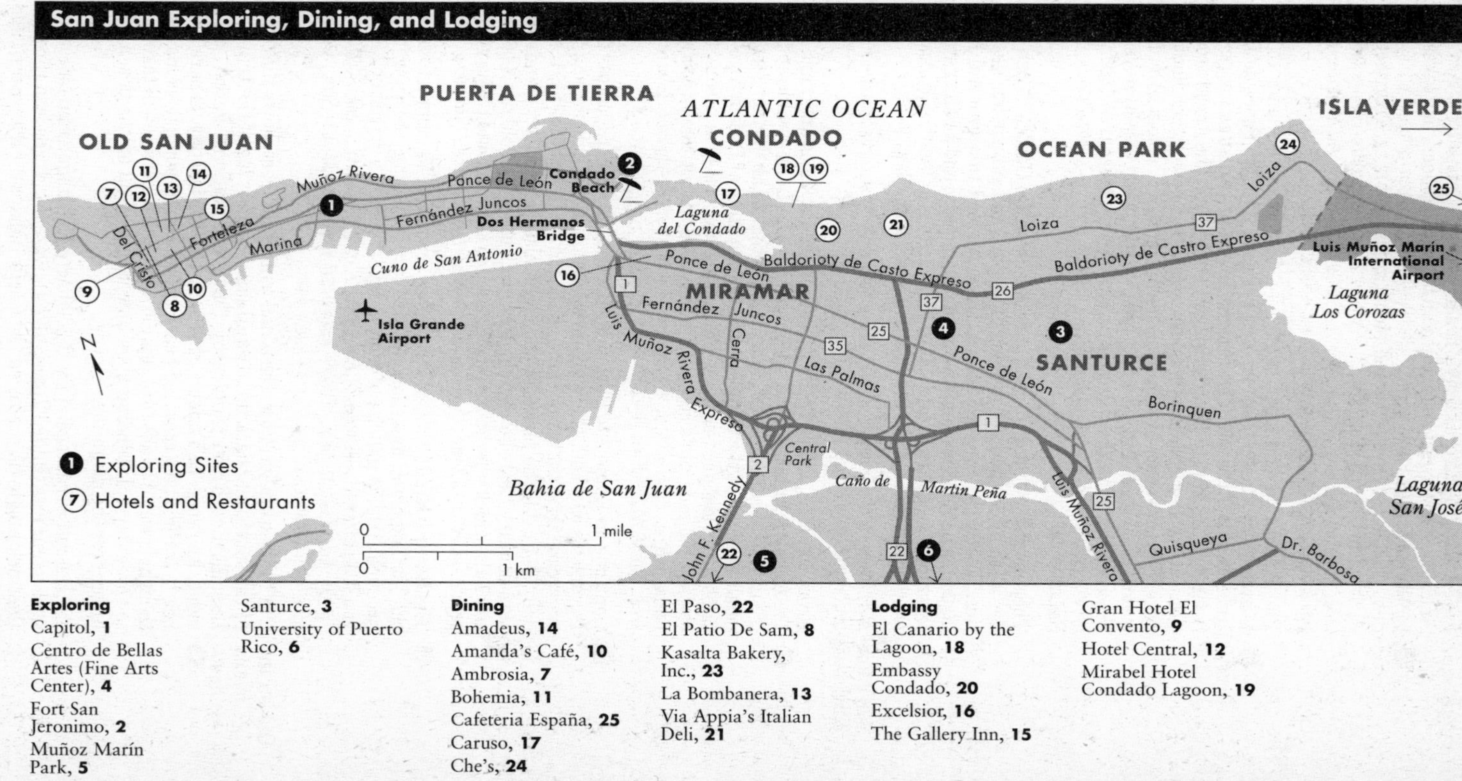

Exploring
Capitol, **1**
Centro de Bellas Artes (Fine Arts Center), **4**
Fort San Jeronimo, **2**
Muñoz Marín Park, **5**
Santurce, **3**
University of Puerto Rico, **6**

Dining
Amadeus, **14**
Amanda's Café, **10**
Ambrosia, **7**
Bohemia, **11**
Cafeteria España, **25**
Caruso, **17**
Che's, **24**
El Paso, **22**
El Patio De Sam, **8**
Kasalta Bakery, Inc., **23**
La Bombanera, **13**
Via Appia's Italian Deli, **21**

Lodging
El Canario by the Lagoon, **18**
Embassy Condado, **20**
Excelsior, **16**
The Gallery Inn, **15**
Gran Hotel El Convento, **9**
Hotel Central, **12**
Mirabel Hotel Condado Lagoon, **19**

Las Américas Expressway, heading south, goes by Plaza Las Américas, the largest shopping mall in the Caribbean, and takes you
5 to **Muñoz Marín Park,** an idyllic tree-shaded spot dotted with gardens, lakes, playgrounds, and picnic areas. Cable cars connect the park with the parking area. *Next to Las Américas Expressway, west on Av. Piñero, Hato Rey, tel. 809/763–0568. Admission free; parking $1 per vehicle. Open Tues.–Sun. 8–5.*

Río Piedras, a southern suburb of San Juan, is home to the
6 **University of Puerto Rico,** located between Avenida Ponce de León and Avenida Barbosa. The campus is one of two sites for performances of the Puerto Rico Symphony Orchestra. Theatrical productions and other concerts are also scheduled here throughout the year. The **University Museum** has permanent archaeological and historical exhibits and occasionally mounts special art displays. *Next to the university's main entrance on Av. Ponce de León, tel. 809/764–0000 ext. 2452 or 2456. Open Mon.–Wed., Fri. 9–4:30; Thurs. 9–9; Sat. 9–3:30.*

The university's main attraction is the **Botanical Garden,** a lush garden with more than 200 species of tropical and subtropical vegetation. Footpaths through the thick forests lead to a graceful lotus lagoon, a bamboo promenade, an orchid garden, and a palm garden. *Intersection of Rtes. 1 and 847 at the entrance to Barrio Venezuela, tel. 809/763–4408. Admission free. Open Tues.–Sun. 9–5.*

San Juan Environs

Numbers in the margin correspond to points of interest on the Puerto Rico map.

From San Juan, follow Route 2 west toward Bayamón and you'll spot
1 the **Caparra Ruins,** where, in 1508, Ponce de León established the island's first settlement. The ruins are that of an ancient fort. Its small **Museum of the Conquest and Colonization of Puerto Rico** contains historical documents, exhibits, and excavated artifacts. (You can see the museum's contents in less time than it takes to say the name.) *Rte. 2, Km 6.6, Guaynabo, tel. 809/781–4795. Admission free. Open Wed.–Sun. 9–4.*

2 Continue on Route 2 to **Bayamón.** In the Central Park, across from Bayamón's city hall, there are some historical buildings and a 1934 sugarcane train that runs through the park (tel. 809/798–8191, open daily 8–5). On the plaza, in the city's historic district, stands the 18th-century Catholic church of Santa Cruz and the old neoclassical city hall, which now houses the **Francisco Oller Art and History Museum** *Tel. 809/787–8620. Admission free. Open Tues.–Sat. 9–4.*

3 The **Bacardi Rum Plant,** along the bay, conducts 45-minute tours of the bottling plant, museum, and distillery, which has the capacity to produce 100,000 gallons of rum a day. There is a gift shop. (Yes, you'll be offered a sample.) *Rte. 888, Km 2.6, Cataño, tel. 809/788–1500. Admission free. Tours every 20 minutes Mon.–Sat., 9:30–10:30 and noon–4.*

Out on the Island

East and South

Our first excursion out on the island will take us east, down the coast to the south, and back up to San Juan. The first leg of the trip—to Luquillo Beach and the nearby Caribbean National Forest, com-
4 monly known as **El Yunque,** can easily be done in a day. (There'll be heavy traffic and a crowded beach on weekends, when it seems as if the whole world heads for Luquillo.) The full itinerary will take two to three days, depending upon how long you loll on the beach and linger over the mountain scenery.

To take full advantage of the 28,000-acre El Yunque rain forest, go with a tour (*see* Guided Tours, *above*). Dozens of trails lead through the thick jungle (it sheltered the Carib Indians for 200 years), and the tour guides take you to the best observation points, bathing spots, and waterfalls. Some of the trails are slippery, and there are occasional washouts.

If you'd like to drive there yourself, take Route 3 east from San Juan and turn right (south) on Route 191, about 25 miles from the city. The **Sierra Palm Visitor Center** is on Route 191, Km 11.6 (open daily 9–5; until 4 in winter). Nature talks and programs at the center are in Spanish and English and by appointment only—a good reason to go with a tour group.

El Yunque, named after the good Indian spirit Yuquiyu, is in the Luquillo Mountain Range. The rain forest is verdant with feathery ferns, thick ropelike vines, white tuberoses and ginger, miniature orchids, and some 240 different species of trees. More than 100 billion gallons of precipitation fall annually. Rain-battered, wind-ravaged dwarf vegetation clings to the top peaks. (El Toro, the highest, is 3,532 feet.) El Yunque is also a bird sanctuary and the base of the rare Puerto Rican parrot. Millions of tiny, inch-long *coquis* (tree frogs) can be heard singing (or squawking, depending on your sensibilities). *For further information, call the Catalina Field Office, tel. 809/887–2875 or 809/766–5335; or write to the Caribbean National Forest, Box B, Palmer, PR 00721.*

5 To reach **Luquillo Beach,** take Route 191 back to Route 3 and continue east 5 miles to Km 35.4. One of the island's best and most popular strands, Luquillo was once a flourishing coconut plantation. Coral reefs protect its calm, pristine lagoon, making it an ideal place for a swim. The entrance fee is $1 per car, and there are lockers, showers, and changing rooms (*see* Beaches, *below*).

6 Back on Route 3, it's 5 miles to **Fajardo,** a major fishing and sailing center with thousands of boats tied and stacked in tiers at three large marinas. Boats can be rented or chartered here, and the *Spread Eagle* catamaran can take you out for a full day of snorkeling, swimming, and sunning (*see* Boat Tours, *above*). Fajardo is also the embarkation point for ferries to the islands of Culebra and Vieques (*see* Getting Around *in* Staying in Puerto Rico, *above*).

North of Fajardo on Route 987, just past the Seven Seas Recreation-
7 al Area, is the entrance to **Las Cabezas de San Juan Nature Reserve.** Opened in 1991, the reserve contains mangrove swamps, coral reefs, beaches, and a dry forest—all of Puerto Rico's natural habitats rolled into a microcosmic 316 acres. Nineteenth-century El Faro, one of the island's oldest lighthouses, is restored and still functioning; its first floor contains a small nature center that has an aquarium and other exhibits. The reserve is open by reservation only to the general public Friday–Sunday, and to tour groups Wednesday, Thursday, and Friday morning. Tours are given on request (in advance, by telephone) four times a day. *Rte. 987, Km 5.8, tel. 809/722–5882; weekends, 809/860–2560. Admission: $5 adults, $2 children under 12, $2.50 senior citizens.*

A trip to the islands of Culebra or Vieques first involves a trip to Fajardo to catch a ferry. If you're driving, you can park in a local lot (about $3 a day) or take your car on the ferry. Cost for the latter depends upon the size of the car; the cheapest will be $26.50 round-trip to Culebra, $26 round-trip to Vieques. Reservations and payment must be made four days to a week in advance. You can also rent a car on either island. Plan on a full day, with overnight stay, to fully see each island.

8 **Culebra** has lovely white-sand beaches, coral reefs, and a wildlife refuge. In the sleepy town of Dewey, on Culebra's southwestern side, check at the visitor information center at city hall (tel. 809/742–3291) about boat rentals. For car rentals, try **Prestige Car Rental** (tel. 809/742–3242). On **Vieques,** Sun Bay public beach has picnic facilities; Blue Beach is superb for snorkeling; and Mosquito Bay is luminous even on moonless nights. The tourist information center (tel. 809/741–5000) is in the fishing village of Esperanza. For car rentals, contact **Vias Car Rental** (tel. 809/741–8173). Both islands are

havens for colorful "expatriates" escaping the rat race stateside. This is pure old-time Caribbean: fun and funky, the kind of getaway that is fast disappearing.

Back on the main island, resume your ramble on Route 3, heading south past the U.S. Naval Base, and ride through the sugarcane fields to **Humacao.** South of Humacao (take Route 906) is the 2,700-acre Palmas del Mar, the island's largest resort complex.

Stay on Route 3 through **Yabuco,** tucked up in the hills, and on through **Maunabo** and **Patillas,** where you can pick up routes that will take you through the Cayey Mountains. Route 184 north skirts Lake Patillas and cuts smack through the **Carite Forest Reserve.** Stay on Route 184 until it meets Route 1, where you'll shoot northward back to San Juan.

Western Island If you're short of time, drive the 64 miles from San Juan to Ponce. On the Las Américas Expressway, Route 52, which cuts through the splendid mountains of Cordillera Central, the trip takes 90 minutes and costs $2 in tolls.

If time is not a major problem, plan a three- or four-day tour to explore the western regions of the island. This route covers Aguadilla, Rincón, San Germán, and Ponce. There's much to see along the way—caves and coves, karst fields and coffee plantations, mountains, beaches, and even a zoo.

Start out going west on Route 2. In Arecibo, pick up Route 10 and go
9 south. Make a right on Route 111, and you'll find the **Caguana Indian Ceremonial Park,** used 800 years ago by the Taíno tribes for recreation and worship. Mountains surround a 13-acre site planted with royal palms and guava. According to Spanish historians, the Taínos played a game similar to soccer, and in this park there are 10 courts bordered by cobbled walkways. There are also stone monoliths, some with colorful petroglyphs, and a small museum. *Rte. 111, Km 12.3, tel. 809/894–7325. Admission free. Open daily 9–4:30.*

Drive west on Route 111 and then north on Route 129 through the spectacular karst country, an alien landscape of collapsed limestone
10 sinkholes, to Km 18.9, where you'll find the **Río Camuy Cave Park,** a 268-acre reserve that contains one of the world's largest cave networks. Guided tours take you on a tram down through dense tropical vegetation to the entrance of the cave, where you continue on foot over underground trails, ramps, and bridges. The caves, sinkholes, and subterranean streams are all spectacular (the world's second-largest underground river runs through here). Be sure to call ahead; the tours allow only a limited number of people. *Rte. 129, Km 18.9, tel. 809/898–3100 or 809/756–5555. Admission: $10 adults, $7 children under 12. Parking $1. Open Tues.–Sun. 8–4. Last tour starts at 3:40.*

11 Backtrack to Route 111, which twists westward to **Aguadilla** on the northwest coast. In this area, somewhere between Aguadilla and Añasco, south of Rincón, Columbus dropped anchor on his second voyage in 1493. Both Aguadilla and **Aguada,** a few miles to the south, claim to be the spot where his foot first hit ground, and both towns have plaques to commemorate the occasion.

Route 115 from Aguadilla to **Rincón** is one of the island's most scenic drives, through rolling hills dotted with pastel-colored houses. Rincón, perched on a hill, overlooks its beach, which was the site of the World Surfing Championship in 1968. Skilled surfers flock to Rincón from November through March, when the water is rough and challenging. The town is also increasingly popular with divers. Locals boast that the best diving and snorkeling in Puerto Rico (and some say the Caribbean) is off the Rincón coast, particularly around the offshore island of Desecheo, a federal wildlife preserve. Whale-watching is another draw for this town; humpback whales winter off the coast from December through February.

Continue along 115 to Route 2 for the 6-mile drive through
12 **Mayagüez,** Puerto Rico's third-largest city, with a population ap-
proaching 100,000. Due south of Mayagüez, via the coastal Route
13 102, is **Cabo Rojo,** once a pirates' hangout and now a favorite resort
area of Puerto Ricans. The area has long stretches of white-sand beaches on the clear, calm Caribbean Sea, as well as many seafood restaurants, bars, and hotels. There are also several paradors in the region. If you want a side trip, take Route 100 south and then Route 101 to its westernmost point—tiny Boquerón, a funky, pastel village with sidewalk oyster vendors, bars, restaurants serving fresh seafood, and several of the standard T-shirt shops. There are also diving and snorkeling tours at the Boquerón Dive Shop on Main Street. Boquerón's balneario is one of the best beaches on the island. Parking is $1 per car, and two-room cabins are for rent.

14 From Cabo Rojo continue east on Route 102 to **San Germán,** a quiet
and colorful Old World town that's home to the oldest intact church under the U.S. flag. Built in 1606, Porta Coeli (Gates of Heaven) overlooks one of the town's two plazas, where the townspeople continue the Spanish tradition of promenading at night. The church is now a museum of religious art, housing 18th- and 19th-century paintings and wooden statues. *Tel. 809/892–5845. Admission free. Open Tues.–Sun. 9–noon and 1–4.*

The fishing village of **La Parguera,** an area of simple seafood restaurants, mangrove cays, and small islands, lies south of San Germán at
the end of Route 304. This is an excellent scuba-diving area, but the
15 main attraction is **Phosphorescent Bay.** Boats tour the bay, where
microscopic dinoflagellates (marine plankton) light up like Christmas trees when disturbed by any kind of movement. The phenomenon can be seen only on moonless nights. Boats leave for the hour-long trip nightly between 7:30 and 12:30, depending on demand, and the trip costs $8 per person.

From San Germán, Route 2 traverses splendid peaks and valleys; pastel houses cling to the sides of steep green hills. The Cordillera Central mountains run parallel to Route 2 here, and provide a stunning backdrop to the drive. East of Yauco, the road dips and sweeps
16 right along the Caribbean and into **Ponce.** Leave the traffic and strip
malls on Route 2, and wander around Ponce's historic downtown.

The town's 19th-century style has been recaptured with pink marble-bordered sidewalks, gas lamps, painted trolleys, and horse-drawn carriages. You have not seen a firehouse until you've seen the red-and-black-striped **Parque de Bombas,** a structure built in 1882 for an exposition and converted to a firehouse the following year. The city hired architect Pablo Ojeda O'Neill to restore it, and it is now a museum of Ponce's history which, not surprisingly, houses Fire Brigade memorabilia. *Plaza Las Delicias, tel. 809/284–4141 ext. 342. Admission free. Open Mon. and Wed.–Sun. 9:30–6. Closed Tues.*

Ponce's charm stems from its mix of neoclassical, Creole, and art deco styles. Stop in and pick up information about this seaside city at the columned **Casa Armstrong-Poventud,** the home of the Institute of Puerto Rican Culture and Tourism Information Offices (open Mon.–Fri. 8–noon and 1–4:30; use the side entrance). Stroll around the **Plaza Las Delicias,** with its perfectly pruned India-laurel fig trees, graceful fountains, gardens, and park benches. View **Our Lady of Guadelupe Cathedral,** and walk down Calles Isabel and Christina, lined with turn-of-the-century wooden houses with wrought-iron balconies. Continue as far as Calles Mayor and Christina to the white stucco **La Perla Theater,** fronted by Corinthian columns.

Be sure to allow time to visit the **Ponce Museum of Art,** worth seeing for the architecture alone. The modern, two-story building designed by Edward Durell Stone (who designed New York's Museum of Modern Art) has seven interconnected hexagons, glass cupolas, and a pair of curved staircases. The collection includes late Renaissance and Baroque works from Italy, France, and Spain, as well as contemporary art by Puerto Ricans. *Av. Las Américas, tel. 809/848–0505. Admission: $3 adults, $2 children under 12. Open daily 10–5.*

There are two intriguing historical sights just outside the city. **Hacienda Buena Vista** is a 19th-century coffee plantation, restored by the Conservation Trust of Puerto Rico, with much of the authentic machinery and furnishings intact. Reservations are required for the 90-minute tours; tours in English are given on request (in advance) once a day. *Rte. 10, Km 16.8, north of Ponce, tel. 809/722–5882 weekdays; 809/848–7020 weekends. Admission: $5 adults, $2 children under 12, $2.50 senior citizens. Open Wed.–Fri. to tour groups; Fri.–Sun. to public.*

The **Tibes Indian Ceremonial Center** is the oldest cemetery in the Caribbean. It is a treasure trove of pre-Taíno ruins and burials, dating from AD 300 to AD 700. Some archaeologists, noting the symmetrical arrangement of stone pillars, surmise the cemetery may have been of great religious significance. The complex includes a detailed recreation of a Taíno village and a museum. *Rte. 503, Km 2.2, tel. 809/840–2255. Admission: $2 adults, $1 senior citizens and children. Open Tues.–Sun. 9–4.*

Beaches

All Puerto Rico's beaches are open to the public by law (except for the man-made beach at the Caribe Hilton in San Juan). Many Puerto Rico hotels are within walking distance of beaches, if not right on the sand; other hotels offer transport to beaches. Thirteen government-run *balnearios* (public beaches), have dressing rooms, lifeguards, parking, and in some cases picnic tables, playgrounds, and overnight facilities. Admission is free, parking $1. Most balnearios are open 9–5 daily in summer and Tuesday through Sunday the rest of the year. Listed below are some major balnearios. You can also contact the Department of Recreation and Sports (tel. 809/722–1551 ext. 341).

Boquerón Beach is a broad beach of hard-packed sand, fringed with coconut palms. It has picnic tables, cabin and bike rentals, basketball court, minimarket, scuba diving, and snorkeling. *On the southwest coast, south of Mayagüez, Rte. 101, Boquerón.*

A white sandy beach bordered by resort hotels, **Isla Verde** is lively and popular with city folk. It offers picnic tables and good snorkeling, with equipment rentals nearby. *Near metropolitan San Juan, Rte. 187, Km 3.9, Isla Verde.*

Crescent-shape **Luquillo Beach** comes complete with coconut palms, picnic tables, and tent sites. Coral reefs protect its crystal-clear lagoon from the Atlantic waters, making it ideal for swimming. It's one of the largest and most well-known beaches on the island, and it gets crowded on weekends. *30 mi east of San Juan, Rte. 3, Km 35.4.*

An elongated beach of hard-packed sand, **Seven Seas** is always popular with bathers. It has picnic tables and tent and trailer sites; snorkeling, scuba diving, and boat rentals are nearby. *Rte. 987, Fajardo.*

Sun Bay, a white-sand beach on Vieques, has picnic tables and tent sites, and offers such water sports as snorkeling and scuba diving. Boat rentals are nearby. *Rte. 997, Vieques.*

The famous **Condado Beach,** along Ashford Avenue in San Juan, is accessible from all hotels on the strip and from public walkways located along the road. To reach the long beaches of **Rincón, Cabo Rojo,** or **Parguera,** simply park your car along the road and walk.

Sports and the Outdoors

Bicycling The broad beach at Boquerón makes for easy wheeling. You can rent bikes at **Boquerón Balnearios** (Rte. 101, Boquerón, Dept. of Recreation and Sports, tel. 809/722–1551). In the Dorado area on the north coast, bikes can be rented at the **Hyatt Regency Cerromar Beach** (tel. 809/796–1234) or the **Hyatt Dorado Beach** (tel. 809/796–1234). Bikes are for rent at many of the hotels out on the island, including the **Ponce Hilton** (tel. 809/259–7676) and the **Copamarina Beach Resort** (tel. 809/821–0505). The average rate is $4 an hour.

Boating Virtually all the resort hotels on San Juan's Condado and Isla Verda strips rent paddleboats, Sunfish, Windsurfers, kayaks, and the like. Contact **Condado Plaza Hotel Watersports Center** (tel. 809/721–1000, ext. 1361), the **El San Juan Hotel Watersports Center** (tel. 809/791–1000) or the **Caribe Hilton** (tel. 809/721–0303). Out on the island, your hotel will be able to either provide rentals, or recommend rental outfitters.

Golf There are four Robert Trent Jones–designed 18-hole courses shared by the **Hyatt Dorado Beach** and the **Hyatt Regency Cerromar Beach** hotels (Dorado, tel. 809/796–1234, ext. 3238 or 3016). You'll also find 18-hole courses at **Palmas del Mar resort** (Humacao, tel. 809/852–6000), **Club Ríomar** (Río Grande, tel. 809/887–3964), **Punta Borinquén** (Aguadilla, tel. 809/890–2987), **Berwind Country Club** (Río Grande, tel. 809/876–3056), and **Bahia Beach Plantation** (Río Grande, tel. 809/256–5600). There are two nine-hole courses out on the island, one at the **Club Deportivo del Oeste** (Cabo Rojo, tel. 809/851–8880), and one east of Ponce at the **Aguirre Golf Club** (Aguirre, tel. 809/853–4052). There is a driving range at the **Ponce Hilton** (Ponce, tel. 809/259–7676). Greens fees for nonguests at hotels range from $35 to $50 for 18 holes, and up to $35 for a nine-hole course. Golf carts cost $15–$30 per course; club rental, $15; and shoe rental, $5. Prices are generally lower at clubs, where greens fees and cart can total as little as $28.

Hiking Dozens of trails lace **El Yunque** (information is available at the Sierra Palm Visitor Center, Rte. 191, Km 11.6). You can also hit the trails in **Río Abajo Forest** (south of Arecibo) and **Toro Negro Forest** (east of Adjuntas). Each reserve has a ranger station, where you can get maps, arrange for a guide, and get advice about the difficulty of different routes. Trails are generally harder to hike during and after a rainfall. You'll need hiking shoes, sunblock, insect repellent, a hat, a first-aid kit, a canteen—and a camera and film.

Snorkeling and Scuba Diving There is excellent diving off Puerto Rico's coast. Some outfits offer package deals combining accommodations with daily diving trips. Snorkeling and scuba-diving instruction and equipment rentals are available at **Caribbean School of Aquatics** (tel. 809/728–6606) and **Caribe Aquatic Adventures** (Radisson Normandie, tel. 809/729–2929, ext. 240), **Coral Head Divers** (Palmas del Mar Resort, Humacao, tel. 809/852–6000 or 800/468–3331), **Parguera Divers Training Center** (La Parguera, tel. 809/899–4171), **Capt. Bill's Dive & Surf Shop** (Rte. 413, Rincón, tel. 809/823–0390 or evenings 809/823–2672; hotel/dive packages available), **Parguera Divers Training Center** (Road 304, MM3-2, Lajas, tel. 809/899–4171), **Dive Copamarina** (Copamarina Beach Resort, Rte. 333, Guánica, tel. 809/821-6009; hotel/dive packages available), and **Boquerón Dive Shop** (Main St., Boquerón, tel. 809/851–2155).

Escorted half-day dives range from $35 to $70 and generally include two tanks of air. Packages, which include lunch and other extras, start at $60. Night dives are often available at close to double the price. Snorkeling excursions, which include equipment rental and sometimes lunch, start at $25. Always ask what your tour includes. Snorkel equipment rents at beaches for about $5.

Caution: Coral-reef waters and mangrove areas can be dangerous to novices. Unless you're an expert or have an experienced guide, avoid unsupervised areas and stick to the water-sports centers of major hotels.

Surfing The best surfing beaches are along the Atlantic coastline from Borinquén Point south to Rincón. Surfing is best from November through April. Aviones and La Concha beaches in San Juan and Casa de Pesca in Arecibo are summer surfing spots and have nearby surf shops.

Tennis If you'd like to use the courts at a property where you are not a guest, call in advance for information about reservations and fees.

There are 17 lighted courts at **San Juan Central Park** (Calle Cerra exit on Rte. 2, tel. 809/722–1646); 6 lighted courts at the **Caribe Hilton Hotel** (Puerta de Tierra, tel. 809/721–0303, ext. 1730); 8 courts, 4 lighted, at **Carib Inn** (Isla Verde, tel. 809/791–3535, ext. 6); and 2 lighted courts at the **Condado Plaza Hotel** (Condado, tel. 809/721–1000, ext. 1775). Out on the island, there are 14 courts, 2 lighted, at **Hyatt Regency Cerromar Beach** (Dorado, tel. 809/796–1234, ext. 3040); 7 courts, 2 lighted, at the **Hyatt Dorado Beach** (Dorado, tel. 809/796–1234, ext. 3220); 20 courts, 4 lighted, at **Palmas del Mar** (Humacao, tel. 809/852–6000, ext. 51); 3 lighted courts (and a practice wall) at the **Mayagüez Hilton** (Mayagüez, tel. 809/831–7575, ext. 2150); 4 lighted courts at the **Ponce Hilton** (Ponce, tel. 809/259–7676); and 4 lighted courts at **Punta Borinquén** (Aguadilla, tel. 809/891–8778).

Windsurfing Many resort hotels rent Windsurfers to their guests, including the **El San Juan, Palmas del Mar,** the **Hyatts,** and the **Condado Plaza.** If your hotel doesn't provide them, they can probably help you make other arrangements.

Shopping

San Juan is not a free port, and you won't find bargains on electronics and perfumes. You can find reasonable prices on china, crystal, and jewelry in and around major towns, but for true bargains, stick to local crafts and those from other Caribbean islands.

Shopping for local Caribbean crafts can be great fun. You'll run across a lot of tacky things you can live without, but you can also find some treasures, and in many cases you'll be able to watch the artisans at work. (For guidance, contact the Puerto Rico Tourism Company's Artisan Center, tel. 809/721–2400 ext. 2201, or the Fomento Crafts Program, tel. 809/758–4747 ext. 2291.)

Popular souvenirs and gifts include *santos* (small, hand-carved figures of saints or religious scenes), hand-rolled cigars, handmade lace, carnival masks, and fancy men's shirts called *guayaberas*. Also, some folks swear that Puerto Rican rum is the best in the world.

Shopping Districts **Old San Juan** is full of shops, especially on Cristo, Fortaleza, and San Francisco streets. The **Las Américas Plaza** south of San Juan is one of the largest shopping malls in the Caribbean, with 200 shops, restaurants, and movie theaters. Other malls out on the island include **Plaza del Carmen** in Caguas, the **Plaza del Caribe** in Ponce, and the **Mayagüez Mall.** A new mall is currently under construction in Aguadilla, right on Route 2.

Good Buys *Clothing* You can get discounts on Hathaway shirts and Christian Dior clothing at **Hathaway Factory Outlet** (203 Calle Cristo, tel. 809/723–

8946). Discounts on Ralph Lauren apparel are found at the **Polo/ Ralph Lauren Factory Store** (201 Calle Cristo, tel. 809/722–2136). The **London Fog Factory Outlet** (156 Calle Cristo, tel. 809/722–4334) offers reductions on men's, women's, and children's raincoats. People are lining up to enter the new **Marshalls** (Plaza de Armas, tel. 809/722–0874) in Old San Juan. Try the **Bikini Factory** (3 Palmar Norte, Isla Verde, tel. 809/726–0016) for stylish men's and women's swimwear.

Local Crafts For one-of-a-kind buys, head for **Puerto Rican Arts & Crafts** (204 Calle Fortaleza, Old San Juan, tel. 809/725–5596). You should also pay a visit to the **artisan markets** in Sixto Escobar Park (Puerta de Tierra, tel. 809/722–0369) and Luis Muñoz Marín Park (next to Las Américas Expressway west on Piñero Ave., Hato Rey, tel. 809/763–0568). The **Haitian Gallery** (367 Calle Fortaleza, tel. 809/725–0986) carries Puerto Rican crafts and a selection of folksy, often inexpensive paintings from around the Caribbean. In Ponce, consult the **Casa Paoli Center of Folkloric Investigations** (14 Calle Mayor, tel. 809/840–4115).

Paintings and Sculptures **Galería Gotay** (212 Calle San Francisco, Old San Juan, tel. 809/722–5726) carries contemporary art in many medias. **Galería Botello** (208 Calle Cristo, Old San Juan, tel. 809/723–9987; Plaza Las Américas, tel. 809/754–7430) exhibits and sells antique *santos* (religious sculptures).

Another gallery worth visiting is the **Galería San Juan** (Gallery Inn, 204–206 Calle Norzagaray, Old San Juan, tel. 809/722–1808; *see* Lodging, *below*). **Corinne Timsit International Galleries** (104 Calle San Jose, Old San Juan, tel. 809/724–0994) features work by contemporary Latin American painters.

Dining

Over the past 10 years, phone-book listings of restaurants in Puerto Rico have quadrupled. Included among these are countless unique and inexpensive eateries. You can dine in kiosks set up near beaches, or tiny roadside cafés with Formica tabletops and some of the best food on the island. What you eat will likely be *comida criolla,* a mix of Spanish, African, and West Indian cooking that uses an abundance of tomatoes, garlic, peppers, and cilantro with rice, local vegetables and fruits, and fried seafood. The prices in small cafés are an attraction in themselves: $5 will get you a full plate of empanadillas and *asopao* (chicken or shellfish gumbo with rice).

Puerto Rico has not escaped the global fast-food industry: Even small interior towns you'll find a McDonald's, Burger King or the like. Puerto Rico's own family-style **El Mesón** features American-size burgers as well as *Cubano* sandwiches (made with roast pork, ham, Swiss cheese, pickles, and mustard), breakfast sandwiches, and Puerto Rican coffee. The inexpensive **Taco Maker** chain offers tacos, burritos, enchiladas, and the usual Tex-Mex fare.

Supermarkets and small grocers are located throughout the island, with many prices comparable to stateside's. Sugar, fish, local vegetables, rum, and local coffees are the best deals. In Old San Juan, try the **Capitol Supermarket** or **SJ Supermarket** on Calle San Francisco, across from the Plaza de Armas. **Mother Earth** (Plaza Las Américas, Hato Rey) is a health-food shop that's worth a stop if you're shopping in the mall. **Salud!** (1350 Av. Ashford, Condado) also has an excellent selection of health food. Well-stocked chain supermarkets, such as **Pueblo,** are located in every major center on the island.

A unique aspect of Puerto Rican cooking is its generous use of local vegetables. Plantains are cooked a hundred different ways—*tostones* (fried green), *amarillos* (baked ripe), and chips. Rice and beans with tostones or amarillos are basic accompaniments to every dish. Locals cook white rice with *achiote* (annatto seeds) or saffron, brown rice with *gandules* (pigeon peas), and black rice with *frijoles negros* (black beans). Garbanzos and white beans are served in many daily specials. A wide assortment of yams is served baked, fried, stuffed, boiled, smashed, and whole. *Sofrito*—a garlic, onion, sweet pepper, coriander, oregano, and tomato purée—is used as a base for practically everything.

Beef, chicken, pork, and seafood are all rubbed with *adobo*, a garlic-oregano marinade, before cooking. *Arroz con pollo* (chicken with rice), *sancocho* (beef and tuber soup), and *encebollado* (steak smothered in onions) are all typical plates.

Fritters, also popular, are served in food kiosks along the highways, notably at Luquillo Beach, as well as at cocktail parties. You may find empanadillas, *surrullitos* (cheese-stuffed corn sticks), *alcapurias* (stuffed green banana croquettes), and *bacalaitos* (codfish fritters).

Local *pan de agua* is an excellent French loaf bread, best hot out of the oven. It is also good toasted and should be tried in a Cubano sandwich.

Local desserts include flans, puddings, and fruit pastes served with native white cheese. Home-grown mangoes and papayas are sweet, and *pan de azucar* (sugar bread) pineapples make the best juice on the market. Fresh *parcha* (passion fruit), *guarapo* (sugarcane), and *guanabana* (a fruit similar to papaya) juice are also sold cold from trucks along the highway. Puerto Rican coffee is excellent served espresso-black or generously cut *con leche* (with hot milk).

To sample local cuisine, consult the listing of *mesónes gastronómicos* in the *Qué Pasa* guide. These are restaurants cited by the government for preserving island culinary traditions and maintaining high standards.

Local legend has it that the birthplace of the piña colada is the Gran Hotel El Convento, but you'd be hard-pressed to find a shoddy version of this famous local drink served anywhere. Rum can also be mixed with cola (known as a *cuba libre*), soda, tonic, juices, water, served on the rocks, or even straight up. Puerto Rican rums range from light white mixers to dark, aged sipping liqueurs. Look for Bacardi, Don Q, Ron Rico, Palo Viejo, and Barillito.

Unless stated otherwise, dress is casual at the restaurants listed below, and reservations are not necessary. Highly recommended restaurants are indicated by a star ★.

Category	**Cost***
$$	$15–$25
$	$10–$15
¢	under $10

**per person, excluding drinks and service*

Old San Juan

$$ **Amanda's Cafe.** This airy cafe across from San Cristobal on the north side of the city, offers seating inside or out, with a view of the Atlantic and the old city wall. The cuisine is Mexican, French, and Caribbean, and the nachos, refreshing fruit frappés, and margaritas are the best in town. *424 Calle Norzagaray. AE, MC, V.*

$$ **Bohemia.** If you tire of tropical cuisine, try this Teutonic outpost near the Pablo Casals museum. A basic German menu is peppered with Spanish and French items. Standards are rich Wiener schnitzel, sauerbraten, and a wide range of sausages; imported German wines and beer round out the experience. There's a bar downstairs

that occasionally hosts jazz concerts. *103 Calle San Sebastián, tel. 809/723–1757. MC, V. Closed Mon.*

$–$$ ★ **Amadeus.** In an atmosphere of gentrified Old San Juan, this charming restaurant offers a nouvelle Caribbean menu. The front dining room is attractive—whitewashed walls, dark wood, white napery, and ceiling fans—but go through the outside passage to the back dining room where printed cloths, candles, and exposed brick make for romantic dining. The roster of appetizers includes buffalo wings and plantain mousse with shrimp; entrées range from chicken breast stuffed with sun-dried tomatoes and cheese ravioli with goat cheese-and-walnut sauce to Cajun-grilled mahimahi. *106 Calle San Sebastián, tel. 809/722–863. AE, MC, V. Closed Mon.*

$–$$ **El Patio de Sam.** A welcoming dark-wood and faux-brick interior and a wide selection of beers make Sam's a popular late-night gathering place. The menu is mostly steaks and seafood, with a few native dishes like asopao mixed in. Try the Samueles Special pizza: mozzarella, tomato sauce, beef, pepperoni, and black olives: It feeds two or three adults. The dessert flans melt in your mouth. *102 Calle San Sebastián, tel. 809/723–1149. AE, D, DC, MC, V.*

$ **Ambrosia.** Order frozen fresh fruit drinks at the bar, or have a seat and order from a selection of pastas, veal, and chicken. The daily lunch specials are a good value and usually include quiche and lasagna served with large mixed salads. *250 Calle Cristo, tel. 809/722–5206. AE, MC, V. Closed Sun.*

¢ **La Bombonera.** Established in 1903, this café and restaurant is known for its strong Puerto Rican coffee and *Mallorca*—a Spanish pastry made of light dough, toasted, buttered, and sprinkled with powdered sugar. Full breakfasts are served as well. It's a favorite Sunday-morning gathering place for locals and tourists. *259 Calle San Francisco, tel. 809/722–0658. AE, MC, V. Open daily 7:30 AM–8 PM.*

San Juan

$$ **Che's.** Juicy *churrasco* (barbecued steaks), lemon chicken, and grilled sweetbreads are specialties at this casual Argentinean restaurant. The hamburgers are huge and the french fries are fresh. The Chilean and Argentinean wine list is also decent. *35 Calle Caoba, Punta Las Marias, tel. 809/726–7202. Weekend reservations advised. AE, D, DC, MC, V.*

$ **Caruso.** This bistrolike restaurant across from the Hotel La Concha and Condado Beach offers solid Italian fare in an unassuming atmosphere. Any of the pastas from the extensive list are a good buy; fish dishes are the most expensive menu items. Pizza and takeout are also available. *1104 Av. Ashford, Condado, tel. 809/723–6876. AE, MC, V.*

$ **El Paso.** This family-run restaurant serves genuine Creole food seasoned for a local following. Specialties include asopao, pork chops, and breaded empanadas. There's always tripe on Saturday and arroz con pollo on Sunday. *405 Av. De Diego, Puerto Nuevo, tel. 809/781–3399. AE, DC, MC, V.*

$ **Via Appia's Italian Deli.** The only true sidewalk café in San Juan, this eatery serves pizzas, sandwiches, cold beer, and pitchers of sangria. It is a good place to people-watch, and the staff is friendly. *1350 Av. Ashford, Condado, tel. 809/725–8711. AE, MC, V.*

¢ **Cafeteria España.** Pop into this Spanish cafeteria for strong coffee, assorted croquettes, toasted sandwiches, soups, and a large selection of pastries. Spanish candies, canned goods, and other gourmet items for sale are packed into floor-to-ceiling shelves that add a cozy note. *Centro Commercial Villamar, Baldorioty de Castro Marginal, Isla Verde, tel. 809/727–4517 or 809/727–3860. No credit cards.*

¢ ★ **Kasalta Bakery, Inc.** Make your selection from rows of display cases offering a seemingly endless array of tempting treats. Walk up to the counter and order from an assortment of sandwiches (try the Cubano), meltingly tender octopus salad, savory *caldo gallego* (a soup jammed with fresh vegetables, sausage, and potatoes), cold drinks, strong café con leche, and luscious pastries. *1966 Calle McLeary, Ocean Park, tel: 809/727–7340. AE, MC, V.*

Out on the Island

$$ **Black Eagle.** The inconsistent quality of the food here hasn't dimmed its status as a Rincón dining landmark. It's on the water's edge, and you dine on the veranda, listening to the lapping waves. The steak-and-seafood menu lists breaded conch fritters, a fresh fish of the day, lobster, and imported prime meats. *Rte. 413, Km 1, Rincón, tel. 809/823–3510. AE, DC, MC, V.*

$$ **El Molino del Quijote Restaurante.** Amid beautifully landscaped gardens just off the beach, this festive, colorful restaurant with tile-top tables and local artwork serves Spanish and Puerto Rican cuisine. Try the *bolas de pescado* (fish balls) appetizer and one of the paellas as an entree, or combine several appetizers for a meal. The sangria is highly recommended. Two one-bedroom cabanas are available to rent. *Rte. 429, Km 3.3, Rincón, tel. 809/823–4010. AE, MC, V. Open Fri.–Sun.*

$$ **La Casona de Serafin.** This informal, oceanside bistro is a *mesón gastronómico,* and specializes in steaks, seafood, and Puerto Rican *criolla* dishes. The indoor dining room has bleached walls, mahogany furniture, and subdued red napery. Try the tostones, asopao, and surrullitos, and follow up with the pumpkin-custard dessert. The somewhat dilapidated palm-fringed patio sits right on the beach, so you can listen to the waves lap the shore. *Rte. 102, Km 9, Playa Joyuda, Cabo Rojo, tel. 809/851–0066. AE, MC, V.*

$$ **La Rotisserie.** An institution in Mayagüez, this fine dining room offers the best value for the money in town with its lavish breakfast and lunch buffets. Grilled steaks and fresh seafood are the specialties. A different food festival is featured nightly: Italian, seafood, Latin night. Brunch is served all day on Sunday. A player piano provides the entertainment. *Mayagüez Hilton, Rte. 2, Km 152.5, Mayagüez, tel. 809/831–7575. Reservations advised. AE, D, DC, MC, V.*

$$ **Parador Perichi's.** An extensive wine selection, with most bottles under $20, and fresh seafood distinguish this *mesón gastronómico.* The informal restaurant and lounge is attached to a parador hotel, across the street from Joyuda Beach. The white stucco and dark wood interior is cool in the tropical heat, and the service is excellent. Try the house specialty, a lavish lobster parmesan. *Rte. 102, Km 14.3, Playa Joyuda, Cabo Rojo, tel. 809/851–3131. AE, D, DC, MC, V.*

$$ **Restaurant El Ancla.** The seafood and Puerto Rican specialties here are served with tostones, *papas fritas* (french fries), and garlic bread. The menu ranges from lobster and shrimp to chicken, beef, and asopao. The piña coladas, with or without rum, and the flan are especially good. *Av. Hostos Final 9, Playa-Ponce, tel. 809/840–2450. AE, DC, MC, V.*

$–$$ **El Bohio.** Join the locals at this informal restaurant by the sea, about a 10- to 15-minute drive south of Mayagüez. You can dine on the large, enclosed wooden deck that juts out over the water or in the dining room inside. Selections include steak and a variety of seafood—all cooked just about any way you want it. *Rte. 102, Playa Joyuda, Cabo Rojo, tel. 809/851–2755. AE, DC, MC, V.*

$ **Pastrami Palace.** A favorite expat hangout, this friendly, small restaurant and lunch counter in downtown Rincón serves up American basics from omelettes, pancakes, and sandwiches to homemade pies, ice cream, and excellent coffee. The colorful decor includes local artwork and a small library for lunchtime reading. An outdoor café is being added. *Calle Parque, Rincón, tel. 809/823–0102. No credit cards. Closed for dinner.*

¢ **Fox Delicias Mall.** This mall food court in Ponce, bustling with hungry shoppers and carousing teenagers, is like a scene from home, but with a Puerto Rican twist. Food stalls include Taco Maker; King Fry Chicken; Le Kafe, serving pastries, flans, and strong Puerto

Rican coffee; and Criollisimo, where you can order empanadillas, asopao, and barbecued dishes. *Across Calle Isabel from the Plaza Las Delicias, Ponce. No credit cards.*

Lodging

Accommodations on Puerto Rico come in all shapes and sizes. There are high-rise beachfront hotels in San Juan that cater to the epicurean, and self-contained luxury resorts that cover hundreds of acres out on the island. But these pricey properties are only half the story on Puerto Rico. Affordable lodging abounds, most noticeably in the government-sponsored *paradores*, lodgings modeled after Spain's successful parador system. Some are rural inns, some offer motel-style apartments, and some are large hotels. They are required to meet certain standards, such as proximity to a sightseeing attraction or beach and a kitchen serving native cuisine. Parador prices range from $50 to $125 for a double room. Reservations for all paradors can be made by calling 800/443–0266 in the U.S., 809/721–2884 in San Juan, or 800/981–7575 elsewhere in Puerto Rico.

Guest houses—traditionally either private homes that rent rooms or small inns—can range from charming dwellings with colorful decor and welcoming owners to stark rooms with few or no amenities and indifferent hosts. Villa rentals, while available on Puerto Rico, generally prove more expensive than a small guest house or parador, unless you are traveling with a group and split the cost. However, you can find one- or two-bedroom villas for as little as $450–$750 per week in the off-season (*see* Villa and Apartment Rentals, *below*).

Keep in mind that the terms "guest house" and "villa" are subject to differing interpretations. Either could really be a small inn; sometimes you'll get a self-contained apartment unit, sometimes a studio with kitchen facilities, and sometimes just a standard hotel room. In all cases, call ahead to discern exactly what is being offered.

Most of the hotels below are within walking distance of a beach. An exception is in Old San Juan, where hotels are generally a short taxi ride from Condado Beach. In the few cases when a hotel or inn in a resort town is not on or near the water, transportation to the beach is usually provided (check when you call). However, if you're staying outside the San Juan area, it's best to have a car anyway, for easy access to sights and restaurants around the island.

Very few Puerto Rican hotels are all-inclusive. If you book the hotel yourself, be sure to ask about any packages the hotel may be offering. Many smaller hotels are willing to negotiate, particularly in the off-season. Also inquire whether rates include sports facilities and airport transfers.

Highly recommended lodgings are indicated by a star ★.

Category	Cost*
$$	$75–$125
$	$40–$75
¢	under $40

**All prices are for a standard double room for two, excluding 7% tax (9% for hotels with casinos) and a 10%–15% service charge. To estimate rates for hotels offering MAP/FAP, add about $20–$25 per person per day to the above price ranges.*

Hotels and Resorts
Old San Juan

The Gallery Inn. Owners Jan D'Esopo and Manuco Gandia restored this rambling, classically Spanish house, one of the oldest private residences in the area, and turned it into an inn. It's full of quirky architectural details—winding, uneven stairs, private balconies, and small interior gardens. The rooms are individually decorated and have telephones but no televisions; most are air-conditioned. Views here are some of the best in the old city, a panorama of the El Morro and San Cristóbal forts and the Atlantic. Galería San Juan, a small gallery and working studio in the inn, features work in various medias (including sculpture and silk screen) by Jan D'Esopo, Bruno Lucchesi, and Teresa Spinner. The inn even offers a package that combines a five-night stay with the creation of your portrait bust. There is no restaurant, but meals can be cooked for groups upon request. *204–206 Calle Norzagaray, 00901, tel. 809/722–1808, fax 809/724–7360. 5 rooms, 3 suites. Facilities: self-service bar. AE, MC, V. EP. $$*

★ **Gran Hotel El Convento.** Standard rates at Puerto Rico's most famous hotel are generally out of our price range during high season, but its many specials and discounts make it worth your while to call. The light brown stucco building, with its dark wood paneling and arcades, was a Carmelite convent in the 17th century. All the rooms are air-conditioned, with TVs, phones, and wall-to-wall carpeting. Fourteen rooms have tiny balconies (ask for one with a bay view). The hotel's central location on Calle Cristo across from the San Juan Cathedral puts restaurants and city sights within walking distance. There are 25% discounts for seniors, and children under 18 stay free when sharing their parents' room. *100 Calle Cristo, 00902, tel. 809/723–9020 or 800/468–2779, fax 809/721–2877. 99 rooms. Facilities: pool, restaurant, 2 bars, Jacuzzi, free transport to beach weekdays. AE, D, DC, MC, V. EP. $$*

Hotel Central. The same family has run this no-frills inn since 1932, and it's one of the city's better bargains. The dark-paneled main lobby, reminiscent of grandmother's sitting room, is furnished with an eclectic array of musty furniture that has seen many, and better, days. Rooms are small and sparsely furnished, with private baths and ceiling fans but no air-conditioning, telephones, or TVs. However, they are clean and possess a travel-worn integrity. A stone's throw from the Plaza de Armas (eight rooms have plaza views), the hotel is central to sights, shopping, and some of Puerto Rico's finest restaurants. *202 Calle San Jose, 00901, tel. 809/722–2751 or 809/721–9667. 62 rooms. Facilities: restaurant. No credit cards. EP. ¢*

San Juan

El Canario by the Lagoon. This bright, cheery inn has a convenient location, a block from Condado Beach and close to shopping and restaurants. The standard rooms are sparse but functional, each with a private bath, double or twin beds, balcony, air-conditioning, telephone, and TV. Superior rooms have updated decor and minifridges. Because they're on a higher floor, they also have views of Condado Lagoo. The complimentary breakfast is Continental. *4 Calle Clemenceau, Condado, 00907, tel. 809/722–5058 or 800/533–2649, fax 809/723–8590. 40 rooms. Facilities: breakfast room. AE, DC, MC, V. CP. $$*

★ **Excelsior.** Room decor here is lackluster, but the rates are a bargain. Each room has a phone and a private bath with a hair dryer; some have kitchenettes. Fine carpets adorn the corridors, and sculptures decorate the lobby. Augusto's, one of the hotel's restaurants, is well respected for its international cuisine. Complimentary coffee, newspaper, and shoe shine are offered each morning. *801 Av. Ponce de León, Miramar 00907, tel. 809/721–7400 or 800/223–9815, fax 809/723–0068. 140 rooms. Facilities: 2 restaurants, lounge, pool, fitness room, free parking and free transportation to the beach. AE, DC, MC, V. EP. $$*

Mirabel Hotel Condado Lagoon. From this high-rise, south of Avenida Ashford in the Condado shopping area, you can easily walk to Condado Beach and the Condado Lagoon. Characterless rooms are comfortable but have a homely 1970s look. Each has a double bed, air-conditioning, a small refrigerator, telephone, and TV. There is a restaurant next door. *6 Calle Clemenceau, Condado,*

00907, tel. 809/721–0170, fax 809/724–4356. 46 rooms, 2 suites. Facilities: coffee shop, pool. AE, DC, MC, V. EP. $$

Out on the Island

★ **Hotel Caribe Playa.** The '60s-style buildings of this small charmer sit 90 feet from the water, on 45 lush acres that include a coconut plantation—picturesque indeed. Simple rooms in three two-story buildings face the sea and catch the virtually nonstop breezes, which cool the rooms and keep insects at bay. All rooms sleep four and are clean and comfortable, with kitchenettes, fans, private baths, and balconies or patios. Children under 10 stay free in their parents' room. Restaurants and food stores are nearby, and the owners will cook dinner for guests on request. The hotel is just south of Humacao on Rte. 3. *HC 764, Buzon 8490, Rte. 3, Km 112, Patillas 00723, tel. 809/839–6339 or 800/221–4483, fax 809/839–1817. 32 studios. Facilities: restaurant, library with TV and phone, beachside barbecues. AE, D, MC, V. EP. $$*

Hotel Meliá. This family-owned and operated hotel has been a landmark in Ponce since 1908. Its slightly shabby exterior gives way to the old-world charm of its lobby, with pink stucco walls, ceiling fans, inlaid ceilings, and dark wood furniture. Rooms are clean and air-conditioned, with dark paneling, pastel-print spreads and drapes, telephones, TVs, large closets, and private baths. Six of the rooms are larger, and have balconies overlooking the plaza—well worth the extra $5. The Continental breakfast served on the rooftop terrace consists of cold toast, juice, and tepid coffee: You're better off eating elsewhere. *2 Calle Cristina, Box 1431, Ponce, 00733, tel. 809/842–0260, fax 809/841–3602. 80 rooms. Facilities: restaurant, bar, lounge, rooftop terrace. AE, DC, MC, V. $$*

Parador Villa Parguera. This parador is a stylish hotel on Phosphorescent Bay. Large, colorfully decorated rooms have TV, phone, air-conditioning, private bath, and balcony or terrace. A spacious dining room, overlooking the swimming pool and the bay beyond, serves excellent native and international dishes. Children under 10 stay free in their parents' room. Ask about honeymoon packages. *Rte. 304, Box 273, Lajas 00667, tel. 809/899–3975 or 800/443–0266, fax 809/899–6040. 63 rooms. Facilities: restaurant, lounge, saltwater pool, nightclub, ATM machine. AE, D, DC, MC, V. EP. $$*

Hotel Joyuda Beach. This cheery, beige-stucco parador sits right on the edge of Joyuda Beach. Rooms aren't large, but have air-conditioning, double beds, TV, telephone, and private bath. Ask for an ocean-view room—well worth the extra cash. The beach is long, with good snorkeling at its reef. Isla de Rationes, another popular snorkeling and picnicking spot, is nearby; excursions can be arranged. Continental breakfast for two is complimentary. Children under 12 stay free. *Rte. 102, Km 11.7, Playa Joyuda, Cabo Rojo, 00623, tel. 809/851–5650, fax 809/255–3750. 42 rooms. Facilities: restaurant, beach bar, volleyball net. AE, D, DC, MC, V. $–$$*

Parador Villa Antonio. This family-owned parador on Rincón beach is a sprawling, motel-style apartment-and-cottage complex with landscaped grounds. Most appealing are the cottages, especially those on the beach. Most are two-bedroom; a few have two bedrooms upstairs and two down and are rented as two units. Each unit is air-conditioned and has a kitchen, living room, TV, private bath, and balcony, but there are no phones. Even the most expensive units, the beachfront cottages, are in the $$ range ($ when shared by two couples). A playground and games room keep children occupied. There's no restaurant, but nearby Rincón has many. *Box 68, Rte. 115, Km 12.3, Rincón, 00677, tel. 809/823–2645 or 809/823–2285, fax 809/823–3380. 55 units. Facilities: 2 lighted tennis courts, basketball court, pool, barbecue areas, laundry facilities, gift shop. AE, D, DC, MC, V. EP. $–$$*

Villa Cofresi Hotel. This apartment hotel on Rincón Beach is on the outskirts of Rincón, with its shops and restaurants. It offers studios, one-bedroom, and two-bedroom apartments (the latter can sleep up to a crowded eight). The spotless accommodations are not elegant and lack phones, but do have simple rattan furniture, kitchenettes, private baths, air-conditioning, and TVs. It's a good place for those who like to roll out of bed and onto the beach. Two of the units face the water. *Box 1193, Rte. 115, Km 12.3, Rincón, 00677, tel. 809/823–7045 or 809/823–2450, fax 809/823–7045. 60 units. Facilities: restaurant, lounge, patio bar, pool, gift shop. AE, D, MC, V. EP. $–$$*

Parador Baños de Coamo. On Route 546, Km 1, northeast of Ponce, this mountain inn is located at the hot sulfur springs that are said to be the Fountain of Youth of Ponce de León's dreams. Rooms open onto latticed wooden verandas and have a pleasing blend of contemporary and period furnishings. All are air-conditioned and have private bath. The parador can make arrangements for you to ride Puerto Rico's glorious, unique *paso fino* horses. *Box 540, Coamo, 00769, tel. 809/825–2186 or 800/443–0266, fax 809/825–4739. 48 rooms. Facilities: restaurant, lounge, pool. AE, DC, MC, V. EP. $*

Parador Boquemar. You can walk to the Boquerón (one of the island's best public beaches) from this small parador at the end of Route 101. Rooms are comfortable. Each has air-conditioning, TV, minifridge, phone, and private bath and is decorated in the island uniform of tropical prints and rattan. Ask for a third-floor room with a balcony overlooking the water. La Cascada, a *mesón gastronómico*, is well known for its scrumptious traditional native cuisine. *Box 133, Boquerón, 00622, tel. 809/851–2158 or 800/443–0266, fax 809/851–7600. 64 rooms. Facilities: restaurant, pool, laundry across street, lounge. AE, D, DC, MC, V. EP. $*

Parador Casa Grande. More than 100 lush acres of a former coffee plantation are the grounds of this parador. Reception is in a restored hacienda, and cottages snuggle along wood walkways among lush green hills. Each cottage holds four spacious balconied rooms. Number 9 is way in the back—quiet, with a lovely mountain view. Rooms have no air-conditioning, but the cool mountain air more than suffices. There are trails for hikers, hammocks for loafers, and occasional music for romantics. *Box 616, Km .3, Utuado, 00761, tel. 809/894–3939 or 800/443–0266, fax 809/894–3939. 20 rooms. Facilities: restaurant, lounge, pool. AE, MC, V. EP. $*

★ **Parador Hacienda Gripiñas.** Don't stay here if you're looking for a beach vacation: The sea is more than 30 miles away. This white hacienda is for those looking for a romantic mountain hideaway. Polished wood and beam ceilings warm the interior. Large airy rooms are decorated with native crafts. Relaxation beckons at every turn: Rocking chairs nod in the spacious lounge, hammocks swing on the porch, and splendid gardens invite a leisurely stroll. Your morning coffee is grown on the adjacent working plantation, and its aroma fills the grounds, as does the chirp of the ubiquitous coquis (tree frogs). *Rte. 527, Km 2.5, Box 387, Jayuya, 00664, tel. 809/828–1717, or 800/443–0266, fax 809/828–1719. 19 rooms. Facilities: restaurant, lounge, pool, hiking and horseback-riding trails. AE. EP. $*

Parador Oasis. The Oasis, not far from the town's two plazas, was a family mansion 200 years ago; the lobby retains a taste of the house's history with peppermint-pink walls and white-wicker furniture. The older rooms are convenient—right off the lobby—but show their age. The newer rooms in the rear lack character, but are functional, clean, and a little roomier. All have TV, phone, and air-conditioning. The hotel is 12 miles from the nearest beach. *72 Calle Luna, Box 144, 00683, tel. 809/892–1175 or 800/443–0266, fax 809/892–1175 ext. 200. 52 rooms. Facilities: restaurant, pool, Jacuzzi, lounge, small gym, sauna. AE, D, DC, MC, V. EP. $*

★ **Parador Perichi's.** Joyuda Beach is right across the street, and Mayagüez just minutes away, from this cheery, orange-and-white hotel. Decor is modern, simple, and bright. All rooms have air-conditioning, TV, phone, balcony, and pastel bedspreads and carpets; most have views of the ocean, but ask for one that faces the beach. The award-winning restaurant draws crowds (*see* Dining, *above*).

Look for live bands and dancing on weekends in the open-air bar area. *Rte. 102, Km 14.3, Playa Joyuda, Cabo Rojo, 00623, tel. 809/851–3131 or 800/443–0266, fax 809/851–0560. 25 rooms. Facilities: restaurant, lounge, game room, pool. AE, D, DC, MC, V. EP. $*

Beside the Pointe. Directly on Rincón beach, this small activity-oriented property attracts surfers from around the world, especially from November to April. Two buildings hold studio, one-bedroom, and two-bedroom apartments, the latter sleeping up to five. Room decor is nonexistent, but all units have fans, private bath, and TV; some have kitchen facilities. Room 8 has a balcony overlooking the roof of the patio and the ocean beyond. A small beach bar/restaurant, the Tamboo Tavern, is on the back patio. *Box 4430, Rte. 413, Rincón 00677, tel. 809/823–5683. 3 studios, 9 apartments. Facilities: restaurant, bar, laundry. MC, V. EP. ¢–$*

Guest Houses and B&Bs

Embassy Guest House Condado. A block from Condado Beach in San Juan, this small, modern two-story guest house is in the right place for the right price. The 15 rooms can be combined to make singles, doubles, or suites; all have private bath, air-conditioning, coffeemaker, minifridge, TV, and kitchenette or access to one. Several rooms have fold-out beds to accommodate an extra person. There's also a rooftop sundeck. Across the road, the guest house operates an inexpensive restaurant and bar right on the beach called Panaché. *1126 Seaview, Condado, San Juan 00907, tel. 809/725–8284, fax 809/725–2400. 15 rooms. Facilities: restaurant, bar, rooftop sundeck. AE, MC, V. EP. $–$$*

Sea Gate. John, Ruthye, and Penny Miller are the friendly proprietors of this small whitewashed hotel on a hilltop of Vieques. They'll meet you at the airport or ferry, drive you to the beaches, arrange scuba-diving and snorkeling trips, and give you a complete rundown on the island. Accommodations include three-room units with terraces (some have kitchens) and two 2-bedroom cottages, which offer more privacy. All have fans, but no air-conditioning (the hilltop breezes are just fine), and no phones; TVs are available on request. There is no restaurant, but the owners will cook for you on request. *Box 747, Vieques, 00765, tel. 809/741–4661. 18 units. No credit cards. EP. ¢–$*

★ **The Lazy Parrot.** Clearly one of the best deals in Rincón, this small, bright guest house is in the hills above Rincón's famous surfing beaches. It's owned and operated by Steve and Francia Lantz, transplanted Americans who came to surf and somehow couldn't leave. Rooms are small but comfortable; each has a fan, private bath, writing desk, and refrigerator. All but one have two bunk beds, the remaining room has a double. The common area has a TV, books, and sofas for rainy-day lounging. The new open-air restaurant in back serves steak, seafood, and pasta; it's open for dinner Tuesday–Sunday in high season, Friday and Saturday in low season. The gift shop sells T-shirts and driftwood painted by a local artist. The most recent addition is the Sea Glass Bar, underneath the restaurant. *Rte. 413, Km 4.1, Box 430, Rincón, 00743, tel. 809/823–5654, fax 809/823–0224. 6 rooms. Facilities: restaurant, bar, patio, gift shop. AE, MC, V. EP. ¢*

Villa and Apartment Rentals

Villa and condominium or apartment rentals are becoming increasingly popular in Puerto Rico, particularly outside San Juan. If you are traveling as a family, or even better, with another couple or family, these are often an excellent option. Call the tourist information office in the area you are interested in staying, or try the options listed below.

If you're part of a large group or you'd like to investigate off-season rates at higher-end properties in the Isla Verde area of San Juan, contact **Condo World** (26645 W. Twelve Mile Rd., Southfield, MI 48034, tel. 800/521–2980). For rentals out on the island, try **Island West Properties** (Rte. 413, Km 1.3, Box 700, Rincón 00677, tel. 809/

823-2323, fax 809/823–3254). They have weekly and monthly vacation rentals that fall into the $ to $$ range.

Lemontree Vacation Rentals. These sparkling, large apartments sit right on the beach, with staircases off their decks to reach it. There are four units, each with a fully equipped kitchen, TV, telephone, large deck on the beach with mahogany-topped wet bar and gas grill. The owner/managers, Mary Jeanne and Paul Hellings have put their personal touches on the apartments: Paul creates all the detailed woodwork and Mary Jeanne designs the interiors. The bright tropical decor includes local artists' work on the walls. There is one three-bedroom unit with two baths, one two-bedroom unit, and two brand new one-bedroom units. The new units have wooden cathedral ceilings and picture windows. The beach is small, but larger ones are close by. It's a 10-minute drive to downtown Rincón. The owners hope to accept credit cards soon. *Rte. 429, Box 200, Rincón, tel. 809/823–6452, fax 809/823–5821. 4 units. Facilities: weekly maid service, laundry service available, linens provided. No credit cards. $$*

Desecheo Inn. This house is connected with Captain Bill's Dive & Surf Shop (*see* Sports and the Outdoors, *above*) and often part of dive-accommodation packages. The house is on a hillside and looks over El Faro lighthouse and the surfing beaches. You can roll out of bed each morning and look out the window for a wave check. There are three units: one two-floor, two-bedroom apartment with a large living room and kitchen (sleeps up to eight), and two smaller apartments with kitchenettes (one sleeps four, one sleeps three). The smallest ground-floor unit uses an outdoor shower. The furniture is functional but worn. Each unit has air-conditioning and TV; the top two have balconies. The units share a backyard and a wooden deck with a covered grill and bar. Nightly and weekly rates are available. Check-in is at the Dive Shop. *Rte. 413, Km 2.5, Box 4181, Rincón, tel. 809/823–0390 or 809/823–2672 (evenings), fax 809/823–0390. 3 apartments. Facilities: linens and towels provided, TV, washer/dryer, garage. AE, MC, V. $–$$*

Camping The Puerto Rico Tourism Company currently recognizes 35 camping areas in locations ranging from Natural Resources parks such as El Yunque National Forest to Luquillo Beach and many of the *balnearios* (public beaches) around the island. Camping facilities can include *casetas* (small cottages), huts, lean-tos, and even small trailer homes. Costs range from $5–$12. Tent sites are also available, at an average cost of 50¢ per person. The facilities can be rustic, some with cold showers, some with no water or toilets at all. Contact the **Recreation Department** (tel. 809/722–1771 or 809/722–1551) or the **Department of Natural Resources** (tel. 809/723–1717).

Off-Season Bets Roughly mid-April through mid-December, many of Puerto Rico's more expensive properties drop their prices to qualify in our $$ range. In addition, these and other hotels may offer limited special deals, mid-week rates, or packages, so inquire when you call. In San Juan, try **Hotel La Concha** (Box 4195, Condado, 00905, tel. 809/721–6090 or 800/468–2822) or the **Excelsior** (801 Av. Ponce de Leon, Miramar, 00907, tel. 809/721–7400 or 800/223–9815). The **Hyatt Dorado Beach** (Rte. 693, Dorado 00646, tel. 809/796–1234 or 800/233–1234, fax 809/796–2022) and **Hyatt Cerromar Beach** (Dorado 00646, tel. 809/796–1234 or 800/233–1234, fax 809/796–4647) frequently offer packages, although some of these are pricey even off-season.

The Arts and Nightlife

Qué Pasa, the official visitors guide, has current listings of events in San Juan and out on the island. Also, pick up a copy of the *San Juan Star*, *Quick City Guide*, or *Sunspot*, and check with the local tourist offices and the concierge at your hotel to find out what's doing.

Music, Dance, and Theater

LeLoLai is a year-round festival that celebrates Puerto Rico's Indian, Spanish, and African heritage. Performances take place each week, moving from hotel to hotel, showcasing the island's music, folklore, and culture. Because it is sponsored by the Puerto Rico Tourism Company and major San Juan hotels, passes to the festivities are included in some packages offered by participating hotels. You can also purchase tickets for $10 for the weekly series of events. *Contact the El Centro Convention Center, tel. 809/723–3135. Reservations can be made by telephoning 809/722–1513.*

La Tasca del Callejon (Calle Fortaleza 317, tel. 809/721–1689) is renowned for its tapas bar and the cabaret show (usually including flamenco guitar) performed by its engaging, talented staff.

Bars

Calle San Sebastian in Old San Juan is lined with trendy bars and restaurants; if you're in the mood for barhopping, head in that direction—it's pretty crazy on weekend nights. The Gran Hotel El Convento's **Ponce de León Salon** (tel. 809/723–9020) also has a pleasant bar. The **Blue Dolphin** (2 Calle Amapola, Isla Verde, tel. 809/791–3083) is a hangout where you can rub elbows with some offbeat locals and enjoy some stunning sunset happy hours. While strolling along the Isla Verde beach, just look for the neon blue dolphin on the roof—you can't miss it.

El Patio de Sam (102 Calle san Sebastián, tel. 809/723–1149) is an Old San Juan institution whose expatriate clientele claims it serves the best burgers on the island. The dining room is awash in potted plants and strategically placed canopies that create the illusion of dining on an outdoor patio.

Casinos

By law, all casinos are in hotels, primarily in San Juan. The government keeps a close eye on them. Dress for the larger casinos tends to be on the formal side. The law permits casinos to operate noon–4 AM, but individual casinos set their own hours.

Casinos are located in the following San Juan hotels: **Condado Plaza Hotel, Dutch Inn & Tower, Sands, El San Juan, Holiday Inn Crowne Plaza, San Juan Marriott,** and **Radisson Ambassador.** Elsewhere on the island, there are casinos at the **Hyatt Regency Cerromar Beach** and **Hyatt Dorado Beach hotels,** and at **Palmas del Mar Resort,** the **Ponce Hilton,** the **El Conquistador,** and the **Mayagüez Hilton.**

Discos

Fridays are big nights in San Juan. Dress to party: If you try to go out in jeans, sneakers, and a T-shirt, you will probably be refused entry at most nightclubs.

Young professionals gather at **Peggy Sue** (1 Av. Roberto H. Todd, tel. 809/722–4664), where the design is 1950s and the music includes oldies and current dance hits. In San Juan, the gay crowd flocks to **Krash** (1257 Av. Ponce de León, Santurce, tel. 809/722–1390). **Lazers** (251 Calle Cruz, tel. 809/721–4479) attracts different crowds on different nights. In Condado and Isla Verde, the thirty-something crowd heads for **Sirenas** (La Concha Hotel, tel. 809/721–6090) and **Amadeus** (El San Juan Hotel, tel. 809/791–1000). Out on the island nightlife is hard to come by, but there are discos in the **Mayagüez** and **Ponce Hiltons.**

Nightclubs

The Sands Hotel's **Players Lounge** brings in such big names as Joan Rivers, Jay Leno, and Rita Moreno. Try El San Juan's **El Chico** to dance to Latin music in a western saloon setting. The Condado Plaza Hotel's **La Fiesta Lounge** sizzles with steamy Latin shows, and the **Casino Lounge** offers live jazz Wednesday through Saturday. The El Centro Convention Center offers the festive **Olé Latino** Latin revue (tel. 809/722–8433).

18 Saba

Updated by Marcy Pritchard

This 5-square-mile fairy-tale isle is not for everybody. If you're looking for exciting nightlife or lots of shopping, forget Saba, or make it a one-day excursion from St. Maarten. There are only a handful of shops, even fewer inns and eateries, and the island's movie theater closed with the arrival of cable. Saba has only 1,200 friendly but shy inhabitants; everyone knows everyone and crime is virtually nonexistent, as is unemployment. Beach lovers should also take note that Saba is a beachless volcanic island, ringed with steep cliffs that plummet sharply to the sea.

So, why Saba? Saba is a perfect hideaway, a challenge for adventurous hikers (Mt. Scenery rises above it all to a height of 2,855 feet), a longtime haven for divers, and, for Sabans, heaven on water. It's no wonder that they call their island the Unspoiled Queen. Saba is also one of the Caribbean's most affordable islands. Only four hotels raise their rates during high season, and all hotels offer package deals with diving outfits.

Saba may be the prettiest island in the Caribbean. It's certainly the most immaculate. An uncomplicated lifestyle has persevered: Saban ladies still hand-embroider the very special, delicate Saba lace and brew the potent rum-based liquor, Saba Spice, sweetened with secret herbs and spices. In tiny, toylike villages, narrow paths are bordered by flower-draped walls and neat picket fences. Tidy houses with red roofs and gingerbread trim are planted in the mountainside among the bromeliads, palms, hibiscuses, orchids, and Norwegian pines.

Saba is part of the Netherlands Antilles Windward Islands and is 28 miles—a 15-minute flight—from St. Maarten. The island is a volcano, extinct for 5,000 years (no one even knows where the crater was). Sabans are a hardy lot. To get from Fort Bay to The Bottom, the early Sabans carved 900 steps out of the mountainside. Everything that arrived on the island, from a pin to a piano, had to be hauled up.

Those rugged steps remained the only way to get about the island until The Road was built by Josephus Lambert Hassell (a carpenter who took correspondence courses in engineering) in the 1940s. An extraordinary feat of engineering, the handmade road took 25 years to build, and if you like roller coasters, you'll love it. The 9-mile, white-knuckle route begins at sea level in Fort Bay, zigs up to 1,968 feet, and zags down to 131 feet above sea level at the airport. This makes a car or scooter the most desirable mode of transportation, although walking is possible (if tiring) and hitchhiking practiced regularly.

What It Will Cost These sample prices, meant only as a general guide, are for high season. A one-bedroom cottage in town rents for about $60 a night; a $ one-bedroom apartment is about $50. Dinner at a $ restaurant will be about $15; lunch at a ¢ restaurant, about $7. A rum punch costs around $2.50; a glass of beer will be $1.50–$2. Rental cars average $40 a day. A taxi from Windwardside hotels to local dive shops is about $10; from hotels in the Bottom to dive shops, $6. Expect to pay about $45 for a single-tank dive; snorkel equipment rents for about $5 a day.

Before You Go

Tourist Information For help planning your trip, contact the **Caribbean Tourism Organization** (20 E. 46th St., New York, NY 10017-2452, tel. 212/682–0435) or the **Saba Tourist Office** (Windwardside, tel. 599/4–62231, fax 599/4–62350). In Canada, contact **New Concepts in Travel** (2455 Cawthra Rd., Suite 70, Mississauga, Ontario L5A 3PI, tel. 905/803–0131, fax 905/803–0132).

Arriving and Departing

By Plane Unless you parachute in, you'll arrive from St. Maarten via **Windward Islands Airways** (tel. 599/5–54210) at Juancho E. Yrausquin Airport.

From the Airport Your only transportation option from the airport is to take a cab; to Windwardside, it's about $5.

By Boat ***The Edge,*** a high-speed ferry, leaves St. Maarten's Pelican Marina in Simpson Bay three times weekly at 9 AM and returns by 5 PM. The trip to Saba's Fort Bay takes an hour, and the round-trip fare is $60 (tel. 599/5–42640 in St. Maarten).

Passports and Visas U.S. citizens need proof of citizenship. A passport is preferred, but a birth certificate or voter registration card will do (a driver's license will *not* do). British citizens must have a British passport. All visitors must have an ongoing or return ticket.

Language Saba's official language is Dutch, but everyone on the island speaks English.

Precautions Take along insect repellent, sunscreen, and sturdy, no-nonsense shoes that get a good grip on the ground.

Staying in Saba

Important Addresses **Tourist Information:** The amiable Glenn Holm is at the helm of the **Saba Tourist Office** (Windwardside, tel. 599/4–62231, fax 599/4–62350) weekdays 8–noon and 1–5 and Sunday 10–2. If needed, the tourist office will help secure accommodations in guest houses.

Emergencies **Police:** call 599/4–63237 in The Bottom, 599/4–62221 in Windwardside. **Hospitals:** The **A.M. Edwards Medical Center** (The Bottom, tel. 599/4–63288) is a 10-bed hospital with a full-time physician. **Pharmacies:** The **Pharmacy** (The Bottom, tel. 599/4–63289).

Currency U.S. dollars are accepted everywhere, but Saba's official currency is the Netherlands Antilles florin (also called guilder). The exchange rate fluctuates but is around NAf 1.80 to U.S. $1. Prices quoted here are in U.S. dollars unless noted otherwise. **Barclays Bank** and **Commercial Bank** in Windwardside are the island's only banks; Barclays is open weekdays 8:30–2; Commercial 8:30–4.

Taxes and Service Charges Hotels collect a 5% government tax. Most hotels and restaurants add a 10%–15% service charge to your bill. You must pay a $2 departure tax when leaving Saba for either St. Maarten or St. Eustatius.

Getting Around Saba is easily explored by car, if you're a good driver and don't mind the road's dips, twists, and nearly vertical stretches. You can see the villages on foot (if you're in good shape), but between them you're better off in a car.

Rental Cars Saba's one and only road—The Road—is a serpentine affair with many a hairpin (read hair-raising) curve. If you dare to drive it, contact **Doc's Car Rentals** (Windwardside, tel. 599/4–62271), **Scout's Place** (Windwardside, tel. 599/4–62205), or **Johnson's Rent A Car** (Juliana's, Windwardside, tel. 599/4–62469). A car rents for about $40 per day, with a full tank of gas and unlimited mileage. (If you run out of gas, call the island's only gas station, down at Fort Bay, tel. 599/4–63272. It closes at noon.) Scooters can be rented at **Steve's Rent A Scoot** (tel. 599/4–62507), next to Sandra's Salon & Boutique, for $10 per hour or $30 per day, less by the week.

Hitchhiking Carless Sabans get around the old-fashioned ways—walking and hitchhiking (very popular and safe). If you choose to get around by thumbing rides, you'll need to know the rules of The Road. To go from The Bottom, sit on the wall opposite the Anglican Church; to go from Fort Bay, sit on the wall opposite Saba Deep dive center, where the road begins to twist upward.

Telephones and Mail To call Saba from the United States, dial 011 plus 599 plus 4 followed by the five-digit number, which always begins with a 6. On the island, it is only necessary to dial the five-digit number. Telephone communications are excellent on the island, and you can dial direct long distance. There are no pay phones on the island.

To airmail a letter to the United States costs NAf 1.30; a postcard, NAf .60.

Opening and Closing Times Businesses and government offices on Saba are open weekdays 8–5. Most shops are closed on Sunday.

Guided Tours All 12 of the taxi drivers who meet the planes at Yrausquin Airport also conduct tours of the island. The cost for a full-day tour is $8 per person with a minimum of four people. If you're just in from St. Maarten for a day trip, have your driver make lunch reservations for you at **Scout's Place** or the **Captain's Quarters** (*see* Dining, *below*) before starting the tour. After a full morning of sightseeing, your driver will drop you off for lunch, complete the tour afterward, and return you to Yrausquin in time to make the last flight back to St. Maarten. Guides are available for hiking. Arrangements may be made through the tourist office.

Exploring Saba

Numbers in the margin correspond to points of interest on the Saba map.

Touring the island's sights by car will take only half a day. Guided tours here make for a pleasant introduction to Saba, but the island is so small that you shouldn't have any problem driving on your own. Begin your tour with a trip from Flat Point, at the airport, up to Hell's Gate. Because there is only one road, we'll continue along its hairpin curves up to Windwardside, and then on to The Bottom and down to Fort Bay.

There are 20 sharp curves on The Road between the airport and Hell's Gate. On one of these curves, poised on Hell's Gate's hill, is

1 the stone **Holy Rosary Church,** which looks medieval but was built in 1962. In the **community center** behind the church, village ladies sell blouses, handkerchiefs, tablecloths, and tea towels embellished with delicate Saba lace. These same ladies also turn out innocent-sounding Saba Spice, each according to her own family recipe. The rum-based liqueur will knock your socks off.

The Road spirals past banana plantations, oleander bushes, and
2 stunning views of the ocean below. In **Windwardside,** the island's second-largest village, perched at an altitude of 1,968 feet, you'll find rambling lanes and narrow alleyways winding through the hills and a cluster of tiny, neat houses and shops.

On your right as you enter the village is the **Church of St. Paul's Conversion,** a colonial building with a red-and-white steeple. Your next stop should be the **Saba Tourist Office** (just down the road), for brochures and books. You may want to spend some time browsing through the **Square Nickel,** the **Breadfruit Gallery,** the **Weaver's Cottage, Saba Tropical Arts,** and **Around The Bend** (*see* Shopping, *below*).

The **Saba Museum,** surrounded by lemongrass and clover, lies just behind the Captain's Quarters. There are small signs marking the way to the 150-year-old house, which has been set up to look much as it did when it was a sea captain's home. Period pieces on display include a handsome mahogany four-poster bed with pineapple design, an antique organ, and, in the kitchen, a rock oven. You can also look at old documents, such as a letter a Saban wrote after the hurricane of 1772, in which he sadly says, "We have lost our little all." The first Sunday of each month, the museum holds croquet matches on its grounds; all-white attire is requested at this formal but fun social event. *Windwardside, no phone. Admission: $1 donation requested. Open weekdays 10–4*

Near the museum are the stone and concrete steps—1,064 of
3 them—that rise to **Mt. Scenery.** The steps lead past giant elephant ears, ferns, begonias, mangoes, palms, and orchids, up to a mahogany grove at the summit: six identifiable ecosystems in all. Signs name the trees, plants, and shrubs, and the tourist office can provide a field guide describes what you'll see along the way. On a cloudless day the view is spectacular. Begin this three-hour excursion in the early morning; bring a picnic lunch (your hotel will pack one), sturdy shoes, a jacket, and water.

Zigzag downhill from Windwardside, past the small settlement of
4 St. John's, to **The Bottom,** which sits in its bowl-shape valley 820 feet above the sea. The Bottom is the seat of government and the home of the lieutenant-governor. The gubernatorial mansion, next to Wilhelmina Park, has fancy fretwork, a high, pitched roof, and wraparound double galleries. In 1993, Saba University opened a medical school in The Bottom, at which about 70 students are enrolled.

On the other side of town is the **Wesleyan Holiness Church,** a small stone building, dating from 1919, with bright white fretwork. Stroll by the church, beyond a place called The Gap, to a **lookout point** where you can see the rough-hewn steps leading down to Ladder Bay. Ladder Bay and Fort Bay were the two landing sites from which Saba's first settlers had to haul themselves and their possessions. Sabans sometimes walk down to Ladder Bay to picnic. If you follow suit, remember there are 400 steps back *up* to The Road.

5 The last stop on The Road is **Fort Bay,** which is the jumping-off place for all of the island's dive operations (*see* Scuba Diving and Snorkeling, *below*) and the location of the St. Maarten ferry docks. There's also the gas station, a 277-foot deep-water pier that accommodates the tenders from ships that call here, and the information center for the **Saba Marine Park** (*see* Scuba Diving and Snorkeling, *below*). On

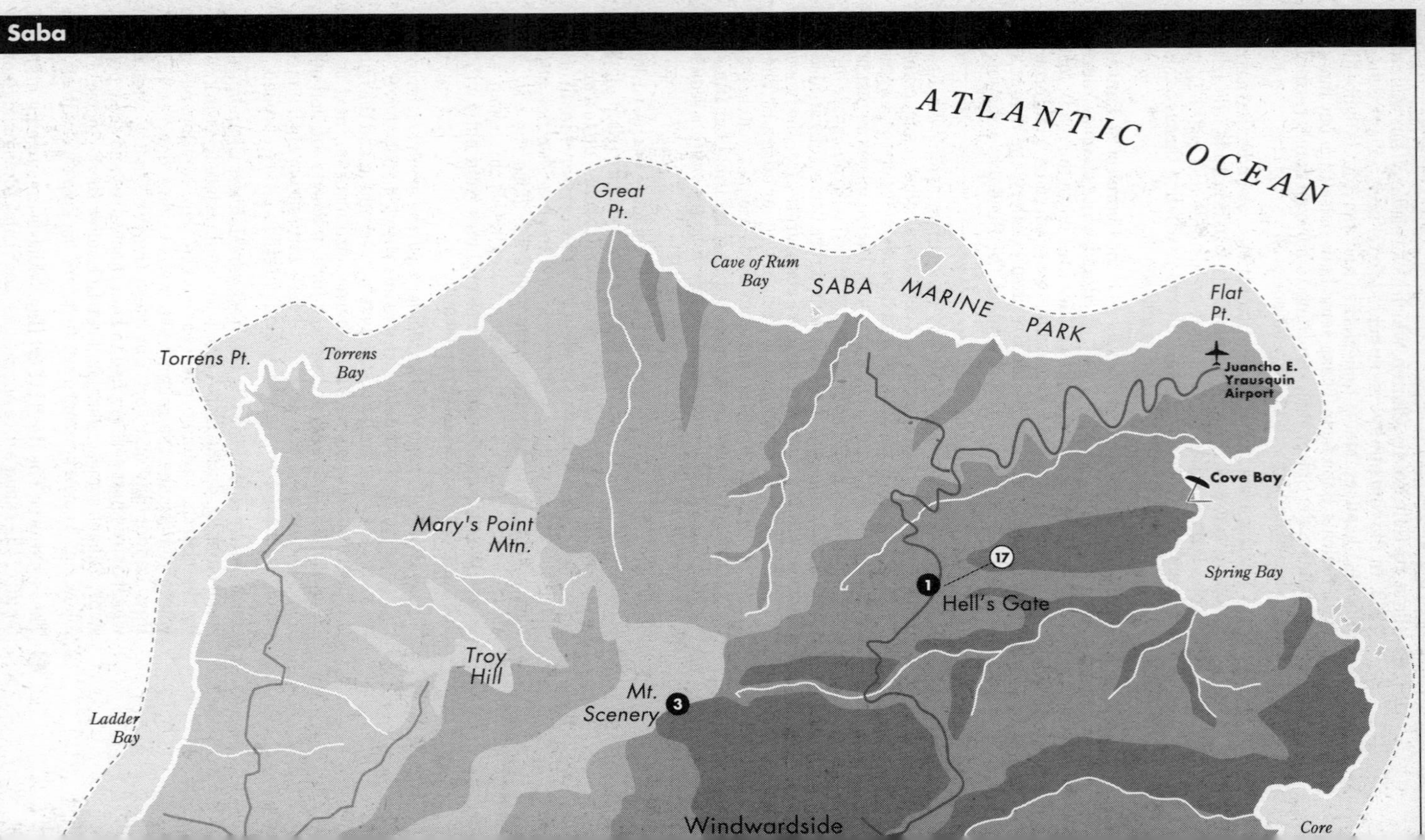
Saba
ATLANTIC OCEAN
SABA MARINE PARK
Great Pt.
Cave of Rum Bay
Flat Pt.
Juancho E. Yrausquin Airport
Cove Bay
Spring Bay
Torrens Pt.
Torrens Bay
Mary's Point Mtn.
Troy Hill
Mt. Scenery
3
1
17
Hell's Gate
Ladder Bay
Windwardside
Core

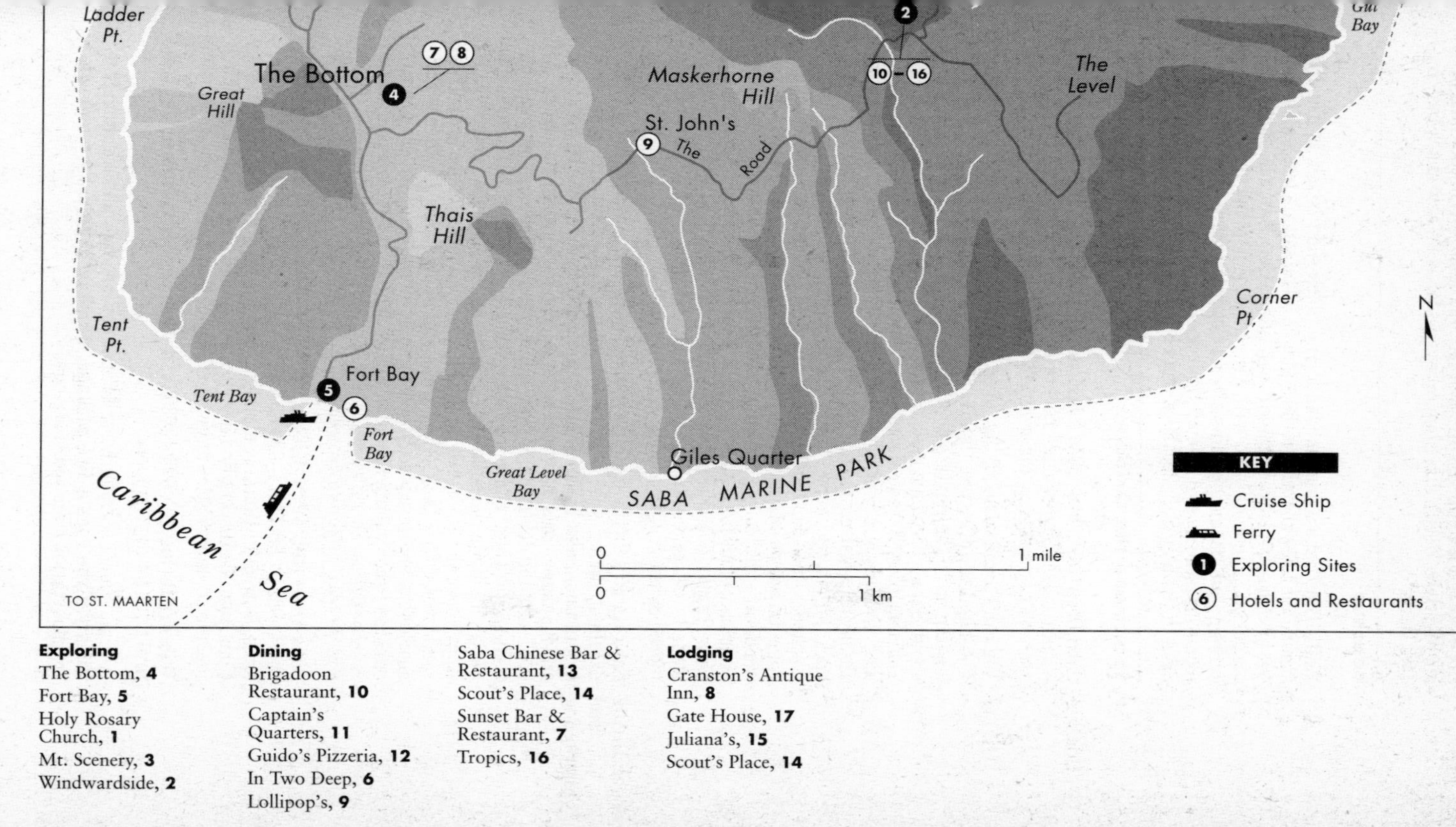

Exploring
The Bottom, **4**
Fort Bay, **5**
Holy Rosary Church, **1**
Mt. Scenery, **3**
Windwardside, **2**

Dining
Brigadoon Restaurant, **10**
Captain's Quarters, **11**
Guido's Pizzeria, **12**
In Two Deep, **6**
Lollipop's, **9**
Saba Chinese Bar & Restaurant, **13**
Scout's Place, **14**
Sunset Bar & Restaurant, **7**
Tropics, **16**

Lodging
Cranston's Antique Inn, **8**
Gate House, **17**
Juliana's, **15**
Scout's Place, **14**

the quay is a recompression chamber, one of the few in the Caribbean, and **Saba Deep's** dive shop, above which is its new snack bar, **In Two Deep.**

Beaches

Well's Bay, Saba's famous wandering black-sand beach, is usually around for a few months in the summer. (The sand is washed in and out by not-always-predictable ocean tides.) **Cove Bay,** a 20-foot strip of rocks and pebbles laced with gray sand, is now the only place for sunning (and moonlight dips after a Saturday night out). There's a picnic area there, and a small tidal pool encircled by rocks for children to swim in. Saba locals swim in Fort Bay, just off the road.

Sports and the Outdoors

Boating **Saba Deep** (tel. 599/4–63347) occasionally conducts one-hour round-island cruises that include cocktails, hors d'oeuvres, and a sunset you won't soon forget, for around $25 a person.

Hiking You can't avoid some hiking, even if you just go to mail a postcard. The big deal, of course, is Mt. Scenery, with 1,064 slippery steps leading up to the top (*see* Exploring Saba, *above*). For information about Saba's recommended botanical hiking trails, check with the Tourist Office. Botanical tours are available upon request. A guided hike through the undeveloped back side of Mt. Scenery, a strenuous, all-day trip, will cost about $50. With the exception of the one on the back of Mt. Scenery, trails throughout the island are clearly marked. Other popular hikes include The Ladder (very steep, with splendid views of the coastal bluffs), the Maskehorne Hill Trail (moderate difficulty, offering magnificent panoramic views and abundant plant life), and the moderately difficult, rambling Sandy Cruz Track. The Old Sulphur Mine Walk from Lower Hell's Gate leads to bat caves—with typical sulfuric stench—that can be explored by the truly intrepid. Exercise caution!

Scuba Diving and Snorkeling **Saba Bank,** a fertile fishing ground 3 miles southwest of Saba, is an excellent diving spot because of its coral gardens and undersea mountains. **Saba Marine Park** was established in 1987 to preserve and manage Saba's marine resources. The park circles the entire island, dipping down to 200 feet, and is zoned for diving, swimming, fishing, boating, and anchorage. One of the unique features of Saba's diving is the submerged pinnacles (islands that never made it) at about the 70-foot depth mark. Here all forms of sea creatures rendezvous. The park offers talks and slide shows for divers and snorkelers and provides brochures and literature. (Divers are requested to contribute $2 a dive to help maintain the park facilities.) *Harbor Office, Fort Bay, tel. 599/4–63295. Open weekdays 8–5. Call first to see if anyone's around.*

Saba Deep (tel. 599/4–63347, fax 599/4–63397) and **Sea Saba** (tel. 599/4–62246, fax 599/4–62362) will take you to explore Saba's 26 dive sites. Both offer rental equipment and SSI- (Scuba Schools International) and PADI-certified instructors, as well as dive packages that include accommodation anywhere on the island.

Wilson's Diving (tel. 599/4–63334) in Fort Bay specializes in shorter dive trips for day-trippers.

A single-tank excursion costs $45 per person. You can save about $50 weekly if you book a dive package, which includes daily round-trip transportation from your lodgings.

Shopping

Gift Ideas The island's most popular purchases are Saba lace and Saba Spice. Every weekday Saban ladies display and sell their creations at the community center in Hell's Gate. Many also sell their wares from their houses; just follow the signs. Collars, tea towels, napkins, purses, and other small items are relatively inexpensive, ranging from $8–$20, but larger items, such as tablecloths, can be pricey. You should also know that the fabric requires some care—it is not drip-dry.

Saba Spice may *sound* as delicate as Saba lace, and the aroma is as sweet as can be. However, the base for the liqueur is 151-proof rum, and all the rest is window dressing.

Shops Saba's famed souvenirs can be found in almost every shop. While you're wandering around Windwardside, stop in at **Saba Tropical Arts,** the **Square Nickel, Peggy's Boutique, Lynn's Gallery,** the **Breadfruit Gallery, Windwardside Gallery, Around the Bend,** the **Variety Store,** the **Little Shop,** the **Yellow Store,** and **Cotton Pickins.** Most of the shops (with the exception of Around The Bend) are closed on Sunday. In The Bottom, the **Saba Artisan Foundation** (tel. 599/4–63260) turns out hand-screened fabrics that you can buy by the yard or already made into resort clothing for men, women, and children. They also sell printed T-shirts, spices, and clothing. Look also for the superlative *Saban Cottages: A Book of Watercolors,* sold at the tourist office and several stores.

Dining

In most of Saba's restaurants you pretty much have to take potluck. If you don't like what's cooking in one place, you can check out another. However, it won't take you long to run out of options, and it's tough to find gourmet cooking.

The markets carry a limited selection of canned goods, produce, and toiletries. Best are **Saba Drug and Superette** (Windwardside) and **My Store** (The Bottom). There are daily fresh produce markets at The Bottom and the Agricultural Garden in Booby Hill. You'll also find posted flyers advertising everything from freshly baked bread to frozen fish fillets. The **Corner Deli and Gourmet Shop** (Windwardside) is *the* place to pick up tasty picnic provisions, with a sophisticated selection of fresh salads, breads, roast chicken, and charcuterie.

Unless stated otherwise, restaurants listed below do not require reservations; dress is always casual. Highly recommended restaurants are indicated by a star ★.

Category	Cost*
$$	$20–$25
$	$10–$20
¢	under $10

**per person, excluding drinks and service*

$$ ★ **Captain's Quarters.** Dining is comfortable on a breezy porch surrounded by flowers and mango trees. The chef's cuisine artfully blends Dutch, Indonesian, French, and Creole influences. Try chicken breast in spicy Indonesian-style peanut sauce. The fish (whatever's fresh that day) is prepared with a variety of sauces, including lime butter. On Saturday night the owner takes over the grill and barbecues steaks, chicken, and fish. Service is pleasant,

but can be slow. *Windwardside, tel. 599/4–62201. Reservations advised. AE, MC, V.*

$$ **Tropics.** A black-and-white-checked floor, crisp black and white napery, and gleaming silver flatwear create a chic, if not exactly tropical, atmosphere in this poolside restaurant. The entrées, a mix of Continental and West Indian dishes, can be on the bland side; stick with the steaks and simply prepared fresh seafood. Try the croquette appetizer: a spicy blend of meat lightly breaded and deep-fried. *Windwardside, tel. 599/4–62469. Reservations advised. MC, V. Closed Sun. No dinner Mon.–Tues.*

$–$$ ★ **Brigadoon Restaurant.** Dining in this open-front restaurant, on the first floor of a colonial building, you can enjoy the passing action on the street. Fresh fish grilled and served with a light Creole sauce is the specialty, but there are also chicken and steak dishes, lobster, and flavorful creations such as shrimp encrusted with salt and pepper. Monday night is Mexican night. *Windwardside, tel. 599/4–62380. AE, D, MC, V. Closed lunch.*

$–$$ **Lollipop's.** Owner Carmen was nicknamed Lollipop in honor of her sweet disposition. Sample her fine land crab, goat, and fresh grilled fish. Meals are served on the outdoor terrace, where stonework and a charming aqua-and-white trellis create a tranquil atmosphere. If you make a reservation, Carmen will pick you up and drop you off at your hotel after dinner. *St. John's, tel. 599/4–63330. No credit cards.*

$–$$ **Scout's Place.** Chef and manager Diana Medero cooks up braised steak with mushrooms, curried goat, and chicken cordon bleu. You can also opt for a simple sandwich—the crab is best. Tables covered with flowered plastic cloths are arranged on the porch and have stunning views of the water. Wednesday breakfast serves as the unofficial town meeting for expatriate locals. There is a lunch seating at 12:30 and a dinner seating at 7:30; only snacks and drinks are served during the rest of the day. *Windwardside, tel. 599/4–62295. Reservations required for the scheduled seatings. MC, V.*

$ **Saba Chinese Bar & Restaurant.** In this plain little house with plastic tablecloths, you can get, among other things, sweet-and-sour pork or chicken, cashew chicken, and some curried dishes. *Windwardside, tel. 599/4–62268. Reservations advised. No credit cards. Closed Mon.*

¢–$ **In Two Deep.** The owners of Saba Deep run this delightful harborside spot, with its stained-glass window and mahogany bar. The soups, sandwiches (especially the Reuben), and smoothies (try the lemon pucker) are excellent. The bar is plastered with humorous sayings, and customers are usually high-spirited—most have just come from a dive. *Fort Bay, tel. 599/4–63438. MC, V.*

¢–$ **Sunset Bar & Restaurant.** Artificial flowers and colorful place mats brighten this humble, homey place. Authentic Creole food—heavenly johnnycakes, bread tart pudding, and lip-smacking ribs—is served. *The Bottom, tel. 599/4–63332. No credit cards.*

¢ **Guido's Pizzeria.** The menu is tacked to the wall at this pleasant, no-frills spot. In addition to pizza, you can order burgers and fish-and-chips. *Windwardside, tel. 599/4–62230. No credit cards. No lunch Sun.*

Lodging

Like everything else on Saba, most of the hotels and guest houses are tiny and tucked into tropical gardens. The selection is limited, but there is something to fit every budget. Accommodations are reasonably priced, and many include breakfast. Keep in mind that Windwardside is the area most centrally located, and near restaurants and shops.

Highly recommended lodgings are indicated by a star ★.

Category	Cost*
$$	$75–$100
$	$50–$75
¢	under $50

**All prices are for a standard double room for two, excluding 5% tax and a 10%–15% service charge.*

Hotels

$$ **Gate House.** Two ex–New Yorkers run this six-room inn in the tiny village of Hell's Gate. The secluded location, between the airport and Windwardside, makes this somewhat of a getaway, even for Saba. Spacious rooms have whitewashed walls and tile floors and are decorated with crisp pinstriped and checked fabrics and colorful art. Two units have kitchenettes. The new restaurant off the lobby looks out to the sea, and is creating an admiring buzz on the island. Chef Beverly changes the menu of local specialties daily; the prix fixe dinner is $20. *Hells Gate, tel. 599/4–62416, in U.S. 708/354–9641; fax 599/4–62415. 6 rooms. Facilities: restaurant. MC, V. CP, MAP.*

$$ **Juliana's.** Juliana and Franklin Johnson's comfortable, tidy studios have tile floors, light wood furnishings, and floral print spreads. One has a queen-size bed; the others have doubles or twins. There's also a 2½-room apartment (Flossie's Cottage) with a kitchenette, a living/dining room, and a bedroom, as well as a large porch facing the sea. Almost every window has fabulous views of the Caribbean. Across the street is the pool, and the café, Tropics (*see* Dining, *above*). *Windwardside, tel. 599/4–62269; in the U.S., 800/223–9815; fax 599/4–62289. 11 studios, 1 2½-bedroom apartment. Facilities: restaurant, pool. MC, V. EP.*

$–$$ **Scout's Place.** Accurately billed as "Bed 'n' Board, Cheap 'n' Cheerful," Scout's Place makes up in convenience and value what it lacks in luxury. Staying here puts you in the center of Windwardside, within walking distance of Sea Saba dive center. The four original rooms are extremely plain and have no hot water; two even share a bath. Ten newer rooms do have hot water (in private bathrooms), as well as four-poster beds and balconies. The restaurant serves a full breakfast. *Windwardside, tel. 599/4–62205, fax 599/4–62388. 14 rooms, 12 with private bath. Facilities: restaurant, bar, pool, gift shop, car rentals. MC, V. EP, CP.*

$ **Cranston's Antique Inn.** The six rooms of this slightly run-down spot are popular digs for the diving set. The shared baths are far from luxurious (dingy decor à la the early '70s), but the rooms have attractive hardwood floors and are neatly decorated with pink or blue fabrics and dark wood antiques; most have four-poster beds. The pool bar is festive, and the Inner Circle disco is practically across the street. There are plans to add private baths, but don't expect them anytime soon. *The Bottom, tel. and fax 599/4–63203. 6 rooms, 1 with private bath. Facilities: restaurant, bar, pool. D, MC, V. EP.*

Apartment Rentals

More than 20 apartments, cottages, and villas are available for weekly and monthly rentals. For listings, check with the **Saba Tourist Office** (*see* Important Addresses, *above*). Most of these are pleasant and well-maintained. The most expensive properties, scattered in the hills outside the towns, have spectacular ocean views and luxurious settings; these cost $100–$175 a night for two people. Three- and four-bedroom cottages with pools are around $250–$275 a night for three or four couples. Units in Windwardside and The Bottom range from $40–$100 a night.

Off-Season Bets

Some properties drop their rates from mid-April to late December. Contact the tourist office for help in finding one in your budget.

The Arts and Nightlife

Guido's Pizzeria (Windwardside, tel. 599/4–62330) is transformed into the Mountain High Club disco on Friday and Saturday nights, and you can dance till 2 AM. Do the nightclub scene at the **Inner Circle** (The Bottom, tel. 599/4–62240), or just hang out at **Scout's Place** or the **Captain's Quarters.** Consult the bulletin board in each village for a listing of the week's events.

19 St. Barthélemy

Updated by Marcy Pritchard

Scale is a big part of St. Barthélemy's charm: a lilliputian harbor; red-roof bungalows dotting the hillsides; minimokes—really glorified golf carts—buzzing up narrow roads or through the neat-as-a-pin streets of Gustavia; and exquisite coves and beaches, most undeveloped, all with pristine stretches of white sand. Just 8 square miles, St. Barts is for people who like things small and perfectly done. It's for Francophiles, too. The French cuisine here is tops in the Caribbean, and gourmet lunches and dinners are rallying points of island life. A French *savoir vivre* pervades, and the island is definitely for the style-conscious—casual but always chic. This is no place for the beach-bum set.

Nor is St. Barts, generally, a destination for the budget-minded. Development has largely been in luxury lodgings and gourmet restaurants, and, with the decline in the dollar, island-wide prices have increased sharply in recent years. There is no public transportation on St. Barts, so getting anywhere other than on foot isn't cheap either. If you're on a budget, but are determined to come to St. Barts, there are ways to save. What you have to remember, however, is that *affordable* here is a relative term. It could mean spending $150 a night for a no-frills hotel, or sharing a modest villa ($1,000–$2,000 a week) with another couple and using minimokes to get to the beach. You can definitely save money by cooking at home, restricting yourself to the occasional splurge meal (well worth it on St. Barts).

Longtime visitors speak wistfully of the old, quiet St. Barts. While development *has* quickened the pace, the island has not been overrun with prefab condos or glitzy resorts. There are no high-rise hotels: The largest hotel has fewer than 100 rooms. The tiny airport accommodates nothing bigger than 19-passenger planes, and there aren't any casinos or flashy late-night attractions.

When Christopher Columbus "discovered" the island in 1493, he named it after his brother, Bartholomeo. A small group of French colonists arrived from nearby St. Kitts in 1656 but were wiped out by the fierce Carib Indians who dominated the area. A new group from Normandy and Brittany arrived in 1694 and prospered—with the help of French buccaneers, who took full advantage of the island's strategic location and well-protected harbor. The island is still a free port today, and, as a dependency of Guadeloupe, is part of an overseas department of France. Dry, sunny, and stony, St. Barts was never one of the Caribbean's "sugar islands" and thus never developed an industrial slave base. Most natives are descendants of those tough Norman and Breton settlers of three centuries ago.

Timing is everything, when planning a vacation to St. Barts. A larger number of hotels and restaurants here have seasonal closings than on other islands. From August until the end of October, your selection of hotels and restaurants will be limited. Fortunately, the gorgeous beaches never close. The advantage of traveling in the off season is enormous savings—sometimes half of the high season rate.

What It Will Cost These sample prices, meant only as a general guide, are for high season. A $ one-bedroom villa or a hotel room costs about $150 a night. Dinner at a $ restaurant is about $30; a snack lunch, $8–$10. Groceries to cook a dinner for two will run about $25; a bottle of wine, such as a vin du pays or beaujolais, will be around $10. A rum punch or cocktail at a restaurant is around $4; a glass of wine, about $3; and a beer, $2.50. Taxi fare between Gustavia and major beach areas is about $10, up to $15 from the airport to the farthest hotel. Jeep or minimoke rental is $40–$45 a day. A single-tank dive averages $55; snorkel equipment rents for about $12 a day.

Before You Go

Tourist Information Information can be obtained by writing to the **French West Indies Tourist Board** (610 5th Ave., New York, NY 10020) or by calling France-on-Call at 900/990–0040 (50¢ per minute). You can also write to or visit the **French Government Tourist Office** (444 Madison Ave., 16th Floor, New York, NY 10022; 9454 Wilshire Blvd., Suite 303, Beverly Hills, CA 90212; 645 N. Michigan Ave., Suite 3360, Chicago, IL 60611; 1981 McGill College Ave., Suite 490, Montreal, Québec H3A 2W9, tel. 514/288–4264; 30 St. Patrick St., Suite 700, Toronto, Ontario M5T 3A3, tel. 416/593–4723; and 178 Piccadilly, London W1V OAL, tel. 0171/629–9376).

Arriving and Departing

By Plane The principal gateway from North America is St. Maarten's Juliana Airport, where several times a day you can catch a 10-minute flight to St. Barts on either **Windward Islands Airways** (tel. 590/27–61–01 or tel. 599/5–4230) or **Air St. Barthélemy** (tel. 590/87–73–46 or 599/5–3150). **Air Guadeloupe** (tel. 599/5–4212 or 590/87–53–74) and Air St. Barthélemy offer daily service from Espérance Airport in St. Martin, the French side of the same island. Air Guadeloupe also has direct flights to St. Barts from Guadeloupe, Antigua, and San Juan, while **Air St. Thomas** (tel. 590/27–71–76) operates daily flights between St. Barts and both St. Thomas and San Juan. You must confirm your return interisland flight, even during off-peak seasons, or you may very well lose your reservation.

From the Airport Airport taxi service costs $5 to $15 (to the farthest hotel). Since the cabs are unmetered, you may be charged more if you make stops on the way. Cabs meet all flights, and a taxi dispatcher (tel. 590/27–66–31) operates from 8:30 AM until the last flight of the day arrives. Several major car rental companies have airport desks. Few affordable hotels offer complimentary transfers, but by all means inquire when booking.

By Boat Catamarans leave Philipsburg in St. Maarten at 9 AM daily, arriving in Gustavia's harbor around 11 AM. These are one-day, round-trip excursions (about $50, including open bar), with departures from St. Barts at 3:30 PM. If there's room, one-way passengers ($25) are often taken as well. The seas can be choppy and it is not uncommon for passengers to get seasick. Contact **Bobby's Marina** in Philipsburg (tel. 599/5–23170) for reservations. The ***St. Barth Express,*** (tel. 590/27–77–24) sails between Gustavia, Philipsburg (Bobby's Marina) and Marigot (Port la Royale) at 7:30 AM, and leaves Marigot at 3:30 PM for the return trip (stopping at Philipsburg). The ***Dauphin II*** (tel. 590/27–84–38) leaves Gustavia for Mairgot at 7:15 AM and 3:45 PM; the crossing takes a little over an hour. The boat departs from Marigot at 8:45 AM and 5:15 PM and goes directly to St. Barts. One-way fare is $35 and round-trip $50. **St. Barth Yachting Service** (tel. 590/27–64–49), **Sibarth** (tel. 590/27–62–38), **Marine Service** (tel. 590/27–70–34), and **OceánMust Marina** (tel. 590/27–62–25) in Gustavia have boats for private charter.

Passports and Visas U.S. and Canadian citizens need either a passport (one that expired no more than five years ago will suffice) or a notarized birth certificate with a raised seal accompanied by photo identification. A valid passport is required for stays of more than three months. British and other EU citizens need a national identity card. All visitors need a return ticket.

Language French is the official language, though a Norman dialect is spoken by some longtime islanders. Most hotel and restaurant employees speak some English.

Precautions Roads are narrow and sometimes very steep, so check the brakes and gears of your rental car *before* you leave the lot. St. Barts drivers seem to be in some kind of unending grand prix and keep their minimokes (the car of choice on this island) maxed out at all times. Prepare yourself for cars charging every which way, making sudden changes in direction while honking wildly, and backing up at astonishingly high speeds. They pause for no one. Some hillside restaurants and hotels have steep entranceways and difficult steps that require a bit of climbing or negotiating. If this could be a problem for you, ask about accessibility ahead of time.

Staying in St. Barthélemy

Important Addresses **Tourist Information:** The **Office du Tourisme** (tel. 590/27–87–27, fax 590/27–74–47) is in a white building on the Gustavia pier; the people who work there are most eager to please. Hours are weekdays from 8:30 to 6 and Saturday from 9 to noon.

Emergencies **Hospitals: Gustavia Clinic** (tel. 590/27–60–35) is on the corner of rue Jean Bart and rue Sadi Carnot. For the doctor on call, dial 590/27–76–03. **Pharmacies:** There is a pharmacy in Gustavia on quai de la République (tel. 590/27–61–82), and one in St. Jean at the La Savane Commercial Center (tel. 590/27–66–61).

Currency The French franc is legal tender. Figure about 5.20F to the U.S. dollar. U.S. dollars are accepted in most establishments, but you may receive change in francs. Credit cards are accepted at most shops, hotels, and restaurants. Note: Prices quoted here are in U.S. dollars unless indicated otherwise.

Taxes and Service Charges A 10F tax is charged for departure to other French islands, and a 16F departure tax is charged to all other destinations. Some hotels add a 10%–15% service charge to bills; others include it in their tariffs. Most restaurants include a 15% service charge in their published prices. It is especially important to remember this when your credit-card receipt is presented to be signed with the tip space blank (just draw a line through it), or you could end up paying a 30% service charge.

Most taxi drivers own their vehicles and do not expect a tip.

Getting Around

Taxis Taxis are expensive and not particularly easy to arrange, especially in the evening. There are two taxi stations on the island, in Gustavia and at the airport. You may also arrange cab service by calling 590/27–66–32, 590/27–60–59, or 590/27–63–12. There is a flat rate of 25F for rides up to five minutes long. Each additional three minutes is 20F. Note: Fares are 50% higher from 8 PM to 6 AM and on Sundays and holidays. Fares average $10 between Gustavia and major beach areas.

Rental Cars A car is not a necessity if you're staying on the water, although you'll find a vehicle gives you freedom for beach- and restaurant-hopping. If you're staying in the hills, you'll have to have a car. The small hotels do not offer shuttle service (unless you befriend the staff).

The island's steep, curvy roads require careful driving. Check the rental car's brakes before you drive away. Jeeps, sturdier than the chic but rickety minimokes, are preferable. **Avis** (tel. 590/27–71–43), **Budget** (tel. 590/27–67–43), **Hertz** (tel. 590/27–71–14), and **Europcar** (tel. 590/27–73–33) are represented at the airport, among others. Check with several of the rental counters for the best price. **Mathew Aubin** (tel. 590/27–73–03) often has special discounts. All accept credit cards. You must have a valid driver's license, and in high season there may be a three-day minimum. Suzuki Jeeps, open-sided Gurgels (VW Jeep), and minimokes—all with stick shift only—rent in season for $40–$45 a day, with unlimited mileage and limited collision insurance. Car-rental reservations are advised, especially during February and around Christmas. Some hotels have their own car fleets; reserve one when you book. Many hotels offer 24-hour emergency road service, which most rental companies do not. Note that there are only two gas stations on the island, one near the airport and one in Lorient. They are not open on Sunday or after 5 PM, but you can use the one near the airport with a credit card at any time.

Motorbikes These rent for about $30 per day and require a $100 deposit. Call **Rent Some Fun** (tel. 590/27–70–59).

Hitchhiking Hitching rides is a popular, legal, and interesting way to get around; it is widely practiced in the more heavily trafficked areas on the island.

Telephones and Mail To phone St. Barts from the United States, dial 011 plus 590 and the local number. To call the United States from St. Barts, dial 19, then 1, the area code, and the local number. For St. Martin, dial just the six-digit number; for St. Maarten, dial 3 plus the five-digit number. For local information, dial 12. Public telephones do not accept coins; they accept Telecartes, a type of prepaid credit card that you can purchase from the post offices at Lorient, St. Jean, and Gustavia, as well as at the gas station next to the airport. Making an international call with a Telecarte is less expensive than making the call from your hotel. You can purchase Telecartes in amounts from 31F to 93F.

Mail is slow. It can take up to three weeks for correspondence between the United States and the island. Post offices are in Gustavia, St. Jean, and Lorient. It costs 3.10F to mail a postcard to the United States, 3.90F to mail a letter.

Opening and Closing Times Businesses and offices close from noon to 2 during the week and are closed on weekends. Shops are generally open weekdays 8:30–noon and 2–5, and until noon on Saturday. Some of the shops across from the airport and in St. Jean also open on Saturday afternoons and until 7 PM on weekdays. The banks are open weekdays 8–noon and 2–3:30.

Guided Tours Tours are by minibus or taxi. An hour-long tour costs about $40 for up to three people; $50 for up to eight people. There are three tours offered by the tourist office (45 minutes, one hour, and 1½ hours in length); these are less expensive—about $10 per person for the shortest one—than the private tours. A private five-hour island tour costs about $100 per vehicle. Itineraries are negotiable. Tours can be arranged at hotel desks, through the tourist office, or by calling any of the island's taxi operators, including **Hugo Cagan** (tel. 590/27–61–28) and **Florian La Place** (tel. 590/27–63–58). If you don't speak French, be sure to request a driver whose English is good.

Exploring St. Barthélemy

Numbers in the margin correspond to points of interest on the St. Barthélemy map.

You're best off renting a car if you want to explore the island at your own pace. If you're staying on or near a major beach, and won't need a car to get to the water, you may want to take a guided half-day tour as an introduction to the island's charms.

Gustavia and the West

1 With just a few streets on three sides of its tiny harbor, **Gustavia** is easily explored in a two-hour stroll, including time to browse through shops or visit a café. This will leave you the rest of the afternoon for a trip to the west coast to enjoy a picnic and a swim.

Park your car harborside on the rue de la République, where flashy catamarans, yachts, and sailboats are moored, then head to the **tourist office** on the pier. Here you should pick up an island map and a free copy of *St. Barth Magazine,* a monthly publication on island happenings. Then settle in at either **Bar de l'Oubli** or **Le Select** (*see* Nightlife, *below*), two cafés at the corner of rue de la France and rue de la République, for coffee and croissants and a quick leaf through the listings of the week's events.

As you stroll through the little streets, you will notice that plaques sometimes spell out names in both French and Swedish, a reminder of the days when the island was a Swedish colony. You'll see ultrachic boutiques along **rue du Roi Oscar II, rue de la France, rue du Bord de Mer,** and **rue du Général de Gaulle.**

Enjoy the colorful spectacle of the local **market,** where ladies from Guadeloupe and Dominica preside over their tropical fruit and vegetable arrangements. And if you feel like a swim, drive around the end of the harbor, turn onto rue Victor Hugo, turn right on rue de l'Eglise, and follow the road to **Petit Anse de Galet.** This quiet little *plage* is also known as Shell Beach because of the tiny shells heaped ankle-deep in some places.

On the other side of the harbor, at the point, the new **Municipal Museum** details the island's history. *Tel. 599/27–89–07. Admission: 10F. Open Mon.–Thurs. 8–noon and 1:30–5:30, Fri. 8–noon, 1:30–5, Sat. 8:30–noon. Closed Sun.*

Head south back the way you came and turn off at the sign for Lurin. The views up the winding road overlooking the harbor are spectacular. After about five minutes, look for a sign to Plage du Gouverneur. A small rocky route off to the right will take you bumping and grinding down a steep incline to **Anse du Gouverneur,** one of St. Barts's most beautiful beaches, where pirate's treasure is said to be buried. If the weather is clear, you will be able to see the islands of Saba, St. Eustatius, and St. Kitts.

Corossol and Flamands

Starting at the intersection on the hilltop overlooking the airport (known as Tourmente), take the road to Public Beach and on to
2 **Corossol,** a two-street fishing village with a little beach. Corossol is where the island's French provincial origins are most evident. Residents speak an old Norman dialect, and some of the older women still wear traditional garb—ankle-length dresses, bare feet, and starched white sunbonnets called *quichenottes* ("kiss-me-not" hats). The women don't like to be photographed, but they're not shy about selling you some of their handmade straw work—handbags, bas-

St. Barthélemy

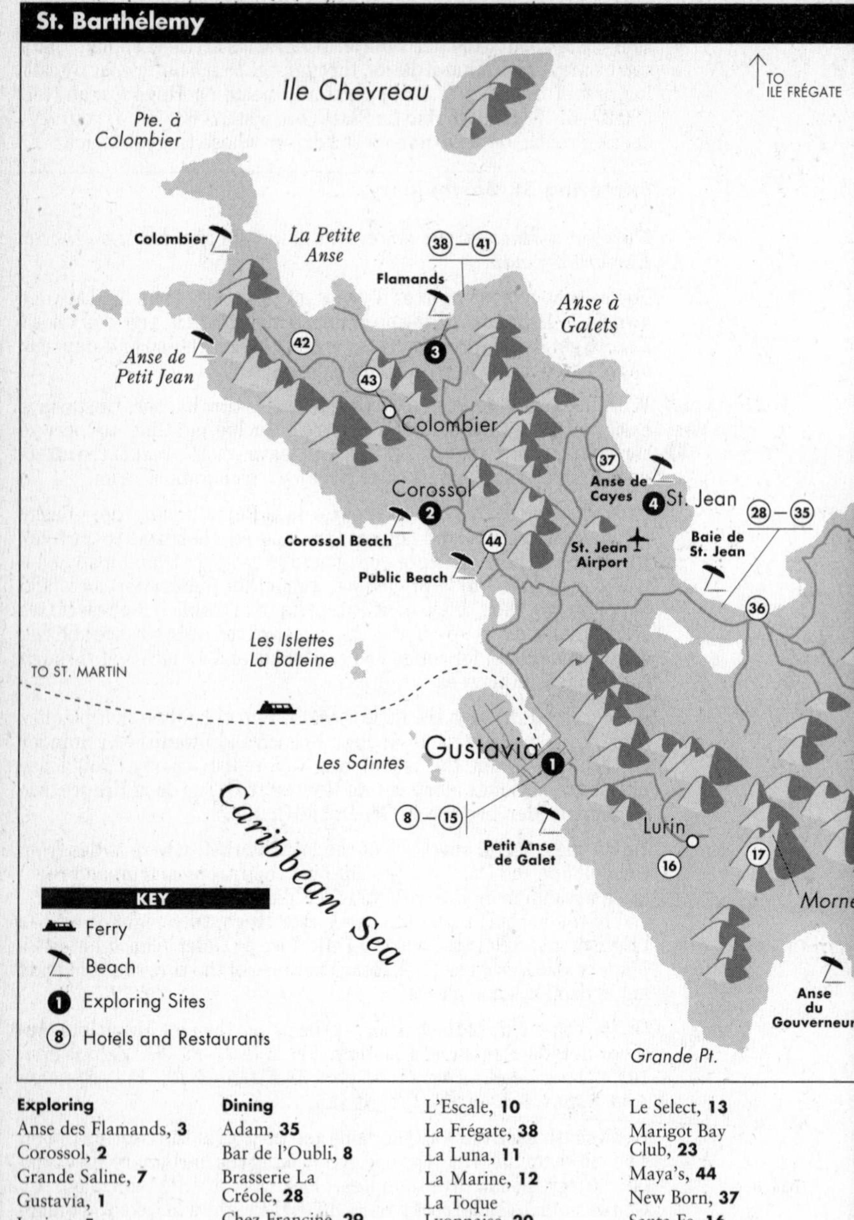

Exploring
Anse des Flamands, **3**
Corossol, **2**
Grande Saline, **7**
Gustavia, **1**
Lorient, **5**
St. Jean, **4**
Toiny coast, **6**

Dining
Adam, **35**
Bar de l'Oubli, **8**
Brasserie La Créole, **28**
Chez Francine, **29**
Chez Pompi, **18**
Eddy's Ghetto, **9**
Gloriette, **19**
L'Escale, **10**
La Frégate, **38**
La Luna, **11**
La Marine, **12**
La Toque Lyonnaise, **20**
Le Patio, **30**
Le Pelican, **33**
Le Rivage, **21**
Le Select, **13**
Marigot Bay Club, **23**
Maya's, **44**
New Born, **37**
Santa Fe, **16**
Topolino, **32**

TO ILE TOC VERS

ATLANTIC OCEAN

Les Grenadiers

La Tortue

Pte. Milou

26 27

Lorient

Marigot

Marechal Beach

23

24

19—22

Marigot

Grand Cul de Sac

Lorient

5

Petit Cul de Sac

18

25

Vitet

Toiny

Morne de Grand Fond

Morne Vitet

6

Morne de Grand Fond

Grande Saline

7

Pt. à Toiny

Anse de Grand Fond

N

ne Lurin

Grande Saline

0 1 mile

0 1 km

ur

Pt. du Gouverneur

Lodging

Auberge de la Petite Anse, **42**

Baie des Anges, **39**

Baie des Flamands, **40**

Castelets, **17**

Eden Rock, **36**

Grand Cul de Sac Beach Hotel/St. Barths Beach Hotel, **22**

Hostellerie des Trois Forces, **25**

La Normandie, **26**

Le P'tit Morne, **43**

Les Mouettes, **27**

Marigot Bay Club, **23**

La Presqu'ile, **14**

Sea Horse Hotel, **24**

Sunset Hotel, **15**

Tropical Hotel, **31**

Village St. Jean, **34**

White Sand Beach Cottages, **41**

kets, broad-brim hats, and delicate strings of birds—made from lantania palms. The palms were introduced to the island 100 years ago by farsighted Father Morvan, who planted groves in Corossol and Flamands, thus providing the country folk with a living that is still pursued today. Here, too, is the **Inter Oceans Museum,** with a small but excellent collection of marine shells from around the world. *Tel. 590/27–62–97. Admission: 20F. Open daily 9–5.*

3 From Corossol, head down the main road about a mile to **Anse des Flamands,** a wide beach with several small hotels and many rental villas. From here, take a brisk hike to the top of what is believed to be the now-extinct volcano that gave birth to St. Barts. From the peak you can take in the gorgeous view of the islands.

A drive to the end of Flamands Road brings you to a rocky footpath that leads to the island's most remote beach, **Anse de Colombier.**

St. Jean, Grand Cul de Sac, Saline

Brimming with bungalows, bistros, sunbathers, and windsurfing sails, the half-mile crescent of sand at **St. Jean** is the island's most famous beach. Lunch at a beachside bistro, such as **Chez Francine**
4 (*see* Dining, *below*), perhaps interrupted by a swim in the surf, is de rigueur, followed by a stroll through nearby boutiques.

5 Leaving St. Jean, take the main road to **Lorient.** On your left are the royal palms and rolling waves of Lorient Beach. Lorient, site of the first French settlement, is one of the island's two parishes, and a newly restored church, historic headstones, a school, post office, and gas station mark the spot.

Turn right before the gleaming white Lorient cemetery. In a short while you'll reach a dusty cutoff to your right. The pretty little Creole house on your left is home to Ligne de Cosmetiques M (*see* Shopping, *below*). Behind it is one of St. Barthélemy's treasured secrets, **Le Manoir.** The 1610 Norman manor was painstakingly disassembled, shipped from France and reconstructed in 1984 by the charming Jeanne Audy Rowland in tribute to the island's Viking forebears. The tranquil surrounding courtyard and garden contain a waterfall and a lily-strewn pool. Mme. Rowland graciously allows visitors; you don't need an appointment, but you do need to speak some French, as Madame speaks little English.

Retrace your route back to Lorient and continue along the coast. Turn left at the Mont Jean sign. Your route rolls around the island's pretty windward coves, past **Pointe Milou,** an elegant residential colony, and on to **Marigot,** where you can pick up a bottle of fine wine at **La Cave.** The bargain prices may surprise you (*see* Shopping, *below*).

The winding road passes through the mangroves, ponds, and beach of **Grand Cul de Sac,** where there are plenty of excellent beachside restaurants and water-sports concessions. Over the hills beyond
6 Grand Cul de Sac is the much photographed **Toiny coast.** Drystone fences crisscross the steep slopes of Morne Vitet along a rocky shoreline that resembles the rugged coast of Normandy. The road turns inland and up the slopes of Morne de Grand Fond. At the first fork (less than a mile), the road to the right leads back to Lorient. A left-hand turn at the next intersection will bring you within a few
7 minutes to a dead end at **Grande Saline.** The big salt ponds of Grande Saline are no longer in use, and the place looks desolate, but climb the short hillock behind the ponds for a surprise—the long arc of **Anse de Grande Saline.**

Beaches

There are nearly 20 *plages*, each with a distinctive personality and all of them public. Even in season, it is possible to find a nearly empty beach. Topless sunbathing is common, but nudism is forbidden. Here are the main attractions:

St. Jean is like a mini Côte d'Azur—beachside bistros, bungalow hotels, bronze beauties, and lots of day-trippers. The reef-protected strip is divided by Eden Rock promontory, and there's good snorkeling west of the rock. Lorient is popular with St. Barts's families and surfers, who like its rolling waves. Marigot is a quiet fishing beach with good snorkeling along the rocky far end. Shallow, reef-protected Grand Cul de Sac is especially nice for small children and windsurfers; it has excellent lunch spots and lots of pelicans. Around the point, next to the Guanahani Hotel, is tiny Marechal Beach, which offers some of the best snorkeling on the island. Secluded Grande Saline, with its sandy ocean bottom, is just about everyone's favorite beach and is great for swimmers. Despite the law, young and old alike go nude on this beach. It can get windy here, so go on a calm day. Anse du Gouverneur is even more secluded and equally beautiful, with good snorkeling and views of St. Kitts, Saba, and St. Eustatius. A five-minute walk from Gustavia is Petit Anse de Galet, named after the tiny shells on its shore. Both Public Beach and Corossol Beach are best for boat- and sunset-watching. The beach at Colombier is the least accessible but the most private; you'll have to take either a rocky footpath from La Petite Anse or brave the 30-minute climb down a cacti-bordered trail from the top of the mountain behind the beach. Flamands is the most beautiful of the hotel beaches—a roomy strip of silken sand. Back toward the airport, the surf at Anse de Cayes is rough for swimming, but great for surfing.

Sports and the Outdoors

Boating St. Barts is a popular yachting and sailing center, thanks to its location midway between Antigua and St. Thomas. **Marine Service** (Quai du Yacht Club, Gustavia, tel. 590/27–70–34) offers full-day outings on a 40-foot catamaran to the uninhabited Ile Fourchue for swimming, snorkeling, cocktails, and lunch; the cost is $90 per person. They also offer one-hour cruises on the glass-bottom boat *L'Aquascope*; cost is about $35 a person, $16 for children under 12.

Diving and Snorkeling **Marine Service** (tel. 590/27–70–34) operates a PADI diving center, with scuba-diving trips for about $50 per person, gear included. Small groups should call **St. Barth Plongée** (tel. 590/27–63–33) in Gustavia for dive or snorkeling excursions. CMAS-certified **Club La Bulle** (tel. 590/27–62–25) and PADI-certified **Dive with Dan** (tel. 590/27–64–78) are other scuba options. Snorkeling off the beaches here is not wonderful; you might want to consider splurging on a snorkel excursion. These cost around $50 a person (gear, drinks, and snacks usually included); contact Marine Service. A single-tank dive on St. Barts averages $55; snorkel equipment rents for about $12 a day.

Tennis If you wish to play tennis at a hotel at which you are not a guest, be sure to call ahead to inquire about fees and reservations. There are two lighted tennis courts at the **Guanahani** (tel. 590/27–66–60), **Le Flamboyant Tennis Club** (tel. 590/27–69–82), and the **Sports Center of Colombier** (tel. 590/27–61–07). There is one lighted court each at the **Hotel Manapany Cottages** (tel. 590/27–66–55), the **Taiwana** (tel. 590/27–65–01), the **St. Barth's Beach Hotel** (tel. 590/27–60–70), and the **St. Barth Isle de France** (tel. 590/27–61–81), which also has the island's only squash court. **Les Ilets de la Plage** (590/27–62–38) has one unlighted court.

Windsurfing Windsurfing fever is high here. Boards can be rented for about $20 an hour at water-sports centers along St. Jean and Grand Cul de Sac beaches. Lessons are offered for about $40 an hour at **St. Barth Wind School** (St. Jean, tel. 590/27–71–22), and **Wind Wave Power** (St. Barths Beach Hotel, tel. 590/27–60–70).

Shopping

Befitting St. Barts's chic reputation, you'll find superb duty-free items here, but few really good buys. Often you can get better prices back home for such items as perfume and designer clothes. The best bargains are crafts such as straw work and pottery.

Shopping Areas Shops are clustered in **Gustavia, St. Jean's Commercial Center,** and the **Villa Creole,** a cottage complex also in St. Jean. More shops are located across from the airport at **La Savane Commercial Center.**

Good Buys

Island Crafts Stop in Corossol to pick up some of the intricate straw work (wide-brim beach hats, mobiles, handbags) that the ladies of Corossol create by hand (*see* Exploring St. Barthélemy, *above*). In Gustavia, look for hand-turned pottery at **St. Barts Pottery** (tel. 590/27–62–74). You'll see coral and exotic shell jewelry at the **Shell Shop** (no phone). Superb local skin-care products are available at **Ligne de Cosmetiques M** (tel. 590/27–82–63) in Lorient (*see* Exploring St. Barthélemy, *above*). Gustavia also has a new market, **Le 'Ti Marché,** dedicated to art and crafts handmade on the island. Open every day except Sunday, the market is set up in stalls on the corner of rue du Roi Oscar II near the city hall. The much-sought-after Belou's P line of aromatic oils is available here. For details call 590/27–83–72 or the tourist office.

Wine and Gourmet Shops Wine lovers will enjoy **La Cave** (Marigot, tel. 590/27–63–21), where an excellent collection of French vintages is stored in temperature-controlled cellars. Also check out **La Cave du Port Franc** (tel. 590/27–65–27), on the far side of the harbor, for vintage wines, contemporary paintings, and objets d'art.

For exotic groceries or picnic fixings, stop by the fabulous gourmet delis in Gustavia: **La Rotisserie** (tel. 590/27–63–13) on rue du Roi Oscar II (branches in Villa Creole and Pointe Milou) and **Taste Unlimited** (tel. 590/27–70–42) on rue du Général de Gaulle. In Grand Fond, stop by **La Cuisine de Michel** (tel. 590/27–90–49), a simple shack that doles out delectable $10 take-out meals.

Dining

Dining out is a ritual on St. Barts. The quality of fare is generally high, and so are the prices, which are among the steepest in the Caribbean. The stiff tariffs reflect both the island's culinary reputation and the difficulty of obtaining fresh ingredients. Several top restaurants offer prix-fixe lunch menus that, while less elaborate than dinner, amply display their chefs' culinary expertise. One is the elegant **Carl Gustav** (tel. 590/27–82–83), perched high above Gustavia harbor; the $35 lunch menu costs less than half what you'd pay at dinner. Generally, the island's Italian, Creole, and French-Creole restaurants tend to be less expensive than the French establishments.

If you're renting a villa, you'll save by eating at home. **Le Mono Shop** (Marigot) and **JoJo Alimentation** (Lorient) are small but well-stocked supermarkets with a good selection of produce. **Chez JoJo,** next door to the latter, is a popular burger stand with great fries. Across from the airport you'll find **Match**, the largest supermarket on the island. For impromptu picnics, you can't do better than **La Cuisine de Michel** (*see* Shopping, *above*) or the higher-priced **La Rotisserie** (*see* Shopping, *above*). The latter also has a few tables to enjoy fine pizzas and salads for $10–$15.

Accras (salt cod fritters) with Creole sauce (minced hot peppers in oil), spiced christophine (a kind of squash), *boudin Créole* (a very spicy blood sausage), and a lusty *soupe de poissons* (fish soup) are some of the delicious and ubiquitous Creole dishes.

Dress code is for the most part casual, although long pants for men and a skirt or dress for women are usually de rigueur in the tonier spots. Some restaurants close in September and October, so call ahead. Reservations are always recommended; on weekend nights in season, they're required almost everywhere. Highly recommended restaurants are indicated by a star ★.

Category	Cost*
$$	$30–$45
$	$20–$30
¢	under $20

**per person, excluding drinks, service, and 4% sales tax*

$$ ★ **Adam.** Vincent Adam, a graduate of the Culinary Academy of France, opened this haute cuisine gem in the hills just off St. Jean beach. Dinner is served each evening in the Creole-style house or in the garden. Many locals insist that it's one of the top restaurants on the island. There are both an à la carte menu with wonderful choices and a very reasonably priced prix-fixe menu (about $38). The prix-fixe menu will keep this spot in the $$ category. Offerings include lobster tabouli, salmon tartare with caviar and oysters, terrine of sweetbreads, and fillet of beef. Vegetarian selections are also available. *St. Jean, tel. 590/27–93–22. Reservations suggested. AE, MC, V. No lunch.*

$$ **Chez Pompi.** This delightful cottage on the road to Toiny, might have sprung from a Cézanne canvas. Pompi (a.k.a. Louis Ledée) is an artist of some repute whose naive paintings clutter the walls of his tiny studio. You can browse and chat with M. Pompi while enjoying his fine Creole and country French cuisine. Daily specials might include stewed chicken or beef bourguignonne. *Petit Cul de Sac, tel. 590/27–75–67. No credit cards. Closed Sun.*

$$ **La Frégate.** Thierry and Jean-Pierre are the inventive chefs at this casual restaurant decorated with nautical paraphernalia. You may order something from the grill (selecting one of 11 sauces) or opt for the fine regular menu. There are also two reasonable prix fixe Creole menus. *Anse des Flamands, tel. 590/27–66–51. Reservations advised. MC, V.*

$$ ★ **Le Patio.** Some of the best classic Italian food on the island is served by candlelight at this pleasant hillside restaurant, where you can dine inside or on the terrace. Entrées change weekly, but you may find grouper medallions rolled in black peppercorns with a light ginger and lime sauce or salmon fillet with both a mustard and a crushed tomato sauce, in addition to six or seven pasta offerings. Children will enjoy holiday menus—such as red snapper in phantom sauce at Halloween. There are nice views of the bay, and the atmosphere is romantic and intimate. Service is unhurried, despite the remarkably reasonable prices. *Village St. Jean Hotel, tel. 590/27–61–39. MC, V. Closed Wed. and June. No lunch.*

$$ **Le Pelican.** This seashore restaurant is a lunch hot spot. Starters, such as baby-shrimp-stuffed avocado, and a wide range of seafood entrées are served at picnic tables set up under awnings. A more elaborate (and more expensive) dinner menu is offered in the indoor dining room. Selections include Creole bouillabaisse and lobster gratin. A pianist and chanteuse serenade diners. Locals cluster around the piano bar for late-night desserts long after other restaurants have locked their doors. *St. Jean Bay, tel. 590/27–64–64. AE, MC, V. Closed Sun.*

$$ **Maya's.** Locals, visitors, and celebs keep returning to this informal, open-air restaurant just outside of Gustavia on the north end of Public Beach; it's one of the hippest and most celebrity-studded eateries on the island. Relax in a colorful deck chair and watch the boats

heading in and out of Gustavia's harbor as you contemplate the Creole, Oriental, Vietnamese, and Thai menu. You choose from five selections for each course. The menu changes nightly, but you might find christophine au gratin, several fresh salads, canard à l'orange, salmon teriyaki, and shrimp curry. Scrumptious cakes and pies are baked on the premises. The schizophrenic service can move from haughty to harried to helpful all in one evening. *Public Beach, tel. 590/27-75-73. Reservations advised. AE, D, MC, V. Closed Sun. and June-Oct. No lunch.*

$$ **New Born.** For authentic Creole cuisine, head down the bumpy road that leads to the Hotel Manapany. The dark wood restaurant is somewhat devoid of decoration except for a large aquarium in the back; ask for a table near it if you want to watch the sharks, turtles, and tropical fish swim while you eat. The fresh seafood is caught at the beach just steps away. This is the place to sample such Creole specialties as accras, boudin, curried goat or shrimp, and salt cod salad. For dessert try the coconut custard or bananas flambées. *Anse des Cayes, tel. 590/27-67-07. Reservations advised. AE, MC, V. Closed Sun. in off season. No lunch.*

$-$$ ★ **Eddy's Ghetto.** The combination of imaginatively prepared, modestly priced fare—crab salad, ragout of beef, crème caramel—served in a disarmingly fun-loving atmosphere has made this open-air restaurant a hit. The crowd is lively, the wine list impressive. *Gustavia, just off rue du Général de Gaulle, no phone. Reservations advised. No credit cards.*

$-$$ **Gloriette.** Visit this beachside bistro for crunchy accras, grilled red snapper with Creole sauce, and other delicious local dishes. Light salads and Creole dishes are served at lunch, and the house wine is always good. *Grand Cul de Sac, tel. 590/27-75-66. No credit cards. No dinner Sun.*

$-$$ **La Marine.** Mussels from France arrive on Thursday and in-the-know islanders are there to eat them at the very popular dockside picnic tables. The lunch menu always includes fresh fish, hamburgers, and omelets; dinner adds more grilled meat and fish. *Rue Jeanne d'Arc, Gustavia, tel. 590/27-70-13. No credit cards.*

$-$$ ★ **Le Rivage.** Bathing suits are acceptable attire at this popular and very casual Creole establishment on the beach at Grand Cul de Sac. Delicious lobster salad, sandwiches, and fresh grilled fish are served at indoor and outdoor tables. The relaxed atmosphere and surprisingly low prices can make for an enjoyable meal, but the service gets frantic when the restaurant is busy. *Grand Cul de Sac. tel. 590/27-82-42. Reservations advised. AE, MC, V. Closed Thurs.*

$-$$ ★ **L'Escale.** Great food, ambience, and views draw locals and visitors alike to this open-air restaurant, at the water's edge on the far side of Gustavia's harbor. The varied menu includes a wide range of pasta (lasagna, tortellini, ravioli, plus spaghetti with marinara, Bolognese, and other sauces), as well as fresh local fish, veal scallopine in an assortment of sauces, steak tartare, chicken, and 12 kinds of pizza. Many dishes are cooked in a wood-burning oven. *Gustavia, tel. 590/27-81-06. Reservations required in season. MC, V. No lunch.*

$-$$ **Marigot Bay Club.** Have a seat at the dark-wood bar or at a table on the beam-ceiling patio, and take in the views of the colorful sailboats moored in the bay. The owner of this casual spot loves to fish, and often reels in the catch of the day himself. It might be grouper, tuna, red snapper, or yellowtail, and it's frequently served with a Creole sauce. Other specials here include veal sautéed with mushrooms and wine, filet mignon with green peppercorn sauce, chicken breast in creamy lime sauce, and fresh local lobster baked in the shell with Gruyère cheese. In season, lunch is also served. *Marigot, tel. 590/27-75-45. Reservations required. AE, MC, V. No dinner Sun; no lunch Mon. in season.*

$–$$ **Topolino.** This lesser-known but excellent (and very reasonably priced) Italian restaurant is set back from the road, within easy walking distance of St. Jean Beach. Linen tablecloths, freshly cut flowers, and dim lighting create a romantic evening atmosphere. The menu includes fresh seafood, grilled chicken and steaks, various veal dishes, a number of pasta choices, and thin-crusted pizzas. There is a happy hour from 6 to 7, and live entertainment almost every night. The wine list has a number of fine, inexpensive choices. *St. Jean, tel. 590/27–70–92. Reservations advised. MC, V. No lunch.*

¢–$ **Brasserie La Créole.** Right in the center of the St. Jean shopping arcade is this casual brasserie with indoor seating, a comfortable bar, and outdoor umbrella tables. Drop by in the morning for freshly baked croissants and magnificent coffee. At lunch try the *croque-monsieur,* a hot sandwich of thin-sliced ham and Gruyère cheese. There is a full breakfast menu, and from noon until late in the evening the restaurant serves sandwiches, salads, and various beef, chicken, and fish entrées. *St. Jean, tel. 590/27–68–09. AE. Open daily 7 AM–midnight.*

¢ **Bar de l'Oubli.** This strategically located bistro/bar is a favorite watering hole of French expatriates and a great spot for people-watching. Come for delicious omelets, salads, and croques-monsieurs. *Gustavia, corner of rues de la France and de la République, no phone. No credit cards.*

¢ **La Luna.** This tiny restaurant with terrace is rapidly becoming an early evening hot spot. Locals love the "ambience très sympathique" and the Mexican/Creole fare, including sensational salads. Try the conch or Cannonball (crab, conch, and cheese). *Gustavia, no phone. No credit cards.*

¢ **Le Select.** Catty-corner from Bar de l'Oubli on the busiest corner in town, this atmospheric spot is popular with a crowd of Americans and nautical types. The bar is decorated with assorted memorabilia, including postcards from exotic ports of call and yellowing magazine covers. Cheeseburger in Paradise, a snack bar named for the song by honorary St. Barthian Jimmy Buffet, occupies the adjoining garden and serves typical fast-food fare. *Gustavia, corner of rues de la France and de la République, tel. 590/27–86–87. No credit cards.*

¢ **Santa Fe.** The hamburgers are the island's best and the view of the sunset is almost as good. On Sunday afternoons the place is jammed with Americans and Brits cheering their favorite sports teams on the TV. *Morne Lurin, tel. 590/27–61–04. No credit cards. Closed Mon.*

Lodging

Expect to be shocked at accommodation prices here. You pay for the privilege of staying on the island rather than for the hotel. Even at $500 a night, bedrooms tend to be small, but that does not diminish the lure of St. Barts for those who can afford it. Away from the beaches are a number of small hotels and a multitude of rental bungalows that offer less expensive accommodations, though staying at these means you'll need a car to get to the beach. For cheaper lodging on or within walking distance of a beach, head for St. Jean. It (and to a lesser extent Flamands and Grand Cul de Sac) offers the greatest variety of accommodations, as well as restaurants, shops, and activities. Unlike some islands, St. Barts has few charming guest houses. It does have villas, however; more modest ones offer a tremendous savings, especially if you're willing to forgo a pool, TV, or ocean view. Most of the top hotels close for a month or two during the off-season, but that shouldn't concern budget travelers: Even the 50% discount these offer when they *are* open during off-season won't bring their rates below astronomical. Most hotels here offer Continental (CP) or European (EP) meal plans, although the Modified American Plan (MAP) is sometimes available.

Hotels may have as many as six different rate periods during a year. The highest rates are in effect from mid-December to early January, and hotels are booked far in advance for this holiday period. Rates used for the listings below are for the second highest period, early January through April—still in season, but not the holiday peak. At all other times, rates are usually lower. If you are flexible in your planning, you can save a good deal of money.

Highly recommended lodgings are indicated by a star ★.

Category	Cost*
$$	$175–$225
$	$125–$175
¢	under $125

**All prices are for a standard double room, excluding a 10%–15% service charge; there is no government room tax. To estimate rates for hotels offering MAP, add about $50–$60 per person per day to the above price ranges.*

Hotels

$$ **Eden Rock.** Set on a craggy bluff that abruptly splits St. Jean Beach is St. Barts's first hotel, opened in the '50s by Rémy de Haenen and lovingly restored by his granddaughter. The six rooms have been spiffed up with four-poster beds, tropical print fabrics, mosquito netting, sparkling silver fixtures, and minibars. The terra-cotta floors are original, as are the stunning views of St. Jean Bay. You can breakfast in the restaurant or in your room. The open-air bar and French-Creole barbecue restaurant, which stretch along the top of the rock, are great places to enjoy the sea breeze and watch the frigate birds dive for fish. *St. Jean 97133, tel. 590/27–72–94, fax 590/27–88–37. 6 rooms. Facilities: restaurant, bar. MC, V. CP.*

$$ **Grand Cul De Sac Beach Hotel** and **St. Barths Beach Hotel.** These side-by-side properties stretch out on a narrow peninsula between lagoon and sea. Both are comfortable, unpretentious, and popular with families and tour groups, who take advantage of the full range of sports available on the hotels' beach. Upper-level rooms are best at the two-story St. Barths Beach Hotel; the best rooms at Grand Cul de Sac Beach Hotel, a group of small air-conditioned bungalow units with kitchenettes, are right on the beach. There's limited parking for cars not rented through the owner's agency. *Box 81, Grand Cul de Sac 97133, tel. 590/27–60–70, fax 590/27–75–57. 36 rooms. Facilities: 2 restaurants, bar, saltwater pool, tennis court, gym, windsurfing school and water-sports center, TV/library room, car rental, boutique. AE, MC, V. EP.*

$$ **Marigot Bay Club.** Jean Michel Ledee's pleasant apartments across from his popular seaside restaurant have comfortable furniture, tile floors, louvered doors and windows, air-conditioning, twin beds, living areas with kitchenette, and large terraces (no phones). It's a 5- to 10-minute walk to the nearest beach. The art gallery on the property is well worth a visit. *Marigot 97133, tel. 590/27–75–45, fax 590/27–90–04. 6 apartments. Facilities: restaurant, bar. AE, MC, V. EP.*

$$ **Sea Horse Hotel.** This secluded, quiet property has four buildings set in a beautifully landscaped garden. All suites have a living room, fully equipped kitchen, and a large terrace with a view of Marigot Bay, and are decorated with pastel floral drapes and spreads. They're not elegant or brand new, but they're a good value. There's a barbecue area for guests to use. Children under 12 are free. The beach is within walking distance. The management is enthusiastic and friendly. *Marigot 97133, tel. 590/27–75–36 or 800/932–3222, fax 590/27–85–33. 11 suites. Facilities: pool, bar, snorkeling gear, complimentary airport transfers, baby-sitting. AE, MC, V. EP.*

$$ **White Sand Beach Cottages.** The road in front of the place is a little ramshackle, but the tiny cottages are pleasant, air-conditioned, and have kitchenettes and semi-private terraces. There are steps down to a beautiful stretch of beach. The cottage on the beach is the best. A three-bedroom villa is also available. *Anse des Flamands 97133, tel. 590/27–82–08, fax 590/27–70–69. 4 cottages, 1 villa. Facilities: sundeck, AE, MC, V. EP.*

$–$$ **Baie des Anges.** These one-room coral and white cottages fronting Flamands Beach are simply but pleasantly appointed, with high beamed ceilings, wooden furniture, crisp white bedspreads, air-conditioning, kitchenettes, TVs, and phones. The pricier ones open onto the beach; less expensive cottages have partial water views and are only steps from the beach. A St. Barts family manages the property, and the warm atmosphere wins many repeat guests. Jean-Yves Froment, *the* artist of the island, has his studio here. *Anse de Flamands, tel. 590/27–63–61, fax 590/27–83–44. 9 cottages. Facilities: complimentary airport transfers, snack bar. MC, V. EP, CP.*

$–$$ **Baie des Flamands.** Families and tour groups frequent this motel-style hotel. Upper-level rooms have balconies, and lower-level ones, which are right on the beach, have terrace kitchenette units. All rooms have phones and air-conditioning, but upper-level rooms do not have TVs. One of the first hotels on the island, it is still run by a St. Barts family and has a gentle, laid-back island ambience. It has a good restaurant—La Frégate—and an outstanding beach location. A rental car is often included in the rate, and children under eight stay free with a parent. *Box 582, Anse des Flamands 97098, tel. 590/27–64–85 or 800/447–7462, fax 590/27–83–98. 24 rooms. Facilities: restaurant, bar, pool, rental cars. AE, MC, V. CP.*

$–$$ **Tropical Hotel.** You can walk downhill to St. Jean's Beach from this cozy pink-and-white gingerbread complex. Rooms are in long, low, motel-style buildings that encircle a lush garden and small pool. All have air-conditioning, TV, telephone, and minifridge. Red tile floors contrast nicely with either fresh pastel or sparkling white furnishings. The ambience is friendly. *Box 147, St. Jean 97095, tel. 590/27–64–87, fax 590/27–81–74. 20 rooms. Facilities: bar, small pool, snack bar. AE, MC, V. CP.*

$–$$ ★ **Village St. Jean.** The second generation of the Charneau family now runs this popular cottage colony, which has acquired a strong following over the years. The accent is on service and affordability, and this is one of the best values on the island. Air-conditioned cottages are spacious, although a bit sparsely furnished (except for the newly refurbished two-bedroom cottages), and have open-air kitchenettes and patios. There are also six hotel rooms without kitchenettes but with refrigerators. Rooms are slowly being done over with elegant natural fabrics and dark wood furniture, including some teak pieces from Bali; some have beam ceilings and cheerful striped awnings and most have king-size beds. Renovations should be completed by press time. Units have a variety of views, from full ocean to almost none, and the units closest to the road are subject to the ongoing noise of minimoke engines struggling with the steep terrain. The open-air restaurant, Le Patio (*see* Dining, *above*), serves excellent Italian fare. From the hotel it is an easy five-minute walk down to popular St. Jean Beach and to a variety of stores and restaurants (the walk back up is a bit more strenuous). *Box 23, St. Jean 97098, tel. 590/27–61–39, fax 590/27–77–96. 6 rooms, 20 cottages. Facilities: restaurant, bar, pool, small grocery, boutique, game room, library. MC, V. EP.*

¢–$$ **Castelets.** The views are breathtaking at this exclusive retreat atop Morne Lurin. Antiques-furnished rooms are in terraced chalets (with the exception of two in the main house) connected by steep paths. The sizes of the rooms vary greatly, as do their prices: The smallest are actually in the ¢ category, while the large suite is astronomically priced. Since the hotel is inland and off by itself, you will need a car. It's a very steep five-minute drive down to Gustavia or the nearest beach. The well-known hotel restaurant now features lighter (and less expensive) fare than in the past. *Box 60, Morne Lurin 97133, tel. 590/27–61–73 or 800/223–1108, fax 590/27–85–27. 10 rooms, 1 2-bedroom suite. Facilities: restaurant, small pool. AE, MC, V. CP.*

$ **Auberge de la Petite Anse.** Rooms in the eight bungalows here may be short on decor, but they're and have terraces, kitchenettes, and air-conditioning. There's a small beach just below the property, down a rocky path; and the gorgeous strip of Anse des Flamands beach is only a five-minute walk away. A grocery store, bar, and restaurant are also within walking distance. *Box 117, Anse des Flamands, tel. 590/27–64–60, fax 590/27–72–30. 16 bungalows. AE.*

$ ★ **Hostellerie des Trois Forces.** This rustic, fairly isolated mountaintop inn is an idiosyncratic delight, with a string of tiny, gingerbread-trimmed West Indian–style cottages charmingly decorated according to astrological color schemes (Libra is soft blue; Leo, bright red; etc.). All have a minibar, a terrace with a breathtaking ocean view, and air-conditioning or a ceiling fan. Most have four-poster beds. The tinkle of chimes floats through the pleasant restaurant. Astrologer Hubert de la Motte (he's a Gemini, by the way) is the personable owner and talented chef, and he may even arrange a reading for you.* *The slogan of the rustic restaurant is Food is Love. *Morne Vitet, tel. 590/27–61–25, fax 590/27–81–38. 8 rooms. Facilities: restaurant, bar, pool. AE, MC, V. EP.*

$ ★ **Le P'tit Morne.** There is good value in these modestly furnished mountainside studios, each with a private balcony, air-conditioning, and panoramic views of the coastline below. Small kitchenettes are adequate for cooking light meals or making picnic lunches, and there's a snack bar that serves breakfast. It's relatively isolated here, and the beach is a 10-minute drive away. In the low season, this rates are in the ¢ category. *Box 14, Colombier 97133, tel. 590/27–62–64, fax 590/27–84–63. 14 rooms. Facilities: small pool, snack bar, reading room. AE, MC, V. CP.*

¢–$ **La Normandie.** This small inn offers reasonably priced rooms, a restaurant, and dancing in the evening on a glass floor set over the pool. Ask for one of the two air-conditioned rooms. You can walk to the beach from here (about 10 minutes). *Lorient 97133, tel. 590/27–61–66, fax 590/27–68–64. 8 rooms. Facilities: pool, restaurant. V. EP.*

¢–$ ★ **Les Mouettes.** Six spacious bungalows overlook the island's best surfing beach. Each has a bathroom with shower, a kitchenette, a patio, two double beds, and a twin bed or foldout sofa. A good bet for families. *Lorient 97133, tel. 590/27–60–74. 6 rooms. Facilities: car rental. No credit cards. EP.*

¢ **La Presqu'ile.** This slightly dilapidated hotel is on the far side of the Gustavia marina. Rooms are small, basic, and unadorned, but they are clean and air-conditioned. All have shower baths, and most have refrigerators. The brightest rooms are those with a marina view. Shell Beach is a 10-minute walk away. *Gustavia, tel. 590/27–64–60, fax 590/27–72–30. 12 rooms. No credit cards. EP.*

¢ **Sunset Hotel.** This basic hotel is located on the main drag of Gustavia, overlooking the marina. Spartan rooms are clean and have air-conditioning, shower baths, and refrigerators. The smaller rooms have no view, but are quieter. It's a 15–20-minute walk to Shell Beach. *Gustavia, tel. 590/26–77–21, fax 590/27–83–40. 8 rooms. MC, V. CP.*

Villas, Condos, Apartments

For the price of an inexpensive hotel room, you can get your own little cottage, and for the price of a room at an expensive hotel, you'll get a villa with several bedrooms and your own swimming pool. Moreover, the island's restaurants are so expensive that having a kitchen of your own makes sense. What you sacrifice in room service and the amenities of a hotel, you'll gain in privacy, more room, and money saved. Don't forget to factor in the almost always necessary cost of car rental. Villas, apartments, and condos can be rented through **Sibarth** (tel. 590/27–62–38), which handles more than 200 properties. **WIMCO** (tel. 800/932–3222) is the agency's representative in the United States. Rents range from $900 to $2,000 per week for one-bedroom villas, $1,600–$7,00 for two- and three-bedroom villas.

Off-Season Bets As noted above, very few of the expensive properties qualify as $$ during the off-season, even at 50% reductions. Among the charming hotels whose prices drop sufficiently in low season are the casually chic **El Sereno Beach Hotel and Villas** at Grand Cul de Sac Beach (Box 19, Grand Cul de Sac 97095, tel. 590/27–64–80); **Filao Beach** (Box 667, St. Jean 97099, tel. 590/27–64–84), a member of the prestigious Relais & Châteaux group; and the colonial-style François Plantation (Colombier 97133, tel. 590/27–78–82), in the hills above Flamands. Note that many of the top hotels here close in September and October.

Nightlife

St. Barts is a mostly-in-bed-by-midnight island—there are no casinos, no movie theaters, and only a few discos. There are many special places to go for the cocktail hour, and some of the hotels and restaurants provide late-night fun. Cocktail hour finds a crowd at **Le Repaire** (Gustavia, tel. 590/27–72–48). The barefoot boating set gathers in the boisterous garden of Gustavia's **Le Select** (tel. 590/27–86–87). Those in search of quiet conversation and some gentle piano at the day's end head up the hill to the **Carl Gustaf** (tel. 590/27–82–83), which is Gustavia's best sunset-watching spot. Both the **Manapany** (tel. 590/27–66–55) and the **Guanahani** (tel. 590/27–66–60) also have piano bars. After dinner, the locals head to **Le Pélican** (St. Jean, tel. 590/27–64–64) for live music. The retro-hip (there's a 1968 Cadillac Eldorado outside and lots of neon inside) **American Bar** (tel. 590/27–86–07) at L'Escale restaurant is another after-dinner hangout. There's a popular *après-dîner* cabaret show nightly at **Club La Banane** (tel. 590/27–68–25). For real late-night activity, head to Gustavia's **Le Petit Club** (tel. 590/27–66–33) and **Bar de l'Oubli** (tel. 590/27–70–06). On Friday and Saturday you can also check out the **Why Not?** (tel. 590/27–68–61) disco, near Gustavia.

20 St. Eustatius

Updated by Marcy Pritchard

The flight approach to the tiny Dutch island of St. Eustatius (often called Statia, which is pronounced *stay*-sha), in the Netherlands Antilles, is almost worth the visit itself. The plane circles The Quill, a 1,968-foot-high extinct volcano that encloses a stunning primeval rain forest within its crater. Here you'll find giant elephant ears, ferns, flowers, wild orchids, fruit trees, wildlife, and birds hiding in the trees. The entire island is alive with untended greenery—bougainvillea, oleander, and hibiscus.

Sleepy Statia is one of the few "undiscovered" Caribbean destinations left, which translates into superb bargains. There's no official high season; all but the three priciest properties offer the same year-round rates. You won't find high-rise developments, traffic lights, cruise ships, or package deals (they'd be redundant on a tropical isle whose rates are already a steal). You *will* find splendid hiking and diving, friendly people, and deserted black-sand beaches. Most visitors are content with a day visit from nearby St. Maarten. But should you stay over, you'll discover an unusual island that attracts a funky mix of European expatriates and young Dutch on holiday. Perhaps the locals are the best reason to visit this island. Statians are warm, welcoming, and happy to stop and chat. People still say hello to strangers here—when passing drivers beep or wave, return the gesture. This is one of the very few remaining islands where tourists will not feel that locals resent their perceived wealth and luxurious lifestyle.

Statia is in the Dutch Windward Triangle, 178 miles east of Puerto Rico and 35 miles south of St. Maarten. Oranjestad, the capital and only "city" (note quotes), is on the western side facing the Caribbean. The island is anchored at the north and the south by extinct volcanoes, like the Quill, that are separated by a central plain. The island is a wonderful playground for hikers and divers. Myriad ancient ships rest on the ocean floor alongside 18th-century warehouses that were slowly buried in the sea by storms.

This 12-square-mile island, past which Columbus sailed in 1493, had prospered almost from the day the Dutch Zeelanders colonized it in 1636. In the 1700s, a double row of warehouses crammed with goods stretched for a mile along the bay, and there were sometimes as many as 200 ships tied up at the duty-free port. The island was called the Emporium of the Western World and Golden Rock. Holland, England, and France fought one another for possession of the island, which changed hands 22 times. In 1816, it became a Dutch possession and has remained so to this day.

During the American Revolution, when the British blockaded the North American coast, food, arms, and other supplies for the revolutionaries were diverted through the West Indies, notably through neutral Statia. On November 16, 1776, the brig-of-war *Andrew Doria*, commanded by Captain Isaiah Robinson of the Continental Navy, sailed into Statia's port flying the Stars and Stripes and fired a 13-gun salute to the Royal Netherlands standard. Governor Johannes de Graaff ordered the cannons of Fort Oranje to return the salute, and that first official acknowledgment of the new American flag by a foreign power earned Statia the nickname "America's Childhood Friend." In retaliation, British Admiral George Rodney attacked and destroyed the island in 1781. Statia has yet to recover its prosperity, which, ironically, ended partly because of the success of the American Revolution: The island was no longer needed as a transshipment port, and its bustling economy gradually came to a stop.

What It Will Cost An inexpensive efficiency apartment with bath and kitchenette will cost about $50 a day. For a moderately priced dinner, expect to pay about $20; picnic fixings for two are about $10. A glass of wine or a rum punch at a restaurant costs about $2.50; two beers and live music at a local spot will be about $5. Car rental is $40–$45 daily. A taxi from the airport to town is about $3.50. A single-tank dive is about $40 a person; snorkel equipment rents for about $5.

Before You Go

Tourist Information Contact the **Caribbean Tourism Organization** (20 E. 46th St., New York, NY 10017-2452, tel. 212/682–0435). You may also contact the **tourist board** on the island (Oranjestad, St. Eustatius, Netherlands Antilles, tel. 599/38–2433) which is very willing to advise you on any aspect of planning a trip to Statia. Although telephone communications are good, it can take several weeks for mail to get through.

Arriving and Departing
By Plane **Windward Islands Airways** (Winair, tel. 599/5–54230 or 599/5–54210) makes the 20-minute flight from St. Maarten five times a day, the 10-minute flight from Saba daily, and the 15-minute flight from St. Kitts twice a week. Be sure to confirm your flight a day or two in advance, as schedules can change abruptly.

From the Airport Planes put down at the **Franklin Delano Roosevelt Airport,** where taxis meet all flights and charge about $3.50 for the drive into town. There's an Avis outlet at the airport, should you decide to rent a car (*see* Getting Around, *below*).

Passports and Visas All visitors must have proof of citizenship. A passport is preferred, but a birth certificate or voter registration card will do. (A driver's license will *not* do.) British citizens need a valid passport. All visitors need a return or ongoing ticket.

Language Statia's official language is Dutch (it's used on government documents), but everyone speaks English. Dutch is taught as the primary language in the schools, and street signs are in both Dutch and English.

Staying in St. Eustatius

Important Addresses **Tourist Office:** The **St. Eustatius Tourist Office** is at the entrance to Fort Oranje (3 Fort Oranjestraat, tel. 599/38–2433). Office hours are weekdays 8–noon and 1–5.

Emergencies **Police:** tel. 599/38–2333. **Hospitals: Queen Beatrix Medical Center** (25 Prinsesweg, tel. 599/38–2211 and 599/38–2371) has a full-time licensed physician on duty.

Currency U.S. dollars are accepted everywhere, but legal tender is the Netherlands Antilles florin (NAf). Florins are also referred to as guilders. The exchange rate fluctuates but is about NAf 1.75 to U.S. $1. Prices quoted here are in U.S. dollars unless noted otherwise.

Taxes and Service Charges Hotels collect a 7% government tax. All hotels, and most restaurants, add a 10–15% service charge. The departure tax is $5 for flights to other islands of the Netherlands Antilles and $10 to foreign destinations. You may be asked at the airport to contribute your leftover guilders to the latest cause.

Getting Around If you stay in or around Oranjestad, you can get by without a car. Most of the historical sites, restaurants, and Smoke Alley Beach are easily accessible on foot. Public transportation is nonexistent. A car is advisable if you're staying outside Oranjestad, although most people seem to hitchhike (it's considered completely safe here). The hardy can walk virtually everywhere. The island is so small that any taxi ride will cost no more than $10. To explore the island (and there isn't very much), car rentals are available through the **Avis** outlet at the airport (tel. 599/38–2421 and 800/331–1084) for $40–$45 per day. **Rainbow Car Rental** (tel. 599/38–2811) has several Hyundais for rent. **Brown's** (tel. 599/38–2266) and **Lady Ama's Services** (tel. 599/38–2451) rent cars and Jeeps. Statia's roads are pocked with potholes, and the going is slow and bumpy. Goats and cattle have the right-of-way. Bikes are not recommended here.

Telephones and Mail Statia has microwave telephone service to all parts of the world. To call Statia from the United States, dial 011 + 599 + 38 + the local number. When making a local call within Statia, just dial the last four digits. Direct dial is available. There are two pay phones on the island, one in Landsradio, and one near the airport. Airmail letters to the United States are NAf 1.30; postcards NAf .60.

Opening and Closing Times Most offices are open weekdays 8–noon and 1–4 or 5. **Barclays Bank** is open weekdays 8–2; **Windward Islands Bank** is open Monday–Thursday 8:30–noon and 1–3:30, Friday 8:30–noon and 2–4:30. Both are in Upper Town.

Guided Tours All 10 of Statia's taxis are available for island tours. A full day's outing costs $35 per vehicle, usually including airport transfer.

Exploring St. Eustatius

Numbers in the margin correspond to points of interest on the St. Eustatius map.

The major attractions of Statia are Oranjestad and The Quill. A guided island tour (*see above*) can be accomplished in about three hours.

Oranjestad
1 Statia's capital and only town, **Oranjestad** sits on the western coast facing the Caribbean. It's a split-level town: Upper Town and Lower Town. History buffs will enjoy poking around the ancient Dutch Colonial buildings, which are being restored by the Historical Foundation. Both Upper Town and Lower Town are easily explored on foot.

The first stop is the **Tourist Office,** which is right at the entrance to Fort Oranje. You can pick up maps, brochures, and a listing of 12 marked hiking trails. You can also arrange for guides and guided tours.

2 When you leave the Tourist Office, you will be at the entrance to **Fort Oranje.** With its three bastions, the fort has clutched these cliffs since 1636. In 1976, Statia participated in the U.S. bicentennial celebration by restoring the old fort, and now the black cannons point out over the ramparts. In the parade grounds a plaque, presented in 1939 by Franklin D. Roosevelt, reads, "Here the sovereignty of the United States of America was first formally acknowledged to a national vessel by a foreign official." The post office used to be in the fort, but it burned in 1991. There are plans under way to rebuild the structure to house boutiques and restaurants.

From the fort, cross over to Wilhelminaweg (Wilhelmina Way) in the center of Upper Town. The award-winning **St. Eustatius Historical Foundation Museum** is in the Doncker/de Graaff house, a lovely building with slim columns and a high gallery. British Admiral Rodney, who captured Oranjestad and confiscated islanders' possessions in the 18th century, set up his headquarters here. The house, acquired by the foundation in 1983 and completely restored, is Statia's most important intact 18th-century dwelling. Exhibits trace the island's history from the 6th century to the present. The basement exhibit details Statia's pre-Columbian history with the results of archaeological digs on the island. Ruins and artifacts of a newly discovered tribe called the Saladoid have been excavated. *12 Van Tonningenweg, tel. 599/38–2288. Admission: $2 adults, $1 children. Open weekdays 9–5, weekends 9–noon.*

The museum also sells a sightseeing package, which includes a guided walking tour, a booklet detailing the sites on the tour, and museum admission. The tour begins in Lower Town at the Marina and ends at the museum. You can take the tour on your own with the book (there are corresponding numbered blue signs on most of the sites), but a guide may prove more illuminating.

Return to Fort Oranjestraat (Fort Orange St.) and turn left. Continue to Kerkweg (Church Way) and turn right. A little further on the right you'll find the **Dutch Reformed church,** built in 1775. It has been partially restored and has lovely stone arches facing the sea. Ancient tales can be read on the gravestones in the 18th-century cemetery adjacent to the church.

Continue on Kerkweg and take the next two left turns onto Synagogepad (Synagogue Path) to **Honen Dalim** ("She Who Is Charitable to the Poor"), one of the Caribbean's oldest synagogues. Dating from 1738, it is now in ruins, but is slated for restoration by groups from the United States and Holland.

Follow Prinsesweg back to the main square and zigzag down the cobblestone Fort Road to Lower Town. Most of the 18th-century warehouses and shops here are in disrepair, but the restoration of the 18th-century cotton mill on the land side of Bay Road, now the **Old Gin House Hotel,** is impressive. The palms, flowering shrubs, and park benches along the water's edge are the work of the Historical Foundation members. All along the beach are the crumbling ruins of 18th-century buildings, dating from Statia's period of prosperity. The sea, which has slowly advanced since then, now surrounds many of the ruins, making for fascinating snorkeling.

3 **The Quill,** the volcanic cone rising in the southern sector, is 3 miles south of Oranjestad on the main road. Most people drive to the slopes and then park their cars alongside the road; the main trails begin from Welfare Road. Most of the various routes are fairly easy, and all afford sensational views of Oranjestad and surrounding Caribbean islands. The truly challenging treks are the Panoramic route surrounding the crater and those descending into the rain for-

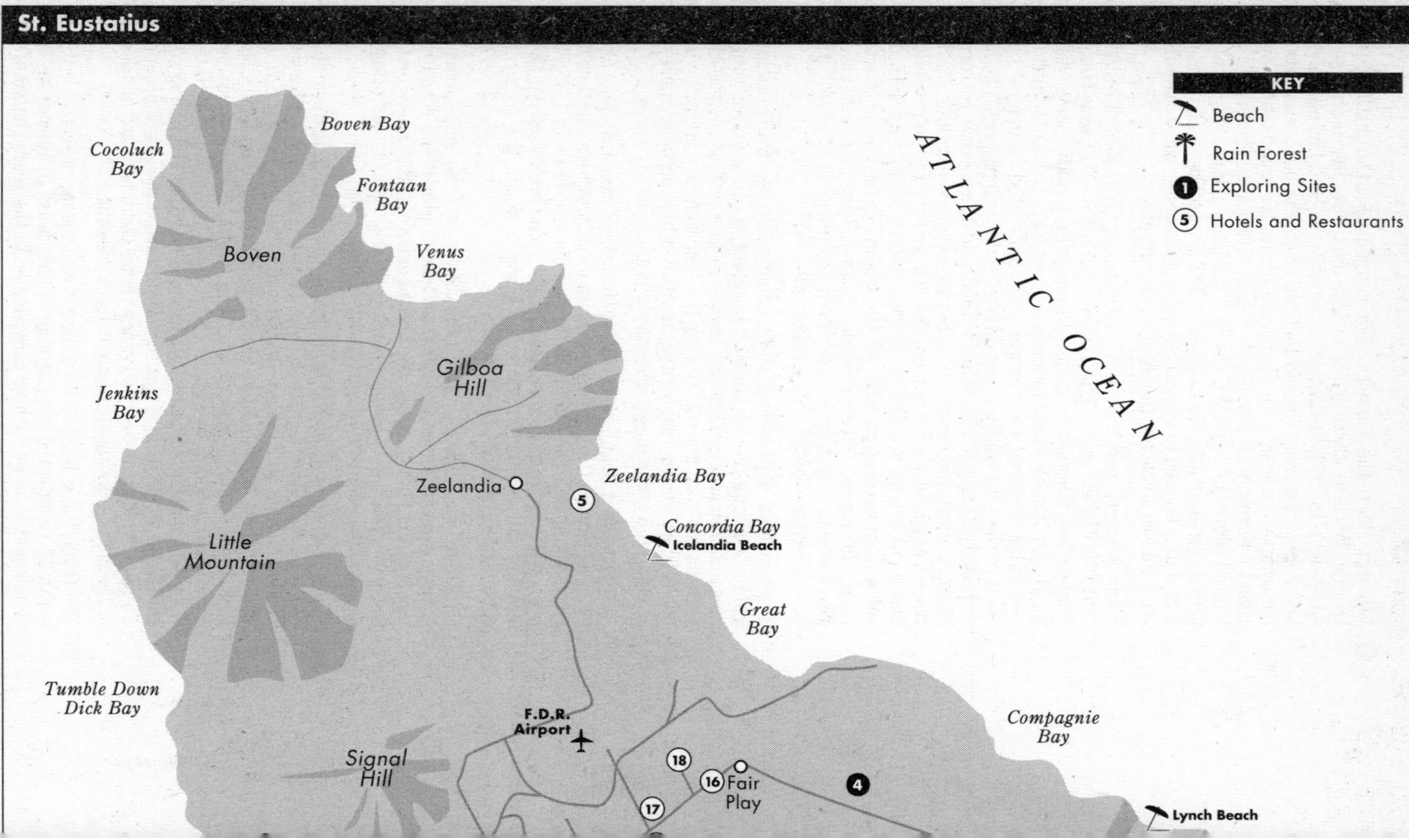
St. Eustatius
KEY
Beach
Rain Forest
Exploring Sites
Hotels and Restaurants
ATLANTIC OCEAN
Boven Bay
Cocoluch Bay
Fontaan Bay
Boven
Venus Bay
Gilboa Hill
Jenkins Bay
Zeelandia
5
Zeelandia Bay
Concordia Bay
Icelandia Beach
Little Mountain
Great Bay
Tumble Down Dick Bay
F.D.R. Airport
Compagnie Bay
Signal Hill
18
16
Fair Play
4
17
Lynch Beach

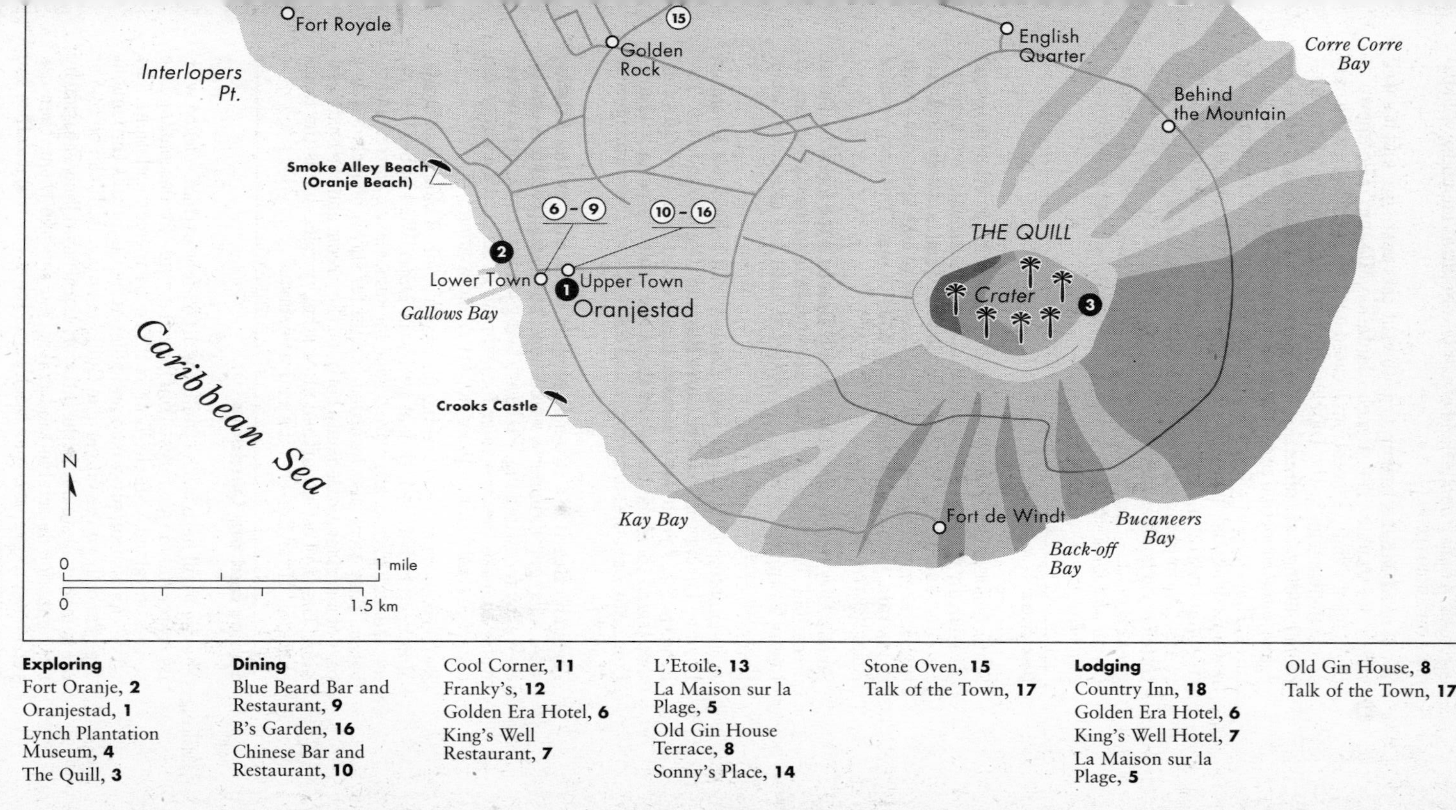

Exploring
Fort Oranje, **2**
Oranjestad, **1**
Lynch Plantation Museum, **4**
The Quill, **3**

Dining
Blue Beard Bar and Restaurant, **9**
B's Garden, **16**
Chinese Bar and Restaurant, **10**
Cool Corner, **11**
Franky's, **12**
Golden Era Hotel, **6**
King's Well Restaurant, **7**
L'Etoile, **13**
La Maison sur la Plage, **5**
Old Gin House Terrace, **8**
Sonny's Place, **14**
Stone Oven, **15**
Talk of the Town, **17**

Lodging
Country Inn, **18**
Golden Era Hotel, **6**
King's Well Hotel, **7**
La Maison sur la Plage, **5**
Old Gin House, **8**
Talk of the Town, **17**

est itself, a dense wonderland of exotic vegetation including wild banana and lime trees.

You'll need either a taxi or a car to visit this next site, and it's well
4 worth the trouble. The **Lynch Plantation Museum,** also known as the Berkel Family Plantation, located out in Lynch Bay, is the only domestic museum in the Dutch Caribbean. It consists of two one-room buildings, set up as they were almost 100 years ago. There's a remarkable collection preserving this family's history—family pictures, Bibles, spectacles, a sewing machine, original furniture, and some farming and fishing implements that give a detailed perspective of life in Statia. Ismael Berkel guides tours of the houses, and if you ask, he might proudly show you his two medals of honor from the Dutch royal families for his conservation efforts. Be sure to sign the guest register. *Lynch Bay, tours by appointment (call the Tourist Office at 599/38–2209 to arrange). Admission free; donations accepted.*

Beaches

Statia is not an island for beach lovers. Beaches are rather poky and occasionally rocky. The nicest are on the Atlantic side, but here the water is generally too rough for swimming. Sand is mainly black (actually varying shades of gray). It is possible to hike around the coast at low tide, though a car is recommended to reach the more remote Atlantic stretches.

Smoke Alley Beach (also called **Oranje Beach**) is the nicest and most accessible. The beige-and-black-sand beach is on the Caribbean, off Lower Town, and is relatively deserted until late afternoon, when the locals arrive.

A 30-minute hike down an easy marked trail behind the Mountain Road will bring you to **Corre Corre Bay** and its gold-sand cove. Two bends north, **Lynch Bay** is somewhat protected from the wild swells that pound the Atlantic side of the island. Here, especially around Concordia Bay, the surf is rough and there is sometimes a dangerous undertow.

Zeelandia Beach is a two-mile strip of black sand on the Atlantic side. A dangerous undertow runs here, but a small section is considered okay for swimming. Plans are being made to construct a breakwater to make the area safer for swimming. As is, it's a lovely and deserted stretch for sunning, walking, and wading.

Beachcombers enjoy searching for Statia's famed blue glass beads. Manufactured in the 17th century by the Dutch West Indies Company, the blue glass beads were traded for rum, slaves, cotton, and tobacco. They were also awarded to faithful slaves or included as a part of marriage settlements between the groom and the bride's father. They're best unearthed after a heavy rain, but as the locals chuckle, "If you find one, it's a miracle, man."

Sports and the Outdoors

Hiking The big thrill here is The Quill, the 1,968-foot extinct volcano with its crater full of rain forest. You'll need a guide for descending into the crater (about $20); the Tourist Office has recommendations. The office can also supply a map and a list of marked trails throughout the island. If you're hiking The Quill, wear layers: It can be cool at the summit and steamy in the interior. Local boys climb The Quill by torchlight for delectable sand crabs. You can join them, then ask your hotel to prepare your catch for dinner. The tourist office can make arrangements.

Horseback Riding Eric and Sabra Pressman (tel. 599/38–2760) run a stable and offer trail rides, beach rides, and lessons.

Scuba Diving Statia has more than 30 dive sites, including **Barracuda Reef,** where barracudas swim around colorful coral walls, and **Double Wreck,** where coral has taken on the shape of the two disintegrated ships. **Dive Statia** (tel. 599/38–2435, fax 599/38–2539), a fully equipped and PADI-certified dive shop offering certification courses, is operated by Rudy and Rinda Hees out of a warehouse just down the road from the Old Gin House. Several hotels offer dive packages with Dive Statia, including the Golden Era, the Old Gin House, Kings Well, and Talk of the Town. Courses are also available in underwater photography, night diving, and multi-level diving. Count on spending $40–$50 for single-tank dives. Buying a week package will get you a discount.

Snorkeling Crooks Castle has several stands of pillar coral, giant yellow sea fans, and sea whips. Jenkins Bay and Venus Bay are other favorites with snorkelers. For equipment rental, contact **Dive Statia** (*see* Scuba Diving, *above*). Daily rentals are about $5; trips about $20.

Spectator Sports Cricket and soccer matches are played at the Sports Complex in Upper Town. Statia hosts teams from other Caribbean islands on weekends; admission is free. Call the office of the Sports Coordinator (tel. 599/38–2209) for schedules.

Tennis At the **Community Center** (tel. 599/38–2249) there's a lone tennis court that's even lighted at night. It has changing rooms, but you'll have to bring your own rackets and balls. The cost is $2. Volleyball and basketball are also played here.

Shopping

Shopping on Statia is duty-free and somewhat limited. Barbara Lane shows her own sophisticated ceramic pieces, together with paintings and woven sculptures by local artists, at **The Park Place Gallery** (tel. 599/38–2452) across from the Cool Corner in the center of town. **Mazinga Gift Shop** (tel. 599/38–2245) on Fort Oranjestraat in Upper Town is a small department store selling jewelry, cosmetics, liquor, beachwear, sports gear, stationery, books, and magazines. The **Paper Store** (Van Tonningen Weg, Upper Town, tel. 599/38–2208) sells magazines, a few books, and stationery supplies. Check out **The Fun Shop** (Van Tonningen Weg, Upper Town, tel. 599/38–82253) for toys and souvenirs.

Dining

Just about everything here is affordable, especially local eateries. You'll likely run into the same crowd wherever you go. The variety of cuisines here is unexpected, given the size of the island. Besides the traditional West Indian fare, you can find French and Chinese food. All restaurants are casual, but do cover up your beachwear.

If you'd rather cook in, there are five supermarkets concentrated around the capital. Best are **Windward Islands Agencies** (Heiligerweg, tel. 599/38–2372) and **Duggin's Shopping Center** (DeWindtweg, tel. 599/38–2241). Go on Monday or Tuesday for the best selection. Bread fanatics should stop by the **Sandbox Tree Bakery** (Kirk Weg, Upper Town, tel. 599/38–2469) for pastries, breads, pizza, and sandwiches.

Highly recommended restaurants are indicated by a star ★.

Category	Cost*
$$	$20–$25
$	$10–$20
¢	under $10

per person, excluding drinks and service

$$ **B's Garden.** This patio spot in the courtyard next to the tourist office serves sandwiches and burgers—good enough to satisfy any homesick American—at lunch, and local cuisine, such as baked snapper with shrimp sauce and tenderloin steak with green peppercorn sauce, at dinner. The courtyard is surrounded by the beautiful old stone Fort and government buildings. *Oranjestraat, Upper Town, tel. 599/38–2733. No credit cards. Lunch daily, dinner Tues. and Sat.*

$$ **Golden Era Hotel.** The restaurant and bar of this establishment are somewhat stark, but the Creole food is excellent and the large dining room is right on the water. Sunday-night buffets, a steal at $14, are popular, served outside by the pool and ocean, with a local band providing entertainment. *Bay Rd., Lower Town, Oranjestad, tel. 599/38–2345. AE, D, MC, V.*

$$ **King's Well Restaurant.** "Good food, cold drinks and easy prices" reads the hand-painted sign at this breezy terrace eatery overlooking the sea, run by a fun-loving expatriate couple. The steaks are from Colorado, the lobster is fresh, and the *rostbraten* (roast beef) and schnitzels are authentic—one of the owners is German. *Bay Rd., Lower Town, Oranjestad, tel. 599/38–2538. Reservations advised. MC, V.*

$$ **La Maison sur la Plage.** The view here is of the Atlantic, and the fare is French. The two chefs (one the owner, the other is well-known in St. Barts restaurant circles) prepare some of the finest cuisine on the island. For dinner, start with the escargots and move on to the veal terrine with mushrooms and an herb sauce, served with a pastry top, or try the lamb medallions broiled with Roquefort cheese. Pastas are also available. Renovations under way in the restaurant will add a waterfall and a dark blue ceiling with lights simulating a starry night. *La Maison sur la Plage hotel, Zeelandia Rd., Zeelandia, tel. 599/38–2256. Reservations advised. MC, V.*

$$ ★ **Old Gin House Terrace.** Dining is delightful on the oceanside terrace across from the hotel. The menu may include lightly breaded stuffed crab, chicken salad, linguini Alfredo, New York strip steak, grouper fillet in lemon-dill sauce, and sandwiches. Lunch is more casual and offers lighter fare; dinner is by candlelight. Hearty breakfasts are also available. If renovations go as planned, dinner will soon be served in the old mansion, in an elegant, candlelit, brick dining room full of antiques. Call ahead to check—prices may rise out of our $$ range. *Lower Town, Oranjestad, tel. 599/38–2319. Reservations advised. DC, MC, V.*

$$ **Talk of the Town.** Breakfast, lunch, and dinner are served at this pleasant restaurant midway between the airport and town. Pink tablecloths, an abundance of hanging plants, and softly seductive calypso music in the background weave a romantic spell. Local, Continental, and American dishes are offered, with seafood (predictably) the standout. *L.E. Sadlerweg, near Upper Town, tel. 599/38–2236. AE, D, MC, V.*

¢–$$ ★ **Blue Bead Bar & Restaurant.** A friendly Dutch expatriate couple runs this new restaurant with spectacular water views—don't miss a sunset cocktail here. Meals are served on a cheery blue-and-yellow-trimmed veranda amid potted plants; the fare runs the gamut of influences: West Indian, Indonesian, Dutch, and American. The daily specials are recommended, as is anything made with owner and chef Phil's own satay sauce—a spicy, peanutty heaven. A steel band plays here on Saturday nights; the bar swings long after the kitchen closes. *Bay Rd., Lower Town, tel. 599/38–2873. No credit cards.*

$ **Chinese Bar and Restaurant.** Owner Kim Cheng serves up tasty Oriental and Caribbean dishes—*bamigoreng* (Indonesian chow mein), pork chops Creole—in hearty portions at his unpretentious establishment. Dining indoors can be slightly claustrophobic, but just ask your waitress if you may tote your Formica-top table out onto the terrace. She'll probably be happy to lend a hand and then serve you under the stars. *Prinsesweg, Upper Town, Oranjestad, tel. 599/38–2389. No credit cards.*

$ ★ **Franky's.** Come here for good local barbecue: ribs, chicken, lobster, and fish served later than at most other places on Statia. Try the bull-foot soup and the goat-water stew. The less adventurous can get pizza. Weekend nights there's live music, and the Sunday evening happy hour is popular. *Ruyterweg, Upper Town, Oranjestad, tel. 599/38–2575. No credit cards.*

$ **L'Etoile.** West Indian dishes, such as spicy stuffed land crab and goat meat, are served at this simple snack bar/restaurant. You can also order hot dogs, hamburgers, and spareribs. *Heiligerweg, Upper Town, Oranjestad, tel. 599/38–2299. No credit cards.*

¢–$ **Stone Oven.** A Spanish couple runs this cozy little eatery, offering such West Indian specialties as goatwater stew. You can eat either indoors in the little house or outside on the palm-fringed patio. *16A Feaschweg, Upper Town, Oranjestad, tel. 599/38–2543. Reservations required. No credit cards.*

¢ **Cool Corner.** Grab a beer and some Chinese fare and join in the local gossip. This friendly bar/restaurant is right in the center of Upper Town, near the Tourist Office. *Fort Oranjestraat, tel. 599/38–2523. No credit cards. Closed Sun.*

¢ **Sonny's Place.** The enticing aromas of conch fritters and rotis emanate from this cheery open-air gazebo that often swings with live music on weekends and has a popular Sunday afternoon happy hour. Try the scrumptious fresh fruit juices for a quick pick-me-up. *Fort Oranjestraat, tel. 599/38–2609. No credit cards.*

Lodging

There are no luxury accommodations on Statia; as a rule, cheerful is the best you can expect. Many of the properties include breakfast, making most of them quite affordable.

Highly recommended lodgings are indicated by a star ★.

Category	Cost*
$$	$75–$100
$	$50–$75
¢	under $50

**All prices are for a standard double room for two, excluding 7% tax and a 10%–15% service charge.*

Hotels

$$ **Golden Era Hotel.** This is a harborfront hotel whose rooms are neat, air-conditioned, and motel-modern, with minifridges, TVs, and phones, and simple (sometimes old) furniture. All have little terraces, but only half have a full or partial view of the sea; the rest look out over concrete or down onto the roof of the restaurant. There is little that is aesthetically attractive about this hotel, but at least it is central, by the water, and enjoys a cheerful clientele and an accommodating and friendly staff. *Bay Rd., Box 109, Lower Town, Oranjestad, tel. 599/38–2345 or 800/223–6510, fax 599/38–2445. 19 rooms, 1 suite. Facilities: restaurant, bar, saltwater pool. AE, D, MC, V. EP.*

$$ **La Maison sur la Plage.** The main attraction of this isolated area is the Atlantic, whose wild waters slap the 2-mile crescent of gray sand. The undertow for much of the strip here can be dangerous, but there is a safer area a few minutes' walk down the beach. The hotel's cozy lobby has rattan furnishings, a checkerboard on the coffee table, and shelves filled with books. There's a stone-and-wood bar, and a *très* gourmet French restaurant bordered by a trellis and greenery. Owners Therese and Michel Viali are repainting, adding new roofs and louvered windows, renovating the restaurant (*see* Dining, *above*), and redecorating each of the five spartan cottages with pastel print spreads and drapes, natural wood furnishings, and ceiling fans. Rooms do not have TVs or phones. Continental breakfast is served on the porch of the main building, overlooking the water. *Zeelandia Rd., Box 157, Zeelandia, tel. 599/38–2256, fax 599/38–2831. 10 rooms with bath. Facilities: restaurant, bar, lounge, saltwater pool, volleyball on beach, putting green. MC, V. CP.*

$$ **Old Gin House.** This property, fashioned by American expatriate John May out of the ruins of an 18th-century cotton-gin factory and warehouse, was once known as one of the finest inns in the Caribbean. With brand new ownership (a resort interest from St. Kitts), hopes are high for major restoration and renewed luster. The main building is two stories high and has bougainvillea-swathed double balconies that overlook a secluded pool and courtyard. At press time, renovations of the elegant indoor dining room here were slated for completion by late 1995. Across the street, overlooking the sea, are the highly acclaimed Old Gin House Terrace restaurant and another building containing an additional six rooms. All the rooms, individually decorated with lovely antiques and artwork from the former owner's collection, have balconies. There are no phones, TV, or air conditioners—ceiling fans and ocean breezes cool the rooms. *Box 172, Oranjestad, tel. 599/38–2319. 20 rooms. Facilities: 2 restaurants, bar, lounge, pool, library. AE, D, DC, MC, V. EP.*

$–$$ **Kings Well Hotel.** Perched on the cliffs between Upper Town and Lower Town, this small hotel offers four rooms, each with water views, a balcony, minifridge, TV, and bath with shower only. The rooms are pleasant but sparsely furnished and don't have phones. The two back rooms are more spacious, offer the best views, have ceiling fans, and offer queen-size waterbeds—well worth the extra $20. The hotel is in the first stages of renovation; a new dining area and a combination pool-Jacuzzi were under construction at press time. The owners, an expatriate couple, hope to attract a sailing clientele; they will lease their yacht-charter license to interested parties and will also arrange sailing lessons. The restaurant serves a complimentary Continental breakfast, as well as lunch and dinner (*see* Dining, *above*). *Bay Rd., Lower Town, Oranjestad, tel. and fax 599/38–2538. 4 rooms. Facilities: bar, restaurant. MC, V. CP.*

$–$$ ★ **Talk of the Town.** These simple but bright rooms are decorated with locally handcrafted furnishings, dark carpeting, beamed ceilings, floral spreads, and local art. Four tidy cottages (nine rooms total) with red roofs and coral trim surround the pool. All rooms have air-conditioning, gleaming white baths with shower only, cable TV, and direct-dial phone. There is a swimming pool, a deck with lounge chairs, and a restaurant downstairs. The hotel is on the road between the airport and town, an excellent choice for those who don't need a water view. Breakfast is included. Children under 12 stay free. *L.E. Saddlerweg, tel. 599/38–2236, fax 599/38–2640. 18 rooms, 2 with kitchenettes. Facilities: restaurant, bar, pool. MC, V. CP.*

$ **Country Inn.** Cows graze in the pasture outside Iris Pompier's comfortable guest house. Simply furnished rooms have cable TV, air-conditioning, and shower baths. Iris does her utmost to make you feel at home, even offering impromptu additions to the Continental breakfasts and lifts into town. The clientele is an appealing mix of students and nature lovers; it's about a five-minute drive to

Oranjestad. *Concordia, tel. and fax 599/38-2484. 6 rooms. Facilities: breakfast room. No credit cards. CP.*

Apartment Rentals Statia has only a handful of apartments, though a spate of small developments and guest houses have sprung up recently to meet demand. Most of these average $50 or less per night. The apartments are very basic by most American standards: It's a good idea to make an inspection before committing to a stay. Check with the Tourist Office for listings.

Nightlife

Statia's five local bands stay busy on weekends. **Talk of the Town** (*see* Lodging, *above*) is the place to be for live music on Friday night. Saturday nights **Cool Corner** (*see* Dining *above*) and the **Exit Disco** at the Stone Oven restaurant (*see* Dining, *above*) have dancing and occasionally host live bands. Sometimes the **community center** (*see* Sports and the Outdoors, *above*) has a dance. Sunday nights find everyone at the **Golden Era Hotel** (*see* Lodging, *above*) for live music. Crowds are found all weekend at **Franky's** (*see* Dining, *above*) and the **Lago Heights Club and Disco** (at the shopping center in Chapelpiece, no phone), known to all as Gerald's, which has dancing and a late-night barbecue.

21 St. Kitts and Nevis

Updated by Jordan Simon

Tour groups are not attracted to islands that have no nonstop flights from the United States, virtually no glittering nightlife or shopping, and no high-rise hotels. Visitors here tend to be self-sufficient, sophisticated types who know how to amuse themselves and appreciate the warmth and character of country inns.

As you might expect, this atmosphere of understated luxury comes at a price: Both St. Kitts and Nevis are expensive. Their resorts and plantation-house hotels attract the upscale traveler. Moreover, the islands are small and offer fewer cheap lodging and dining alternatives than larger, more diverse destinations. Nevertheless, St. Kitts does have a few mid-priced hotels and some condominiums with kitchen facilities, as well as one all-inclusive resort that represents good value. Nevis has two affordable plantation-house hotels and—for those on a tighter budget—a few simple cottage complexes and guest houses.

Tiny though it is, St. Kitts, the first English settlement in the Leeward Islands, crams some stunning scenery into its 65 square miles. The island is fertile and lush with tropical flora and has some fascinating natural and historical attractions: a rain forest replete with waterfalls, thick vines, and secret trails; a central mountain range dominated by the 3,792-foot Mt. Liamuiga, whose crater has been long dormant; and Brimstone Hill, the Caribbean's most impressive fortress, which was known in the 17th century as the Gibraltar of the West Indies. The island is home to 35,000 people and hosts some 60,000 visitors annually. The shape of St. Kitts has been variously compared to a whale, a cricket bat, and a guitar. It's roughly oval, 19 miles long and 6 miles wide, with a narrow peninsula trailing off toward Nevis, 2 miles across the strait.

Nevis (pronounced *nee*-vis) rises out of the water in an almost perfect cone, the tip of its 3,232-foot central mountain smothered in clouds. It's lusher and less developed than its sister island. Nevis is known for the beauty of its long white- and black-sand beaches and lush greenery, for a half-dozen mineral spa baths, and for the restored sugar plantations that now house some of the Caribbean's most elegant hostelries. Although you can mountain climb, swim, play tennis, horseback ride, or go snorkeling, the going is easy here: Pick a hammock and snooze, indulge at a beachside lobster bake, or enjoy a quiet dinner on a romantic veranda.

Nevis is linked with St. Kitts politically. The two islands, together with Anguilla, achieved self-government as an Associated State of Great Britain in 1967. In 1983, St. Kitts and Nevis became a fully independent nation. Nevis papers sometimes run fiery articles advocating independence from St. Kitts, and the two islands may separate someday. However, it's not likely that a shot will be fired, let alone one that will be heard around the world.

What It Will Cost These sample prices, meant only as a general guide, are for high season. On St. Kitts, a $$ hotel will be about $150 a night; a ¢ one-bedroom condominium costs about $85 a night. On Nevis, a room at one of the more affordable plantation-house hotels costs $185 a night. A room at a ¢ guest house is about $45–$65 a night. Dinner at a $ restaurant on either island is about $15; a sandwich lunch is $1.50–$3. A rum punch is $3–$4 on either island; a beer is about $2.50. Figure on $35–$40 a day for car or Jeep rental. On St. Kitts, cab fare from the airport to Basseterre is only about $6, but fare to more distant hotels can approach $20. On Nevis, cab fare from the airport to the Mt. Nevis hotel is $8; from Charlestown to Oualie Beach, it's about $9. A single-tank dive on both islands costs around $45; snorkel equipment rents for about $10.

Before You Go

Tourist Information Contact the **St. Kitts & Nevis Tourist Board** (414 E. 75th St., New York, NY 10021, tel. 212/535–1234, fax 212/734–6511; 8700 West Bryn Mawr, Suite 800S, Chicago, IL 60631, tel. 312/714–5015, fax 312/714/–4910) or the **St. Kitts & Nevis Tourist Office** (11 Yorkville Ave., Suite 508, Toronto, Ontario, Canada M4W 1L3, tel. 416/921–7717, fax 416/921–7997; 10 Kensington Ct., London W8S 5DL, tel. 0171/376–0881, fax 0171/937–3611).

Arriving and Departing

By Plane **American** (tel. 800/433–7300) and **Delta** (tel. 800/221–1212) fly from the United States to Antigua, St. Croix, St. Thomas, St. Maarten, and San Juan, Puerto Rico, where connections can be made on regional carriers such as **American Eagle,** part of the **American Airlines** system (tel. 800/433–7300); **LIAT** (tel. 809/465–2511, or tel. 212/251–1717 in NY); **Windward Island Airways** (tel. 809/465–0810); and **Air BVI** (tel. 800/468–2485). **British Airways** (tel. 800/247–9297) flies from London to Antigua, **Air Canada** (tel. 800/422–6232) flies from Toronto to Antigua, and American flies from Montreal to San Juan. **Air St. Kitts-Nevis** (tel. 809/465–8571), **Nevis Express** (tel. 809/469–9755), and **Carib Aviation** (tel. 809/465–3055, St. Kitts; 809/469–9295, Nevis; fax 809/469–9185) are reliable air-charter operations providing service between St. Kitts and Nevis and other islands.

From the Airport Taxis meet every flight at the airports on both islands. The taxis are unmetered, but fixed rates, in E.C. dollars, are posted at the airport and at the jetty. On St. Kitts the fare from the airport to the closest hotel in Basseterre is E.C. $16 (U.S. $6); to the farthest point, E.C. $56 (U.S. $21). On Nevis, a taxi from Newcastle Airport to Golden Rock is about U.S. $15; to Pinney's Beach Hotel, it's about U.S. $12. Be sure to clarify whether the rate quoted is in E.C. or U.S. dollars.

By Boat The 150-passenger, government-operated ferry MV *Caribe Queen* makes the 45-minute crossing from Nevis to St. Kitts daily except Thursday and Sunday. The schedule is a bit erratic, so confirm departure times with the tourist office. Round-trip fare is U.S. $8. A new, air-conditioned, 110-passenger ferry, MV *Spirit of Mount Nevis,* makes the run twice daily except Wednesday. The fare is U.S. $12 round-trip. Call **Nevis Cruise Lines** (tel. 809/469–9373) for information and reservations.

Passports and Visas Although it is always wiser to travel in the Caribbean with a valid passport, U.S. and Canadian citizens need only produce proof of citizenship in the form of a voter registration card or birth certificate (a driver's license will not suffice). British citizens must have a passport; visas are not required. All visitors must have a return or ongoing ticket.

Language English with a West Indian lilt is spoken here.

Precautions Visitors, especially women, are warned not to go jogging on long, lonely roads.

St. Kitts

Staying in St. Kitts

Important Addresses **Tourist Information: St. Kitts/Nevis Department of Tourism** (Pelican Mall, Bay Rd., Box 132, Basseterre, tel. 809/465–2620 and 809/465–4040, fax 809/465–8794) and the **St. Kitts-Nevis Hotel Association** (Box 438, Basseterre, tel. 809/465–5304, fax 809/465–7746).

Emergencies **Police:** Call 911. **Hospitals:** There is a 24-hour emergency room at the **Joseph N. France General Hospital** (Basseterre, tel. 809/465–2551). **Pharmacies:** In Basseterre, **Skerritt's Drug Store** (Fort St., tel. 809/465–2008) is open Monday–Wednesday 8–5, Thursday 8–1, Friday 8–5:30, and Saturday 8–6; closed Sunday; **City Drug** (Fort St., Basseterre, tel. 809/465–2156) is open Monday–Wednesday and Friday–Saturday 8–7; Thursday 8–5, Sunday 8–10 AM. In Frigate Bay, **City Drug** (Sun 'n' Sand, Frigate Bay, tel. 809/465–1803) is open Monday–Saturday 8:30–8, Sunday 8:30–10:30 AM and 4–6 PM.

Currency Legal tender is the Eastern Caribbean (E.C.) dollar. At press time, the rate of exchange was E.C. $2.60 to U.S. $1. U.S. dollars are accepted practically everywhere, but you'll almost always get change in E.C. dollars. Prices quoted here are in U.S. dollars unless noted otherwise. Most large hotels, restaurants, and shops accept major credit cards, but small inns and shops usually do not.

Taxes and Service Charges Hotels collect a 7% government tax and add a 10% service charge to your bill. In restaurants, a tip of 10%–15% is appropriate. The departure tax is $10. There is no departure tax from St. Kitts to Nevis, or vice versa.

Getting Around If you are adventurous and don't mind driving on the left, you'll save money by renting a vehicle rather than relying on guided tours and cabs to transport you. (A full day's rental is $35–$40, while a half-day taxi tour costs $50.) Even one day of car rental gives you time to explore the island and still have time to visit some beaches. You can do without renting a car for the rest of your trip if your hotel includes transfers to and from the airport and a shuttle to the beach (if it's not within walking distance). To visit restaurants and shops, however, it's best to have a car throughout your stay.

Taxis Taxis are unmetered here; fixed rates are posted at the airport and the jetty. The fare from Ocean Terrace Inn in Basseterre to Dieppe Bay, near the Golden Lemon is $18; from Basseterre to Sandy Point near Brimstone Hill, $12. There is a 50% surcharge for trips between 10 PM and 6 AM.

Buses A privately owned minibus circles the island. Fare is E.C. 25¢ per mile. Check with the tourist office about schedules.

Rental Cars and Scooters Driving is on the left here. Roads are in reasonably good condition; the 6½-mile South East Peninsula Road was completed in 1990. You'll need a local driver's license, which you can get by presenting yourself, your valid driver's license, and E.C. $30 at the police station on Cayon Street in Basseterre. Rentals are available at **Avis** (tel. 809/465–6507), **Holiday** (tel. 809/465–6507), and **Caines** (tel. 809/465–2366, fax 809/465–6172). **Economy Car** (tel. 809/465–8449) also rents scooter bikes. **TDC Rentals** (tel. 809/465–2991, fax 809/469–1329) rents minimokes, as well as cars, and offers the best service. At press time, the price of gas was U.S. $2 per gallon. You can make arrangements ahead of time for a rental car representative to meet you at the airport; call or fax the company before you leave home.

Telephones and Mail To call St. Kitts from the United States, dial area code 809, then access code 465 or 469 and the local number. Telephone communications are as clear as a bell, and you can make direct long-distance calls. To make an intra-island call, dial the seven-digit number. A local call costs E.C. 25¢.

Airmail letters to the United States and Canada cost E.C. 80 per half ounce; postcards require E.C. 50¢. Mail takes at least 7–10 days to reach the United States. St. Kitts and Nevis issue separate stamps, but each also honors the other's. The beautiful stamps are collector's items.

Opening and Closing Times Although shops used to close for lunch from noon to 1, more and more establishments are remaining open Monday–Saturday 8–4. Some shops close earlier on Thursday. Hours vary somewhat from bank to bank but are typically Monday–Thursday 8–3 and Friday 8–5. St. Kitts & Nevis National Bank is also open Saturday 8:30–11.

Guided Tours **Tropical Tours** (tel. 809/465–4167) can run you around the island ($12 a person) and take you to the rain forest ($35 a person). **Kriss Tours** (tel. 809/465–4042) offers rain-forest tours with lunch and a drink for $35 a person, and volcano tours, also with lunch and drink, for $40. **Greg Pereira** (tel. 809/465–4121) offers a full-day hike to Mt. Liamuiga, including lunch and an open bar, for $45 a person. He also offers a half-day rain-forest hike, including lunch and open bar, for $35; and a plantation tour with West Indian lunch for $45.

Exploring St. Kitts

Numbers in the margin correspond to points of interest on the St. Kitts map.

Basseterre

1 The capital city of **Basseterre,** set in the southern part of the island, is an easily walkable town, graced with tall palms and small, beautifully maintained houses and buildings of stone and pastel-colored wood. You can see the town's main sights in a half hour or so.

Your first stop is at the **St. Kitts Tourist Board** (Tourism Complex, Bay Rd.) to pick up maps. Turn left when you leave there and walk past the handsome Treasury Building. It faces the octagonal **Circus,** which contains a fanciful memorial to Thomas Berkeley, a former president of the Legislative Assembly. Duty-free shops fill the streets and courtyards leading off from around the Circus. The **St. Kitts Philatelic Bureau** (open weekdays 8–4) is nearby on the second floor of the Social Security Building (Bay Rd.).

The colorful **Bay Road produce market** is open on weekends only. On the waterfront, next to the Treasury Building, is the air-conditioned **Shoreline Plaza,** and nearby is the landing for the ferries to Nevis.

From the Circus, Bank Street leads to **Independence Square,** with lovely gardens on the site of a former slave market. The square is surrounded on three sides by Georgian buildings.

Exploring
Basseterre, **1**
Black Rocks, **7**
Bloody Point, **2**
Brimstone Hill, **5**
Middle Island, **4**
Romney Manor, **3**
Sandy Point Town, **6**

Dining
Arlecchino, **12**
Atlantic Club, **24**
Ballahoo, **13**
Blue Horizon, **19**
Chef's Place, **15**
Coconut Cafe, **22**
Fisherman's Wharf, **14**
The Golden Lemon, **8**
J's Place, **9**
Ocean Terrace Inn, **14**
Olivee's, **11**
OTI Turtle Beach Bar and Grill, **28**
Pizza's Place, **16**
PJ's Pizza, **26**

Lodging
Bird Rock Beach Resort, **20**
Colony's Timothy Beach Resort, **22**
Fairview Inn, **10**
Fort Thomas Hotel, **17**
Gateway Inn, **23**
Inter Grande Frigate Bay Beach Hotel, **21**
Jack Tar Village Beach Resorts and Casino, **27**
Morgan Heights Condominiums, **24**
Ocean Terrace Inn, **14**
Palms Hotel, **18**
Sun 'n Sand Beach Village, **25**

St. Kitts

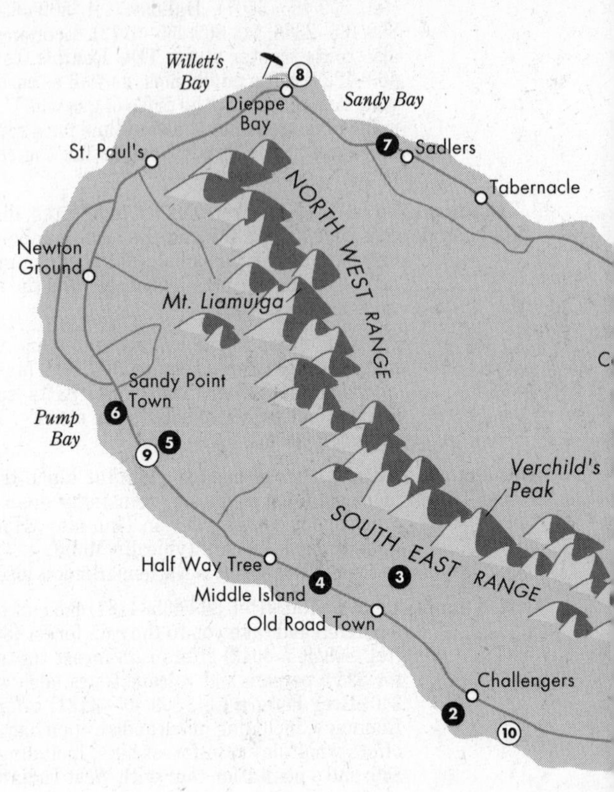

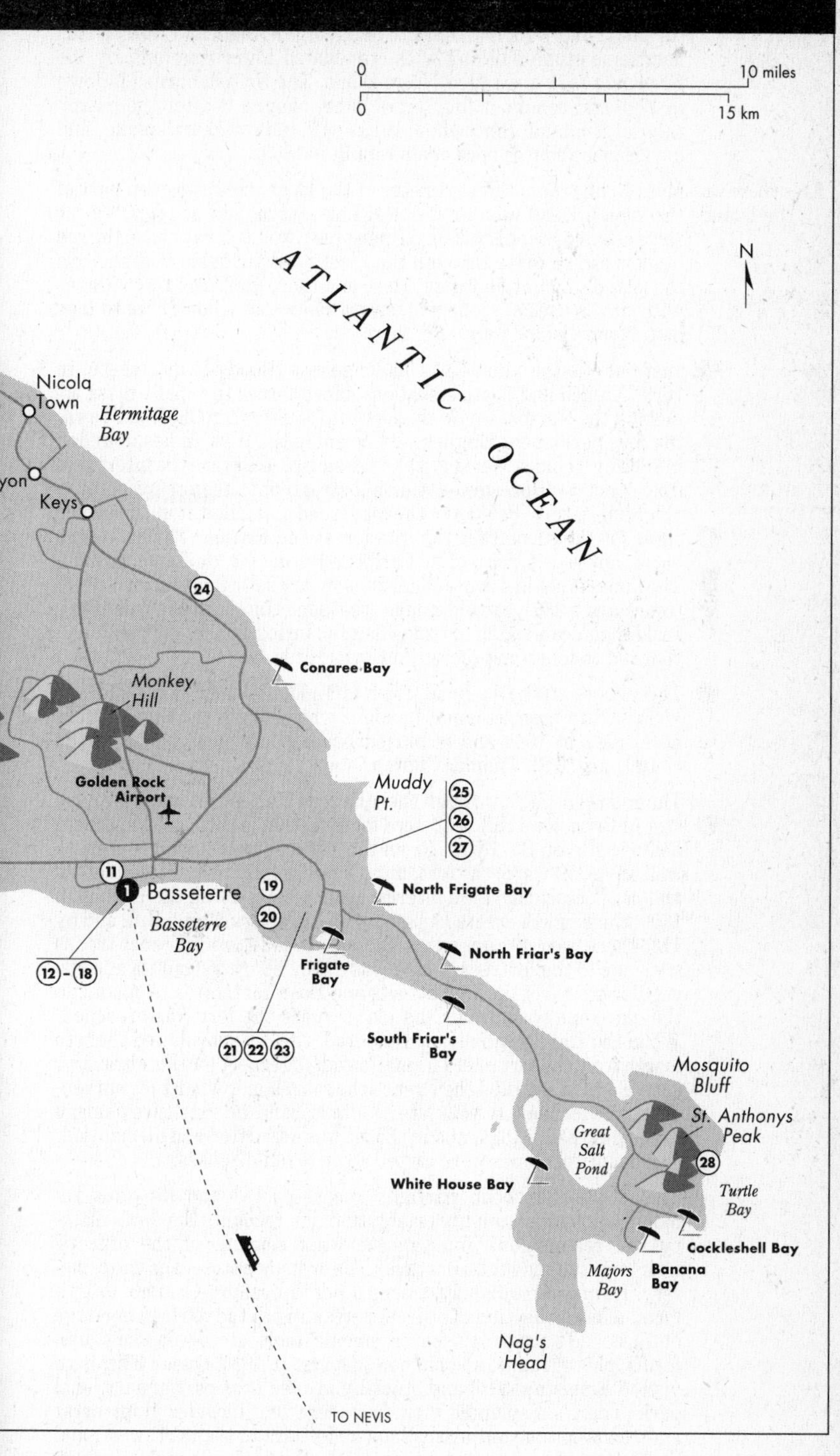

0
10 miles
0
15 km
N
ATLANTIC OCEAN
Nicola Town
Hermitage Bay
yon
Keys
24
Conaree Bay
Monkey Hill
Golden Rock Airport
Muddy Pt.
25
26
27
11
1 Basseterre
19
20
Basseterre Bay
12-18
North Frigate Bay
Frigate Bay
North Friar's Bay
South Friar's Bay
21 22 23
Mosquito Bluff
St. Anthonys Peak
Great Salt Pond
28
White House Bay
Turtle Bay
Cockleshell Bay
Majors Bay
Banana Bay
Nag's Head
TO NEVIS

Walk up West Square Street, away from the bay, to Cayon Street, turn left, and walk one block to **St. George's Anglican Church.** This handsome stone building with crenellated tower was built by the French in 1670 and called Nôtre Dame. The British burned it down in 1706 and rebuilt it four years later, naming it after the patron saint of England. Since then, it has suffered fire, earthquake, and hurricanes and was once again rebuilt in 1859.

Elsewhere on the Island

Main Road traces the perimeter of the large, northwestern part of the island. Head west on it out of Basseterre, and be prepared for some stunning scenery. For the most part, you'll always have the sea in view as you drive through the acres of sugar fields that encircle the island's mountain range. Here and there you'll see tiny villages with tiny houses of stone and weathered wood. Allow three to four hours for an island tour.

2 Just outside the village of Challengers is **Bloody Point,** where, in 1629, French and British soldiers joined forces to repel a mass attack by the Caribs. Be on the lookout for signs for **Old Road Town,** the first permanent English settlement in the West Indies, founded in 1624 by Thomas Warner. Take the side road toward the interior to find some well-preserved Carib petroglyphs, testimony of even older habitation. Return to the main road and follow it until you see
3 signs for the turnoff for the rain forest and **Romney Manor,** where batik fabrics are printed at **Caribelle Batik** (*see* Shopping, *below*). The house is set in 6 acres of gardens, with exotic flowers, an old bell tower, and a 350-year-old saman tree (sometimes called a rain tree). Inside, you can watch artisans hand-printing fabrics by the 2,500-year-old Indonesian process known as batik.

4 The village after Old Road Town is **Middle Island,** where Thomas Warner, the "gentleman of London" who brought the first settlers here, died in 1648 and is buried beneath a green gazebo in the churchyard of **St. Thomas Church.**

The road continues through the village of Half-Way Tree to well-re-
5 stored **Brimstone Hill,** a 38-acre fortress that is the most important historic site on St. Kitts. From the parking area it's quite a steep walk up to the top of the fort, but it's well worth it if military history and/or spectacular views interest you. After routing the French in 1690, the English erected a battery on top of Brimstone Hill, and by 1736 there were 49 guns in the fortress. In 1782, 8,000 French troops lay siege to the fortress, which was defended by 350 militia and 600 regular troops of the Royal Scots and East Yorkshires. A plaque in the old stone wall marks the place where the fort was breached. When the English finally surrendered, the French allowed them to march from the fort in full formation out of respect for their bravery. (The English afforded the French the same honor when they surrendered the fort a mere year later.) A hurricane did extensive damage to the fortress in 1834, and in 1852 it was evacuated and dismantled. The beautiful stones were carted away to build houses.

The citadel has been partially reconstructed and its guns remounted. A seven-minute orientation film recounts the fort's history and restoration. You can see what remains of the officers' quarters, the redoubts, barracks, the ordnance store, and the cemetery. Its museums display, among other things, pre-Columbian artifacts, a new collection of objects pertaining to the African heritage of the island's slaves (masks, ceremonial tools, etc.), weaponry, uniforms, photographs, and old newspapers. In 1985, Queen Elizabeth visited Brimstone Hill and officially opened it as part of a national park. There's a splendid view from here that includes Montserrat and Nevis to the southeast, Saba and Statia to the northwest, and St. Barts and St. Maarten to the north. Nature trails snake through the tangle of surrounding hardwood forest and savannah (a fine spot to catch the green vervet monkeys skittering about). *Main Rd.,*

Brimstone Hill. Admission: $5 adults, $2.50 children. Open daily 9:30–5:30.

Continuing on through seas of sugarcane, past breadfruit trees and
6 old stone walls, you'll come to **Sandy Point Town.** The houses here
are West Indian–style raised cottages. The **Roman Catholic church**
has lovely stained-glass windows.

Farther along, just outside the village of **Newton Ground,** are the remains of an old sugar mill and some ancient coconut palms. Outside
the village of **St. Paul's** is a road that leads to **Rawlins Plantation,** a
restored sugar plantation that's popular for dining and lodging. The
fishing town of **Dieppe Bay** is at the northernmost point of the island.
Its tiny black-sand beach is backed by **The Golden Lemon,** one of the
7 Caribbean's most famous inns. **Black Rocks** on the Atlantic coast
just outside the town of Sadlers, in Sandy Bay, are lava deposits,
spat into the sea ages ago when the island's volcano erupted. They
have since been molded into fanciful shapes by centuries of pounding
surf. The drive back to Basseterre around the other side of the island is a pleasant one, through small, neat villages with centuries-
old stone churches and pastel-colored cottages.

Beaches

All beaches on the island are free and open to the public, even those occupied by hotels. The powdery white-sand beaches are all at the southern end of the island and on the peninsula. The best way to see the beaches is to rent a vehicle for a day, take your swimsuit and a picnic lunch, and make the rounds.

The South East Peninsula Road leads from the foot of Timothy Hill to Major's Bay on the southern tip of the island, providing access to some of the island's best beaches. Among them are the twin beaches of **Banana Bay** and **Cockleshell Bay,** which together cover more than 2 miles, marred somewhat by the skeletal remains of abandoned hotel developments.

Locals consider the Caribbean side of **Friar's Bay** the island's finest beach. You can haggle with fishermen here to take you out snorkeling off the eastern point. The waters on the Atlantic side are rougher, but the beach itself has a wild, desolate beauty. **White House Bay** is rocky, but the snorkeling, which takes in several reefs surrounding a sunken tugboat, is superb. A tiny dirt road, virtually impassable after heavy rains, leads to **Sandbank Beach** on the Atlantic side. The shallow coves are protected here, making it ideal for families, and it's usually deserted.

Beaches elsewhere on the island are of gray-black volcanic sand. **Conaree Bay** on the Atlantic side is a narrow strip where the water is good for bodysurfing (no facilities). Snorkeling and windsurfing are good at **Dieppe Bay,** on the north coast, where the Golden Lemon Hotel is located.

Sports and the Outdoors

Boating Sunfish and Hobie Cats can be rented at **Tropical Surf** (Turtle Bay, tel. 809/496–9086) and **Mr. X Watersports** (Frigate Bay, tel. 809/465–4995) for $20–$30 an hour.

Golf The **Royal St. Kitts Golf Club** (tel. 809/465–8339) is an 18-hole championship course in the Frigate Bay area. It costs $35 to play here, with cart rental an additional $40. There is a nine-hole course at **Golden Rock** (tel. 809/465–8103).

Hiking Trails in the central mountains vary from easy to don't-try-it-by-yourself. **Greg Pereira** (tel. 809/465–4121), Oliver Spencer at **Off the**

Beaten Track (tel. 809/465–6314), and **Kriss Tours** (tel. 809/465–4042) lead guided hikes (*see* Guided Tours, *above*).

Scuba Diving and Snorkeling Kenneth Samuel of **Kenneth's Dive Centre** (tel. 809/465–7043 or 809/465–2670) is a PADI-certified dive master who takes small groups of divers with C cards to nearby reefs. Auston MacLeod, a PADI-certified dive master/instructor and owner of **Pro-Divers** (tel. 809/465–3223), offers resort and certification courses. He also has Nikonos camera equipment for rent. A single-tank dive costs $45; a double is about $70. Snorkel equipment rents for about $10.

There are more than a dozen excellent dive sites on St. Kitts, all with a variety of sea life and color. **Coconut Tree Reef,** one of the largest in the area, includes sea fans, sponges, and anemones. **Black Coral Reef** features the rare black coral tree. **Brassball Wreck** is a shallow-water wreck, good for snorkeling and photography. **Redonda Bank** is an extensive area of reef that's just beginning to be explored. The shallow **Tug Boat** is a good spot for snorkelers.

Sea Excursions **Leeward Island Charters** (tel. 809/465–7474) offers day and overnight charters on two catamarans—the 47-foot *Caona* or the 70-foot *Spirit of St. Kitts*. Day sails are from 9:30 to 4:30 and include barbecue, open bar, and snorkeling equipment. **Tropical Tours** (tel. 809/465–4167) offers moonlight cruises on the 52-foot catamaran *Cileca III* and glass-bottom-boat tours. ***Jazzie II*** (tel. 809/465–3529) is another glass-bottom boat that cruises the southeastern coast. Half-day snorkeling tours are $30. ***Tropical Dreamer*** (tel. 809/465–8224) is another catamaran available for day and sunset cruises. For the ultimate underwater trip, call **Blue Frontier Ltd.** (tel. 809/465–4945); owner Lindsey Beck will take even nondivers for a half-hour ride off Frigate Bay in his two-man submarine.

Tennis There are four lighted courts at **Jack Tar Village Beach Resorts** (tel. 809/465–8651), two lighted courts at **Sun 'n' Sand Beach Village** (tel. 809/465–6221), as well as one court each at **Bird Rock Beach Hotel** (tel. 809/465–8914), the **Golden Lemon** (tel. 809/465–7260), and **Rawlins Plantation** (tel. 809/465–6221). Hotel courts are free during the day; night play on lighted courts costs about $5.

Waterskiing and Windsurfing **Tropical Surf** (tel. 809/469–9086) at Turtle Bay rents Windsurfers, surfboards, and boogie boards. **Mr. X Watersports** (Frigate Bay, tel. 809/465–4995) has windsurfing and waterskiing equipment. Windsurfing costs $15 an hour; waterskiing is $15 for 15 minutes.

Shopping

Worth a splurge are the batik fabrics, scarves, caftans, and wall hangings of Caribelle Batik; cost of batik wall hangings ranges from $25 to $70. Locally produced jams, jellies, and herb teas make good gifts, as do handcrafts of local shell, straw, and coconut. CSR (Cane Spirit Rothschild) is a drink that's distilled from fresh sugarcane right on St. Kitts.

Shopping Districts Most shopping plazas are near the Circus in downtown Basseterre. Some shops have outlets in other areas, particularly in Dieppe Bay. The **Pelican Mall** has 26 stores, a restaurant, tourism offices, and a bandstand. This shopping arcade is designed to look like a traditional Caribbean street. **TDC Mall** is just off the Circus in downtown Basseterre. **Shoreline Plaza** is next to the Treasury Building, right on the waterfront in Basseterre. **Palms Arcade** is on Fort Street, also near the Circus.

Good Buys **TDC** (TDC Plaza, on Bank St., tel. 809/465–2511) carries fine china and crystal, along with cameras and other imports.

Slice of the Lemon (Palms Arcade, tel. 809/465–2889) carries fine perfumes but is better known for its elegant jewelry. **Lemonaid**

(Dieppe Bay, tel. 809/465–7359) has select Caribbean handicrafts, antiques, and clothing by John Warden.

Island Crafts and Gifts **Caribelle Batik** (Romney Manor, tel. 809/465–6253) sells batik wraps, T-shirts, dresses, wall hangings, and the like. **Island Hopper** (The Circus, tel. 809/465–2905) is a good place for island crafts, especially woodcarvings. **Palm Crafts** (Palms Arcade, tel. 809/465–2599) sells a variety of goodies, including savory Caribbean jams and jellies. **Spencer Cameron Art Gallery** (N. Independence Sq., tel. 809/465–1617) has historical reproductions of Caribbean island charts and prints, in addition to owner Rosey Cameron's popular Carnevale clown prints and a wide selection of exceptional works by Caribbean artists. They will mail anywhere, so you don't have to lug home something that catches your eye. The **Plantation Picture House** (Fort St., tel. 809/465–7740) showcases the enchanting silk pareus, jewelry, prints, and papier mâché works of Kate Spencer (who also has a studio at the Rawlins Plantation). **Rosemary Lane Antiques** (7 Rosemary La., tel. 809/465–5450) occupies a beautifully restored 18th-century town house and is crammed with superlative, affordable antiques and objets d'art from throughout the Caribbean. They will gladly ship any purchases. **Splash** (TDC Plaza, Bank St., tel. 809/465–9279) carries colorful beachwear by local designers. **Music World** (The Circus, tel. 809/465–1998) offers a vast selection of island rhythms—lilting soca and zouk, pulsating salsa and merengue, wicked hip hop, and mellow reggae and calypso.

Dining

Dining in St. Kitts can be affordable if you avoid plantation dining rooms. There are a number of good restaurants with reasonably priced menu items. Most restaurants offer a variety of West Indian specialties, such as curried mutton, Arawak chicken (seasoned chicken, rice and almonds served on a breadfruit leaf), pepper pot, and honey-glazed garlic spare ribs.

There's little in the way of fast food here, but quick, cheap lunches can be had at the temporary snack stands set up on beaches around the island. Try also **Chick-A-D's Chicken and Ribs/Kenbo's Pizzas** (Fort Thomas Hotel, tel. 809/465–5454) for cheap takeout. If you're cooking in, **Ram's Supermarket** and **Scotch House** in Basseterre have provisions; in the Frigate Bay area, try **City Drug Store.** You can buy picnic fare at **Ocean Terrace Inn** (*see below*).

Highly recommended restaurants are indicated by a star ★.

Category	Cost*
$$	$25–$35
$	$15–$25
¢	under $15

**per person, excluding drinks and service*

$$ ★ **The Golden Lemon.** Although it's out of our price range for dinner, come here for the excellent Sunday brunch ($15 for the likes of banana pancakes and rum beef stew) and reasonably priced lunches ($10 lobster sandwich). Owner Arthur Leaman creates the recipes himself for the West Indian, Continental, and American cuisines served in his hotel, and he never repeats them more than once in a two-week period. The patio, lush with bougainvillea and ferns, is a popular spot. *Dieppe Bay, tel. 809/465–7260. Reservations required. AE, MC, V.*

$$ **Ocean Terrace Inn.** The local elite frequent this spot. Dinner is by candlelight, in the inn's dining room or on a small balcony or terrace overlooking the bay. The chef's special, which includes appetizer,

soup, entrée, vegetables, dessert, and coffee, costs $35—a price that barely makes it into our $$ category, but is an excellent value. The lunch menu includes sandwiches for $5–$9. At the Friday-night buffet, a lobster and steak barbecue alternates with West Indian specialties. The 7:30 dinner is followed by entertainment and dancing. *Fortlands, Basseterre, tel. 809/465–2754. Reservations required. AE, MC, V.*

$$ ★ **Olivee's** Robert Cramer and Ian Smith have converted their traditional West Indian home, filled with antiques acquired on their extensive travels, into the island's most charming, convivial eatery. Drinks are served on the hillside terrace, set amid fragrant tropical gardens with smashing views of Basseterre and the Caribbean below. Robert serves as maitre d' and Ian as chef. The prix fixe menu, $20–$40 depending on entree (beef is most expensive), includes delectable homemade sourdough bread, soup or salad, appetizer, entrée, vegetables, dessert, and tea or coffee. Among Ian's savory Continental selections, delicately spiced with island flair, are saltfish fritters with red pepper coulis, sweet potato pâté, herb-stuffed chicken breast in kumquat glaze, and grilled lime-marinated swordfish with guava and red onion relish. Most of the fruits and vegetables are organically grown on the property. The bittersweet chocolate torte with gooseberry sauce is sublime. You can choose from their well-considered wine list. Olivee's also functions as a B&B, with two rooms, priced at $75 and $90 a night, beautifully furnished with antiques, local crafts, and beds swaddled in mosquito netting. *Upper Buckley's, Basseterre, tel. 809/465–3662. Reservations advised. AE, MC, V. Restaurant closed May 15–Nov. 15.*

$–$$ **Arlecchino.** The shaded courtyard of this breezy trattoria is a pleasant place to while away the afternoon or evening. Enjoy a sublime minestrone, fresh pastas, creative pizzas, and excellent veal parmigiana, then top off the meal with the best cappuccino and *tiramisu* on St. Kitts. *Cayon St., Basseterre, tel. 809/465–9927. AE, MC, V. Closed Sun.*

$–$$ **Blue Horizon.** On the cliffs of Bird Rock, this unassuming restaurant affords a panoramic view of Basseterre and Nevis and of spectacular sunsets. The charming menu is written in five languages (including English) on dinner plates, and the tables, with red-and-white checked tablecloths, are placed to catch the breezes. The chef is Austrian, so specials such as Wiener schnitzel are often found on the menu alongside fresh local fish dishes.*Bird Rock (just outside Basseterre), tel. 809/465–5863. Reservations advised. AE, MC, V.*

$–$$ **Coconut Cafe.** Pop music blares at this cheerful beachfront restaurant at the Colony's Timothy Beach Resort. Breakfast, lunch, and dinner are all served, but only dinner comes with a beautiful sunset. Among the better offerings are chicken *chasseur* (with cheese, bananas and tangy calypso sauce) and snapper in lobster sauce. *Frigate Bay, tel. 809/465–3020. AE, D, MC, V.*

$–$$ ★ **Fisherman's Wharf.** Part of the Ocean Terrace Inn (head straight rather than up the hill to the hotel's main building), this extremely casual waterfront eatery is decorated in swaggering nautical style, with rustic wood beams, rusty anchors, cannons, and buoys. It serves fresh grilled lobster and seafood and excellent conch chowder in the evening. Finish off your meal with a slice of the memorable banana cheesecake. The tables are long, wooden affairs and it's generally lively, especially on weekend nights. *Fortlands, Basseterre, tel. 809/465–2754. AE, MC, V. No lunch.*

$ **Ballahoo.** Curried conch, rotis, salads, and sandwiches are served in a delightful upstairs gallery overlooking Pelican Gardens and the Circus in the heart of town. The list of well-priced entrées includes beef madras and chicken Creole. The specialty is (no kidding) banana and rum sandwiches for dessert. Lilting calypso and reggae on the sound system, whirring ceiling fans, potted palms, and colorful island prints enhance the tropical ambience. *Fort St., Basseterre, tel. 809/465–4197. AE, MC, V. Closed Sun.*

$ **OTI Turtle Beach Bar and Grill.** Simple but scrumptious cuisine has made this informal restaurant a popular daytime watering hole. Taste treats include honey-mustard ribs, calypso chicken, coconut-shrimp salad, and grilled stuffed lobster. The glorified shack is on an isolated beach at the south end of the South East Peninsula Road: Just look for the signs. Business cards from around the world plaster the bar, and the room is brightly decorated with a small sailboat, colorful crusted bottles dredged from the deep, and painted wooden fish, turtles, and toucans. You can rent a kayak, Windsurfer, or mountain bike here to help you work off your meal, or schedule a deep-sea fishing trip. *Turtle Bay, tel. 809/469–9086. Dinner reservations required. Dinner Fri. and Sat. only. AE, MC, V.*

¢–$ **The Atlantic Club.** Everything from West Indian cuisine to club sandwiches is served for lunch at this oceanside eatery. It's on the island's east coast, next to the Morgan Heights Condominiums. The portions are hearty, the piña coladas divine, and the prices can't be beat. *Morgan Heights Condominiums, Main Rd. near Basseterre, tel. 809/465–8633. AE, D, MC, V. Closed Sun.*

¢–$ **PJ's Pizza.** "Garbage pizza" may not sound too appetizing, but this pie, topped with everything but the kitchen sink, is a favorite here. You can also choose from 10 other varieties of pizza or create your own. Sandwiches and other Italian standards are available (lasagna is a house specialty). Finish your meal with delicious, moist rum cake. This casual spot borders the golf course and is open to cooling breezes. The atmosphere is always boisterous. *Frigate Bay, tel. 809/465–8373. AE. Closed Mon. and Sept.*

¢ **Chef's Place.** Inexpensive West Indian meals are the draw here. Try the local version of jerk chicken (more moist than the original) or the goat stew. The best seats are outside on the wide white veranda. *Upper Church St., Basseterre, tel. 809/465–6176. No credit cards. Closed Sun.*

¢ **J's Place.** Chattering monkeys in a cage greet you at the entrance to this simple terrace eatery across from Brimstone Hill. Goatwater stew, conch and chips, and other local dishes are staples. The lobster salad's the best on the island, and at $12 ($17.50 for a grilled crustacean), it's a fantastic buy. Everything else is under $10, with burgers at $1.50 and chicken and chips for $3.50. J's turns into a popular disco weekend nights. *Sandy Point, tel. 809/465–6264. No credit cards. Closed Sun.*

Lodging

St. Kitts does not have an abundance of hotels, and what it has are mostly expensive. You'll have to bypass the unique resorts and restored plantations the island is known for and concentrate on more modest properties, located for the most part in Basseterre and in the Frigate Bay area. Apartment rentals are another possibility (*see below*).

Highly recommended lodgings are indicated by a star ★.

Category	Cost*
$$	$115–$175
$	$90–$115
¢	under $90

**All prices are for a standard double room for two, excluding 7% tax and a 10% service charge. To estimate rates for hotels offering MAP, add about $35 per person per day to the above price ranges. For all-inclusives, add about $75 per person per day.*

Hotels
$$ **Colony's Timothy Beach Resort.** If you don't mind trading some atmosphere for modern comfort at a good price, this could well be the

ideal spot for a beach-oriented vacation. Set at the end of the Frigate Bay beach, this casual hotel overlooks the Caribbean. Simple beige stucco buildings hold comfortable, adequately furnished rooms and suites. Larger units have kitchens and multiple bedrooms, and every room has air-conditioning, phone, and minifridge. Opt to stay in one of the original buildings, which sit right on the beach; they have better views than the recent additions and are larger and airier. You can choose from a wide variety of sports activities. Greens fees for the nearby golf course are included in the room rate. The hotel's Coconut Cafe is a local favorite. However, rates are based on EP, so you can sample the cuisine around St. Kitts. The management is attentive and friendly. *Box 81, Frigate Bay, tel. 809/465–8597 or 800/621–1270, fax 809/465–7723; Colony Reservations Worldwide, 800/777–1700. 60 rooms. Facilities: restaurant, pool, water-sports center. AE, MC, V. EP.*

$$ **Jack Tar Village Beach Resorts and Casino.** A lively atmosphere pervades this appealing all-inclusive resort. A slew of sports are available, each day has a schedule of recreational activities and contests, and there are supervised programs for children. Two pools are a nice touch: One is for the volleyball and water aerobics crowd, the other for those who want a quiet, relaxing dip. Live entertainment, a disco, and the island's only casino keep the action going late into the night. Guest rooms are freshly decorated with floral linens, boating prints, and jade carpets. All have a small terrace or balcony, cable TV, safe, and phone. About 10% of the rooms, booked at least 60 days in advance, go for $139 per person during high season; once these are filled, the remaining rooms cost $170 a person. (The two suites are out of our price range.) You can walk to the nearby Atlantic beach, or take the free shuttle to a beach on the Caribbean side. *Box 406, Frigate Bay, tel. 809/465–8651 or 800/999–9182, fax 809/465–8651. 240 rooms, 2 suites. Facilities: 2 restaurants, 3 bars, casino, 2 pools, 4 lighted tennis courts, facilities for guests with disabilities, shuffleboard, Ping-Pong, basketball, scuba lessons, minigym, spa, massage, water-sports center, access to golf course, supervised children's activities. AE, MC, V. All-inclusive.*

$$ ★ **Ocean Terrace Inn.** Referred to locally as OTI, this is a rarity: a stylish, intimate business hotel. The main building, which houses the fancier restaurant, reception, a pool with a swim-up bar, and many of the rooms, is set high on a hill overlooking the ocean, amid lovingly tended gardens dotted with gazebos. Condominium units are farther down the hill but also have water views. Accommodations range in size from smallish standard rooms to one- and two-bedroom condos with full kitchens. All are air-conditioned, have cable TV, phone, and minibar, and are handsomely decorated in rattan and bright fabrics. Fisherman's Wharf, waterfront at the bottom of the hill, is a casual seafood restaurant. The hotel's Pelican Cove Marina has its own fleet of boats that you can take out or charter. There is a daily shuttle to the hotel's beach at pretty Turtle Bay (a good 20 minutes away), where you'll find all the water sports and a restaurant/bar that's also owned by OTI. *Box 65, Basseterre, tel. 809/465–2754, 800/223–5695, or 800/524–0512, fax 809/465–1057. 54 units. Facilities: 3 restaurants, 3 bars, 2 pools, outdoor Jacuzzi, fleet of boats, water-sports center. AE, MC, V. EP, MAP.*

$$ **Sun 'n' Sand Beach Village.** This simple complex is on the beach at North Frigate Bay, on the Atlantic side of the island. Studios in two-story buildings and two-bedroom, self-catering units in pretty, Antillean-style wood-and-stucco cottages, stretch back from the beach. Decor is simple and tropical, with rattan furnishings, island prints and batiks, and tile floors. Studios are air-conditioned; each has twin or queen-size beds, cable TV, phone, bath with shower, and a private terrace. The cottages have a convertible sofa in the living room and a fully equipped kitchen; there's a window air conditioner in the bedroom and a ceiling fan in the living room. *Box 341, Frigate Bay, tel. 809/465–8037 or 800/223–6510, fax 809/465–6745. 32 studi-*

os, 18 2-bedroom cottages. Facilities: restaurant, pool, children's pool, 2 lighted tennis courts, grocery store, gift shop. AE, D, MC, V. CP, MAP.

$–$$ **Bird Rock Beach Resort.** Perched on a bluff overlooking its own beach a few miles from the airport and downtown, this rather plain-looking resort has been expanding every year, with a new dive shop and casual beach grill slated to open by fall 1995. Two-story buildings contain air-conditioned rooms and suites with direct-dial telephone, cable TV, and balcony with ocean view. Suites also have kitchenettes. The tile-floored rooms are simply furnished with rattan and wicker furniture and floral fabrics. An informal dining room is next to the pool, and there is shuttle service to the gourmet Lighthouse Restaurant, which is owned by the hotel. There is particularly excellent snorkeling and diving in the waters just off the resort's golden-sand beach. Golf and the larger Frigate Bay beaches are just five minutes away. *Box 227, Basseterre, tel. 809/465–8914 or 800/621–1270, fax 809/465–1675. 38 rooms. Facilities: 2 restaurants, 3 bars, 2 pools, tennis court, shuttle service to golf. AE, DC, MC, V. EP, MAP.*

$–$$ **Inter Grande Frigate Bay Beach Hotel.** The third fairway of the island's golf course adjoins this property (guest here get discounts on greens fees), and the two nearby beaches—Caribbean and Atlantic—are reached by complimentary shuttle buses (the Caribbean beach is also easily reached by following the path from the far end of the pool, along the edge of the golf course). The whitewashed, air-conditioned buildings contain standard rooms as well as condominium units with fully equipped kitchens. There are hillside and poolside units; the latter are preferable. Rooms and condos have navy tile floors and are decorated with fresh floral linens and sailing prints. All have cable TV, phone, ceiling fans, and sliding glass doors leading to a terrace or balcony. There's an Olympic-size pool with swim-up bar and a terraced restaurant overlooking the pool. Packages of all sorts are available. *Box 137, Basseterre, tel. 809/465–8935, or 800/266–2185, fax 809/465–7050. 64 rooms. Facilities: restaurant, bar, pool. AE, D, MC, V. EP, MAP.*

$ **Fairview Inn.** The main building of this old, quiet, and rather simple inn is an 18th-century great house, with graceful white verandas and Oriental rugs on hardwood floors. The rooms are in little cottages sprinkled around the backyard, in the shadow of a looming mountain. The rooms are tiny and have functional furnishings (they look rather like a motel room that you might find in the middle of nowhere in the United States), with either twin or double beds, private patios, and radios. All have private baths with showers or bathtubs. Some have air-conditioning, some fans, and some neither. Those in the converted stables have the most character, with exposed stone walls. Banks of yellow allemanda climb the trellises surrounding the delightful pool, which has an ocean view. The hotel restaurant serves West Indian cuisine. *Box 212, Basseterre, tel. 809/465–2472 or 800/223–9815, fax 809/465–1056. 30 rooms. Facilities: restaurant, 2 bars, pool. AE, D, MC, V. EP, MAP.*

$ **Fort Thomas Hotel.** The new Canadian owners of this hotel, which has long been popular with business travelers and tour groups, have sunk a great deal of money into much-needed renovations. It's built on the site of an old fort, on a hillside overlooking Basseterre and the harbor. Unfortunately, the cannons anchoring the driveway and a few ramparts scattered about the grounds near the pool are the only reminders of its storied past. The building resembles an antiseptic stateside motel, but the rooms are spacious, with seashell colors and wicker furnishings. All have two double beds, telephone, private bath, air-conditioning, and radio; most have cable TV. The second-floor rooms have far better views and are worth the minimal surcharge. There's a free shuttle bus to the Frigate Bay beaches, and you can walk to town and to the stores at Pelican Mall. The pool enjoys a splendid prospect of Basseterre and the ocean. A fine, afford-

able local restaurant is part of the hotel, and there's a reasonable barbecue/pizza shop franchise on the premises. *Box 407, Basseterre, tel. 809/465–2695, fax 809/465–7518. 64 rooms. Facilities: restaurant, bar, pool, game room. AE, D, MC, V. EP, MAP.*

¢–$ ★ **Palms Hotel.** A prime location in Palms Arcade makes this delightful new all-suites hotel a good base for those wishing to explore Basseterre. Air-conditioned units are decorated mainly in corals and teals, with bright throw rugs, pastel floral linens, and art deco-style fixtures, including elaborate chandeliers. Even the smaller junior suites, which fall into the ¢ category, have cable TV, minifridge, coffeemaker, and phone. The only drawbacks are the 10-minute drive to the nearest beach and the noise that comes along with the central location (*don't* stay here during Carnival or other major festivals). *Box 64, The Circus, Basseterre, tel. 809/465–0800, fax 809/465–5889. 10 units. Facilities: bar, shops. AE, MC, V.*

Condo and Apartment Rentals

The **St. Kitts Tourist Board** (Box 132, Basseterre, St. Kitts, tel. 809/465–2620) has information on condominium and apartment rentals.

¢–$ **Morgan Heights Condominiums.** A laid-back atmosphere and reasonable prices are found at this complex along the Atlantic (although not on the beach), 10 minutes from Basseterre. The rooms are clean and comfortable, with simple contemporary white wicker furniture and ceramic tile floors. All are air-conditioned and have direct-dial phone, fully equipped kitchen, cable TV, and private bath. Covered patios overlook the water. The buildings are along a main highway and can be rather noisy during the day. The Atlantic Club serves excellent local cuisine and piña coladas with a punch. *Box 536, Basseterre, tel. 809/465–8633 , fax 809/465–9272. 5 2-bedroom units that can be rented as 1-bedroom units and individual hotel rooms. Facilities: restaurant, pool, beach shuttle. AE, D, MC, V. EP, MAP.*

¢ **Gateway Inn.** Located at the entrance to Frigate Bay, this inn has 10 air-conditioned apartments, each with kitchen, patio, washer and dryer, telephone, and cable TV. Decor is rather worn and drab in earth tones and rattan. It's a 10-minute walk to the beach or the public golf course. *Box 64, Frigate Bay, tel. 809/465–7155/7158/7159, fax 809/465–9322. 10 rooms. EP.*

Guest Houses

There are at least 20 guest houses available to visitors. The quality varies, so it's a good idea to inspect your room and be prepared with an alternate hotel should you not like what you see. Although many guest houses provide charming accommodations, warm service, and even fine cooking, the clear advantage is the cost, which can be as low as $30 a night. Most of the best properties are located in Basseterre, including **Llewellyn's Haven** (Infirmary Rd., Basseterre, tel. 809/465–2941), **On the Square** (14 Independence Sq., Box 81, Basseterre, tel. 809/465–2485/2071), **Park View Guest House** (Box 64, Basseterre, tel. 809/465–2100), **Rose's Guest House** (New Pond Site, Basseterre, tel. 809/465–4651/2434), and **Windsor Guest House** (Box 122, Basseterre, tel. 809/465–2894).

Off-Season Bets

Although the expensive properties on St. Kitts are generally out of our price range even in the off-season, more moderately priced establishments listed above become even cheaper, with rates averaging 20% lower. At **Jack Tar Village** (*see above*), for instance, all-inclusive rates per person per night start at $89. Many St. Kitts hotels also offer packages with various amenities; these offer considerable savings over standard room rates and separate amenity payments. For instance, **Ocean Terrace Inn** (*see above*) offers a variety of seven-night packages, including windsurfing ($458 per person), diving ($649 per person), and honeymoon/romantic break ($495 per person) packages.

Nightlife

Most of the Kittitian nightlife revolves around the hotels, which host folkloric shows and calypso and steel bands.

Casinos The only game in town is at the **Jack Tar Village Casino** (*see* Lodging, *above*), where you'll find blackjack tables, roulette wheels, craps tables, and one-armed bandits. Dress is casual, and play continues till the last player leaves. Note: You do not need to purchase Jack Tar passes to play, even though the casino entrance is in the hotel lobby.

Discos On Saturday night head for the **Turtle Beach Bar and Grill** (Turtle Bay, tel. 809/469–9086), where there is a beach dance-disco. Play volleyball into the evening, then dance under the stars. At **J's Place** (across from Brimstone Hill, tel. 809/465–6264), you can dance the night away with locals on Friday and Saturday. **Reflections Night Club** (tel. 809/465–6000), upstairs at Flex Fitness Center, is the hottest Kittitian nightspot. It's open Tuesday through Sunday from 9 until well past midnight. Cover charge is E.C. $10 Thursday, Friday, and Saturday nights. Another disco popular with locals is the **Cotton House Club** (Canada Estate, no phone), open weekends from 10 PM. Weekends, **Kool Runnins** (Morris Paul Dr., Pond Industrial Site, tel. 809/466–5665) serves up jerk chicken, rotis, and goat-water stew to the accompaniment of live local bands in an open-air gazebo. The hot spot for happy hour (free eats and occasional live music) is the tropical bar of **Stonewalls** (Princes St., Basseterre, tel. 809/465–5248).

Nevis

Staying in Nevis

Important Addresses **Tourist Information:** The **Tourism Office** (tel. 809/469–5521) is on Main Street in Charlestown. The office is open Monday and Tuesday 8–4:30 and Wednesday–Friday 8–4.

Emergencies **Police:** Call 911. **Hospitals:** There is a 24-hour emergency room at **Alexandra Hospital** (Charlestown, tel. 809/469–5473). **Pharmacies: Evelyn's Drugstore** (Charlestown, tel. 809/469–5278) is open weekdays 8–5, Saturday 8–7:30, and Sunday 7 AM–8 PM; the **Claxton Medical Centre** (Charlestown, tel. 809/469–5357) is open Monday–Wednesday and Friday 8–6, Thursday 8–4, Saturday 7:30–7, and Sunday 6–8 PM.

Currency Legal tender is the Eastern Caribbean (E.C.) dollar. The rate of exchange fluctuates but hovers around E.C. $2.60 to U.S. $1. The U.S. dollar is accepted everywhere, but you'll almost always get change in E.C.s. Prices quoted here are in U.S. dollars unless noted otherwise. Credit cards are accepted at most hotels and restaurants on the island, though some of the inns will take only personal checks.

Taxes and Service Charges Hotels collect a 7% government tax, and most add a 10% service charge to your bill. In restaurants, a 15% tip for good service is the norm. The departure tax is $10. Taxi drivers typically receive a 10% tip.

Getting Around
Rental Cars You may not want to drive here. The island's roads are pocked with crater-size potholes; driving is on the left; goats and cattle crop up out of nowhere to amble along the road; and if you deviate from Main Street, you're likely to have trouble finding your way around. That said, cars can be rented from the following companies: **Avis** (Stoney Ground, tel. 809/469–1240) provides Suzuki jeeps and Nissan cars. **Striker's Car Rental** (Hermitage, tel. 809/469–2654) have minimokes and compacts. **Nisbett Rentals Ltd.** (Charlestown, tel. 809/469–1913 or 809/469–6211) rents cars, minimokes, and Jeeps. None of these companies charge for mileage, and all of them accept major credit

cards. You'll need a valid driver's license; your car-rental agency will help you obtain a local license at the police station. The cost is E.C. $30 (about U.S. $12). Rental costs about $40 a day for a Jeep and about $25 for a minimoke.

Taxis Taxi service (tel. 809/469–5621; after dark, 809/469–5515) is available at the airport and by the dock in Charlestown. Sample taxi rates: from the airport to Mt. Nevis Hotel, about $17; from the airport to Charlestown, $14; from Charlestown to Oualie Beach near Hurricane Hill, about $10; from the ferry to Golden Rock, $12. Be sure to clarify whether the rate quoted is in E.C. or U.S. dollars.

Telephones and Mail To call Nevis from the United States, dial area code 809, followed by 469 and the local number. Communications are excellent, both on the island and with the United States, and direct-dial long distance is in effect. A local call costs E.C. 25¢.

Airmail letters to the United States and Canada require E.C. 80¢ per half ounce; postcards, E.C. 50¢. It takes 7–10 days for mail to reach home. Nevis and St. Kitts have separate stamp-issuing policies, but each honors the other's stamps.

Opening and Closing Times Shops are open Monday–Saturday 8–noon and 1–4; some are open on Saturday. Banking hours vary but are generally Monday–Thursday 8–2; Friday 8–5. **St. Kitts & Nevis National Bank** and the **Bank of Nevis** are open Saturday 8:30–11 AM.

Guided Tours The **taxi driver** who picks you up will probably offer to act as your guide to the island. Each driver is knowledgeable and does a three-hour tour for $50. He can also make a lunch reservation at one of the plantation restaurants, and you can incorporate this into your tour. **Fitzroy "Teach" Williams** (tel. 809/469–1140) is particularly recommended.

All Seasons Streamline Tours (tel. 809/469–5705 or 809/469–1138, fax 809/469–1139) has a fleet of air-conditioned, 14-seat vans and uniformed drivers to take you around the island at a cost of $75 for three hours.

Another tour option is **Jan's Travel Agency** (Arcade, Charlestown, tel. 809/469–5578), which arranges half- and full-day tours of the island.

Exploring Nevis

Numbers in the margin correspond to points of interest on the Nevis map.

Charlestown

1 About 1,200 of the island's 9,300 inhabitants live in **Charlestown,** the capital of Nevis. It faces the Caribbean, about 12½ miles south of Basseterre in St. Kitts. If you arrive by ferry, as most people do, you'll walk smack onto Main Street from the pier. You can tour the capital city in a half hour or so, but you'll need three to four hours to explore the entire island.

Turn right on Main Street and look for the **Nevis Tourist Office** (on your right as you enter the main square). Pick up a copy of the Nevis Historical Society's self-guided tour of the island and stroll back onto Main Street.

Although it is true that Charlestown has seen better days—it was founded in 1660—it's easy to imagine how it must have looked in its heyday. The buildings may be weathered and a bit the worse for wear now, but there is still evidence of past glory in their fanciful galleries, elaborate gingerbread, wooden shutters, and colorful hanging plants.

The stonework building with the clock tower at the corner of Main and Prince William streets houses the **courthouse** and **library.** A fire in 1873 severely damaged the building and destroyed valuable records. The current building dates from the turn of the century. You're welcome to poke around the second-floor library (open Mon.–Sat. 9–6), a cooling retreat. If you intend to rent a car, go to the **police station** across from the courthouse for your local driver's license.

The little park opposite the courthouse is **Memorial Square,** dedicated to the fallen of World Wars I and II.

When you return to Main Street from Prince William Street, turn right and go past the pier. Main Street curves and becomes Craddock Road, but keep going straight and you'll be on Low Street. The **Alexander Hamilton Birthplace,** which contains the **Museum of Nevis History,** is on the waterfront, covered in bougainvillea and hibiscus. This Georgian-style house is a reconstruction of the statesman's original home, which was built in 1680 and is thought to have been destroyed during an earthquake in the mid-19th century. Hamilton was born here in 1755. He left for the American colonies 17 years later to continue his education; he became secretary to George Washington and died in a duel with political rival Aaron Burr. The **Nevis House of Assembly** sits on the second floor of this building, and the museum downstairs contains Hamilton memorabilia and documents pertaining to the island's history, as well as fascinating displays on everything from the island's geology to its cuisine. *Low St., no phone. Admission $2 adults, $1 children under 18. Open weekdays 8–4, Sat. 10–noon. Closed Sun.*

Elsewhere on the Island

The main road makes a 20-mile circuit, with various offshoots bumping and winding into the mountains. Take the road south out of Charlestown, passing **Grove Park** along the way, where soccer and cricket matches are played.

2 About ¼ mile from the park you'll come to the ruins of the **Bath Hotel** (built by John Huggins in 1778) and **Bath Springs.** The springs—some icy cold, others with temperatures of 108°F—emanate from the hillside. Huggins's 50-room hotel, the first hotel in the Caribbean, was adjacent to the waters. Eighteenth-century accounts reported that a stay of a few days, bathing in and imbibing the waters, resulted in miraculous cures. It would take a minor miracle to restore the decayed hotel to anything like grandeur—it closed down in the late 19th century—but the Spring House has been partially restored, and some of the springs are as hot and restorative as ever. *Bathing costs $2. Open weekdays 8–noon and 1–3:30, Sat. 8–noon. Closed Sun.*

3 On Bath Road is the **Nelson Museum,** containing memorabilia from the life and times of Admiral Lord Nelson, including letters, documents, paintings, and even furniture from his flagship. Nelson was based in Antigua, but came to Nevis often to court, and eventually marry, Frances Nisbet, who lived on a 64-acre plantation here. *Bath Rd., tel. 809/469–0408. Admission: $2 adults ($1 if admission paid to Nevis History Museum), $1 children. Open weekdays 9–4, Sat. 10–1.*

4 About 2 miles from Charlestown, in the village of Fig Tree, is **St. John's Church,** which dates from 1680. Among its records is a tattered, prominently displayed marriage certificate that reads: "Horatio Nelson, Esquire, to Frances Nisbet, Widow, on March 11, 1787."

5 At the island's east coast, you'll come to the government-owned **Eden Brown Estate,** built around 1740 and known as Nevis's haunted house, or, rather, haunted ruins. In 1822, apparently, a Miss Julia Huggins was to marry a fellow named Maynard. On the day of the wedding the groom and his best man had a duel and killed each other. The bride-to-be became a recluse, and the mansion was closed down. Local residents claim they can feel the presence of . . .

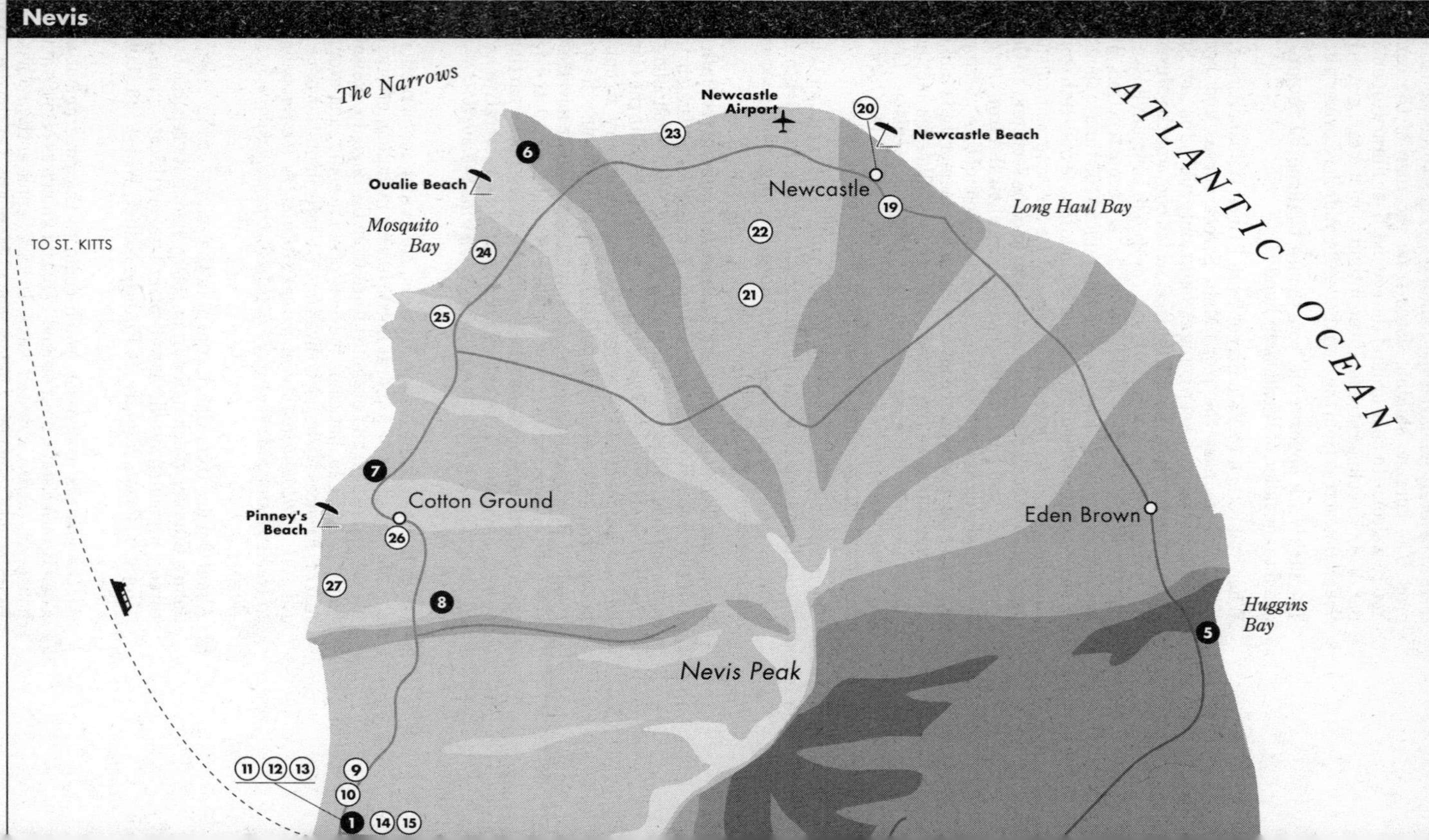
Nevis
The Narrows
Newcastle Airport
Newcastle Beach
ATLANTIC OCEAN
Oualie Beach
Newcastle
Long Haul Bay
Mosquito Bay
TO ST. KITTS
Cotton Ground
Pinney's Beach
Eden Brown
Huggins Bay
Nevis Peak
6
23
20
19
22
21
24
25
7
26
27
8
5
11
12
13
9
10
1
14
15

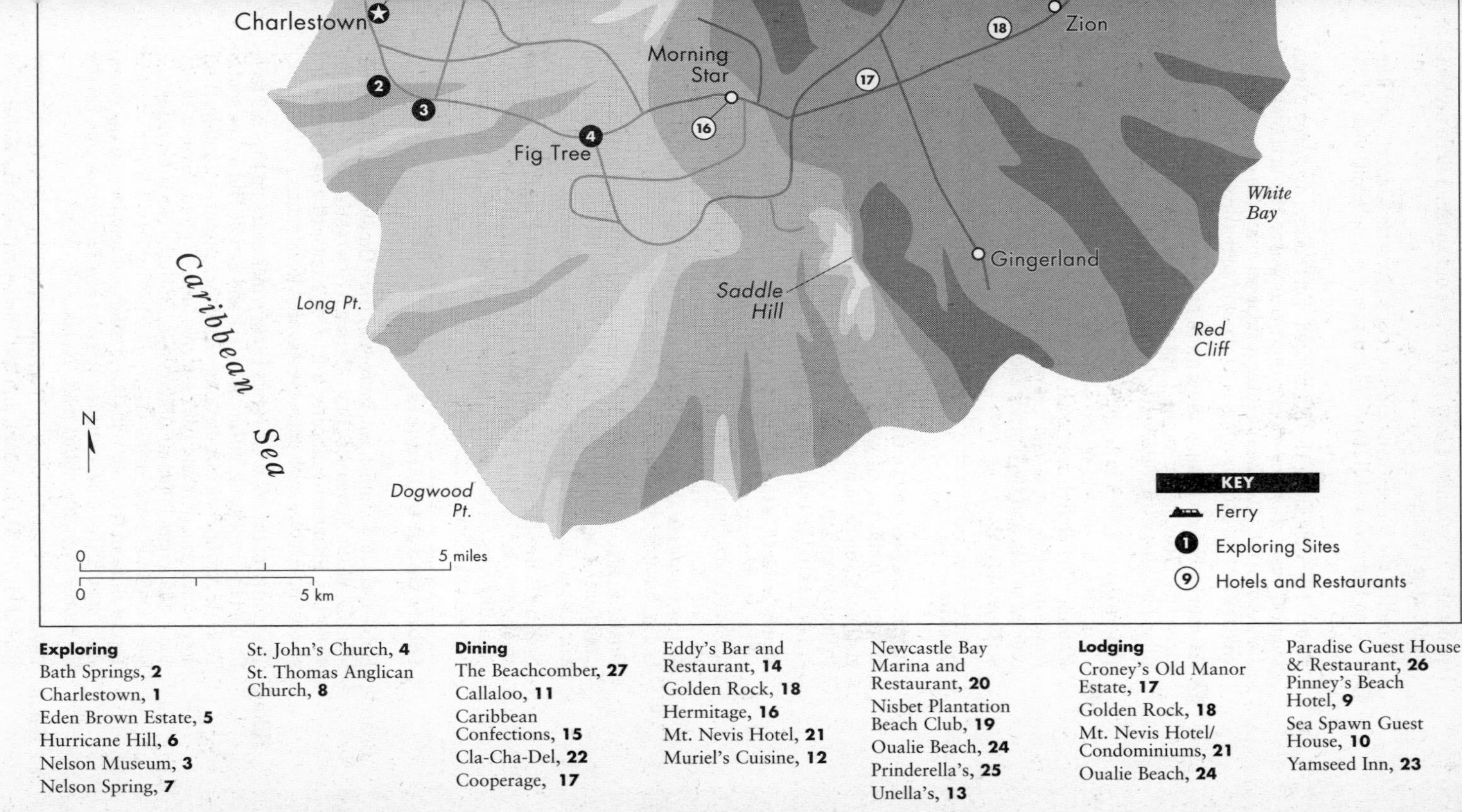

Exploring
Bath Springs, **2**
Charlestown, **1**
Eden Brown Estate, **5**
Hurricane Hill, **6**
Nelson Museum, **3**
Nelson Spring, **7**
St. John's Church, **4**
St. Thomas Anglican Church, **8**

Dining
The Beachcomber, **27**
Callaloo, **11**
Caribbean Confections, **15**
Cla-Cha-Del, **22**
Cooperage, **17**
Eddy's Bar and Restaurant, **14**
Golden Rock, **18**
Hermitage, **16**
Mt. Nevis Hotel, **21**
Muriel's Cuisine, **12**
Newcastle Bay Marina and Restaurant, **20**
Nisbet Plantation Beach Club, **19**
Oualie Beach, **24**
Prinderella's, **25**
Unella's, **13**

Lodging
Croney's Old Manor Estate, **17**
Golden Rock, **18**
Mt. Nevis Hotel/ Condominiums, **21**
Oualie Beach, **24**
Paradise Guest House & Restaurant, **26**
Pinney's Beach Hotel, **9**
Sea Spawn Guest House, **10**
Yamseed Inn, **23**

someone . . . whenever they go near the old house. You're welcome to drop by. It's free.

Rounding the top of the island, west of Newcastle Airport, you'll ar-
6 rive at **Hurricane Hill,** from which there is a splendid view of St.
Kitts.

About 1½ miles along the Main Road, **Fort Ashby,** overgrown with tropical vegetation, overlooks the place where the settlement of Jamestown fell into the sea after a tidal wave hit the coast in 1680. Needless to say, this is a favored target of scuba divers.

7 At nearby **Nelson Spring,** the waters have considerably decreased
since the 1780s, when young Captain Horatio Nelson periodically
filled his ships with fresh water here.

Before driving back into Charlestown, a little over a mile down the
8 road, stop to see the island's oldest church, **St. Thomas Anglican
Church.** The church was built in 1643 and has been altered many
times over the years. The gravestones in the old churchyard have
stories to tell, and the church itself contains memorials to the early
settlers of Nevis.

Beaches

All the beaches on the island are free to the public. There are no changing facilities, so you'll have to wear a swimsuit under your clothes. If you're doing a cab tour, you may arrange with your driver to drop you off at the beach and pick you up later. Most hotels are either located on the beach or provide transportation.

Pinney's Beach is the island's showpiece. It's almost 4 miles of soft, white sand backed by a magnificent grove of palm trees, and it's on the calm Caribbean Sea. The palm-shaded lagoon is a scene right out of *South Pacific*. The Four Seasons Resort is now here, and several of the mountain inns have private cabanas and pavilions on the beach, but it is, nevertheless, a public beach.

Oualie Beach, at Mosquito Bay, just north of Pinney's, is a black-sand beach where Oualie Beach Club (tel. 809/469–9518) can mix you a drink and fix you up with water-sports equipment.

Newcastle Beach is the beach location of Nisbet Plantation. Popular among snorkelers, it's a broad strand of soft, white sand shaded by coconut palms on the northernmost tip of the island, on the channel between St. Kitts and Nevis.

Sports and the Outdoors

Boating Hobie Cats and Sunfish can be rented from **Oualie Beach Club** (tel. 809/469–9518).**Newcastle Bay Marina** (Newcastle, tel. 809/469–9395) has Phantom sailboats, a 23-foot KenCraft powerboat, and several inflatables with outboards available for rent.

Hiking The center of the island is Nevis Peak, which soars up to 3,232 feet, flanked by Hurricane Hill on the north and Saddle Hill on the south. To scale Nevis Peak is a daylong affair that requires a guide. Your hotel can arrange it and pack a picnic lunch for you. Expect to pay about $45 a person for an all-day hike. Both the **Nevis Academy**(tel. 809/469–2091, fax 809/469–2113), headed by David Rollinson, and **Top to Bottom** (tel. 809/469–5371) offer ecorambles (slower tours) and hikes. Three-hour rambles or hikes are $20 per person, $30 for the more strenuous climb up Mt. Nevis.

Tennis There are 10 tennis courts at the **Four Seasons Resort Nevis** (tel. 809/469–1111; fee $15 an hour), and 2 at **Pinney's Beach Hotel** (tel. 809/469–5207; fee $2 an hour). **Hermitage** (tel. 809/469–3477) and **Golden Rock** (tel. 809/469–3346) offer courts to nonguests at no charge.

Water Sports The village of **Jamestown** was washed into the sea around Fort Ashby; the area is a popular spot for snorkeling and diving. Reef-protected **Pinney's Beach** offers especially good snorkeling.

Snorkeling and waterskiing trips can be arranged through **Scuba Safaris** (at the Oualie Beach Club, tel. 809/469–9518) and **Newcastle Bay Marina** (tel. 809/469–9395). Windsurfers can also be rented at both places. Scuba Safaris offers resort and NAUI-certification courses and a five-day dive package with two dives per day for $300 a person. The average cost of a single-tank dive on Nevis is $45, $80 for a two-tank dive. Snorkel equipment rents for about $10 a day.

Winston Crooke (tel. 809/469–9615) rents windsurfing equipment and provides instruction. A two-hour beginners class is $50 per person. Equipment rental is $12 an hour.

Shopping

Rare is the traveler who heads for Nevis on a shopping spree. However, there are some surprises, notably the island's stamps and batik and hand-embroidered clothing.

For dolls and baskets handcrafted in Nevis, visit the **Sandbox Tree** (tel. 809/469–5662) in Evelyn's Villa, Charlestown. Among other items available here are hand-painted chests. This is an appealing shop even if you are only browsing. The **Nevis Handicraft Co-op Society** (tel. 809/469–5509), next door to the tourist office, offers work by local artisans, including clothing, woven goods, and homemade jellies. Heading out of town, just past Alexander Hamilton's birthplace, you'll see the **Nevis Crafts Studio Cooperative** (no phone). Here Alvin Grante, a multitalented Nevisian artisan, displays his works and those of Ashley Phillips: hand-blocked prints and watercolors of the local landscape and architecture, hand-painted T-shirts, and baskets.

Stamp collectors should head for the **Philatelic Bureau,** just off Main Street opposite the tourist office. St. Kitts and Nevis are famous for their decorative, sometimes valuable, stamps. An early Kittitian stamp recently brought in $7,000.

Other local items of note are the batik caftans, scarves, and fabrics found in the Nevis branch of **Caribelle Batik** (in the Arcade of downtown Charlestown, tel. 809/469–1491). Kate Spencer's lovely island paintings and silk scarves and pareus are on sale at the **Plantation Picture House** (Main St., Charlestown, tel. 809/469–5694). **Amanda's Fashions** (Prince William St., Charlestown, tel. 809/469–5774) will custom make hand-painted sarongs and T-shirts. **Knick Knacks** (The Courtyard, off Main St., Charlestown, tel. 809/469–5784) showcases top local artisans, including Marvin Chapman (stone and wood carvings) and Jeannie Digby (exquisite dolls). They also sell whimsical hats, silk and cotton beach wraps and glazed pottery.

Dining

Nevis is known for its memorable plantation dinners, ranging from candlelit meals in elegant dining rooms to family-style dinners and West Indian buffets. Although not all of these are affordable, there are three plantations on the island that serve prix-fixe dinners costing $25–$35 per person, including wine. Another option is to visit at lunch, when some serve less expensive à la carte items. Besides these dining rooms, the island has a number of casual eateries serving inexpensive lunches and dinners. If you're renting a place with a kitchen, you can get fresh produce from the public market in Charlestown. **Super Foods** sells liquor as well as groceries.

Highly recommended restaurants are indicated by a star ★.

Category	Cost*
$$	$25–$35
$	$15–$25
¢	under $15

per person, excluding drinks and service

$$ **Cooperage.** An old stone dining room provides an elegantly rustic setting. This is classic Caribbean hotel dining, old-fashioned and drowned in butter but very good. For lunch you can order Jamaican jerk chicken or pork, burgers, conch, and sandwiches of lobster, tuna, and chicken salad. The pricier dinner menu includes green-pepper soup, curried chicken breasts, coconut shrimp, and veal in champagne morel sauce. The lobster, at $20, is the most expensive item. *Croney's Old Manor Estate, tel. 809/469–3445. Reservations required. AE, D, MC, V.*

$$ **Golden Rock.** Affordable lunches are served alfresco at umbrella-shaded tables. Lobster and shrimp, chef, chicken, and tuna are among the array of salads, and a list of sandwiches includes lobster, shrimp, ham, tuna, and chicken. Dinner here is a more opulent and expensive affair. Tables are set with pink cloths and arranged in a romantic, dimly lit room with walls of fieldstone that date from when this was a plantation house. Local Nevisian cuisine is the specialty; affordable house favorites include chicken in a raisin curry, grilled snapper with tania (a type of tuber) fritters, and green papaya pie. *Golden Rock, tel. 809/469–3346. Reservations required. AE, MC, V. Closed Sun.*

$$ **Mt. Nevis Hotel.** The airy 60-seat dining room, where white wicker tables are draped with coral napery and set with fine china and silver, opens onto the terrace and pool. During the day, there is a splendid view of St. Kitts in the distance. The menu is one of the island's most creative, thanks to head chef James de Barbieri. Dinner barely qualifies as $$, even with careful ordering. Starters include grilled portobello mushrooms with goat cheese and black olives in sherry vinaigrette, and lobster bisque. Entrées may include yellowtail fragrant with coriander, mango, and ginger; penne with smoked chicken, shiitakes, and roast peppers; or veal chop stuffed with spiced walnuts in caper sauce. The $15 Sunday buffet brunch with live music is a great buy. *Mt. Nevis Hotel/Condominiums, Newcastle, tel. 809/469–9373. Reservations advised. AE, D, MC, V.*

$–$$ **The Beachcomber.** This laid-back seaside eatery is a popular place to hang out and watch the sun drift across the sky. Reggae blasts on the sound system, locals commandeer the pool table, and live bands entertain on Tuesday, Thursday, and Friday, all of which makes food seem extraneous. It's very good, nonetheless, with standouts including mozzarella en carozza, flying fish and chips, and snapper en papillote. The staff is ultrafriendly. *Pinney's Beach, tel. 809/469–1192. MC, V.*

$–$$ **Prinderella's.** This casual open-air restaurant enjoys a stunning setting on Tamarind Bay, with views across the channel to St. Kitts. A lovely mural behind the bamboo bar suffices for decor. Seafood is the obvious specialty, although the English owners, Ian and Charlie Mintrim, do a proper shepherd's pie and roast beef with Yorkshire pudding. Yachties (it has a great anchorage) buzz around the bar, there's wonderful snorkeling right around the point, and Friday brings a boisterous happy hour, with free finger food like salmon mousse, hummus, and chicken wings. The ambiance is the farthest thing from stuffy. Ask Charlie to tell you the story behind the restaurant's name; it features Prinderella, a cince and a gairy frogmother. You'll want a bouble dourbon when she's finished. *Jones Bridge, tel. 809/469–1291. AE, MC, V. Closed Mon. June–Sept. (Mon.–Wed. in Oct., Nov., and April 15–May 31).*

$ **Eddy's Bar and Restaurant.** Colorful flags flutter from the veranda of this white-on-white second-story restaurant overlooking Memorial Square in the center of Charlestown. A local artist designed the tablecloths and bright, boldly colored wall hangings. You'll find fine stir-fried dishes and local West Indian specialties, such as cream of cauliflower soup and tender, crispy conch fritters with just the right amount of sass in the sauce. Eddy's mom, Eulalie Williams makes the terrific hot sauce, on sale at the Main Street Supermarket down the street. His wife Sheila is an amiable hostess. Stop by between 5 and 8 on Wednesday for happy hour, when drinks are half-price and snacks are free. *Main St., Charlestown, tel. 809/469–5958. Reservations advised. AE, MC, V. Closed Thurs., Sun., and Sept.*

$ **Oualie Beach.** This low-key, casual bar and restaurant on Oualie Bay is the perfect stop for authentic Nevisian fare after a long day on the beach. Try the delicious homemade soups, including ground-nut or breadfruit vichyssoise. Then move on to Creole conch stew, lobster crepes, or chicken breasts stuffed with spinach. The atmosphere is rollicking on weekends, with live music and local crowds. *Oualie Beach, tel. 809/469–9735. AE, D, MC, V.*

$ **Unella's.** The atmosphere is nothing fancy, just simple tables set ona second-floor porch overlooking the waterfront in Charlestown, but the fare is good West Indian. Stop here for exceptional curried lamb, island-style spareribs, and steamed conch, all served with local vegetables, rice, and peas. Unella opens shop around 9 in the morning, when locals and boaters appear waiting for breakfast; she stays open all day. *Waterfront, Charlestown, tel. 809/469–5574. No credit cards.*

¢–$ **Callaloo.** This simple but pretty eatery, run by genial Abdul Hill who learned to cook with typical French-Creole flair on St. Martin, is another local standout. Delicious rotis make a quick, cheap lunch. Or opt for the yummy grilled kingfish in lemon butter, conch Creole, curried goat, or ribs, all served with generous side portions of rice and beans, salad, and "provisions" (local foods such as yams and cassava). *Government Rd. and Main St., tel. 809/469–5389. D, MC, V. Closed Sun.*

¢–$ **Caribbean Confections.** Drop by this friendly Charlestown establishment for local color and good food. Sandwiches, homemade pastries, cookies, and popcorn are great for a quick bite. There's also a full menu of local dishes served with peas, rice, and salad. On Saturdays, free hors d'oeuvres at 6 PM are followed by a courtyard buffet dinner and entertainment for $19 a person. The restaurant also serves breakfast. *Main St. (across from tourist office), Charlestown, tel. 809/469–5685. Reservations advised for Sat. buffet. MC, V.*

¢–$ **Cla-Cha-Del.** Locals frequent this place for the authentic West Indian fare and informal atmosphere. The appealing dining room is dressed with painted parrots on ocher walls, lace tablecloths, and flower pots. Seafood is particularly good here, with freshly caught kingfish or snapper and conch swimming in a Creole or light lemon butter sauce. Sides might include scrumptious tania fritters or macaroni pie. The four-course dinners, ranging from $10 (chicken or ribs) to $30 (lobster), are an amazing bargain. On Saturdays, try the goatwater or bullhead stew. *Shaw's Rd., Newcastle, tel. 809/469–9640. Dinner reservations required. MC, V. No lunch Sun.*

¢–$ ★ **Muriel's Cuisine.** Hanging plants, local still lifes and scarlet carnations on the tables dress up this simple eatery. Three meals are served daily, except Sunday. Bountiful entrées are served with mounds of rice and peas and fresh local vegetables, a side salad, and garlic bread. The subtly spiced jerk chicken would pass muster in many a Jamaican kitchen, and the goat-water and beef stews are fabulous: full-bodied and fragrant with garlic and coriander. Muriel St. Jean is the gracious hostess. Her restaurant attracts a very local clientele—women in hair curlers and young men who come to flirt shyly with the waitresses. *Upper Happy Hill Dr., Charlestown, tel. 809/469–5920. AE, D, MC, V. Closed Sun.*

¢ **Newcastle Bay Marina and Restaurant.** The pizza here is excellent, as is the sea view from the deck. Try the conch chowder, a sandwich, or a salad. This complex, part of the Mt. Nevis hotel, will soon include a fitness facility and live entertainment on certain evenings. *Newcastle Bay Marina, tel. 809/469–9395. AE, D, MC, V. Closed Wed. and mid-Apr.–mid-Dec.*

Lodging

Restored sugar plantations are Nevis's trademark lodging. Two of the island's five plantations have rates that fall into the top end of our $$ category in high season. You'll do better in low season (*see* Off-Season Bets, *below*), when more of the plantations become affordable. Most of these operate on the Modified American Plan (MAP; breakfast and dinner included in room rate). Besides these fairly pricey accommodations, choices are somewhat limited, with only a handful of budget hotels and guest houses.

Highly recommended lodgings are indicated by a star ★.

Category	Cost*
$$	$125–$200
$	$90–$125
¢	under $90

**All prices are for a standard double room, excluding 7% tax and a 10% service charge. To estimate rates for hotels offering MAP, add about $35–$40 per person per day to the above price ranges.*

$$ **Croney's Old Manor Estate.** Vast tropical gardens surround this restored sugar plantation in the shadow of Mt. Nevis. Many of the enormous guest rooms have high ceilings, gorgeous stone or tile floors, marble vanities, exposed wood beams, king-size four-poster beds, and colonial reproductions, but some units are a bit gloomy and dark, with old-fashioned dowdy madras settees and soiled carpets. The appealing air throughout is one of faded, slightly shabby elegance. The outbuildings, such as the smokehouse and jail, have been imaginatively restored, and the old cistern is now the pool. This is the home of the Cooperage, a well-respected restaurant (*see* Dining, *above*). There's transportation to and from the beach. The hotel is not recommended for children under 12. *Box 70, Charlestown, tel. 809/469–3445, 800/223–9815, or 800/892–7093, fax 809/469–3388. 14 rooms. Facilities: pool, 2 restaurants, 2 bars. AE, MC, V. EP, MAP.*

$$ **Golden Rock.** Co-owner Pam Barry runs this inn, which was built by her great-great-great-grandfather over 200 years ago. She has decorated the 16 units with four-poster beds of mahogany or bamboo, native grass rugs, rocking chairs, and island-made floral-print fabrics. All rooms have a private bath and a patio. The restored sugar mill is a two-level suite (with a glorious wood-and-bamboo staircase) for honeymooners or families and the old cistern is now a spring-fed swimming pool. Although charming, many of the rooms are somewhat worn. The estate covers 150 mountainous acres and is surrounded by 25 acres of lavish tropical gardens, including a sunken garden. Enjoy the Atlantic view and cooling breeze from the bar. The Saturday night West Indian buffet, held December –June, is very popular. Barry also organizes historical and nature hikes. *Box 493, Gingerland, tel. 809/469–3346, fax 809/469–2113. 16 rooms. Facilities: restaurant, bar, pool, tennis court. AE, MC, V. EP, MAP.*

$$ **Mt. Nevis Hotel/Condominiums.** Air-conditioned standard rooms and suites at this hotel are done up with handsome white wicker furnishings, southwestern pastel fabrics, glass-top tables, and colorful island prints. Suites, which are just outside our $$ category, have

full, modern kitchens and dining areas. All units have a balcony, minifridge, direct-dial phone, cable TV, and VCR. The main building houses the casual restaurant and bar, which open onto a terrace that overlooks the pool and St. Kitts beyond. Shuttle service is provided to the water-sports center and outdoor restaurant at Newcastle Beach. The hotel has its own ferry, used for moonlight cruises when it's not carrying passengers to and from St. Kitts. *Box 494, Newcastle, tel. 809/469–9373 (collect), fax 809/469–9375. 32 rooms. Facilities: pool, restaurant, bar, water sports, beach club, boutique. AE, D, MC, V. EP, MAP.*

$$ ★ **Oualie Beach.** Every few years this beachside spot builds a few more charming West Indian–style cottages, and there are now 22 rooms, including air-conditioned deluxe rooms with mahogany four-poster canopy beds and marble vanities. Even these are in the $$ range, one of the island's best buys. All rooms look across the water to stunning views of neighboring St. Kitts. The rooms are bright, airy, and simply furnished and have refrigerator, cable TV, phone, and safe. Studio units have a full kitchen. There is a full dive shop here offering NAUI-certified instruction, and dive packages are available. Sunfish and Windsurfers may be rented, and the hotel just introduced Skimmer waterborne rowing machines. Breakfast, lunch, and dinner are served at an informal restaurant and bar. *Oualie Beach, tel. 809/469–9735, fax 809/469–9176. 22 rooms. Facilities: restaurant, bar, water-sports and dive center. AE, D, MC, V. EP, MAP.*

$–$$ **Pinney's Beach Hotel.** These bungalows and rooms are smack on Pinney's Beach, a short walk from Charlestown. Unfortunately, the accommodations are rather worn. Rooms in the $ range are in cottages that face the garden. For an extra $25–$40, you get a newer and slightly more spacious room in one of the beach cottages. All rooms are air-conditioned and have cable TV, phone, and minifridge. More expensive units also have a microwave. *Pinney's Beach, tel. 809/469–5207 or 312/699–7570 in the U.S. 36 rooms. Facilities: restaurant, bar, 2 tennis courts, pool. AE, D, MC, V. EP, MAP.*

$ **Yamseed Inn.** A very rough access road leads to this pale yellow bed-and-breakfast overlooking St. Kitts, tucked away from resort and plantation hotels on its own private patch of glittering white sand. Friendly innkeeper Sybil Siegfried offers four rooms in her house right by the sea, nestled amid beautiful grounds (Sybil's an avid gardener). Chirping hummingbirds welcome you into the stylish reception area. Each room has a private bath and is handsomely appointed with a mahogany bed, wood-panel ceiling, throw rugs, white-tile floors, and antiques. Breakfast includes delicious homemade muffins and grated coconut muesli. Sybil is a gracious hostess, having lost neither her Southern accent nor her charm. The only flaw in paradise is Yamseed's location near the airport, which puts it in the flight path (fortunately, air traffic isn't busy). You'll need a car to get to restaurants and shops. *On the beach, Newcastle, tel. 809/469–9361. 4 rooms. 3-night minimum. No credit cards. BP.*

¢ **Paradise Guest House and Restaurant.** This pretty whitewashed inn with powder blue trim opened in October 1994. The eight upstairs rooms are simple but clean and fresh. All have fans or ceiling fans, private shower baths, crisp blue floral curtains, and upholstery and bedspreads made of boldly colored abstract pattern fabrics. Ask for one of the front rooms, which open onto a terrace with ocean view. The downstairs restaurant has a few immaculately set tables on the terrace and indoors, with sky blue napery, and a distant view of the water. Prices for the solid local cuisine are ¢ to $. *Across the main road from Pinney's Beach, tel. 809/469–0394. 8 rooms. Facilities: restaurant. No credit cards.*

¢ **Sea Spawn Guest House.** If you're willing to forsake all extras, this place is among the least expensive on the island. Rooms are bare but clean. Guests pay $7 to use a communal kitchen. Breakfast, lunch, and dinner are served in the restaurant. It's a two-minute walk to Pinney's Beach and a 10-minute walk to downtown Charlestown. Service is not especially friendly. *Old Hospital Rd., Charlestown, tel. 809/469–5239, fax 809/469–5706. Facilities: dining room, lounge, beach cabana, common kitchen. MC, V. EP.*

Villa and Cottage Rentals Nevis has several villa and cottage complexes that offer an affordable alternative to hotels and guest houses. Among them are **Pinney's Village Complex** (Box 508, Charlestown, tel. 809/469–1811; \$31–\$65 a night); **Hurricane Cove Bungalows** (Mosquito Bay, tel. 809/469–9462; \$75–\$115 a night); and **Castle Bay Villas** (Newcastle, tel. 809/469–9088/9490; \$125–\$150 a night).

Off-Season Bets Although the plantations tend to be expensive, an off-season visit brings more of these charming properties within reach, including the **Hermitage** (St. Johns, Figtree Paris, tel. 809/469–3477) and **Nisbet Plantation Beach Club** (Newcastle, St. James Parish, tel. 809/469–9325).

Nightlife

The hotels usually bring in local calypso singers and steel or string bands one night a week. On Friday night the Shell All-Stars steel band entertains in the gardens at **Croney's Old Manor** (tel. 809/469–3445). The **Golden Rock** (tel. 809/469–3346) brings in the Honeybees String Band to jazz up the Saturday-night buffet. Have dinner and a dance on Wednesday nights at **Pinney's Beach Hotel** (tel. 809/469–5207). The **Oualie Beach** hotel (tel. 809/469–9735) throws a popular Saturday night buffet with live string band and masquerade troupe. **Eddy's Bar and Restaurant** (tel. 809/469–5958) holds raucous West Indian nights with theme buffet and live string band Fridays and Saturdays.

Apart from the hotel scene, there are a few places where young locals go for late-night calypso, reggae, and other island music. **Club Trenim** (no phone), on Government Road in Charlestown, has disco dancing starting at 8:30 every night except Tuesday. **Dick's Bar** (no phone) in Brickiln has live music or a DJ on Friday and Saturday evenings.

22 St. Lucia

Updated by Kate Sekules

Oval, lush St. Lucia, 27 miles long and 14 miles wide, sits at the southern end of the Windward Islands. It has two topographical features, apart from its beaches, that earn it a special place in the Caribbean tableau of islands: the twin peaks of the Pitons (Petit and Gros), which rise to more than 2,400 feet, and the bubbling sulfur springs in the town of Soufrière, part of a low-lying volcano that erupted thousands of years ago and now produces highly acclaimed curative waters.

Thanks to its startling natural beauty, St Lucia is often referred to as "the Helen of the West Indies", and its coastline is familiar to sailors and divers alike—the reefs near the Pitons at Anse Chastanet being especially sought-after scuba sites. In between the populous north and the gorgeous south runs a sometimes tortuously winding road passing lush valleys, rain forest, banana plantations, secluded bays, and small villages. In its less secluded regions, St Lucia is noticeably sophisticated, hosting not only the usual carnival, but also its world-renowned Jazz Festival in late spring, and filled with a glittering selection of all-inclusive resorts, many of them very fancy indeed.

If you think this renders St Lucia among the less affordable islands, you're right—to a point. Less pricey inns and apartments do exist, however, and some of the finest hotels drop their rates so far in the off-season (*see* Off-Season Bets, *below*) that they become accessible to budget travelers. Consider also the potential savings represented by an all-inclusive rate—there are reasons why this form of accommodation is so popular around here. One way you can save with this is to glue yourself to the resort and not go around much. Renting a car here is pricey, and public transportation not the best, though there are minivan taxis that ply fixed routes cheaply.

The history of this 238-square-mile island resembles that of many in the Caribbean. After a 150-year struggle between the French and the English for control of St. Lucia, during which the island changed hands 14 times, the British took permanent possession in 1814. On February 22, 1979, St. Lucia became an independent state within the British Commonwealth of Nations, with a resident governor-general appointed by the queen, though the French occupation is remembered in the island patois, the Creole cuisine, and the names of the places and the people. Nowadays, bananas and tourism are neck-and-neck as top revenue earners, with tourism coming out on top for the first time in 1993. This pleases the savvy St Lucians, who are working hard to avoid ruining their island with opportunistic overbuilding—as has happened on many other islands—while remaining the friendliest people for miles around.

What It Will Cost These sample prices, meant only as a general guide, are for high season. Expect to pay $125 a night or more at a $ full-service hotel, though it is possible to spend less than that. A $$ all-inclusive resort will cost about $300 per couple per night. Transportation, be it taxi or rental car, is also expensive: A car costs about $60 a day. Public transportation is limited, but a minivan, or route taxi, from Castries to Rodney Bay is about $2; from Castries to Vieux Fort, it's about $5.50. If you have a kitchen of your own, you can save on local produce, especially if you're in range of Castries market, where fresh fish, fruit and vegetables are very reasonably priced. However, imported goods, such as coffee, are expensive. Expect to pay about $20 a person for a modest dinner; at least $5 for lunch at an inexpensive café. Wine is prohibitively expensive; stick to local rum punches or beer, which start at about $1.75 in restaurants, and remember that rum is cheaper and more plentiful than water, for which resorts charge as much as $5 a bottle. A single-tank scuba dive is about $45; snorkel equipment rents for about $5 a day.

Before You Go

Tourist Information Contact the **St. Lucia Tourist Board** (820 2nd Ave., 9th Floor, New York, NY 10017, tel. 212/867–2950 or 800/456–3984, fax 212/370–7867; in Canada: 4975 Dundas St. W, Suite 457, Etobicoke "D," Islington, Ontario, tel. 416/236–0936 or 800/456–3984, fax 416/236–0937; in the United Kingdom: 10 Kensington Court, London W8 5DL, tel. 0171/937–1969, fax 0171/937–3611)

Arriving and Departing

By Plane There are two airports on the island. Wide-body planes use Hewanorra International Airport, on the southern tip of the island. Vigie Airport, near Castries, handles interisland and charter flights. **BWIA** (tel. 800/327–7401) has direct service from Miami and, on Sunday, New York. **American** (tel. 800/433–7300) has a nonstop service to St. Lucia from New York on Saturday and Sunday, plus daily service from most major U.S. cities, with a transfer in San Juan. (**American Eagle** flights from San Juan land at Vigie Airport.) **Air Canada** (tel. 800/776–3000; in Canada, 800/268–7240) has direct weekend service from Toronto. **British Airways** (tel. 0181/897–4000) has service from London to St. Lucia with a stop in Antigua on Thursdays, Saturdays, and Sundays. **LIAT's** (tel. 809/462–0701) small island-hoppers fly into Vigie Airport, linking St. Lucia with Barbados, Trinidad, Antigua, Martinique, Dominica, Guadeloupe, and other islands.

From the Airport Taxis are unmetered, and although the government has issued a list of suggested fares, these are not binding. Negotiate with the driver *before* you get in the car, and be sure that you both understand whether the price you've agreed upon is in E.C. or U.S. dollars. The drive from Hewanorra to Castries takes about 75 minutes and should cost about U.S. $50—almost as much as a full day's car rental. A taxi to Castries from Vigie Airport, on the other hand, is only about $5. If you plan to rent a car for your entire stay, consider picking it up at the airport.

Passports and Visas U.S., Canadian, and British citizens must produce a valid passport and a return or ongoing ticket.

Language The official language is English, but you'll also hear the local French-influenced patois.

Precautions Bring along industrial-strength insect repellent to ward off the mosquitoes and sand flies. If you happen to step on a sea urchin, its long black spines may lodge under the skin; don't try to pull them out, because you could cause infection. Apply ammonia or an ammonia-based liquid as quickly as possible, and the spine will retreat, allowing you to ease it out. Don't touch or even sit under a manchineel tree, whose poisonous fruit and leaves cause skin blisters; these trees are usually marked on hotel property. The waters on the Atlantic (east) coast can be rough, with dangerous undertows—avoid swimming there. Tropical Storm Debbie in 1994 contaminated the water supply slightly, so ask before you drink from the faucet.

Staying in St. Lucia

Important Addresses **Tourist Information: St. Lucia Tourist Board** is based at the Pointe Seraphine duty-free complex on Castries Harbor (tel. 809/452–4094 or 809/452–5968). The office is open weekdays 8–4:30. There is also a tourist information desk at each of the two airports (Vigie, tel. 809/452–2595, and Hewanorra, tel. 809/454–6644).

Emergencies **Police:** Call 999. **Hospitals:** Hospitals with 24-hour emergency rooms are **Victoria Hospital** (Hospital Rd., Castries, tel. 809/452–2421) and **St. Jude's Hospital** (Vieux Fort, tel. 809/454–6041), a privately endowed hospital run by nuns, which is said to have the better equipment. **Pharmacies:** The largest pharmacy is **Williams Pharmacy** (Williams Bldg., Bridge St., Castries, tel. 809/452–2797).

Currency The official currency is the Eastern Caribbean dollar (E.C.$). Figure about E.C. $2.60 to U.S. $1. U.S. dollars are readily accepted, but you'll usually get change in E.C. dollars. Major credit cards are widely accepted, as are traveler's checks. Prices quoted here are in U.S. dollars unless indicated otherwise.

Taxes and Service Charges Hotels collect an 8% government tax. Hotels and most restaurants add a 10% service charge to your bill. Tip taxi drivers 10%. There is no sales tax. The departure tax is $11, or E.C. $27.

Getting Around Discovering St. Lucia using public transportation is difficult. You will probably want to budget for either renting a car for at least two days or taking a guided tour (*see below*).

Buses There's no organized service, but minivans, or route taxis, cruise the island and, like taxis, will stop when hailed. You can also catch a minivan in Castries by hanging around outside Clarke Cinema (corner Micoud and Bridge Sts.). This is the cheapest way to get around the island. The fare varies according to distance. A ride from Castries to Rodney Bay is E.C. $5; to Vieux Fort, E.C. $15. Be sure you are being charged the minivan and not the private taxi rate.

Taxis Taxis are always available at the airport, the harbor, and in front of the major hotels. Most hotels post the names and phone numbers of drivers and a table of fares set by the taxi commission. Learn the fare before you agree to a journey. Taxi drivers have usually undergone some training, and make excellent tour guides.

Rental Cars Driving is on the left. Roads are congested around Castries and in the north; to the south, traffic is light, but the road surface is not always smooth, and the hairpin bends can be surprising. To rent a car, you have to be over 25 and hold a valid driver's license and a credit card. You must buy a temporary St. Lucian license at the airports or police headquarters (Bridge St., Castries) for $16. Rental agencies include **Avis** (tel. 809/452–2700 or 800/331–1212), **Budget** (tel. 809/452–0233 or 800/527–0700), **Dollar** (tel. 809/452–0994), and **National** (tel. 809/452–8028 or 800/328–4567). Rates are high—from $60 a day.

Telephones and Mail

To call St. Lucia from the United States, dial area code 809, access code 45, and the local five-digit number. You can make direct-dial long-distance calls from the island, and the connections are excellent. To place interisland calls, dial the local five-digit number. A local call costs E.C. 25¢.

Postage for airmail letters to the United States, Canada, and Great Britain is E.C. 95¢ for up to 1 ounce. Postcards are E.C. 75¢ to the United States and Canada; E.C. 85¢ to Great Britain.

Opening and Closing Times

Shops are open weekdays 8–4, Saturday 8–noon. Banks are open Monday–Thursday 8–3, Friday 8–5, and, at a few branches in Rodney Bay, Saturdays 9–noon.

Guided Tours

Taxi drivers take special guide courses and offer the most personalized way to see the island. Four can share a car and cut rates; otherwise, costs are steep. A six-hour tour around the island costs $120 (tip additional). Hourly taxi rates are about $20. **Carib Touring** (tel. 809/452–6791) and **Sunlink International** (tel. 809/452–8232) offer a variety of half- and full-day tours. A full-day tour of southern St. Lucia, including the Pitons and Mt. Soufrière, costs $25 per person. **Barnard's Travel** (tel. 809/452–2214) and **St. Lucia Representative Services Ltd.** (tel. 809/452–3762) also offer half- and full-day island tours.

Exploring St. Lucia

Numbers in the margin correspond to points of interest on the St. Lucia map.

Castries

Castries, on the northwest coast, is a busy city with a population of
1 about 60,000. It lies on the shore of a sheltered bay surrounded by green hills. Ships carrying bananas, coconuts, cocoa, mace, nutmeg, and citrus fruits for export leave from **Castries Harbour,** one of the busiest ports in the Caribbean. Cruise ships dock here, too, though most go to **Pointe Seraphine,** a Spanish-style cruise ship complex that includes duty-free shops. The tourist board is here, so you may want to drop by to collect free maps and brochures. It is also the starting point for many island tours.

The John Compton Highway connects the duty-free complex to downtown Castries. To reach the downtown center from Pointe Seraphine's transportation terminal, you can stroll for 20 minutes or take a cab.

Castries, with Morne Fortune (the Hill of Good Luck) rising behind it, has had more than its share of bad luck over the years, including two hurricanes and four fires. As a result, it lacks the colorful colonial buildings found in other island capitals. Most of the buildings are modern, and the town has only a few sights of historical note.

Head first to **Derek Walcott Square,** a green oasis ringed by Brazil, Laborie, Micoud, and Bourbon streets. Formerly Columbus Square, it was renamed in 1993 after Nobel poet and St. Lucian son Derek Walcott, one of the island's two Nobel laureates, the other being the late economist Sir Arthur Lewis. At the corner of Laborie and Micoud streets there is a 400-year-old saman tree. A favorite local story is of the English botanist who came to St. Lucia many years ago to catalogue the flora. Awestruck by this huge old tree, she asked a passerby what it was. "Massav," he replied, and she gratefully jotted that down in her notebook, unaware that "massav" is patois for "I don't know." Directly across the street is the Roman Catholic **Cathedral of the Immaculate Conception,** which was built in 1897. Some of the 19th-century buildings that managed to survive fire, winds, and rains can be seen on Brazil Street, the southern border of the square.

Head north on Laborie Street and walk past the government buildings on your right. On the left, William Peter Boulevard is one of Castries's shopping areas. "The Boulevard" connects Laborie Street with Bridge Street, another shopping street.

Continue north for one more block on Laborie Street and you'll come to Jeremie Street. Turn right, and head a few blocks to the **market** on the corner of Jeremie and Peynier streets. The hot, smelly, and crowded old indoor market is undergoing renovations, and there's a new redbrick semi-open-air produce market with all the color and bustle still intact. The market is most crowded on Saturday mornings, when farmers bring their produce to town.

Elsewhere on the Island

Morne Fortune

You'll need a full day to explore the island south of Castries. A rental car gives you greater flexibility and is cheaper than a guided tour, if shared among three or four people. To reach **Morne Fortune,** head due south on Bridge Street, turning right onto Government House Road. The drive will take you past the **Government House,** the official residence of the governor-general of St. Lucia and one of the island's few remaining examples of Victorian architecture. Also on the road, and worth a stop is **Bagshaw Studios,** producing its instantly recognizable screen-printed clothing and linens in wildly tropical colors and intricate designs—the most distinctive St. Lucian gifts, since Bagshaw's products are not exported. From the top of the hill,
2 at **Fort Charlotte,** you'll see Martinique to the north and the twin peaks of the Pitons to the south.

Fort Charlotte was begun in 1764 by the French as the *Citadelle du Morne Fortune.* It was completed after 20 years of battling and changing hands. Its old barracks and batteries have now been converted to government buildings and local educational facilities, but you can drive around and look at the remains, including redoubts, a guardroom, stables, and cells. At the end of the road you can also walk up to the Inniskilling Monument, a tribute to one of the most famous battles, fought in 1796, when the 27th Foot Royal Inniskilling Fusiliers wrested the Hill of Good Fortune from the French. Stop also in the Military Cemetery, which was first used in 1782; faint inscriptions on the tombstones tell the tales of the French and English soldiers who died here. Six former governors of the island are buried here as well.

South of Castries

The road from Castries to Soufrière travels through beautiful country. The entire West Coast road has been undergoing a widening face-lift since 1992, which, at press time was still underway, having suffered slightly from 1994's Tropical Storm Debbie. Originally planned for completion as far as Soufrière in 1995, it is anyone's guess how far the road has got by now, and you should check its status before you set out for anywhere on the west coast. As it stands, it takes about three hours to drive the whole loop from Castries down the west coast, back up the east coast, and across the Barre de L'Isle Ridge—and that's with ideal conditions and no stops.

3 A few miles south of Castries, stop by **Marigot Bay,** one of the most beautiful natural harbors in the Caribbean. In 1778, British Admiral Samuel Barrington took his ships into this secluded bay within a bay and covered them with palm fronds to hide them from the French. The resort community today is a great favorite of yachtspeople. Parts of *Doctor Doolittle* were filmed here 30 years ago. You can arrange to charter a yacht, swim, snorkel, or lime with the yachting crowd at one of the bars. A 24-hour water taxi connects the various points on the bay.

If you continue south, you'll be in the vicinity of one of the island's two rum distilleries. Major production of sugar ceased here in

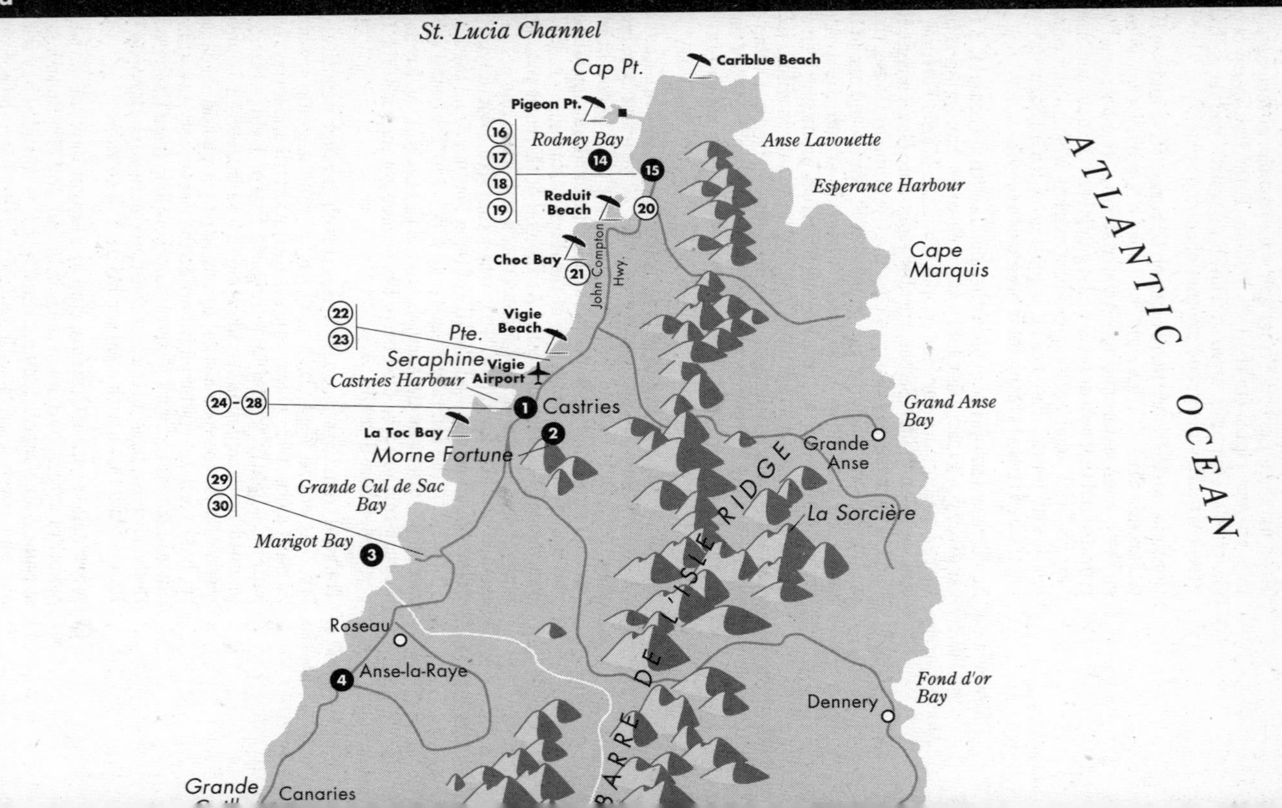
St. Lucia Channel
Cap Pt.
Cariblue Beach
Pigeon Pt.
Rodney Bay
Anse Lavouette
Esperance Harbour
ATLANTIC OCEAN
16
17
18
19
14
15
Reduit Beach
20
Choc Bay
21
John Compton Hwy.
Cape Marquis
22
23
Vigie Beach
Pte. Seraphine
Vigie Airport
Castries Harbour
24-28
Castries
1
La Toc Bay
2
Morne Fortune
Grand Anse Bay
Grande Anse
29
30
Grande Cul de Sac Bay
BARRE DE L'ISLE RIDGE
La Sorcière
Marigot Bay
3
Roseau
4
Anse-la-Raye
Fond d'or Bay
Dennery
Grande
Canaries

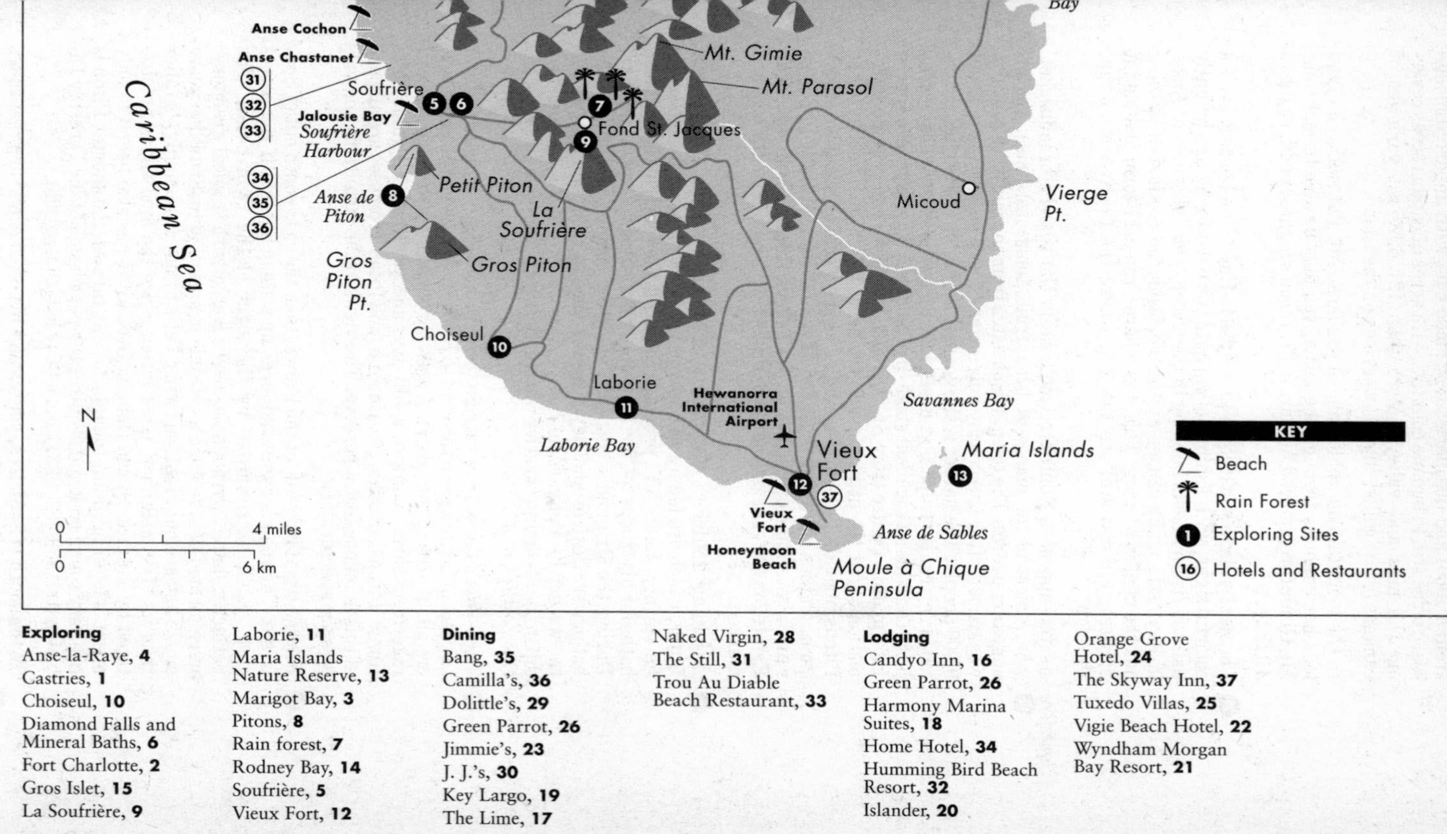

Caribbean Sea
Anse Cochon
Anse Chastanet
31
32
33
Soufrière
Jalousie Bay
Soufrière Harbour
34
35
36
Anse de Piton
Petit Piton
Gros Piton Pt.
Gros Piton
La Soufrière
Fond St. Jacques
Mt. Gimie
Mt. Parasol
Micoud
Vierge Pt.
Choiseul
Laborie
Laborie Bay
Hewanorra International Airport
Savannes Bay
Maria Islands
Vieux Fort
Vieux Fort
Honeymoon Beach
Anse de Sables
Moule à Chique Peninsula
0 4 miles
0 6 km
N
KEY
Beach
Rain Forest
Exploring Sites
Hotels and Restaurants
Exploring
Anse-la-Raye, 4
Castries, 1
Choiseul, 10
Diamond Falls and Mineral Baths, 6
Fort Charlotte, 2
Gros Islet, 15
La Soufrière, 9
Laborie, 11
Maria Islands Nature Reserve, 13
Marigot Bay, 3
Pitons, 8
Rain forest, 7
Rodney Bay, 14
Soufrière, 5
Vieux Fort, 12
Dining
Bang, 35
Camilla's, 36
Dolittle's, 29
Green Parrot, 26
Jimmie's, 23
J. J.'s, 30
Key Largo, 19
The Lime, 17
Naked Virgin, 28
The Still, 31
Trou Au Diable Beach Restaurant, 33
Lodging
Candyo Inn, 16
Green Parrot, 26
Harmony Marina Suites, 18
Home Hotel, 34
Humming Bird Beach Resort, 32
Islander, 20
Orange Grove Hotel, 24
The Skyway Inn, 37
Tuxedo Villas, 25
Vigie Beach Hotel, 22
Wyndham Morgan Bay Resort, 21

around 1960, and distilleries now make rum with imported molasses. You're still in banana country, with acres of banana trees covering the hills and valleys. More than 127 different varieties of bananas (often called "figs") are grown on the island.

In the mountainous region ahead you'll see **Mt. Parasol,** and if you look hard enough through the mists, you may be able to make out **Mt. Gimie** (pronounced "Jimmy"), St. Lucia's highest peak, rising to 3,117 feet.

4 The next village you'll come to is **Anse-la-Raye.** The beach here is a colorful sight, with fishing nets hanging on poles to dry and brightly painted fishing boats bobbing in the water. The fishermen of Anse-la-Raye still make canoes by the old-fashioned method of burning out the center of a log. This was where Tropical Storm Debbie hit hardest; you can still see the gulf where the floodwaters swept through.

Soufrière As you approach **Soufrière,** you'll be in the island's breadbasket,
5 where most of the mangoes, breadfruit, tomatoes, limes, and oranges are grown. The town, which dates from the mid-18th century, was named after the nearby volcano and has a population of about 9,000 people. The harbor is the deepest harbor on the island, accommodating cruise ships that nose right up to the wharf. The nearby jetty contains an excellent small-crafts center. The **Soufrière Tourist Information Centre** (Bay St., tel. 809/459–7200) can provide information about the attractions in the area, which, in addition to the Pitons, include La Soufrière, billed as the world's only drive-in volcano, and its sulfur springs; the Diamond Mineral Baths; and the rain forest. You can also ask at the Tourist Centre about Soufrière Estate, on the east side of town, replete with botanical gardens and minizoo.

6 Adjoining Soufrière Estate are the **Diamond Falls and Mineral Baths,** which are fed by an underground flow of water from the sulfur springs. Louis XVI provided funds for the construction of these baths for his troops to "fortify them against the St. Lucian climate." During the Brigand's War, just after the French Revolution, the baths were destroyed. They were restored in 1966, and you can see the waterfalls and gardens before slipping into your swimsuit for a dip in the steaming curative waters. *Soufrière. Admission: E.C. $5. Open daily 10–5.*

7 The island's dense tropical **rain forest** is most easily accessible from the east of Soufrière on the road to Fond St. Jacques. It actually covers about 10% of the island. A trek through the lush landscape can take from three hours to a full day, and you'll need a guide. Mt. Gimie, Piton Canaries, Mt. Houlom, and Piton Tromasse are all part of this immense forest reserve. The views of the mountains and valleys are spectacular.

8 For the best land view of the **Pitons,** take the road south out of Soufrière. The road is awful and leads up a steep hill, but if you persevere, you'll be rewarded by the sight of the twin peaks. The perfectly shaped pyramidal cones, covered with tropical greenery, were formed of lava from a volcanic eruption 30 to 40 million years ago. They are not identical twins: Petit Piton, confusingly, is taller than its "fat" neighbor, Gros Piton. Since the mud slides precipitated by Tropical Storm Debbie, Gros Piton has also been the only one it is legal to climb, though the way up even the shorter Piton is one very tough trek and requires the permission of the Forestry Division (tel. 809/452–3231) and a knowledgeable guide.

To the south of Soufrière, your nose will note the left turn that takes
9 you to **La Soufrière,** the volcano, and its **sulfur springs.** There are more than 20 pools of black, belching, smelly sulfurous waters and yellow-green sulfur baking and steaming. You walk—behind your

guide, whose service is included in admission—around a fault in the substratum rock, which makes for a fascinating 20-minute experience, but an experience that can be stinking and sweaty as hell (maybe literally) on a hot day. *La Soufrière. Admission: E.C. $3 (including guided tour). Open daily 9–5.*

Follow the road farther south and you'll come next to the coastal
10 town of **Choiseul,** home to wood-carving and pottery shops. At the turn of the road past the Anglican Church, built in 1846, a bridge crosses the river Dorée, so named because the riverbed is blanketed with fool's gold. In La Fargue, just to the south, the **Choiseul Arts & Craft Centre** (tel. 809/452–3226) sells superb traditional Carib handicrafts, including pottery, wickerwork, and braided khus-khus grass mats and baskets.

11 The next stop is **Laborie,** the prototypical St. Lucian fishing village, little changed over the centuries. There's not much to see here, but you can stop to buy cheese, bread, and fish for lunch.

12 Now drive along the southern coast of the island to **Vieux Fort,** St. Lucia's second-largest city and home of Hewanorra International Airport. Drive out on the **Moule à Chique Peninsula,** the southernmost tip of the island. If you look to the north, you can see all of St. Lucia, and, if the day is especially clear, you can spot the island of St. Vincent 21 miles to the south. Looking straight down, you can see where the waters of the Caribbean blend with the bluer Atlantic.

13 The **Maria Islands Nature Reserve,** which has its own interpretive center, consists of two tiny islands in the Atlantic off the southeast coast. The 25-acre Maria Major and its little sister, 4-acre Maria Minor, are inhabited by rare species of lizards and snakes that share their home with frigate birds, terns, doves, and other wildlife. *Moule à Chique, tel. 809/454–5014. Admission: Wed.–Sat. E.C. $3, Sun. E.C. 50¢. Open Wed.–Sun. 9:30–5.*

A road leads from Vieux Fort through the towns on the Atlantic coast. Don't be fooled by its smooth start, it gets bumpier and bumpier as you progress. It takes you past **Honeymoon Beach,** a wide, grassy, flat Anse l'Islet peninsula jutting into the ocean. Drive through Micoud and, a few miles farther north, Dennery, both of which are residential towns overlooking the Atlantic. At Dennery the road turns west and climbs across the Barre de l'Isle Ridge through a tiny rain forest with dense vegetation. There are trails along the way that lead to lookout points where you can get a view of the National Forest Preserve. The road eventually winds back to Castries.

The North End and Gros Islet

The west coast north of Castries is the most developed part of the island and is easy and safe to navigate. Take the John Compton Highway north toward the Vigie Airport. This whole stretch is of far more interest to the hedonist than to the historian, but it features some of the island's best beaches and resort hotels.

14 About 15 minutes north of Castries, **Rodney Bay,** named after Admiral Rodney, is an 80-acre man-made lagoon surrounded by hotels, restaurants, and tourists. The St. Lucian and Royal St. Lucian hotels are in this area, as are Capone's, Lime, and several other popu-
15 lar eateries. North of the lagoon, **Gros Islet** (pronounced grow-zee-*lay*) is a quiet little fishing village not unlike Anse-la-Raye to the south. But on Friday nights, Gros Islet springs to life with a wild and raucous street festival to which everyone is invited (*see* Nightlife, *below*).

Pigeon Point

Pigeon Point, jutting out on the northwest coast, was Pigeon Island until a causeway was built to connect it to the mainland. Tales are told of the pirate Jambe de Bois (Wooden Leg), who used to hide out here. This 40-acre area, a strategic point during the struggles for control of the island, is now a national park, with long sandy beaches, calm waters for swimming, and areas for picnicking.

The **Pigeon Point Museum** includes the ruins of barracks, batteries, and garrisons dating from the French and English battles. *Pigeon Point, no phone. Admission: E.C. $3. Open Mon.–Sat. 9–4.*

Beaches

Beaches are all public, and many are flanked by hotels where you can rent water-sports equipment and have a rum punch. Unlike many islands, St. Lucia does not have any major hotel strip, where property after property lines a single beach. Rather, hotels tend to have their own stretches of sand; visitors usually keep to the beach where they are staying. There are also secluded beaches, accessible only by water, to which hotels can arrange boat trips. It is not advisable to swim along the windward (east) coast, where the Atlantic waters are rough and sometimes dangerous.

Pigeon Point off the northern shore has secluded white-sand beaches, fine for picnicking and swimming. You can walk to the beaches from the main road.

Reduit Beach is a long stretch of beige sand between Choc Bay and Pigeon Point and is home to the St. Lucian and the Royal St. Lucian hotels, which offer numerous water sports. You can walk or drive here from the main road.

Vigie Beach and **Choc Bay,** north of Castries Harbour, have fine beige sand and calm waters. Both are within walking distance of the main road.

La Toc Bay is near Castries Harbour and is accessible by car or taxi. The sand here is beige.

Anse Cochon, on the Caribbean coast, is a black-sand beach accessible only by boat. The waters are superb for swimming and snorkeling.

Anse Chastanet is a gray-sand beach just north of Soufrière, with a backdrop of green hills and the island's best reefs for snorkeling and diving. Anse Chastanet Hotel, located here, has a dive shop, restaurant, and bar on the beach. You'll need a car to travel from Soufrière down the rutted road that leads to the hotel and beach.

Vieux Fort, at the southernmost tip, has a long secluded stretch of gray volcanic sand and waters protected by reefs. **Honeymoon Beach** is another sandy escape just west of Vieux Fort. You'll need a car to reach either one.

Sports and the Outdoors

Most hotels offer Sunfish, water skis, fins, masks, and other water-sports equipment free to guests and for a fee to nonguests.

Golf There are nine-hole courses at **Sandals St. Lucia** (tel. 809/452–3081) and **Cap Estate Golf Club** (tel. 809/452–8523). A caddy is required at the former; greens fees are $15–$20 at either for 18 holes. Club rentals are another $10. These courses are scenic and good fun, but they're not of professional caliber.

Hiking The island is laced with trails, but you should not attempt the challenging peaks on your own. Your hotel, the tourist board, or the **Forestry Division** (tel. 809/452–3231) can provide you with a guide. **The St. Lucia National Trust** (tel. 809/452–5005), established to preserve the island's natural and cultural heritage, tours several sites, including Pigeon Island, the Maria Islands, and Fregate Island.

Jogging You can jog on the beach by yourself or team up with the **Roadbusters** (tel. Jimmie at 809/452–5142 or evenings at 809/452–4790).

Scuba Diving **Scuba St. Lucia** (tel. 809/459–7355), a PADI five-star training facility with dive shops at Anse Chastanet (which is, among aficionados, one of the most highly regarded dive sites anywhere) and the St. Lucian Hotel, offers daily beach and boat dives, resort courses, underwater photography, and day trips. Trips are also arranged through **Buddies Scuba** (tel. 809/452–5288), **Dive Jalousie** (tel. 809/459–7666), the **Moorings Scuba Centre** (tel. 809/451–4357), and **Windjammer Diving** (tel. 809/452–0913). The cost of a single-tank dive starts at $45. Snorkel equipment rents for about $5 a day. **Anse Chastanet** hotel (tel. 809/454–7000 or 800/545–2459) offers seven-day dive packages that include two dives daily.

Sea and Snorkeling Excursions The 140-foot square-rigger ***Brig Unicorn*** (tel. 809/452–6811) sails to Soufrière, with steel bands, a swim stop, rum punch, and soda. Its sister schooner, the ***Buccaneer,*** also does outings. **Captain Mike's** (tel. 809/452–0216) does swimming and snorkeling cruises. **Jacob's Watersports** (tel. 809/452–8281) offers speedboat and snorkeling cruises. Sea and snorkeling excursions can also be arranged through **Mako Watersports** (tel. 809/452–0412) and the **Surf Queen** (tel. 809/452–8351, ext. 515) or through your hotel. These excursions range from $15 for snorkeling to $70 for a lunch cruise.

Squash The **St. Lucia Racquet Club** (adjacent to Club St. Lucia, tel. 809/450–0551) has one court and its own pro, who gives lessons and clinics. It is not air-conditioned, however. **Jalousie Plantation** (tel. 809/459–7666) also has a squash court open to nonguests.

Tennis All the major hotels have their own tennis courts, but many of them prohibit nonguests from playing. Those that do allow nonguests charge about $10 for 45 minutes of court time. Failing that, **St. Lucia Racquet Club** (adjacent to Club St. Lucia, tel. 809/452–0551), with its seven lighted courts, offers temporary memberships to nonguests.

Waterskiing Contact **Mako Watersports** (tel. 809/452–0412). Rentals are also available at most of the hotels for about $20 for 15 minutes.

Windsurfing The **St. Lucian Hotel** is the local agent for Mistral Windsurfers (tel. 809/452–8351). Also contact **Marigot Bay Resort** (tel. 809/453–4357) and **Mako Watersports** (tel. 809/452–0412). Most hotels rent Windsurfers to nonguests for about $10 an hour ($35 for instruction).

Shopping

Shopping on St. Lucia is low-key. The island's best-known products are the unique hand-silk-screened and hand-printed designs of Bagshaw Studios, which are designed, printed, and sold only on St. Lucia. In addition, there are native-made wood carvings, pottery, and straw hats and baskets, which happen to be the best souvenir bargains. Some of the straw baskets at the Castries market, for example, can be had for a few dollars; those filled with spices make good gifts.

Remember that duty-free products such as designer clothing and perfume are not cheap, even without taxes. Check prices in your hometown before your trip: They may be lower than they are in the Caribbean.

Shopping Areas St. Lucia entered the duty-free market with the opening of **Pointe Seraphine,** a Spanish-style complex by the harbor, with shops selling designer perfumes, china and crystal, jewelry, watches, leather goods, liquor, and cigarettes. Native crafts are also sold in the shopping center. Castries has a number of shops, mostly on **Bridge Street**

and **William Peter Boulevard,** selling locally made souvenirs. The new **Castries market** is chockablock with stalls selling crafts and local products, such as hand-sewn dolls and pressed cocoa powder. There is also a shopping arcade at the **St. Lucian** hotel. **Choiseul** is the capital of local arts and crafts.

Good Buys

Fabrics and Clothing

Bagshaw Studios (La Toc Rd., La Toc Bay, tel. 809/452–7570; Vigie Airport, Pointe Seraphine, no phone) sells silk-screened fabrics and clothing. **Windjammer Clothing Company** (tel. 809/452–1041) has its main store at Vigie Cove and an outlet at Pointe Seraphine. **Caribelle Batik** (Old Victoria Rd., the Morne, Castries, tel. 809/452–3785) creates batik clothing and wall hangings. Visitors are welcome to watch the craftspeople at work. The **Batik Studio** at Humming Bird Beach Resort (Soufrière, tel. 809/459–7232) offers superb sarongs, scarves, and wall panels.

Native Crafts

Trays, masks, and figures are carved from mahogany, red cedar, and eucalyptus trees in the studio adjacent to **Eudovic Art Studio** (Morne Fortune, tel. 809/452–2747). Hammocks, straw mats, baskets and hats, and carvings, as well as books and maps of St. Lucia, are at **Noah's Arkade** (Jeremie St., Castries, and Pointe Seraphine, tel. 809/452–2523). **Artsibit** (corner Brazil and Mongiraud Sts., tel. 809/452–7865) features works by top St. Lucian artists. The **Choiseul Art & Craft Centre** (Lafargue, tel. 809/454–3226) has a huge selection of handmade basketware, ceramics (from pots to sculpture), bas-reliefs from local woods, and many small and portable pieces too.

Dining

With so many visitors staying at all-inclusives, the selection of independent restaurants here is limited. You'll find the widest choice of moderately priced places in and around Rodney Bay. The best area for sampling the local fare (mostly spicy barbecue) is Gros Islet, during its Friday-night jump-up (*see* Nightlife, *below*).

If you're planning to cook, you'll find the basics in most grocery stores here. Stores in Rodney Bay supply charter boats and offer better-quality imported goods, such as coffees and canned foods. Buy your breads and pastries at **Bread Baskets** (tel. 809/452–0647) in Rodney Bay or the **Central Bakery Amurbroise** (Marianne St., no phone) in Castries. For vegetables and fruits, don't miss the Castries market on the corner of Jeremie and Peynier streets (*see* Exploring St. Lucia, *above*).

Mangoes, plantains, breadfruits, limes, pumpkins, cucumbers, pawpaws (pronounced poh-poh here, known as papaya elsewhere), yams, christophines (a squashlike vegetable), and coconuts are among the fruits and vegetables that appear on menus throughout the island. Every menu lists the catch of the day (especially flying fish), along with the ever-popular lobster, and you may see the national dish, saltfish and green fig (dried, salted white fish with plantainlike banana), which most agree is an acquired taste. Chicken, pork, and barbecues are also big-time here. Most meat is imported, including beef from Argentina and Iowa and lamb from New Zealand. The French influence is strong in St. Lucian restaurants, and most chefs cook pre–nouvelle cuisine, with a Creole flair.

Highly recommended restaurants are indicated by a star ★.

Category	Cost*
$$	$20–$30
$	$10–$20
¢	under $10

**per person, excluding drinks and service*

$$ **Jimmie's.** This popular, open-air, mom-and-pop-cozy restaurant and bar perched above the bay makes a relaxing daytime stop and becomes a romantic dinner spot when the harbor lights twinkle below. Appetizers on the seafood-dominated menu include a great Creole stuffed crab, while a wise choice of entrée is the special seafood platter with samplings from every part of today's catch; all entrées come with several local vegetables—pumpkin, black beans, christophines, greens—plus garlic bread. Dessert lovers had better be in a banana mood, since the menu lists about 10 options—every single one, from fritters to ice cream, made with St. Lucian "figs." *Vigie Cove, Castries, tel. 809/452–5142. No reservations. AE, MC, V.*

$$ ★ **Trou Au Diable Beach Restaurant.** This beachside open-air lunch spot at the Anse Chastanet hotel is the perfect place to break from a day of diving or sunbathing. The West Indian cuisine is delicious, and many specialties are prepared right before your eyes on a barbecue grill. The *rotis* (Caribbean-style burritos)here are the best on the island, served with homemade mango chutney you could eat by the jar. Try also the island pepper pot—pork, beef, or lamb simmered for many hours with local veggies and spices; or a good old tuna melt in case you're homesick. Dessert always features an unusual flavor of ice cream, maybe soursop or anise seed; try it! There's always a young and lively crowd here, and although the restaurant caters mostly to the resort's guests, everyone is quite welcome. *Anse Chastanet, Soufrière, tel. 809/459–7000. AE, DC, MC, V. No dinner.*

$–$$ **Bang.** The eccentric Brit Colin Tennant (a.k.a. Lord Glenconner), founder of the glamorous hideaway island of Mustique (between the Pitons), came to St. Lucia to open his dream resort, over which he lost control (it's a long story). The resort became Jalousie Plantation, but Tennant stayed on to open this wickedly cute spoof on a Jamaican jerk joint, with ice-cream-color trim, assorted ramshackle wooden chairs and cushion-strewn booths, a cerise velvet-draped stage for music, and a buzz like the early days of Mustique when Jagger was young. Drink rum, eat barbecue from "Ye Olde Jerk Pit," but beware—this place closes at whim. *Next to Jalousie, north of Soufrière, tel. 809/459–7864. Reservations advised. No credit cards.*

$–$$ ★ **The Lime.** Across the street from Capone's, the Lime is a favorite place for "liming" (hanging out). A casual place with lime-colored gingham curtains, straw hats decorating the ceiling, and hanging plants, it offers a businessman's three-course lunch and a buffet of local dishes, like callaloo and lambi (conch). Starters may include homemade pâté or stuffed crab back. Entrée choices may be medallions of pork fillet with the chef's special orange-and-ginger sauce, stewed lamb, or fish fillet poached in white wine and mushroom sauce. The prices are more reasonable than neighboring Capone's, which is perhaps why the expatriates and locals gather here in the evenings. Next door is Late Limes, where they gather when the evening starts turning into morning. *Rodney Bay, tel. 809/452–0761. Dinner reservations advised. MC, V. Closed Tues.*

¢–$$ **Camilla's.** About the only decent restaurant actually in the town of Soufrière, the tiny, second-floor Camilla's is pretty in pink, somewhat under-ventilated on a hot night (apart from the two balcony tables), and friendly as anything. The menu is admirably simple and all local—you can have today's catch as curry, Creole-style, or grilled with lemon sauce, or there's barbecue chicken with garlic sauce and fries, or lobster salad. There's also a list of tropical cocktails that's bigger than the entire restaurant. *7 Bridge St., Soufrière, tel. 809/459–5379. Reservations advised. AE.*

¢–$$ **Key Largo.** Here's where to get brick-oven pizzas, espresso and cappuccino when homesickness strikes. The popular Pizza Key Largo—topped with shrimp, artichokes, and what seems like a few pounds of mozzarella—is tough to pass up. *Rodney Bay, tel. 809/452–0282. MC, V.*

$ **Naked Virgin.** Tucked away in the quiet Castries suburb of Marchand (just opposite the local post office—keep asking), this pleasant hangout offers terrific Creole cuisine, and every guest leaves with a free T-shirt. The owner, Mr. Paul John, has worked in many of the island's major hotels and his rum concoction, the Naked Virgin, could be the best punch you've ever tasted. Shrimp Creole and fried flying fish are highly recommended. *Marchand Rd., Castries, tel. 809/452–5594. Reservations advised. AE, MC, V.*

¢ ★ **J.J.'s.** Not only are the prices right here, but the food is also some of the best on the island. The superbly grilled fish with fresh vegetables is tops. Tables are on a terrace above the road, and the welcome is friendly and casual. On Friday nights the music blares, and the locals come for liming and dancing in the street. *Marigot Bay Rd. (3 mi before the bay), Marigot, tel. 809/451–4076. No reservations. No credit cards.*

Lodging

St. Lucia is known for its upscale, all-inclusive resorts, but it is also home to more moderately priced all-inclusives. Even at lesser-priced properties, however, only the least expensive rooms are what we would consider affordable during high season (*see* price chart, *below*). The island has few options in the strictly budget range. You won't find the inexpensive hotels, guest houses, or apartment and cottage rentals that are plentiful on some Caribbean islands. Given this, you may be better off budgeting most of your money for lodging in order to opt for an all-inclusive, especially because transportation can be expensive if you stay away from the beach in a small hotel. You should reserve four months in advance for a room during high season.

Highly recommended lodgings are indicated by a star ★.

Category	Cost*
$$	$125–$200
$	$60–$125
¢	under $60

**All prices are for a standard double room for two, excluding 8% tax and a 10% service charge. To estimate rates for hotels offering MAP/FAP, add about $35–$40 per person per day to the above price ranges. To estimate rates for all-inclusives, add about $75 per person per day.*

Hotels

$$ **Green Parrot.** The hillside setting is the draw at this hotel, set high up in Morne Fortune above Castries. The motel-like rooms have a patio, phone, air-conditioning, and bath with tub/shower and vanity. In addition to the Green Parrot Restaurant, which is open to the public, hotel guests have a separate dining room with a sunken bar. The hotel arranges boat trips to Jambette Beach for barbecue and snorkeling, and a free bus scoots you to town and the beach. *Box 648, Castries, tel. 809/452–3399, fax 809/453–2272. 60 rooms. Facilities: 2 restaurants, bar, games room, pool, nightclub. AE, MC, V. EP, MAP.*

$$ ★ **Harmony Marina Suites.** Your suite may have a view of the pool or Rodney Bay Marina, but don't fear, Reduit Beach is only 200 yards away. You get an awful lot for a relatively modest sum at this all-suite hotel: quiet air-conditioning, direct-dial phones, cable TV, clock radio, "his and hers" closets, snow-white bathrooms with tubs, hair dryers, and separate toilets. Four of the studios have kitchenettes (worth the extra $10), which are a dream on long stays, especially since there's a well-stocked minimarket on the property. Eight VIP suites were added 1994 and are within this price category off-season. They have coffeemakers and fridges instead of kitchens, huge Jacuzzis instead of walls between bathroom and bedroom, 10-foot sundecks, and four-poster beds. Yet, with all this, they seem smaller overall. For long stays (more than a month) paid in advance, rates are slashed by more than half. *Box 155, Castries, tel. 809/452–8756 or 800/742–4276, fax 809/452–8677. 30 units. Facilities: restaurant, bar, minimarket, pool, water sports, laundry. MC, V. EP, MAP.*

$$ **Tuxedo Villas.** This pristine-white apartment block set around a tiny swimming pool in a peaceful corner close to Reduit Beach is a good value, as long as you insist on one of the newly decorated apartments (the three elderly first-floor ones have dingy '70s decor with louvered closets and sloping pine ceilings). There's individually controlled air-conditioning in all the bedrooms, which are tiny but comfortable, each with its own en suite, tubless, bathroom. Kitchens are well equipped, with full-size fridge-freezers, plus glass-topped bamboo tables, and breakfast bars, while compact lounges have rattan couches, cable TV, phones, and cool white tile floors. There's nothing exciting here, but everything works, everything's spotless, and the staff is friendly. *Box 419, Castries, tel. 809/452–8553, fax 809/452–8577. 10 apartments. Facilities: pool, restaurant, bar. AE, MC, V. EP.*

$ ★ **Candyo Inn.** This small pink hotel, which opened in 1992 in the heart of Rodney Bay, is one of the best buys in the Caribbean. It's a five-minute walk from beaches and several good restaurants, and it has a small pool and lanai decked with the usual plastic lawn furniture and potted palms. A small outdoor bar near the pool serves drinks and snacks. The two-story building and its lush green grounds are carefully looked after and spotless. All 12 rooms have air-conditioning, cable TV, clock radio, direct-dial phone, veranda, white-tile floors, and white contemporary furniture with floral upholstery. The eight suites have kitchenettes, larger sitting areas, and tubs and are worth the extra $15 a night. The atrium lobby has a small convenience shop. The staff is delightful. *Box 386, Rodney Bay, tel. 809/452–0712, fax 809/452–0774. 4 rooms, 8 suites. Facilities: drink/snack bar, minimarket, pool. AE, MC, V. EP.*

$ **Humming Bird Beach Resort.** Choose from a wide range of accommodations at this charming spot at the edge of Soufrière. Rooms are a bit dark and would fare better without the dingy carpeting, but four-poster beds and African sculpture are nice touches. The restaurant is a favorite hangout of locals and expatriates. Joyce Alexander, the owner, is a marvelous, dynamic hostess who, when not making improvements to her small hotel, designs batiks for the adjoining boutique. *Box 280, Soufrière, tel. 809/459–7232, fax 809/459–7033. 10 units. Facilities: restaurant, bar, pool. D, MC, V. EP, MAP.*

$ **Islander.** Step off the U-shaped drive into the bustling lobby, full of notices for German tour groups and calypso music, and you'll already feel more local than if you were across the street at the handsome international Royal St Lucian. Accommodation is in one of the wooden bungalows set in thickly verdant gardens, each with a tall wooden ceiling and skylight and a big front porch. Superior twins have a wacky wicker bar, complete with bar stools for your own cocktail party. Other rooms have kitchenettes, while apartments ($5–10 more) have a full kitchen on the porch. There is air-conditioning throughout, plus phone, cable TV, and clock radio. You won't write home about the decor, but you might about the sound of laughter from the poolside bar, and the friendly staff. *Box 907, Castries, tel. 809/452–8757 or 800/223–9815, fax 809/452–0958. 56 rooms, 6 apartments. Facilities: restaurant, bar, pool, shuttle bus to beach. AE, D, MC, V. EP.*

$ **Orange Grove Hotel.** Up a long hill off the road to Windjammer Landing, you'll come upon this hilltop motel with a nondescript exterior. It looks like an inexpensive accommodation and it is one. Surprisingly, the rooms—which are large, light, and clean—are packed with all the conveniences you'd expect at a large resort: two phones, two cable TVs, air-conditioning, full baths, white-tile floors, and new but typical Caribbean-style furniture. All have separate sitting areas and balconies or patios overlooking the hillside. And although you're away from the beach, guests are welcome to use the beach facilities at Club St. Lucia 15 minutes away—free transportation is available. The hotel tripled in size in 1994 and is getting to be better known among Americans, as well it might when a suite costs less than $80 off-season. The restaurant serves West Indian cuisine for similarly low prices. *Box 98, Castries, tel. 809/452–8213. 51 rooms, 11 suites. Facilities: restaurant, bar, pool. AE, MC, V. EP, MAP.*

$ **The Skyway Inn.** If you're staying in the north but have an early flight to catch from Hewanorra in the morning, this is the ideal place to stay, just 100 yards from the airport and minutes from Vieux Fort and its beaches. The inn is clean and comfortable with air-conditioned rooms, cable TV, meeting facilities, and a free shuttle to the beach. There's an open-air restaurant and bar on the roof and a pool down below. *Box 353, Vieux Fort, tel. 809/454–7111, fax 809/454–7116. 32 rooms, 1 suite. Facilities: restaurant, bar, gift shop. AE, MC, V.*

$ **Vigie Beach Hotel.** A glassed-in bar sits on the mile-long Vigie Beach, and a path leads through gardens up to the hotel. Air-conditioned rooms are spacious, with modern decor, double beds, balconies with garden or beach view, TVs, and phones. You'll be sunning to the sound of small planes, since the hotel is located adjacent to Vigie Airport. The staff seems genuinely unconcerned. *Box 395, Castries, tel. 809/452–5211, fax 809/452–5434. 47 rooms. Facilities: restaurant, 2 bars, pool, Jacuzzi. AE, D, DC, MC, V. EP.*

¢ **Home Hotel.** Expect bare-bones rooms with shared baths and a cheerful welcome in this family home in the center of town, in the shadow of the church steeple. Rooms are clean and basic, each with a double bed, table, and two chairs. There's a kitchen where you can make breakfast and snacks. Small grocery stores and cafés are about a block away. It's only a short walk to the harbor, the bay, and the gray-sand beach. *Soufrière, tel. 809/454–7318. 7 rooms with shared baths. No credit cards. EP.*

Apartment Rentals St. Lucia has limited short-term home and apartment rentals. The **Top of the Morne Apartments** (tel. 809/452–3603, fax 809/453–1433), above Castries, has modern studio units with kitchens and patios overlooking a pool for about $150 a night. **Le Cure Villas** (tel. 800/387–2726) has apartments starting at $190 a night. Comparable units are offered by **Island Hideaways** (tel. 800/832–2302). **Villa Apartments** (tel. 809/452–2691), a local agent, has properties with slightly lower rates. Also contact the **Tourist Board** (tel. 809/452–4094 or 809/452–5968) for additional listings.

Off-Season Bets The following hotels fall within the $$ category from April to October, and are well worth considering. Prices are based on off-season rates, which can more than double during winter.

Wyndham Morgan Bay Resort (Box 2216, Gros Islet, tel. 809/450–2511) is one of the best-priced all-inclusives on St Lucia. Its double rooms-with-everything cost less than $200 off-season. Off-season at **Anse Chastanet Hotel** (Box 7000, Soufrière, tel. 809/459–7000),

$150–$200 buys you a slice of heaven in the form of a Premium or Deluxe room. These meld into the tropical mountainside, with louvered wooden walls open to stunning Piton and Caribbean vistas, or to the deep shady green of the forest. There are also good dive packages here.

Nightlife

Most of the action is in the hotels, which feature entertainment of the island variety—limbo dancers, fire-eaters, calypso singers, and steel band jump-ups. Many offer entertainment packages, including dinner, to nonguests.

Splash (St. Lucian Hotel, tel. 809/452–8351) is a sophisticated place with a good dance floor and suitably splashy lighting effects. It's open Monday–Saturday from 9 PM.

On weekends, locals usually hang out at the **Lime** (Rodney Bay, tel. 809/452–0761); **Capone's** (Rodney Bay, tel. 809/452–0284), an art deco place right out of the Roaring '20s, with a player piano and rum drinks; or **A-Pub** (tel. 809/452–8725), a lounge in an A-frame building overlooking Rodney Bay. The **Charthouse** (Rodney Bay, tel. 809/452–8115) has a popular bar, jazz on the stereo, and live music on Saturday. Young boaters tie up at the **Bistro** (Rodney Bay, tel. 809/452–9494) for drinks, chess, darts, and backgammon. The **Green Parrot** (The Morne, tel. 809/452–3399) is in a class all by itself. Chef Harry Edwards hosts the floor show, which features limbo dancers. Harry has been known to shimmy under the pole himself. There are also belly dancers.

On Friday nights, sleepy Gros Islet becomes like Bourbon Street during Mardi Gras, as the entire village is transformed into a street fair. Vendors and stalls sell beer and fried chicken. At the far end of the street, mammoth stereos loudly beat out sounds as locals and strangers let their hair down. **Club Society** (Grande Rivière, Gros Islet, tel. 809/453–0312) and the **Golden Apple** (Grande Rivière tel. 809/450–0634) are probably the best spots for meeting locals. The **Banana Split** (St. Georges St., Gros Islet, tel. 809/452–8125) offers entertainment and special theme nights, with a perpetual "spring break" atmosphere. It can get rowdy, so it's best to travel in a group and keep your wits about you. Another Friday night street scene and a popular alternate venue for liming can be found just before you enter Marigot Bay. The music is supplied by **J.J.'s Restaurant** (tel. 809/453–4076), and the popular fare is curried goat. More and more locals are choosing to come here instead of the more touristy Gros Islet happening.

23 St. Martin/ St. Maarten

Updated by Marcy Pritchard

There are frequent nonstop flights from the United States to St. Maarten/St. Martin, so you don't have to spend half your vacation getting here—a critical advantage if you have only a few days to enjoy the sun. The 37-square-mile island is home to two sovereign nations, St. Maarten (Dutch) and St. Martin (French), so you can experience two cultures for the price of one (although the Dutch side has lost much of its European flavor).

This island, particularly the Dutch side, is ideal for people who like to stay busy. It's hard to be bored when you're surrounded by sparkling beaches, fine restaurants, duty-free shopping, and activities from water sports to golf, discos to casinos. The island depends on tourism and strives to appeal to the whole spectrum of travelers (anyone can fit in here). This makes bustling St. Martin/St. Maarten much more affordable than its reputation would lead you to believe. The fierce competition between properties translates into package deals, especially in the off-season or for large tour groups—you can save a lot by hooking up with a wholesale travel agent's specials. The island also offers apartments, small inns, and guest houses (those on the French side have more charm but are pricier). Best of all, with few exceptions, even the cheapest accommodations are either on or within walking distance of beaches. If you frequent local Creole restaurants rather than swank French boîtes, you'll be pleasantly surprised by the quality of the kitchens and the fairly low prices.

On the negative side, St. Maarten/St. Martin has been thoroughly discovered and exploited; you are likely to find yourself sharing beachfronts with tour groups or conventioneers. Yes, there is gambling, but the table limits are so low that hard-core gamblers will have a better time gamboling on the beach. It can be fun to shop, and there's an occasional bargain, but many goods, particularly electronics, are cheaper in the United States. The island infrastructure has not kept pace with development. Although there are plans to expand marina, airport, and road services, you will probably run in to congestion at the airport and seemingly endless traffic on the roads.

What It Will Cost These sample prices, meant only as a general guide, are for high season. A $ hotel room on either the Dutch or French side averages $125 a night; a ¢ guest house is about $50. A $ restaurant dinner will be about $25; lunch at a *lolo*, or Creole snack bar, is about $8. A beer or glass of wine costs around $2.50; a rum punch is about $3. A taxi ride from Marigot to the nearest beach is about $5. A round-trip ride between Marigot and Philipsburg is about $20; a bus ride between the two costs 80¢–$2. Car rental is about $35 for a subcompact. Cost for a single-tank dive ranges from $45 to $50; snorkel equipment rents for about $10.

Before You Go

Tourist Information For information about the Dutch side, contact the **tourist office** on the island directly (tel. 599/5–22337), or, in Canada, contact **St. Maarten Tourist Information** (243 Ellerslie Ave., Willowdale, Toronto, Ontario M2N 1Y5, tel. 416/223–3501). Information about French St. Martin can be obtained by writing to the **French West Indies Tourist Board** (610 5th Ave., New York, NY 10020) or by calling France-on-Call at 900/990–0040 (50¢ per minute). You can also write to or visit the **French Government Tourist Office** (444 Madison Ave., 16th Floor, New York, NY 10022; 9454 Wilshire Blvd., Suite 303, Beverly Hills, CA 90212; 645 N. Michigan Ave., Suite 3360, Chicago, IL 60611; 1981 McGill College Ave., Suite 490, Montreal, Québec H3A 2W9, tel. 514/288–4264; 30 St. Patrick St., Suite 700, Toronto, Ontario M5T 3A3, tel. 416/593–4723; and 178 Piccadilly, London W1V OAL, tel. 0171/629–9376).

Arriving and Departing

By Plane There are two airports on the island. **L'Espérance** (tel. 590/87–53–03) on the French side is small and handles only island-hoppers. Bigger planes fly into **Princess Juliana International Airport** (tel. 599/5–4211) on the Dutch side. The most convenient carrier from the United States is **American Airlines** (tel. 800/433–7300), with daily nonstop flights from New York and Miami, as well as connections from more than 100 U.S. cities via its San Juan hub. **Continental Airlines** (tel. 800/231–0856) has daily flights from Newark. **LIAT** (tel. 809/462–0701) has daily service from San Juan and several Caribbean islands including St. Thomas and St. Kitts; **ALM** (tel. 800/327–7230) from Aruba, Bonaire, Curaçao, the Dominican Republic, and from Atlanta and Miami via Curaçao. ALM also offers a Visit Caribbean Pass, which offers savings for traveling to several Caribbean islands. BWIA (tel. 800/327–7401) offers twice-weekly service from Miami. Air Martinique (tel. 596/51–08–09 or 599/5–4212) connects the island with Martinique twice a week. Windward Islands Airways (Winair, tel. 599/5–4230), which is based on St. Maarten, has daily scheduled service to Anguilla, Saba, St. Barts, St. Eustatius, St. Kitts/Nevis, and St. Thomas. Air Guadeloupe (tel. 599/5–4212 or 590/87–53–74) has several flights daily to St. Barts and Guadeloupe from both sides of the island. Air St. Barthélemy (tel. 590/87–73–46 or 599/5–3150) has frequent service between Juliana or Espérance and St. Barts. Tour and charter services are available from Winair and St. Martin Helicopters (Dutch side, tel. 599/5–4287).

From the Airport Taxi rates are government-regulated on both sides; fixed fares to hotels are posted prominently and range from $5 to $25. Some hotels offer free transfers; inquire when you book. Several major car rental companies have desks at Juliana. There is no regularly scheduled public transportation.

By Boat Motorboats zip several times a day from Anguilla to the French side at Marigot ($9 one-way), three times a week from St. Barts. Catamaran service is available daily from the Dutch side to St. Barts ($40 one-way). The high-speed ferry ***Edge*** (tel. 599/5–22167) travels across from Saba three times a week ($45 round-trip).

Passports and Visas U.S. citizens need proof of citizenship. A passport (valid or expired for not more than five years) is preferred. An original birth certificate with raised seal (or a photocopy with notary seal), or a voter registration card is also acceptable. British and Canadian citizens need valid passports. All visitors must have a confirmed room reservation and an ongoing or return ticket. You won't need your passport traveling between the Dutch and French sides of the island; there is no customs.

Language Dutch is the official language of St. Maarten and French is the official language of St. Martin, but almost everyone speaks English. If you hear a language you can't quite place, it's Papiamento, a Spanish-based Creole of the Netherlands Antilles.

Staying in St. Martin/St. Maarten

Important Addresses **Tourist Information:** On the Dutch side, the **tourist information bureau** is on Cyrus Wathey (pronounced watty) Square in the heart of Philipsburg, at the pier where the cruise ships send their tenders. The administrative office is on Walter Nisbeth Road 23 (Imperial Building) on the third floor. *Tel. 599/5–22337. Open weekdays 8–noon and 1–5, except holidays.*

On the French side, there is the smart and very helpful **tourist information office** on the Marigot pier. *Tel. 590/87–57–21, fax 590/87–56–43. Open weekdays 8:30–1 and 2:30–5:30; Sat. 8–noon. Closed holidays and the afternoon preceding a holiday.*

Emergencies **Police:** Dutch side (tel. 599/5–22222), French side (tel. 590/87–50–10). **Ambulance:** Dutch side (tel. 599/5–22111), French side (tel. 590/87–50–06). **Hospital: St. Maarten Medical Center** (Cay Hill, tel. 599/5–31111) is a fully equipped hospital. **Pharmacies:** Pharmacies, which are open Monday–Saturday 7–5, include the **Central Drug Store** (Philipsburg, tel. 599/5–22321), **Mullet Bay Drug Store** (tel. 599/5–52801, ext. 342), and **Pharmacie du Port** (Marigot, tel. 590/87–50–79).

Currency Legal tender on the Dutch side is the Netherlands Antilles florin (guilder), written NAf; on the French side, the French franc (F). The exchange rate fluctuates, but in general it's about NAf 1.78 to U.S. $1 and 5F to U.S. $1. On the Dutch side, prices are usually given in both NAf and U.S. dollars, which are accepted all over the island, as are credit cards. Note: Prices quoted here are in U.S. dollars unless otherwise noted.

Taxes and Service Charges On the Dutch side, a 5% government tax is added to hotel bills. On the French side, a *taxe de séjour* (visitor's tax) is tacked onto hotel bills (the amount differs from hotel to hotel, but the maximum is $3 per day, per person). Departure tax from Juliana Airport is $5 to destinations within the Netherlands Antilles and $10 to all other destinations. It will cost you 15F to depart by plane from l'Espérance Airport or by ferry to Anguilla from Marigot's pier.

In lieu of tipping, service charges (15% on the Dutch side; 10%–15% on the French) are added to hotel bills all over the island, and, by law, are included in all menu prices on the French side. Taxi drivers expect a 10% tip.

Getting Around Chances are, you won't have to rent a car for the duration of your stay here. One day of driving (or a guided tour, roughly the same cost) is sufficient to see the major sights. After that, you can take taxis to Marigot, Philipsburg, and the casinos (if your hotel doesn't have a shuttle service). Most hotels here are on or within walking distance of the beach.

Taxis Taxi rates are government regulated, and authorized taxis display stickers of the St. Maarten Taxi Association. There is a taxi service at the Marigot port next to the Tourist Information Bureau. Fixed fares apply from Juliana Airport and the Marigot ferry to the various hotels and around the island. Fares are 25% higher between 10 PM and midnight, 50% higher between midnight and 6 AM. Sample rates are: Marigot to Philipsburg, $10–$12, Marigot to the nearest beach, $5.

Buses One of the island's best bargains at 80¢ to $2, depending on destination, buses operate frequently between 7 AM and 7 PM (less often from 7–10 PM) and run from Philipsburg through Cole Bay to Marigot. There are no official stops: You just stand by the side of the road and flag the bus down. Exact change is preferred though not required, and drivers don't accept bills over $5.

Rental Cars You can book a car at Juliana Airport, where all major rental companies have booths, but to give taxi drivers work, you must collect the car at the rental offices located off the airport complex. (The Hertz office is closest to the airport, just a quarter-mile away.) There are also rentals at every hotel area. Rental cars are inexpensive—approximately $35 a day for a subcompact. All foreign driver's licenses are honored, and major credit cards are accepted. **Avis** (tel. 800/331–1212), **Budget** (tel. 800/527–0700), **Dollar** (tel. 800/421–6868), **Hertz** (tel. 800/654–3131), and **National** (tel. 800/328–4567) have offices on the island. Scooters rent for $25–$35 a day at **Rent 2 Wheels** (Nettlé Bay, tel. 590/87–20–59).

Telephones and Mail To call the Dutch side from the United States, dial 011 + 599 + the local number; for the French side, 011, 590, and the local number. To phone from the Dutch side to the French, dial 06 plus the local number; from the French side to the Dutch, 011, 5995, and the local number. Keep in mind that a call from one side to another is an overseas call, not a local call. Most hotels have direct-dial phones.

At the Landsradio in Philipsburg, there are facilities for overseas calls and an AT&T USADirect telephone, where you are directly in touch with an AT&T operator who will accept collect or credit-card calls.

On the French side, it is not possible to make collect calls to the United States, and there are no coin phones. If you need to use public phones, go to the special desk at Marigot's post office and buy a Telecarte (it looks like a credit card), which gives you 40 units for around 31F or 120 units for 93F. There is a public phone outside the tourist office in Marigot where you can make credit-card phone calls. The operator takes your credit card number and assigns you a PIN (personal identification number), which you can then use to charge calls to your card.

Calls from anywhere on the island to the United States cost $4 per minute.

Letters from the Dutch side to the United States and Canada cost NAf 1.30; postcards, NAf 60¢. From the French side, letters up to 20 grams, 4.10F; postcards, 3.50F.

Opening and Closing Times Shops on the Dutch side are open Monday–Saturday 8–noon and 2–6; on the French side, Monday–Saturday 9–noon or 12:30, and 2–6. Some of the larger shops on both sides of the island open Sunday and holidays when the cruise ships are in port. Some of the small shops set their own capricious hours.

Banks on the Dutch side are open Monday–Thursday 8:30–3:30 and Friday 8:30–4:40. French banks open weekdays 8:30–1:30 and 2–3 and close afternoons preceding holidays.

Guided Tours A 2½-hour taxi tour of the island costs $35 for one or two people, $10 for each additional person. Your hotel or the tourist office can arrange it for you. **St. Maarten Sightseeing Tours** (Philipsburg, tel. 599/5–22753) uses 20-passenger vans for various tours, including a 2½-hour complete island tour for $15 per person. **Calypso Tours** (Philipsburg, tel. 599/5–42858) offers a half-day island tour for $15 per person. On the French side, both **R&J Tours** (Colombier, tel. 590/87–56–20) and **Hanna Tours** (Marigot, 590/29–29–29) offer island tours. Prices vary with the number of people and the itinerary.

Exploring St. Martin/St. Maarten

Numbers in the margin correspond to points of interest on the St. Martin/St. Maarten map.

You can explore the island in your own rental car or take a guided tour (*see above*). The two are roughly equivalent in cost, and one day is more than sufficient to see the major sights.

St. Maarten

1 The Dutch capital of **Philipsburg,** which stretches about a mile along an isthmus between **Great Bay** and the Salt Pond, has three more-or-less parallel streets: Front Street, Back Street, and Pondfill. Front Street has been recently recobbled. Cars are discouraged from using it, and the pedestrian area has been widened. Shops, restaurants, and casinos vie for the hordes coming off the cruise boats. Head for **Wathey Square** and stroll out on the pier. **Great Bay** is rolled out before you, and the beach stretches alongside it for about a mile. The square bustles with vendors, souvenir shops, and tourists. Philipsburg should be explored on foot, but you'll need wheels to get around the rest of the island.

Directly across the street from Wathey Square, you'll see a striking white building with a cupola. It was built in 1793 and has since served as the commander's home, a fire station, and a jail. It now serves as the town hall, courthouse, and post office.

The square is in the middle of the isthmus on which Philipsburg sits. To your right and left the streets are lined with hotels, duty-free shops, fine restaurants, and cafés, most of them in pastel-colored West Indian cottages gussied up with gingerbread trim. Narrow alleyways lead to arcades and flower-filled courtyards where there are yet more boutiques and eateries.

The **Simart'n Museum** has just moved to a new building on Front Street. It hosts rotating cultural exhibits and a permanent historical display entitled "Forts of St. Maarten/St. Martin," featuring artifacts ranging from Arawak pottery shards to articles salvaged from the wreck of HMS *Proselyte. 9 Front St., Philipsburg, no phone. Admission: $1. Open weekdays 9–4, Sat. 9–noon.*

Little lanes called *steegjes* connect Front Street with Back Street, which has fewer shops and is considerably less congested.

Our drive begins at the western end of Front Street, right before it becomes Sucker Garden Road. Follow the road north along Salt Pond. It begins to climb and curve just outside of town. Take the
2 first right to **Guana Bay Point,** from which there is a splendid view of the island's east coast, tiny deserted islands, and small St. Barts, which is anything but deserted. Sucker Garden Road continues north through spectacular scenery. Continue along a paved roller-coaster road down to **Dawn Beach,** one of the island's best snorkeling beaches.

3 **Oyster Pond,** just north of Dawn Beach on the same road, is the legendary point where two early settlers, a Frenchman and a Dutchman, allegedly began to pace in opposite directions around the island to divide it between their respective countries. Local legend maintains that the obese sweaty Hollander stopped frequently to refresh himself with gin—the reason that the French side is nearly

twice the size of the Dutch. (The official boundary marker is on the other side of the island.)

St. Martin

4 From Oyster Pond, follow the road along the bay and around Etang aux Poissons (Fish Lake), all the way to **Orléans.** This settlement, which is also known as the French Quarter, is the oldest on the island. Noted local artist and activist Roland Richardson makes his home here. He holds open studio on Thursdays from 10 to 6, or by appointment (tel. 590/87–32–24). He's a proud islander, ready to share his wealth of knowledge about the island's cultural history.

A rough dirt road leads northeast to **Orient Beach,** the island's best-known nudist beach. There's even a pricey rustic resort catering to "naturists." Offshore, little **Ilet Pinel** is an uninhabited island that's fine for picnicking, sunning, and swimming.

5 Farther north you'll come to **French Cul de Sac,** where you'll see the French colonial mansion of St. Martin's mayor nestled in the hills. Little red-roof houses look like open umbrellas tumbling down the green hillside. The scenery here is glorious, and the area is great for hiking. There is a lot of construction, however, as the surroundings are slowly being developed. From the beach here, three shuttle boats make the five-minute trip to Ilet Pinel.

The road swirls south through green hills and pastures, past flower-entwined stone fences. Past L'Espérance Airport is the town of
6 **Grand Case.** Though it has only one mile-long main street, it's known as the "Restaurant Capital of the Caribbean": More than 20 restaurants serve French, Italian, Indonesian, and Vietnamese fare, as well as fresh seafood. The budget-minded will appreciate the lolos—barbecue stands along the waterfront. **Grand Case Beach Hotel** is at the end of this road and has two beaches to choose from for a short dip. Better yet, travel down the road about 5 miles toward Marigot, and on the right is a turnoff to **Friar's Beach,** a small, picturesque cove that attracts a crowd of locals. A small snack bar, **Kali's,** owned by a welcoming gentleman wearing dreadlocks, serves refreshments. From here, you can turn inland and follow a bumpy tree-canopied road to **Pic du Paradis,** at 1,278 feet the highest point on the island, affording breathtaking vistas of the Caribbean.

7 Just before entering the French capital of **Marigot,** you will notice a new shopping complex on the left. At the back of it is **Match** (tel. 590/87–92–36), the largest supermarket on the French side, carrying a broad selection of tempting picnic makings—from country pâté to foie gras—and a vast selection of wines. If you are a shopper, a gourmet, or just a Francophile, you'll want to tarry awhile in Marigot. Marina Port La Royale is the shopping complex at the port, but Rue de la République and Rue de la Liberté, which border the bay, are also filled with duty-free shops, boutiques, and bistros. The harbor area has a jumble of stalls selling anything from handmade crafts to fish so fresh they're still mad. Across from these stalls, on pier road leading to the ferries for Anguilla, is the helpful French tourist office, where you can pick up the usual assortment of free maps and brochures.

You are likely to find more creative and fashionable buys in Marigot than in Philipsburg. There is less bustle here, and the open-air cafés are tempting places in which to stop for a rest. Unlike Philipsburg, Marigot does not die at night, so you may wish to stay into the evening. **Le Bar de la Mer** (tel. 590/87–81–79) on the harbor is a popular gathering spot in the evening (it's open 'til 2), though the bar and restaurant are open all day.

The road due south of Marigot to Philipsburg passes the official boundary, where a simple border marker, erected by the Dutch and French citizenry to commemorate 300 years of peaceful coexistence, bears the dates "1648 to 1948." Straddling the border are the mam-

Exploring
French Cul de Sac, **5**
Grand Case, **6**
Guana Bay Point, **2**
Marigot, **7**
Orléans, **4**
Oyster Pond, **3**
Philipsburg, **1**

Dining
Antoine, **55**
Bistrot Nu, **21**
Captain Oliver's, **58**
Cha Cha Cha Caribbean Café, **12**
Cheri's Café, **33**
Chesterfield's, **56**
David's Pub, **22**
Don Camillo da Enzo, **23**
Don Carlos, **34**
The Grill & Ribs Co., **36**
Harbour Lights, **47**
Island Bar and Restaurant, **43**
L'Alabama, **13**
L'Escargot, **48**
La Résidence, **24**
Le Charolais, **25**
Le Marocain, **26**
La Plaisance, **27**
Lolos, **14**
Maison sur le Port, **28**
Mark's Place, **11**
Shiv Sagar, **49**
Surf Club South, **15**
Turtle Pier Bar & Restaurant, **35**
Wajang Doll, **46**
Yvette's, **61**

Lodging
Alizéa, **8**
Beach House, **50**
Captain Oliver's, **58**
Caribbean Hotel, **51**
Chez Martine, **16**
Coralita Beach Hotel, **60**
Divi Little Bay Beach Resort, **44**
Ernest's Guest House, **41**
Golden Tulip St. Martin, **10**
Gracie Mansion Guest House, **59**
Great Bay Beach Hotel & Casino, **45**
Hevea, **17**

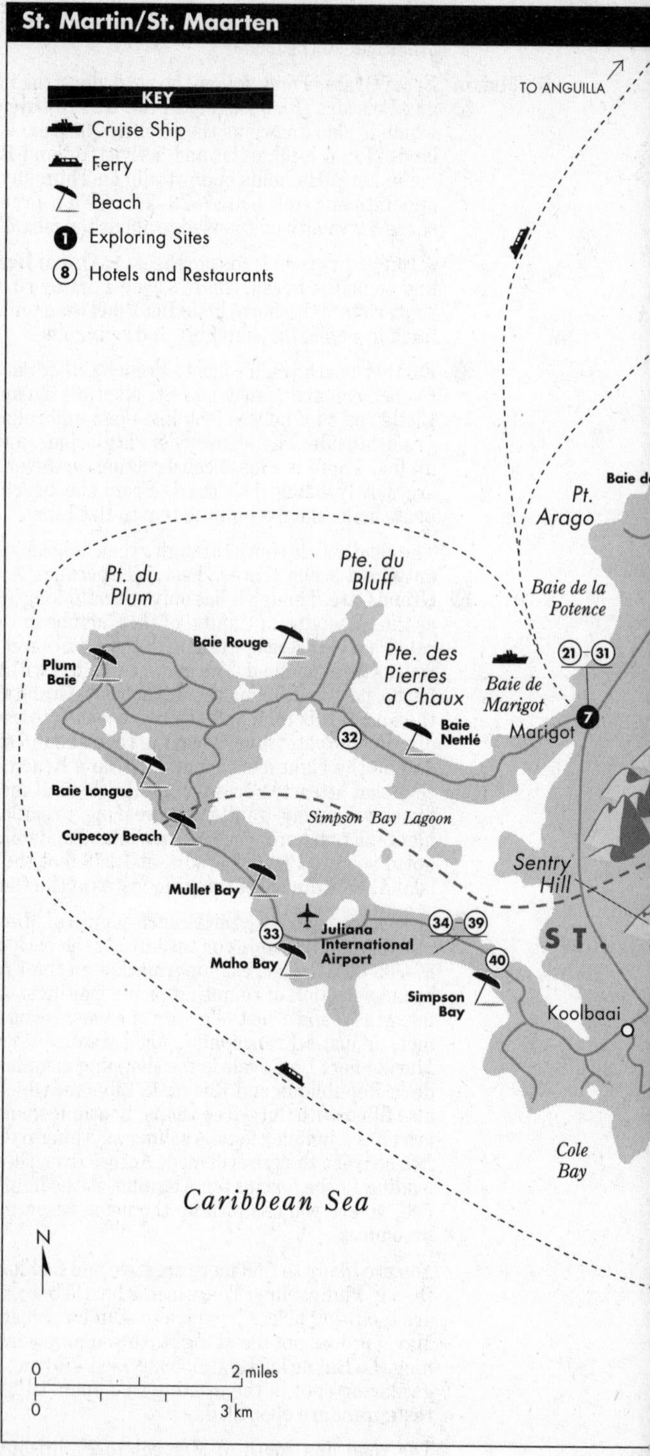

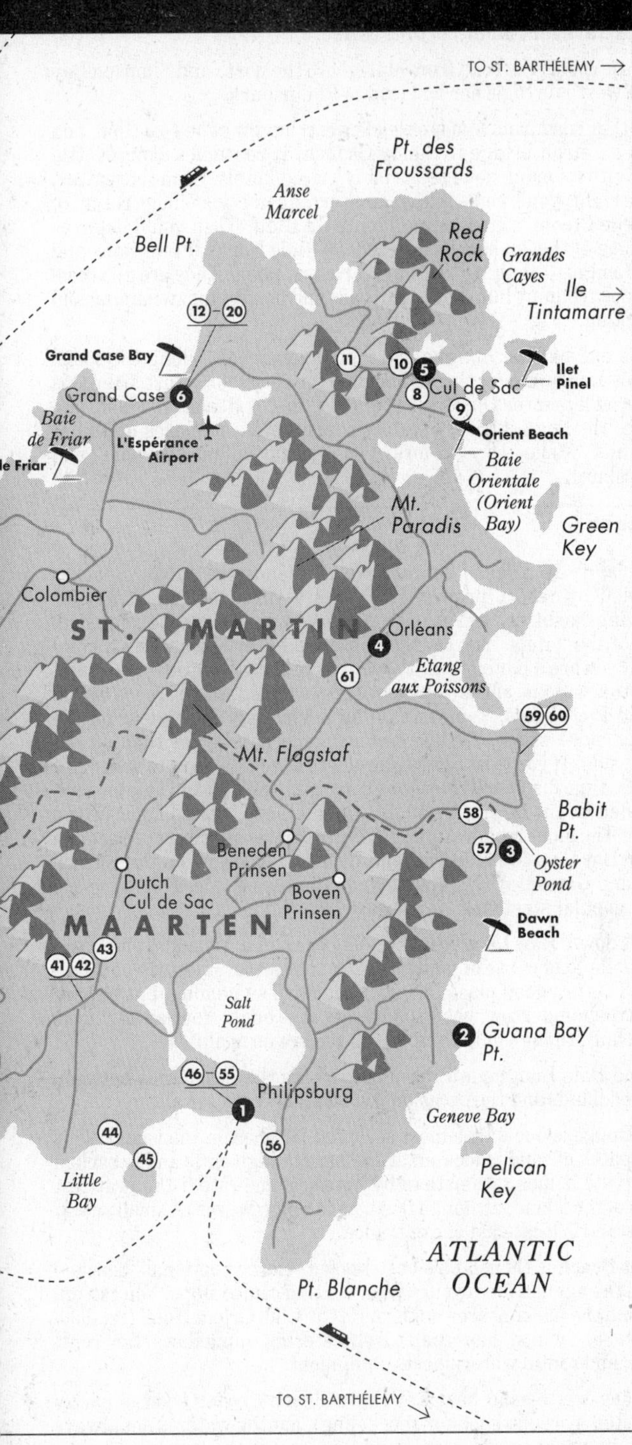

Holland House Beach Hotel, **52**
Horny Toad Guesthouse, **37**
Hôtel l'Atlantide, **20**
Hôtel L'Esplanade Caraibes, **19**
Jardins de Chevrise, **9**
La Résidence, **24**
Le Royale Louisiana, **29**
La Vista, **40**
Le Cigalon, **30**
Marina Royale Hotel, **31**
Marine Hotel Simson Beach, **32**
Mary's Boon, **38**
Oyster Pond Beach Hotel, **57**
Passangrahan Royal Guest House, **54**
Pavillon Beach Hotel, **18**
Residence La Chatelaine, **39**
Sea Breeze Hotel, **42**
Seaview Hotel & Casino, **53**

moth Port de Plaisance condominium hotel complex, and the adjacent extravagant Mont Fortune casino.

At the airport, the road from Marigot to the north and Simpson Bay to the west join together and lead to Philipsburg.

The other road from Marigot leads west, hugging the coastline, and crosses a small bridge to Sandy Ground. It continues along Nettlé Bay, with its many new, reasonably priced hotels. Soon thereafter, on the right, you'll come to the Mediterranean-style village resort of **La Belle Creole,** commanding Pointe du Bluff. Then you'll begin to see some of the island's best beaches—**Baie Rouge, Plum Baie,** and **Baie Longue**—clinging to its westernmost point. They are all accessible down bumpy but short dirt roads and perfect for swimming and picnicking.

At the end of Baie Longue and running eastward along the south coast is **La Samanna,** the fashionable jet-set resort. Just after this hotel you'll reenter Dutch territory at **Cupecoy Beach.** You'll have to endure the huge, garish vacation condo-hotel complexes of Mullet Bay and Maho Bay before you reach Juliana Airport and Philipsburg.

Beaches

The island's 10 miles of beaches are all open to the public. Beaches occupied by resort properties charge a small fee (about $3) for changing facilities, and water-sports equipment can be rented in most of the hotels. You cannot, however, enter a beach via a hotel unless you are a paying guest or will be renting water-sports equipment there. Some of the 37 beaches are secluded, some are located in the thick of things. Topless bathing is virtually de rigueur on the French side, where the beaches are generally better than on the Dutch side. If you take a cab to a remote beach, be sure to arrange a specific time for your driver to return, and don't leave valuables unattended on the beach. Virtually all hotels are located on or near a beach. The more moderately priced properties are clustered around **Nettlé Bay** (outside Marigot) and **Grand Case Beach** on the French side, and **Great Bay** (Philipsburg) on the Dutch side. Following are other popular stretches.

Hands down, **Baie Longue** is the best beach on the island. It's a beautiful, mile-long curve of white sand on the westernmost tip of the island. This is a good place for snorkeling and swimming, but beware of a strong undertow when the waters are rough. You can sunbathe in the buff, though only a few do. There are no facilities.

Beyond Baie Longue is **Plum Baie,** where the beach arcs between two headlands and the occasional sunbather discloses all.

Baie Rouge is one of the most secluded beaches on the island. This little patch of sand is located at the base of high cliffs and is backed by private homes rather than by hotels. Some rate it the prettiest beach of the island, although it can have rough waves. A small snack/soda stand is located at the entrance.

Orient Beach is the island's best-known "clothes optional" beach—it's on the agenda for voyeurs from visiting cruise ships. You can enter from the parking area or through the **Club Orient Hotel** (tel. 590/87–33–85), which has chalet self-catering bungalows for rent, shops, and rental water-sports equipment.

The long white-sand beach at **Dawn Beach–Oyster Pond** is partly protected by reefs (good for snorkeling), but the water is not always calm. When the waves come rolling in, this is the best spot on the island for bodysurfing.

Ilet Pinel is a little speck off the northeast coast, with about 500 yards of beach where you can have picnics and privacy. There are no facilities. Putt-putts (small boats) are available to take you from French Cul de Sac and Orient Beach.

Simpson Bay is a long half-moon of white sand near Simpson Bay Village, one of the last undiscovered hamlets on the island. In this small fishing village you'll find refreshments, the **Ocean Explorers** (*see* Sports and the Outdoors, *below*) for water-sports rentals, and neat little ultra-Caribbean town homes.

Ecru-color sand, palm and sea-grape trees, calm waters, and the roar of jets lowering to nearby Juliana Airport distinguish the beach at **Maho Bay.** Concession stand, beach chairs, and facilities are available.

At **Mullet Bay,** the powdery white-sand beach is crowded with guests of the Mullet Bay Resort.

Cupecoy Beach is a small shifting arc of white sand fringed with eroded limestone cliffs, just south of Baie Longue on the western side of the island, near the Dutch-French border. On the first part of the beach, swimwear is worn, but farther up, sun worshipers start shedding their attire. There are no facilities, but a truck is often parked at the entrance, with a vendor who sells cold sodas and beer.

Sports and the Outdoors

All the resort hotels have activities desks that can arrange virtually any type of water sport.

Boating Motorboats, speedboats, Dolphins, pedal boats, sailboats, and canoes can be rented at **Lagoon Cruises & Watersports** (Mullet Bay Resort, tel. 599/5–52898), **Caribbean Watersports** (Nettlé Bay, tel. 590/87–58–66), and **Caraibes Sport Boats** (Marina Port la Royale, tel. 590/87–89–38). Rates average $15–$20 an hour.

Sun Yacht-Charters (tel. 800/772–3500), based in Oyster Pond, has a fleet of 50 Centurion sailboats for hire. The cost of a week's bareboat charter for a 36-foot Centurion with six berths runs $2,850 in peak winter season. Also in Oyster Pond, **The Moorings** (tel. 800/535–7289 or 590/87–32–55) has a fleet of Beneteau yachts, and bareboat and crewed catamarans. **Dynasty** (tel. 590/87–85–21), in Marigot's Port la Royale Marina, offers an excellent fleet of Dynamique yachts ranging in size from 47 to 80 feet.

Fitness **Le Privilège** (tel. 590/87–37–37), a sports complex at Anse Marcel above Meridien L'Habitation, has a full range of exercise equipment. **Fitness Caraibes** (tel. 590/87–97–04) is a toning center at Nettlé Bay. On the Dutch side, **L'Aqualigne** at the Pelican Resort (tel. 599/5–42426) is a health spa with gym, sauna, and beauty treatments, including manicures, facials, and massages. Day passes average $5.

Jet- and Waterskiing On the Dutch side, rent equipment through the **Divi Little Bay Resort**'s water-sports activity center (tel. 599/5–22333). On the French side, try **Orient Bay Watersports** (tel. 590/87–33–85) or **Laguna Watersports** (tel. 590/87–91–75) at Nettlé Bay. Rental is about $40 for a half-hour.

Parasailing A great high can be arranged through **Lagoon Cruises & Watersports** (tel. 599/5–52898). Cost is $30–$40 for 15 minutes.

Running The **Road Runners Club** meets Wednesday in the parking lot of the Raoul Illidge Sportscomplex for a 5 PM Fun Run and Sunday at 6:45 AM in the parking lot of the Pelican Resort for a 2–15K run. For more information, contact Dr. Frits Bus at 599/5–22467 or Ron van Sittert at 599/5–22842.

Scuba Diving The water temperature here is rarely below 70°F, and there's usually excellent visibility. There are many diving attractions both right around the island, and at numerous off-shore islands. On the Dutch side is Proselyte Reef, named for the British frigate HMS *Proselyte*, which sank south of Great Bay in 1801. In addition to wreck dives, reef, night, and cave dives are popular. Off the northeast coast of the French side, dive sites include Ilet Pinel, for good shallow diving; Green Key, with its vibrant barrier reef; and Tintamarre for sheltered coves and subsea geologic faults.

On the Dutch side, SSI- (Scuba Schools International) and PADI-certified dive centers include **Trade Winds Dive Center** (Bobby's Marina, tel. 599/5–75176), **St. Maarten Divers** (Philipsburg, tel. 599/5–22446), **Leeward Island Divers** (Simpson Bay, tel. 599/5–42268), and **Ocean Explorers Dive Shop** (Simpson Bay, 599/5–45252). On the French side, **Lou Scuba** (Marine Hotel Simson Beach, Nettlé Bay, tel. 590/87–22–58) and **Pelican Dive Adventures** (Pelican Resort Marina, tel. 599/5–42503, ext. 1553) are PADI-certified dive centers. **Blue Ocean** (Marigot, tel. 590/87–89–73) is PADI and CMAS certified. **Octoplus** (Grand Case Blvd., tel. 590/87–20–62) is a complete dive center. Single-tank dives average $45–$50, with package deals available.

Sea Excursions Day sails and cruises average a hefty $65 a person, but they do include snorkel gear, drinks, and snacks. You may want to consider one for a splurge. Half-day sails cost around $30 and cocktail cruises, $35. You can take a daylong picnic sail to nearby islands or secluded coves aboard the 45-foot ketch ***Gabrielle*** (tel. 599/5–23170), the sleek, new 76-foot catamaran ***Golden Eagle*** (tel. 599/5–22167), or the 70-foot schooner ***Gandalf*** (tel. 599/5–45427). The 50-foot catamaran ***Bluebeard II*** (tel. 599/5–52898), moored in Simpson Bay, sails around Anguilla's south and northwest coasts to Prickly Pear, where there are excellent coral reefs for snorkeling and powdery white sands for sunning. The ***Lady Mary*** (tel. 599/5–53892) sails around the island each evening from La Palapa Center on Simpson Bay; $60 per person includes dinner, open bar, and live calypso music. It's tremendous fun. The ***Laura Rose*** (tel. 599/5–70710) offers a variety of half- and full-day sails. The ***Karib One*** glass-bottom boat (tel. 590/87–89–73) makes three cruises daily, including dinner-and-disco trips.

In St. Martin, sailing, snorkeling, and picnic excursions to nearby islands can be arranged through **Orient Bay Watersports** (Club Orient Hotel, tel. 590/87–33–85), **Le Meridien L'Habitation** (tel. 590/87–33–33), **La Belle Creole** (tel. 590/87–66–00), and **La Samanna** (tel. 590/87–51–22).

Snorkeling Coral reefs teem with marine life, and clear water allows visibility of up to 200 feet. Some of the best snorkeling on the Dutch side can be had around the rocks below Fort Amsterdam off Little Bay Beach, in the west end of Maho Bay, off Pelican Key, and the around the reefs off Dawn Beach and Oyster Pond. On the French side, the area around Orient Bay, Green Key, Ilet Pinel, and Flat Island (or Tintamarre) is especially lovely for snorkeling, and should soon be officially classified a regional underwater nature reserve. Arrange rentals and trips through **Ocean Explorers** (tel. 599/5–45252), and **Orient Bay Watersports** (tel. 590/87–33–85). Half- and full-day trips, usually including picnic lunch, run anywhere from $40 to $70 per person. Snorkel equipment rents for about $10 a day.

Tennis If you want to play tennis at a hotel at which you are not a guest, be sure to call ahead to find out whether they allow visitors. You'll probably need to make reservations, and there's usually an hourly fee ($15–$25). There are 2 lighted courts at the **Dawn Beach Hotel** (tel. 599/5–22929); 6 lighted courts at the **Pelican Resort** (tel. 599/5–42503); 3 lighted courts at the **Divi Little Bay Beach Resort** (tel. 599/

5-22333); 4 lighted courts at the **Maho Beach Hotel** (tel. 599/5-52115); 6 lighted courts at **Le Privilège** (Anse Marcel, tel. 590/87-38-38), which also has 4 squash and 2 racquetball courts; 14 courts (7 lighted) at **Port de Plaisance** (tel. 599/5-45222); 4 lighted courts at **La Belle Creole** (tel. 590/87-66-00); 2 lighted courts at the **Mont Vernon Hotel** (tel. 590/87-62-00); 1 lighted court at the **Marine Hotel Simson Beach** (tel. 590/87-54-54); 14 courts at **Mullet Bay Resort** (tel. 599/5-52801); 2 courts at the **Oyster Pond Beach Hotel** (tel. 599/5-22206); and 1 lighted court each at the **Grand Case Beach Club** (tel. 590/87-51-87) and the **Coralita Beach Hotel** (tel. 590/87-31-81).

Windsurfing Rental and instruction are available at **Divi Little Bay Beach Resort** (tel. 599/5-22333, ext. 186) and **Orient Watersports** (590/87-33-85). The new **Nathalie Simon Windsurfing Club** (tel. 590/87-48-16) offers rentals and lessons in Orient Bay. Equipment and lessons cost $15-$30 an hour.

Shopping

About 180 cruise ships call at St. Maarten each year, and they do so for about 500 reasons. That's roughly the number of duty-free shops on the island.

You'll find the best buys on goods manufactured outside the United States. European luxury items can cost 25%-50% less than they do in the United States and Canada, but check stateside prices before you leave home. In general, you will find more fashion on the French side in Marigot.

St. Maarten's best-known "craft" is its guavaberry liqueur, made from rum and the wild local berries (not to be confused with guavas) that grow only on this island's central mountains. Other than that, you're unlikely to find any great local buys.

Prices are quoted in florins, francs, and dollars, and shops take credit cards and traveler's checks. Most shopkeepers, especially on the Dutch side, speak English. Although most merchants are reputable, there are occasional reports of inferior or fake merchandise passed off as the real thing. Generally, if you can bargain excessively, it's probably not worth it.

Shopping Areas In St. Maarten: **Front Street,** Philipsburg, is one long strip lined with sleek boutiques and colorful shops. **Old Street,** near the end of Front Street, has 22 stores, boutiques, and open-air cafés. (If more than one cruise ship is in port, avoid Front Street. It's so crowded you won't be able to move.) There are almost 100 boutiques in the **Mullet** and **Maho** shopping plazas, as well as at the **Simpson Bay Yacht Club** complex.

In St. Martin: Wrought-iron balconies, colorful awnings, and gingerbread trim decorate Marigot's smart shops, tiny boutiques, and bistros in the **Marina Port La Royale** complex and on the main streets, **Rue de la Liberté** and **Rue de la République.**

Island Specialties Caribelle batik, hammocks, handmade jewelry, the local guavaberry liqueur, and herbs and spices are stashed at the **Shipwreck Shop** (Philipsburg, tel. 599/5-22962 and Port La Royale, tel. 590/87-27-37). T-shirts, beach towels, native dolls, Indian glass bangles, and hand-painted delft souvenirs can all be found at **Sasha's** (Philipsburg, tel. 599/5-24331). The restaurant **Le Poisson D'Or** (Marigot, tel. 590/87-72-45) houses a gallery featuring the work of local artists. **ABC Art Gallery** (Marigot, tel. 590/87-96-00) also exhibits the work of local artists. The **Gingerbread Galerie** (Port La Royale, tel. 590/87-73-21) specializes in Haitian art. **Galerie Lynn** (83 Blvd. de Grand Case, tel. 590/87-77-24) sells stunning paintings and sculptures. **Minguet** (Rambaud Hill, 590/87-76-06) carries pictures by the artist Minguet depicting island life. **Greenwith Galleries** (Philipsburg, tel. 599/5–23842) specializes in Caribbean art. **Calabash** (Philipsburg, tel. 599/5–25221) gallery showcases the work of local artists.

Dining

It may seem that this island has no monuments. Au contraire, there are many of them, all dedicated to gastronomy. You'll scarcely find a touch of Dutch; the major influences are French and Italian. This season's "in" eatery may be next season's remembrance of things past, as things do have a way of changing rapidly. The generally steep prices reflect both the island's high culinary reputation and the difficulty of obtaining fresh ingredients. Not surprisingly, the hotel restaurants on the French side are usually more sophisticated, but at prices that would make almost anyone but a Rockefeller go Dutch.

Although most of the haute restaurants are appropriate only for splurges, some offer prix-fixe menus that represent tremendous savings over à la carte prices. Creole restaurants are generally less expensive than their classic and nouvelle French counterparts. The greatest concentration of moderately priced, open-air eateries can be found in Philipsburg and in Marigot's Marina Port La Royale. In addition, look for Creole snack bars serving tasty budget island specialties along Philipsburg's steegjes, and French fast-food cafés and sidewalk croissanteries offering omelets or *steak frîtes* in Marigot.

If you're cooking at your lodgings, the selection, quality, and prices are so good at Marigot's **Match** that it's worth coming over if you're staying on the Dutch side. Otherwise, try **Stop and Shop** (Juliana Airport), either **Food Center** (Bush Road or Cole Bay), or **Ram's Cash and Carry** (Cay Hill).

Except for very informal eateries, reservations are always recommended, particularly in high season. Dress is casual unless stated otherwise. Highly recommended restaurants are indicated by a star ★.

Category	Cost*
$$	$30–$40
$	$20–$30
¢	under $20

**per person, excluding drinks and service*

Dutch Side

$$ **Antoine.** Pay a visit to this elegant, airy terrace overlooking Great Bay for a romantic evening. Candles glow on tables set with crisp blue and white napery and gleaming silver, and the sound of the surf drifts up from the beach. You might start your meal with French onion soup or lobster bisque, then move on to steak au poivre, duck in brandy sauce with cherries, or lobster thermidor. Pastas and Creole specials are also available. For dessert, try the sublime Grand Marnier soufflé. *Front St., Philipsburg, tel. 599/5–22964. AE, MC, V. Reservations required in high season. Closed Sun.*

$$ **Captain Oliver's.** A glorious cockatoo presides over the entrance to this engaging bistro, perched over the marina at Oyster Pond. Although the staff and artfully presented cuisine are French, the restaurant is just over the Dutch border. Seafood is king here, in such dishes as lobster flambéed in cognac or tuna in pink pepper sauce. You can catch your own lobster in the pool. *Oyster Pond, tel. 590/87–30–00. Reservations advised. AE, MC, V.*

$$ **L'Escargot.** A lovely 19th-century house wrapped in verandas is home to one of St. Maarten's oldest classic-French restaurants.

Starters include frogs' legs in garlic sauce and crepes filled with caviar and sour cream. There is also, of course, a variety of snail dishes. For an entrée, try grilled red snapper with red wine and shallot sauce, or *canard de l'escargot* (crisp duck in pineapple and banana sauce). There's a fun cabaret Wednesday night, and you don't have to pay the cover charge if you come for dinner. *84 Front St., Philipsburg, tel. 599/5–22483. AE, MC, V. Reservations advised.*

$–$$ **Island Bar and Restaurant.** This unassuming Caribbean coffee shop serves delectable Creole cooking. Try conch or bullfoot soup, a sultry spicy bouillon, followed by juicy ribs or goat meat. Wash it down with a potent Peanut Punch. *Bush Rd., Cul de Sac, tel. 599/5–25162. AE, MC, V.*

$–$$ **Wajang Doll.** Indonesian dishes are served in the garden of this West Indian–style house. *Nasi goreng* (fried rice) and red snapper in a sweet soy glaze are standouts, but the specialty is rijsttafel, a traditional Indonesian meal of rice accompanied by 15 to 20 different dishes. *137 Front St., Philipsburg, tel. 599/5–22687. AE, MC, V. Closed Sun. No lunch.*

$ **Chesterfield's.** Casual lunches of burgers and salads and more elaborate Continental dinners are served at this informal, nautically themed restaurant at the marina. The dinner menu includes French onion soup, roast duckling with fresh pineapple and banana sauce, and several different preparations of shrimp. The Mermaid Bar is a popular spot with yachtsmen. *Great Bay Marina, Philipsburg, tel. 599/5–23484. No credit cards.*

$ ★ **Shiv Sagar.** Authentic East Indian cuisine, emphasizing Kashmiri and Mughlai specialties, is served in this small mirrored room fragrant with cumin and coriander. Marvelous tandooris and curries are offered, but try one of the less-familiar preparations like *madrasi machi* (red snapper cooked in a blend of hot spices). A large selection of vegetarian dishes is also offered. There's a friendly open-air bar out front. *3 Front St., Philipsburg, tel. 599/5–22299. AE, D, DC, MC, V. Closed Sun.*

$ ★ **Turtle Pier Bar & Restaurant.** Chattering monkeys and squawking parrots greet you at the entrance to this classic Caribbean hangout, teetering over the lagoon and festooned with creeping vines. The genial owner Sid Wathey, whose family is one of the island's oldest, and his American wife, Lorraine, have fashioned one of the funkiest, most endearing places in the Caribbean, with cheap beer on draft, huge American breakfasts, all-you-can-eat ribs dinners for $9.95, and live music several nights a week. A lively crowd gathers at the bar during the daily happy hour, 4–8. *Airport Rd., tel. 599/5–52230. No credit cards.*

¢–$ **Cheri's Café.** Every night terrific live entertainment draws crowds from the neighboring Casino Royale to this hot spot, the closest thing to a classic singles bar on St. Maarten. Food is mostly good old American grub: huge burgers and sandwiches. You can also get grilled fish, including mahimahi and salmon. There's a children's menu, with dinner just $3.75. *Cinnamon Grove Shopping Center, Maho Beach, tel. 599/5–53361. No credit cards.*

¢–$ **Don Carlos.** This plant-filled room adorned with sombreros is a popular local hangout, with surprisingly good Mexican fare and killer margaritas. You can also order excellent local specialties and juicy burgers. Thursdays bring the all-you-can-eat Mexican buffet at just $12.95. *Airport Rd., Simpson Bay, tel. 599/5–53112. No credit cards.*

¢ **The Grill & Ribs Co.** This new venture by the owner of Pizza Hut serves burgers, fajitas, and sandwiches, but specializes in ribs. The all-you-can-eat rib dinner for $10.95 is a tremendous bargain, and the barbecue sauce has just the right spicy-sweet blend. The decor is typical fast-food, but a hungry family probably won't notice. A children's menu is available. *Front St., Phillipsburg, tel. 599/5–24723; Airport Rd., Simpson Bay, tel. 599/5–54498. No credit cards.*

¢ **Harbour Lights.** This modest family-run spot is in a historic building built in 1870. The interior is warm, with peach and coral walls and seafoam-green tablecloths. Rotis and *pilau* (a fragrant, spiced rice dish) are excellent, and stewed or curried chicken, meats, and seafood are even better. Try one of the knockout cocktails made with the local guavaberry liqueur. The tables on the second-floor balcony overlook Back Street, and make for pleasant alfresco dining. *30 Back St., Philipsburg, tel. 599/5–23504. AE, MC, V.*

French Side

$$ ★ **Cha Cha Cha Caribbean Café.** A gaudy decor, with Japanese gardens and loud colors, and an even gaudier clientele haven't stopped Pascal and Christina Chevillot's restaurant from becoming an island hot spot. Of course, the mouthwatering Creole haute cuisine and reasonable prices don't hurt. Try the roasted pork tenderloin with ginger sauce or the grilled snapper with pesto, and wash it down with a Grand Case Sunset—a rum concoction made with fresh orange, grapefruit, and mango juices. *Grand Case, tel. 590/87–53–63. MC, V. Closed Sun. No lunch.*

$$ **La Résidence.** Diners enjoy the intimate setting of this open-air restaurant, with soft lighting and a tinkling fountain. The French and Creole menu includes red snapper in mustard sauce, duck fillet with peaches, and grilled lobster. You'll keep your bill within reason by ordering the prix-fixe *menu gastronomique* for $28, or one of the chicken or fish entrées. The soufflés are sensational. *La Résidence Hotel, Marigot, tel. 590/87–70–37. AE, D, MC, V.*

$$ **Le Marocain.** This exotic oasis in the middle of Marigot resembles a pasha's posh digs, with lush potted plants, intricate mosaics, hand-painted tiles, and wood carvings. The food is as colorful and enticing as the decor, with wonderfully perfumed *tajines* (casseroles of chicken or meat) and *pastillas* (fragrant pastries filled with spices, raisins, and meat or chicken) among the standouts. *Rue de Hollande, Marigot, tel. 590/87–83–11. AE, MC, V.*

$$ **Maison sur le Port.** Watching the sunset from the palm-fringed terrace is not the least of pleasures in this old West Indian house surrounded by romantically lit garden fountains. Try the sautéed duck fillet in passion-fruit sauce or red snapper with beurre blanc. Avoid expensive seafood items to keep dinner in our $$ price range, or order one of the two three-course prix-fixe menus at $21.50 or $29. Lunch, with chef Jean-Paul Fahrner's imaginative salads, is a better value. *On the port, Marigot, tel. 590/87–56–38. AE, D, MC, V. Closed Sun.*

$$ **Mark's Place.** Sunday dinner at this barnlike roadside restaurant is an island institution. You might start with pumpkin soup or stuffed crab, then follow with linguine Bolognese or curried goat. Scrumptious daily specials, including homemade pies and pastries, are posted on a blackboard. *French Cul de Sac, tel. 590/87–34–50. AE, MC, V. Closed Mon.*

$–$$ **Bistrot Nu.** For simple, unadorned fare at a reasonable price, this may be the best spot on the islands. Traditional brasserie-style food—coq au vin, fish soup, snails, pizza, and seafood—is served in a friendly atmosphere. The place is enormously popular; its tables are packed until it closes as 2 AM. *Rue de Hollande, Marigot, tel. 590/87–97–09. MC, V. Closed Sun.*

$–$$ **Don Camillo da Enzo.** Country-style decor and excellent service distinguish this small eatery. Both northern and southern Italian specialties are served. Favorites are the carpaccio, green gnocchi in Gorgonzola cream sauce, and veal medallions in marsala sauce. *Port La Royale, Marigot, tel. 590/87–52–88. AE, MC, V.*

$–$$ **La Plaisance.** The cool strains of jazz waft through this lively open-air brasserie as you sample terrific salads (try the niçoise or landaine—duck, smoked ham, croutons, and fried egg), pizzas (wonderful lobster), pastas (garlic and basil pistou), and fresh grilled seafood at unbeatable prices. This is one of several fine ultracasual eateries at Port La Royale, all offering simple, appetizing food, prix-fixe menus, and happy hours. *Port La Royale, Marigot, tel. 590/87–85–00. AE, MC, V.*

$–$$ **L'Alabama.** This extravagant eatery looks like it was hacked out of the jungle: it's crawling with plants and decorated in lavish florals. The food artfully blends classic French cuisine and island influences in such dishes as minced beef sautéed in orange, red wine, and curry; and red snapper in delicate lime-and-ginger butter sauce. *Grand Case, tel. 590/87–81–66. MC, V.*

$–$$ **Le Charolais.** Steak, steak, and more steak (the chef is a licensed butcher in France) are the specialties at this pleasant, upscale diner. You can also get a tasty leg of lamb Provençal or seafood casserole. The prix-fixe menus are a wonderful bargain. *Rue Felix Eboué, Marigot, tel. 590/87–93–19. MC, V.*

$ **David's Pub.** Presided over by a British expat, it's quintessentially English right down to the dartboard. You can get draft Guinness, fish-and-chips soused in malt vinegar, beef Wellington, and steak-and-ale pie. The raucous trivia nights on Tuesdays and Fridays draw a lively and erudite crowd. *Rue de la Liberté, Marigot, tel. 590/87–51–58. AE, MC, V.*

¢–$ ★ **Yvette's.** The attempts at romance couldn't be more endearing: Classical music plays softly, and the tiny, eight-table room is a symphony in Valentine red, from the curtains, tablecloths, and roses to the hot pepper sauce. Yvette herself couldn't be more down-home, nor her food more delicious. Plates are piled high with lip-smacking Creole specialties, such as *accras* (spicy fish fritters), stewed chicken with rice and beans, and conch and dumplings. This is the kind of place that is so good you're surprised to see other tourists—but word gets around. *Orléans, tel. 590/87–32–03. AE (5% surcharge).*

¢ ★ **Lolos.** These barbecue stands are a St. Martin institution, dishing out heaping helpings of scrumptious grilled lobster, chicken or fish, rice and peas, and johnnycakes on paper plates. You'll find lolos lining Marigot harbor in the marketplace and between the tourist office and Anguilla ferry, but the best are in Grand Case. **Cynthia's** sauce recipe is the most coveted, but **Jimbo** lolo is the hippest. It stays open until midnight for French punks and American wannabes. *Marigot and Grand Case, no phone. No credit cards.*

¢ **Surf Club South.** This friendly beach shack, seemingly held together by business cards and silly photos, is straight from southern California via Jersey City. Run by American expats, it rocks every happy hour, when beer and hot dogs are both a buck. Otherwise, there are filling deli heros, chili, and pastas (all garlic and attitude) for $5–$6. *Grand Case, no tel. No credit cards.*

Lodging

Big, splashy resorts with casinos are prominent here, especially on the Dutch side of the island. Although standard rates at many of these are not affordable for the budget traveler, most offer group package rates through travel wholesalers. Bargains are rife on the Dutch side, which is paying the price of overbuilding with cut-rate tariffs and other incentives.

In general, the French resorts are more intimate and romantic, but Dutch properties compensate with clean, functional, comfortable rooms with lots of amenities. Most of the larger Dutch resorts feature time-share annexes; the units are often available for those vacationers who prefer the condo lifestyle at comparable rates.

Both St. Martin and St. Maarten also have less expensive small inns and guest houses. Often locally owned, these have few of a large hotel's amenities, but they are a cheap and sometimes charming introduction to the local scene. Budget guest houses on the French side usually have more character and ambience than their spartan Dutch counterparts. In addition to inns and guest houses, you'll find many signs here advertising rooms to let in private homes, especially around Grand Case on the French side. These are the cheapest alternative of all ($20–$30 a night), but you are advised to inspect rooms before you commit.

Worth noting on the French side is a coalition of seven small inns called "Les Hotels de Charme." They are dedicated to providing "warmth, individual attention, and homey feeling," with rates that range from $ to $$. In the off season a couple of them hit the ¢ category. Some include breakfast in their rates. The participating hotels are: Alizéa, Panoramic Privilege, L'Hoste, Blue Beach, Hotel du Golf, Chez Martine, and the Sunrise Hotel. For information on any of these inns, call 800/468–6796 in the United states, or 590/87–33–44 in St. Martin.

Keep in mind that truly budget accommodations tend to be a hike from beaches. Those we've recommended are on established bus routes and no more than a half-hour's walk from the nearest major beach. Exceptions are those in Philipsburg and Grand Case, which have their own beaches as well as restaurants and nightlife.

As with most Caribbean islands, you'll save substantially if you travel off-season, although many hotels close for refurbishment during some of these months (usually August/September).

Highly recommended lodgings are indicated by a star ★.

Category	Cost*
$$	$150–$200
$	$80–$150
¢	under $80

**All prices are for a standard double room for two, excluding 5% tax (Dutch side), a taxe de séjour (set by individual hotels on the French side), and a 10%–15% service charge. To estimate rates for hotels offering MAP, add $35–$50 per person per day to the above price ranges. For all-inclusives, add about $75 per person per day.*

Hotels
Dutch Side

Great Bay Beach Hotel & Casino. One of the island's few properties offering an all-inclusive rate, this resort, a 10-minute walk from the center of Philipsburg, has its own stretch of beach and terrific views of the bay. The bustling open-air lobby, with striped awnings overlooking the sea, is more striking than the rooms, which are furnished in typical muted pastels and have the usual amenities, including a TV and phone, but lack any attempt at charm or interest. You do get a private balcony or terrace with an ocean or mountain view. A list of activities is posted each morning, and the hotel staff can arrange virtually any type of island excursion or sport. The clientele is generally friendly, fun-seeking, and active. *Box 910, Philipsburg, tel. 599/5–22446, fax 599/5–23859. 285 rooms, 10 1-bedroom suites. Facilities: 2 restaurants, 3 bars, 2 pools, casino, nightclub, water-sports center, lighted tennis court, gift shop, car rental. AE, DC, MC, V. EP, all-inclusive. $$*

La Vista. On this intimate property, quaint Antillean buildings are connected by brick walkways lined with riotous hibiscus and bougainvillea. All accommodations are air-conditioned suites with cable TV, phone, and balcony. Most have king-size beds; some have a queen or two twins. Guests have the use of the facilities at the adjacent Pelican Resort. *Box 40, Pelican Key, tel. 599/5–43005 or 800/365–8484, fax 599/5–43010. 24 suites. Facilities: restaurant, horseback riding, pool, tennis. AE, MC, V. EP.$$*

★ **Oyster Pond Beach Hotel.** The refined elegance of this hotel is quite out of character with the rest of St. Maarten. The original buildings surround a courtyard furnished with tables and chairs. Two towers with Moorish arches and stone walls hold split-level suites and standard rooms (there are also rooms along the corridors that connect the towers), all with terra-cotta floors, white wicker furnishings, ceiling fans, and pastel French cottons. All rooms have a secluded balcony or terrace and a view of the ocean, the courtyard, or the yacht basin. A newer building offers larger rooms with the same white-wicker furnishings and balconies facing the sea. Rooms in all of the buildings are air-conditioned and have a phone and cable TV. The hotel is a one-minute walk from Dawn Beach, which is excellent for snorkeling, though not for sunbathing or swimming. The dining room opens onto the Atlantic, and the pool is perched right at the water's edge. A PADI-certified dive shop is on the premises. Breakfast is included. *Oyster Pond, Box 239, Philipsburg, tel. 599/5–22206, 599/5–23206, or 800/374–1323; fax 599/5–25695. 40 rooms. Facilities: restaurant, bar, saltwater pool, water-sports center. AE, D, MC, V. BP. $$*

Divi Little Bay Beach Resort. The quaint, red-tile whitewashed buildings are nestled on an emerald hill overlooking the bay and ecru-sand beach. All the spacious rooms have dazzling ocean views, terrace or balcony, cable TV, air-conditioning, and minifridge. Newer deluxe oceanfront rooms also have a Jacuzzi. The decor is pleasing, with aquamarine or terra-cotta tile floors and fresh-looking floral upholstery. *Box 61, Philipsburg, tel. 599/5–22333 or 800/367–3484, fax 599/5–23911. 163 rooms. Facilities: 3 restaurants, 3 bars, 2 pools, car-rental desk, water-sports center, 3 lighted tennis courts, shops, casino. AE, DC, MC, V. EP, FAP, MAP. $–$$*

Holland House Beach Hotel. This is a centrally situated hotel, with the shops of Front Street at its doorstep and a mile-long backyard called Great Bay Beach. Each room has white rattan furnishings with muted-pastel spreads and drapes, balcony, phone, cable TV, and air-conditioning; most have kitchenettes. The huge suites are two large rooms: living room with dining table, sofa, coffee table, chairs, and TV area, and bedroom with king-size bed, a second TV, and phone. Ask for a beach view. The delightful open-air restaurant overlooking the water serves reasonably priced dinners, and the indoor/outdoor patio lounge is a popular and friendly spot to watch the sunset. *35 Front St., Box 393, Philipsburg, tel. 599/5–22572 or 800/223–9815; fax 599/5–24673. 54 rooms, 6 suites. Facilities: restaurant, lounge, meeting room, gift shop, activity desk. AE, D, DC, MC, V. EP. $–$$*

★ **Horny Toad Guesthouse.** This is one of the most charming properties on the island, thanks to the caring touch of owners Bette and Earle Vaughan who keep things as immaculate as if it were their own home (which it is most of the year). Each of the eight apartments on the beach is individually decorated; some have air-conditioning, some have ceiling fans. Many repeat guests request the same apartment. The blue-and-white sun terrace duplicates the patterns of delft china; chirping birds and fresh flowers greet you every morning; and Bette and Earle always treat you like family. There is a barbecue area for guests to use, but no restaurant. *Box 397, Simpson Bay, tel. 599/5–54323, or 800/223–9815, fax 599/5–53316. 2 studios, 6 1-bedroom apartments. Facilities: library, barbecue. No credit cards. EP. $–$$*

Mary's Boon. This informal, out-of-the-way inn sits amid lushly landscaped gardens just off Simpson Bay's big beach. The many repeat guests don't seem fazed by the roar of the jets landing at the nearby airport. Rooms are enormous and have kitchenettes, seaside patios, and ceiling fans, but no phones or TVs. There are two twin beds, sometimes pushed together. Meals are served family-style, and there is an honor bar. *Simpson Bay Rd., Box 2078, Simpson Bay, tel. 599/5–54235 or 800/223–9815, fax 599/5–53403. 12 studios. Facilities: restaurant, bar. No credit cards. EP. $–$$*

Seaview Hotel & Casino. This is another good buy on Front Street and Great Bay Beach. The air-conditioned, twin-bed rooms resemble dormitory rooms, but are cheerful and clean. All have bath (some with shower only), TV, and phone. Ten of the rooms look out on the courtyard, where breakfast is sometimes served; four rooms face the sea. *59 Front St., Box 65, Philipsburg, tel. 599/5–22323 or 800/223–9815; in NY, 212/545–8469; in Canada, 800/468–0023; fax 599/5–24356. 45 rooms. Facilities: breakfast room, casino. AE, D, MC, V. EP. $*

Sea Breeze Hotel. This spotless motel is in a quiet residential area, a 10-minute walk from the beach. The plain but tidy rooms have air-conditioning, phone, cable TV, and minifridge. *Cay Hill, tel. 599/5–26054, fax 599/26057. 30 rooms. Facilities: pool, restaurant, bar, sundry shop. AE, MC, V. EP. ¢–$*

Caribbean Hotel. Frankly, this hotel is recommended more for its funky (some might venture tacky: the curtains look like they could be vintage 1970s, and they don't always match the upholstery) atmosphere, than for its facilities, which are passable and clean. It's on a second floor above Front Street, across the street from Great Bay beach. The rooms have air-conditioning (when it's working), and private baths. Those in the back are quieter. *86 Front St., Box 236, Philipsburg, tel. 599/5–22028. 40 rooms. Facilities: adjacent restaurant and bar. AE, MC, V. EP. ¢*

French Side

Alizéa. The view of Orient Bay from this Mont Vernon hill setting is stunning. There is a path to the beach (a 10-minute walk). An open-air feeling pervades the hotel from its terrace restaurant, where the food is superb, to the 26 guest apartments done up with contemporary light-wood furnishings and pastel floral-print fabrics. Rooms vary in style and design, but all are tasteful and each has a kitchenette and a large private patio balcony. Each also has TV, phone, and large bathroom. A fitness room was slated for completion by the end of 1995. *Mont Vernon 25, 97150, tel. 590/87–33–42, fax 590/87–41–15. 8 1-bedroom bungalows, 18 studios. Facilities: restaurant, bar, gym, pool. AE, MC, V. CP. $$*

★ **Captain Oliver's.** If you want to escape the hustle and bustle of St. Maarten, consider this small hotel. It faces a beautiful horseshoe-shape bay, and rooms have either bay or garden views. Only the standard rooms make into our $$ price range. They are exceptionally clean and air-conditioned and have patio deck, satellite TV, minibar, direct-dial phone, and kitchenette. The property straddles the border: Stay in France, dine in the Netherlands. Sail-and-stay packages can be arranged by the friendly, helpful staff. *Oyster Pond, 97150, tel. 590/87–40–26 or 800/223–9862, fax 590/87–40–84. 50 rooms. Facilities: restaurant, snack bar. AE, DC, MC, V. CP. $$*

Pavillon Beach Hotel. Every room and suite at this small hotel faces the sea and has a private balcony. The spacious studios and one-bedroom suites are decorated in warm pastel colors and have tile floors and elegant rattan furniture. On the balcony is a small kitchenette. Bathrooms come with a hair dryer and shower but no tub. From the ground-level rooms, you can walk right onto the beach through sliding wooden shutters. You may prefer the upper-story rooms, where you can leave the shutters open without as much exposure. The managers, Paul and Marie-Florence, are wonderfully warm-hearted and helpful. Prices are high-end $$. *Plage de Grand Case, RN 7, Grand Case 97150, tel. 590/87–96–46 or 800/223–9815, fax 590/87–71–04. 17 rooms. MC, V. EP. $$*

Hôtel l'Atlantide. This small hotel has four sun-drenched units, ranging in size from a studio to a two-bedroom suite. Private balconies overlook Grand Case Bay and the beach. Each unit has a TV and phone; suites have large living areas and fully equipped kitchens. The decor is airy, with gleaming white tile floors, elegant rattan furniture, and crisp pastel-striped or floral upholstery. There's no restaurant or bar, but the village of Grand Case is known for its lively restaurant scene. *BP 5140, Grand Case 97150, tel. 590/87–09–80, fax 590/87–30–09. 4 units. No credit cards. $–$$*

★ **Hôtel L'Esplanade Caraibes.** Opened in 1992, this complex still sparkles as if brand-new. It's built on a hillside overlooking Grand Case Bay, a three-minute walk from the beach. Two curved stone staircases with inlaid tile and brick lead up from the bougainvillea beds to the open-air reception area. The standard suites are large, with complete kitchens, large private balconies with table and chairs, elegant rattan furniture, king-size beds, gleaming wood ceilings, and ceiling fans; some have an office alcove with a desk. All have phone, TV, and air-conditioning. Duplexes have elegant cathedral ceilings and mahogany staircases, as well as an extra half-bath, an upstairs loft bedroom, and a sleeper sofa in the living room. Upholstery throughout is striped with muted pinks and corals; drapes have crisp tropical prints. There is no restaurant at the hotel, but Grand Case's roster of gourmet spots is just a short walk away. *Box 5007, Grand Case 97150, tel. 590/87–06–55, fax 590/87–29–15. 24 units. Facilities: pool, deep-sea fishing boat for rental. AE, D, MC, V. EP. $–$$*

★ **Marine Hotel Simson Beach.** This sprawling complex may be the best buy on the hotel strip known as Nettlé Bay. Rooms and duplex suites are cheerfully decorated. Most have a view of the water; all have kitchenette, balcony, TV, and phone. The youthful, fun-loving clientele makes sure there's never a dull moment. Budget-conscious Europeans love this place because of the many extras, like a huge breakfast buffet and nightly local entertainment. There are shuttles to Marigot, Philipsburg, and beaches (not complimentary). *Box 172, Nettlé Bay, tel. 590/87–54–54, fax 590/87–92–11. 120 studios, 45 1-bedroom duplexes. Facilities: restaurant, bar, pool, lighted tennis court, beach, water-sports center, activity center, car and bike rental, minimart, gift shop, laundry facilities, dive shop. AE, DC, MC, V. CP. $–$$*

Golden Tulip St. Martin. This new resort, in the somewhat isolated Cul de Sac area, opened in early 1994. It offers a luxury feel for a low price. Clusters of blue bungalows with white gingerbread trim, each housing a suite, are spread out along the water. Garden suites are set farther up from the sea; ocean suites are closer to the beach. Ocean suites are close to/on the beach; garden suites are set farther back. Each unit has a kitchenette, TV, phone, minibar, and a porch facing the sea. The interiors are spacious, with white tile floors, a seating area, and elegant woven-rattan furniture. Pretty floral fabrics are used for the bedspreads, drapes, and upholstery. *BP 5240, Cul de Sac 97072, tel. 590/87–89–98 or 800/344–1212, fax 590/87–35–14. 94 units. Facilities: restaurant, bar, poolside snack bar, water sports, horseback riding, 5 pools, boutique, baby-sitting. AE, DC, MC, V. EP. $*

Jardins de Chevrise. This peaceful little complex is perched on a hill overlooking Orient Bay, a few minutes' (steep) walk from the beach. Simply appointed but appealing efficiencies have small balconies (not all rooms have sea views), kitchenettes, and air-conditioning. Pleasant plant-filled walkways connect the buildings. Children under six stay free. *52 Mont Vernon 97150, tel. 590/87–37–79, fax 590/87–38–03. 30 studios and 1-bedroom bungalows. Facilities: pool, grill. MC, V. CP. $*

★ **La Residence.** The downtown location and soundproof rooms of this Marigot hotel make it a popular place for business travelers. All the accommodations have bath (with shower only), king-size bed, balcony, dark rattan furniture, tile floors, phone, TV, and minibar. You've a choice among single or double rooms, some with mezzanine loft beds. The intimate restaurant offers a good $28 three-course menu. You'll have to take a cab to get to the beach. *Rue du Général de Gaulle, Marigot 97150, tel. 590/87–70–37 or 800/223–9815, fax 590/87–90–44. 21 rooms. Facilities: restaurant, lounge, sundry shop. AE, D, MC, V. MAP, CP. $*

Marina Royale Hotel. This busy little hotel on the Marina Port La Royale is very popular with young French families and businesspeople on holiday. The bright, simple rooms all have kitchenette, cable TV, air-conditioning, and direct-dial phone. The beach is about a 20-minute stroll away; the hotel advises that guest have a car, which is necessary to get to restaurants (the hotel doesn't have one). *Port La Royale, Marigot, tel. 590/87–52–46, fax 590/87–92–88. 62 rooms. AE, MC, V. EP. $*

Coralita Beach Hotel. The entrance is a bit unprepossessing, like something out of a Graham Greene novel about well-bred Europeans down on their luck. But the ultraneat, fresh rooms haven't gone to seed. They are large and breezy, with light woods, tile floors, and pastel fabrics, most with air-conditioning and kitchenette. Sunday brunch is one of the island's liveliest. As the name suggests, the hotel is right on the beach, though you'll need a car for restaurant hopping. The Coralita may be a little worn and way off the beaten path, but it's quite congenial and an excellent bargain. *BP 175, Oyster Pond 97150, tel. 590/87–31–81, fax 590/87–31–20. 24 studios. Facilities: restaurant, bar, pool, lighted tennis court, game room. AE, DC, MC, V. EP. ¢–$*

Ernest's Guest House. The rooms in this nondescript, motel-style facility are spacious, clean, and surprisingly nice for their $45-a-night price tag. They have cable TV, phone, and air-conditioning. The motel is about a 10-minute walk from Great Bay Beach, and there are restaurants, including Pizza Hut, very close by. Children under seven stay free. *Bush Rd., Cay Hill, tel. 599/5–22003. 16 rooms. Facilities: pool. No credit cards. EP. ¢*

Le Royale Louisiana. Located in downtown Marigot in the boutique shopping area, this upstairs hotel is pleasant and pretty. White and pale-green galleries overlook the flower-filled courtyard. There's a selection of twin, double, and triple duplexes, all with air-conditioning, private bath (tub and shower), TV, and phone. You can reach the nearest beach by a 20-minute walk. *Rue du Général de Gaulle, Box 476, Marigot 97055, tel. 590/87–86–51, fax 590/87–96–49. 68 rooms. Facilities: restaurant, snack bar, beauty salon. AE, MC, V. CP. ¢*

Guest Houses
Dutch Side

★ **Passangrahan Royal Guest House.** It's entirely appropriate that the bar here is named Sidney Greenstreet. This is the island's oldest inn, and it looks like a set for an old Bogie-Greenstreet film. The green and white building was once Queen Wilhelmina's residence and the government guest house. Wicker peacock chairs, slowly revolving ceiling fans, balconies shaded by tropical greenery, king-size mahogany headboards, and a broad tile veranda are some of the hallmarks of this guest house. A complimentary afternoon tea is served. There are no TVs or phones in the rooms, and you're offered just a sliver of Great Bay Beach. *15 Front St., Box 151, Philipsburg, tel. 599/5–23588, fax 599/5–22885. 30 rooms, 1 suite. Facilities: restaurant, bar. AE, MC, V. EP. $–$$*

Beach House. This unexpectedly tranquil oasis amid the bustle of downtown Philipsburg gives you the best of both worlds: The beach and the shops and restaurants of Philipsburg are right at your doorstep. Gleaming white halls with gorgeous carved mahogany doors lead to tidy, well-appointed rooms with cable TVs, kitchenettes, ocean-view balconies, and air-conditioning. *161 Front St., Philipsburg, tel. 599/5–22456, fax 599/5–30308. 8 1-bedroom apartments. AE, MC, V. EP. $*

Residence La Chatelaine. This pink and white apartment hotel sits right on the beach and is within walking distance of restaurants. Owner Maryanne Chatelaine floats through the property, and her delicate, slightly frilly touch is evident in the light, pastel rooms with lacy mosquito netting imported from Amsterdam. Each unit has a full kitchen, small bath, and ceiling fan. Extras like air-conditioning, dishwashers, and lovely old mahogany four-poster beds are unevenly distributed. The only TV is in the lounge. There are studios, one- and two-bedroom apartments. Your view depends on the rate you are willing to pay. *Box 2056, Simpson Bay, tel. 599/5–54269, fax 599/5–53195. 16 units. Facilities: pool. AE, MC, V. EP. $*

French Side **Chez Martine.** The rooms in this green and white Antillean-style house on Grand Case Bay are modestly furnished with wicker and pastel prints. All are air-conditioned and have minifridge and hand-held showerhead. There are no ocean views from the rooms, but you can see the water from the shared terrace. There is a full kitchen for guest use. Personable owners Elaine and Jean-Pierre Bertheau tell fascinating tales of their days in Morocco. You're right on Grand Case Beach, with lots of restaurants nearby. Regrettably, the property's own very fine restaurant is quite expensive. *Box 637, Grand Case 97150, tel. 590/87–51–59, fax 590/87–87–30. 5 rooms. Facilities: restaurant, laundry service. DC, MC, V. EP. $*

★ **Hevea.** This small white guest house with smart striped awnings is across the street from the beach in the heart of Grand Case. The rooms are dollhouse small but will appeal to romantics. There are beam ceilings, washstands, and carved-wood beds with lovely white coverlets and mosquito nets. The five air-conditioned rooms, studios, and apartment are on the terrace level; three fan-cooled studios and apartments are on the garden level. Hotel guests can get a special "house" dinner at the delightful gourmet restaurant for $30. *163 Blvd. de Grand Case, Grand Case 97150, tel. 590/87–56–85 or 800/423–4433, fax 590/87–83–88. 8 units. Facilities: restaurant. MC, V. EP. $*

Gracie Mansion. The whitewashed walls, teal roofs, and coral balconies of this immaculate little guest house contrast brilliantly with the azure sky and water. It's a peaceful retreat. Units are furnished in tasteful but idiosyncratic fashion, and have kitchenette, terrace, small shower baths, satellite TV, and fans. The house is on Oyster Pond, a three-minute drive from the beach (it's difficult to get to on foot). You'll want a car. *Baie Lucas 97150, tel. and fax 590/87–41–56. 19 units. AE, MC, V. EP. ¢*

Le Cigalon. Look behind drying wash and luxuriant, barely contained gardens to find this somewhat ramshackle, rambling old house. You pass through a flower-draped arbor into a welcoming little restaurant, which serves superb local food (you can get dinner with wine for about $20). All rooms have private shower baths and are air-conditioned; the nicest have hand-painted murals. Nothing fancy, no TVs or phones, but as inexpensive as they come—$46 for a double—and well worth the 20-minute trek it takes to get to the beach. *Rue de Fichaut, Marigot 97150, tel. 590/87–08–19. 11 rooms. Facilities: restaurant, bar. No credit cards. EP. ¢*

Home and Apartment Rentals Both sides of the island offer a variety of homes, villas, condominiums, and apartments. Information in the United States can be obtained through **WIMCO** (Box 1461, Newport, RI 02840, tel. 800/932–2222), **Caribbean Home Rentals** (Box 710, Palm Beach, FL 33480, tel. 407/833–4454), **Jane Condon Corp.** (211 E. 43rd St., New York, NY 10017, tel. 212/986–4373), or **St. Maarten Villas** (707 Broad Hollow Rd., Farmingdale, NY 11735, tel. 516/249–4940). On the island, contact **Carimo** (tel. 590/87–57–58) or **St. Martin Rentals** (tel. 599/5–54330; in the U.S., tel. 800/872–8356). Both tourist boards publish lists of recommended villas and guest houses that meet minimum standards in various price categories. The least expensive apartment complexes are located in Grand Case; all are fairly basic, clean, and priced in the ¢–$ range.

Off-Season Bets While the most glamorous properties remain outside our price range, several top resorts lower their rates by up to 50% during the off-season. It also pays to inquire about special packages that can make an otherwise pricey property affordable. Most of the megaresorts on the Dutch side, as well as their sister time-share developments, are good off-season bets. You'll be where all the activity is, with a tremendous range of facilities at your disposal. Foremost among these are **Mullet Bay Resort** (Mullet Bay, tel. 599/5–52801), **Pelican Resort** (Simpson Bay, tel. 599/5–42503 or 800/626–9637), and **Maho Beach Hotel & Casino** (Maho Bay, tel. 599/5–52115 or 800/223–0757). The elegant **Oyster Pond Beach Hotel** (Oyster Pond, tel. 599/5–22206 or 800/374–1323) is a quieter property with great charm. On the French side, good bets are the bustling **Mont Vernon** (Baie Orientale, tel. 590/87–62–00 or 800/223–0888) and the pretty and popular **Anse Margot** (Nettlé Bay, tel. 590/87–92–01 or 800/742–4276). Most are on lovely stretches of beach.

Nightlife

To find out what's doing on the island, pick up any of the following publications: *St. Maarten Nights, What to Do in St. Maarten, St. Maarten Events,* or *St. Maarten Holiday*—all distributed free in the tourist office and hotels. *Discover St. Martin/St. Maarten,* also free, is a glossy magazine that includes articles about the island's history and the latest on shops, discos, restaurants, and even archaeological digs.

Each of the resort hotels has a Caribbean spectacular one night a week, replete with limbo and fire dancers and steel bands.

Casinos are the main focus on the Dutch side, but there are discos that usually start late and keep on till the fat lady sings.

Bars and Nightclubs

Cheri's Cafe (across from the Maho Beach Hotel, tel. 599/5–53361) is a local institution, with cheap food and great live bands. **Turtle Pier Bar & Restaurant** (Airport Rd., tel. 599/5–52230) always hops with a lively crowd. **Coconuts Comedy Club** (Maho Plaza, tel. 599/5–52115) headlines top comedy acts Sunday–Friday. **David's Pub** (Rue de la Liberté, Marigot, tel. 590/87–51–58) is run by an expatriate Brit; its wild Tuesday and Friday trivia nights are legendary. **Bamboo Cocktail Bar** (Rue de la Liberté, Marigot, tel. 590/29–01–00) is the place for karaoke fans. On Grand Case Boulevard, happy hours rock at the American-owned **Surf Club South** (no phone), and **Jimbo Lolo** (no phone) stays open until midnight for French punks and American wanna-bes, who then head over for a nightcap at **Cha Cha Cha Caribbean Café** (tel. 590/87–53–63). The friendly **News Music Cafe** (Airport Rd., Simpson Bay, tel. 599/5–42236) serves food into the wee hours.

Casinos

All the casinos have craps, blackjack, roulette, and slot machines. You must be 18 years old or older to gamble. The casinos are located at the **Great Bay Beach Hotel & Casino, Divi Little Bay Beach Resort, Pelican Resort, Mullet Bay Resort, Seaview Hotel & Casino** and the **Coliseum** in Philipsburg; **Port de Plaisance;** and **Casino Royale at Maho Beach.**

Discos

Last Stop (A.T. Illidge Rd., no phone) and the **Tropics** (by Madame Estate in the Royal Inn Motel, no phone) are hot, somewhat rowdy discos frequented by locals. There have been reports of drug activity at the latter. **Studio 7** (Mullet Bay, tel. 599/5–42115) attracts a young crowd of locals and visitors Tuesday through Saturday. **Casino Royale,** across from the Maho Beach Hotel, produces the splashy "Paris Revue Show," and **La Luna** is Maho's disco, popular with young people. French nationals and locals flock to the **Copacabana** disco (tel. 87–42–52) in Marina Royale in Marigot for salsa and soca. **Night Fever** (Colombier, outside Marigot, no phone) attracts a young crowd of locals who gyrate to the latest Eurodisco beat.

24 St. Vincent and the Grenadines

Updated by Kate Sekules

St. Vincent and the Grenadines is a nation comprising 32 lush, mountainous islands and cays. St. Vincent, only 18 miles long and 9 miles wide, sits just over 13° north of the equator, with the Grenadines lined up like a tadpole tail for 45 miles to the southwest. They are, each in a different way, islands for the demanding escapist, devoid of all-inclusive resorts, glitzy disco clubs, and duty-free shopping malls, but rich in natural beauty.

St. Vincent itself produces most of the world's arrowroot, though its major export is bananas, and these plants, along with coconut palms and breadfruit trees crowd, more of the island than the 99,000-person population does. This has obvious charm for the nature lover, who can spend weeks hiking St. Vincent's not always well-paved trails, perhaps sighting the rare St. Vincent parrot in the Vermont Valley, or climbing the Caribbean's most active volcano, La Soufrière, which last erupted in 1979. Below sea level, snorkeling and scuba landscapes are similarly exciting, both off St. Vincent and around the Grenadines.

Despite its unspoiled beauty, most people don't linger long in St. Vincent, using it as a stop-off en route to their preferred Grenadine. That has a lot to do with the beaches, which are narrow and mostly black—in contrast to the Grenadines' picture-postcard expanses of powdery white sand—and with the fact that St. Vincent is not really set up for tourists. This can be an advantage for the budget traveler, since prices have not been artificially hiked. It is also possible to go the self-catering route, living like a local instead of being confined to tourist ghettos, as visitors often are on very developed islands.

The Grenadines offer some of the most exclusive, expensive, and snazzy accommodations in the Caribbean, created expressly as playgrounds for rich visitors. You should not, for instance, bother to alight at Mustique or Petit St. Vincent, nor Young and Palm Islands. On the other hand, Bequia is one of the Caribbean's most charmingly affordable small islands, and if you keep away from the jet-setters, you'll find the islands generally very supportive of a budget-minded existence. You can take minivans instead of renting a car or using taxis, cook your own meals in your simple kitchenette, walk to the beach (not always viable on St. Vincent, unless you're staying at Villa Beach), and hike through the gorgeous landscapes for kicks. Bareboats are available for charter at reasonable cost, and groups of four or six will find even a crewed yacht within their budget on St. Vincent. Thanks to the friendly, unpretentious atmosphere, visitors with even minimal charm and manual dexterity often find themselves invited to day-sail by the many yacht owners or bare-boaters who frequent the Grenadines.

Remember, though, that unspoiled involves tradeoffs: no shopping, no nightlife, and often no hot water in the clean but bordering-on-primitive budget hotels. Getting anything accomplished (even buying groceries) always takes more time and effort than you think . . . but sooner or later, everything seems to work out.

What It Will Cost These sample prices, meant only as a general guide, are for high season. Expect to pay from \$50 to \$80 a night for a ¢ hotel or a B&B for two. A two-bedroom apartment rents for \$300–\$600 a week. Plan on about \$6 for a ¢ restaurant meal, about \$5 for a sandwich lunch. Supermarket prices are higher than in the United States, as most food must be shipped in. A beer costs about \$1.75 here. A glass of house wine or rum punch can be anywhere from \$1.50 to \$3. Car rental is about \$45–\$50 a day for a stick-shift model. Taxi fares cost about \$3–\$4 around Kingstown, about \$8 from Kingstown to Villa Beach, a minivan ride on that route costs E.C. \$1.50, or about 50¢. A single-tank dive here is about \$50; snorkel equipment rents for around \$8 a day.

Before You Go

Tourist Information The **St. Vincent and the Grenadines Tourist Office** (801 2nd Ave., 21st Floor, New York, NY 10017, tel. 212/687–4981 or 800/729–1726, fax 212/949–5946; or 6505 Cove Creek Pl., Dallas, TX 75240, tel. 214/239–6451, fax 214/239–1002. In Canada: 100 University Ave., Suite 504, Toronto, Ontario M5J 1V6, tel. 416/971–9666, fax 416/971–9667. In the United Kingdom: 10 Kensington Court, London W8 5DL, tel. 0171/937–6570, fax 0171/937–3611). Write for a visitor's guide, filled with useful, up-to-date information.

Arriving and Departing

By Plane Most U.S. visitors fly via **American** (tel. 800/433–7300) into Barbados or St. Lucia, then take a small plane to St. Vincent's E.T. Joshua Airport or to Bequia. Other airlines that connect with interisland flights are **BWIA** (tel. 800/538–2942), **British Airways** (tel. 800/247–9297), **Air Canada** (tel. 800/776–3000), and **Air France** (tel. 800/237–2747).

LIAT (Leeward Islands Air Transport, tel. 809/462–0700; in NY, 212/251–1717; elsewhere in the U.S., 800/253–5011), **Air Martinique** (tel. 809/458–4528), and **SVGAIR** (tel. 809/456–5610; fax 809/458–4697) fly interisland. Delays are common, but usually not outrageous. A surer way to go is with **Mustique Airways** (tel. 809/458–4380 or 809/458–4818. In the United States, contact Stratton Travel, 795 Franklin Ave., Franklin Lakes, NJ 07417, tel. 201/891–3456, or 800/223–0599). Its six- or eight-seat charter flights meet and wait for your major carrier's arrival even if it's delayed.

From the Airport Taxis and/or buses are readily available at the airport on St. Vincent and Bequia. A taxi from the E.T. Joshua airport to Kingstown, St. Vincent, will cost about \$6; bus fare is less than 75¢. If you have a lot of luggage, it might be best to take a taxi—buses (actually minivans) are very short on space.

Passports and Visas U.S. and Canadian citizens must have a passport; all visitors must hold return or ongoing tickets. Visas are not required.

Language English is spoken everywhere in the Grenadines, often with a Vincentian patois or dialect.

Precautions Insects are a minor problem on the beach during the day, but when hiking and sitting outdoors in the evening, you'll be glad you brought industrial-strength mosquito repellent.

Beware of the manchineel tree, whose little green apples look tempting but are toxic. Even touching the sap of the leaves will cause an uncomfortable rash. Most trees on hotel grounds are marked with signs; on more remote islands, the bark may be painted red. Hikers should watch for Brazil wood trees/bushes, which look and act similar to poison ivy.

When taking photos of market vendors, private citizens, or homes, be sure to ask permission first and expect to give a gratuity for the favor.

There's relatively little crime here, but don't tempt fate by leaving your valuables lying around or your room or car unlocked.

Staying in St. Vincent and the Grenadines

Important Addresses **Tourist Information:** The **St. Vincent Board of Tourism** (tel. 809/457–1502) is in the new financial complex, close to the port on Upper Bay Street.

Emergencies **Police:** tel. 809/457–1211. **Hospitals: Kingston General Hospital** (tel. 809/456–1185). **Pharmacies: Deane's** (tel. 809/456–2877) and **Reliance** (tel. 809/456–1734), both in Kingstown; on Bequia **Bequia Pharmacy** (tel. 809/458–3296).

Currency Although U.S. and Canadian dollars are taken at all but the smallest shops, Eastern Caribbean currency (E.C.$) is accepted and preferred everywhere. At press time, the exchange rate was U.S. $1 to E.C. $2.67; banks give a slightly better rate of exchange.

Price quotes on the islands are normally given in E.C. dollars; however, when you negotiate taxi fares and such, be sure you know which type of dollar you're agreeing on. Note: Prices quoted here are in U.S. dollars unless indicated otherwise.

Taxes and Service Charges The departure tax from St. Vincent and the Grenadines is $8 (E.C. $20). Restaurants charge a 5% government tax, and if a 10% service charge is included in your bill, no additional tip is necessary. Hotels charge a 5% tax and an additional 10% for service.

Getting Around The islands' roads make San Francisco's look almost flat, and they're not always well-maintained. For those not used to driving on the left, the whole experience can be unnerving. You may prefer to spend money on taxis or minibuses.

Taxis Fares run $3–$4 around Kingstown, $8 from Kingstown to Villa Beach. You can hire a taxi and driver for sightseeing (*see* Guided Tours, *below*) at $15 an hour.

Minivans Public buses in St. Vincent come in the form of brightly painted minivans with names like "Easy Na," "Irie," and "Who to Blame." Fares are E.C. $1–$6; the higher rate will take you from the bottom to the top of the island. Just wave from the road, and the driver will stop for you, then pay the man by the door on the way out, with the correct change in E.C.$ coins, if at all possible. In Kingstown, buses leave from the Terminus in Market Square.

On Bequia, most taxis are pickup trucks with benches in the back and canvas covers for when it rains.

Rental Cars Rental cars cost $45–$50 per day; driving is on the left. Many roads are not well marked or maintained. We recommend a taxi or minibus tour before going out on your own in order to familiarize yourself with directions and road conditions.

To rent a car you'll need a temporary Vincentian license (unless you already have an International Driver's License), which costs E.C. $20. Among the rental firms are **Johnson's U-Drive** (tel. 809/458–4864) at the airport and **Kim's Auto Rentals** (tel. 809/456–1884), which has a larger selection of slightly more expensive rental cars that must be rented by the week.

Telephones and Mail The area code for St. Vincent and the Grenadines is 809. If you use Sprint or MCI in the United States, you may need to access an AT&T line to dial direct to St. Vincent and the Grenadines. From St. Vincent, you can direct-dial to other countries; ask the hotel operator for the proper country code and the probable charge, surcharge, and government tax on the call. Local information is 118; international is 115.

When you dial a local number from your hotel in the Grenadines, you can drop the 45 prefix. Few hotels have phones in the rooms. Pay phones are best operated by the prepaid card available from stores, and usable in several Caribbean islands.

Mail between St. Vincent and the United States takes two to three weeks. Airmail postcards cost 45¢; airmail letters cost 65¢ an ounce.

Opening and Closing Times Stores and shops in Kingstown are open weekdays 8–4. Many close for lunch from noon to 1 or so. Saturday hours are 8–noon. Banks are open weekdays 8–noon, 2, or 3, Friday from 2 or 3 to 5. The post office is open weekdays 8:30–3, Saturdays 8:30–11:30.

Guided Tours Tours can be informally arranged through taxi drivers who double as knowledgeable guides. Your hotel or the tourism board will recommend a driver. When choosing a driver/guide, look for the Taxi Driver's Association decal on the windshield and talk with the driver long enough to be sure you can understand his patois over the noise of the engine. Settle the fare first ($15 per hour is the going rate). To prearrange a taxi tour, contact the Taxi Driver's Association (tel. 809/457–1807).

St. Vincent

Exploring St. Vincent

Numbers in the margin correspond to points of interest on the St. Vincent map.

Kingstown's shopping/business district, cathedrals, and sights can easily be seen in a half-day tour. Outlying areas, botanical gardens, and the Falls of Baleine will each require a full day of touring. City maps are in the "Discover SVG" booklet, available everywhere.

Kingstown

1 The capital and port of St. Vincent, **Kingstown** is at the southeastern end of the island. It is very much a working city with no concessions made to tourists, or to cruise line day-trippers. The **harbour** is far more likely to be hosting a freight liner than a passenger ship anyway, but what few gift boutiques there are can be found nearby, on and around Bay Street. Here you will also find the **financial complex**, a cool and tall structure, of which the island is inordinately proud. Among its official duties, it houses the tourist office.

The most exciting thing to do in Kingstown is browse among the 2,000 varieties of breadfruit-like root vegetables and soursoplike fruits (only kidding) in **Kingstown Market.** There are outdoor and indoor sections, the latter featuring many homemade-lunch stalls around the periphery, and though the bustle is greatest on Saturdays before 11 AM, there is usually a seething and frenetic crowd. Take a look at the indoor **fish market** too. This was a gift from the Japanese people who also donated ecological deep sea fishing lessons.

There isn't much actually to buy, unless you have a kitchenette in your hostelry, in which case you'll be spending a lot of time here. For gifts, try the **Philatellic Bureau** on Lower Bay Street, or the **post office** on Granby Street east of Egmont. St. Vincent is known worldwide for its particularly beautiful and colorful issues, which commemorate flowers, undersea creatures, and architecture.

Follow Back Street (also called Granby Street) west past the Methodist Church to **St. George's Cathedral,** a yellow Anglican church built in the early 19th century. The dignified Georgian architecture includes simple wood pews, an ornate hanging candelabra, and stained-glass windows. The gravestones tell the history of the island.

Across the street is **St. Mary's Roman Catholic Cathedral,** built in 1823 and renovated in the 1930s. The renovations resulted in a strangely appealing blend of Moorish, Georgian, and Romanesque styles in black brick.

A few minutes away by bus is St. Vincent's famous **Botanical Gardens.** Founded in 1765, it is the oldest botanical garden in the Western Hemisphere. Captain Bligh—yes, the captain of the *Bounty*—brought the first breadfruit tree to this island, a direct descendant of which you can see today in the gardens. St. Vincent parrots and green monkeys are housed in cages, and unusual trees and bushes cover the well-kept grounds. Local guides offer their services for $2–$4 an hour. *Information: c/o Minister of Agriculture, Kingstown, tel. 809/457–1003. Open weekdays 7–4, Sat. 7–11 AM, Sun. 7–6.*

The tiny **National Museum** just inside the entrance to the gardens houses a series of maps tracing the migrations of the Ciboney, the very first Vincentians, who arrived around 4000 BC, plus pre-Columbian Indian clay pottery found by Dr. Earle Kirby, St. Vincent's resident archaeologist, and the museum's director. Dr. Kirby's historical knowledge is as entertaining as it is extensive. Contact him for a guided tour, since the labels in the museum offer little information. *Tel. 809/456–1787. Admission free (suggested donation: $1). Open Wed. 9:45–noon, Sat. 4–6.*

2 Flag another taxi for the 10-minute ride to **Fort Charlotte,** built in 1806 to keep Napoleon at bay. The fort sits 636 feet above sea level, with cannons and battlements perched on a dramatic promontory overlooking the city and the Grenadines to the south, Lowman's Beach and the calm east coast to the north. The fort saw little military action; it was used mainly to house paupers and lepers. Nowadays it is the island's women's prison.

Outside Kingstown

The coastal roads of St. Vincent offer panoramic views and insights into the island way of life. Life in the tiny villages has changed little in centuries. This full-day driving tour includes Layou, Montreal Gardens, Mesopotamia Valley, and the Windward coast. Be sure to drive on the left, and honk your horn before you enter the blind curves. Note that you can make the same tour—albeit more slowly—by minibus. Start from Market Square, where the buses wait in ranks next to Leeward and Windward signs. Take a Leeward bus, making sure it's going as far as you want to go.

About 45 minutes north of Kingstown is **Layou,** a small fishing village.
3 Just north of the village are **petroglyphs** (rock carvings) left by the Caribs 13 centuries ago. If you're seriously interested in archaeological mysteries, you'll want to stop here. Phone the tourism board to arrange a visit with Victor Hendrickson, who owns the

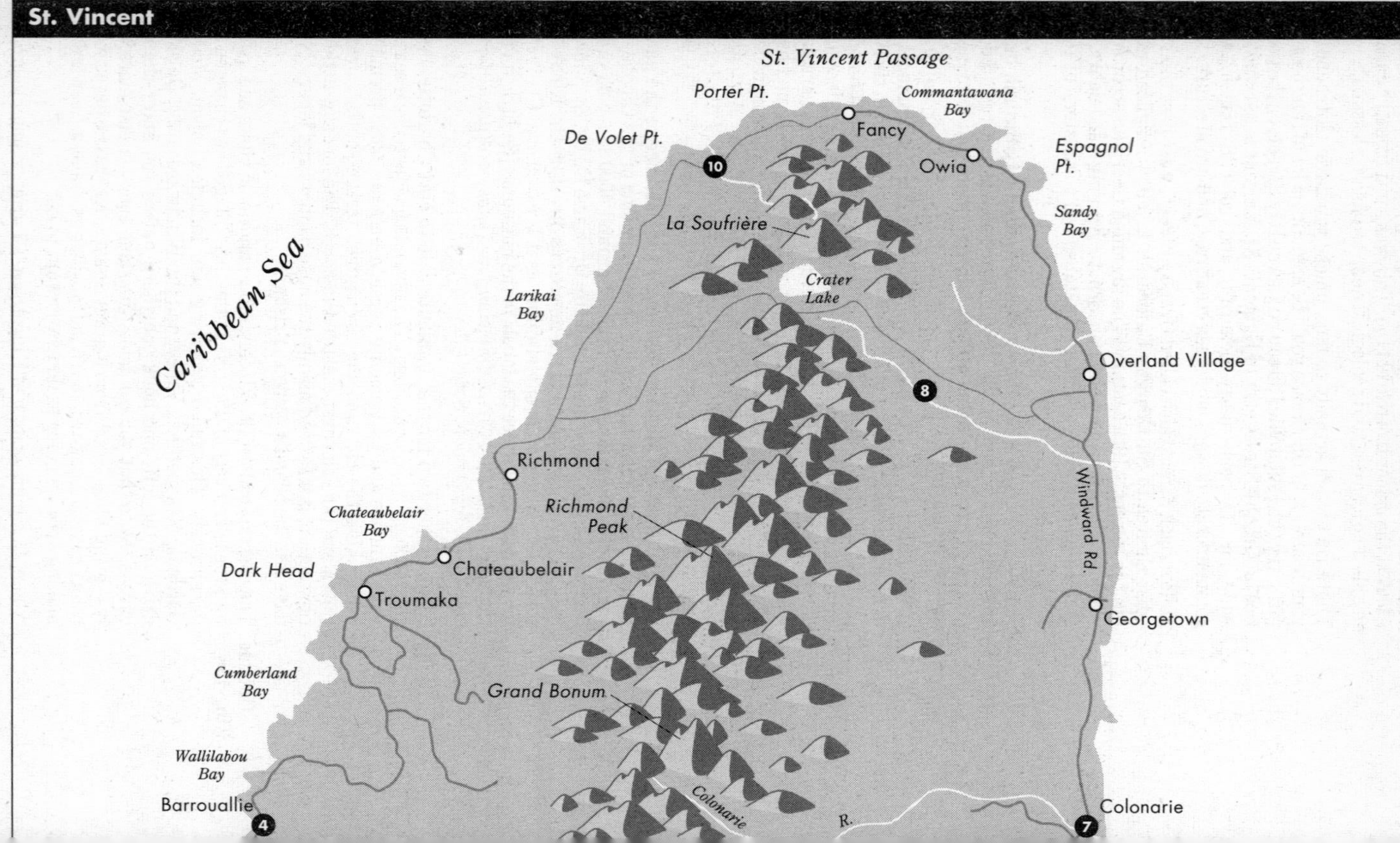
St. Vincent
St. Vincent Passage
Porter Pt.
Commantawana Bay
Fancy
De Volet Pt.
Espagnol Pt.
Owia
Sandy Bay
La Soufrière
Caribbean Sea
Crater Lake
Larikai Bay
Overland Village
Richmond
Richmond Peak
Windward Rd.
Chateaubelair Bay
Chateaubelair
Dark Head
Troumaka
Georgetown
Cumberland Bay
Grand Bonum
Wallilabou Bay
Barrouallie
Colonarie
R.
Colonarie
10
8
4
7

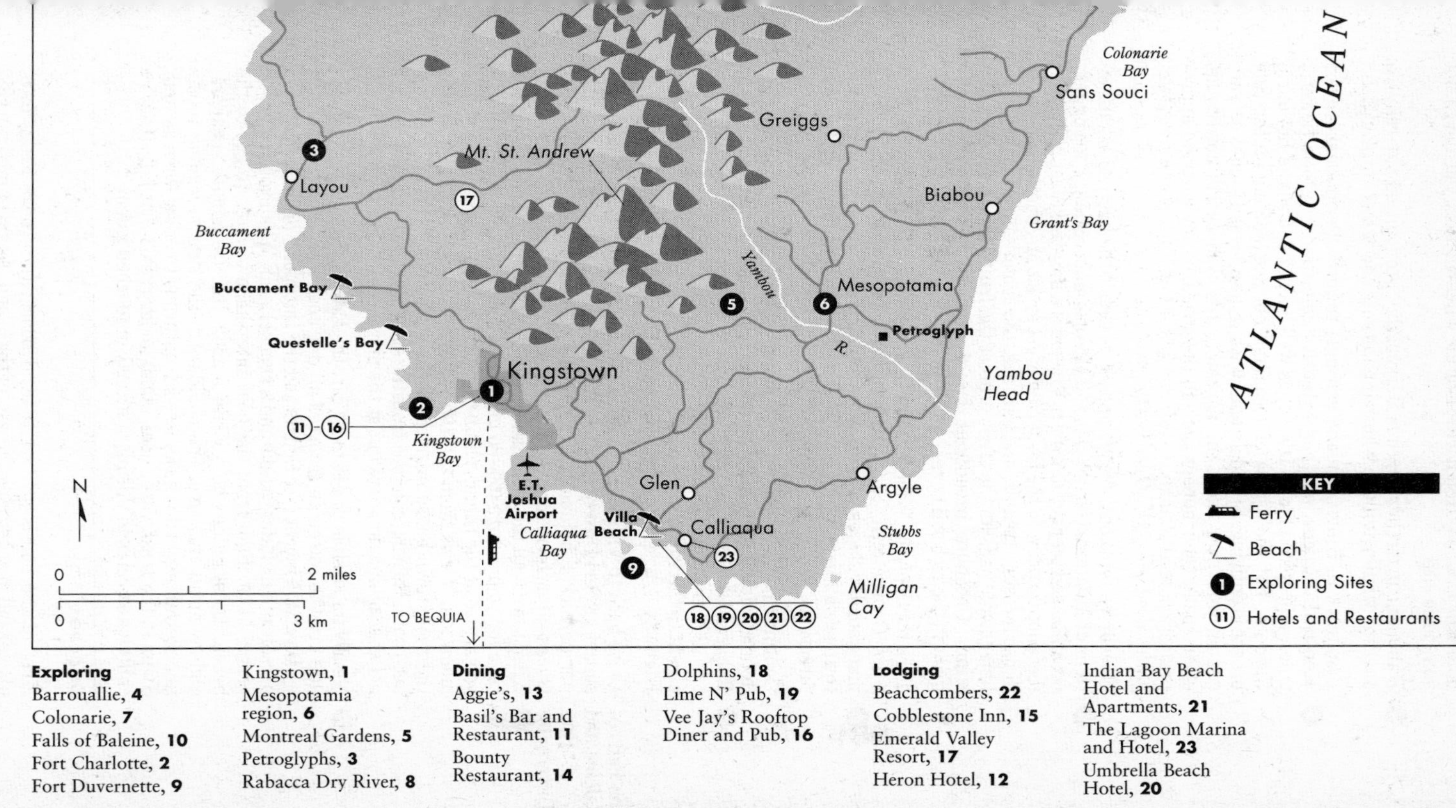
ATLANTIC OCEAN
Colonarie Bay
Sans Souci
Greiggs
Mt. St. Andrew
Layou
Biabou
Grant's Bay
Buccament Bay
Buccament Bay
Yambou R.
Mesopotamia
Petroglyph
Questelle's Bay
Kingstown
Yambou Head
Kingstown Bay
E.T. Joshua Airport
Glen
Argyle
Villa Beach
Calliaqua
Calliaqua Bay
Stubbs Bay
Milligan Cay
TO BEQUIA
0 2 miles
0 3 km
N
KEY
Ferry
Beach
Exploring Sites
Hotels and Restaurants
Exploring
Barrouallie, 4
Colonarie, 7
Falls of Baleine, 10
Fort Charlotte, 2
Fort Duvernette, 9
Kingstown, 1
Mesopotamia region, 6
Montreal Gardens, 5
Petroglyphs, 3
Rabacca Dry River, 8
Dining
Aggie's, 13
Basil's Bar and Restaurant, 11
Bounty Restaurant, 14
Dolphins, 18
Lime N' Pub, 19
Vee Jay's Rooftop Diner and Pub, 16
Lodging
Beachcombers, 22
Cobblestone Inn, 15
Emerald Valley Resort, 17
Heron Hotel, 12
Indian Bay Beach Hotel and Apartments, 21
The Lagoon Marina and Hotel, 23
Umbrella Beach Hotel, 20

land. For E.C. $5, Hendrickson or his wife will meet you and escort you to the site.

4 Half an hour farther north is **Barrouallie** (pronounced *bar*-relly), a onetime whaling village whose inhabitants now trawl for blackfish.

Backtrack to Kingstown and continue toward Mesopotamia to the
5 **Montreal Gardens,** another extensive collection of exotic flowers, trees, and spice plants. It's not as well maintained as the Botanical Gardens, but the aroma of cocoa and nutmeg wafting on the cool breeze is enticing. Spend an hour with well-informed guides or wander on your own along the narrow paths. Vincentian newlyweds often spend their honeymoons in the garden's tiny cottage, appropriately named Romance. *Tel. 809/458–5452. Admission free (suggested donation: $1). Open daily.*

Now drive southeast (roads and signs aren't the best, so ask direc-
6 tions at Montreal Gardens) to the **Mesopotamia region.** The rugged, ocean-lashed scenery along St. Vincent's windward coast is the perfect counterpoint to the lush, calm west coast. Mesopotamia is full of dense forests, streams, and bananas, the island's major export. The blue plastic bags on the trees protect the fruit from damage in high winds. Coconuts, breadfruit, sweet corn, peanuts, and arrowroot grow in the rich soil here.

Turn north on the Windward Highway up the jagged coast road toward Georgetown, St. Vincent's second-largest city. You'll pass
7 many small villages and the town of **Colonarie.** In the hills behind the town are hiking trails. Signs are limited, but locals are helpful with directions.

Continue north to **Georgetown,** amid coconut groves and the long-defunct Mount Bentinck sugar factory. A few miles north is the
8 **Rabacca Dry River,** a rocky gulch carved out by the lava flow from the 1902 eruption of La Soufrière. Here hikers begin the two-hour ascent to the volcano. Return south to Kingstown via the Windward Highway.

The Falls of Baleine and Fort Duvernette

Drive back to Villa Beach, south of Kingstown, in time to catch the sunset at **Fort Duvernette,** the tiny island that juts up like a loaf of pumpernickel behind Young Island Resort. Take the *African Queen*–style ferry for a few dollars from the dock at Villa Beach near
9 Kingstown (call the boatman from the phone on the dock) and set a time for your return (60–90 minutes is plenty for exploring). When you arrive at the island, climb the 100 or more steps carved into the mountain. Views from the 195-foot summit are terrific, but avoid the overgrown house near the top, where you'll encounter (harmless) bats. Rusting cannons from the early 1800s are still here, aimed not at seagoing invaders but at the marauding Caribs.

10 Nearly impossible to get to by car, the **Falls of Baleine** are an absolute must to see on an escorted all-day boat trip. A motorboat ride by **Dive St. Vincent** (*see* Sports and the Outdoors, *below*) costs $40 a person and includes drinks and a snorkel stop. When you arrive, be prepared to climb from the boat into shallow water to get to the beach. Local guides help visitors make the five-minute sneakers-and-swimsuit trek over the boulders in the stream leading to the falls; a walkway allows the less adventurous to enjoy them as well. Swim in the freshwater pool, climb under the 63-foot falls (they're chilly), and relax in this bit of utterly untouched Eden.

Beaches

Most of the hotels and white-sand beaches are near Kingstown; black-sand beaches ring the rest of the island. A taxi or minivan ride is necessary to get to most beaches, unless you're staying on Villa Beach. The placid west coast includes the island's main beach (although it's hardly big enough to merit such a title), the white sand **Villa**, with the adjacent, slightly rocky **Indian Bay.** Farther up the westward (leeward) coast are the black sand **Questelle's** (pronounced keet-*ells*) **Bay,** next to the Camden Park Industrial Site, and tiny **Buccament Bay**, which is good for swimming. The beaches at Villa and the CSY Yacht Club are small but safe, with dive shops nearby. The exposed Atlantic coast is dramatic, but the water is rough and unpredictable. No beach has lifeguards, so even experienced swimmers are taking a risk. The windward side of the island has no beachfront facilities.

Sports and the Outdoors

Hiking Dorsetshire Hill, about 3 miles from Kingstown, rewards you with a sweeping view of city and harbor; picturesque Queen's Drive is nearby. Mt. St. Andrew, on the outskirts of the city, is a pleasant climb through a rain forest on a well-marked trail.

The queen of climbs is La Soufrière, St. Vincent's active volcano (which last erupted, appropriately enough, on a Friday the 13th in 1979). Approachable from both windward and leeward coasts, this is *not* a casual excursion for inexperienced walkers; you'll need stamina and sturdy shoes for this climb of just over 4,000 feet. Be sure to check the weather before you leave; hikers have been sorely disappointed to reach the top only to find the view completely obscured by enveloping clouds.

Climbs are all-day affairs; a Land Rover and guide can be arranged through your hotel. The four-wheel-drive vehicle takes you past Rabacca Dry River through the Bamboo Forest. From there it's a two-hour hike to the summit, and you can arrange in advance to come down the other side of the mountain to the Chateaubelair area. Expect to pay about $25 a person.

Sailing and Charter Yachting The Grenadines are the perfect place to charter a sailboat or catamaran (bareboat or complete with captain, crew, and cook) to weave you around the islands for a day or a week. Boats of all sizes and degrees of luxury are available. **Barefoot Yacht Charters** (tel. 800/677–3195) and **Nicholson Yacht Charters** (tel. 809/460–1530, 809/460–1059 or 800/662–6066) offer bareboats and crewed yachts of varying sizes. Prices vary, but expect to pay around $1,900 a week ($1,300 off-season) for a 32-foot bareboat that sleeps four to six. A 36-foot bareboat sleeping six to eight is $2,850 a week ($2,350 off-season). The **Lagoon Marina** (tel. 809/458–4308) in St. Vincent offers 44-foot captained sailboats for $400 a day ($300 off-season).

Much more common on St. Vincent than formal charter companies are individuals who live on their boats and charter when they can, on an informal basis. Every hotel and yacht service office can refer you to competent captains. Realize that for lower rates (about $140 a day per person for a crewed charter) and short notice, you may forgo formal contracts and insurance. If you go this route, be very clear about what you want and expect, and what the boat and captain offer in terms of itinerary, food, and activities. Agree on costs, and get it in writing, even if it's penciled on the back of an envelope.

Hotels can refer you to the many privately owned boats that will take you on a day-sail to nearby islands for about $50 a person (lunch and drinks often included).

Water Sports The constant trade winds are perfect for windsurfing, and 80-foot visibility on numerous reefs means superior diving. Many divers find St. Vincent and Bequia far less crowded and nearly as rich in marine life as Bonaire and the Caymans; snorkeling in the Tobago Cays is among the world's best.

Dive St. Vincent (tel. 809/457–4714), on Villa Beach, just across from Young Island, is where NAUI instructor Bill Tewes and his staff offer beginner and certification courses, and dive/hotel packages. A single-tank dive is about $50. Based at the Lagoon Marina Hotel, NAUI instructor Perry Hughes's **St. Vincent Dive Experience** (tel. 809/456–9741) offers all levels of training and certification, plus night dives, snorkeling, and tours. A single-tank dive is about $40.

Depending on the weather, Young Island has some of the area's most colorful snorkeling. Nonguests of this private island can phone the resort (tel. 809/458–4826) for permission to take the ferry and rent equipment from the resort's water-sports center.

Shopping

St. Vincent isn't a duty-free port, but appealing local crafts (batik, baskets) and resortwear can be found at **Noah's Arkade** (tel. 809/457–1513) on Bay Street. The **St. Vincent Craftsmen Center** (tel. 809/457–1288), in the northwest end of Kingstown on James Street above Granby Street, sells grass floor mats and other woven items. Swiss watches, crystal, china, and jewelry can be found at **Stecher's** (tel. 809/457–1142) on Bay Street in the Cobblestone Arcade (a branch is at the airport).

Dining

West Indian food is the best and least expensive way to eat in St. Vincent. Dishes include callaloo soup, made from a spinachlike vegetable; goat stew; *rotis* (burritos filled with curried potatoes and meat or conch); "salt fish and bakes" (salty, spiced and flaked fish in a fried biscuit); seasonal seafood, including lobster, kingfish, snapper, and dolphin ("not Flipper," as everyone assures you, but dolphin*fish*); local vegetables such as christophines, breadfruit, and eddoes; and exotic fruit ranging from sugar apples and soursop to pineapple and papaya. Fried chicken and burgers are available everywhere, but look for the "imported beef" note on the menu; local beef is not aged, so it tends to be extremely chewy. The local lager, Hairoun, is brewed at Camden Park on the leeward coast, according to a German recipe.

Highly recommended restaurants are indicated by a star ★.

Category	Cost*
$$	$10–$20
$	$6–$10
¢	under $6

**per person, excluding drinks and 5% sales tax*

$$ **Basil's Bar and Restaurant.** This air-conditioned restaurant, downstairs in the Cobblestone Inn, is owned by the infamous Basil of Mustique but has little else in common with that laid-back Grenadine glitterati hangout. This is the Kingstown power-lunch venue, serving a daily buffet of local fish dishes, plus the likes of seafood pasta and chicken in fresh ginger and coconut milk, to local businessmen and yachties for about $12 an entrée. *Bay St., Kingstown, tel. 809/457–2713. Reservations advised. AE, MC, V.*

$–$$ **Lime N' Pub.** Although this sprawling, waterfront, indoor-outdoor restaurant and bar is named after the *pursuit* of liming (hanging out), its decor happens to feature a great deal of virulent green, which could prove painful after several cocktails. An eclectic menu caters to burger- and pizza-eaters as well as seafood fans, and even provides for more adventurous diners if they're brave enough to order the smoked sailfish pizza. Good rotis and coconut shrimp go down well with Hairoun. Shop before dinner at the swimwear-and-batik boutique, or stay late and dance on weekends, when the place resembles a singles bar. *Opposite Young Island, tel. 809/458–4227. AE.*

¢–$$ ★ **Dolphins.** Next to the Lime N' Pub is this welcome addition to the Villa scene. The well-traveled, Scottish-born father and son owners insist on fresh local ingredients for everything on the Dolphins menu, and from the kingfish, snapper, lobster, conch, and shrimp to the dressing on the chef's salad, nothing is bottled, canned, or artificial. Sit on the large covered terrace or take up residence in the bar, with its separate menu, old-fashioned Naugahyde booths, and barkeep who mixes a mean punch. Local musicians play (Friday and Saturday), and the work of local artists, including former classical violinist owner Austin Patterson, decks the walls. Dolphins is also the pioneer of St. Vincent home delivery, so note the number if you're staying nearby. *Villa Beach, tel. 809/457–4337. MC, V.*

¢–$$ **Vee Jay's Rooftop Diner & Pub.** This local dive above Roger's Photo Studios (have your pix developed while you eat), nearly opposite the Cobblestone Hotel, offers downtown Kingstown's best port view from beneath its green corrugated plastic roof. Among "authentic Vincie cuisine" specials chalked on the blackboard are mutton or fish stew; chicken, vegetable, or liver rotis; or not remotely Vincie sandwiches and burgers, which can be authentically washed down with mauby (a bittersweet drink made from tree bark—an acquired taste), linseed, peanut punch, or sorrel cordials. Lunch is buffet-style. *Upper Bay St., Kingstown, tel. 809/457–2845. Dinner reservations required. AE, MC, V.*

¢–$ **Aggie's.** Up on the second floor opposite the Sardine Bakery on Grenville, the Kingstown shopping street, is this casual bar and restaurant, with a swimming-pool-blue ceiling and trellised arches. It serves local seafood dishes, like conch souse and kingfish steak, various soups, including callaloo and pumpkin, rotis, and salads, right up to midnight. There's a Friday happy hour from 4 to 6. *Grenville St., Kingstown, tel. 809/456–2110. No credit cards.*

¢–$ **Bounty Restaurant.** Rotis, fried meat patties, homemade soursop ice cream, and other West Indian dishes are offered in this popular city liming spot. *Halifax St., Kingstown, tel. 809/456–1776. No credit cards.*

Lodging

Affordable lodging in St. Vincent—of which there is plenty—is often simple to the point of primitive: a bed, a nightstand, a place to hang your clothes, maybe a dresser. Bring your own shampoo. Hot water is a rarity (although how cold can the water get in 84-degree weather?). Most visitors report 24 hours of mild shock and frustration until they settle into island time, and realize that the simple life really does offer its own rewards. Gorgeous hibiscus and bougainvillea grow outside your window, the sea is usually steps away, and most managers of small hotels treat guests as valued friends.

Villa Beach, where most affordable hotels are located, is the only white-sand beach on St. Vincent. It's a 10-minute minivan ride to Kingstown for groceries, though the island's best restaurant, the French (too expensive for our listings, but a recommended splurge), plus two of the top liming hangouts, the Lime N' Pub and Dolphins (*see* Dining, *above*) are right here.

Highly recommended lodgings are indicated by a star ★.

Category	Cost*
$$	$80–$130
$	$60–$80
¢	under $60

**All prices are for a standard double room for two, excluding 5% tax and a 10% service charge. To estimate rates for hotels offering MAP/FAP, add about $35 per person per day to the above price ranges.*

$$ ★ **The Lagoon Marina and Hotel.** The only hotel overlooking sheltered Blue Lagoon Bay may well be the friendliest hotel on the island. Thanks to its full-service yacht marina, complete with the best-equipped marine shop in St. Vincent, there are usually seafaring types liming in the terrace bar, and plenty of yacht traffic to watch from your big, comfortable balcony with its two couches. Sliding patio doors lead onto these from the high wood-ceilinged, carpeted rooms; you can practically dive into the sea from Numbers 1–9, which hang over the wooden quay and face the sunset; 10–20 overlook the narrow, curved, black-sand beach. Basic wooden furniture, twin beds, rather dim lighting, phones, tiled bathrooms, and ceiling fans provide an adequate level of comfort; about half the rooms have air-conditioning (for a few dollars extra), but don't expect luxury. Sloping garden grounds contain a secluded two-level pool and the St. Vincent Dive Experience Headquarters, and there's a pretty, candlelit terrace restaurant. *Box 133, Blue Lagoon, St. Vincent, tel. 809/458–4308, fax 809/457–4716. U.S. agent: Charms Caribbean Vacations, tel. 800/742–4276. 19 rooms. Facilities: restaurant, bar, yacht marina, yacht charter, beach, pool, conference room, scuba, and water sports. AE, V. EP.*

$ ★ **Beachcombers.** At Villa, next to Sunset Shores, Flora and Richard Gunn have built a tiny and darling village on their sloping lawns, with a pair of chalet buildings containing the guest rooms, an open-terraced bar-restaurant, and the reception area, which includes a shop and a library. You could eat breakfast (included) off the floor of any bedroom here, such is the standard of housekeeping, though some rooms are prettier than others. Numbers 1–3 are prime, since they face the sea, and No. 1, in top-to-toe dark-wood paneling, has a kitchenette, too, for $5 extra; 4–6 are in back of these, with no view to speak of. The other building, containing Rooms 7–12, faces the "Bridal Bridge" (they do weddings) and the garden's frenzy of flowers and has a communal red-tile terrace in front. There's air-conditioning in Numbers 2, 5, and 7; ceiling fans elsewhere. Bathrooms lack tubs, and rooms lack phones or soft lighting, but these are insignificant privations when the welcome is this warm and the rates this low. Room 11 is not usually bookable, because Flora uses it for her other career—as beauty and massage therapist. Yes, this is the only Vincentian B&B featuring top-class aromatherapy, reflexology, and facials. *Box 126, Villa Beach, St. Vincent, tel. 809/458–4283. 12 rooms. Facilities: restaurant, bar, beauty treatments, shop, library. AE, MC, V. BP.*

$ **Cobblestone Inn.** Downtown in the city, as Vincentians call Kingstown, this 1814 stone-built onetime sugar warehouse has a delightful, sunny interior courtyard and arched passageways and a popular rooftop bar-restaurant for breakfast and soup-salad-burger lunches (come dinnertime, Basil's is downstairs). All the rooms have air-conditioning, phones, small, sparkling bathrooms, exposed stone walls painted white, and rattan furniture. Number 5 at the front is lighter and bigger than most of the other rooms, but noisier too, and many are rather dark, with a faint, not unpleasant, smell of dungeon emanating from the stones. Next to Basil's downstairs is an array of shops selling local craftwork and fashions. The staff is lackadaisical but efficient enough. *Box 867, Kingstown, St. Vincent, tel.*

809/456–1937. 19 rooms. Facilities: restaurant, bar. AE, D, MC, V. CP.

$ **Emerald Valley Resort.** The rural, rain-forested Penniston Valley, half an hour by road from Kingstown, is the unlikely setting for the Grenadines' only casino, which is, equally improbably, attached to this newly renovated family-friendly 5-acre resort. Two pairs of Brits toiled for two years to bring a run-down property up to very high standards, installing air-conditioning, fans, satellite TV, VCRs, phones, locally made wood-frame king-size or twin beds, stone-floored terraces, and (stoveless) kitchenettes in the 12 chalets. In the garden grounds are an outdoor bar, a two-level pool bisected by a wooden bridge and diving platform, a stage for local bands on weekends, a tennis court (pro lessons available), a nine-hole golf course (make sure this is finished before you book), and the pretty Valley restaurant. What you don't get, of course, is a beach, and the nearest groceries are in Kingstown, but the Vermont Nature Trail is 2½ miles away, and you can gamble till the small hours. *Penniston Valley, Box 1081, St. Vincent, tel. 809/456–7140, fax 809/456–7145. 12 chalets. Facilities: restaurant, bar, casino with bar, 2 tennis courts, grass volleyball court, croquet, pool. AE, MC, V. EP.*

¢ **Heron Hotel.** Steps away from the Grenadines wharf, on the second floor above a Georgian plantation warehouse that now contains shops but once provided lodgings for the plantation bosses, the Heron now caters mostly to stopover island-hoppers. It has managed to retain an old-fashioned atmosphere, maybe due to the grouchy manager, or the radio tuned faintly to a religious station, or the rooms themselves, which are straight out of a '50s boardinghouse, with thin, wine red or navy carpets; billowing faded floral drapes; single beds; bentwood chairs; and tiny cream-color bathrooms. Rooms have air-conditioning and phones and fan out from a palm-filled central courtyard, with tables set on a veranda for breakfast (light lunches, drinks, and West Indian dinners are also available). There's also a corner TV lounge with rows of wooden armchairs, black floorboards, and two giant ficus plants. *Box 226, Kingstown, St. Vincent, tel. 809/457–1631, fax 809/457–1189. 12 rooms. Facilities: dining room, courtyard, lounge. MC, V. CP.*

¢ **Indian Bay Beach Hotel and Apartments.** This pretty, whitewashed, two-story building sits on Indian Bay, with its small, sheltered, somewhat rocky, white-sand beach that's good for snorkelers. The simple apartments have either one or two bedrooms, air-conditioning, and kitchenettes; the best overlook the bay, with use of a large terrace on top of the restaurant, A La Mer—an airy space with white-trellised arches and a sapphire-blue awning. Both baby-sitting and lower weekly rates are available, making this spot useful for families. *Box 538, Kingstown, St. Vincent, tel. 809/458–4001, fax 809/457–4777. 12 apartments. Facilities: restaurant, bar, beach, water sports nearby. AE, MC, V. EP, CP, MAP.*

¢ **Umbrella Beach Hotel.** If you're prepared to sacrifice gorgeous bedroom decor for the sake of your pocketbook but still want to be well located, this very simple cluster of small apartment rooms may fit the bill. All are clean and equipped with ceiling fan, phone, kitchenette with fridge and Calor gas stove, and shower-only bathroom, but, make no mistake, they're dark and plain, with white walls, red marble-chip floors with a rush mat, and plastic chairs at a small Formica table. Steps away are Villa Beach, across from Young Island (ask permission to take the ferry over), the Lime N' Pub, and the French, where you could spend the cash you saved on the room. *Villa Beach, St. Vincent, tel. 809/458–4651, fax 809/457–4930. 9 rooms. Facilities: beach, water sports nearby. MC, V. EP.*

Apartment Rentals

Apartments for short-term rental are bare-bones simple; architecture and design are, well, undistinguished. Each has at least a small porch, but none have ocean views, air-conditioning, or meal plans. None take credit cards either. Services and amenities are limited to linens and a few functional kitchen implements (you might want to bring your favorite omelet pan). Whichever one you stay in, you'll need a car to get to the beach and main tourist areas. Kingstown is usually a 10- to 15-minute ride away. Apartments include: **Belleville Apartments** (Box 746, St. Vincent, tel. 809/458–4776), **Breezeville Apartments** (Box 222, St. Vincent, tel. 809/458–4004), **Paradise Inn** (Box 1286, Villa Beach, St. Vincent, tel. 809/457–4795), **Macedonia Rock Apartments** (Cane Hall, Box 1070, tel. 809/458–4076), and **Tranquility Beach Apartments** (Box 71, Indian Bay, St. Vincent, tel. and fax 809/458–4021).

Off-Season Bets In terms of cost, there isn't much of an off-season here; lower shoulder and summer rates at the luxury resorts are still too high for budget travelers. However, some budget hotels trim their already affordable rates even further; it pays to make inquiries.

Nightlife

Don't look for fire-eaters and limbo demonstrations on St. Vincent. Nightlife here consists mostly of hotel barbecue buffets and jump-ups, so called because the lively steel-band music makes listeners jump up and dance.

The Attic (1 Melville St., above the Kentucky Fried Chicken, tel. 809/457–2558), a jazz club with modern decor, features international artists and steel bands. There is a small cover charge; call ahead for hours and performers.

Young Island (tel. 809/458–4826) hosts sunset cocktail parties with hors d'oeuvres once a week on Fort Duvernette, the tiny island behind the resort. On that night, 100 steps up the hill are lit by flaming torches, and a string band plays. Reservations ($15) are necessary for nonguests.

The **Emerald Valley Casino** (tel. 809/456–7140) has the homey atmosphere of an English pub, but offers bar, food, and all the gaming of Vegas—three roulette tables (the only single-zero ones in the Caribbean), three blackjack, one Caribbean stud poker, one craps, five video slots, three slots—and is open daily (except Tuesday) 9 PM–3 AM; until 4 AM on Saturday.

The Grenadines

The Grenadines are wonderful islands to visit for fine diving and snorkeling opportunities, good beaches, and unlimited chances to laze on the beach with a picnic, waiting for the sun to set so you can go to dinner. Travelers seeking privacy, peace and quiet, active water sports, or informal socializing will be happy on a Grenadine. But for those on a budget, the choice is limited. Some of the Grenadines, such as Palm Island and Petit St. Vincent, contain nothing but one very expensive resort. Mustique, that tony society hideaway where the average beach cottage costs $3 million, is no place for the shoestring traveler trying to stretch a dollar. In fact, only two of the several islands that have tourist accommodations are what we consider truly affordable, and we devote our space to these. In addition, day sails to the tiny, uninhabited Tobago Cays for world-class snorkeling, as well as to Canouan and Union islands, are another fairly inexpensive option.

Arriving and Departing

By Plane **Mustique Airways** (tel. 809/458–4380 or 809/458–4818) flies into Bequia's airport daily from Barbados. Flights from St. Vincent cost about E.C. $45 one way. There are up to three flights daily. A shared taxi from Mitchell Airstrip to Friendship Bay is around $6; to Port Elizabeth, $10.

By Ferry The MV *Admiral I* and the MV *Admiral II* motor ferries leave Kingstown for Bequia weekdays at 9 AM, 10:30 AM, 4:30 PM, and, depending on availability, 7 PM. Saturday departures are at 12:30 PM and 7 PM; Sunday, 9 AM and 7 PM. Schedules are subject to change, so be sure to check times upon your arrival. All scheduled ferries leave from the main dock in Kingstown. The trip takes 70–90 minutes and costs $4.

The MV *Snapper* mail boat travels south on Saturdays, Mondays and Thursdays at about 10:30 AM, stopping at Bequia, Canouan, Mayreau, and Union, and returns north on Tuesdays and Fridays, departing Bequia at about 11 AM. The cost is less than $10.

Weekday service between St. Vincent and Bequia is also available on the island schooner *Friendship Rose,* which leaves St. Vincent at about 12:30 PM and returns from Bequia at 6:30 AM. Fare is $4.

The "Discover St. Vincent and the Grenadines" booklet, available in hotels and at the airport, has complete interisland schedules.

Bequia

Nine miles south of St. Vincent is Bequia, the second-largest Grenadine. Admiralty Bay is one of the finest anchorages in the Caribbean. With superb views, snorkeling, hiking, and swimming, the island has much to offer the international mix of backpackers and luxury yacht owners who frequent its shores.

Important Addresses **Tourist Information:** The **Bequia Tourism Board** (tel. 809/458–3286) is on the main dock.

Emergencies **Police:** tel. 809/456–1955. **Medical Emergencies:** tel. 999. **Hospital: Bequia Hospital:** tel. 809/458–3294.

Getting Around Bicycle and scooter rentals can be found at the **Almond Tree Boutique** (no phone) on the main waterfront street in Port Elizabeth. Costs range from $20 to $35 a day. Drive on the left and use caution: Road improvements have made for overly speedy traffic.

Guided Tours To see the views, villages, and boat-building around the island, hire a taxi (Gideon, tel. 809/458–3760, is recommended) and negotiate the fare in advance. Expect to pay about $25–$30 for a two-hour tour. Water taxis, available from any dock, will take you by Moonhole, a private community of stone homes with glassless windows, some decorated with bleached whale bones. The fare is about $11.

For those who prefer sailboats to motorboats, Arne Hansen and his catamaran *Toien* can be booked through the **Frangipani Hotel** (tel. 809/458–3255). Day sails to Mustique run $35–$40 per person, including drinks. *Friendship Rose,* a large, hand-built schooner, will ferry you to the Tobago Cays for an all-day excursion that includes lunch; snorkeling; and beer, wine, or soft drinks. Cost is $60 a person; book through the **Local Color Boutique** (tel. 809/458–3202).

In addition, you'll see several signs on boats in the bay advertising day sails and charter. Ask your hotel for recommendations, then discuss price and itineraries thoroughly with your chosen captain before deciding (*see* Sailing and Charter Yachting in St. Vincent, *above*).

Beaches A half-hour walk from the Plantation House Hotel will lead you over rocky bluffs to **Princess Margaret Beach,** which is quiet and wide, with a natural stone arch at one end. Though it has no facilities, this is a popular spot for swimming, snorkeling, or simply relaxing under palms and sea-grape trees. Snorkeling and swimming are also excellent at **Lower Bay,** a wide, palm-fringed beach that can be reached by taxi or by hiking beyond Princess Margaret Beach; wear sneakers, not flip-flops. Facilities for windsurfing and snorkeling are here, and the **De Reef** restaurant has waiters who will eventually find you on the sand when your lunch is ready. **Friendship Bay** can be reached by land taxi and is well equipped with windsurfing and snorkeling rentals and an outdoor bar. **Industry Bay** boasts towering palm groves, a nearly secluded beach, and a memorable view of several uninhabited islands. The tiny three-room Crescent Bay Lodge is here; its huge bar offers drinks and late lunches (tel. 809/458–3400).

Sports and the Outdoors

Water Sports

Of Bequia's two dozen dive sites, the best are **Devil's Table,** a shallow dive rich in fish and coral; a sailboat wreck nearby at 90 feet; the 90-foot drop at **The Wall,** off West Cay; the **Bullet,** off Bequia's north point for rays, barracuda, and the occasional nurse shark; the **Boulders** for soft corals, tunnel-forming rocks, and thousands of fish; and **Moonhole,** shallow enough in places for snorkelers to enjoy.

Dive Bequia (tel. 809/458–3504, fax 809/458–3886) and **Sunsports** (tel. 809/458–3577, fax 809/458–3031) offer one- and two-tank dives, night dives, and certified instruction, plus snorkel excursions and equipment rental. Single-tank dives are about $50; snorkel gear rents for about $15 a day.

If you'd like to go snorkeling on your own, water taxis are available at any jetty along Admiralty Bay. These can take you to most snorkel spots, including Moonhole. Be sure to negotiate the fare in advance, including whether it's in U.S. or E.C. dollars, and arrange a pickup time. A trip to Moonhole costs about $4 each way.

Shopping

All Bequia's shops are along the beach and are open weekdays 10:30–5 or 6, Saturdays 10:30–noon.

Best Buys

Handmade model boats (you can special-order a replica of your own yacht) are at **Mauvin's** (¼ mile down the road to the left of the main dock, no phone). Along Admiralty Bay, hand-printed and batik fabric, clothing, and household items are sold at the **Crab Hole** (tel. 809/458–3290). You can watch the fabrics being made in the workshop out back. **Solana's** (tel. 809/458–3554) offers attractive beachwear, saronglike pareus, and handy plastic beach shoes. The **Bequia Bookshop** (tel. 809/458–3905) has an exhaustive selection of Caribbean literature, plus cruising guides and charts, beach novels, souvenir maps, and exquisite hand-carved whalebone penknives. **Local Color** (tel. 809/458–3202), above the Porthole restaurant in town, has an excellent and unusual selection of handmade jewelry, wood carvings, and resort clothing. Next door is **Melinda's By Hand** (tel. 809/458–3409), with hand-painted cotton and silk clothing and accessories.

Dining

Dining on Bequia ranges from West Indian to gourmet cuisine, and it's consistently good. Moderately priced barbecues at Bequia's hotels mean spicy West Indian seafood, chicken, or beef (although it is usually tougher than Hulk Hogan), plus a buffet of spicy side dishes and sweet desserts. Restaurants are occasionally closed on Sundays; phone to check. Most waterfront cafés fall into our ¢ category. For price information on restaurants and hotels, *see* the price charts *in* Dining *and* Lodging *in* St. Vincent, *above.*

$–$$ **Dawn's Creole Garden.** The walk up the hill is worth it for the delicious West Indian lunches and dinners, especially the Saturday-night barbecue buffet and the major five-course, two-entrée dinners, including the fresh christophine and breadfruit accompaniments that Dawn's is known for. There's a wonderful view and live guitar entertainment most Saturday nights. *At the far end of Lower Bay beach, tel. 809/458–3154. Dinner reservations required. No credit cards.*

$–$$ **De Reef Restaurant.** This duo of a restaurant and a café on Lower Bay is the essential feeding station for long, lazy beach days, with the restaurant taking over when the café closes at dusk, as long as

you've made reservations. For lunch or dinner, conch, lobster, whelks, and shrimp are treated the West Indian way, and the mutton curry is famous. For breakfast (from 7 AM), or light lunch, the café bakes its own breads, croissants, coconut cake, and cookies and blends fresh juices to accompany them. *Lower Bay, tel. 809/458–3447. Dinner reservations required. No credit cards.*

$–$$ ★ **Mac's Pizzeria.** The island's best lunches and casual dinners are enjoyed amid fuchsia bougainvillea on the covered outdoor terrace overlooking the harbor. Choose from lobster pizza, quiche, pita sandwiches, lasagna, home-baked cookies, and muffins. *On the beach, Port Elizabeth, tel. 809/458–3474. Dinner reservations required. No credit cards.*

$–$$ ★ **Theresa's Restaurant.** On Monday nights, Theresa and John Bennett offer a rotating selection of enormous and tasty Greek, Indian, Mexican, or Italian buffets. West Indian dishes are served at lunch and dinner the rest of the week. *At the far end of Lower Bay beach, tel. 809/458–3802. Dinner reservations required. No credit cards.*

¢ **The Kingfisher.** It serves genuine West Indian fast food for those with no cholesterol worries. Try a salt fish and bake at this tiny, lunch-only spot on the main street. *Port Elizabeth, no phone. No credit cards. No dinner.*

Lodging

$$ **Gingerbread Apartments.** This complex, including restaurant, bar, café, and dive shop, is on the posh side for the Bequia apartment scene, maybe because it belongs to the prime minister's wife. Beach bums and gossips will particularly like the location, a stroll from all Bequia's hot spots, and all should appreciate the porch, kitchen, and hot water in every apartment. *Admiralty Bay, Box 1, Bequia, St. Vincent, tel. 809/458–3800, fax 809/458–3907. 3 apartments. Facilities: restaurant, bar, café, tennis, scuba and water sports, boutique. No credit cards. EP.*

¢–$$ ★ **The Frangipani Hotel.** The Frangipani, which has gained the status of venerable institution partly because its owner is St. Vincent's prime minister, James Mitchell, who lives here on Bequia, is a local gossip center for international yachties and tourists. (The PM's wife, Pat, by the way, owns the nearby Gingerbread. Why don't they live together? Listen to the local Calypso for the whole story.) Surrounded by flowering bushes, the garden units are built of stone, with private verandas and baths. Four simple, less-expensive rooms are in the main house, only one with a private bath. A two-bedroom house with a patio and another apartment with a large bedroom and kitchen are nearby. String bands appear on Mondays, with folksingers on Friday nights during tourist season. The Thursday-night steel-band jump-up at the beachfront bar is a must; the bar, with its huge, white-painted wooden armchairs facing the sunset, is probably the nicest around. Main tourist beaches are a $3 taxi ride away. *Box 1, Bequia, St. Vincent, tel. 809/458–3255, fax 809/458–3824. 13 rooms, 4 with shared bath. Facilities: restaurant, bar, tennis, water-sports center, yacht services. MC, V. EP.*

¢–$ **Isola and Julie's Guest House.** Right on the water in Port Elizabeth, these two separate buildings share a small restaurant and bar. Furnishings (which are few) run to early Salvation Army, but the food is great and the rooms are airy and light, with private baths; some have hot water. *Box 12, Bequia, St. Vincent, tel. 809/458–3304, 809/458–3323, or 809/458–3220. 25 rooms. Facilities: restaurant, bar. No credit cards. EP, MAP.*

¢–$ **Kingsville Apartments.** A few minutes' stroll from lovely, lively Lower Bay Beach, these two-bedroom apartments with kitchens and hot water are short on furniture and style, but they're more than adequate for a budget vacation. There's no air-conditioning, but you will find linens and kitchen utensils. From here it's a half-hour walk to town. *Lower Bay, Box 41, Bequia, St. Vincent, tel. 809/458–3404. 2 apartments. No credit cards.*

Dining
- Dawn's Creole Tea Garden, **8**
- De Reef Restaurant, **5**
- Dennis Hideaway, **12**
- The Kingfisher, **1**
- Mac's Pizzeria, **2**
- Theresa's Restaurant, **7**

Lodging
- De Reef Apartments, **9**
- Dennis Hideaway, **12**
- The Frangipani Hotel, **4**
- Gingerbread Apartments, **11**
- Isola and Julie's Guest House, **3**
- Keegan's Guest House, **6**
- Kingsville Apartments, **10**

The Grenadines

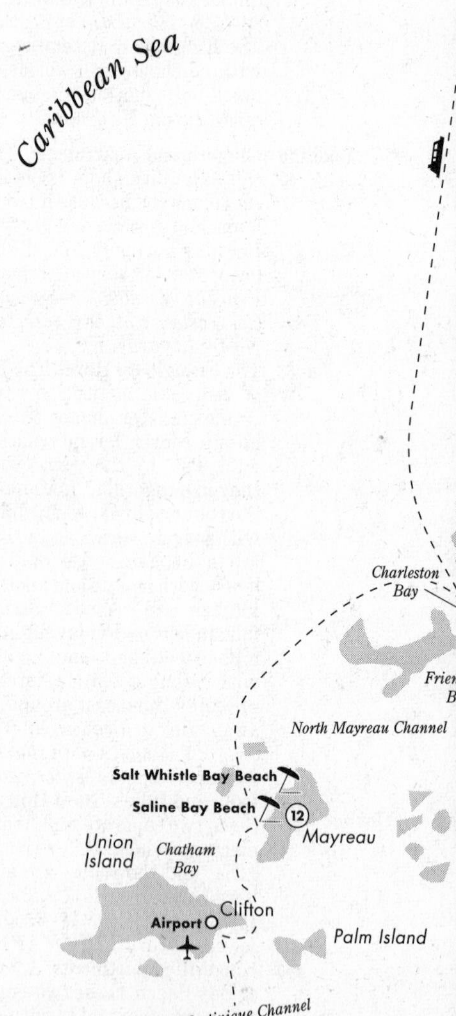

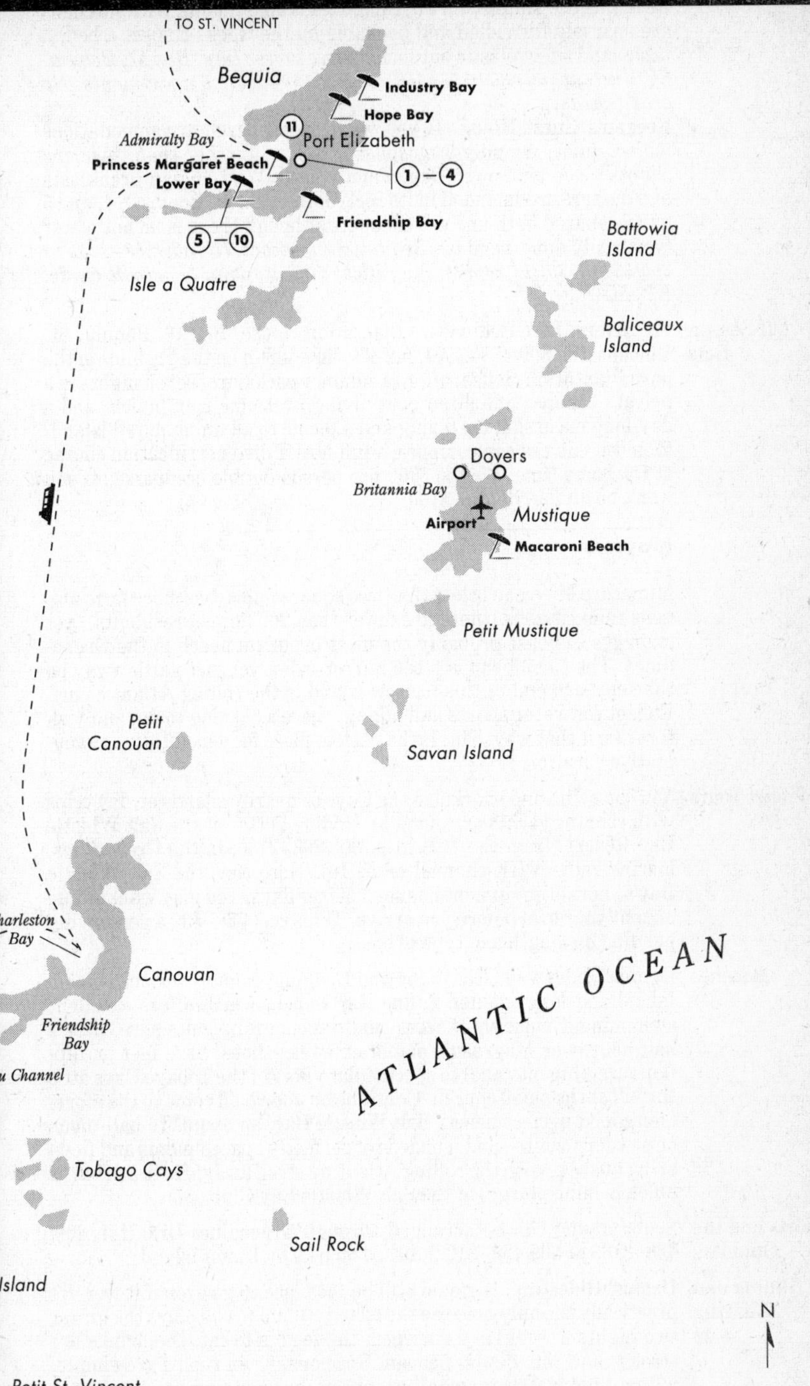
TO ST. VINCENT
Bequia
Industry Bay
Hope Bay
Admiralty Bay
Port Elizabeth
Princess Margaret Beach
Lower Bay
Friendship Bay
Isle a Quatre
Battowia Island
Baliceaux Island
Dovers
Britannia Bay
Mustique
Airport
Macaroni Beach
Petit Mustique
Petit Canouan
Savan Island
Charleston Bay
Canouan
Friendship Bay
ATLANTIC OCEAN
Tobago Cays
Sail Rock
Island
N
Petit St. Vincent

¢ **De Reef Apartments.** Just 100 yards from gorgeous Lower Bay Beach, these simple, un-air-conditioned apartments with kitchens are sparsely furnished and bookable by the week. Expect a bed, a table, and a few plastic outdoor chairs. *Lower Bay, Box 47, Bequia, St. Vincent, tel. 809/458–3484 or 809/458–3447. 5 apartments. No credit cards.*

¢ **Keegan's Guest House.** If you want cheap beach accommodations with a quiet, friendly atmosphere, look no further than this *very* simple place on Lower Bay. Family-style West Indian breakfasts and dinners are included in its rock-bottom rates. Rooms 3, 4, and 5 have a shared bath and are cheaper, although there is no hot water (you really don't need it). *Bequia, St. Vincent, tel. 809/458–3254 or 809/458–3530. 11 rooms. Facilities: dining room. No credit cards. EP, MAP.*

Off-Season Bets For divers, **Dive Bequia** (c/o Plantation House, Box 16, Bequia, St. Vincent, tel. 809/458–3504, fax 809/458–3886), on the grounds of the posh Plantation House, offers a summer package of seven nights in a private cabana, unlimited boat diving, welcome rum punch, and a day-long excursion for diving and a picnic to an uninhabited island. Would-be divers can complete a full NAUI dive-certification course at the same time. Cost is $700 per person double occupancy; if you won't be diving, deduct $100.

Mayreau

Miniature Mayreau is less than two square miles, has more farm animals than citizens (there are fewer than 200 human residents), yet manages to boast probably the most beautiful beach in the Grenadines. The Caribbean is often mirror-calm, yet just yards away on the southern end of this narrow island is the rolling Atlantic surf. Except for water sports and hiking, there's nothing to do, and visitors like it that way. This is the perfect place for a meditative or vegetative vacation.

Guided Tours You can swim and snorkel in the Cays or nearby islands on day trips with charter yachts arranged by Undine Potter at the Salt Whistle Bay Resort (from the U.S., tel. 800/263–2780; in the Grenadines, marine radio VHF channel 68 or 16). Note that the Salt Whistle Bay's snorkel equipment has seen better days. You may want to buy or rent your own before you arrive. Trips cost $20–$30 a person, depending on length and type of boat.

Beaches Dennis' Hideaway (*see* Dining and Lodging, *below*) overlooks Union Island and long, golden **Saline Bay Beach,** which offers excellent swimming. Cruise ships occasionally anchor for picnics here. Hike a half-hour over Mayreau's mountain (wear shoes; bare feet or flip-flops are a big mistake) to spectacular views of the Tobago Cays atop the hill at the small church. Continue on and you'll come to the aforementioned perfect beach, **Salt Whistle Bay,** an exquisite half-moon of powdery white sand, shaded by perfectly spaced palms and flowering bushes, with the rolling Atlantic a stroll away. Have a drink or lunch (a minisplurge) at the Salt Whistle Bay Club.

Sports and the Outdoors Scuba diving can be arranged through **Grenadines Dive** (tel. 809/458–8138 or 809/458–8122), based on nearby Union Island.

Dining and Lodging *$–$$* **Dennis' Hideaway.** It would still be *the* place to go even if it weren't practically the only place on the island. Dennis (who plays the guitar two nights a week) is a charmer, the food is great, the drinks are strong, and the view is heaven. Spacious, clean rooms are simple, without hot water or amenities, but with private baths. A separate building houses the restaurant, where West Indian prix-fixe dinners are served. *Saline Bay, tel. 809/458–8594. 3 rooms. Facilities: restaurant ($$). Reservations advised. No credit cards. EP.*

25 Trinidad and Tobago

Updated by Barbara Hults

Good news from the most southerly islands in the Caribbean: Trinidad has changed radically and Tobago has not. Trinidad, once an island on no one's list, has emerged from many of its problems with a fresher outlook, a cleaner capital, and, wonder of wonders, a newly renovated airport. The general spirit of the island is good, and many new entrepreneurial businesses in the capital, Port-of-Spain, seem to be doing well. Another bit of good news for the island is that major carrier BWIA has begun to take itself seriously as a tourist airline. Sparkling new planes and better-trained flight attendants are offering much improved service to Trinidad.

Around 51,000 of Trinidad's 1.3 million residents—Africans, Indians, Americans, Europeans, and Asians, each with their own language and customs—live in the capital city of Port-of-Spain, one of the most active commercial cities in the West Indies. However, you have to leave the capital to find a good beach, and most visitors are still business travelers. Trinidad has known prosperity from oil (it's one of the biggest producers in the Western Hemisphere), a steel plant, natural gas, and a multiplicity of small businesses. The island is also home to a spectacular Carnival and is the birthplace of steelband music.

Because Trinidad has not been developed as a resort island, prices are lower than on other Caribbean islands, though this also means fewer tourist facilities. The most economical way to stay in a Port-of-Spain hotel is to buy an air fare-accommodation package through American Airlines or BWIA. Along the north coast, near the best beaches, there are inexpensive guest houses and strands of roti stands and humble eateries where you can get generous portions of Indian and West Indian food for a few dollars. Thanks to the diverse population, there's a good selection of affordable ethnic restaurants throughout the island.

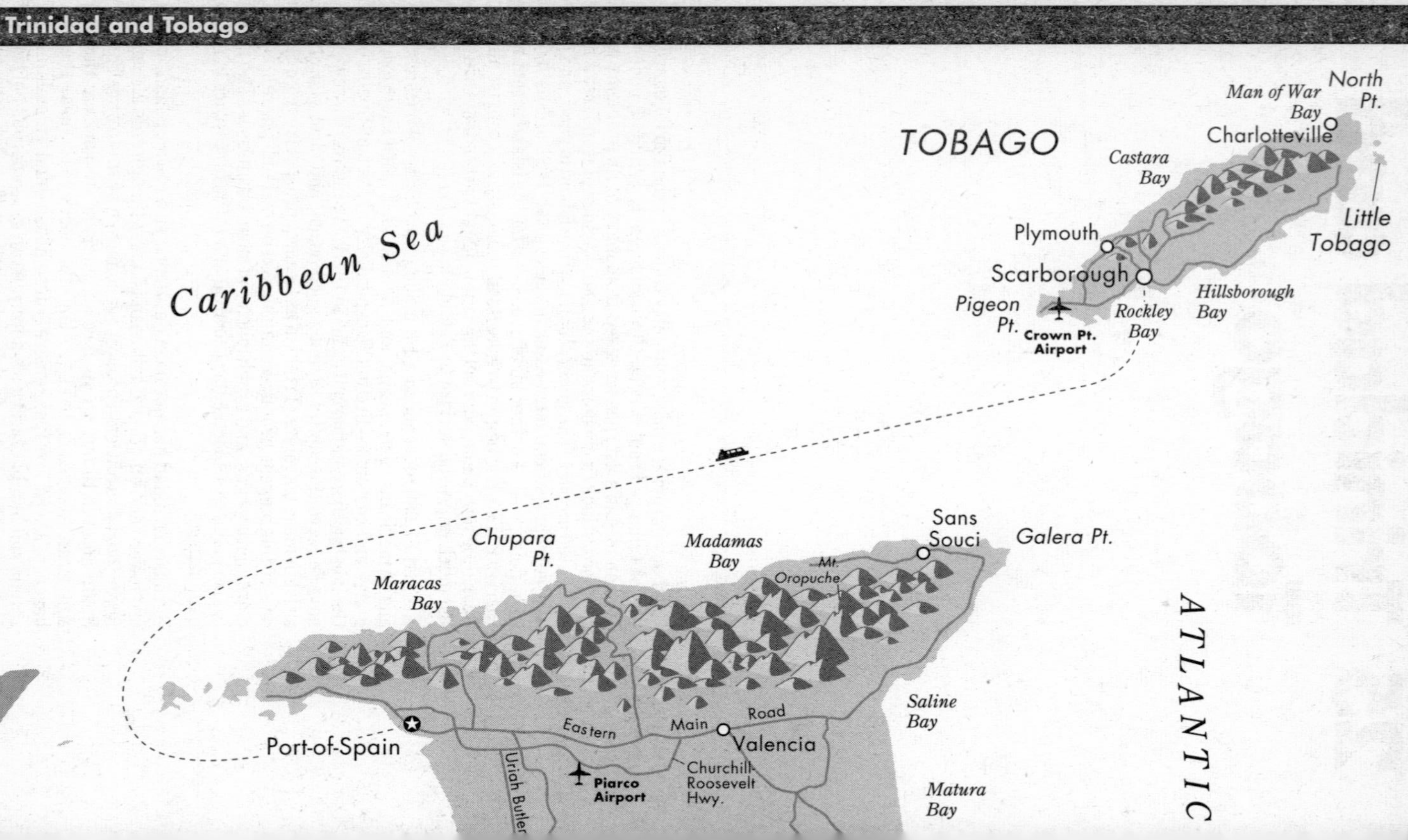
TOBAGO
Man of War Bay
North Pt.
Charlotteville
Castara Bay
Little Tobago
Plymouth
Scarborough
Pigeon Pt.
Crown Pt. Airport
Rockley Bay
Hillsborough Bay
Caribbean Sea
Chupara Pt.
Madamas Bay
Sans Souci
Galera Pt.
Mt. Oropuche
Maracas Bay
ATLANTIC
Saline Bay
Eastern
Main
Road
Valencia
Port-of-Spain
Uriah Butler
Piarco Airport
Churchill-Roosevelt Hwy.
Matura Bay

Chaguanas
Hwy.
OCEAN
Manzanilla Bay
Gulf of Paria
Tabaquite
Oropuche Lagoon
Pierreville
Mayaro Bay
Los Irois Bay
La Brea
Penal
Guayaguayare
Cedros Bay
San Francique
Moruga
Guayaguayare Bay
Erin Bay
Erin Pt.
Icacos Pt.
TRINIDAD
KEY
Ferry
N
VENEZUELA
0
20 miles
0
30 km

Tobago, an island almost unknown to American tourists, has begun to realize the advantages of unspoiled rain forests, a mostly undeveloped coastline, and a colorful population of birds that would keep the most avid bird-watcher happy for years. Buccoo and Speyside reefs are underwater wonderlands for scuba divers and snorkelers. The island has delightful hotels and restaurants, and now direct air service from Miami and Barbados has made getting there easier, without the need to change planes in Trinidad. However, with all those wide-bodied planes delivering tourists, new hotels are being planned, and without careful control, the island could lose its Robinson Crusoe wilderness. Now is the time to savor an island that would charm Gauguin.

You'll find fewer opportunities to save on Tobago, where many of the hotels are expensive beach resorts. You can skip the pricey hotel dining rooms, however, in favor of the many good, reasonably priced local restaurants. Most resorts are on the beach, so you don't have to rent a car.

The islands together have more than 600 species of birds, more than 200 species of plants, and more than 100 species of mammals—within pristine rain forests, lowlands and savannahs, and fresh- and saltwater swamps. Birdsong, a disappearing music in the rest of the world, is easily heard, since restaurants often hang feeders outside their porches, as much to keep the birds away from your food as to provide a chance for observation.

Columbus reached these islands on his third voyage, in 1498. Three prominent peaks around the southern bay of Trinidad prompted him to name the land La Trinidad, after the Holy Trinity. Trinidad was captured by British forces in 1797, ending 300 years of Spanish rule. Tobago's history is more complicated. It was "discovered" by the British in 1508. The Spanish, Dutch, French, and British all fought for it until it was ceded to England under the Treaty of Paris in 1814. In 1962, both islands—T&T, as they're commonly called—gained their independence within the British Commonwealth, finally becoming a republic in 1976.

In 1986, the National Alliance for Reconstruction (NAR) won a landslide victory, toppling the People's National Movement (PNM), which had been in power for 30 years but had brought the country to the brink of economic ruin. Then, in the 1991 elections, power was returned to the PNM. The new government, especially because of the decline in oil prices, seems eager to create a new tourist economy without spoiling the great tourist advantages that lack of development has brought.

What It Will Cost These sample prices, meant only as a general guide, are for high season (mid-December–mid-April) for Tobago, and year-round for Trinidad, which has no high season outside Carnival (*see* Carnival, *below*). On Trinidad, a room in a comfortable guest house may be had for $55 a night; in an international hotel, it's about $125. Meals run from $30 for dinner at a fine establishment to $1 for a roti (a kind of East Indian burrito, usually filled with curried chicken and potatoes) from a stand, while a buffet Indian curry meal costs less than $10. Locally made beer is about $1.25 in a rum shop (local bar), about $2.50 in a classier place. If you are willing to use local transportation, getting around Trinidad can be cheap: $3 for an hour's trip. A rental car is about $40 a day. A single-tank dive costs about $40; daily snorkel equipment rental, about $5.

On Tobago, a night's lodging is around $50 for a modest accommodation a few minutes from the shore and $120 for a beach hotel with resort facilities. Many new mini-apartments have kitchenettes, keeping cooking costs low. Not all hotel dining here is expensive and there are good local restaurants in Scarborough, Plymouth,

Charlotteville, and Speyside. If you're not gastronomically adventurous, it makes sense to take a meal plan at your hotel.

Before You Go

Tourist Information For information on Trinidad in the United States, call 800/748–4224 or send a fax to 201/869–7628. In the United Kingdom and Canada, contact the very helpful and efficient **Trinidad and Tobago Tourism Development Authority** (8a Hammersmith Broadway, London W6 7AL, tel. 0181/741–4466, fax 0181/741–1013; 40 Holly St., Suite 102, Toronto, Ontario M4S 3C3, tel. 416/486–4470 or 800/268–8986, fax 416/440–1899).

Arriving and Departing
By Plane There are daily direct flights to Piarco Airport, about 30 minutes east of Port-of-Spain, from New York, Miami, Toronto, and London on **BWIA** (tel. 800/538–2942), Trinidad and Tobago's national airline. **American** (tel. 800/433–7300) offers direct flights from Miami to Trinidad. They also offer connecting service, through Miami or San Juan, from all of the cities they serve in the United States. **Air Canada** (tel. 800/422–6232) flies to Trinidad from Toronto via Miami or San Juan. There are numerous interisland flights in the Caribbean on BWIA and **LIAT** (tel. 809/462–0701). All flights to Trinidad alight at Piarco Airport. BWIA and Air Caribe flights from Trinidad to Crown Point Airport in Tobago take about 15 minutes and depart 6 to 10 times a day. For those wishing to circumvent Trinidad entirely, LIAT has direct service from Barbados and Grenada to Tobago, and BWIA flies direct from Miami to Tobago. **Caledonia Airways** (0293/567–1000) also flies to Tobago from London.

Package tours aren't generally touted as heavily as they are for other Caribbean islands, but there are bargains to be had, especially around Carnival. One particularly good tour operator is **Pan Caribe Tours** (Box 3223, Austin, TX 78764, tel. 512/266–7995 or 800/525–6896; fax 512/266–7986). BWIA also has a variety of Caribbean tours.

From the Airport A taxi ride from the airport to downtown Port-of-Spain costs TT $80 (about U.S. $15) hour into South Quay Bus Terminal for TT $5, but you will probably need a taxi from there to your hotel, and that may run another TT $40 (about U.S. $9.50).

By Boat The Port Authority maintains daily ferry service between Trinidad and Tobago, although flying is preferable, because the sea can be very rough. The ferry leaves once a day, and the trip takes about five hours. Round-trip fare is TT $60, cabin fare (one-way double occupancy) is TT $22, with an extra charge for vehicles. Tickets are sold at offices in Port-of-Spain (tel. 809/625–3055) and at Scarborough, in Tobago (tel. 809/639–2417).

Passports and Visas Citizens of the United States, the United Kingdom, and Canada who expect to stay for less than two months may enter the country with a valid passport. A visa is required for a stay of more than two months.

Language The official language is English, although no end of idiomatic expressions are used by the loquacious Trinis. You will also hear smatterings of Hindi (Trinidad's population is about one-quarter Indian), French, Spanish, and Chinese.

Precautions Insect repellent is a must during the rainy season (June–December) and is worth having around anytime. If you're prone to car sickness, bring your preferred remedy. Trinidad is only 11 degrees north of the equator, and the sun here can be intense. Even if you tan well, it's a good idea to use a strong sunblock, at least for the first few days.

Staying in Trinidad and Tobago

Important Addresses **Tourist Information:** Information is available from the **Trinidad & Tobago Tourism Development Authority** (134–138 Frederick St., Port-of-Spain, tel. 809/623–1932, fax 809/623–3848; Piarco Airport, tel. 809/664–5196). For Tobago, contact the **Tobago Division of Tourism** (N.I.B. Mall, Scarborough, tel. 809/639–2125, fax 809/639–3566), or drop in at its information booth at Crown Point Airport (tel. 809/639–0509).

Emergencies **Police:** Call 999. **Fire and Ambulance:** Call 990. **Hospitals: Port-of-Spain General Hospital** is at 169 Charlotte Street (tel. 809/625–7869). **Tobago County Hospital** is on Fort Street in Scarborough (tel. 809/639–2551). **Pharmacies: Oxford Pharmacy** (tel. 809/627–4657) is at Charlotte and Oxford streets near the Port-of-Spain General Hospital. **Ross Drugs** (tel. 809/639–2658) is in Scarborough.

Currency The Trinidadian dollar (TT$) has been devalued twice in recent years. The current exchange rate is about U.S. $1 to TT $5.50. The major hotels in Port-of-Spain have exchange facilities whose rates are comparable to official bank rates. Most businesses on the island will accept U.S. currency if you're in a pinch. Note: Prices quoted here are in U.S. dollars unless indicated otherwise.

Taxes and Service Charges Restaurants and hotels add a 15% value-added tax (VAT). Many also add a 10% service charge to your bill. If the service charge is not added, you should tip 10%–15% of the bill for a job well done. The airport departure tax is TT $75, or about U.S. $15.

Getting Around In Port-of-Spain, where the streets are often jammed with traffic and drivers who routinely play chicken with one another, taxis are your best bet. Once away from the congestion of downtown, however, a car is by far the easiest way to travel. Though it's possible to get to the north coast by route taxi, you'll need a car to explore from one point to another. In Tobago you will be better off renting a car or Jeep than relying on taxi service, which is less frequent and much more expensive.

Route Taxis Route—or shared—taxis ply fixed routes to and from Port-of-Spain. They collect and drop off passengers anywhere along a set route and serve as a better alternative to buses. Route taxis come in two sizes: minibuses (often referred to as maxi-taxis) and regular sedans. The maxi-taxis are marked with stripes and are easy to recognize, but the only way to identify the sedans as taxis is by the H at the start of the license plate. Although this will tell you whether the vehicle is a taxi, it does *not* distinguish whether it is a route taxi or a private taxi (*see below*). Therefore it is essential to make sure what you are getting in is a route taxi, or you'll end up paying private taxi fare. Fares are nominally fixed, but unless you have knowledge of the proper fare, you'll likely pay a dollar or two above what a local would pay. From Port-of-Spain, the departure point is at the corner of Prince and George streets. Fare to Maracas Bay is TT $7 and to Blanchisseuse Bay, TT $15.

Private Taxis When you choose a private taxi instead of a route taxi, you are hiring all the seats, and your driver goes straight to the destination you specify. Private taxis are useful for longer trips or trips to more remote destinations not covered by route taxis. There are set rates, though they are not always observed, particularly at Carnival. To be sure, pick up a rate sheet from the tourism office. An average ride within Port-of-Spain costs TT $20 (U.S. $5).

Buses Buses cover the island and are inexpensive, but they are very old and very crowded. Travelers generally opt for a route taxi (*see above*) instead. The South Quay Bus Terminal is the main departure point for buses.

Rental Cars/ Scooters Car-rental services include **Auto Rentals** (tel. 809/675–7368, fax 809/675–2258), with many locations, and **Kalloo's Auto Rental and Taxi Service** (tel. 809/622–9073). Mr. Kalloo goes out of his way to help, and his cars are reliable. As befits one of the world's largest exporters of asphalt, Trinidad's roads are generally good, although you may encounter roadwork in progress as major resurfacing is done. In the outback, roads are often narrow, twisting, and prone to washouts in the rainy season. Inquire about conditions before you take off, particularly if you're heading toward the north coast. Never drive into downtown Port-of-Spain during afternoon rush hour.

In Tobago you might be better off renting a Jeep than relying on taxi service, which is much more expensive. A four-wheel-drive vehicle is far better and safer than a car, because many roads, particularly in the interior or on the far coast near Speyside and Charlotteville, are bumpy, pitted, winding, and/or steep (though the main highways are smooth and fast). Ask your hotel about rentals and taxis, or contact **Sweet Jeeps** (tel. 809/639–8391, fax 809/639–8495) or **Singh's Auto Rentals** at Grafton Beach Resort (tel. 809/639–0191, ext. 53). Various tours are also offered by rental agencies on both islands, and rates are negotiable. All agencies require a credit-card deposit, and in season you must make reservations well in advance of your arrival. Figure on paying $40–$60 per day. Don't forget to drive on the left.

Telephones and Mail The area code for both islands is 809. For telegraph, telefax, teletype, and telex, contact **Textel** (1 Edward St., Port-of-Spain, tel. 809/625–4431). Faxes can be sent from major hotels.

To place a local call, dial the local seven-digit number. To reach the United States, dial 1, the appropriate area code, and the local number.

Postage for first-class letters to the United States is TT $2.25; for postcards, TT $2.

Opening and Closing Times Most shops open Monday–Thursday 8–4, Friday 8–6, and Saturday 8–noon. Banking hours are Monday–Thursday 8–2 and Friday 8–noon and 3–5.

Guided Tours One of Trinidad's best tour operators is the **Travel Centre** (Box 1254, Port-of-Spain, tel. 809/625–1636, fax 809/623–5101). Their office is also American Express's cardmember service office, for check-cashing and other matters. For a personal guide in Trinidad who speaks German as well as English, contact **Maria Lopez** (3 Palm Ave. W, Petit Valley, tel. 809/637–3642). On Tobago, **Helen Grant** (tel. 809/639–3581) gives tours in English. You can also ask the tourism office in Tobago for a list of guides. Almost any **taxi driver** in Port-of-Spain will be willing to take you around the town and to the beaches on the north coast. It costs around $70 for up to four people to go Maracas Bay beach, plus $20 per hour extra if you decide to go farther; you may be able to haggle for a cheaper rate. For a complete list of tour operators and sea cruises, contact the tourism office.

Carnival

Trinidad always seems to be either anticipating, celebrating, or recovering from a festival, the biggest of which is **Carnival.** Carnival occurs each year between February and early March. Trinidad's version of the pre-Lenten bacchanal is reputedly the oldest in the Western Hemisphere; there are festivities all over the country, but the most lavish is in Port-of-Spain.

Carnival officially lasts only two days, from *J'ouvert* (sunrise) on Monday to midnight the following day. If you're planning to go, it's a good idea to arrive in Trinidad a week or two early to enjoy the events leading up to Carnival. Not as overwhelming as its rival in

Rio or as debauched as Mardi Gras in New Orleans, Trinidad's fest has the warmth and character of a massive family reunion.

Carnival is about extravagant costumes: Individuals prance around in imaginative outfits. Colorfully attired troupes—called *mas*—that sometimes number in the thousands march to the beat set by steel bands. You can visit the various mas "camps" around the city where these elaborate costumes are put together—the addresses are listed in the newspapers—and perhaps join one that strikes your fancy. Fees run anywhere from $35 to $100; you get to keep the costume. Children can also parade in a Kiddie Carnival that takes place on Saturday morning a few days before the real thing.

Throwing a party is not the only purpose of Carnival, it's also a showcase for calypso performers. Calypso is music that mixes dance rhythms with social commentary, sung by characters with such evocative names as Shadow, the Mighty Sparrow, and Black Stalin. As Carnival approaches, many of these singers perform nightly in calypso tents, which are scattered around the city. You can also visit the pan yards of Port-of-Spain, where steel orchestras such as the Renegades, Desperadoes, Catelli All-Stars, Invaders, and Phase II rehearse their arrangements of calypso.

For several nights before Carnival, costume makers display their talents, and the steel bands and calypso singers perform in spirited competitions in the grandstands of the racetrack in Queen's Park, where the Calypso Monarch is crowned. At sunrise, or J'ouvert, the city starts filling up with metal-frame carts carrying steel bands, flatbed trucks hauling sound systems, and thousands of revelers who squeeze into the narrow streets. Finally, at the stroke of midnight on "Mas Tuesday," Port-of-Spain's exhausted merrymakers go to bed. The next day everybody settles back to business.

Understandably, prices escalate during Carnival. Lodging rates are about 45% higher, and hotels usually require a minimum three-night stay. Reservations should be made far in advance.

Exploring Trinidad

Numbers in the margin correspond to points of interest on the Trinidad map.

Port-of-Spain Port-of-Spain has improved greatly in the past few years. Many new malls and a generally happier mood are obvious. Start this walking tour early in the day, as the city becomes hot by mid-afternoon. It is
1 not really surprising that a sightseeing tour of **Port-of-Spain** begins at the port. Though it is no longer as frenetic as it was during the oil boom of the 1970s, **King's Wharf** entertains a steady parade of cruise and cargo ships, a reminder that the city started from this strategic harbor. Across Wrightson Road is **Independence Square,** not a square at all, but a wide, dusty thoroughfare crammed with pedestrians, car traffic, taxi stands, and peddlers of everything from shoes to coconuts—not a pleasant walk for lone females, though not really unsafe. Flanked by government buildings and the familiar twin towers of the Financial Complex (familiar because its facade also adorns one side of all TT dollar bills), the square is representative of this city's chaotic charm.

Walk all the way west along the square to Wrightson Road, where stands the Gothic-style Cathedral of the Immaculate Conception. On the south side is the Cruise Ship Complex, full of duty-free shops, forming an enclave of international anonymity with the Holiday Inn. Alternatively, at the midpoint of Independence Square, head north up Frederick Street. This is the main shopping drag, a market street of scents—corn roasting and Indian spices—and crowded shops. At the corner of Prince Street, look across **Woodford Square** toward the magnificent **Red House,** a Renaissance-style building that takes up an entire city block. Trinidad's House of Parliament takes its name from a paint job done in anticipation of Queen Victoria's Diamond Jubilee in 1897. Woodford Square has served as the site of political meetings, speeches, public protests, and occasional violence. The original Red House, in fact, was burned to the ground in a 1903 riot. The present structure was built four years later. The chambers are open to the public.

The view of the south side of the square is framed by the Gothic spires of **Trinity,** the city's other cathedral, and, on the north, by the impressive **public library** building, the **Hall of Justice** and **City Hall.**

Continue north along Pembroke Street and note the odd mix of modern and colonial architecture, gingerbread and graceful estate houses, and stucco storefronts. After five blocks, Pembroke crosses Keate Street at **Memorial Park,** from which a short walk north leads to the greater green expanse of **Queen's Park,** more popularly called the **Savannah.**

The **National Museum and Art Gallery,** at the southeast corner of the Savannah, is worth a visit, if only to see the Carnival exhibits, the Amerind collection and historical re-creations, and the fine 19th-century paintings of Trinidadian artist Cazabon.

Buy a cool coconut water from any of the vendors operating out of flatbed trucks along the Savannah. For about 50¢, he'll lop the top off a green coconut with a deft swing of the machete and, when you've finished drinking, lop again, making a bowl and spoon of coconut shell for you to eat the young pulp—the texture of a boiled egg white. According to Trinis, "It'll cure anyt'ing dat ail ya, mon."

Proceeding west along the Savannah, you'll come to a garden of architectural delights: the elegant lantern-roof **George Brown House;** what remains of the **Old Queen's Park Hotel;** and a series of astonishing buildings constructed in a variety of 19th-century styles, known as the **Magnificent Seven.**

Notable among these buildings are **Killarney,** patterned (loosely) after Balmoral Castle in Scotland, with an Italian-marble gallery surrounding the ground floor; **Whitehall,** constructed in the style of a Venetian palace by a cacao-plantation magnate, and currently the office of the prime minister; **Roomor,** a flamboyantly baroque colonial-period house with a preponderance of towers, pinnacles, and wrought-iron trim that suggests an elaborate French pastry; and the **Queen's Royal College,** in German renaissance style, with a prominent tower clock that chimes on the hour.

The **racetrack** at the southern end of the Savannah is no longer a venue for horse racing, but it is still the setting for music and costume competitions during Carnival and, when not jammed with calypso performers, tends toward quietude.

The northern end of the Savannah is devoted to plants. A rock garden, known as the **Hollow,** and a fish pond add to the rusticity. The **Botanic Gardens,** across the street, date from 1820. The official residences of the president and prime minister are on these grounds.

Way east on Picton Road in the scruffy, industrial district of Laventille, are **Fort Chacon** and **Fort Picton,** erected to ward off invaders by the Spanish and British regimes, respectively. The latter is a martello tower with a fine view of the gulf.

Out on the Island

The intensely urban atmosphere of Port-of-Spain belies the tropical beauty of the countryside surrounding it. It is truly stunning, but you will need a car and three to eight hours (if you include the Caroni swamp) to get into the real countryside. The Caroni Swamp route keeps mainly to the northern section of the island. The central and southern portions of Trinidad are mostly endless sugar plantations

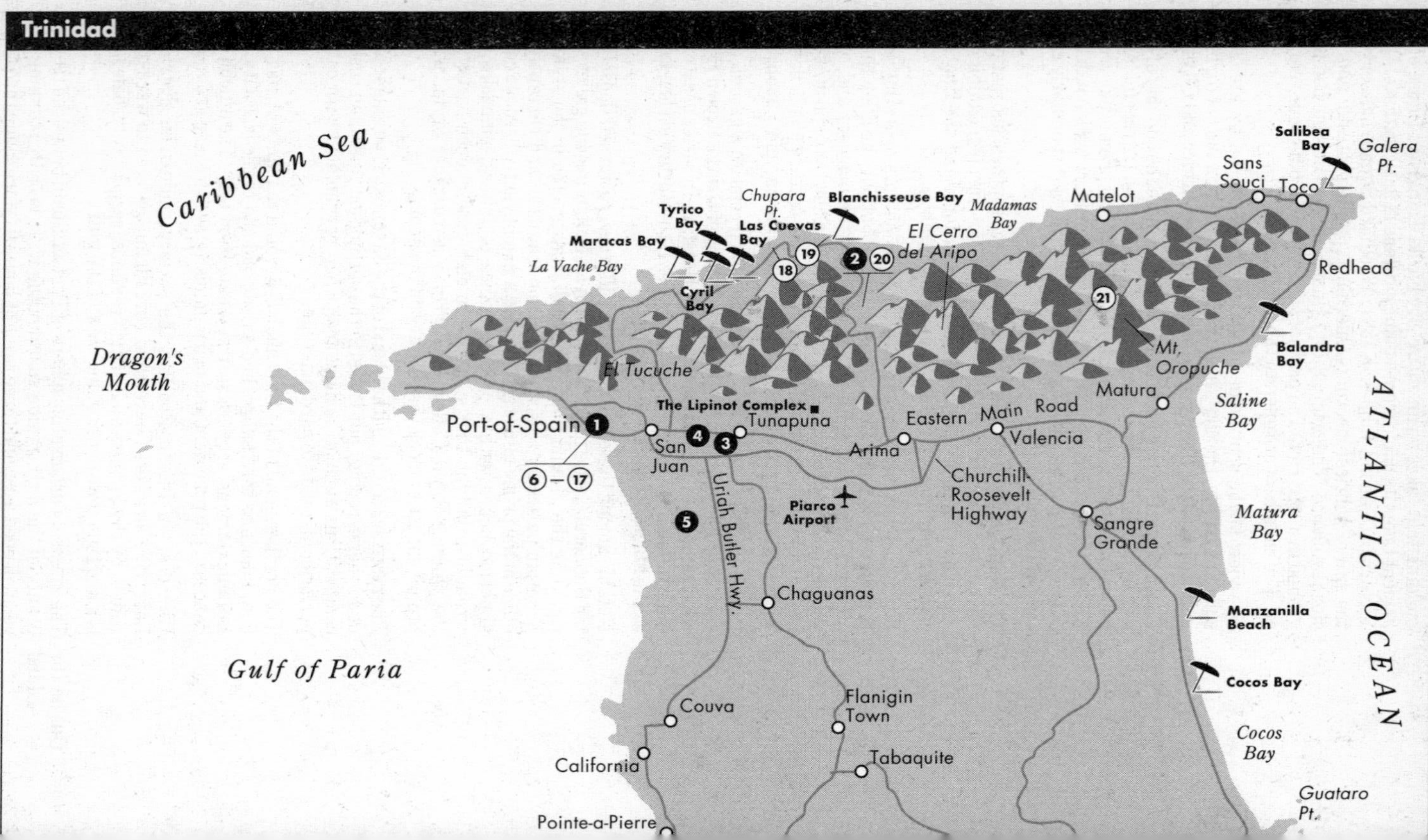
Trinidad
Caribbean Sea
Dragon's Mouth
Gulf of Paria
ATLANTIC OCEAN
La Vache Bay
Maracas Bay
Tyrico Bay
Cyril Bay
Las Cuevas Bay
Chupara Pt.
Blanchisseuse Bay
Madamas Bay
El Cerro del Aripo
Matelot
Sans Souci
Toco
Salibea Bay
Galera Pt.
Redhead
Balandra Bay
Mt. Oropuche
Saline Bay
Matura
El Tucuche
The Lipinot Complex
Port-of-Spain
San Juan
Tunapuna
Arima
Eastern Main Road
Valencia
Churchill-Roosevelt Highway
Piarco Airport
Uriah Butler Hwy.
Sangre Grande
Matura Bay
Manzanilla Beach
Cocos Bay
Cocos Bay
Guataro Pt.
Chaguanas
Couva
California
Pointe-a-Pierre
Flanigin Town
Tabaquite

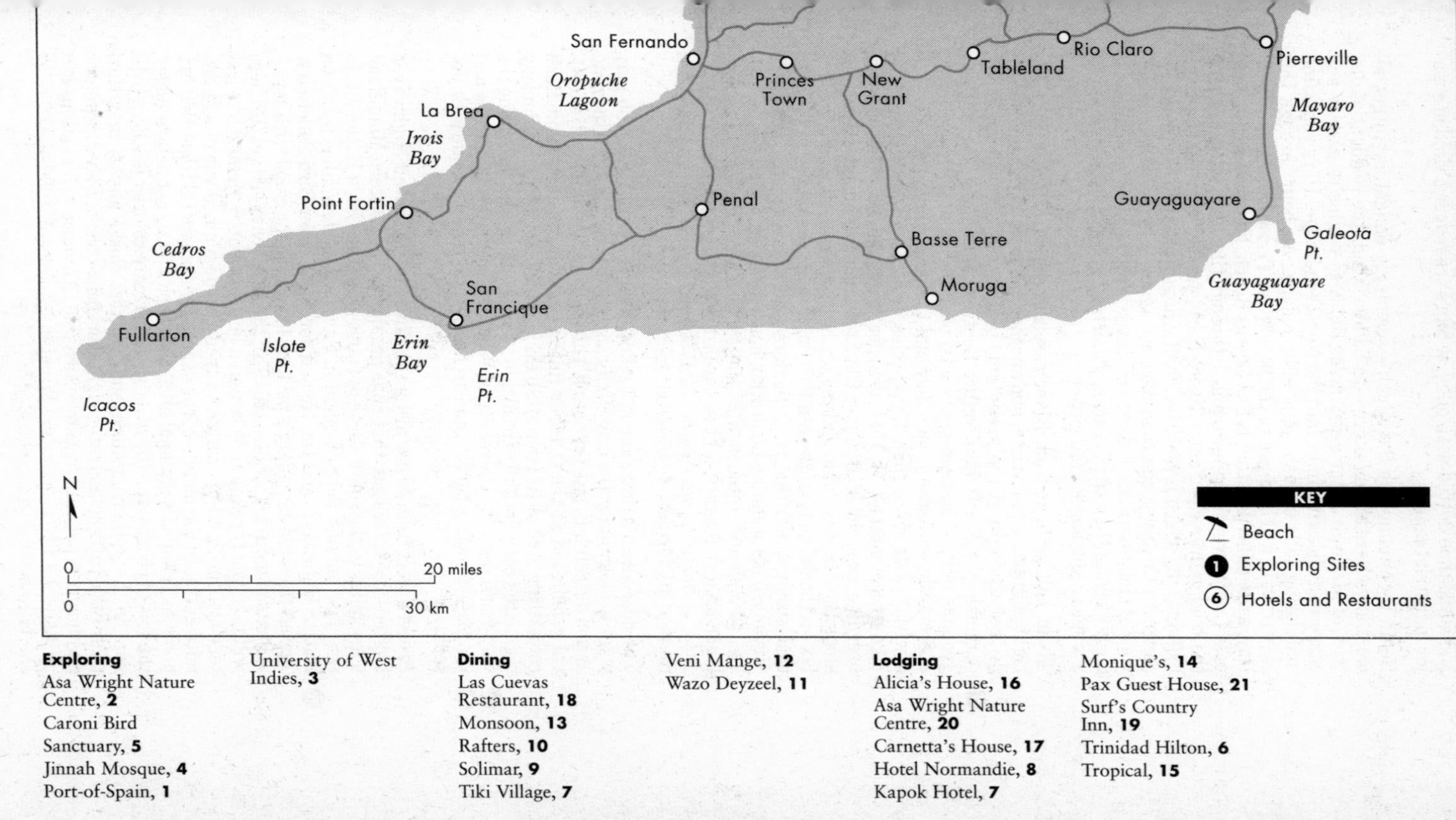

Exploring
Asa Wright Nature Centre, **2**
Caroni Bird Sanctuary, **5**
Jinnah Mosque, **4**
Port-of-Spain, **1**
University of West Indies, **3**

Dining
Las Cuevas Restaurant, **18**
Monsoon, **13**
Rafters, **10**
Solimar, **9**
Tiki Village, **7**
Veni Mange, **12**
Wazo Deyzeel, **11**

Lodging
Alicia's House, **16**
Asa Wright Nature Centre, **20**
Carnetta's House, **17**
Hotel Normandie, **8**
Kapok Hotel, **7**
Monique's, **14**
Pax Guest House, **21**
Surf's Country Inn, **19**
Trinidad Hilton, **6**
Tropical, **15**

and a coastline dotted with oil rigs. San Fernando is Trinidad's major industrial center.

Begin by circling the Savannah—seemingly obligatory to get almost anywhere around here—to Saddle Road, the residential district of **Maraval.** After a few miles the road begins to narrow and curve sharply as it climbs into the Northern Range. Here you'll find undulating hills of lush, junglelike foliage. An hour through this hilly terrain will lead you to the beaches at **Tyrico Bay** and **Maracas Bay;** a few miles past that is **Las Cuevas Beach.** Follow the same road past Las Cuevas for several miles, through tiny La Fillete, crossing the bridge over the Yarra River. Here, washerwomen hang their laundry out, which is how the small village of **Blanchisseuse** got its name. In this town the road narrows again, winding through canyons of moist, verdant foliage and mossy grottoes. As you painstakingly execute the hairpin turns, you'll begin to think you've entered a tropical rain forest. You have.

About half an hour from Blanchisseuse, the road forks. Take the right, signposted to Arima, and another half hour on this road (and a *very* sharp right at the green hut) brings you to a bird-watcher's
2 paradise, the **Asa Wright Nature Centre** (*see* Lodging, *below*). The grounds (almost 500 acres) are a tropical paradise of plants, trees, and multihued flowers, and they and the surrounding acreage are atwitter with more than 170 species of birds, from the gorgeous blue-green motmot to the rare nocturnal oilbird. The oilbirds' breeding grounds in Dunston Cave are included among the sights along the center's guided hiking trails. If you're feeling languid, relax on the veranda of the inn here and watch the diversity of birds that swoop about the porch feeders—an armchair bird-watcher's nirvana. This stunning plantation house looks out to the Arima valley, as lush and untouched as the earth offers. You can also have lunch or stay for the night in old-fashioned splendor. *Tel. 809/667–4655. Admission: $6 adults, $4 children. Open daily 9–5. Guided tours at 10:30 and 1:30, reservations necessary.*

The descent to **Arima,** about 7 miles, is equally pastoral. You may want to look out for the tiny Hindu shrine on the left side of the road as you descend. In late October it's lit with candles for Divali, a festival celebrated at the October full moon. The Eastern Main Road connecting Arima to Port-of-Spain is a busy, bumpy, and densely populated corridor full of roadside stands and businesses. Along the
3 way you'll pass the **University of West Indies** campus in Curepe and
4 the majestic white turrets and arches of the **Jinnah Mosque in St. Joseph.**

Proceed west from Arima along the Churchill-Roosevelt Highway, a limited-access freeway that runs parallel to the Eastern Main Road a few miles to the south. Both avenues cross the Uriah Butler Highway just outside Port-of-Spain in San Juan. A few miles south on
5 Butler Highway, take the turnoff for the **Caroni Bird Sanctuary.** Across from the sanctuary's parking lot is a sleepy canal with several boats and guides for hire ($6–$15; the small ones are best). These will take you through the Caroni, a large swamp with mazelike waterways bordered by mangrove trees, some plumed with huge termite nests. In the middle of the sanctuary are several islets that are home to Trinidad's national bird, the scarlet ibis. Just before sunset the ibis arrive by the thousands, their richly colored feathers brilliant in the gathering dusk, and, as more flocks alight, they turn their little tufts of land into bright Christmas trees. Bring a sweater and insect repellent for your return trip. Advance reservations can be made with boat operators Winston Nanan (tel. 809/645–1305) or David Ramsahai (tel. 809/663–4767).

If you have more time to explore Trinidad, use it to travel farther along the northwest coast, with its numerous coves, until you reach

Sans Souci and **Salibea Bay**. This area is likely to become a hotel resort playground in the future, but for now the beaches are deserted except for a few fishing boats drawn up on the sand.

Exploring Tobago

Numbers in the margin correspond to points of interest on the Tobago map.

A driving tour of Tobago, from Scarborough to Charlotteville and back, can be done in about four hours, but you'd never want to undertake this spectacular, and very hilly, ride in that time. Plan to spend a night at the Speyside end of the island and give yourself a chance to enjoy this largely untouched country and seaside at leisure. Buy the guides to trees, flowers, and birds of the Caribbean so that you can see the poinsettia before it goes north for Christmas, the nutmeg tree, the coconut palm that may be 80 feet tall, the sea date tree, the cashew, cocoa, breadfruit, pawpaw (papaya), soursop, tamarind, pink or yellow pui, banyan, scarlet cordia, or the traveler's tree that looks like a large green fan.

1 **Scarborough** is a sleepy place that is undergoing an awakening as Tobago's residents travel and bring home new ideas for hotels and restaurants. It's nestled around **Rockley Bay,** was settled two centuries ago, and lacks the pastel glamour of many Caribbean ports. A little exploration will take you to wonderful restaurants and shops.

The road northeast from Scarborough soon narrows as it twists
2 through **Mount St. George,** a village that clings to a cliff high above the ocean. Fort King George is a lovely, tranquil spot commanding sweeping views of the bay, with a restored 18th-century English fort and barracks, a fine arts center, and lush landscaped gardens.

The sea dips dramatically in and out of view as you pass through a series of small settlements and the town of Roxborough. If you want to cross the island here, the drive through the forest to Parlatuvier is a glorious trip. Otherwise, about an hour's drive will take you to
3 **King's Bay,** an attractive crescent-shape beach. Just before you reach the bay there is a bridge with an unmarked turnoff that leads to a gravel parking lot; beyond that, a landscaped path leads to a waterfall with a rocky pool where you can refresh yourself. You may meet enterprising locals who'll offer to guide you to the top of the falls, a climb that you may find not worth the effort.

After King's Bay the road rises sharply; just before it dips again
4 there's a marked lookout with a vista of **Speyside,** a small fishing village, and the lovely offshore islands Bird of Paradise and Little Tobago, the latter one of the Caribbean's most important seabird sanctuaries. The red-billed tropic birds dazzle explorers from October through June. The Blue Waters Inn can arrange a tour, or you can strike your own arrangement with local boatmen.

Past Speyside the road cuts across a ridge of mountains that separates the Atlantic side of Tobago from the Caribbean. This forest reserve is the oldest in the Western Hemisphere, established in 1764, soon after the island came under British rule. Trips can be arranged
5 through tour operators. On the far side is **Charlotteville,** a remote community that's one of the prettiest fishing villages in the Caribbean. Fishermen here announce the day's catch (usually flying fish, red fish, or bonito) by sounding conch shells. The paved road ends a few miles outside Charlotteville, in Camberton. Returning to
6 Speyside, take a right at the sign for **Flagstaff Hill.** Follow a well-traveled dirt road for about 1½ miles to a radio tower. It's one of the highest points in Tobago, surrounded by ocean on three sides and with a view of the hills, Charlotteville, and Bird of Paradise Island in the bay.

Tobago

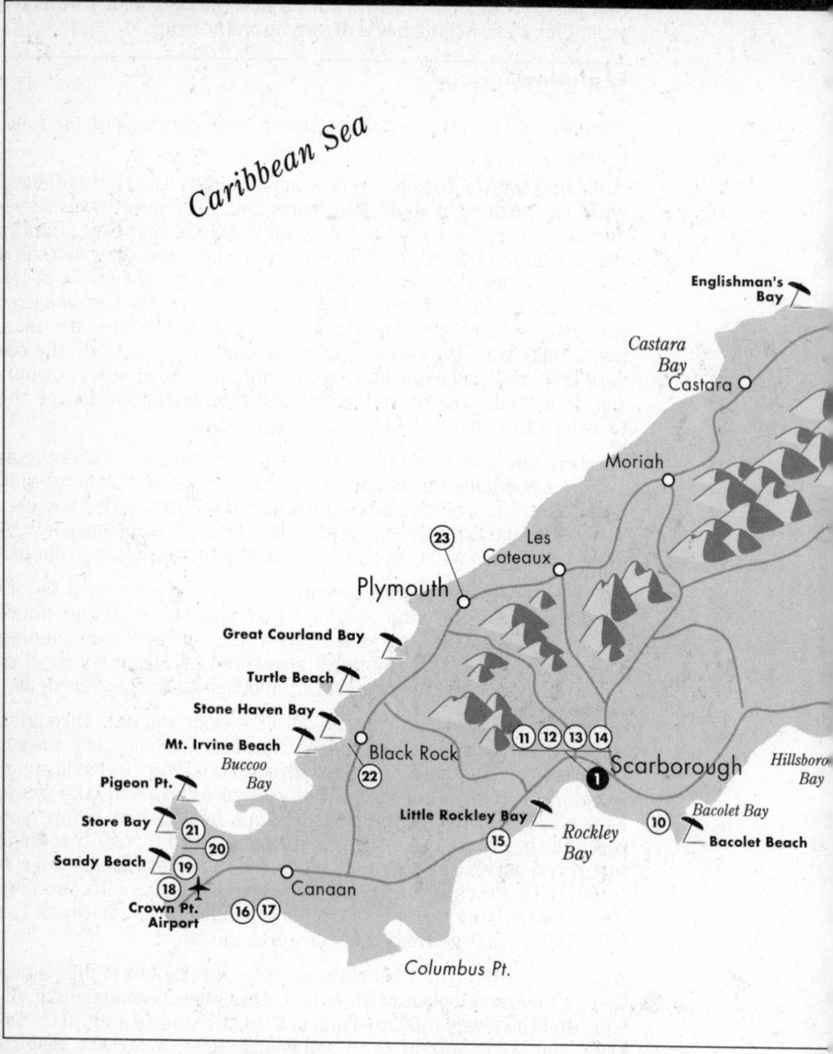

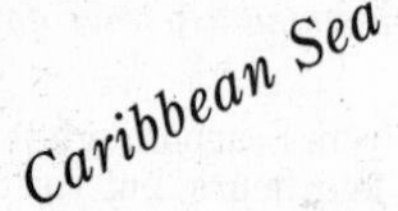

Exploring
Charlotteville, **5**
Flagstaff Hill, **6**
King's Bay, **3**
Mt. St. George, **2**
Scarborough, **1**
Speyside, **4**

Dining
Blue Crab, **11**
Cocrico Inn, **23**
Jemma's Village Kitchen, **8**
The Old Donkey Cart House, **12**
Papillon, **22**
Rouselles, **13**
Store Bay Centre, **20**
Mount Marie, **15**
Kariwak Village, **16**

Lodging
Blue Waters Inn, **7**
Cocrico Inn, **23**
The Golden Thistle Hotel, **17**
Harris Cottage, **10**
Kariwak Village, **16**

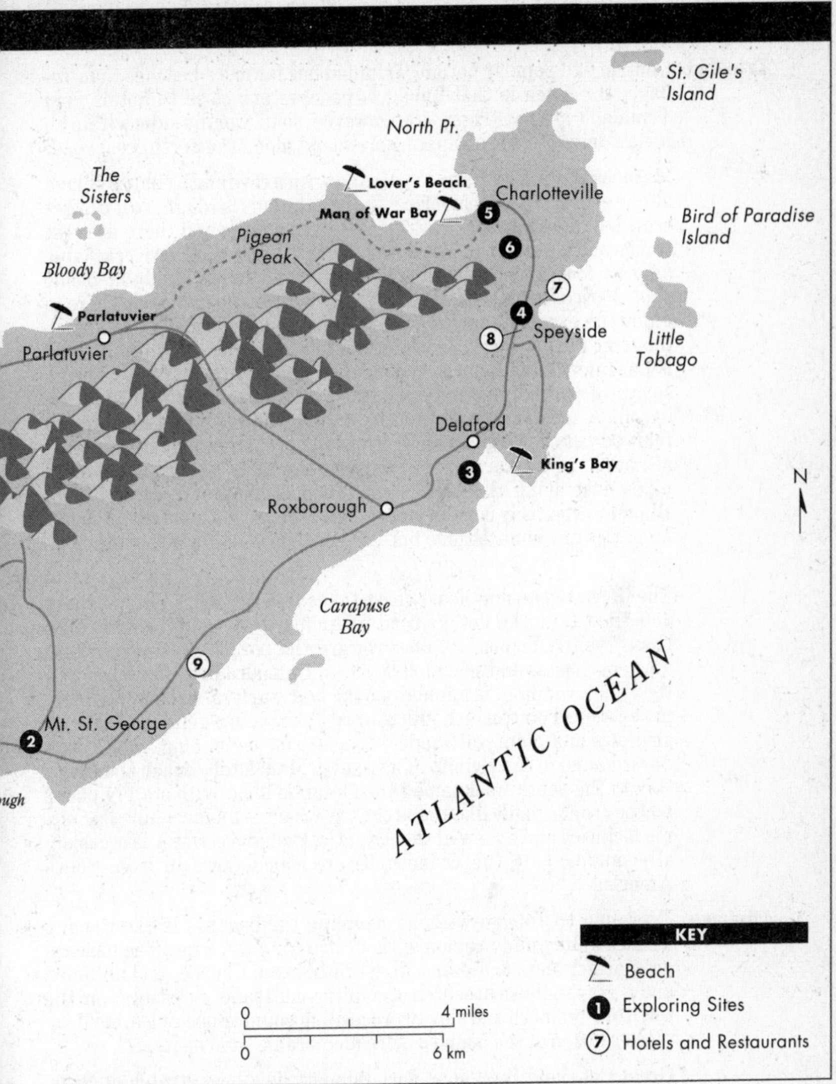
St. Gile's Island
North Pt.
The Sisters
Lover's Beach
Charlotteville
Man of War Bay
Bird of Paradise Island
Pigeon Peak
Bloody Bay
Parlatuvier
Parlatuvier
Speyside
Little Tobago
Delaford
King's Bay
Roxborough
Carapuse Bay
ATLANTIC OCEAN
Mt. St. George
KEY
Beach
Exploring Sites
Hotels and Restaurants
0
4 miles
0
6 km

Beaches

Trinidad Contrary to popular notion, Trinidad has far more beaches than Tobago; the catch is that Tobago's beaches are close to hotels, and Trinidad's are not. There are, however, some worthy sites within an hour's drive of Port-of-Spain, spread out along the north coast road.

Maracas Bay is a long stretch of sand with a cove and a fishing village at one end. It's a local favorite, though the surf is rough, so it can get crowded on weekends. Parking sites are ample, and there are rest rooms and a snack bar. **Cyril Bay,** a pebble-and-sand cove reachable only by foot, is laced with small waterfalls and is an idyllic picnic spot. **Tyrico Bay** is a small beach lively with surfers who flock here to enjoy the excellent surfing. The strong undertow may be too much for some swimmers. A few miles farther along the north coast road is **Las Cuevas Bay,** a narrow, picturesque strip of sand named for the series of partially submerged and explorable caves that ring the beach. A food stand offers tasty snacks, and vendors hawk fresh fruit across the road. It's less crowded here, and seemingly serene, although, as at Maracas, the current can be treacherous. About 8 miles east along the north coast road is another narrow beach. **Blanchisseuse Bay** is palm-fringed and the most deserted of the lot. Facilities are nonexistent, but the beach is ideal for a romantic picnic.

The drive to the northeast coast takes several hours. To get there you must take the detour road to Arima, but "goin' behind God's back," as the Trinis say, does reward the persistent traveler with gorgeous vistas and secluded beaches. **Balandra Bay,** sheltered by a rocky outcropping, is popular among bodysurfers. **Salibea Bay,** just past Galera Point, which juts toward Tobago, is a gentle beach with shallows and plenty of shade— perfect for swimming. Snack vendors abound in the vicinity. The road to **Manzanilla Beach** and **Cocos Bay** to the south, nicknamed the Cocal, is lined with stately palms whose fronds vault like the arches at Chartres. Manzanilla has picnic facilities and a view of the Atlantic, though its water is occasionally muddied by the Orinoco River, which flows in from South America.

Tobago Traveling to Tobago without sampling the beaches is like touring France's Burgundy region without drinking the wine. The beaches are perfection to those in search of Robinson Crusoe, and untamed and messy to those in search of country-club sand. Starting from the town of Plymouth and slowly proceeding counterclockwise, we'll explore a dozen of the island's more memorable sand spots.

Great Courland Bay, near Fort Bennett, is a long stretch of clear, tranquil water, bordered on one end by **Turtle Beach,** named for the turtles that lay their eggs here at night between April and May. A short distance west, there's a side road that runs along **Stone Haven Bay,** a gorgeous beach that's across the street from Grafton Beach Resort, a luxury hotel complex.

Mt. Irvine Beach, across the street from the Mt. Irvine Beach Hotel, is an unremarkable setting that has great surfing in July and August. It's also ideal for windsurfing in January and April. There are picnic tables surrounded by painted concrete pagodas and a snack bar.

Pigeon Point, an astonishingly beautiful beach not far from the airport, is the locale inevitably displayed on Tobago travel brochures. It's the only privately owned beach on the island, part of what was once a large coconut plantation, and you must pay admission (about $2) to enter the grounds. The beach is lined with royal palms, and there are bathing and changing facilities, a food stand, a gift shop, and paddleboats for rent. The waters are calm.

Store Bay, where boats depart for Buccoo Reef, is probably the most socially convivial setting in the area. The beach is little more than a small sandy cove between two rocky breakwaters, but six shacks sell delectable rotis, *pilau* (rice and peas), and messy but marvelous crab and dumplings. Miss Jean's is the most popular; try Miss Esmie's crab, though. Farther west along Crown Point, **Sandy Beach** is abutted by several hotels. You won't lack for amenities around here.

Just west of Scarborough, take Milford Road off the main highway to the shores of **Little Rockley Bay.** The quiet beach is craggy and not much good for swimming, but offers a pleasing view of Tobago's capital across the water.

After driving through Scarborough, continue south on Bacolet Street 4 miles to **Bacolet Beach,** a dark-sand beach that was the setting for the films *Swiss Family Robinson* and *Heaven Knows, Mr. Allison.*

The road from Scarborough to Speyside has plenty of swimming sites. **King's Bay Beach,** surrounded by steep green hills, is the most appealing—the bay hooks around so severely that you feel as if you're swimming in a lake. It's easy to find, because it's marked by a sign about halfway between Roxborough and Speyside.

Windward Road turns across the island toward **Man of War Bay,** which is flanked by Charlotteville, one of the prettiest fishing villages in the Caribbean. You can lounge on the sand and purchase the day's catch for your dinner. Sunset from the hills is worth the trip. Farther west across the bay is **Lover's Beach,** so called because of its pink sand and because it can be reached only by boat. You can hire one of the locals to take you across.

Parlatuvier, also on the north side of the island, is best approached via the road from Roxborough, which crosses the massive rain forest at Tobago's center. The beach here is a classic Caribbean crescent, a scene peopled by villagers and local fishermen. The next beach over, **Englishman's Bay,** is equally seductive and completely deserted.

Sports and the Outdoors

Bird-Watching You don't have to watch to see hundreds of birds, even on your hotel terrace. The rough cry of the cocrico, the national bird, will awaken you at dawn, as raucous as the green parrots in the rain forests. At dusk the motmots line up their tennis-racket–shaped tails on telephone wires. Hummingbirds whirl like dervishes and sugar birds wait for you to leave your breakfast table to polish off sweet morsels. Bird-watchers can fill up their books with notes on the variety of species to be found in Trinidad at the **Asa Wright Nature Centre,** the **Caroni Bird Sanctuary** (*see* Exploring Trinidad, *above*), and the **Pointe-à-Pierre Wild Fowl Trust,** which is located within the confines of a petrochemical complex (42 Sandown Rd., Pt. Cumana, tel. 809/637–5145). **Mount St. Benedict** has 600 acres of marked trails and about 100 species to spot (*see* Pax Guest House *in* Lodging, *below*). In Tobago, naturalist **David Rooks** offers walks inland and trips to offshore bird colonies (tel. 809/639–4276). A morning's walk with a small group of no more than eight is TT $55 (U.S. $13). **Little Tobago,** off Speyside is one of the best spots to bird-watch, and locals, or the Blue Waters Inn, can arrange a boat trip for about $5 per person.

Golf There are nine golf courses in the country, the best of which are the **Mt. Irvine Golf Club** (tel. 809/639–8871) in Tobago and **St. Andrew's Golf Club** in Trinidad (tel. 809/629–2314), just outside Port-of-Spain. Greens fees average TT $60 (U.S. $14).

Scuba Diving Tobago draws scuba-diving aficionados from around the world. You can get supplies and instruction at **Dive Tobago** (tel. 809/639–0202),

Tobago Marine Sports Ltd. (tel. 809/639–0291), **Man Friday Diving** (tel. 809/660–4676), and **Viking Dive and Sail/Yacht Charter** (tel. 809/639-9209). In Trinidad, contact **Scuba Shop Ltd.** (Mirabella, tel. 809/658–2183). Cost of a single-tank dive averages $40.

Snorkeling The best spots for snorkeling are on Tobago, of which **Buccoo Reef** is easily the most popular—perhaps too popular. Over the years the reef has been damaged by the ceaseless boat traffic and by the thoughtless visitors who take pieces of coral for souvenirs. Even so, it's still a trip worth experiencing, particularly if you have children. For $8 (tickets are available in almost any hotel), you board a Plexiglas-bottom boat at either Store Bay or Buccoo Beach. The 15-minute trip to the reef, 2 miles offshore, is made only at low tide. Operators provide rubber shoes, masks, and snorkels but not fins, which are helpful in the moderate current.

There is also good snorkeling by the beach near the **Arnos Vale Hotel** and at **Blue Waters,** and the government is slowly developing reefs around Speyside that rival, if not surpass, Buccoo's. Most beachside hotels on Tobago rent snorkeling equipment; the cost is around $5 a day.

Tennis The following private tennis courts allow nonmembers or nonguests to play: in Trinidad, the **Trinidad Hilton** (tel. 809/624–3211), the **Trinidad Country Club** (tel. 809/622–3470), the **Tranquility Square Lawn Tennis Club** (Victoria Ave., Port-of-Spain, tel. 809/625–4182); on Tobago, **Turtle Beach** (tel. 809/639–2851), **Mt. Irvine** (tel. 809/639–8817), and the **Blue Waters Inn** (tel. 809/660–4341). The fees vary and sometimes can be negotiated.

Shopping

Thanks in large part to Carnival costumery, there's no shortage of fabric shops on the islands. The best bargains for Asian and East Indian silks and cottons can be found in downtown Port-of-Spain, on **Frederick Street** and around **Independence Square.** Other good buys are such duty-free items as Angostura Bitters and Old Oak or Vat 19 rum, all widely available.

Local Crafts The tourism office can provide an extensive list of local artisans who specialize in everything from straw and cane work to miniature steel pans. A charming experience is to be had at Monica Monceaux's **Craft Boutique** (corner of Adam Smith Sq. S and Murray St. in the Woodbrook section of Port-of-Spain, tel. 809/627–2736). Monica's house is a delight in gingerbread wood tracery. Almost every inch of the house is utilized by Monica and her craftspeople, who make carnival and folk dolls, Christmas ornaments (even those for the Hilton tree), crocheted picture frames, preserves, and dozens of other items in merry disarray. At the new Ellerslie Plaza behind the Kapok Hotel, stop at **Bonga!** (tel. 809/624–8819) for smart T-shirts, carryalls, shorts, and bathing suits. **Poui Boutique** (Ellerslie Plaza, tel. 809/622–5597) has stylish handmade wax batik wear and Ajoupa pottery, an attractive local terra-cotta pottery. The **Market** (Nook Ave. by the Hotel Normandie) is a mall with several shops that specialize in indigenous fashions, crafts, jewelry, basketwork, and ceramics. On Tobago, the **Cotton House** on lovely Bacolet Street in Scarborough (tel. 809/639–2727) is a good bet for jewelry and imaginative batik work. Paula Young runs her shop like an art school. You can visit the upstairs studio; if it's not too busy, you can even make a batik square at no charge. A good line (Forro brand) of homemade tamarind chutney, marmalade of lime or lemon, hot sauce, and guava or golden apple jelly can be found at **Forro's** (Wilson Rd., across from the Scarborough market, tel. 809/639–2979) or at the airport in Tobago. Mrs. Eileen Forrester, wife of the Anglican priest at St. David's in Plymouth, supervises a kitchen full of good cooks who boil and bottle the condiments and pack them in little straw baskets.

Most jars are small, easily carried, and very inexpensive. Straw baskets and other crafts are sold at the **Souvenir and Gift Shop** (Port Mall, Scarborough, tel. 809/639–5632).

Records For the best selection of calypso and soca music, check out **Rhyner's Record Shop** (54 Prince St., 809/623–5673; Cruise Ship Complex, tel. 809/627–8717) in Port-of-Spain.

Dining

Dining can be very inexpensive. Small stands and cafés throughout Port-of-Spain sell such snacks as rotis (a kind of East Indian burrito, usually filled with curried chicken and potatoes) for less than an American dollar. Fewer budget options exist on Tobago, where dining is primarily in hotel restaurants, but even here prices are reasonable. If your lodgings include kitchen facilities, you'll find plenty of minimarkets on Trinidad that are well-stocked with local and imported foods; stores are few and far between on Tobago.

Trinidad Port-of-Spain doesn't lack for variety when it comes to eateries, with imaginative hybrids of European, Asian, East Indian, and Caribbean fare. In addition to the establishments below, there are plenty of East Indian and Chinese restaurants and pizzerias (don't expect New York–style pizza).

Trinidadians are particularly fond of *callaloo*, a soup or stew of dasheen leaves (similar to spinach) and okra, flavored with anything from pork to shrimp and coconut, pureed and served at every restaurant on the island. It's hard to believe anything this green and swampy-looking can taste so delicious. Other items in a Trinidadian menu worth sampling are *coocoo*, a dumpling of cornmeal and coconut (similar to polenta); roti; pilau; tamarind ball, a dessert made from the sweet-sour tamarind; and peanut shake, a peanut butter–flavored milk shake.

No Trinidadian dining experience can be complete, of course, without a rum punch with fresh fruit and the legendary Angostura Bitters, made by the same company that produces the excellent Old Oak rum. Carib beer and Stag are recommended for washing down the spicier concoctions. Dark-beer aficionados can try Royal Extra Stout (R.E.), which is even sweeter than Guinness.

Tobago With few exceptions, the restaurants in Tobago are in hotels and guest houses; several of the large resort complexes also offer some form of nightly entertainment. The food isn't as eclectic as on Trinidad, generally favoring local styles, but in terms of quality and service Tobagonian "home cooking" more than holds its own.

Highly recommended restaurants are indicated by a star ★.

Category	Cost*
$$	$20–$30
$	$10–$20
¢	under $10

**per person, excluding drinks, service, and 15% sales tax*

Trinidad *$$* **Rafters.** Behind a stone facade with green rafters stands a pub that has become an urban institution. Once it was a rum shop; currently it's a bar and a restaurant. The pub is the center of activity, especially Friday night. In late afternoons the place begins to swell with Port-of-Spainers ordering from the tasty selection of burgers, barbecues, and burritos and generally loosening up. The Seafood Medley platter (seasonal fin and shellfish, including shrimp and conch) is served with baked potato and tartar sauce for about $8 (TT $45). In the evening an unexpectedly romantic candlelit restaurant opens in another part of the delightful old building. *6A Warner St., Port-of-Spain, tel. 809/628–9258. AE, DC, MC, V. No lunch weekends.*

$$ **Solimar.** Dining here is oddly, but not unpleasantly, like dining under the Caribbean, thanks to the huge turquoise-lit fish tank, jungle of greenery, and candlelight. The chef offers a menu that tries to travel the world in one meal: You can eat shrimp tempura, Irish smoked salmon, Hawaiian barbecued mahimahi, Greek salad, linguine Alfredo, or Zwiebel Schnitzel, all while listening to John Denver singing "I think I'd rather be a cowboy." Best bets are the day's specials—seafood mixed grill, perhaps (which is not, in fact, grilled, but fried, like everything else on Trinidad), then hot chocolate soufflé with chilled coconut cream. You'll have to avoid high-end à la carte dishes to keep the tab in the $$ range. Solimar is popular with expat types and tends toward careful casualness. *6 Nook Ave., St. Ann's, Port-of-Spain, tel. 809/624–1459. AE, DC, MC, V. Closed Sun.*

$$ **Tiki Village.** Cosmopolitan Port-of-Spainers are as passionate about their Asian food as New Yorkers and San Franciscans are. Everyone touts their favorite, but this eatery, a serious (nonkitsch) version of Trader Vic's, is the most reliable. It's high under the rafters atop the Kapok Hotel, air-conditioned, clean-lined, and sunlit. Fine Asian food is served, including the very popular dim sum, which you order by checking off your picks on a multiple-choice card. *Kapok Hotel, 16–18 Cotton Hill, Port-of-Spain, tel. 809/622–6441. Reservations advised. AE, D, DC, MC, V.*

$–$$ ★ **Veni Mange.** The best lunches in town are served inside this small stucco house. Credit Allyson Hennessy, a Cordon Bleu–trained cook who has become a celebrity of sorts because of a TV talk show she hosts, and her sister-partner Rosemary Hezekiah. The cuisine here is Creole. *13 Lucknow St., St. James, Port-of-Spain, tel. 809/622–7533. No credit cards. No dinner.*

$ **Wazo Deyzeel.** Wazo ("oiseaux des isles"—get it?) is adored by all for its setting, high up in the hills of St. Ann, with Port-of-Spain spread out below; its live bands and dancing on weekends; its friendliness; and its prizewinning cocktails (the cucumber-lime-rum-syrup Wazo Combo is essential); as well as for its food. The Thursday night all-you-can-eat Caribbean buffet might include grouper, flying fish, red snapper, macaroni pie, coo-coo, *bhajia* (East Indian spinach fritters), and savory pumpkin pie, and at about $10 is probably the best bargain in the city. Other nights (except Monday–Wednesday) you could go for a seafood platter or a beef pot roast, all cooked by three Jamaican ladies. Candy-colored director's chairs, white walls, a big, open-air terrace for admiring the view, wining (a naughty dance style), and liming (hanging out) set the tone. *Carib Way, 23 Sydenham Ave., St. Ann's, Port-of-Spain, tel. 809/623–0115. MC, V. Closed Mon.–Wed.*

¢ **Las Cuevas Restaurant.** This local fishermen's hangout doubles as a beachside snack bar. The menu is limited; your best bet is a wholesome and tasty bake 'n' shark (shark burger). If you want a full meal, go for the fish of the day. It was probably caught this morning. *Las Cuevas, no phone. No credit cards. Open 11–7.*

¢ **Monsoon.** Dark green Formica tables, lavender walls, and a few sprigs of flowers comprise the simple decor of this Indian restaurant. The specialties are curries: goat, shrimp, chicken, and beef, made with spices imported from India and served with chutney, potatoes, and chickpeas. Wednesday evenings bring a special buffet. *Corner of Tragerete Rd. and Picton St., Newtown, Port-of-Spain, tel. 809/628–7684. AE, DC, MC, V. Closed Sun.*

Tobago

$$ ★ **Blue Crab.** Alison Sardinha is Tobago's most ebullient and kindly hostess, and her husband, Ken, one of its best chefs. He cooks "like our mothers cooked," serving the local food with heavy East Indian influence, a bit of Portuguese, and occasionally Asian too. There

might be rolled flying fish, *katchowrie* (spiced split pea patties, a little like falafel), curry chicken, or long-cooked suckling pig. There's always a callaloo, differently flavored on different days, fine rotis and coocoo, and sometimes a "cookup"—pelau-type rice, with *everything* in it. The place is only officially open on Wednesday and Friday nights, but Miss Alison will open up on other evenings (and for weekend lunches, too) even for one table, if you call in the morning. The setting, on a wide, shady terrace overlooking the bay, is just about perfect, and there's a bar for cocktails. Two guest rooms (the front one's a beauty) in the Sardinhas' home are also available. If you want to see the joy of Caribbean cooking in one presentation, ask Alison how to make one of the dishes: her expressions, gestures, and advice should be exported. They epitomize the joy of living. *Corner of Main and Fort Sts., Scarborough, tel. 809/639–2737. AE, MC, V. No dinner except Wed. and Fri.*

$$ **Cocrico Inn.** A café with a bar against one wall, the Cocrico offers delectable home cooking. The three rotating chefs use fresh fruits and vegetables grown in the neighborhood. They zealously guard their recipes, including a marvelous coocoo and lightly breaded, subtly spiced grouper. There is nothing fancy here, just delicious food and cool air-conditioning. *Corner of North and Commissioner Sts., Plymouth, tel. 809/639–2661. AE, V.*

$$ ★ **Kariwak Village.** Steel-band music (on tape) plays gently in the background at this romantic candlelit spot. In a bamboo pavilion created by her architect-husband to resemble an Amerindian round hut, Christine Clovis orchestrates a very original four-course menu. Changing daily, the choices may include christophine soup, curried plantain, kingfish with shrimp sauce, and coconut cake. Whatever it is, it will be full of herbs and vegetables freshly picked from Christine's own organic garden, and everything will be bursting with flavor, including the home-baked breads. It's a treat for vegetable lovers, because Kariwak knows how to honor the simple squash and green beans. The nonalcoholic drinks are wonderful, even the iced coffee, which is more like a frozen coconut cappuccino. Saturday buffets, with live jazz or calypso, are a Tobagonian highlight. *Kariwak Village, Crown Pt., tel. 809/639–8442. AE, DC, MC, V.*

$$ **The Old Donkey Cart House.** The name is something of a curiosity, since this restaurant is set in and around an attractive green-and-white colonial house (2 miles south of Scarborough). There's outdoor dining in a garden with twinkling lights. The cuisine is standard Caribbean, nothing special, but German side dishes and an extensive selection of Rhine and Moselle wines set it apart. *Bacolet St., Scarborough, tel. 809/639–3551. AE, V. Closed Wed.*

$$ **Papillon.** Named after one of the proprietor's favorite books, this seafood restaurant is a homey room with an adjoining patio. Lobster Buccoo Bay is marinated in sherry and broiled with herbs and garlic-butter sauce. Seafood Casserole au Gratin means chunks of lobster, shrimp, fish, and cream, all seasoned in ginger wine. Baby shark is marinated in rum and lime. Or you can just enjoy some good broiled chicken or pork cutlets with pineapple. *Buccoo Bay Rd., Mt. Irvine, tel. 809/639–0275. AE, DC, MC, V. No lunch Sun.*

$–$$ ★ **Rouselle's.** An enchanting terrace high above Scarborough Bay with a big, congenial bar, Rouselle's was just a liming spot until friends and regulars demanded proper food. Bet they didn't expect food that could compete with big-city cuisine, though. The small menu varies from day to day; you may find grouper, broiled and served with a fresh Creole sauce and several vegetables—garlicky green beans, carrots with ginger, a raw bok choy salad, and potato croquette with spices and celery—or dolphinfish with white wine sauce, or lobster, steamed just so, which is very hard to procure. Whatever there is, you can trust that it'll be delicious. A sizable *amuse-gueule* (appetizer), hot garlic bread, plus dessert (save room for pineapple pie or homemade ice cream) are included in the entrée price, and don't forgo the Rouselle's punch. The recipe's a secret, but the lovely, welcoming co-owners Bobbie and Charlene will probably let you in on it. *Old Windward Rd., Bacolet, tel. 809/639–4738. AE, MC, V. Lunch by reservation only.*

$ **Mount Marie.** If you want a spotlessly clean, air-conditioned restaurant in Scarborough that serves good local and international fare, look no further. The menu changes according to what's available at the market, but usually includes pasta and seafood dishes. The place is owned by the local police pension fund and managed by the very stylish and efficient Petunia Thomas. Best of all, the place is a real bargain. *Mount Marie, near the Rockley Bay harbor just off Claude Noel Hwy., tel. 809/639-2014. MC, V.*

¢ **Jemma's Village Kitchen.** Just outside of Speyside on the main road, this local house perches on stilts by the ocean's shore. Jemma produces tasty Tobagonian cooking spiced with Indian herbs—the chicken is a popular choice. Decor is as basic as can be, but the ocean views are inspiring. *Speyside, tel. 809/660–4066. No credit cards.*

¢ **Store Bay Centre.** In a small park across the road from the beach are a collection of small take-out restaurants serving fish burgers, rotis, fried chicken, and other local-style fast food. Make your selection and carry it to one of the tables set under a thatched roof. If you're with a group, each person can select from one of several restaurants and together enjoy a large, varied meal for little money. *Store Bay, no phone. No credit cards. Open 11 AM–7 PM.*

Lodging

If you're looking for a full-service hotel, the best way to save money is to take a package deal. BWIA offers excellent air fare-hotel combinations. Port-of-Spain hotels also offer bargain packages, usually with a minimum stay of several nights. Recent offerings have included stays at the Kapok hotel for $54 per night for a single and $60 for a double and the Holiday Inn for $40 single and $74 double. Lodging prices in Trinidad and Tobago are among the lowest in the Caribbean, and Trinidad's are slightly lower than Tobago's. Even taken at full rate, Trinidad's top city hotel, the Trinidad Hilton, falls just within our $$ category for a standard double room. When booking the top hotels at their lowest prices, do not expect their best rooms. They should be acceptable, but usually without the best view. However, the facilities of the hotel are yours. On Trinidad, most lodging is located within the vicinity of Port-of-Spain, far from any beach. The larger Port-of-Spain hotels cater mainly to the business traveler or convention groups. As a consequence, a number of small inns and guest houses have sprung up to meet the needs of tourists. These offer a congenial, family-type atmosphere.

Unlike Trinidad's properties, almost every one of Tobago's hotels is on or within walking distance of the ocean. Recent BWIA package rates at the Grafton, Tobago's top-of-the-line hotel, were less than $100 per night for single or double rooms. An inclusive package, with all meals and drinks, came to $475 for two nights. At Palm Tree Village, a two-bedroom villa costs under $75 per person for a double.

On both islands, private homes have begun opening their doors to paying guests. These rooms can be reserved through the tourist offices on either island, or contact the **Trinidad and Tobago Bed and Breakfast Association** (Box 3231, Diego Martin, Trinidad, tel. 809/663–4413, fax 809/627–0856; on Tobago, c/o Federal Villa, 1–3 Crooks River, Scarborough; tel. 809/639–8836, fax 809/639–3566), which only admits members after an inspection for safety and cleanliness. We recommend that you only consider those listed with this organization or the tourist office. Most private homes are away from the beach.

During Carnival week and Christmas, you should book reservations far in advance; expect to pay about 40%–50% more for lodging at these times. From mid-December to mid-April, Tobago's hotel rates average 30% higher than the rest of the year.

Most establishments offer a choice of EP, CP, or MAP meal plans. Since most of the Trinidad accommodations listed below are a few blocks from any breakfast shop, you may want to elect for a CP plan, but an MAP plan on Trinidad will limit your dinner options. On Tobago, however, MAP is a sensible choice if you don't have a car; it's an especially good idea on the east side of the island, where there is a dearth of restaurants. Lodgings with cooking facilities are the exception rather than the rule.

Highly recommended lodgings are indicated by a star ★.

Category	Cost*
$$	$100–$150
$	$50–$100
¢	under $50

**All prices are for a standard double room for two, excluding 15% tax and a 10% service charge. To estimate rates for hotels offering MAP/FAP, add about $25–$35 per person per day to the above price ranges.*

Trinidad
$$ **Hotel Normandie.** Built by French Creoles in the 1930s on the ruins of an old coconut plantation, the Normandie has touches of Spanish, English Colonial, and even postmodern architecture. The standard rooms, set around a pretty pool courtyard, have beige textured-vinyl walls, wood floorboards and trim, TV, phone, noisy but efficient air-conditioning, and very little light. The 13 loft rooms are far better: For $25 more, you get a towering duplex with simple wood furniture, exposed eaves, and a bigger bathroom. Number 236 is especially bright and beautiful, with a big window upstairs, and 231 has extra space. These are great for families, since two under-12s can share for free. The conference facilities ensure a steady flow of convention groups, who also like the quiet location, set back from residential St. Ann's Road in the center of an artsy mall of crafts and clothes shops and galleries. Service is friendly and efficient. The Market shopping gallery here has a small café for light meals, but the hotel's main restaurant, La Fantasie, makes for expensive dining. You can catch one of the buses that run along the nearby main road for the 10-minute ride to downtown. *10 Nook Ave., St. Ann's Village, Port-of-Spain, tel. and fax 809/624–1181 or 800/223–6510. 48 rooms, 13 loft rooms. Facilities: restaurant and bar, café, pool, gallery, shops, car rental, taxi service. AE, DC, MC, V. EP. MAP.*

$$ ★ **Kapok Hotel.** This hotel has been run by the Chan family for years and gleams with cheerful efficiency. The rooms, done in pink and white, are spotless, spacious, and sunlit, with rattan furniture and Polynesian prints the colors of highlighting markers. Front ones are best for the view over the Savannah—the Kapok is next to it, but away from the hubbub—and even better are the studios, with kitchenette included for the same price as a room. Request a refrigerator when you book, and a hair dryer (they're built into about a quarter of the bathrooms); all rooms have quiet air-conditioning, satellite TVs, push-button phones with an extra fax-friendly jack, and full-length mirrors. Suites are vast, and fine for families, who will also like the laundry facilities and the birds and monkeys who live by the pool. The Café Savanna may stretch your budget, but do sample the Chinese and Polynesian specialties at Tiki Village, especially the dim sum. (*see* Dining, *above*). *16–18 Cotton Hill, Port-of-Spain, tel. 809/*

622–6441 or 800/333–1212, fax 809/622–9677. 71 rooms. Facilities: 2 restaurants, pool, taxi service. AE, DC, MC, V. EP.

$$ ★ **Trinidad Hilton.** Perched above Port-of-Spain, the newly expanded Hilton radiates the feeling of comfort and competence. This is Port-of-Spain's most stylish hotel, with prices to match: Everything but the standard rooms here exceeds our $$ price range. (Check with BWIA for package rates.) Each room has a balcony, which either opens to either a fine view of Queen's Park, the city, and sea beyond or overlooks the inviting Olympic-size pool, shaded by trees. La Boucan, the hotel's formal restaurant, tends to be expensive, but the Pool Terrace, where there's live entertainment on Monday nights, is more reasonable. The bar is decorated with wonderful, dramatically lit carnival masks. The hotel frequently bustles with conventioneers, which may be its only drawback. Ask for a special corporate rate when you book. *Lady Young Rd., Box 442, Port-of-Spain, tel. 809/624–3211, fax 624–4485. 442 rooms. Facilities: 2 restaurants, bar, satellite TV, pool, health club, 2 lighted tennis courts, drugstore, gift shops, car rental, taxi service. AE, DC, MC, V. EP.*

$–$$ **Asa Wright Nature Centre.** Bird-watchers and nature photographers are frequently among the guests at this handsome lodge. Built in 1908, it's set in a lush rain forest (about 90 minutes east of Port-of-Spain) populated by nearly 200 species of birds. There are impressive views of the verdant Arima Valley and the Northern Range from the veranda, where tea is served each afternoon. Just inside is an elegant, comfortable lounge with black lacquered floorboards, bookcases, antiques, and ornithological memorabilia. The two huge bedrooms on the main floor share its romantic atmosphere, with fans turning slowly on tall ceilings, hardwood closets, and antique beds. All other rooms are in modern lodges near the house, simply outfitted with marble floors, spartan wood furniture, and private covered terraces. You'll feel that you're miles from anywhere and, actually, you are, so you'll need the three meals a day and evening rum punch that are included in the rates. A car is essential, unless bird-watching at the center and being alone are your sole aims, in which case airport transfers cost $40. Reserve at least six months in advance. (For more information about the center, *see* Exploring Trinidad, *above*.) *Write to the lodge at 20 Farfan St., Arima, Trinidad, tel. 809/667-4655, fax 809/667-0493; or write to Caligo Ventures, 156 Bedford Rd, Armonk, NY 10504, tel. 914/273–6333 or 800/426–7781. 23 rooms. Facilities: restaurant. No credit cards. FAP.*

$ **Alicia's House.** The Govias managed to keep the family atmosphere when they converted their home for guests, so all here is welcoming and reassuring. The enormous, breezy lounge has squashy sofas, round tables, cane chairs, a piano, and a tank of fish; it leads into the dining area, where you may take breakfast, and other meals if you ask. Rooms vary greatly. "Admiral Rooney" (a local flower) is a big one with mahogany furniture, a cute garden-view desk, and a giant bathtub; the "Back Room" is very small but also very bright, and has a private spiral staircase to the pool; "Alicia's Room" (she's the Govias' daughter) is a petite apartment with twin cherry-red sofas, many windows, an acre of closets, a pink bathroom with a huge bathtub, and mirror tiles over the bed. Extras—which you shouldn't expect for the low rates but get anyway—include a hot tub and a water cooler by the pool, 14-channel U.S. cable TV, air-conditioning, private bathrooms, and push-button phones in every room. It's a 10-minute walk from the Savannah, very near the Normandie. *7 Coblentz Gardens, St. Ann's, Port-of-Spain, tel. 809/623–2802, fax 809/622–8560. 16 rooms. Facilities: breakfast room, pool, lounge, Jacuzzi. MC, V. EP, CP, MAP.*

$ **Carnetta's House.** When Winston Borrell retired as director of tourism for Trinidad and Tobago, he and his wife, Carnetta, opened their suburban two-story house to guests. One guest room is on the upper floor, the same level as the lounge and terrace dining room.

The other four are on the ground floor, with the choice room, Le Flamboyant, opening onto the garden's patio. All rooms have a private bathroom with shower, telephone, radio, and TV. And, although there is air-conditioning, cool breezes usually do the trick. Unfortunately, the doors need to be shuttered at night for security reasons. Winston is a keen gardener, and his garden has a sampling of plants that are a fascinating introduction to tropical flowers and herbs. Carnetta uses the herbs in her cooking, and she can prepare some of the best dinners that you may find in Port-of-Spain. Equally important is the fund of information that both Carnetta and Winston can offer on what to see and do in Trinidad and the necessary arrangements they can make to do it. *28 Scotland Terr., Andalusia, Maraval, Port-of-Spain, tel. 809/628–2732, fax 809/628–7717. 5 rooms. Facilities: dining room, lounge, laundry facilities, car-rental, airport transfers. AE, DC, MC, V. EP, BP, MAP.*

$ ★ **Monique's.** Mike and Monique Charbonné really *like* having guests, as they have been proving for more than 10 years. In fact, they like it so much, they've built an annex close to their house, with a further 10 rooms. Rooms are sizable, spotless, and, mostly, light. Each has air-conditioning, phone, and private bathroom; the newer rooms also have TV and kitchenette. Numbers 25 and 26 are enormous and can sleep up to six. They're darker than the other rooms, but each has a little sunken red stone patio where you can soak up some sun. Breakfast is in the parlorlike dining room, where you can ask to have dinner, too. The airy, marble-floored lounge is a great place to hang out—with the hosts, often as not. Mike sometimes organizes a picnic to the couple's 100-acre plantation near Blanchisseuse. *114 Saddle Rd., Maraval, Port-of-Spain, tel. 809/628–3334, fax 809/622–3232. 26 rooms. Facilities: dining room, common-room area with TV. AE. EP, CP, MAP.*

$ **Pax Guest House.** Aptly named for peace, this is a marvelous place to reconnect with nature and listen to the wind and the birds while exploring Mount Saint Benedict's 600 acres of marked trails. The Benedictine order came to Trinidad in 1912 and established the original monastery, whose ruins can be explored on Mt. Tabour. Guests come, regardless of religion, to enjoy the peace (pax) to be found on this Northern range, 800 feet above the lowlands. The guest house is simple but comfortable, and popular with bird-watchers and biologists, who use its lab facilities. The rate includes breakfast and dinner, but lunch will be served on request. The lack of phones and TV is a plus with ecotourists. Every day, the tea shop serves "Pax Tea" from 3 to 6 PM, the original meal, complete with brown bread and honey, and one of 22 teas made with spring water. Plans are in the offing to expand the tea menu to a luncheon menu. *Call or fax the manager, Mr. Ram Sawak, at 809/662–4084. 14 rooms. MAP.*

¢ **Surf's Country Inn.** The location, on a hillside on the north coast, makes this a good spot to overnight after a day of swimming and surfing. Six guest rooms are in buildings adjoining a popular fish restaurant. *Blanchisseuse, tel. 809/669–2475. 6 rooms. Facilities: restaurant, bar. No credit cards. EP, BP.*

¢ **Tropical.** Crazy-paved steps take you into a pretty reception area with a clicking ceiling fan, murmuring TV, pea-green chairs, white arches, and white wrought-iron gates shielding a central, cloister-like courtyard. That's about it for the grounds, except for the small pool. Rooms, too, are spartan, if psychedelic, with their fuchsia-and-tomato drapes, bedcovers, and shower curtains. Most are big, and all have air-conditioning and bathrooms. Big pluses are the excellent restaurant-bar and club attached, serving local food, and the low rates. *6 Rookery Nook, Maraval, Port-of-Spain, tel. 809/622–5815, fax 809/622–4249. 16 rooms. Facilities: restaurant, pool. AE. EP.*

Tobago

$$ ★ **Blue Waters Inn.** If your dream of the tropics is a simple place as close to the waves as possible, set amid 46 acres of greenery, including massive gnarled beach plum trees that seem to hold up the house, this is for you. A good 90-minute drive from Scarborough and up a bumpy driveway bring you to this beach hotel and its villas on the northeast Atlantic coast, with Little Tobago and Bird of Paradise islands across Bateaux Bay. From your bedroom balcony, you'll see a little beach fringed with mangos, palms, and hardy twisted sea grape trees. Rooms have little more than the basics, but you're guaranteed the sounds of waves all night and a chorus of bright birds to greet the dawn. The bungalows have one or two bedrooms, living room, and kitchen. The "self-catering" apartments, oddly enough, have no real kitchens. Do your shopping in Scarborough before you set out, if possible: Local stores are small. But there is a good bar and restaurant. Bring along books and binoculars: This is more a place for bird-watchers, nature lovers (and lovers), than it is for those who want TV or nightlife. *Batteaux Bay, Speyside, Tobago, tel. 809/660–4341, fax 809/660–5195. 23 rooms. Facilities: restaurant, bar, 2 tennis courts, dive instruction, gift shop. AE, DC, MC, V. EP, MAP.*

$$ **Richmond Great House.** This is a restored late-18th-century plantation house on a 1,500-acre citrus estate. The common rooms have a great view, but what holds your gaze are the original wood, the golden cloth on the walls, and furniture collected by the professor who owns the place. You can choose one of the two rooms in the main house or one of four guest cottages. The beach is a 10-minute drive away, so you'll probably need a car here. Even if you're not staying here, you can visit for lunch (call for reservations in the morning). Although the house is exquisite, staff changes have been inordinately frequent, so you might want to visit before reserving. *Belle Garden, Tobago, tel. 809/660–4467. 6 rooms. Facilities: dining room, pool, TV lounge. MC, V. MAP.*

$–$$ ★ **Kariwak Village.** People fall helplessly in love with Allan and Christine Clovis's cabana village, which is to the average hotel as the scarlet ibis is to the city pigeon. You enter a bamboo, raw teak, and coral stone lobby and bar area. Outside, in a bamboo pavilion, is the highly respected restaurant (*see* Kariwak Village *in* Dining, *above*). Nine large, round palm-thatched cabanas, each containing two bedrooms, are in a semicircle around a pretty pool. Rooms are simple and air-conditioned, with loft-height dark-wood ceilings, carpeted floors, and wicker armchairs; each has a separate bathroom and dressing area and a little terrace outside the patio doors. Lush flora makes a fairly small site seem more spacious, and an herb-and-vegetable garden out back, which furnishes Christine's kitchen with ingredients, provides a place for an extra stroll. The best breakfast around—fresh cocoa made with local chocolate, homemade yogurt, granola, whole-wheat bread, and spice tea—plus the best rum punches and local bands playing on weekends make this a favored liming spot as well as a lively holiday base. It's very near the airport (where the main activity is the hourly small plane from Trinidad), Store Bay, and Pigeon Point. *Crown Pt., Tobago, tel. 809/639–8442; write to Box 27, Scarborough, Tobago; fax 809/639–8441. 18 rooms. Facilities: restaurant, bar, shuttle service to beach, pool. AE, DC, MC, V. EP, MAP.*

$ **Cocrico Inn.** Named after the national bird of Tobago, this inn built around a courtyard and small pool is set on a quiet side street in the village of Plymouth. Although the impression is a little like a roadside motel, with large rooms, rather drab furnishings, and stained carpets, the hosts are genuinely welcoming, the restaurant serves a combination of good local and American fare (*see* Dining, *above*), and you can walk to the village, the marina, and beaches. *North and Commissioner Sts., Box 287, Plymouth, Tobago, tel. 809/639–2961, fax 809/639–6565. 16 rooms. Facilities: restaurant, bar, pool, gift shop. AE, MC, V. EP, MAP.*

$ **Old Grange Inn.** You're a 10-minute drive from the beach here, and you can see the Mt. Irvine Golf Course from your windows. It's more like an American motel than an inn, but rooms are stylishly furnished, clean, and air-conditioned, with balconies. A big plus is the Papillon restaurant (*see* Dining, *above*) and the Grotto Ticino, run by the same family, in an adjoining building. Bikes and motor-scooters can be rented. *Box 297, Scarborough, Tobago, tel. 809/639–0275, fax 809/639–9395. 20 rooms AE, DC, MC, V.*

$ **Sandy Point Beach Club.** Spacious, modern villas have all the amenities, including air-conditioning and closed-circuit TV. The 22 apartments have one bedroom and a lounge that can double as sleeping quarters for another couple. The laid-back attitude and friendliness of the staff is infectious, and activities from volleyball on the beach to festive dinners encourage guests to join in the party spirit. The beach is so close that the sea actually washes the base of the bar. The village of Crown Point is within walking distance. *Crown Point, Tobago, tel. 809/639–8533 or 800/223–6510, fax 809/639–8495. 22 apartments. Facilities: restaurant, 2 bars, 2 pools, car rentals, dive shop, boutique, laundry. DC, MC, V. EP.*

$ **Tropikist.** This amiable, gleaming-white little hotel spread out across Store Bay attracts a fun, youngish crowd who appreciate its bargain prices, sparkling cleanliness, and beachfront location. The lively atmosphere is generated by the gaiety of the guests rather than the hotel's austere architecture and plain decor. *Store Bay, tel. 809/639–8512, fax 809/638–1110. 30 rooms. Facilities: beach, pool, restaurant, bar, disco, volleyball. AE, DC, MC, V. EP.*

¢ **The Golden Thistle Hotel.** The look here is that of a respectable 1950s motel. All rooms include kitchenettes. You can make the 15-minute walk to the beach and local eateries, but a rental bike may give you more flexibility. Store Bay Rd., Crown Point, Tobago, tel. and fax 809/639–8521. 36 rooms. Facilities: restaurant, bar, pool. DC, V. EP.

¢ **Harris Cottage.** Unlike most of the guest houses on Tobago—old clapboard homes converted on an ad hoc basis to accept boarders—Harris Cottage is a new stone-and-stucco structure built on a half-acre of land. This is a family home, the kind of place where kids run in and out. The comfortable, air-conditioned rooms with private baths are in an addition abutting the house. Breakfast is served on a small terrace, and meals are by request throughout the day. It's about 10 minutes by bicycle from Scarborough, and a 10-minute walk from the beach. *Bacolet, near Scarborough, tel. 809/639–8810. 8 rooms. Facilities: dining room, TV lounge. No credit cards. BP.*

¢ **Mount Marie.** Sparkling clean and new, in the middle of Scarborough, is a wonderful new hotel, with bar and restaurant (*see* Dining, *above*). This charming little place has air-conditioned rooms, a nice, breezy terrace looking out to sea, and a staff willing to do anything. The police pension fund is the owner, and members of the force made much of the furniture. *Mt. Marie, Scarborough, tel. 809/639–2014, fax 809/639–1129. 11 rooms. Facilities: restaurant. MC, V.*

¢ **Store Bay Holiday Resort.** Close to the airport and less than a mile from the beach, this impersonal, motel-like property has air-conditioned rooms that look out on a pool. Furnishings are plain and the carpets somewhat worn, but rooms have fully equipped kitchens. *Store Bay Rd., Crown Point, tel. 809/622–2141, fax 809/639–8810. 15 rooms. Facilities: snack bar, pool. MC, V. EP.*

¢ **Viola's Place.** New but already homey, this friendly place is run by a Tobago crafts teacher, whose attractive works can be seen in the adjoining gift shop/general store. The sparkling rooms, some with loft beds, are either air-conditioned or have ceiling fans. All have well-equipped kitchenettes and maid service. A modern supermarket is across the street. Prices are apt to increase as this place becomes known. TVs or cribs can be arranged, as can baby-sitting. *Birchwood Triangle, Lowlands, Tobago, tel. 809/624–8765; evenings, 809/664–3670. 10 rooms. No credit cards.*

Off-Season Bets Other than Carnival time, Trinidad does not have a high season, and consequently no off-season when hotel rates dip. On Tobago, prices drop by about 30% from mid-April to mid-December. Among affordable hotels at this time is **Grafton Beach Resort** (Black Rock, Tobago, tel. 809/639–0191, fax 809/639–0030), the best-run resort on the island. It's on the beach and has a large swimming pool, tennis and squash courts, and good restaurants.

The Arts and Nightlife

Trinidad Trinidadian culture doesn't end with music, but it definitely begins with it. Although both calypso and steel bands are best displayed during Carnival, the steel bands play at clubs, dances, and fêtes throughout the year. There's no lack of nightlife in Port-of-Spain. A type of music that's popular right now is "sweet Parang," a mixture of Spanish patois and calypso sung to tunes played on a string instrument much like a mandolin.

The Blue Iguana (no phone) is the place to go. It's about 20 minutes west of town in Chaguanas, so get a party together from your hotel and hire a cab. It opens at 10 PM, Wednesday through Sunday. **Mas Camp Pub** (corner of Ariapata and French Sts., Woodbrook, tel. 809/627–8449) is Port-of-Spain's most comfortable and dependable nightspot. There are tables, a bar, an ample stage in one room, and an open-air patio with more tables and a bar with a TV. There's a kitchen if you're hungry, and **Hush,** which makes delicious fruit-flavored ice cream, is right next door. **Cricket Wicket** (149 Tragarete Rd., tel. 809/622–1808), a popular watering hole with a cupola-shape bar in the center, is a fine place to hear top bands, dance, or just sit and enjoy the nocturnal scenery. **Wazo Deyzeel** (23 Sydenham Ave., St. Ann's, tel. 809/623–0115; closed Mon.–Wed.) is the current fave with a mixed age group for its music, dancing, drinking, views, and great food cooked by three Jamaican ladies. The **Pelican** (2–4 Coblentz Ave., St. Ann's, tel. 809/627–6271), an English-style pub, gets increasingly frenetic as the week closes, with a singles bar atmosphere. Collect gossip over a beer at **Smokey & Bunty** (Western Main Rd. and Dengue St., St James, no phone), which calls itself a sports bar but is really just the essential liming corner. Finally, **Moon Over Bourbon Street** (Southern Landing, Westmall, Westmoorings, tel. 809/637–3448) has comedy or music most nights, plus long, long happy hours.

There are several excellent theaters in Port-of-Spain. Consult local newspapers for listings.

Tobago People will tell you there's no nightlife on Tobago. Don't believe them. Some kind of organized cabaret-style event happens every night at the **Grafton Beach Resort** (tel. 809/639–0191). Even if you hate that touristy stuff, check out Les Couteaux Cultural Group, who do a high-octane dance version of Tobagonian history. Performances are held at the **Grafton** and at the **Turtle Beach Hotel** (tel. 809/639–2851), where similar shows are staged Wednesday and Sunday. Hip hotel entertainment, frequented as often by locals as tourists, is found at the **Kariwak Village** (tel. 809/639–8441) Friday and Saturday night—almost always one of the better local jazz/calypso bands. But the most authentic nightlife of all is anywhere in downtown Scarborough, any weekend. The entire town throbs with competing sound systems and impromptu or prearranged parties, any of which will welcome extra guests.

Between the two extremes, the **Starting Gate** (Shirvan Rd., tel. 809/639–0225), an indoor-outdoor pub, is the venue for frequent party-discos, while Sunday night at Buccoo there is an informal hop, affectionately dubbed Sunday School, at **Henderson's disco** (no phone). It's great fun. "Blockos" (spontaneous block parties) spring up all over the island; look for the hand-painted signs. Tobago also has Harvest parties on Sunday, when a particular village opens its doors to visitors for hospitality. These occur throughout the year and are a great way to meet the locals; the tourist office can let you know when and where they'll be taking place.

26 Turks and Caicos Islands

Updated by Anna Moschovakis

The Turks and Caicos Islands are relatively unknown except to scuba divers and aficionados of beautiful beaches, who religiously return to these waters year after year. First settled by the English more than 200 years ago, the British Crown Colony of Turks and Caicos is renowned in two respects: Its booming banking and insurance institutions lure investors from the United States and elsewhere; and its offshore reef formation entices divers to a world of colorful marine life surrounding its 40 islands and small cays, only eight of which are inhabited. The total landmass is 193 square miles; the population of the eight inhabited islands and cays is some 12,350.

The Turks and Caicos are two groups of islands in an archipelago lying 575 miles southeast of Miami and about 90 miles north of Haiti. The Turks Islands include Grand Turk, which is the capital and seat of government, and Salt Cay, with a population of about 200. According to local legend, these islands were named by early settlers who thought the scarlet blossoms on the local cactus resembled the Turkish fez.

Approximately 22 miles west of Grand Turk, across the 7,000-foot-deep Christopher Columbus Passage, is the Caicos group, which includes South, East, West, Middle, and North Caicos and Providenciales (nicknamed Provo). South Caicos, Middle Caicos, North Caicos, and Providenciales are the only inhabited islands in this group; Pine Cay and Parrot Cay are the only inhabited cays. "Caicos" is derived from *cayos*, the Spanish word for cay, and is believed to mean "string of islands."

These islands are one of the few places in the Caribbean where visitors can still experience a small-town ambience along with their sun, sea, and sand, but, alas, small town does not mean low prices. There are no fast-food restaurants or budget motel franchises on Turks and Caicos, and the hefty importation tax is reflected in everything from orange juice to room rates. Island-hopping among the Turks and Caicos is relatively expensive: a $30 round-trip on the ferry, plus taxi hire once you get there. Generally, these islands are best traveled by tourists who can pay at least $$ prices. Nevertheless, the recent introduction of major airlines and hotels has given rise to affordable niches. (Provo, for instance, now claims a bed-and-breakfast that charges $65 for up to two people.) Cost-conscious travelers willing to ferret out the smattering of affordable restaurants and rooms will find the islands accessible.

With an eye toward tourism dollars to create jobs and increase the standard of living, the government has devised a long-term development plan to improve the Turks' and Caicos' visibility in the Caribbean tourism market. Mass-tourism on the scale of some other island destinations, however, is not in the cards; government guidelines promote a "quality, not quantity" policy towards visitors, including conservation awareness and firm restrictions on building heights and casino construction.

What It Will Cost These sample prices, meant only as a general guide, are for high season. A $$ small inn or hotel within walking distance of the beach is $125–$150 a night. Dinner at a $$ restaurant costs about $25; it's $10 or less at a ¢ spot. A rum punch is about $4 at a restaurant; a glass of wine averages $3.25, and a beer, about $2.50. Car rental is about $40 a day. A bus into town from most hotels on Providenciales runs $2–$4 one-way. A new public bus system on Grand Turk charges 50¢ one-way to any scheduled stop. Single-tank dives cost $30–$35; snorkel equipment rents for $7–$15 a day.

Before You Go

Tourist Information The **Turks and Caicos Islands Tourist Board** has a toll-free number on the islands (tel. 800/241–0824). **The Caribbean Tourism Organization** (20 E. 46th St., New York, NY 10017, tel. 212/682–0435) is another reliable source of information. In the United Kingdom, contact **Morris-Kevan International Ltd.** (International House, 47 Chase Side, Enfield, Middlesex EN2 6NB, tel. 0181/367–5175).

Arriving and Departing
By Plane **American Airlines** (tel. 800/433–7300) flies daily between Miami and Provo. **Turks & Caicos Islands Airlines** (tel. 800/845–2161 or 809/94–64255) flies nonstop several days a week from Miami to both Provo and Grand Turk. It also serves Provo from Nassau four days a week. Both **Turks & Caicos Islands Airlines** and **InterIsland Airways** (tel. 809/94–15481) provide regularly scheduled service between Provo and Grand Turk.

From the Airport Taxis are available at the airports; expect to share a ride. Rates are fixed. A trip between Provo's airport and most major hotels is about $15. On Grand Turk, a cab from the airport to town is about $5; to hotels outside town, $6–$11. **Executive Tours** (tel. 809/94–64524, fax 809/94–15391) offers shuttle service on Provo between town and 11 key hotels and destinations for between $2 and $4. On Grand Turk, some hotels will arrange a pickup at the time you make reservations.

Passports and Visas U.S. citizens need some proof of citizenship, such as a birth certificate, plus a photo ID or a current passport. British subjects require a current passport. All visitors must have an ongoing or return ticket.

Language The official language of the Turks and Caicos is English.

Precautions Petty crime does occur here, and you're advised to leave your valuables in the hotel safe-deposit box. During the rainy season bring along a can of insect repellent: The mosquitoes can be vicious.

If you plan to explore the uninhabited island of West Caicos, be advised that the interior is overgrown with dense shrubs that include manchineel, which has a milky, poisonous sap that can cause painful, scarring blisters.

In some hotels on Grand Turk, Salt Cay, and South Caicos, there are signs that read, "Please help us conserve our precious water." These islands have no freshwater supply other than rainwater collected in cisterns, and rainfall is scant. Drink only from the decanter of fresh water your hotel provides; tap water is safe for brushing your teeth or other hygiene uses.

Staying in Turks and Caicos Islands

Important Addresses **Tourist Information:** The **Government Tourist Office** (Front St., Cockburn Town, Grand Turk, tel. 809/94–62321; and Turtle Cove Landing, Provo, tel. 809/94–64970) is open Monday–Thursday 8–4:30, Friday 8–5.

Emergencies **Police:** Grand Turk, tel. 809/94–62299; Providenciales, tel. 809/94–64259; North Caicos, tel. 809/94–67116; South Caicos, tel. 809/94–63299. **Hospitals:** There is a 24-hour emergency room at **Grand Turk Hospital** (Hospital Rd., tel. 809/94–62333) and the **Providenciales Health-Medical Center** (Leeward Hwy. and Airport Rd., tel. 809/94–64201). **Pharmacies:** Prescriptions can be filled at the **Government Clinic** (Grand Turk Hospital, tel. 809/94–62040) and in Provo, at the **Providenciales Health-Medical Center** (Leeward Hwy. and Airport Rd., tel. 809/94–64201).

Currency The unit of currency is U.S. dollars.

Taxes and Service Charges Hotels collect a 7%–8% government tax and add a 10%–15% service charge to your bill. In a restaurant, a tip of 10%–15% is appropriate; some establishments add it to your bill, so check carefully. Taxi drivers expect a small tip. There is no sales tax. The departure tax is $15.

Getting Around If you're more interested in swimming and diving than in exploring, you'll find that a cab to and from the airport is probably the only transportation you need. Major hotels are within walking distance of a beach, and others offer shuttle service. However, ¢ restaurants and other attractions on Provo are about a $10 taxi trip from most hotels, making a scooter or rental car advisable if you're not taking a meal plan at your hotel.

Taxis Taxis are unmetered, and rates, posted in the taxis, are regulated by the government. A trip between Provo's airport and most major hotels runs $15. On Grand Turk, a trip from the airport to town is about $5; from the airport to hotels outside town, $6–$11.

Ferries **Caicos Express** (tel. 809/94–67111) offers two scheduled interisland ferries between Provo, Pine Cay, Middle Caicos, Parrot Cay, and North Caicos daily except Sunday. Tickets cost $15 each way. Caicos Express also offers various guided tours to the outer islands (*see* Guided Tours, *below*).

Rental Cars On Provo, **Turks & Caicos National** (809/94–64701) offers the lowest rates. On Grand Turk, try **Dutchie's Car Rental** (tel. 809/94–62244). Rates average $40–$50 per day.

Scooters Scooters are available at the **Honda Shop** (tel. 809/94–64397) and **Scooter Rental** (tel. 809/94–64684) for $25 per 24-hour day.

Buses A bus into town from most hotels on Providenciales runs $2 one-way. A new public bus system on Grand Turk charges 50¢ one-way to any scheduled stop.

Telephones and Mail You can call the islands direct from the United States by dialing 809 and the number. To call home from Turks and Caicos, dial direct from most hotels, from some pay phones, and from **Cable and Wireless,** which has offices in Provo (tel. 809/94–64499) and Grand Turk (tel. 809/94–62200), open Monday–Thursday 8–4:30 and Friday 8–4. You must dial 0, followed by the country code (1 for the United States and Canada; 44 for the United Kingdom), area code, and local number. To make local calls from public phones, you must purchase debit cards. Available in increments of $5, $10, and $20, these are inserted into phones like credit cards.

Postal rates for letters to the United States, Bahamas, and the Caribbean are 50¢ per half-ounce; postcards, 35¢. Letters to the United Kingdom and Europe, 65¢ per half-ounce; postcards, 45¢. Letters to Canada, Puerto Rico, and South America, 65¢; postcards, 45¢.

Opening and Closing Times Most offices are open weekdays from 8 or 8:30 till 4 or 4:30. Banks are open Monday–Thursday 8:30–2:30, Friday 8:30–12:30 and 2:30–4:30.

Guided Tours The cheapest and easiest way to see Provo is by bus. **Executive Tours** (tel. 809/94–64524) and **Turtle Tours** (tel. 809/94–65585) offer bus tours for $10 a person that take in all major sights and include a stop for drinks. Make reservations at least one day in advance. Although a bus tour is cheaper if you're traveling solo, the $25 it costs for an hour's tour by taxi (you can see the main sights of Providenciales in an hour) can be split by four or five passengers. If you do travel by cab, note that a full tour of the Conch Farm can take an hour, so you should go there last. Contact **Paradise Taxi Company** (tel. 809/94–13555). There are no bus tours on Grand Turk, but a one-hour taxi tour is sufficient to see the island. Cost is $30 ($25 for each additional hour) for up to four people. Another good way to see the island is by bicycle (*see* Sports and the Outdoors, *below*).

If you'd like to tour any of the other islands, you'll find it's cheaper to go with an organized tour than to try to do it on your own. You can take a ferry to Pine Cay, Parrot Cay, or North Caicos, but you'll need to hire a cab to get to the main attractions and beaches. **Caicos Express** (tel. 809/94–67111) offers various tours to and around these islands. Round-trip ferry passage to Middle Caicos, a two-hour cavern tour, land transportation, and swimming at Mudjian Harbour costs $76 per person—less than round-trip airfare alone would be, and a lot less hassle than going by yourself. A tour of North Caicos for $85 a person begins with a ferry tour of the Caicos Cays, followed by either a guided tour of North Caicos or a rental car to explore on your own, lunch at the island's leading hotel, and a guided tour of the Caribbean king crab farm. For $60 a person, Caicos Express's *Express Island Hopper* departs Turtle Cove Yacht Club for a six-hour boat run down the beaches of Provo, Pine, and Big Water Cays, a stop to feed the wild iguanas at Little Water Cay, a viewing of the submerged cannons off Ft. George's Cay National Park, shelling and swimming at Dellis Cay, and lunch with rum punch or soda.

Exploring Turks and Caicos Islands

Numbers in the margin correspond to points of interest on the Turks and Caicos Islands map.

Grand Turk Horses and cattle wander around as if they owned the place, and the occasional donkey cart clatters by, carrying a load of water or freight. Front Street, the main drag, lazes along the western side of
1 the island and eases through **Cockburn Town,** the colony's capital and seat of government. Buildings in the capital reflect the 19th-century Bermudian style of architecture, and the narrow streets are lined with low stone walls and old street lamps, now powered by electricity.

The **Turks & Caicos National Museum** opened in 1993 in the restored Guinep House. One of the oldest native stone buildings in the islands, the museum now houses the Molasses Reef wreck of 1513, the

Turks and Caicos Islands

Mary Cays
Caicos Passage
Parrot Cay
Fort George Cay
Pine Cay
Big Water Cay
Little Water Cay
North Caicos
Spanish Point
Highas Cay
Juniper Hole
Providenciales
Middle
South Bluff
Jubber Point
Northwest Point
Ocean Hole
Vine Point
West Caicos
CAICOS ISLA
Southwest Point
CAICOS BANK
N
0 14 miles
0 21 km
White Cay

Exploring
Balfour Town, **2**
Cockburn Harbour, **3**
Cockburn Town, **1**
Conch Bar Caves, **5**
East Caicos, **4**
Flamingo Pond, **6**
Kew, **7**
Providenciales, **9**
Sandy Point, **8**

Dining
Banana Boat, **21**
Caicos Café, **22**
Dora's, **11**
Hey, José, **13**
Hong Kong Restaurant, **14**
Jimmy's Dinner House & Bar, **15**
The Poop Deck, **27**
Pub on the Bay, **23**
Regal Begal, **30**
Salt Raker Inn, **28**
Sandpiper, **29**
Sharney's Restaurant and Bar, **12**
Top O'The Cove Gourmet Delicatessen, **10**
Turk's Head Inn, **35**
The Water's Edge, **32**

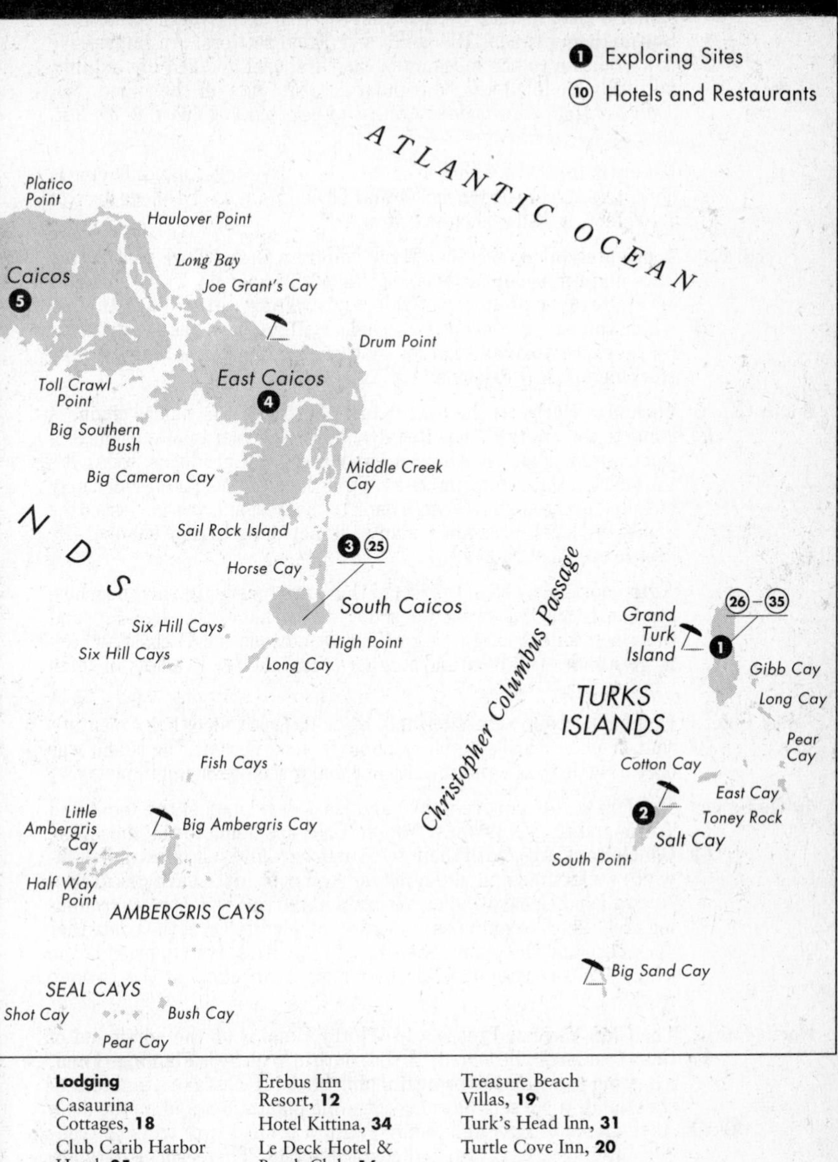

Lodging
Casaurina Cottages, **18**
Club Carib Harbor Hotel, **25**
Club Vacanze Prospect of Whitby Hotel, **24**
Coral Reef Resort, **26**
Erebus Inn Resort, **12**
Hotel Kittina, **34**
Le Deck Hotel & Beach Club, **16**
Louise Fletcher's, **17**
Ocean View Hotel, **33**
Salt Raker Inn, **28**
Treasure Beach Villas, **19**
Turk's Head Inn, **31**
Turtle Cove Inn, **20**

earliest shipwreck discovered in the Americas, and natural history exhibits that include artifacts left by African, North American, Bermudian, French, Hispanic, and Taino settlers. An impressive new addition to the museum is the coral reef and sea life exhibit, faithfully modeled after a popular dive site just off the island. *Tel. 809/94–62160. Admission: $5. Open weekdays 9–4 (Wed. 9–6), Sat. 10–1.*

Fewer than 4,000 people live on this 7½-square-mile island. Diving is definitely the big deal here. Grand Turk's Wall, with a sheer drop to 7,000 feet, is well known to divers.

Salt Cay A privately hired boat can ferry you from Grand Turk to this tiny 2½-square-mile dot that's home to about 200 people. The island was once a leading producer of salt, and visitors can still see the old
2 windmills, salt sheds, and salt ponds. **Balfour Town** has a few restaurants where you can stop for lunch and a drink, and a few stores stocking picnic provisions.

South Caicos **Cockburn Harbour,** the best natural harbor in the Caicos chain, is
3 home to the South Caicos Regatta, held each year in May. This 8½-square-mile island was once an important salt producer; today it's the heart of the fishing industry. Spiny lobster and queen conch may be found in the shallow Caicos bank to the west and are harvested for export by local processing plants. Bonefishing here is some of the best in the West Indies.

At the northern end of the island there are fine white-sand beaches; the south coast is great for scuba diving along the drop-off; and there's excellent snorkeling off the windward (east) coast, where large stands of elkhorn and staghorn coral shelter a variety of small tropical fish.

East Caicos Uninhabited and accessible only by boat, **East Caicos** has a magnifi-
4 cent 17-mile beach stretching along its north coast. The island was once a cattle range and the site of a major sisal-growing industry.

Middle Caicos The largest (48 square miles) and least-developed of the inhabited Turks and Caicos Islands, Middle Caicos is home to the limestone
5 **Conch Bar Caves,** with their eerie underground salt lakes and milk-white stalactites and stalagmites. Archaeologists have discovered Arawak and Lucayo Indian artifacts in the caves and the surrounding area. Since telephones are a rare commodity here, the boats that dock here and the planes that land on the little airstrip provide the island's 270 residents with their main connection to the outside world.

North Caicos The **Club Vacanze Prospect of Whitby Hotel** is on the north end of
6 this 41-square-mile island. To the south of Whitby is **Flamingo Pond,** a nesting place for the beautiful pink birds. If you take a taxi tour of the island, you'll see the ruins of the old plantations and, in the little
7 8 settlements of **Kew** and **Sandy Point,** a profusion of tropical trees bearing limes, papayas, and custard apples. The beaches here are superb for shelling and lolling, and the waters offshore offer excellent snorkeling, scuba diving, and fishing.

Providenciales In the mid-18th century, so the story goes, a French ship was wrecked near here and the survivors were washed ashore on an island they gratefully christened La Providentielle. Under the Span-
9 ish, the name was changed to **Providenciales.**

Provo's 44 square miles are by far the most developed in the Turks and Caicos. With its rolling ridges and 12-mile beach, the island is a prime target for developers. More than two decades ago, a group of U.S. investors, including the DuPonts, Ludingtons, and Roosevelts, opened up this island for visitors and those seeking homesites in the Caribbean. In 1990 the island's first luxury resort, the **Ramada Turquoise Reef Resort & Casino,** opened, and with it, the island's first gourmet Italian restaurant. The luxurious **Ocean Club,** a condominium resort at Grace Bay, was also completed in 1990, and was followed by the upscale **Grace Bay Club** resort in 1992. The competition created by the new resorts spurred many of the older hotels to undertake much-needed renovations. About 8,000 people live on Provo, a considerable number of whom are expatriate U.S. and Canadian businesspeople and retirees.

Provo is home to the **Island Sea Center** (on the northeast coast, tel. 809/94–65330), where you can learn about the sea and its inhabitants. Here you'll find the **Caicos Conch Farm** (tel. 809/94–65849), a major mariculture operation where the mollusks are farmed commercially. The farm's tourist facilities include a video show, boutique, and a "hands-on" tank. A geodesic dome, housing natural history exhibits, was severely damaged in a 1993 fire but is slated to reopen by late 1995. Established by the PRIDE Foundation (Protection of Reefs and Islands from Degradation and Exploitation), the **JoJo Dolphin Project,** named after a 7-foot male bottlenose dolphin who cruises these waters and enjoys playing with local divers, is also here. You can watch a video on JoJo and learn how to interact with him safely if you see him on one of your dives.

Beaches

There are more than 230 miles of beaches in the Turks and Caicos Islands, ranging from secluded coves to miles-long stretches. Most beaches are soft coralline sand. Tiny uninhabited cays offer complete isolation for nude sunbathing and skinny-dipping. Many are accessible only by boat. All hotels in Provo and Grand Turk are within walking distance of a beach.

Big Ambergris Cay, an uninhabited cay about 14 miles beyond the Fish Cays, has a magnificent beach at **Long Bay.**

East Caicos, an uninhabited island accessible only by boat, has a beautiful 17-mile beach along its north coast.

Governor's Beach, a long white strip on the west coast of **Grand Turk,** is one of the nicest beaches on this island.

The north and east coasts of **North Caicos** are bordered by great beaches for swimming, scuba diving, snorkeling, and fishing.

Pine Cay, a private upscale retreat, has a 2½-mile strip of beach—the most beautiful in the archipelago.

A fine white-sand beach stretches 12 miles along the northeast coast of **Providenciales.** Other splendid beaches are at **Sapadilla Bay** and rounding the tip of the northwest point of the island.

There are superb beaches on the north coast of **Salt Cay,** as well as at **Big Sand Cay** 7 miles to the south.

Only in **South Caicos** are the beaches small and unremarkable, but the vibrant reef makes it a popular destination for divers.

Sports and the Outdoors

Bicycling Much of Provo is steep, and the many unpaved roads kick up clouds of dust with each passing motorist (there aren't many). Still, there is very little on the island that can't be seen by bike, and it's an inexpensive way to explore. Bikes can be rented at the **Island Princess** hotel at the Bight (tel. 809/94–64260) for $10 per day, through **Turtle Inn Divers** (Turtle Cove Inn, tel.809/94–15389) for $12 a day and $60 a week, or at the **Ramada Turquoise Reef Resort & Casino** (Grace Bay, tel. 809/94–65555) for $14 a day. In Grand Turk, both the **Salt Raker Inn** (Duke St., tel. 809/94–62260) and the **Hotel Kittina** (tel. 809/94–62232) rent bikes for $10 per day, $40 per week.

Boating **Dive Provo** (Ramada Turquoise Reef Resort, Provo, tel. 809/94–65040) rents single-seater kayaks for $10 an hour and two-seaters for $15 an hour. They also rent laser sailboats for $20 an hour and provide beginner instruction for the sailboats for $40 (up to two hours).

Golf A 6,529-yard golf course opened on Providenciales in late 1991. **Provo Golf Club** (tel. 809/94–695991) is an 18-hole, par-72 championship course designed by Karl Litten that is sustained by a desalination plant that produces 250,000 gallons of water a day. The turf is sprinkled in green islands over 12 acres of natural limestone outcroppings, creating a desert-style design of narrow "target areas" and sandy waste areas—a formidable challenge to anyone playing from the championship tees. Fees are $65 plus $15 for a mandatory electric cart. A pro shop, driving ranges, and a restaurant and bar round out the club's facilities.

Scuba Diving Diving is the top attraction here. (All divers must carry and present a valid certificate card.) These islands are surrounded by a reef system of more than 200 square miles—much of it unexplored. Grand Turk's famed wall drops more than 7,000 feet and is one side of a 22-mile-wide channel called the Christopher Columbus Passage. From January through March, an estimated 6,000 eastern Atlantic humpback whales swim through this passage en route to their winter breeding grounds. There are undersea cathedrals, coral gardens, and countless tunnels. Among the operations that provide instruction, equipment rentals, underwater video equipment, and trips are **Sea Eye Divers** (Grand Turk, tel. 809/94–61407), **Blue Water Divers** (Salt Raker Inn, Grand Turk, tel. 809/94–62432), **Off the Wall Divers** (Grand Turk, tel. 809/94–62159 or 809/94–62517), **Dive Provo** (Ramada Turquoise Reef Resort, Provo, tel. 809/94–65040), **Flamingo Divers** (Provo, tel. 809/94–64193), **Provo Turtle Divers** (Provo, tel. 809/94–64232 or 800/328–5285), and **Porpoise Divers** (Salt Cay, tel. 809/94–66927). Single-tank dives cost $30–$35, two-tank dives average $60, and night dives run about $40. Scuba gear rental costs about $15 when you book a boat dive.

Note: A modern hyperbaric decompression chamber is located on Provo (tel. 809/94–64242) in the **Menzies Medical Centre** on Leeward Highway. Divers in need on Grand Turk are airlifted to Provo—a 30-minute flight.

Sea Excursions The ***Ocean Outback*** (tel. 809/94–64080), a 70-foot motor cruiser, does barbecue-and-snorkel cruises to uninhabited islands. Both the 37-foot catamaran ***Beluga*** (tel. 809/94–15196, $39 per half day) and the 56-foot trimaran ***Tao*** (tel. 809/94–65040) run sunset cruises, as well as sailing and snorkeling outings. A full-day outing on the *Tao* is $59 per person, including snorkel rental and lunch. For $20 per person, **Dive Provo** (Ramada Turquoise Reef Resort, tel. 809/94–65040 or 800/234–7768) gives two-hour glass-bottom-boat tours of the spectacular reefs. **Turtle Inn Divers** (Turtle Cove Inn, tel. 809/94–15389) offers full-day Sunday excursions for divers for $64.50 per person ($25 per person for nondivers and snorkelers). The ***Turks and Caicos Aggressor*** (tel. 504/385–2628 or 800/348–2628, fax 504/384–0817) offers luxury six-day dive cruises with full accommodations.

Snorkeling **Dive Provo** (Provo, tel. 809/94–65040), **Blue Water Divers** (tel. 809/94–62432), **Sea Eye Divers** (Grand Turk, tel. 809/94–61407), **Provo Turtle Divers** (Provo, tel. 809/94–64232), and **Flamingo Divers** (Provo, tel. 809/94–64193) offer snorkeling, boat trips, and equipment rentals. Boat trips cost $25–$35 and include all snorkel gear. Gear rental alone costs $7–$10.

Tennis There are two lighted courts at **Turtle Cove Inn** (Provo, tel. 809/94–64203), eight courts (four lighted) at **Club Med Turkoise** (Provo, tel. 809/94–65500), two lighted courts at the **Erebus Inn** (Provo, tel. 809/94–64240), and two courts at the **Ramada Turquoise Reef Resort**

(Provo, tel. 809/94–65555). Guests at all of the resorts play free. Nonguests can play at the Erebus Inn for $10 an hour (day), $20 an hour (evening). Club Med Turkoise has a half-day tennis package for nonguests for $50.

Waterskiing Water-skiers will find the calm turquoise water ideal for long-distance runs. **Dive Provo** (Ramada Turquoise Reef Resort, Provo, tel. 809/94–65040) charges $35 for a 15-minute run.

Windsurfing Rental and instruction are available at the **Club Vacanze Prospect of Whitby Hotel** (North Caicos, tel. 800/346–67119) and **Dive Provo** (Ramada Turquoise Reef Resort, Provo, tel. 809/94–65040). The latter offers the Mistral School program for $20 an hour and rents boards for the same price.

Shopping

These are not shop-'til-you-drop islands. The exception to the rule is Provo, where new shops and franchises open every month. Most of these stores can be found in four main shopping complexes: Market Place, Central Square, and Caribbean Place, all on Leeward Highway, and Turtle Cove Landing, in Turtle Cove. The only craft items native to the Turks and Caicos are the beautiful baskets woven from the indigenous top plant; these are sold at the airport.

The **Bamboo Gallery** (Market Place, Provo, tel. 809/94–064748) sells all types of Caribbean art, from vivid Haitian paintings to wood carvings. **Greensleeves** (Central Square, Provo, tel. 809/94–64147) is the place to go for paintings by local artists, island-made rag rugs, baskets, jewelry, and sisal mats and bags. **Local Color** (Governor's Rd., Grace Bay, Provo, no phone) sells art and sculpture made by local artists as well as native basketry, hand-painted tropical clothing, tie-dyed pareus, and silk-screened T-shirts. On the ground floor of **Pelican's Pouch/Designer I** (Turtle Cove Landing, Provo, tel. 809/94–64343), you'll find resortwear, sandals, Provo T-shirts, perfumes, and gold jewelry; head upstairs for basketry, sculpture, and watercolors. **Paradise Gifts/Arts** (Central Square, Provo, tel. 809/94–64637) has a ceramics studio on the premises; in addition to ceramics, jewelry, T-shirts, and paintings by local artists are sold here. **Royal Jewels** (Leeward Highway, Provo, tel.809/94–64885; Ramada Turquoise Reef Resort, Provo, tel. 809/94–65311; Airport, Provo, tel. 809/94–65311) sells gold and jewelry, designer watches, and perfumes, all at significant savings.

Dining

Like everything else on these islands, dining out is a laid-back affair, which is not to say that it is cheap. Because of the high cost of importing all edibles, the cost of a meal is usually higher than that of a comparable meal in the United States. The most reasonably priced dishes are usually the local conch and the catch of the day. Reservations are not required, and dress is casual.

As recently as seven years ago, grocery shopping was limited to what the twin-engine plane delivered from Miami once a week. Today, however, Provo's grocery stores, **Island Pride Supermarket** (Butterfield Sq.) and nearby **BWI Trading** offer such delicacies as fresh arugula. Prices reflect the ubiquitous import tax, but as high as they seem, they remain the budget alternative to eating out. Gourmet items and whole-bean coffee ground to order are available at **Top O' the Cove** on Leeward Highway. On Grand Turk, get groceries at **Sarah's Shopping Centre** (Frith St.).

Highly recommended restaurants are indicated by a star ★.

Category	Cost*
$$	$15–$25
$	$10–$15
¢	under $10

**per person, excluding drinks, service, and 7% sales tax*

Grand Turk

$$ **Salt Raker Inn.** Starters at this rustic, informal patio restaurant include tomato and mozzarella salad and melon with ginger. Lobster in cream and sherry sauce, barbecued steak, and seafood curry are oft-ordered entrées. For dessert, try the tasty apple pie. The Sunday dinner and sing-along is popular. *Salt Raker Inn, tel. 809/94–62260. AE, D, MC, V.*

$–$$ **Sandpiper.** Candles flicker on the Sandpiper's terrace beside a flower-filled courtyard. Blackboard specialties may include pork chops with applesauce, lobster, filet mignon, or seafood platter. *Hotel Kittina, tel. 809/94–62232. AE, D, MC, V.*

$–$$ **Turk's Head Inn.** The menu changes daily at this lively restaurant, touted by many residents as the best on the island. Some staples include escargot, pâté, and a handful of other delectables, including local grouper fingers perfectly fried for fish and chips. Look for lobster, quiche, steaks, and homemade soups on the blackboard menu. You may not want to leave after your meal—come nightfall, the inn's bar is abuzz with local gossip and mirthful chatter. *Turk's Head Inn, Duke St., tel. 809/94–62466. AE, MC, V.*

$ **The Water's Edge.** Relaxed waterfront dining awaits you at this pleasantly rustic eatery. The limited menu covers the basics with a twist—from barbecued grouper to a fresh seafood crepe. A children's menu is also available. The food is authentic and filling, and the view at sunset breathtaking, but the irresistible homemade pies are enough to justify a visit. *Duke St., tel. 809/94–61680. MC, V. Closed Mon.*

¢ **The Poop Deck.** Known for its savory island fare, this restaurant serves conch in a variety of guises. The 25 seats fill up fast with locals and expats who come for the spicy island-fried chicken. Dinners cost $7–$10, and come with rice or potato and a salad. *Front St., no phone. No credit cards.*

¢ **Regal Beagle.** Drop by this popular local eatery for native specialties such as cracked conch, minced lobster, and fish-and-chips. The atmosphere is casual and the decor unmemorable, but the portions are large and the prices easy on your wallet. *Hospital Rd., tel. 809/94–62274. No credit cards.*

Providenciales

¢–$$ ★ **Dora's.** At this popular local eatery, they serve up island fare—turtle, shredded lobster, spicy conch chowder—seven days a week, from 7 AM until the last person leaves the bar. Plastic print and lace tablecloths, hanging plants, and Haitian art add to the island ambience. Soups ($4) come with homemade bread, and entrées such as fish-and-chips, conch Creole, and grilled pork chops come with a choice of vegetable. Be sure to come early for the packed Monday- and Thursday-night all-you-can-eat $20 seafood buffet. The price includes round-trip transportation to your hotel. *Leeward Hwy., tel. 809/94–64558. No credit cards.*

¢–$$ ★ **Sharney's Restaurant and Bar.** Although most of the prices at this restaurant in the Erebus Inn are in our $$ range, you can enjoy a less expensive lunch or dinner here by ordering from the abbreviated bar menu. Served from 10 to 10, the menu offers gourmet ravioli with fillings that change daily ($6), hamburgers ($7), finger foods, and regional favorites such as conch chowder and conch fritters. You can also order English favorites. The lunch of fish-and-chips ($10) doesn't disappoint: moist chunks of native grouper lightly battered and served with crisply thin, skin-on potatoes. The view from the restaurant is incomparable, and a band provides music on Friday

nights. *Erebus Inn, Turtle Cove Rd., tel. 809/94–64204. AE, D, MC, V.*

$ **Banana Boat.** Buoys and other sea relics deck the walls, and white plastic chairs surround colorful, well-spaced tables, but what this restaurant lacks in elegance it makes up for in hospitality. You could stay here all night, munching on pizza, burgers, and various finger food, then washing down your meal with those famous, tropical, rum-filled cocktails. *Turtle Cove, tel. 809/94–15706. AE, MC, V.*

$ **Caicos Cafe.** Elegant street lanterns line the walkway to this popular restaurant, and there's a pervasive air of celebration in the uncovered outdoor dining area. Choose from a selection of local and American cuisine, including lobster sandwiches, hamburgers, and a variety of excellent salads. *Across from the Ramada, tel. 809/94–65278. No credit cards.*

$ ★ **Hey, José.** This restaurant claims to serve the island's best margaritas. Customers also return for the tasty Tex-Mex treats: tacos, tostados, nachos, burritos, fajitas, and José's special-recipe hot chicken wings. Creative types can build their own pizzas. *Central Square, tel. 809/94–64812. AE, MC, V. Closed Sun.*

$ **Pub on the Bay.** If beachfront dining is what you're after, it doesn't get much better than this. Located in the Blue Hill residential district, a five-minute drive from downtown Provo, this restaurant serves fried or steamed fish, chicken and pork, various sandwiches, calamari, fried zucchini, and even turtle steak. There is no air-conditioning inside the restaurant, so you may as well cross the street to one of three thatched roof "huts," which stand quite literally on the beach. *Blue Hill Rd., tel. 809/94–14309. AE, MC, V.*

$ **Top O' the Cove Gourmet Delicatessen.** You can easily walk to this tiny café on Leeward Highway from the Turtle Cove and Erebus Inns. Don't be put off by the location in the Napa Auto Parts plaza—the restaurant's interior is not at all garagelike! You can order breakfast, deli subs, sandwiches, or salads to go or have a seat at a bistro table topped with a colorful tropical cloth. This is one of the few places on the island that serves a potable cup of coffee, as well as genuine espresso and frothy cappuccino—and it's open every day (except Christmas and New Year's) from 7 AM to 3:30 PM. *Leeward Hwy., tel. 809/94–64694. No credit cards.*

¢–$ **Hong Kong Restaurant.** A no-frills place with plain wood tables and chairs, the Hong Kong offers dine-in, delivery, or takeout. The menu includes lobster with ginger and green onions, chicken with black-bean sauce, sliced duck with salted mustard greens, and sweet-and-sour chicken. Peking duck is a house specialty. *Leeward Hwy., tel. 809/94–65678. AE, MC, V. No lunch Sun.*

¢ **Jimmy's Dinner House & Bar.** Locals favor this spot, filling the polished oak chairs around tables covered with red-checked cloths. The menu includes pizza, pasta, ribs, and steaks. Early bird specials, served 5:30–7:30 PM for $9.95, include panfried grouper, charbroiled sirloin steak, and a hot beef sandwich served with salad. *At Turtle Cove, tel. 809/94–15575. AE, MC, V. No lunch.*

Lodging

In general, Provo hotels and inns are a bit more expensive than those on Grand Turk, Middle Caicos, or South Caicos. North Caicos and Salt Cay both tend to have either inexpensive guest houses or expensive hideaway resorts, with few or no moderately priced inns. Although we do list a couple of properties on the out islands, most affordable lodging is located on Provo or Grand Turk. Rustic places on the more remote islands are rustic indeed, and in most cases we do not recommend them.

Affordable accommodations here range from renovated properties with charm, air-conditioning, and modern amenities to basic digs with simple furnishings and few extras. Most budget inns and guest houses are not on the beach, although those on Provo and Grand Turk are usually within walking distance or are a short bus ride away. These cheaper properties generally do not have a restaurant or meal plans. On Provo, where inexpensive restaurants are usually off the beaten track, you will need to rent a car to get to your meals, or consider staying at a more expensive hotel and taking a meal plan. If you're staying in town on Grand Turk, you'll be within walking distance of several inexpensive restaurants.

If you're a diver, you can save money by taking advantage of one of the many packages offered by properties here. These provide considerable savings, so inquire when you call.

Highly recommended lodgings are indicated by a star ★.

Category	Cost*
$$	$110–$140
$	$95–$110
¢	under $95

**All prices are for a standard double room for two, excluding 7% tax and a 10% service charge. To estimate rates for hotels offering MAP, add $30–$45 per person per day to the above price ranges.*

Grand Turk

$$ ★ **Hotel Kittina.** This family-owned hostelry, the largest hotel on Grand Turk, is split in two by the town's main drag. On one side, comfortable, lodge-style rooms and sleek balconied suites with kitchens sit on a gleaming white sand beach. Across the street, the older main house holds a lively dining room and rooms that ooze island atmosphere. Behind the house are the pool and garden. Tile floors and air-conditioning were added to all of the rooms and suites in 1994. Be sure to catch the occasional Friday-night poolside barbecue. *Duke St., Box 42, tel. 809/94–62232 or 800/548–8462, fax 809/94–62877. 43 rooms and 2 suites. Facilities: 2 restaurants, 2 bars, pool, boutique, Omega Dive Shop, T&C Travel Agency, scooter and bicycle rentals, windsurfing, baby-sitting, room service, boat rentals. AE, MC, V. EP, MAP.*

$ ★ **Coral Reef Resort.** One- and two-bedroom units here have complete kitchens, air-conditioning, and contemporary furnishings. The resort is a short drive from town, and the beach is a few steps from your door. *Box 10, Grand Turk, tel. 809/94–62055 or 800/243–4954, fax 809/94–62911. 18 rooms. Facilities: restaurant, bar, lighted tennis court, pool, boutique, mini-fitness center, water sports arranged with dive operations. AE, MC, V. EP, MAP.*

$ **Ocean View Hotel.** A white picket fence, slightly worn wood and rattan furniture, and hand-stencilled walls and doors give this popular hotel a home-sweet-home atmosphere. Guest rooms are individually decorated and have cool tile floors and clean white walls. Hearty homemade meals are served in the breezy dining area, and the lively bars stay open until midnight or until the last person goes home (whichever comes later). The beach is right across the street. *Box 97, tel. 809/94–62517. 14 rooms and 3 suites. Facilities: restaurant, 2 bars, bicycle rentals, horseback riding, dive packages with Sea Eye Diving and Omega Diving. AE, D, MC, V. MAP.*

$ **Salt Raker Inn.** Across the street from the beach, this galleried house was the home of a Bermudian shipwright 180 years ago. The rooms and suites are not elegant, but are individually decorated and have a homey atmosphere; each has a minifridge. The three garden rooms are desirable for their screened porches and ocean views. *Duke St., Box 1, Grand Turk, tel. 809/94–62260, fax 809/94–62817. In U.K., 44 Birchington Rd., London NW6 4LJ, tel. 0171/328–6474. 10 rooms, 2 suites. Facilities: restaurant, bar, dive packages with Blue Water Diving. AE, D, MC, V. EP.*

$ **Turks Head Inn.** Built in 1850 by a prosperous salt miner, this classic Bermudian building has had incarnations as the American consulate and as the governor's guest house (the Queen reportedly took a room here on her last visit to the island). Now run by a Frenchman known as Mr. X, the inn has acquired a strong European flavor. A plethora of Brits and other expat Europeans make it their stomping ground. The seven distinctive rooms are lovingly furnished with antiques and island artifacts, and the owner's own drawings and detailed maps adorn many of the walls. In the front courtyard, an oversized hammock provides the perfect vantage point from which to admire the well-tended garden. The beach is only a few strides away. The bar and restaurant area bustle at night. *Duke St., Box 58, Grand Turk, tel. 809/94–62466, fax 809/94–62825. 6 units. Facilities: restaurant, bar, dive packages. AE, MC, V. CP.*

Providenciales

$$ ★ **Le Deck Hotel & Beach Club.** This 27-room pink hostelry was built in classic Bermudian style around a tropical courtyard that opens onto a tiki hut- and palm tree-dotted beach on Grace Bay. It offers clean rooms with a tile floor, color TV, phone, and air-conditioning. Le Deck is especially popular with divers, and its atmosphere is informal and lively, with a mostly thirtysomething-and-over crowd. *Grace Bay, Box 144, Provo, tel. 809/94–65547 or 800/528–1905, fax 809/94–65770. 25 rooms, 2 suites. Facilities: restaurant, bar, pool, boutique, water sports. AE, D, MC, V. CP, MAP.*

$–$$ ★ **Erebus Inn Resort.** All units in this modest resort have two double beds, modern wicker furnishings, and original island artwork, including some lovely and unique Haitian wall hangings. Rooms in the older chalet cost under $110 a night double occupancy in the winter. For those preferring creature comforts, we recommend the units in the newer section ($$); each has air-conditioning, cable TV, and phone. The hotel sits on a cliff overlooking Turtle Cove and has wonderful views of the marina and the Caribbean beyond. Frequent bus shuttles take gueststo a nearby beach. The restaurant and bar, always one of Provo's liveliest spots, has a menu of French and Caribbean cuisine. Five affordable restaurants are within walking distance, as are a shopping center and several dive operations. *Turtle Cove, Box 238, Provo, tel. 809/94–64240, fax 809/94–64704. 30 rooms. Facilities: restaurant, bar, 2 pools (1 saltwater), fitness center, water aerobics, 2 lighted tennis courts. AE, MC, V. EP, MAP.*

$–$$ **Turtle Cove Inn.** A marina, a free-form pool, a dive shop with equipment rentals and instruction, and lighted tennis courts attract the sporting crowd to Turtle Cove. There's a free boat shuttle to the nearby beach and snorkeling reef. All rooms have a TV, phone, and air-conditioning, and eight also have minifridges. A handful of good restaurants are within walking distance. *Box 131, Provo, tel. 809/94–64203 or 800/887–0477, fax 809/94–64141. 30 rooms, 1 suite. Facilities: 2 restaurants, 2 bars, lounge, game room, 2 lighted tennis courts, pool, marina, 3 dive shops nearby. AE, D, MC, V. EP.*

¢ **Louise Fletcher's.** The ambience at Provo's only bed-and-breakfast is more utilitarian British than quaint New England. With "natural" air-conditioning and a nearby pay phone, this tidy house with beach-towel curtains is not for those bent on luxury, but you will get clean lodging at a cheap price. The property is 200 yards from the beach. The two apartments have separate entrances, and each has a private bath and kitchen. The guest room also has a private bath, and guests there have access to the owner's kitchen. Continental breakfast and the company of the charming Canadian proprietress's dogs and cats are included for the $75-a-day ($495 a week) price for two people. Bicycles are available for rent. *Box 273, Provo, tel. 809/94–65878. 2 apartments, 1 room. Facilities: bicycle rental. No credit cards; personal checks accepted. CP.*

North Caicos

$$ ★ **Club Vacanze Prospect of Whitby Hotel.** Italian resort chain Club Vacanze took over this secluded retreat in 1994. Seven miles of beach are yours for sunbathing, windsurfing, or snorkeling. Spacious

guest rooms have a simple but elegant Mediterranean theme; in true getaway fashion, they lack both TVs and radios. Both the service and the restaurant here are superb. *Kew Post Office, North Caicos, tel. 809/94–67119, fax 809/94–67114. 28 rooms and 4 suites. Facilities: restaurant, bar, pool, 1 tennis court, windsurfing, dive shop, baby-sitting, tour desk. AE, MC, V. EP, MAP.*

South Caicos
$–$$ **Club Caribe Harbor Hotel.** Cockburn Harbour, the only natural harbor in the Turks and Caicos islands, is a prime setting for this hotel. The 17 beachfront villas, which can be rented as studios or as one-, two-, or three-bedroom apartments, have cool tile floors and kitchenettes equipped with minifridge and microwave. Half of the rooms don't have air-conditioning, but they get a nice breeze around the clock. The 24 harbour rooms are smaller than the others but have air-conditioning and wall-to-wall carpeting. There's a dive shop with a full-time instructor. *Box 1, South Caicos, tel. 809/94–63446. 40 rooms. Facilities: restaurant, bar. D, MC, V. EP, MAP.*

Villa and Apartment Rental
Most of the rentals on Turks and Caicos are on Provo, although you can find a few cottage rentals on the out islands. For more information on villa rentals, contact the tourist office (tel. 809/94–62321).

$$ **Casaurina Cottages.** Overlooking the south side of Providenciales are these pleasant one- and two-bedroom apartments. Each has a kitchen, twin beds, a sofa bed in the living room, weekly maid service, cable TV, a phone, and a ceiling fan. The lack of air-conditioning can make them uncomfortable in the summer. Chairs and lounges are provided for use on the adjacent beach or large sun deck. *Provo, tel. 809/94–64687, fax 809/94–64895. 3 units. No credit cards.*

$–$$ **Treasure Beach Villas.** These one- and two-bedroom self-catering apartments have fully equipped kitchens, fans, and Provo's 12 miles of white sandy beach for beachcombing and snorkeling. It's best to have a car or scooter here, but you can take the bus to the nearby grocery store and restaurants. *The Bight, tel. 809/94–64325, fax 809/94–64108. Mailing address: Box 8409, Hialeah, FL 33012. 8 single, 10 double rooms. Facilities: pool, tennis court. AE, D, MC, V. EP.*

Off-Season Bets
Late April to the end of November is off-season here, when hotel rates drop 15%–20%. **Ramada Turquoise Reef Resort & Casino** (Box 205, Provo, tel. 809/94–65555 or 800/228–9898) and the **Club Med Turkoise** (Provo, tel. 809/94–65500 or 800/258–2633) are two upscale resorts that have rooms available in our $$ range.

Nightlife

On Provo, a full band plays native, reggae, and contemporary music on Thursday night at the **Erebus Inn** (tel. 809/94–64240). **Le Deck** (tel. 809/94–65547) offers one-armed bandits every night. A lively lounge can be found at the **Ramada Turquoise Reef Resort** (tel. 809/94–65555), where a musician plays to the mostly tourist crowd. The Ramada is also the location of **Port Royale** (tel. 809/94–65508), the island's only gambling casino. **Bacchus** (opposite the Ramada Turquoise Reef Resort, tel. 809/94–65214) is open Thursday, Friday, and Saturday night for drinks and dancing. **Disco Elite** (Airport Rd., tel. 809/94–64592) has strobe lights and an elevated dance floor. The newest hot spot here is **Casablanca** (next to Club Med, tel. 809/94–65449), a Monte Carlo–style nightclub complete with mirrors and a decked-out crowd. On Grand Turk, Xavier Tonneau (a.k.a. Mr. X) leads sing-alongs in his bar at the **Turk's Head Inn** almost every night (tel. 809/94–62466), and there's music at the **Salt Raker Inn** (tel. 809/94–62260) on Wednesday and Sunday nights. For a lively bar filled with local color, try **Smokey's on the Beach** (near Le Deck hotel, tel. 809/94–13466). Night owls can head over to the **Lady** for dancing (at the former Naval base, no phone) or to the **Rack Room** (Back Salina, tel. 809/94–61802) for music and gaming.

27 The U.S. Virgin Islands

St. Thomas, St. Croix, St. John

Updated by Pamela Acheson and Gail Gillen de Haas

It is the combination of the familiar and the exotic found in the United States Virgin Islands that defines this "American Paradise" and explains much of its appeal. The effort to be all things to all people—while remaining true to the best of itself—has created a sometimes paradoxical blend of island serenity and American practicality in this U.S. territory 1,000 miles from the southern tip of the U.S. mainland.

The postcard images you'd expect from a tropical paradise are here: Stretches of beach arc into the distance, and white sails skim across water so blue and clear it stuns the senses; red-roof houses add their spot of color to the green hillsides' mosaic, along with the orange of the flamboyant tree, the red of the hibiscus, the magenta of the bougainvillea, and the blue stone ruins of old sugar mills. The other part of the equation are all those things that make it so easy and appealing for Americans to visit this cluster of islands. The official language is English, the money is the dollar, and there's cable TV, Pizza Hut, and McDonald's.

Your destination here will be St. Thomas (13 miles long); its neighbor St. John (9 miles long); or, 40 miles to the south, St. Croix (23 miles long). A pro/con thumbnail sketch of these three might have it that St. Thomas is bustling (hustling) and the place for shopping and discos (commercial glitz and overdevelopment); St. Croix is more Danish, picturesque, and rural (more provincial and duller, particularly after dark); and St. John is matchless in the beauty of its National Park Service–protected land and beaches (a one-village island mostly for the rich or for campers). Surely not everything will suit your fancy, but chances are that among the three islands you'll find your own idea of paradise.

With all this diversity, the budget traveler has plenty of options. Amid the glittering, $300-a-night resorts on St. Thomas, you'll find small hotels, bed-and-breakfasts, and condominium rentals. Those staying at campgrounds on St. John, where a bare site on the beach can be had for as little as $15 a night, share the same magnificent parkland and beaches as are enjoyed by guests at luxury resorts. On St. Croix, small inns and less-expensive properties are the rule rather than the exception.

The U.S.V.I. offer other ways to save. Plenty of nonstop flights to St. Thomas, with direct service to St. Croix, mean you won't have the additional cost of an island-hopper flight. (St. John is just a $3 ferry ride from Charlotte Amalie, St. Thomas.) On St. Thomas you can find cheap eats (if you don't mind fast food) and a fairly good bus system that can get you around much of the island.

What It Will Cost These sample prices, meant only as a general guide, are for high season. Expect to pay around $90 a night for a $ hotel. Bed-and-breakfast places can be as low as $55 for two (with shared bath); for a private bath, prices climb to $75–$135 for two. A two-bedroom villa sleeping four rents for $1,500–$3,000 a week. You can pay as little as $15 a night for a tent site on St. John, but it's about $80 for one of the lovely tent-cottages at Maho Bay Camp. On St. Thomas, a ¢ lunch costs about $6; a dinner, about $10. At the West Indian and Latin restaurants on St. Croix and St. John, a filling dinner can be had for $5–$7. Rum punches cost around $3.50; a glass of house wine ranges from $3 to $4.50; a glass of beer, $2.50–$3. Car rental prices on all three islands range from $45 to $55. A taxi ride from Charlotte Amalie to the beach is about $4 a person for two people sharing a cab. A single-tank dive costs about $55 (including all equipment rental) on St. Thomas, a little less on St. Croix and St. John. Snorkel equipment rents for about $10 a day.

Before You Go

Tourist Information Information about the United States Virgin Islands is available through the following **U.S.V.I. Government Tourist Offices** (225 Peachtree St., Suite 760, Atlanta, GA 30303, tel. 404/688–0906, fax 404/525–1102; 500 N. Michigan Ave., Suite 2030, Chicago, IL 60611, tel. 312/670–8784, fax 312/670–8789; 3460 Wilshire Blvd., Suite 412, Los Angeles, CA 90010, tel. 213/739–0138, fax 213/739–2005; 2655 Le Jeune Rd., Suite 907, Coral Gables, FL 33134, tel. 305/442–7200, fax 305/445–9044; 1270 6th Ave., Room 2108, New York, NY 10020, tel. 212/332–2222, fax 212/332–2223; 900 17th Ave. NW, Suite 500, Washington, DC 20006, tel. 202/293–3707, fax 202/785–2542; 1300 Ashford Ave., Condado, Santurce, Puerto Rico 00907, tel. 809/724–3816, fax 809/724–7223; and 2 Cinnamon Row, Plantation Wharf, York Place, London, England SW11 3TW, tel. 0171/978–5262, telex 27231, fax 0171/924–3171).

You can also call the Division of Tourism's toll-free number (tel. 800/878–4463).

Arriving and Departing

By Plane One advantage of visiting the U.S.V.I. is the abundance of nonstop flights that can have you at the beach in a relatively short time (three to four hours from most East Coast departures). You may fly into the U.S.V.I. direct via **Continental** (tel. 800/231–0856), **Delta** (tel. 800/221–1212), or **American** (tel. 800/433–7300), or you may fly via San Juan on all the above plus **American Eagle** (tel. 800/474–4884).

From the Airport On both St. Thomas and St. Croix you will need to take a taxi from the airport to your hotel. Public taxi vans, which line up in front of the airports, charge a flat fee and will often take several people headed in the same direction. On St. Thomas the per-person rate ranges from $3 into Charlotte Amalie to $10 to East End resorts and Red Hook. On St. Croix a taxi for one or two people will cost around $10 to most hotels on the island.

St. John travelers will fly into St. Thomas and take a taxi to either the Charlotte Amalie waterfront (near the Coast Guard dock) or

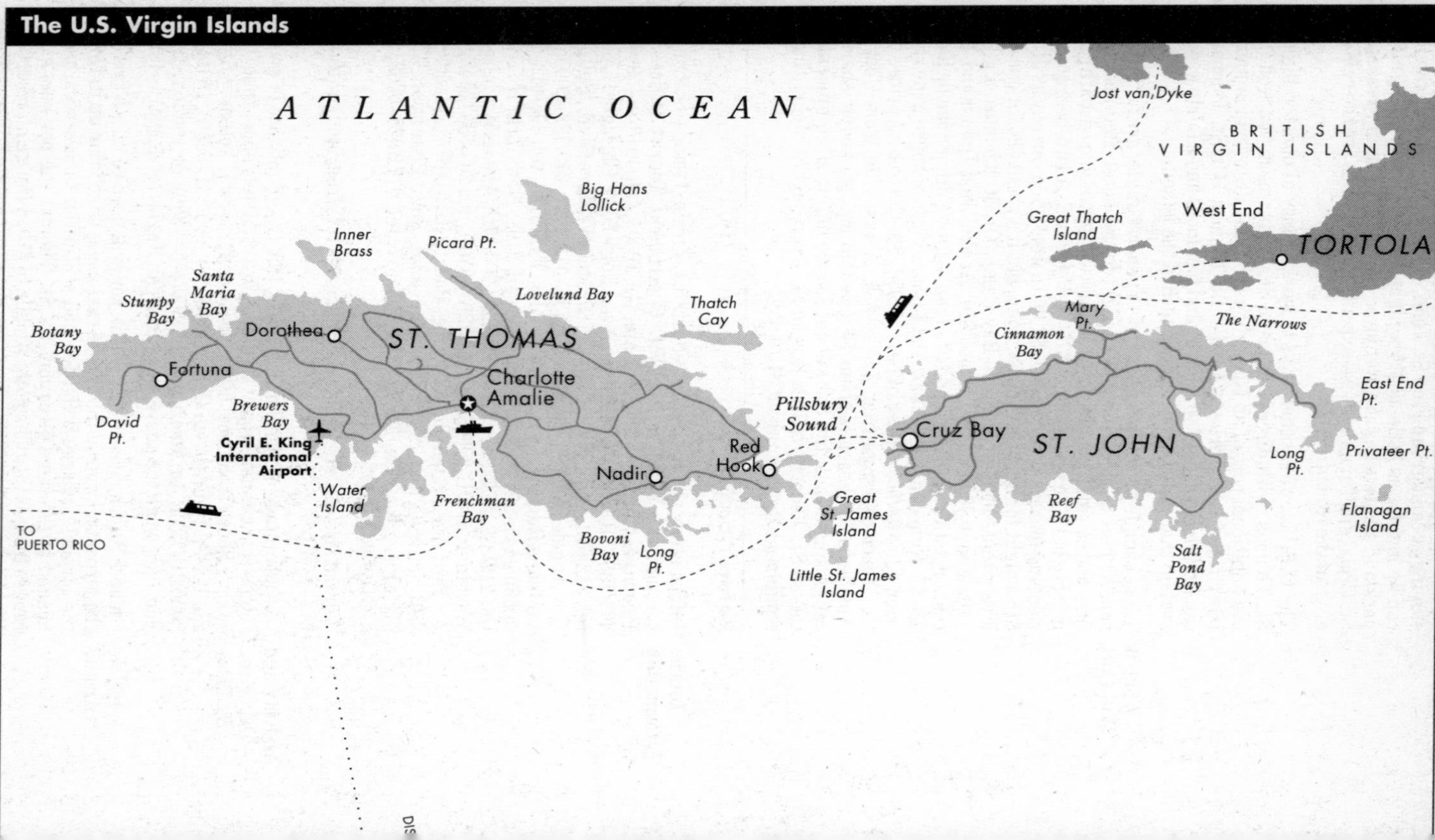

The U.S. Virgin Islands
ATLANTIC OCEAN
Jost van Dyke
BRITISH VIRGIN ISLANDS
Big Hans Lollick
Great Thatch Island
West End
TORTOLA
Inner Brass
Picara Pt.
Santa Maria Bay
Stumpy Bay
Lovelund Bay
Thatch Cay
Mary Pt.
The Narrows
Botany Bay
Dorothea
ST. THOMAS
Cinnamon Bay
Fortuna
Charlotte Amalie
East End Pt.
Brewers Bay
Pillsbury Sound
David Pt.
Cruz Bay
ST. JOHN
Cyril E. King International Airport
Red Hook
Long Pt.
Privateer Pt.
Nadir
Water Island
Frenchman Bay
Great St. James Island
Reef Bay
Flanagan Island
TO PUERTO RICO
Bovoni Bay
Long Pt.
Salt Pond Bay
Little St. James Island

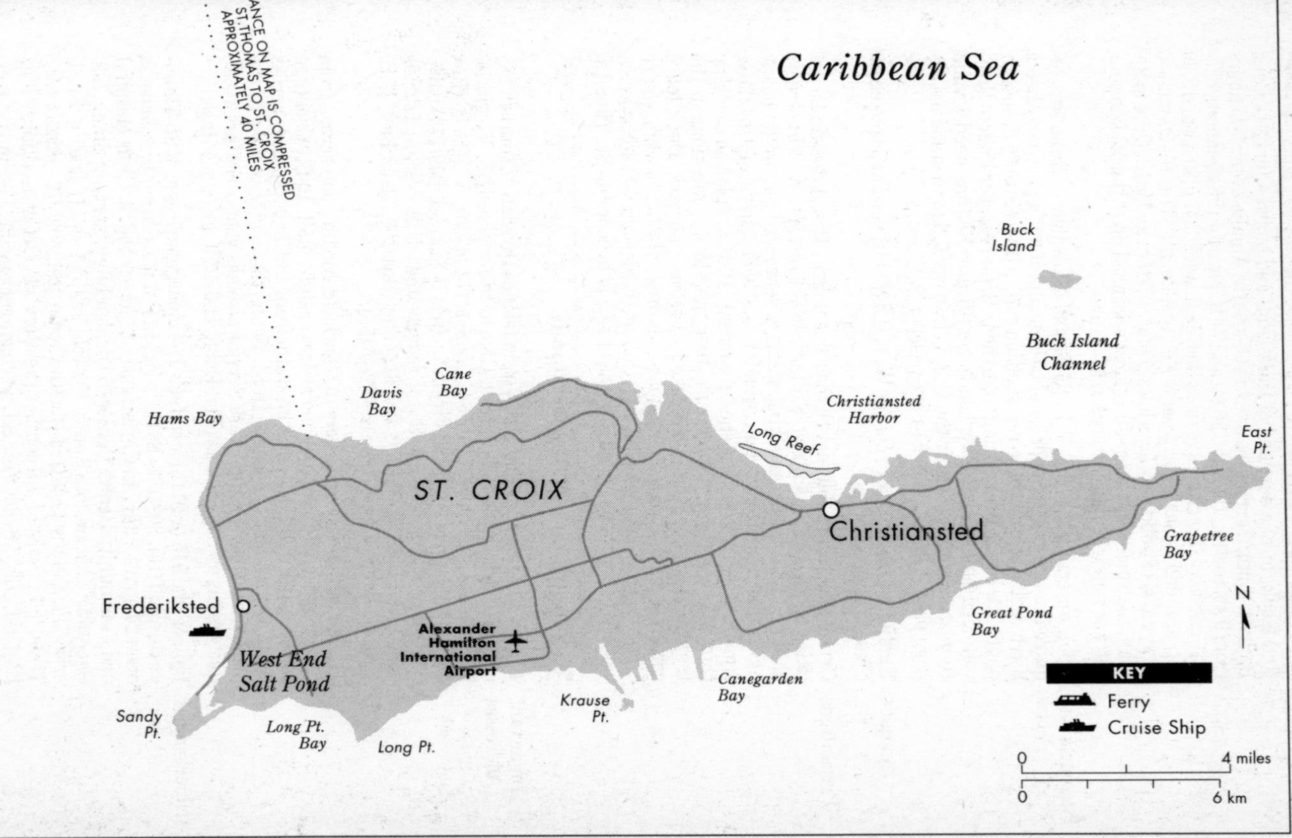
ANCE ON MAP IS COMPRESSED
ST.THOMAS TO ST. CROIX
APPROXIMATELY 40 MILES
Caribbean Sea
Buck Island
Buck Island Channel
Hams Bay
Davis Bay
Cane Bay
ST. CROIX
Long Reef
Christiansted Harbor
Christiansted
East Pt.
Grapetree Bay
Frederiksted
Alexander Hamilton International Airport
West End Salt Pond
Great Pond Bay
N
Canegarden Bay
Krause Pt.
Sandy Pt.
Long Pt. Bay
Long Pt.
KEY
Ferry
Cruise Ship
0 4 miles
0 6 km

Red Hook, on the east end of the island, and board a ferry to Cruz Bay, St. John. Ferries leave from Charlotte Amalie every two hours from 9 AM to 3 PM, then at 5:30 PM and 7 PM. Fare for the 45-minute ride is $7 one-way. Ferries leave from Red Hook weekdays 6:30 AM and 7:30 AM, and daily each hour from 8 AM to midnight. The 15–20-minute ferry ride is $3 one-way for adults, $1 for children under 12. Once in St. John, take one of the open-air safari buses lined up at the dock to your hotel or campground (per person $3–$10).

Passports and Visas Upon entering the U.S.V.I., U.S. and Canadian citizens are required to present some proof of citizenship, if not a passport then a birth certificate or voter-registration card with a driver's license or photo ID. If you are arriving from the U.S. mainland or Puerto Rico, you need no inoculation or health certificate. Britons need a valid 10-year passport to enter the U.S.V.I. (cost: £15 for a standard 32-page passport, £30 for a 94-page passport).

Language English, often with a Creole or West Indian lilt, is what's spoken on these islands.

Precautions Crime exists here, but not to the same degree that it does in larger cities on the U.S. mainland. Still, it's best to stick to well-lit streets at night and use the same kind of street sense that you would in any unfamiliar territory (don't wander the back alleys of Charlotte Amalie after five rum punches, for example). If you plan on carrying things around, rent a car, not a Jeep, and lock possessions in the trunk. Keep your rental car locked wherever you park. Don't leave cameras, purses, and other valuables lying on the beach while you're off on an hour-long snorkel, whether at the deserted beaches of St. John or the more crowded Magens and Coki beaches on St. Thomas.

Staying in the U.S. Virgin Islands

Important Addresses **Tourist Information:** The **U.S. Virgin Islands Division of Tourism** has offices in St. Thomas (Box 6400, Charlotte Amalie, U.S. Virgin Islands 00804, tel. 809/774–8784, fax 809/774–4390), St. Croix (Box 4538, Christiansted, U.S. Virgin Islands 00822, tel. 809/773–0495, and on the pier, Strand St., Frederiksted, U.S. Virgin Islands 00840, tel. 809/772–0357), and St. John (Box 200, Cruz Bay, U.S. Virgin Islands 00830, tel. 809/776–6450).

There are two **visitor centers** in Charlotte Amalie: one across from Emancipation Square and one at Havensight Mall. In St. Croix, go to the Old Scale House at the waterfront in Christiansted, across from Fort Christiansvaern. In St. John, the center is next to the post office. The **National Park Service** also has visitor centers at the ferry areas on St. Thomas (Red Hook) and St. John (Cruz Bay).

Emergencies **Police:** Dial 915 or 911. **Hospitals:** The emergency room of **St. Thomas Hospital** (tel. 809/776–8311) in Sugar Estate, Charlotte Amalie, is open 24 hours a day. In Christiansted there is the **St. Croix Hospital and Community Health Center** (6 Diamond Bay, north of Sunny Isle Shopping Center, on Route 79, tel. 809/778–6311, and in Frederiksted, the **Frederiksted Health Center** (tel. 809/772–1992 or 809/772–0750). On St. John contact the **Morris F. DeCastro Clinic** (Cruz Bay, tel. 809/776–6400) or call an **emergency medical technician** (tel. 809/776–6222).

Air Ambulance: Bohlke International Airways (tel. 809/778–9177) operates out of the airport in St. Croix. **Air Medical Services** (tel. 800/443–0013) and **Air Ambulance Network** (tel. 800/327–1966) also serve the area from Florida.

Coast Guard: For emergencies on St. Thomas or St. John, call the **Marine Safety Detachment** (tel. 809/776–3497) from 7 to 3:30 weekdays; on St. Croix, call 809/778–2692. If there is no answer, call the

Rescue Coordination Center (tel. 809/729–6800 ext. 140–145) in San Juan, open 24 hours a day.

Pharmacies: Sunrise Pharmacy has two branches on St. Thomas, one in Red Hook (tel. 809/775–6600), and another in the Wheatley Center (tel. 809/774–5333). **Drug Farm Pharmacy's** main store (tel. 809/776–7098) is across from the General Post Office; another branch (tel. 809/776–1880) is next to St. Thomas Hospital. On St. Croix, try **People's Drug Store, Inc.** (tel. 809/778–7355) in Christiansted and at Sunny Isle Shopping Center (tel. 809/778–5537) or **D&D Apothecary Hall** (tel. 809/772–1890) in Frederiksted. On St. John, contact the **St. John Drug Center** (tel. 809/776–6353) in Cruz Bay.

Currency The U.S. dollar is the medium of exchange.

Taxes and Service Charges An 8% tax is added to hotel rates. Some hotels and restaurants add a 10% or 15% service charge to your bill, generally only if you are part of a group of 15 or more. There is no sales tax in the U.S.V.I. Departure tax for the U.S.V.I. is included in the cost of your airplane ticket.

Getting Around Although sprawling St. Thomas is not a walker's island, you can get by here without a car. Most hotels and condominium complexes are on or near a beach, and those that aren't often provide a beach shuttle (free or for a few dollars). Most of the less-expensive B&Bs and inns are in the old historic district downtown or scattered throughout the hills above Charlotte Amalie; both locations are a short taxi or bus ride from some of the island's best beaches. You may find a car necessary for trips to restaurants and shops, though. Even if you opt not to rent a car for your entire vacation, you may want to rent one for a day in order to explore the less-frequented areas of the island.

St. Croix is a big island, and visitors usually find their freedom severely curtailed without a car. The public taxi runs only between Christiansted and Frederiksted along Centerline Road, not to any of the hotels along the coast, and buses only go from east and west to town and back. On St. John, you can get by without renting a car if you stay in Cruz Bay or one of the more popular hotels where taxis are likely to stop. If you are renting a private house or condo, you'll probably need a car to come down out of the hills.

Car Any U.S. driver's license is good for 90 days here; the minimum age for drivers is 18, although many agencies won't rent to anyone under the age of 25. Driving is on the left side of the road (although your steering wheel will be on the left side of the car). Many of the roads are narrow and the islands are dotted with hills, so there is ample reason to drive carefully. Jeeps are particularly recommended on St. John, which has well-paved main roads but many dirt side roads.

On St. Thomas, you can rent a car from **ABC Rentals** (tel. 809/776–1222 or 800/524–2080), **Anchorage E-Z Car** (tel. 809/775–6255 or 800/524–2027), **Avis** (tel. 809/774–1468), **Budget** (tel. 809/776–5774), **Cowpet Rent-a-Car** (tel. 809/775–7376 or 800/524–2072), **Dependable** (tel. 809/774–2253 or 800/522–3076), **Discount** (tel. 809/776–4858), **Hertz** (tel. 809/774–1879), **Sea Breeze** (tel. 809/774–7200), **Sun Island** (tel. 809/774–3333), or **Thrifty** (tel. 809/775–7282). Average cost is $52 a day (unlimited mileage), but you can get a standard shift car without air-conditioning for $43.

On St. Croix, call **Atlas** (tel. 809/773–2886), **Avis** (tel. 809/778–9355), **Budget** (tel. 809/778–9636), **Caribbean Jeep & Car** (tel. 809/773–4399), **Hertz** (tel. 809/778–1402), **Olympic** (tel. 809/773–2208), and **Thrifty** (tel. 809/773–7200). Economy cars on St. Croix average $40–$45 a day.

On St. John, call **Avis** (tel. 809/776–6374), **Budget** (tel. 809/776–7575), **Cool Breeze** (tel. 809/776–6588), **Delbert Hill Taxi and Jeep** (tel. 809/776–6637), **Hertz** (tel. 809/776–6695), **O'Connor Jeep** (tel.

809/776–6343), **St. John Car Rental** (tel. 809/776–6103), or **Spencer's Jeep** (tel. 809/776–7784). Economy rental cars on St. John average $25–$30 a day.

Taxis Taxis of all shapes and sizes are available at various ferry, shopping, resort, and airport areas on St. Thomas and St. Croix and respond quickly to a call. U.S.V.I. taxis do not have meters, but rather a list of standard per-person fares to popular destinations. Rates are lower if more than one person is traveling to the same destination. Sample fares to popular tourist destinations on St. Thomas: town to Havensight Mall, $2.50; town to Magens Bay, $6.50 for one, $4 per person for more than one; town to Red Hook, $9 for one, $5.50 per person for more than one. In Charlotte Amalie, taxi stands are across from **Emancipation Gardens** (in front of Little Switzerland behind the post office) and along the waterfront. Away from Charlotte Amalie, you'll find taxis available at all major hotels, at such public beaches as Magens Bay and Coki Point, and at the ferry dock in Red Hook. Calling taxis will work, too, but allow plenty of time.

Taxis on St. Croix, generally station wagons or minivans, are a phone call away from most hotels and are available in downtown Christiansted, at the Alexander Hamilton Airport, and at the Frederiksted pier during cruise-ship arrivals. Rates, set by law, are prominently displayed at the airport. The public taxi van, running along Centerline Road between Frederiksted and Christiansted, costs $1.50 one way. Private taxis (the same vans, but they don't stop to pick up other passengers along the way) typically cost $10 for a trip from the airport to Christiansted or to most North Shore hotels.

On St. John, buses and taxis are the same thing: open-air safari buses. You'll find them congregated at the Cruz Bay Dock, ready to take you to any of the beaches or other island destinations, but you can also pick them up anywhere on the road by signaling. Taxis from Cruz Bay to the popular North Shore beaches cost around $5 per person. It's a bit more expensive to reach the attractions on the other side of the island: A ride to Annaberg Plantation or Coral Bay can run $10 per person.

Buses Service is minimal, but the deluxe mainland-size buses on St. Thomas and St. Croix are a reasonable and comfortable way to get from east and west to town and back. Fares are $1 between outlying areas and town and 75¢ in town. St. John has no public bus system, and residents rely on the kindness of taxi vans and safari buses for mass transportation.

Ferries Ferries ply two routes between St. Thomas and St. John—either between the Charlotte Amalie waterfront and Cruz Bay or between Red Hook and Cruz Bay. The schedules for daily service between Red Hook, St. Thomas, and Cruz Bay, St. John: Ferries leave Red Hook weekdays 6:30 and 7:30 AM, and all week long hourly 8 AM–midnight. They leave Cruz Bay for Red Hook hourly 6 AM–10 PM and at 11:20 PM. The 15–20 minute ferry ride is $3 one way for adults, $1 for children under 12. Ferries leave from Charlotte Amalie every two hours from 9 AM to 3 PM, then at 5:30 PM and 7 PM. They leave Cruz Bay for Charlotte Amalie every two hours from 7:15 AM to 1:15 PM, and also at 3:45 PM and 5:15 PM. Fare for the 45-minute ride is $7 one-way.

Telephones and Mail The area code for all the U.S.V.I. is 809, and there is direct dialing to the mainland. Local calls from a public phone cost 25¢ for each five minutes. On St. John, the place to go for any telephone or message needs is **Connections** (tel. 809/776–6922). On St. Thomas, it's **Islander Services** (tel. 809/774–8128), behind the Greenhouse Restaurant in Charlotte Amalie, or **East End Secretarial Services** (tel. 809/775–5262, fax 809/775–3590), upstairs at the Red Hook Plaza. On St. Croix, visit **AnswerPLUS** (5005B Chandler's Wharf, Gallows Bay, tel. 809/773–4444) or **Worldwide Calling** (head of the pier in Frederiksted, tel. 809/772–2490).

You may notice that on St. John and St. Croix, some of the telephone exchanges stray from the normal 77-something prefix. The exchanges 693 for St. John and 692 for St. Croix are being integrated into the system to serve the islands' growing needs.

The main U.S. Post Office on St. Thomas is near the hospital, with branches in Charlotte Amalie, Frenchtown, and Tutu Mall; there are post offices at Christiansted, Gallows Bay, Sunny Isle, and Frederiksted on St. Croix and at Cruz Bay on St. John. Postal rates are the same as elsewhere in the United States: 32¢ for a letter, 20¢ for a postcard to anywhere in the United States, 50¢ for a half-ounce letter mailed to a foreign country.

Opening and Closing Times

On **St. Thomas,** Charlotte Amalie's Main Street–area shops are open weekdays and Saturday 9–5. Havensight Mall (next to the cruise-ships dock) shop hours are the same, though shops sometimes stay open until 9 on Friday, depending on how many cruise ships are staying late at the dock. You may also find some shops open on Sunday if a lot of cruise ships are in port. American Yacht Harbor stores are open weekdays and Saturdays 9–6. **St. Croix** store hours are usually weekdays 9–5, but you will find some shops in Christiansted open in the evening. On **St. John,** store hours are similar to those on the other two islands, and Wharfside Village shops in Cruz Bay are often open into the evening.

Guided Tours

On St. Thomas, the **V.I. Taxi Association City-Island Tour** (tel. 809/774–4550) gives a two-hour tour aimed at cruise-ship passengers that includes stops at Drake's Seat and Mountain Top. You can join an air-conditioned taxi-van tour for about $12 a person or pay $35 for two people and have your own taxi. **Tropic Tours** (tel. 809/774–1855 or 800/524–4334) offers half-day shopping and sightseeing tours of St. Thomas by bus six days a week for $20 per person and full-day snorkeling tours to St. John daily for $50 per person (including lunch). It picks up at all the major hotels. For a chance to wait hidden on a St. Croix beach while the magnificent hawksbill turtles come ashore to lay their eggs in the spring, write or call the **St. Croix Environmental Association** (Box 3839, St. Croix 00822, tel. 809/773–1989); there is no charge to participate.

Van tours of St. Croix are offered by **St. Croix Safari Tours** (tel. 809/773–6700) and **Smitty's** (tel. 809/773–9188). The tours, which depart from Christiansted and last about three hours, cost from $20 per person. You might also try to strike a bargain with one of the taxi-van drivers you'll see congregating on King Street in Christiansted, outside the tourist office. Their prices are likely to be comparable to those of the safari tour, but if you get enough people together you could save money.

On St. John, contact the **St. John Taxi Association** (tel. 809/776–6060) for tours of the island. The **park service** (St. John National Park Visitor Center, Cruz Bay, tel. 809/776–6201) also conducts guided tours on- and off-shore. Prices range from a $3 hike to Reef Bay to a $40 Round-the-Island snorkel tour. Taxi drivers are your best bet for an informal driving tour of the island. You'll find a multitude of these personable men gathered at the clock in Cruz Bay. A couple can take a two-hour tour for $30; three or more people bring the price down to $12 a person.

Exploring St. Thomas

Numbers in the margin correspond to points of interest on the St. Thomas map.

Charlotte Amalie

1

This tour of historic (and sometimes hilly) Charlotte Amalie and environs is on foot, so wear comfortable shoes, start early, and stop often to refresh. A note about the street names: In deference to the island's heritage, the streets downtown are labeled by their Danish names. Locals will use both the Danish name and the English name (such as Dronnigen's Gade and Main Street).

Begin at the waterfront. Waterfront and Main streets are connected by cobblestone-paved alleys kept cool by overhanging green plants and the thick stone walls of the warehouses on either side. The alleys (particularly Royal Dane Mall and Palm Passage, Main St. between the post office and Market Sq., and Bakery Sq. on Back St.) are where you'll find the unique and glamorous—and duty-free—shops for which Charlotte Amalie is famous (*see* Shopping, *below*).

At the end of Kronprindsens Alley north of the waterfront is the cream-color Roman Catholic **Cathedral of St. Peter and St. Paul,** consecrated as a parish church in 1848. The ceiling and walls of the church are covered in the soft tones of murals painted in 1899 by two Belgian artists, Father Leo Servais and Brother Ildephonsus. The San Juan–marble altar and side walls were added in the 1960s. *Tel. 809/774–0201. Open Mon.–Sat. 8–5.*

At **Market Square,** east of the church on Main Street, try to block out the signs advertising cameras and electronics and imagine this place as it was in the early 1800s, when plantation owners stood on wrought-iron balconies and chose from the slaves for sale below. Today in the square, a cadre of old-timers sell papaya, taina roots, and herbs, and sidewalk vendors offer a variety of African fabrics and artifacts, tie-dyed cotton clothes at good prices, and fresh-squeezed fruit juices. Go east on Back Street, then turn left on Store Tvaer Gade; walk a short block, and take a left on Bjerge Gade.

As you walk up Bjerge Gade, you'll end up facing a weather-beaten but imposing two-story red house known as the **Crystal Palace,** so named because it was the first building on the island to have glass windows. The Crystal Palace anchors the corner of Bjerge and Crystal Gade. Here the street becomes stairs, which you can climb to Denmark Hill and the old Greek Revival **Danish Consulate building** (1830)—look for the red-and-white flag.

Descend to Crystal Gade and go east. At Number 15, you'll come to the **Synagogue of Beracha Veshalom Vegmiluth Hasidim.** Its Hebrew name translates as the Congregation of Blessing, Peace, and Loving Deeds. Since the synagogue first opened its doors in 1833, it has held a weekly Sabbath service, making it the oldest synagogue building in continuous use under the American flag, and the second-oldest (after the one on Curaçao) in the Western Hemisphere. *15 Crystal Gade, tel. 809/774–4312. Open weekdays 9–4.*

One block east, down the hill, you'll come to the corner of Nye Gade. On the right corner is the St. Thomas **Dutch Reformed Church,** founded in 1744, burned in 1804, and rebuilt to its austere loveliness in 1844. The unembellished cream-color hall exudes peace—albeit monochromatically. The only touches of another color are the forest green shutters and carpet. *Tel. 809/776–8255. Open weekdays 9–5 (call ahead of time as the doors are sometimes locked).*

Continue on Crystal Gade one block east and turn left (north) on Garden Street. The **All Saints Anglican Church** was built in 1848 from stone quarried on the island. Its thick, arched window frames are lined with the yellow brick that came to the islands as ballast aboard merchant ships. The church was built in celebration of the end of slavery in the Virgin Islands in 1848. *Tel. 809/774–0217. Open Mon.–Sat. 6 AM–3 PM.*

Return down Garden Street and go east on Kongen's Gade. Keep walking up the hill to the east and you'll find yourself at the foot of the **99 Steps,** a staircase "street" built by the Danes in the 1700s. (If you count the stairs as you go up, you'll discover, like thousands before you, that there are more than 99.)

Up the steps you'll find the neighborhood of **Queen's Street.** The homes are privately owned except for one guest house—**Blackbeard's Castle.** Its tower was built in 1679 and is believed to have been used by the notorious pirate Edward Teach. The castle is now the site of a charming guest house, a good restaurant, and a swimming pool open to customers. Here you can lunch and sit by the pool, taking in the view from the terrace.

Go back down the steps and continue east to **Government House.** This elegant home was built in 1867 and is the official residence of the governor of the U.S.V.I. The first floor is open to the public. The staircases are carved from native mahogany, as are the plaques hand-lettered in gold with the names of the governors appointed and, since 1970, elected. The three murals at the back of the lobby were painted by Pepino Mangravatti in the 1930s as part of the U.S. government's Works Projects Administration (WPA). The murals depict Columbus's landing on St. Croix during his second voyage in 1493, the transfer of the islands from Denmark to the United States in 1917, and a sugar plantation on St. John.

Return west on Norre Gade (Main Street) toward town. In the block before the post office you'll pass the **Frederick Lutheran Church,** the second-oldest Lutheran church in the Western Hemisphere. The inside is highlighted by a massive mahogany altar. The pews, each with its own door, were once rented to families of the congregation. *Tel. 809/776–1315. Open Mon.–Sat. 9–4.*

Directly across from the Lutheran Church, through a small side street, you'll see **Fort Christian.** Built between 1672 and 1687, it is St. Thomas's oldest standing structure and a U.S. national landmark. The clock tower was added in the 19th century. This remarkable redoubt has, over time, been used as a jail, governor's residence, town hall, courthouse, and church. The building is currently undergoing renovation, so the interior is not open to the public.

Across from the fort is **Emancipation Garden,** which honors the freeing of slaves in 1848. On the other side of the garden is the **legislature building,** its pastoral-looking lime-green exterior concealing the vociferous political wrangling going on inside. Built originally by the Danish as a police barracks, the building was later used to billet U.S. Marines, and much later it housed a public school.

Stop in the **post office** to contemplate the murals of waterfront scenes by *Saturday Evening Post* artist Stephen Dohanos. His art was commissioned as part of the WPA in the 1930s. Behind the post office, on the waterfront side of Little Switzerland, are the hospitality lounge and **V.I. Visitor's Information Center.**

As you head back toward **Market Square** along Main Street, you'll pass the **Tropicana Perfume Shop,** between Store Tvaer Gade and Trompeter Gade. The building the shop is in is also known as the **Pissarro Building** because it was the birthplace of French Impressionist painter Camille Pissarro.

The South Shore and East End

Exploring St. Thomas by car gives you the freedom to see the sights at your own pace. You can tour the island outside Charlotte Amalie in a day and even take an hour or so to linger on a beach. If you prefer a cheaper alternative, take a guided tour (*see* Guided Tours, *above*). Leaving Charlotte Amalie, take Veterans Drive (Route 30) east along the waterfront. Once you bear to the right at **Nelson Mandela Circle** (Yacht Haven is on your right), you'll make quicker progress.
2 You may want to stop at **Havensight Mall,** across from the dock. This

St. Thomas

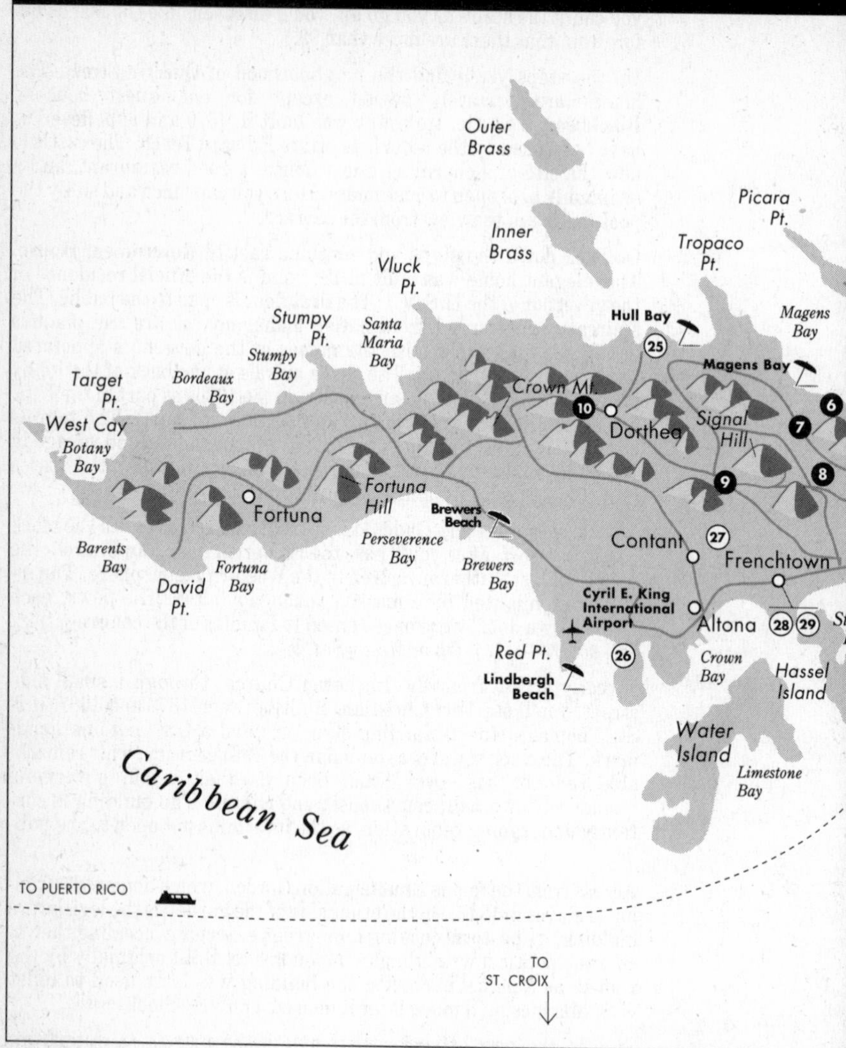

Exploring
Charlotte Amalie, **1**
Coral World, **4**
Drake's Seat, **6**
Fairchild Park, **8**
Four Corners, **9**
Havensight Mall, **2**
Mountain Top, **7**
Red Hook, **3**
Tillet's Gardens, **5**
U.S. Department of Agriculture Inspection Station, **10**

Dining
Alexander's Cafe, **28**
Bryan's Bar and Restaurant, **25**
The Chart House, **29**
Eunice's Terrace, **24**
For the Birds, **17**
Grateful Deli, **20**
Little Bopeep, **11**
Señor Pizza, **21**
Wok and Roll, **19**
Zorba's Cafe, **12**

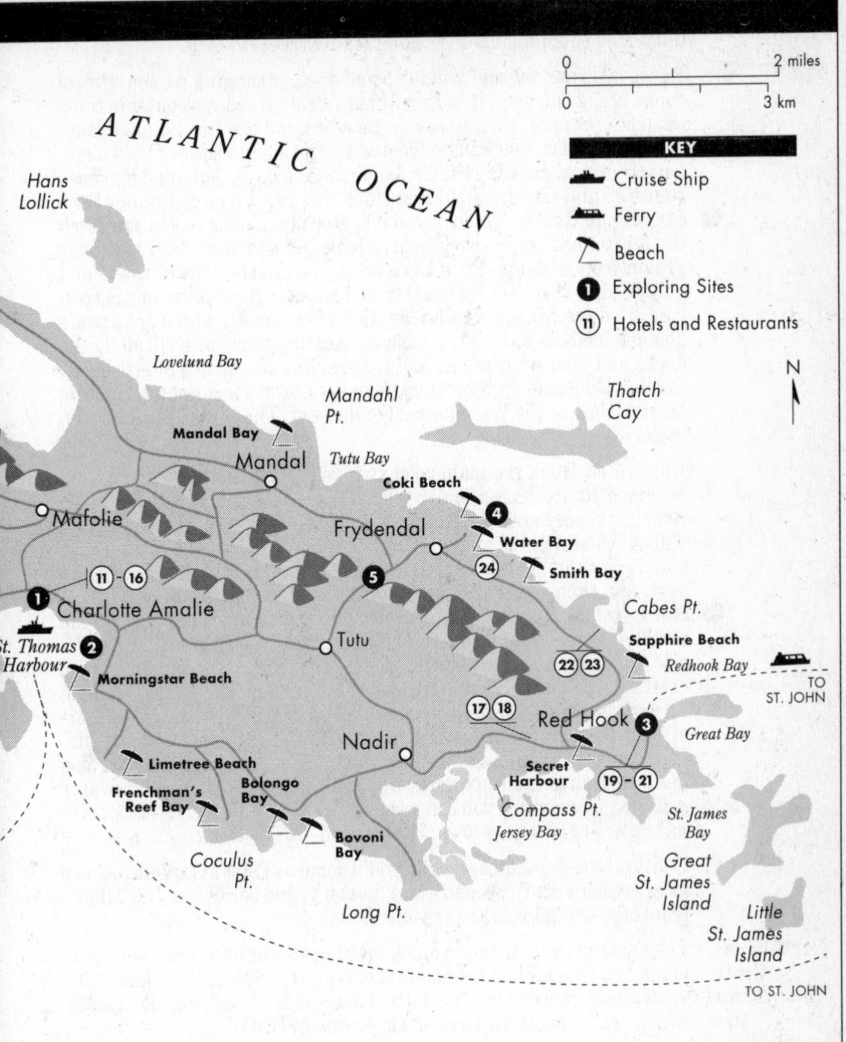

Lodging
Crystal Cove, **22**
Hotel 1829, **12**
Island Beachcomber, **26**
Island View Guest House, **27**
Ramada Yacht Haven Hotel & Marina, **14**
Sapphire Village, **23**
Sea Horse Cottages, **18**
Villa Blanca Hotel, **13**
Villa Santana, **15**

shopping center is a less crowded (and less charming) version of the duty-free shopping district along Main Street in town.

Route 30 is narrow and winds up and down, changing names several times along the way; it is Frenchman's Bay Road just outside town (sharp left turn), then becomes Bovoni Road around Bolongo Bay. As you travel it, you will be treated to southerly vistas of the Caribbean Sea (and possibly St. Croix, 40 miles away). The road becomes Route 32 and then is called Red Hook Road as it passes Benner Bay.
3 Staying on Route 32 brings you into **Red Hook,** where you can catch the ferry to St. John (parking available for $5 a day). Red Hook has grown from a sleepy little town connected to the rest of the island only by dirt roads (or by boat) to an increasingly self-sustaining village. Browse through **American Yacht Harbor,** a waterfront arcade housing branches of many Charlotte Amalie shops, or walk along the docks and visit with sailors and fishers. You can have a bite to eat at Tickles Dockside Pub or Mackenzies, or stop for a beer at Piccola Marina Cafe or the Warehouse. For dessert, The Big Chill has frozen yogurt.

Above Red Hook the main road swings toward the north shore and becomes Route 38, or Smith Bay Road, taking you past Sapphire Beach, a resort and restaurant with water-sports rentals and a popular snorkeling and windsurfing spot. As you come to Smith Bay, you'll pass the lush green landscaping of Stouffer Grand Beach Resort, and then you'll see a turn-off to the right for Coki Point Beach
4 and **Coral World,** with its three-level underwater observatory, the world's largest reef tank, and an aquarium with more than 20 TV-size tanks providing capsulized views of sea life. A semisubmarine (a craft that is half-submarine, half-boat, allowing passengers to come up on deck) offers 20-minute undersea tours for $12 per person. Coral World's staff will answer your questions about the turtles, iguanas, parrots, and flamingos that inhabit the park. The complex also has a restaurant, a souvenir shop, and the world's only underwater mailbox, from which you can send postcards. *Tel. 809/775–1555. Admission: $16 adults, $10 children ages 3–12. Open daily 9–6.*

5 Continue west on Route 38 and you'll come to **Tillet's Gardens,** where local artisans craft stained glass, pottery, and ceramics. Jim Tillet's paintings and fabrics are also on display.

North Shore, Center Islands, and West

The north shore is home to many inviting attractions, not to mention much lusher vegetation than is found on the rest of the island. The most direct route from Charlotte Amalie is Mafolie Road (Route 35), which can be picked up east of Government Hill.

6 In the heights above Charlotte Amalie is **Drake's Seat,** the mountain lookout from which Sir Francis Drake was supposed to have kept watch over his fleet, looking for enemy ships of the Spanish fleet. Magens Bay and Mahogany Run are to the north, with the British Virgin Islands and Drake's Passage to the east. Off to the left, or west, are Fairchild Park, Mountain Top, Hull Bay, and such smaller islands as the Inner and Outer Brass islands. The panoramic vista is especially breathtaking (and romantic) at dusk, and if you arrive late in the day you'll miss the hordes of day-trippers on taxi tours who stop at Drake's Seat to take a picture and buy a T-shirt from one of the vendors there. The vendors are gone by the afternoon.

7 West from Drake's Seat is **Mountain Top,** not only a mecca for souvenir shopping, but also the location of the establishment that claims to have invented the banana daiquiri. There is a restaurant here, and, at more than 1,500 feet above sea level, some spectacular views as well.

8 Below Mountain Top is **Fairchild Park,** a gift to the people of the U.S.V.I. from the philanthropist Arthur Fairchild.

If you head west from Mountain Top on Crown Mountain Road
9 (Route 33) you'll come to **Four Corners.** Take the extreme right turn and drive along the northwestern ridge of the mountain through **Estate Pearl, Sorgenfri,** and **Caret Bay.** There's not much here except peace and quiet, junglelike foliage, and breathtaking vistas. You may want to stop at one of the inviting plant stores. Near Bryan's
10 Plants you'll pass the **U.S. Department of Agriculture Inspection Station.** If you buy a plant, be sure to stop here to get the plant's roots sprayed for diseases and to get a certificate to present to U.S. customs when you leave the territory. Continue west to Brewer's Bay, then follow Route 30 east back to Frenchtown and Charlotte Amalie.

Exploring St. Croix

Numbers in the margin correspond to points of interest on the St. Croix map.

You can see some of St. Croix's sights by public transportation—the taxi-van route goes from Christiansted, the heart of the island past the St. George Botanical Gardens, Whim Greathouse, and on to Frederiksted—and you can get off and on the taxi anywhere along the line. But you should plan on renting a car for at least one day to tour the coastal roads and explore the lush rain forest on the West End. If you don't dally too long at some sandy stretch of beach, one day should be plenty to see the main points of interest.

1 This tour starts in the historic, Danish-style town of **Christiansted,** St. Croix's commercial center. Many of the structures, which are built from the harbor up into the gentle hillsides, date from the 18th century. An easy-to-follow walking tour begins at the **visitor's bureau,** at the harbor. The building was constructed in 1856 and once served as a scale house, where goods passing through the port were weighed and inspected. Directly across the parking lot, at the edge of D. Hamilton Jackson Park (the park is named for a famed labor leader, journalist, and judge), is the **Old Customs House.** Completed in 1829, this building now houses the island's national park offices. To the east stands yellow **Fort Christiansvaern.** Built by the Danish from 1738 to 1749 to protect the harbor against attacks on commercial shipping, the fort was repeatedly damaged by hurricane-force winds and was partially rebuilt in 1772. It is now part of the National Historic Site and is the best-preserved of the remaining Danish-built forts in the Virgin Islands. Five rooms, including military barracks and a dungeon, have been restored to demonstrate how the fort looked in the 1840s, when it was at its height as a military establishment. There is also an exhibit that documents the Danish military's 150-year presence in Christiansted. *Tel. 809/773–1460. Admission: $2 (includes admission to Steeple Building); free to children under 16 and senior citizens. Open daily 8–5, except Christmas, Easter, and Thanksgiving.*

Cross Hospital Street from the customs house to reach the post office building. Built in 1749, it once housed the Danish West India & Guinea Company warehouse. To the south of the post office, across Company Street, stands the maroon-and-white **Steeple Building.** Built by the Danes in 1754, the building once housed the first Danish Lutheran church on St. Croix. It is now a national-park museum and contains exhibits documenting the island's habitation by Native Americans through an extensive array of archaeological artifacts. There are also displays on the architectural development of Christian sted and the African-American experience in the town during Danish colonial rule. *Box 160, Christiansted 00822, tel. 809/773–1460. Admission: $2 (includes admission to fort). Open Tues.–Thurs. and weekends 9–4.*

One of the town's most elegant buildings is **Government House,** on King Street. Built as a home for a Danish merchant in 1747, the

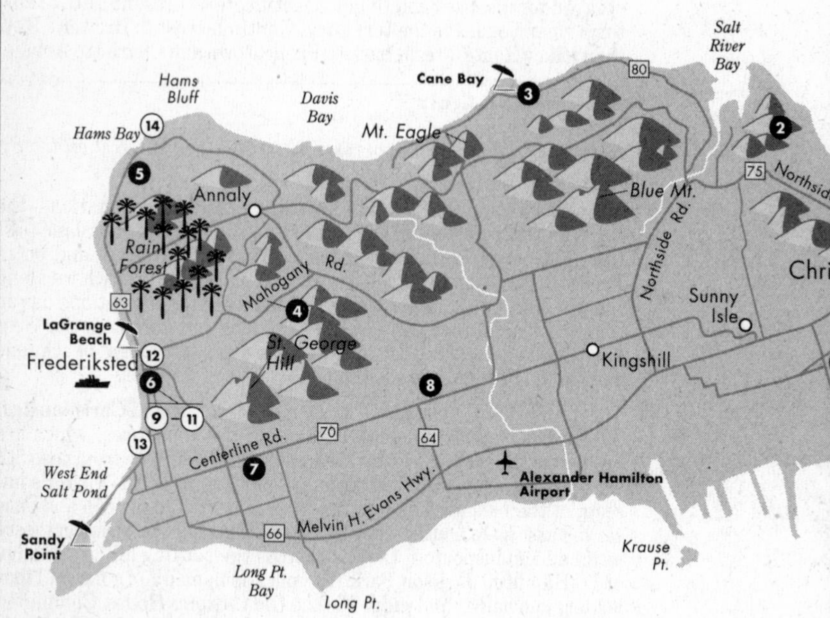

Exploring
Cane Bay, **3**
Christiansted, **1**
Estate Mount Washington Plantation, **5**
Estate Whim Plantation Museum, **7**
Frederiksted, **6**
Judith's Fancy, **2**
Mahogany Road, **4**
St. George Village Botanical Gardens, **8**

Dining
Blue Moon, **9**
Camille's, **16**
La Guitarra, **18**
LaGrange Beach Club, **12**
Le St. Tropez, **11**
Stixx on the Waterfront, **17**

Lodging
Cottages by the Sea, **13**
The Frederiksted, **10**
Hilty House, **15**
Paradise Sunset Beach, **14**
The Pink Fancy, **19**

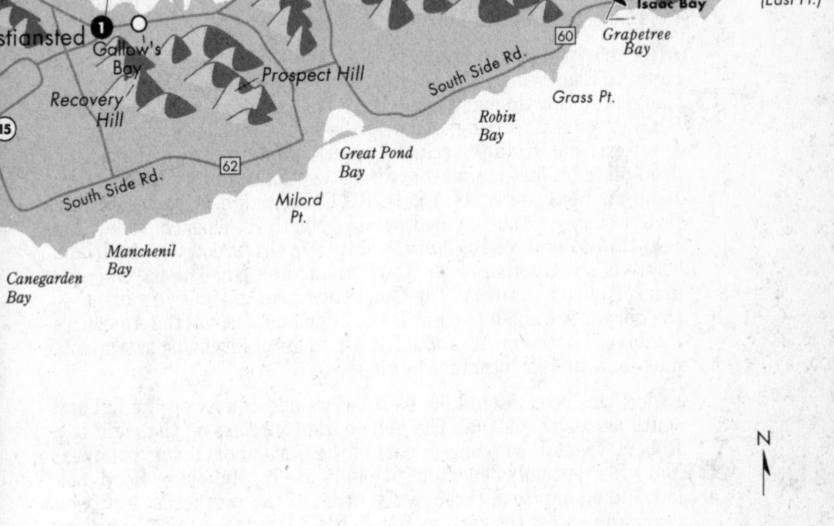
Buck Island
Buck Island Beach
Long Reef
Christiansted Harbor
Green Cay
Pull Pt.
Tamarind Reef Beach
Coakley Bay
Teague Bay
Cramer Park
Cottongarden Pt.
Reef Beach
Sugarloaf Hill
Pt.Udall (East Pt.)
East End Rd.
82
16
19
Rd.
1
stiansted
Gallow's Bay
Isaac Bay
60
Grapetree Bay
Prospect Hill
South Side Rd.
Recovery Hill
Grass Pt.
15
Robin Bay
Great Pond Bay
62
South Side Rd.
Milord Pt.
Manchenil Bay
Canegarden Bay
N
0
2 miles
0
3 km

building today houses U.S.V.I. government offices and the U.S. district court. Slip into the peaceful inner courtyard to admire the still pools and gardens. A sweeping staircase leads visitors to a second-story ballroom, still the site of official government functions.

To leave Christiansted and begin a driving tour, take Hospital Street from the tourist office and turn right onto Company Street. Follow Company Street for several blocks and turn right with the flow of traffic past the police station. Make a quick left onto King Street, and follow it out of town. At the second traffic light, make a right onto Route 75, Northside Road. A few miles up the road, you can make a side trip by turning right, just past the St. Croix Avis building, onto Route 751, which leads you past the St. Croix by the
2 Sea hotel to **Judith's Fancy,** where you can see the ruins of an old great house and the tower left from a 17th-century château that was once home to the governor of the Knights of Malta. The "Judith" comes from the first name of a woman buried on the property. From the guardhouse at the entrance to the neighborhood, follow Hamilton Drive to its end for a view of Salt River Bay, where Christopher Columbus anchored in 1493.

After driving back to Route 75, continue west for 2 miles and turn right at Tradewinds Road onto Route 80, which quickly returns to
3 the grassy coastline and **Cane Bay.** This is one of St. Croix's best beaches for scuba diving, and near the small stone jetty you may see a few wet-suited, tank-backed figures making their way out to the drop-off (a bit farther out there is a steeper drop-off to 12,000 feet). Rising behind you is Mt. Eagle, St. Croix's highest peak, at 1,165 feet. Leaving Cane Bay and passing North Star beach, follow the beautiful coastal road as it dips briefly into the forest, then turn left. There is no street sign, but you'll know the turn: The pavement is marked with the words "The Beast" and a set of giant paw prints—the hill you are about to climb is the infamous Beast of the America's Paradise Triathalon, an annual St. Croix event in which participants must bike up this intimidating slope.

Follow this road, Route 69, as it twists and climbs up the hill and south across the island. The golf course you pass on the right is a Robert Trent Jones course, part of the Carambola resort complex.
4 You will eventually bear right to join Route 76, **Mahogany Road.** Follow Mahogany Road through the heart of the rain forest until you reach the end of the road at Ham's Bluff Road (Route 63), running along the west coast of the island. Turn right and, after a few miles,
5 look to the right side of the road for the **Estate Mount Washington Plantation** (tel. 809/772–1026). Several years ago, while surveying the property, the owners discovered the ruins of a historic sugar plantation buried beneath the rain forest brush. The grounds have since been cleared and opened to the public. A free, self-guided walking tour of the animal-powered mill, rum factory, and other ruins is available daily, and the antique shop located in the old stables is open on Saturdays.

6 Double back along Ham's Bluff Road to reach **Frederiksted,** founded in 1751. A single, long cruise-ship pier juts into the sparkling sea from this historic coastal town, noted less for its Danish than for its Victorian architecture (dating from after the uprising of former slaves and the great fire of 1878). A stroll around will take no more than an hour.

Begin your walking tour at the **visitor center** (tel. 809/772–0357) on the pier. From here, it's a short walk across Emancipation Park to **Fort Frederik** where, in 1848, the slaves of the Danish West Indies were freed by Governor General Peter van Scholten. The fort, completed in 1760, houses a number of interesting historical exhibits as well as an art gallery. *Tel. 809/772–2021. Admission free. Open weekdays 8:30–4:30.*

Stroll along King Street to Market Street and turn left. At the corner of Queen Street is the Market Place, where fresh fruits and vegetables are sold in the early morning, just as they have been for more than 200 years. One block farther on the left is the coral-stone **St. Patrick's Church,** a Roman Catholic church built in 1842.

Head back to King Street and follow it to King Cross Street. A left turn here will bring you to Apothecary Hall, built in 1839, and on the next block, **St. Paul's Episcopal Church,** a mixture of classic and Gothic Revival architecture, built in 1812. Double back along King Cross Street to Strand Street and the waterfront. Turn right and walk along the water to the pier, where the tour began.

Back in your car, take Strand Street south to its end, turn left, then bear right before the post office to leave Frederiksted. Make a left at the first stoplight to get on Centerline Road (Queen Mary High-
7 way). A few miles along this road, on the right, is the **Estate Whim Plantation Museum.** The lovingly restored estate, with a windmill, cook house, and other buildings, will give you a true sense of what life was like on St. Croix's sugar plantations in the 1800s. The oval-shaped, high-ceilinged great house, built of stone, coral, and lime, has antique furniture, decor, utensils, and the largest apothecary exhibit in the West Indies. Notice the fresh and airy atmosphere: The waterless moat around the great house was used not for defense but for gathering cooling air. You will also find a museum gift shop. *Box 2855, Frederiksted 00841, tel. 809/772–0598. Admission: $5 adults, $1 children. Open Mon.–Sat. 10–4.*

Continue along Centerline Road to the St. George Estate. Turn left
8 here to reach the **St. George Village Botanical Gardens,** 17 acres of lush and fragrant flora amid the ruins of a 19th-century sugarcane plantation village. *Box 3011, Kingshill 00851–3011, tel. 809/772–3874. Admission: $5 adults, $1 children. Open daily 9–4.*

Continue east along Centerline Road all the way back to Christiansted.

Exploring St. John

Numbers in the margin correspond to points of interest on the St. John map.

St. John may be small, but the roads are narrow and wind up and down steep hills, so don't expect to get anywhere in a hurry. Bring along your swimsuit for stops at some of the most beautiful beaches in the world.

1 **Cruz Bay** town dock is the starting point for just about everything on St. John. Take a leisurely stroll through the streets of this colorful, compact town: There are plenty of shops to browse in, and plenty of watering holes where you can stop to take a breather.

Follow the waterfront out of town (about 100 yards) to another dock at the edge of a parking lot. At the far side of the lagoon here you'll find the **National Park Service Visitors Center** (tel. 809/776–6201), where you can pick up a handy guide to St. John's hiking trails and see various large maps of the island. If you see an island map featuring Max the Mongoose, grab it; it's full of information.

Begin your driving tour traveling north out of Cruz Bay. You'll pass **Mongoose Junction,** recently expanded to include Mongoose Junction II, one of the prettiest shopping areas in the Caribbean. At the half-mile mark you'll come to the well-groomed gardens and beaches of **Caneel Bay,** purchased from the Danish West India Company and developed in the 1950s by Laurance Rockefeller, who then turned over much of the island to the U.S. government as parkland. Caneel Bay Beach (home of two friendly stingrays) is reached by parking in

St. John

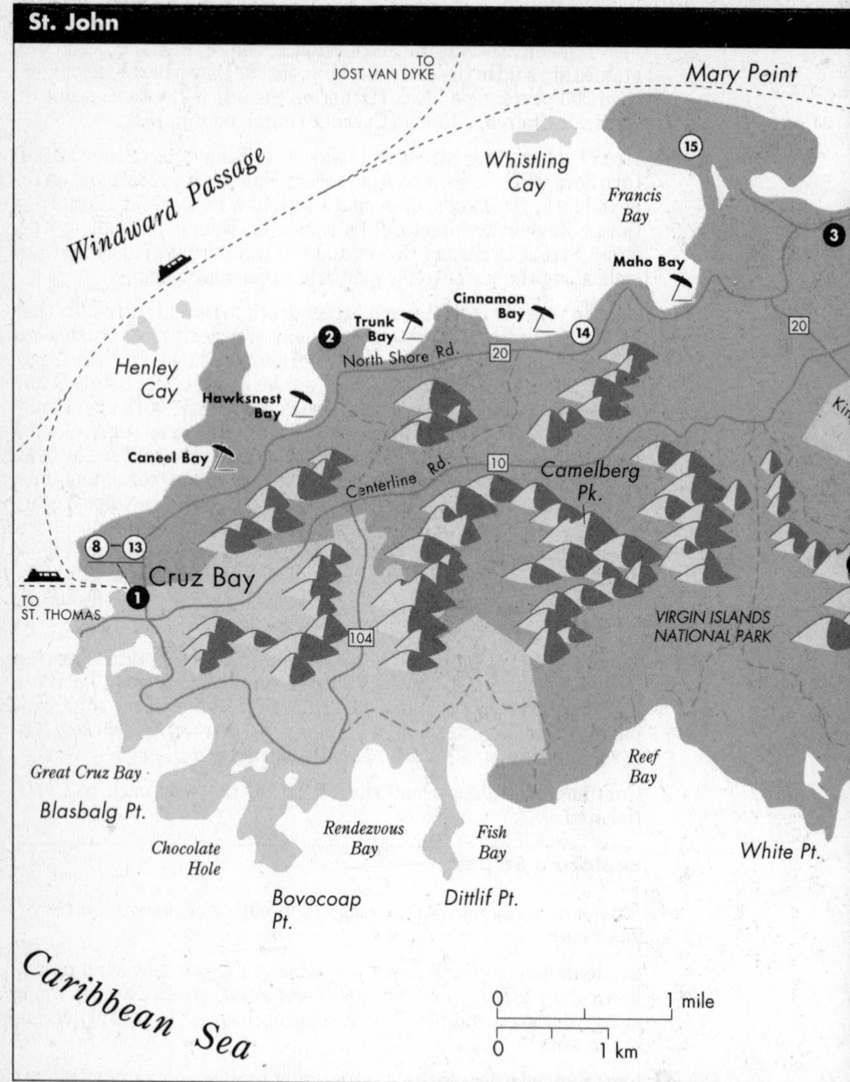

Exploring
Annaberg Plantation, **3**
Bordeaux Mountain, **7**
Christ of the Caribbean statue, **2**
Coral Bay, **4**
Cruz Bay, **1**
East End, **5**
Salt Pond, **6**

Dining
Etta's, **10**
The Fish Trap, **8**
Lime Inn, **9**
Luscious Licks, **12**
Shipwreck Landing, **16**

Lodging
Cinnamon Bay Campground, **14**
Cruz Inn, **13**
The Inn at Tamarind Court, **10**
Maho Bay Camp, **15**
Raintree Inn, **11**

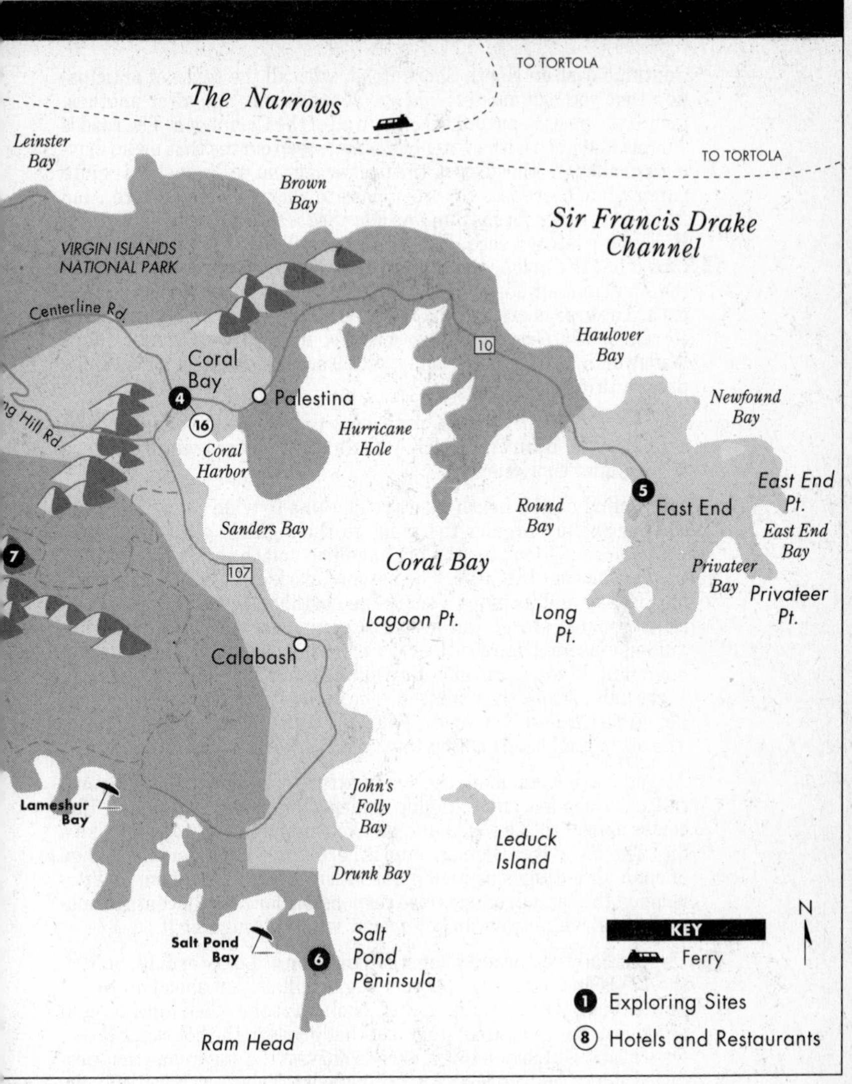

TO TORTOLA
The Narrows
Leinster Bay
TO TORTOLA
Brown Bay
Sir Francis Drake Channel
VIRGIN ISLANDS NATIONAL PARK
Centerline Rd.
10
Haulover Bay
Coral Bay
4
Palestina
Newfound Bay
16
Hurricane Hole
Coral Harbor
5
East End Pt.
East End
Round Bay
Sanders Bay
East End Bay
7
Coral Bay
Privateer Bay
Privateer Pt.
107
Lagoon Pt.
Long Pt.
Calabash
John's Folly Bay
Lameshur Bay
Leduck Island
Drunk Bay
N
KEY
Salt Pond Bay
Salt Pond Peninsula
6
Ferry
Exploring Sites
Hotels and Restaurants
Ram Head

the Caneel parking lot and walking through the grounds (ask for directions).

Continue east on North Shore Road, with all the sense of anticipation that you can muster; you are about to see, one after another, four of the most beautiful beaches in all of the Caribbean. The road is narrow and hilly with switchbacks and steep curves that make driving a challenge. **Hawksnest,** the first beach you will come to, is quite narrow but there is a fine reef close to shore. This is where Alan Alda shot scenes for his film *The Four Seasons*. Just past Hawksnest Hill, swing left to Peace Hill, sometimes called Sugarloaf Hill, to the
2 ***Christ of the Caribbean* statue** and an old sugar-mill tower. Park in the small unmarked parking lot and walk about 100 yards up a rocky path. The area is grassy, and views do not get much better than this. *Christ of the Caribbean* was erected in 1953 by Colonel Julius Wadsworth and donated, along with 9 acres of land, to the national park in 1975.

Your next stop, and that of quite a few tourist-filled safari buses, is **Trunk Bay,** a beautiful beach with an underwater trail that's good for beginner snorkelers.

Continuing on the beach hunt, you'll come to wide **Cinnamon Bay.** The snorkeling around the point to the right is good unless the waves are up—look for the big angelfish and the swarms of purple triggerfish that live here. The national-park campground is at Cinnamon Bay and includes a snack bar, bathhouse, boutique, restaurant, general store, water-sports equipment rental, and a self-guided museum. Across the road from the beach parking lot is the beginning of the Cinnamon Bay hiking trail; look for the ruins of a sugar mill to mark the trailhead. The nature trail here takes you on a flat circle through the woods, following signs that identify the flora. The other trail heads all the way up to Centerline Road.

As you leave Cinnamon, the road flattens out, and you'll find yourself on a shaded lane running under flowering trees. **Maho Bay** comes almost to the road here, and you may want to stop and take a dip. The Maho Bay Campground is here, too—a wonderful mélange of open-air cottages nestled in the hillside above. The team that developed the campground is also responsible for the adjacent Harmony, a hotel where you can be "green" without roughing it.

3 The partially restored **Annaberg Plantation** at Leinster Bay, built in the 1780s and once an important sugar mill, is just ahead on North Shore Road. As you stroll around, look up at the steep hillsides and imagine cutting sugarcane against that grade in the hot sun. Slaves, Danes, and Dutchmen toiled here to harvest the sugarcane that produced sugar, molasses, and rum for export. There are no official visiting hours, no charge for entry, and no official tours, although some well-informed taxi drivers will show you around. For more information on talks and cultural demonstrations, contact the National Park Service Visitors Center (tel. 809/776–6201).

From Annaberg keep to the left and go south, then uphill, and bear
4 left at the junction to Route 10, to **Coral Bay,** named for its shape rather than for its underwater life. The community at the dry, eastern end of the island is the ultimate in laid-back style. The small wood-and-stucco West Indian homes house everyone from families born here to newer residents who offer palm readings and massage.

The road forms a loop around Coral Bay. Head northeast along
5 Route 10 to Hurricane Hole at the remote and pristine **East End,** only a 15-to 20-minute ride from Coral Bay, where Arawak Indians are believed to have first settled on the island 2,000 years ago. At **Haulover Bay,** only a couple of hundred yards separate the Atlantic Ocean from the Caribbean.

6 Route 107 takes you south to the peninsula of **Salt Pond,** which is only about 1 foot above sea level. If you're weary of driving, you can hike the trail south to the spectacular cliffs of **Ram Head.** In any case, you or your rented car can't proceed much farther on 107 without venturing onto a truly rocky road that heads west. Be sure at least to get a view of **Lameshur Bay,** one of the best snorkeling places on St. John and an area used for underwater training by the U.S. Navy.

Once you've run out of road on Route 107, retrace your route to Coral Bay and go west (left) on Route 10 again, which takes you over the heights of the island toward Cruz Bay. On your left is the turnoff for
7 **Bordeaux Mountain,** at 1,277 feet St. John's highest peak. This is also an area of rain forest. Crackle a leaf from a bay tree, and you'll get a whiff of the spicy aroma that you may recognize from St. John's famous bay rum. To appreciate the Bordeaux Mountain region fully, save some time during your stay to hike the **Reef Bay Trail.** Join a hike led by a National Park Service ranger, who can identify the trees and plants on the hike down, fill you in on the history of the Reef Bay Plantation, and tell you about the carvings you'll find in the rocks at the bottom of the trail. You can continue straight back into Cruz Bay on Route 10.

Beaches

All beaches on these islands are open to the public, but often you have to walk through a resort to reach them. Once there, you'll find that resort guests may have access to lounge chairs and beach bars that are off limits to you; for this reason, you may feel more comfortable at one of the beaches not associated with a resort. Whichever one you choose, remember to remove your valuables from the car.

St. Thomas The majority of St. Thomas's beaches are on the eastern half of the island. The closest to Charlotte Amalie is **Morningstar Beach,** in the shadow of the huge Marriott's Frenchman's Reef Hotel. Snorkeling is good here when the current doesn't affect visibility. Take a taxi or the hotel's *The Reefer* ferry, which plies the waters of the harbor from downtown every half hour (fare: $3.50 one-way). World-famous **Magens Bay** is just a taxi ride over the hill behind Charlotte Amalie. Nestled between two peninsulas, this lively, popular beach has a spectacular half-mile arc of white sand and calm, protected waters. **Coki Beach,** next to Coral World, is a popular snorkeling spot for cruise-ship passengers. If you are visiting Coral World, you can use the lockers and changing rooms for free. **Sapphire Beach,** at Sapphire Beach Resort and Marina, has excellent snorkeling and a lovely view of St. John and the British Virgin Islands. Water-sports gear is available for rent here. Among the coves of the southeast tip of the island is **Secret Harbour** beach, a quiet spot with good snorkeling, near the low-key condo resort set among palm trees.

St. Croix **Buck Island** and its reef, which is under environmental protection, can be reached only by boat; still, it's a must on any visit to St. Croix. Its beach is beautiful, but its finest treasures are those you can see when you plop off the boat and adjust your face mask, snorkel, and flippers. The waters are not always gentle at **Cane Bay,** a breezy north shore beach, but the scuba diving and snorkeling are wondrous, and there are never many people around. Just swim straight out to see elkhorn and brain corals. Less than 200 yards out is the drop-off or so-called Cane Bay Wall. **Tamarind Reef Beach** is a small but attractive beach east of Christiansted. Both Green Cay and Buck Island seem smack in front of you and make the view arresting. Snorkeling is good. There are several popular West End beaches along the coast north of Frederiksted. Tiny **LaGrange Beach** is connected to a casual restaurant/bar of the same name, and **Rainbow Beach,** the beach at the West End Beach Club, features a bar, water sports, and volleyball. It's a bit of a hike, but if you don't have a car you can take the taxi-van to Frederiksted and walk to these two beaches—if you're friendly with the driver, he may drop you off for free. South of Frederiksted, try the beach at the **On the Beach Resort,** where palm trees can provide plenty of shade for those who need it, and there is a fine beachside restaurant for a casual lunch on weekends.

St. John **Caneel Bay** is actually seven white-sand beaches on the north shore, six of which can be reached only by water if you are not a hotel guest. The main beach (ask for directions) provides easy access to the public. **Hawksnest Beach** is becoming more popular every day; it's narrow and lined with sea-grape trees. There are rest rooms, cooking grills, and a covered shed for picnicking. It's popular for group outings and is the closest beach to town, so it is often fairly crowded. **Trunk Bay** is probably St. John's most photographed beach, and the most popular spot for beginning snorkelers, because of its underwater trail. It's the St. John stop for cruise-ship passengers who choose a snorkeling tour for the day. To avoid the crowd, check cruise-ship listings in *St. Thomas This Week* to find out when the fewest are in port. There are changing rooms, a snack bar, picnic tables, a gift shop, telephones, small lockers, and snorkeling equipment for rent. **Cinnamon Bay,** a long, sandy beach facing beautiful cays, serves the adjoining national-park campground. Facilities (showers, toilets, commissary, restaurant, beach shop gift shop, small museum, kayak and windsurfing rentals) are open to all. There's good snorkeling off the point to the right, and rental equipment is available. These north shore beaches are all accessible by public taxi from Cruz Bay, for about $5 one way. **Salt Pond Bay,** on the southeastern coast of St. John, is a scenic area with a beach designed for the adventurous. It's a short hike down a hill from the parking lot, and the only facility is an outhouse. The beach is a little rockier here, but there are interesting tide pools and the snorkeling is good. Take special care to leave nothing valuable in the car; reports of thefts are numerous here.

Sports and the Outdoors

Golf On St. Thomas, scenic **Mahogany Run** (tel. 809/775–5000), with a par-70, 18-hole course and a view of the B.V.I., lies to the north of Charlotte Amalie and has the especially tricky "Devil's Triangle" trio of holes. Greens fees are $85 per person in high season. On St. Croix, **The Buccaneer's** (tel. 809/773–2100) 18-hole course is just east of Christiansted with a greens fee of $35 per person. Yet more spectacular is **Carambola** (tel. 809/778–5638), in the valleyed northwestern part of the island, designed by Robert Trent Jones (greens fee $55). **The Reef Club** (tel. 809/773–8844), at the northeastern part of the island, has nine holes. In the summertime, greens fees are $10 to $20 less per person, which may or may not include cart rental.

Hiking The very developed St. Thomas has little hiking to recommend. Similarly, options on St. Croix are limited to the dirt roads that wind up through the rain forest (try joining the scenic road either in the hills above Carambola or from Creque Dam Road on the West End). St. John, on the other hand, is hikers' heaven. The staff at the park ranger station in Cruz Bay will be happy to help direct you to a trail suitable to your abilities. Some of the more popular are the 1-mile Lind Point trail that runs from behind the visitor center to Salomon Beach; the Cinnamon Bay nature trail; and the 3-mile Reef Bay trail, which leads downhill to the south shore.

Scuba Diving/ Snorkeling There are numerous dive operators on the three islands, and some of the hotels offer dive packages. Many of the operators listed below also offer snorkeling trips; call for details. The typical cost of a two-tank dive is $80; a single-tank dive, $55; and a night dive, $65.

St. Thomas **Aqua Action Watersports** (6501 Red Hook Plaza, Suite 15, 00802, tel. 809/775–6285) is a full service, PADI five-star shop with all levels of instruction. They also rent sea kayaks and Windsurfers.

Joe Vogel Diving Co. (505 Crown Bay Marina, 00801, tel. 809/775–7610 for the shop), the oldest certified diving operation in the U.S.V.I., leaves from the West Indies Inn for day or night, reef or wreck dives. It has both PADI and NAUI instructors and will dive even if only one person shows up.

St. Thomas Diving Club (Box 7385, St. Thomas, U.S.V.I. 00801, tel. 809/776–2381), a divers' resort at Bolongo Bay, has a PADI five-star facility with sales, rentals, and introductory and certification courses.

Underwater Safaris (Box 8469, St. Thomas, U.S.V.I. 00801, tel. 809/774–1350) is conveniently located in Long Bay at the Ramada Yacht Haven Marina—which is also home to the U.S.V.I. charter boat fleet. It is a PADI five-star dive operation that specializes in Buck Island dives to the wreck of the World War I cargo ship *Cartenser Sr.*

St. Croix **Dive Experience, Inc.** (Box 4254, Strand St., Christiansted 00822-4254, tel. 809/773–3307 or 800/235–9047) is a PADI five-star training facility providing the range from certification to introductory dives.

Dive St. Croix (59 King's Wharf, Box 3045, Christiansted 00820, tel. 809/773–3434 or 800/523–3483, fax 809/773–9411), takes divers to walls and wrecks—more than 50 sites—and offers introductory, certification, and PADI, NAUI, and SSI C-card completion courses. It has custom packages with five hotels and is the only dive operation on the island allowed to run dives to Buck Island.

V.I. Divers, Ltd. (Pan Am Pavilion, Christiansted 00820, tel. 809/773–6045 or 800/544–5911) is a PADI five-star training facility with a 35-foot dive boat and hotel packages.

St. John **Cruz Bay Watersports Co., Inc.** (Box 252, 00830, tel. 809/776–6234 or 800/835–7730; fax 809/693–8720) is a PADI five-star diving center with two locations in Cruz Bay. Owner/operators Patty and Marcus Johnston offer regular reef, wreck, and night dives aboard three custom dive vessels.

Low Key Water Sports (Box 716, 00830, tel. and fax 809/693–8999), located at the Wharfside Village, offers PADI certification and resort courses, one- and two-tank dives, wreck dives, and specialty courses.

St. John Watersports (Box 70, 00830, tel. 809/776–6256) is a five-star PADI center in the Mongoose Junction shopping mall.

Sea Excursions and Day Sails

On St. Thomas, **Coconut Charters** (Red Hook Plaza, Suite 202, 00802, tel. 809/775–5959) has a sunset sail for $35 a person. **Tropic Tours** (tel. 809/774–1855 or 800/423–4334) offers a full-day snorkeling trip to St. John for $50 a person; cost includes snorkel gear and lunch. Call at least a day ahead for reservations.

On St. Croix, try Mile-Mark Charters (Box 3045, 59 King's Wharf, Christiansted 00822, tel. 809/773–2628 or 800/524–2012, fax 809/773–9411) or **Big Beard's Adventure Tours** (Box 4534, Pan Am Pavilion, Christiansted 00822, tel. 809/773–4482) for trips to the underwater snorkeling trail at Buck Island. Cost is $35–$40, including snorkel gear, but you'll need to bring your own lunch. Captain Heinz's trimaran, the *Teroro II* (Box 2881, Christiansted, tel. 809/773–3161) departs for full- ($40 a person) or half-day ($30 a person) Buck Island trips from Green Cay Marina.

On St. John, **Connections** (Box 37, 00831, tel. 809/776–6922) represents a dozen of the finest local boats; many of its employees have worked on the boats they book.

Small Powerboat Rentals This is an interesting—and surprisingly affordable—way to see the islands. **Club Nautico** (American Yacht Harbor, St. Thomas 00802, tel. 809/779–2555) and **Nauti Nymph** (American Yacht Harbor, St.

Thomas 00802, tel. 809/775–5066) both have a variety of 21- to 27-foot boats.

Tennis
St. Thomas Most hotels rent time to nonguests for $9–20 an hour. For reservations call **Bluebeard's Castle Hotel** (tel. 809/774–1600, ext. 196), **Marriott's Frenchman's Reef Tennis Courts** (tel. 809/776–8500 ext. 486), **Mahogany Run Tennis Club** (tel. 809/775–5000), or **Sugar Bay Plantation Resort** (tel. 809/777–7100). There are two public courts at **Sub Base** (next to the Water and Power Authority), open on a first-come, first-served basis.

St. Croix There are courts open to nonguests ($7–$10 an hour) at **The Buccaneer** (tel. 809/773–2100), **Chenay Bay Beach Resort** (tel. 809/773–2918), **St. Croix by the Sea** (tel. 809/778–8600), **The Reef** (tel. 809/773–9250), and **Club St. Croix** (tel. 809/773–4800) hotels. Public courts can be found at **Conegata Park** (two) and **Fort Frederik** (two), though they may not be in the best condition.

St. John The **Hyatt Regency** (tel. 809/776–7171) has six lighted courts, open to nonguests for $10 an hour, and a pro shop.

Shopping

St. Thomas Most people would agree that St. Thomas lives up to its self-described billing as a shopper's paradise, but duty-free doesn't necessarily mean bargain shopping. You can, however, find certain items that cost 20%–30% less than they do stateside. Among the best buys are liquor, linens, imported china, crystal (most stores ship), perfume, and cosmetics. Island crafts, at reasonable prices, offer good value.

Most stores take major credit cards, and there is no sales tax in the U.S.V.I.

Shopping Districts The prime shopping area in **Charlotte Amalie** is between Post Office and Market squares and consists of three parallel streets running east to west (Waterfront, Main Street, and Back Street) and the alleyways connecting them. A new addition is **Vendors Plaza.** Located on the waterfront at Emancipation Gardens, this is a centralized location for all the vendors who used to clog the sidewalks with their merchandise. Best bets here are T-shirts and locally made jewelry.

Havensight Mall, next to the cruise-ship dock, has parking and many of the same stores as Charlotte Amalie, though it's not as charming. West of town, the pink stucco **Nisky Center** is more of a hometown shopping center than a tourist area, but there's an excellent bookstore (next to a bakery and yogurt shop), as well as a bank, gift shops, and clothing stores.

Out east, in Red Hook, **American Yacht Harbor** is a waterfront shopping arcade with branches of some Charlotte Amalie stores as well as a deli, candy store, and a few restaurants.

Books and Magazines **Dockside Bookshop** (Havensight Mall, Bldg. IV, tel. 809/774–4937) has a wide selection of books, including those written in and about the Caribbean and the Virgin Islands, from literature to chartering guides to books on seashells and tropical flowers.

China and Crystal **A.H. Riise Gift Shops** (Riise's Alley off Main St.; Havensight Mall; tel. 809/776–2303) carries Waterford, Wedgwood, Royal Crown, and Royal Doulon at good prices. Outside the Charlotte Amalie branch are local art and hand-painted postcards.

The English Shop (Waterfront, tel. 809/776–5399, and Havensight Mall, tel. 809/776–3776) sells china and crystal from major European and Japanese manufacturers.

Little Switzerland (locations at Main St., Emancipation Park, Havensight Mall, and American Yacht Harbor, tel. 809/776–2010) carries crystal from Lalique, Baccarat, Waterford, Riedel, and Orrefors, and china from Villeroy & Boch and Wedgwood, among others.

Clothing **Java Wraps** (American Yacht Harbor, Red Hook, tel. 809/777-3450)) specializes in Indonesian batik creations and offers a complete line of beach cover-ups, swimwear, and leisurewear for women, men, and children.

Local Color (Garden St., tel. 809/774-3727) sells cool cotton T-shirts and other casual clothing with the designs of St. Thomas artist Kerry Topper. Brightly printed sundresses, shorts, and shirts by Jams; big-brim straw hats dipped in fuchsia, turquoise, and other tropical colors; and unique jewelry are also for sale here.

Crafts and Gifts **The Caribbean Marketplace** (Havensight Mall, Bldg. III, tel. 809/776-5400) is the place to look for Caribbean handicrafts, including Caribelle batiks from St. Lucia; bikinis from the Cayman Islands; and Sunny Caribee spices, soaps, teas, and coffees from Tortola.

The Gallery (Veteran's Dr., tel. 809/776-4641) carries Haitian art, along with works by a number of Virgin Islands artists.

Jim Tillet's Gardens (Estate Tutu, tel. 809/775-1405) is an oasis where you can watch craftspeople and artisans produce silk-screened fabrics, pottery, candles, watercolors, and more.

Down Island Traders (Bakery Sq., Veteran's Dr., and Frenchman'sReef, tel. 809/776-4641) deals in hand-painted calabash bowls ($10); finely printed Caribbean note cards; jams, jellies, spices, and herbs; and herbal teas made of rum, passion fruit, and mango.

Linens **Mr. Tablecloth** (Main St., tel. 809/774-4343) has a friendly staff who will help you choose from a floor-to-ceiling array of linens.

Shanghai Linen (Waterfront, tel. 809/776-2828) does a brisk trade in linens.

Shanghai Silk and Handicrafts (Royal Dane Mall, tel. 809/776-8118) has frames, figurines, and other Asian crafts on sale. It also carries silk fabric and silk clothing; scarves that cost less than $15 each make distinct, packable gifts.

Liquor and Wine **A.H. Riise Liquors** (Riise's Alley off Main St.; Havensight Mall; tel. 809/776-2303) offers a large selection of liquors, cordials, wines, and tobacco, including rare vintage cognacs, Armagnacs, ports, and Madeiras. They also stock imported cigars, fruits in brandy, and barware from England.

Al Cohen's Discount Liquor (across from Havensight Mall, Long Bay Rd., tel. 809/774-3690) is a warehouse-style store with a large wine department.

Music **Parrot Fish Records and Tapes** (Back St., tel. 809/776-4514) stocks standard stateside tapes and compact discs, along with a good selection of music by Caribbean artists, including local groups. For a catalogue of calypso, soca, steel band, and reggae music, write to Parrot Fish (Box 9206, St. Thomas 00801).

Perfumes **Tropicana Perfume Shoppes** (2 Main St., tel. 809/774-0010, and 14 Main St., tel. 809/774-1834) has the largest selection of fragrances for men and women in all of the Virgin Islands; both shops give small free samples to customers.

St. Croix Although it doesn't offer the shopping opportunities of St. Thomas, St. Croix has an array of smaller stores with unique merchandise. In Christiansted, the best shopping areas are the Pan Am Pavilion and Caravelle Arcade off Strand Street and along King and Company streets.

China and Crystal At the **Royal English Shop** (5 Strand St., Frederiksted, tel. 809/772–4886) Natchman and Beyer crystal cost significantly less than on the mainland.

Little Switzerland (Hamilton House, 56 King St., Christiansted, tel. 809/773–1976), the St. Croix branch of this Virgin Islands institution, features a variety of Rosenthal flatware, Lladro figurines, Waterford and Baccarat crystal, Lalique figurines, and Wedgwood and Royal Doulton china.

Clothing **Wayne James Boutique** (42 Queen Cross St., tel. 809/773–8585) is the venue of an engaging Crucian who has designed vestments for the pope and evening wear for the queen of Denmark. His bright, savvy clothes are inspired by island traditions and colors.

Crafts and Gifts **American West India Company** (1 Strand St., Christiansted, tel. 809/773–7325) offers a range of goods from St. Croix and around the Caribbean, including Jamaican allspice and Haitian metalwork.

Folk Art Traders (1B Queen Cross St. at Strand St., Christiansted, tel. 809/773–1900) has energetic owners who travel to Haiti, Jamaica, Guayana, and elsewhere in the Caribbean to find the treasures sold in their shop, including baskets, masks, pottery, and ceramics.

Green Papaya (Caravelle Arcade No. 15, Christiansted, tel. 809/773–8848), a new store, sells unusual hand-crafted furniture and accessories for the home. Oriental baskets and lovely wrought-iron lamps and hurricanes with handblown teardrop lanterns are among the selection.

Liquor **Grog and Spirits** (Chandlers Wharf, Gallows Bay, tel. 809/773–8485) is a conveniently located shop with a good selection of liquor.

Woolworth's (Sunny Isle Shopping Center, Centerline Rd., tel. 809/778–5466) carries a huge line of discount, duty-free liquor.

Perfumes **St. Croix Shoppes** (53AB Company St., Christiansted tel. 809/773–2727) is two side-by-side shops. One specializes solely in Estée Lauder and Clinique products, while the other carries a full line of fragrances, all at lower-than-stateside prices.

St. Croix Perfume Center (1114 King St., Christiansted, tel. 809/773–7604) offers an extensive array of fragrances, including all major brands.

St. John You won't find many bargains on pricey St. John, but you'll enjoy strolling through the lovely shopping centers here anyway. Several levels of cool stone-wall shops, set off by colorfully planted terraces and courtyards, make **Mongoose Junction** one of the prettiest shopping malls in the Caribbean. **Wharfside Village,** on the other side of Cruz Bay, is a painted-clapboard village with shops and restaurants.

Dining

Almost every cuisine you can imagine is available in the U.S.V.I. In upscale hotels, prices are comparable to those in expensive international cities, but local eateries serving delicious, filling, and inexpensive West Indian cuisine provide plenty of alternatives. St. Thomas has a variety of delis and Chinese restaurants, and all islands have their fair share of fast food.

St. Thomas, the most cosmopolitan of the islands, has the most diverse restaurant scene. While eating dinner in full-service restaurants can be expensive, lower-priced lunch menus let you enjoy pricey ambience with an affordable bottom line. Two that serve up a spectacular view with good food are **Blackbeard's Castle** (tel. 809/776–1234), which overlooks Charlotte Amalie Harbor and offers a moderately priced Sunday brunch, and the **Seagrape** restaurant (tel. 809/775–6100), a few steps from the surf at Sapphire Beach Resort and Marina. Fast-food eateries on St. Thomas include Burger King, Arby's, McDonald's, Pizza Hut, and Kentucky Fried Chicken.

If you are renting a house or a condo and doing your own cooking, check out the **Pueblo** supermarket chain, with locations at Sub Base; Long Bay, across from Havensight Mall; and at the Four Winds and Lockhart Gardens Shopping Centers. **Gourmet Gallery,** at Yacht Haven Marina, has an excellent and fair-priced wine selection, as well as condiments, cheeses, and specialty ingredients for everything from tacos to curries to chow mein. For fresh fruits and vegetables, go to the **Fruit Bowl,** at Wheatley Center. On the East End, shop at **Marina Market** in Red Hook for the island's freshest meats and seafood.

On St. Croix and St. John, dozens of West Indian and Latin restaurants will serve you a filling dinner of fish or goat with a salad, vegetable, and potato, rice, or plantain for $5–$7. These include **La Guitarra** (tel. 809/692–9069), **Vel's** (tel. 809/772–2160), **Motown** (tel. 809/772–9882), and **Stars of the West** (tel. 809/772–9039), on St. Croix; and **Fred's** (tel. 809/776–6363) on St. John. Cheap lunches are available at the many little coffee shops and roadside lunch trucks on St. Croix and St. John. Rotis (here, hot meat- or fish-filled pastries) or johnnycakes (deep-fried pastries), washed down with locally bottled Brow soda, make an authentic and very inexpensive meal.

For a fast-food fix on St. Croix, visit the Pizza Hut or Burger King in Christiansted, and the Wendy's or Kentucky Fried Chicken in Frederiksted. St. John has a Subway in Cruz Bay. Christiansted and Frederiksted on St. Croix do not have supermarkets; you'll have to make do with a few corner stores. There are supermarkets at the **Villa LaReine** and **Sunny Isle** shopping centers. On St. John, the **Pine Peace Mini-Mart,** in Cruz Bay, has the best prices and selection on the island. Also in Cruz Bay is **Smiling Al's Natural Food Store,** which stocks unusual items.

Highly recommended restaurants are indicated by a star ★.

Category	Cost*
$$	$15–$25
$	$10–$15
¢	under $10

*per person, excluding drinks and service

St. Thomas

$$ ★ **Alexander's Cafe.** This charming restaurant is a favorite with the people in the restaurant business on St. Thomas—always a sign of quality. Local media types and wine aficionados (the always-changing wine list offers the best value on the island) are often among the relaxed crowd that packs this place. Alexander is Austrian, and the schnitzels are delicious and reasonably priced; the baked-brie-and-fruit plate and pasta specials are fresh and tasty. Save room for strudel. *24A Honduras, Frenchtown, tel. 809/776–4211. Reservations advised. AE, D, MC, V. Closed Sun.*

$$ **The Chart House.** Fresh fish, teriyaki dishes, lobster, Hawaiian chicken, and a large salad bar are all on the menu at this old great house. The early-bird specials (5:30–6:30) are somewhat limited, but they're delicious, less expensive, and the view—from the tip of the Frenchtown peninsula—is just as good. *Villa Olga, Frenchtown, tel. 809/774–4262. Reservations accepted for 10 or more. AE, D, DC, MC, V.*

$$ **Eunice's Terrace.** Eunice is deservedly famous for her excellent West Indian cooking. Her roomy two-story restaurant has a spacious bar and a menu of native dishes, including *callaloo* (a West In-

dian soup), conch fritters, fried fish, local sweet potato, *funghi* (a polentalike dish), and plantain. *Rte. 38, near Stouffer's Grand Beach Resort and Coral World, Smith Bay, tel. 809/775–3975. AE, MC, V.*

$$ **For the Birds.** The beer is served in mason jars, and margaritas are available in 46-ounce servings. You can also have sizzling fajitas, barbecued baby-back ribs, seafood, or steak at this beach restaurant whose disco floor is hopping by 10. For children there are coloring place mats and crayons. Come Friday night for happy hour drinks and a free pub-grub buffet. *Scott Beach, near Compass Point, East End, tel. 809/775–6431. Reservations required for 6 or more. AE, MC, V. No lunch.*

$$ **Little Bopeep.** Inside this unpretentious restaurant is some of the best West Indian food on the island. Try the curried chicken, conch in Creole sauce, sweet potato stuffing, and fried plantains. Bring a group of six and one person gets a meal for only 10¢. *Barbel Plaza, Charlotte Amalie, tel. 809/774–1959. AE, MC, V.*

$$ **Zorba's Cafe.** Tired of shopping? Summon up one last ounce of energy and head up Government Hill to Zorba's. Sit and have a cold beer or bracing iced tea in the 19th-century stone-paved courtyard surrounded by banana trees. Greek salads and appetizers, moussaka, and an excellent vegetarian plate top the menu. If you're dining with kids, you may order anything on the menu in a child's portion at a lower cost, but be sure to specify this when ordering. *Government Hill, Charlotte Amalie, tel. 809/776–0444. AE, MC, V. No lunch Sun.*

$–$$ **Bryan's Bar and Restaurant.** Located high on the cool north side of the island, overlooking Hull Bay, this surfer's bar offers some of the best food on the island. The chefs surf by day and cook by night, serving up gargantuan portions of grilled fish, steaks, and burgers. You dine by lantern light at wood booths inside or at picnic tables outside. A local hangout complete with pool table, it's casual and reasonably priced—definitely one of the island's best values. *Hull Bay, tel. 809/774–3522. No credit cards. No lunch.*

$ **Wok & Roll.** Tucked in a corner just below the Warehouse Bar in Red Hook, this nook has brought tasty take-out Chinese to the East End. You'll find all the standards, from fried rice and chow mein to sweet and sour pork, at good prices. *Red Hook, across from the ferry dock, tel. 809/775–6246. No credit cards.*

¢ **Grateful Deli and Coffee Shop.** For a beach picnic or lunch on the run, visit this gourmet delicatessen. Offerings include freshly made deli salads, specialty sandwiches, and vegetarian fare as well as daily specials that will make your mouth water. *Red Hook Plaza, tel. 809/775-5160. No credit cards. Closed Sun.*

¢ **Señor Pizza.** Want to have great pizza or calzones and support U.S.V.I. Olympic bobsledders? Sink you teeth into the island's only $8.88 value pizza, sold at this red, green, and white trailer, and feel good knowing that all proceeds go to the team. There's free delivery anywhere on the island. *Red Hook, across from the ferry dock, tel. 809/775–3030. No credit cards.*

St. Croix

$$ **Blue Moon.** This terrific little bistro in Frederiksted, popular for its live jazz on Friday nights, has an eclectic, often changing menu that draws heavily on Cajun and French influences. Try the hearty seafood chowder as an appetizer or a light meal. Leave room for the bittersweet chocolate torte. *17 Strand St., Frederiksted, tel. 809/772–2222. AE. No lunch. Closed July–Sept. and Mon.*

$$ **Le St. Tropez.** A dark-wood bar and soft lighting add to the Mediterranean atmosphere at this pleasant bistro, tucked into a courtyard off Frederiksted's main thoroughfare. Diners seated either inside or on the adjoining patio order from a menu of light French fare, including quiches, salads, brochettes, and crepes. Daily specials often take advantage of fresh local seafood. *67 King St., Frederiksted, tel. 809/772–3000. AE, MC, V. Closed Sun.*

$ ★ **Camille's.** This tiny, lively spot is perfect for lunch or a light supper. Sandwiches and burgers are the big draw here, though the daily seafood special, often wahoo or mahimahi, is also popular. *Queen Cross St., Christiansted, tel. 809/773–2985. No credit cards. Closed Sun.*

$ **LaGrange Beach Club.** Take a seat just steps from the lapping surf and soak in the unbeatable views while you order a casual, well-prepared meal. A quick beachside lunch might include potato skins, chili, or burgers. At dinner, check the daily specials (seafood is emphasized). The restaurant is a 10-minute walk along Rte. 63 north from Frederiksted. A children's menu is available. *Rte. 63, Frederiksted, tel. 809/772–5566. MC, V.*

$ **Stixx on the Waterfront.** You can't beat a $10 Sunday brunch buffet with unlimited mimosas and Bloody Marys. Good pizza, burgers, and daily specials make for casual dining at other times, all served on a deck overlooking the harbor in Christiansted. Try the rum Hurricane, served in a variety of strengths. *Pan Am Pavilion, Christiansted, tel. 809/773–5157. AE.*

¢ **La Guitarra.** To sample authentic West Indian/Latin cooking, head for this small restaurant. Choose from stew beef, conch stew, or fried pork chops, all served with rice, beans, and salad. *39–40 Queen Cross St., Market Square, Christiansted, tel. 809/692–9096. No credit cards. Closed Sun.*

St. John

$$ ★ **The Fish Trap.** There are several rooms here, all open to the breezes, and all busy with happy diners. This local favorite serves up six kinds of fresh fish nightly, along with tasty appetizers, such as conch fritters and Fish Trap chowder. The menu also includes steak, pasta, chicken, and hamburgers. *Downtown, Cruz Bay, tel. 809/693–9994. AE, D, MC, V. No lunch. Closed Mon.*

$$ ★ **Lime Inn.** This busy, roofed, open-air restaurant has an ornamental garden and beach-furniture chairs. There are several shrimp and steak dishes and such specials as sautéed chicken with artichoke hearts in lemon sauce. On Wednesday night there's an all-you-can-eat shrimp feast. *Downtown, Cruz Bay, tel. 809/776–6425. No reservations. AE, MC, V.*

$ **Shipwreck Landing.** Start with a house drink, perhaps a concoction of fresh-squeezed lime, coconut, and rum, then move on to hearty taco salads, fried shrimp, teriyaki chicken, and conch fritters. The birds keep up a lively chatter in the bougainvillea that surround the open-air restaurant, and there's live music on Sunday nights in season. *Coral Bay, tel. 809/693–5640. MC, V.*

¢ ★ **Etta's.** The courtyard restaurant at the Inn at Tamarind Court has long been a local favorite. Terrific West Indian lunches—conch, grouper, or mutton served with plantains, potato salad, and sweet potatoes—are just $5. The menu also features callaloo soup, goat water, funghi, great curries, and other local specialties. *Centerline Rd. north, bear right at Texaco, tel. 809/693–8246. No reservations. No credit cards.*

¢ **Luscious Licks.** This funky hole-in-the-wall serves mostly healthful foods, such as all-natural fruit smoothies, veggie pita sandwiches, and homemade muffins. For those who've gotta have them, specialty coffees and Ben & Jerry's ice cream are also sold here. Be sure to check the blackboard for the day's advice. *Cruz Bay, tel. 809/693–8400. No credit cards.*

Lodging

Although it's common to associate the U.S.V.I. with pricey resorts chock-full of activities and amenities, the islands are also home to inexpensive hotels, small inns, campgrounds, and affordable rental properties. On St. Thomas, most moderately priced hotels and condominium complexes are on or near a beach. Guest houses and smaller hotels are not typically on the water, but many offer pools and shuttle service to nearby beaches. If you're staying in Charlotte Amalie and your hotel does not offer shuttle service to the beach, you can take a bus to nearby beaches or take the *Reefer* ferry across the water to Morningstar Beach.

In keeping with its small-town atmosphere, St. Croix offers a number of modest small hotels and guest houses. You'll need a car at these. There are no beaches in Christiansted, but those staying in town can take a quick ferry to Cay Beach across the harbor (it's cheaper than a taxi to beaches outside town).

St. John has a handful of inexpensive inns in downtown Cruz Bay, a short safari-bus ride ($8–$13 a couple one-way) from nearby beaches. Many budget visitors, however, head straight for one of the two campgrounds here, where accommodations range from bare sites to breezy open-air tent-cabins. Both campgrounds have eating facilities and are on beautiful beaches, with National Park hiking all around. (Maho Bay guests must walk down a hill to get to the beach.) If you're traveling with a group or another couple, you may find you can afford one of the upscale villas on St. John, though hillside locations make a car mandatory.

Highly recommended lodgings are indicated by a star ★.

Category	Cost*
$$	$110–$200
$	$75–$110
¢	under $75

**All prices are for a standard double room, excluding 7.5% accommodations tax. To estimate rates for hotels offering MAP/FAP, add about $30–$40 per person per day to the above price ranges.*

St. Thomas
Hotels and Resorts

Island Beachcomber. Although a fence and careful landscaping shield the nearby airport from view, they cannot keep out the sound of departing planes (usually between 2 and 5 PM daily). The hotel *is* right on Lindbergh Beach, however, and has a casual, laid-back ambience that attracts an unpretentious clientele. The beach is on a shallow bay with a gentle surf that makes it ideal for children. Eleven rooms are right on the water; the others open onto a courtyard with the ocean visible through the trees. All rooms have refrigerators, air-conditioning, and ceiling fans. A reasonably priced restaurant rests under the palms a few feet from the surf. At least once a year this hotel runs a two-for-one deal, kids for free, or something else. Packages and times vary, so be sure to ask when you make reservations. *Box 2579, 00803, tel. 809/774–5250 or 800/982–9898, fax 809/774–7675. 48 rooms. Facilities: restaurant, water sports. AE, D, DC, MC, V. EP. $$*

Ramada Yacht Haven Hotel & Marina. This pink landmark anchoring the outer edge of Charlotte Amalie is part of sprawling Yacht Haven Marina. It's a lively spot, with a variety of shops, restaurants, bars, and a deli. Many of the clean, simple rooms—some with balcony—overlook the ever-changing vista of marina, cruise dock, and harbor. Morningstar Beach is a short cab ride away. Children under 17 stay free with their parents, and there are special couples rates in the fall. *5400 Long Bay Rd., Charlotte Amalie 00802, tel. 809/774–9700 or 800/228–9898. 151 rooms. Facilities: 3 restaurants, bar, swim-up bar with seating, freshwater pool. AE, DC, MC, V. EP. $$*

Villa Blanca Hotel. Above Charlotte Amalie and surrounded by an attractive garden on Raphune Hill sits this secluded hotel. Its modern, balconied rooms have rattan furniture, kitchenettes, cable TVs, and ceiling fans (six have air-conditioning). All of the rooms have eastern views of Charlotte Amalie Harbor, and partial westerly views of Drake's Channel and the B.V.I. Ask about summertime specials when you call to make reservations. Children under five stay free. *Box 7505, Charlotte Amalie 00801, tel. 809/776–0749 or 800/237–0034, fax 809/779–2661. 12 rooms. Facilities: pool, honor bar. AE, D, DC, MC, V. EP. $$*

Hotel 1829. This historic Spanish-style inn is popular with visiting government officials and people who have business at Government House down the street. It's on Government Hill, at the edge of Charlotte Amalie's shopping area. Rooms on several levels range from elegant and roomy to quite small, but they are priced accordingly, so there is one for every budget (be advised, however, tht some exceed the upper range of our $$ category). All have a refrigerator, TV, and air-conditioning. Author Graham Greene is said to have stayed here, and it is easy to imagine him musing over a drink in the small, dark bar. There's a tiny pool for cooling off. *Box 1567, Charlotte Amalie, 00801, tel. 809/776–1829 or 800/524–2002. 15 rooms. Facilities: restaurant, pool. AE, D, DC, MC, V. EP. $–$$*

Guest Houses and B&Bs

Villa Santana. Built by General Santa Anna of Mexico, circa 1857, this villa still provides a panoramic view of Charlotte Amalie Harbor along with plenty of age-old West Indian charm. Guests at this St. Thomas landmark, which is a five-minute walk from town, have a choice of five different villa-style rooms. Dark wicker furniture, white plaster and stone walls, shuttered windows, cathedral ceilings, and interesting nooks contribute to the feeling of romance and history. Villas La Torre and La Mansion are split level with spiral staircases, and all units have full kitchens and either four-poster or cradle beds. Rooms are kept cool by ceiling fans and natural trade winds and do not have telephones. In the summer months, stay for seven days, and pay for six. *Denmark Hill, Charlotte Amalie 00802, tel. and fax. 809/776–1311. 5 villa-style rooms. Facilities: pool, croquet field. AE. $$*

Sea Horse Cottages. This simple, quiet retreat rests on a hillside overlooking Nazareth Bay on the East End, a world away from the bustle of Charlotte Amalie. Island-style rooms with shuttered windows and screened-in porches all have private bath. Steps going down a hillside from the pool lead to a sunning platform built into the rocks and a cove for snorkeling and swimming. Although you may want to rent a car in this somewhat isolated spot, you can get by without one if your agenda is purely one of relaxation. All rooms have kitchen facilities, and Red Hook grocery stores and restaurants are a $5 taxi ride away. Here you'll find a room to fit any budget. *Box 2312, 00803, tel. 809/775–9231. 15 cottages. Facilities: freshwater pool. No credit cards. EP. $–$$*

Island View Guest House. This lovely, clean guest house near Frenchtown rests amid tropical foliage on the south face of 1,500-foot Crown Mountain, the highest point on St. Thomas. Guests get a sweeping view of Charlotte Amalie harbor from the pool and shaded terrace, where breakfast is served. All rooms have ceiling fans and at least a partial view; half are air-conditioned, and three have kitchenettes. The nearest beach is Lindbergh, about a 10-minute drive away. *Box 1903, 00801, tel. 809/774–4270 or 800/524–2023. 12 rooms with bath, 2 with shared bath. Facilities: pool. AE, MC, V. CP. ¢–$*

Condominium and Villa Rentals

These are plentiful on St. Thomas. Almost all condominium complexes on the island are on or near a beach on the East End, a short taxi ride from a supermarket but across the island from the bustle and shopping in Charlotte Amalie. Most villas on St. Thomas are nestled into the hillside and have a pool, but are far from beaches. Although rental units tend to be pricey, they are affordable—even economical for those who cook—for a family or two or more couples traveling together. Rental prices drop significantly during off-season (*see* Off-Season Bets, *below*). You can arrange rentals on St. Thomas and St. John through several agents, including **Leisure Enterprises** (Box 11192, 00801, tel. 809/775–3566 or 800/843–3566);

McLaughlin-Anderson Vacations (100 Blackbeard's Hill, Suite 3, 00802, tel. 809/776-0635 or 800/537-6246); and **Ocean Property Management** (Box 8529, 00801, tel. 809/775-2600 or 800/874-7897). The following condominium and apartment complexes are good rental bets:

Crystal Cove. One of the older condo complexes on the island, Crystal Cove was built as part of a Harvard University-sponsored architectural competition. The unassuming buildings blend into the Sapphire Beach setting so well that egrets and ducks are right at home in the pond in the center of the property. There are studio, one-, and two-bedroom units, each with a porch or balcony. Good snorkeling is nearby. In the summer, stay for six nights and only pay for five. *Reservations: Property Management Caribbean, Rte. 6, 00802, tel. 809/775-6660 or 800/524-2038. Facilities: saltwater pool, 2 lighted tennis courts. AE,**D, DC, MC, V. $$*

Sapphire Village. Be prepared for a swinging-singles atmosphere, since many of the units are rented out long-term to refugees from northern winters working here for the season. The best units overlook the marina and St. John; the beach is in sight and just a short walk down the hill. *Tel. 809/775-6100. Reservations: Property Management Caribbean, Rte. 6, 00802, tel. 809/775-7531 or 800/524-2038. 35 units. Facilities: restaurant, pub, 2 pools. AE, MC, V. $$*

Off-Season Bets

Besides the up-to-50% drop in prices, you'll find even bigger savings with one of the many hotel packages available during the off-season. The "Summer Lovers Special" offered by **McLaughlin-Anderson** (100 Blackbeard's Hill, 00802, tel. 809/776-0635 or 800/537-6246) offers two people a private villa with pool for $1,500 a week—it's twice that in high season. At **Bolongo Inclusive Beach Resort** (50 Estate Bolongo, 00802, tel. 809/779-2844 or 800/524-4746), the off-season "Club Everything" includes a beachfront room; full breakfast; airport transfers; shuttle to town; use of tennis courts, snorkel gear, canoes, Sunfish sailboats, windsurfing equipment, and paddleboats; and vouchers for an all-day sail, a cocktail cruise, and a half-day snorkel tour on one of the resort's yachts—all for a daily rate of $190 for two. At **Sugar Bay Plantation** (Estate Smith Bay, 00802, tel. 809/777-7100 or 800/465-4329, fax 809/777-7200), Holiday Inn's new Crowne Plaza Resort, an off-season rate of $165 for a double includes a daily full breakfast buffet with champagne; use of tennis, health club, and snorkel equipment; and a nightly cocktail party. Other luxury hotels that enter the affordable range in off-season include **Bluebeard's Castle** (Box 7480, Charlotte Amalie, 00801, tel. 809/774-1600 or 800/524-6599) and **Marriott's Frenchman's Reef and Morningstar Beach Resorts** (Box 7100, 00801, tel. 809/775-6550 or 800/627-7468), both of which rest on hills high above Charlotte Amalie and the harbor. For a more intimate atmosphere, try **Blackbeard's Castle** (Box 6041, Charlotte Amalie, 00801, tel. 809/776-1234), an upscale inn and premier sunset-watching spot built on a hill just above town.

St. Croix
Hotels, Inns, and B&Bs

Cottages by the Sea. Reminiscent of some lakeside bungalow complex from the 1950s, these cottages on a beach just outside Frederiksted are a good deal, as long as you don't mind dark paneling and somewhat shabby decor. The small cinder-block units all have porches, and there is a community barbecue area at the edge of the sand (one of the nicest beaches around). The atmosphere is friendly and familiar—most of their business is from repeat guests. You can save plenty by stocking up on food and barbecuing here often; the restaurant next door is also very good. Ask about summer specials when making reservations. *Box 1697, Frederiksted, 00840, tel. 809/772-0495. 20 units. Facilities: barbecue, restaurant/bar next door. AE, D, MC, V. EP. $*

The Frederiksted. This modern four-story inn is your best bet for lodging in Frederiksted. Yellow-stripe awnings and tropical greenery create a sunny, welcoming atmosphere. The bright, pleasant guest rooms are outfitted with tiny balconies, refrigerators, and sinks, and decorated with light-color rattan furniture and print bedspreads. Bathrooms are on the small side (most have shower baths) but are bright and clean. Though you can walk to the beach at La-Grange, north of town, you're better off driving. Ask about their summertime weekend getaway specials for two. *20 Strand St., Frederiksted 00840, tel. 809/772–0500 or 800/524–2025, fax 809/778–4009. 40 rooms. Facilities: restaurant, bar, outdoor pool, sundeck. AE, D, DC, MC, V. EP. $*

Hilty House. This small hilltop bed-and-breakfast is a tranquil alternative to the island's many beach resorts. Follow a rutted dirt road up the hill to a shaded courtyard, and pass through picturesque iron gates to reach the inn's gardens. The house is a rambling, one-story affair that was once a rum distillery. The immense, high-ceilinged living room has a Mediterranean flavor; hand-painted Italian tile lines the walls, and the giant fireplace accommodates a spit. The four guest rooms, each based on a specific color scheme, are all lovely (the peach bedroom is the roomiest). There are also three cottages that afford more privacy. On the other side of the main house is a large pool with hand-painted tile. You must have a car to get anywhere—including beaches—from here. *Box 26077, Gallows Bay 00824, tel. 809/773–2594. 4 rooms, 1 with bath across the hall, 3 cottages. Facilities: pool. No credit cards. CP. $*

★ **The Pink Fancy.** This homey, restful place is a few blocks west of the center of town in a much less touristy neighborhood. The oldest of the four buildings here is a 1780 Danish town house, and old stone walls and foundations enhance the setting. The inn's efficiency units are some of the loveliest guest rooms in town. Clean and well tended, all rooms feature hardwood floors, tropical-print fabrics, wicker furniture, and air-conditioning. Ask about summertime specials when making reservations. *27 Prince St., Christiansted 00820, tel. 809/773–8460 or 800/524–2045, fax 809/773–6448. 12 rooms. Facilities: bar, pool. AE MC, V. CP. $*

Paradise Sunset Beach. You'll need a car to get to beaches and restaurants from this remote pink hotel, tucked away on a cliff on the island's northwest corner. The rooms are on the small side, and the furnishings are nothing special, but you will have air-conditioning and TV, as well as a pool and bar out on the common deck. Wander behind the hotel to visit the ruins of an old sugar mill. *Box 1788, Frederiksted 00840, tel. 809/772–2499. 15 rooms. Facilities: bar, pool. AE, MC, V. EP. ¢–$*

Off-Season Bets

Many hotels here knock $20–$50 off their prices during the off-season. At the lovely **Caravelle** (44A Queen Cross St., Christiansted, tel. 809/773–0687), prices drop to around $100. Off-season rooms at the **King Christian** (Box 3619, Christiansted, tel. 809/773–2285) also go for $100. At **Club St. Croix** (3280 Estate Golden Rock, Christiansted, tel. 809/773–4800), studios go for about $165, and four can share a one-bedroom suite for $185. **Hibiscus Beach Hotel**'s (4131 La Grande Princesse, tel. 809/773–4042 or 800/442–0121) $190 Superior rooms are just $135 in low season. **The Waves at Cane Bay** (Box 1749, Kingshill, tel. 809/778–1805) offers $85 rooms with kitchenettes during the summer.

St. John

Hotels

Raintree Inn. If you want to be in the center of town and bunk at an affordable, island-style place, go no farther. The dark-wood rooms, some with air-conditioning, have simple, tropical-cabin decor. Lower floor rooms are very small. Three efficiencies have kitchens and a comfortable sleeping loft—reached by climbing an indoor ladder. The Fish Trap restaurant is next door, and you can take a safari bus to north coast beaches. This is a no-smoking property. *Box 566, Cruz Bay, 00831, tel. and fax 809/693–8590 or 800/666–7449. 11 rooms. AE, DC, MC, V. EP. ¢–$*

The Cruz Inn. This cozy inn is within walking distance of docks, stores, and restaurants. Rooms are small but bright and airy, some are air-conditioned, and most share baths. There are also several suites with private baths and kitchenettes. *Box 566, 00831, tel., 809/693–8688, fax 809/693–8590. 7 rooms, 5 suites. AE, DC, MC, V. ¢*

The Inn at Tamarind Court. Decor reflects prices, with mismatched and somewhat shabby furnishings, but you will save money. Choose among traditional hotel rooms (some with shared bath), suites, or a one-bedroom apartment. The front-courtyard bar is a friendly hangout that attracts singles, as well as home to one of Cruz Bay's best West Indian restaurants (*see* Dining, *above*). *Box 350, Cruz Bay 00831, tel. 809/776–6378. 20 rooms, some with shared bath. Facilities: restaurant, bar. AE, D, MC, V. CP. ¢*

Villa and Apartment Rentals

Generally, renting a private apartment or villa on St. John is not cheap. What you save by doing your own cooking you'll quickly spend on car rental, which you'll need at the hillside properties far from beaches. If you are traveling with a group, however, renting is an affordable option. Try **Caribbean Villas and Resorts Management Company** (Box 458, Cruz Bay 00831, tel. 809/776–6152 or 800/338–0987, fax 809/779–4044), the island's largest rental agent. Although their luxurious, multibedroom homes are expensive, they can accommodate a large number of people. At **Jaden Cottages** (tel. 809/776–6423), you'll find two inexpensive cottages just five minutes outside Cruz Bay. The apartments at **Serendip** (Box 273, Cruz Bay 00831, tel. 809/776–6646) are a bit shabby, but a good budget option.

Campgrounds

Maho Bay Camp. Eight miles from Cruz Bay, this private campground is a lush hillside community of three-room tent cottages (canvas and screens) linked by boardwalks, stairs, and ramps that also lead down to the beach. The 16-by-16-foot shelters have beds, dining table and chairs, electric lamps (and outlets), propane stoves, ice coolers, kitchenware, and cutlery. It's nicer than most campgrounds you'll come across, and prices reflect this: You'll pay $80 a night to rough it in style. The camp has the chummy feel of a retreat and is very popular, so book well in advance. *Cruz Bay, 00830, tel. 212/472–9453 or 800/392–9004. 113 tent cottages. Facilities: restaurant, commissary, barbecue areas, bathhouses (showers, sinks, and toilets), water sports. No credit cards. $*

Cinnamon Bay Campground. Tents, cottages with four one-room units in each cottage, and bare sites are available at this National Park Service location surrounded by jungle and set at the edge of big, beautiful Cinnamon Bay Beach. The tents are 10 feet by 14 feet, with flooring, and come with living, eating, and sleeping furnishings and necessities; the 15-by-15-foot cottages have twin beds. Bare sites, which can be reserved up to a year in advance and fill quickly in high season, come with a picnic table and a charcoal grill. The bare sites are cheap—at press time they were $15 a site—but tents and cottages range from $86 to $95 in season for two people per night. Security is minimal so be careful with your belongings. *Cruz Bay, 00830–0720, tel. 809/776–6330 or 800/223–7637. 44 tents, 40 cottages, 26 bare sites. Facilities: commissary, bathhouses (showers and toilets), cafeteria, water sports. AE, MC, V. ¢–$*

Off-Season Bets

Many individual real estate companies here run special deals on house rentals during the off-season. For instance, a house renting for $1,300 a week during high season may go for $850 in the summer. The price for a bay-view condo at **Lavender Hill Estates** (Box 8306, Cruz Bay, tel. 809/776–6969) drops from $210 to $125 per night; a two-bedroom penthouse sleeping four is just $150 a night. Similar price breaks are available at **Gallows Point** (Box 58, Cruz Bay, tel. 809/776–6434 or 800/323–7229), where summer rates are typically 50% off. Inexpensive hotels become even more inexpensive: Rooms at the **Raintree Inn** (*see above*) and the **Inn at Tamarind Court** (*see above*) are around $60. The price of a tent at **Cinnamon Bay** (*see* *above*) drops from $62 to $40; at **Maho Bay** (*see above*), an $80 tent-cottage is $55.

Nightlife

St. Thomas
Night Spots

Barnacle Bill's (tel. 809/774–7444), Bill Grogan's Crown Bay landmark with the bright-red lobster on its roof, is a musicians' home away from home.

Castaways (tel. 809/774–8446) is the watering hole and dance floor for the crews, owners, and those chartering the fleet of boats anchored at Yacht Haven.

Club Z (tel. 809/776–4655) is a disco-style club at the top of Crown Mountain Road, behind the Nisky area, with a spectacular view of glittering harbor lights from the terrace.

The Greenhouse (tel. 809/774–7998) resembles a T.G.I. Friday's. A restaurant by day, once this establishment puts away the salt and pepper shakers, it becomes a rock-till-you-drop late-night spot. It's a drink and dance place—and a loud one.

The Old Mill (tel. 809/776–3004) located in—you guessed it— an old mill, is a lively spot with a small dance floor and a good sound system.

Piano Bars

Provence (tel. 809/777–5600) in Frenchtown, and **Grand Palazzo** (tel. 809/775–3333), offer piano bars, each with its own flavor. The player at Provence has been entertaining with his show "Gray, Gray, Gray" for many years and shouldn't be missed.

St. Croix

Christiansted has a lively and eminently casual club scene near the waterfront. At **Mango Grove** (53 King St., tel. 809/773–0200) you'll hear live guitar and vocals in an open-air courtyard with a bar and Cinzano umbrella–covered tables. The upstairs **Moonraker Lounge** (43A Queen Cross St., tel. 809/773–8492) presents a constant calendar of live music. To party under the stars, head to the **Wreck Bar** (tel. 809/773–6092), on Christiansted's Hospital Street, for crab races as well as rock-and-roll.

Although less hopping than Christiansted, Frederiksted restaurants and clubs have a variety of weekend entertainment. **Blue Moon** (17 Strand St., tel. 809/772–2222), a waterfront restaurant, is the place to be for live jazz on Friday 9 PM–1 AM. The **Lost Dog Pub** (King St., tel. 809/772–3526) is a favorite spot for a casual drink, a game of darts, and occasional live rock-and-roll on Sunday nights. For another outdoor lime, head up to Mahogany Road to the **Mt. Pellier Hut Domino Club** (50 Mt. Pellier, tel. 809/772–9914). Listen to a variety of local bands Friday through Sunday.

St. John

Some friendly hubbub can be found at the rough-and-ready **Backyard** (tel. 809/693–8886), the place for sports-watching as well as grooving to Bonnie Raitt et al. There's rock and jazz on Friday at **Fred's** (tel. 809/776–6363).

Index